The Push WHICH UNIVERSITY 2002

Edited by: Johnny Rich

Written by: Kieron McCaffrey and Katryn Refaussé

9th Edition
Project Editors: John Barratt and Liz Friend-Smith.

Executive Editors: Sophie Dennis, Rachael Reeves, Johnny Rich, Andy Robinson.

Editorial Assistants: Louise Dobrin, Sereen El-Jamal, Liz Friend-Smith, Jenny Gordon, Stuart Hazell, Kieron McCaffrey.

Researchers (2002 edition): Helen Adtoun, Scott Appleton, Wendy Atkins, Matthew Barker, Penny Brereton, Martin Burrows, Roma Cassidy, Jenny Clark, Joanna Clarke, Emma Clegg, Jon Clements, Sally Cockerton, Helen Cooper, Jane Cosher, James Diamond, Rebbeca Dickinson, Amy Donnellan, Emily Fowke, Ben Gelblum, Katy Harrison, Jeanette Hurdle, Jessica Jacobs, Sudip Kar-Gupta, Jennifer lee, Sophie Lloyd, Rowena Macdonald, Paula McManus, Joanne O'Connel, Nick O'Meally, Anna Perkins, Joanna Quinn, Nikki Ratcliffe, Skeena Rathor, Arlene Russo, Elaine Sinclair, Kate Sleeman, Kathryn Smith, Ben Spriggs, James Toner, Paula Vincent, Mike Williams.
Special thanks to: Ian Carter, Ben Rich, Ed Suthon, Kevin White.

Design by: Colleen Crim

Published by: The Stationery Office

Push Online: www.push.co.uk

Copyright (c) Push Partnership 1992, 1993, 1994, 1995, 1996, 1997, 1998, 1999, 2001.

Ninth edition published in 2001 as The PUSH Guide to Which University 2002.
ISBN 0 11 702832 0
First published in 1992 as PUSH 93 (The Polytechnic & University Students' Handbook).
No part of this publication may be copied or reproduced, stored in a retrieval system or transmitted in any form or by any means electronic or mechanical or by photocopying, recording or otherwise without prior permission of the copyright owners.

Flunk rates:
Calculated by PUSH from data provided by the Higher Education Funding Council for England. Source of data: HEFCE Performance indicators in Higher Education, Tables of Indicators, 1997-1998, Table T5
Data used by permission of the Higher Education Funding Council for England. HEFCE cannot accept responsibility for any inferences or conclusions derived from the data by third parties.

Editorial:
PUSH
The Stationery Office
Nine Elms Lane
London SW9 5DR

Ordering:
The Stationery Office
PO Box 29, St Crispins House
Duke Street
Norwich NR3 1GN
Telephone: 0870 600 5522
Fax: 0870 600 5533

E-mail: editor@push.co.uk   E-mail: esupport@tso.co.uk
Push Online: www.push.co.uk Website: www.clicktso.co.uk

Push on

CONTENTS

4	*Push* power – **All about PUSH**
5	*Push* start – **Foreword by the NUS President**
6	*Push*over – **How to use PUSH**
15	*Push*links – **Other services from PUSH**
16	Applied *Push*ed – **Applying to university**
18	Hard *Push*ed – **Money matters**
22	*Push*ing out the boat – **Taking a year out**
24	*Push*ing on a bit – **Mature students**
25	Pleased as *Push* – **Welfare**
26	*Push*ing back the frontiers – **Students with disabilities**
27	*Push*grads – **Postgraduate students**
28	United we *Push* – **Students' Unions**
29	*Push*ing the pennies – **Charity Rags**

College profiles

687	*Push* other institutions
714	*Push*, of course – **Index of courses A-Z**
734	**Entry Requirements**
743	**Clubs & sports tables**
750	**Vital statistics tables**
756	**Top 10's**
758	When *Push* comes to shove – **Glossary**
769	Short, sharp *Push* – **Abbreviations**
770	*Push*ing on – **useful books and websites**
776	**Maps**
779	**Index**

Push power

Push is an independent organisation that collects the largest ever resource of information about student life in the UK.

Push distributes that information through five services:

The *Push* Guide to Which University – the best-selling guidebook (tip: you're reading it): essential facts, figures and opinions on every university in the UK.

The *Push* Guide to Choosing a University – top advice about choosing the right university for you.

The *Push* Guide to Money: Surviving as a Student – the lowdown on what you'll have to spend, what you'll have to spend it on and how the cost varies at each of the UK's universities.

The *Push* Online Guide to UK Universities (www.push.co.uk) – the website: the comprehensive interactive guide to finding your perfect university.
Push Visits – the personal touch: *Push* experts visit schools and colleges to give specialist advice.

DID YOU KNOW?

Over the past eight years, *Push* has employed more than 300 researchers, photographers and writers.
Push researchers visit every university in the UK.
Push's research probes the universities themselves, students' unions, public and Government bodies and thousands of students.
Each year *Push* generates over 10,000 pages of research.
Push's entire database of information is fully updated every year.
Push information has all been checked three times.
Push researchers and staff are high-flying students and recent graduates.
Push is the UK's most widely used resource to student life, used by students, teachers, careers advisers, parents, universities, Government bodies, political parties, media organisations and many others.
Push always strives to provide the most up-to-date information in the most accessible style at an affordable cost.

Everything we do is by students for students.

Push start

Foreword by Owain James, President of the National Union of Students

As a student today you have to make a lot of decisions. The first one is choosing the university that suits you best. Of course every institution will be happy to tell you what courses they offer, where their services are located and how many students graduate every year. But you want to know more than that. That's where *Push* comes in.

Push has developed a reputation for providing no-nonsense advice. Their guide is compiled by students and graduates who know what you need to know because they've been in the same position. They're good judges of the accommodation, entertainments, sports and welfare facilities that you could soon be using. *Push* is a lively and valuable resource.

You'll find contact details for students' unions in the guide. I recommend visiting some before you decide on a university, because it's in the union that you'll also get a down-to-earth view. Students' unions are at the centre of student life. NUS, representing three million students across the UK, plays a big part as well. Both are there for you to get involved in.

Wherever you choose to go I wish you all the best. Enjoy using *Push* and enjoy your time at university.

Owain James
NUS President

Push over

Using *The Push Guide* is a pushover. A 5-year old child could understand it, but before you rush out to find a 5-year old child because you can't make head nor tail of it, here's the idiots' guide to *The Push Guide* – also invaluable for gifted 5-year olds, vastly over-qualified academics and you...

The Push Guide has been designed and devised to make it as easy to use as possible, whatever you want to do with it.

Well, maybe if you want to use it as a pet, you're probably better off with a goldfish, but as a guide to real life at the UK's universities and colleges, it's the best there is.

The Push Guide isn't trying to replace UCAS or the colleges' own prospectuses. We're just lending a hand in what is frankly the sort of decision that has most people reaching for the pin cushion. *The Push Guide* provides the sort of information you really want to know in order to decide, not all that stuff about course codes and quotas which appears everywhere else.

And don't let anyone tell you your decision doesn't matter. Manchester Metropolitan, Warwick University and Christ's College, Cambridge may each do a maths course, but students are letting themselves in for more than algebra and calculus. Differentiation and integration mean something quite different when your chosen college becomes your home for the next few years.

Push tells you the real story and tells it straight. But there's no point just telling you that one college is the best and that everyone should go there. Everyone wants something different and every college offers something unique. What *The Push Guide* does is match you with the college of your dreams... or near enough.

The Push Guide backs up nearly everything with facts, figures and statistics and when nothing tells it better than an honest opinion, we're not ashamed to admit that it's a personal view – even if it is the best informed opinion available anywhere. In fact, we slap it in italics just so you know. Although our judgements are scrupulously researched and representative, we still advise a pretty hefty accompanying dose of salt. After all, even *Push's* opinion is still only an opinion.

With *The Push Guide* you can make comparisons and pin-point the features that you're looking for. The symbols, charts and maps give a quick and easy reference to the sort of factors that might really sway your decision, not just courses. The profiles for each college make it possible to check out whether they make the grade in the important parts other colleges cannot reach.

WHEN TO USE THE PUSH GUIDE:

Choosing a course is obviously one of the first things to do and *The Push Guide* provides a table of all courses on offer (see '*Push*, of course', page 714). Since you don't want to see essentially the same course listed under 93 different names in 203 different places, *Push* has standardised the names and listed them alphabetically by subject areas.

This means that you don't have to wade through pages of different institutions to find the few that offer the course you're looking for. A word of warning: the standardisation of nearly 10,000 degree courses means that some get grouped together in a way which would perhaps be objectionable to those who appreciate the

How to use Push

finer differences between Phonic Linguistics and Linguistic Phonemics. For exact details of any course, its contents and with which other courses it may be combined, check availability with the institutions themselves, their prospectuses or UCAS's listings.

If you know more or less what course you want to study and that course is not unusual – like Maths or English Literature, but not Cartesian Astrophysics with a side order of Sewage Managment – then, no problem, you can choose entirely on the strength of other factors as outlined in each college's *Push* profile. However, if the course is only offered at a few colleges, you should make a shortlist from the '*Push*, of course' lists (page 714) and then turn to the profiles for the clinching factors: Where is it? Is there any social life beyond a non-alcoholic cocktail bar and regular bus-spotting conventions? Is there a croquet club? Will it be possible to buy cigarettes at 3 in the morning?

Even for quite unusual courses, there are so many colleges to choose from that you should take the opportunity to get pushy – to demand exactly what you want, or as near as damn it.

But maybe you don't know what course you want to study, don't care or just haven't quite finalised it yet (it's still a toss up between Fine Art or Chemical Engineering, for example). Well, then there are no constraints – you can choose entirely on the basis of where you'd like to study and in what environment, rather than what you'd like to study.

Either way, *The Push Guide* is the best key to all the vital factors students have to put up with on a day-to-day basis. It's easy enough to chose the right course from a list of titles on a page, but to chose a place to live, to work, to rest, to play, to eat Mars bars, *The Push Guide* is needed, like bread.

NAMES AND CROSS-REFERENCING:
When all the old polytechnics became universities way back at the start of the 90s, we suddenly found ourselves with lorry-loads of universities with wacky names like De Montfort University (formerly Leicester Poly) and Liverpool John Moores University (formerly Liverpool Poly) which is named after the bloke who founded the Littlewoods Pools. However, since old habits die hard, if you look up a college under the old name you will find it cross-referenced to its new name anyway.

All the profiles are arranged alphabetically (ignoring the words 'University' or 'University of'), but some places like UEA (University of East Anglia) are sent simply to try the brains behind *Push*. Should it be U for 'UEA'? E for 'East'? Or A for 'Ah, we're in Norwich'? Well, if you can't beat 'em... put it under all three. However you try to look up even the most awkward of names you should find it cross-referenced.

THE PUSH SYMBOLS:
On the inside back cover, you'll find the key to the *Push* symbols – handy and at hand.

GLOSSARY & ABBREVIATIONS:
It's a jargon jungle out there. Everything in higher education would be so easy to understand if the colleges didn't insist on using acrid acronyms and tedious terminology all the time. In fact, it's a plot to stop the unemployed from becoming professors, but that's another (paranoid) story. *Push* unleashes the lingo in its 'Short, sharp *Push*' (Abbreviations, page 769) and 'When *Push* comes to shove' (Glossary, page 758).

OTHER OPTIONS:
Even though all the old polytechnics are now universities, you should still remember that higher education doesn't begin and end there. The choice for prospective students is bigger than Chris Evan's bar tab. We've included most of the non-university institutions which offer their own degree courses in a separate chapter (see page 687). There's thousands more universities abroad. And how about vocational training, rather than a degree? Free your mind and your pants will follow.

The Push Guide can't include all the options – it would be thousands of pages long, years out of date, cost the earth and be impossible to pick up, let alone read. Apart from that, we like the idea.

GETTING IN TOUCH:
We crave feedback. We love it. We would crawl naked over splintered glass to hear what you have to say about *Push*. Unless, that is, you just want to slag us off or sue us for libel. Please then keep your comments to yourself. (Unfettered and pointless flattery is very welcome.) However, assuming you have some worthwhile and constructive response, not necessarily positive, please feel free to write to *Push*, TSO, Nine Elms Lane, London, SE1, or e-mail us at editor@push.co.uk.

For next year's edition, we will again need researchers with an unassailable sense of duty and a streak of masochism – if you think we might not slam the door in your face whilst doubling up in fits of giggles, please drop us a line with reasons why you meet *Push's* exacting standards.

Making the most of the college profiles

NAMES:
As a headline, *The Push Guide* uses the name most students use or the most convenient title. So, for example, LSE is LSE, not the London School of Economics & Political Science. The college's exact name is used in the address, if you really need to know.

ADDRESSES:
For each college, *The Push Guide* lists the address and telephone number of the administration and of the students' unions, as well as any fax numbers or e-mail addresses there might be. If there is more than one site, the address of the main site is given, or if there is more than one main site, we say, what the hey, and give them all.

GENERAL

STATISTICS
All statistics were right up to the minute of going to press and *Push* is really, really cut up if they're wrong later, but, hell, that's the way it goes. Some institutions, for various reasons, don't release certain statistics. Although we are not known for willingly taking 'no' for an answer, *Push* follows the old journalistic maxim, 'If in doubt, leave it out'. We suggest readers should follow the cynics' maxim, 'What are they trying to hide?'

Founded: Many colleges have hazy histories either too deep in the clouds of time or involving too many complicated mergers and changes of name to have just one founding year. Some newer institutions, desperate to appear venerable and ivy-covered, prefer to give the founding date of an obscure technical college on the other side of town that eventually morphed into the current institution after 14 name changes and multiple mergers. *Push*, however, has used the latest techniques (a step beyond the 'Eeny-Meeny-Miny-Mo Principle') to select just one year and, if further clarification is worthwhile, it's explained elsewhere in the profile.

Full-time u'grads: This includes students on sandwich courses, which are nothing to do with learning what to put between slices of bread, but courses where some time is spent not actually studying but on a work placement.

Part-time: Those on undergraduate courses only.

Postgrads: Full-time postgraduate students (who've already taken a degree).

Non-degree: Often HND (Higher National Diploma) students but all sorts of vocational, access and pre-degree courses might be offered, especially at newer universities. Again, figures are for full-time students.

Ave course: Strictly speaking, for the pedantic statisticians out there, this is the modal length of courses. Or, in English, the most common course length.

Ethnic: Some institutions prefer not to ask their students to classify themselves into one racial box or another; others are concerned to keep tabs on the ethnic origins of students, in order to ensure no bias or discrimination is occurring. Criteria for definition will vary but this figure should give a pretty good idea of the cultural mix at a particular institution.

Private school: The proportion of undergraduates educated at a privately-funded secondary school. Nationally, the proportion of students from private schools is about 20%.

Flunk rate: This is an indication of the percentage of full-time undergraduates who, for one reason or another, don't successfully complete their course by being awarded a degree or even dropping to a lower qualification such as an HND. The national average is 15.7% (more than 1 in 6) with figures for individual institutions ranging from 1.3% to 38.1% – yes, that's right, at some institutions well over a third of students don't get a degree.

Our flunk use data supplied by HEFCE, the Higher Education Funding Council of England. These figures project how many students who started in 1997-98 will not gain a degree and doesn't count those who transfer to another university.

Mature students: Those aged 21 or over at the time of starting their courses. Postgrads are not included.

Overseas students: Includes EU students from outside the UK.

Disabled students: These figures are obtained from the colleges who, if they keep records at all, often define 'disabled' differently. Some include only registered disabled students, others extend the definition to students with dyslexia, asthma or any students who, for whatever reason, choose to define themselves as disabled.

'Text in italics is Push's point of view – take it or leave it.'

ATMOSPHERE:
This section in the profiles, more than any other, gives the real feel of the place.

TRAVEL:
Trains & buses: Fares given are the best we've been able to find at the time of writing (though it can be beyond even *Push* to get a straight answer out of National Rail Enquiries at times). That means the cheapest possible return journey with a student discount card or apex ticket. Some of these don't apply at certain times of the day and apex tickets have to be bought at least 2 weeks in advance.
Hitching: *Push* would like to warn readers that if they don't know that hitching can be dangerous, then there is something wrong with them. *Push* accepts no responsibility for students who have bad experiences when thumbing it, such as waiting 6 hours in the rain for a lift, being picked up by Capri-driving 'X-Files' obsessives or being made to listen to Billie Piper on the car stereo.

FAMOUS ALUMNI:
A bit of celebrity gossip – who went where. Just so students can boast that they're going to same college as that famous 1920s Swiss serial killer or whoever.

FURTHER INFORMATION:
Prospectuses are absolutely essential if you're seriously considering applying to an institution and invaluable for seeing what the college would like you to think of them. They are sales documents and whilst almost every word will be true, it will not be the truth, the whole truth and nothing but the truth. They are available from the address at the top of each profile.

On the other hand, some students' unions publish 'alternative' prospectuses, which present the point of view of students at the college. Also worth getting, although the views contained are almost exclusively biased and, since the writers have rarely visited a representative number of colleges, not very comparative.

We've also listed any videos, CD-roms, websites or other sources of information. Some are just prospectuses dumped on the 'net – others are more revealing. Where possible we give the address for the SU website, as well as the official university one. If you've got the time and the facilities, check them out.

The teaching standard is:

 barely hovering

 flying

 soaring high

ACADEMIC STATS:

Staff/student ratios: This isn't as straightforward as it may appear. Part-time staff and students can muddy the statistical waters. But it gives you a rough idea of whether tutorials are going to be cosy little sherry sessions a deux, or rugby scrums with the tutor as the ball.

Range of points required for entrance: You'll need to know whether you're likely to be able to get in and so here's the top and bottom benchmarks that the college uses based on the UCAS points tariff (see '*Push* in: Entrance Requirements', page 734). Not every course requires the same points though. You may need 300 points to get into a university's law degree, for instance, but be able to get into the same place to do catering and tourism with just 80. But it's not as cut and dried as some people make out. It depends how you gather your points – what qualifications and in what subjects. For example, AS levels aren't really worth as much as the UCAS points tariff claims and you can have 360 points in English, French and history A Levels, but it won't get you in to study physics even if they claim to only want 200 points. In the end, you'll have to double check with the university anyway about what points they'd want from you for an individual course.

Clearing: The percentage of students who entered through the UCAS clearing system. Some institutions have (sometimes undeserved) reputations as UCAS dumping grounds. This figure should give an idea of the number of students whose presence isn't entirely by choice. UCAS don't release figures for individual institutions and understandably, some universities are a little coy about revealing this figure.

Number/length of terms/semesters: Different colleges split up the year differently. Some have three short terms, others have two long ones. It may not seem all that important, but, apart from anything else, if the vacations are shorter, odds are you won't be earning as much money in the vacations.

Research: The average figure for the college based on the last Government-funded Research Assessment Exercise (which was in 1996). It's judged on a scale of 1 to 7 where 1 is crap and 7 means they're international research superstars. For undergrads, the level of research isn't as directly important as colleges would like you to think, but it is a good general indicator of a top notch department.

LIBRARIES:

Unless otherwise stated, we give the total number of books in all the college libraries, not just the main library.

COMPUTERS:

For study places and computer workstations, we give the number available for general use and don't include places or terminals set aside exclusively for students on a particular course.

A lecturer at Newcastle brought the whole admissions procedure to a standstill with his Newcastle United Supporters' website.

ENTERTAINMENT

Beer is:

 expensive

 average

 cheap

BEER & WINE:
Prices of beer and wine are given as the average at student bars and in towns. There are of course likely to be the usual guest ales and local specials.

SOCIAL & POLITICAL

The SU's activities and facilities are:

 frozen stiff

 lukewarm

 hot, hot, hot

CLUBS & SOCS:
Clubs and societies have been split into sporting and non-sporting, which isn't always easy. *The Push Guide* has put them under whichever heading the college uses and you'd be well advised to check under both headings if the existence of a certain club is really important to you. Since it would get a bit repetitive otherwise, we've missed out the ones which crop up just about everywhere in the college profiles, but to be sure that the club you want is at the college you're looking at, turn to the 'clubs & societies' tables at the back (page 744). The only ones usually missed out are the course-related societies (for sucking up to tutors).

Of course, if you've decided that somewhere is perfect apart from the fact that it doesn't have a 'South Park' Fan Club, you shouldn't dismiss it out of hand. At most colleges it's fairly easy to start a society – you only need to find between 20 and 50 others to say they want to join and the SU may well give you a packet to spend on parkas, overpriced merchandising and that vital sight-seeing trip to Colorado.

SPORTS

Student sport is:

 slobbish

 average

 active and triumphant

ACCOMMODATION

The average rent is:

 expensive

 average

 cheap

ACCOMMODATION:
Colleges tend to transform mysteriously into conference centres the moment vacations start, so if you're in halls you may well get turfed out with all your belongings to allow some pantyhose salesman to attend a corporate beerfest. *The Push Guide* gives a weekly cost and how many weeks you're going to be paying. Also given are the percentages of full-time undergraduates living in catered and self-catered accommodation. Bear in mind that 'catered' can mean anything from the full-board of 3 square meals a day and a Harrods hamper for your picnics, to a single 'pay-as-you-eat' canteen which you have to catch a bus to get to and which serves cockroaches in the soup.

As well as costs, *The Push Guide* also gives you details of the availability and standard of college accommodation and the kinds of security arrangements you can expect. As if that weren't enough there's even information on local housing.

```
The Trinity Foot Beagles at Cambridge kill
hares. The Trinity Foot Bagels, however, smear
each other with cream cheese.
```

WELFARE

The welfare provisions is:

 poor

 passable

 pampering

FINANCIAL:
Access funds: When student loans were introduced in 1990, the Government made some money available to colleges to help avoid the problems that were likely to arise for students who were less able to pay. The figures given are the total amount each college is currently allocated. Students who want a slice of the cake should apply annually to their college, but not until they get there. Other sources of available income are listed below this figure.
Successful applications: The number of students who get a slice of the cake gives an indication of how large a slice they each got. Some colleges were only willing or able to provide figures as a percentage. Others couldn't give us any figures at all, or wouldn't because they're 'orrible.

A former member of Glamorgan University Rag holds the world record for standing in a bucket of maggots.

Push Links: Other services from Push

Push is an independent organisation that does more annual research into UK student life than anyone else.

The Push Guide to Which University is just one of the services we provide to university applicants and, since all of them are designed to work together to help you make the best decision and to support you once you've made it, we might as well take this opportunity for a plug.

THE *PUSH* GUIDE TO CHOOSING A UNIVERSITY
You may be wondering why you need to bother with half the information contained in The Push Guide to Which University. Stuff like the price of beer - that's obviously important, but why, for instance, should you care how many staff the careers service has or whether the accommodation is catered or self-catering?
 The answer is that these are the very things that really affect student life and mean that not only are no two universities the same, they all differ radically, with strengths weaknesses and mediocrities.
 The Push Guide to Choosing a University explains all those difference, why they matter and how they affect your life as a student. It's also jam-packed with tips about choosing and it dissects the application process, student funding and, perhaps best of all, has Push's unique Choosing a Uni Questionnaire to help you design your ideal institution and find which comes closest.

PUSH ONLINE - WWW.PUSH.CO.UK
The ultimate interactive guide to UK universities. Get the Push lowdown on every UK university, links to university and student websites, and like it is information and advice on every aspect of being a student and applying to university.
 For subscribers, our interactive tools take the guess work out of finding the perfect university. Punch in your preferences for an instant shortlist, then go head-to-head with your top choices to compare entertainment, accommodation, sport, travel, and every other aspect of student life with Push's in-depth university profiles.
 There's loads of free information - including short, sharp profiles of every UK univesrity - plus extra goodies for those that part with some cash. If your school, college or careers service isn't a subscriber yet, they should be soon. Nag them for us, would you?

THE *PUSH* GUIDE TO MONEY: STUDENT SURVIVAL
 Perhaps the biggest issue for students today is the cost of it all. In Push's unique tell-it-like-it-is-style, we explain what you'll have to spend, what you'll have to spend it on and how to get by.
 The Push Guide to Money also gives unique details of how important costs differ at every university in the UK.
 More coming soon...
 Push's ongoing commitment to applicants means that we'll not rest until we've provided everything goddamn thing we can think of to help you pick the right university for you.
 Already our experts give talks in schools and colleges throughout the country and we'll be launching yet more new books and services soon. Watch this space.

FOR MORE INFORMATION ABOUT PUSH OR PUSH SERVICES
Please contact...
The Stationery Office
PO Box 29
ST Crispins House
Duke Street
Norwich NR3 1GN
Telephone: 0870 600 5522
Fax: 0870 6005533
Web: www.clicktso.com
...or visit www.push.co.uk

Applied *PUSH*: Getting in to university

So. How do you get into university? Some say you need a degree to understand how to apply for a degree. *Push* cuts through the jargon and tells you how it really works.

The first piece of jargon you need to learn is UCAS (pron 'you-cass'), the Universities and Colleges Admissions Service. They manage the application process for most universities and colleges in the UK, though they don't have anything to do with deciding who actually goes where.

Every May they send out application forms to schools and colleges and a handbook or CD-rom listing all the universities and all the courses available. The form has spaces for applying to up to 6 courses, but you don't have to use them all. You can apply to the same course at up to 6 different universities, 6 different courses at the same university, or, indeed, 6 different courses at 6 different universities. The first technique is usually the one to go for, as universities like to feel you've got at least some idea of what you want to do.

You'll also be asked all sorts of questions about what grades you've got in the past, what exams you're taking in the future and how you justify your existence to date. It's your main chance to convince the universities how committed you are to the course you've chosen, how brilliant you'll be at it and what a generally fab person you'd be to have around.

There's also a section that the school fills in where they either sing your praises or chant your funeral dirge. They'll also say what they think you're likely to get in your A Levels, Highers or other exams. Unfortunately, you don't get to see what they've said about you because when they've added their comments, they send the form straight back to UCAS.

UCAS starts accepting forms from the end of September. If you're applying for Oxford or Cambridge it'll need to be in by 15th October, otherwise you've got until 15th December to get your act together. If it arrives after that UCAS will still process your application, but they'll probably spill coffee on it and write insults all over it. More seriously, the universities will only consider your application if they've got places left.

You should get an acknowledgement fairly quickly that UCAS have received your form and another within the next six weeks which gives you an application number and a record of what UCAS thinks you've applied for.

Meanwhile the universities get copies of your form and write to you direct with their decisions.

They'll either make you a conditional offer, effectively saying that if you get certain grades in your A levels or other forthcoming exams, then they'll take you.

Or they might make an unconditional offer, saying they'll take you whatever your grades, but this isn't likely unless you've already done some A Levels, Highers or equivalent.

Or they might turn you down outright.

Or they'll ask you for interview. In which case you get a good chance to check out the place.

If you get an interview, be prepared. Be keen. Be enthusiastic. Above all, be yourself. If you're worried about it, grab your careers adviser or nearest friendly teacher and insist they help you. Remind them that they chose their atrociously paid profession for love rather than money.

After the interview, the university will either make you a conditional or unconditional offer or they'll reject you. If you don't get in, console yourself with the fact that thousands of other hopeful students also got turned down and besides, you didn't want to go to that nasty dump anyway.

UCAS will send you a note of the universities' decisions as they make them. Whatever they say, you don't have to respond until you've got a full set of replies from all the universities you applied to. You should hear from them all, one way or another by, at the latest, the end of April and, when you hear from the last one, UCAS will send you a summary of all the responses.

If you've got any unconditional offers, you can reject them right away or accept one, go away, relax and prepare to start that course at the beginning of the next year.

If you've got more than two conditional offers, then you've got to dump some. You've also got to say which is your favourite and firmly accept it. That means that if you manage to meet whatever conditions they've made then that's where you're off to. You are allowed to keep a back up (or 'insurance') offer by provisionally accepting another offer with easier conditions. That means if you don't make the grades for your first choice, you've still got somewhere to go.

It is possible that none of your choices will make you offers, or maybe that you'll decide after an interview that you don't like the place. Alternatively, maybe you just won't make the grade for either of the two offers you've kept. In this case, you've got two choices. Either take a year out and go through the whole process again. Or try to go through clearing.

Clearing is the mad scramble that takes place between the day the exam results come out and the first day of the universities' new terms, where students without a university place try to get matched up with university courses that don't have enough students. Although it's all masterminded by UCAS in theory, in practice they don't have much to do with it and this time you get to approach universities directly.

Be careful, though, if you end up in Clearing, not just to jump at the first place you get offered. Clearing gets the iciest maidens hot and bothered and it's easy to end up on a course you don't like at a university you hate.

It's important to pick a course and a university that suit you as an individual – if you don't, you may live to regret it. More than 1 in 6 students don't successfully complete the course they start and the proportion is highest among those who get in through clearing.

If you're not at school or college in the UK you can get your UCAS form and courses listings from UCAS, Fulton House, Jessop Avenue, Cheltenham, Gloucs, GL50 3SH. Tel: 01242 227788. You can also order copies on their website (www.ucas.ac.uk).

Students from outside the EU should apply directly to the universities they are interested in. The same applies to most postgraduate and some specialist arts courses.

Hard *PUSH*ed

Nowadays, being a student is almost the same as being in debt, but there are ways of stashing the cash and diverting the debts.

If you're thinking about embarking on a course of study at a UK university or college, you should be thinking about debt at the same time. The two go together like cream cheese and bagels (only not so tasty). Debt has become such a fact of life for most students that some fall into a state of paralysis about the whole thing and never really deal with the problem. *Push* can't wave a magic cliché and make debts disappear but we can come up with a few ideas to help students make the best out of a situation roughly equivalent to swimming the Atlantic with Pavarotti strapped to your knees.

At the brink of a promising career, starting with being accepted to university or college, most students don't want to think of the poverty they are going to have to put up with until they land that cushy job in merchant banking, marketing or medicine. Still less, if they are looking forward to a career where the greatest reward will be job satisfaction, such as teaching, social work or even acting.

However, there is little point starting a course you are not going to be able to afford to finish. Students have to ask themselves, 'How am I going to make ends meet?'.

If the answer is that your parents are so phenomenally wealthy and indulgent that they'll give you all the cash you need, then your problems are over. But, for those on this side of the rainbow, there are a number of issues to consider.

In fact, there are so many that we've produced a book all about it – *The Push Guide to Money: Student Survival*. It covers everything to do with student finance – what you'll have to spend, what you'll have to spend it on and how to put the fun back into funding. Rush out and steal a copy now (it's only £7.99, but you might as well start saving now).

If you didn't take that advice and you're still reading the following brief guide may help till you realise you need that truly excellent publication.

ECONOMISE

Whatever other options you take, economy is always the one that puts shoes on your feet. Decide what's important and pay for that. Then see how much money you have left and decide what else you'd like if possible. Plan expenditure – on a weekly basis if your income's tight – and stick to your plan.

Be pessimistic. Optimistic students don't check their balance when they shove their cards in the cash machine and sooner or later their card gets swallowed. Realists check their balance and then get out half the amount they wanted. Pessimists don't bother going to

 slobbish

 average

 active and triumphant

 expensive

 average

 cheap

the cashpoint because they know the hole-in-the-wall has been designed to swallow them. Hence they preserve enough readies to live a miserly, but not miserable existence.

As with most things, sensible moderation is the key. Students who are so desperate to economise that they never set foot in the SU bar and don't buy anything not directly related to food, shelter or academic survival may well come out the other end with a first class degree and a bank balance in the black but they might have missed out on many of the life experiences that make a degree course worthwhile. Students usually have to accept that Maserati and Armani aren't going to be on the shopping list for the next 3 or 4 years but the odd pint of beer or the next Chemical Brothers album aren't going to cast you into the fires of debt hell either.

GOVERNMENT FUNDING

Few things in life get quite so confusing as the current student funding situation over the last few years. *Push*, as ever, is here to help you tell the wood from the deforestation trucks and find out how you'll be affected.

First off, grants may rest in peace. From now on, you may have to find money for tuition fees and you'll certainly have to find your living costs or maintenance.

TUITION FEES

It will come as news only to those who have been in Timbuktu with their heads buried in an elephant's bottom, that the Government has introduced means-testing for tuition fees for undergraduate courses. This means that your local LEA (local education authority or equivalent) may no longer pay the full cost of your tuition at university.

How much lolly you have to fork out will usually depend on how much your parents earn. If your parents' income is about £30,000 before tax or more, you'll have to pay £1,075 towards your fees. If your parents' income is less than that, but more than about £20,000, you'll have to pay between £45 and £1,075. If your parents' income is less than £20,000, you won't have to pay fees at all and your LEA will pay the full whack.

There are a few exceptions to the rules outlined above:
(1) Scottish students on courses at Scottish universities and colleges don't have to pay fees. Instead they pay an 'endowment' of £2,000 when they graduate. However, students from the rest of the UK who study at Scottish institutions will have to pay fees for the whole of their course (including the extra year that most degrees last in Scotland).
(2) Students on a course or industrial placement year will pay a reduced fee of up to £535 (again, dependent on income) for that year.
(3) Overseas students will have to pay fees, except students from Europe who will probably qualify to get their fees paid.

Whatever the case and whatever your parents' income, you should still apply to your LEA for tuition fees awards, or you'll end up paying rather more than £1,000.

LOANS

A loan is money borrowed and don't you forget it. There are two fundamental problems with borrowing money: (i) sooner or later, whoever lent it will want it back, and (ii) they will want more than they lent in the first place. This applies whether it is borrowed from a bank, the Student Loans Company, a building society, whoever.

There are two possible exceptions. If they can afford it, students' parents often give them interest-free loans and many recognise that the likelihood of seeing it again is somewhat smaller than meeting June Whitfield at a death metal concert. On average, more than a fifth of a student's debt is to their parents. Sometimes, friends can be persuaded to lend each other a few quid to get by, but this is usually the quickest way to lose friends. Especially if they're students too, because the chances are they'll have financial problems of their own.

Student bank accounts often offer free overdraft facilities of £1,000 and even more. After the limit though, interest rates can be gob-stoppingly high, especially if the overdraft is unagreed. Students who intend to exceed their agreed limit, should tell the bank about it first. It's frightening as hell, but they're much nicer when they know what's going on and they send fewer rude letters and charge lower interest. They might, of course, say no, but they rarely cut students off without a penny so long as they've shown a responsible attitude.

Each year, almost all students can also apply for a Government-funded Student Loan from the inspiringly titled Student Loans Company. This is to cover living costs and, if they have to pay them, their tuition fees.

It's not, as rumour sometimes has it, interest-free. Interest is fixed at the rate of inflation; it's a cheaper loan than most, but it's not just a grant which has to be paid back. Repayments will start when a student has graduated and is earning £10,000 a year. However, the amount they have to pay back each month is linked to how much they earn, rather than how much they've borrowed.

To get a Student Loan you need to apply to your LEA as part of the process of applying for them to pay a share of your tuition fees. They'll confirm that you're eligible and tell you how much you can claim, though you have to ask the Student Loans Company for the actual dosh. This means that you can get everything sorted before you start your course, which should be handy for paying your first rent cheque.

Student Loans aren't available to postgraduates or overseas students and if in any doubt, check on your eligibility.

In 2001-2 all students will be entitled to the following amounts for each full year and for the final year (which doesn't include the summer):

	Full year	Final year
Students living away from their parents:		
in London	£3,525	£3,055
elsewhere	£2,860	£2,485
Students living with their parents:	£2,265	£1,975

Part of the new loan will be also be means-tested, ie. they'll look at what your parents earn and decide whether you need extra. All students will be able to claim the amounts above, but if your family is on a low income, you may be eligible for more money (an extra 25%), up to the following maximum amounts:

	Full year	Final year
Students living away from their parents:		
in London	£4,700	£4,075
elsewhere	£3,815	£3,310
Student living with their parents	£3,020	£2,635

There are other operations students can borrow from such as credit card companies and loan sharks, but if you do go down this path, check out the interest rates first and see what advance Satan will give on your soul. (It may be a better offer.)

JOBS, SPONSORSHIPS AND MORE

Earning a bob or two helps maximise income and, since working time can't be spent spending, it can even help minimise outgoings. The problem is finding a good job. For those who can find work from the employment agencies which don't have 'No Students' signs in the windows, too often it's a toss-up between valuable work experience for less than a condom machine earns in a convent, or dreadful drudgery for only reasonable readies.

There's also the problem of a job interfering with study. Students rarely find time to do more than a little bar work during term and just because some people call that five week period between terms 'the holidays', it doesn't mean they don't have dissertations, essays, field trips, projects and so on. Some unions and colleges run their own employment agencies or offer work to their own students – obviously they're much more likely to be sympathetic about the need to juggle paid work with academic commitments.

Earning extras is all very well, but except for those with a specially marketable talent (such as being bilingual, able to type at 80 wpm or having insider knowledge about the 2:30 at Chepstow), students should never rely on what they might make. Therefore, pessimism intact, it's best to leave it out of the equation when calculating budgets.

Some employers offer schemes whereby students are subsidised for the duration of their courses, usually in exchange for work during the vacation or after graduation. The armed forces and science/technology based organisations are usually the best bet for this – if you're one of those admirably and unfeasibly sussed people who mapped out what they wanted to do with their lives at the age of 12 it could be worthwhile contacting employers in your chosen field and seeing what they have to offer.

Some universities and colleges also have their own set of sponsorships and bursaries, many of which are dependent on studying a certain subject or having been born in a particular county on a Thursday when Aquarius was in the ascendant. There might not be much available but, again, it's always worth checking out the possibilities. In many cases, these schemes are being restructured to help students meet tuition fees and living costs in the wake of the new funding developments.

For some students, financial salvation comes in the form of a sandwich course. These involve doing a work placement at some point in the course for periods of anything from a few months up to a whole year. Apart from getting work experience, sandwich students usually get paid while they're working. It may not clear all their debts, but it can certainly fill a pretty big hole at the bank.

TOP TIPS

Finally a couple of cunning ploys to employ...
(1) Make a budget. Work out how much you're going to get from your loan, your parents and any other sources of income and then subtract your rent, allowances for food, bills, travel, clothes, books and other stuff you need for your course, insurance and even a bit for beer money. This will probably be a scary and educational process, striking such fear into you that you tak a sensible attitude to money

throughout your student career. If it isn't scary, either you're very rich, very brave or you've got your sums wrong.

(2) Whether they think they need it or not, students should take up a student loan. You almost certainly will and it's better to have the money in the bank when you need it than realise your stony broke and only then start the application process which, if you're desperate for cash seems to take forever. It's certainly better than making futile attempts to stay in the black. They won't work and they won't last.

(3) Even if you definitely don't need one, take out a student loan anyway. Borrow the money and invest it elsewhere. The interest charged on a student loan is pegged to the rate of inflation, currently 2.6%pa. In most building societies, it's easy enough to earn at least twice that in interest on investments over £500. ISAs can pay slightly more at 6.5% with 45 days notice. So you're quids in, whatever.

(4) Students who can apply for state benefits, should do. Unfortunately, when student loans were introduced, students also became the only members of society not entitled to normal benefits because of their occupation. Students are not allowed to collect either unemployment benefit during their vacations if they cannot find work and are not allowed to claim housing benefit. In London, where rents are often well over £65 a week, this has proved particularly harsh. It doesn't take much maths to realise that at that level, rent alone is £3,380, leaving a princely sum of £1,100 for books, travel, food and so on – and that's assuming you get the full loan. However, students with disabilities or with dependents will still find they can claim some benefits.

(5) Stay friends with your bank. Never go beyond your overdraft limit without getting permission. They'll send you rude letters and – to add insult to injury – they'll charge you for them. They'll also fine you for breaking the rules and whack a big interest rate on your borrowings.

(6) Get advice. Banks are always willing to provide a pearl or two of wisdom on budgeting and the like and students' unions have all sorts of resources to help make the most of money and to lend a hand if things get too hot to handle.

(7) Use *The Push Guide to Which University* 2002 to choose a university that suits your budget. Not all universities cost the same.

(8) Now read *The Push Guide to Money: Student Survival* to become more of an expert on student finance than you ever thought possible (or ever wanted to be).

*Push*ing out the boat

A look at the pros and cons of taking a year out before going on to higher education.

Why do students consider taking a year off? They're young once, so why waste time not getting on with life? Why don't they just get a degree, get a job and get an income? Why don't they choose life, choose a pension plan, choose 2.4 kids, a Tesco charge account and a 34-inch telly with surround sound with a boob-job thrown in? Why don't they take the short cut and just coat themselves in compost and rot?

Why? Because it's more fun to spend a year getting up to the kind of thing they can only do when they've got the youth and the opportunity, when they haven't got kids and when slumming it round the Amazon basin doesn't leave bits of mosquito in their dentures.

But it's not all fun and opportunity-seizing, there are real practical advantages too. Far from the old view that time out is worthless bumming around, a constructive year off is now an immense asset in the competitive job market. An extended CV is better than a brown envelope stuffed with used fifties when it comes to sending out job applications. Students who've taken a year out or spent their long vacations broadening their horizons, have got more to offer to a potential employer. They stand out from the crowd at every opportunity and not just because they smell funny. It won't get them a position for which they're not qualified, but all things being equal, it helps.

With little or no real work experience, employers will have to make judgements based on qualifications and nobody's fooled for a moment into thinking that a degree in politics or an A level in physics is relevant to a career in marketing, management or merchant banking. If they can find something to pick a student out from the rest of the pack, they'll home in like wasps on spiked lager. Many employers even discriminate against students who spent long summer vacations living with their parents, staying in bed and watching 'Teletubbies'.

Another reason some students take a year out is simply to work and store up their cash to see them through university. There are very few ways to avoid being in debt after graduation, but one of them is to have cash before you start. NUS estimates that the current average student debt on graduation is around £13,000. You might not be able to stash that sort of money away in one year before college, but you could make a dent.

But during a year out, time can be even more valuable than money. Even if money's tight, with time, you can always find a way to get away or get up to something worthwhile. Time is necessary – money isn't. Even a bout of globe-trotting doesn't have to cost the earth. It's all too easy to think cash is needed for a good time and so students sit around waiting for a job that doesn't turn up. They'd be better off using that waiting time to get out of the rut and out of the country.

Of course, some ventures do require money – for example, for a six-month expedition across Africa, several hundred quid minimum up front would be needed. But there are also ways of getting overseas for less than £100, such as crewing on a yacht to the Caribbean, being a youth leader at an American summer camp or picking fruit on a kibbutz in Israel. One thing leads to another and other opportunities open up. Travel breeds confidence, which breeds success.

If you plan to work and travel overseas, it's worth pausing to consider aims and objectives. To promote the environment? To conserve wildlife? To make some money? Or simply have a unique experience, filled with self discovery? These things are all very well, but never forget the fun factor.

You shouldn't worry about what you think you should do – you should do what you really want to. Time out doesn't have to be politically correct – a year spent ski bumming in Switzerland is not inferior to one spent helping orphans in India or saving a rain forest in South East Asia.

Whatever you end up doing – even if you eventually decide to stay at home and get work experience (or re-sit exams) – you shouldn't expect non-stop action. You're unlikely to complete a trans-Africa expedition without getting stomach problems, very unlikely to sail across the Atlantic without getting sea sick and there's no chance of going to Australia without getting hungover. But new friends, knowledge, self-confidence and experience will make the sacrifices worthwhile.

When, after a year out, a student becomes a fresher, you can always tell they're not straight from school. They're the ones for whom new challenges are not quite such a fresh experience. Or maybe just the insufferably arrogant ones.

*Push*ing on a bit: Mature students

A few wise words for mature students and returners to higher education.

First off, a mature student is not necessarily someone who wears cardigans and shakes their greying or balding head in a responsible way saying, 'It's not like it was in my day'. Nor necessarily are they pushing on a bit.

Students can be classified as mature from as young as 21. That means if you were alive on this earth the first time 'Star Wars' was released, let alone old enough to have actually seen it, you'll be classed as a mature student. The only generally accepted definition is that mature students are not the same age as conventional students and they are (with a few exceptions) not coming to higher education straight from school.

If you are returning to education, there are special considerations to be taken into account which vary enormously from one college to another. There's no need to accept sloppy seconds and just make do when it comes to higher education – there's enough choice to put your foot down and set an agenda according to your own specific needs.

Most students' unions (SUs) provide some facilities for mature students such as common rooms, mature student groups and specialised welfare advice. Make a checklist of needs from housing through to entertainment which will make a difference to which college you choose.

Although mature students often have roots and ties which may be an incentive to look no further than the most local college, many will find that special provisions for mature students may make a broader search worthwhile.

Some colleges provide specialised packages which are centred on people who have not just left the parental home. For example, many offer off-campus self-catering accommodation, others have specialised flats for mature students with their partner (usually only if married) and even their children, though it's rare to find places that can accommodate more than one child per couple. The college will probably also provide house hunting info for those who'd rather go it alone. The Accommodation Officer will be most handy for this – SU's accommodation help is generally geared mainly to conventional students.

As for social life, most entertainments centre around the SU rather than the college. *The Push Guide* gives the low-down on the goings-on, but bear in mind that bars may be full of students who for the first time don't have to prove their age to buy a pint and discos will be aimed at groovy young things who think Depeche Mode is a setting on their hi-fi (though you can always wow them with your intimate knowledge of 80s pop lyrics on retro night). From gigs to grub, what do you want to do? And does the college you're looking at provide it?

If appropriate, check about childcare facilities as many colleges are only beginning to develop services in this area. *The Push Guide* tells you whether there's a creche, but under that description can be anything from well-staffed care at subsidised cost for children from 6 months to 5 years old to some nobody who fancied a spot of babysitting, swamped by squawking brats and tipped up paint pots. In most colleges, the SU is either the main provider of childcare facilities on campus or knows best what provisions are available and will give an honest opinion of how good they are. Either get in touch in person – talk to the Welfare Officer – or ask for a copy of the SU handbook or alternative prospectus.

Although many students are aged over 21, the mainstream of facilities still caters for the 18+ age range. Mature students can feel isolated and so it's useful if there are others in the same boat and a forum for them to meet. Some SUs provide better support than others and many mature student groups organise their own functions. Under the Welfare section, *The Push Guide says* whether there is a mature students' association.

Also in the vital statistics panel in the general section of each college profile, we provide figures for the percentage of matures students. Naturally enough, this is one of the best indicators of how well geared up the university may be for mature students. After all, there's safety in numbers. Or failing that, other people to moan with.

Pleased as *Push*: Welfare

Student life has its ups and downs and welfare is the safety net for the down times, the support system provided by universities and colleges for students to help with their health, happiness and fortunes.

Universities do worry about students beyond whether get their essays in and pay their tuition fees on time. They also worry about their welfare. After all, if students aren't healthy, wealthy (or solvent) and happy, they're hardly likely to get their essays in or pay their tuition fees on time.

Most provide services to look after students: (a) their health, including doctors, nurses and, sometimes, physiotherapists, chiropracters, psychiatrists and so on; (b) their well-being and happiness, including councellors and advisers trained to deal with all the problems likely to be faced by students, including exam stress, depression and sexual problems; and (c) their finance, including debt counsellors, hardship funds, emergency loans, bursaries and some scholarships. Most universities also have services to help student find housing and deal with accommodation problems and some have advice systems for legal difficulties.

Often some or even all of these services are provided by the students' union or they provide complementary services, such as academic appeals representation, financial help and nightline – a Samaritans-style free and confidential phone service, staffed by trained students.

As well as the provisions from the universities and unions (found in the Welfare section of each college profile), here are some other helpful contacts:
Alchoholics Anonymous: Local groups of recovered alcoholics provide support for those wishing to stop drinking. Local lines in each area manned by volunteers.

Bisexual Phoneline: Offers listening and referral to local and national groups. 0131 557 3620 (Thurs 7.30pm-9.30pm).
Brook Centre: Provides free, confidential sex advice and contraception to people under 25. 0800 0185 023
Eating Disorders Association (EDA): Offers support and mutual care to those suffering from Anorexia or Bulimia Nervosa, and their families. 01603 765050 (Youth Helpline 4pm-6pm) 01603 621414 (General Helpline 9am-6.20pm).
Get Connected: A free confidential helpline for young people that will put them in touch with the right help they need. 0800 096 0096 (Every day from 5pm till late).
Lesbian Youth Support Information Service: Runs a service to support young lesbians. 01706 817235 (Helpline 7pm-9pm Weds only and Admin during office hours).
London Lesbian and Gay Switchboard: National service for lesbians, gays and anyone needing support regarding their sexuality. Information, advice, listening and referral. 0171 837 7324 (24 hours).
Narcotics Anonymous: Society of recovering addicts who meet regularly to help each other stay clean. 020 7730 0009.
National Aids Helpline: For anyone concerned about HIV/Aids. Offers information and advice. Can make referrals. 0800 567 123 (24 hours).
National Drugs Helpline: Helpline for anyone concerned about drug misuse, including users, families, friends and carers. 0800 776600 (24 hours) also available in some languages other than English.
NHS Direct: National 24 hour nurse-led helpline providing confidential healthcare and advice. 0845 4647.
Release: Provides health, welfare and legal services to meet the needs of drug users, their families and friends. 020 7729 9904 (24 hours)
The Samaritans: Providing confidential, emotional support to anyone in need. 0345 90 90 90. E-mail: jo@samaritans.org or anonymously: samaritans@anon.twwells.com
Sexwise: Information, advice and guidance for young people on sexual health and sexuality. 0800 282930 (7am-12midnight).
Skill: Promotes opportunities for young people and adults with any kind of disability in post-16 education. Voice 0800 328 5050, text 0800 068 2422.

*Push*ing back the frontiers

Having a disability doesn't mean your needs can't be met at University. Skill (the National Bureau for Students with Disabilities) points the way...

Being disabled doesn't mean going to higher education will be different for you – the other information in *The Push Guide* is as relevant to you as anyone else – but if you do have a disability, medical condition or specific learning difficulty, you may have a few more things to think about before you apply.

As a disabled student, you will need to know if your disability related needs can be met in colleges, but don't be tempted to make disability the only criteria you use when making choices – remember that the subject you are going to study, the social life and so on are all just as important to you as to a non-disabled student.

Skill produces a guide called 'Higher Education and Disability' which gives advice about applying and also includes profiles of some universities' facilities for disabled students. The courses database ECCTIS 2000 includes information about access and facilities for disabled students in all UK HE establishments, as well as named contacts. It's usually available in careers offices and some schools and colleges.

Don't be afraid to contact colleges before applying. If you're not sure what's available, never be afraid to ask. All colleges of Higher Education produce disability statements – so if something doesn't make you feel welcome, let them know.

It's a good idea to visit colleges before applying. 'Information visits' are a good way for you to check out the university's facilities and attitude. Consider all areas of student life – it may be just as important for you socially to get into the bar and meet other students as it is for you academically to get into the library and find books.

If you are eligible for a financial support as a student (awards and loans – see 'Hard Pushed', p18), there is a disabled students' allowance split into 3 components to help with disability related costs in studying. Skill produces a lot of information about these allowances and how to apply for them.

There's no need for you to do everything on your own. There are college advisers and union welfare officers. Some SUs have disability officers and some colleges have disabled students' groups for support and campaigning. NUS nationally has a disabled students' committee.

Skill's Information Service is available for telephone/minicom enquiries on 0800 328 5050 between 1:30pm and 4:30pm Monday to Thursday, or write to Skill, Chapter House, 18-20 Crucifix Lane, London, SE1 3JW. Alternatively, if you have internet access you can visit the website at www.skill.org.uk. Skill also has a membership scheme and a newsletter written by and for students called 'Notes and Quotes'. So if you've any questions, hit any problems or if you'd like to be involved in Skill's work, why not get in touch?

Push grads

Some students become addicted to student life and think, what the hell, I'll do another degree. But life as a postgrad is very different from the lazy hazy daze of days as first degree students and it can be just as troubled financially. Here are some of the pitfalls for postgrads.

Whether it's because they don't think they'll get a job or not the job they want, or they want to postpone it, or being a student is just too much fun, or maybe because of a sheer commitment to their subject, more than 100,000 undergrads either stay on after graduating or return to take postgraduate courses.

But students simply expecting an extension of undergraduate life are sorely misled. Postgrads study all year round with no long holidays to recharge batteries or bank accounts.

Funding, too, is harder to come by – very few postgrads are guaranteed financial support for any course (trainee teachers are one notable exception). This applies not just to maintenance costs (postgrads aren't allowed to apply for student loans), but also to tuition costs, all of which postgrads have to meet themselves, regardless of income. What grants are available are awarded on a competitive basis and so it's a good idea to have a pretty damn impressive first degree (even a good 2:1 may be cutting it fine for humanities and arts subjects ebcause there's less funding about). It also helps if you're able to apply to a funding council who're more generous with grants.

There are also Government-subsidised Career Development Loans, mostly for courses which can claim some kind of vocational element (translating obscure Abyssinian limericks probably doesn't count), which can be large enough to pay course fees.

At the end of the day, a postgraduate qualification may solve the financial problems it creates. Postgrads stand out from the crowd to potential employers and can expect to earn more. However, many employers prefer to train recent undergraduates and postgrads can find themselves overqualified. Many postgrads become professional academics, but the financial rewards alone are not likely to be a temptation.

Postgraduate courses split into 2 broad types – those that centre on research and those that are taught.

Students must research for 1 or 2 years to get a Masters degree or MPhil, or 3 years for a Doctorate. However, these are minimum periods – many students take a bit longer. Funding for research is available from Research Councils, charities or on research contracts from the institutions themselves. Commercially valuable research can often attract industrial sponsorship and delving into new types of plastic is likely to be less financially fraught than examining the philology of Philo.

Although there's no teaching, postgrads' research is supervised and it's important the supervisor is appropriately clued up. Postgrads should interview whoever will be supervising them before accepting a place – it's important not only that supervisors are able to appreciate the subtleties of their postgrads' work, but also that they get on well.

As for taught courses, they are usually part of an extended career ladder or a stepping stone to a research degree. They are either for students who want to specialise in a particular field or want to convert their qualifications to a different area. Conversion courses in particular vary greatly in what they offer, so students should be sure not just that it's suitable, but also why it is. Grants for these courses are available from the same sources as for research degrees.

United we *Push*

Call them talking shops, bop shops, shopping centres or advice centres, what are students' unions? Who are they? Over to the NUS...

Inescapable, unavoidable and absolutely essential. Within minutes of arriving at university you'll find yourself in your students' union and frankly, till the day you graduate, you'll want it.

Students' unions (SUs) form the collective voice of the student body. Each student is a member of the students' union, automatically, and each student will be involved in running the union through general meetings and electing executive officers. It costs you zero and you can't get much cheaper than that. The union represents you and your interests and whatever you want to do, you can, because you own and run your union and you can make it happen.

Students' unions work in different ways. If you want to know where to find accommodation, contraception, more money, even how to get a job, they have trained staff and student officers to help. If you want to disco till dawn, eat, drink and be merry, this is the place to be. But it's more than top bands, cheap drink, decent food and good advice. If you want to join any one of the thousands of different student sporting, social, political, cultural or special interest clubs and societies, from tiddlywinks to the lambada, then get down to the union.

And if you have a particular gripe, if there aren't enough books in the library, minibuses for the hockey teams, halls of residence or similar, then union officers will meet with the college administrators and sort it out for you. They represent your views at college meetings and make sure the student voice is heard.

Your union will also probably be a member of the National Union of Students. NUS is a confederation of unions representing over 3 million students in the UK. NUS gives you national representation, letting Parliament and the press know exactly what you think and lobbying for change. NUS also provides back-up and training for all your individual elected union officers.

*Push*ing the pennies

They're a generous bunch these students. Penniless themselves they give and raise millions each year for charity. Really it's an excuse for often obscene, often illegal and always fun activity in the name of a good cause. This is how you get from charity Rags to riches...

It's big and throbbing. Lots of people get excited about it. Much beer is drunk, many songs are sung and pots of dough are raised for charities. In fact, millions of pounds are raised every year by charity Rags across the UK.

Ten years ago or so, Rags were seen as a group of students indulging in light-hearted pranks, concentrated into one week of general debauchery. Oh yes, some money was usually given to worthwhile causes as an excuse for such orgiastic goings on.

But these days, some Rags are highly motivated and remarkably professional and run by students indulging in light-hearted pranks, concentrated into one week of general debauchery.

This week is known as 'Rag Week'. It's exact timing and content varies (and that even includes how many days make a week) from college to college. More often than not, there are beerfests, floats processions, collections, stunts, gungings, hit squads, parties, bands and much more. The big differences are that these days Rags focus as much on funds as fun and carry on their collection campaigns almost all year round.

It may help you to understand what a Rag is when you know that they were part of the inspiration for Comic Relief and Red Nose Day.

When students first get to college, they usually find themselves joining half a dozen societies or more. Rag is generally one of the very few that is completely free to join. At most places, students can find themselves at the heart of activities or on the organising committee early in the first term.

Rag is a most peculiar occupation. You somehow convince yourself that standing on a windy street corner asking Joe Public for a donation is good fun. It's not that easy, but it is a laugh. Meeting folks, chatting up the old dears, going for 'a' pint afterwards. It's all part of the job and it's addictive. Students only have to go on one 'Rag raid' (collection trip) to get caught up in it all. Before they know it, they're badgered into writing the Rag Mag (usually full of coarse humour), publicising the next big event or scrounging prizes for the raffle.

For many, Rag becomes the centre of their social life. Joining the course clubs is all well and good, but there is only so much fun that the Chemistry Society can generate and it doesn't do much to ease overloaded social consciences.

Most colleges have a Rag of some description. Of course, they're very different and *The Push Guide* details them all. As students themselves have got poorer in recent years, the amounts raised have dropped off a bit. However, they're all guaranteed to raise a laugh, a pint glass, and not an insignificant amount of money for charity.

Don't slip up choosing your university

Push Online

is the ultimate interactive guide

to finding the right university for you

Push.co.uk
independent profiles of every UK university • advice • opinions • comprehensive university guide • links • statistics • shortlisting • course search • university search • head-to-head comparisons • interactive map • facts • figures • information • student life • choosing a university • money • welfare • accommodation • why university? • how to apply • surviving clearing • top tens • university and student websites • budget planner • freshers' guide • competitions • jargon buster

Push
college
profiles

University of Aberdeen
....

University of Abertay Dundee
....

Aberystwth University
....

African Studies see <u>SOAS</u>
....

Anglia see <u>University of East Anglia</u>
....

Anglia Polytechnic University
....

Aston University
....

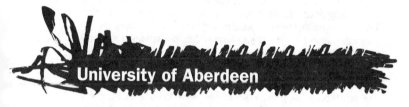

University of Aberdeen

University of Aberdeen, Kings College, Aberdeen, AB24 3FX.
Tel: (01224) 272090. Fax: (01224) 272576.
E-mail: srs@admin.abdn.ac.uk
Students' Representative Council, University of Aberdeen,
50/52 College Bounds, Aberdeen, AB24 3DS. Tel: (01224) 272965.
Fax: (01224) 272977. E-mail: office@ausa.org.uk

GENERAL

The first university in the alphabet is way up north in the *affectionately named* Granite City. The old stone city *(marginally warmer than Pingu's behind)* is also home to <u>Robert Gordon University</u>. It lies on the east coast of Scotland, suitably placed to be the oil capital of Europe and *spanned all round by spectacular castles and coastline, beaches and lochs*, the Grampians and the Cairngorms. The city itself's a *pretty place* too with flowers, parks and *smashing* architecture *in every wee nook and cranny*. The University is based on three sites which once made up two separate universities. In fact, Aberdeen had 2 universities at a time when that was the total in the whole of England. The larger, main site is King's College in Old Aberdeen, *a satisfying eyeful* of 15th-century buildings, modern blocks, green space and cobbled streets, ¾ mile north of the city centre where Marischal College is situated. The Medical School at Foresterhill is further inland to the west.

Sex ratio(M:F): 48%:52%	Founded: 1495
Full time u'grads: 7,866	Part time: 568
Postgrads: 1,163	Non-degree: 624
Ave course: 4yrs	Ethnic: 3%
Private school: 20%	Flunk rate: 16.1%
Mature students: 19%	Overseas students: 14%
Disabled students: 5%	

ATMOSPHERE:
As well as Scottish students, Aberdeen attracts many English *who often find themselves further from home and more isolated than*

Aberdeen

they'd anticipated. However, the University offers plenty of excitement of its own in a beautiful and relaxed environment, but students do complain that the only mixing they do is in the student accommodation within their own year (oh, mixing wine with beer).

THE CITY:
- Population: 201,099 • London: 410miles • Edinburgh: 103miles
- Dundee: 75miles

Aberdeen is busy to the point of congestion, but it's clean and relatively prosperous thanks to North Sea oil. The trade in black slippery stuff attracts a varied cultural cocktail from all over the UK, as well as big industry and tankers. Meanwhile, the traditional fishing fleet is on the rocks. *But Aberdeen is no sprawling waste, not by a long shot, and it's easy to burst out into splendid countryside and onto sandy beaches.* Miles from anywhere, the city has more than enough shops to spend a student loan, which takes about 34 seconds since it's not a cheap town. It has bookshops and banks (most major branches) and several museums, including the City Art Gallery and the Maritime Museum (Aberdeen's oldest building).

TRAVEL:
Trains: *Despite being so far north* (the same latitude as St Petersburg), rail connections are quite good, if expensive. Among others, services are offered to London (£52.15), Glasgow (£19.15) and Dundee (£10.55).
Buses: National Express coach services to for example, London (£37), Glasgow (£19.50), Dundee (£9). For coach journeys within Scotland the company is Scottish Citylink, Stagecoach also run services.
Car: A92, A93, A94 and A96. 2 miles to the nearest junction.
Air: Inland flights around the UK and to some European cities.
Ferries: There's a ferry service to Lerwick in the Shetlands.
Hitching: *The A92 is fairly major and once hitchers have got to the M90, it's plain sailing. But the hitch of hitching is that it's a long, long road and going west inland is nigh impossible.*
Local: Good bus services run anywhere in the city from 35p, *useful for getting into the centre from King's.*
Taxis: *Useful late at night, but expensive* - £4 from the station to King's, £8 from the airport.
Bicycles: Despite the heavy traffic and the cold winds, many students take to cycling. Some halls are only ¾ mile from the campuses so pedal power can be just the ticket. Incidentally, bike theft is as rare as any other crime in Aberdeen, which has the lowest crime rate in Britain for a city its size.

CAREER PROSPECTS:
- Careers Service • No of staff: 4 full/3 part
- Unemployed after 6mths (1996): 4%

SPECIAL FEATURES:
• When James IV of Scotland applied to the Pope for permission to found a university in Aberdeen, he said the area contained 'men who are rude, ignorant of letters and almost barbarous' and that, by providing education, 'the ignorant would become informed and the rude become learned'.
• Clarissa Dickson-Wright (TV's Fat Lady chef) is the rector.

FAMOUS ALUMNI:
Nicky Campbell (DJ); Iain Crichton-Smith (poet); Iain Cuthbertson (actor); Alistair Darling MP (Lab); Sandy Gall (ITV newsreader); Denys Henderson (Chair of ICI); Kenneth McKellar (singer); David McLean

MP (Con); James Naughtie (BBC 'Today' presenter).
FURTHER INFO:
Prospectuses for undergrads and postgrads, a handbook for international students, a website (www.abdn.ac.uk).

The only UK university offering a course in Belgian law *(so all about chocolate trading then)*.

staff/student ratio: 1:14
Range of points required for entrance: 320-200
Percentage accepted through clearing: 10%
Number of terms/semesters: 3
Length of terms/semesters 12 wks
Research: 3.9

LIBRARIES & COMPUTERS:
• Books: 1,050,000 • Study places: 1,700
There are 6 libraries, including one at the Medical School.

COMPUTERS:
• Computer workstations: 772
24-hour computer access for 208 terminals, office hours for the rest.

THE CITY:
• Price of a pint of beer: £1.90 • Glass of wine: £1.80
Cinemas: There are 4 cinemas: the Odeon (with 8 screens), the UGC cinema (a multiplex), the Lighthouse and the Belmont (independent and foreign films).
Theatres: His Majesty's Theatre attracts big time ballet and opera on tour as well as less elite delights like pantos. The Aberdeen Arts Centre is smaller and hosts more fringey shows.
Pubs: *A mixture of old men's pubs and pretentious glittery bars with little dance floors.* Pushplugs: The Illicit Still; The Bobbin; Machar Bar.
Clubs/discos: Whilst not exactly bop city, Aberdeen has enough clubs to keep hip hips moving. Pushplugs: Mudd Club at the Palace (hard rock/indie); Glow 303 (dance); Ministry (techno/house); L'Akimbo at Exodus (hard house); Glider at Pelican (Britpop/acid jazz); Amadeus at The Beach (free buses on student nights).
Music venues: Many pubs have regular folk or rock performances, *but the top student-oriented venues are the Music Hall, Beach Ballroom and the Lemon Tree.* The Exhibition Centre pulls in bigger names.
Eating Out: Eating out is *expensive compared to most of Scotland.* Fish is a local speciality. Pushplugs: Gio's, Littlejohn's, Royal Thai, Café 52. Ashvale chippy is the best.

UNIVERSITY:
• Price of a pint of beer: £1.60 • Glass of wine: £1.50
Bars: 6 bars in the Union: *The Dungeon* (home to free entertainment throughout the week); the *Sivell's* (large, airy, domed, art deco *with murals*); Factory (*industrial look*, main venue); Associates (non-smoking bar); the Seasons Café bar; the Loft (club/comedy/film venue).

Theatres: Performers perform and actors act in the University theatre, often to critical acclaim *(and not just by their mums)*. The Charities Campaign *(Aberdeen's Rag)* runs an *acclaimed* show each year.
Cinema: 3 films a week, *nothing too esoteric*.
Music venues: The Elf (cap 473), the Factory (cap 521) and Liquid Loft (cap 483) host live bands, Toploader, Tailgunner, Michael Kilkie. Folk music free in the Union on Wednesdays.
Clubs/discos: The Elf, Factory, Liquid Loft and the Dungeon *share the flashing-light chores*.
Cabaret: Fortnightly comedy slots at the Elf; Parrot and Alan Parker have trekked up in the past.
Food: The Central Refectory at Kings offers *good value chow* 9am to 6pm and New Seasons Café bar does *great* grub all day.
Other: In the Dungeon, Monday night is quiz night, on Tuesdays, bingo's in the house. Many departmental balls *(Land Economy is supposed to be the best)* and a casino night.

SOCIAL & POLITICAL

STUDENTS' ASSOCIATION:
• <u>4 sabbaticals</u> • <u>Turnout at last ballot: 17%</u> • <u>NUS member</u>
Aberdeen's Union, SRC and Athletics Association have all merged to become one big happy Students' Associaton. *Students, though, despite being quite aware and sound, are rarely stirred into action, but when they do, ooh, when they do... It must be all the porridge. A respectable 500 students attended a recent demo against Tuition Fees in Edinburgh.*

SU FACILITIES:
The lively Union Building (the second largest in Scotland) is in the city centre near Marischal, although it also has a mini-market at Hillhead Halls and a general shop. In the Union itself, there are 2 bars, a restaurant, 2 disco venues, a disco for hire, showers, photocopying, games room (with pool table, games machines and table football), welfare shop, large snooker hall, vending machine, cashpoint, launderette, music practice room, dark room and meeting rooms.

CLUBS (NON SPORTING):
AUSNA (Scots Nationalists); Bird; Bridge; Buddhist; Celtic; Centre Stage; Cocktail Society (COKSOC); CND; Creative Writing; Duke of Edinburgh; Documentary; Dungeons & Dragons; Exploration; Feminist; Fine Art; Gilbert & Sullivan; Arabian Gulf Students; HELP (Scotland); Hellenic; Hungarian Dining; Hong Kong Students; Jordanean; Korean; Law Mooting (legal debating); Live Music; Malaysian; Malt Whisky; Methodists; Pakistan; Parents Co-op; Red Cross; Role-playing; Re-enactment; Revelation; Ring of Fire; Scots Leid Quorum; Scroll; SNP; Scottish Socialist Party; Sri Lankan; Sticky Toffee Pudding Appreciation Society; Street Drummers; Street Entertainers; Taiwanese; Tap Dancing; Ten Pin Bowling; Tibet; Treading The Boards (musicals); Wine.

OTHER ORGANISATIONS:
Debater: Along with the Students' Association, students become members, automatically and for free, of a fourth organisation when they join Aberdeen University. Namely, Debater, one of the country's oldest mooting societies that does nothing but host discussions on topics of every hue and cry and come to conclusions (or not) about them. *It's popular fun and not as pompous as the Oxbridge debating unions.*
Others: The weekly student newspaper is 'Gaudie'. As part of the Charities Campaign, the annual Torcher Parade is the largest

torchlight parade in Europe. Students have 16 hours to design and make their own float and then process through the streets with folks throwing money at them. SCA stands for Student Community Action and is the energetic local help organisation run by student volunteers.

RELIGIOUS:
- 3 chaplains (RC, CofS, Episcopal)

2 chapels and a small mosque in the University. Locally, apart from St Mary's Cathedral (Catholic), St Andrew's Cathedral (Episcopal) and St Machar's Cathedral (Presbyterian), there are local places of worship for Catholics, Anglicans, Methodists, Mormons, Christian Scientists, Quakers and, of course, members of the Church of Scotland.

PAID WORK:
A free job agency has the usual part-time and vacation work. Students can sometimes find work in the oil industry, particularly those whose studies are in some relevant field.

SPORTS

- Recent successes: men's football, rowing, rugby, triathlon, women's basketball

Sports are organised by the Students' Association, which has a sabbatical officer responsible for sport, indicating the seriousness with which sport is taken. There's even a sports bursary scheme whereby athletes are given financial help. *However, some students are better at getting involved for a bit of a giggle than competing successfully. They are currently very proud that their blokey football team* won the British Shield football final.

SPORTS FACILITIES:
Most facilities are based on 2 sites. The Butchart Recreation Centre at King's has been refurbished and contains a sports hall, gym, cardiovascular equipment, fitness and testing room, weights room, 4 squash courts and a climbing wall. Also at King's, there are 2 more squash courts, playing fields, 3 all-weather tennis courts (or sometimes 1 all-weather pitch instead) and a swimming pool. However, the main sports fields are at Balgowery, 2 miles north, where there are more playing fields (bringing the total to just under 20 acres), a running track, golf course and dry ski slope. Elsewhere, the University has a boathouse on the River Dee, a glider at Aboyne and a mountain hut at Lochnagar.

SPORTING CLUBS:
Aikido; Athletics; Archery; Boat; Boxing; Curling; Gaelic Football; Gliding; Gymnastics; Inline Hockey; Jiu-Jitsu; Lacrosse; Life Saving; Nordic Ski; Octopush; Potholing and Caving; Shinty; Small Arms; Table Tennis; Trampoline; Triathlon; Weightlifting; Windsurfing.

ATTRACTIONS:
The local football team is one-time Scottish giants Aberdeen FC, alias 'the Dons'.

Edwina Currie is an honorary member of Liverpool Guild of Students.

ACCOMMODATION

IN COLLEGE:
- Catered: 14% • Cost: £74-88 (32wks) • Self-catering: 21%
- Cost: £41-63 (32-50wks)

Availability: All 1st years that want it are provided with accommodation. Many 2nd years live in as well, but students are usually on their own for the last 2 years. The halls themselves, in 3 groups, *are well equipped modern blocks set in picturesque grounds.* The Hillhead Halls are the largest set, about ¾ of a mile north of King's, a mixture of halls *(with tiny rooms)* and flats. *The very popular Hillhead is the most spirited hang-out, as well as being cheapest.* Dunbar and Crombie-Johnston Halls are closer and dearer. The self-catering accommodation is split between blocks of flats, shared between 6 to 8 students, and local flats and houses either owned or leased by the University, a few of which are available for married couples.

Car parking: *Enough free parking with a permit, but only just.*

EXTERNALLY:
- Ave rent: £50

Availability: Local landlords ignore the student trade preferring the better income from the oil industry. There is still just about enough to go round, but it's expensive. There are cheap areas like Sandilands, but it's too rough to make it worth it. Students are better off in Ferryhill, Seaton, King St, George St, Urquhart Rd and Rosemount, for example.

WELFARE

SERVICES:
- Nursery • Lesbian & Gay Society • Minibus
- Self-defence classes

Apart from the 3 part-time trained staff of the University's Counselling Service, which is the universal shoulder for crying on, students can also get advice and support from their personal adviser, the welfare officer or the finance adviser at the SRC. For leprous outbreaks and dismembered limbs, the student health centre has 4 doctors, a dentist and a nurse. A night taxi scheme is now in operation where students can pay back their fare to the SRC the following day.

Women: In addition to the Women's Group, there's an action group and a women's campaigning week. Seaton Park should be avoided at night.

Disabled: Newest halls have wheelchair access, *but the SA's campaign for improvement is making headway.* The library has a book scanner for sight-impaired students. All departments have a disabilities co-ordinator and there's a disabilities support group. The University regent provides an ombudsman service.

FINANCE:
- Access fund: £236,137 • Successful applications: 927

There are about 150 endowments, bursaries, external grants and trusts available for school leavers coming to Aberdeen University. *Some are very obscure,* for example, for one, applicants must be from Cabrach (a tiny village 40 miles away) and promise not to drink or smoke throughout their degree.

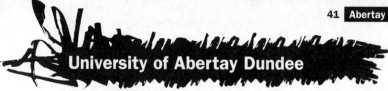

University of Abertay Dundee

• *Formerly Dundee Institute of Technology*
University of Abertay Dundee, 40 Bell Street, Dundee, DD1 1HG.
Tel: (01382) 308000. Fax: (01382) 308081.
E-mail: iro@abertay-dundee.ac.uk
University of Abertay Dundee Students' Association, 158 Marketgait, Dundee, DD1 1NG. Tel: (01382) 227477. Fax: (01382) 206569.

GENERAL

Dundee's newest university has three sites, all about 2 minutes' walk from the town centre. The large labyrinthine main building is set around a *fluffy* grassy quad but other buildings are a *weird* mix of Edwardian and 70s architecture. 500 metres away is the *pretty drab* Marketgait annexe. Once upon a time it was a jute mill, then it became a bowling alley, now it houses the Students' Association (there are plans to build a new home for the SA), laboratories and teaching rooms over a garage. Summer 2001 sees the refurbishment of the old college which will house the Dundee Business School

Sex ratio(M:F): 49%:51%	Founded: 1994
Full time u'grads: 3,448	Part time: 374
Postgrads: 386	Non-degree: 228
Ave course: 4yrs	Ethnic: 2%
Private school: 3%	Flunk rate: 15.8%
Mature students: 35%	Overseas students: 10%
Disabled students: 7%	

ATMOSPHERE:
Many students are local and most are techies of some description. They seem happy to be at Abertay although some nurse a grudge against Dundee University. For the time being, the small numbers and cosy atmosphere mean that student/staff relations are particularly good.

THE CITY: see University of Dundee

TRAVEL: see University of Dundee
Dundee station is 10 minutes' walk from the University. The *very comprehensive* local bus service is well used by students. The bus fare from the halls to the University is 80p.

CAREER PROSPECTS:
• Careers Service • No of staff: 1 full/2 part
• Unemployed after 6mths (1997): 2.3%

FAMOUS ALUMNI:
David Jones (invented Lemmings computer game); Maurice Malpass (Dundee Utd); Andy Nicoll, Craig Redpath, Tom Smith (rugby international); George Simpson (Chief Executive, GEC), Brian Souter (Stagecoach Chairman).

FURTHER INFO:
Prospectus, video, open days, course, accommodation, finance leaflets, a drop-in centre and a website (www.abertay.ac.uk).

ACADEMIC

Among its more unusual departments, Abertay is home to the Urbanwater Technology Centre (probably exactly what you're thinking it is) and the Scottish Institute for Wood Technology. The University has an International Centre for computer games and virtual entertainment (www.ic-cave.com). It's so impressive that the Scottish Games Alliance moved themselves here from Glasgow.

staff/student ratio: 1:17
Range of points required for entrance: 280-120
Percentage accepted through clearing: 5%
Number of terms/semesters: 2
Length of terms/semesters: 15 wks
Research: 1.9

LIBRARIES:
• Books: 130,000 • Study places: 705
The library is available for limited use by the public and by Dundee University and St Andrews students and Abertay students get to use the library at Dundee University and St Andrews University.

COMPUTERS:
• Computer workstations: 1,500
A recent £8Mn development has provided excellent library and computer facilities with 24-hour access during exams and a virtual reality computer suite.

ENTERTAINMENT

THE CITY: see University of Dundee

UNIVERSITY:
• Price of a pint of beer: £1.30 • Glass of wine: £1.50
Bars, clubs/discos & music venues: In the union bar, murals and royal blue velour seating *à la airport lounge* have replaced the previous pink and purple design a *definite improvement*. More are being completed as we write. *Despite the aesthetic change the entertainments side of things is weak and the bar struggles to pull in the punters although it does fill up a bit for the 2 discos a week and the bands* (Britney Spears Tribute). Anne Savage the Dance DJ (famous all over the globe for her hard house and Trance), also puts in an appearance.
Food: The University refectory, in the Kydd building, is open mornings and lunchtimes and the Union bar does lunch, dinner and snacks. *Nothing special but it's cheap and does the job.*
Others: *Individual departments and clubs host balls.*

SOCIAL & POLITICAL

UNIVERSITY OF ABERTAY DUNDEE STUDENTS' ASSOCIATION:
• 3 sabbaticals • Turnout at last ballot: 13% • NUS member
Relations between the SA, the University administration and the student body are pretty friendly, helped by the small size of the place. The SA has a stronger presence than in the past although they still

struggle to make an impact on the laid back student body and the administration. However the Union will be moving into a lovely shiny new £4.25Mn building.

SU FACILITIES:
Gym; snooker and pool tables; hospitality suite; games & vending machines; satellite TV; two meeting rooms; launderette.

OTHER ORGANISATIONS:
'Writers Block' is the SA-produced newspaper. No Rag week but there's a local primary school tutoring scheme.

CLUBS (NON SPORTING):
Dancing in Outer Space; Christian Union; Dance; Games Console; Goth; Hellenic; Hippy and Groovers; Jazz; Role Play; Sci Fi and Fantasy; SNP; Ten-pin bowling; Vampyre.

RELIGIOUS:
• 5 local chaplains (RC, CofS, Episcopalian)
A brand new Chaplaincy centre with 5 Honorary Chaplains representing the main denominations, the policy is to be available for students of 'all faiths and none'. There is also a Muslim Prayer Room.

PAID WORK: see University of Dundee
The University Careers Service offers a service called SCOPE (Student Centre for Opportunities and Part-time Employment) which assists students in finding part-time work, casual or vacation work

• Recent successes: gaelic football
Given its recent successes *it's surprising that*, apart from a new gym, Abertay doesn't have any sporting facilities to rave about, but those students who are destined for sporting greatness can take advantage of the Elite Athletes programme proving information on nutrition, coaching etc. Students can purchase a £13 card giving access to council facilities such as the Olympia Complex and the international sports centre for free or at reduced rates.

SPORTING CLUBS:
Badminton; Basketball; Gaelic Football; Golf; Hillwalking; Jiu-Jitsu; Kung Fu; Mountain Bike; Paintball; Parachute; Rowing; Rugby; Snowboarding; Street Hockey.

ATTRACTIONS: see University of Dundee

IN COLLEGE:
• Self-catering: 21% • Cost: £36-54 (36-52wks)
Availability: All 1st years who want to live in can do so, but this is helped by the 60% of students who live within a 20 mile radius, so they're usually sorted anyway. The accommodation ranges from modern purpose-built halls to converted Victorian terraces. The halls have single sex flats available for 1st years through to 4th years. 2-8 people share a kitchen.
Car parking: *Adequate* free parking near the accommodation.

EXTERNALLY: see University of Dundee
Housing help: Student Services allocates the University's own places, but also gives advice on private housing.

WELFARE

SERVICES:
• Lesbian & Gay Society • Mature SA • Overseas SA • Postgrad SA
Health services are provided by a visiting doctor and nurse who come to the University each day. Student Services employs 2 counsellors. Study skills workshops are available. An SA-run minibus operates late at night from the town to all halls.
Disabled: There's a dedicated student adviser. *Disabled access has improved, particularly* the new library and some halls. However *there is no decent access to the Union.* All buildings have lifts and 'Phonic ears' are provided for hearing-impaired students until the new building opens.

FINANCE:
• Access fund: £223,000 • Successful applications: 462
Other sources of financial assistance (administered by the Student Services Unit) are available in the form of local trusts and legacies. There is a centenary scholarship (£1,000) and there are a few bursaries for part-timers and overseas students.

Aberystwyth, University of Wales

• **The College is part of <u>University of Wales</u>.**
University of Wales Aberystwyth, Old College, King Street, Aberystwyth, Ceredigion, SY23 2AX. Tel: (01970) 622021.
Fax: (01970) 627410. E-mail: undergraduate-admissions@aber.ac.uk
The Guild of Students, The Union, University of Wales Aberystwyth, Penglais Campus, Aberystwyth, SY23 3DX. Tel: (01970) 621700.
Fax: (01970) 621701.

GENERAL

On the coast of mid-Wales is a small market town with a promenade of brightly painted houses on the sea front, a pier, the ruins of a 12th-century castle and an unspellable name. *It's a remote place and chilly when the winter winds whistle across Cardigan Bay, but there is a human warmth and relaxed tone about the town. Apart from the sea front, it's not quite as quaint as it sounds,* although the mountains (*well, big hills*) spreading inland make for an *inspiring* landscape. Up the side of one of these hills, less than a mile from the town centre, sits the University's Penglais campus. *The panoramic view is splendid:* the whole bay, the hills and the Afon Rheidol flowing through the town below. Aber, as it's known to those in the know, was one of the first Welsh colleges and the oldest buildings are *classic* Victorian stuff, but mostly it's 1960s concrete blocks, *although they're nicely spaced and you'd be surprised how interesting concrete can be with a bit of effort.* The second site, a couple of miles outside town at the village of Llanbadarn, *is a pleasant scene and a secluded one, even by Aber's standards.*

Aberystwyth

800 students are based here (doing Information & Library Studies and Rural Studies) and they travel frequently to the main site and the town centre.

Sex ratio(M:F): 50%:50%	Founded: 1872
Full time u'grads: 5,500	Part time: 400
Postgrads: 780	Non–degree: 230
Ave course: 3yrs	Ethnic: 6%
Private school: n/a	Flunk rate: 9.5%
Mature students: 12%	Overseas students: 8%
Disabled students: 5%	

ATMOSPHERE:
Because the campus is small and there are relatively few students, it's hard to avoid bumping into friends and foes constantly, particularly when crossing the paved concourse in the middle of the campus. This is great as the students are a really friendly crowd and even though it's not the most pulsating night-spot in the hemisphere, the warmth of the local welcome makes up for the less hospitable weather conditions.

THE TOWN:
Aberystwyth is one of the major towns in the Welsh region of Ceredigion. *But that's a bit like saying a puddle is the largest expanse of water in the Sahara.* There are various museums, the castle ruins and public libraries with ancient Celtic records, all mixed in with the banks, bookshops (several second-hand), supermarkets and all the standard stores in the shopping centre as well as a covered and a street market. Tourists often pass through, popping into the port and holiday centre and making the *obligatory* visit to the castle and gardens. Students make the most of the *beautiful* beaches when the sun comes out and the wind dies down. *They take their books to the seashore where amazingly they seem to absorb knowledge by just lying on their backs wearing sunglasses.*

TRAVEL:
Remoteness is one of Aber's advantages – getting away from it all – but it's a downer when it comes to getting about.
Trains: Aberystwyth station is about ½ a mile from the main campus. Direct main-line connections to London (£29.55), Birmingham (£21.65) and Manchester (£23.15).
Coaches: Trans Cambria and National Express services – London (£18.25), Birmingham (£15.25), Cardiff (£14.80).
Car: A487 and A44 – *not exactly Spaghetti Junction.*
Hitching: *Without any major roads to Aber, it's mainly thumbs down, although the Welsh do take pity on hitchers.*
Local: *Reliable* local buses run until 11pm. Every 20 mins, services run from the station to the main campus and to Llanbadarn. Both trips cost 50p. Britain's longest electric cliff railway, which leads to a camera obscura on the headland cliff, is strictly for the tourists.
Taxis: £2 from the station.
Bicycles: *Students need legs like girders to pedal up the hills – worth it for those who are into pain.*

CAREER PROSPECTS:
- Careers Service • No of staff: 3 full
- Unemployed after 6 mths : 5.8%

FAMOUS ALUMNI:
Prince Charles (prince); Neil Hamilton (ex-Con MP); Dr Jeremy Leggat (Greenpeace); John Morris QC (Attorney General); Simon Thorpe (editor, Viz).

FURTHER INFO:
Prospectuses, video and departmental brochures all free from the admissions office. Website (www.aber.ac.uk).

ACADEMIC

Students don't have to decide what course they're studying until they've already been doing it for a year. The course is fairly general for the 1st year, after which students specialise.

staff/student ratio: 1:21
Range of points required for entrance: 300-160
Percentage accepted through clearing: 19%
Number of terms/semesters: 2
Length of terms/semesters: 15 wks
Research: 4.2

LIBRARIES:
• Books: 650,000 • Study places: 1,100
The Hugh Owen Library and 3 others for separate departments. The National Library of Wales, a copyright library (*it has a copy of every book printed in the UK*), is free to Aber students.

COMPUTERS:
• Computer workstations: 560
Computing facilities have 24-hour access.

ENTERTAINMENT

TOWN:
• Price of a pint of beer: £1.70 • Glass of wine: £1.40
Pubs: Warm, cosy and somewhat pricey. Pushplugs: Rummers, Boar's Head and, for Welsh-speakers, the Llew-Du (Welsh-speaking), Lord Beechings, The Cambrian.
Cinemas: 1 mainstream.
Theatres: A small theatre by the harbour hosts touring productions, everything from cabaret to Brecht, and performances by local professional groups which also appear at the University's arts centre (see below).
Clubs/discos: *Aber is not exactly cutting edge. Pier Pressure, K2 and the Footie are all pretty run-of-the-mill. The Bay has occasional indie/grunge aspirations.*
Music venues: Local bands play at a couple of the pubs and, in the true Welsh spirit, Aber has its own male voice choir. There's also an annual Jazz festival.
Eating out: An *excellent* variety of local restaurants, especially for fresh fish. *Don't expect high health after closing time* – chips till 3am from the kebab van or Chinese till midnight. Pushplugs: The Tree House, Royal Pier Tandoori, Gannets, Spartacus, Agra (curry house), Little Italy.

UNIVERSITY:
• Price of a pint of beer: £1.40 • Glass of wine: £1.35
Bars: The Cwrt Mawr is packed all day but there's also the Penglais Bar, aka The Joint (events 7 nights a week) and the refurbished Outback Bar in Llanbadarn in the evenings (*more relaxed, if you can cope with occasional karaoke, that is*).
Theatres: (2) The Arts Centre is *dead swish* and has a customised theatre, used by students and 'proper' companies. The drama students give their all in their studio theatre, including Welsh language productions.
Clubs/discos: The floors burn up 3 nights a week, everything from the Loaded dance night to the monthly Spank for rare groovers. The Wednesday Loveshack (retro) is *pretty popular*.
Music venues: The Penglais Bar tempts tunesmiths such as Cartoon, Therapy, Catatonia and Space.
Cabaret: *Rarely* – has included Ben Elton and Lee Hurst, *but not for a while*.
Food: Most students who live in chow down in the dining rooms in their halls (pay-as-you-eat). Munchies and Joint Food in the Union provide alternatives, as does the Refectory.
Other: Annual May Ball takes place out of town.

ABERYSTWYTH GUILD OF STUDENTS/URDD Y MYFYRWYR:
• 6 sabbaticals • Turnout at last ballot: 25% • NUS member
The Guild has a good relationship with the college authorities and its students. Politics comes in a fairly left-wing form, although round these parts PC means Plaid Cymru rather than Political Correctness. Only 1 in 7 students speak Welsh, which sometimes makes the bilingual policy a tad hard to enforce.

GUILD FACILITIES:
2 shops; a pizza bar; travel agent; print shop; insurance; HSBC Bank; car/van hire; games & vending machines; second-hand bookshop once a week. At Llanbadarn, there's a bar, shop, common room and refectory.

CLUBS (NON SPORTING):
Anti-Apartheid; Asian Society; Bell Ringers; Birdwatching; Chess; Chinese; CND; Comedy; Debating; Dining; Elizabethan Madrigal Singers; Fantasy & Sci-Fi; Film/TV; Friends of the Earth; Hellenic; Irish; Islamic; Jewish; Kite; Meditation; Methodists; Pakistani; Photographic; Real Ale; Red Cross; Wargames; Women's Group.

OTHER ORGANISATIONS:
Aber Rag is one of Europe's biggest. They regularly raise 5-figure sums, but then, they do have 4 minibuses which shoot off round the country every weekend to hassle strangers for cash. The *excellent* Community Action group is called 'Dim Prob' which is not a reflection on the intellect of the participants, but Welsh for 'No Problem'. Bay Radio is the new student station. 'The Courier' is Aber's twice termly student magazine and there's also the Welsh language 'Yr Utgorn'.

RELIGIOUS:
The College has its own chapel and several chaplains. The town has churches for most Christian denominations and a mosque is under construction. The Christian Union meets outside college after it got kicked out of the Guild.

PAID WORK:
Somewhere as small as Aberystwyth can't provide jobs for 6,000+ students, but things improve in the summer, when the tourists move in. A shopping complex provides opportunities for retail operatives (*ie. shelf-stackers*).

SPORTS

- Recent successes: Women's football

Sport is a friendly affair (the attitude is 'have a go') and half the students are members of the Athletics Union. There's an £18 charge for an AU card, which gives access to all facilities.

SPORTS FACILITIES:
Impressive: 52 acres of playing fields around the outskirts of town; 7 footy pitches, 4 rugby, 4 cricket, 3 hockey (2 grass, 1 artificial), 1 American football; 9 tennis courts; floodlit all-weather pitch; 2 tennis courts; 3 squash courts; 2 sports halls (with 9 badminton courts, volleyball and basketball); swimming pool; cardiovascular gym and weights room. The town doubles up on many of the University's amenities, adding a bowling green and a golf course (with a special student deal). Water sports enthusiasts whet their whistles with willing both in the river (Rheidol) and the sea (Irish). These aquatic activities also provide an attraction for those who'd rather watch than do.

SPORTING CLUBS:
American Football; Ai-Kido; Caving; Clay Pigeon; Expedition; Ladies Cricket & Rugby; Lacrosse; Paintballing; Running; Sky-diving; Surfing; Ultimate Frisbee; Water Polo; Wind-surfing.

ACCOMMODATION

IN COLLEGE:
- Catered: 19% • Cost: £54-67 (30wks) • Self-catering: 37%
- Cost: £42-54 (30-48wks)

Availability: All 1st years can live in and 65% of finalists come back into the halls, but 2nd years are usually on their own. The main sets of halls are Penbryn and Penglais with 958 places in the student village at Pentre Jane Morgan. Students speak or learn Welsh at Pantycelyn Hall (260) which also houses Welsh treasures such as paintings and musical instruments. 4.5% of rooms are shared, but none after the 1st year. *Conditions are variable, but a refurb will be finished by the time you read this.*
Car parking: There's a large permit car-park on the Penglais campus (£15/yr for a permit) and *parking's not too hard around town, provided you remember your hand-brake.*

EXTERNALLY:
- Ave rent: £45

Availability: The reason the University has built more accommodation is not so that a higher percentage will be able to live in, but rather because, like many other places, the intake has expanded recently. *Aber's a bit too dinky to support all its student population and, as a result, finding places to live out isn't the easiest job in the world.*
Housing help: The University's residential office is lumbered with the task of helping house students. Its 4 full-time staff produce a newsletter and bulletin board.

WELFARE

SERVICES:
• Nursery • Lesbian & Gay Society • Mature SA • Overseas SA
• Women's Officer • Self-defence classes

In addition to the above services, there's a Welsh language group and the town provides a rape crisis line. The Guild operates a welfare department employing 2 full-time and 3 part-time counsellors. The Student Health Centre (with doctor, nurse and secretary) provides a service exclusively for students, in addition to local GPs. The Medical Officer also offers counselling. Nursery places for 63 little 'uns (6mths-4yrs).
Women: Cost-price attack alarms available.
Disabled: *Wheelchair access is problematic for geographical and historical reasons. The University has a welcoming attitude, but short of flattening the whole town, there's not much they can do.* Disabled applicants are encouraged to get in touch for an individual assessment. *Facilities for sight-impaired students are good, though.*

FINANCE:
• Access fund: £216,000 • Successful applications: 400

The Student Financial Support Office provides help and advice for all matters fiscal. 90 scholarships are available (worth up to about £3,000 apiece) by sitting Aber's own exam. There's the Hardship Fund and music bursaries at £400 per year, per successful applicant.

African Studies

see SOAS

Anglia

see University of East Anglia

Anglia Polytechnic University

• **Formerly Anglia Polytechnic, CCAT, Essex IHE**
(1) Anglia Polytechnic University, Chelmsford Campus, Bishop Hall Lane, Chelmsford, Essex, CM1 1SG. Tel: 0845 271 3333.
E-mail: answers@apu.ac.uk
(2) Anglia Polytechnic University, Cambridge Campus, East Road, Cambridge, CB1 1PT. Tel: (01223) 460008. Fax: (01223) 356558.
Anglia Students' Union, Victoria Road South, Chelmsford, Essex, CM1 1LL. Tel: (01245) 258178. Fax: (01245) 267653.
E-mail: ausutc@asu.apu.ac.uk

GENERAL

Along with Ulster, De Montfort and Cranfield, *this is as close as different sites get to being separate colleges.* In fact, Anglia

Polytechnic University's two main campuses were separate colleges - Cambridge College of Art & Technology (CCAT) and the Essex Institute of Higher Education in Chelmsford - until they merged in 1989, became a poly in 1991 and a university in May 1992. All in the time it takes to get a degree. *'Merged' that is, in the loosest sense, because they're still geographically and socially quite distinct.* The courses taught at each site are different, but to confuse matters, there is another campus at Danbury. It's the last institution in the UK to retain the *dreaded* 'P' word in its name although most people refer to it as Anglia or APU.

Sex ratio(M:F): 39%:61%	Founded: 1989
Full time u'grads: 10,445	Part time: 2,077
Postgrads: 3,386	Non-degree: n/a
Ave course: 3yrs	Ethnic: 11%
Private school: 5%	Flunk rate: 27.1%
Mature students: 40%	Overseas students: 16%
Disabled students: 5%	

ATMOSPHERE:
The spirit at each site varies as much as the place names on the train tickets and there's no common overtone.

SITES:
Chelmsford: (11,564 students - business, law, construction, nursing, product design, land management, IT) The administrative centre of the University is housed on this site, composed of 4 buildings *(squat, 60s, ugly, shabby and drab inside and out)* around a token patch of grass and set in the main town of Essex, *built with depressingly great concern for practicality. However in 2002 a brand spanking new campus will be completed 10 minutes away at Rivermead. This is definitely the site for party people and sporty sorts, but not political vultures or those who mind others knowing their business. The place feels a bit like a school*, not surprising since that's what it once was.

Cambridge: (4,678 - arts, maths, music) Since Cambridge is 37 miles north-west of Chelmsford, students at the Cambridge campus have less to do with students from the other sites, socially speaking, than with those from Cambridge University, whose clubs they can join and whose entertainment they can attend. The campus buildings themselves are a small collection of mostly modern red-brick blocks, *looking functional, smart and impressively like the home of eminent technical insight. The main problem is that there are really too many students for what's essentially a small site. It's artier, more attractive and greener than Chelmsford, but socially quieter, despite the vibrant local student population.*

Danbury: (590 – part-time graduate study) 4 miles east of Chelmsford, this is a conference centre with a few management courses added on.

CAMBRIDGE:
see University of Cambridge

CHELMSFORD:
• Population: 92,479   • London: 37miles
Chelmsford isn't exactly Thrill City but nor is it dullsville. It's a run-of-the-mill commuter town (which of course means that London's accessible enough when things get too turgid) with an adequate selection of clubs and pubs. It isn't a student city in the sense of

Cambridge and unless the students are able to integrate with the local community they might as well stay on campus for three years.

TRAVEL:
see University of Cambridge

TRAVEL: CHELMSFORD:
Trains: Chelmsford Station, 2 minutes from the campus, direct trains into London Liverpool Street (£5.00) and *it is easy enough to change* to services to Manchester (£30.35) and all over the country.
Coaches: Chelmsford by National Express services, which, among other places, go to London (£6), Bristol (£23) and beyond.
Car: Chelmsford is on the A12 out of London. Parking isn't a problem in the town and many students use cars.
Air: Stansted, London's third airport, is 14 miles north-west of Chelmsford and offers inland and international flights.
Hitching: *This is good hitching territory, mainly because Essex lads want to show off their turbo-powered nob substitutes.*
Local: Buses and Network SouthEast trains keep commuters commuting, shoppers shopping and students on the move.
Taxis: *Expensive, but you could have guessed that.*
Bicycles: *Bikes are too earthy and unnecessary in Chelmsford.*

CAREER PROSPECTS:
- Careers Service • No of staff: 4 full/5 part
- Unemployed after 6mths (2000): 5.4%

Some of the careers staff also work in the welfare department.

FAMOUS ALUMNI:
Adam Ant (80s pop icon); Fluck & Law (creators of 'Spitting Image'); Kim Howells MP (Lab); Ronald Searle (cartoonist); Patricia Scotland QC (first black female judge); Tom Sharpe (writer); Mike Smith (TV presenter, Smashie and Nicey type).

FURTHER INFO:
Prospectuses for undergrads and postgrads, audio, Braille and enlarged versions for blind people, PC disk, web site (www.anglia.ac.uk). *Everything short of Morse code, really.*

ACADEMIC

staff/student ratio: 1:11
Range of points required for entrance: 320-120
Percentage accepted through clearing: 24%
Number of terms/semesters: 3
Length of terms/semesters: 14 wks
Research: 2.2

LIBRARIES:
- Books: 310,000 • Study places: 1,060

Space is a problem, but the new Rivermead campus has eased matters a little.

COMPUTERS:
- Computer workstations: 1,000

```
The head of the law course at Thames Valley
University also teaches kite flying
```

ENTERTAINMENT

CAMBRIDGE:
see University of Cambridge

CHELMSFORD:
• Price of a pint of beer: £2.00 • Glass of wine: £1.60
Cinemas: 2, the 8-screen Odeon and one in Brentwood.
Theatres: Chelmsford has one mainstream theatre, the Civic, plus the Cramphorn and the Old Court for less commercial and amateur productions.
Pubs: They rely on commuters more than student trade. *Pushplugs: The Sheep; The Roundhouse; The Bayhorse; The Rat and Parrot; The Plough; The Ship; Yates.*
Clubs/discos: *Mostly towny. Dukes (house); Zeus (student nights); Y Club (indie); Enigma (Gothy, runs buses to London).*
Music venues: Some pubs host live bands (especially the Army & Navy) and some of the clubs above also ditch the decks for a few minutes. Hylands Park (509 acres) has made a pitch for the festival season, doing large-scale gigs by Blur and The Prodigy recently. *Pushplugs: The Basement (various theme nights eg Blues).*
Eating out: Not the most thrilling selection. *Pushplugs: Duke Street Tandoori; Cod Father (late night chippy); Chicago's (nice but pricey); Back in Time; The Spice.*

UNIVERSITY:
• Price of a pint of beer: £1.50 • Glass of wine: £1.30
Bars: *The cheap and tacky Placcy (cap 250) at Chelmsford is still the friendliest bar in town.* There's also a bar at Rivermead *which is much nattier* (and non-smoking) *but seems permanently dead. Go figure.* Cambridge has two bars (300 and 200).
Theatres: The theatre in the Mumford Building at Cambridge *is excellent - well equipped and big for a student theatre* (the biggest in Cambridge). *Standards of am dram reflect this - and contrast with the thespian dead zone that is Chelmsford.*
Clubs/discos/music venues: Chelmsford pumps up various volumes in the Placcy and the Gym (800) 3 nights a week. Cambridge's Big Bar has live music (Atomic Kitten, Roni Size and Lightening Seeds, recently) and discos twice a week.
Food: The college refectory at Chelmsford serves a *good value range* of meals and snacks and the Placcy does more of the same. The SU runs a canteen at Cambridge.
Others: The Anglia Summer Ball and two or three all-nighters a year at Cambridge.

SOCIAL & POLITICAL

ANGLIA STUDENTS' UNION:
• 6 sabbaticals • Turnout at last ballot: 16% • NUS member
ASU operates on all sites and each branch is as distinct as the sites themselves. Campaigning concentrates on charity fundraising and awareness of issues such as Aids, drugs etc. The SU describes itself as centre left, *whatever that means these days*. Cambridge students are allowed to join Cambridge University's clubs. *However, the initiative is in their hands - the clubs don't come looking for them. Relations between the SU and the University staff are good,*

especially at Cambridge. Eight out of ten students who expressed a preference said they thought the SU was okay - but many don't have a preference.

SU FACILITIES:
Chelmsford: Bar; photocopying; minibus hire; general shop; games room; common room; vending machines.
Cambridge: Canteen; bar; catering; general shop; photocopying; minibus hire; launderette.

CLUBS (NON SPORTING):
Drum n' Bass; European Cinema; Exhibition; Groove; Hellenic; Japanese; Law; Optics; Philosophy; Role Playing; St Lukes; Theatre; Writers.

OTHER ORGANISATIONS:
SU newspaper 'Apex' (circ 2,500) is distributed on all sites.

RELIGIOUS:
• 3 chaplains (2 CofE, 1 Catholic)

PAID WORK:
University employment office with bar work, restaurants, etc.

• Recent successes: rugby, football
At Cambridge, students have access to Cambridge University's facilities. APU itself has 22 acres of playing fields in total and all facilities are free, *if a bit dilapidated*.

SPORTS FACILITIES:
Chelmsford: Gym; two hockey pitches; badminton and basketball courts; sports hall; playing fields.
Cambridge: two hard tennis courts; playing fields; sports centre; cricket pitches; the small multigym has been moved and resited (brick by brick?) to make way for an accommodation block.

SPORTING CLUBS:
Aerobics; Badminton; Basketball; Body Toning; Climbing; Cross country; Fencing; Football; Golf; Health and Fitness; Ice Skating; Lacrosse; Mountain Bike; Rowing; Rugby; Tae Kwon Do; Table Tennis; Yoga.

IN COLLEGE: CAMBRIDGE:
• Self-catering: 15%   • Cost: £63-68 (40wks)
The halls in Cambridge are *rather good*, but they have to be bolstered by local flats and houses, under a head tenancy arrangement and 60 places in the YMCA.

IN COLLEGE: CHELMSFORD:
• Self-catering: 15%   • Cost: £46-62(40wks)
The housing at Chelmsford is good quality but overpriced. The *plush* new Rivermead development has proved popular *despite the costly rooms*. There's no University housing at Danbury.

EXTERNALLY: CAMBRIDGE:
see University of Cambridge

EXTERNALLY: CHELMSFORD:
• Ave rent: £42-70
Availability: Chelmsford is adapting to its expanded student

population, so some landlords are still a bit wary of renting to people perceived as doped-up traffic-cone shaggers. Most places are safe but the Broomfield estate is best avoided.
Housing help: Accommodation Services at Chelmsford and Cambridge. They keep registers of vacancies and post lists on bulletin boards. They also provide help and advice on contracts.

WELFARE

SERVICES:
• Creche • Mature SA • Overseas SA • Women's Officer
• Self-defence classes

With the exception of the nurse and health clinic, ASU (which has one University-wide welfare adviser and one at each teaching site) is just about it. No doctor at the Rivermead site but a local surgery is close to the halls. The University-run counselling unit employs 3 full-time counsellors, 4 part-timers and a registered doctor. Study skills are taught on all sites.

Disabled: Cambridge students can apply to live at St Bridget's Hall (*full care support see* Cambridge University). *Access is good in Cambridge and Rivermead. Induction loops are installed in lecture theatres.*

FINANCE:
• Access fund: £691,486 • Successful applications: 1,600
Small welfare fund for short-term loans.

Aston University

Aston University, Aston Triangle, Birmingham, B4 7ET.
Tel: (0121) 359 3611. Fax: (0121) 333 6350.
E-mail: prospectus@aston.ac.uk
Aston Students' Guild, Aston Triangle, Gosta Green, Birmingham, B4 7ES. Tel: (0121) 359 6531. Fax: (0121) 333 4218.
E-mail: president@aston.ac.uk

GENERAL

About a Steve Backley welly-lob (or 10 minutes' walk) from the centre of Birmingham is the Aston Triangle. In fact it's a parallelogram but don't tell anyone. The 'Triangle' is the modern green landscaped campus of brown brick buildings which make up Aston University. The campus's more *thoroughly modern excesses* include the startling red and blue glass entrance with 2 towering *futuristic* sky lifts on the outside. Despite being so compact, the campus has room for the Vice-Chancellor's Lake.

```
The Warwick University sports teams' anthem is
called 'Warwick Wanking Men Are We'
```

Aston

Sex ratio(M:F): 51%:49%
Full time u'grads: 4,751
Postgrads: 589
Ave course: 4yrs
Private school: 15%
Mature students: 8%
Disabled students: 14%

Founded: 1966
Part time: 0
Non≠degree: 0
Ethnic: 24%
Flunk rate: 6.9%
Overseas students: 5%

ATMOSPHERE:
It's unusual to find a university that's always been a university (*as opposed to a former poly*) that has such a large vocational element to its courses. *This sets the tone for the students - they have a heavy workload and are career-minded, refined and business-like. When students do lift their bloodshot, baggy eyes from the screen to have a spot of fun, the advantages of being in an environment this size show through - it's small enough to be cosy but large enough to let them avoid the people they can't stand.*

THE CITY: see University of Birmingham

TRAVEL: see University of Birmingham
New Street is Aston's nearest station, 12 mins away.

CAREER PROSPECTS:
• Careers Service • No of staff: 5 full
• Unemployed after 6mths (1996): 3%
The vocational nature of the courses, as well as the business placements scheme, *gives Aston students a definite edge.*

FAMOUS ALUMNI:
Jeff Rooker MP (Lab). Jasper Carrott has an honorary scroll.

FURTHER INFO:
Undergrad and postgrad prospectuses, open days. Alternative prospectus is free by e-mailing j.r.seymour@aston.ac.uk. Website (www.aston.ac.uk).

ACADEMIC

Most courses are linked to careers and usually involve a year on a work placement. 75% of students are on a sandwich or language programme.

staff/student ratio: 1:17
Range of points required for entrance: 340-240
Percentage accepted through clearing: 9%
Number of terms/semesters: 3
Length of terms/semesters: 10wks
Research: 4.6

LIBRARIES:
• Books: 215,000 • Study places: 600
Bones of contention include not enough books.

COMPUTERS:
• Computer workstations: 750

> 'Hamlet is a completely sad man he's Danish and a perpetual student.' - Arthur Smith.

ENTERTAINMENT

THE CITY: see University of Birmingham

UNIVERSITY:
• Price of a pint of beer: £1.65 • Glass of wine: £1.60

Bars: The drinking-holes include the refurbished Einstein's (capacity 250, *pubby and popular*, hosts balti night, Wednesdays); Sack of Potatoes (really is a pub); the Blue Room (loads of mixed music); Dream Team; Moneypennies (resident ABBA tribute band) The Loft and the new Bar Lago.

Clubs/discos/music venues: The Guild Hall (940) caters for all dancey tastes 4 nights a week (£2-3). This includes Euphoria (dance), Disco 2000 (indie), Slide (R n B, Hip Hop, garage), Revive (70s & 80s) and Club Soda (anything at all). They get big names for the Balls (Louise, Olive) *but not much beyond that.*

Food: Einstein's does pub grub and balti night on Wednesdays, Bar Lago also does its fast food thing and La Serre offers takeaway baguettes.

Others: Balls are held several times a year, including the Freakers' Ball (perverse) and the May Ball (fireworks, fairgrounds and featuring acts like GodsKitchen and the Honeyz). There are other one-off events, such as Pyjama Hops (*Rag-related bops in jim-jams*) and so on. *Also runs one of the best Freshers Weeks around.*

SOCIAL & POLITICAL

ASTON STUDENTS' GUILD:
• 5 sabbaticals • Turnout at last ballot: 24% • NUS member

The Guild is pretty apolitical and a decent rep with the students and, increasingly, the University authorities. The campaigns against tuition fees cobbled together 1,000 signatures and 200 attendees to a demo. Might not sound much, but it's better than most. The recent vote for NUS re-affiliation scored a record-breaking 1,062 in favour.

SU FACILITIES:
The purpose-built Guild Building contains a general shop, print shop, advice centre, photo booth, vending machines, pool tables, post office, NatWest Bank, Barclays and Link cash machines, hairdresser, second-hand bookshop, travel centre, cafeteria, games room and launderette.

CLUBS (NON SPORTING):
AIESEC; Artificial Intelligence (drum & bass); Asian; Ballroom Dancing; Chinese; CU; Drama; European Affairs; Fusion; Hellenic; Hindu; India; Irish; Islamic; Jewish; Juggling; Law; Lesbian, Gay, Bisexual; Links (First Aid); Mary Jane (Soul Swing); Motorsport; New Musicians; Oddsoc; Optics; Psychology; Rail and Transport; Retro; Rock Music; Sikh; Singapore; Smelly Green; Sociology; Wargames and Roleplay; Twisted Logic; Young Engineers; Zulu Warriors.

OTHER ORGANISATIONS:
'Helios' is the Guild's student magazine, and there's a weekly info sheet, 'Wot's Up?'. The student Community Action scheme is run by a Volunteers Officer organising events like kids' football tournaments. Rag raised £27k in just three months recently and has been commended by Help the Aged.

RELIGIOUS:
Chaplains operate on a non-denominational basis. There is a Muslim prayer room.

PAID WORK:
The Aston Students' Guild runs a jobshop.

SPORTS

- Recent successes: rugby, football

Reasonably successful and popular but nothing extraordinary.

SPORTS FACILITIES:
95 acres: 2 indoor playing fields; outdoor all-weather pitch; swimming pool; 2 squash courts; solarium; 2 multigyms; snooker and table tennis tables and sports shop. At Shustoke: 15 playing fields; 2 hard all-weather pitches; 3 tennis and 4 squash courts; cricket square; a large pavilion with 3 bars and social facilities.

SPORTING CLUBS:
Aikido; American Football; Ballroom Dancing; Canoe; Caving; Dance; Handball; Ice-Skating; Jiu-Jitsu; Lacrosse; Mountaineering; Parachuting; Rifle; Rollerblading; Ski and Snowboard; Skydiving; Snooker; Surfing; Swimming and Waterpolo; Ten Pin Bowling; Thai Boxing; Weight Training; Windsurfing.

ATTRACTIONS: see University of Birmingham

ACCOMMODATION

IN COLLEGE:
- Self-catering: 45%   • Cost: £49-71 (40-52wks)

Availability: All college accommodation is now on the Aston campus following the selling off of Handsworth Village. All 1st years and most finalists are guaranteed accommodation (if they apply in time) in three 20-storey towers and four low-rise blocks of self-catering flats, which have phones, and at the new Lakeside halls of residence (2,147 places, all of which are single rooms). Most 2nd years will need to find their own places - 3rd years tend to be out on placements. There is no longer any provision for married couples on campus but the Students' Guild provides 19 places for couples at nearby Aston Brook Green. Car parking is available for the disabled only.

EXTERNALLY: see University of Birmingham
For those students who regard Selly Oak as too much of a trek across town, Erdington is regarded as a cheap alternative only 3 miles from the campus with a regular bus service.
Housing help: The Student Advisory Centre offers standard contracts, help with landlords and checks safety certificates.

WELFARE

SERVICES:
- Creche   • Lesbian & Gay Society   • Mature SA   • Overseas SA
- Postgrad SA   • Minibus   • Welfare Officer   • Self-defence classes
- Nursery   • Day Care Centre

The Guild's Students' Advice Centre, run by a full-time welfare manager and student sabbatical, is the prime source of help and advice for students. The Health Centre on campus provides a counselling service for students employing 1 full-time and 2 part-time professional counsellors.

Disabled: A Disabilities Officer has been appointed; provisions and access are better than average, with a small number of specially adapted rooms for disabled students on the campus and departmental provisions for sight-and hearing-impaired students.

FINANCE:
- Access fund: £276,000   • Successful applications: 728

Guild hardship fund (up to £3,000 per person), two other hardship funds, help with childcare costs. There's the opportunity to get a bursary before you even start your course and there are emergency loans.

Bangor, University of Wales

University of Bath

Bath Spa University College

Bedford College see <u>De Montfort University</u>

Bedford New College see <u>Royal Holloway, London</u>

Belfast Queen's University see <u>The Queen's University of Belfast</u>

Birkbeck College, London

University of Birmingham

Birmingham Conservatoire see <u>University of Central England</u>

Birmingham Poly see <u>University of Central England</u>

Bishop Grosseteste College see <u>Other Institutions</u>

Bolton Institute of Higher Education

Bournemouth University

University of Bradford

Bretton Hall see <u>Other Institutions</u>

University of Brighton

University of Bristol

Bristol Poly see <u>Bristol, University of the West of England</u>

Bristol, University of the West of England

Brookes University see <u>Oxford Brookes University</u>

Brunel University

University of Buckingham

Buckinghamshire Chilterns University College

```
Legend has it that students who are standing
under the Birmingham University's Old Joe
clock tower when it chimes will fail their
finals.
```

Bangor, University of Wales

- *The College is part of <u>University of Wales</u>.*
University of Wales Bangor, College Road, Bangor, Gwynedd, LL57 2DG. Tel: (01248) 351151. Fax: (01248) 370451.
E-mail: admissions@bangor.ac.uk
Students' Union, University of Wales Bangor, Deiniol Road, Bangor, Gwynedd, LL57 2TH. Tel: (01248) 388000. Fax: (01248) 388020.
E-mail: undeb@undeb.bangor.ac.uk

GENERAL

Squeezed between the *magnificent* mountains of the Snowdonia National Park, an official area of outstanding natural beauty, and the Menai Strait (the broad stretch of water cutting off the Isle of Anglesey from mainland Wales), is Bangor. Officially, it's a city (qualifying on the strength of its 8th century cathedral), but with a tiny population *who all seem to know each other, it's more like a small town*. It's a *pretty* fishing port with a few shops *(although the Victoria Beckhams of this world may find it insufficient)* and some cutesy features: the harbour, pier, scenic views of Anglesey and the mountains. The main University buildings rest on a hill in town, resembling a grand Victorian hotel. The rest of the buildings (almost all within ½ mile of each other) are a mixture of more modern stone and concrete constructions, *the most attractive being the arts building* which gets mistaken for a cathedral.

Sex ratio(M:F): 46%:54%	Founded: 1884
Full time u'grads: 5,408	Part time: 156
Postgrads: 902	Non-degree: 41
Ave course: 3yrs	Ethnic: n/a
Private school: n/a	Flunk rate: 14%
Mature students: 16%	Overseas students: 7%
Disabled students: n/a	

ATMOSPHERE:
Strong on environmental courses and well stocked locally with the wonders of nature, the University attracts the outdoor type, more at home in a cagoule than a Babe Power T-shirt and, bearing in mind the rugged environment, that's only sensible. Nevertheless they keep themselves fairly busy and know how to have a good time.

OTHER SITES:
Faculty of Education: (493 students) Until 1996 this was a separate teacher training college. The faculty is based just outside Bangor near the Menai Bridge.
Wrexham: (350 students) Radiography is taught at Wrexham Maelor Hospital, but since that's 63 miles from Bangor, *the students get left out of the social equation.*

THE TOWN:
- Population: 15,000 • London: 236miles
- Cardiff: 180miles • Manchester: 85miles

Bangor is a true rural harbour town which attracts plenty of tourists. Such a *cosy* community and such *beautiful* scenery make it a *fine place* to live as well as visit. Its amenities are *okay for everyday needs* and apart from the usual high street shops it more or less ends there: a museum, renovated Victorian pier, supermarkets, first- and second-hand book shops, a few shops open as late as midnight, banks and a street market.

TRAVEL:
Trains: Bangor station is ½ mile from the main buildings. To get almost anywhere, it's got to be via Crewe (£16.65). London (£35) is possible without changing.
Buses: National Express services to London (£26), Birmingham (£18.25), Cardiff (£35.75) and other destinations.
Car: *Despite being a bit out on a limb, the roads to Bangor (A5, A55 & A487) are quite direct and very scenic.*
Hitching: *Quite easy.* The A55 to Chester and then the M56, which goes within 2 miles of the city centre.
Ferries: £6 rtn to Ireland from Holyhead (½ hr by train).
Local: The buses are *fairly regular* and for a quid it's possible to get about 6 miles out of town till 11pm. They also go all over Gwynedd (the county). Trains run every hour to towns all along the coast of north Wales and there's an *incredible* journey by a single carriage steam train up Wales's highest mountain on the Snowdon Mountain Railway, *a journey to absolutely nowhere, but worth it.*
Taxis: *Bangor's small enough to make taxis an affordable option for group trips or for getting home after the buses.*
Bicycles: Bangor is hillsville, *but for those with thighs on a mission, a bike is handy. There are plenty of sheds and stands and theft is a rarity.*

CAREER PROSPECTS:
• Careers Service • No of staff: 3 full
• Unemployed after 6mths (1999): 5.6%

SPECIAL FEATURES:
• Obsessive Beatles fans may be interested to know that the Fabs were staying in Bangor with the Maharishi Mahesh Yogi when Brian Epstein (their manager) died.

FAMOUS ALUMNI:
Frances Barber (actress); Ann Clwyd MP (Lab); John Sessions (comedian/actor); Roger Whittaker (cheesy singer).

FURTHER INFO:
Prospectuses for undergrads and postgrads and videos (all bilingual) from the Marketing and Public Relations Office. The SU does an info pack. Further information on the website (www.bangor.ac.uk/home.html).

ACADEMIC

Many courses have a green conservation-based tinge.

Staff/student ratio: 1:12
Range of points required for entrance: 300-120
Percentage accepted through clearing: 13%
Number of terms/semesters: 2
Length of terms/semesters: 15wks
Research: 3.6

LIBRARIES:
- Books: 660,000 • Study places: 1,038

2 big faculty and 6 small departmental libraries.

COMPUTERS:
- Computer workstations: 153

There is a newly refurbished computer centre but having your own PC is handy.

CITY:
- Price of a pint of beer: £2.05 • Glass of wine: £1.90

Cinemas: The Plaza has 2 screens. The Gwynedd Theatre shows regular films.

Theatres: The Gwynedd Theatre hosts touring shows from music to mime and plays in both English and Welsh.

Pubs: The key pubs by the quay and on the High Street are *small and personable*. Pushplugs: Fat Cats (trendy); Y Glôb (Welsh); Patrick's. Try Upper Bangor and the High Street for the obligatory pub crawl.

Clubs/discos: Most students rely on the University for club sounds and sways, although the Octagon has student nights.

Music venues: Local bands play in a few local pubs and at Powis Hall.

Eating out: *The best value is probably pub grub.* Pushplugs: Bella Pasta; Fat Cats.

UNIVERSITY:
- Price of a pint of beer: £1.60 • Glass of wine: £1.80

Bars: 4 bars frequented, not only by students but also, as with all the University entertainments, by locals who recognise that *the student ents are the most happening thing around*. Three are run by the SU: Jocks Bar (capacity 250, *often packed with Trekkies and sporties watching Sky, although they are two totally immiscible groups*); the Main Bar (350, *uninspiring, popular during evenings*).

Theatres: The Gwynedd Theatre (see above) is right next door. There are 4 student groups (Soola, Big Nasty Carrot, Rostra and the English Dept) who often hire it, providing them with an *excellent* venue for student drama.

Cinemas: SU film club shows 2 cult or classic films a month.

Clubs/discos/music venues: 'Time' is a new nightclub, which cost £1m, and hosts big dance nights by the likes of MoS, Moneypennies and Cream; *looks like a ferry*. About 5 times a week, a club of some sort is held here or in the Main Bar. The LGB society throws a Fruit Salad together and comes up with a club night every so often. Mansun, Big Leaves and Sasha stopped off here recently.

Cabaret: Various comedy shows to tickle your fancy.

Food: Freddy's, the SU's fast food outlet, keeps the pizzas pumping out, Mrs P's is a deli and Mrs Q's does hot meals. *Ceris' Diner is also a good bet.*

BANGOR STUDENTS' UNION/COLEG PRIFYSGOL GOGLEDD CYMRU UNDEB Y MYFYRWYR:
- 6 sabbaticals • Turnout at last ballot: 11% • NUS member

Party affiliations aren't bandied around although there's a general leaning to Labour and Plaid Cymru, but the SU's most direct influence on students is through its services.

SU FACILITIES:
The new SU building has some *smart* facilities: 4 bars; cafeteria; snack bar & deli; restaurant; NatWest (plus cashpoint); night club; library; launderette; showers; travel agency; general shop; bookshop; print shop; photocopying; photo booth; pool & snooker tables; 6 minibuses for hire; parking; games room; creche; vending machines; juke box.

CLUBS (NON SPORTING):
Archaeology; Bangor Concert Band; Big Nasty Carrot Performers; Bird; Duke Of Edinburgh; Hellenic; Japanese; Marine Archaeology; Malaysian; Methodist; Pakistan; Plaid Cymru; Roleplay; Second Language; Wargames.

OTHER ORGANISATIONS:
Weekly free English language magazine, 'Seren', and 'Y Ddraenen' in Welsh once or twice a term. The Rag has been relaunched with pancakes and bungees. The *highly active* student community group employs a full-time co-ordinator, has over 300 members and works on projects from stuff for kids to hospital radio and meals on wheels.

RELIGIOUS:
• Team of chaplains
The College has Catholic and Anglican chaplaincies. The latter also has 28 self-catered rooms for the really keen and an ecumenical centre where followers of all faiths can drop in. Local ministers of various denominations can be contacted in times of spiritual need. Locally, there's the Cathedral and Catholic, Methodist, Church of Wales and Baptist churches, a Quaker house and a mosque.

PAID WORK:
Apart from the usual bar work and restaurant waiting, there's the local Outdoor Pursuits Centres and other tourist spots which offer jobs to the early bird. Student Services runs a Student Opportunities Centre with employment bureau and volunteer agencies.

SPORTS

• Recent successes: canoeing, gaelic football, sailing
With the Menai Strait and Snowdonia, it comes as no surprise that Bangor offers exceptional opportunities for outdoor sports like climbing, mountaineering and all sorts of water sports. The priority is wide involvement but they're no strangers to triumph. With a Union card, amenities aren't too expensive.

SPORTS FACILITIES:
Bangor is very compact, nudged from every side by geographical limitations, and all the facilities are right on campus and next to the residential halls. It boasts a newly refurbished School of Sport, Health & Exercise Science, 50 acres of playing fields (8 soccer, 4 hockey and 3 rugby pitches) and a floodlit all-weather pitch, 2 sports halls, athletics tracks, 2 gymnasia, squash and tennis courts, archery range, multigym and, of course, the Menai Straits where the rowing club has a boathouse and the mountains. The new sports hall provides badminton, netball, squash and floodlit tennis courts, fitness studio, cardiovascular room, climbing wall, weights, 2 gyms and an Astroturf pitch. *We're knackered just thinking about it.* The town has a leisure centre, a swimming pool, golf course, bowling

green and, about ½ hour from the campus, the Outdoor Pursuits Centres. Also, at Llandudno, a few miles along the coast, there's a ski slope.

SPORTING CLUBS:
Caving; Dance; Gaelic Football; Gymnastics; Jiu Jitsu; KiAikido; Lacrosse; Lifeguard; Octopush; Rifle & Pistol; Rowing; Surf; Table Tennis; Thai Boxing; Water Polo; Women's rubgy and football.

ACCOMMODATION

IN COLLEGE:
- Catered: 15% • Cost: £67-74(31wks)
- Self-catering: 29% • Cost: £41-56(37wks)

Availability: 80% of 1st years live in, 10% of 2nd years and finalists. There are 3 catered halls of residence or 'Neuadds' in Welsh; 1 all-female and 2 others. There are 7 self-catering buildings. For those who want a room with a view, odds on it'll happen. Nobody has to share. Keycards and nightporters keep the unwanted out.

Car parking: Permits are required, which are 70p per month. Cars are only really useful in Bangor for students who find themselves living out of town.

EXTERNALLY:
- Ave rent: £40

Availability: Rentable accommodation in a town this small is finite and *many students find themselves living further out than they would wish.* Landlords tend to own more than one house, so accommodation shifts by word of mouth as much as anything. *Upper Bangor is a popular area with students. The local population tends to be friendly but Maesgeirchen is a bit hostile, as well as hard to say.*

Housing help: The University Accommodation Office provides a landlord and vacancy lists on the internet, seminars on safety and rights, a bulletin board and friendly staff to moan to.

WELFARE

SERVICES:
- Creche • Nightline • Lesbian Gay & Bisexual Society • Mature SA
- Overseas SA • Minibus • Women's Officer • Self-defence classes

The new Student Services Centre unit brings together welfare, careers and accommodation assistance with 1 full- and 2 part-time counsellors and a Finance Adviser. Free condoms and pregnancy tests dispensed for the fornicating feckless.

Disabled: *Despite being quite hilly, an effort has been made for better access, particularly in the Arts faculty* which has ramps and lifts. Some accommodation has been specially designated. Good facilities are also being developed for sight and hearing-impaired students (loops, sign language, white lines on steps). The Dyslexia Unit is internationally renowned.

FINANCE:
- Access fund: £311,000 • Successful applications: 278

Help may be sought from a small welfare budget in emergency cases. Otherwise there are scholarships for the brilliant only.

University of Bath

University of Bath, Claverton Down, Bath, BA2 7AY.
Tel: (01225) 826826. Fax: (01225) 826366.
E-mail: admissions@bath.ac.uk
Bath University Students' Union, Claverton Down, Bath, BA2 7AY.
Tel: (01225) 826612. Fax: (01225) 444061.
E-mail: union@union.bath.ac.uk

GENERAL

The Romans may have built the first settlement in Bath, but it was in Georgian times that it became the *truly beautiful* city it now is. The *glorious* golden local stone is everywhere with hardly a brick building to be seen. The many tourists don't come just to see the Roman Baths and *pretty* city (site of so many swoons in the novels of Jane Austen), but also the local countryside the Mendip Hills, the Cotswolds and the Severn Estuary. *Unfortunately*, the University, being on a small 60s campus 2 miles from the city centre, *shares very little of this elegance. It's a disorienting place at first, with no immediately apparent focus or entry point.* The buildings, *with all the concrete charm of a shopping precinct, are definitely not the University's best feature, but students soon become used to them.* After all, there's loads of grassy and leafy bits to frolic in as well as the *itsy bitsy* University lake, *compensating somewhat for the remote, windy situation.*

Sex ratio(M:F): 59%:41%	Founded: 1966
Full time u'grads: 8,482	Part time: 0
Postgrads: 1,179	Non-degree: 329
Ave course: 3/4yrs	Ethnic: 12%
Private school: 20%	Flunk rate: 7.7%
Mature students: 10%	Overseas students: 13%
Disabled students: 3%	

ATMOSPHERE:
The campus is a bit isolated from the city (which isn't exactly Sodom and Gomorrah to start with) and the students tend to be quite serious about their studies. They know how to use their limited spare time, though – sport and other extracurricular goings on are popular diversions. The Uni has gone through a frenzied building phase resulting in the following new facilities: a chemistry building, an engineering building, residencies in the city and sports facilities.

THE TOWN:
• Population: 79,900 • London: 100miles • Bristol: 11miles
Tourism not only means that Bath has *plenty* of amenities, museums, galleries and the like, but also *that these things cost a lot.* The Roman Baths must be visited at some time and the Assembly Rooms, Holborne Museum, Victoria Art Gallery and The Royal Photographic Centre are *all worth a look.*

TRAVEL:
Trains: Bath Spa station offers services to London Paddington (£19.80), Bristol (£3.10), Birmingham (£17.80) and beyond.

Buses: National Express and Badgerline services from Bath to various destinations including London (£11), Bristol (£3.25).
Car: Bath is 9 miles off the M4 down the A46 and on the A4.
Air: Bristol Airport 18 miles away has flights inland and to main European destinations.
Hitching: *Many students cadge lifts up the hill to the University and the M4's good for thumbing down to London.*
Taxis: *Not cheap, but special offers for students.*
Bicycles: *Bath's a humpy bumpy ride, okay for turbo-powered limbs and it does mean it's not worth nicking bikes.*
Local: The SU has negotiated a bus service which operates between the town, Bath University and Bath Spa.

CAREER PROSPECTS:
- Careers Service • No of staff: 2 full/5 part
- Unemployed after 6mths: 3.2%

FAMOUS ALUMNI:
Neil Fox (Capital Radio DJ); Russell Senior (exPulp guitarist).

FURTHER INFO:
Undergrad and postgrad prospectuses and an alternative one from the SU. Website (www.bath.ac.uk).

ACADEMIC

The University is strongest on professional courses, particularly in sciences, management and languages; many students do a placement in industry that counts towards their degree.

staff/student ratio: 1:15
Range of points required for entrance: 340-240
Percentage accepted through clearing: 2%
Number of terms/semesters: 2
Length of terms/semesters: 15wks
Research: 5.1

LIBRARIES:
- Books: 410,000 • Study places: 950

Library services have been improved and expanded.

COMPUTERS:
- Computer workstations: 380

IT services have been revamped and expanded, with computing facilities open 24hours in term-time.

ENTERTAINMENT

TOWN:
- Price of a pint of beer: £2.00 • Glass of wine: £1.80

For a more diverse selection of fun, the short trip to Bristol is worth the effort.
Cinemas: (3) Cannon Beau Nash, Robins Cinema and Little Theatre. Bath Film Festival is becoming more high profile.
Theatres: The *elegant* old Theatre Royal presents highbrow arts like opera, ballet and pre-West End runs, but isn't above the occasional lowbrow dross.
Pubs: *Quaint and plentiful with many a potent pint, but expensive.*

Many are designed purely to part the tourist trade from their money, but most are welcoming enough. Pushplugs (or maybe bathplugs): The Boater; The Huntsman; the Pulteney Arms; the Porter; the Pig & Fiddle.

Clubs/discos: Not a huge deal going on, but things are more lively than the staid, touristy image might suggest. Pushplugs: Cadillacs (very pink, Monday is student night); Hush (funky); Moles (live music and DJs); Babylon.

Music venues: The Moles Club is a *pretty good indie* hangout and the recently opened Porter Cellar Bar hosts live music.

Eating out: The dozens of chintzy tea rooms aimed at tourists have been replaced by various chain coffe outlets, *but they go down just as well with visiting parents (and their wallets).* Other, more student-friendly Pushplugs: Café Retro (lively and cheap); Eastern Eye and Pria do good curries. Try Sally Lunn's - totally touristy, but everything comes with a traditional Bath bun.

UNIVERSITY:
- Price of a pint of beer: £1.50 • Glass of wine: £1.90

Bars: (5) The main bar, The Plug (cap 250), is a *classic* student boozer. There's also a bar in the Venue which isn't open as often, but can now hold more hot and sweaty bods, and the Sports Bar in the Training Village.

Theatres: Despite the fact that there are no real artists *(a few linguists, though),* the students still muster a little amusement from the muses. The Arts Barn has a fully equipped studio theatre and rehearsal space for drama, dance and music and an arts workshop. Regular trips to the Edinburgh Fringe.

Cinemas: There's a 200 seat, stereo-equipped cinema, showing 2 classic, culty or new released films a week.

Clubs/discos: The Venue (500) does its bit for the disco dollies and sets the stage for karaoke, dance, cheese etc.

Music venues: Recent bands include: Terrorvision and Brandon Black.

Food: The main University refectory is backed up by smaller departmental facilities and the SU run Melting Pot *(great baguettes)* and Strollers (deli).

Others: Plenty of balls and occasional cabaret from the likes of George Dawes, Rory McGrath, Jeff Green and Craig Charles.

SOCIAL & POLITICAL

BATH UNIVERSITY STUDENTS' UNION:
- 7 sabbaticals • Turnout at last ballot: 29% • NUS member

BUSU's quite carefully apolitical even though its representative role is important and the exec is quite vocal about bringing grievances to the University's notice.

SU FACILITIES:
BUSU is based in Norwood House where it offers 2 bars and a venue, a coffee bar, travel agency, shop, 4 minibuses for hire, printing & photocopying, photo booth, games and vending machines, TV lounge, pool tables and a juke box. All 4 major banks also have branches on campus (with cash machines).

CLUBS (NON SPORTING):
Adventure Gaming; ARCE (architects and civil engineers); Astrosoc; Backstage; Bahai; BANG (religious); Bath Forum; Bodysoc; BUGS; Chamber Choir; Chinese; Clubbing; Cocksoc; CNRG; Folk The Force (engineering); Dance Ceilidh; Football Supporters; Hellenic; Motorcycle; Nemesis; Orchestral & Choral; Samba; Scandinavian; Spanish; Tarts; Visual Arts; Wine.

OTHER ORGANISATIONS:
BUSU publishes the weekly 'Sponge' and 'Spike' runs University Radio Bath, the successful and well equipped student radio station. Campus Television (CTV) broadcasts its own programmes and movies to campus, courtesy of satellite stations. Students take part in the Bath area charity Rag which has a sabbatical co-ordinator and raised a *whopping* £55,000 in 2000. They also operate their own Community Action group which runs a number of projects in the local area and is currently planning an aid trip to Eastern Europe.

RELIGIOUS:
- 8 chaplains (CofE, RC, Baptist, Methodist, Quaker, Orthodox, United Reformed)

The Chaplaincy Centre is the base for all religions (but with a Christian slant) and there's a Muslim prayer room. The city, or Bristol at a pinch, provide for most other religious needs.

PAID WORK:
Tourism always provides seasonal work.

SPORTS

- Recent successes: ballroom dancing, athletics

Sport takes a high priority at Bath - none of this wimpy crap about 'it's only a game'. The facilities, the expert tuition and the fact that there are no charges for any amenities are enough to make you want to run and jump and wave your athletic support in the air. There is a sports scholarship scheme where students of exceptional standards take an extra year to do their degrees which are combined with intensive training. The University was recently declared a Regional Centre for Sporting Excellence.

SPORTS FACILITIES:
The excellent amenities are all on campus: sports hall; 95 acres of playing fields; 50m pool; squash court; Astroturf pitches; four indoor tennis courts; two all-weather pitches; athletics field; tennis courts; climbing wall; weight room; multigym. Next door there's a golf course and in town further facilities like a bowling green, river and so on. Expansion plans are in the pipeline.

SPORTING CLUBS:
American Football; Ballroom Dancing; Boxing; Chess; Claverton Academicals; Gliding; Gymnastics; Hot Air Balloon; Jiu Jitsu; Korfball; Lacrosse; Life Saving; Motor; Mountain Bike; Mountaineering; Parachuting; Paragliding; Rifle; Rowing; Skate hockey; Snooker; Surfing; Table Tennis; Tai Chi Chuan; Triathlon; Water Polo; Windsurfing; Yoga.

ATTRACTIONS:
Bath Rugby Club for the cauliflower-eared. Bath City FC is in the Vauxhall Conference. *Lucky Vauxhall Conference.*

ACCOMMODATION

IN COLLEGE:
- Self-catering: 42% • Cost: £42-54(33-50wks)

Availability: All 1st years are offered a place in the University housing, mostly on campus, though the Uni also has some *rather nice* converted terraces in town. Few others live in. Each block has its own launderette and one even has a hairdresser. Kitchens are shared between 8 and 13 students but many can't be bothered to

cook and make regular use of the refectory. The top-price rooms have en suite bathrooms and phone lines, with all campus residences networked by September 2002. CCTV and entry-phones operate.
Car parking: T*he parking on campus is inadequate* and a permit is needed for which there is a charge. Clamps abound.

EXTERNALLY:
• Ave rent: £49

Availability: Bath is a wealthy town and house prices reflect it but it's still possible to find the odd habitable hovel. Provided students put any thought of the gracious Regency terraces out of their minds and concentrate on the less central areas, living out is manageable. Oldfield Park and Coombe Down are good bets, but avoid smeggy Twerton.

Housing help: The University Accommodation Office has 8 full-time and 4 part-time staff who help with the annual home hunt (or more often if it comes to it), provide a landlord accreditation scheme and advise on the pitfalls of renting. The SU runs a housing forum for 1st years and various other accommodatory accoutrements.

WELFARE

SERVICES:
• Creche • Nightline • Lesbian & Gay Society • Mature SA
• Overseas SA • Postgrad SA • Minibus • Women's Officer
• Self-defence classes

The University employs 5 counsellors and every student has a personal tutor. The Medical Centre has 3 doctors, a dentist and a psychiatrist. There's also a money advice centre.

Disabled: *Wheelchair access on campus isn't great and the library is a nightmare to negotiate but things are improving slowly.* Talking-book facilities exist for sight-impaired students.

FINANCE:
• Access fund: £271,888 • Successful applications: 220
Students who have to do vacation and field study can apply for special awards. There's a hardship fund.

Bath Spa University College

• *Formerly Bath College of Higher Education*
(1) Bath Spa University College, Newton St Loe, Bath, BA2 9BN.
Tel: (01225) 875875. Fax: (01225) 875444.
E-mail: enquiries@bathspa.ac.uk
Bath Spa University College Students' Union, Newton Park, Bath, BA2 9BN. Tel: (01225) 872603. Fax: (01225) 874765.
E-mail: students_union@bathspa.ac.uk
(2) Bath Spa University College, Sion Hill, Lansdown, Bath, BA1 5SF.
Tel: (01225) 875684. Fax: (01225) 875666.

Researchers at Sheffield University have developed a contraceptive pill for squirrels.

Bath Spa

GENERAL

Like Bath University, the main site of Bath Spa isn't actually in Bath, *one of the most beautiful, unspoilt cities in England (although, as all you tight-trouser fans will know, Jane Austen considered it 'a monstrosity of epic proportion' but then set half her novels there – so what does she know).* The main site of Bath Spa isn't even in the town of Keynsham. In fact, the centre of either Bath or Keynsham is as far as 5 miles away with *the main Newton Park site amidst hilly countryside more National Trust than NUS.* The buildings themselves are, for the most part, built with the golden-coloured Bath stone, in the classic Regency style *(lovely indeed).* The unwritten rule obeyed by all the students, that no one drops litter, preserves the beauty of the place *(debatable, if you like wrappers and stuff).* The second smaller site at Sion Hill is 5 miles away and much further into Bath in a different part of the city. It has some residences, a library and canteen in a converted Georgian crescent and a main 1960s building housing the College's Art & Design subjects and a purpose-built sculpture studio.

Sex ratio(M:F): 30%:70%	Founded: 1983
Full time u'grads: 2,552	Part time: 48
Postgrads: 519	Non-degree: 178
Ave course: 3yrs	Ethnic: 4%
Private school: n/a	Flunk rate: 11.8%
Mature students: 43%	Overseas students: 5%
Disabled students: 4%	

ATMOSPHERE:
The high percentages of female (70%) and mature students has a significant effect, shifting the focus from traditional alcoholic boisterousness towards a more quiet and friendly little college, where everyone knows everyone else. It's the sort of place that you wouldn't mind having in your own backyard, if you had a backyard big enough. Although the Sion Hill site is, in some ways, the poor relation, many students prefer its city centre location to being out on a limb at Newton Park. In fact, most Newton Parkies who don't live in find somewhere in town and commute. The campus dies socially at weekends, adding to the isolation of those who live there.

THE TOWN: see University of Bath
The Newton Park area itself is somewhere close to nowhere, but there's the occasional pub worth visiting en route to Bath.

TRAVEL: see University of Bath
Buses are the best way of getting from Newton Park into Bath. There are 2 an hour, quite reliably, until around 2:30am. The Orange Bus runs between town, Bath Spa and Bath University and does season tickets (£7.50 for 10 journeys, £170pa). A bus also runs between Newton Park and Sion Hill.

CAREER PROSPECTS:
- Careers Service • No of staff: 1 full-time
- Unemployed after 6mths: 10%

SPECIAL FEATURES:
The Newton Park campus is built on Duchy of Cornwall land so, although there is plenty of space, *getting planning permission for new buildings is nearly impossible.*

FAMOUS ALUMNI:
Andy Bradshaw (novelist); Howard Hodgkin (painter); Anita Roddick (Body Shop).

FURTHER INFO:
Prospectuses from the College. Websites (www.bathspa.ac.uk and www.bathspa.ac.uk/su1.html).

ACADEMIC

Staff/student ratio: 1:10
Range of points required for entrance: 200-80
Percentage accepted through clearing: n/a
Number of terms/semesters: 2
Length of terms/semesters: 16wks
Research: n/a

LIBRARIES:
• Books: 173,117 • Study places: 205
There's a library at each site.

COMPUTERS:
• Computer workstations: 136

ENTERTAINMENT

TOWN: see University of Bath
COLLEGE:
• Price of a pint of beer: £1.50 • Glass of wine: £1.20
Bars: (2) *The Newton Park bar (cap 250) is especially popular on Fridays. Sion Hill bar (cap 250) is fab.*
Clubs/discos: There are 1 or 2 dance nights a week in the SU at Newton Park which has a recently revamped sound system: Frisky (cheesy pop), Bubblicious (70s) and band/society nights.
Music venues: The Michael Tippett Centre (250) is the College's serious sound saloon, but bands also strut their stuff in the SUs at Sion Hill and Newton Park. Recent gigs include: Bentley Rhythm Ace (BRA); Artful Dodger; James Taylor Quartet.
Cabaret: Occasional cabaret evenings in the Newton Park SU.
Food: Somerset Place at Sion Hill is the spot for salivating students. The canteen at the main site staves off starvation *in an uninspiring fashion.*
Others: 3 balls a year, climaxing in the Summer *extravaganza.*

SOCIAL & POLITICAL

BATH SPA UNIVERSITY COLLEGE STUDENTS UNION:
• 3 sabbaticals • Turnout at last ballot: 10% • NUS member
Branches of the SU are on both sites. *If they've any political leanings, they enjoy them in the privacy of their own homes.*

SU FACILITIES:
2 bars; minibus hire; 1 shop; Natwest cashpoint; photocopiers; pool table; juke box; vending machines; satellite TV; meeting and function rooms; customised nightclub.

CLUBS (NON SPORTING):
Aerobics; Black Sheep; Clubbing; Drinking; Equestrian; Follicle Awareness (promoting the growth of facial hair); Human Rights; Music; Pagan; Poetry; Pool; Positive Vibrations.

OTHER ORGANISATIONS:
The SU produces the 'Bath Spa Experience' and 'Indent' magazines; there is a Rag organised in conjunction with Bath University, which successfully raises several grand a year.

RELIGIOUS:
- 2 chaplains (CofE and RC).

PAID WORK:
The Uni has a Jobshop and there are the usual suspects in town.

- Recent successes: hockey
More aesthetes than athletes.

SPORTS FACILITIES:
Sports hall; football, rugby, and 5-a-side grass pitches; gym; multigym. The tennis courts have been turned into a car park.

SPORTING CLUBS:
5-a-side football; Hockey; Horse-riding; Jiu Jitsu; Mountain biking; Netball; Rowing; Women's rugby and football; Swimming.

ATTRACTIONS: see University of Bath

IN COLLEGE:
- Self-catering: 22% • Cost: £48-71 (38-40wks)

Availability: The College has places in halls or shared houses for 575 students and aims to house 5% of 1st years *(demand outstrips supply by loads)*, very few others. At Newton Park there are 3 courts built a few years ago and five 60s courts, of which 2 are single sex only. At Sion Hill, *the beautiful* converted Georgian Crescent provides 100 spaces. Overall, 5% share. 24-hour patrols watch over your lava lamps and stuff.

Car parking: Free parking is available but not for 1st years.

EXTERNALLY: see University of Bath
Housing help: The College and SU Accommodation Offices employ 2 full-time staff who can help with emergency housing, blacklisted landlords and properties *and most other impediments to inhabitancy.*

SERVICES:
- Nursery • Lesbian & Gay Society • Mature SA • Overseas SA
- Minibus • Women's Officer • Self-defence classes

3 part-time counsellors employed by the College and a weekly surgery on the campus with a doctor and resident nurse.

Disabled: *The listed buildings don't help, but access is improving.* The college can arrange dyslexia assessment. There is a full-time Disability Officer.

FINANCE:
- Access fund: £220,000 • Successful applications: 800

Bedford College
see De Montfort University

Bedford New College
see Royal Holloway, London

Belfast Queen's University
see The Queen's University of Belfast

Birkbeck, University of London

• **The College is part of University of London and students are entitled to use its facilities.**
Birkbeck, University of London, Malet Street, London, WC1E 7HX.
Tel: 0845 601 0174. Fax: (020) 7631 6270.
E-mail: admissions@bbk.ac.uk
Birkbeck Students' Union, Malet Street, London, WC1E 7HX.
Tel: (020) 7631 6335. Fax: (020) 7631 6349.
E-mail: president@bcsu.bbk.ac.uk

Birkbeck College was founded as the London Mechanics' Institution in a pub on the Strand, in 1823. It is part of the complex of London University buildings in Bloomsbury, handy for ULU and Senate House and just a mile from Trafalgar Square. It specialises in courses for mature students with jobs or other daytime commitments, although quite a few are unemployed. Almost all undergraduates are part-time and teaching takes place in twilight hours, between 6 and 9pm (3 days a week for most courses). The main building is a redbrick block, *starkly Bauhausian, or, if you prefer, just stark, but don't be put off – courses have an excellent reputation and results are good. Everyone's friendly enough, but it's a long way from the standard student scenario.* Since most students have pretty heavy commitments (such as jobs and families), not everyone gets involved, but those who do have a sense of community. Often the reason they're studying is that they want to develop professionally or switch careers and a degree helps with that kind of stuff. *Students have a great sense of loyalty to the College because, for many, it offers a life-changing opportunity.* The staff return the compliment. The work ethic is strong as most students have had to make sacrifices to study, but there is a quiet vitality which springs from such a diverse collection of individuals. Any real social buzz has to be picked up from other nearby colleges by osmosis but there are plenty of them (including UCL and SOAS). Transport links are *good*: Euston Station is just 700 metres away; Goodge St (Northern) and Russell Square (Piccadilly) are the nearest tube stations (but there are several others within a few minutes' walk) and there are plenty of buses (nos 10, 14, 14A, 24, 29, 73 and 134 and night buses N1, N2, N5, N9, N29, N73 and N90).

Sex ratio(M:F): 46%:54%	Founded: 1823
Full time u'grads: 7	Part time: 3,544
Postgrads: 532	Non-degree: 9,000
Ave course: 4yrs	Ethnic: 25%
Private school: n/a	Flunk rate: n/a
Mature students: 99%	Overseas students: >1%
Disabled students: 4%	Staff/student ratio: 1:13
Clearing: n/a	

2 libraries: The Main Library and the Gresse Street Library (235,000 volumes, 316 study places total); 150 computers. Careers service with 1 part-time adviser. Bar (run by ULU, beer £1.50, wine £1.50, cap 100) *good for a swift drink before heading home, but not much more*; SU organises discos and/or bands in the bar on occasions; the snack bar and dining club are the main scoff stops. SU (1 sabb, 2% turnout, NUS member) *but students tend to be too busy to exert much energy in political activity;* common room (JCR); TV room; pool table; photocopier; shop; 'Lamp & Owl' magazine. *Sports are almost purely recreational and not seriously competitive*, although Birkbeck has sports clubs of its own (as well as access to University facilities). No accommodation of its own but with its peculiar role of teaching predominantly part-timers, it's not a problem and besides, the University has intercollegiate housing. Creche; nightline; SU operates some welfare services including 3 part-time counsellors, an advice centre and academic learning support; other support through the University of London's services; *college goes as far as it can in making disabled provisions on an individual basis* (new Disability Officer); ramps, lifts and other facilities in main building; *other buildings not so hot, but no worse than usual*; induction loops; IT equipment for the partially sighted. Access fund £442,325 (545 successful applicants last year), entrance fees awards scheme and a hardship fund.

FAMOUS ALUMNI:
Philippa Forrester (Tomorrow's World *babe*); Sandy Shaw (barefooted 60s *babe*); Helen Sharman (first British astronaut *babe*); Laurie Taylor (media sociologist); Tracey Thorn (Everything but the Girl *babe*). Oh, and Ramsay MacDonald (former PM, but not really a *babe*).

FURTHER INFO:
Prospectus for undergrads and postgrads, and www.bbk.ac.uk

University of Birmingham

University of Birmingham, Edgbaston, Birmingham, B15 2TT.
Tel: (0121) 414 6679. Fax: (0121) 414 3850.
E-mail: schoolsliaison@bham.ac.uk
Birmingham University Guild of Students, Edgbaston Park Road, Edgbaston, Birmingham, B15 2TU. Tel: (0121) 472 1841.
Fax: (0121) 471 2099. E-mail: enquiries@guild.bham.ac.uk

Pembroke College, Cambridge has the oldest bowling green in Europe.

GENERAL

Birmingham, midway between Manchester and Bristol and *almost as far from the coast as it's possible to be in Britain*, is arguably the second largest city in Britain. This depends on how you count, because, together with the surrounding towns, the Birmingham conurbation covers a huge expanse of land, even by London's standards. Until the early 90s it was famous for its urban splat and sprawl: stinking factories, stagnant canals and that aptitude for sociopathic traffic planning. But now the city's moving on, moving up, developing and redeveloping and consequently, with only a little hesitation, we would actually go so far as to say it's an ... *attractive city*. The landscaped University Campus is about 2½ miles from the centre of Birmingham in Edgbaston in a little island of green trees and grassy banks, *close to an abundance of shops, pubs and markets*. The buildings are redbrick, *although there's some modern concrete thrown in for bad measure*. The campus is dominated by the Old Joe clock tower, nicknamed after Joseph Chamberlain, a local hero turned politician.

Sex ratio(M:F): 45%:55%	Founded: 1900
Full time u'grads: 13,905	Part time: 473
Postgrads: 3,466	Non-degree: 25,000
Ave course: 3yrs	Ethnic: 10%
Private school: 25%	Flunk rate: 5.2%
Mature students: 11%	Overseas students: 10%
Disabled students: 3%	

ATMOSPHERE:
If variety is the spice of life, Birmingham University is the vindaloo. Although Birmingham itself is a big place, the University is large enough to dominate its own chunk of the city, creating a touch of antipathy among a few. Most, however, reciprocate the cheerful, chummy nature of the student body, unlikely to get worked up about much except sport. Also, the Uni has been pouring £20m into a new building programme – *this place will be smokin'*.

THE CITY:
- Population: 2,200,000 • London: 105miles
- Manchester: 75miles • Bristol: 75miles

Thanks mainly to EC cash, Birmingham is like a phoenix rising from the ashes of the Industrial Revolution, coughing and spluttering and spreading brand new space-age wings. The many canals *(despite rumours there are not more in Birmingham than Venice)* have been cleaned up. *Grotty alleys have been cobbled or paved.* The city was designed for cars with a Bull-ring centre, *but lo and behold, the council has decided that cars don't work in the city centre and there are now provisions for pedestrianisation (and often dehumanisation as a result)*. The Broad Street area in the centre now has the Convention Centre, *one of the best venues for miles with some of the best acoustics*. It has the Birmingham Rep Theatre *and one of the best club scenes in the UK*, an indoor arena and a modern modish piazza full of well cool cafés and chic shops. Birmingham Museum and Art Gallery has the kind of collection (particularly Pre-Raphaelites) *that makes Loyd Grossman drool*. The Sadlers Wells Ballet has moved back to 'Brum' and the D'Oyly Carte Opera has joined them here. *The Bull Ring shopping centre, the ugliest ever (currently being demolished), and monstrosities are being replaced by swish shopping centres like* the Pallisades (incorporating New Street Station), the Pavilions and City Plaza, which has usually, as well as a big new Tower Records, a man playing Grand Piano at the bottom of the escalator. The new tarted-up centre will soon be graced by a Selfridges (my, my, what more can we say?). Most residential areas of the Birmingham conurbation have always tended to shelter those who can't afford to lugubriate in luxurious largesse, and now they house a friendly multiracial, multicultural society and a student population of over 40,000. *Brum lacks one main feature pretension, unlike Manchester, it's spent too long in the dumps to start preaching or teaching other cities how to be hip. The message is: forget your prejudices, Brum is brilliant. Owroight?*

TRAVEL:
Trains: Being the belly button of Britain, Brum is *brilliantly* placed for rail links. Mainline links from London (£19.60), Manchester (£15.85), Edinburgh (£50.15) and just about every city in the country come into New Street Station.
Buses: National Express services to London (£11), Manchester (£8.20), Edinburgh (£26) *and, well, all over the shop, really.* Also West Midlands Travel and London Liner.
Car: From: north-west and north Wales: M6, M54, A41; south-west and south Wales: M5, A38, A456; London and south-east: M6 (to the M1), M40, A45. From north-east: M42, A38. *Avoid driving on Mondays unless you like sitting in a car-park for hours - like Reebok's Belly, the traffic's gonna git ya.*
Air: Birmingham International Airport, 9 miles from the campus to the east of the city, operates flights to the USA, Europe and Ireland as well as inland services.
Hitching: *Well located for branching out to the whole country. Plenty of traffic and a motorway ring road all around the city.*
Local: *Bus services are comprehensive, but too often crowded (especially in rush hour). However, while there are plenty of services from the outskirts to the centre, it's quite difficult to skirt the edge.* They run late into the night (85p from campus to town). The Guild and the University between them run a bus service between halls and campus (40p for the round trip). Overground trains run around the city – *they're faster than buses, but more expensive and very unreliable. Not worth using, except by students who live in Selly Oak.*
Taxis: *The cowboy outfits are cheaper than the black cabs but when God invented taxis, he wasn't thinking of students.* Usually costs around £3.50 from town to college.
Bicycles: *Routes are juggernaut jungles but cycle lanes are appearing.*

CAREER PROSPECTS:
- Careers Service • No of staff: 19 full
- Unemployed after 6mths: 3.6%

FAMOUS ALUMNI:
Hilary Armstrong MP (Lab); Mark Cameron (Sean the chef in 'Emmerdale'); Tim Curry (Rocky Horror star); Philippa Forrester ('Tomorrow's World' presenter); Simon Le Bon (Duran Duran); Desmond Morris (zoologist); Chris Tarrant (TV and radio presenter); Victor Ubogu (rugby player); Ann Widdecombe MP (Con); Victoria Wood (comedian).

FURTHER INFO:
Prospectuses for undergrads and postgrads, alternative prospectus (£3.50) from the Guild. Also, a website (www.bham.ac.uk) and a Guild site (www.guild.bham.ac.uk).

Staff/student ratio: 1:15
Range of points required for entrance: 340-240
Number of terms/semesters: 3
Percentage accepted through clearing: 1%
Length of terms/semesters: 10wks
Research: 4.9

LIBRARIES & COMPUTERS:
• Books: 2,600,000 • Study places: 2,350
The Main Library is massive and there are various other site libraries, 12 in all. Students still complain about overcrowding,

COMPUTERS:
• Computer workstations: 2,500
Computer provisions are satisfactory.

CITY:
• Price of a pint of beer: £1.90 • Glass of wine: £1.50
Cinemas: In and around the city, there are 4 multiplexes with a total of 38 screens and various smaller cinemas, including specialist Indian cinemas and the *artyish* Electric. *If students can't find a film they want to see, they're impossible to please.*
Theatres: *The Birmingham Rep is one of the best rep companies in the country, but it's not the only one in the city* there's also the Alexandra Theatre and the Hippodrome for ballet *as well as numerous leftfield, shoestring operations.*
Pubs: *Brum pubs are plentiful, varied and vital.* Pushplugs: The Groove; The Brook (both in Selly Oak); Three Horseshoes; Gun Barrels; It's a Scream. The Station is best avoided, as students are less than welcome.
Clubs/discos: *A place this size is guaranteed to have umpteen shimmy palaces. There is a truly awesome club scene that has developed recently.* Pushplugs: Renaissance; God's Kitchen (Fridays); Miss Moneypenny's, Babooshka (spanking new); Sundissential.
Music venues: *The trouble with Brum's music scene is the lack of a decent medium-sized venue. For most decent acts the NEC and Aston Villa Leisure Centre are too big and indie venues like The Foundry, the Sanctuary and the Jug of Ale are too pokey. Nevertheless, the city has managed to spawn acts as diverse as Duran Duran, Ocean Colour Scene and, um... UB40.* The Hibernian and the Irish Centre feature Irish music, Ronnie Scott's caters for jazzers, and there's a Jazz festival come the summer. The Symphony Hall is home to Sakari Oramo (conductor), but can adapt itself to less classical delights.
Eating out: *Birmingham deserves special culinary kudos for introducing balti, a coriander-heavy style of Indian cookery accompanied by vast, duvet-like naan breads, to the Western world (Selly Oak is full of it, that's naan breads, okay). But there's more,* check out Brindle Place for top tucker and bars and the Hurst Street Chinese places and numerous fast food stations, many open until dawn. Pushplugs go to: Circo; Magic Bean (cheap veggie); The Mud Café (good value Italian); Selly Sausage (huge portions); House of Phoenix (Persian).

Others: *Other ways to pass the time include the Silver Blades Ice Rink and Merry Hill (out of town), which is one of the largest shopping centres in Europe and houses a multiplex cinema and a bowling alley. The Glee Club is a big comedy club, recently offering Harry Hill and Jenny Éclair's meretricious mirth.*

UNIVERSITY:
- <u>Price of a pint of beer: £1.65</u> • <u>Glass of wine: £1.30</u>

Bars: There are 12 bars around the University including 1 in each hall of residence and the Guild bars: *Joe's (capacity 700, rowdy); All Bar One; Berlin's (400, doubles as a club/venue); the new Café Connection is non-smoking.*

Cinemas: The Black Lodge society shows a mix of cult movies and recent releases in the Debating Hall 4 times a week.

Theatres: The Studio Theatre is frequently used by the Guild Theatre Group, Guild Musical Theatre Group, BU Dance Society and the Drama Department. Also, 2 other theatres around the campus. *Trips to Edinburgh Fringe have been known to occur.*

Clubs/discos/music venues: *Acts to play the Uni read like a who's who:* Tim Westwood; Scott Mills; Goldfinger; Timmy Magic; Tony Blackburn; Mark Goodier. *There's a funster Club Night at the Guild; Fab; Joe's (with a request policy); Slammers (£2) and Berlin's (Cheese) both on Wednesdays; Berlin's also covers Thursdays with ample dance and sticky cheese; Frenzy (£4 on Fridays); Space and Bubble Up (Saturdays).*

Cabaret: *The Joke Joint at Berlin's fronts a fistful of funnies, such as the ubiquitous smeghead Craig Charles.*

Food: *The bars produce all manner of solid fuel. Café Connection is trendy, Harry Ramsden's chippie is good for fish-killers, Amigo's for fast food and Derrecks is a classic greasy-spoon. All Guild outlets are franchised, so the quality costs.*

SOCIAL & POLITICAL

BIRMINGHAM UNIVERSITY GUILD OF STUDENTS (BUGS):
- 7 sabbaticals • <u>Turnout at last ballot: 15%</u> • <u>NUS member</u>

Most students perceive the Guild *as a building where fun things happen*, rather than as BUGS see themselves – *a big, cheerful, all-inclusive band of diverse people out to battle for student interests*. Facilities take precedence over political intrigue, indeed the Guild has been concentrating on letting students know they're there. *Some say that confused students can't be convinced that creepy crawly bugs could ever be helpful, (specialist help may be required here).*

SU FACILITIES:
The Guild building provides 3 bars, student shopping mall, cafeterias, sandwich bar, SPAR shop, CD shop, advice centre, student travel agency, photo shop, print shop, box office, media centre, Waterstones, opticians, hairdressers, a greengrocers, IT shop, Endsleigh Insurance office, car and bus hire, meeting rooms, debating chamber, customised club venue, Midland, Halifax & Co-op banks, Blockbuster video rental machine, juke box, vending and games machines.

CLUBS (NON SPORTING):
ACAB; Alternative Performing Arts; Astronomical; Ba hai; Ballroom Dancing; Bangladesh; Black Lodge (films); Bodsoc (cartoons); Change Ringers; Chess; Child Advocacy; Chinese; Chinese Christian; Circus; Club Latino; Comedy; Cypriot; Duke of Edinburgh; Egyptian; Equisoc (horses); Football Supporters; Hellenic; Hindu; Indonesian; Italian; Japan; Jazz;

Korean; Krishna; Living Marxism; Manga Anime; Methodist; Motor; Musical Theatre; Navigators; Nigerian; Pakistan; Plonkers (wine app); Prolife; Prosession (muso); Radio; Recycling; Roleplay; Scout and Guide; Sikh; Singapore; Speleological; Square Circle (philosophy); Steam; Stratford; Student Staff; Taiwan; Talking Hands; Thai; Treasure Trap; Turkish; Wargames; Wayfarers; Welsh Women.

OTHER ORGANISATIONS:
Based at the impressive Media Centre, the student magazine *'Redbrick' is unusual and professional.* 'B15' is the Guild's info-sheet. BURN FM broadcasts for 2 months a year *to great popular acclaim and is angling for a permanent licence; Guild TV wins awards but is less popular with students because of limited transmission.* A successful Community Action Group and an annual charity carnival. RAG is known as 'Carnival' *and does silly things like 'blind date' and Dublin hikes. Sillier still (arguable), organised carnage takes place with a student pub crawl through Brum.*

RELIGIOUS:
The University's St Francis Hall is a multi-denominational centre, catering for all Jewish and Christian hues. There's also a new Buddhist chaplain and a Muslim prayer room. Birmingham itself is a multicultural city and so not only has cathedrals and churches of all types, but also mosques, temples and synagogues.

PAID WORK:
The Guild's the best bet for a fuller pocket, employing around 430 students on a casual basis at any one time; check out the job Zone too.

- Recent successes: across the board

Both the city and the University are full of facilities for those who like nothing better than sliding through mud, zooming round tracks and building pecs. The University's record in just about every sport is among the best in the country. This emphasis on achievement is not to the detriment of the less able athletes who can take part on a broad level even if they don't win. Departments will even shift their timetables to allow participation in the University's Active Lifestyle's Programme. As for facilities, they would ease a decathlete's soul and the ones that aren't free are cheap (eg tennis court hire £2 per court).

SPORTS FACILITIES:
On campus the Munrow Sports Centre has a *humungous* sports hall, martial arts dojo, squash courts, 2 gyms, dance studio, a pool, a 4,500 sq feet fitness suite *(cor-blimey)* and facilities for all manner of indoor sports. Near the Centre are outdoor amenities such as an all-weather athletics track, gymnastics centre, floodlit pitches, Astroturf pitches and tennis courts. There are another 50 acres of fields further afield on various sites close to the Uni. Out on a limb about 180 miles north, at Coniston Water in the Lake District, the University has a centre *for cable-knit sweater sports* like sailing and rock climbing. There are about a dozen scholarships for serious contenders.

SPORTING CLUBS:
American Football; Clay Pigeon; Gymnastics; Jiu Jitsu; Korfball; Kung Fu; Lacrosse; Lifesaving; Ninpo Budo (no idea either); Parachuting; Rowing; Surf; Table Tennis; Ten Pin Bowling; Thai Boxing; Water Polo; Wing Chun.

ATTRACTIONS:
Footie fans will of course know all about local teams, Aston Villa and

Birmingham City, *and nobody can ignore* the cricket at Warwickshire's main ground at Edgbaston. There's also Moseley Rugby Football Club (now based at the Uni), the Alexander Athletics Stadium, the Horse of the Year Show, figure skating at the NEC, and athletics at the Indoor Arena.

ACCOMMODATION

IN COLLEGE:
- Catered: 18% • Cost: £76-106 (30-40wks)
- Self-catering: 19% • Cost: £44-66 (40wks)

Availability: Most 1st years live in (and all who want to can), after which most students choose to live out. The halls themselves are mainly on the Vale Campus about 10 minutes from the main campus. Others are spread around the south-west area of Birmingham within 2 miles of the campus. There is one, University House, the smallest, actually on the edge of the campus with some facilities for students with disabilities. Students can choose between all-male, all-female or mixed blocks. 10% of rooms are shared. There are also 6 blocks of self-catering student flats. A new block of 620 en-suite rooms is due to be ready for this September. Security comes in the form of CCTV, burglar alarms and night porters.

EXTERNALLY:
- Ave rent: £42

Availability: *Accommodation is cheap and easy to find, and the quality's improving. Selly Oak and Selly Park are the most student infested. Moseley is also popular, but less of a ghetto.* Edgbaston is Brum's poshest part, but the part of Edgbaston that's near the cricket ground *is a red light district, quite run down, poor, multiracial and being so cheap, it's ideal for students. The scuzzier parts of Balsall Heath, Northfield and North Birmingham are generally best avoided.*

Housing help: The University Housing Service provides info on accommodation available, and the Guild produces helpful guides to student housing in Birmingham.

WELFARE

SERVICES:
- Nursery • Nightline • Lesbian & Gay Society • Mature SA
- Overseas SA • Minibus • Women's Officer • Postgrad SA
- Self-defence classes

The Advice and Representation Centre offers 4 full-time and 5 part-time counsellors, the SU offers 3. The student health clinic provides medical support from full-time doctors and nurses. Info room with pamphlets about the city, services, welfare and cash. Attack alarms are provided, and there's a women's common room.

Disabled: A Mobility Map is available for wheelchair users, showing the location of ramps, lifts etc. *All new buildings have good access but there are still no-go areas, which completely preclude study of some subjects.* Provision for sight-impaired and dyslexic students is very good.

FINANCE:
- Access fund: £875,448 • Successful applications: 1183

In addition to numerous scholarships and prizes there's a hardship fund administered jointly by the University and BUGS and special support to help student parents.

Birmingham Conservatoire
see University of Central England

Birmingham Poly
see University of Central England

Bishop Grosseteste College
see Other Institutions

Bolton Institute of Higher Education

Bolton Institute of Higher Education, Deane Road, Bolton, BL3 5AB.
Tel: (01204) 900600. Fax: (01204) 399074.
E-mail: enquiries@bolton.ac.uk
Bolton Institute Students' Union, Deane Road, Bolton, BL3 5AB.
Tel: (01204) 900850. Fax: (01204) 900860.
E-mail: bisu@bolton.ac.uk

GENERAL

Bolton grew up amidst the urban giants of the north-west and if it had been among less towering company, it would have gained more credit as a sizeable civic centre on its own merits. Between Liverpool, Preston and Manchester (including Salford), there are now 8 universities, with Bolton Institute being the newest. The Institute's main site, the Deane Campus, is outside the town centre on 2 main roads, consisting of a high glass tower and lower surrounding blocks built in the late 60s. *Apart from a scruffy stretch of grass in front of the tower, there isn't a lot of greenery.*

Sex ratio(M:F): 55%:45%	Founded: 1982
Full time u'grads: 3,033	Part time: 1,406
Postgrads: 417	Non-degree: 1,094
Ave course: 3yrs	Ethnic: 12%
Private school: 1%	Flunk rate: 31.7%
Mature students: 72%	Overseas students: 15%
Disabled students: 7%	

ATMOSPHERE:
The tone is set by the massive proportion of mature students. Conventional student activities and adolescent high jinks still take place, but not on a huge scale. People are friendly but focused. They tend to come in for their lectures and then leave fairly rapidly. If life gets dull, Manchester is only 10 miles away.

THE SITES:
Deane Campus: The main campus, see above.
Chadwick Street Campus: (2,000 students – Humanities, Education, Art & Design) ½ mile from the main campus on the outskirts of Bolton.

TOWN:
- Population: 253,300 • London: 182miles
- Manchester: 10miles • Blackpool: 35miles

Bolton is *blessed* with lots of modern amenities including a large shopping centre with 3 arcades and branches of all the major chains. *The Market Place development has given modern fronts to various old shop buildings.* Relics of the cloth industry include the Tonge Moor Textile Museum. Also worth a look, the Last Drop Village, an 18th-century converted farmhouse extended to create a *picturesque* village with cottages, pub, restaurant, hotel, craft shops and other would be tourist traps (if there were any tourists).

TRAVEL:
Trains: The Institute is ½ mile from Bolton mainline station with connections to Manchester (£2.15) every 15 minutes, Blackpool, Wigan, Blackburn. Via Manchester, you can go anywhere: London (£27.70), Birmingham (£14.50).
Coaches: National Express and Timeline Travel run services to Manchester (£2.35), London (£19), Birmingham (£9.85).
Car: The *devilish* A666, M61, M62 and A679 all serve Bolton.
Air: Manchester Airport is only a 30-minute drive.
Hitching: *A good selection of main roads nearby to chose from, but students don't really try.*
Local: Students often use the buses which go from the Institute to the halls every 10 or 15 minutes until 11.30pm. A nightbus from Manchester pulls in at 1am or 2.30am on Fridays and Saturdays. There are also plans to expand Manchester's *excellent* Metro service to Bolton.
Taxis: On average, taxis cost £2 from the town to the halls.
Bicycles: *Not many students use bikes – the town centre is very busy and has no cycle lanes. Nevertheless, people still seem to find reason to steal bikes regularly.*

CAREER PROSPECTS:
- Careers Service • No of staff: 1 full-time
- Unemployed after 6mths (1997): 36%

A diminutive Careers Service, run jointly by students and Uni.

FURTHER INFO:
Prospectuses for undergrads and postgrads; SU handbook; website (www.bolton.ac.uk).

ACADEMIC

The Institute is constantly campaigning for university status and can already award its own degrees.

staff/student ratio: 1:15
Range of points required for entrance: 60-180
Percentage accepted through clearing: 10%
Number of terms/semesters: 2
Length of terms/semesters: 15wks
Research: 1.9

LIBRARIES:
- Books: 170,000 • Study places: 510

Libraries at Deane Street and Eagle Mill. Not really enough books.

COMPUTERS:
- Computer workstations: 548

Or enough computers, for that matter. Computer access is 24-hour and more computers are held in individual departments.

TOWN:
- Price of a pint of beer: £1.70 • Glass of wine: £1.80

When Bolton falls short, Manchester never fails to satisfy.
Pubs: *Bolton has a goodly selection of pubs, and while some in the town centre don't welcome students (especially at weekends), there are plenty that do.* Pushplugs: Durty Nellie's; Cattle Market (close to halls); The Hogs; Three Crowns; Old Man & Scythe; O'Neill's.
Theatres & cinema: The Octagon puts on a mixture of modern plays, the occasional Shakespeare and Xmas panto. Flicks include a Virgin megaplex and a Warner Bros (5 miles out).
Clubs/discos: The Ritzy and the Crown & Cushion do student nights and Hawthorn's is an indie hang-out. Pushplugs: Atlantis and IKON (weekly student nights); Revolution (vodka bar). *The tarty Temple hosts dance nights with Kiss FM.*
Music venues: Various venues with anything from rock to Ravel. *Pushplugs: Oscar's Café (jazz, blues, rock); Gypsy's Tent (alternative); Albert Hall Complex (classical, blues).*
Eating out: *Gourmey delights beyond the filet-o-fish are thin on the ground, but there are a few reasonable restaurants.* Pushplugs: Tiggi's (pizza); Patagonia (chillout zone); Taj Mahal (Indian); Cook in the Books (veggie vendor).

INSTITUTE:
- Price of a pint of beer: £1.20 • Glass of wine: £1.25

Facilities are based in the new SU building at Derby Street.
Bars: (2) The Spinners Bar is the main daytime hang-out, Bob Ins is used in the evenings and when there are ents on. There are plans for a new venue.
Theatres & cinema: Pavilion Performances use the theatre at Chadwick Street for student shows. 12 free films a week.
Clubs/discos/music venues: The North Bar (cap 275) is the main venue. Friday night is DJ night, recent gigs on Saturday include: Bodixa, Dan Bailey and Steve Sutherland as well as Irish and karaoke themes, plus occasional special events and local bands. Bogie at the Venue (cap 400), Trolley (Tuesdays with a £10 entry fee ouch, but includes some free drinks) and Temple on Wednesdays.
Food: The Institute spent £100K on revamping one of the 3 refectories, but forgot the pots and pans. *Some students think the food's crap.* The bars serve spuds and pizzas.
Others: Quiz and sports nights and 2 balls a year. Cabaret occurs *but occasionally.*

Lancaster University owns a peahen and two peacocks which wander around the campus.

SOCIAL & POLITICAL

BOLTON INSTITUTE STUDENTS' UNION:
• 3 sabbaticals • Turnout at last ballot: 15% • NUS member
Politics is a no-go, but things can get a bit juicier when it comes to campaigning for better ents.

SU FACILITIES:
Bars; cafeteria; minibus hire; travel agency; printing services; bookshop; welfare centre; general shop; bank (Co-op); photocopiers; library; games room; pool table; juke box; fax service; vending machines.

CLUBS (NON SPORTING):
Anti-racism; Beer and Crisps; Christian Union; Irish; Islamic; Mature Students; Music; Roleplay.

OTHER ORGANISATIONS:
'Fresh' is the *optimistically titled* student mag. The Union is involved in Community Action Groups and Safer City projects The Rag has its own mag.

RELIGIOUS:
• 1 chaplain (CofE)
A multi-faith facility is being created, *but it'll take more than seven days*. Local prayer places for Muslims, Hindus, CofE, Baptists, RC, Methodists, URC, Quakers and Scientologists.

PAID WORK:
Usual bar and shop work, etc, *but not much of it*. There is a jobshop run by the careers service.

SPORTS

• Recent successes: gaelic football
Charges for the use of facilities are minimal. All students are eligible for a Bolton Leisure Card which costs £2.00.

SPORTS FACILITIES:
Sports hall; athletics field; tennis court; climbing wall; rowing machines and 3 acres of sports fields. Recent Health & Fitness centre. Bolton adds a swimming pool and a leisure complex at the Centretainment Park.

SPORTING CLUBS:
Archery; Badminton; Basketball; Climbing; Cricket; Fencing; Football; Gaelic Football; Hockey; Hung Kuen; Netball; Paintball; Rugby; Skiing; Snowboarding; Squash; Surfing; Tae Kwon Do; Tai Chi.

ATTRACTIONS:
Bolton Wanderers FC and their stadium, and Bolton Harriers (athletics).

ACCOMMODATION

IN COLLEGE:
• Self-catering: 23% • Cost: £46 (40wks)
Availability: Accommodation for 383 is sited on the *nice* Orlando village, in 'The Hollins' halls on the Chadwick campus and more off campus. *1st years have guaranteed accommodation on campus to look forward to and, bearing in mind that most mature students look after themselves and many others are local, these provisions leave*

few in the lurch. Security is provided by security guards and intercoms in the Hollins Halls *(which are in the the red-light area)*.
Car parking: Adequate free parking at the halls.

EXTERNALLY:
- Ave rent: £38

Availability: *Accommodation is reasonably easy to find, but some students have to live further out than they might have hoped.* In the Great Home Quest, the first clue is to look for a shared house preferably in Chorley Old Rd, Chorley New Rd, Heaton Park Road, Queen's Park Road or just Park Road. Avoid rough Darcyleaver and the crime-ridden Mencroft Avenue area, unless you're Robocop.

WELFARE

SERVICES:
- Nursery • Lesbian & Gay Society • Minibus
- Mature SA • Overseas SA • Women's Officer

There is a full-time counsellor and several other advisers.
Disabled: Facilities include a Special Needs Adviser, *easily readable signs (also handy for drunk students)*, lots of braille, ramps and alarms around the Institute. *The SU building is very good.*

FINANCE:
- Access fund: £317,471 • Successful applications: 523

The access fund is concentrated on child-care support.

Bournemouth University

- *Formerly Bournemouth Polytechnic, Dorset Institute*

Bournemouth University, Fern Barrow, Poole, Dorset, BH12 5BB.
Tel: (01202) 524111. Fax: (01202) 595287.
E-mail: enquiries@bournemouth.ac.uk
Students' Union at Bournemouth University, Fern Barrow, Poole, Dorset, BH12 5BB. Tel: (01202) 523755. Fax: (01202) 535990.
E-mail: subu@bournemouth.ac.uk

GENERAL

Bournemouth is the largest of three towns rolled into one, with Poole to the west and Christchurch to the east and a collective population of 350,000. Following the coast east, the New Forest stretches inland. The University is technically in Poole, 2½ miles from Bournemouth town centre. It's a modern campus University, *resembling beige Lego linked by brick pathways.* This is reflected in its vocational, *single-minded* career-oriented remit.

> 'How can you have student cool? It's like having student sex.' - David Quantick, NME.

- Sex ratio(M:F): 43%:57%
- Full time u'grads: 6,471
- Postgrads: 632
- Ave course: 4yrs
- Private school: n/a
- Mature students: 22%
- Disabled students: 5.6%
- Founded: 1976
- Part time: 480
- Non-degree: 3,550
- Ethnic: 5.7%
- Flunk rate: 16.5%
- Overseas students: 7%

ATMOSPHERE:
The student body tends to be middle-class, politically apathetic, clean-cut and car-owning, the most radical style statement being the occasional surf dude look. It's a high spec world, teeth gritted for the free market, a more economic plastic substitute for the original ivory tower.

OTHER SITES:
Bournemouth House: (health and community studies, business) In the town centre, 1,800 students are based here.
Studland House: (design, engineering, computing) Also a high rise block, in the centre of town.

TOWN:
- Population: 154,400
- London: 100miles
- Southampton: 26miles
- Bristol: 60miles

In summer, Bournemouth's a bristling, bustling town full of tourists, little hotels, sandy beaches, sea and ice-cream melting down your wrist. It doesn't totally close down in winter, but there's definitely less fun to be had. It does have 2,000 acres of parks in town, though, and has enough shops to keep students kitted out, although for the true shopaholic, a big city trip is needed. The urban village of Winton, ⅔ mile from the campus has shops for *mundane necessities*.

TRAVEL:
Trains: From Bournemouth station, 2 miles from the campus, to London (£17.15), Brighton (£14.70) and all over.
Coaches: National Express: London (£11), Brighton (£10.50).
Car: The A38, A31 and A35. Many Bournemouth students have cars, despite parking shortages.
Air: Bournemouth airport has internal and continental flights.
Ferries: Ferries from Poole's busy port to the Channel Islands and France.
Hitching: The ferries attract quite a lot of long distance travel and so, from out of town or the ferry port, *chances are fair*.
Local: Buses run regularly until about 11pm. Trains stop frequently along the coast, *but few students bother*. The uni runs free buses between town and college in term-time.
Taxis: Numerous firms charging £1.40 minimum fare and about £4 from the campus to the station.
Bicycles: *Even more students cycle than drive* and there's space to park 600 bikes on campus.

CAREER PROSPECTS:
- Employment Centre
- No of staff: 4 full/2 part
- Unemployed after 6mths: 18%

FAMOUS ALUMNI:
Rick Adams (ex 'Big Breakfast' presenter); Nick Knight (fashion photographer); Stuart Miles (ex 'Blue Peter' presenter).

FURTHER INFO:
Prospectuses for undergrads, part-timers and postgrads. 24hr infoline (01202 595551); website (www.bournemouth.ac.uk).

ACADEMIC

The University is the home of the National Centre for Computer Animation. Most courses have a 6 week to yearlong placement period.

Staff/student ratio: 1:21
Range of points required for entrance: 300-60
Percentage accepted through clearing: 15%
Number of terms/semesters: 3
Length of terms/semesters: 10wks
Research: 1.9

LIBRARIES:
• Books: 200,000   • Study places: 1,200

COMPUTERS:
• Computer workstations: 1,000
Despite all those computers being available 24 hours a day, shortages still occur because students are expected to do most of their coursework on them.

ENTERTAINMENT

TOWN:
• Price of a pint of beer: £1.85   • Glass of wine: £1.60
Cinemas: (5) Bournemouth - IMAX, ABC, ODEON; Poole - UCI, the Arthouse.
Theatres: The Pavilion and Pier Theatres *are more interesting in winter, since with tourists in town, it's just one long summer spectacular run.* The Bournemouth International Centre and the Bryanson and Poole Arts Centres offer *better* prospects.
Pubs: *The local brew, Old Thumper, is a pint with punch. Places near the clubs are becoming more student oriented. Pushplugs: the Slug; Inferno; Litten Tree; Legend (gay-friendly).*
Clubs/discos: *Don't think that Bournemouth is just blue-rinse foxtrots and the Roly Polys' summer season. There's real dancing to be done. Pushplugs: The Opera House (mainstream); Elements (studenty); Urban; the Great Escape; Club Blah Blah; Jazz Juice.*
Music venues: *Pushplugs: Showbar (on the pier); the Bournemouth International Centre ('BIC' is the town's biggest venue); Poole Arts Centre (a bit smaller and more eclectic).* Some clubs also host live sounds.
Eating out: *For those at the main site, Bournemouth is a bit too far to pop out to lunch. Apart from the standard array of Indian, Chinese and fast polystyrene, Pushplugs go to: HotRocks (on the seafront); Coriander; DNA (Caribbean); ASK (pizza).* The Old Christchurch Road offers eats till at least 2am.
Others: In summer, the tourist delights include sailboarding on the beach and seaside fairs.

UNIVERSITY:
• Price of a pint of beer: £1.40   • Glass of wine: £1.30

Bars: (3) The SU's Fire Station (1,200) in the centre of town used to be a real fire station and has the longest brass pole in Britain. *It also has the largest bar. Alternatives on campus are the D 2 Café and the smokey but characterful Dylan's.*

Clubs/discos/music venues: Thrice a week the Fire Station turns into a sweaty pool of wiggling bodies. Artful Dodger, Chicane and Brandon Block have appeared here recently. There are DJs at the Old Fire Station every Friday; Lollipop on Friday's will give you a free lolly (it's not that obvious).

Food: *The uni's refectory is less than scintillating, but the SU's Thomas Hardy restaurant offers more to the Madding Crowd.* D 2 does Mediterranean-style food, while Dylan's dollops out breakfasts.

Balls: At least 3 balls a year. Comedy at the Old Fire Station.

SOCIAL & POLITICAL

STUDENTS' UNION AT BOURNEMOUTH UNIVERSITY (SUBU):
• 3 sabbaticals • Turnout at last ballot: 10% • NUS member
Bournemouth is not a hotbed of radicalism, Trotskyism or any kind of ism. Except maybe careerism.

SU FACILITIES:
In the SU building, there is a variety of sporting facilities, a new travel agent, a Waterstones, Endsleigh Insurance, cafeteria, hall, bar, video games, pool tables and 7 minibuses. Elsewhere on campus, there's a Barclays Bank with cashpoint and, of course, the Fire Station in town.

CLUBS (NON SPORTING):
Afro-caribbean; Amnesty; Animal Rights; Asian; Bunac; Catholic; Chess; Chinese; Christian Union; Cinema; Concert Band; Conservation; Conservative; Dance; Debating; Drama; Duke of Edinburgh; Gig; Green; Guiness Appreciation; House music; Islamic; Law; SF and Fantasy; Star Trek; Student Newspaper; Student Radio; Student TV.

OTHER ORGANISATIONS:
The SU publishes the fortnightly 'Nerve' mag and there's also the student-run Nerve FM. 'C6' is the campus TV channel that could do with a few more programmes. Rag is big and its ball has featured big DJs.

RELIGIOUS:
• Team of chaplains (CofE, RC, Free Church, Jewish, Muslim)

PAID WORK:
Tourism brings many vacancies for deckchair attendants, ice cream vendors and hotel work, but most students go home in summer. Some teach English to foreigners. There's a Work Bank and a job noticeboard.

SPORTS

• Recent successes: swimming, sailing
The most popular athletic pursuit is probably trying to create 'Baywatch' on Bournemouth beach but some teams put in solid performances. The Uni's insistence on scheduling lectures on Wednesday afternoons hampers activity. What do they think this is, an educational institution?

SPORTS FACILITIES:
The Uni has recently installed a £60,000 all-singing-all-dancing

climbing wall and the gym facilities have been totally overhauled. There's also a sports hall; ICCAS sports centre; squash courts; badminton; all-weather pitch; floodlit Astroturf. Students pay for a Sports Card (£10 for a year).

SPORTING CLUBS:
Aerobics; Badminton; Basketball; Canoeing; Caving; Cricket, Cross Country; Cycling; Fitness & Training; Golf; Hill-walking; Hockey; Horse-riding; Karate; Martial Arts; Netball; Orienteering; Rugby; Sailing; Skiing; Squash; Sub-aqua; Swimming; Tae Kwon Do; Tennis; Trampolining; Volleyball; Watersports; Women's rugby; Yoga.

ATTRACTIONS:
Bournemouth FC. Also some speedway and various leisure, sports and swimming centres.

ACCOMMODATION

IN COLLEGE:
• Self-catering: 14%   • Cost: £60-64 (34–40wks)
Availability: The student village on campus only has places for 250 1st years (ie a few) with a quarter of them sharing. The houses in the non-smoking village, *which look like the set of 'Brookside', are shared between 4, 5 or 7 students. They're not cheap though, and a bit far from shops – a bit far from anything except the campus for that matter.* Cranborne (500 students) and Hurn House (250 students) are both based in Lansdowne and are *more popular* than the student village, despite being 2 miles from the main site.
Car parking: *Adequate but expensive permit parking.*

EXTERNALLY:
• Ave rent: £55
Availability: The University helps the 1st years it can't fit in the student village to find their feet. 120 are housed in University-approved hotels and B&Bs in Boscombe and Bournemouth (which can cost up to £77 a week all in). It also manages 250 private houses in Bournemouth and Poole under its UNILET scheme. By the time the summer season is over, there is so much housing that landlords sometimes have to advertise for tenants. *The best areas are Winton and Charminster (both near the campus) and Lansdowne (near the Fire Station).*
Housing help: The SU advises on contracts and how best to hunt. The main help is from the accommodation service with 1 full- and 2 part-time staff who run an accreditation scheme.

WELFARE

SERVICES:
• Nursery • Nightline • Lesbian & Gay Society
• Minibus • Self-defence classes
Counselling and advice services are contracted out to the local authority (1 part-/2 full-time advisers). The medical centre in Talbot House has a doctor and nurses and is also home to the day nursery. No Women's Officer *(a result of apathy).*
Disabled: The Uni *shows concern* for students with any form of special need including epileptics, students with dyslexia, partially sighted students. There's a Disability Co-ordinator, specially adapted accommodation on campus. *Access to all buildings is good.* A disability fund is also available.

FINANCE:
- Access fund: £384,087 • Successful applications: 732
SUBU runs a small emergency loan fund.

University of Bradford

University of Bradford, Richmond Road, Bradford, West Yorkshire,
BD7 1DP. Tel: (01274) 233081. Fax: (01274) 236260.
E-mail: enquiries@bradford.ac.uk
University of Bradford Students' Union, Richmond Road, Bradford,
West Yorkshire, BD7 1DP. Tel: (01274) 233300.
Fax: (01274) 235530. E-mail: ubu@bradford.ac.uk

GENERAL

In a gap in the Pennines, not far from the Yorkshire Dales, is a city that bloomed and boomed during the Industrial Revolution because of sheep or, more accurately, wool. The main campus is less than a mile from the city centre *and the mega roundabouts which trap cars in ever repeating circles. It's as compact as a Swiss Army knife (although it can't get a pebble out of a horse's hoof).* Most of the modern building blocks rise into the sky leaving room to park cars in between. There's also the School of Management at Emm Lane which consists of a former religious training college and 2 modern extensions.

Sex ratio(M:F): 47%:53%	Founded: 1966
Full time u'grads: 6,161	Part time: 1,708
Postgrads: 705	Non-degree: 603
Ave course: 3-4yrs	Ethnic: 24%
Private school: 9%	Flunk rate: 15.5%
Mature students: 20%	Overseas students: 11%
Disabled students: 5%	

ATMOSPHERE:
Bradford's a small, friendly and relatively quiet University. Having one main self-contained campus helps keep student spirit from dissipating into the city which would otherwise swallow it with friendliness. Students at Emm Lane are less a part of the party. There's an air of hardworking practicality – students are either working, on their way to work or maybe having a swift half while they think about what work they should do next.

THE SITES:
Emm Lane: (1,000+ students) The School of Management 3 miles from the main campus, *in the posher suburbs of Bradford,* has a refectory and accommodation for 25 students but for most entertainments, the main site is where you'll want to go. Sadly, only a regular bus service during the day is provided.

THE CITY:
- Population: 449,100 • London: 180miles
- Leeds: 9miles • Manchester: 30miles

Bradford is one of the cheapest places to live in the whole country, but there are still any number of ways to blow what little money you have. It has all the trappings of cosmopolitan commerce and culture, with a *rich and vibrant* ethnic mix. The streets are criss-crosses of Victorian terraced housing, except in the city centre, a jigsaw of big civic centres and buildings including the *brilliant* National Museum of Photography and the fantastic Alhambra Theatre. *If it does get a bit dull, don't forget Leeds and Manchester are almost on the doorstep.*

TRAVEL:
Trains: Services from Bradford Interchange to London (£39.95), Manchester (£7.55), Birmingham (£23.90).
Coaches: National Express services to, among other places, London (£16.75) and Manchester (£6.50).
Car: Just a few minutes off the M62 down the M606, on the A58, A658 and A650.
Air: Leeds & Bradford Airport (6½ miles away) operates flights inland and to Europe, Ireland and North America.
Hitching: *Not too many lifts – the beginning of the M606 is the place to try though. Pushplug: try and look like Harry Potter – a pair of spectacles works wonders. Of course, if you are Harry Potter you're reading the wrong section, see above.*
Local: Regular and *cheap* bus services from the campus to the city centre, but everybody walks if it isn't raining. There are 3 stations around the city (including neighbouring Shipley) which are useful for getting to Leeds (80p). A West Yorkshire Metrocard gives unlimited travel on trains and buses – students can get one for a *bargain* £29.70 a month.
Taxis: *Not too expensive*, costing £3 from the campus to the station. Bradford is compact and local journeys are cheap.
Bicycles: *Bradford and the campus are a bit hilly so students need to be riding something with as many gears as spokes.*

CAREER PROSPECTS:
- Careers Service • No of staff: 4 full/1 part
- Unemployed after 6mths: 6%

Bradford's vocational training makes it popular with employers, especially in engineering and technology sectors.

SPECIAL FEATURES:
- *Goths still haunt Bradford streets in admirable numbers.*
- A register of romances has been set up to keep track of staff/student relationships. *No comment.*

FAMOUS ALUMNI:
Roland Boyes MP, David Hinchliffe MP, Alice Mahon MP, Ann Taylor MP (all Lab), John Hegley (poet); Rt Hon Lord Viscount Sir Earl Baron etc (*we can't remember which*) David Puttnam has an honorary scroll.

FURTHER INFO:
Prospectuses for undergrads, postgrads and part-time students, course booklets, information for international students, websites (www.bradford.ac.uk and www.ubu.brad.ac.uk) *and, quite probably by now, an interactive movie starring Kate Winslett as the Vice-Chancellor.*

ACADEMIC

Most students are involved in science and technology based subjects, with 50% on sandwich courses.

staff/student ratio: 1:14
Range of points required for entrance: 320-120
Percentage accepted through clearing: 20%
Number of terms/semesters: 2
Length of terms/semesters: 15wks
Research: 4.1

LIBRARIES:
• Books: 600,000 • Study places: 1,400
The main book repository is the J B Priestley Library, plus smaller libraries at Emm Lane and in the School of Health Studies.

COMPUTERS:
• Computer workstations: 320
Every room in halls has a computer socket for linking up to the University network.

ENTERTAINMENT

THE CITY:
• Price of a pint of beer: £1.60 • Glass of wine: £1.80
Cinemas: One multiplex. The Bradford Playhouse burned down and is now the J B Priestley Centre, with art-house cinema and a theatre. The Pictureville shows arty films. The National Museum of Photography, Film & Television has an *enormous* Imax screen (the second largest cinema screen in the UK), a *beezer* digital multimedia gallery and studio, and the only Cinerama auditorium still in existence.
Theatres: (3) The Alhambra, with *excellent* foyer facilities, features some of the best shows outside the West End.
Pubs: Some of the country's *finest* bitters are native to Yorkshire: Theakstons, Tetleys, Websters, Timothy Taylors and Sam Smiths as well as less well-known local brews. New pubs have been springing up between campus and the city. *Pushplugs: The Delius; The Peel; Varsity; Hogshead.*
Clubs/discos: Pushplugs go to Rio's (alternative) and Solutions (indie, pop and house).
Music venues: St George's Hall hosts a mix of classical, MOR, comedy and bands; Club Rio has largish (*ie. crap*) indie bands.
Eating out: Locally, curry is the predominant aroma, most Indian restaurants are *phenomenally* cheap and *amazing* quality and, what's more, there are 38 places within the campus area alone many open till 4am. But the choice is wider: there's every kind of restaurant including cheap chippies and value veggie joints. *Pushplugs: Mr Papadom's (balti); Omars (biggest naan in Yorkshire); Kashmir; Karachi; Shezan (best of the Indians); Angelo's Pizza; Hansa's (Asian); The Love Apple (groovy veggie).*

UNIVERSITY:
• Price of a pint of beer: £1.40 • Glass of wine: £1
Bars: (5) The SU bars are even cheaper than local pubs. The SU's Biko Bar is recommended by CAMRA for its range of real ales. JB's

(recently refurbished, *dingy though atmospheric*, about the only smoking venue on campus) is situated below Student Services. There's also the Escape, the Colours Bar (both heading up café street) and the Basement.
Cinema: Bradford Student Cinema (cap 900) shows mainstream and cultish fare 4 or 5 times a week and gets new films a month after release.
Theatre: *Drama's a big deal, especially for a place with no drama department.* The Theatre Group runs 2 venues at the Edinburgh Fringe and also arranges exchanges with Eastern European groups. The Theatre In the Mill on campus hosts student and pro productions.
Clubs/discos/music venues: The Basement has a capacity of 1,400, large enough to attract *biggish* names - recently, Dave Pierce, LTJ Bukem and Stereophonics. Regular clubs include the self-evident Friday Night Discos (FND), Escape hosts hip hop and dance, while Colours does pop and dance.
Cabaret: 2 or 3 gag-gigs a term. Craig Charles visited recently.
Food: The Refectory opens for lunch (11.45 am - 1.40pm) and Colours and Escape churn out the chow.

SOCIAL & POLITICAL

BRADFORD UNIVERSITY STUDENTS' UNION:
• 6 sabbaticals • Turnout at last ballot: 20% • NUS member
Students tend to be too wrapped up in their work to agitate, unless their personal finances are under threat, although awareness campaigns for issues such as breast cancer have met with some success.

SU FACILITIES:
Facilities are centred in the Commie, the University's social centre, where the SU has offices, 3 bars (with satellite TV), printing and photocopying, a common room, shop, NatWest bank (with cashpoint), photo booth, pool tables, juke boxes, vending and games machines, customised night club and meeting rooms. In the Richmond Building, the University's administrative centre, the Union runs the Biko Bar; kiosk and a shop.

CLUBS (NON SPORTING):
Cult TV; Vampyre.

OTHER ORGANISATIONS:
Somebody must have been selling off a bulk load of newsprint round here. There's the *charmingly* titled union paper, 'Scrapie'; 'Ram', a daily message sheet; 'Shout', for women. There's also an independent student radio station, 'Ramair'. BUSCA, the Community Action group, provides practical help for the young, the old, the disabled and so on. The *hitherto modest* Rag has ambitions.

RELIGIOUS:
• 3 chaplains (RC, CofE, Methodist)
The University has a quiet room and a Muslim prayer room and the city has an Anglican cathedral and other places of worship for Christians of all sorts, Jews, Muslims, Sikhs and Hindus.

PAID WORK:
The University runs a jobshop. Having plenty of pubs and restaurants also spells opportunity.

SPORTS

- Recent successes: basketball, tae kwon do, football

Bradford has a few Corinthians but most students are persuaded to don trainers only on the off-chance of post-match debauchery. There is a one-off charge to students for facilities.

SPORTS FACILITIES:
The campus sports centre includes badminton and squash courts; climbing wall; dance/martial arts studio; pool; gym; sauna; solarium and *seriously flash* Nautilus suite. Just off campus, there are outdoor facilities at Laisteridge Lane: 4 tennis courts; floodlit hockey/football pitch and there are 35 acres of grass pitches 4 miles away at Woodhall. Locally and in the region students can also enjoy the delights of a bowling green, golf course, ski slope, a go-karting track, an ice rink and hills.

SPORTING CLUBS:
Jiu Jitsu; Rowing; Weightlifting.

ATTRACTIONS:
Bradford City FC is the local team and there's also Bradford Bulls Rugby League and the Bradford Bulldogs (ice hockey).

ACCOMMODATION

IN COLLEGE:
- Self-catering: 30% • Cost: £42-61 (30wks)

Availability: All rooms are single. Two of the halls have blocks devoted to single sex accommodation for both men and women and elsewhere all corridors are segregated. Intercoms and swipe cards help to keep out unwanted guests. Kitchens are shared between as few as 7 or as many as 23. *The private market is cheaper.*
Car parking: Adequate permit parking, *but cars aren't needed.*

EXTERNALLY:
- Ave rent: £33

Availability: Cheap and easy. Popular areas are Great Horton and Laisteridge Lane which are close and Heaton which is attractive. *In Buttershaw, even the muggers go in pairs.*
Housing help: The University Accommodation Office's 2 staff help and advise in the search.

WELFARE

SERVICES:
- Creche • Lesbian & Gay Society • Mature SA • Overseas SA
- Minibus • Women's Officer • Self-defence classes

The University has 3 full-time counsellors, the Union 2 advisers. The Health Centre has 4 doctors and several nurses.

Disabled: Ramp access and a chair lift to the Richmond Building, *extensive* braille facilities and loop systems in some lecture theatres. *Otherwise, wheelchair access is poor. There's not a comprehensive approach and there are a lot of problems, but improved since the setting up of* a Disability Office with 3 staff members, including a Disability Co-ordinator. 5p of each drink sold in the Union goes to the Disability Fund.

FINANCE:
• Hardship fund: £385,141 • Successful applications: 850
The University operates its own hardship fund and there's a £10,000 trust fund for female students.

Bretton Hall
see Other Institutions

University of Brighton

• *Formerly Brighton Polytechnic*
University of Brighton, Mithras House, Lewes Road, Brighton, BN2 4AT. Tel: (01273) 600900. Fax: (01273) 642825. E-mail: admissions@brighton.ac.uk
University of Brighton Students' Union, Cockcroft Building, Lewes Road, Brighton, BN2 4GJ. Tel: (01273) 642746. Fax: (01273) 600649. E-mail: ubsu@bton.ac.uk

GENERAL

Once every year a rally of vintage cars drives from central London over the South Downs to Brighton on the coast. The ones that make it have a party in one of the many hotels on the sea front, which is dashed all along with pebble beaches and marked by the Palace Pier. Hundreds of cyclists make the same pilgrimage in aid of charity, and thousands of tourists in the name of sea air *and the town's unique mix of shabby gentility and pulsating subculture.* Less joyfully, Brighton has a very large proportion of homeless. *However, the permanent residents are not all homeless, nor are they retired old fuddy duddies. A throbbing youth culture and a wholesome happening scene makes Brighton a good place for a University – it's fun and genteel, if a little shabby, and the weather's good.* However, one of the Unis is a bit outside town and the other (this one) isn't entirely in Brighton either. Okay, so 3 of the 4 sites are, but the fourth is east along the south coast in Eastbourne – Brighton's similar, but more *posh, bath chaired cousin. Each site is distinctly different – characters, building styles and courses.* None can claim to be the main site *and it would be a bad move for students to apply without knowing where they'd be based.*

Sex ratio(M:F): 38%:62%	Founded: 1976
Full time u'grads: 8,791	Part time: 935
Postgrads: 752	Non-degree: 2,695
Ave course: 3yrs	Ethnic: 11%
Private school: 5%	Flunk rate: 17%
Mature students: 27%	Overseas students: 18%
Disabled students: 4%	

ATMOSPHERE:
The social mix varies between sites but overall it's a vibrant, cosmopolitan mix, with a more creative bent than some of the other new universities. When facilities in the University fail to come up to scratch, temptations in town can take the strain.

THE SITES:
Grand Parade: (1,436 students – art, design, humanities) The site in the centre of Brighton and *the most attractive* consists of a large 60s block with a small grassy central courtyard and a few other older buildings. *It's full of arts students being pseudo-radical and creative (but friendly) poseurs.*

Moulsecoomb: (5,495 students – engineering, pharmacy, IT, business studies, sciences, accountancy, maths, interior design, building, architecture) In one of Brighton's less grand suburbs, 3 miles from the town centre, this site comprises 2 small tower blocks of light brick, white concrete and glass and a converted factory. *Characterless and little more than a busy work place,* most overseas students are based here.

Falmer: (2,747 students – community studies, library studies, multicultural studies, languages, education) Just over the rail line from the large campus of Sussex University are the post-war buildings of this greenfield site. It's 3 miles from the city centre and *feels vaguely remote despite the easy rail connection. Even less character than Moulsecoomb,* but has a new nursing building and student restaurant/café.

Eastbourne: (1,825 students – sports, PE, physiotherapy, podiatry, hotel & catering management) The Eastbourne site is split into several buildings around the town centre: a mixture of Victorian mock Tudor and newer buildings in some *pleasant* gardens within a brisk walk of the seashore. *A lot of students here are sporty and many display a little disappointment about having applied to Brighton, but ending up relatively far away, in an area cruelly, but not inaccurately, known to some as Crumblybourne; some end up loving it, though –* especially those who prefer it with the older man or woman.

THE TOWN:
- Population: 250,000
- London: 55miles
- Southampton: 56miles
- Eastbourne: 26miles

Brighton: Sometimes called 'London by the sea', *Brighton is a truly cosmopolitan town that feels a bit like a city crushed into a village,* because of the local variety and life. Homeless people beg outside swanky antique shops and leather-clad representatives of the large gay community stroll alongside well-dressed country ladies of a certain age. It's not as tacky as you might expect of the kiss-me-quick and candy floss coastal resorts – it's a bit too posh for all that. Most of the touristy bits are of the quaint, craft work variety rather than bedazzling unsubtlety. Brighton has all the daily trade and shopping stocks for most needs. There's North Laines (*vastly preferable*) with *terminally trendy* clothes, jewellery and antique shops, cafés and buskers. Some of the more notable features include the *excellent* selection of second-hand bookshops, the *bizarre* Brighton Pavilion (Indian colonial throwback) and the Palace Pier with its permanent funfair.

EASTBOURNE:
- Population: 83,200
- London: 57miles

In many ways just like Brighton, but less so. It's smaller for a start and, with the exception of the sea front, is less quaint. It has a *deserved reputation as part of the Costa Geriatrica, but mauve rinses aren't compulsory.* It has plenty of shops, an Arndale Shopping Centre and a number of second-hand spending spots. *What nightlife there is, is student-oriented, and although it's not as pulsating as Brighton, it's still better than picking out Chris Moyles' navel fluff with your tongue.*

TRAVEL:
Trains: Connections from Brighton station to London (£6.60), Bristol (£23.75), Sheffield (£38.30) and elsewhere.
Coaches: All over the country including London (£10.50), Bristol (£32), Sheffield (£25).
Car: The A23 connects Brighton with London. Within Brighton beware the voucher system and zealous wardens.
Air: Gatwick is 23 miles north on the A23.
Ferries: Ferries from Newhaven (8 miles east) to Dieppe.
Hitching: *Best results on hot summer days by the beautiful, for the rest (or on the other 322 days of the year) try the five options above.*
Local: The local buses are *reliable but take forever*. Trains provide a comprehensive local service inland and along the coast linking Brighton and Eastbourne.
Taxis: *Not the country's cheapest.*
Bicycles: *New cycle lanes have improved matters but the traffic's a bit mad and the hills are a bit hilly.*

CAREER PROSPECTS:
- Careers Service • No of staff: 5 full/2 part
- Unemployed after 6mths (1999): 6%

FAMOUS ALUMNI:
Kate Allenby (Olympic bronze – Modern Pentathlon); Helen Chadwick (artist); Norman Cook aka Fat Boy Slim (musician, DJ, father of Woody Cook); Harvey Goldsmith (promoter); Helen Rollason (late BBC sports reporter); Jo Whiley (R1 DJ).

FURTHER INFO:
Prospectuses for undergrads and postgrads; guides to housing and for International students from the Registry; a video (for schools and careers offices); and the SU has an alternative prospectus on the University's website (www.brighton.ac.uk).

ACADEMIC

Brighton puts a special emphasis on job-based study, and runs some very unusual courses, such as a BA in Editorial Photography and a BSc in Podiatry (that's feet).

staff/student ratio: 1:20
Range of points required for entrance: 300-160
Percentage accepted through clearing: 5%
Number of terms/semesters: 3
Length of terms/semesters: 10wks
Research: 2.8

LIBRARIES:

- Books: 573,000 • Study places: 1,213

There's a major library on each site and 3 support libraries.

COMPUTERS:
- Computer workstations: 1,500

ENTERTAINMENT

TOWN:
- Price of a pint of beer: £1.95 • Glass of wine: £1.45

Cinemas: 3 cinemas including an Odeon, ABC and an MGM multiplex and the Duke of York's arthouse cinema club.

Theatres: Theatre Royal puts on pre-West End runs, summer spectaculars and Xmas pantos. The Gardner Arts Centre (owned by Sussex University) hosts *less mainstream* productions and there are several smaller venues as well.

Pubs: *Expensive but* Pushplugs: Hector's Horse; The Bear; AliCats; Zanzibar and the Marlborough (gay).

Clubs/discos: Brighton has a *brilliant, banging, booming, bon...(enough) club-scene, clubs include the trendy, cavernous* Zap Club with its cabaret and gay nights (*£6-8 though and attracts rich, dim Sloanes*); The Beach (home of 'The Big Beat Boutique', *legendary hip-hang-out* – 2nd & 4th Friday monthly); The Escape (indie nights). The Event and Paradox *are popular student stuffstrutting stables.*

Music venues: *For a bit of Brighton rock: the Event and the Brighton Centre are the big name venues; the Theatre Royal does classical and opera; and the Richmond pub, the Concorde and the Zap provide indie and dance stuff – also the Dome, the Pavilion and Fresher's Point.*

Eating out: Brighton has a choice *as wide as Tony Blair's cheesiest grin*, including fish and chips and seafood, veggie and wholefood, pizzas and burgers, Indian, Thai, Chinese, Mongolian and of course, traditional British restaurants to *every degree of daintiness. It's almost as good and almost as expensive as London.* Pushplugs: Donatello's (student specials); Cactus Canteen (Mexican); Food For Friends (veggie); Blind Lemon Alley; Dorset bar; Sanctuary Café.

Other: The Brighton Festival each May is one of the country's biggest arts and entertainment festivals – *an excellent distraction from exams.* The Festival Radio station employs a fair few students. Also in May is the Essential Music Festival, the *start of the naked mud-rolling outdoor music season.*

UNIVERSITY:
- Price of a pint of beer: £1.40 • Glass of wine: £1.20

Bars: There are 2 bars run by the SU at Falmer and Eastbourne and 2 smaller boozers at Moulsecoomb.

Theatres/cinema: There are 2 *enthusiastic* drama societies who use the Komedia (*tiny* cap 90), plus the uni-owned Sallis Benney Theatre. 2 film societies play with projectors.

Clubs/discos/music venues: Ents facilities are somewhat hampered with no main venue, but the SU makes the best use of the local bars and clubs.

Cabaret: Thursdays are braided with badinage from the likes of the *execrable* Craig Charles and the *excellent* Adam Bloom.

Food: All SU bars do a *wide* range of grub, as do the *expensive* University-run refectories.

Others: Eastbourne and Brighton sites host annual balls, and last year's Fresher's ball took place on Palace Pier.

SOCIAL & POLITICAL

UNIVERSITY OF BRIGHTON STUDENTS' UNION:
• 5 sabbaticals • Turnout at last ballot: 1% • NUS member
Students as a whole are too apathetic to organise politically. There are at least some facilities on each site.

SU FACILITIES:
Falmer: bar, shop, meeting room. Eastbourne: SU office, bar, satellite TV.

CLUBS (NON SPORTING):
Cinema; Film; Hindu; Interior design; Nursing; Punjab.

OTHER ORGANISATIONS:
'Babble' is the monthly glossy mag and there's also the self explanatory 'Visual Culture' magazine.

RELIGIOUS:
• 2 chaplains (CofE, RC)
Students can find all the world's major religions represented locally.

PAID WORK:
Although the jobs are no different from other towns, prospects are more hopeful, especially during the tourist season. The SU's Work Shop can find function for fidgeting fingers.

SPORTS

• Recent successes: netball, football
Facilities at Eastbourne are good (thanks to sports studies) and not bad at Falmer either. Elsewhere, nothing to rave about. Participation is high, especially in women's sports.

SPORTS FACILITIES:
3 sports halls; playing fields; athletics track; 50m Olympic-size swimming pool (at Eastbourne) – for something bigger try the sea, 50+miles to France); floodlit tennis courts; floodlit 5-a-side football pitch; floodlit netball court; climbing wall; gyms; multigym; putting green; sauna; cardiovascular gym (at Moulsecoomb); Sport & Racquet club (£10 membership for students at Falmer).

SPORTING CLUBS:
Contemporary dance; 4-a-side football; Lacrosse; Low-impact aerobics; Mixed hockey; Sailing; Sauna; Sub-aqua; Tai Chi; Track & field; Yoga.

ATTRACTIONS:
Brighton & Hove Albion is the *dire* local football team and of course, there's also Sussex County cricket and Brighton races.

ACCOMMODATION

IN COLLEGE:
• Catered: 1% • Cost: £77-81 (32wks)
• Self-catering: 16% • Cost: £45-62 (38-50wks)
Availability: Uni accommodation is almost all snapped up by 1st years and with other options, 68% of them are housed, with 3% sharing. The buildings range in size from the Varley Halls (495) in Brighton to the Whitworth house in Eastbourne (40). There are also 377 places in University-run head tenancy schemes. CCTV and codepad entry at some halls.

Car parking: Free spaces if students can find them.

EXTERNALLY:
- Ave rent: £48

Availability: *It used to be hell trying to find affordable accommodation, but things have become easier (a number of agencies now deal with students) although prices are still steepish. Hopeful spots for bedsits and shared houses are London Rd (near station and the best pubs), Lewes Rd/Elm Grove (good for Falmer), Seven Dials (near another station and the town centre) and Kemptown (just 'cos it's nice). Hove is a bit far and Moulsecoomb is a bit rough. Having a car doesn't help – there's nowhere to park it.*

Housing help: The Student Services organisation allocates the University's spaces and lends a hand in finding places in the private market as do a number of private agencies.

WELFARE

SERVICES:
- Playscheme • Nightline • Lesbian & Gay Society
- Mature SA • Postgrad SA • Overseas SA • Minibus
- Women's Officer • Self-defence classes

Student Services has 4 full-time and 1 part-time counsellors and SU Welfare Unit surgeries tour around the sites. There are doctors' surgeries and a nurse on each site, and an Aids Awareness worker jointly funded by Sussex University. *Drugs (particularly cannabis and ecstasy) are especially prevalent locally.*

Disabled: *Facilities are pretty feeble at Falmer and Eastbourne.* The University insists the situation is improving and has recently provided 6 specially designed rooms, a Special Needs Co-ordinator and Hearing Impaired Welfare Officer.

FINANCE:
- Access fund: £731,492 • Successful applications: 1,441

Hardship loans up to £500.

Bristol University

University of Bristol, Senate House, Tyndall Avenue, Bristol, BS8 1TH.
Tel: (0117) 928 9000. Fax: (0117) 925 1424.
E–mail: admissions@bris.ac.uk
University of Bristol Union, Queens Road, Bristol, BS8 1LN.
Tel: (0117) 954 5800. Fax: (0117) 954 5817.
E–mail: president–ubu@bris.ac.uk

GENERAL

Just as the mouth of the Severn begins to yawn, before being swallowed by the Bristol Channel, the Avon river drops off into the south–west of England. Within a few miles it flows through the heart of Bristol before reaching the *traumatically spectacular* Avon Gorge at Clifton. It's an *attractive* mix of old and new buildings, surrounded by green hills, *which can only be described as countryside*. In the middle of all this is the University Precinct and *no one can forget it, what with the splendid gothic tower of the Wills Memorial Building dominating the city skyline*. Many of the other buildings are *equally inspiring such as the large tea-with-crooked-pinkie* Victorian houses converted to form the arts departments and the 18th-century mansion, Royal Fort House. The Union Building, however, *lets the side down – an ugly, concrete, squat, grey, eminently demolishable tower block.*

Sex ratio(M:F): 50%:50%
Full time u'grads: 9,989
Postgrads: 2,179
Ave course: 3yrs
Private school: 37%
Mature students: 10%
Disabled students: n/a

Founded: 1876
Part time: 32
Non-degree: n/a
Ethnic: 9%
Flunk rate: 5.9%
Overseas students: 15%

ATMOSPHERE:
Bristol is trying to shed its image as one of the so-called green welly universities but it is nevertheless still popular with Sloanes and Oxbridge rejects (although most students would rather be here than Oxbridge any day). It's big enough and the SU is buzzing enough, to blur the edges of any social stereotypes that might be encountered. The two great social unifiers are sport and alcohol – especially on Wednesdays.

THE CITY:
- Population: 370,300 • London: 111miles
- Birmingham: 77miles • Cardiff: 29miles

Bristol is effectively the capital of the south–west. It was, until the 19th century, as important as the big boys like London, Brum or Manchester, but the old maritime industry has gone now and the docks have been redeveloped with offices for yuppies. *Bristol's highlights include:* the Cabot Tower (which, from below, can be seen from almost anywhere and, from the top of which, almost anything can be seen) and the *outrageous* Clifton Suspension Bridge, designed by Brunel. Also designed by Brunel in 1843 is the SS Great Britain, now in dry dock at the Maritime Heritage Museum. *For science with knobs on,* try @bristol on the waterfront, for art and nature, the City Museum & Art Gallery and, for caged animals, Bristol Zoo. *In some ways, Bristol is the British San Francisco (surely the other way round, this isn't the New World); beautiful, quirky, culturally thriving, slightly hippy-dippy and too many hills.*

TRAVEL:
Trains: Bristol Temple Meads is one of the country's centres for mainline routes: London (£27.15), Birmingham (£20.45) and elsewhere. Bristol Parkway for Wales.
Coaches: Bristol is *similarly well* served by coach services, including National Express buses to, among other places, London (£15), Birmingham (£12.75) and Cardiff (£6.50). Arrow and Bakers Dolphin also offer cheap return trips to London.
Car: *How do you get two whales in a mini? Down the M4.* On the way to the Severn Bridge, the M4 also bypasses Bristol with the M32 going into the city. The M5 comes down from the Midlands, and the A38, A4 and A37 also all visit Bristol.
Air: Bristol Airport, 7 miles outside the city centre, has flights inland and to Europe.

Hitching: *The M4 and M5 are good for distance thumbsters.*
Local: There are several British Rail stops in and around the city providing *a reliable, frequent and comprehensive service without staggering cost.* Local buses fill in where trains can't go, costing £1 from Temple Meads Station to the Union.
Taxis: At about £1 per mile, useful for late night tripping.
Bicycles: *The hilly city presents ups and downs, but busy roads present downright danger, although there is an increasing number of cycle lanes. Nevertheless pedalling is a popular pastime if you can hold onto your trusty bike for long enough.*

CAREER PROSPECTS:
- Careers Service • No of staff: 13 full/11 part
- Unemployed after 6mths: 3%

SPECIAL FEATURES:
- Bristol has some of the best recycling facilities and one of the highest proportions of local ex-students of any British city.

FAMOUS ALUMNI:
Paul Boateng MP (Lab); Alex Cox (film director); Dominic Diamond (Gamesmaster who was always destined for the Channel 5 graveyard shift); Frances Horovitz (poet); Sue Lawley (broadcaster); Matt Lucas (aka George Dawes); Chris Morris ('Jam' and 'Brass Eye' *comic genius*); Trude Mostue (TV vet); Alistair Stewart (newsreader); Chris Woodhead (ex-schools inspector); Charlotte Uhlenbrock (nature prog TV presenter).

FURTHER INFO:
General prospectus from the University and alternative prospectus from UBU (not free); websites (www.bris.ac.uk and www.ubv.org.uk).

Staff/student ratio: 1:13
Range of points required for entrance: 360-160
Percentage accepted through clearing: 1%
Number of terms/semesters: 3
Length of terms/semesters: 11wks
Research: 5.2

LIBRARIES:
- Books: 1,200,000 • Study places: 2,100

Students complain that the library's too small – plenty of students at other universities would disagree.

COMPUTERS:
- Computer workstations: 1,050

24-hour access to computers, plus network links in most residential hall rooms.

TOWN:
- Price of a pint of beer: £2.00 • Glass of wine: £2.00

Cinemas: (12) A wide range of flicks in all kinds of picture palaces. *Some of the specially special include the Arts Centre Cinema, The Watershed and the Arthouse Cinema at the city's superlative*

dockside arts complex, the Arnolfini. There's also a Warners at the Cribs Causeway shopping complex.
Theatres: The Old Vic (the country's oldest working theatre) hosts high profile high-brow shows. The Hippodrome (West End re-runs, pantos, occasional ballet and opera) and the Arnolfini again. Several fringe theatres as well.
Pubs: *Local ciders and Smiles Brewery beers are worth a sip. Pushplugs: Berkeley (huge, cheap and close); It's a Scream.*
Clubs/discos: *Bristol used to be a dozy layby on the UK's musical autobahn but local dance acts such as Portishead, Roni Size, Tricky and Massive Attack have caused ripples worldwide. It's not just trip-hop, though – Pushplugs: Steam Rock; the Maze on the Waterfront the Roo Bar; Henry J Beans. 'The Strip' is a mile-long stretch on Whiteladies Road, containing 41 nightspots of varying tack levels.*
Music venues: The Bierkeller, Louisiana, Fleece & Firkin and New Trinity all keep live sounds pumping, *often of an indie persuasion.* Colston Hall (more mainstream) and St George's Hall (free at lunchtimes) are the scene of classical concerts.
Eating out: A wide range of eateries, some doling out the munchies till the early hours. *Pushplugs: Cotham Hill area generally; Hullabaloos; York Café (legendary English breakfast); Boston Tea Party (bohemian); Mud Dock Café (voted Café of the Year 1998 by... someone); Henry Africa's Hothouse.*

UNIVERSITY:
• Price of a pint of beer: £1.15 • Glass of wine: £1.00
Bars: The Epicurean ('The Epi', cap 650) on the 3rd floor of the Union Building, *is the gravitational centre of student social life (which probably explains why so many are lying on the floor).* The Avon Gorge Bar is on the 5th floor with roof garden and events. The University runs a number of other bars in the halls.
Theatres: *(4) Budding actors burst into full bloom at Bristol, one of the strongest universities for student theatre.* Winston Theatre and Lady Windsor Studio are both run by the Union. The drama department uses the Glynn Wickham Studio and the Victoria Rooms (700) are used for large scale productions. Bristol usually sends something to the Edinburgh Fringe.
Cinemas: Bristol Filmhouse and the Fine Film society show anything and everything in the Union's Winston Theatre.
Clubs/discos: The Union can be used by ravesters on a roll, as can the larger Anson Room (900) and occasionally the Epi.
Music venues: The Anson Room attracts biggies like Roni Size, David Gray and Coldplay.
Food: Café Zuma is the focus for face-fillers, offering a *vast range* including its *famous* all-day breakfast (£2).

SOCIAL & POLITICAL

UNIVERSITY OF BRISTOL UNION (UBU):
• 7 sabbaticals • Turnout at last ballot: 20% • NUS member
UBU's building is one of the largest and best equipped in the country. The Union has a significant say in the Uni, but it still doesn't attract much interest from students – it's a bit out of the way and dead in the day. Campaigns include trying to get the Union moved, which would require a very big crane.

SU FACILITIES:
At the Union Building: 3 bars; restaurant; snack bar; vending machines; travel agent; huge new general shop; second-hand bookshop; NatWest and Lloyds Bank cash machines; video arcade; market stalls; swimming pool; 2 dark-rooms; music rooms; pottery workshop; art studio; pool; 2 theatres; launderette; hairdresser and barber; study rooms; photo booth.

CLUBS (NON SPORTING):
Art; Balloon Debates; Baptist; Bewilderebeeste ('Monty Python' appreciation); Bottled Beer; Buhabs (ballooning); Chinese; ChocSoc; Christian Science; Circus; CND; Dr Who; 007; Duke of Edinburgh; Expeditions; Hellenic; Hispanic; Malaysian; Marxist; Massage; Meditation; Methodist; Mr Men; Opera; Panto; Pottery; Rag Morris (silly bells and bouncing for charity); Red Cross; Scandinavian; Silly Walk; Speleological; Tibet; Turkish; War Games; Welsh.

OTHER ORGANISATIONS:
UBU's 2 regular (free) publications are 'Epic', the fortnightly newsletter and 'Epigram', the *excellent* fortnightly newspaper. Burst FM is the student radio station. Do-gooders do good through the Bristol-wide charity Rag and the active Students Community Action, involved in over 20 local projects.

RELIGIOUS:
• Chaplains (most flavours)
Ecumenical University chaplaincy centre. In town, worshippers of every species can worship anywhere from Sikh temples and the Salvation Army to the Vedanta Movement and synagogues.

PAID WORK:
There's always go-go dancing, but otherwise just the normal limited selection of bar work and restaurants. The SU runs a student employment office.

• Recent successes: across the board
Pull on your boots, flex those pecs – this is one of those places where students are as likely to be carrying Deep Heat as they are hot dope. Bristol came 9th in last year's BUSA league and the emphasis is firmly on sports for the sporty, but even slobby couchers can turn into Mr Motivator in this environment.

SPORTS FACILITIES:
If a sport's worth playing, facilities are probably slotted in for it somewhere around the University. The sports centre at Woodland House by the main University buildings houses a gym and facilities for many indoor sports. Under the Union Building is a swimming pool and further out, by the halls of residence at Stoke Bishop and at Coombe Dingle there are 38 acres of playing fields, a floodlit artificial pitch and 16 grass tennis courts. Hockey is played on an Astroturf pitch and there is an indoor tennis centre (also to be used by the LTA). There are further sports provisions at the halls including squash and tennis courts. Sailors swing their booms down at the Baltic Wharf Marina near the city centre and rowers pull their oars at the boathouses on the Avon.

SPORTING CLUBS:
Aikido; Boat Club; Clay Pigeon; Combat Karate; Cricket; Explorers; Hang Gliding; Jiu Jitsu; Korfball; Kuro Hebi; Lacrosse (mixed as well); Mountain Bike; Mountaineering; Polo; Riding; Rifle; Shorinji Kempo; Sky Diving; Snooker; Snow-boarding; Surf; Waterpolo; Triathlon; Ultimate Frisbee; Waterski; Weightlifting; Windsurfing; X-Games.

ATTRACTIONS:
Rugby and football keep the fans flapping. There's Bristol Rugby Club, the Bristol Packers, the local American Football team, and, with round balls, Bristol Rovers and Bristol City FC. Nevil Road is the main ground for Gloucestershire County Cricket Club and other balls fly at the Redland Lawn Tennis Championship. Greyhounds race at Eastville Stadium.

ACCOMMODATION

IN COLLEGE:
- Catered: 16% • Cost: £65–92 (30wks)
- Self-catering: 9% • Cost: £35–60 (30–38wks)

Availability: 90% of 1st years live in halls (5% can't, even if they beg), but few after that. The choices are based in 3 areas: 6 large halls at Stoke Bishop (just under 2 miles north of the University Precinct); 3 halls near the *gorgeous* gorge in Clifton (⅔ mile west); and student houses in and around the Precinct itself, which are all self-catering *and scarce*. There are 5 catered halls *(whose food is 'orrible)*, 4 self-catering halls *(2 of which are blocks of shared flats)* and 19 houses for between 9 and 125 students. 6% have to share and some corridors in some halls and some student houses are single sex. *Night porters do the Dirty Harry bit with intruders.*

Car parking: The demand for spaces is kept down by requiring drivers to buy a permit, which means that parking is *adequate at most, if not all,* halls for those who can afford it.

EXTERNALLY:
- Ave rent: £50

Availability: *Finding suitable accommodation in Bristol is nigh on a pushover, although the relative affluence of students has edged prices up a bit. Although local relations are quite good, some areas of Bristol are ruff'n'tuff. St Paul's has drug dealers on street corners but some students live there for the gutter cred. Avoid South Bristol in favour of Bishopston, Cotham, Clifton and Redland (where external scenes for 'The Young Ones' were shot). Wherever students lay their hat, they find it hard to park their car.*

Housing help: The University Accommodation Office's 6 staff keep a vacancies register and database and provide general help, a landlord blacklist and advice in home-hunting.

WELFARE

SERVICES:
- Creche • Lesbian & Gay Society • Mature SA • Overseas SA
- Minibus • Women's Officer • Self-defence classes

The University employs 2 counsellors and UBU enlists the services of several part-time volunteers. The University Health Service has 5 doctors and nursing staff and the physical recreation centre keeps students fit in the first place.

Disabled: *Bristol is quite hilly, making it very difficult for students with mobility problems to get between the buildings where, ironically, access is quite good.* The University has an integrated service called the Access Unit for Deaf and Disabled Students.

FINANCE:
• Access fund: £516,355   • Successful applications: 548

Bristol Poly
see Bristol, University of the West of England

Bristol: University of the West of England

• *Formerly Bristol Polytechnic*
University of the West of England, Frenchay Campus, Coldharbour Lane, Bristol, BS16 1QY. Tel: (0117) 965 6261.
Fax: (0117) 344 2810. E-mail: admissions@uwe.ac.uk
Students' Union, University of the West of England,
Frenchay Campus, Coldharbour Lane, Bristol, BS16 1QY.
Tel: (0117) 344 2577. Fax: (0117) 344 2675.
E-mail: union@uwe.ac.uk

GENERAL

The University has 4 sites with its main campus 5 miles north of the city centre at Frenchay. It was purpose-built in 1975 *in a style that suggests that built with a purpose means 'built with an excuse' – although things have been improved with a bit of 'landscaping'*. The other campuses, described below, are spread out around Bristol nearer the centre. They have their own courses and are *roughly self-contained*, although all students are allowed to use the facilities of the main site.

Sex ratio(M:F): 44%:56%	Founded: 1969
Full time u'grads: 13,390	Part time: 1,583
Postgrads: 1,155	Non-degree: 5,465
Ave course: 3yrs	Ethnic: 7%
Private school: n/a	Flunk rate: n/a
Mature students: 15%	Overseas students: 7%
Disabled students: 4%	

ATMOSPHERE:
The University lacks a single focal point for all students at all campuses – Frenchay ends up ignoring the others a bit and the advantages of Bristol as an attractive and fun city come into play. There's a relatively high proportion of students from private schools for an ex-poly. Some, aiming for social cachet, see UWE as the next best thing to Bristol University, *without the unnecessarily stringent A-level requirements.*

THE SITES:
Frenchay: (9,500 students – most courses) The main campus.
Glenside: (5,000 students – Health & Social Care) This is the former Avon & Gloucestershire College of Health, which before that was a psychiatric hospital. It's an imposing Victorian edifice, 1½ miles from Frenchay.

St Matthias: (1,800 students – Humanities, Psychology) 2½ miles from Frenchay with 2 halls of residence, *by far the best looking site with a gothic style listed building and sunken lawn. A tight-knit community and almost a college in its own right.*

Bower Ashton: (1,300 students – Art, Media & Design) 2 miles from the city centre near the Clifton Suspension Bridge, *but with the advantage of being in a student area.* 7½ miles from Frenchay, this is an *overwhelmingly white concrete and glass oblong, not built to appeal to the aesthetic nature of the students based here. Surrounded by pleasant fields, students consider themselves almost entirely separate from the main campus.*

THE CITY: see University of Bristol

TRAVEL: see University of Bristol
Bus services link the Frenchay campus to the city centre (£1.35 rtn) and run between the sites *(which isn't often necessary)*. *Local buses have improved* with a new late night service that runs every hour from the city centre but only on weekends. The most convenient station for Frenchay is Bristol Parkway.

CAREER PROSPECTS:
• Careers Service • No of staff: 4 full-time
• Unemployed after 6mths: 5.5%
Among its other services, the careers office publishes a service on the net (www.uwe.ac.uk/careers/).

FAMOUS ALUMNI:
Kyran Bracken, Victor Obogu and Steve Ojomoh (England Rugby Union); Ian Cognito (comedian); Dawn Primarolo MP (Lab); Jack Russell (cricketer); Geoff Twentyman (ex-footballer now BBC sports presenter).

FURTHER INFO:
Undergraduate prospectus and websites (www.uwe.ac.uk and www.uwe.ac.uk/union).

ACADEMIC

staff/student ratio: 1:28
Range of points required for entrance: 300-120
Percentage accepted through clearing: 12%
Number of terms/semesters: 3
Length of terms/semesters: 12wks
Research: 3.1

LIBRARIES:
• Books: 666,300 • Study places: 2,142
There are libraries on all campuses relating to the studies based there.

COMPUTERS:
• Computer workstations: 1,987
The University's extensive computer provision is spread around the sites, open 24 hours a day, 7 days a week.

Students from Bangor Rag once 'closed' the island of Anglesey by erecting an 'Anglesey Full' sign.

ENTERTAINMENT

CITY: see University of Bristol
UNIVERSITY:
• Price of a pint of beer: £1.30 • Glass of wine: £1.30
Bars: (6) The Escape Bar is the primary social hub but the Venue hosts events and St Matts is popular. The Bower is gaining ground as a venue.
Theatre: Topcat Productions put on several performances a year, and the performing arts group do *lavish* musicals.
Clubs/discos/music venues: *Don't hang out here if you think dance music is a lot of banging with no tunes.* 'Fried' brings on that Friday feeling at Frenchay (cap 700) and is popular, being free and having the cheapest late bar in Bristol. The Venue bar hosts live music and karaoke. Space, LTJ Bukem and local band, The Wurzels have played here in recent months.
Food: The SU's main food stop, in the Escape Bar, is usually packed out. St Matts does the *best toasties on earth* and there's also Pizza Towers (pizza and nachos). The University-run Refectory is *cheap but the food is pretty drab. Sign of the times: 'budget meals' for hard-up students*. Local eateries are fewer, *further between and duller* away from the city centre.
Others: 3 balls a year and occasional comedy.

SOCIAL & POLITICAL

UNIVERSITY OF THE WEST OF ENGLAND STUDENTS' UNION:
• 6 sabbaticals • Turnout at last ballot: 10% • NUS member
The SU has at least an office on each campus and usually a bar and common room as well, but the main centre is on the Frenchay campus. Relations with the university administration are practically post-coital. UWESU produced a 40ft petition for the NUS Student Rights Charter – the longest in the country.

SU FACILITIES:
With most facilities at Frenchay, the collected provisions of the SU include: 4 bars; minibus for hire; training centre; post office; advice centre; 4 general shops; NatWest Bank (with cashpoint at Frenchay); Endsleigh Insurance office; photocopying; library; photo booth; games and vending machines; pool and snooker tables; juke box; jobshop; computing facilities.

CLUBS (NON SPORTING):
Band; Bowerhouse (magazine); Buddhist; Chinese; Exhibition; Hempology; Hong Kong; House & Garage; Internet; Juggling; Law & Debating; Malaysian; Radiobase; Role Play & Gaming; Salsa; Spanish; Top Cat Productions (drama); Welsh.

OTHER ORGANISATIONS:
The SU publishes 'Westworld', *the name referring to location rather than the android western*, plus each site has its own mag. They're also working on Radio Base. There's a charity Rag and a Student Community Action group which involves students in local help activities.

RELIGIOUS:
The 'Octagon' houses the University's chaplaincy centre for all versions of Christianity and is available for use by other faiths such as Muslims and Jews, also separate Islamic prayer room.

SPORTS

- Recent successes: rugby, equestrian

Despite the fact that the Uni has been in the shadow of its notoriously sporty neighbour for some time and facilities aren't really up to much, UWE has produced a few individual champions.

SPORTS FACILITIES:
Frenchay: 3 squash courts; training room; floodlit artificial pitch. Redland: small gym. St Matthias: small gym; 2 soccer pitches; cricket square. *The Uni had the bright idea of building a car-park on the netball pitch. Great PR move, guys. Perhaps they can make up for it by building the swimming pool everyone wants.*

SPORTING CLUBS:
Aikido; American football; Athletico Glenside; Duke of Edinburgh; Gliding; Jiu Jitsu; Karting; Kickboxing; Lacrosse; Mountain Bike; Paintball; Parachute; Paragliding; Rowing; Shadwell Rovers; Surf; Table tennis; Ultimate Frisbee; Water polo; Waterski; Windsurf; Zen Shorin Do.

ATTRACTIONS: see University of Bristol

ACCOMMODATION

IN COLLEGE:
- Self-catering: 15% • Cost: £46-51 (40-46wks)

Availability: 70% of 1st years can be accommodated. There are halls at Glenside and St Matthias, a student village at Frenchay and some new developments in the city centre (*better for all the fun of Bristol, worse for making that 9am lecture*). There are strict rules for those in halls regarding 'guests'.
Car parking: *Not entirely adequate (despite the loss of the netball pitch).* Permit required.

EXTERNALLY: see University of Bristol
Availability: *Accommodation works out just a bit cheaper than for those at Bristol University, because they can live further out and still be close to the campus, but otherwise, details of housing in Bristol remain the same. A car certainly helps.*
Housing help: The 19 full-time staff of Student Accommodation Services provide aid and advice.

WELFARE

SERVICES:
- Nursery • Lesbian & Gay Society • Postgrad SA • Minibus
- Women's Officer • Self-defence classes

The University's Centre for Student Affairs' 4 full-time counsellors provide help and advice. The SU also has its own advice centre and staff. 2 nurseries for those too young to be at university on their own merit.
Disabled: *Frenchay has good access, but elsewhere for every ramp, there seems to be an annoying hump.* The Disability Resource Centre attempts to even out the odds.

FINANCE:
- Access fund: £910,535 • Successful applications: 1,123

Brookes University
see Oxford Brookes University

Brunel University

Brunel University, Uxbridge, Middlesex, UB8 3PH.
Tel: (01895) 274000. Fax: (01895) 232806.
E-mail: courses@brunel.ac.uk and admissions@brunel.ac.uk
Union of Brunel Students, Cleveland Road, Uxbridge, Middlesex,
UB8 3PH. Tel: (01895) 462200. Fax: (01895) 462300.
E-mail vp.communications@brunel.ac.uk

GENERAL

Fettered by London's influence, Uxbridge is *a metallic satellite-town with space-age offices, a slick, spick'n'span shopping mall and a few quaint streets.* A mile south of Uxbridge proper are the redbrick and grey concrete buildings of the main campus of Brunel University. *They were designed to be more practical than sexy, although grassy patches and a stream (the optimistically titled 'River' Pinn) help create a feeling of space.* There are also three smaller sites, none within walking distance.

Sex ratio(M:F): 53%:47%	Founded: 1966
Full time u'grads: 8,817	Part time: 808
Postgrads: 2,119	Non-degree: 479
Ave course: 3/4yrs	Ethnic: 39%
Private school: 10%	Flunk rate: 15.1%
Mature students: 23%	Overseas students: 7%
Disabled students: 3.7%	

ATMOSPHERE:
Brunel used to be overrun with geeks who told maths jokes no one ever got. This image is no longer accurate as in recent years more students are studying humanities (they can tell pretty dodgy jokes too). However, students still tend to be focused on careers rather than careering through student scrapes. Split sites create a slightly disparate social set-up although most ents are based at Uxbridge.

THE OTHER SITES:
Twickenham & Osterley: (3,611 students – arts, education, health, sport, geography) The former Brunel University College (and, before that, West London Institute) is split between 2 sites in Middlesex, 13 and 11 miles from Uxbridge. Because of the different subjects, *the mood is anything but techie and female students outnumber the blokes.*
Runnymede: (474 students – design) 65 acres including beautiful 19th century gardens and Victorian buildings, situated in Egham, 11 miles from Uxbridge. See Royal Holloway College to find out how *crap* Egham is.

TOWNS:
Uxbridge is a modern town with all the latest mod cons, like Tesco's, Sainsbury's, banks and so on. The host-towns for the smaller sites are pretty similar and all equally accessible to London, which is necessary for any serious stimulation.

THE CITY: see University of London

LOCAL TRAVEL:
Trains: West Drayton and Hayes are the BR stations nearest to the Uxbridge site both a short bus ride away (Uxbridge tube station is closer). There are trains to Bristol, Cardiff, Slough and other cities in the south-west served by trains out of London Paddington (at least 45 minutes away). For other services, the *quickest route is usually via* London mainline stations. For trains to and from Egham, which is the nearest station to the Runnymede site, see Royal Holloway College.

Buses: National Express and London Country coach services bypass both Uxbridge and Egham. The nearest stop is Heathrow Airport (25 minutes by bus). Connections with London are *good enough* to make London Victoria a possibility.

Car: Both sites are on the London escape route to the west, near the M25 (2 miles), and on the M4, M40, A4, A40 and A30.

Air: Heathrow is 4 miles from the Uxbridge campus.

Hitching: *No shortage of main roads (although hitchers have to get on to them to start with), but drivers round here are not too enthusiastic and pick-ups take time.*

Local: Uxbridge is still within London's local transport network, *which is convenient but expensive.* It's served by buses 207, 222, U3, U4, Express Coach 607 and Night Bus N89 (which goes right into London's West End). On the London Underground, Uxbridge station (a mile from campus) is the last stop on the Metropolitan and Piccadilly Lines *and offers a fast but expensive service into London.* The Uni runs a bus service between Uxbridge and Runnymede, *which isn't quite enough.*

Taxis: Cabs charge London and Heathrow prices, but £2 from the campus to Uxbridge *is okay between a couple of people.*

Bicycles: *Bikes are useful for local trips although the busy roads can make it hell.*

TRAVEL: see University of London

CAREER PROSPECTS:
- Careers Service   • No of staff: 4 full/1 part
- Unemployed after 6mths: 4%

Since so many students go on placements they have a *useful* mix of qualifications and experience.

FAMOUS ALUMNI:
Linford Crawford (first black barrister on the Bar Council); Jo Brand (comedienne); James Cracknell (olympic gold coxless 4); Audley Harrison (boxing olympic gold medallist); Alan Pascoe, Marcia Richardson, Kathy Smallwood (athletics); Iwan Thomas (400m).

FURTHER INFO:
Prospectuses for undergrads and postgrads, departmental brochures; call (01895) 203267 for open days or see the websites (www.brunel.ac.uk), (www.ubsonline.net).

ACADEMIC

Brunel has traditionally taught sciences, social sciences and engineering, usually in the form of so-called 'thin sandwich' courses. There are now more arts and humanities courses. Half of the students study 'thin sandwich' courses. These are made up of a slice of industrial placement for 2 semesters out of the 6 in the first 3 years of 4-year courses, and slices of academic study for the rest of the time.

> staff/student ratio: 1:16
> Range of points required for entrance: 320-200
> Percentage accepted through clearing: 24%
> Number of terms/semesters: 2
> Length of terms/semesters: 13wks
> Research: 4.1

LIBRARIES:
• Books: 402,000 • Study places: 1,056
One library on each campus. There are plans to upgrade the libraries at Osterley and Twickenham and to expand the library at Uxbridge. The SU insists that this will still not address all the access problems.

COMPUTERS:
• Computer workstations: 1,000

ENTERTAINMENT

UXBRIDGE:
• Price of a pint of beer: £2.20 • Glass of wine: £2
Pubs: *Local pubs are expensive and students tend to steer clear. The Good Yarn is an exception.*
Cinemas: The Odeon in Uxbridge does 10% student discounts.
Theatres: The Beck Theatre in Hayes (1½ miles away) *is outshone by London's bright lights, but it still serves up a regular diet of musicals, plays and jazz and classical concerts.*
Music venues: *Royale is a tacky pick-up joint. Students prefer to go into London to the more expensive pick-up joints.*
Eating out: *Pub grub is usually a good deal. Pushplugs: Grand Union (steaks); Nona Rosa (Italian).*

IN LONDON: see University of London

UNIVERSITY:
• Price of a pint of beer: £1.60 • Glass of wine: £1.75
Bars: (5) The main Union bar (cap 400) is at Uxbridge.
Theatres: The addition of Performing Arts students from BUC has raised Brunel's performing profile. There are several productions in conjunction with the University arts centre.
Music venues: The Academy (600) is the University's largest site for sounds.
Clubs/discos: Decades at Uxbridge; Heavy Cheddar at Runnymede; *the SU's 'Meltdown' R&B and Garage extravaganza and The Birds and the Bees pulls potential bees into the Beehive every Friday and makes them buzz in a vaguely rhythmic manner.*
Cabaret: Brunel is a *serious spot* on the alternative comedy circuit, with recent *mirthsters* including Lee & Herring, Bill Bailey, Craig Charles.

Food: The Uni-run Refectory and the SU's Gallery Café provide the full meal scenario while the Pinn Inn, Chompers and the sandwich bar serve snacks. SU outlets are much cheaper than the Uni's.
Other: Balls at all sites and in *posh* hotels, regular fireworks at Runnymede.

SOCIAL & POLITICAL

UNION OF BRUNEL STUDENTS:
• 6 sabbaticals • Turnout at last ballot: 9% • NUS member
Emphasis and energy is devoted to clubs and societies, which maintain a broad involvement in the Union's gamut of goings on and go some way to uniting the disparate sites. Politically speaking, Brunel students are notoriously uninterested.

SU FACILITIES:
In the Students' Union at Uxbridge there are 2 bars, 2 catering outlets, The Academy nightclub, Information and Advice centre, Endsleigh Insurance office, launderette, 4 minibuses, photobooth, vending and games machines, juke box, pool tables, conference and function rooms. There's also a travel agent, mini supermarket (open at weekends), Waterstones bookshop and HSBC Bank (cash machine). Runnymede site has a bar/venue, barbecue, campus shop, pool table, games and vending machines. Osterly & Twickenham has 2 bars, 2 venues, information and advice service, mini supermarket, games and vending machines, pool tables, 3 minibuses.

CLUBS (NON SPORTING):
Arabic; Artists United; Ballroom Dancing; Contemporary Dance; First Aid; Gaming; Hellenic; Motor; Multicultural; Music & Drama; Oriental; Pakistani; Planet 21 st; Punjabi; Radio; Salsa; Sikh; Tamil; Thinker's Forum; Unicultural.

OTHER ORGANISATIONS:
The SU's magazine is 'Route 66', a slick glossy and the B1000 radio station has some pretty flash equipment. The Community Action Group is funded by the SU to help the elderly and the young.

RELIGIOUS:
• 6 chaplains
The Meeting House chaplaincy at Uxbridge welcomes believers of all faiths and there is a mini mosque in one of the university buildings, plus chaplaincy rooms at Osterley and Twickenham. There are local churches for most flavours of Christian, *but for specialities like chocolate chutney and for different religions altogether, a pilgrimage to London is required.*

PAID WORK:
Even with the placements, students find it necessary to earn an extra buck, which is unfortunate, since local opportunities are only slightly more common than the local amphibious giraffes.

SPORTS

• Recent successes: rugby, athletic, women's football, hockey, boxing, rowing
For a small university, Brunel has some big-time facilities and has had several successes in recent years.

SPORTS FACILITIES:
The sports centre has, a sports hall with scoreboards, a gymnasium, 7 squash courts, a brilliant climbing wall, solarium, multigym and free weights. Outside, there are 2 floodlit pitches (1 artificial grass), netball courts, cricket nets, 6 tennis courts, an Astroturf pitch and many acres of playing fields. (Watch out for the nominal charges.) Osterley has a sports centre, badminton courts, netball pitches and a running track. Students who like their sports wet can either use the Queen Mother Reservoir, 7 miles from the campus (windsurfing and sailing), the boathouse on the Thames at Runnymede (rowing, canoeing) or the pavilion bar. Badminton courts and netball pitches at Twickenham also. As if that weren't enough, locally there's an ice rink, an artificial ski slope, a golf course, Thorpe Park water world and so on...

SPORTING CLUBS:
Boxing; Canoe; Chinese Boxing; Climbing; Gaelic Football (male & female); Gymnastics; Jiu Jitsu; Karate; Karting; Lacrosse; Outdoor Pursuits; Rugby League; Running; Sailing; Skydiving; Softball; Sub Aqua; Surf; Table tennis; Tae Kwon Do; Ten Pin Bowling; Triathlon; Trogs; Ultimate Frisbee; Women's rugby and football.

ATTRACTIONS:
The MCC's second cricket ground is in Uxbridge and Queen's Park Rangers are the local football team. Twickenham is, of course, the home of English rugby. For a flutter on the nags, there's nearby Kempton and Sandown.

ACCOMMODATION

IN COLLEGE:
- Catered: 4% • Cost: £48 - 60 (37-52wks)
- Self-catering: 27% • Cost: £43 (37wks)

Availability: All students at Runnymede can be accommodated in halls, but only 1st years and postgrads at the other sites can be housed. Catered halls at Osterley and Twickenham only include 5 main meals per week. Faraday and Fleming Hall are the *most sought after*, with big ensuite rooms. *Some are left out in the cold* and 3% have to share. Swipe cards, code access and CCTV *to help you feel safe.*

Car parking: *Plenty of free parking (permit required) but students will insist on trying to park as close to the hall doors as possible and complain if they have to walk 10 yards.*

EXTERNALLY:
- Ave rent: £65

Availability: Many students set up camp in Hayes, within 3 miles of the campus, mostly in shared houses and flats. *There are enough vacancies for students to have some choice in the matter. Uxbridge is not enormously welcoming, but not as bad as Egham. Twickenham is more expensive. Hounslow may be a more realistic option for students based here.*

Housing help: The University operates an Accommodation Office with full-time staff. *Students get 3 names and have to go back if none of them come up trumps (which is none too helpful).* The SU helps with contracts and produces an annual housing pack.

WELFARE

SERVICES:
- Nightline • Lesbian & Gay Society • Mature SA
- Overseas SA • Postgrad SA • Equal Opportunities Officer

There are 4 full- and 3 part-time counsellors. The SU operates an Information and Advice Service with 3 full- and 1 part-time counsellors. The Medical Centre for students' ailments is an NHS-run practice with 3 doctors (1 female), 2 nurses, a night nurse and psychiatrist. They offer a students only surgery for a couple of hours a day.

Disabled: Toilets and some rooms have been adapted for wheelchairs and a few ramps have been installed. Together with a Disability Office, these make Brunel, *well, a notch above adequate*.

FINANCE:
- Access fund: £558,193 • Successful applications: 1,546

Welfare loans (up to £150) from the SU. *Sponsorships and placement pay can ease the financial burden for many.*

University of Buckingham

University of Buckingham, Buckingham, MK18 1EG.
Tel: (01280) 814080. Fax: (01280) 822245.
E-mail: admissions@buckingham.ac.uk
Students' Union, Tanlaw Mill, University of Buckingham,
Hunter Street, Buckingham, MK18 1EG.
Tel: (01280) 822522. Fax: (01280) 812791

GENERAL

The county of Buckinghamshire stretches from the northwest of London and contains many towns larger than Buckingham – not least, Milton Keynes (the largest) or Aylesbury (the county town). For over 1,100 years, the county has been named after *what is little more than a village retreat for city folk but then, Milton Keynesshire really doesn't have the same ring*. The University, based on two 8 acre sites on the edge of town, *is unique*. For a start, it is Britain's only private university – that is to say, it gets no Government funding and so most students end up paying over £9,000 a year in fees alone. The Hunter Street site has the University's main facilities and shares departments with Verney Park. The buildings are mostly modern, *but very attractive*, with a converted mill and chapel, some purpose-built new blocks and one of the sites set amidst the banks of the Ouse. *Fields, trees and old stone buildings make it all seem a far cry from anywhere.*

Buckingham

Sex ratio(M:F): 45%:55%
Full time u'grads: 458
Postgrads: 140
Ave course: 2yrs
Private school: n/a
Mature students: 33%
Disabled students: 10%
Founded: 1974
Part time: 60
Non-degree: 66
Ethnic: n/a
Flunk rate: n/a
Overseas students: 72%

ATMOSPHERE:
Imagine what sort of people can afford £20,000 over two years, with little time to earn money in the meantime. Students fall into three groups – either (1) overseas students, (2) rich students or (3) a mixture of the above. There are, of course, exceptions such as the few local students who get a scholarship (or students with big bank loans), but that rather proves the rule, doesn't it? Because of the 2-year courses, it actually works out cheaper for those overseas students who'd have to pay whatever university they decided to attend. But these courses mean the workload is heavy and, in their own words, long vacations are 'perceived as an obsolescence'. Students rise to the challenge of the burden, often because they're footing the bill. The short courses also mean there's a lot less time to get involved in non-academic stuff – fine for those who believe that getting a degree is all that being a student is about. There is, however, a variety of extracurricular activities, although political activism is zilch. Being itsy bitsy, it's easy to get to know almost all the other students and staff and having so many overseas students makes it almost incomparably multicultural.

TOWN:
- Population: 12,620 • London: 50miles
- Milton Keynes: 14miles • Oxford: 21miles

Buckingham may look pretty but it ain't up to much when it comes to fun and convenience: a 24-hour Tesco's and high street shops, including Londis open till 10pm; bookshop; banks, beauticians and boutiques; and a street market. For glitzy glamour gladrags and funky threads try catching a plane to Milan. Milton Keynes (or, as it's known, 'MK'), on the other hand, is all convenience, but has the urban charm of a large eggbox. Its greatest attraction is one of the country's largest cinema multiplexes. Bicester is 11 miles in the other direction, but doesn't offer much more than Buckingham except a station.

TRAVEL:
Trains: The nearest stations are at Bicester and MK (London to MK £8.20 day rtn).
Buses: Buses take 20 minutes to get to MK and National Express services go from there all over the country. The X5 hourly Stagecoach Express goes between Oxford and Cambridge, taking in Buckingham, Bedford and MK en route. Also 2 coaches a day to Northampton and Leicester, 1 a day to Nottingham.
Car: *Students who can afford UB's fees can often afford a car as well.* Parking presents few problems. Routes often involve the M1, which bypasses MK, the A5, going straight through it, or the A43. Direct roads include A413, A421 and A422.
Air: Luton Airport, 36 miles away, is the closest international airport offering flights to most major destinations.
Hitching: *Hitching in the home counties is like eating spaghetti through a straw it's - just about possible, but it takes a long time and there are easier ways.*

Local: A shuttle runs betwixt bus station, campus and Tesco's.
Taxis: Several companies offer student discounts, *but still, it's quite a journey to MK or anywhere else that students might want to go and distance makes the fares grow bigger.*
Bicycles: *What with the quality and quantity of fresh air, the rural rarity of traffic and the ½ mile between the 2 sites, a bike is a handy asset indeedy.*

CAREER PROSPECTS:
- Service   • No of staff: 1 full
- Unemployed after 6mths: 17%

The careers service is open to the public, for a small charge, of course *(all in the best free market tradition).*

SPECIAL FEATURES:
- Most courses start at the beginning of the calendar year which leaves the Autumn term before the 1st year for other activities. Many students go abroad, often on programmes in Europe arranged by the Uni or as far as Japan. Overseas students often arrive early for courses to improve their English.
- Baroness Thatcher was the University Chancellor *(a kind of mascot).*

FAMOUS ALUMNI:
Marc Gene (Formula 1 driver); Leopold Mills II (Secretary to the Cabinet, Government of Bermuda); Alex Tovy (film director), you get the picture.

FURTHER INFO:
Prospectuses for undergrads and postgrads and course leaflets. Website (www.buckingham.ac.uk).

ACADEMIC

Courses are only 2 years long, with four 10-week terms in each year. This, along with the facts that students are customers first and foremost and UB's independent status means it requires less rigorous inspection and supervision from outside bodies, has led to accusations that a degree here is somehow of less value than others. But exams are externally graded, so degrees should be just as good.

staff/student ratio: 1:10
Range of points required for entrance: 240-160
Percentage accepted through clearing: n/a
Number of terms/semesters: 4
Length of terms/semesters: 10wks
Research: 2.1

LIBRARIES:
- Books: 92,703 • Study places: 219

As far as the 2 libraries go, *Buckingham suffers from one of the disadvantages of small universities: it may have more books per head, but it doesn't help the breadth of choice.*

COMPUTERS:
- Computer workstations: 130

24-hour access to some computers.

ENTERTAINMENT

TOWN:
- Price of a pint of beer: £2.10 • Glass of wine: £1.75

For a fix of fun or culture, Buckingham is as happening as a pork chop in a synagogue. In fact, for films, students go to MK, for night clubs to Oxford (see University of Oxford) and for a treat to London (see University of London).

Theatres: *Serious-minded* local amateur dramatics and more theatres in MK.

Pubs: There are 12 pubs within walking distance of the University, *but many are expensive.* Pushplugs: Grand Junction; New Inn; Mitre; the White Hart.

Music venues: Stowe School and the Community Centre host classical concerts and Seven Stars in Twyford, 6 miles away, has live rock'n'roll. Pubs have occasional bands and the Radcliffe centre is worth a look.

Eating out: *Not a great deal to tempt the discerning budget diner but 'budget' isn't always a relevant concept round here.* Pushplugs: Buckingham Tandoori (student discounts); Chen Du, Beijing (Chinese); Dipalee (popular Indian); Da Martino (Italian).

UNIVERSITY:
- Price of a pint of beer: £1.20 • Glass of wine: 95p

Bars: *George's Bar (cap 70) is open lunchtimes and evenings. The academic pace is evidently too intense for all-day quaffing sessions.* There are usually small events on every Friday.

Theatres: *Rare* productions in the Radcliffe Centre (250) or the open air.

Clubs/discos: The Refectory (cap 220), uncannily, is used as the refectory during the day, turns into a disco 3 times a week in term time (cap 200), often with a theme. Also the Francisenn Cellars (cap 100).

Music venues: Local and student bands appear at the Tanlaw Mill Bar. Classical concerts crop up at the Radcliffe centre.

Food: The University-run Refectory provides *reasonably priced* meals till 4.30pm with snacks in the afternoons.

Others: Karaoke, quizzes and the *posh* Graduation Ball.

SOCIAL & POLITICAL

UNIVERSITY OF BUCKINGHAM STUDENTS' UNION:
- 1 sabbatical • Turnout at last ballot: 35%

Political agitation is a non-starter. The student body is either apolitical or devoted to the free market ideals which underpin the Uni's existence. With the restricted amount of leisure time and the exec being changed twice a year, rather than annually as in every other institution, there's not a lot the SU can do. It provides services, co-ordinates clubs and runs the annual Rag week and Ball, but beyond that, students aren't aware of its existence.

SU FACILITIES:
The SU is based on the Hunter St site in the converted Tanlaw Mill which also houses the refectory and some indoor sports amenities. The SU runs a travel information service, bar, Sky TV, games machines, disco and pool tables.

CLUBS (NON SPORTING):
Aviation; Caribbean; Chinese; Christian Union; Film; Greek; Islamic; Law; Malaysian; Nigerian.

OTHER ORGANISATIONS:
There's Rag week. Er, that's it.

RELIGIOUS:
The Islamic Society has access to a prayer room. Several Christian denominations are catered for in Buckingham.

PAID WORK:
Nothing original here and fewer opportunities for conventional student jobs than most places but very few UB students need fast cash or have the time to earn it. That comes later.

- Recent successes: nothing special

Courses are so intense many students don't find the time to hit the pitch, but this means that those who play sports can do so for fun without suffering any serious competitive urges (racket rage and stuff).

SPORTS FACILITIES:
In the Tanlaw Mill: fitness centre (£35/year); aerobics and martial arts room; a snooker room. There are also table tennis tables, basketball, netball and tennis courts, all-weather 5-a-side pitch, a floodlit training area and 32 acres of playing fields. Local sports centres cost cash, but provide a broader choice of provisions including a swimming pool.

SPORTING CLUBS:
Aerobics; Basketball; Cricket; Football; Golf; Health & Fitness; Kick boxing; Rugby; Snooker; Table Tennis; Tai Chi; Tennis; Volleyball.

IN COLLEGE:
- Self-catering: 87% • Cost: £57-100 (52wks)

Availability: All 1st years live in and 30% of finalists. *The rooms themselves are comfy and pleasant and no one has to share. Students prefer the accommodation at the Hunter St site because Verney Park has no bar or refectory and few other facilities.* For a price, students can have phones connected in their rooms. All the accommodation is mixed and there is little provision for married couples.
Car parking: *Adequate, but a permit's needed.*

EXTERNALLY:
- Ave rent: £80

Availability: *Local housing is limited, which pushes prices up* and the University requires that students live within 10 miles. *Since many have cars and/or cash though, housing problems don't worry many students.* Some have funds to buy a place.
Housing help: The Accommodation Officer forges links with local estate agents for renting.

WELFARE

The University has a student counsellor and a Learning Support Adviser and the SU provides a few scant provisions for students' welfare. There is a dyslexia specialist. For help with your health there are weekly drop-in surgeries in town.

Disabled: Converted buildings have very poor access. Modern buildings are just a little better.

FINANCE:

Average debts vary beyond belief. Some students owe nothing while others are in debt to the tune of their entire course costs. Being a private university, Buckingham has no Government access fund provisions. Instead, scholarships are available and a limited hardship fund provides up to £750 to students who can present a good case.

Buckinghamshire Chilterns University College

(1) Buckinghamshire Chilterns University College, Queen Alexandra Road, High Wycombe, Bucks, HP11 2JZ. Tel: (01494) 522141.
Fax: (01494) 524392. E-mail: marketing@buckscol.ac.uk
Buckinghamshire Chilterns University College Students' Union, Queen Alexandra Road, High Wycombe, Bucks, HP11 2JZ.
Tel: (01494) 446330. Fax: (01494) 538195.
E-mail: vpcommunications@bcuc.ac.uk
(2) Buckinghamshire Chilterns University College, Wellesbourne Campus, Kingshill Road, High Wycombe, Bucks, HP13 5BB.
Tel: (01494) 522141. Fax: (01494) 465432.
(3) Buckinghamshire Chilterns University College, Chalfont Campus, Gorelands Lane, Chalfont St Giles, Bucks, HP8 4AD.
Tel: (01494) 522141. Fax: (01494) 871954.

GENERAL

Buckinghamshire Chilterns University College is named after the county rather than the town, that honour is reserved for University of Buckingham which is an entirely different thing. It is based in High Wycombe, a town that grew out of the industrial age although parts of it date back to the 13th century. Granted the power to award degrees as recently as 1996, it's one of those *chimeric beasts* called a 'University College'. The Chilterns part of the name is a nod to those rolling hills that start rolling nearby and *are one of the most beautiful areas in the country*. The two other sites are Wellesbourne, just outside town and Chalfont St Giles, a small village about 9 miles away. John Milton moved to Chalfont St Giles when the plague broke out in London and wrote 'Paradise Lost' *because there was nothing better to do there. In that respect, it has changed much since.*

Buckinghamshire

Sex ratio(M:F): 43%:57%
Full time u'grads: 5,990
Postgrads: 187
Ave course: 3yrs
Private school: n/a
Mature students: 48%
Disabled students: 6%
Founded: 1893
Part time: 2,282
Non-degree: 3,130
Ethnic: 10%
Flunk rate: 16.7%
Overseas students: 10%

ATMOSPHERE:
The students' evident commitment to their courses doesn't stop them chilling out. The rampant careerism and ambition evident at other colleges with an equally middle-class make-up doesn't apply here. Frolics are based around the College, especially the SU, since all High Wycombe offers in the way of diversion is a chair museum.

THE SITES:
Wellesbourne Campus: (1,000 leisure and tourism) About 2 miles away on the outskirts of town are some mainly 60s buildings which pass for Wellesbourne Campus. There are buses to the main site every 10 minutes (£1 return).

Chalfont Campus: (2,500 business, health studies) Students based in this 18th-century mansion don't have to travel to High Wycombe for their course, *but might want to if they want a life outside the college*, since woods and farmland are the only diversion here. Evening minibuses will get them home free if they do go to the main site where the main SU events take place.

TRAVEL:
Trains: High Wycombe station is ¼ of a mile from campus. London (£5.20) is 35 minutes by train.
Coaches: One National Express service a day to London (£2.50), Bristol (£28.50) or Heathrow (£3.30). Local buses go to Oxford, Cambridge, Reading and all over.
Car: High Wycombe's handy for the A40 and M40. Chalfont is right by the M25. The M4 is close by to the south.
Air: Heathrow is 40 miles away.
Hitching: *Don't bother hitching unless you're interested in spending the rest of your life on junction 4 of the M40.*
Local: *Good local buses but where are you going to go?*
Taxis: £2 from station to campus. *High Wycombe isn't a big place, so sharing makes taxis viable.*
Bicycles: *Okay around town, but the surrounding area is rather hilly. Theft isn't much of a problem.*

CAREER PROSPECTS:
- Careers Service • No of staff: 2 full/1 part
- Unemployed after 6 mths: 8%

The UEA Union Financial Officer for 1995-6 was John Holmes (aka Gonch Gardner from 'Grange Hill').

FAMOUS ALUMNI:
Howard Jones (80s teen idol); Zandra Rhodes (Fashion designer).

FURTHER INFO:
Undergrad, postgrad and part-time prospectuses, course leaflets, video, handbook and website (www.buckscol.ac.uk).

ACADEMIC

There's a unique Music Industry Management course *for any potential pony-tailed coke-heads who haven't got a clue what young people want.*

staff/student ratio: n/a
Range of points required for entrance: 220-140
Percentage accepted through clearing: 19%
Number of terms/semesters: 2
Length of terms/semesters: 15wks
Research: n/a

LIBRARIES & COMPUTERS:
• Books: 186,555   • Study places: 821

COMPUTERS:
• Computer workstations: 165
Students seem perfectly content with the computer provision even though there aren't that many. They can be booked for half-hour sessions.

ENTERTAINMENT

TOWN:
• Price of a pint of beer: £2   • Glass of wine: £1.80

Cinemas: There's a UCI 6-screen job in town and another at Gerard's Cross.

Theatres: As well as *low-brow* theatre, the Wycombe Swan hosts comedy nights.

Pubs: *High Wycombe isn't what you'd call a student town, but one or two pubs offer bibulous benefits.* Pushplugs: Antelope; Firkin; Hobgoblin. *Avoid the White Horse and Saracen's Head unless you want to eat fist pie.*

Clubs/Discos: Club Eden has a student night on Mondays (dance, free before 10.30pm) *but that's about it.*

Music venues: The Nag's Head hosts a bit of rock and indie, *but for anything big, go to London.*

Eating out: *More belly-filling than bohemian.* Pushplugs: Bella Pasta; Francesco's (Italian); all-you-can-eat-for-a-fiver at Pizza Hut is popular. The Disraeli and Wendover Arms do good pub grub.

> In a poll at Robert Gordon University 70% of students said that the communal fridge is the biggest cause of student flat disputes.

UNIVERSITY:
• Price of a pint of beer: £1.55 • Glass of wine: £1.80
The SU makes up for lack of entertainment in High Wycombe.
Bars: (3) Footprints and Junction 4 are both in The Venue at the main site. The Final Whistle at Wellesbourne *is more cosy and intimate* and there's an SU bar at Chalfont.
Film: One usually arty or student flick a week.
Music venues/clubs/discos: Junction 4 in The Venue is the nightclub: Friday night is club night, Wednesday night is run by clubs and societies, while Saturday varies between drum'n'bass and soul and swing. Robbie Williams and Divine Comedy have played recently.
Food: The Solar Café does breakfast till 11.30 *and otherwise standard meals*. The Grapevine does baguettes and *alternative healthy options*. Newland Park has Megabites, the burger bar, and there are refectories at each site.
Other: The May Ball is the big deal.

SOCIAL & POLITICAL

STUDENTS' UNION:
• 4 sabbaticals • Turnout at last ballot: 6% • NUS member
The SU enjoys a good relationship with the Uni, since they concentrate mainly on ents, though a successful demo against poor accommodation got them a better deal last year.

SU FACILITIES:
Bars; nightclub; photocopier; payphone; video games; fax; juke box; sandwich bar; late-night minibus; vending machines; photobooth; pool tables.

CLUBS (NON SPORTING):
Afro-Caribbean; Dance; Drama; Media; Playstation; U'grad Clubbing.

OTHER ORGANISATIONS:
'Intercourse' magazine comes out every month. Rag raises rabbles for charity.

RELIGIOUS:
• 1 chaplain (CofE)
Places of worship for Christians, Muslims and Sikhs.

PAID WORK:
More than half the students have jobs and there are plenty in this home-counties suburbia if you don't mind a bit of temp work or shelf-stacking. The Uni runs a jobshop.

```
The catering staff and Chemistry Department at
Sheffield University have appeared on a TV
soap powder advert with Carol Vorderman
```

SPORTS

- Recent successes: nothing special

Sport isn't a big thing here and participation is recreational rather than competitive.

SPORTS FACILITIES:
A recreation card (£30/year) gets you access to all facilities.
High Wycombe: Fitness, aerobics and weights room; gym; tennis courts; football pitches. In the local area: leisure centre; golf course; sauna and solarium; dry ski-slope.
Chalfont Campus: Sports hall; swimming pool; multigym; tennis courts; athletics field; all-weather pitch; gym.

SPORTING CLUBS:
Archery; Badminton; Basketball; Canoeing; Fencing; Football; Golf; Hockey; Netball; Rugby; Sailing; Tennis; Surf.

ACCOMMODATION

IN COLLEGE:
- Self-catering: 20% • Cost: £56-68 (38wks)

25% of 1st years live in (40% can't) and about a quarter of the students in each of the other years get a place too. Brook Street Hall and John North Hall house 500 students in High Wycombe town centre and there are 700 places at Newland Park. Self-catering kitchens are shared between 5 to 9 students (not all at once). Some halls have CCTV and guards.
Car parking: *Dire at Wycombe, but okay at Newland Park.*

EXTERNALLY:
- Ave rent: £57

Availability: *For upwards of £40, it's possible to get decent accommodation in the area. The most popular areas are Wycombe town, Desborough, Green St and Upper Street. Avoid West Wycombe like you would a plague-ridden corpse.*
Housing help: The accommodation office has a team of staff *who try to make sure everyone's housed. There are lists for vacancies and recommended and blacklisted landlords, a notice board, legal help and advice, emergency housing and safety checks.*

```
The installation ceremony for the rector of
Aberdeen University involves being wheeled
around on the back of a model bull called
Angus.
```

WELFARE

SERVICES:
- Lesbian & Gay Society • Overseas SA

The College's Student Advisery Service has one full-time counsellor. There's a GP referral programme, sports and therapeutic massage service, legal surgeries every month and support groups for women.
Disabled: *Reasonable* disabled access to most of the buildings. *Vague support for dyslexic students.*

FINANCE:
- Access fund: £150,000 • Successful applications: 650

Six of the MPs elected in Labour's 1997 landslide were former presidents of the National Union of Students.

'The Constitution of the NUS is meant to be the bible of the Union but I've never got past the first page.'
- Jim Murphy, former NUS President.

Caledonian University see Glasgow Caledonian University

Camberwell College of Arts see The London Institute

Camborne School of Mines see University of Exeter

University of Cambridge
Christ's College, Cambridge
Churchill College, Cambridge
Clare College, Cambridge
Corpus Christi College, Cambridge
Downing College, Cambridge
Emmanuel College, Cambridge
Fitzwilliam College, Cambridge
Girton College, Cambridge
Gonville & Caius College, Cambridge
Homerton College, Cambridge
Jesus College, Cambridge
King's College, Cambridge
Lucy Cavendish College, Cambridge
Magdalene College, Cambridge
New Hall, Cambridge
Newnham College, Cambridge
Pembroke College, Cambridge
Peterhouse, Cambridge
Queen's College, Cambridge
Robinson College, Cambridge
St Catharine's College, Cambridge
St John's College, Cambridge
Selwyn College, Cambridge
Sidney Sussex College, Cambridge
Trinity College, Cambridge
Trinity Hall, Cambridge

Canterbury see University of Kent at Canterbury

Canterbury Christ Church University see Other Institutions

Cardiff, University of Wales

Cardiff Institute see Other Institutions

Caythorpe see De Montfort University

CCAT see Anglia Polytechnic University

University of Central England

University of Central Lancashire

Central St Martins College of Art see The London Institute

Charing Cross & Westminster Hospital see Imperial College, London

Charlotte Mason see Lancaster University

Chelsea College of Art see The London Institute

Cheltenham & Gloucester College of Higher Education

continued next page

Chester College see Other Institutions

University College Chichester see Other Institutions

Cirencester see Royal Agricultural College

City of London Poly see London Guildhall University

City University

Coleraine see University of Ulster

Courtauld Institute of Art, London

Coventry University

Cranfield University

Caledonian University
see Glasgow Caledonian University

Camberwell College of Arts
see The London Institute

Camborne School of Mines
see University of Exeter

University of Cambridge

University of Cambridge, Intercollegiate Applications Office, Kellet Lodge, Tennis Court Road, Cambridge, CB2 1QJ.
Tel: (01223) 333308. Fax: (01223) 366383.
E-mail: ucam-undergraduate-admissions@lists.cam.ac.uk
Cambridge University Students' Union, 11/12 Trumpington Street, Cambridge, CB2 1QA. Tel: (01223) 356454. Fax: (01223) 323244.
E-mail: info@cusu.cam.ac.uk

GENERAL

If it weren't for the University, Cambridge would have remained pretty much as the Romans left it: a fairly insignificant village, surrounded by flat fenlands, where East Anglia starts to bulge from the rest of England. It would just have been blown by cold winds from Siberia in winter and the river Cam would have flowed through gently, uncluttered by tourists' punts in summer. However, about a century after the trend started in Oxford, higher education sprouted in Cambridge and now, more than 700 years later, these are the *most* famous, most highly revered and possibly the most extraordinary universities in the world. The University remains (much more than at Oxford) the focal point of the city, *which is very pretty, with lots of attractive buildings* in light golden stone. The University buildings are its colleges – 31 in all (depending what you count as a college) – and they are as *attractive* examples of English architecture spanning 8 centuries as are likely to be found anywhere. *The area they cover is remarkably compact and has an utterly surreal feel about it, aided and abetted by the bizarre (to an outsider) language at play – backs, cuppers, bedders, bumps. These words occupy this separate world inhabited by the elite – a controversial word to which the University objects. They are elite not necessarily because of their astonishing intellect, social background and astounding talent in sport, music, drama or whatever (although many possess at least one of these), but elite by the mere fact that they are students here.* More or less, the centre point of Cambridge (for the purpose of distances to the colleges in Push entries, at any rate) is the breath-takingly beautiful King's Parade with a view of King's and Caius.

Sex ratio(M:F): 53%:47%	Founded: 1284
Full time u'grads: 11,627	Part time: 0
Postgrads: 4,892	Non-degree: 0
Ave course: 3yrs	Ethnic: 11%
Private school: 47%	Flunk rate: 1.3%
Mature students: 6%	Overseas students: 11%
Disabled students: 2.5%	

ATMOSPHERE:
Okay, so Cambridge and Oxford are more similar than Uma Thurman and a piece of papaya. If you want someone to say they're completely different, go look in their prospectuses. Push, however, is quite happy to concede that, whilst they have their similarities, (1) it is not sufficient to dismiss them both as 'Oxbridge', (2) they are unlike each other in as many respects as they are alike, and (3) 'Hillbilly Rock, Hillbilly Roll' by the Woolpackers isn't a very good record. Like Oxford, most of the students' social concerns and the intense academic life revolve around the colleges which run themselves and arrange their own admissions. However, unlike Oxford, there are plenty of opportunities to switch courses and an even stronger sense that this is a student city.
Three years at Cambridge is one of the most intense educational experiences you can hope to have with your clothes on. There is virtually no escape. It can be challenging, it can be claustrophobic and it can be compared to watching every episode of 'ER' end to end. The city (the beauty of which cannot be praised too much) is overwhelmed by the University. It offers little by way of diversion that is not connected somehow and it's rare for students to walk through the streets without meeting faces they know at every other step. But despite the tourist friendly image, Cambridge does have its nasty side and ambling drunkenly through town is not the carefree delight it once was, at least not on your own.
Students have no spare time, not because they're working (although, in Cambridge, the words 'doss' and 'course' rarely go together), but because their leisure time is spent buzzing away in some hive of activity: sport; drama; journalism; music; politics; archaic drinking clubs; whatever. Cambridge students do a lot of whatever. They need to have good time management skills or learn them pretty quick.

Life in the colleges is even more cosseted, closeted and all-consuming: ranging in size from Lucy Cavendish with under 80 undergrads, to Trinity College with over 600. *Most colleges have around 400 undergraduates (slightly larger than Oxford on average) and many students experience a little shock when they enter the big bad real world. The colleges themselves vary enormously and it's a foolhardy fool who uses the pinprick method of picking.* Odd ceremonies and traditions persist, and it remains the case that students from atypically 'Cambridge' backgrounds (state schools, women, ethnic minorities) may take longer to adjust than others, whatever the prospectuses may say.

The following Push entries expose the naked truth and the neatly garbed falsehoods about each of the undergraduate colleges. Push doesn't cover Darwin, Hughes Hall, St Edmund's or Wolfson, which are postgrad colleges. We suggest you write to the above address or the colleges themselves if this upsets you (letters of complaint to Push will be duly noted and used as coffee filters).

THE CITY:
- Population: 100,000 • London: 58miles • Oxford: 77miles
- Norwich: 57miles

People in Cambridge seem to be either students or tourists. *The permanent residents just get lost in the throng, although there are all the basic ingredients you'd expect in a relatively prosperous city of Cambridge's size.* Superficially, at least, most of the shops are trying to appeal to a passing trade: quaint shops and tea rooms, pubs with horse brasses, that sort of thing. *The river Cam couldn't have been better designed if it had been put there especially for tourism. It's littered with ducks and drunken punters at almost every turn.* On a more sober note, the local amenities include the Grafton Shopping Centre, big book shops (new and second-hand), a street market, the Kettles Yard Art Gallery and a mass of museums. There is, however, a shortage of supermarkets (one small and busy Sainsbury's) and convenience shops in the city centre.

TRAVEL:
Trains: Cambridge Station connects to London King's Cross and Liverpool Street (£8.45), Birmingham (£30.60), Bristol (£41) and more. Incidentally, the station is some way beyond the city centre because the *University authorities didn't want rough common London folk coming too close to the sensitive young undergraduates.*
Coaches: Plenty of competitive services, for example, Greenline, Premier Travel and National Express who offer runs to London (£7.50), Bristol (£17) and elsewhere.
Car: Just a few minutes off the M11 from London. Also A428, A10 and A14.
Air: There's Cambridge Airport, *but unless you own your own jet, you'd better think more in terms of Stansted,* 23 miles down the M11 and on a direct train link.
Hitching: Variable – aim towards M11 junctions, or A10/Trumpington Road for London.
Local: The local buses, *which are regular as prunes,* go round the surrounding villages, the station and the outer colleges. *Cambridge is too small to need much more.*
Taxis: *They work out quite cheap (mainly because it doesn't take too long to get anywhere).* Some colleges have free taxi arrangements at night. See separate entries.
Bicycles: *The Cambridge student on a bike, college scarf flapping in*

the breeze, has been a cheesy stereotype for so long, it came as
something of a shock when a bike ban was imposed in the city centre
and around the Grafton. This ban is still largely ignored, though the
police also take great pleasure in hauling cyclists up for having no
lights.

CAREER PROSPECTS:
• Careers Service • No of staff: 8 full/3 part
• Unemployed after 6mths: 4%
Although '(Cantab)' after your name might not be the sure-fire
guarantee of a top job it once was, a Cambridge education rarely
does harm on a CV and, supposedly, employers find Cambridge
students more down to earth than those from Oxford (who must
surely then be abject space cadets). Although Cambridge was the
spawning ground for most of the spies on every side of the Iron
Curtain during the Cold War, vacancies for budding Bonds and
Burgesses are not advertised on the careers vacancies board (though
you might want to try the national press).

SPECIAL FEATURES:
• Undergrads have to 'keep term' which means that they may not live
more than 3 miles from the city centre and they must get permission
before going away during term time.
• An expansion masterplan is afoot which would site the University's
science and technology departments on a campus 1½ miles west
of King's.

FAMOUS ALUMNI:
See individual colleges. *Cambridge seems particularly strong on
spies, Tory MPs and comedians. Draw your own conclusions.*

FURTHER INFO:
Prospectuses for undergrads from the Cambridge Intercollegiate
Applications Office (*aka CIAO... cue bad Italian joke*), and postgrads
from the Board of Graduate Studies, 4 Mill Lane, Cambridge
CB2 1RZ, tel: (01223) 766302. Also from the individual colleges
and a website (www.cam.ac.uk). CUSU also produces an alternative
prospectus, costing £3.50.

ACADEMIC

To get in to Cambridge, most students do a Cambridge exam after
A Levels/Highers – STEP (Sixth Term Examination Paper). See the
prospectus for details or contact the STEP Office, OCR, 1 Hills Rd,
Cambridge, CB1 2EU. *The terms are only 8 weeks, but this doesn't
mean an easy life – exams and work pressure manage to ruin all
hopes of long vacations with nothing to do.* All undergraduate degree
courses (except a BEd for education and a 4-year MEng in Engineering)
lead to a BA, and, 3 years after graduation, students can claim an MA
without any further work. *That's where the easy life comes in.*

staff/student ratio: 1:12
Range of points required for entrance: 360-240
Percentage accepted through clearing: n/a
Number of terms/semesters: 3
Length of terms/semesters: 8wks
Research: 6.3

LIBRARIES:
- Books: 6.3 million • Study places: 988

The University Library is one of 5 copyright libraries in the country and as such has the right to claim a copy of every new book published in the UK. Every year, the number of new additions, if laid end to end, would extend the collection by a mile. *As if that weren't enough*, every college has its own library and there are more than 30 libraries devoted to individual subjects – *quite a few books, then.*

COMPUTERS:
- Computer workstations: 2,800

The general level of computer facilities is good but varies between colleges.

ENTERTAINMENT

THE CITY:
- Price of a pint of beer: £2.30 • Glass of wine: £1.70

Cinemas: (2) The Arts and a 10-screen Warner multiplex in the Grafton Centre.

Theatres: Apart from student venues, the Corn Exchange does a wide mixture of thespy stuff.

Pubs: *Cambridge has many good pubs, despite the fact they're pretty expensive.* The pubs along the riverside are most popular among students. Push would just like to plug the places where we've fallen over most often: The Mill; Anchor (watch fat American tourists fall off their punts); The Eagle; Town & Gown (gay-friendly); King's Run. Some town centre boozers should be treated with caution at weekends.

Clubs/discos: Considering a local student population of something over 20,000, Cambridge is poorly equipped in this field. Pushplugs: Big Holy Noise at Fifth Avenue (cheesy but cheery); Fez; Po Na Na's.

Music venues: The Junction (cap 700) is a purpose-built venue *with as much character as a goldfish, although the big (especially indie) names make it worthwhile*. The Corn Exchange has a capacity of 1,500 and has a more mainstream roster. The Boat Race is more geared to local bands – Cambridge, contrary to outside appearances, has a thriving indie scene.

Eating out: *It's customary to take out one's parents or at least their credit cards.* Many cafés are just pricey tourist traps but several curry houses in Castle Hill offer sound value. Pushplugs: Henry's Café; Livingstone's.

Other: Strawberry Fair is an annual *small-scale festival of moozic and booze*.

UNIVERSITY:
- Price of a pint of beer: £1.30 • Glass of wine: £1.20

Bars: Each college has at least one bar, *often shamefully cheap*, although some don't allow anyone but college members and their guests (but it's never too hard to crash). Usually the bar is the gravitational centre of college life, which may explain the number of people lying on the floors (physics joke). Rumour has it that some of the jukeboxes still take half-crowns and play 78rpm records...

Theatres: Drama is all over the place in Cambridge. *The pokey but well-kitted out* ADC (cap 250) is run professionally for student productions and aims at a wider audience than simply students. Between ADC, Fitzpatrick Hall (in Queens' College) and the Robinson Theatre a *handsome* number of pretty big shows are performed each

term of *an extremely variable standard*. There's also an enormous proliferation of other smaller venues throughout the University and more experimental productions continue virtually non-stop all year.
Cinemas: Most colleges have their own film club, which usually amounts to rented videos in the JCR, although some are more professional (especially at St John's, Queens', Peterhouse and the Cambridge Union Society). Being run by students, these, of course, show just about anything students might want to see and *often just what the projectionist wants to see (The 'Ooh, let's do 'Star Wars' again' factor)*.
Clubs/discos: The biggest regular club night is the weekly Big Holy Noise held at Fifth Avenue (800) run by CUSU (and often attended by Anglia Poly University students) but students can usually rely on a rave five or six times every week by doing the rounds of the college bops.
Cabaret: The Cambridge Footlights Revue has given birth to *some of the world's best chuckle-mongers* including half the Monty Python Team, Peter Cook & Dudley Moore, Smith & Jones, Fry & Laurie, Clives Anderson and James, Emma Thompson, Tony Slattery and so on ad ridiculum, *although the talent scouts haven't been so ready with their chequebooks in recent years. Cambridge Comedy is unkillable, though, and the Footlights show goes on (and on and...).*
Music venues: The University Concert Hall (650) hosts mainly classical concerts including the University's many orchestras, choirs and chapel music groups. For more contemporary sound-waves the one to watch is Queens' Fitzpatrick Hall (again) with a capacity of 300.
Balls: *Oo-er, sounds a bit rude. Wild parties in penguin suits and ball frocks which usually end up covered in strawberries and vomit. Most colleges have one (or share one with another college) and some are huge (such as Trinity's). The one thing they almost all have in common is a discussion with the bank manager – a double ticket can cost in excess of £140 (plus the dry-cleaning bill). Some colleges have cheaper versions by cutting back the thrills and frills. Balls are the crunching ground for really top names in music and cabaret, as the organisers are often willing to splash out on chart bands. The odd thing is the balls are almost all in June and yet are called May Balls. Answers on a postcard... May Week also includes 'Suicide Sunday' – not, as some presume, anything to do with exam pressure but a day to begin alcoholic consumption at 9am and carry on until oblivion.*
Others: *Terribly civilised entertainments flourish, such as garden parties and cocktail parties and cheese and wine parties and possibly even S&M Tupperware parties for all we know. Students should remember to pack their cravats and Laura Ashley dresses.*
Food: Livers-in generally eat lunch in the college dining halls, but there are also cafeterias and sandwich bars in some of the departments and the University Library. Evening meals are provided by the colleges. *They're cheap* but that's because they're subsidised by the Kitchen Fixed Charge that all students pay at the beginning of term. So, even if you go out for the other kind of KFC, you've paid for your meal already. The big, candle-lit, roast-pig-with-fruit-rammed-up-every-orifice type of Cambridge dinner still goes on but it's not an everyday occurrence.

The rock music diploma course at Thames Valley University has a strict 'no grunge' policy.

SOCIAL & POLITICAL

CAMBRIDGE UNIVERSITY STUDENTS' UNION:
• 5 sabbaticals • Turnout at last ballot: 30% • NUS member
The colleges' JCRs and MCRs have really plugged the gap that students' unions usually fill and CUSU (which, to be fair, is good at what it does) doesn't have a huge profile. CUSU co-ordinates many Uni campaigns such as Target Schools, Green and so on. It also handles Uni-wide events such as trips to the Ministry of Sound. They have also attracted bands like Toploader to play at the Uni. *Amazingly,* CUSU is one of the poorest student unions in the country and its sabbaticals are amongst the poorest paid.... *Its facilities also don't reflect Cambridge's stature.* CUSU publishes various handbooks (Societies Guide, Diary, Alternative Prospectus, termly paper, Sex Guide and Green Guide) *and lashings of political hackery. However, the politics is limited, because most students get all the (non-party) politics they need through their own JCR. On the quiet, CUSU does all sorts of valiant representation and welfare work in the University,* trains and advises JCR officers and co-ordinates more societies than there are days in the academic year.

SU FACILITIES:
CUSU facilities include: *cheap* photocopier, shop, fax, stationery, condoms; minibus hire. Practically speaking, it aims at providing for JCRs who then provide amenities for individual students.

CLUBS (NON-SPORTING):
This list doesn't include college-based societies. What do you want, the moon on a stick?
Abacus; Action Aid; Air Squadron; Anglo-Japanese; Anti-Bloodsports; Archimideans; Art; Assassin's Guild; Baby Milk Action; Backgammon; Baha'i; Ballet; Bangladesh; Birders; Black & Asian Caucus; Bone Marrow; Brass Band; Bridge (community); Buddhist; Campus Children's Holidays; Canadian; Canal; Cannabis Legalisation; Ceilidh; Chamber Choir; Chocolate; Christian Music; Christian Science; Cobblers; Cognitive Science; Comic (the paper variety not stand-up); Community Church; Computer; Contact (helping the elderly); Cuba; Cycle Safety; Dance; Detective Fiction; Diamond Way; Diplomacy (game); Disabilities; Dr Who; Duke of Edinburgh Award; Early Music; Eating Disorders; Enterprise (Star Trek); Environment Action; Esperanto; Essex; European; European Theatre Group (international touring company); Excitium; Explorers & Travellers; Field Sports; Film & TV; First Aid; Fisher Society (Catholic); Footlights; Freaky Comics; Free (libertarian); Freemasonry; French; Friends of the Earth; Gamelan (gongs); German; Go (game); Greenlink; Grimsco (professional Northerners); Hellenic; Heraldic; Hillwalking; Hindu; Hispanic; Holistic Medicine; Hong Kong & China; Hungarian; Imfundo (South African Educational Trust); India; International; Iran; Israel; Italian; Jews & Christians; Jomborg the New (fantasy); Jugglers; Kettle's Yard (visual arts); Light Entertainment; Link Africa; Linkline; Literary; Madhouse Theatre; MahJong; Malaysia & Singapore; Marlowe Dramatic; Massage; Medical Action; Methodist; Middle East; Mummers; Mystical; Officers' Training Corps; Opera; Orthodox; Overlanders (rough travel); Oxfam; Pakistan; Poetry; Pottery; Progressive Jewish; Punjabi; Quorum; Radio; Railway; Raleigh; Revolver & Pistol; Roleplaying; RN; Science Fiction; Scientists for the Earth; Scottish & Irish; Scouts & Guides; Seres (Chinese magazine); Sheila & Her Dog (relapse into childhood); Slavonic & East European; Sri Lanka; Strathspey & Reel (Scottish dancing); Student Christian Movement; Support for the Homeless; Survival (tribal rights); Tibet Support; Tolkien; Transcendence; Troubadors; Ugandan Children; Underwater Exploration; Union Society; Union Society Boycott; United Nations; Up Shit Creek Without A Paddle (ignore exams); Visual Arts; Welsh; West End; Wine; Young Friends (Quakers).

OTHER ORGANISATIONS:
Media: The award-winning 'Varsity' was the first student paper to go full colour and now produces an annual Year Book, a new rival to 'Varsity', 'The Cambridge Student' . Endless other magazines rise and die, some surviving longer than others – 'Spark' (arts), 'Quorum' (politics), 'Sprocket' (film) and 'Corridor' (feminist) deserve a

mention. *College magazines are often no more than crude gossipy muck-rakers.* Cambridge University Radio broadcasts from Churchill to a very small area although expansion is in the air waves.

Cambridge Union Society: The second oldest university debating society (after Oxford) and a right-wing stronghold. With a few student facilities (bar, café, reading room, etc) *the Union can lay some claim to having scuppered CUSU. But the Union's on a rocky road itself these days, not attracting speakers of quite the same calibre any more and membership flagging (partly 'cos it costs a packet to join). The Cambridge Union Boycott Society looks on, grinning.*

Rag: Colleges compete in raising money for the University's charity Rag. With competition spurring them on, they raise vast sums every year.

Student Community Action: You'll notice from the list above that there's a number of Cambridge clubs with a conscience. Some of these and other organisations – in all about 50 – do voluntary work in all sectors of the community.

Music: Cambridge offers *the perfect chance to get together and make sweet music,* mostly of the classical variety with the Chamber Orchestra (CUCO), the Music Society (CUMS) or in any of the many college orchestras, choirs, etc. Contemporary musicians, ie poppers and rockers, either form bands the usual way or use the Musicians Directory to find each other. If they're any good or know the student ents officer concerned or both, student bands can reckon on a gig or two at college bops. Jazz is also pretty big, *but not like it was in the late fifties, daddio.* And the list goes on, opera, Gilbert & Sullivan, Christian singers, brass bands, bells, gongs, guitars, Tibetan nose flutes and so on.

RELIGIOUS:

It's not enough to say Anglican Christianity is the norm although it's true that most colleges have a CofE or interdenominational chapel and chaplain – Corpus Christi has a mosque. Even Anglicanism takes every form from *incense swingers to rockin' vicars.* Every denomination of Christianity is here and virtually no religion is unrepresented (including a few religious orders started by students wanting to avoid poll tax in the 90s). Try the following for some *communal God squadding:* The Christian Union (Anglican); the Fisher Society (Catholic); the Methodists; the Islamic Society (linked to local mosque); not one, but two Jewish societies, Progressive and Orthodox (with a synagogue, rabbi and kosher restaurant of their own) and so on. There are local places of worship for Hindus, Sikhs and Buddhists.

PAID WORK:

The tourist trade provides the only opening beyond the ordinary.

```
A building at New Hall, Cambridge, was funded
by businessman Yasuto Kaetsu, who was director
of the Japanese anti-student riot police in
the 1960's.
```

SPORTS

- Recent successes: rowing, rugby, etc

Face it, Cambridge breeds many more than its fair share of sports gods. Many of the rulers of rugby, captains of cricket and angels of athletics have come running from Cambridge's sporting fields. But all this is for a few bionic heroes at a University-wide level. Cambridge and its colleges also encourage even the weediest wimp to exert themselves in anything from tiddlywinks to boxing, but most often, rowing. Whatever the game, it's probably played in a college society or team and, if not there, in the University as a whole.

SPORTS FACILITIES:
Every college has its own facilities to a varying degree, so read their individual entries for details. The University doesn't actually have all that many facilities to call its own, beyond endless playing fields. But if there's something somebody wants to do, there's funding galore to redress any deficiencies. Anyone for competitive plate-spinning?

SPORTING CLUBS:
American Football; Boxing; Caving; Clay Pigeon Shooting; Croquet; Drag Hunt; Eton Fives; Field Sports; Gymnastics; Hang Gliding; Hill Walking; Korfball; Lacrosse; Life Saving; Parachuting; Pétanque; Polo; Power Lifting; Rambling; Real Tennis; Revolvers & Pistols; Rifles; Rugby League; Surf Squad; Trampoline; Ultimate Frisbee.

ATTRACTIONS:
As if the University's own sports didn't satisfy every possible desire to watch sport, there's always Cambridge United Football and Rugby Clubs. The more Sloaney set can don their toff hats and pop off to Newmarket for the races *and lose all daddy's money.*

ACCOMMODATION

IN COLLEGE:
- Catered: 95%

Availability: Even more so than at Oxford, *one of Cambridge's best features* is being able to live in college accommodation. Most colleges have room for all 1st years and finalists, and 2nd years who can't be squeezed into the college itself will usually be offered some kind of college-owned housing nearby. *The rooms vary from palatial suites to pokey cupboards without central heating, although most are fairly impressive.* Older rooms around the college courts can look *spectacular* from the outside, *but the more modern rooms tend to offer better living conditions.* It's rare to have to share a room, but sets (2 linked rooms) are fairly common. There is only limited availability for couples and even less for students with children. Each college makes its own arrangements and for the petty particulars, check the college entries.

Car parking: Students aren't technically allowed to bring cars to their colleges, but, in fact, some outer colleges (where parking is less impossible) don't bother too much.

EXTERNALLY:
- Ave rent: £55

Availability: With so many students based in a city not purpose-built for them, accommodation can be tough to source. *The hand-me-down housing method has kept the severest problems at bay but students do have to keep an eye open for a few landlords who're willing to make* *a fast buck from a student's bad luck.* Usually livers-out share houses but digs (a room in a landlord's house) are not uncommon. *Relations with the local community are generally pretty good and there are no student ghettos, although Mill Rd and Huntingdon Rd are popular. The only place students should rule out is the north of the city, because it's easy enough to find something closer.* For fast relief students can refer to the Accommodation Syndicate (18 Silver Street) who keep a list of suitable accommodation, *often a little pricier than those on the open market but always up to scratch.* Students who choose to live out have to find somewhere within 3 miles of the city centre.

WELFARE

SERVICES:
• Nightline • LesBiGay Society • Mature SA • International SA
• Postgrad SA • Women's Officer • Anti-racisim officer

Although the University has no creche of its own, it supports the local one, which is used by students. In addition to the above, there are support groups for AIDS/HIV and ethnic minorities. For individual problems, every student has a personal tutor who can always refer them to the Welfare Officer at CUSU, the University Counselling Service or anyone else who might be able to help. CUSU doesn't have full-time welfare staff. This is delegated to the colleges. Most colleges have their own nurses or even doctors and the University operates a dental service for students' toothy pegs.

Women: Most colleges have only started to allow women students over the last two decades and *some are still reeling from the shock. As female numbers grow the situation and the facilities improve,* but the academic staff of many departments and colleges are still ominously all male. *The prevailing chauvinism is that of a previous generation and some women end up pedalling on a lower gear just to show they can. The most blatant m-c-piggery rears its head in college bars where the tone can be frankly oppressive.* But, in the face of aggression, women have taken steps. There's a Women's Council, Women's Executive, Women's Handbook, free rape alarms and strong campaigns.

Lesbian/Gay/Bisexual: Cambridge has the largest LGB Society in the UK and *there's a long tradition of relative sexual tolerance in the University. Gay icons such as EM Forster, Ian McKellen and Stephen Fry have passed through its portals.*

Disabled: Cambridge was not originally built with wheelchairs in mind, although it is blessed with a lack of hills. However, a fair amount of building has been going on over the last 20 years and there has been a genuine attempt to make these new buildings accessible at least. Bridget's hostel, on Tennis Court Road, has special facilities for people with disabilities, offering ground floor accommodation, a care attendant and an independent life and a new full-time disability adviser. Professor Stephen Hawking is a regular sight in his electric chair. For sight-impaired students, large print or Braille exam papers are available.

FINANCE:
Financial assistance usually comes from individual colleges.

> The Sheffield Rag once tried to paint a zebra crossing on the M1.

Christ's College, Cambridge

• *The College is part of <u>University of Cambridge</u> and students are entitled to use its facilities.*
Christ's College, Cambridge, CB2 3BU. Tel: (01223) 334953.
Fax: (01223) 334967. E-mail: admissions@christs.cam.ac.uk
Christ's College Students' Union, Cambridge, CB2 3BU.
Tel: (01223) 334900.
Website: www.christs.cam.ac.uk

Christ's is only 300 yards from King's Parade and is slap bang in the middle of the city, right by the shops and the bus station (and Burger King). It is one of the older and *most beautiful* colleges, built around 4 courts (with some parts dating back to the 15th century), except for 'the Typewriter', the 1970s accommodation block, *which, visually, is a poke in the eye, but, socially, a pat on the back*. Academic standards are very high which can cause pressure, but there's a cheerful, supportive, sociable atmosphere.

Sex ratio(M:F): 62%:38%	Founded: 1448
Full time u'grads: 395	Postgrads: 100
Private school: 42%	Mature students: 2%
Overseas students: 15%	Disabled students: n/a

Buttery Bar (cap 100) closes early; new Late Night Bar opens 8.30-11pm; 2 bops/term, biennial balls; theatre/venue (200); film soc; Plumb auditorium for recitals; *drama strong*. 'Christ's Pieces' for gossip and an SU newsletter; Milton Society for dining/debating. 3 libraries (120,000 books); 75 computers, 24hr. *Strong* Christian Union; CofE chapel. Successes in football and rowing; squash courts on site, but most sports facilities 1 mile away. All live in College or in Jesus Lane hostels. Canteen and formal meals. CCTV, college sick bay; nurse; free rape alarms.

FAMOUS ALUMNI:
Sacha Baron Cohen aka 'Ali G' (boo yakka cha); Charles Darwin (revolutionary evolutionary); John Milton (poet); Lord Mountbatten; CP Snow (writer); Richard Whiteley ('Countdown' love god).

Churchill College, Cambridge

• *The College is part of <u>University of Cambridge</u> and students are entitled to use its facilities.*
Churchill College, Cambridge, CB3 0DS. Tel: (01223) 336202.
Fax: (01223) 336180. E-mail: admissions@chu.cam.ac.uk
Junior Common Room, Churchill College, Cambridge, CB3 0DS.
Tel: (01223) 465545.
Website: www.chu.cam.ac.uk

Just under a mile from King's Parade, Churchill is one of Cambridge's larger, more modern, *progressive* and less central colleges. The buildings are *stark modern blocks* (but still Grade II listed), based on the old college format of courts and staircases, set in large grounds. *The modernity offers some advantages over Cambridge's more traditional colleges in terms of facilities and space*. There are more scientists at Churchill than most colleges and also more state-educated students *which means poncing about like a Cambridge stereotype attracts funny looks more than admiration*.

Sex ratio(M:F): 70%:30%	Founded: 1960
Full time u'grads: 427	Postgrads: 220
Private school: 26%	Mature students: 2
Overseas students: 8%	Disabled students: 1

2 bars, bops on Fridays, happy-hour at weekends, termly event with Fitzwilliam, spring ball; film theatre (cap 300; film soc voted best by 'Varsity'); sound-proof rooms for music practice/recitals; party room. 'Winston' mag for gossip; College-based university radio. 4 libraries (45,000 books); 40 computers, 24hr; free language and computing courses offered to all students. Chapel. *Sport good, but better pool teams.* Everyone lives in, 10% in rented college houses; some smoking areas; phone and computer sockets in all rooms; cafeteria and access to self-catering; veggie option; *kitchens reasonable.* CCTV, swipe cards, *good* SU welfare; nurse; *okay* disabled access; scholarships, hardship and travel grants.

Clare College, Cambridge

- The College is part of <u>University of Cambridge</u> and students are entitled to use its facilities.

Clare College, Cambridge, CB2 1TL. Tel: (01223) 333200.
E-mail: admissions@clare.cam.ac.uk
Union of Clare Students, Junior Common Room, Clare College, Cambridge, CB2 1TL. Tel: (01223) 333200.
Website: www.clare.cam.ac.uk

About 100 yards from King's Parade, Clare is Cambridge's second oldest college. Its buildings are traditional, focused around the 17th century Old Court and spanning both sides of the river (linked by Cambridge's oldest bridge) on the Cambridge 'Backs' (the college-crusted banks of the River Cam). The College is *unpretentious, relaxed* and has a *good social mix.*

Sex ratio(M:F): 50%:50%	Founded: 1326
Full time u'grads: 430	Postgrads: 175
Private school: 45%	Mature students: 0%
Overseas students: 8%	Disabled students: 1.2%

Atmospheric cellars (bar cap 200) give a university-wide ents reputation; 2 venues include the bar and a chill out room; pool table, jukebox; weekly theme nights, DJs and jazz; *extensive* gardens used for annual May Ball attended by 950 students (*most romantic in Cambridge*). 2 libraries (33,000 books); 30 computers. CofE chapel used for classical recitals; semi-professional choir. Sports fields (4 acres) 1½ miles away; *women's football and rugby strong.* 1st to 3rd years are guaranteed rooms but a few 2nd years live out. Most students eat in the dining hall (Italian bias with veggie option). CCTV; SU welfare officers, nurse; counselling; hardship fund, travel and book grants.

FAMOUS ALUMNI:
Sir David Attenborough (TV naturalist); Chris Kelly (ex 'Food and Drink'); Peter Lilley MP (Con); Paul Mellon (philanthropist); Matthew Parris (exMP, 'Times' sketch writer); Siegfried Sassoon (poet); Cecil Sharp (folk music historian); Richard Stilgoe (entertainer/lyricist); James Watson (discovered DNA); Andrew Wiles (proved Fermat's Last Theorem).

Corpus Christi College, Cambridge

- *The College is part of <u>University of Cambridge</u> and students are entitled to use its facilities.*

Corpus Christi College, Cambridge, CB2 1RH. Tel: (01223) 338000.
Fax: (01223) 338061. E-mail: admissions@corpus.cam.ac.uk
Junior Common Room, Corpus Christi College, Cambridge, CB2 1RH.
Website: www.corpus.cam.ac.uk

Corpus Christi, founded by and for the townsfolk, is found downtown (on the King's Parade). The 'Old Court' is mid-14th century and its hardly modern equivalent 'New Court' was completed in 1827 by the designer of The National Gallery. It's one of the smallest colleges and *retains a strong identity.*

Sex ratio(M:F): 62%:38%	**Founded: 1352**
Full time u'grads: 249	**Postgrads: 180**
Private school: 42%	**Mature students: 1%**
Overseas students: 15%	**Disabled students: 1%**

Playroom theatre; student bands in bar (190); new lecture theatre/concert venue; film soc; biennial May Ball. 2 libraries (over 100,000 books including largest collection of Medieval manuscripts in UK); 15 computers. CofE chapel. *Active* JCR. Sports fields (3 acres) 10 mins away; squash courts, ergo machines, outdoor swimming pool, snooker room. All students can live in; most rooms have network and phone connections; cafeteria, 3 formals/week, veggie option. 3 rooms with wheelchair access; *sympathetic* Senior Tutor; hardship funds and scholarships.

FAMOUS ALUMNI:
Christopher Isherwood (writer); Christopher Marlowe (playwright); Lord Sieff (Marks & Spencer); EP Thompson (historian).

Downing College, Cambridge

- *The College is part of <u>University of Cambridge</u> and students are entitled to use its facilities.*

Downing College, Cambridge, CB2 1DQ. Tel: (01223) 334826.
Fax: (01223) 362279. E-mail: admissions@dow.cam.ac.uk
Junior Common Room, Downing College, Cambridge, CB2 1DQ.
Tel: (01223) 334825. Fax: (01223) 358674.
E-mail: jcrofficers@dow.cam.ac.uk
Website: www.dow.cam.ac.uk

A little over 500 yards from King's Parade is the *elegant* Downing College, an expanse of *spacious* lawns and classical architecture from the last 200 years. *It's noted for sporting achievements, but there's plenty of opportunity at a lower level if your idea of exertion is feeding the vast squirrel population. Social indulgence can take precedence over banner-waving, but Downing students are active on the University-wide hack scene as well. Music is also increasingly strong.*

Sex ratio(M:F): 54%:46%	**Founded: 1800**
Full time u'grads: 391	**Postgrads: 206**
Private school: 50%	**Mature students: 1%**
Overseas students: 2%	**Disabled students: 7%**

Large *plush* bar, longest hours in the Uni; student bands in Howard Building (theatre, cap 120) and Dining Hall (400); bops weekly in Party Room (100), cheesy/jazz/theme discos and karaoke; music practice rooms; annual June 'event' (cap 1,200). *Active* JCR; 'Griffin' college mag bi-termly. Library (47,000 books); 40 computers, 24hr. CofE chapel. Successes in rowing, football, rugby and others; sports fields (9 acres) 1 mile away; *good* facilities on site. Almost all 1st, 2nd and 3rd yrs live in; 'net connections in rooms. Pay-as-you-eat dining hall (KFC £106); 3 formals/week; veggie option. CCTV, entry-phones; nurse; counselling; free taxi service for women; rape alarms; room for disabled student; hardship fund; travel grant.

FAMOUS ALUMNI:
Michael Apted ('James Bond' director); Mike Atherton (former England cricket captain); Quentin Blake (illustrator); John Cleese (former funnyman); Thandie Newton (actress); Trevor Nunn (theatre director); Michael Winner (director/restaurant critic).

Emmanuel College, Cambridge

• **The College is part of <u>University of Cambridge</u> and students are entitled to use its facilities.**
Emmanuel College, Cambridge, CB2 3AP. Tel: (01223) 334291.
Fax: (01223) 334426. E-mail: admissions@emma.cam.ac.uk
Emmanuel College Students' Union, Junior Common Room, Cambridge, CB2 3AP. Tel: (01223) 314790.
E-mail: ecsu@emma.cam.ac.uk.
Website: www.emma.cam.ac.uk

'Emma' (as Emmanuel is affectionately known), 500 yards from King's Parade, is a collection of *dignified* buildings from the 16th century, 1960s accommodation blocks, *elegant* gardens and a duck pond (into which freshers are ritually ducked), replete with 50 resident ducks and cute but stupid ducklings every spring. *Emmanuel is perceived by other students as unpretentious and approachable and its students are well represented in University activities.*

Sex ratio(M:F): 44%:56%	Founded: 1584
Full time u'grads: 471	Postgrads: 173
Private school: 48%	Mature students: n/a
Overseas students: 9.5%	Disabled students: n/a

Refurbished bar (cap 200); ball/event every year; theatre in new Queen's building; films, DJ nights, quizzes, live funk every week; college music and drama societies. 'Roar' mag. Library (54,000 books); 30 *decent* computers, 24hr. CofE chapel designed by Sir Christopher Wren. Sports fields (2½ acres) 20mins away; squash courts; *okay sporting reputation*, basketball and rowing *strong*. Most undergrads live in; College owns houses nearby; internet connections in most rooms. Optional formals daily; veggie option. CCTV; 2 part-time nurses; part-time counsellor; free condoms; bursaries and scholarships.

FAMOUS ALUMNI:
Graham Chapman ('Monty Python's' Brian); Michael Frayn (playwright); Eddie George (ex-Governor, Bank of England); Griff Rhys Jones (comic); FR Leavis (lit crit); Lord Cecil Parkinson (Tory).

Fitzwilliam College, Cambridge

- **The College is part of University of Cambridge and students are entitled to use its facilities.**
Fitzwilliam College, Huntingdon Road, Cambridge, CB3 0DG.
Tel: (01223) 332030. Fax: (01223) 332057.
E-mail: admissions@fitz.cam.ac.uk
Junior Members' Association, Fitzwilliam College, Huntingdon Road, Cambridge, CB3 0DG. Tel: (01223) 332000.

Fitz isn't a typical Cambridge college. For a start, its main buildings are modern and redbrick. It admits more state school students than most. *It's friendly, down to earth and not at all claustrophobic or overwhelming.* It's also set apart from the other colleges, a mile from King's Parade at the top of Cambridge's only 'hill' (shallow slope) next to New Hall in the city's businessy area.

Sex ratio(M:F): 62%:38%	Founded: 1869
Full time u'grads: 453	Postgrads: 167
Private school: 30%	Mature students: 1%
Overseas students: 8%	Disabled students: 3%

Large *departure-loungey* bar; small theatre; Fitz Entz (£6) twice a term *big and very popular*; jazz on Sundays; concerts in dining-hall; regular theatre; termly 'events' (miniballs). Good JCR facilities; 'Fitz News'. Library (37,000 books); 40 computers, 24hr; cyber café. Chapel. Good sports fields (7 acres) including a boathouse ⅓ mile away plus facilities on site; tennis courts, squash courts, multigym; football *success*. All years can live in College or College-owned houses; internet points in rooms. Most students eat in; *decent* food, veggie option. CCTV, swipe cards; shared nurse, welfare officers; free taxis and attack alarms; travel grants, and hardship funds.

FAMOUS ALUMNI:
Nick Clarke (broadcaster); Charlotte Hudson ('Watchdog' presenter); Norman Lamont (ex-Chancellor); Christopher Martin-Jenkins (cricket commentator); Derek Pringle (cricketer); Dr David Starkey *(unpleasant historian).*

Girton College, Cambridge

- **The College is part of University of Cambridge and students are entitled to use its facilities.**
Girton College, Cambridge, CB3 0JG. Tel: (01223) 338972.
Fax: (01223) 338939.
Junior Combination Room, Girton College, Cambridge, CB3 0JG.
Tel: (01223) 338898.
Website: www.girton.cam.ac.uk

Girton is 2¼ miles from King's Parade and the city centre *(a bike is pretty much compulsory).* It started life as a women-only college, before going mixed in 1977. *Nowadays, it's one of Cambridge's most liberal, relaxed and actively fun colleges.* Being out of town gives it over 50 acres of grounds with gothic redbrick buildings *and the distance means integration with the rest of the University is rare,* although Girtonians seem quite proud of their distinctive lifestyle.

Sex ratio(M:F): 48%:52%	Founded: 1869
Full time u'grads: 493	Postgrads: 196
Private school: 39%	Mature students: 1%
Overseas students: 9%	Disabled students: 1%

2 bars; 3 bops/term; annual garden party; annual revue; biennial balls. JCR newsletters: termly 'Angle' and fortnightly 'Bog Sheet'; *green* JCR policies. 2 libraries (95,000 books); 44 computers, 24hr. Chapel. Sports facilities on site and the bike ride into town keeps Girtonians fit (JCR lends some bikes); rugby *success*. Rooms guaranteed to all years either in College or in College-owned housing; cafeteria of *celebrated standard; good* self-catering. 2 nurses; counsellors; self-defence classes; various financial help.

FAMOUS ALUMNI:
Queen Margarethe of Denmark; Joan Robinson (economist); Arianna Stassinopoulos (writer); Angela Tilby (writer & TV producer); Sandi Toksvig (short comedian); Baroness Warnock (of Warnock Committee fame).

Gonville & Caius College, Cambridge

- **The College is part of <u>University of Cambridge</u> and students are entitled to use its facilities.**
Gonville & Caius College, Cambridge, CB2 1TA. Tel: (01223) 332447. Fax: (01223) 332456. E-mail: admissions@cai.cam.ac.uk
GCSU, Gonville & Caius College, Cambridge, CB2 1TA.
Tel: (01223) 332400.
Website: www.cai.cam.ac.uk

The most important thing about Gonville & Caius is to pronounce its name correctly. Gonville's okay, apart from sounding like a Muppet character and most people drop that bit anyway, but Caius is pronounced 'keys'. Caius is based on 2 sites, 8 mins walk apart. The main building is at one end of King's Parade and is centred on the *fine* old renaissance Caius Court, next to Tree Court, the only college court in Cambridge with, er, trees. The other site is Harvey Court, the 1st year accommodation, designed in the 1960s in concrete and grey brick (*and the worse for it*) and situated on the other side of the river on the Backs (meadow banks). *It's one of the friendliest colleges with a good social mix.*

Sex ratio(M:F): 62%:38%	Founded: 1348
Full time u'grads: 470	Postgrads: 269
Private school: 48%	Mature students: 1%
Overseas students: 9%	Disabled students: 0

2 bars; Shreddies dance night 3 or 4 times a term (*cheese and theme*); Bateman concert room; biennial ball. Newsletter twice a term; many drinking/dining clubs; *active* music soc. Library (40,000 books); 50 computers, some 24hr. Chapel. *Good* sports facilities in College and ¼ mile away (3 acres and a bar). All 1st and 3rd years live in hall, 2nd years in College hostels; most of the rooms have internet points; *was worst food in Cambridge, getting better.* Swipe cards; nurse; hardship funds, travel and study grants.

FAMOUS ALUMNI:
Harold Abrahams (runner in 'Chariots of Fire'); Kenneth Clarke MP (Con); Francis Crick (Nobel prize-winning geneticist); Sir David Frost (broadcaster); William Harvey (who discovered circulation of blood); Sir Nevill Mott (Nobel prize-winning physicist); Dr Venn (as in 'Venn diagram').

Homerton College, Cambridge

• *The College is part of <u>University of Cambridge</u> and students are entitled to use its facilities.*
Homerton College, Cambridge, CB2 2PH. Tel: (01223) 507114. Fax: (01223) 507140. E-mail: nt204@cus.cam.ac.uk
Homerton Union of Students, Homerton College, Cambridge, CB2 2PH. Tel: (01223) 507235.
Website: www.homerton.cam.ac.uk

Homerton is probably the least 'Cambridgey' Cambridge college, because of its location (2 miles out of town) and its academic set-up (education and nursing students). It's less rich than some other colleges and some feel undue emphasis has been put on the conference trade. Students tend to socialise in College, but Homerton types have made their University-level mark in sport, journalism and more.

Sex ratio(M:F): 19%:81%	Founded: 1695
Full time u'grads: 684	Postgrads: 500
Private school: 30%	Mature students: 5%
Overseas students: 2%	Disabled students: 3%

2 bars; bops and live bands in the Main Hall (300); dance/drama studio; annual ball. 'Hush' College mag. Library (70,000 books); 70 computers. Sports fields (10 acres) on site; *sport for fun rather than glory*. All-day buttery; dining hall; *food can still get better*. Accommodation for 95% of 1st yrs, 10% of other yrs, *very expensive but good quality*. Nurse; travel grants, hardship fund, bursaries and childcare fund.

FAMOUS ALUMNI:
Julie Covington (actress/singer); Nick Hancock ('They Think It's All Over' – *wish he were*); Cherie Lunghi (actress); Ben Oakley (British windsurfing coach).

Jesus College, Cambridge

• *The College is part of <u>University of Cambridge</u> and students are entitled to use its facilities.*
Jesus College, Cambridge, CB5 8BL. Tel: (01223) 339339.
Fax: (01223) 339313. E-mail: jesusadmissions@lists.cam.ac.uk
JCSU, Jesus College, Cambridge, CB5 8BL.
E-mail: jcsupresident@jesus.cam.ac.uk

Sleepy Jesus College, built around an old convent with buildings dating from the 12th century, is 5 mins walk from King's Parade and the 1140 chapel is the oldest building in Cambridge. Jesus combines sporting enthusiasm with a liberal, if not radical, ethos and it makes a genuine effort to recruit more women and students from state schools. The bar is the social suction point and is usually full by nightfall.

Sex ratio(M:F): 61%:39%	Founded: 1496
Full time u'grads: 451	Postgrads: 190
Private school: 51%	Mature students: 0
Overseas students: 6%	Disabled students: 0

Bar (cap 175) - *cliquey*; classical concerts in the Chapel (250); May Ball and lower-key 'event' on alternate years; music practice rooms; venue closed - *college thought it was too distracting*. Students holding music awards have *high quality* tuition provided; *excellent drama and music*. College mags: 'Red & Blackmail' and 'Peripheral Vision'. Library (25,000 books); 25 computers, 24hr. CofE chapel. *Excellent* sports; sports fields (4 acres) and facilities on site. All 1st and 3rd years can live in; 2nd years in converted houses on College perimeter; eat in dining hall; 'net connections in rooms. CCTV, entry-phones; nurse; subsidised rape alarms, self-defence courses; no disabled facilities; hardship fund and loans.

FAMOUS ALUMNI:
ST Coleridge (poet); Alistair Cooke (broadcaster); Thomas Cranmer (former Archbishop of Canterbury); Ted Dexter (cricketer); Prince Edward (showbiz impresario); Wilfred Hadfield (invented double yellow lines); Nick Hornby (writer); Richard Lacey (food safety guru); Thomas Malthus (economist).

King's College, Cambridge

- *The College is part of University of Cambridge and students are entitled to use its facilities.*

King's College, Cambridge, CB2 1ST. Tel: (01223) 331417.
Fax: (01223) 331193.
E-mail: undergraduate-admissions@kings.cam.ac.uk
King's College Student Union, King's College, Cambridge, CB2 1ST.
Tel: (01223) 331454.
Website: www.kings.cam.ac.uk

King's College, on King's Parade, has many a dreaming spire and the famous King's chapel (started in 1446). *There's a good mix of all Cambridge's different types, with the same staid hierarchy. Despite this, and the awe-inspiringly ancient surroundings, King's has a somewhat leftist tradition, relaxed and down to earth* with an unusually high proportion of state school students.

Sex ratio(M:F): 55%:45%	Founded: 1441
Full time u'grads: 396	Postgrads: 244
Private school: 13%	Mature students: <1%
Overseas students: 5%	Disabled students: <1%

Biggest college bar in Cambridge (cap 300); Cellar Bar (150); VAC bar (4 days a week); all bars and Keynes Hall (200) are used for D'n'B and hip hop events – *more hip than a pelvis joint*. Every term there's a 'Mingle' (a mini ball); 'June Event' is a deluxe 'Mingle'. Termly 'Red Dragon Pie' student mag. 2 libraries (67,000 books); 33 computers, 24hr. Ecumenical chapel. Sports fields (6 acres) 15 mins walk; multigym; squash courts; *enthusiastic but not one of the big winners*. All students can live in and eat in the dining hall; self-catering provision. Entry-phones; nurse; a few rooms for wheelchair users.

FAMOUS ALUMNI:
David Baddiel (comedian?); Martin Bell MP (Ind); Rupert Brooke

(poet); EM Forster (writer); John Maynard Keynes (economist); Michael Mates MP (Con); Salman Rushdie (writer).

Lucy Cavendish College, Cambridge

• *The College is part of <u>University of Cambridge</u> and students are entitled to use its facilities.*
Lucy Cavendish College, Cambridge, CB3 0BU. Tel: (01223) 330280. Fax: (01223) 332178. E-mail: lcc-admission@lists.cam.ac.uk
Students' Association, Lucy Cavendish College, Cambridge, CB3 0BU. Tel: (01223) 332190. E-mail: lcc-admin@lists.cam.ac.uk
Website: www.lucy-cav.cam.ac.uk

Four of the buildings of Lucy Cavendish College (½ mile from King's Parade) date from the end of the 19th century, the rest are modern, including a new library. Only women over 21 years old are admitted and the average age is 30. The site is full of trees, *tranquil and quite beautiful*, complete with a tiny Anglo-Saxon herb garden - *perfect for peaceful study*. It's a refreshingly diverse and progressive college with dedication, creativity and flexibility rated higher than early educational success. There's a healthy dose of partying along with the intellectual exertions, though, and students are increasingly making their mark on the wider University stage.

Sex ratio(M:F): 0%:100%	Founded: 1965
Full time u'grads: 90	Postgrads: 127
Private school: 10%	Mature students: 100%
Overseas students: 25%	Disabled students: 3%

Bar; karaoke and theme nights; 2 bops/term. Music and meditation room. Library (20,000 books); 28 computers, 24hr. 'Lucy News' College mag; 24hour gym; *solid* sporting record. All students who want to be are accommodated in college or town (80% in all); self-catering facilities; weekly formals; *food and rooms are good*. Entry-phones; nurse; 2 rooms for disabled students; hardship fund, travel grants and bursaries. Permit car parking.

Magdalene College, Cambridge

• *The College is part of <u>University of Cambridge</u> and students are entitled to use its facilities.*
Magdalene College, Cambridge, CB3 0AG. Tel: (01223) 332135. Fax: (01223) 462589. E-mail: magdadmissions@lists.cam.ac.uk
Junior Common Room, Magdalene College, Cambridge, CB3 0AG.
Website: www.magd.cam.ac.uk

If you want to cause a sudden embarrassed hush at parties say 'Maggdalleen'. To flow with wit and wisdom pronounce it correctly as 'Maudlin' - to be in the in crowd, call it 'The Village'. The atmosphere at this college, 700 yards from King's Parade and with more river frontage than any other, *is certainly not maudlin and the social scene, which revolves around the bar, is simply spinning*. Magdalene is one of the smaller colleges *and tradition and camaraderie pervade*. The College features medieval and 15th- and 16th-century courts and Pepys' Library, but *unfortunately*, it hasn't escaped clumsy post-war architecture for some residential blocks.

Sex ratio(M:F): 56%:44%
Full time u'grads: 335
Private school: 50%
Overseas students: 17%

Founded: 1542
Postgrads: 165
Mature students: 1%
Disabled students: 1%

Bland bar and own pub; classical and jazz concerts in Benson Hall (cap 100); 3 discos a term; biennial ball (*one of the best, very posh*). 'Ars Magna' termly College mag and weekly 'Magd Out' newsletter. 3 libraries (26,000 books in main one); 20 computers, 24hr. CofE chapel. Good sports fields (8 acres) 500 yards away shared with St John's; boathouse shared with Queens'. All students live in; most eat *mediocre* food in Ramsay Hall (daily formal *better - candlelit because there's no electricity in Hall*); all rooms networked. CCTV, electronic entry (*do they know something we don't?*); nurse; hardship funds, scholarships, travel grants and prizes; subsidised rape alarms.

FAMOUS ALUMNI:
William Cash (journalist); Katie Dereham (ITN newsreader, *sweetie*); Bamber Gascoigne (quizmaster, writer); Gavin Hastings (former Scottish rugby captain); Anthony Jay (writer, 'Yes Minister'); Charles Kingsley (author); CS Lewis (author); Charles Stewart Parnell (19thC Irish nationalist); Samuel Pepys (diarist); Alan Rusbridger (editor, 'The Guardian'); John Simpson (TV reporter).

New Hall, Cambridge

• *The College is part of University of Cambridge and students are entitled to use its facilities.*
New Hall, Huntingdon Road, Cambridge, CB3 0DF.
Tel: (01223) 762229. Fax: (01223) 763110.
E-mail: admissions@newhall.cam.ac.uk
New Hall Union, New Hall, Huntingdon Road, Cambridge, CB3 0DF.
Tel: (01223) 762100.
Website: www.newhall.cam.ac.uk

³/₄ mile from King's Parade, most of New Hall's white brick buildings were built in the 60s. A huge dome dominates the centre of the College, *and is, shall we say, an acquired taste*. In the grounds there's a display of women's 20th-century art and sculpture; *generally loathed by students, but the college adores it*. Apart from the freedom from history and tradition, New Hall differs from many other Cambridge institutions in maintaining its single-sex women-only status. The students seem pretty happy with this but most look beyond the college walls for entertainment and socialising.

Sex ratio(M:F): 0%:100%
Full time u'grads: 360
Private school: 40%
Overseas students: 11%

Founded: 1954
Postgrads: 70
Mature students: 0.6%
Disabled students: 0.3%

Bar (cap 100, open 4 times a week, giant TV); concerts and student bands at the Dome (300), Vivien Stewart Room (60), Fellows' Drawing Room (45 and a Steinway) or the Party Room (80); 3 major ents per term. Music room. Fortnightly JCR newsletter 'Little Juicy Bits'. 1 library (60,000 books); 24 computers, 24hr. Art room (largest collection of modern women's art in Europe); darkroom. *Strong* boat club; multigym; squash and tennis courts. All 1st and 3rd yrs and 90% of 2nd yrs live in or in College-run properties; 6% of rooms are shared; almost all rooms have internet and phone connections; pay-as-you-eat canteen (*could be better but good for veggies*), formals once a week; permit parking. Some CCTV, swipe cards; nurse; various support funds *but it's not one of the richest colleges*.

FAMOUS ALUMNI:
Jocelyn Bell Burnell (discoverer of pulsars); Frances Edmonds (writer); Joanna MacGregor (pianist); Sue Perkins (out of Mel & Sue); Tilda Swinton (actress).

Newnham College, Cambridge

• *The College is part of University of Cambridge and students are entitled to use its facilities.*
Newnham College, Cambridge, CB3 9DF. Tel: (01223) 335783.
Fax: (01223) 357898. E-mail: adm@newn.cam.ac.uk
Junior Combination Room, Newnham College, Cambridge, CB3 9DF.
Tel: (01223) 335700.
Website: www.newn.cam.ac.uk

Newnham is a warm brick Victorian college with distinctive white window frames set in huge gardens, ¾ mile from King's Parade near the arts faculties (*beyond most tourists' curiosity*). Being female is the only stereotype you can apply to Newnham students and the all-female cast exudes more confidence than counterparts in mixed Colleges. The College is supportive and liberal – students are thoroughly involved and successful in University-wide activities but still come 'home' to put their feet up.

Sex ratio(M:F): 0%:100%	Founded: 1871
Full time u'grads: 405	Postgrads: 144
Private school: 45%	Mature students: 2%
Overseas students: 15%	Disabled students: <1%

Boilerhouse bar; classical concerts and bops of every hue in the College Hall (cap 250); performing arts studio; biennial ball; garden parties; plays performed in hall or garden. Observatory; library (85,000 books); 35 computers, 24hr. Fortnightly JCR 'NFiles' magazine. Success at rowing, footie and rugby; sports fields on site; multigym and tennis courts. Almost all students live in; *food is edible*; *good* self-catering facilities; 80% of rooms have data points. Nurse; rooms for wheelchair users; grants for books, sport and travel; scholarships and hardship funds.

FAMOUS ALUMNI:
Dianne Abbot MP, Patricia Hewitt MP (Lab); Joan Bakewell (broadcaster); Eleanor Bron, Emma Thompson (actresses); AS Byatt, Margaret Drabble, Germaine Greer (writers); Rabbi Julia Neuberger (writer, medical ethicist and all-rounder); Sylvia Plath (poet); Baroness Seear (Lib Dem).

The Bar at Emmanuel, Cambridge has been renamed the Parkinson/Yeo, to commemorate two of its more notoriously heterosexual alumni.

Pembroke College, Cambridge

- **The College is part of <u>University of Cambridge</u> and students are entitled to use its facilities.**
Pembroke College, Cambridge, CB2 1RF. Tel: (01223) 338154.
Fax: (01223) 766409. E-mail: admissions@pem.cam.ac.uk
Junior Parlour, Pembroke College, Cambridge, CB2 1RF.
Tel: (01223) 338100.
Website: www.pem.cam.ac.uk

Pembroke's buildings range from 14th-century dreaming spires to 50s redbrick and more recent buildings of an *indeterminate* 90s style, just off King's Parade and surrounded by beautiful gardens. *Students are fairly well-integrated with University life, but also get a bit insular here. Sport, drama, music and alcohol are the main pastimes, not necessarily in that order.*

Sex ratio(M:F): 54%:46%	**Founded: 1347**
Full time u'grads: 400	**Postgrads: 170**
Private school: 47%	**Mature students: 2%**
Overseas students: 7%	**Disabled students: 1%**

Bar; Old Reader (cap 50, theatre); concerts in Old Library (90); student bands in Junior Parlour (80) and New Cellars (80), also used for twice termly discos; annual 'ball-like event'. Library (50,000 books); music room; 50 computers, 24hr. CofE chapel. 'Pembroke Street' newsletter, 'Pem' arts; Pembroke runs a community centre in South London (where students can stay). Success in rowing; sports fields (4½ acres) 1½ miles away; oldest bowling green in Europe; multigym. All students live in College or College houses; all rooms have data points; students eat in canteen (*appropriately* named 'Trough'); optional formal every night; *good chef and good veggie option*; *limited* self-catering in college. Night porters; nurse; grants and scholarships; subsidised attack alarms and self-defence classes for women.

FAMOUS ALUMNI:
Tim Brooke-Taylor, Bill Oddie ('Goodies'); Peter Cook (comedy god); Raymond Dolby (audio inventor); Thomas Gray, Ted Hughes, Edmund Spenser (poets); Eric Idle ('Monty Python'); Clive James (writer, presenter); Jonathan Lynn (writer, director); Pitt the Younger (PM); Tom Sharpe (writer); Chris Smith MP (Lab).

Peterhouse, Cambridge

- **The College is part of <u>University of Cambridge</u> and students are entitled to use its facilities.**
Peterhouse, Cambridge, CB2 1RD. Tel: (01223) 338223.
Fax: (01223) 766147. E-mail: admissions@pet.cam.ac.uk
Junior Common Room, Peterhouse, Cambridge, CB2 1RD.
Website: www.pet.cam.ac.uk

Peterhouse, 500 yards from King's Parade, is Cambridge's smallest and oldest college, *with beautiful and well-kept gardens. The old Peterhouse image of reactionary posh kids is fading and there's room for everybody although teetotallers might get a bit bored. Because the college is so small, energetic movers and shakers tend to use their talents on the wider University stage.*

Sex ratio(M:F): 70%:30%	Founded: 1284
Full time u'grads: 248	Postgrads: 100
Private school: 59%	Mature students: 1%
Overseas students: 10%	Disabled students: 2.5%

Bar; Music Room (cap 100) for discos and student bands *but college tutors not too keen on big events*; theatre (180) for drama and classical concerts; biennial ball; dining and debating societies. Termly mag 'The Sex'. Library (45,000 books); 10 computers. CofE chapel. Sports facilities (8 acres shared with Clare College), 1 mile away; squash court; gym. All students live in or in housing arranged or maintained by College; most eat in *gorgeous* dining hall; *limited* self-catering (*best at Parkside off-site housing*). Nurse; women's advisers; hardship fund, generous prizes and scholarships.

FAMOUS ALUMNI:
Charles Babbage (computing pioneer); Thomas Campion (poet), Stephanie Cook (Olympic gold, modern pentathlon); Richard Crashaw (poet); Sir Christopher Cockerell (invented the hovercraft); Colin Greenwood (Radiohead); Michael Howard MP (Con); James Mason (actor); Sam Mendes (director); Michael Portillo MP (Con, Shadow Chancellor); Frank Whittle (inventor of the jet engine).

Queens' College, Cambridge

• *The College is part of University of Cambridge and students are entitled to use its facilities.*
Queens' College, Cambridge, CB3 9ET. Tel: (01223) 335540. Fax: (01223) 335522. E-mail: admissions@quns.cam.ac.uk

Junior Combination Room, Queens' College, Cambridge, CB3 9ET. Tel: (01223) 335567. E-mail: jcr_ctte@quns.cam.ac.uk
Website: www.quns.cam.ac.uk

Queens' College's Elizabethan and early 17th-century buildings, 200 yards from King's Parade, are a *good-looking and convenient place to be*, close to The Anchor pub. *The bar is a strong magnet, aesthetically unappealing as it may be. Students are getting more involved in the University than they used to (especially in drama and music) but always return to the laid-back charm of their college. Recent years have seen a strong emphasis on applications from state schools.*

Sex ratio(M:F): 58%:42%	Founded: 1448
Full time u'grads: 494	Postgrads: 288
Private school: 45%	Mature students: 0
Overseas students: 8%	Disabled students: 0

Bar; Fitzpatrick Hall (380, theatre) for student bands *and the best college club nights in Cambridge* as well as Jingles (cheese); films; biennial ball; 3 music rooms. 'The Drain' student mag; JCR newsletter. Successful Rag raised £10,000. 2 libraries (70,000 books); 13 computers, 24hr. CofE chapel. Multigym and squash courts on site; *big* sports fields (15 acres shared with Robinson) ½ mile away; very modern boathouse; success in hockey, tennis and rowing. All undergraduates can live in except a few 4th years; eat in dining hall; *very limited* self-catering. Nurse; creche; hardship fund (usually pays creche fees); scholarships.

FAMOUS ALUMNI:
Erasmus (Renaissance scholar); Mike Foale (first Brit in space); Stephen Fry (the inimitable writer, actor and comedian); Michael Gibson, John Spencer (rugby players); Graham Swift, TH White (writers).

Robinson College, Cambridge

- *The College is part of <u>University of Cambridge</u> and students are entitled to use its facilities.*
Robinson College, Cambridge, CB3 9AN. Tel: (01223) 339143.
Fax: (01223) 339743.

E-mail: undergraduateadmissions@robinson.cam.ac.uk
Robinson College Students' Association, Robinson College, Cambridge, CB3 9AN. Tel: (01223) 339100.
Website: www.robinson.cam.ac.uk

The only Cambridge college (so far) to be founded by a TV salesman-cum-horse fancier, Robinson College is one of the youngsters and mainly redbrick. It is set in *good* gardens ½ mile from King's Parade, handy for the arts faculties and the University Library. *Although it lacks the grand buildings of some other colleges, it also lacks their affectations and reflects the policy of admitting those who'll contribute most to College life.* The catering and the rooms are good, there's a large common room and an *excellent* auditorium.

Sex ratio(M:F): 61%:39%	Founded: 1979
Full time u'grads: 390	Postgrads: 109
Private school: 39%	Mature students: 3%
Overseas students: 8%	Disabled students: 1%

2 bars; bands, concerts and plays in the Auditorium (cap 250); frequent club nights. Fortnightly newsletter, termly mag. 2 libraries (48,000 volumes); 30 computers, 24hr. Chapel with famous organ. Sports fields (15 acres shared with <u>Queens'</u>) ¾ mile away; some facilities on site. All students live in; *good* rooms, most ensuite with phone and 'net connections, *good* self-catering. Doctor and nurse; *good* JCR welfare; free rape alarms and taxis for the stranded; financial tutor and various funds and scholarships; *excellent* disabled access.

FAMOUS ALUMNI:
Morwenna Banks ('Absolutely' comedian); Adrian Davies (Welsh rugby); Charles Hart (lyricist); Gary Sinyor (film director).

St Catharine's College, Cambridge

- *The College is part of <u>University of Cambridge</u> and students are entitled to use its facilities.*
St Catharine's College, Cambridge, CB2 1RL. Tel: (01223) 338300.
Fax: (01223) 353074.

Junior Common Room, St Catharine's College, Cambridge, CB2 1RL. Tel: (01223) 338300.
Website: www.caths.cam.ac.uk

Catz, as it's known, is at the beginning (or the end) of King's Parade *conveniently close to most major facilities*. It was founded in 1473 and its buildings bear witness to the many centuries since, including the last 50 years. *There's a strong sporting tradition, but non-jocks will not feel excluded. Political agitation is limited to campaigning for a new ironing board.*

Sex ratio(M:F): 49%:51%
Full time u'grads: 437
Private school: 38%
Overseas students: 12%

Founded: 1473
Postgrads: 147
Mature students: 3%
Disabled students: 4%

Bar; bops every 3 weeks; The Octagon theatre (cap 150) and chapel (100) used for concerts; biennial ball. Catzeyes magazine. 2 libraries (410,000 books); 25 computers, 24 hr; record library. CofE chapel. Sports fields (3 acres) ¾ mile; only Astroturf pitch in a Cambridge college; success in football and rugby. All students live in (all 2nd years in the octagonal St Chad's building); eat in dining halls; *self-catering*. CCTV; nurse; sick bay; 5 rooms for wheelchair users; *good* access; some financial support; prizes.

FAMOUS ALUMNI:
Peter Boizot (founded Pizza Express); Kevin Greening (Radio 5 Live); Sir Peter Hall (director); Malcolm Lowry (writer); Ian McKellen (actor); Jeremy Paxman (BBC newscaster); Steve Punt (*cat's-bum-mouthed comedian*).

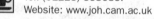

St John's College, Cambridge

- *The College is part of* <u>University of Cambridge</u> *and students are entitled to use its facilities.*

St John's College, Cambridge, CB2 1TP. Tel: (01223) 338703. Fax: (01223) 766419. E-mail: admissions@joh.cam.ac.uk
Junior Combination Room, St John's College, Cambridge, CB2 1TP. Tel: (01223) 338685.
Website: www.joh.cam.ac.uk

St John's College, 200 yards from King's Parade, is the home of the Bridge of Sighs, a tourist Mecca. It's one of the 'River Colleges' old, large and set in majestic grounds. *Its courts harmonise tunefully (as does the famous choir), until, that is, you reach the Cripps Building, which looks as bad as it sounds. There's a posh, sporty stereotype but it's not much more true than anywhere else. Its size and wealth means there's a niche for everyone and usually funds to fill it. The bar has more pulling power than Britney Spears.*

Sex ratio(M:F): 62%:38%
Full time u'grads: 556
Private school: 45%
Overseas students: 13%

Founded: 1511
Postgrads: 313
Mature students: <1%
Disabled students: 2.5%

Bar; Pythagoras Building (theatre); art and music rooms; Palmerston Room (cap 350) for bands; Old Music Room (100) for concerts; Boiler Room (120) for fortnightly drum 'n' bass and hip hop; annual ball. Weekly JCR newsletter and twice termly 'Cripptic' magazine; cable TV. 2 libraries (120,000 books); 45 computers, 24hr. *Large* cathedral-like CofE chapel. *Large* on-site sports hall, *superb* hockey club and *extensive* sports fields 200 yards away; cardiovascular gym. Everyone lives in or in hostels; *good* self-catering. CCTV, swipe cards; nurse; *very good* disabled access and provisions. *Excellent* financial support, grants and scholarships (*well, they can afford it*).

FAMOUS ALUMNI:
Douglas Adams (late author, 'Hitch Hiker's Guide to the Galaxy'); Rob Andrew (former England rugby player); Thomas Clarkson, William Wilberforce (antislavery campaigners); Derek Jacobi (actor); Lord Palmerston (PM); William Wordsworth (poet).

Selwyn College, Cambridge

- **The College is part of <u>University of Cambridge</u> and students are entitled to use its facilities.**
Selwyn College, Cambridge, CB3 9DQ. Tel: (01223) 335896.
Fax: (01223) 331720. E-mail: admissions@sel.cam.ac.uk
JCR Society, Selwyn College, Cambridge, CB3 9DQ.
Tel: (01223) 335846.
Website: www.sel.cam.ac.uk

Selwyn College is on the outskirts of Cambridge, ½ mile from King's Parade, adjacent to the University Arts and Mathematics Faculties and <u>Newnham</u>. Old Court, the focal point of the College, is an *attractive* example of neogothic Victorian architecture. A more recent addition, the Cripps Building has won an award, *but not from Push*. Selwyn is 10 minutes from other colleges, and has good involvement in university sports and drama. Students are easy-going and there's a fun, relaxed atmosphere.

Sex ratio(M:F): 55%:45%	Founded: 1882
Full time u'grads: 360	Postgrads: 170
Private school: 53%	Mature students: 2%
Overseas students: 6%	Disabled students: 1%

3 bars (2 for events only); theatre and 23 bops a term in Selwyn Diamond (cap 175), also live music and in Main Hall (200) and JCR (100); themed events; alternate May balls and Snowball at Xmas. *Excellent* college mag 'Kiwi'. Library (40,000 books); 20 computers. CofE chapel. Sports facilities ¼ mile away, shared with other colleges; *rowing, netball and basketball strong*. Most students live in; *very limited* self-catering; 3 formals a week (non-compulsory). Nurse; sickbay; hardship fund, scholarships, prizes; free attack alarms; parenting; *some disabled facilities*.

FAMOUS ALUMNI:
Clive Anderson (TV host, lawyer); John Gummer MP (Con); Simon Hughes MP (Lib Dem); Hugh Laurie (comedian, actor); Malcolm Muggeridge (journalist); Rob(ert) Newman (comedian, novelist).

Sidney Sussex College, Cambridge

- **The College is part of <u>University of Cambridge</u> and students are entitled to use its facilities.**
Sidney Sussex College, Cambridge, CB2 3HU. Tel: (01223) 338872.
Fax: (01223) 338884.
Students' Union, Sidney Sussex College, CB2 3HU.
Website: www.sid.cam.ac.uk

Behind the dreaming spires of Sidney Sussex's 16th-century buildings there lurks red brick. The College is central (200 yards from King's Parade; its proximity to the supermarket has led to the nickname Sidney Sainsbury's – and helped them to field the entire university team for the 'cam vs ox bean-eating competition'). It's also small and *familiar – one of the friendliest of Cambridge's colleges. It has some of the best sports grounds in Cambridge and one of the most active JCRs with considerable say in the running of the College. Sidney students also venture forth into the University, especially for drama and Rag. Academic standards are also high.*

Sex ratio(M:F): 58%:42%	Founded: 1596
Full time u'grads: 328	Postgrads: 131
Private school: 47%	Mature students: 2%
Overseas students: 5%	Disabled students: 2%

Only student-run bar in Cambridge (cap 175) used for fortnightly bops; Knox Shaw Room (40 seated); biennial ball. 'Sid News' and 'El Sid' mags, Yearbook and their own Rag mag. Library (40,000 books); 36 computers, 24hr. Chapel. Sports fields (22 acres) 1½ miles; *success in women's football and pool*. Majority of students live in, with most 2nd years in College-owned housing; eat in dining hall (food *improving*, veggie option); *adequate self-catering*. CCTV; nurse; hardship fund, bursaries, book grants, prizes; 1 room for a disabled student, some lifts.

FAMOUS ALUMNI:
Asa Briggs (historian); Oliver Cromwell (Lord Protector); Lord Owen (ex-SDP leader); Carol Vorderman (mathematician and sex symbol, *but no fashion icon*).

Trinity College, Cambridge

• *The College is part of <u>University of Cambridge</u> and students are entitled to use its facilities.*
Trinity College, Cambridge, CB2 1TQ. Tel: (01223) 338400.
Fax: (01223) 338584.
Students' Union, Trinity College, Cambridge, CB2 1TQ.
Tel: (01223) 367424.
Website: www.trin.cam.ac.uk

Trinity is Cambridge's largest College, situated a hop, skip and jump from King's Parade. *It's grand and imposing, with a prestigious history. Trinity is big enough for all individuals to find somewhere to fit in. They're keen to attract more state school and female students, but they could hardly have had fewer. The flip side is that Trinity's so rich that less well-off students will always be assured of some level of assistance. There's a strong academic reputation, especially in sciences.*

Sex ratio(M:F): 67%:33%	Founded: 1546
Full time u'grads: 679	Postgrads: 357
Private school: 50%	Mature students: 3%
Overseas students: 10%	Disabled students: 2%

Bar; Chapel (200) and Combination Room (100) for live music (*prestigious* choir) and fortnightly sweaty bops in Wolfson Party Room (150); biggest annual ball (2,000 tickets); regular jazz and comedy. SU newsletter 3 times a term. 2 libraries (300,000 books); 70 computers, 24hr. CofE chapel; 3 chaplains; charity fund-raising. *Extensive* sports fields ½ mile from College; success in rowing, rugby, hockey, women's football. Everyone lives in; most rooms have network points; rooms vary (attics with oak beams, grand rooms with high ceilings, modern with en suite facilities); mixed sex couples can choose to share; eat in dining hall (optional formal dinner every night), wine cellar. CCTV, swipe cards; nurse; *generous* financial support; rooms for wheelchair access.

FAMOUS ALUMNI:
Francis Bacon (artist); Lord Byron (mad, bad poet); Prince Charles; Lord Hurd (former Foreign Secretary); Lord Macaulay (historian);

Vladimir Nabokov (writer); Isaac Newton (scientist); Enoch Powell (ex-MP); Bertrand Russell, Ludwig Wittgenstein (philosophers); Tennyson (less mad poet); Lord Whitelaw (ex Tory minister).

Trinity Hall, Cambridge

- **The College is part of <u>University of Cambridge</u> and students are entitled to use its facilities.**
Trinity Hall, Cambridge, CB2 1TJ. Tel: (01223) 332510.
Fax: (01223) 332537. E-mail: admissions@trinhall.cam.ac.uk
Junior Common Room, Trinity Hall, Cambridge, CB2 1TJ.
Tel: (01223) 332534.
Website: www.trinhall.cam.ac.uk

'Tit Hall', as Trinity Hall is widely (*but not abusively*) known, is a 'River' college, 200 yards from King's Parade in the centre of town, but away from the shops. It's the fourth smallest - *nice and intimate* (*ie short on privacy*) - with a Georgian courtyard and 17th-century buildings and shouldn't be confused with its larger, richer neighbour, <u>Trinity College</u>. *It's a friendly place where academic pursuits don't get in the way of drinking and messing about in boats.*

Sex ratio(M:F): 54%:46%	Founded: 1350
Full time u'grads: 343	Postgrads: 276
Private school: 49%	Mature students: 1%
Overseas students: 10%	Disabled students: <1%

Bar; indie and dance bands; fortnightly Global nights with London DJs; lecture theatre for drama and music (cap 270). 'New Moon' mag, weekly newsletter; *active* Rag. 2 libraries (85,000 books); 20 computers, 24hr. CofE chapel. Sports fields (3 acres) 1 mile away; *'boaty'* reputation. Most live in; accommodation split between college and Huntingdon Road, 1 mile away. Nurse; hardship fund, book loans and scholarships.

FAMOUS ALUMNI:
Lord Howe (former Cabinet Minister); Nicholas Hytner (theatre/film director); Donald Maclean (spy); JB Priestley (writer); Tony Slattery (*chunky* comedian); Terry Waite (former hostage).

Canterbury
see <u>University of Kent at Canterbury</u>

Canterbury Christ Church University
see <u>Other Institutions</u>

```
Heinz Wolff, the professor of bio-engineering
at Brunel University, has posed with glamour
model Joanne Guest in the pages of 'Loaded'
magazine.
```

Cardiff University

- **The College is part of <u>University of Wales.</u>**
Cardiff University, PO Box 921, Cardiff, CF10 3XQ.
Tel: (029) 20 874839. Fax: (029) 20 874457.
E–mail: prospectus@cardiff.ac.uk
Cardiff University Students' Union, Park Place, Cardiff, CF10 3QN.
Tel: (029) 20 781400. Fax: (029) 20 781518.
E–mail: studentsunion@cf.ac.uk

GENERAL

Cardiff, over the Channel from Bristol, is Wales's largest city and, since 1955, its capital. Around the northern outskirts is industry and housing, *built with cash from the coalmines.* Nearer Cardiff's centre, impressive Victorian and Georgian buildings are set off by *loads of trees and other green stuff.* The place is full of museums and buildings of architectural note, including most of the University's buildings, *which are pretty fancy*. Some are more modern, but still have gardens and leafy walkways, *perfect for the odd frisbee and sunbathing session (well maybe not the sun bit).*

Sex ratio(M:F): 46%:54%	**Founded: 1883**
Full time u'grads: 12,014	**Part time: 0**
Postgrads: 3,329	**Non–degree: 0**
Ave course: 3yrs	**Ethnic: n/a**
Private school: n/a	**Flunk rate: 11.6%**
Mature students: 12%	**Overseas students: 17%**
Disabled students: 3%	

ATMOSPHERE:
Cardiff is a vibrant, action-packed city with students to match, who party hard and don't care who gets caught in the headlights. There are plenty of ways of passing one's days with a wide range of facilities and activities. You might even bump into the odd celeb or film crew – the film 'Human Traffic' was set in the city. The Students' Union spends more time being a successful multi-million pound company than a political fighting force.

THE CITY:
- <u>Population: 272,600</u> • <u>London: 143miles</u> • <u>Bristol: 30miles</u>
- <u>Swansea: 40miles</u>

The University along with the civic buildings dominates the city centre, most of which is closed to cars. But the traffic flows through usually rage-free and the streets are *amazingly litter-light (wrapper collectors will be disappointed).* As the major urban centre for the whole of Wales, Cardiff is *well kitted out*: shopping malls and supermarkets; banks and book shops (including second-hand) and late-night shopping. It is also extremely chuffed with its Millennium Stadium and the development at Cardiff Bay. It has many provisions designed for the tourists, including lots of museums and galleries (National Museum of Wales, Turner House Gallery, Welsh Industrial & Maritime Museum, etc) and the Castle (half Roman, half Norman, half medieval, half mathematical impossibility).

TRAVEL:
Trains: Direct trains from Cardiff Central: London (£17.15); Birmingham (£13.20); Manchester (£25.10) and so on.
Coaches: National Express to most places: London (£18), Birmingham (£14.50) and all over.
Car: Parts of the city centre are for pedestrians only. To get to Cardiff, there's the M4, A470 and A48. *A car's not really necessary since the invention of feet but it's nice for reaching the South Wales countryside, just 5 miles away.*
Air: Cardiff International Airport has flights to the Channel Islands, Ireland, and even the USA, as well as inland trips.
Hitching: The A48's a bonus – only 5 mins walk from the campus – and the Welsh are willing.
Local: Local bus services run every 20–30 mins all round town. They're reliable with an average trip costing 50p.
Taxis: Lots of firms will happily extort about £1.60 for the privilege of a ride it'd take 10 mins to walk.
Bicycles: *Everything's within cycling distance and there are sheds at all the halls. Bikes have been known to ride off by themselves, though.*

CAREER PROSPECTS:
• Careers Service • No of staff: 7 full • Unemployed after 6mths: 5%

FAMOUS ALUMNI:
Huw Edwards (BBC TV news reader); Richie Edwards (missing Manic); Arwel Hughes (conductor); Karl Hyde, Rick Smith (Underworld); Lord Jenkins (Lib Dem); Neil and Glenys Kinnock (Europe's First Couple); Sian Lloyd (weatherperson); Philip Madoc (actor); Sian Philips (actress); Bernice Rubens (Booker Prize winner); Tim Sebastian (BBC reporter).

FURTHER INFO:
Undergraduate prospectus (call (029) 20 874899), video and websites (www.cardiff.ac.uk).

ACADEMIC

Apart from a regular range of courses, students can study Welsh or, indeed, in Welsh, but they have to make special arrangements.

staff/student ratio: 1:9
Range of points required for entrance: 340-240
Percentage accepted through clearing: 2%
Number of terms/semesters: 2
Length of terms/semesters 15wks
Research: 5.0

LIBRARIES:
• Books: 1,250,000 • Study places: 2,800
There are 10 libraries in all but only 3 main ones: Arts & Social Studies, the Aberconway and Science. Co-stars: Law and Architecture.

COMPUTERS:
• Computer workstations: 5,000
24-hour access to some computer labs.

ENTERTAINMENT

THE CITY:

- Price of a pint of beer: £1.90 • Glass of wine: £1.40

Cinemas: (6) 5 mainstreamers and the Chapter Arts Centre (arty alternative flicks and 80 different bottled beers).

Theatres: Cardiff has 4 theatres with everything from panto to Pinter, including the Chapter Arts Centre (which also has a dance studio, exhibition centres and so on), the New Theatre (home of the Welsh National Opera) and the Sherman Theatre.

Pubs: *Some excellent boozers. Pushplugs: Clancey's (Irish, good fun); Rat & Carrot; The Woodville Arms (aka the Woody – very studenty); Sam's Bar; Macintosh (skittles in the summer), the redeveloped docks area is now full of pubs and clubs which are now vastly more friendly towards students. Beware the tacky theme pubs that aren't worth the effort.*

Clubs/discos: *There's a high proportion of naff flesh arcades but, despite this, Pushplugs: Solvs (cap 1,900); Zeus (70s on Thursdays); Emporium and Blah Blah's (cheese); Club Ifor Bach (aka the Welsh Club) is popular on Wednesdays; the Square and Hippos ('proper' dance music).*

Music venues: Really big bands include the International Arena and the Millennium Stadium on their tours (Cardiff Arms Park is currently closed) but, for more down to earth tunes, there's St David's Hall, the Jazz bar and plenty more. The Corrs, Robbie Williams and All Saints are among the acts who have played Cardiff recently.

Eating out: You want it, you got it, including the obligatory post-club kebab at 4am. *Pushplugs: Ethnic Deli (£10 for 5 dishes); Las Iguanas & Old Orleans (Tex–Mex); Ramone's (greasy spoon); Friend's Café; The Pear Tree (Cathays community centre); Taurus (steakhouse).*

UNIVERSITY:

- Price of a pint of beer: £1.60 • Bottle of wine: £1.50

The Union has some of the best facilities in the country, but is currently working on dissuading rowdy students from disturbing the locals lest they lose their late licence. A sackful of fun bursts every week during term-time with frequent clubs and socs bashes and bops, Rag romps and theme parties as well as the usual fare of ents.

Bars: (22) Six in the Union and each residential hall has its own bar. The most popular is the stained-glass-enhanced, oak-beamed Tafarn, which is also the only one open before 9pm.

Theatre and film: The Act One drama group puts on four or five productions annually.

Clubs/discos: Five regular, mainstream club nights a week in Solus (cap 1,900), with 70s cheese nights being very popular. *More sophisticated party people prefer the occasional pleasure of guest DJs such as Judge Jules, Dave Pearce and Danny Rampling.*

Music venues: The Great Hall (1,500) is the main live auditorium but the newly refurbished Solus (1,900) also does its bit. Between them they can pull in big league acts to make most SUs go pale green, recent examples being Coldplay, Leftfield, David Gray and Pete Tong. Seren Las (320) puts on lower-key events.

Food: During the day the university refectories serve full meals and snacks and the snack bars in the Union do a fine but not exactly cheap spread of filled rolls, baked spuds and stuff.

Other: Several balls, culminating in the June Ultimate event. Weekly comedy at Solus.

SOCIAL & POLITICAL

CARDIFF UNIVERSITY STUDENTS' UNION:
• 8 sabbaticals • Turnout at last ballot: 20% • NUS member
This Union's plat du jour is business-like and commercial rather than political but the emphasis has been shifting in recent years. The current factional focus is against tuition fees and better housing. The Union has a Welsh language policy and all signs and many publications are bilingual. Every year there's a Welsh Awareness Week (*maybe for people who think they're actually in Belgium*).

SU FACILITIES:
Ready, steady, go... 9 bars, 5 cafeterias/sandwich bars, minibus hire, printing and photocopying, 2 shops (general, food, stationery, new and second-hand books), HSBC Bank, travel centre, payphones, phone messaging service, photobooth, video games and vending machines, juke box, 8 pool tables, 4 snooker tables, media suite, volunteer suite, job shop, IT suite, study rooms, TV lounges, function rooms, conference hall, nightclub, Endsleigh Insurance and probably a small sub-continent in the basement.

CLUBS (NON-SPORTING):
Bellringing; Duke of Edinburgh; Hellenic; Hindu; Jazz; Live music; Methodist; Motorcycle; Real Ale; Scout & Guide.

OTHER ORGANISATIONS:
The Union publishes the award-winning newspaper 'Gair Rhydd' (meaning 'Free Word') which is distributed to other colleges in Cardiff and Xpress Radio broadcasts to the Union and twice a year for a month on FM and all year round on the internet. The Cardiff charity Rag (Caerdydd) raised over £18,000 last year with the usual pranks. Student Community Action performs many a good deed locally, *helping to ease occasionally frayed town/gown relations*. It has a full-time organiser and a high level of involvement.

RELIGIOUS:
Cardiff has 2 cathedrals (Anglican and Catholic) and churches of most sorts, including Church of Scotland, Orthodox, Methodist, Quaker, United Reform. There are also places of worship for Muslims, Jews, Hindus, Sikhs and Buddhists.

PAID WORK:
Cardiff, particularly during the tourist season, has lots of opportunities for casual cash and the SU runs a Jobshop. *Unfortunately, there are truckloads of students going for jobs.* The Union employs 700 students every year.

SPORTS

• Recent successes: waterpolo, women's rugby
The level of involvement has been low-key recently, despite getting their spanking new sports hall. Student sports are run by the SU Athletic Union.

SPORTS FACILITIES:
4 sports centres; 33 acres of playing fields for all the usual field games; small athletics track; floodlit artificial pitch; Astroturf pitch; tennis and squash courts. Expert advice, including fitness assessment, is usually to hand. Refurbished indoor facilities at

Talybont, one of the residential complexes (about a mile from the main campus), include 2 sports halls, a fitness studio, free weights room and 5-a-side soccer pitch. The Union has facilities for table-tennis, squash, fencing, darts, snooker and pool. Other facilities, such as a swimming pool, shooting range, sailing centre and boathouse, are hired locally by the University. The local area also adds an ice rink, ski slope, bowling green and the mountains of the surrounding countryside. For water sports, there's the River Taff, the Bristol Channel and a lake – a fair choice. Facilities are such that a full body work-out can be arranged for disabled students.

SPORTING CLUBS:
American Football; Dance; Karate; Lacrosse.

ATTRACTIONS:
There's also round ball action at Ninian Park, Glamorgan Cricket Club at Sophia Gardens and the Cardiff Devils ice hockey team. There's rugby at Cardiff Arms Park home to Cardiff RFC, Internationals are played at the Millenium Stadium which also steps up as Wembley's replacement.

ACCOMMODATION

IN COLLEGE:
• Catered: 4% • Cost: £55–67(39wks) • Self–catering: 31%
• Cost: £39–58(39–52wks)
Availability: All non-clearing 1st years are guaranteed accommodation. There are 11 halls (including the all-female Aberdare) within a mile of campus and 7 more up to 2 miles away. £40m has been spent on accommodation recently *and the standard's pretty good, especially in the flash halls* with en suite facilities. Nobody needs to share. There are also 363 places in College-owned housing. CCTV is watching.
Car parking: There's limited parking and cars need permits.

EXTERNALLY:
• Ave rent: £46
Availability: *Houses can get a bit grungy, given that they've housed students before you. The search is most fruitful on the north side of town – eg the Cathays student ghetto and Roath (good for pubs and chippies) in shared houses and flats. Splott also looks damn good as an address.* Push recommends avoiding Grange Town and nearby Riverside.
Housing help: The University operates a Residence Office with 2 full-time staff who provide vacancy and landlord lists. They also help students get legal advice.

SERVICES:
• Creche • Lesbian & Gay Society • Mature SA • Overseas SA
• Postgrad SA • Minibus • Women's Officer • Self–defence classes
The University counselling service has 4 full-time and 2 part-time staff, with the Union adding its own welfare provision. The University also runs a Health Centre with 3 doctors and 3 nurses. Special provision is made for overseas students.

Disabled: *Access is pretty good all round but improvements could still be made in the SU and halls of residence.* There's also a Dyslexia Resource Centre.

FINANCE:
- Access fund: £612,492
- Successful applications: 701

The Oldfield Davies Trust can help women with health problems and there are also short–term loans up to £100 and small grants, usually limited to finalists.

Cardiff Institute
see Other Institutions

Caythorpe
see De Montfort University

CCAT
see Anglia Polytechnic University

University of Central England

- *Formerly Birmingham Polytechnic*

University of Central England, Perry Barr, Birmingham, B42 2SU.
Tel: (0121) 331 5595. Fax: (0121) 331 6740.
E-mail: recruitment@uce.ac.uk
Students' Union, University of Central England, Perry Barr, Birmingham, B42 2SU. Tel: (0121) 331 6801.
Fax: (0121) 331 6802. E-mail: union.president@uce.ac.uk

GENERAL

Perry Barr is an area of Birmingham 3 miles to the north of the centre. UCE's main site is planted here and half the students are here. There are nine sites in all, most around the city centre but one *out on a limb* at Bournville. *Sites differ in atmosphere and looks as much as the Hilton and a Happy Eater, from the elegant Victorian gothic College of Art in Margaret Street to the brown brick and dark glass slab at Perry Barr. Over the last few years, UCE has undergone the kind of face-lift that would make Cher jealous.*

Sex ratio(M:F): 44%:56%	Founded: 1971
Full time u'grads: 8,236	Part time: 2,419
Postgrads: 1,071	Non-degree: 8,349
Ave course: 3yrs	Ethnic: 34%
Private school: n/a	Flunk rate: 25.3%
Mature students: 30%	Overseas students: 12%
Disabled students: 9%	

ATMOSPHERE:
The University offers many FE courses and free part-time courses to the unemployed, *so the social mix isn't just the usual array of undergrads.* As for University facilities, there's the Union services and... okay, so they're limited, but that just broadens students' horizons. Doesn't it? Maybe not, but it does mean they have to get out and explore their city.

THE SITES:
Perry Barr: (4,376 – most courses) Despite being the main site, it isn't all that big and its students are very business-like. Perry Barr is a *fairly scruffy, grubby part of the city (although the campus itself is a large enough and pleasant enough island).* Its best features are a good number of local shops, a greyhound stadium (opposite the campus) and a station to get you out of there.
Westbourne Rd/Edgbaston: (6,589 – education and nursing) 6 miles from Perry Barr, one of the main benefits of this site seems to be the crammed Edge Bar, which attracts students from all over.
Bournville: (785 – art & design) 4 miles from the centre, near the choccy factory, Bournville is one of 4 sites housing art & design courses, and unsurprisingly, the students here are arty and exciting.
Others: Gosta Green (1,721 – art & design), Margaret St (415 – art & design), the Birmingham Conservatoire (498 – music) and the Jewellery School (478) in the city's Jewellery Quarter which is turning touristy.

THE CITY: see University of Birmingham

TRAVEL: see University of Birmingham
No inter-site transport laid on by the university.

CAREER PROSPECTS:
• Careers Service • **No of staff: 4 full** • Unemployed after 6mths: 6%

FAMOUS ALUMNI:
Apache Indian (Bhangra muffin); Zoë Ball (TV and radio presenter and Mrs Fat Boy Slim); Alfred Bestall (Rupert Bear's creator); Betty Jackson (fashion designer); Larry (cartoonist); Jas Mann (Babylon Zoo); Judy Simpson (Nightshade in 'Gladiators'); Frank Skinner (comedian).

FURTHER INFO:
Prospectuses for undergrads, postgrads and part-timers, faculty videos and a website (www.uce.ac.uk).

ACADEMIC

The University has one helluva range of courses grouped into nine faculties: the Birmingham Conservatoire; the Birmingham Institute of Art and Design; Built Environment; Business School; Computing; Information & English Technology; Innovation Centre; Health & Community Care; Law & Social Sciences. Many of the courses are career-related and part-time and sandwich students are common.

staff/student ratio: 1:14
Range of points required for entrance: 260-160
Percentage accepted through clearing: 10%
Number of terms/semesters: 3
Length of terms/semesters: 11wks
Research: 2.2

LIBRARIES:
- Books: 680,924 • Study places: 759

The main Kenrick Library is at Perry Barr with 7 specialist libraries on other sites for the courses based there. *Students are happy with the library except when they all have to fight over the same book.*

COMPUTERS:
- Computer workstations: 900

There are computer rooms at each site.

CITY: see University of Birmingham

UNIVERSITY:
- Price of a pint of beer: £1.45 • Glass of wine: £1.25

Bars: (8) The Union Club (cap 600), The Edge at Westbourne Rd (350) and The Village Inn (cap 200), a pub in Handsworth Wood. There are also bars at Moor Lane and the Conservatoire.

Theatre/cinema: A drama group that does stuff like 'Grease'. The film club shows recent hits, world cinema and cult faves twice a week.

Clubs/discos/music venues: Club nights at: Perry Barr; Bar 42 (cap 600); the Edge (cap 200); The Union Club (cap 600). DJs include Fergie and Lisa Lashes.

Cabaret: Fortnightly *foppery.*

Food: There are eateries at all sites. *Variety is improving* and you can now eat kosher or vegan.

Others: 2 sports balls a year, various faculty/society events and Sunday pub quizzes.

UNIVERSITY OF CENTRAL ENGLAND STUDENTS' UNION (UCESU):
- 7 sabbaticals • Turnout at last ballot: 13% • NUS member

UCESU was the first student union to become a limited company with the sabbaticals as directors. *So far this has failed to impress the punters, as the voting figures indicate. Split sites, limited facilities and downright disorganisation don't help to foster a spirit of cohesion either.* Decentralisation of the Union's structure is being considered to redress this. Awareness campaigns go down well.

SU FACILITIES:
The Union has facilities on 5 sites. At the Union's main centre at Perry Barr, there's a cheap bar, shop, advice centre, Endsleigh Insurance office, games machines, photobooth and photocopier. There's also a NatWest bank.

CLUBS (NON SPORTING):
Archaos (architecture and... um... chaos); Cedd House (religious and secular forum); Podiatry (feet).

OTHER ORGANISATIONS:
'Spaghetti Junction' is the student newspaper, published by the Union. *The charity Rag is charitably raggy.* The Community Action Group is involved in projects to help the homeless among others.

RELIGIOUS:
- 5 chaplains (2 CofE, 3 RC)

In addition to the chaplaincy there is a Muslim prayer room.

SPORTS

- Recent successes: rugby league

Having virtually no facilities of its own currently, the University isn't going to take on the big boys and girls and win hands down, though there is excellent hockey and tennis. However, there's a new £3m sports academy being built. This will be followed by a new sports hall and pitches in the next 2 years. *So things are on the up;* unlike many universities Wednesday afternoons aren't kept free for sporting endeavours, *which gives them even less of a chance.* But the Union has a student sports sabbatical, whose job it is to spend a large proportion of the Union's annual budget hiring local facilities so students can actually take part in competitions. Charges for facilities vary between 30p and £2.

SPORTING CLUBS:
Aerobics; Boardriders; Intra-university sports; Jiu Jitsu; Kick Boxing; Lacrosse; Surf; Ten-Pin Bowling; Thai Boxing.

ATTRACTIONS: see University of Birmingham

ACCOMMODATION

IN COLLEGE:
- Catered: 2% • Cost: £60(40wks) • Self-catering: 24%
- Cost: £45-66 (40-52wks)

Availability: The self-catering halls are based at Westbourne Road and in The Coppice in Perry Barr with refurbished catered and self-catered accommodation at the Hampstead site. Overseas students get special preference at Cambrian Hall in the city centre. There's also a student village with 650 study bedrooms at Perry Barr and university-leased houses and flats for 850 students. 3% share. Entry-phones and CCTV.

Car parking: Easy enough, *but a car isn't really necessary.*

EXTERNALLY: see University of Birmingham
Housing help: The Accommodation Service runs the head tenancy scheme and there's a register of approved private housing.

WELFARE

SERVICES:
- Nursery • Lesbian & Gay Society • Mature SA • Overseas SA
- Minibus

The University's Student Services Section provides 1 full- and 4 part-time counsellors for all kinds of problems except medical ones, which are dealt with by nurses based on 3 of the sites or by the usual NHS practices. There are 2 nurseries (at Westbourne Road and Perry Barr) for children aged 12 months to 5 years.

Disabled: A Disability Action Officer has made improvements to access. There's also a Student Services Co-ordinator for students with special needs and library facilities for sight- and hearing-impaired students.

Central Lancashire

FINANCE:
- Access fund: £778,045 • Successful applications: 2,174

UCE has decent support systems with its own non-Government Access Fund and there are Chaplaincy and Hardship Funds and bursaries for students from low income and disadvantaged backgrounds.

University of Central Lancashire

- *Formerly Preston Polytechnic, Lancashire Polytechnic*

University of Central Lancashire, Preston, PR1 2HE. Tel: (01772) 892400. Fax: (01772) 892935. E-mail: c.enquiries@uclan.ac.uk
University of Central Lancashire Students' Union, University of Central Lancashire, Fylde Road, Preston, PR1 2TQ. Tel: (01772) 513200. Fax: (01772) 908553. E-mail: s.u.soc@uclan.ac.uk

GENERAL

Preston, on the River Ribble, is the second largest town in Lancashire and the county's administrative capital. It's bigger than Lancaster, the county town, but not as big as Blackpool, which illuminates England's north-west coast. Preston is old *and attractive*, with mature parks stuffed between some *interesting* buildings and churches. The University is almost in the heart of Preston set in a 38-acre campus in 2 main blocks of buildings encompassing a variety of modern styles (mostly red brick, concrete and glass; *smart, but about as cutting edge as a rubber knife*) with paved squares and a few outpost buildings. *In the midst of the campus there are a few noteworthy features*, such as the Arts Centre – a converted church – and the SU Building, a *stumpy* russet place with odd angles and a light pyramid on top.

Sex ratio(M:F): 43%:57%	Founded: 1828
Full time u'grads: 10,722	Part time: 2,081
Postgrads: 450	Non–degree: 9,152
Ave course: 3yrs	Ethnic: 12%
Private school: n/a	Flunk rate: 25.9%
Mature students: 45%	Overseas students: 7%
Disabled students: 3%	

ATMOSPHERE:
The student body is made up of two largely immiscible groups: mature students who tend to knuckle down, but not hang around; and their younger, thrusting colleagues, who, when not thinking about beer, sex and sport, see everything as a potential line on the ol' CV.

TOWN:
- Population: 147,109 • London: 202miles • Blackpool: 15miles
- Manchester: 25miles

Granada TV awarded Preston the staggering accolade of being the *'best and cheapest shopping centre in Britain with a marvellous mixture of modern and old style shops and an excellent market hall'.*

And who are we to argue with the company that gave us Richard and Judy? It is true that the cost of living in Preston is low and the quality of life high. Its long history goes further back than its boom time as a cotton town during the Industrial Revolution. It's been redeveloped in recent years, particularly the centre and the docks.

TRAVEL:
Trains: Preston Station, ½ mile from the campus, runs direct trains to London (£28.40), Manchester (£6.55) and beyond.
Coaches: National Express services to, among other places, London (£18.50), Manchester (£3.40).
Car: Preston is on the A6, A49, A59 and A677, and just off the M6, M55 and M61.
Hitching: *The A6 and M6 offer excellent opportunities for thumbing north or south.*
Local: Local buses keep to an exact fare system (no change given). Discounted Rambler tickets (anywhere in town, £5.20/week) are available.
Taxis: *Cheap enough even for students, occasionally.*
Bicycles: *There's many a hump and bump in Preston and there's rain and poor bike parking facilities. Nevertheless, bikes are popular for getting round the campus.*

CAREER PROSPECTS:
• Careers Service • No of staff: 3 full • Unemployed after 6mths: 5%

FAMOUS ALUMNI:
Mark Beaumont (NME hack); Joe Lydon (rugby league); Phil MacIntyre (pop promoter); Tjinder Singh, Ben Ayres (Cornershop).

FURTHER INFO:
Prospectuses for undergrads, part-timers and postgrads, website (www.uclan.ac.uk), Union handbook. Open day info: (01772) 892700.

ACADEMIC

Most courses include a sandwich year, working in industry in a course-related field. *A recent survey indicated that 25% of students would not return to Central Lancashire if they could choose again – on the other hand, that's 75% who would.*

staff/student ratio: 1:18
Range of points required for entrance: 300-80
Percentage accepted through clearing: 20%
Number of terms/semesters: 2
Length of terms/semesters: 15 wks
Research: 2.5

LIBRARIES:
• Books: 350,000 • Study places: 1,732
The library, centrally placed on campus, is one of the most modern buildings (built in 1979) *but the consensus is that they need more books. And,er, free beer would be nice too.*

COMPUTERS:
• Computer workstations: 1,100

ENTERTAINMENT

TOWN:
• Price of a pint of beer: £1.70 • Glass of wine: £1.40
Pubs: Pubs are student-friendly, or at least tolerant, especially those near the University. Pushplugs: Roper Hall; O'Neill's; The Adelphi; The Ship.
Cinemas: (2) 17 screens between them.
Theatres: The Charter Theatre, 15 minutes' walk from campus, offers *a fairly straightforward bill of Shakespeare 'n' stuff.*
Clubs/discos: Several offering *good* student fare. Pushplugs: The Mill (alternative, free bus service); Squires (Mondays); Tokyo Jo's (Wednesdays).
Music venues: The Guild Hall hosts anything you *might wish to tap a toe to (and plenty you wouldn't)*. The Adelphi is the indie HQ. A new event called Prest Fest is organised by the University and various local venues in October/November.
Eating out: Preston's culinary scene is varied and *usually very cheap*. There are plenty of ethnic eateries and burger bars to satisfy those post-midnight longings. Pushplugs: Isis Café bar; ultimate student friendly ChillOut Zone; Tiggi's (50% student discount); Bella Pasta (half-price on Wednesdays).

UNIVERSITY:
• Price of a pint of beer: £1.10 • Glass of wine: £1.50
Bars: The SU has 3 *popular* bars. The Polygon (cap 400) and Union Square (400) are open all day. The *aptly* named Venue (900) only opens when an event is on.
Cinemas: 2 films a week, varying between mainstream new(ish) releases and theme weeks.
Theatres: The Crumpet Theatre Company sends a play to the Edinburgh Fringe every year and even to the Ukraine last year. There is an Arts Centre on campus *for all sorts of arty things*.
Clubs/discos/music venues: The Venue hosts 3 or 4 club nights a week, with Futurfunk (D'n'B and hip hop) and Feel (garage/house) on alternate Fridays and Saturdays. Recent acts include Atomic Kitten, Judge Jules, Freestylers and Cream Live.
Food: During the day students choose their chews in the University's 3 refectories, open all day, the SU's 3 eateries (Mr Nibbles for sarnies, the Polygon for pub lunch and Union Square for all-day breakfast) and local pubs.

SOCIAL & POLITICAL

UNIVERSITY OF CENTRAL LANCASHIRE STUDENTS' UNION:
• 7 sabbaticals • Turnout at last ballot: 3% • NUS member
The University's growth in numbers has rather outstripped its resources, but the SU and the University are doing an okay job, working together to deal with some of the fall-out. Issues are more important than political labels with environmental and racial concerns being particularly high on the agenda. Most students are more concerned with their own life plans, though.

SU FACILITIES:
The modern SU Building has 3 bars, a cafeteria, sandwich shop, service restaurant, 4 minibuses for hire, printing service, 3 shops

(selling stationery, sweets and general goods), HSBC Bank and cashpoint, photocopying, photo booth, games, video and vending machines, pool tables and juke boxes and TV lounge.

CLUBS (NON SPORTING):
Celtic; Computer; Deaf; Film; Franglais; Hellenic; Juggling; Scientific Expedition, Spanish.

OTHER ORGANISATIONS:
'Pluto' is the Guardian/NUS student media winning SU tabloid (every fortnight) and other media goes on in an academic sort of way at the Journalism Department, who also produce 'The Reporter'. The do-gooders of the student community group do good all over the place – priority is given to local charities. Rag organises pub-crawls including putting people in stocks.

RELIGIOUS:
• 1 chaplain
The Multi-Faith Centre is available for all religions to do their thing. Locally, there's the Cathedral, churches and places of worship for Muslims, Hindus, Sikhs, Buddhists and Jews.

PAID WORK:
Jobshop called 'The Bridge'. *There's an abundance of pubs and restaurants hungry for part-time staff.*

SPORTS

• Recent successes: gaelic football
The sports facilities are limited, but students make use of anything they can find locally. There's an annual Lancashire Cup competition against Lancaster University, but if you want to expand beyond intra-county rivalry to fight against ye old Yorkist enemy across the border and compete in the annual War of the Roses competition, then you'll have to change university and enrol at either York or Lancaster – *sorry.*

SPORTS FACILITIES:
On campus, in the small sports centre, there's a sports hall, activities room, multigym and fitness area. A new £12m outdoor multi-sport complex has been built, on a 65-acre site. Preston adds goodies like tennis courts, a golf course and the Forest of Bowland nearby. Mobile phones are provided for dangerous sporting activities, *such as grenade-hurling and croquet.*

SPORTING CLUBS:
Baseball; Jiu Jitsu; Kung Fu; Mountaineering; Parachuting; Snowboarding; TenPin Bowling; Windsurfing.

ATTRACTIONS:
Preston North End FC are the local football heroes and the town is also the home of the National Museum of Football. Also Preston Grasshoppers RFC.

ACCOMMODATION

IN COLLEGE:
• Self-catering: 14% • Cost: £45-53(37wks)
Availability: The University can house 60% of 1st years (7% who want to, can't live in) and few others. The University promises to have phone sockets in all on-campus rooms. There are also 120 places in

local houses owned by the University and rented to students, but, still, almost everything goes to 1st years. 1% of livers-in have to share. The wary can be reassured by CCTV and a campus cop.
Car parking: There is limited, permit-only parking (£36 per year).

EXTERNALLY:
• Ave rent: £36
Availability: *Preston is not too heavily pressed to provide housing and students should find something adequate with merely most moderate hassle. Plungington and Broadgate are the most popular areas. Deepdale and Ashton are bits to avoid.*
Housing help: The University Accommodation Service has 13 full- and 1 part-time staff whose collective mission in life is to provide students with vacancy lists, bulletin boards, contract advice and rat 'n' rising-damp checks of student housing.

SERVICES:
• Creche • Lesbian & Gay Society • Mature SA • Nightline
• International SA • Postgrad SA • Ethnic Minorities SA
• Overseas SA • Minibus • Women's Officer • Self-defence classes
Troubled students head for the SU Welfare Unit or to see one of the 4 full-time counsellors. There are also 4 doctors and 2 nurses at the health service on campus.
Disabled: *Wheelchair access is no worse than most places, but facilities for hearing-impaired and, more particularly, sight-impaired students are good.* The University became a member of NFAC (National Federation of Access Centres) in 1997.

FINANCE:
• Access fund: £710,000
• Successful applications: 700
There's also a Hardship Fund and postgraduate bursaries.

Central St Martins College of Art
see The London Institute

Charing Cross & Westminster Hospital
see Imperial College, London

Charlotte Mason
see Lancaster University

Chelsea College of Art
see The London Institute

```
Newnham College, Cambridge contains the
second-longest corridor in Europe.
```

Cheltenham & Gloucester College of Higher Education

Cheltenham & Gloucester College of Higher Education, PO Box 220, The Park, Cheltenham, Gloucestershire, GL50 2QF.
Tel: (01242) 532825. Fax: (01242) 543334.
E-mail: admissions@chelt.ac.uk
Cheltenham & Gloucester College Students' Union, PO Box 220, The Park, Cheltenham, Gloucestershire, GL50 2QF. Tel: (01242) 532848. Fax: (01242) 261381.

GENERAL

Cheltenham and Gloucester are two towns of similar size, of similar style (*mostly elegant Regency stone, Gloucester less so*) and similarly placed. They're less than 7 miles apart in the *tumbling humps* of Gloucestershire, beyond the end of the Bristol Channel, where it gives up being the Severn Estuary *and resorts to being the not-so humble Severn River*. Cheltenham and Gloucester is a college of higher education. The main site, the Park Campus (originally a botanic and zoological garden), is an *urban island* 1½ miles from Cheltenham town centre with *elderly* buildings, *elegant* grounds and an *extraordinary* garden. Among the tennis courts and the large pond where the ducks occasionally allow students to row, it's one of the few places in England where Wellingtonia trees can be found. *They have very soft bark, which can be punched or head-butted without fear of pain – handy for students wandering home drunk.* This is one of three main sites, all of which are in Cheltenham – a new site in Gloucester is due to open in 2002, *so the name might finally be appropriate.*

Sex ratio(M:F): 43%:57%	Founded: 1990
Full time u'grads: 5,362	Part time: 1,119
Postgrads: 389	Non-degree: 2,613
Ave course: 3/4yrs	Ethnic: 10%
Private school: n/a	Flunk rate: 10.4%
Mature students: 40%	Overseas students: 31%
Disabled students: n/a	

ATMOSPHERE:
The separateness of the sites tends to create a slightly fragmented community, but each site is a fun place to be, full of keen, helpful and quite sporty people. Relations with the nice, Laura Ashley-clad folk of 'Chelters' are OK, because (1) the students bring money with 'em and (2) the students know not to push it.

THE SITES:
Pittville: (1,500 – art, design) This *unfortunately* named site, 2.4 miles from the main Park Campus, has dedicated studio space, a media centre and 274 self-catered rooms.
Francis Close Hall/Hardwick: (1,000 – environment, sport, religion, education, catering, geography, geology) 1.8 miles from Park Campus, FCH is picturesque and classically *academic-looking. The diversity of the students here make this a very interesting campus indeedy.*

Cheltenham & Gloucester

TOWN:
- Population: 107,300 • London: 95miles • Bristol: 40miles
- Birmingham: 43miles

Cheltenham is famous for 3 things: (1) its racecourse; (2) its spa; and, *ironically, since it's supposed to be clouded in secrecy* (3) GCHQ. The spa more than the spies were responsible for its growth in the early part of the 19th century into what is now a very safe, *Middle England town with a satisfactory number of amenities (but certainly not a glut).* Among the *serene* sights are the art gallery in the centre of town, the numerous parks and the Pittville Pump Rooms *where the water is brown and tastes disgusting* – although push is not sure whether we were drinking from the right outflow.

TRAVEL:
Trains: Cheltenham Spa station is 2 miles from Park Campus, offering direct links to London (£23.10), Birmingham (£9.40), Manchester (£20.70) and elsewhere.
Coaches: National Express, Marchants and Swanbrook operate coach services from Cheltenham; a return trip to London will cost £16.50.
Car: Main road links to the A40, M5 and M40.
Local: The College runs its own free bus service between all the sites. It's quite reliable and runs until 11.30pm. Local buses take up the slack and run till midnight, but cost 65p from Park Campus to the town centre.
Bicycles: *Most students like to get the real feel of a wheel between their thighs.* The College offers a subsidy to students who want to buy bikes.

CAREER PROSPECTS:
- Careers Service • No of staff: 6 part-time
- Unemployed after 6mths: 6%

FAMOUS ALUMNI:
Chris Broad (cricketer); David Bryant (bowls champion); Jonathan Callard (rugby international); Beverley Knight (pop star); Roger Lovegrove (wildlife broadcaster); PH Newby (writer); Sarah Potter (cricketer).

FURTHER INFO:
Prospectuses for undergrads and postgrads, video for schools, website (www.chelt.ac.uk).

ACADEMIC

staff/student ratio: **1:30**
Range of points required for entrance: **240-140**
Percentage accepted through clearing: **13%**
Number of terms/semesters: **3**
Length of terms/semesters: **11wks**
Research: **2.9**

LIBRARIES:
- Books: 250,000 • Study places: 920 • 3 libraries (1 at each site)

COMPUTERS:
- Computer workstations: 300

ENTERTAINMENT

TOWN:
- Price of a pint of beer: £2.20 • Glass of wine: £1.80

Pubs: A fairly typical mix of pubs and wine bars, most of which at least tolerate students. *Pushplugs: Norwood; Restoration; Slug & Lettuce; Frog & Fiddle; Pepper's. Try the Montpellier Run – a string of good pubs near the College.*

Theatres: (2) An annual 6-night production by the college is put on at the Everyman, which hosts all kinds of productions *and is a bit more ambitious than the Playhouse.*

Cinemas: There's a 7-screen Odeon *but discerning cinéastes trek to the Guildhall in Gloucester.*

Clubs/discos: *Time is chart/dance oriented; Embassy is more indie.* Both do student nights.

Music venues: The Town Hall presents mainstream acts, while the Gloucester Guildhall has a more *left-field* programme. Cheltenham hosts three annual music festivals: Jazz, Folk and Classical, *if that's your thang.*

Eating out: There are the usual fast food chains and plenty of pubs *do better than average grub. Pushplugs: Café Uno; Il Bottelino; Norwood; Valentino's; Casa.*

COLLEGE:
- Price of a pint of beer: £1.40 • Glass of wine: £1.30

Bars: The Park SU Bar (capacity 840) *is the centre of most activities and is usually heaving*, although it closes between 2 and 5pm. There are also bars at FCH (180; *small and cosy*) and Pittville (220). *A union policy is to have free entry for all SU events (except balls).*

Cinema: Each site has a big video screen, *showing a mix of arty and mainstream fare as well as sporting action.*

Theatre: As well as the annual show in town, there is also the Sweet Charity Drama Group who make the odd trip to the Fringe.

Music venues: The Park Bar and the Refectory (500) are the main venues but the biggest names (eg Coolio, B*witched, Atomic Kitten) tend to be restricted to the Summer Ball.

Clubs: There are 4 club events a week, 2 in the Park Bar and 2 in Pittville and the SU gets a number of late licences each term *which adds to the fun stuff.*

Food: *The food is good but pricey in a service station kind of way. There is food at the bars too, plus the training restaurant at Francis Close, which is also open to the public.*

Other: The annual Freshers', Xmas and Rag Balls pack 'em in, but the Summer Ball is the biggie with a capacity of 7,000.

SOCIAL & POLITICAL

CHELTENHAM & GLOUCESTER COLLEGE OF HIGHER EDUCATION STUDENTS' UNION:
- 4 sabbaticals • Turnout at last ballot: 15% • NUS member

The bright and welcoming SU is on a mission to entertain and politics would be a hindrance. There are facilities on all sites. The SU headquarters is based in a plush new building.

SU FACILITIES:
Park Campus: Bar; shop; photocopying; games, video and vending machines; pool table; juke box; launderette; computers.
Pittville: Bar; photocopier; disco; juke box; vending machines; pool table.
Francis Close Hall: Bar; shop.

CLUBS (NON SPORTING):
Parapsychology; Pittville degree (art, design, fashion and drinking).

OTHER ORGANISATIONS:
The SU publishes a *pretty good* newspaper 'Space'. The Student Community Action group has a permanent staff co-ordinator and is involved in various schemes to help local children.

RELIGIOUS:
The College was originally an Anglican institution and has its own CofE chapel. Most shades of Christian are represented locally and there's a mosque in Gloucester. There's a Muslim prayer room provided too.

PAID WORK:
UCAS, the University applications processing body, has its headquarters locally and during the vacations it often takes on temporary clerical help. The racecourse sometimes uses casual labour, *but don't put your grant cheque on a sure-fire tip for the 2.30. The employment policies of GCHQ are a different matter.* The Student Employment Centre will help you find part-time work locally.

- Recent successes: rugby, running, athletics, waterpolo, hockey, kendo

Successes across the board. Facilities are pretty good, and are free, and sport is much higher on the agenda than in most colleges of HE. The new annual Varsity rugby match against Royal Agricultural College *helps raise cash for Oxfam.*

SPORTS FACILITIES:
3 football pitches; 2 rugby pitches; 3 hockey pitches; sports hall; swimming pool; multigym. The town provides facilities for most other sports.

SPORTING CLUBS:
Aerobics; Gaelic Football; Korfball; Lacrosse; Rugby League.

ATTRACTIONS:
Cheltenham Racecourse; Gloucester Cricket Ground; Cheltenham Town FC; Gloucester Rugby Club; Gloucestershire County Cricket Club.

IN COLLEGE:
- Self-catering: 14% • Cost: £49-59(41wks)

Availability: Accommodation provision is split across the Park and Pittville sites, with further digs very close to Francis Close Hall. Most of this accommodation is brand *new and v. comfy.* There are also 720 places in head tenancy schemes. Nobody has to share, though some

students live at a different site to where they study. Wardens and porters *keep out the bogeymen*.
Car parking: There's roadside parking only, but livers-in *aren't supposed to bring cars and no one really needs them*.

EXTERNALLY:
• Ave rent: £44
Availability: *Housing comes on the market on a very seasonal basis, which means students need to get in there quick for the best shot, although places tend to be of a decent standard. Leckhampton, St Paul's, Pittville Gates or Bath Road are the places to be. There are student pockets, but no ghetto.*
Housing help: The College Accommodation Office lends a hand with contracts and vacancy lists and they also provide a list of recommended properties (currently around 800) which have all been vetted by the college.

WELFARE

SERVICES:
• Pre-school Centre • Lesbian & Gay Society • Mature SA
• Overseas SA • Gender Awareness Officer • Minibus
The SU has a drop-in welfare and advice centre providing leaflets on useful topics, but the main welfare provisions are from Student Services where there are 1 full- and 2 part-time counsellors. There are also 3 part-time nurses and a pool of visiting doctors on site based at the new medical centre.
Disabled: College Disability Officer; overall, the college has good disabled access and 10% of college accommodation is specially adapted. There are induction loops.

FINANCE:
• Access fund: £382,766 • Successful applications : 1,143
Student Services provides small short-term emergency loans.

Chester College
see Other Institutions

University College Chichester
see Other Institutions

Cirencester
see Royal Agricultural College

City of London Poly
see London Guildhall University

```
Queen's College Cambridge hosts the world
tiddlywinks championships.
```

City University

City University, Northampton Square, London, EC1V 0HB.
Tel: (020) 7040 5060. Fax: (020) 7477 8560.
City University Students' Union, Northampton Square, London,
EC1V 0HB. Tel: (020) 7505 5600. Fax: (020) 7505 5601.
E-mail: cusu@city.ac.uk

GENERAL

Northampton Square, 2 miles north-east of Trafalgar Square, *just too far north of the square mile of the City of London, Britain's financial heartland, to be part of it, is nevertheless itself rather trendy.* This is the site of City University's main buildings with the rest dotted around the area, all within a mile of the Square, *which is the University's most attractive part.* Its redbrick buildings surround a small tree-lined grassy patch, space enough for students to sunbathe in summer. Some of the University's other buildings *are less good-looking*. The University's listed administration building, which also houses some teaching and research was hit by a bad fire in the summer of 2001 (however no disruption to teaching). *How quickly they'll make good the damage is anyone's guess.*

Sex ratio(M:F): 48%:52%	Founded: 1894
Full time u'grads: 4,741	Part time: 515
Postgrads: 1,785	Non–degree: n/a
Ave course: 3/4yrs	Ethnic: 39%
Private school: n/a	Flunk rate: 16.8%
Mature students: 43%	Overseas students: 26%
Disabled students: n/a	

ATMOSPHERE:
The work ethic is strong at City. Top priority is to get a degree (preferably a good one) and the schedule doesn't allow for much free time. Extra-curricular activities take second place and political posturing comes last and definitely least. The University is fragmented, with a high proportion of postgrads and competition from the strong draw of London's own entertainments. But the common cause does create a certain sympathy and a lot of friendliness around the halls of residence. A new £50m business school is due to open in September 2002.

THE CITY: SEE University of London

LOCAL AREA:
There are enough expensive wine bars and chintzy sandwich bars to blow a serious hole in anybody's pocket, let alone a student's. Clerkenwell has some marginally more affordable hang-outs including: wholemeal cafés, antique shops, the Chapel Market and *groovy* pubs. It is largely residential and, *if you keep your ambitions on a leash, possibly affordable (well not really).* The West End is just a bus ride or brisk walk away.

TRAVEL: SEE University of London
Trains: Liverpool Street and King's Cross mainline stations are both within 20 minutes' walk of the University.
Buses: 4; 19; 30; 38; 43; 55; 56; 73; 171; 196; 214; 243; 279; 341 and 505.

Night buses: N19; N21; N73; N92; N96.
Car: *Parkers beware:* clamps and tickets.
Underground: Angel (Northern Line), Farringdon or Barbican (both on the same lines: Hammersmith & City; Circle; Metropolitan; Thameslink).

CAREER PROSPECTS:
- Careers Service • No of staff: 3 full/3 part
- Unemployed after 6 mths: 3.9%

The University's vocational emphasis is rewarded by a *good* graduate employment rate.

SPECIAL FEATURES:
City's motto is 'To Serve Mankind' – *Push wonders how the women students feel about that.*
The University validates degrees at colleges as diverse as the Guildhall School of Music & Drama and the Laban Centre, London.

FAMOUS ALUMNI:
Michael Fish (weatherman); Dermot Murnaghan (newsreader); Jack Warner (Dixon of Dock Green - ask your gran).

FURTHER INFO:
Prospectuses, SU prospectus and websites (www.city.ac.uk and www.cusu.city.ac.uk).

ACADEMIC

City was one of the first universities to leap whole-heartedly into vocationally relevant courses. Its journalism department, for example, is world renowned.

Staff/student ratio: 1:18
Range of points required for entrance: 340-180
Percentage accepted through clearing: 18%
Number of terms/semesters: 3
Length of terms/semesters: 10wks
Research: 3.7

LIBRARIES:
- Books: 350,000 • Study places: 905

Two main libraries as well as various departmental libraries. *Facilities are very good following recent expansion.*

COMPUTERS:
- Computer workstations: 630

ENTERTAINMENT

IN LONDON: see University of London

THE CITY, CLERKENWELL AND ISLINGTON:
In Clerkenwell, the Crown Tavern on Clerkenwell Green is popular as is the Turnmills club on Clerkenwell Road and the Aquarium. For cultural carousing, the Sadlers's Wells Theatre is close by and, further South, the Barbican contains theatres, cinemas, restaurants, bars and *not enough loos,* all under one roof. *In Islington the Leopard, Central Bar on Old Street and the King's Head are all good for a pint or five.* The Hope & Anchor has indie bands while the Bull &

Gate has dance nights. The Fabric at Smithfields.

UNIVERSITY:
• Price of a pint of beer: £1.60 • Glass of wine: £2

Bars: The new SU building houses 2 bars, the *countryfied* Saddlers and the *clubby* Wonderbar.

Theatre & film: One major production a year plus a trip to the Fringe. 1 or 2 films a week.

Music venues/clubs/discos: The Wonderbar (cap 550) has been revamped and hosts live gigs (mainly tribute bands) and doubles as a dance venue with a weekly dose of DJs, 70s themes, swing, hiphop and more chart-oriented noise. DJ Spoony and Artful Dodger ventured here recently.

Comedy: *The slapstick scene has improved with* occasional shows courtesy of the Newcastle Brown Comedy Network.

Food: The University runs two refectories *(with a good vegetarian range)* throughout the day. Ponchos in the Wonderbar serves Mexican food, while the Saddlers Bar serves snacks and sandwiches – *try saying that after 7 pints and a tuna bap.*

Others: The Union tries to keep up a programme of at least 3 events per week and *generally churns out some worthwhile budget fun.*

SOCIAL & POLITICAL

CITY UNIVERSITY STUDENTS' UNION (CUSU):
• 4 sabbaticals • Turnout at last ballot: 14% • NUS member

The new SU building has done a lot to put entertainments and socialising centre stage and the Union's extra efforts to liven up the party have been fairly successful (not hard, since it was as fevered as a fossilised flatworm in the past). A new Ents manager has helped too, although the facilities still suffer by comparison with ULU, which City students aren't entitled to use *(but many do).*

SU FACILITIES:
2 bars; general shop; games area; minibus hire; committee room; snooker and pool tables; vending machines and video games; travel shops; second-hand book stall.

CLUBS (NON SPORTING):
Chinese; Film; Malaysian; Motorcycle; Punjabi; Role Play; Singaporean; Vedic.

OTHER ORGANISATIONS:
The glossy student mag, 'Massive', is out 6 times a year and is also available on the net (www.cusu.city.ac.uk/massive). There is a Rag and various charity events coincide with awareness campaigns.

RELIGIOUS:
• Chaplain

The University has some active religious clubs and a Muslim prayer room, but otherwise, students rely on London's religious amenity overload.

PAID WORK: see University of London

SPORTS

• Recent successes: sailing, netball, basketball

For a small civic university, City has access to some fairly good facilities but the overall level of interest is pretty mediocre.

SPORTS FACILITIES:
City shares facilities for rugby, hockey, football, tennis and cricket located all over north London. Close to Northampton Square, the University owns the Saddler's Sports Centre, 2 squash courts, gym, sports hall, martial arts room, multi-gym, sauna and solarium. There's a boathouse for the rowing club on the Thames at Chiswick and sailors and surfers can use facilities at the Queen Mary Sailing Club.

SPORTING CLUBS:
Extreme Sports (bungee, parachuting, stock car); Hiking; Rowing; Shorinji Kempo; Table Tennis.
ATTRACTIONS: see University of London

ACCOMMODATION

IN COLLEGE:
• Catered: 7% • Cost: £90 (39 wks) • Self-catering: 14%
• Cost: £77 (39-42 wks)
Availability: The University guarantees accommodation to 1st years subject to some *fairly* strict conditions (early application, non-Londoners only). In practice, about 40% live in leaving few places for 2nd years, finalists and postgrads. There are 2 catered halls and 3 blocks of self-catering flats (mainly for postgrads and not available for 1st years). *The centres of sociability and spirit in the University revolve around the halls, or, more precisely, around the halls' bars. Accommodation is very expensive but this reflects property costs locally.* Security guards, entry-phones and CCTV operate.
EXTERNALLY: see University of London
• Ave rent: £75
Housing help: The University Accommodation Office helps students find housing. *Camden, Finsbury Park and Manor House are popular and cheaper than the immediate locality, but you can also try Hackney and Stoke Newington.*

WELFARE

SERVICES:
• Lesbian & Gay Society • Mature SA • Overseas SA • Postgrad SA
• Minibus • Women's Officer • Self-defence classes
• Anti-racism Officer
The University runs a student counselling service which is the *principal problem post* for students, employing 7 part-time and 2 full-time advisers. CUSU also has 2 student advisers. The health service has 2 doctors and a nurse.
Disabled: All new buildings are wheelchair accessible *and things are improving in the older ones.* Some accommodation has been adapted. There is a Disability Officer.

FINANCE:
• Access fund: £260,000
There is a hardship fund and the SU can make short-term loans of £50.

Coleraine
see University of Ulster

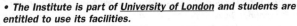
Courtauld Institute of Art, London

- **The Institute is part of <u>University of London</u> and students are entitled to use its facilities.**

The Courtauld Institute of Art, Somerset House, Strand, London, WC2R 0RN. Tel: (020) 7848 2645. Fax: (020) 7848 2410. E-mail: ugadmission@courtauld.ac.uk
Courtauld Students' Union, Somerset House, Strand, London, WC2R 0RN. Tel: (020) 7848 2717.

Courtauld Institute of Art is *appropriately* housed in one of Europe's *most elegant* 18th-century public buildings – Somerset House, located on a *huge* site between the north bank of the Thames and the Strand. This used to be the main offices of the Inland Revenue, *but they've since been kicked out (hurrah)* to open up the building to more public use – cafés, restaurants and art, including the Courtauld Collection. The Institute is the UK's only college specialising solely in teaching the history of art. Somerset House is strewn with *splendid* sculptures and architectural features and the Institute's *remarkable* collection of art, books and manuscripts is open to the public. To the east are Fleet Street and the City (London's financial centre), to the west, the West End and, about 500 metres away at the other end of the Strand, Trafalgar Square and the National Gallery. It's also close to Covent Garden and, over the Thames, the South Bank Complex (National Theatre, National Film Theatre, Royal Festival Hall etc). *It's extremely well served for entertainments and culture, but this is the heart of London and it's an expensive place to buy a canned drink, let alone bread and cheese.* The nearest mainline BR stations are Waterloo, Charing Cross and Blackfriars, there's Covent Garden (Piccadilly Line); Temple (Circle and District Lines) for the tube and loads of buses (nos 1, 4, 25, 68, X68, 76, 168, 171, 176, 188, 341, 501, 505 and 521, and night buses N1, N175 and N176). *Women outnumber men three to one and the intake from the private education sector is high which leaves a subtle hint of Swiss finishing schools – better than an odour of Swiss cheese.* The main influences on the atmosphere, however, are its small size, its intimacy, its proximity to King's (which makes up for the Institute's lack of facilities) and the shared interests of the students.

Sex ratio(M:F): 25%:75%	Founded: 1932
Full-time u'grads: 116	Part-time: 0
Postgrads: 174	Non-degree: 0
Ave course: 3yrs	Ethnic: n/a
Private school: 30%	Flunk rate: n/a
Mature students: 14%	Overseas students: 9.5%
Disabled students: 4.5%	

The libraries (140,000 volumes, 139 study places) are among the country's major sources for art history with over 1.6 million reproductions and 800,000 photographs, *however, specific undergraduate course books are in short supply;* only 12 computers but students have access to those at <u>King's College, London</u> next door. No bar, so Courtauld students pop into the <u>King's College</u> bar next door and it's only a bus ride/tube trip/energetic walk to ULU, whose facilities Courtauld students are entitled to use; <u>LSE</u> is also just round the corner; there's a bit of a party once a term, but that's about it. For food, there's a glass-roofed refectory (cap 100) with contract caterers or there's always King's. The SU (no sabbs, NUS member) is *in theory an entertainment-based organisation, but in practice does bugger all; representatives are rumoured to attend staff meetings but are never around to verify it;* lounge; *very popular* pool table; no Rag. No sports facilities of its own; students are entitled to use ULU and London University facilities, *but don't*; sporadic attempts at mixed-sex football crop up and someone played hockey for the University – once – we think. No accommodation of its own but students can apply for University of London's intercollegiate housing. Student welfare officer; access to University of London Central Health Service and counselling; no disabled students at present but there are lifts and *wheelchair access is good; used to have a bit of a reputation for accommodating a loud gay clique, but things are quieter of late – no LGB Society, but the atmosphere is more tolerant than many;* access fund £20,000, travel grants, course trips are subsidised.

FAMOUS ALUMNI:
Anita Brookner (writer); Andrew Graham-Dixon (art historian); Neil MacGregor (National Gallery); Vincent Price (actor); Nicholas Serota (Tate Gallery); Brian Sewell (*oh so posh and poncy* art critic). Anthony Blunt (spy) was the Director here for several years, before he was fingered.

FURTHER INFO:
Prospectuses for undergrads and postgrads and a website (www.courtauld.ac.uk).

Coventry University

- *Formerly Coventry Polytechnic*

Coventry University, Priory Street, Coventry, CV1 5FB. Tel: (024) 7688 7688. Fax: (024) 7688 8638. Email: education.cor@coventry.ac.uk
Coventry University Students' Union, Block E, Priory Street, Coventry, CV1 5FT. Tel: (024) 7657 1200. Fax: (024) 7655 9146. Email: suexec@coventry.ac.uk

GENERAL

Coventry has a much longer history than most cities in the Midlands and, *what with good connections all over the country, being sent to Coventry is far from the isolation it's supposed to be.* This is where Lady Godiva did her famous bareback horse ride, but trotting naked through the streets has fallen off somewhat as a local sport since the city was almost completely destroyed in a single night's bombing during the 2nd World War. *Despite the speed with which it was resurrected, there was some thought involved and it's interesting to look at if not exactly attractive - a huge futuristic machine with giant chimneys and intestinal roads woven among the buildings. The city's heart is a shopping centre maze (although wheelchair access is among the best in the country).* This is where the University campus is spread, across 35 acres, near other civic buildings like the sports centre, the Art Gallery & Museum and the very *impressive* Cathedral opposite the SU Building. The University buildings are made of red bricks and look modern, *but are not brash. An effort has been made to make them blend*. There are lots of sculptures, flowerbeds, paved squares and, *bizarrely*, gravestones.

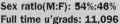

Sex ratio(M:F): **54%:46%**
Full time u'grads: **11,096**
Postgrads: **627**
Ave course: **3/4yrs**
Private school: **n/a**
Mature students: **37%**
Disabled students: **<1%**

Founded: **1843**
Part time: **3,218**
Non–degree: **838**
Ethnic: **28%**
Flunk rate: **24.4%**
Overseas students: **17%**

ATMOSPHERE:
The silly but fun, first-freedom-from-home attitude is now increasing due to the influx over recent years of art-based students looking to have a good time. Students are here to get a qualification, preferably job-related. Relations with the locals are reserved but better than they once were.

COVENTRY:
• Population: 322,573 • London: 88miles • Birmingham: 16miles
Rebuilt, Coventry's a new city with an old spirit, which doesn't let the modern design interfere with the ancient heritage. There are archaeological digs on view close to the campus and in the city centre. There's a mile-long pedestrianised shopping centre, *big enough to provide more shops than a student grant can withstand* (including several bookshops and a number of stores open after 10pm). The local heritage can be viewed in the city's museum and tourist attractions *(although Coventry is hardly what you might call a holiday resort),* notably the Herbert Art Gallery, the Toy Museum, the Museum of British Road Transport, the Cathedral (restored and built anew by Basil Spence), the olde world shops, Lunt Roman Fort and statue of Lady Godiva. *It's hoped that a project currently underway will transform Coventry into a truly cosmopolitan 24-hour city, which, if successful, will be an astounding feat of triumph over adversity.* The plans include 'The Millenium Initiative' with a complete transformation of Fairfax Street, and a whole new lower precinct.

TRAVEL:
Trains: The Grade II listed Coventry Station is about 1 mile from the Coventry University campus and on the main London (£11.80) to Birmingham (£2.30) line.
Coaches: National Express, Bharat and Harry Shaw services all over the place, including London (£12), Birmingham (£4), Manchester (£11) and more.
Car: *The usual Midlands ease of accessibility,* via the M6, M69 and M45/A45, and just a few miles from the M1, M40, M42 and A5. *The one-way streets aren't good for the blood pressure.*
Air: *Coventry Airport isn't terribly helpful,* but Birmingham International is a big one, 9½ miles away.
Local: There are three BR train stops within the confines of Coventry, but the reliable local bus services are *more useful for getting to places students haven't got the welly to walk to.*
Taxis: Coventry's small enough to mean £2 will get students a *worthwhile whack* across town by taxi.

Bicycles: *The roads are busy, the thefts frequent. But it's flat.*
Others: Summer brings 'Lady Godiva Topless Tours'; for £3.50, visitors can tour Coventry in an open-topped bus (but they're allowed to keep their vests on).

CAREER PROSPECTS:
- Careers Service • No of staff: 3 full/2 part
- Unemployed after 6 mths: 16%

The Careers Office is off campus (about 5 minutes walk) and many students seem unaware of its existence.

FAMOUS ALUMNI:
John Kettley (is a weatherman, a weatherman, a weatherman); Steve Mattin (designed Mercedes A & S Series); Andrea McLean (GMTV Presenter); Michael Rodber (designed the distinctly unprofitable Eurostar); Alison Snowden (Oscar-winning animator); Chris Svenson and Piere Webster (designed Ford Ka); David Yelland (Talk Radio Owner).

FURTHER INFO:
Prospectuses, individual course leaflets, open days, alternative prospectus, a video and a website (www.coventry.ac.uk and www.coventry.ac.uk/su).

ACADEMIC

Staff/student ratio: 1:21
Range of points required for entrance: 300-160
Percentage accepted through clearing: n/a
Number of terms/semesters: 3
Length of terms/semesters: 12wks
Research: 2.3

LIBRARIES:
- Books: 400,000 • Study places: 1,200

The new library and resource centre has improved the look but the contents could be improved.

COMPUTERS:
- Computer workstations: 1,579

ENTERTAINMENT

COVENTRY:
- Price of a pint of beer: £1.80 • Glass of wine: £1.90

Cinemas: The New Skydome complex houses 10 screens with another two 10-screen multiplexes on the edge of town.
Theatres: The Belgrade Theatre offers *competent* dramatic fare.
Pubs: Some pubs are no-go areas; the local name for them is 'playschool pubs', *because you have to guess which window you're going to be chucked through. Wise students have their own supping sanctuaries. Pushplugs: Oak Inn; The Campbell; The Lanes; Gringos; Old Orleans; the Golden Cross.*
Clubs/discos: The drum 'n' bass scene is still going strong. *Pushplugs: Colosseum (mainstream); Diva; Icon; Scholars (towny); Dog and Trumpet.*

Music venues: Not exactly throbbing. *Pushplugs: West Indian Centre (world music); Dog & Trumpet; Collosseum; Hand and Heart.*
Eating out: *Cheap and cheerful or overpriced offal, Coventry has something to offer any gourmet. Pushplugs: Brown's (parent-friendly); Pizza Express; TGI Friday's; Varsity; Yate's; The Litten Tree (upmarket – take your parents).*

UNIVERSITY:
• Price of a pint of beer: £1.45 • Glass of wine: £1.30
Bars: The brand spanking new Cox Street venue houses Casbar the main union bar, with a chillout lounge surprisingly called The Chiller and unusually an alcohol-free bar, Universe. There's also a bar in the SU building at Priory Street, the Elephant and Castle (former working men's club).
Theatre: Performing Arts puts on lots of productions *but extra-curricular drama is pretty well non-existent.*
Music venue: Britpop is alive and well in Coventry with Ocean Colour Scene and Paul Weller.
Clubs/discos: Club nights every week: Phase (the big student night) and Trollied (cheese). Recent names to visit include: Spiller, Black Legend.
Food: Basement Jakks serves the *standard* student fayre with hot and cold pub food available in Casbar and Universe; Also around college are the Best Cellar, Fads, the Pavilion Bar and the William Morris Bistro, *named with an alarming absence of irony.*
Others: 1 ball a year, Unbelieverball.

SOCIAL & POLITICAL

COVENTRY UNIVERSITY STUDENTS' UNION (CUSU):
• 5 sabbaticals • Turnout at last ballot: 10% • NUS member
CUSU has been making a real effort to stir the student body from its cryogenically-frozen attitude to politics. Now they're just apathetic and uninformed, which is a vast improvement.

SU FACILITIES:
The SU Building provides: general shop; bars; activities and development centre (nicknamed 'the Junction' with a music rehearsal room, print and copy shop, meeting rooms, IT, printing and fax facilities); travel agency; 4 minibuses for hire; photo booth; video games; hairdresser; vending machines; pool tables; juke boxes and 2 meeting rooms. Elephant and Castle Venue.

CLUBS (NON SPORTING):
Ba'hai; Choir; Clubbing; Friends of Palestine; Pacific Soul; Role-play; Sikh.

OTHER ORGANISATIONS:
The student magazine is called 'Source' and pops off the presses every month and there's Source student radio. The Community Action group does *much needed* good for students' local image by raising funds and helping volunteer projects.

RELIGIOUS:
• 3 chaplains (CofE, RC, Free Church)
There's a Muslim prayer room. Locally, Coventry has many a prayer palace and creed cabin for god-squadders of every hue, *most notably,* the Anglican Cathedral.

PAID WORK:
CUBE (Coventry University Bureau of Employment) is run by students to help them find part-time and vacation work, from bar work to market research.

SPORTS

- Recent successes: volleyball, swimming, women's and men's rugby

Coventry students get more interested in sport than in politics, but that's not saying much. Facilities are okay though, and the rugby and footie teams recently toured in the States.

SPORTS FACILITIES:
Westwood Heath: 37 acres of playing fields (3 football pitches, 3 rugby pitches, cricket pitch, etc); floodlit hockey pitch; cricket nets; 9-hole golf course; 4 tennis courts. Alma St: gym; weights; martial arts dojo; table tennis; sunbed. Coventry makes up for any shortfalls by providing student discount rates for use of the local sports centre including the Olympic standard swimming pool and squash courts.

SPORTING CLUBS:
American Football; Handball; Jiu Jitsu.

ATTRACTIONS:
Coventry City FC are the local footie boys. There's also horse racing at Warwick and 2 council-owned golf courses. Millennium developments will provide a new arena and leisure complex.

ACCOMMODATION

IN COLLEGE:
- Catered: 6% • Cost: £71 (40-52 wks) • Self-catering: 10%
- Cost: £45-57 (40-52 wks)

Availability: 4 halls of residence and 1,000 places in head tenancy schemes. Priority is given to 1st years but 5% are unlucky. Lots of local and mature students are already sorted. 2% have to share. 60% of accommodation is single sex. Most hall places are in Priory Hall on campus, with Singer Hall being the *nicest* (600), although Caradoc Hall (64 single bedsits and 62 twin flats) is 3 miles away and there are 350 places in University-owned houses in town. The new Quadrant hall has 100 places. There are security patrols overnight.
Car parking: Like Monopoly - occasional free parking.

EXTERNALLY:
- Ave rent: £35-40

Availability: *With a bit of work, students can find somewhere suitable and when they do, the cost is sweet. The best areas are Earlsdon, Stoke, Cheylesmore, Radford and Chapelfields. Hillfields is Coventry's Bronx. The cost and availability of parking spaces renders cars pointless.*
Housing help: The Accommodation Office checks out every place it recommends on its list of houses and also offers a handbook, bulletin board, full-time staff and contract advice.

```
One of the sites of Oxford Brooks was once
lived in by Robert Maxwell.
```

WELFARE

SERVICES:
• Creche • Nightline • Lesbian & Gay Society • Mature SA
• Overseas SA • Minibus • Women's Officer • Self-defence classes
The SU runs an excellent Advice Centre which offers to help students with anything. The University also employs 2 full- and 5 part-time counsellors. The Medical Centre on the campus has 6 doctors and 1 nurse.

Women: The SU produces a women's rights booklet. Women get priority on the free minibus, though men are allowed to use it too, *but it can be irregular and could run later sometimes.*

Disabled: Disabled Students' Forum. The Disabilities Office has 4 staff and facilities for students with various forms of disability, especially those with sight impairments. *Wheelchair access has improved considerably over the last few years.*

Drugs: *The city was getting a bit of a reputation for drug gangs and associated nastiness but things seem to be changing.* The University remains relatively untouched.

FINANCE:
• Access fund: £740,427 • Successful applications: 634
As well as the access fund there's a small welfare fund for the desperate, short term loans of up to £50 and arts and sports bursaries worth £500 each.

Cranfield University

(1) Royal Military College of Science, Shrivenham, Swindon, Wiltshire, SN6 8LA. Tel: (01793) 785400. Fax: (01793) 783966.
Association of Students, Royal Military College of Science, Shrivenham, Swindon, Wiltshire, SN6 8LA. Tel: (01793) 785702. Fax: (01793) 783966.
(2) Silsoe College, Silsoe, Bedfordshire, MK45 4DT.
Tel: (01525) 863319. Fax: (01525) 863316.
Student Union Society, Silsoe College, Silsoe, Bedfordshire, MK45 4DT. Tel: (01525) 863075. Fax: (01525) 863001.
Email for both sites: recruitment@cranfield.ac.uk

GENERAL

Push has visited several multi-site universities but few as odd as Cranfield. Not only are the two sites separated by more than 100 miles, but they're as unalike as two peas in a pod aren't. They have their own social peculiarities which may put off some potential applicants, but the academic and vocational reputation compensates for many. *Silsoe is the gentle, Yin bit,* sometimes known as the School of Agriculture, Food and the Environment (SAFE). It's a rural backwater between Luton and Bedford, *without much in the way of high calibre entertainments. The Yang side,* RMCS (Royal Military

College of Science), as the name suggests, revolves around the scientific requirements of the armed forces *and is more akin to a military establishment than a university* (although civilians are admitted). It's about 8 miles from Swindon, *again not exactly at the social heart of things.*

Sex ratio(M:F): 75%:25%
Full time u'grads: 744
Postgrads: 562
Ave course: 3/4yrs
Private school: 10%
Mature students: 20%
Disabled students: 4%

Founded: 1948
Part time: 0
Non–degree: 2,185
Ethnic: 12%
Flunk rate: 14.1%
Overseas students: 20%

ATMOSPHERE:
Silsoe is a quiet, contemplative place, where students tend to be very committed to their courses and social activity rarely extends beyond a few pints on a Saturday night. It's a tight-knit, supportive atmosphere and if things start to get claustrophobic, a car is indispensable. Shrivenham is equally remote and tight-knit, but considerably less quiet. Although not all the students have specifically military connections, the dominant ethos is that of the forces personnel and potential students who aren't into rules, regulations and dress codes should think long and hard before applying. Students at each site appear to go about their business in blissful ignorance of their nominal peers at the other and they probably wouldn't have that much in common if they did meet up.

TOWNS:
Silsoe Village itself has little going beyond a couple of pubs. For the nearest thing to fun see Luton University and, for Bedford, De Montfort University. Swindon, the nearest centre of population to Shrivenham, is another commuter commune for London and the historical home of the Great Western railway. It has all the usual accoutrements – pubs, clubs, supermarkets and so on – *but it's not a 'student town' in the conventional sense. Not that RMCS people are conventional students.*

TRAVEL:
At both sites non-drivers are at a distinct disadvantage. Silsoe's nearest train station is Flitwick, 3 miles away, but it's way off any beaten track, so Luton's *the best bet. The A6 passes through the village. Local buses supposedly run every hour or so (£2.70 rtn to Luton), but don't count on it. Shrivenham is even more remote, but at least Swindon has rail and coach connections to most major cities. London is £13.85 by train, £12.75 by coach. The A420 runs near the college and local buses go from the main gate every hour.*

CAREER PROSPECTS (SILSOE):
- Careers Service • No of staff: 1 full/2 part
- Unemployed after 6mths: 4%

CAREER PROSPECTS (RMCS):
- Careers Service • No of staff: 1 part • Unemployed after 6mths: 0%

Although the armed forces have been cutting back in recent years, Shrivenham graduates don't appear to have been touched.

FAMOUS ALUMNI:
Prince Andrew.

FURTHER INFO:
Prospectuses from both sites. Silsoe has an Alternative Prospectus. Websites (www.silsoe.cranfield.ac.uk and www.rmcs.cranfield.ac.uk).

staff/student ratio: 1:9
Range of points required for entrance: 280-120
Percentage accepted through clearing: 1.5%
Number of terms/semesters: 2
Length of terms/semesters: 15wks
Research: 4.8

LIBRARIES (SILSOE):
• Books: 65,000 • Study places: 79

LIBRARIES (RMCS):
• Books: 125,000 • Study places: 239

The Ministry of Defence provides free stationery and books for students at Shrivenham.

COMPUTERS (SILSOE):
• Computer workstations: 200

COMPUTERS (RMCS):
• Computer workstations: 272

SILSOE VILLAGE:
• Price of a pint of beer: £1.90 • Glass of wine: £1.90

Silsoe is not the sort of place that attracts coachloads of up-for-it clubbers. There are 2 good pubs: the Nelson and the Star & Garter. That's it. Try Luton or Bedford for burning off excess energy.

SHRIVENHAM VILLAGE:
• Price of a pint of beer: £1.80 • Glass of wine: £1.20

Shrivenham's much the same, if a bit bigger. The Royal Oak and the Eagle sometimes host live music. *The Indian Brasserie is expensive but worth a splurge once in a while. Go to Swindon for flicks and clubs (Mission, Route 66).*

COLLEGE: SILSOE:
• Price of a pint of beer: £1.60 • Glass of wine: £1.40

Bar: (cap 350). Open lunchtimes and evenings only.
Clubs/discos/music venues: The common room and bar host free discos every other Friday and occasional local bands.
Food: A food card (£200/term) entitles students to eat in the one cafeteria. *It's okay but limited, especially for vegetarians, and there isn't much alternative, barring a sandwich bar.*
Others: 4 balls a year, plus International Week.

COLLEGE: RMCS:
• Price of a pint of beer: £1.20 • Glass of wine: £1.10

Bars: (3) *The main social magnet for the student body, especially the army types. You have to dress smart in the mess bars or you'll be court-martialled, soldier.*

Theatre: 4 productions a year, plus a panto and 2 or 3 shows from the choral society.
Clubs/discos/music venues: 1 foot-moving fiesta a week, plus some obscure bands once a month.
Food: The Mess (note military terminology) comes up with four 5-course meals a day. Dress codes are enforced at all times, even for non-military students. There is also a café.
Others: 3 balls a year.

SOCIAL & POLITICAL

STUDENTS' UNION:
• <u>Turnout at last ballot: 68%</u> • <u>NUS member</u>
Politics is an irrelevance at both sites, although the private opinions of RMCS students, unsurprisingly, tend rightwards. The Union's officers are non-sabbatical, *so they're juggling the intensive workload too. There's an occasional undercurrent of tension between the civvies and the millies.*

SU FACILITIES:
Silsoe: Cafeteria; shops; TV lounge; student society house; snooker & pool tables; launderette; minibus hire.
RMCS: TV lounge; photocopier; launderette; function rooms.

CLUBS (NON SPORTING):
Silsoe: International; Motor; Music.
RMCS: Arts; Bridge; Choral; Flower; Good Neighbours; Military; Record Collectors; Scottish Country Dancing; Shrivenham; Young Engineers (not Village People appreciators).

OTHER ORGANISATIONS:
Silsoe has the 'Nameless Newsletter' (*so non-descript that the name fits*), a Rag week and a charity called SAFAD (Student Aid For Appropriate Development) which raises funds for projects abroad. RMCS has a Rag and a number of periodicals, including 'Student Matters'. *Neither site has picked up any creative name awards recently.*

RELIGIOUS:
Silsoe: 1 CofE chaplain and a Muslim prayer room.
RMCS: 2 chaplains (1 CofE, 1 RC) and a multi-denomination prayer room.

SPORTS

• <u>Recent successes: rugby</u>
Students pay £1/month towards the sports fund. *Sporting success is hampered by low numbers, but facilities and attitude are good, especially at RMCS. The fact that there's not much else to do may help.*

> In 1994 students at Portsmouth were housed temporarily in a naval barracks and subjected to naval discipline.

SPORTS FACILITIES:
Silsoe: Sports Hall with climbing wall; rowing machine; courts for squash, badminton, tennis; rugby, football and hockey pitches; gym.
RMCS: Astroturf pitch; gym with jogging, rowing and step machines, swimming pool.

SPORTING CLUBS:
Silsoe: Gun; Shooting.
RMCS: Beagling; Shooting.

ACCOMMODATION

IN COLLEGE (SILSOE):
- Catered: 80% • Cost: £60(30 wks) • Self-catering: 20%
- Cost: £40-67(40-50 wks)

All undergrads can be housed, except for those on work placements. CCTV, guards and entry-phones.

IN COLLEGE (RMCS):
- Catered: 14% • Cost: £81 (32wks) • Self-catering: 13%
- Cost: £35-55 (52wks)

Again, all who want to live in can do so, mostly in the Mess or its Annexe. Night-porters and soldiers protect.

EXTERNALLY:
- Ave rent: £50

Silsoe & RMCS: *There's plenty of attractive housing for those who choose to strike out on their own, although at this point the status of a car moves from handy to indispensable. The housing around RMCS is a bit more expensive than at Silsoe.*

WELFARE

SERVICES:
- Nightline • Overseas SA • Women's Officer • Overseas SA

FINANCE:
Silsoe:
- Access fund: £110,000 • Successful applications: 80

RMCS:
- Access fund: £4,550 • Successful applications: 20

Many RMCS students are sponsored by the forces.

```
The Northumberland building at the University
of Northumbria was going to be powered by the
biggest solar panels in Europe until a passing
student pointed out they were facing the wrong
way.
```

Dartington College of Arts see Other Institutions

De Montfort University

University of Derby

Distributive Trades see The London Institute

DIT see University of Abertay Dundee

Dorset Institute see Bournemouth University

University of Dundee

Dundee Institute of Technology see University of Abertay Dundee

University of Durham

Darlington College of Arts
see Other Institutions

De Montfort University

- *Formerly Leicester Polytechnic*

Telephone hotline to all campuses: (0645) 454647.
E-mail: enquiry@dmu.ac.uk
(1) De Montfort University Leicester, The Gateway, Leicester, LE1 9BH. Tel: (0116) 255 1551. Fax: (0116) 255 0307.
De Montfort University Students' Union, 4 Newarke Close, Leicester, LE1 9BH. Tel: (0116) 255 5576. Fax: (0116) 257 6309.
(2) De Montfort University Bedford, 37 Landsdowne Road, Bedford, MK40 2BZ. Tel: (01234) 211688. Fax: (01234) 347357.
(3) De Montfort University Lincoln, School of Agriculture and Horticulture, Caythorpe Court, Caythorpe, Grantham, Lincolnshire, NG32 3EP. Tel: (01400) 272521. Fax: (01400) 272722.
(4) De Montfort University Lincoln, School of Applied Art and Design, Lindum Road, Lincoln, LN2 1NP. Tel: (01522) 512912. Fax: (01522) 895147.

GENERAL

When Leicester Polytechnic stopped being Leicester Polytechnic in the early 90s, the powers that be obviously had bigger ideas than their colleagues at the other 'new universities' and started putting feelers out way beyond to Bedford, Lincoln and Milton Keynes. So DMU currently has 4 centres in all, 3 of which in turn have more than one site. *However, the Milton Keynes site will be closing in 2003 – so much for those feelers and has stopped recuiting undergraduates for this site. Students don't need to travel between the various towns for their courses and the sites are pretty much separated institutions. The advantage to DMU's 'distributed' status is that it can offer one of the widest ranges of courses in the UK. The drawback is that there's no sense of a central university identity except in name.*

Sex ratio(M:F): 47%:53%
Full time u'grads: 13,775
Postgrads: 1,325
Ave course: 3yrs
Private school: n/a
Mature students: 25%
Disabled students: 3%

Founded: 1969
Part time: 1,750
Non-degree: 2,375
Ethnic: 29%
Flunk rate: n/a
Overseas students: 7%

ATMOSPHERE:
Students tend to be committed to having a good time, getting a good degree then going on to a good job. The University is just too spread out to make generalisations, however, so see 'The Sites' below.

THE SITES:
Leicester: (16,950 students – most courses) The large City Campus, *in the groovy bit of town, is pretty ugly in a 60s brutalist way,* although it does include the medieval Trinity building. There are also sites at Scraptoft, 6 miles away, in a *rather nice* wooded setting *but with fairly basic facilities,* and the Charles Frears Campus (for nursing) *a brisk walk away.* There are regular bus services between the Leicester sites.
Bedford: (2,625 – humanities, education, sports, leisure, performing arts) 65 miles from Leicester, there are two campuses, 2 miles apart, Lansdowne (sporty) and Polhill (less so).
Lincoln: (1,175 – agriculture, horticulture, art and design, FE courses). Approximately 60 miles from Leicester. The artists are based in the city of Lincoln itself, with the various diggers and planters in Caythorpe, Riseholme and Holbeach in the Lincolnshire countryside. It's planned that students at this site will become part of the University of Lincolnshire and Humberside.

THE CITY: see University of Leicester

TRAVEL: see University of Leicester

CAREER PROSPECTS:
• Careers Service   • No of staff: 4 full/4 part-time
• Unemployed after 6mths: 4%
The Careers Service publishes the fortnightly 'Grapevine', listing job opportunities, which is distributed to all sites. They also arrange workshops and talks from employers.

SPECIAL FEATURES:
De Montfort takes its name from Simon De Montfort, the 13th-century Earl of Leicester. The Earl, banned Jews from Leicester, tried to overthrow the King, led the baronial revolt, kidnapped Henry III and his son, all before he finally got his head chopped off and put on a spike. His father, also called Simon, fought in the Fourth Crusade slashing his way through Jews and Muslims. His son, er, also called Simon, may or may not have fornicated his way through Kent. None of them, however, had any firm policies on lifelong education, the rights of all to get academic and professional qualifications, or indeed the merits of charity shop clothing.

FAMOUS ALUMNI:
Charles Dance (actor); Engelbert Humperdinck (*cheesy* 60s singer); Prolapse (indie band); Janet Reger (nice knicks); Kendra Slawinski (netball player); Liz Tilberis (Editor, 'Vogue'); Simon Wells (Spielberg director).

FURTHER INFO:
Prospectuses for undergrads, postgrads and part-timers. Website including interactive prospectus (www.dmu.ac.uk).

ACADEMIC

Includes Golf Studies.

staff/student ratio: 1:17
Range of points required for entrance: 320-120
Percentage accepted through clearing: 27%
Number of terms/semesters: 3
Length of terms/semesters: 10 wks
Research: 3.1

LIBRARIES:
- Books: 660,000 • Study places: 2,200
1 library on each site. New £6Mn library at Bedford.

COMPUTERS:
- Computer workstations: 550

ENTERTAINMENT

THE CITY: see University of Leicester
De Montfort's smaller outposts tend to be based in towns less cosmopolitan and student-oriented than Leicester.
Bedford: Student faves include the Bankers Draft, The Rose, Enigma, Foresters, Chicago's clubs and Gulshan's Tandoori. Also Aspects Complex near Polhill with a 6-screen cinema and ten-pin bowling; an annual regatta and *notorious* beer festival.
Lincoln: Lincoln is never going to challenge Leeds or Manchester as a student Mecca, but University of Lincolnshire and Humberside's site has increased the number of fun-seekers, so the level of entertainment should progress in coming years. Those based at the rural outposts have to hike to the city or put up with May-pole dancing and satanic worship.

UNIVERSITY:
- Price of a pint of beer: £1.30 • Glass of wine: £1.50
Bars: At Leicester the main lunchtime boozer is the Lava Lounge but the *space-age, chrome-effect* Arena (rather better and voted fourth best venue by 'The Guardian') takes over for events. There are bars at the other main centres.
Theatres: The DTC put on performances in the Y Theatre and often take shows to Edinburgh. At Bedford the Bowen West Centre on the Lansdowne site is run by DMU. The University drama course is based at Scraptoft.
Clubs/discos: The Arena has recently been expanded to a capacity of 1,200 with an *ear-scraping* sound system. Regulars range from the Big Cheese (Saturdays, 70s, 80s and 90s cheese) to Kinky Afro

(70s, *erm*, cheese). There are 2 club nights a week at Polhill (Bedford) and discos at other sites.
Music venues: The Arena can pull in big names of the calibre of Atomic Kitten, Coldplay and the Cream tour. John Peel has called it the best student venue for live bands in the country *and we wouldn't want to contradict His Holiness.*
Food: At Leicester the Lava Lounge and the Servery fulfil most hot and cold requirements, but there are also facilities at Shack in the Arena. MK has a *pretty expensive* refectory, run by outside caterers. Bedford has a canteen on each site – *the Polhill bacon rolls come recommended.* The Caythorpe, Risehome and Lincoln sites all have canteens.
Other: 2 balls a year.

SOCIAL & POLITICAL

DE MONTFORT UNIVERSITY STUDENTS' UNION:
• 10 sabbaticals • Turnout at last ballot: 10% • NUS member
The Global Union (*which sounds like something created to fight the Dark Side*) represents students on all sites, but is based in Leicester, but there are also site specific officers responsible for the individual sites.

SU FACILITIES:
City Centre Union Building: 2 bars; 1 café; coffee bar; restaurant; 2 minibuses; travel agent; printing services and photocopier; general shop (including newsagent); games, vending and video machines; photobooth; pool tables; juke box; meeting room.
Scraptoft: 2 bars; 1 coffee bar; photocopying; game machines; pool table; juke box; TV lounge; launderette; parking.
Bedford: Bar; 2 shops; 2 games rooms; video machines; pool table; juke box; 2 minibuses.
Lincoln: 2 bars.

CLUBS (NON SPORTING):
Hellenic; Hindu; Malay; Melting Pot; Pagan; Salsa; Sikh; Theatre.

OTHER ORGANISATIONS:
Fusion magazine (monthly). Demon FM broadcasts 2 months a year and won Radio 1's best on-air marketing award, *for what that's worth.* No Rag at the moment due to *shamefully poor* sums raised in the past.

RELIGIOUS:
• Chaplains at all sites (2 CofE, RC, Jewish, Methodist)
There's a Centre for Religion for Catholics, Anglicans and Muslims next to the Union. **Religion in Leicester:** see Leicester University.

PAID WORK: see University of Leicester.
The Workbank operates from Leicester but caters for all sites.

SPORTS

• Recent successes: football, netball, ladies' rugby
Again, distance precludes University-wide enthusiasm. Sport is popular at Leicester, but Bedford is the prime pillar of sporting success (women's teams are particularly strong) along with Caythorpe (for posh country pursuits, especially).

SPORTS FACILITIES:
Leicester: There are sports facilities at both Leicester sites, but at Scraptoft, it *only* amounts to 7 acres of playing fields and a gym. At the John Sandford Sports Centre, a few minutes walk from the City site, there are squash and badminton courts, a sports hall, a multigym and sauna and a newly refurbished fitness suite. The River Soar which runs by the campus is *useful* for watersports.
Bedford: *Huge* sports hall, swimming pool, 3 gyms, fitness suite, dance studio, astroturf, cricket, football & rugby pitches.
Lincoln: Riseholme has a fitness suite, swimming pool, sports hall, pitches and a golf course, *handy for those doing the course in Golf Studies*. Caythorpe has a pool. Students also have access to pitches and sports halls in the locality.

SPORTING CLUBS:
Leicester: Aikido; American Football; Knockdown Budo; Moutaineering; Parachuting; Rowing; Snooker & Pool; Snowboarding.
Bedford: Lacrosse; Martial Arts; Rowing; Rugby League.
Lincoln: Polo (at Caythorpe).

ATTRACTIONS: see University of Leicester

ACCOMMODATION

LEICESTER:
- Catered: 7% • Cost: £59 (30wks)
- Self-catering: 8% • Cost: £41-51 (38wks)

Only about ¾ of 1st years are accommodated in halls at the moment. 3% have to share.

BEDFORD:
- Catered: 21% • Cost: £53 (35-39wks)
- Self-catering: 1% • Cost: £43 (35-39wks)

Most places at Bedford are catered and usually only people with special dietary requirements will get into a self-catered hall. *Not liking the canteen food probably doesn't qualify.* Limited head tenancy schemes. 370 are housed in total.

LINCOLN:
- Catered: 23% • Cost: £65-79 (31-32wks)

Halls are at Riseholme and Caythorpe and there are a number of head tenancy schemes. *Caythorpe also houses under-18s so you'd better set a good example.*

The figures above show percentages of full-time undergrads at each site who are in college accommodation. Overall, 19% of De Montfort full-time undergrads are housed. Many are local anyway, especially in Leicester, and so are alright for digs. *Security provision tends towards the feeble across the board.*

EXTERNALLY: see University of Leicester
Housing help: The University Accommodation Office at all sites has a bulletin board and newsletter, the SU helps and advises.

If you have any comments about push or fancy being involved in the next edition, please write to Push, The Stationery Office, 15 Nine Elms Lane, London, SW8 5DR

WELFARE

SERVICES:
- Creche • Nightline • Lesbian & Gay Society • Mature SA
- Overseas SA • Minibus • Women's Officer • Self-defence classes

The Union and University provide welfare services on all sites. They are organised by the Union's Student Support Unit and Welfare Officer and the University's Counselling & Welfare Service (with 4 full-time and 3 part-time counsellors), Law Clinic, Student Health Centre (with 2 doctors and nurses) and the sick bay run in conjunction with Leicester University (costing students £7 a year). Free pregnancy tests are provided. The creche is at Bedford only.

Disabled: *Poor access at Leicester* - there are chair lifts and ramps, but ramps are designed for goods rather than people. It has a Disabilities Committee, *which is nice. Bedford is okay.*

FINANCE:
- Access fund: £1,500,000 • Successful applications: 1,563

Bursaries are available in science and engineering subjects. Debts are higher overall at Leicester, *maybe because there are more spending temptations in town.*

University of Derby

- *Formerly Derbyshire College of Higher Education*

University of Derby, Kedleston Road, Derby, DE22 1GB. Tel: (01332) 590500. Fax: (01332) 294861.
University of Derby Students' Union, University of Derby, Kedleston Road, Derby, DE22 1GB. Tel: (01332) 591507.
Fax: (01332) 348846. E-mail: udsu@derby.ac.uk

GENERAL

At the southern tip of the *beautiful* Derbyshire Peak District is the *less beautiful* city of Derby, in the north of the Midlands. The University is based at seven sites around the city, the main one being the Kedleston Road campus just outside town to the north-west amidst rather pleasant open countryside. Having taken the leap from a College of Higher Education to University in 1992, *it is still undergoing tremendous changes.* Over the past few years in particular, a complete face-changing programme has been underway – and it's still not finished.

Sex ratio(M:F): 47%:53%	Founded: 1851
Full time u'grads: 8,567	Part time: 2,369
Postgrads: 223	Non-degree: 1,388
Ave course: 3yrs	Ethnic: 22.9%
Private school: n/a	Flunk rate: 24.7%
Mature students: 40%	Overseas students: 5%
Disabled students: 7%	

ATMOSPHERE:
The Kedleston campus is a friendly, buzzing environment. The large fashion department polarises students into those who look cool and those who wear anoraks. But even among those who still think terylene is trendy, there's a generally good buzz.

OTHER SITES:
The *much-improved* bus service has made inter-site travel much easier.
Mickleover: (1,000 – health & community studies, education, social science) A mainly concrete site, 2 miles to the west of the city centre, with some halls of residence. It used to be the Bishop Lonsdale College for Teacher Training.
Green Lane: (300 – film & TV) Right in the city centre, 3 miles from Kedleston, is this listed Victorian building – a purpose-built art college.
Britannia Mill: (500 – art & design) Arty atmosphere in a converted mill, also in the city centre. *There are rumours of a new base for art students.*
Cedars: (200 – occupational therapy) *An Edwardian building and modernist chunk* side by side, 3 miles from the main site.
Jackson's Mill: (100 – art & design) Close to the halls of residence at Bridge St, but students have to take the 20-minute walk to the main campus for books, food and beer.

THE CITY:
- Population: 220,681
- London: 120 miles
- Birmingham: 37 miles
- Nottingham: 14 miles

Those who dismiss Derby as being as ugly as a warthog are missing the historical significance of the place. After all, Derby played an important role in the Jacobite Rebellion and a crucial part in the Industrial Revolution. It has 600 listed buildings, a good number of parks, lots of *useful* shops and amenities, including a number of bookshops (not least a Waterstones at the Kedleston campus). Derby has three museums – the Derby Museum, Industrial Museum and Pickford House – and attractions like the Arboretum Park and, outside town, Elvaston Castle, Shipley Country Park and Chatsworth House. Note for American readers: it's pronounced 'Darrby', not 'Derrby'.

TRAVEL:
Trains: Derby BR station is 2 ½ miles from Kedleston Road: London (£23.10), Sheffield (£4.75) and beyond.
Coaches: National Express and other services operate to London (£15.75) and Sheffield (£5), among other places.
Car: Derby is 8m from the M1 and on the A6, A38, A50, A52.
Air: East Midlands is the closest airport, 8 miles south east of town, with flights inland and to Europe.
Hitching: *Kindly motorists on long hauls on the main roads.*
Local: *Reliable* buses run every 15 minutes to the town centre from the main campus. Weekly passes are available.
Taxis: £2-3 between sites and city centre – several companies offer 10% student discounts.
Bicycles: Plans for a bike link between city and sites are still plans: *roads are too busy for all but the most stubborn cyclist.*

CAREER PROSPECTS:
- Careers Service
- No of staff: 5 full/4 part
- Unemployed after 6mths: 10%

SPECIAL FEATURES:
• 42% of Derby students are local to the area.

FAMOUS ALUMNI:
Cedric Brown (former BG fatcat); Jyoti Mishra (White Town).

FURTHER INFO:
Prospectuses for undergrads and part-timers, course leaflets for some departments, video and website (www.derby.ac.uk).

ACADEMIC

staff/student ratio: 1:20
Range of points required for entrance: 260-140
Percentage accepted through clearing: 20%
Number of terms/semesters: 3
Length of terms/semesters: 11 wks
Research: 1.9

LIBRARIES:
• Books: 323,000 • Study places: 1,680
Five libraries, one at each site. Study space is pretty cramped but the new Learning Centre at Kedleston has added more space. Green Lane and Cedars Libraries are closed at weekends.

COMPUTERS:
• Computer workstations: 850
All halls of residences are networked to the Uni and students can subscribe.

ENTERTAINMENT

THE CITY:
• Price of a pint of beer: £1.80 • Glass of wine: £1.40
Cinemas: There are two multiplexes with 22 screens between them, as well as the artier Metro.
Theatres: The Derby Playhouse has its own repertory company.
Pubs: Nearby Burton is the brewing capital of England. *Pushplugs: Ryan's; O'Neil's; The Flamingo & Firkin. The Ashbourne Mile is a renowned bar crawl.*
Clubs/discos: Derby is picking up speed on the club front. The SU runs Union one and Union two in town. Other *Pushplugs include: Blue Note (indie/jazz); Future (alternative); Eclipse (dance); Curzons (gay-friendly, disco).*
Music venues: *No massive venues, but several large enough to attract more than local strummers and drummers.* Victoria Inn and the Flower Pot and the Loft host live *muzak*. The Assembly Rooms has major bands *but they charge the earth.*
Eating out: The pizza chains do student discounts. Curzon Street and Normanton Road provide the curry nexus. *Pushplugs: Friargate (Cantonese); Excelsior (Chinese); Moghul (Indian); Plug Tonic (posh); Antibo's (Italian); Cactus Café (Mexican); New Normanton 10 minutes from city centre is good for all sorts of restaurants.*

UNIVERSITY:
- Price of a pint of beer: £1.20 • Glass of wine: £2

Bars: The Riverside (cap 700) next to Britannia Mill is *a social focus for the student body* plus the Union Arms at Kedleston Road. Smaller outlets at Mickleover and in halls of residence.
Theatres: (1) Mickleover Student Theatre do several shows.
Cinema: Derby's Metro Cinema is on the Green Lane site.
Clubs/discos/music venues: Union One and... wait for it... Union Two are the top venues, luring the likes of Bentley Rhythm, Judge Jules and Atomic Kitten recently. There's also some sort of dance event every night.
Food: The Atrium in the large entrance hanger at Kedleston does *inexpensive* snacks and meals, and other outlets at most sites.
Others: Three balls a year, plus various club and society dos and an annual beer festival. 'Week in the Sun' is a theme week in the summer. Fortnightly comedy and an Arts Fayre showcase.

SOCIAL & POLITICAL

UNIVERSITY OF DERBY STUDENTS' UNION:
- 7 sabbaticals • Turnout at last ballot: 14% • NUS member

Relations with the Uni have slipped from cosy to strained since the Vice-Chancellor's outspoken views that are a bit uncomfortable for students and the decision to charge the SU rent on two of its bars, now that they've become so successful. Oh, the price of success.

SU FACILITIES:
At Kedleston and in the Mickleover Students' Union Block: bars; Natwest bank; Waterstones; minibuses for hire; general and stationery shops; advice centre; fax service; payphone; photocopier; games and vending machines; pool tables; juke box; TV lounge; conference hall; parking.

CLUBS (NON SPORTING):
Grape & Grain; Hellenic; Heritage Conservation; Masters; Mind Games; Pagan; Sikh; Student Chamber of Commerce; Writing.

OTHER ORGANISATIONS:
There's 'Eclipse' magazine *(which is pretty good)* and a charity Rag which *raises a few pennies* (£6,000 in 2000). There's now a permanent member of staff in charge of Rag, so the figures are growing. A radio station was launched a couple of years ago and the Community Development Area *gets up to a lot of good*.

RELIGIOUS:
- 2 chaplains (CofE, RC)

The Spirit Zone houses advisers from Anglican, Roman Catholic, Free Church, Hindu, Muslim, Sikh, Jewish, Bahai and Buddhist faiths. The Religious Resource & Research Centre has prayer facilities at both Kedleston and Mickleover and there's a Muslim prayer room at Kedleston. In Derby, there's an Anglican cathedral and provisions for Christians of every hue and Hindus, Muslims, Sikhs and Jews.

PAID WORK:
There's a Student Employment Service to assist in the search for part-time work.

SPORTS

- Recent successes: football, rugby

Facilities are cramped but a new 21-acre site has been acquired. Things were supposed to perk up, but the SU is currently upset about the lack of facilities, and is also causing disruption to get Wednesday afternoons freed for sports.

SPORTS FACILITIES:
Facilities are based at Mickleover. Riverside Health Club; 6 football pitches; athletics field; swimming pool; all-weather pitch; climbing wall; multigym; running track; badminton court; American football pitch; hockey pitch. Derbyshire adds various other goodies like golf courses, cricket facilities, the river and, of course, the Peak District.

SPORTING CLUBS:
Aerobics; American Football; Bodytone; Dance; Jiu Jitsu; Mountainbiking; Mountaineering; Muay Thai; Parachuting; Polo; Snowboarding; Surf; Table Tennis; Yoga.

ATTRACTIONS:
Derby County FC, and Derbyshire Cricket Club as well.

ACCOMODATION

IN COLLEGE:
- Self-catering: 29% • Cost: £51-63 (35-52 wks)

Availability: 8% of 1st years can't be accommodated. The residences are purpose-built in the last few years, *all a healthy walk away* from the main campuses. *St Christopher's Court is a groovy cosmopolitan place to live. Students should beware late-payment fines, which are strictly observed. As are people passing the CCTV and the 24-hour watch scheme.*

Car parking: Space for parking is at a premium and not available to most students.

EXTERNALLY:
- Ave rent: £40

Availability: *The rental market has calmed down after student numbers exploded and encouraged pretty sub-standard flats into the scene. The West End, Ashbourne Road and Kedleston Road are the main pockets of student habitation. Normanton and Peartree are the red-light districts - if that's of any interest one way or the other.*

Housing help: The six staff in the Residential Services Department can offer advice and assistance, as can the SU.

WELFARE

SERVICES:
- Nursery • Nightline • Lesbian & Gay Society • Mature SA
- Minibus • Women's Officer • Self-defence classes

The Uni has 5 personal counsellors and 2 nurses who offer services to students. There is a 90-place nursery available for kidlet care.

Disabled: Wheelchair access is variable according to the site - *all new developments are excellent*. The University is rightly proud of its Deafness Studies Unit and there's help available for students with dyslexia.

FINANCE:
- Access fund: £928,366 • Successful applications: 1,295

Distributive Trades
see The London Institute

DIT
see University of Abertay Dundee

Dorset Institute
see Bournemouth University

University of Dundee

University of Dundee, Dundee, DD1 4HN. Tel: (01382) 344000.
Fax: (01382) 201604. E-mail: secretary@dundee.ac.uk
Dundee University Students' Association, Airlie Place, Dundee,
DD1 4HP. Tel: (01382) 221841. Fax: (01382) 227124.
E-mail: jvp@dvsa.co.uk

GENERAL

On the northern side of the Firth of Tay, down the eastern coast of
Scotland from Aberdeen, is Dundee. The Tay estuary, the surrounding
miles of beaches and the highlands rising inland are *very picturesque
– unfortunately, the same cannot be said for Dundee. It's a fairly
dour city, a hotch-potch of architecture.* In an area of town with *some
lovely views* over the Tay, a mile west of the city centre, is the self-
contained campus of Dundee University. Its buildings *have sprouted
like mung beans* over the last 100 years or so and provide examples
of most styles over that period – *some of the best and worst
excesses*. The Union Building, for example, is a *modernist glass-
fronted thingy*. Despite a sense of space, there are few green areas,
but the sports fields of Riverside are only ¼ mile away.

Sex ratio(M:F): 41%:59%	Founded: 1967
Full time u'grads: 7,452	Part time: 1,018
Postgrads: 669	Non-degree: 1,295
Ave course: 4yrs	Ethnic: 6%
Private school: 4%	Flunk rate: 13.5%
Mature students: 32%	Overseas students: 8%
Disabled students: 3%	Staff/student ratio: 1:10

ATMOSPHERE:
*The campus is compact and the University untraditional. The mix of
students on campus is broad – full of normal, unpretentious people
and, although there is fun to be had, the atmosphere isn't exactly*

rocking. By all rights, the main centre of activity should be the Union, but it feels a bit flat and characterless. So students find their own entertainment, forming clubs and losing themselves in their work.

THE CITY:
- Population: 148,920 • London: 384 miles
- Edinburgh: 50 miles • Aberdeen: 60 miles

The city has recently had a long overdue facelift including the new £150Mn city centre shopping complex. The Tay itself, Riverside and the port area have *certain attractions* and there are 1,300 acres of parkland including golf courses, a zoo and a nature trail. There are two bridges over the Tay – a railway and a road bridge, both of which are *more successful* than the first bridge which collapsed in 1879 shortly after it was built, killing 75 people (*as described in the, er, profoundly moving poem by McGonagall). The people are friendly enough too.* The city has several museums, galleries and historic buildings including Bonar Hall (a University-owned exhibition centre). *Worth a mention* are the Observatory on Balgay Hill and Captain Scott's ship 'Discovery'.

TRAVEL:
Trains: Dundee BR has services to London (£54.90), Glasgow (£14.40) and routes to most parts of Scotland and England.
Coaches: National Express, Stagecoach and Citylink services including London (£32), Glasgow (£11) and Edinburgh (£10).
Car: From the south, the M90 goes up to Perth (19 miles west) from where there's the A90, or the A914 which crosses the Tay. From the north, there's the A92, A929 and A923.
Air: Dundee (Riverside Park) Airport.
Hitching: *Not easy. Around Dundee there are too many roundabouts where hitchers can get stuck all day. The best bet is to get a lift on the A92 along the coast and, if heading south, to try to pass close by Edinburgh.*
Local: There's a good bus service *and it's fairly cheap* (80p across town), but the last is at around 11.15pm. There's only one train stop in Dundee – one line comes along the Tay from Perth and the other crosses the Tay heading south.
Taxis: *Cheapest in Scotland.*
Bicycles: *Not too hilly and theft isn't a major problem, but bikes aren't really that necessary.*

CAREER PROSPECTS:
- Careers Service • No of staff: 3 full
- Unemployed after 6mths: 2%

Despite lots of resources available and the Careers Office open in vacations, personal help is felt to be in short supply.

SPECIAL FEATURES:
- Tony Slattery is the Rector of the University, *which is sad, as his predecessor, Stephen Fry, is much funnier.*
- Jerry Sadowitz describes Dundonians: 'They're so thick, if you pour hot water on their heads, you get Pot Noodle.'

FAMOUS ALUMNI:
Sir James Black (Nobel laureate, medicine; current Chancellor); Brian Cox (actor); George Robertson (Secretary General, NATO).

FURTHER INFO:
Prospectuses for undergrads and postgrads SA Handbook, and websites (www.dundee.ac.uk and www.dundee.ac.uk/dusa).

ACADEMIC

The University has taken over the School of Nursing and Midwifery with campuses in Dundee, Kirkcaldy and Fife, about 30 miles away.

staff/student ratio: 1:10
Range of points required for entrance: 340-140
Percentage accepted through clearing: 10%
Number of terms/semesters: 3
Length of terms/semesters: 10 wks
Research: 4.1

LIBRARIES:
- Books: 690,000 • Study places: 1,569

More than ½ of the books are in the Main Library, but there are 3 others specialising in Medicine, Art and Law, as well as departmental libraries.

COMPUTERS:
- Computer workstations: 1,000

ENTERTAINMENT

THE CITY:
- Price of a pint of beer: £1.80 • Glass of wine: £2

Cinemas: 10-screen Odeon and 2 screens at the new contemporary art gallery just off campus.
Theatres: The Dundee Rep hosts transfers from the West End, Scottish plays, Xmas pantos and so on, often starring household names. On Sundays it has comedy nights.
Pubs: *Being Scotland, pubs are open virtually all the time. Pushplugs: The Globe (friendly, good food); Tally-Ho (beer yard). Avoid the Speedwell and the Taybridge – old men alert.*
Clubs/discos: *Dundee's clubs may not be world-renowned, nor indeed cheap, but that doesn't stop students having a good time. Pushplugs: Fat Sam's; Mardi Gras; Enigma*
Music venues: The Union and Fat Sam's do gigs. Recent acts to do it in Dundee include Cast, the Charlatans and Radiohead. Caird Hall hosts classical and pop while the West Port pub *swings* to cajun and Mexican sounds.
Eating out: *Pubs are usually a good starting-point – most of the student favourites do food beyond the pork scratchings stage. Other Pushplugs: Raffles; Visocchi's.*
Others: *For fun before nightfall*, there are the zoo and wildlife sanctuary and, beaches.

UNIVERSITY:
- Price of a pint of beer: £1.30 • Glass of wine: £1.50

Bars: The Union has four bars: The Liar, with a view over the Tay; the smaller Tav Bar (200, *revamped but still cosy*); Pete's Bar and The Main Hall, mainly used for ents.
Theatres: (2) There are theatres in the Union and the Bonar Hall (500), which is run as a commercial venture by the University. There are *active* student drama and opera troupes.
Cinema: *One arty, culty, fringey or world-cinema-y film a week.*

Music venues: The Main Hall and Pete's Bar both pull in *okay* live acts – recently, Judge Jules, Neil Anthony and various tribute bands. *The trend is towards DJs.*
Clubs/discos: Lots of theme nights such as Club Tropicana (80s and 90s), Superfly (70s), Mono (cap 650), Satisfaction (60s). Big (80s and 90s) *'snog-city'*) and Dallas (70s and 80s) are regular sell-outs.
Food: The Filling Station is open for breakfast and lunches.
A pizza/snack bar, the Liar and the Tav do *good value* meals.
Others: Annual 12-hour 'event' with fairs, circus acts *and the usual gubbins;* faculty balls and termly, *less dressy affairs.*

SOCIAL & POLITICAL

DUNDEE UNIVERSITY STUDENTS' ASSOCIATION:
• <u>3 sabbaticals</u>   • <u>Turnout at last ballot: 12%</u>
The Union is the name of the *horribly* mirrored building where DUSA, the representative and organisational body is based. *The students can be a bit complacent about the services they get out of the SA. Politically, most students don't care if they're right, left or hanging from the ceiling by their ankles, so long as the beer doesn't run out.*

SU FACILITIES:
In the Union: four bars; coffee lounge; off-licence; advice centre; meeting room; minibuses; travel agency; photocopying and printing service; banks & cashpoints (Clydesdale & Royal Bank of Scotland); pool tables; swimming pool; bookshop; launderette; hairdressers; photo booth; vending machine; large games room; juke-box. Also on campus is a general shop.

CLUBS (NON SPORTING):
African; Animal Action; Charities; Chinese; Dare; Debating Union; Cumbrian Roads; European; Free For All (free education); Hellenic; Ideological (religious); Lip Theatre; Malaysian; Operatic; Role Playing; Scottish Country Dance; SGI (Buddhist).

OTHER ORGANISATIONS:
The official, DUSA-sponsored paper is the thrice-weekly 'Student Times'.

RELIGIOUS:
• <u>8 chaplains (CofE, RC, Baptist, Methodist, CofS, Jewish)</u>
In the University, there are a large chaplaincy (which also hosts things like line-dancing events), an inter-denominational chapel and a Muslim prayer room. In town, there are other churches and places of worship, catering for most types of Christian, as well as Muslims, Jews, Sikhs and Hindus.

PAID WORK:
Some seasonal work at the local Outdoor Pursuits Centre and tourist spots across the Tay in Fife. Local part-time work *is as hard to find as a good heart,* but the SU employs up to 200.

SPORTS

• <u>Recent successes: water polo, Gaelic football</u>
Despite good facilities there is little corresponding interest.

SPORTS FACILITIES:
The Riverside sports facilities include 33 acres of playing fields and an all-weather pitch. On campus, there are 2 refurbished sports halls,

4 squash and tennis courts, a gym, a swimming pool and a sauna. Overall Dundee has the most extensive indoor facilities of any Scottish university. At Newport, there is a watersports centre. There's a set of bursaries from the St Andrews Royal & Ancient Golf Club worth £1,500 each to eight students hot with a 3-iron.

SPORTING CLUBS:
Boat; Boxing; Free Fall; Frisbee; Gaelic Football; Jiu Jitsu; Kickboxing; Roller Hockey; Rucksack; Sunday League; Swimming & Water-polo; Women's Football & Rugby.

ATTRACTIONS:
Dundee United and Dundee FC are the local soccer heroes. There are also 3 local sports centres.

ACCOMMODATION

IN COLLEGE:
- Catered: 7% • Cost: £72 (31wks)
- Self-catering: 14% • Cost: £37-58 (38-52wks)

Availability: All 1st years who live outside Dundee are guaranteed accommodation and 65% of 1st years live in, *but it gets a bit tougher after that*. Halls tend to be for freshers only *and the catered food is dire*. Then there's self-catering accommodation, some of it *newish and flash*, with en suite, *good security and everything*. There's also rooms and a number of leased houses around the city that the University administers. 1% have to share. Entry-phones, security patrols and night porters.

Car parking: *There's a desperate shortage of parking on and around the campus.* Permits, at £50 a year, are needed.

EXTERNALLY:
- Ave rent: £45

Availability: Many students who live out live in their parents' or their own homes and *so they're alright, Jack. There's enough choice around for students to be able to pick somewhere near where they have to study. Good places include Perth Road, but even this is getting to be quite expensive, and students are moving further and further out. The east side and city centre are a bit too rough for more sensitive souls. Certainly, it's better to be safe than sorry.*

Housing help: The University Residences Office, apart from allocating University places, offers bulletin boards, advice and booklets, provided by eight staff.

WELFARE

SERVICES:
- Nursery • Lesbian & Gay Society • Mature SA • Minibus
- Women's Officer • Self-defence classes

2 full-time counsellors at the University Counselling Service deal with all manner of troubles and the new Student Advisory Service concentrates on financial matters. There are drop-in lunchtime sessions, police and solicitor's clinics. The Student Health Service has visiting doctors and a nursing officer.

Women: Attack alarms are subsidised.

Disabled: *The University has a good record for making provision for sight-impaired students, but wheelchair access isn't so great.* One

hall has some specialised rooms. There is also a Disabled Support
Unit, a Special Needs Adviser and 'Dudes' Support Group.

FINANCE:
• Access fund: £520,000 • Successful applications: 903
The University doles out various bursaries and DUSA has its own
hardship fund.

Dundee Institute of Technology
see University of Abertay Dundee

University of Durham

(1) The University of Durham, Old Shire Hall, Old Elvet, Durham,
DH1 3HP. Tel: (0191) 374 2000. Fax: (0191) 374 7250.
Durham Students' Union, Dunelm House, New Elvet, Durham,
DH1 3AN. Tel: (0191) 374 3310. Fax: (0191) 374 3328.
E-mail: student.union@durham.ac.uk
(2) University of Durham Stockton Campus, University Boulevard,
Thornaby, Stockton-on-Tees, Cleveland, TS17 6BH.
Tel: (01642) 335300. Fax: (01642) 618345.
University of Durham Stockton Campus Students' Union, University
Boulevard, Thornaby, Stockton-on-Tees, Cleveland, TS17 6BH.
Tel: (01642) 335344.

GENERAL

Durham City, laced by the River Wear, lies in the heart of the
Geordie-speaking North East, near the Northumbrian moors,
10 miles from the North Sea and 52 south of the Scottish border.
The University is *planted* in the middle of the ancient, small city, *and
on weekdays during term time, students dominate it socially as much
as the cathedral and castle do physically.* The Castle is one of the
University's colleges, which are spread out in three main groups
giving the advantages of a collegiate, a civic and a campus university.

Sex ratio(M:F): 50%:50%	**Founded: 1832**
Full time u'grads: 9,167	**Part time: 544**
Postgrads: 1,500	**Non-degree: 572**
Ave course: 3yrs	**Ethnic: 4.9%**
Private school: 38%	**Flunk rate: 5.5%**
Mature students: 26%	**Overseas students: 10%**
Disabled students: 5%	

ATMOSPHERE:
*As England's third oldest university, there's something of the
Oxbridge about Durham, with its traditions, its formal dinners and
balls (the black-tie variety). One major difference though is the
strength of its central SU. Although the weather's chilly, the hearts
are warm. The college system and the size of the city certainly create*

a communal atmosphere that some find claustrophobic, but the city's becoming more student friendly, so there's more chance to escape.

THE COLLEGES:
Much of a student's social life is centred around the college where they eat, sleep and drink. However, unlike Oxbridge, teaching is not college–based. The colleges are grouped into three areas *and each group has a flavour of its own. It is important to pick the right college – they do vary.* The oldest colleges are on 'the Peninsula', along 'the Bailey', *and they appeal particularly to those who admire their architecture and tradition, if not their facilities, and to Sloanes.*

University College or 'Castle' (616 students): Predominantly public school, *students sacrifice a few creature comforts* to live in a castle in their 3rd year. The Castle (founded in 1072) is the oldest building used for student accommodation in the country *and can get a bit Sloaney.*
Hatfield (619): *Rugby and beer. Don't come here to be quiet.*
St Chad's (296): *Croquet and Pimms. Small but with character.*
St John's (352): *Church links, largely Christian.*
St Cuthbert's Society (910): *80% live out of college. Many mature students but this is balancing out.*
'The Hill Colleges', near the science departments, were mostly built in the 60s *and tend to be more progressive:*
St Aidan's (735): *Motivated and progressive students; they have to be to climb that hill and still party.*
Van Mildert (737): *Like Aidan's, but very blue, perhaps less motivated and not on a hill. Most cosmopolitan college.*
Trevelyan (566): *Honeycomb maze architecture and rather arty.*
St Mary's (531): *All female, knitting and nighties or sporty party monsters.*
Grey (704): *Slightly more character than its name suggests.*
Collingwood (902): *Media hacksville but unpretentious.* The third area is the hilly north bank of the Wear.
Hild/Bede (1,084) stands alone, *a mixture of all sorts, accused variously of being too insular or too dominant.*
There are also **The Graduate Society** (945) for postgrads and **Ushaw College** (4), a Catholic seminary 4 miles outside the city.
The 15th college, **University of Durham Stockton Campus**, *is completely unlike the main site, in terms of atmosphere, history and geography. It only accepted its first intake in 1992.* It has 1,370 undergraduates, many from the local area, and about 40% mature. Stockton is about 21 miles south of Durham, and 3 miles from Middlesbrough. *Basically it feels like a separate institution.*

THE CITY:
• Population: 85,000 • London: 240 miles • Newcastle: 15 miles
Durham used to be the epicentre of the north-east's mining tradition. There was a time when the annual Durham Miners' Gala (pronounced GAY–ler) was the country's largest Labour meeting – recently though, it has only attracted 5,000 people and no Labour leaders. *Nowadays, there's not much in Durham that isn't connected to the University or the Cathedral:* a shopping mall, lots of quaint shoppes, DLI (army) and arts museums, and open air and covered markets. *Things are picking up a bit but fun–seekers and money–spenders take themselves to Newcastle.*
Stockton: Stockton is part of the Teesside conurbation and was the birthplace of commercial passenger railways in 1825. *It's now a*

stream of urban renewal with a couple of shopping malls and easy access to Middlesbrough (see University of Teesside).

TRAVEL:
Trains: Mainline connections to London King's X (£47.50), Newcastle (£2.60) and more.
Coaches: National Express and Blue Line services to many destinations: London (£25.50), Newcastle (£3) and so on.
Car: 5 mins off the A1.
Air: Newcastle Airport on the A691 – flights to London, Northern Ireland and Europe.
Hitching: *Good grooving from the A1*.
Local: Good buses around town and surrounds *which lazy students use to get to the hill colleges*. Fares from 32p. No trains around the city but a *useful* service into Newcastle.
Taxis: *Some of Britain's cheapest taxis* (minimum fare £1; only £15 to Newcastle, making it a *worthwhile* share).
Bicycles: *A bit hilly for bikes*.

CAREER PROSPECTS:
- Careers Service • No of staff: 7 full/3 part
- Unemployed after 6 mths: 5.4%

SPECIAL FEATURES:
- A new £30 million, 17-acre science park and a new college at Howlands Farm just opened.
- A Japanese university has a campus in Durham for the purpose of forging cultural links with British students.

FAMOUS ALUMNI:
George Alagiah, Jeremy Vine (BBC reporters); Nasser Hussain (England cricket captain); Biddy Baxter (ex–producer of 'Blue Peter'); Will Carling, Phil de Glanville (England rugby captains); Jack Cunningham MP, Mo Mowlam MP (Lab); Hunter Davies (journalist); Jonathan Edwards (triple jumper); Harold Evans (ex-Sunday Times editor); Will Greenwood (England rugby centre); Cmdr Tim Lawrence (Princess Anne's hubby); Edward Leigh MP (Con); James Wilby (actor); Glenda Jackson (actress and MP); Johnny X (Kenickie).

FURTHER INFO:
Prospectuses for undergrads, postgrads and adult students. SU Handbook. Alternative Prospectus from SU (£3.50). Websites (www.dur.ac.uk and www.dur.ac.uk/DSU).

ACADEMIC

Durham has one 9-week and two 10-week terms. 2001 sees the first intake of medical students at the Stockton campus, in a joint programme with the University of Newcastle.

Staff/student ratio: 1:15
Range of points required for entrance: 340-240
Percentage accepted through clearing: 10%
Number of terms/semesters: 3
Length of terms/semesters: 9 wks
Research: 4.8

LIBRARIES:
- Books: 1,140,000 • Study places: 1,200

In addition to the main library there are four other libraries (education, ecclesiastical texts and special collections) and each college and many departments have their own library too.

COMPUTERS:
- Computer workstations: 620

Despite there being six classrooms of computers, computer rooms in most colleges and a 24-hour computer centre, *access to computers can get difficult at peak times.*

ENTERTAINMENT

THE CITY:
- Price of a pint of beer: £1.80 • Glass of wine: £1.75

Durham is too small to provide a thrilling roster of ents and what's there isn't really geared to a student market. For big thrills, students tend to go to Newcastle.

Pubs: Although students aren't welcomed everywhere, there are still plenty of traditional northern pubs serving bitters with bite like the ubiquitous 'dog' (Newcastle Brown). Pushplugs: Colpitts; The Shakespeare; Dun Cow (real ale); Market Tavern; New Inn; Saints (Internet café); Scruffy Murphy's. The aptly-named Fighting Cocks is best avoided.

Cinemas: An independent with four screens, Robin's Cinema on North Street has a student night and shows *arty stuff*.

Clubs/discos: Café Rock is a chart-bound venue. *Pushplugs: Funky Slug (indie); Riverside; Club Elysium (Drum'n'Base).*

Music venues: No big venues, but local bands play at the Working Men's Club and local pubs *(plenty of folk and R&B).*

Eating out: *Not a great deal of choice but one or two places to take your mind off college food for a few hours. Pushplugs: La Spaghetatta (Italian); Market Tavern (great pies); The Court Inn (good grub).*

UNIVERSITY:
- Price of a pint of beer: £1.30 • Glass of wine: £1.20

Bars: (17) (4 in student Union, 13 colleges). Each college has its own bar, *where college spirit comes in doubles.* The Kingsgate Bar in Dunelm House (the SU) is open on a regular basis, *but the seating is bad, music too loud and the staff rubbish.* There's a club bar at DUS (not the same as DSU, see below).

Theatre: Durham Student Theatre *is very active*, putting on big productions in the University theatre and the Fringe. The Castle Shakespeare Theatre Co and Fountains Theatre Co based at Grey College are *developing quite a reputation*.

Cinemas: Hild/Bede and the SU each show recent films.

Clubs/discos/music venues: Ballroom (cap 750); Riverside Café (cap 150); Dunelm House has three halls to use as club and live music venues (caps 750, 250, 100) and colleges have smaller facilities *but round these parts 'bangin' choons' means hitting menthol sweets, though St Aidan's puts on a good dance night. Visiting bands are conspicuous by their absence, though larger name DJs pop up.*

Food: In Dunelm House, Kingsgate does *pretty standard stuff*, while the Riverside does veggie breakfasts.

Balls: Each college has at least one ball a year, costing from a few quid to £130 for a double ticket at Castle's elitist June bash. The SU also holds a Freshers' Ball. *Durham's 'Rah' contingent (chinless*

posh kids) use these as an opportunity to behave badly in expensive frocks. As if they need an excuse.
Comedy: Comedy is *irregular* but recent giggle–givers include Craig Charles as well as the Union's own Durham Revue.
Others: Musicon organises classical and more populist shows (but not pop) in the Cathedral and around the University.

SOCIAL & POLITICAL

DURHAM STUDENTS' UNION (DSU):
• 3 sabbaticals • Turnout at last ballot: 17% • NUS member
DSU is a politically shrewd union with a representative voice in the Uni, but active members don't often have party allegiances (at least not on their sleeves, though many feel the sabbatical posts are just stepping stones for political careers). Conversely, the exec feel the students forget who provides the many services. There are seven JCR Chair sabbaticals and the three in the executive. Stockton has its own Union.

SU FACILITIES:
The large union building, Dunelm House, is placed right in the middle of the city where it offers: three bars; a ballroom; Riverside Room cafeteria; small hall; shop; travel agent; launderette; stationery shop; second-hand bookshop; advice centre; ticket agency; pool tables; minibuses; car & van hire; fax; print and photocopier service; meeting rooms; games and vending machines; juke box; public phones; photo booth.

CLUBS (NON SPORTING):
Anglo–Japanese; Archaeology; Assassins; Beatles; Belly-dancing; Blondes; Buddhist Meditation; Change Ringers; Choral; Circus; Club Scene; Football Supporters; Free Tibet; Hellenic; Hot Curry; Indie; Industrial; Line Dancing; Mah Jong; Merhaba; Methodist; Motor Sports; Oriental; Real Ale; Rock; Russian; Ruth First (South African links); Scouts & Guides; Tibet; Treasure Trap; Walking; Wine; Wodehouse (as in PG). Each college also has its own set of societies.

OTHER ORGANISATIONS:
DSU publishes the *excellent* independent student newspaper 'Palatinate', 'ON', the *similarly impressive* student arts mag, 'The Score' ents listings mag and 'Hogwash', a *satirical rag*. There's also Purple FM radio. The charity Rag was banned in 1976 for breaking into Durham's top security prison and so students just changed the name to 'DUCK' (Durham University Charity weeK). Student Community Action acts as an umbrella group for town-gown projects including SPARK which promotes work with local youngsters. The Durham Union Society (DUS) is the long-standing debating society which offers more than just debating – *often seen as a right-wing*

```
The Jesus and Mary Chain appeared at the Poly
(now University) of North London in the mid
80's. They performed for 15 minutes and
refused to do an encore. The crowd rioted.
```

alternative to DSU or a refuge for the sophisticated Sloane – either way it costs £35 to get in. It runs a bar, TV room, café and a range of events.

RELIGIOUS:
There is a 1,500 year-old Christian heritage, *so finding a church is easy*: as well as the Cathedral there are Anglican, Catholic, Methodist, Quaker and United Reformed churches. Most colleges have their own chapel. For Muslims, a prayer room is provided, but the nearest mosque is in Sunderland. Anyone else has to venture to Newcastle for places to worship.

PAID WORK:
Few openings, although the SU runs a job-shop. Recently, 700 sought work through the shop and 350 of them were blessed.

SPORTS

- Recent successes: men's and girlies cricket, fencing, mountaineering

Durham has an excellent sporting record as a glance at the alumni list will testify. *The large amount of money spent on sports by the University may have something to do with this*. There's a sabbatical student sports president. In 2000 the Uni appointed a full-time rowing coach, ex-olympian and alumnus Wade Hall-Craggs *(they don't do things by halves)*.

SPORTS FACILITIES:
Sports hall; 60 acres of playing fields; all-weather pitch; multigym; athletics and running track; gym; croquet lawn and bowling green; tennis and squash courts and the River Wear. Outdoor pitches are floodlit. Durham City also has a public baths and an ice rink. Stockton, by contrast, has no facilities of its own, but a public sports centre is being built nearby.

SPORTING CLUBS:
Bridge; Chess; Croquet; Fives; Free Fall; Gliding; Golf; Guns; Hang Gliding; Ice Hockey; Ice Skating; Kendo; Lacrosse; Mountaineering; Real Tennis; Rowing; Rifles; Speleological (caving); Tang Soo Do; Ten-pin Bowling; Water Polo; Windsurfing. Each college also has its own sporting clubs, including a boat club each.

ATTRACTIONS:
The Durham Regatta is one of the top annual university rowing events *(Henley and the Varsity Boat Race are more top)*. The Uni doesn't organise it itself, but Uni crews compete in it. The ice rink is the home of the Durham Wasps ice-hockey team and *Durham is now a first class cricketing county (but not a very good one)*. Some of Durham's Sloanes like to flutter daddy's money on the geegees at Thirsk. As with most things, Newcastle offers more.

```
York University hasn't had a central music
venue since the Boomtown rats (Bob Geldof's
old band) played in 1979. The fans danced so
hard the building began to slip into the lake.
```

ACCOMMODATION

IN COLLEGE:
- Catered: 48% • Cost: £93 (28wks) • Self-catering: 10%
- Cost: £45–55 (29wks)

Availability: Almost all 1st years live in and some colleges can provide accommodation for at least one further year. Overall, 17% have to share. Except in St Mary's, all accommodation is mixed. 48% of postgrads are already housed and another hall is being planned for them. The Stockton Campus has self-catering accommodation for 512 students.

Catering: *Living in means suffering the variable standards of mass-catering. (University College is the worst, Collingwood the best – bring your vitamin supplements, either way).* Except for the self-catering places (post–grads and Stockton only), the shared kitchens are only adequate for tea and toast.

Amenities: Launderettes; bars; libraries; chapels; common rooms; TV and games rooms; music rooms; some colleges also have halls and large theatre–style venues. CCTV, entry–phones, keypads and night porters.

Car parking: Permit required for the *limited* spaces.

EXTERNALLY:
- Ave rent: £48

Availability: *It's difficult but feasible to find private housing for rent.* Some choose to *resort* to the surrounding villages where rents are lower and places are more available. What there is is in Victorian houses shared between three to five. *The Viaduct is a sought after spot, closely followed by Bowburn and Langley Moor. The surrounding pit villages should be avoided. Cars are unnecessary and are the cause of much local tension, but many still bring them.*

Housing help: DSU employs one part-time accommodation officer who runs an office with vacancy lists, standard contracts, legal help and postgrad house-hunting days. St Cuthbert's Society gives a bit of a boost to its own students.

WELFARE

SERVICES:
- Creche • Lesbian & Gay Society • Mature SA • Overseas SA
- Postgrad SA • Minibus • Women's Officer • Self-defence classes

There is a student health centre run by the University with a doctor, a psychotherapist and nurses. Students are also allocated to local NHS practices by their colleges. There's an *excellent* welfare service employing eight full-time counsellors. Each student is also assigned a 'moral' tutor by their college and there's even a legal advice surgery, run by a local solicitor. Race Awareness Officers are a recent introduction.

Disabled: Special provisions have been made for hearing-impaired students and, with a few partially sighted students, they make up most of the University's disabled population. However, the city's *topsy topography makes it a toughie for students with mobility difficulties.* Students with physical disabilities are allowed to use the women's minibus.

FINANCE:
- Ave debt per year: £1,850 • Access fund: £442,571
- Successful applications (1999): 390

There's a hardship fund of £30,000 but *a student has to be in seriously deep poo to benefit from it. There are also scholarships, bursaries and prizes galore.*

Bangor have been the British wargames champions for five of the last six years.

'If you want a sound education in Britain, the safest way is to buy it. That's no way to run a country at the end of the 20th century.' - George Walden MP.

Ealing College see Thames Valley University

East Anglia see University of East Anglia

East European Studies see SSEES

University of East London

Economics see LSE

Edge Hill see Other Institutions

University of Edinburgh

Edinburgh College of Art see Heriot-Watt University

University of Essex

Essex IHE see Anglia Polytechnic University

University of Exeter

Ealing College
see Thames Valley University

East Anglia
see University of East Anglia

East European Studies
see SSEES

University of East London

- *Formerly Polytechnic of East London, North East London Polytechnic*
(1) University of East London, Barking Campus, Longbridge Road, Dagenham, Essex, RM8 2AS. Tel: (020) 8223 3000.
Fax: (020) 8590 7799.
University of East London Students' Union, Longbridge Road, Dagenham, Essex, RM8 2AS. Tel: (020) 8223 2420.
(2) University of East London, Stratford Campus, Romford Road, London, E15 4LZ.
(3) University of East London, Docklands Campus, Royal Albert Way, London, E16 2QT. Tel (020) 8223 3000.

'Advice for Push: Never mix grain and grape and never eat newspaper.' - Stephen Fry.

GENERAL

For general information about London: see University of London. The University of East London (UEL) isn't just in east London. In fact, it's in 6 places, grouped into UEL's 3 main sites, 4 miles from each other: the Stratford Campus (*nothing to do with Avon or Shakespeare*); the Barking Campus (*nothing to do with dogs – sorry*) in the huge area of *sprawling suburbia*, east of London, that is Ilford and Barking; and the new Docklands Campus. 5½ miles north-east of Trafalgar Square at Stratford is the Main Building – *a fine example of Victorian municipal architecture* (a listed building), surrounded by London's East End, which, with *toned down stereotypes, is pretty well represented by a certain well-known soap*. The Barking site is bigger and *more attractive, despite the surrounding area*. This is partly because it is set in Goodmayes Park, *an oasis in this part of Essex*.

Sex ratio(M:F): 50%:50%	Founded: 1970
Full time u'grads: 8,000	Part time: 1,750
Postgrads: 2,800	Non-degree: 800
Ave course: 3yrs	Ethnic: 51%
Private school: n/a	Flunk rate: 32.1%
Mature students: 80	Overseas students: 19.5%
Disabled students: 2.5%	

ATMOSPHERE:
Probably the best part of UEL is that students can get on with their own lives without being bothered with the delights and distractions of student culture. A real disappointment for those in quest of the cliché lifestyle of beer (lager), totty (pronounced bird in Essex – for her, or geezer – for him), beans-on-toast (whowoooph!), and books (wot libraries have); but a definite bonus for some, particularly the huge proportion of students who qualify as mature, which means they're returners to education, not that they smell of cheese. In fact, although facilities may be wanting, the social mix is an interesting cocktail – more than half of the students come from ethnic minority backgrounds and many come from the local area. There's a positive atmosphere of vibrant tolerance, but most people see this as a friendly environment in which to study, rather than as a political statement.

BEING A STUDENT IN LONDON: see University of London

THE SITES:
There's a fair amount of travelling between sites (by London's public transport, see below). It is, however, important for students to check out which site their courses are based at and what's there: Docklands (electrical, manufacturing, engineering, media studies, cultural studies, art and design); Barking (civil engineering, business and social sciences); Maryland; Duncan House (management); Holbrook (architecture). *As sites go, the Stratford campus is a bit incohesive, while Barking is much more bustley.*

THE CITY: see University of London

THE EAST END AND DAGENHAM:
Stratford and the rest of London's East End are, traditionally, the home of London's dispossessed: first, Jews; nowadays, Asians and yuppies. *The lively community atmosphere is hard to find elsewhere in inner city London.* Petticoat Lane market *may be a bit more*

gimmicky than it used to be, but Brick Lane *is an overdose for the shopaholic, even late night.*
Barking and Ilford are the classic home of Essex Girl, where Essex Man used to park his Capri. There are shops and pubs, but the variety and culture pale beside Stratford.

TRAVEL: see University of London
Local travel: *One thing that would really make UEL seem like a real University would be a decent bus service between sites and this may happen one day. Until then students often bring cars, but parking pressure causes friction with the locals.*
Trains: For Stratford the nearest rail station is Maryland (10mins from London Liverpool St). Barking Station is 13 minutes from London Fenchurch St Station.
Buses: The only buses that run between Stratford and Barking are the 238 and the 25 (more or less), which run from Oxford Circus (in the West End), past the Stratford site's Main Building to Ilford. Other buses for Stratford include 69, 173, 241, 262 and some night buses. For Barking: 5, 87, 162, 287 and N95.
Docklands Light Railway: The DLR runs services into the City and Docklands and is being extended into South London. The Docklands campus has its very own DLR station which runs directly to the campus at Stratford. *Beware the service is patchy during the day and even worse at night.*
Underground: Stratford is on the Central Line. Barking (District Line and, at peak hours, the Hammersmith & City) and Plaistow (same lines) are useful for some buildings.
Hitching: *Impossible from inside London – hitchers have to get to the outskirts, but Essex is a no go area for the thumb traveller, even the freight terminal near the University.*
Bicycles: *For those students who can stand the filth and traffic, biking it is a great deal cheaper than public transport, until they have to replace their stolen bike.*

CAREER PROSPECTS:
- Careers Service • No of staff: 3 full/4 part
- Unemployed after 6mths: 11%

Many of the courses are vocationally based which doesn't necessarily mean students get jobs, but does increase their chances of going into certain areas.

FAMOUS ALUMNI:
Hilary Armstrong MP (Lab); Garry Bushell ('Sun' TV 'critic'); Mark Frith (editor, Heat magazine); Imran Kahn (lawyer); Ken Russell (film director); Sir Alex Trotman (chairman Ford Motors); Christopher Wenner (ex-Blue Peter presenter).

FURTHER INFO:
Prospectuses for undergrads and postgrads. Website (www.uel.ac.uk).

ACADEMIC

Many of the courses are vocationally based.

staff/student ratio: 1:19
Range of points required for entrance: 300-140
Percentage accepted through clearing: n/a
Number of terms/semesters: 2
Length of terms/semesters: 15 wks
Research: 2.3

LIBRARIES:
- Books: 307,840 • Study places: 1,158

COMPUTERS:
- Computer workstations: 704

ENTERTAINMENT

CITY: see University of London

EAST LONDON:
- Price of a pint of beer: £1.90 • Glass of wine: £2.20

Cinemas: Multiplexes at Romford and Gant's Hill, Ilford (10 screens in all), and a 4-screen cinema at Stratford.

Theatres: The Theatre Royal Stratford East has many productions which transfer to the West End – those who have the foresight to see them here first, see them cheaper.

Pubs: *In the East End there are plenty of pubs passing cheerfully for the stereotypical (and fictional) Queen Vic; Viz's Cockney Wankah would be comfy in many. In Barking every pub's a pitiful pulling joint for Essex Men and Girls. These are outrageously unfair generalisations and at least they're cheaper than most London pubs.* Pushplugs: the King Edward, Princess Alice and The Pigeons are all earmarked as student pubs.

Eating out: The best local cuisine comes from the Indian, Chinese and other ethnic restaurants in the East End. Other Pushplugs: Sombrero Steak House (Ilford); Raj (Barking).

Clubs/discos: *Endless nightclubs in east London score highly on the snog, vomit and fight factor. Most students avoid them like a sewage dump in summer.* They flock instead to Benjy's on the Mile End Road, the Princess Alice (indie nights) or The Pigeons pub, which tends to deliberately complement SU events and has indie, gay & lesbian and student nights.

UNIVERSITY:
- Price of a pint of beer: £1.50 • Glass of wine: £1.50

Bars: (3) 2 in Barking, 1 in Stratford. Maryland House (800) *is a popular drinking den, but the Barking Bar* (600) *is more ents-related. The bars are a refuge from unfriendly local pubs.*

Cinema: 1 film is shown every fortnight (*not the same one*) by the student film society 'Reels'.

Clubs/discos/music venues: Weekly Sabotage night (techno/house) in the Barking Bar. Bands aren't so common.

Cabaret: Regular acts in Maryland House and Barking SU bar.

Food: Refectories and snack bars at several sites; the A Block at Barking; one half of the SU bar in C Block; the top floor at the Stratford Main Building (*where the mural is more memorable than the food*); the *friendly* coffee bar at Greengate House; Holbrook House; the Green and the *best one* at the swish management course centre at Duncan House.

Others: Quiz nights; Freshers and May Ball; cultural nights.

The Vice-Chancellor of the University of the West of England is a keen skateboarder.

SOCIAL & POLITICAL

UNIVERSITY OF EAST LONDON STUDENTS' UNION:
• 6 sabbaticals • Turnout at last ballot: 11% • NUS member
The dingy, graffitied C Block is the SU's administrative, advice/information and finance centre. Ents, communications and more welfare are based on the ground floor at Maryland House. It operates a satellite service around the other sites. *The Union is particularly strong on welfare and specific issues such as racism and the 'no means no' campaign.*

SU FACILITIES:
Collectively, the various sites of the SU offer 2 bars, 2 cafeterias, bookshops at both sites, minibus hire, general shop, Barclays bank, Endsleigh Insurance office, photocopying, phones, pool table, vending machines and juke box.

CLUBS (NON SPORTING):
African; Barking Union Student Staff; Bengali; Beer Appreciation; Chinese Oriental Cookery; Cultural Awareness; European Students; Fashion; Finnish; Indian; Italian; Kegites; Law; Live Music; Malaysian; Meditation; Nursery; Punjabi; Reels (film); Rock Musicians; Samba; Scientific; Sikh; Social Equality.

OTHER ORGANISATIONS:
The SU's 'FUEL' magazine is good-looking, if sloppily written.

RELIGIOUS:
• 1 chaplain (CofE)
The Christian Union is large and active, but apart from the Muslim prayer room in Barking's T Block, students rely on East London's *plentiful* religious facilities. There's a particularly strong Asian community and corresponding religions.

PAID WORK: see University of London
A jobshop has been introduced.

SPORTS

• Recent successes: Women's netball
The sporting record is okay, but The Guinness Book isn't about to show an interest. Facilities priced at about £1 a session.

SPORTS FACILITIES:
Most facilities are around Goodmayes Park at the Barking site, where there's a sports centre, swimming pool, 2 gyms, 1 squash court, multigym, weights, minibus, sauna and solarium, tennis courts (football pitches have been sold-off and the canoes stolen).
Optimistically, there's an Injuries Clinic with built-in physio. For other sports look to London and the nearby Newham Sports Centre. Near both sites there's a dry ski slope, athletics track and amenities for most sports.

SPORTING CLUBS:
Callanetics; Jiu Jitsu; Mountaineering; Mountain Bike; Parachuting; Paragliding.

ATTRACTIONS:
West Ham is the local football team, but there's also Leyton Orient. Sports fans can fan their fanaticism all over London, see University of London for details.

ACCOMMODATION

IN COLLEGE:
• Self-catering: 18% • Cost: £40-66 (52wks)
Availability: Pressure is eased by the majority of local students. There are 3 developments, with a total of 1,062 places. Park Village (next to an international freight terminal) is about 20mins walk from the Stratford site. There are 508 places on the Barking site, including some purpose-built rooms for disabled students. Kitchens are shared between 6 people. The new Docklands campus will provide more accommodation.
Car parking: *It's far enough from central London to be free and adequate, although a permit is needed.*

EXTERNALLY: see University of London
Local Availability: Most mature students have their homes already sorted. East London is cheaper than many other parts of the capital and at UEL, it's possible to live quite far out (and so more cheaply) and still be on the doorstep. *Stratford itself is a likely locale, as are Leyton, Forest Gate and East Ham. Also Leytonstone and Walthamstow, but they're quite a trek.*
Housing help: There are 3 accommodation offices, which between them employ 6 full- and 3 part-time staff. They provide vacancies boards and newsletters.

WELFARE

SERVICES:
• Nursery • Lesbian & Gay Society • Mature SA • Overseas SA
• Postgrad SA • Women's minibus • Women's Officer
• Self-defence classes

Student Services Department provides advice on all sorts of problems, employing 2 counsellors and 5 welfare advisors. The SU is very *eager* to help with a range of issues, although it has no professional counsellors so concentrates on financial, legal and academic advice and representation. Medical centres are on both sites, staffed by nurses, offering GPs and family planning.
Women & ethnic minorities: UEL has a crusading equal opportunities policy, reflected in the high proportion of students from ethnic minorities and the equal gender balance, *which is particularly important given local racial and social tensions.* The Women's Unit run by the SU is *strong* and the student Women's Officer is a sabbatical. There's also a Black Mentor scheme to pair up black students with successful black people in their chosen career and a race officer.
Disabled: The University employs a disability advisor and provides *fairly good access.* New housing takes students' disabilities into account. The largest library has 2 Arkenstone readers for the sight-impaired and Minicom equipment for the hearing-impaired. Workshop for students with dyslexia.

FINANCE:
• Access fund: £303,000 • Successful applications: 1,324
There are 7 scholarships for part-time unwaged students, as well as partial fee remission schemes.

Economics
see LSE

Edge Hill
see Other Institutions

University of Edinburgh

The University of Edinburgh, Old College, South Bridge, Edinburgh, EH8 9YL. Tel: (0131) 650 1000. Fax: (0131) 650 2147.
Edinburgh University Students' Association (EUSA),
5/2 Bristo Square, Edinburgh, EH8 9AL. Tel: (0131) 650 2656. Fax: (0131) 668 4177. E-mail: eusa.enquiry@ed.ac.uk

GENERAL

It's on the east coast of Scotland. It's the country's capital. *It's one of the most cultural, beautiful and vibrant cities in the world. It's been called 'the most ideal city to live in'.* It is Edinburgh. Enough from the Tourist Office, see below for a fuller advert... Edinburgh has four universities: Napier, Heriot-Watt, Queen Margaret College, and, of course, the University of Edinburgh, itself – the sixth oldest in Britain, situated in buildings throughout the city. There are three main areas, but departments and halls are dotted all over the place. Many departments are concentrated in the George Square/Old College area of the city centre with almost as many at King's Buildings (the science & engineering campus) 2 miles south. The largest group of residences, the Pollock Halls, are east of the centre near Holyrood Park. The University buildings have steadily developed over the last two centuries, many appearing in the last 40 years, *but almost all have been built in local stone with a care for the city's beauty.*

Sex ratio(M:F): 46%:54%	Founded: 1582
Full time u'grads: 15,604	Part time: 599
Postgrads: 2,375	Non-degree: 695
Ave course: 4yrs	Ethnic: n/a
Private school: n/a	Flunk rate: 8.7%
Mature students: 13%	Overseas students: 10%
Disabled students: 5%	

ATMOSPHERE:
There are over 50,000 students from various colleges in Edinburgh and just as the University buildings are spread throughout the city and reflect its beauty, so the students are a part of the city, rather than simply in it, reflecting its lively culture, combining study and fun as if there aren't enough hours in the day. Students are often from the south – 40% are English – but get on with the locals nevertheless.

THE CITY:
- Population: 421,213 • London: 391 miles
- Glasgow: 44 miles • Newcastle: 93 miles

Edinburgh is a stunning city with a tremendous heritage. Like all the best cities, it's built on seven hills, overlooked by Arthur's Seat, a mini-mountain. The centre hill is peaked by the castle and old city walls. There are over 16,000 listed buildings (*mostly in the local stone that picks up something ethereal in the quality of the light*) which date mainly from two periods of expansion: the formation of the centre from the 11th-century onwards and later, the New Town, mainly to the north. The *broad* streets, garden squares, cobbled alleys, parks and awesome views are *well* planned (all by one guy, George Drummond) with three main roads running parallel (Queen Street, George Street and Princes Street). The Royal Mile, a straight stretch of linked roads, runs through the city's heart. Four-storey tenements line the Royal Mile. The Old Town is *unique in its ability to look as though Nature intended it to be there and the names paint some pretty pictures*: Grassmarket; Lawnmarket; The Pleasance; Cowgate; The Mound. Among the first sites on any tour of the city should be Holyrood Palace, the new Museum of Scotland, the Royal Museum of Scotland, the National Gallery, the Castle and lots more. The latest addition to the city is the Scottish Parliament building, a stone's throw from the University. *Despite the history all around, it's a living, breathing 24-hour city with a pumping nightlife. There's always somewhere to be seen at any time, day or night. It's not just a tourist trap of course, there are rough areas that don't turn up on the lids of shortbread gift boxes. But stay safe and it's one hell of a place to be a student.*

TRAVEL:
Trains: Edinburgh Waverley Station is the most central in Edinburgh with a direct line to Glasgow (£4.95) and others to the north and the south (via Newcastle and York) to London (£50.80). Connections also to Birmingham and Bristol.
Coaches: National Express, Stagecoach and Citylink services to London (£27.25), Glasgow (£5) and so on.
Car: The M8 and M9 connect with the A8 to the west. There are also the A1, A7, A68, A70, A71, A702, A703 and A90.
Air: Edinburgh (Turnhouse) Airport, 5½ miles west of the city centre, has a range of international and internal flights (from £69 return to London).
Hitching: *The A1 is a popular road for hitchers. Unfortunately, this part isn't so popular with the sort of driver who gives lifts. But the lifts will come eventually. It's easier to get into the city than out.* The M8 and M9 are good for Glasgow and Perth.
Local: *Bus services are good all round the city and quite cheap* (from 50p). They run less frequently between 7pm and midnight.
Taxis: Useful at night, *extravagant otherwise* (£3 across town).
Bicycles: *Useful, but remember Edinburgh is built on seven hills. Bicycles also have a tendency to wheel themselves away.*

CAREER PROSPECTS:
- Careers Service • No of staff: 6 full/6 part
- Unemployed after 6mths: 4.2%

SPECIAL FEATURES:
- Past Rectors (elected every three years by the students) have included Magnus Magnusson, Winston Churchill, Muriel Gray, Donnie

Munro (of Runrig), Sir David Steel and James Robertson Justice (the fat bearded one in the 'Doctor' movies).
• The Moray House Institute of Education (education and 'people-centred profession' courses) merged with Edinburgh University in 1998. 2,000 students are based at Moray House's two campuses, one at the end of The Royal Mile near Edinburgh's city centre, the other on the seashore. Accommodation for 300 students is about 2 miles away.

FAMOUS ALUMNI:
James Barrie, Arthur Conan Doyle, Walter Scott, Robert Louis Stevenson (writers); Dr Barry (world's first qualified woman doctor who impersonated a man in order to study and practice); David Brewster (who invented the kaleidoscope); Gordon Brown MP, Robin Cook MP (Lab); Thomas Carlyle (historian/philosopher); Charles Darwin (revolutionary evolutionary); David Hume (philosopher, who had a nervous breakdown shortly after graduating); Eric Liddell ('Chariots of Fire' runner) and Ian Charleson, who played him; Lord Mackay of Clashfern; Julius Nyerere (ex-President, Tanzania); Malcolm Rifkind (ex-minister, ex-MP); Peter Roget (of Thesaurus fame); Kirsty Wark (TV presenter); James Watt (engineer/inventor); and so on.

FURTHER INFO:
Prospectuses for undergrads, postgrads, mature and overseas students. Website (www.ed.ac.uk and www.eusa.ed.ac.uk).

ACADEMIC

staff/student ratio: n/a
Range of points required for entrance: 340-220
Percentage accepted through clearing: 5%
Number of terms/semesters: 3
Length of terms/semesters: 10 wks
Research: 4.9

LIBRARIES:
• Books: 2,690,125 • Study places: 3,500
There's an enormous Main Library and six other more specialised ones (Divinity; Law; the Europa Institute; Medicine; Music; Science & Veterinary Medicine).

COMPUTERS:
• Computer workstations: 1,500

ENTERTAINMENT

CITY:
• Price of a pint of beer: £2.40 • Glass of wine: £2
Festivals: *Edinburgh is never short of entertainments*, but there is a *positive festglut* during August, not just the main Edinburgh Festival (in itself the largest arts event in the world), but at the same time the Fringe *(which includes hundreds of student productions)*, Film, Dance, Jazz, TV and Book Festivals and probably many others. *(The whole thing has been described by Robert Llewellyn (aka Kryten from 'Red*

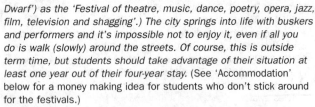

Dwarf') as the 'Festival of theatre, music, dance, poetry, opera, jazz, film, television and shagging'.) The city springs into life with buskers and performers and it's impossible not to enjoy it, even if all you do is walk (slowly) around the streets. Of course, this is outside term time, but students should take advantage of their situation at least one year out of their four-year stay. (See 'Accommodation' below for a money making idea for students who don't stick around for the festivals.)

Cinemas: Seven cinemas with a total of 40 screens. The *arty* Filmhouse and Cameo host the Edinburgh Film Festival.

Theatres: Strictly speaking, there are 13 theatres, but each year the Festivals find literally hundreds of venues. *The Festivals have a knock-on effect and Edinburgh brims with exciting and experimental theatre and dance, as well as mainstream arts, throughout the year.* The Royal Lyceum, King's Theatre and the relocated Traverse are among the hardy perennials and the *magnificent* new Festival Theatre does everything from Rocky Horror to Sing-a-long-a Sound of Music.

Pubs: Most pubs are open till 1am. *Students who want to make the most of an Edinburgh education will develop a taste for whisky.* The best places to do it are most pubs around Grassmarke; Maggie Dicksons (good grub), Sneaky Pete's and Whistlebinkies (for the serious quaffer), Iguana, Bar Kohl (studenty), Black Bo's (cheap), The Kitchen (funky music) and Jekyll & Hyde (in the New Town).

Clubs/discos: Just because there's lots of fun for audiences, doesn't mean Edinburgh slacks on more active entertainment. Pushplugs: Pure (legendary hardcore at The Venue, £6-7); Mercado (dance of all sorts); Joy (gay/Hi-NRG) and Bound To Please (house) at the New Calton Studios; Café Graffiti; JP's.

Music venues: *The remarkable thing about the number of live music venues is how they can all continue to make a profit. Maybe they don't. Maybe they do it for fun.* Apart from the following, live music spills out from many a pub and club. Pushplugs: Usher Hall (classical, including the Scottish National Opera); Queen's Hall (indie and more); Playhouse (AOR); The Venue (indie); Rocking Horse (metal mayhem).

Eating out: Some of Scotland's best restaurants are in Edinburgh, serving everything from cordon bleu cuisine to brown sauce cookery. The only drawback is that eating out in Edinburgh will unfill students' pockets faster than it fills their stomachs. Pushplugs (among many others): Henderson's (veggie hang-out); Pierre Victoire and Chez Jules (bistro); Mamma's (value Italian); Kalpna (gorgeous Indian veggie).

Others: Among the *endless* entertainments, there's cabaret galore and the Tattoo, a military parade at the castle. *Americans and old people seem to like it best of all.*

UNIVERSITY:
- Price of a pint of beer: £1.55

Bars: 12 bars around EUSA's various sites (see below). The major ones are the Teviot main bar, the Potterrow union bars and the *pubby* Pleasance Bar.

Theatres: There are three theatres around the University and its students staged more shows at last year's Edinburgh Fringe Festival than any other university, *but then, it does have a slight geographical advantage.* The Bedlam Theatre Company runs its own theatre.

Cinemas: The University film club, the largest in the country with more than 2,500 members, shows about two films a week, a broad range *beyond the usual pap.* Annual membership also gets you cheap tickets to the Cameo *arty* cinema.

Clubs/discos: There are dance venues all over the place in EUSA's various centres, including the 'Bristo Square' experience which links up Teviot Row (capacity 1,800) and the Potterrow (capacity 1,200) for Edinburgh's biggest Friday night. EUSA also hosts the usual indie, funk, soul and cheese nights.
Music venues: The Union at Potterrow is now a 1,200-capacity music venue on two levels. The Potterrow features regular live bands including recently Toploader as well as local wannabes.
Cabaret: Weekly cabaret nights at the Pleasance, which was voted best student comedy venue in the UK recently.
Food: The University itself doesn't actually provide any eateries, but there are cafeterias in all EUSA's main sites open from 8.30am till late at night. In total, there are 13 EUSA food outlets.
Others: Regular quiz nights and several balls a year, the *highspot* being the Societies ball in February.

SOCIAL & POLITICAL

EDINBURGH UNIVERSITY STUDENTS' ASSOCIATION:
• <u>4 sabbaticals</u> • <u>Turnout at last ballot: 10%</u>
Forget any other structures of student representation and services, Edinburgh is different. EUSA is an umbrella for the SRC (Student Representative Council) which does political and representative work and The Union which provides student services. *To make matters more complicated,* there's also the Sports Union which is separate, although membership is simultaneous with automatic free membership of EUSA. This entitles students to use the Union centres (see below). There's also 'The Advice Place' (see Welfare below), which is particularly important as EUSA is not affiliated to NUS (but often campaigns with NUS Scotland on big issues) and doesn't have its services as a back-up. *Enthusiasm pervades the Unions (as with everything else) and students appreciate the choice of service centres.*

SU FACILITIES:
Teviot Row: Five bars; juke boxes; snack bar; two cafeterias; restaurant; showers; games room; music room; satellite TV; shop; launderette; free showers.
King's Buildings House: KBH offers sports facilities, mature, international and postgrad students' lounge, welfare advice, a shop and a bar as well as being the largest catering outlet in the university.
Potterrow: Newly refurbished Potterrow offers a 1,200-capacity nightclub and music venue, games room and eateries is a popular lunchtime meeting place and has the biggest and busiest EUSA shop.
The Pleasance: Bar; Societies Centre; catering; technical equipment hire; theatre (cap 270); meeting/function rooms.
Also: Print service; five shops; NatWest and Bank of Scotland cashpoints; library; photo booths; pool tables; games and vending machines; TV lounges; meeting rooms; launderettes.

CLUBS (NON SPORTING):
A-ha Revival; American; Asylum & Immigration Bill; Celtic Supporters; Chess; Children's Holiday Venture; Chinese Cultural; Cyborg; Duke of Edinburgh Award; European; Fabian; Folk Song; Football Supporters; Footlights (revue); Friends of Edinburgh Direct Aid; Games & Recreational; GEAS (roleplaying); Goth & Rock; Hearts Supporters; Hellenic; Help (Scotland); Highland; Hispanic; Huggabugga Jaffa Cake Appreciation; Hungarian; Indonesian; Japanese; Jazz Orchestra; Juggling; Korean; Malaysian Students; Methodist; Mooting; Motorcycle; New Philosophy; New Scotland Country Dance; Norwegian Students; Opera; Perfidious Albion; Pie Eaters; Piping; Poetry; Politics; Rajayoga Meditation; Red Cross; Reel; Renaissance

Singers; Revelation; Savoy Opera; Scottish Militant; Sign Language; Singaporean; SNP; Sri Chimnoy; Student Action for Refugees; Student Christian Movement; Suave; Tibet Support; Turf; UNICEF; Untapped Talent; Up the Kilt Productions; Virtual Trading & Investment; Wargames; Water of Life (whisky appreciation); Wind Ensemble; Wind (kiteflying); Wine; Yoga.

OTHER ORGANISATIONS:

EUSA produces a number of *excellent* publications including the weekly 'Hype' and many student society magazines. Among Edinburgh's other award-winning media are 'Student' (independent newspaper) and Fresh Air FM (24 hours, 2 months a year). Another couple of acronyms to learn: ESCA, the charities appeal which, despite the more reserved name, is *wackier* than many of the wildest rags and SCAG (the Student Community Action Group), the high-profile local help organisation. Other groups include 'Settlement', a help group that, together with members of the community, provides for the deprived and disadvantaged in the local area. The Debates Committee is a *popular* talk shop and much more than just another club.

RELIGIOUS:

There is a chaplaincy centre staffed by Anglican, Church of Scotland, Methodist and Catholic chaplains. Local worship shops include all manner of churches as well as facilities for Sikhs and Jews. A gospel choir, Revelation, has been formed.

PAID WORK:

The Uni/Union-run Student Employment Service helps with part-time and vacation work with students making up many of the union employees and there's always plenty of work around the Festivals for those who get in early enough.

SPORTS

• Recent successes: archery, ladies rugby, skiing, weightlifting
Edinburgh students are stronger at cultural pursuits than sporting ones, but that isn't to say they don't have facilities or successes. It's just that with all the other distractions, sport isn't quite the collective obsession to be found in some other universities.

SPORTS FACILITIES:

The University has outdoor facilities at Peffermill Sports Ground (including 25 acres of playing fields and three clay tennis courts), the playing fields include a floodlit synthetic grass pitch, tennis courts and golfing facilities. At the Uni Sports Centre (10 minutes from Pollock Halls) there's a sports hall, a small hall, fitness room, 10 squash courts, table tennis studios, a combat salle, a rifle and archery range. Further outdoor amenities at the Firbush Point Field Centre, 80 miles from Edinburgh, including sailing, canoeing, skiing and hills to walk. The city has many golf courses, a large swimming pool, ice rink and the Meadowbank Stadium. 50% of the city is made up of parks and open spaces (including Queen's Park and Arthur's Seat).

SPORTING CLUBS:

Angling; Boat; Boxing; Curling; Hare & Hounds; Hot Air Balloon; IMSA; K Shotokan; K Shotokai; Korfball; Lacrosse; Motorsport; Mountaineering; RDVAC; Rifle; Shinty; Sky Diving; Table Tennis; Ultimate Frisbee; Weightlifting; Wind Surfing.

ATTRACTIONS:

Hearts and Hibs FCs' home turfs are in Edinburgh and there's Murrayfield rugby, athletics at Meadowbank and speedway.

ACCOMMODATION

IN COLLEGE:
- Catered: 15% • Cost: £84-97 (30wks)
- Self-catering: 28% • Cost: £52-67 (including heating) (30-50wks)

Availability: It's almost exclusively 1st years who live in the *popular modern catered rabbit-warren-like Pollock Halls of Residence which house 1,794 students in 10 halls, ½ mile from the city centre.* The half of 1st years who can't get into Pollock are spread between student houses, which accommodate nine to 77 students each, and the University-owned flats. Only 1% have to share. There's room for about 20% of students from other years, particularly in the flats, but also in Mylne's Court, a *beautiful* old building on The Royal Mile housing 230 students, mainly postgrads and 2nd years. Most of the older halls have been refurbished.

Car parking: Because so much of Edinburgh's residential housing is in tenements, there is a tremendous parking problem all round the city. Limited permits are available for £39 a year at Pollock Halls or £15 at the King's Buildings.

EXTERNALLY:
- Ave rent: £55

Availability: *Living out presents as many options as living in. Most students rent flats (some are very good value), but some end up* (for at least part of a year) in lodgings with a live-in landlord/lady who cooks and cleans. This can be like a home from home, but more usually, rather than making students homesick, it makes them sick of home. Talking of home, many students are local and live with their parents and/or families. *With all these options, most of the year, it's not too difficult to find somewhere, until September when everybody else is looking or August when landlords with any sense don't want to know, because all their properties are on profitable short-term rents to Festival-goers.* Students with nous can get a piece of this action themselves: avoid the crush by renting from the beginning of the summer (ensuring subletting's allowed). Then get some am dram group doing a show in the Fringe Festival to pay £50 per person per week, cram in a cast of 20, and suddenly student debt is a thing of the past. *The best places are Marchmont, Bruntsfield and Newington, particularly student areas, close to the centre with high quality housing. Niddrie, Pilton and Wester Hailes are a bit rough.*

Housing help: The four full-time staff of the Accommodation Service, apart from allocating and managing University-run properties, keep a register of approved flats and lodgings, help negotiate contracts and provide general advice.

WELFARE

SERVICES:
- Creche • Nightline • Equal Opportunities Officer
- Self-defence classes

EUSA's Advice Place operates as a drop-in centre providing help of a high standard. The University, however, does have some services of its own, including the Legal Dispensary, the Student Counselling Service, which employs two full- and six part-time counsellors, and the Student Health Centre, which has six doctors, as well as nurses, a psychologist, physiotherapist, pharmacist and a family planning unit. Edinburgh itself has a large gay and lesbian community, *which, although it doesn't necessarily make coming out any easier, means there's more fun to be had for those who have.*

Disabled: *The access is inherently restricted by the nature of the many old buildings,* but the University has a disability office and a Special Needs committee who, if informed early enough, will do what they can to meet the needs of individuals, even to the point of making some structural changes to buildings. Many lecture theatres have audio loops. There is a Dyslexia Study Adviser.

FINANCE:
- Access fund: £997,940 • Successful applications: 995

EUSA can offer a small crisis loan (up to £100) on a 6-month repayment scheme and limited grants are available from the University Common Bursaries Fund. There are also 50 bursaries of £1,000 each per year as well as 25 open bursaries.

Edinburgh College of Art
see Heriot-Watt University

University of Essex

University of Essex, Wivenhoe Park, Colchester, CO4 3SQ.
Tel: (01206) 873666. Fax: (01206) 873423.
E-mail: admit@essex.ac.uk
Essex University Student Union, Wivenhoe Park, Colchester, CO4 3SQ.
Tel: (01206) 863211. Fax: (01206) 870915.
E-mail: su@essex.ac.uk

GENERAL

Forget the Essex Girl jokes – the University isn't in the famously maligned part of Essex, *full of parked Ford Capris and peroxide blondes.* It's 2½ miles from Colchester, a thoroughly modern Roman town, a bit further from London. It's the smallest fully fledged university in England and Wales according to student numbers, but it's set amidst three large lakes in 200 acres of *scenic* parkland designed to hold a much larger institution – the University slowed its ambitious expansion a few years after it was founded. It has remnants of the big plans, though: the campus contains shops, eating places and facilities *which betray the grander designs for the place.* They're all arranged in a *confusing* series of interlinked courtyards and modern concrete buildings, flanked by towering multi-storey residential blocks.

```
The Guild Buildings at Liverpool house
Europe's largest toilet complex.
```

Essex

Sex ratio(M:F): 52%:48%	Founded: 1964
Full time u'grads: 4,600	Part time: 0
Postgrads: 1,395	Non-degree: 0
Ave course: 3yrs	Ethnic: 16%
Private school: n/a	Flunk rate: 17%
Mature students: 20%	Overseas students: 32%
Disabled students: n/a	

ATMOSPHERE:
Being such a small university, based in a big campus (if you include the parkland), there's quite a sense of community. This can either be seen as friendly solidarity or as busy-body nosiness, close-knit groups or cliques. Whatever, most of the atmosphere is tightly focused on the bars. Less gregarious students can have a hard time and relations with the locals aren't particularly warm, particularly the large contingent from the nearby barracks.

COLCHESTER:
• Population: 88,847 • London: 40 miles • Ipswich: 16 miles
Like we said, Colchester is a thoroughly modern Roman town – that is to say, the Romans started the place, although they went home some time ago. It's the oldest recorded town in the country – *and the town plan hasn't been greatly changed since.* But, as when all the bits of a car have been replaced so many times that you have a new car, Colchester has established many modern pockets: shopping centres and light industry, busy roads and modern architecture and now a leisure centre. There are still many *pretty* parts, old houses and ancient buildings, not least the original Roman Wall and the castle (built by William the Conqueror) which houses the town's Museum. *The area's most recent claims to fame, ex-Mods/reborn slackers Blur, have left less of an impression on the town.*

TRAVEL:
Trains: The nearest mainline station to the campus is Colchester, 3 miles away (there are 2 other stations in town). Direct services run into London Liverpool Street (£8.70). Connections via London are possible all over the country including Birmingham, Bristol and Edinburgh.
Coaches: National Express services to London (£6.75), Birmingham (£16.75) and more.
Car: Colchester is visited by the A120, A12, A133, and A604.
Air: Stansted International is 32 miles west on the A120.
Ferries: To the continent from Harwich and Felixstowe, 16 miles away.
Hitching: *The slip roads of the A12 are the best bet, but trying to get a lift in Essex is basically the same as waving a thumb at passing cars.*
Local: *Buses are expensive* (£1 return to the town centre), *but they are reliable and* they tour the local villages *which is useful for those living there.*
Taxis: Some firms are less expensive than others, *but Push wouldn't use the word 'cheap' for any of them.* From £4 from the station to the campus.
Bicycles: There's a cycle network around Colchester. *Essex is quite flat, which is nice, but means there are no big hills to fly down.*

CAREER PROSPECTS:
- Careers Service • No of staff: 3 full/3 part
- Unemployed after 6mths: 3%

SPECIAL FEATURES:
- There are a lot of ducks on the three lakes and around the campus there are more rabbits than students. Each year, much to the distress of the students, the University carries out a bunny cull.

FAMOUS ALUMNI:
Oscar Arias (former President of Costa Rica & Nobel Prize winner); Tony Banks (Genesis); John Bercow MP, Virginia Bottomley MP (Con); Ivor Dembina (comedian); Brian Hanrahan (BBC reporter); Jane Heptonstall (actress); Ben Okri (writer, Booker Prize winner); Chandra Sonic (Asian Dub Foundation).

FURTHER INFO:
Prospectuses for undergrads and postgrads; video and website (www.essex.ac.uk), SU website planned.

ACADEMIC

Essex offers *flexible* degree courses and it is possible to change courses at the end of the first year. They've just introduced part-time degrees, which take 6 years rather than 3-4 for the full-timers.

staff/student ratio: 1:16
Range of points required for entrance: 320-120
Percentage accepted through clearing: 15%
Number of terms/semesters: 3
Length of terms/semesters: 10 wks
Research: 5

LIBRARIES:
- Books: 820,000 • Study places: 1,000

The Albert Sloman Library has a Paternoster lift, just step on and step off while the open lift keeps moving.

COMPUTERS:
- Computer workstations: 260

If you ever get bored of the library lift you can use the computer terminals in the library and in 9 departmental libraries. However, *access is not always easy.*

ENTERTAINMENT

THE TOWN:
- Price of a pint of beer: £1.90 • Glass of wine: £1.40

Cinemas: The Odeon shows mainstream films and St Mary's Arts Centre sometimes features more arty flicks.
Theatres: The Mercury Theatre hosts a rep company.
Pubs: *Students more usually stick to their own bars or the pubs close by, since the local pubs are full of soldiers. A few Pushplugs: The Lamb (noisy); The Flag; Hole in the Wall; Wig & Pen; Horse & Groom (aka the Doom & Gloom).*
Clubs/discos: *The real stiletto-heeled, mini-skirted cattle markets are in Southend (28 miles away) and Chelmsford (24 miles). Colchester's*

clubs are slower lane, more down-to-earth, but still tacky. Students often don't bother. Terrace (student DJs but no student groovers, sadly); Hippodrome (large, crowded, £5); Club Valentino's (small, a bit Costa Del Sol, £2); L'Aristo's (expensive) are all Sharon Central. The housier King's Club earns a Pushplug out of desperation.
Music venues: The Hippodrome has naff PAs. Better stick to Oliver Twist (blues and rock), Arts Centre (indie, reggae), Charterhall (various). Better still, stick to London.
Eating out: Colchester has restaurants of every description – *worth checking out those with student discounts* – and junk yards of fast food. Pushplugs: Food on the Hill (veggie); Jade Garden (cheap Chinese); Chicago's; Rose & Crown for parental purchasing; Playhouse, Wig & Pen (cheap pub grub); Sloppy Joe's (Tex-Mex). Some kebab shops and the like are open till 4am.

UNIVERSITY:
• Price of a pint of beer: £1.25 • Glass of wine: £1.00
Bars: (4) The SU's Main Bar is, *unsurprisingly, the chief quaffing spot*, holding 1,000 thirsty people when it's chocka. *The Level 2 bar is a bit posh and cocktaily for an SU boozer* although the Underground Bar is now open twice weekly.
Theatres: The University is *well-equipped* and the Lakeside Theatre has many visits from national companies. Student shows are also *enthusiastically* produced.
Cinemas: 3 mainstream films a week.
Clubs/discos: The main, charty club night is Tonic on Fridays (£3) and there are other, less regular dance events, including recent visits from the likes of Digweed, Judge Jules and Danny Rampling.
Music venues: Underground (850) is the main live venue but there are also frequent band nights in the bar and the Party Room. Recent giggers include Mansun, Shed Seven and Embrace. The various student music societies put on concerts and there is a weekly classical music concert.
Food: *The meals in the Hexagon restaurant and the snacks in the Blue's Cafe and the Top Bar are beyond the pockets of many students*, who tend to stock up on eats in the Main Bar.
Others: The University has a purpose-built exhibition gallery. Loads of balls organised by societies, with a main one in the summer.

SOCIAL & POLITICAL

UNIVERSITY OF ESSEX STUDENTS' UNION (UESU):
• 5 sabbaticals • Turnout at last ballot: 25% • NUS member
Essex had a radical reputation as a red-hot hot-bed, then became known for a few blue-eyed Thatcherites, but the students are somewhat more apathetic nowadays, although UESU was a major player in the campaign against tuition fees.

SU FACILITIES:
In SU Building: 2 bars; 5 minibuses for hire; printing services; general shop; Lloyds/NatWest cashpoint; Endsleigh Insurance office; function room (cap 100); TV room; 3 meeting rooms; and a *bloody* Lottery terminal. On campus, there is another general shop, jointly run with the University to challenge the *huge* Tesco's at the bottom of the hill.

CLUBS (NON SPORTING):
1960s; Ballroom Dancing; Buddhist; Comedy Workshop; Choir; Chinese; Christian; Classical; Cocktail; Cypriot; DiscWorld Companions; DJ; Fifth Monarchists; Film Society; Gigsoc; Goth;

Gregsoc; Hellenic; Human Rights; Italian; Japan; Jungle; Latin American; Magic Gathering; Malaysian; Mexican; Musoc; Nigerian; Poetry; Silly; Soul; Star Trek; Stop the Fees; Turkish; Wine & Beer.

OTHER ORGANISATIONS:
The student media include the SU's newspaper 'Parklife' and URE (University Radio Essex), which broadcasts 24 hours a day. ESCA, the Community Action group, started up last year.

RELIGIOUS:
- 2 chaplains (RC, CofE)

There is a worship area in the University chaplaincy centre for use by all religions. During term, there are Anglican services each Sunday and Mass 3 times a week. The Islamic Society organises a prayer schedule and has a deep freeze with Halal meat. A kosher kitchen supplies the general shop.

PAID WORK:
The SU has a policy of giving students paid work in shops and bars.

SPORTS

- Recent successes: rugby, judo

As with many other things, the University has sports facilities that were intended for somewhere much larger. But who's complaining? The number of students means that the University is less likely to boast as many bionic men and women as larger colleges, but it still holds its own (and sometimes other people's) in competitions, while maintaining a good overall level of participation.

SPORTS FACILITIES:
A new purpose-built sports science laboratory currently takes pride of place while 40 acres of the parkland are used for sports including: playing fields; a grass athletics track; a floodlit synthetic sports pitch; 3 all-weather tennis courts; 4 new squash courts; new fitness room; archery range; an exercise circuit ('the Squirrel Run'); the only 18-hole frisbee golf course in the country; and, of course, the 3 lakes. Also a gym and sports hall including 6 badminton courts, another tennis court, a climbing wall (largest in the south-east), 6 squash courts (4 elsewhere on campus), weights and other indoor sports facilities. Colchester also provides swimming pools and a roller rink.

SPORTING CLUBS:
Canoeing; Jazz Dance; Kickboxing; Korfball; Step Aerobics; TenPin Bowling; Trampolining; Yoga.

ATTRACTIONS:
Colchester United is the local football team, also Essex County Cricket Club.

ACCOMMODATION

IN COLLEGE:
- Self-catering: 65%   • Cost: £36-57 (39wks)

Availability: There are 6 tower blocks on campus which are the highest brick buildings in the whole of Essex. *Apparently,* the architect was a bit *eccentric* and based the campus design on an Italian hill town. Also 934 rooms in the low level court and houses, 351 places in off-campus halls and flats and 3 houses off-campus for overseas postgrads. *Not a bad selection, meaning that the University is able to guarantee accommodation* (usually on the campus) to all 1st years who apply in time and 60% of all other students too. All rooms are single, mostly in shared flats for between 4 and 6 students. *Many are quite spacious and well-equipped, but the room numbering system is quite incomprehensible.* Most flats are mixed, although some single-sex flats are available. No loud music is allowed after midnight. The 39-week rentals have the advantage that students aren't required to move their lives out of their rooms at the end of every term, but on the down side, it stretches the cost through the two short vacations.

Car parking: Automotive students living on or near campus have to pay and display.

EXTERNALLY:
• Ave rent: £40

Availability: The University runs a contract housing scheme where it rents from private landlords and then sublets to students on favourable terms. In this way it currently provides space for 444 students. But anyway, finding suitable accommodation in Colchester, Wivenhoe or other surrounding villages presents few problems. Students should avoid Lexden (too close to the barracks) and Tollgate is just too far. If living out, a car is handy, but the cost of parking should be brought into the reckoning.

Housing help: The University Accommodation Office, apart from running the contract housing scheme and providing general help, approves some houses and flats and can fix students up in lodgings (with live-in landlord/lady).

WELFARE

SERVICES:
• Day nursery • Nightline • Mature SA
• Lesbian, Gay & Bisexual Society • Overseas SA
• Postgrad SA • Minibus • Women's Officer

The SU Advice Centre provides help and referral for students with all manner of difficulties. It is staffed by student volunteers, trained and supported by professional staff. The University has a welfare advisor in the Student Support Office and the Health Centre provides 1 full- and 2 part-time counsellors, 3 nurses, 5 doctors, 2 physiotherapists and an administrator. *In general, the welfare provision is extensive and well-structured at every level.* There is both a University-run nursery and a Union-run creche. *A nursery is for toddlers and a creche is for babies. Both can get smelly.*

Disabled: There are special provisions and representative channels for students with all forms of special needs, including a Braille map of the campus, induction loops in lecture theatres and adapted housing for wheelchair users in the houses on campus. *Accessibility and provisions are generally among the best in the country.* Colchester Council recently gave the University an award by way of recognition.

FINANCE:
Hardship funds are available from the Student Support Office and the SU provides loans.

Essex IHE

see Anglia Polytechnic University

University of Exeter

(1) University of Exeter, Northcote House, The Queen's Drive, Exeter, EX4 4QJ. Tel: (01392) 263263. Fax: (01392) 263108.
E-mail: registry@exeter.ac.uk
Guild of Students, Exeter University, Devonshire House, Stocker Road, Exeter, EX4 4PZ. Tel: (01392) 263540. Fax: (01392) 263531.
(2) Camborne School of Mines, Pool, Redruth, Cornwall, TR15 3SE. Tel: (01209) 714866. Fax: (01209) 716977.

GENERAL

The River Exe flows out into the English Channel in a wide estuary with the golden, sandy beaches of south Devon all round. The river springs inland amidst the windy wilds of Exmoor, in the heart of the West Country 9 miles from the coast. And where the river starts to widen, there's Exeter, not a big city, but a *pretty* one. Although the city was almost wiped out by a single night's bombing in World War II, the Luftwaffe didn't manage to destroy any major landmarks, such as the ancient cathedral (built in 1050), the city walls (built by the Romans) or the Guild Hall. Among the other things not destroyed by bombing was the University – mainly because it wasn't built until 1955. Some of the University's buildings date from the last century though, but most were built in the 50s and 60s and are *low-rise blocks* in light stone. The University is about a mile from the city centre in a particularly hilly and green area. *The setting is stunning, perfect for both town and country*, with two streams and ponds dotted about the campus. There are two other sites: St Luke's, 1½ miles away, is the School of Education; and the Camborne School of Mines in Redruth, Cornwall, is now part of the University.

Sex ratio(M:F): 48%:52%
Full time u'grads: 7,126
Postgrads: 3,156
Ave course: 3yrs
Private school: n/a
Mature students: 9.9%
Disabled students: 3%

Founded: 1955
Part time: 2,571
Non-degree: 1,144
Ethnic: 2%
Flunk rate: 6.5%
Overseas students: 11%

ATMOSPHERE:
Exeter has a reputation for attracting rich kids who couldn't make it to Oxbridge. As with most reputations this is probably overstating things but there is a higher-than-average concentration of GTis and double-barrelled names. Despite this, it's a very friendly place and there are plenty of real people as well. The gorgeous setting is also more than enough compensation for the odd bit of social friction.
Students are tolerated by the local populace (maybe because they

spend so much) rather than welcomed with open arms. The local endearment 'm'lover' isn't as romantic as it sounds.

THE SITES:
St Luke's: (1,426 students – education, sport sciences) Although it's only 1½ miles from the main campus, opposite the police station, this site feels a bit like a separate institution and there's a constant battle to include the 'Lukies' in Guild activities, though it does have a community spirit all of its own. St Luke's Hall has housing for 209 students.
Camborne School of Mines: (231 students) Camborne covers courses like geology, engineering and so on. It's 100 miles from Exeter in the *pretty* countryside near Camborne and Redruth and teaches 350 students in purpose-built blocks *thrown up* in the mid 70s. *The students have no practical connection with Exeter or the University's main site.* They have their own Student Club with a bar and *limited* social and sporting facilities, although the Guild provides welfare and counselling services. There is accommodation for 65 students and plenty of rented places nearby.

EXETER:
- Population: 101,100 • London: 170miles
- Bristol: 69miles • Plymouth: 46miles

Exeter is *quaint and quiet* and, according to the EC, has the highest quality of life of any English city. In part, this must be due to the *ample* selection of high street shops, supermarkets and banks, and to the *numerous wholesome cafes and cute little hippy-dippy shops run by people who came to Glastonbury 25 years ago and haven't moved far away.* Tourist attractions include the ancient cathedral, the historic Guild Hall and various museums, including the Royal Albert Museum and Art Gallery, with its *amusing* giraffe.

TRAVEL:
Trains: Exeter St Davids Station is ½ mile from the University. There are direct lines to London (£26.40), Bristol (£10.90), Birmingham (£30.35) and connections all over.
Buses: National Express services all over the country, include London (£22), Birmingham (£22.50) and more.
Car: Exeter is at the southern end of the M5, or there's the A30, A377 and A38.
Air: Exeter Airport (6 miles) offers inland and European flights.
Hitching: *The M5 is good for heading north.*
Local: *Local buses are reliable and quite comprehensive, but not cheap. The same can be said of local trains – there are four stations around the city, but they're not very usefully placed.*
Taxis: *Numerous, reliable and relatively cheap.*
Bicycles: *The city's not the flattest around and the University's in the hilly part, but students with legs like steam pistons find bikes useful.*

CAREER PROSPECTS:
- Careers Service • No of staff: 3 full-time
- Unemployed after 6mths: 3%

FAMOUS ALUMNI:
Toby Amies (MTV VJ); Emma B (radio 1 presenter); Anastasia Cooke (BBC presenter); Paul Downton, Richard Ellison (England cricketers); Richard Hill (former England rugby captain); J.K. Rowling (Harry Potter creator); Paul Jackson (TV producer/bigshot); Juliet Morris (TV presenter); Stewart Purvis (ITN chief exec); Sam Smith (tennis player); David Sole (former Scotland rugby captain); Thom Yorke (Radiohead).

FURTHER INFO:
Prospectuses for undergrads, postgrads; websites (www.exeter.ac.uk and www.guildex.ac); video and alternative prospectus from Guild (£1.50). Free factfile from the registry.

ACADEMIC

staff/student ratio: 1:18
Range of points required for entrance: 320-220
Percentage accepted through clearing: 10%
Number of terms/semesters: 3
Length of terms/semesters: 10 wks
Research: 4.3

LIBRARIES:
• Books: 1,000,000 • Study places: 1,733
The main library (9am to 10pm) now has 690 places and the rest are in the departmental libraries.

COMPUTERS:
• Computer workstations: 1,050
Five computer rooms have 24-hour access, with a special emphasis on computers in Arts departments (aka Project Pallas).

ENTERTAINMENT

THE CITY:
• Price of a pint of beer: £1.70 • Glass of wine: £1.80
Cinemas: There's a three-screen Odeon and the *arty* Picture House.
Theatres: The Northcott on campus is the main regional theatre, but the Barnfield and the Arts Centre *encourage less commercial fare*.
Pubs: *Pushplugs: Victoria Inn; Jolly Porter; Mount Radford (for Lukies); Double Locks (a bit far, but worth it in summer); Black Horse (sportsnights); Bowling Green (live music); Walkabout Inn (Aussie theme pub). Avoid the Turk's Head (it's a Royal Marines pub).*
Clubs/discos: Most clubs, such as Warehouse and Volts, are mainstream; *Pushplugs: Rococco's; The Cavern and Timepiece (eclectic indie).*
Music venues: West Point is a big venue and the University is also a main venue for the town, but again The Cavern provides a *more intimate, less mainstream alternative*.
Food: *Not a huge selection of cheap eats but you won't starve either. Late night food can be hard to come by unless you're near a 24-hour garage. Pushplugs: Waterfront (vast, good value pizzas); Mad Meg's (supposedly haunted by a medieval cook); Herbies (veggie); House of Wong; Double Locks (pub lunches by the river).*
Others: Exeter Arts Centre has reopened after a £2.4 million re-fit. Bowling alley. *Exeter shuts down when the pubs close.*

UNIVERSITY:
• Price of a pint of beer: £1.30 • Glass of wine: £1.40
Bars: The Ram is *hugely popular* throughout the day. There are two Union bars and four non-Union ones. The Lemon Grove (Lemmy) has a varied programme of events including big screen sport and games evenings (jolly good).

Theatres: Northcott Theatre (cap 433) is based on campus and student companies put on occasional productions there, as well as jaunts to Edinburgh and other parts of the country.
Cinema: CinSoc shows three films a week, mostly mainstream.
Clubs/discos/music venues: The Lemon Grove (cap 750) hosts varied club nights twice a week. Live sounds *pound* there and in the Great Hall (cap 1,700), which doesn't actually belong to the Guild, but is regularly borrowed from the University and is one of the biggest venues in the South West. Recent bands: Lightning Seeds, Jools Holland; The Levellers; Reef; James; Leftfield; Jimmy Somerville; Fun Lovin Criminals.
Cabaret: Occasional comic stops, past offenders being Harry Hill, Lee Hurst and Paul Merton.
Food: The Refectory opens for lunch and dinner and the *good-value* Coffee Bar *is popular all day.* The Ram bar does a *good* freshly-cooked food and snacks in the evenings and there's even an on-campus pizza delivery service.
Others: *According to the SU 'we're big on balls', the high spot being the Summer do.*

SOCIAL & POLITICAL

UNIVERSITY OF EXETER GUILD OF STUDENTS:
• 7 sabbaticals • Turnout at last ballot: 20% • NUS member
If pushed, many students would describe themselves as more right-wing than their contemporaries elsewhere but nobody can be bothered to push them, so let's put that one down as 'don't know', shall we? They recently took a stalwart stand against tuition fees though, which almost qualifies as political activity. The Guild's facilities are based in Devonshire House, shared with various University activities

SU FACILITIES:
Advice centre; two bars; a shop; creche; travel agency; coffee shop; launderette; second-hand bookshop.

CLUBS (NON SPORTING):
Arts & Crafts; Ballroom Dancing; Change Ringing; Circus Skills; Cocktail; Debates; Folk Dance; Gilbert & Sullivan; Malaysian; Out of Doors; ProLife; Turkish; Welsh; Wine; XTV; Yoga.

OTHER ORGANISATIONS:
There's a newspaper, 'Exeposé', the XTV station broadcasting to the bars, a great website (www.guild.ac.uk) and an *excellent* award-winning radio station. There is also a charity RAG (which raises loads) and a major league Community Action organisation, which manages 36,000 hours of voluntary work a year, including work with kids' camps. EXTRA is the Guild's training team, and offers a programme of CV-enhancing so-called key skills training to all students and to those involved in running socs, clubs and so on.

'Political Correctness is a creatures of silly women and people badly educated at polytechnics as universities - Brian Sewell, art critic.

RELIGIOUS:
Anglicans and Catholics don't have to leave the campus to find a place to bow their heads and there are numerous chaplains too for most Christian denominations as well as a Muslim prayer room. The town churches also keeps the faithful prayerful and there's an Anglican Cathedral.

PAID WORK:
A few local jobs for students in the tourist trade and some bar and clerical work in the Guild. Also an on-line bulletin board has just been set up and is available at www.ex.ac.uk/jobsurfing

- <u>Recent successes: athletics, football and across the board</u>
Exeter has an excellent sporting reputation and facilities. *Athletics and football.*

SPORTS FACILITIES:
Two all-weather pitches; 2 gyms (at St Luke's); climbing wall; indoor cricket nets; 8 squash courts; a multigym; indoor swimming pool (at St Luke's); a *beezer* outdoor swimming pool at the main site. *The sea and moors are also assets.* Exeter has sports bursaries for the gamesomely gifted.

SPORTING CLUBS:
Aikido; American Football; Boardsailing; Boat (rowing); Fives; Gliding; Golf; Jiu Jitsu; Kendo; Kuk Soo Woon; Lacrosse; Nin Jitsu; Rifle; Sailing; Ski Racing; Snooker; Speleology (caving); Sport Parachute; Street Hockey; Surf; Table Tennis; Ultimate Frisbee; Waterpolo; Weightlifting; Windsurfing.

ATTRACTIONS:
Exeter FC is the local footy team and there are rugby and hockey outfits as well. The races are also popular round here – horses at Newton Abbott, speedway, dogs and people in town.

IN COLLEGE:
- <u>Catered: 26%</u> • Cost: £82.50-99.80 (31wks)
- <u>Self-catering: 30%</u> • Cost: £42.90-77.60 (34-50wks)

Availability: All 1st years are guaranteed a place in University accommodation if they want it and there's still space for over half the students from other years. The 1st years live in the catered halls, which, with the exception of St Luke's Hall (which has housing for

> 'If I was called upon to mention the prettiest corner of the world, I should draw athoughtful sigh and point the way to the gardens of Trinity Hall.' - Henry James.

209 students), are right next to the campus and vary in style from 19th-century buildings to new *very plush* halls. 10% of 1st years have to share. Most students who live in after their 1st year are housed in the self-catering flats, including a new development near St Davids Station. *Prices are steep but standards, especially in the newer accommodation, are very high.* There are also 142 places in a head tenancy system.

Car parking: Permit parking is only available for students living more than 1½ miles from campus or those with a medical excuse.

EXTERNALLY:
- Ave rent: £47

Availability: Finding private accommodation in Exeter doesn't present a major problem. Some car-owners travel quite a way into the countryside *(but find beautiful country homes there)*. The best places are St James and Pennsylvania near the campus and Newtown nearer the St Luke's site.

Housing help: The Accommodation Office keeps a list of lodgings.

WELFARE

SERVICES:
- Creche • Nightline • Lesbian & Gay Society • Mature SA
- Overseas SA • Postgrad SA • Minibus • Women's Officer

The Guild has a Student Advice Centre with a Welfare Officer who helps with all sorts of upsets and an Education Officer. Personal tutors are assigned to each student and there are two full- and three part-time counsellors. *For a game of doctors and nurses, join the staff of the health centre.*

Disabled: *Wheelchair access is not good – the hilly campus doesn't help.* Bearing that in mind, there are officers for the disabled and some halls/houses have adapted facilities. Provisions are pretty good for students with sight or hearing problems.

FINANCE:
- Access fund: £295,000 • Successful applications: 990

There are sports scholarships and bursaries of £1,000 for some education courses.

The murals in the Sivell's Bar at Aberdeen University were originally nudes, but they were thought a bit racy for the 1930s, so clothes were added.

George's Hospital see St George's Hospital Medical School, London

University of Glamorgan

Glasgow Univesity

Glasgow Caledonian University

Glasgow Poly see Glasgow Caledonian University

Gloucester see Cheltenham & Gloucester College of Higher Education

Goldsmiths College, London

Gordon University see Robert Gordon University

University of Greenwich

Guildhall see London Guildhall University

Guy's Hospital see King's College, London

George's Hospital

see St George's Hospital Medical School, London

University of Glamorgan

- *Formerly Polytechnic of Wales*

University of Glamorgan, Treforest, Pontypridd, Mid Glamorgan, CF37 1DL. Tel: 0800 716 925. Fax: (01443) 480558.
E-mail: enquiries@glam.ac.uk
University of Glamorgan Union, Forest Grove, Treforest, Pontypridd, Mid Glamorgan, CF37 1UF. Tel: (01443) 408227.
Fax: (01443) 491589.

GENERAL

In South Wales, up the Taff Valley from Cardiff, is the market town of Pontypridd. A mile away is the slate and stone village of Treforest and overlooking it on a steep hillside are the 70 acres of the University of Glamorgan campus. It's a mixture of building styles with *a few attempts to prettify the place,* such as piazza steps and seating areas. *Students complain that money is being spent on making the place more 'attractive' when it could be better spent elsewhere, like replacing some of the staff who've left.* The main attraction isn't the University itself, but the extraordinary views it affords over the valley, especially when it's not raining. Those who are struck with a desire to listen to Tom Jones singing 'Green Green Grass of Home' will be forgiven.

Sex ratio(M:F): 50%:50%
Full time u'grads: 9,915
Postgrads: 632
Ave course: 4yrs
Private school: n/a
Mature students: 37%
Disabled students: n/a

Founded: 1913
Part time: 5,501
Non-degree: 6,846
Ethnic: 15%
Flunk rate: 27.2%
Overseas students: 10%

ATMOSPHERE:
It's a fairly self-contained place and the high proportion of business and technology students makes for a pretty down-to-earth environment. The only real social outlet is sport, but amongst students there's a friendly, almost family atmosphere, especially because relations with the locals aren't too wonderful. This can be reassuring to nervous newcomers, but it does mean everybody knows who you copped off with last night. It's a weekend ghost-town, though.

PONTYPRIDD:
- Population: 35,000 • London: 145miles • Cardiff: 15miles
- Birmingham: 90miles

There are 3 towns to consider: (1) Treforest. Corner shop, post office, train station. *Consider it considered.* (2) Pontypridd (pronounced 'Pontipreeth'), which is, of course, Welsh for 'the bridge near the earthen cottage', and is familiarly known as 'Ponty'. It's an old town, built mainly on the money of local coal mining in the last century *which has now been spent, leaving a depressed, working-class community.* Although it's still small, Ponty's got enough amenities for daily needs: shops, supermarket, book shops, banks, market and a local history museum for the sizeable tourist trade. And (3) Cardiff. Only 20 minutes away by train. See Cardiff, University of Wales.

TRAVEL:
Trains: From Treforest station, only 400 yards from the campus, trains go every 20 minutes to Cardiff (£1.60). Unfortunately the last return train is just after 10pm. London (£24.60), Swansea (£8.80), Manchester (£26.20).
Coaches: National Express to London (£16.00). *Cardiff is a better bet for getting elsewhere.*
Car: Treforest is on the A470 and about 8 miles off the M4.
Hitching: *The Welsh take pity on hitchers and once on the M4 prospects are good (except if dropped in the home counties).*
Local: There are local bus services going every 20 minutes to Ponty and every 25 minutes to Cardiff – last bus from Cardiff is at 11.30pm. A free shuttle bus within a 10-mile radius of the campus is run for students after 10.30pm.
Taxis: Cabs to Ponty work out at about £1.50.
Bicycles: The roads have hills and holes and *bike theft is a bit of a problem.*

CAREER PROSPECTS:
- Careers Service • No of staff: 8 full/2 part
- Unemployed after 6mths: 7.2%

FAMOUS ALUMNI:
Max Boyce (comedian, singer); Ian Hamer (Olympic athlete, known to sing); Nigel Davies, Jonathan Humphreys, Rupert Moon (Welsh rugby union caps, which they had to sing for first).

FURTHER INFO:
There are prospectuses for undergrads and part-timers and a website (www.glam.ac.uk/home.html).

ACADEMIC

staff/student ratio: **1:16**
Range of points required for entrance: **300-140**
Percentage accepted through clearing: **13%**
Number of terms/semesters: **3**
Length of terms/semesters: **11 wks**
Research: **2.2**

LIBRARIES
- Books: 225,000 • Study places: 808

The Learning Resources Centre contains the main library (open until 11.45pm), a bookshop, TV and sound studios and photographic darkroom. *Could do with some more books, too — indeed some students end up going to Cardiff's library.*

COMPUTERS
- Computer workstations: 1,000

Only 170 computers are available for open access, the others are available when not booked for teaching.

ENTERTAINMENT

TOWN (PONTYPRIDD):
- Price of a pint of beer: £1.90 • Glass of wine: £1.20

Entertainment in Ponty goes about as far as a drink in one of the pubs, a little music or a stroll through the very pleasant park or maybe a ramble in the hills. These limitations and the somewhat cold local shoulder mean that most students resort to the resort of Cardiff (see Cardiff, University of Wales*).*
Cinema/theatre: *The Muni Arts Centre puts on community-based shows and arty films.*
Pubs: *With a few exceptions, students tend to stick to the SU. Pushplugs: The Otley (full of photos of local boyo Tom Jones), Pick & Shovel, The Forest. Just don't act like a Student.*
Clubs/discos/music venues: *Clwb-y-bont has the Clwb phwt student night (in desperate need of vowels – please send any spares), but for anything else, go to Cardiff. Avoid Silks like a ebola-ridden corpse.*
Eating out: *Beyond the usual variants on unidentifiable meat, grease and chips, not a lot of variety, especially for veggies and health-food freaks. There's an Indian and 4 Chinese restaurants. Pushplugs: The Knot Inn; John & Maria's (Italian); Prince's Café; Pick & Shovel.*

```
Gourmet students at St Andrew's can join the
Friends of Fondue and the Tunnocks Caramel
Wafer Appreciation Society.
```

UNIVERSITY:

- Price of a pint of beer: £1.50 • Glass of wine: £1.10

Even though it's none too big, the SU building is a well-equipped, modern, yet atmospheric venue for a variety of ents, but that's about as far as the entertainment on campus goes.

Bars: (3) *The SU bars provide a cosy refuge from the sort of reception students might face in Ponty pubs.* They are the George Knox Tavern (cap 200, *Irish-esque*, named after the first principal, who happened to be teetotal), Smith's Café Bar (500, named after the late John Smith MP) and Shafts Disco Bar (500).

Theatres: 1 studio theatre. Shows often make it to the Edinburgh Fringe and the National Student Drama Festival.

Cinemas: Movies every month in Shafts.

Clubs/discos: Every night is dance night in Shafts and just about every taste is catered for.

Music venues: Shafts is also the main site for live gigs, Robbie Williams being a recent visitor. Jazz nights once a month in Smith's.

Cabaret: Once a month featuring circuit comedians such as JoJo Smith.

Food: The refectory does a range of main meals and salady things. The SU responds with a sandwich bar plus a veggie range in Smith's.

Others: Quizzes, karaokes and 4 annual balls.

SOCIAL & POLITICAL

UNIVERSITY OF GLAMORGAN UNION/ UNDEB PRIFYSGOL MORGANNWG:

- 6 sabbaticals • Turnout at last ballot: 10% • NUS member

The SU focuses most of its energies on its campaigning, especially on issues close to home, such as the University's facilities. Even this goes over the heads of most of the students. Recent meningitis scares have provoked an awareness campaign.

SU FACILITIES:

The facilities don't need much management because they're generally pretty successful and limited by the size of the SU building (although expansion is on the agenda). *Plenty of goodies*: 3 bars; cafeteria; media training centre; restaurant; customised night club/theatre; 4 minibuses for hire; travel agency; general shop (also sells new books); cashpoints; minibus; Endsleigh Insurance office; photocopier; photo and phone booths; video and vending machines; pool tables; juke box and launderette.

CLUBS (NON SPORTING):

Chinese; Ghost & Paranormal; Girl-Guides and Scouts; Hellenic; Malaysian.

OTHER ORGANISATIONS:

'Leek', the monthly independent student tabloid, *is good for a free publication*. A talking newspaper is produced for the blind. *Involvement in Rag is good*, raising money for leukaemia research and youth disability. A Community Action Group has been set up to redeem the University's image in the locality.

RELIGIOUS:

- 2 chaplains (Christian, Jewish)

In college there's an Anglican and a Catholic Chapel and a Mosque. Locally, there are churches for all flavours of Christian endeavour from Methodist to Ben & Jerry's Rainforest Crunch. For other godly grace, a trip to Cardiff is called for.

PAID WORK:
A Union-run employment service finds students jobs at open days and in college bars, but that's about your lot.

SPORTS

- Recent successes: football, karate, basketball

Everyone is very proud of the sports facilities and not without reason. The 3-storey Recreation Centre makes muscles bulge in the strangest places just looking at it. A new sports science course can only add to the influx of pec-flexers.

SPORTS FACILITIES:
30 acres of playing fields (some flood-lit); all-weather pitch; flood-lit trim trail; sports hall; 4 squash courts; climbing wall; fitness room with multigym; sauna/solarium/steam suite; 2 gyms; golf practice area; archery range; boules, bowls and croquet lawns; flood-lit tennis court; astroturf pitch. All for a £15 membership fee. And locally: mountains; caves; lakes; the River Taff among others; golf course; and in Ponty, a swimming pool.

SPORTING CLUBS:
Aerobics; Aikido; Gaelic football; Hurling; Jiu Jitsu; Mountaineering; Sub-Aqua; Women's football & rugby.

ATTRACTIONS:
Rugby union in Pontypridd.

ACCOMMODATION

IN COLLEGE:
- Catered: 1% • Cost: £78 (37wks)
- Self-catering: 9% • Cost: £35-55 (37wks)

Availability: *The new Glamorgan Court development has eased things a little, but it's still not enough – 30% of 1st years can't live in let alone other students. There are other developments on campus and 2 halls 3 miles away. CCTV is in operation. Big Brother is watching.*
Car parking: *Permits are needed although there's a lack of space around the halls. There's a car park just down the hill, which means that parking on campus doesn't present dilemmas of any epic proportion.*

EXTERNALLY:
- Ave rent: £38

Availability: *Most students try to get a place in Treforest, it being nearest the campus (Queen St is the golden prize), but inevitably many end up in Ponty which is not only further, but also not that welcoming and the houses themselves can be a bit crappy. Merthyr is worse. With a car, the surrounding villages become an alternative and it's quite useful for jaunts to Cardiff, Ponty or the surrounding hills. Parking isn't too easy in Treforest.*
Housing help: *The University Accommodation Office has 1 full-timer who offers a very friendly service, trying to set students up with approved landlords and negotiated contracts, with help from an outside consultancy.*

WELFARE

SERVICES:
• Creche • Lesbian & Gay Society •Mature SA • Overseas SA
• Postgrad SA • Minibus • Women's Officer • Self-defence classes

Both the University and the SU offer welfare provisions. In the SU, there's the Welfare sabbatical and the University employs 3 full- and 2 part-time counsellors and a number of nurses to staff the campus sick bay. Free attack alarms are provided.

Disabled: *There is a desire to do better* which has meant that the newest buildings (for example, the Union Building and Recreation Centre) have improved access and there are now ramps and toilets in most buildings. *Unfortunately, there's still been a lack of funds to do anything about the older buildings.* A special effort has been made for sight-impaired students who should find the facilities *pretty good*.

FINANCE:
• Access fund: £753,511 • Successful applications: 809

There's a specialist finance advisor in the Department of Student Services. Bursaries.

Glasgow University

Glasgow University, Glasgow, G12 8QQ. Tel: (0141) 339 8855. Fax: (0141) 330 4808.
Student Representative Council, John McIntyre Building, University of Glasgow, University Avenue, Glasgow, G12 8QQ.
Tel: (0141) 339 8541. Fax: (0141) 337 3557.
E-mail: www.enquiries@src.gla.ac.uk

GENERAL

We'll get in trouble with the Glaswegians if we describe their city as Scotland's second, so we'll just say it's the largest and the unofficial capital of the west of Scotland. It's an industrial city with a ring of tower blocks and factories around the outside, but more upmarket in the city centre with a spattering of large busy parks. It's been going through something of a mini retail boom and now boasts a new shopping centre. To the north of just such a park, 2 miles west of the city centre on Gilmorehill, is the campus of Glasgow's oldest and the UK's fourth oldest university. (Glasgow also has Strathclyde University, Glasgow Caledonian University and, a few miles out of town, Paisley University.) Here nestles the Gilmorehill Centre which offers a *state-of-the-art theatre and cinema complex to thrill you*. Some campus buildings were erected in the 50s and 60s, but many date back to when the University relocated to its present site in 1870. The older buildings of particular note include the *splendid* chapel (built in 1921), set by secluded quadrangles. The Landmark Gilbert Scott Building houses the academic centre as well as the Hunterian Museum.

Sex ratio(M:F): 44%:56%	Founded: 1451
Full time u'grads: 14,820	Part time: 3,023
Postgrads: 1,813	Non-degree: 4,440
Ave course: 4yrs	Ethnic: n/a
Private school: n/a	Flunk rate: 12.8%
Mature students: 11%	Overseas students: 8%
Disabled students: 4%	

ATMOSPHERE:
Glasgow students are almost as much people of this city as the Glaswegians. Both groups get on famously, partly because 48% of the students live at home locally and partly because the University happens to be in a formerly middle-class (now fairly déclassé) area. It'd be interesting to see how students coped in the city's rougher areas. However, we don't want to give the impression there is any pretentiousness about the students – there isn't. The University has the odd advantage of being very near the city centre while at the same time being an exclusive haven, which makes for a friendly campus community. Students make less use of the city than those at the other universities nearby.

THE OTHER SITES:
There's the **Garscube site**, at Bearsden (faculty of Veterinary Medicine), about 4 miles away.
St Andrews site (faculty of Education), about 6 miles away, but soon to be moved to the main site.
Chrichton campus (faculty of Arts), based about 70 miles from the main site with its own accommodation block, swimming pool, gym, and get this, a 9-hole golf course. There are also video links to the main campus to supplement any teaching by the on-site lecturers.

THE CITY:
• Population: 654,542 • London: 367miles • Edinburgh: 52miles
The Clyde flows out to sea from Glasgow to its Firth and towards the Isle of Arran. Inland, the city is surrounded by the rolling hills of Strathclyde. It used to be a centre for shipping and steel, *before the city dropped into a recession as deep as a saying by Confucius. With enormous effort in recent years, Glasgow has been dragging itself up by the bootstraps and has shown itself to be a thoroughly cultural, modern European city.* It was 1999's City of Architecture and Design reflecting the *magnificent* architecture in the city centre (with many buildings designed by home-grown Charles Rennie Mackintosh) and there are 35 museums and art galleries, including notably the Art Gallery & Museum in Kelvingrove Park, the Burrell Collection, the McLellan Galleries, the Tobacco Lords House and many National Trust properties. *You might expect a city of this size to have loads of shops, public amenities and stuff like that – you wouldn't be wrong.* In the under-belly of Glasgow life, especially around the East End, there is a considerable amount of drug abuse with both hard and soft drugs easily available. There is a considerable problem with related crime.

TRAVEL:
Trains: Queen's Street and Central Stations are the mainline stops and run regular services to London (£41.60), Edinburgh (£9.60), Birmingham (£32) and most other major stops.
Coaches: Services to London (£27.25), Birmingham (£28.75) and all over Scotland and beyond.

Car: *Good* connections all over the country by road, including the M74, A8/M8, A80/M80, A82, A77 and A736.
Air: Direct flights to Europe and the US, as well as shuttle links to Heathrow and Gatwick (London £69), from Glasgow Abbotsinch Airport, 8 miles from the city centre.
Hitching: *If you bus it out to the main roads, you may be okay, but it's not a thumber's paradise.*
Local: *Buses are frequent with cheap and comprehensive* fares from 45p to 90p to the city centre. The local trains are *fast and efficient*, with several stops around the city. A 10-week Zonecard covering all travel in the city costs £339.
Underground: There's an *efficient* underground system (aka the Clockwork Orange) costing 80p a trip.
Taxis: *Only worth it late at night.*
Bicycles: *Glasgow is hilly and traffic is heavy. Bikes are useful, but not essential.*

CAREER PROSPECTS:
• Careers Service • No of staff: 3 full-time
• Unemployed after 6mths: 5%
The Careers Service holds information about part-time work as well as opportunities after graduation. It also offers a temping agency for students hunting out term-time jobs.

SPECIAL FEATURES:
• The Rector (the senior student representative) used to be Ross 'Grant Mitchell' Kemp. However, the Uni forced the *meanster* to resign because of his poor attendance on campus. Now it's Ges Hempill (TV comedian).

FAMOUS ALUMNI:
William Boyd, AJ Cronin (writers); Menzies Campbell MP (Lib Dem), Donald Dewar (Scotland's late First Minister); the Delgados; James Herriot (vet and writer); Pat Kane (Hue & Cry); Joseph Lister (pioneer of antiseptics); John Logie Baird (invented TV); Anne Louise McIlroy (pioneer of women in medicine); Adam Smith (economist); John Smith (late Labour leader); James Watt (inventor).

FURTHER INFO:
Undergraduate prospectus and various handbooks from the various unions. Website (www.gla.ac.uk).

ACADEMIC

The teaching week runs from Monday to Saturday.

Staff/student ratio: 1:13
Range of points required for entrance: 340-200
Percentage accepted through clearing: 2%
Number of terms/semesters: 3
Length of terms/semesters: 10 wks
Research: 2.8

LIBRARIES:
• Books: 1,500,000 • Study places: 3,200
There are something over 50 libraries in departments around the University as well as a main library.

COMPUTERS:
- Computer workstations: 2,200

Computer facilities are excellent. The only problem seems to be that students don't know about them.

ENTERTAINMENT

THE CITY:
- Price of a pint of beer: £1.90 • Glass of wine: £1.60

Cinemas: (8) *Enough cinemas to keep eyes squared for ages, including everything from 21st century multiplexes to old-fashioned flea pits.* There are a few which specialise in *arty* flicks including the Glasgow Film Theatre.

Theatres: Take your pick from the Theatre Royal (classical repertoire, Scottish Opera), King's (mainstream and musicals), Citizens' (special offers for students), Tramway (avant-garde), Tron (studio) and any number of fringe and amateur set-ups.

Pubs: *Some of the city's best beer bars are more fun than a jelly-fight on a bouncy castle.* Pushplugs (among many others): Bon Accord (real ales); O'Neill's (Irish). Ashton Lane for Cul De Sac and Jinty McGuinty's. Don't try your luck in the East End if you're English.

Clubs/discos: *Glasgow's clubs may not be cheap but they're varied.* Many have student nights. Pushplugs: The Garage; Trash; Ark at the Tunnel (hard house); Ice at Archaos (garage/techno).

Music venues: Many local bands have made it big, often starting out at some of the *vibe-ridden venues.* Pushplugs: Barrowlands, King Tut's Wah Wah Hut, The Garage (all indie hang-outs) and the vast SECC.

Eating out: Glasgow has plenty of restaurants but *Ainsley Harriott wouldn't get hyperactive over the ones that students can afford.* Pub lunches offer the best value. Pushplugs: Maw Broom's (traditional Scottish); Fire Station (student discounts); California Gourmet (eat standing up).

UNIVERSITY:
- Price of a pint of beer: £1.50 • Glass of wine: £1.35

Bars: (7) There are bars at both of the University's two unions (see 'Social & Political' for an explanation). The most popular are Deep Six (with a pre-club bar and karaoke) and the Beer Bar (sporty), at GUU, and Jim's Bar at QM (*friendly,* hosts bands and karaoke).

Theatres & cinema: The University's theatre hosts regular productions. Students take shows to the Edinburgh Fringe regularly (*but it's not such an effort for them is it?*). The University drama course is *highly regarded* and over-subscribed. The Gilmorehill Centre has facilities for theatre, TV and film studios as well as public performances.

Clubs/discos: Qudos (capacity 1,100) has four regular boogie-fests per week at QM and The Hive at GUU (1,100) hosts three club nights a week, with cheese, indie and dance themes. *Cheeze at The Hive creates the most pungent perspiration.* Cream has the first regular residency in Glasgow; Bugged Out 'voted the best underground club in the UK by Musik Magazine'; Bedlam 'alternative rock and goth'; Cheezy Gold '70s and 80s fun for all'.

Music venues: QM has a definite edge on the live action front, recent names attracted to play Glasgow include Divine Comedy, Shed Seven, Ash, Badly Drawn Boy, Mansun, Roni size, Reprozant, Coldplay, Bewitched, Moloko and Cast.

Food: The Hub offers *slightly pricey* snacks and full meals from 12-2. There's also the Food Factory (9-8) and the Qudos Café at QM (10-5). GUU has a new coffee bar.

Others: The *highlight* of the ents year is 'Daft Friday', the last day of the first term, when GUU holds a posh ball for its members only. In *retaliation*, QM started the 'Dafter Friday Ball' which is much less formal and geared around bands and discos. Both unions have other occasional events like the *unavoidable* karaoke and so on. Friday night is Newky Brown comedy night at QM. QM runs a comedy night every other Thursday, featuring comedians from Glasgow and Edinburgh. Recent names to appear include Phil Kay.

SOCIAL & POLITICAL

STUDENT REPRESENTATIVE COUNCIL/GLASGOW UNIVERSITY UNION/QUEEN MARGARET UNION:
• 3 sabbaticals • Turnout at last ballot: 25%

Glasgow has the most confusing set of student organisations in the country, but you can always rely on Push to un-muddy. In Glasgow, there are five student unions, with two in competition. First, there's the Student Representative Council (all students are automatically members when they first come to Glasgow), which organises student representation, welfare and the student clubs and societies. *It's gently left-wing and not very high profile.* Next come the two services unions. A student can be a member of only one of these and they must choose in their first few weeks. The rivalries are not too distinct and students can use the facilities at both most of the time, but can only vote in their own union and if you don't join either you can't use either's facilities, *so there*. Glasgow University Union, originally a men-only affair, is bigger (*37% of students to QM's 25% – the rest obviously couldn't give two hoots to a monkey*) with a large centre in a listed building near the centre of the campus. It organises debates, as well as services, and rates with the Oxbridge Unions for the speakers it attracts. *Fans of Queen Margaret Union (formerly the women's union) would argue that, despite its size, it's where the cool people who don't like rugby hang out and ents are given priority over laddish drinking games.* The fourth union is the Sports Association (see Sports below). Finally, there is the Postgraduate Research Club called GUSA. None of the unions is a member of NUS, but they are members of Northern Services, a buying consortium, *i.e. cheap beer*.

SU FACILITIES:
SRC: Printing; second-hand bookshop; vending machines.
GUU: Five bars; cafeteria; restaurant; minibus; travel agency; nine bars; six pool tables; 10 snooker tables; canteen shop; 24-hour student facilities; print shop; photocopying; games machines; pool; juke box; vending machines; 2 libraries; meeting and conference rooms; launderette; Bank of Scotland and Royal Bank of Scotland cashpoints.
QM: Two bars; cafeteria; restaurant; sandwich bar; print shop; photocopying; shop; games and vending machines; two pool tables; study rooms; juke box; snooker room (members only); TV lounge; meeting rooms; customised nightclub; launderette; Bank of Scotland cash machine.

CLUBS (NON SPORTING):
Alchemists; Alexandrian; Debating; Dialectic; East Timor & Indonesia; Gaming; Humanist; Lion and Unicorn Club (Uni traditions); Monty Python; Pakistani; Roleplay; SNP.

OTHER ORGANISATIONS:
The SRC publishes 'The Guardian' newspaper (no, not that one) and there's also the independent Glasgow University Magazine (GUM). The student TV station, GUST, and Sub City radio (with an FM licence 2 months a year and official radio station of the 'T in the Park' festival) have both won national awards.

RELIGIOUS:
• Team of chaplains
There are Anglican, Methodist, Free Church, Baptist, Catholic and Church of Scotland chaplaincies. In town there are enough churches of different *denominations to wear out the knees of any good pair of jeans*, including, *notably*, Glasgow Cathedral (Church of Scotland) and St Andrew's Cathedral (Catholic). There are other places of worship locally for Muslims, Jews, Buddhists, Hindus and Sikhs.

PAID WORK:
Glasgow has been heaving itself out of the doldrums for more than a decade now and is still heaving. There is work around in bars and so on but there are others than students looking for it. There is a jobshop run by the SRC to help out, and Student Templine, a University supported temp agency.

SPORTS

• Recent successes: hockey, tennis
Glasgow has had a fair amount of sporting success, but the organisational structure doesn't invite broad involvement. Membership of the Sports and Recreation Service and of the Sports Association costs £5 giving access to all of the sports facilities but it isn't automatic.

SPORTS FACILITIES:
Indoor facilities are available on campus in the Stevenson Building where there are squash courts, a swimming pool, saunas, multigym and a sports hall. Just a short way off is the Kelvin Hall sports centre with an indoor running track, fitness rooms, climbing wall and multigym. At the Garscube site: three artificial tennis courts, exercise studio and conditioning suite, two squash courts, football and rugby pitches, synthetic pitch and cricket wicket. A new sports hall is being developed and will open next year.

SPORTING CLUBS:
Aikido; Curling; Gaelic Football; Lacrosse; Parachuting; Shinty; Shorinji Kempo; Trampolining; Ultimate Frisbee.

ATTRACTIONS:
Glasgow is one of the world's great football battlefields housing both Rangers and Celtic FCs and Glaswegians won't understand it if soft southern students can't say which team they support. There are eight lovely golf courses around town feeding the Scottish habit and a dry ski slope locally.

Baywatch icon Pamela Anderson has turned down an invitation to stand for the Presidency of Stirling University Students' Association.

ACCOMMODATION

IN COLLEGE:
- Catered: 5% • Cost: £66-89 (31wks)
- Self-catering: 12% • Cost: £45-64 (38-52wks)

Availability: Rent costs include a block insurance policy. 24% of 1st years are housed in the University accommodation. The rest are mostly 'home students', i.e. they live either with their parents or in their own homes. 15% have to share. The halls of residence are all within 20 minutes' walking distance of the campus, with the exception of Wolfson Hall 3 miles away (which has a shuttle bus in the evening). There are 11 student houses, housing between eight and 28 students in self-catering places. There are 1,875 digs to be had in flats which the University rents to students on a private basis but on favourable terms (housing 1st years and a few 2nd and 3rd years). There are also 70 flats for couples (140 places) and the Murano Street student village (1,100 places) with a shop, the village is 15 minutes' walk from the campus (*downhill*) and 25 minutes back (*uphill*). Self-catering accommodation offers an all female block. There are also 240, five-person flats with single study bedrooms and en-suite facilities; Wolfson Hall also has some en-suite bits. Queen Margaret Hall is to be re-developed, to include en-suite facilities. CCTV and porters.

Car parking: *Parking for residents only is limited but adequate. A £15 permit is needed for the Hillhead area.*

EXTERNALLY:
- Ave rent: £55

Availability: *For those students not living at home or in University accommodation, it's best to look as early as possible. Around September, all the students who don't heed our wise advice will be looking just when it's getting toughest. Despite its run-down image, housing in Glasgow is far from cheap, although it's possible to get good value in suburban tenement flats. Glasgow has its rough areas, but gentrification is cleaning up some of the former slums and students can live happily, although there are still some no-go areas. Parking is not easy and having a car is more hassle than help.*

Housing help: The massive Accommodation Office has a centralised Private Accommodation Database which caters to all students in Glasgow over the Internet. Also, weekly vacancy lists (daily in the peak period), bulletin boards, selective advertising on landlords' behalf, standard renting contracts and various other *pearls of advice and help.*

WELFARE

SERVICES:
- Creche • Lesbian & Gay Society • Mature SA
- Minibus • Women's Officer

The SRC runs a welfare service, but it suffers from the division of resources across the unions. That said, it is helpful on all sorts of problems and runs the LGB Pride week. The Accommodation Office also offers debt counselling and the University has a Counselling Service with three part- and two full-time counsellors. The Student Health Service employs a doctor, a psychiatric counsellor, a nursing sister and a visiting psychiatrist and the new student village has its own health centre.

Disabled: The University is spending £50,000 a year on making buildings more accessible, including much-needed improvements to the library, which has also benefited from a suite for those with visual impairments. Hearing loops in lecture theatres.

FINANCE:
• Access fund: £894,508 • Successful applications: 1,584
Student Hardship Fund as well as the access fund. Also, plenty of little grants and bequests.

Glasgow Caledonian University

• *Formerly Glasgow Polytechnic*
Glasgow Caledonian University, City Campus, Cowcaddens Road, Glasgow, G4 0DA. Tel: (0141) 331 3000. Fax: (0141) 331 3005. E-mail: rhu@gcal.ac.uk
Glasgow Caledonian University Students' Association, Cowcaddens Road, Glasgow, G4 0BA. Tel: (0141) 332 0681. Fax: (0141) 353 0029. E-mail: gcusagcal.ac.uk

GENERAL

For general information about Glasgow: see University of Glasgow. The University has two sites. One is *slap bang in the heart of Glasgow* near the main shops and various housing estates. The other is the City Campus made up of four 1960s' concrete and glass towers and a *mish-mash* of 70s through to newly-built *oddities*.

Sex ratio(M:F): 40%:60%	Founded: 1971
Full time u'grads: 14,836	Part time: 2,883
Postgrads: 849	Non-degree: 262
Ave course: 4yrs	Ethnic: n/a
Private school: n/a	Flunk rate: 5.2%
Mature students: 38%	Overseas students: n/a
Disabled students: n/a	

ATMOSPHERE:
Many of the students are locals and/or mature students, which tends to make the place feel like a means to an end rather than a cohesive, self-contained environment. Students are here to do a course and everything else is secondary. Interestingly, the Uni used to be a lunatic asylum and is referred to by local press as the Loony Uni. On the up side, Miss Scotland 2000 is a student here.

THE CITY: see University of Glasgow

TRAVEL: see University of Glasgow
Queen Street station is 10 minutes' walk from the City Campus.

CAREER PROSPECTS:
• Careers Service • No of staff: 7 full-time
• Unemployed after 6mths (1998): 10.5%
The service is rather under-used because it's rather under-publicised.

FAMOUS ALUMNI:
Eric Cullen (the late lamented 'Wee Bernie' from Rab C Nesbitt); Jim Delahunt, Louise White (of Scottish TV); Pat Nevin (footballer).

FURTHER INFO:
Prospectuses for undergrads, postgrads and part-timers and a handbook for mature students. The SA does a fresher's handbook and a Rough Guide to Glasgow. Website (www.gcal.ac.uk and www.sa.gcal.ac.uk).

ACADEMIC

The Caledonian Business School is the largest in Scotland and was opened, *bizarrely*, by Michael More – *the hugely adored inventor of the cleavage-enhancing Ultimo bra (hooray for Michael).*

Staff/student ratio: 1:18
Range of points required for entrance: 300-140
Percentage accepted through clearing: n/a
Number of terms/semesters: 2
Length of terms/semesters: 15 wks
Research: 2.8

LIBRARIES:
• Books: 335,102 • Study places: 1,367
There's a library on both sites. *The main library doubles as a social venue, so a studious atmosphere is hard to maintain.*

COMPUTERS:
• Computer workstations: 1,550
Pressure on computer facilities can be a tad intense, but the recent opening of the Caledonian Library & Information Centre should ease the strain.

ENTERTAINMENT

THE CITY: see University of Glasgow

UNIVERSITY:
• Price of a pint of beer: £1.50 • Glass of wine: £1.20
Bars: (4) There are 3 bars on the City Campus – the Refuge, the Haven and the Lounge.
Cinema: Big video screen at City Campus *but this is used as much for sporting events as for arty movies.*
Clubs/discos/music venues: *Clubbing seems to be the only form of social activity that can keep students on campus beyond nightfall* and to that end there are two big club nights in the Asylum (650, refurbished 'cos it burnt down, adm £3) with regular events including X-rated and 70s cover bands every month. Daphne & Celeste and God's Kitchen have played here recently.
Food: *The City Campus Refectory is pretty expensive but the Park Café and the Asylum are more realistic. The training restaurant at Park Campus is worth a try.*
Others: At least three balls a year and the Final Fling – another all-nighter. Also quiz nights, karaoke and occasional cabaret.

SOCIAL & POLITICAL

GLASGOW CALEDONIAN UNIVERSITY STUDENTS' ASSOCIATION:
• 4 sabbaticals • Turnout at last ballot: 20% • NUS member
The SA's campaigning has woken up a generally politics-free student body to the extent that they're peeping drowsily over their duvets and looking curiously at the fried breakfast of agitation. The sabbs here, if not the students, are prime movers in the Scottish end of the Free Education Movement.

SU FACILITIES:
The Association is housed in the Union at the City Campus with a few further facilities at Park Campus.
City Campus: Three bars; cafeteria; pizza cafe; two shops (general and stationery); games, video and vending machines; pool table; TV; conference hall; publications office; customised nightclub; welfare centre.

CLUBS (NON SPORTING):
Branston Pickle Appreciation; Campus TV; Homer Simpson Appreciation (doh! Students!); SNP; Stop the Fees.

OTHER ORGANISATIONS:
The SA publishes 'UNI' the monthly student newspaper. They also come up with Re:union magazine and about an hour's worth of campus TV every week.

RELIGIOUS:
• 1 chaplain
As well as a chaplaincy there is a Muslim prayer room.

PAID WORK: see University of Glasgow
Student job shop run by the Welfare department helps to find the *odd bit of shit-shovelling.*

SPORTS

• Recent successes: football, rugby, hockey
Apart from a committed hardcore, no one knows where the sports hall is. There's a *lovely, glittery* new £4Mn sports centre, erected in 2000, which comprises two gyms, two sports halls and conference facilities.

SPORTS FACILITIES:
City: A sports hall with multigym. **Park:** Multigym.

SPORTING CLUBS:
Boxing; Handball; Gokarting; Snowboarding; Table Tennis.

ATTRACTIONS: see University of Glasgow

ACCOMMODATION

IN COLLEGE:
• Catered: 1.3% • Cost: £64 (37wks)
• Self-catering: 5.1% • Cost: £38-55 (37wks)
Availability: 1st years get priority in the University's *haphazard mix* of accommodation, which ranges from the study bedrooms at Gibson Hall (*needs a load of TLC*) to 320 self-catering flats just off City Campus in Caledonian Court (*which is of a pretty high standard*).

There are also 340 spaces in a head tenancy scheme but in all, provisions aren't great – 50% who want to can't live in and 20% of those who do have to share. CCTV, entry phones and night-porters keep away the bed-bugs.
Car parking: Staff and disabled students only.

EXTERNALLY: see University of Glasgow
Housing help: Student Services provides an accommodation service with one full- and one part-time member of staff who allocate the University-managed rooms and can help with rent difficulties. *Compared to services at other universities, this is more of an internal than an external accommodation service*, although some work is done housing students in the private sector – er, they have a database, for instance.

WELFARE

SERVICES:
• Creche • Nightline • Mature SA • Overseas SA • Postgrad SA
The Counselling Service has seven full-time counsellors while the SA has one advisor. The University Health Service provides a nurse and visiting doctor. Tutors are also a *good* source for help. Still no special provision for women (such as a room, group, attack alarms – *perhaps they're all hard as nails*).
Disabled: *Access is improving, slowly.* There is a Disability Advisor and induction loops in the largest lecture theatres. The University, together with the Royal National Institute for the Blind, has established a Visual Resource Centre for sight-impaired students and help is available for those with dyslexia.

FINANCE:
• Access fund: £241,715 • Successful applications: 1,003
University Hardship Fund and Childcare Fund.

Glasgow Poly
see Glasgow Caledonian University

Gloucester
see Cheltenham & Gloucester College of Higher Education

Goldsmiths College, London

• **The College is part of University of London and students are entitled to use its facilities.**
Goldsmiths College, New Cross, London, SE14 6NW.
Tel: (020) 7919 7171. Fax: (020) 7919 7113.
E-mail: admissions@gold.ac.uk
Goldsmiths College Students' Union, New Cross, London, SE14 6NW.
Tel: (020) 8692 1406. Fax: (020) 8694 9789.
E-mail: gcsu@gold.ac.uk

GENERAL

New Cross, 5 miles south-east of Trafalgar Square, is a *shabby* part of London, *with traffic trundling through interminably. It's a bit like a tattered teddy bear, torn at the seams, but still with character. Some nearby areas, such as Greenwich, are lively cultural toy boxes, but most are busted Airfix models and broken Tonka toys, such as Lewisham, Catford, Deptford and New Cross itself.* Goldsmiths College, in the midst of all this, *is a veritable Buzz Lightyear.* The main building is *clean (considering its location), attractive,* 3 storeys and redbrick with a big, busy, white-pillared entrance at the front and creeper-covered walls and a flat lawn to the rear. The rest of the College's buildings are more modern and in keeping with *the surrounding urban sprawl, but unassuming enough to be ignored.* The Millennium Dome can be seen from the top floor of the library. Most of the students are arty types from a collage of different backgrounds.

Sex ratio(M:F): 34%:66%	Founded: 1891
Full time u'grads: 2,677	Part time: 823
Postgrads: 966	Non-degree: 482
Ave course: 3yrs	Ethnic: 31%
Private school: n/a	Flunk rate: 17%
Mature students: 61%	Overseas students: 13%
Disabled students: 6%	

ATMOSPHERE:
Goldsmiths is unique in London. It combines a buzzing and vividly vibrant student culture with local community links. The College is friendly, open and bristling with fun, a self-contained oasis of *expressive, creative people and most are doing courses because they're interested rather than as a means to an end. Earnest careerists in suits are noticeably absent.*

THE CITY: see University of London

NEW CROSS, LEWISHAM, GREENWICH:
New Cross, Lewisham and most of the surrounding areas are *dingily residential, with shops on every corner and paving stones cracked and littered. They're not inner-city hellhole, though (there are plenty of green spaces). What they lack in tourist appeal, they make up for with a friendly, vibrant local community and a relatively low cost of living (by London standards).* Greenwich provides *culture*: the famous park with the Observatory and Planetarium; the Maritime Museum; the Cutty Sark; a *fun* Sunday market; *and one of London's best theatres outside the West End.*

TRAVEL: see University of London
Local Trains: Trains from New Cross and New Cross Gate go straight into London Bridge, Waterloo and Charing Cross in less than 15 minutes.
Buses: 21, 36, 142, 171 (to the West End), 225 and Night Buses N21, N36, N53, N70 and N81.
Car: Close to the South Circular (the bottom bit of London's inner ring road), which helps. *Parking is easier than in some parts of London, but still harder than brie in sunshine.*

Underground: *Oddly ill-served by the tube;* the East London Line ends with stations at New Cross and New Cross Gate, but it's not a very direct route into London. The Jubilee Line and DLR are nearby.
Bicycles: *A lot of theft and pollution, but many students use bikes because they're more sound (and cheaper) than cars.*

CAREER PROSPECTS:
- Careers Service • No of staff: 2 full
- Unemployed after 6 mths: 5%

Despite its arts bias, Goldsmiths' employment record is better than many 'vocational' universities. Students also have access to London University's careers service.

FAMOUS ALUMNI:
Most of Blur; Martin Brabbins (conductor); John Cale (Velvet Underground); Julia Carling (TV presenter); Vic Charles (karate champ); Julian Clary (comedian); Wendy Cope (poet); Lucien Freud, Damien Hirst, Tom Keating, Bridget Riley (artists); Tessa Jowell MP (Lab); Linton Kwesi Johnson (dub poet); Malcolm MacLaren (Sex Pistols manager, manipulator); Brian Molko (Placebo); Molly Parkin (writer); Mary Quant (designer); Lord Merlyn-Rees (former Home Secretary); Gillian Wearing (Turner prize-winner 1997); Colin Welland (playwright/actor).

FURTHER INFO:
Prospectuses for undergrads, postgrads and part-timers. Website (www.goldsmiths.ac.uk).

ACADEMIC

Goldsmiths is one of the UK's leading universities in creative, cultural and social subjects.

staff/student ratio: 1:17
Range of points required for entrance: 300-180
Percentage accepted through clearing: 13%
Number of terms/semesters: 3
Length of terms/semesters: 10 wks
Research: 4.1

LIBRARIES:
- Books: 240,000 • Study places: 768

The library is housed in the shiny new Rutherford Information Services Building.

COMPUTERS:
- Computer workstations: 435

ENTERTAINMENT

IN LONDON: see University of London

NEW CROSS:
- Price of a pint of beer: £1.90 • Glass of wine: £1.60

Cinemas: *For most entertainments – not least movie-going – the West End has more to offer than the locality,* which offers multiscreens at Greenwich, Peckham and Surrey Quays.

Theatres: Again the West End, although local venues include Lewisham Theatre, Greenwich Theatre, Royal George Pub Theatre, Brockley Jack in Brockley, Birds Nest and the Albany Theatre in Deptford.

Pubs: *A few are worthwhile.* Pushplugs: New Cross Inn, Marquis of Granby, Rosemary Branch, Paradise Bar.

Clubs/discos/music venues: *Live music and spinning sounds are soundest in some of the less unwholesome local pubs and clubs.* Pushplugs: Rivioli Ballroom; The Venue (tribute bands); Je Suis Music; Amersham Arms; Up the Creek (regular comedy).

Eating out: *Most tuck shops are cheap and there's a good range of ethnic and cultural taste experiences to be had.* Pushplugs: The Thailand (one of the best in London); The Turkish Place; Moonbow Jakes; Marie's Café, Gem's (greasy spoons); Mr Cheung, Raj Bhujan.

COLLEGE:
- Price of a pint of beer: £1.40
- Glass of wine: £1.30

Bars: (2) *The main SU bar is usually packed, but everything closes down at weekends.*

Theatres: *With lots of drama and arts students, it's not surprising that Goldsmiths is well-equipped:* a proscenium stage in the George Wood Theatre and 3 studios used for thespian pursuits by the Players, *though recent years have seen a decline in their extra-curricular use.*

Cinema: 2 arty shows every week, as well as occasional blockbusters.

Clubs/discos/music venues: Two regular club nights: 'Club Sandwich' (weekly); 'Lollipop' (fortnightly). Live acts, including recent performances by Freestylers, Fabio, Grooverider and former students Blur, do their stuff at the top of the SU building, *but with decreasing regularity.*

Food: Loafer's Corner and the Refectory *are surprisingly health-oriented, but pricey. The more junk-laden Revolution, run by the SU, is cheaper.* Students' artwork adorns the eateries.

Cabaret: Regular comedy nights were recently graced by Lee Mack and Noel Fielding, *as well as a strange man who used a gun, some string and his own nipples to unexpectedly comic effect.*

Others: At least 4 balls a year, plus hall and society events. Karaoke and quiz nights have proved very popular.

SOCIAL & POLITICAL

GOLDSMITHS COLLEGE STUDENTS' UNION (GCSU):
- 5 sabbaticals
- Turnout at last ballot: 15%
- NUS member

Goldsmiths' SU is one of the most politically vocal in London but the broad left consensus within the ranks of the hacks doesn't necessarily translate to the student body in general – they're more likely to be getting down to studying and partying. The Union is big on awareness campaigns and were instrumental in getting Damon Albarn to appear in the House of Commons to talk about tuition fees.

SU FACILITIES:
It's quite a trek to Bloomsbury from New Cross so Goldsmiths students rarely use the University and ULU facilities, but, in its own Tiananmen Building, GCSU provides the Revolution Bar and Coffee Shop, 2 other bars, a general shop, photocopier, launderette, 4 pool

tables, games machines, CD juke box and 2 minibuses. On campus there's a Waterstones bookshop and a NatWest Bank.

CLUBS (NON SPORTING):
Broad Left; Chiaroscuro (film); Chinese; Hellenic; Hip Hop; Japan International; Sound; Student Assembly Against Racism; Young Socialists.

OTHER ORGANISATIONS:
The monthly 'Smiths' magazine is an *excellent example* of what can be *achieved without gloss and gimmick*. Rag this year raised money for Oxfam and the Terence Higgins Trust.

RELIGIOUS:
• 4 chaplains (CofE, RC, Methodist, United Reformed)

PAID WORK: see University of London

• Recent successes: football, martial arts
Sporting enthusiasm at Goldsmiths has taken an up-turn lately although the facilities leave something to be desired. Fortunately, students are entitled to use University of London amenities.

SPORTS FACILITIES:
Facilities are poor with only a small gym on site, 21 acres of playing fields at the Loring Sports ground in Sidcup, Kent (8 miles away). Wavelengths Baths in Deptford are just down the road.

SPORTING CLUBS:
Aerobic; Aikido; Kickboxing; Nin Po; Self-Defence; Women's Football.

ATTRACTIONS:
The local football team is Millwall. Also nearby are Crystal Palace and Charlton Athletic.

IN COLLEGE:
• Catered: 4% • Cost: £65 (39wks)
• Self-catering: 20% • Cost: £60-80 (39-50wks)
Availability: All 1st years who want it are accommodated in halls close to campus. Chances for other years are less good and less than 10% of finalists lived in last year. Nobody needs to share.
Car parking: Parking facilities at two halls. Further parking available for disabled students.

EXTERNALLY: see University of London
Availability: South London usually works out cheaper than North because of the capital's own topsy-turvy north/south divide. *Brockley, Lewisham and Brixton are all quite popular.*
Housing help: The College runs an accommodation office in addition to the University's.

SERVICES:
• Creche • Nightline • Lesbian & Gay Society • Mature SA
• Postgrad SA • Minibus • Women's Officer • Self-defence classes

London University provides some services but so does Goldsmiths itself and the SU. Health services (from doctors and nurses) are based at the College's Medical Centre just round the corner and there are 1 full-time and 2 part-time counsellors available. There is also a tutor support system. The International Office takes particular care of overseas students.

Women: Men are in the minority and the *provisions for women are excellent.* The SU issues attack alarms and provides women's safe transport after events.

Disabled: *Wheelchair access is good in the Learning Centre and the SU, but elsewhere you have to cope with stairs and old Victorian houses.* Braille signs have been fitted and there are induction loops in some teaching rooms. One bar has been specially adapted. A Dyslexia Support Group is in place.

FINANCE:
- Access fund: £363,656
- Successful applications: 655

Gordon University

see Robert Gordon University

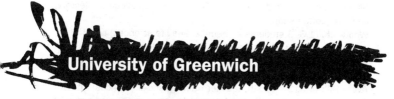

University of Greenwich

- *Formerly Thames Polytechnic*

University of Greenwich, Old Royal Naval College, Park Row, London, SE10 9LS. Tel: 0800 005 006. Fax: (020) 8331 8145.
E-mail: courseinfo@gre.ac.uk
University of Greenwich Students' Union, Bathway, Woolwich, London, SE18 6QX. Tel: (020) 8331 8268. Fax: (020) 8331 8591.

GENERAL

Don't be fooled by the name 'Greenwich'. (Only Americans pronounce it 'green-witch'. It's *'grennidge' – get it right.*) The University has acquired the *stunning* Royal Naval College and is now the main site for the University, which really is in Greenwich, *so at least the name is vaguely appropriate, but none of the other sites are in the area.* Other sites include the *un-touristy* Woolwich, 8½ miles east of Trafalgar Square, and some sites aren't even in the Borough of Greenwich, such as Dartford (in Kent). In all, the sites are spread over 23 miles, never far from the river, *which seems to suggest that the old name (Thames Poly) was closer to the mark.* The different sites offer different courses and students considering applying should check where they'd be based, *since they're largely self-contained and as different as chalk and chutney.*

> The mascot of City University Rag is a lifesize carrot which went to the lord Mayor's Ball and met Mr Blobby.

Sex ratio(M:F): 48%:52%	Founded: 1890
Full time u'grads: 14,050	Part time: 6,716
Postgrads: 13,526	Non-degree: 3,839
Ave course: 3yrs	Ethnic: 33%
Private school: 5%	Flunk rate: 26.6%
Mature students: 40%	Overseas students: 16%
Disabled students: 5%	

ATMOSPHERE:
The two major SU venues, particularly the Bar Lattitude in Greenwich and Deep End at Woolwich, provide a social focus which would otherwise be lost in the distances between sites. This and the social melting pot of many ethnic groups help to provide a sense of fun and an extra-curricular buzz that's missing at some of the other 'new' universities.

THE SITES:
Greenwich: (9,168 – IT, maths, post-compulsory education, law, business) Latest addition to the collage of colleges, based in the *elegant* Georgian former Royal Naval College on the edge of Greenwich Park. There's the *glamour* of the Cutty Sark, the Maritime Museum and the Sunday markets. Other facilities include a refectory, café and coffee shop.
Woolwich: (1,313 students – chemical and life sciences) Local attractions include the Thames Barrier (the world's largest flood gate), the Woolwich Ferry across the Thames and the Woolwich Arsenal.
Avery Hill: (4,312 – health, teacher training, social sciences) An *attractive site*, 3 miles south of Woolwich, set in an 86-acre park with a listed mansion as the main building. The nearest major shopping area is Eltham, a mile away.
Dartford: (1,926 – architecture, surveying, civil engineering) In Kent, 13 miles from Woolwich (40 minutes by train from Charing Cross), it's a collection of *modern rectangles* with 5 halls of residence and some amenities including *good sports facilities*. It's actually about a mile from Dartford. Dartford is a *fast expanding industrial town* with a few shops and a direct escape route by train into London and is close to Bluewater.
Medway: (1,334 – earth sciences, engineering) A relatively new development in association with the Natural Resources Institute.

THE CITY: see University of London

TRAVEL: see University of London
Trains: For Woolwich – Woolwich Arsenal Station (25 mins to central London); for Dartford – Dartford Station (40 mins); for Avery Hill – Falconwood or New Eltham (both 30 mins travel + 15 mins walk). Chatham station for Medway. There's a DLR station 'Cutty Sark' at Greenwich.
Buses: All sites, except Dartford and Medway, are served by a wide range of regular London bus services including night buses. Dartford is connected by Green buses with central London. The uni runs buses between sites *but Push has never managed to catch one*.
Car: Dartford is just within the M25 (London's outer ring road) on the M2/A2. Medway is 3 miles from the M2.
Bicycles: *Your life in the hands of juggernaut drivers*.

CAREER PROSPECTS:
- Careers Service • No of staff: 3 full
- Unemployed after 6mths: 7%

Poorly advertised careers services at each site, but good job shop and website.

FAMOUS ALUMNI:
Hale & Pace (*unamusing* double act); Rachel Heyhoe Flint (cricketer); Prof Charles Kao (inventor of fibre optics); Graham Ingham (BBC TV reporter); Brian Jacks (former judo champ); Matt James (Gene drummer); William G Stewart (Fifteen to One).

FURTHER INFO:
Prospectuses for undergrads and postgrads, guide for mature students. Website (www.greenwich.ac.uk).

staff/student ratio: 1:15
Range of points required for entrance: 260-120
Percentage accepted through clearing: 38%
Number of terms/semesters: 2
Length of terms/semesters: 15 wks
Research: 3

LIBRARIES:
- Books: 600,000 • Study places: 1,600

Students aren't exactly jumping over the moon about library facilities, given the scrums over primary texts and the fact that they're closed on Sundays.

COMPUTERS:
- Computer workstations: 1,250

IN LONDON: see University of London

LOCAL AREAS:
Except Greenwich itself there is little to do outside college as the sites are not in London's most jumping joints. There's more or less the level of entertainment facilities you might reckon to find in London's inner cities and outermost commuter reaches. Many students avoid the local pubs, especially those popular with local squaddies. Pushplugs: Earl of Chatham in Woolwich; The Ordnance; The Trafalgar in Greenwich. For other ents, the SU and the West End provide more than enough compensation.

UNIVERSITY:
- Price of a pint of beer: £1.60 • Glass of wine: £1.20

The main SU hang-outs are at Woolwich and Avery Hill but there's a presence at the other sites, especially Dartford.
Bars: (13) The major ones are Bar Lattitude at Greenwich, the Deep End at Woolwich (*drab, but with heart-beat*) and the Jesters bar in the Dome at Avery Hill (*dead expensive and just dead*).
Cinema: 1 blockbuster a week on a 15ft screen at Woolwich.
Clubs/discos: There are 3 or 4 club nights a week for every taste.

Music venues: The Deep End at Woolwich and the Dome at Avery Hill can hold 1,000 punters each and the Zone at Dartford can take 300. Recent acts have included Brian Harvey.
Cabaret: Every other Monday Jesters plays host to the Comedy Network presenting the best up and coming student comics.
Food: A range of eateries across the expanse, *the best being Woolwich's Snorkels Cafe.*
Others: 2 main balls (Christmas and May) and the more outlying sites do their own spherical things.

SOCIAL & POLITICAL

UNIVERSITY OF GREENWICH STUDENTS' UNION:
• 5 sabbaticals • Turnout at last ballot: 8% • NUS member
The concentration of SU facilities at Woolwich and Avery Hill tends to leave the further-flung members somewhat out of the equation. The entertainment facilities are well used, but politics isn't really on the agenda – 5 people turned up to a fees rally and they were the sabbs.

SU FACILITIES:
13 bars (on 5 sites); 2 minibuses; 3 shops; vending and games machines; pool tables; half-term play-scheme; juke box; library; photocopying; STA travel; hair and beauty centre; 3 meeting rooms.

CLUBS (NON SPORTING):
DJ; Hellenic; Malaysian; Socialist Worker (obviously not working very hard); Tamil.

OTHER ORGANISATIONS:
There's a monthly student magazine, the 'Sarky Cutt'. The fortnightly ents sheet is called 'Get Out'. *Rag is dormant.*

RELIGIOUS:
• 3 chaplains (CofE, RC, multi-faith)
Prayer rooms available on all sites for students of any denomination. Muslim prayer room at Woolwich.

PAID WORK: see University of London

SPORTS

• Recent successes: rugby, football
For a university mostly inside the M25, Greenwich has some pretty good sports facilities, but only a certain proportion of the students get into the spirit. Most sites have something to offer. *Successes tend to be individual rather than team efforts.*

SPORTS FACILITIES:
Avery Hill: (£10/year membership) sports centre with multigym, squash courts, snooker tables; gym; football, rugby, hockey pitches; tennis courts; running track.
Woolwich: Sports hall; fitness room; 2 squash courts.
Dartford: Swimming pool; sports hall; netball and tennis courts; playing fields; cricket nets.
Medway: Sports hall.

ATTRACTIONS:
Charlton Athletic, Millwall and Gillingham are the local football teams.

ACCOMMODATION

IN COLLEGE:
- Catered: 3% • Cost: £75 (34-46wks)
- Self-catering: 20% • Cost: £46-84 (40-50wks)

Availability: The University guarantees to house all 1st years who request it, although this might mean private accommodation (head tenancy or housing association schemes). The majority of Uni-owned housing is at Avery Hill but there's something at each site – *Woolwich is a bit pants, but everywhere else is fine*. All sites have disabled facilities, CCTV, entry-phones and 24-hour security.

EXTERNALLY: see University of London
- Ave rent: £58

Availability: *East and South-East London, especially Woolwich and Plumstead, are cheaper than north of the river, but you get what you pay for. Some parts, such as Thamesmead, are a bit deficient on the safety front.*

Housing help: The University runs an accommodation service with a vacancies board and an approval scheme.

WELFARE

SERVICES:
- Creche • Lesbian & Gay Society • Overseas SA
- Women's Officer

The SU runs a welfare and advice department with 4 advisors and the University runs a counselling service employing 5 full- and 6 part-time staff, *easily accessible on the larger sites only*. They organise workshops for coping with stress, anxiety and so on. The Medical Service operates at Woolwich, Dartford and Avery Hill offering a nurse and medical officer. *Sadly, the minibus doesn't run late.*

Disabled: There are a few ramps, designated parking spaces and faulty lifts, *but generally the facilities have discouraged disabled students*. A new disability advisor is working to reverse this. They do have an aromatherapist and hypnotherapist for referral, though, *so that's okay.*

FINANCE:
- Access fund: £1 million • Successful applications: 1,243

Guildhall

see London Guildhall University

Guy's Hospital

see King's College, London

> 'I think that's the problem with a University education. You just end up thinking too much'
> – Ed O'Brien (Radiohead).

Hallam see Sheffield Hallam University

Harper Adams see Other Institutions

Hatfield see University of Hertfordshire

Heriot-Watt University

University of Hertfordshire

Heythrop College, London

Holloway College see Royal Holloway, London

Homerton College see University of Cambridge

University of Huddersfield

University of Hull

University of Humberside see University of Lincolnshire & Humberside

Hallam

see Sheffield Hallam University

Harper Adams

see Other Institutions

Hatfield

see University of Hertfordshire

Heriot-Watt University

Heriot-Watt University, Riccarton, Edinburgh, EH14 4AS.
Tel: (0131) 449 5111. Fax: (0131) 449 5153.
E-mail: edu.liaison@hw.ac.uk
Heriot-Watt University Students' Association, The Union, Riccarton, Edinburgh, EH14 4AS. Tel: (0131) 451 5333. Fax: (0131) 451 5344.

GENERAL

For general information about Edinburgh: see Edinburgh University. Heriot-Watt is based on a 380-acre parkland site 6½ miles outside Edinburgh at Riccarton – *beautiful for some, plain for others*. This green and wooded campus, which was only completed in 1992, is on the site of an old mansion. The gardens of the mansion remain, surrounding the library which now stands where the house once did.

The University buildings, built mostly from *smart* light brick in the 70s and 80s, lie among the old trees and around an artificial lake or, *since this is Scotland*, artificial loch with *bad-tempered* swans. The campus is still growing and now includes the Edinburgh Conference Centre. *The countryside around the campus is not exactly the purple flower of Scotland's thistle. It's fairly uninteresting*. There is also an associated college of the University based in Edinburgh centre and another campus – in Galashiels, 38 miles away.

Sex ratio(M:F): 61%:39%	Founded: 1966
Full time u'grads: 4,458	Part time: 155
Postgrads: 896	Non-degree: 66
Ave course: 4yrs	Ethnic: 18%
Private school: 10%	Flunk rate: 11.2%
Mature students: 15%	Overseas students: 17%
Disabled students: 5%	

ATMOSPHERE:
By Scottish university standards, Heriot-Watt is quite cosmopolitan: only 59% of students are native Scots and there is a large number of overseas students who take an active role in student life. It's a science-based, nine-to-five type place and most students who live off campus don't hang around come tea-time, leaving the place a bit bleak except for the lesser-spotted fresher who can be spotted, flitting nervously through his (and it's mainly blokes) brick habitat. That said, things are becoming a teensy bit more sociable with the numerous watering holes and sporty bits.

THE SITES:
Edinburgh College of Art: (architecture, landscape, planning & housing, art & design) Situated in Edinburgh's centre, *the 1,700 students here are very arty. Funny, that. Although the associated college is technically part of Heriot-Watt, students often try to disown their 'big brother' institution, regarding it as a bit techy.* Students are entitled to use HW facilities but few do.

The Scottish Borders Campus: (fashion, clothing, textile technology, management & computing) SBC (as it's abbreviated) formerly known as the Scottish College of Textiles. There are 700 students based here, some of whom study for part of their courses at the Edinburgh campus. SBC is in Galashiels, a small but *attractive* town, 38 miles from the Edinburgh campus and *somewhat limited in facilities*.

THE CITY: see University of Edinburgh

TRAVEL: see University of Edinburgh
Local buses: Buses to the city centre cost 90p and take 25 minutes. There is a night service until 4.30am.
Car: The Edinburgh campus is about one mile outside the A720 Edinburgh ring road, just off the A71 on its way out of the city. There are parking spaces on the campus.
Taxis: By taxi to Waverley Station in the city centre only takes about 15 minutes but costs around £7.
Hitching: *Not a safe way of getting into town and so most students take the bus.*
Bicycles: *A bit far to the city centre ($6^1/_2$ miles) but the opening of the union canal and other cycle paths has improved access to the city centre. Although Edinburgh is generally too hilly and windy (but that's Scotland for you).*

CAREER PROSPECTS:
• Careers Service • No of staff: 9 full/1 part
• Unemployed after 6mths: 5%

SPECIAL FEATURES:
•The name Heriot-Watt has nothing to do with TV vet James Herriot. James Watt (1736-1819) was one of the innovators of the Industrial Revolution with his work on steam engines. George Heriot (1563-1623), known as 'Jinglin' Geordie', was a jeweller and financier to James VI of Scotland (James I of England).

FAMOUS ALUMNI:
Craig Joiner (rugby player); Archy Kirkwood MP (Lib Dem); Henry McLeish (First Minister of Scotland); Martin O'Neill MP (Lab); Irvine Welsh ('Trainspotting' author).

FURTHER INFO:
Prospectuses for undergrads and postgrads and website (www.hw.ac.uk). SU website www.hwusa.org

ACADEMIC

The country's only degree course in Brewing & Distilling. *Cheers.*

staff/student ratio: 1:13
Range of points required for entrance: 280-160
Percentage accepted through clearing: 7.7%
Number of terms/semesters: 3
Length of terms/semesters: 12 wks
Research: 4.5

LIBRARIES:
• Books: 200,000 • Study places: 750
There's a main library at the Edinburgh campus where, apparently, Irvine Welsh wrote most of Trainspotting. Just imagine what effect the place will have on your essays. There are, also, collections in some departments and at least one library at each of the other sites.

COMPUTERS:
• Computer workstations: 1,070

ENTERTAINMENT

TOWN: see University of Edinburgh

UNIVERSITY:
• Price of a pint of beer: £1.30 • Glass of wine: £1.15
Bars: (4) Three in the Union, which are Liberty's (170), Zero Degrees (450) and the popular Jinglin' Geordies (cap 250), and one in the Conference Centre. The Edinburgh College of Art also has its own bar arrangements.
Clubs/discos/music venues: The recently refurbished Zero Degrees is the dance dive two or three times a week (£3) with theme nights from acid jazz to mainstream chart fodder. Names to appear include Mr C and Brandon. The Conference Centre (452) hosts occasional gigs (recently Arkana and the Dharmas). *Jam is one big party fest* and runs across all the bars on Fridays.

Food: The University refectory does three meals a day *at reasonable prices* and the SA bars also serve hot and cold food.
Others: There are weekly pub quizzes, occasional balls and the *usual posse* of hypnotists.

SOCIAL & POLITICAL

HERIOT-WATT UNIVERSITY STUDENTS' ASSOCIATION:

• 4 sabbaticals • Turnout at last ballot: 14% • NUS member
Politics is generally a bigger turn-off for Heriot-Watt students than a tongue sandwich from Mr Bean, although this was one of the first unis to overturn top-up fees and admin charges on tuition fees. Students regard their Student Association first and foremost as a services organisation.

SU FACILITIES:
The Student Association's building is called the Student Union (*so that's 'the Association' 'that's the organisation and 'the Union' is the building, got that?*): three bars; disco; cafeteria; shop; travel agency; PA hire; welfare library; meeting rooms. The Scottish Borders campus has a brand new union building designed by SBC students.

CLUBS (NON SPORTING):
Aussie Travellers; Brewing (biggest beer fest in Scotland); Bookworm; Celtic Supporters; Collectable Card Players; Clubbing; Distortion; Film; Freedom for Fish; Four-by-Four Club; French Students; German Theatre; Hong Kong Students; International Banking and Finance; Orkney; Parthenon Hellenic; Vegetarian; Venture Scouts.

OTHER ORGANISATIONS:
The free student newspaper, 'Watt's On', comes out three times a term. A Community Action Group is being set up.

RELIGIOUS:
• 6 chaplains
Multi-faith chaplaincy centre (with 6 honorary chaplains of various denominations) and a Muslim prayer room.

PAID WORK: see University of Edinburgh
A jobshop has been set up.

SPORTS

• Recent successes: badminton, football, rugby, skiing
With such large grounds, the University has provided some *excellent* sporting facilities *which have attracted a fair number of muscle-bound Olympians*. There's a multi-purpose sports hall and building is underway for a football academy – Student sports are co-ordinated by the Sports Union (independent of the SA). Sports scholarships are available for badminton, golf and squash.

SPORTS FACILITIES:
The Edinburgh campus boasts the *impressive* National Squash Centre, but also has a number of large playing fields (6 football, 2 rugby, 1 cricket), a floodlit training area, jogging track, 3 tennis courts and a sports hall, climbing wall, 2 multigyms, golf driving nets, croquet pitch, weights and fitness rooms and indoor sports courts. A new pool is being built.

SPORTING CLUBS:
Curling; Gaelic Football; Rifle; Skate; Table Tennis; Windsurfing.

ATTRACTIONS: see University of Edinburgh

ACCOMMODATION

IN COLLEGE:
- Catered: 6% • Cost: £55 (33wks)
- Self-catering: 40% • Cost: £30-56 (35-50wks)

Availability: All 1st years from outside the region can be accommodated and most of those from other years who want it (about 20%). The accommodation is divided into four 'phases', I to IV, which differ according to cost *and levels of concreteness*. There are also new halls with phone and internet sockets. There's also a head tenancy scheme, whereby the University rents out 100 flats in town. Night patrols hunt out Gremlins.

Car parking: Car ownership is increasing *and the situation sometimes approaches a shoehorn/vaseline scenario, with some pressure being relieved with the building of an extra car park.*

EXTERNALLY: see University of Edinburgh

Housing help: The *excellent* Accommodation Office has five staff providing a bulletin board, approval scheme and advice.

WELFARE

SERVICES:
- Nursery • Lesbian & Gay Society • Overseas SA
- Women's Officer • Minibus • Self-defence classes

The Student Association has a drop-in advice centre. The University provides 'mentors', tutors or members of staff with some welfare training, as well as one full- and one part-time counsellor. The Health Service at Edinburgh has doctors, nurses and a dentist, plus a sports doctor and physiotherapist on site.

Disabled: *Access to some departments and buildings is very good and there is a good degree of awareness, but considering how modern a campus this is, there have been some omissions.* The Union has been refurbished to improve access. There is some specially adapted accommodation and there's a Special Needs Adviser.

FINANCE:
- Access fund: £301,982 • Successful applications: 883

The Student Association runs a crisis fund and there are sports bursaries worth between £500 and £1,500. Also a hardship fund.

University of Hertfordshire

- ***Formerly Hatfield Polytechnic***

University of Hertfordshire, College Lane, Hatfield, Hertfordshire, AL10 9AB. Tel: (01707) 284800. Fax: (01707) 284870.
University of Hertfordshire Students' Union, Hatfield Campus, College Lane, Hatfield, AL10 9AB. Tel: (01707) 285000. Fax: (01707) 286151.

GENERAL

Hatfield is hardly outside London, less than 8 miles from the outskirts. *It's an uninteresting satellite*, but Hertfordshire is one of the *less trite* Home Counties with *many pretty* rural villages and attractive St Albans. *The University's main campus seems divorced from everything but the A1*, which runs right along one edge. It's a couple of miles away from the train station in Hatfield – and *in Hatfield, the station is all you'll want*. The campus buildings are uninspiring blocks from the last 30 years (which to be fair, are gradually being phased out), dotted *spaciously* around the green and wooded site. *Fortunately*, this is just the main campus out of four, not including the Bayfordbury site where a field centre is based.

Sex ratio(M:F): 50%:50%	Founded: 1952
Full time u'grads: 13,000	Part time: 3,000
Postgrads: 2,900	Non-degree: 3,800
Ave course: 3/4yrs	Ethnic: 26%
Private school: 5%	Flunk rate: n/a
Mature students: 55%	Overseas students: 10%
Disabled students: 6%	

ATMOSPHERE:
The fact that the immediate vicinity isn't the most socially happening slab of commuter-land hasn't dampened students' spirits. In fact, it galvanises them to build fun factories of their own. This doesn't, however, distract them from the main purpose of coming to Herts which is the old 'choose university, choose degree, choose career' progression. *Perhaps not the most spiritually fulfilling prescription for life but this lot seem to be doing all right.*

THE SITES:
Changes are on the way, a new campus at Hatfield will be up and jogging in 2003, leading to the closure of the Watford and Hertford campuses, with new facilities including leisure centre, swimming pool and theatre.

Hatfield: (all courses not based at other sites) This 93 acre site is the main campus, but the *least attractive – it's the sort of place that will take over the world when the Orwellian nightmare begins*. Among the more recent additions are some *modern* brick student houses on the edge of the campus, *brightly adorned* with colourful drainpipes.

Hertford Campus: (1,500 students – Business School) *A stunningly beautiful and seemingly remote site*, ½ mile from Hertford and 11 miles from the Hatfield campus. Its main building is a mansion dating from 1640, edged by some *inconspicuous* more modern buildings and 100 acres of parkland, ponds, topiaried hedges and so on, known as Balls Park (*and yes, thanks, they've heard all the jokes*).

Watford: (1,900 students – Education, Humanities) Rural site at the village of Aldenham near the little town of Radlett, about 2 miles from Watford (the most north-westerly tip of London) and 12 miles from Hatfield. Like Hertford it has a mansion as its main building. This one looks like a castle and, having been built in 1799, is modern by comparison. *The grounds are pleasant indeed and the contemporary additions are imposing.*

St Albans: About a mile from Hatfield is the *pretty* Roman town of St Albans, which houses the Law faculty. *Leisure facilities on site* aren't that great, but it's so close to the main campus this rarely matters.

Bayfordbury: 5 miles east of the Hatfield campus, in the grounds of yet another mansion (Bayfordbury House). This time only a *mildly grand* white affair, host to the University's observatory and biology field station.

THE TOWNS:

None of the nearby towns are totally devoid of attractions; conversely, none are so well-provided that London's proximity isn't a bonus.

HATFIELD: *The only part of Hatfield that has any real character is Old Hatfield with some village charm and an almost separate identity.* Hatfield House is here, an Elizabethan palace. The new town is larger, but *pretty nondescript, except that (or, perhaps, because)* it is at the centre of the UK pharmaceutical and computing industries, which is useful for the many students on sandwich placements. *Lots of grass verges are a nice idea, but they are a nightmare for residential parking.* The massive Galleria shopping mall on a bridge above the A1 on the outskirts of town has distracted shoppers (*although it is pretty good*).

HERTFORD: 7 miles away, Hertford is a *sleepy, middle-class market town, which despite a long history, hasn't got much of a story to tell. It's not the largest, nor the most important, nor the most exciting town in Hertfordshire*, despite providing the county with its name. However, it has a surprisingly *good number of shops and is a pretty town surrounded by lovely countryside*.

OTHERS: St Albans is prettier still. Watford may have its architectural fans but *Push* isn't one of them.

TRAVEL:

Trains: Hatfield station is 1½ miles from the main campus, useful for the direct service to London King's Cross to the south and Stevenage to the north. From these stations, there are also direct services all the way to York, Newcastle and Edinburgh and connections to the rest of the country. Hertford station is about ½ hour from London (£8.90).

Coaches: No National Express service to Hatfield or Hertford. The nearest stops are London's Victoria Coach Station and Luton (12 miles away). London Country and Greenline buses run services to and from London.

Car: The A1(M) runs right by the campus (*but through a cutting, so the noise and fumes aren't too bad*). The A1000 passes through Hatfield, as does the A414 which also goes to Hertford. All sites are within 5 miles of the M25.

Air: Luton Airport, offering international and inland flights, is 11 miles north-east.

Hitching: *The Home Counties as a rule are not good for picking up lifts, but if that's where you've gotta hitch from, the A1 is just about the best road to be on.* Try the junction with the M25, 6 miles down the road.

Local: *Buses aren't the cheapest in the country, but are useful for quick trips into Hatfield.* The University also provides a bus service between sites, 90p for students on all routes. Also has routes from Hatfield to St Albans, Stevenage, Watford and Welwyn Garden City.

Taxis: Numerous firms, *but they work out expensive beyond any of the town boundaries.*

Bicycles: *Provided you've got a hefty padlock, a bike's a useful way of rolling around the campuses.*

CAREER PROSPECTS:
- Careers Service • No of staff: 1 full/4 part
- Unemployed after 6mths: 5.2%

SPECIAL FEATURES:
- Students who can claim a loan can claim a bigger one at the Watford campus because it is 2 miles within the M25 ring road and qualifies as London (*despite the fact that Hertford's more expensive*).

FAMOUS ALUMNI:
Sanjeer Bhaskar (Goodness Gracious Me); Ian Dowie (footballer); Helen Lederer (comedian); Lady Parkinson (wife of Cecil); Jayne Zito (mental health campaigner).

FURTHER INFO:
Prospectuses for full- and part-time undergrads and postgrads, alternative prospectus, faculty booklets, video, websites (www.herts.ac.uk and www.uhsu.herts.ac.uk). The undergrad prospectus is also available in enlarged print, braille and on tape and disk.

ACADEMIC

staff/student ratio: 1:18
Range of points required for entrance: 320-160
Percentage accepted through clearing: 15%
Number of terms/semesters: 2
Length of terms/semesters: 15 wks
Research: 3.5

LIBRARIES:
- Books: 293,390 • Study places: 1,600

The Learning Resources Centre at Hatfield is one of the main features of the campus. Other campus libraries relate to the subjects taught at each site.

COMPUTERS:
- Computer workstations: 800+

ENTERTAINMENT

TOWN:
- Price of a pint of beer: £2.20 • Glass of wine: £1.90

Hatfield and Hertford are pretty minimally equipped for entertainments. Welwyn Garden City (3 miles up the A1 and easily accessible by train) offers more by way of a good time and there's also the garish Stevenage Leisure Park, St Albans and (sorry about this) London.

Cinemas: At the Galleria, there's a 9-screen multiplex offering student discounts during the week. There's also a *nice* 9-screener at Watford and a multi-screen at Stevenage.

Theatres: The Gordon Craig Theatre offers everything from films to tribute bands.

Pubs: Pushplugs: *The Eight Bells* in Hatfield, *The Philanthropist & Firkin* in St Albans and *The White Hart* in Hertford are worth a wet whistle stop. Some other places are less than welcoming to the student population.

Clubs/discos: *Destiny in Watford is the nearest club with any merit. Zero's (house/garage) is the closest thing to a non-mainstream dance venue round here, so most serious party animals seek their kicks in London. Batchwood is the club in St Albans. Eros in Enfield. All clubs do bus runs from the University sites.*
Music venues: Wembley and Knebworth are both within ½ an hour's drive (not that Wembley's open right now).
Eating out: Students chase a chomp at the Galleria's many eateries (*including McDonald's and other plastic food in plastic packs*). Hatfield has a few restaurants (Indian, Italian, Greek and Chinese) and snack shops, such as burger bars, chippies and spud places, but there's nothing to make a seasoned gourmet drop her foie gras butty. St Albans, Hertford and Watford have some yumshus but somewhat expensive eateries.

UNIVERSITY:
- Price of a pint of beer: £1.60 • Glass of wine: £1.40

Bars: (4) The Font Bar (cap 1,000) at the main site is the most popular; Hutton Hall (cap 580) at Hatfield; the Boathouse at Hertford (cap 350), the Wall Hall (cap 360) at Watford.
Theatres: *Pretty strong dramatic activity and a theatre.*
Cinemas: New releases on different days across the sites.
Clubs/discos/music venues: Regular nights include, Fisson – Drum n' Bass night, Fever – 70's, Roobarb and Custard – 80's. Musical maestros to have hit the Hub recently include: Damage, Dane Bowers, Blue, Dave Pierce.
Cabaret: Occasional comedy at the Elephant House in Hatfield and the Font.
Food: The Elephant House does all manner of speedy snacks, *which usually work out cheaper than the Uni Refectory*. The Hertford bar serves snacks and top Sunday lunches.
Others: 3 balls a year at each campus (except St Albans).

SOCIAL & POLITICAL

HERTFORDSHIRE UNIVERSITY STUDENTS' UNION:
- 5 sabbaticals • Turnout at last ballot: 18% • NUS member

The Elephant House is the SU's own building, but it also has offices in the University's Hutton Block. *Where the Font Bar is the low-ceilinged venue for some of the University's most lively moments.* However, if the students were any more middle of the road they'd be white lines (there are no political societies on campus). Potential hacks have been known to stand for SU posts on a platform of introducing telephone ticket booking, but the SU *has gotten a bit more in-yer-face recently* and won a reduction in rent for those living in the Balls Park portacabins. There are facilities on all the teaching sites.

SU FACILITIES:
Bars, snack bar, Union shops, Endsleigh Insurance office, letting office; travel office, games and vending machines, satellite TV, juke boxes, fax, printing, blockbuster vending machine, photo booth, photocopier, 2 meeting rooms, 2 conference halls. There are regular stalls *flogging* CD's, posters, jewellery and so on. All SU facilities are due for new developments in the near future.

CLUBS (NON SPORTING):
Hellenic; Cypriot; Malaysian; Morpheus Project Gaming; AfCab; Alternative Music; Asian; Clubbing; Sikh; Drama; St Johns Links.

OTHER ORGANISATIONS:
'Universe' is the SU-published newspaper, out every month. CRUSH radio station broadcasts daily to all the halls and houses on the main site and has regular slots in the Union bars. It's been running for over 20 years. There's also a charity Rag which raised £4,000 last year.

RELIGIOUS:
On campus there are facilities for Muslim and Christian worship, including an ecumenical chaplaincy and a full-time chaplain at Hatfield and part-time at the other sites. In Hatfield, there are Anglican, Catholic and Evangelical churches. The Uni has opened the Key Centre as a new Multifaith Centre.

PAID WORK:
There are many local temping agencies and the Galleria offers some hope for shop and café jobs but luck still plays a large part. The SU Studentemps agency can offer part-time work within the Union and the local area.

SPORTS

- Recent successes: Judo, American football

Quite good facilities + overall level of keenness = some not bad results. To help pulses to race a bit faster, there are plans for a new development which will revamp the facilities.

SPORTS FACILITIES:
Hatfield: There's a large sports hall with facilities for all manner of indoor sports and a viewing balcony, which can be curtained off for other sports such as aerobics. There's also a climbing wall, 2 squash courts, minigym, trim trail, 2 floodlit tennis/netball courts and playing fields. Further playing fields are 15 minutes walk away at Angerland Common. There's a natural rock climbing wall or you can get yourself pampered at the Therapy Shop which offers *weary students physiotherapy, aromatherapy, massage and reflexology.* Hatfield has a leisure centre 10 minutes' walk from the campus.
Hertford: Swimming pool; gym; tennis and netball courts; cricket pitch; trim trail; golf practice area.
Watford: Fitness centre; tennis; netball and basketball courts; grass pitches.

SPORTING CLUBS:
American Football; Flying; Gaelic Football; and lots of Martial Arts.

ATTRACTIONS:
Wembley Stadium is just 20 minutes drive away but it's closed for the time being. Choose between Barnet, Luton and Watford for the local footie team and Saracens for rugby.

ACCOMMODATION

IN COLLEGE:
- Self-catering: 22% • Cost: £42-59 (38-52wks)

Availability: There is accommodation on 3 sites. On the Hatfield campus, the choice includes single rooms in halls, flats with 2-6 places or shared houses for 7 in the new student village, *or, if you draw a very short straw,* a Balls Park portacabin. All 1st years are

accommodated, but few others. The houses and flats are quite *plush*, but many of the hall rooms are *quite small*. The flats (in Chantry Court) are let to couples. Other areas are all mixed sex.
Car parking: There is *inadequate* free parking – a permit is needed. *Cars are useful, but parking all round is a problem.*

EXTERNALLY:
- Ave rent: £60

Availability: *Finding places in September, when most people look, can be difficult and students may well not start the academic year in the same place that they finish it. By November, it gets a bit easier.* The University comes to the rescue of a large proportion of students with its head tenancy scheme, whereby it rents local accommodation for 1,000 students. The University also has arrangements with landlords/ladies placing 300 students in digs, living with their host. *South Hatfield and St Albans are the best places to look.*

Housing help: The Accommodation Office has 5 full-time staff who, apart from running the head tenancy scheme, provide advice and help in the house hunt. *The SU lettings office is also handy in finding hassle-free accommodation that's actually habitable.*

WELFARE

SERVICES:
- Creche • Nightline • Lesbian, Gay and Bisexual Society
- Mature SA • Overseas SA • Postgrad SA • Minibus
- Women's Officer • Self-defence classes

A full-time welfare adviser and a trained sabbatical officer at the SU provide help *(usually for cases where the University's help might be inappropriate, such as appeals)* and the University runs the excellent Student Services Unit, which employs 10 staff including a legal adviser and one full-time and four part-time counsellors. On each site there is a Medical Centre, staffed by nurses and doctors who hold surgeries daily at Hatfield, as well as facilities such as Alexander technique, aromatherapy and First Aid training.

Disabled: The Hatfield campus has *comparatively excellent access* and special accommodation provisions, including rooms for carers. *Other sites aren't too bad either.* What's more, there are various amenities for hearing- and sight-impaired students. All main switchboards are equipped with minicoms and *there's good support for dyslexics* done in conjunction with the local Access Centres.

FINANCE:
- Access fund: £727,393 • Successful applications: 1,974

There's also a hardship fund of £500 and a fee waiver system.

```
One of the modern sculptures at Southampton
University was designed to moan in the wind
but it disturbed the law department so the
holes were blocked up.
```

Heythrop College, London

- **The College is part of <u>University of London</u> and students are entitled to use its facilities.**

Heythrop College, Kensington Square, London, W8 5HQ.
Tel: (020) 7795 6600. Fax: (020) 7795 4200.
E-mail: r.bolland@heythrop.ac.uk
Heythrop Students' Union, Kensington Square, London, W8 5HQ.
Tel: (020) 7795 4248. Fax: (020) 7795 4200.

Heythrop, one of London University's smallest colleges, moved in 1993 to an *attractive* Victorian campus-style site, sharing facilities with several other institutions, including an American college, various other religious groups and LAMDA drama school, in Kensington, 3 miles west of Trafalgar Square. *The college buildings and the surrounding area are posher than many of the University's other constituent colleges*, within easy reach of Kensington Gardens and the Kings Road, *but don't be thinking the students are vacuous Sloanes*. Heythrop teaches theology and philosophy and was originally founded in Louvain, Belgium, moving through Liége, Stonyhurst, North Wales and Oxfordshire, finally rolling into London in 1970. There are two 12-week terms and one of 6 weeks and tutorials mostly on a one-to-one basis. Although it accepts students of any religion, *the overall feel of the place reflects its Catholic (specifically Jesuit) roots. This is not the first place to start looking for Shi'ite Muslim fundamentalists, devil worshippers or Ian Paisley.* Many of the students and staff are members of religious orders or hoping to join one. *It's a very cosy, informal, largely Catholic community, with a significant number of mature students and postgrads, which means the distinction between staff and students is less important. The presence of other institutions on site adds to the social pot-pourri. Being so few in number and having so much in common means everyone is very friendly, familiar and homely. The flipside, of course, is that claustrophobia can set in.*

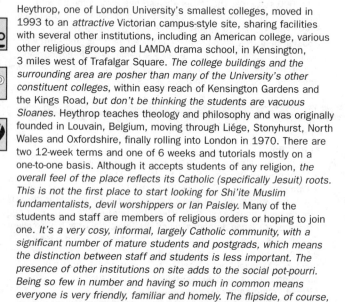

Sex ratio(M:F): 60%:40%	Founded: 1614
Full time u'grads: 150	Part time: 1
Postgrads: 324	Non-degree: 17
Ave course: 3yrs	Ethnic: n/a
Private school: 20%	Flunk rate: n/a
Mature students: 20%	Overseas students: 6%
Disabled students: 1%	Staff/student ratio: 1:6
Clearing: 15%	

KENSINGTON:
Kensington is very posh (London's royal borough), very respectable (high concentration of embassies) and very beautiful (the palace, gardens, leafy streets, and residences). There are a number of *cosy old pubs*, some in unaffordable residential roads, but others are *achingly trendy*, especially on Kensington Church St. Earl's Court, just down the road, is more down-to-earth, *as is Victoria* (15 minutes by bus or tube). *For drama-lovers the Royal Court Theatre (Sloane Square) is particularly useful.* Kensington has a Garfunkels, numerous pizza places and the Next café is good (*and cheap by local*

standards) for coffee and squidgy cakes. *Pushplugs: Greyhound (theologians); Builders' Arms (philosophers)*. Nearest mainline stations: Victoria, Paddington. Nearest tubes: High Street Kensington (District & Circle), Gloucester Rd (District, Circle & Piccadilly). Bus nos 9, 10, 27, 28, 31, 49 and the *bonus number*, 52.

IN COLLEGE:
Largest theological library in the country (250,000 volumes, 60 study places), *so be prepared to share the aisles with nuns*; 20 computers and access to the *far more impressive* facilities at Imperial College. Access to University of London careers service. *For a life in the clergy or teaching religion a Heythrop degree goes a long way*. No bar, but students make use of Imperial College and ULU; occasional evenings lubricated with the sale of bottled beers; Summer Ball held at the Kensington Park Hotel; jazz band at Christmas; £15 membership of the JCR gets you free newspapers, tea and coffee; The Maria Assumpta Centre provides *good-value* meals during the day. SU (no sabbs, *pathetic* 7% turnout, SU forging links with NUS, Imperial College and ULU) *organises social events, especially at the beginning and end of term, but has little political role*; smoking and non-smoking common rooms; kitchen; TV; pool tables; table football; drinks machines. There's a Rabbit Sanctuary run by a bicycling nun – as seen on TV's 'Animal Hospital'. *The football team knocks around the London intercollegiate league but students' minds are generally on higher things than high jumps*; pool; ping-pong tables; tennis courts for those living at Maria Assumpta; a bit of a one-sided agreement with Imperial College, London. Only about 15% of students request college accommodation, which is handy because Heythrop only has catered halls for 18 people, but there is access to University of London intercollegiate halls; *accommodation in Kensington is exorbitant (unless you have access to the Vatican bank)* – Earl's Court (*Australians and not just behind bars*), Notting Hill (*rastas and rich kids slumming it, snogging Julia Roberts is not compulsory*), Battersea (*yuppies, dogs*) and Hammersmith are nearby and considerably cheaper. Access to ULU and University of London welfare facilities; College welfare office; chaplain, Catholic/Ecumenical chapel, optional weekly Mass; creche; nightline; Mature, Overseas and Postgrad SAs; occasional signing during lectures and meetings; Dyslexia Teaching Centre; *wheelchair access is a bit of a problem in the stair-crazy college buildings*; no access fund, small bursary fund for fee-paying students.

CLUBS (NON SPORTING):
Justice & Peace; Liturgy (music for Eucharist services).

FAMOUS ALUMNI:
Frederick Copleston (philosopher); Gerard Manley Hopkins (poet); Nick Stuart (TV presenter).

FURTHER INFO:
Prospectus, website (www.heythrop.ac.uk).

Holloway College

see Royal Holloway, London

Homerton College

see University of Cambridge

University of Huddersfield

- *Formerly Huddersfield Polytechnic*
University of Huddersfield, Queensgate, Huddersfield, HD1 3DH.
Tel: (01484) 422288. Fax: (01484) 516151.
E-mail: schools.prospectus@hud.ac.uk
Huddersfield University Union, University of Huddersfield, Queensgate, Huddersfield, HD1 3DH. Tel: (01484) 538156. Fax: (01484) 432333.

GENERAL

Huddersfield is on the eastern side of the Pennines in the middle of northern England and in the centre of town is one of the two main sites of Huddersfield University. The other, St Peter's, is due to move to the main campus soon. The main building is *a big brown concrete thing with convoluted steps and walkways* and a bridge arching over a part of a canal. There's another building a short walk from the central campus at Larchfield Mills, with light brick and glass 70s architecture, *but not too bad*. Other assorted buildings date from the Victorian period and later. The Uni is renovating the 70s architecture and has redeveloped the Old Mill to form the headquarters of the School of Education & Professional Development.

Sex ratio(M:F): 66%:34%	Founded: 1841
Full time u'grads: 7,764	Part time: 4,140
Postgrads: 936	Non-degree: 4,404
Ave course: 3/4yrs	Ethnic: 17%
Private school: n/a	Flunk rate: 29.1%
Mature students: 30%	Overseas students: 5%
Disabled students: 4%	

ATMOSPHERE:
If it's possible to be laid-back with attitude that's what Huddersfield students are; they want to get on with their courses and wash them down with several pints. As long as nobody gets in the way they're a happy, hospitable, cosmopolitan bunch.

THE TOWN:
- Population: 148,544 • London: 174miles
- Leeds: 14miles • Manchester: 23miles

Huddersfield grew up as an industrial town peddling textiles, *although cloth has turned to economic sloth* and various recessions over the last century left the town in considerable recession by the 80s. *In the last few years, however, things have been looking up with rapid development*, new jobs and *trendy* bars springing up *like Hear'say tribute bands*. There's even a new £50Mn shopping complex. *There's now a slow and aged pace about the place, some might even say boring*, definitely not a bright-lights-big-city, but still friendly. Leeds is close enough for those who need some serious action. The architecture reflects the tone – *rather grand, though sooty*, Georgian buildings, co-existing with the more modern features of the shopping centre. *When God created Huddersfield, he was going through a hilly phase.*

TRAVEL:
Trains: The main site is 10 minutes walk from Huddersfield BR station which has direct lines to Leeds (£2.80) and Manchester (£5.80) every 30 mins. Trains to London (£29.60) via Wakefield.
Coaches: National Express services to London (£16.75), Birmingham (£13.75) and elsewhere.
Car: A few minutes off the M62, on the A62, A642, A629 and A616.
Air: Manchester Airport (International), 30 miles away.
Hitching: *Locals will pick up hitchers even if they're pretty smeggy. The A62 is probably the best pick-up point or take a bus to Junction 24 of the M62.*
Local: *Buses are comprehensive*, charging between 60p and £1.30. A Metrocard *is a worthwhile investment.*
Taxis: £3 to get most of the way across town.
Bicycles: *Heavy traffic, hellish hills and plenty of rain, so much stamina is required even going downhill.* And then there are the usual problems with theft.

CAREER PROSPECTS:
- Careers Service • No of staff: 4 full/2 part
- Unemployed after 6mths: 4.9%

FAMOUS ALUMNI:
Gorden Kaye (René in 'Allo, Allo'); Wilf Lunn (eccentric inventor); Patrick Stewart (Capt Piccard in 'Star Trek TNG').

FURTHER INFO:
Prospectuses for undergrads, part timers and postgrads, plus a video. Netties can find out more at www.hud.ac.uk

ACADEMIC

staff/student ratio: 1:18
Range of points required for entrance: 300-140
Percentage accepted through clearing: 16%
Number of terms/semesters: 3
Length of terms/semesters: 12 wks
Research: 2.5

LIBRARIES:
- Books: 350,000 • Study places: 800

The recently refurbished Central Library includes a new Media Centre, with dead good audio-visual resources, DTP facilities and 24 hour access during term time. There are 3 smaller libraries: education; a music library; and a chemistry periodicals library.

COMPUTERS:
- Computer workstations: 1,500

There's 24-hour computer access in the Schools of Computing and Mathematics.

ENTERTAINMENT

TOWN:
- Price of a pint of beer: £1.80 • Glass of wine: £1.70

Pubs: Some good real ale pubs – this is Yorkshire after all – and generally welcome to student custom. *Pushplugs: Revolution (vodka*

bar), College Arms, O'Neill's, Thirsty Scholar (all near the University) and a Rat & Parrot right outside.
Cinemas: There's a new UCI multiplex 10 minutes bus-ride from the Uni.
Theatres: The Lawrence Batley Theatre is mainstream, while the Cellar does more off-beat stuff, including comedy nights.
Clubs/discos: Many local clubs are *truly naff and the many students who frequent them do so with their tongues firmly planted in their cheeks.* Pushplugs: Visage; retro nights at Hotshots.
Music venues: The Alfred McAlpine Stadium hosts occasional mega-gigs (eg REM) but for a wider choice Leeds, Manchester and Bradford are *an easy trip*. Classical music fans are better catered for at the Huddersfield and St Paul's Concert Halls.
Eating out: Local eateries are not plentiful and offer more by way of value than quality. Some are worth Pushplugging anyway: Mensahib (cheap student Indian); Shamus O'Donnell's (best of a good pub grub selection); Caspian takeaway; Blue Rooms (veggie).

UNIVERSITY:
• Price of a pint of beer: £1.40 • Glass of wine: £1.20
Bars: The 2 SU bars are the Roland and Cellar Bars, aka the Milton Hall bars. There are also University-run *dens of iniquity* at Storthes Hall.
Films: The film club shows two cult films a month.
Clubs/discos/music venues: Big names on the club circuit recently include Tim Westwood, Mark and Lard, Shanks and Bigfoot.
Comedy: Mirth bits courtesy of the Carlsberg ICE Comedy Network.
Food: The Milton Hall coffee bar is *cheap and cheerful* and the Refectory serves *school dinner-style permutations* of pies, chips and beans all day. Eden serves fast food.
Other: Various balls and dinners, *providing a good range*, all revolving around alcohol and usually with drinks promotions.

SOCIAL & POLITICAL

UNIVERSITY OF HUDDERSFIELD STUDENTS' UNION:
• 5 sabbaticals • Turnout at last ballot: 12.5% • NUS member
The Union is pretty sussed but things can get tense where budget is concerned. The student body as a whole doesn't seem particularly concerned or even aware about politics but they're very happy with the booze and boogie side of things.

SU FACILITIES:
Its collective facilities include: bars and coffee bars; cafeteria; printing service; general shop; photocopying; pool room; games and vending machines; juke box; function rooms.

CLUBS (NON SPORTING):
Bahrain; Capoeira; Duke of Edinburgh; Film; Juggling; Medieval; Rapid; Roleplay; Students against Racism.

OTHER ORGANISATIONS:
'Ay-Up' is the student newspaper. There's a student radio station too. UNITY is a campaigning organisation which holds an annual festival for Community Action and does *good stuff* with local residents (OAP visits, cleaning up the canal, etc), plus a busy Rag week and ball.

RELIGIOUS:
- 3 chaplains (RC, CofE, Free Church)

There is an interdenominational chaplaincy centre and a Muslim prayer room. The town caters for Christians of 6 different flavours as well as Muslim, Hindu, Sikh, Buddhist and Jewish.

PAID WORK:
Local unemployment keeps opportunities limited, but the SU employs over 500 students and the Uni runs a professionally managed jobshop to help the rest get some readies.

SPORTS

- Recent successes: basketball

The University has little to offer by way of its own sports arrangements – sports hall on campus and astroturf at Storthes Hall – but this is somewhat compensated for by the town's very good facilities which the students use frequently. To get in the pink, a Kirklees Passport (£6/yr) is recommended, giving discounted access to local facilities.

SPORTS FACILITIES:
There are 15 acres of playing fields, 2 miles from the campus, a sports hall, athletics field, astroturf pitch, squash courts, multigym and newish fitness gym. The town doubles up on all of these and also has a croquet lawn, bowling green, running track, swimming pool, golf courses, tennis courts, saunas and an all-weather pitch. Close by there are also a lake, river and hills.

SPORTING CLUBS:
Caving; Jiu Jitsu; Kung Fu; Motorsport; Mountain Bike; Outdoor Pursuits; Parachute; Snowboard; Surf; Table Tennis.

ATTRACTIONS:
Huddersfield Town FC and Huddersfield Rugby League both play at the Alfred McAlpine stadium which also has great facilities including a fitness centre and golf driving range.

ACCOMMODATION

IN COLLEGE:
- Self-catering: 25% • Cost: £38-60 (41wks)

Availability: There are 6 halls in all, *a mere short crawl from the main campus,* although the new Storthes Hall development is 4 miles away (but free transport is laid on). *Storthes is popular because of its student village feel.* 7% have to share (no mixed quarters) and 13% of 1st years who want to can't live in. Single sex flats and houses are available as are single gender corridors in St Peter's Hostel and the Central Services Building.

EXTERNALLY:
- Ave rent: £38

Availability: *As the accommodation office points out, the further away students are prepared to look, the better value they will find.* The best student nests are Bradford Road, Springrove, Newsome, Birkby and Lockwood. Sheepridge, Deighton and Fartown are a bit rough, though, and worth avoiding.

Housing help: The Accommodation Office allocates places in halls and, for those living out, can offer legal advice, vacancy lists, recommended landlords and safety checks.

WELFARE

SERVICES:
- Nursery • Nightline • Lesbian & Gay Society • Overseas SA
- Minibus • Women's Officer • Self-defence classes

The University offers one full- and one part-time counsellor, the Union two and one respectively. The University Health Centre has two visiting local GPs with another two on job-share, and three nurses.

Disabled: *What with the hills wheelchair-users don't have it easy to start with. New buildings are well thought out* but the Union is a Grade II listed building *which makes access difficult.* Some halls of residence are specially designed for wheelchairs. Text-phone facilities are available for hearing-impaired students.

FINANCE:
- Access fund: £678,634 • Successful applications: 906

The Union offers emergency welfare loans of about £30/week, and there's money available for disabled and overseas students.

University of Hull

University of Hull, Hull, HU6 7RX. Tel: (0870) 1262000.
Fax: (01482) 442290. E-mail: admissions@admin.hull.ac.uk
Hull University Union, University House, Cottingham Road, Hull, HU6 7RX.
Tel: (01482) 465361. Fax: (01482) 466280.

GENERAL

Hull's full name is Kingston-upon-Hull and it's Britain's 3rd largest port, a *sprawling city (but not sprawling very far)* on England's north-east coast, surrounded by miles of flat, flat land. The River Hull flows down from the north to join the huge estuary of the Humber. The surrounding coastline is *stunning* and the Victorian city centre is also *quite attractive*, even if the outskirts and harbours are heavily industrialised. The University is 2 miles from the centre in a *pleasantly* leafy Victorian/Edwardian residential area. The large campus (94 acres) is a collection of municipal architecture from the last 100 years, but principally from the 30s and 60s. Those 60s bits in *dull* brick *damage* the overall picture, which would *otherwise be a good-looking, low-lying campus with broad spreads of paths, paving and even grass and trees.* In August 2000, there was a merger with University College Scarborough (40 miles away from the main site). 1,300 students are based in the Schools of Art and Education, the Centre for Internet Computing, the Centre for Coastal Studies and the Centre for Business and Leisure Management.

Sex ratio(M:F): 41%:59%
Full time u'grads: 6,695
Postgrads: 1,447
Ave course: 3yrs
Private school: 10%
Mature students: 25%
Disabled students: 3.5%

Founded: 1927
Part time: 513
Non-degree: 6,718
Ethnic: 3.4%
Flunk rate: 14.2%
Overseas students: 8.3%

ATMOSPHERE:
Hull University is a classic example of a civic campus university. It has the friendly camaraderie of a self-contained campus, but, being in a city, isn't stifling, because there's escape into the welcoming anonymity of the centre (most students don't bother escaping). *Fun facilities are better than average; any more and the students would be approaching meltdown.*

TOWN:
- Population: 250,000 • London: 165 miles
- York; 34 miles • Leeds: 50 miles

Back in the 19th-century, fish were responsible for the growth of *Hull (the fishing industry rather than a school of particularly adept mackerel)*. This century, trade has shifted to industries, particularly chemical ones. *In a weird twist of the old adage, Hull is an okay place to live, but you wouldn't want to visit there. It hasn't got much to attract tourists, but has all the paraphernalia that attend daily existence*: shops, banks, VD clinics and so on (including a Waterstones bookshop). The local sights include the docks and marina, the Hull Fair, several art galleries and the Humber Suspension Bridge (the largest central span in the world). Hull is also the only town in Britain to have its own telephone system.

TRAVEL:
Trains: Hull Paragon rail station runs services to London via Doncaster or York (£19.20) and other connections to Newcastle (£20.15) and Birmingham (£24.95).
Coaches: Clipper and National Express services all over the country including London (£22.50), Birmingham (£17.75) and Newcastle (£16.75).
Car: From the south the M18 connects the M1 with the local Hull motorway, the M62. From the north, take the M1 then M62 which leads into the A63, then look out for the A1079.
Air: Humberside Airport, 12 miles south across the Humber is mainly for inland flights, although it has some to Europe.
Ferries: To Holland and Scandinavia.
Hitching: *There's a semi-official hitch pitch on the A63 that all traffic has to pass.*
Local: There are two *fiercely competitive* bus companies running until midnight-ish. There are three train stops in Hull, two of which are useful for students, since one is in the city centre and the other is in Cottingham.
Taxis: *Sharing taxis is often cheaper than catching a bus or train.*
Bicycles: Hull is very flat with straight wide roads between the residential and functional parts of the University. *However, theft is rife.*

CAREER PROSPECTS:
- Careers Service • No of staff: 3 full/2 part
- Unemployed after 6mths: 3%

FAMOUS ALUMNI:
Lord Dearing (of Dearing Report fame); Sarah Greene (TV ex-sex goddess and Mrs Mike Smith); Jonathan Harvey (playwright); Lord Hattersley; John McCarthy (former hostage) & Jill Morrell (his campaigning ex-partner); Roger McGough (poet); Anthony Minghella ('English Patient' director); Juliet Morris, Jenni Murray (broadcasters); Tom Paulin (TV arts critic); John Prescott MP (Lab); Michael Stock (S****, Aitken & Waterman); Ben Watt & Tracey Thorn (Everything But The Girl).

FURTHER INFO:
Prospectuses for undergrads and postgrads, plus an alternative prospectus from the Union. Not to mention departmental pamphlets and website (www.hull.ac.uk). Except we just did.

ACADEMIC

staff/student ratio: 1:15
Range of points required for entrance: 320-140
Percentage accepted through clearing: 12%
Number of terms/semesters: 2
Length of terms/semesters: 15 wks
Research: 4.0

LIBRARIES:
• Books: 1,031,448 • Study places: 1,880
It may have quite a few books, but given that most students anywhere spend their library time staring out of the window, Hull's main library is a *good* one – the top floor gives spectacular views over the Humber Estuary. There are 3 subsidiary libraries as well.

COMPUTERS:
• Computer workstations: 800

ENTERTAINMENT

TOWN:
• Price of a pint of beer: £1.75 • Glass of wine: £1.60
Cinemas: (4) 2 multiplexes with 8 screens each, one of which is in St Andrew's Quay. Also another cinema with 4 screens; and another 9-screener at Kingswood. Also, the Film Theatre, next to the City Library, for arty flicks.
Theatres: (2) *The more highbrow* is the New Theatre for *posh* plays, opera and ballet. Spring Street Theatre is a rep base, the home of the *excellent* Hull Truck Theatre company and also hosts cabaret nights.
Pubs: Being a port, Hull has *no shortage of pubs*, some of which have stuffed fish on the walls and glass balls in nets, but most are less naff. *Pushplugs:* Gardner's Arms (packed with students); Haworth Arms; The Cranborough; The Piper; Foxhill & Firkin; Scruffy Murphy's. The Bev Road Run, a 12-pub crawl, is a good bet for the hollow-legged.
Clubs/discos: Hull's selection of dance palaces leaves much to be desired. Student nights offer the best value. Pushplugs: The Room (voted 7th best club in UK by Sky); Spiders (Goth/trash); Silhouette (theme nights, gay-friendly, £2); Eclipse (cheesy house).

Music venues: *Things are better on the live front, especially for indie fans.* Pushplugs: The Room, The Adelphi (small-scale gigs); City Hall, Tower Ballroom (bigger draws); Hull Arena.
Eating out: A good range, *if a little lacking on the late night snacking front.* Pushplugs: Hitchcock (veggie); Zoo Café (hippy); Chaplin's (Tex-Mex, all-you-can-eat buffet £4); Old Grey Mare (good value pub grub).

UNIVERSITY:
• Price of a pint of beer: £1.25 • Glass of wine: £1.35

Bars: (5) The Resnikov Bar is the main one, *especially popular* at lunchtime and weekends. The John McCarthy is the main venue boozer in the evenings. The Chico Mendes (named after a Brazilian environmental campaigner and, *ironically, decorated with hardwood) is* mainly used for society functions. The Continental isn't, especially. Continental, that is. While the Sports Bar is a bit poo, even when it's open.

Theatres: Drama students put on 10 major shows a year in the *flash* Gulbenkian Theatre and the Z Theatre Company takes regular productions to Edinburgh. *Thespian things are thuperb especially since the merger with Scarborough.* This brought with it links with the Stephen Joseph Theatre, home of the National Student Drama Festival, which also features the premiers of all Sir Alan Ayckbourne's plays.

Cinemas: one cult film a week.

Clubs/discos: Two main club nights a week in the Union Main Hall (cap 1,485); the indie of Big Beat and the two-room dance/nostalgia mix that is Twisted, costing £1.50 each. The monthly drum'n'bass do New Horizons is also popular. *Things get a bit more exciting when the occasional Industry night attracts big names such as LTJ Bukem.*

Music venues: The Union Main Hall is the main live music venue, luring the likes of Terrorvision, Grooverider, Gene and Mansun, Toploader, Embrace, The Lightning Seeds and S Club Heaven (tribute band to the S Club Seven lot) recently. The John McCarthy Bar also hosts jazz nights fortnightly.

Food: The Main Hall has yet another guise; it's a *greasy* Refectory during the day, doling out *reasonably priced chips* 'n' pizza-type stuff to willing gannets. There's also a new continental style bar serving *above-average* student munchies. The Resnikov has a *less enthralling* menu of fry-ups and sarnies.

Cabaret: Fortnightly *farce from would-be Festes* such as Craig Charles, Brendan Burns, Alan Parker and Phil Kaye.

Others: Numerous termly balls, annual Athletic and St Patrick's Day Events, etc.

HULL UNIVERSITY UNION:
• 8 sabbaticals • Turnout at last ballot: 20% • NUS member

The Union's main roles are welfare provision and commercial acumen. The building is big and the facilities are impressive, but politics of the soapbox variety seldom intrudes. A boycott of Nestlé is still in place, however.

SU FACILITIES:
A £5.3Mn revamp of the Union building is planned, to include new bars, a purpose-built venue, a nightclub and shops. Currently, Union facilities are based in University House: three bars; mini-mart shop

(and another mini-mart with limited opening hours at the Lawns Centre – see below); gift shop; travel agency; dark room; launderette; photocopying; DTP unit; Lloyds and Midland cash-points; games machines room; vending machines; pool tables; function rooms (including 4 large halls); minibus hire. The sports centre is one of only two Union-run centres in the country.

CLUBS (NON SPORTING):
AIDEC; Backfire (motorbikes); Ballroom Dancing; Beatroot (DJ); Buddhist; Change ringing; Chinese; Cock (cocktails); CRAIC (Ceilidh, Rave & Irish Culture); Drum'n'Bass; Dutch/Flemish; European football supporters; Evangelical; Gilbert & Sullivan; Hellenic; Hempology; Italianissima; Jazz; Kabbadi (probably something to do with fighting); Links First Aid; Malaysian; Mediterranean; Methodist; Music.

OTHER ORGANISATIONS:
The Union-financed, but editorially independent 'Hullfire' is the main student newspaper and has notched up more than its share of national awards. The student radio station JAM1575 broadcasts on AM and has a 24-hour licence. There's also a student TV station. HUSSO, the country's largest student community group, runs some *extremely active and worthwhile* projects. It employs a sabbatical coordinator, a full-time secretary and involves over 1,000 students.

RELIGIOUS:
• <u>10 chaplains (CofE, RC, Orthodox, Methodist, Baptist, URC, Friends, Jewish)</u>
There's a chapel sort of thing under the Arts building and a Muslim prayer room. In Hull, most versions of Christianity are represented and there is a small Jewish community.

PAID WORK:
Hull has got a pretty bad unemployment problem, and students aren't first in the queue, facing resentment if they try to push in, but the SU-run Job Exchange provides details of sits vac for those trying to get in the back door.

SPORTS

• <u>Recent successes: cricket, rugby, women's badminton</u>
In the past, Hull didn't have the facilities to attract anybody who took sport too seriously. Things have improved, and *the Uni is now a premier coaching centre (awarded by the National Coaching Foundation)*. However, it's still not one of those places where winning's all that important. There is a good level of participation, though.

SPORTS FACILITIES:
At the Sports & Fitness Centre: indoor sports; fitness and weight training; 2 multigyms; sauna and solarium; jacuzzi. At the Sports Centre (5 minutes' walk from the Union): gym; 2 sports halls; badminton and 7 squash courts; all-weather pitch; climbing wall. 11 playing fields on the campus and near the Lawns Halls, an athletics and running track, 11 tennis courts and a boathouse at Beresford Avenue. New netball/5-a-side courts. The city also provides a swimming pool nearby and an ice rink; recreation passes (£4.50) allow students to use many facilities for free during the day. There is a new sports bursary scheme.

SPORTING CLUBS:
Aikido; Jiu Jitsu; Karting; Ken Po Karate; Latin and Ballroom Dancing; Rowing; Speleological; Ten Pin Bowling; Ultimate Frisbee; Yoga.

ATTRACTIONS:
Hull has two major rugby league clubs plus soccer and ice hockey teams. There is also a race track in Beverley.

ACCOMMODATION

IN COLLEGE:
- Catered: 22% • Cost: £61-79 (33wks)
- Self-catering: 19%
- Cost: £39-56 (33-50wks), doesn't include fuel costs

Availability: There are three types of University accommodation: the six Lawns Halls, on a baby greenfield site, 3 miles from the University itself; the three traditional halls (behind the Botanical Gardens, halfway between the campus and the Lawns); but the largest number of places are in shared houses, most of which are close to the campus. All 1st years can be accommodated. 15% have to share, but some of those are *judiciously partnered* in halls. Catered accommodation ranges from providing seven to 15 meals per week. The Lawns Halls (one is self-catering) are accompanied by the Lawns Centre featuring all sorts of facilities. There are also 480 places in a head leasing scheme and 44 in a Housing Association scheme. Thwaite Hall offers single-sex accommodation on certain corridors; some other provisions are also available in student houses. *There are the everyday problems with burglary*, but action through the Uni's Crime Prevention Panel is attempting to address this.

Car parking: Permit parking only – get on your bike.

EXTERNALLY:
- Ave rent: £35

Availability: *Finding housing is easy enough. Students could do worse than Beverley Rd, Cottingham Rd, Newland Avenue and Prince's Avenue.*

Housing help: Information on private housing is available from the Advice Centre of the SU. The Uni has close links with private landlords.

WELFARE

SERVICES:
- Creche • Nightline • Lesbian & Gay Society • Mature SA
- Overseas SA • Postgrad SA • Minibus • Women's Officer
- Self-defence classes

The Union and University give troubled and miserable students the metaphorical spoonful of sugar at the Welfare and Counselling Service, which employs one full- and four part-time counsellors and a student sabbatical adviser. There isn't a late minibus laid on, but there is an arrangement with a local bus company to shuttle between campus and town till 2.30am Thurs–Sat.

Disabled: There is a disability support service manned by four staff. Only the major buildings are adapted with wheelchair access in mind. Dyslexia, however, is well covered.

FINANCE:
- Access fund: 593,822 • Successful applications: 1,002

The Vice Chancellor's Hardship Fund dishes out loans as does the SU in emergencies.

University of Humberside

see University of Lincolnshire & Humberside

Imperial College, London

Imperial College, London

- **The College is part of University of London and students are entitled to use its facilities.**

Imperial College of Science, Technology & Medicine (University of London), London, SW7 2AZ. Tel: (020) 7594 8014. Fax: (020) 7594 8004. E-mail: admissions@ic.ac.uk
Imperial College Union, Prince Consort Road, London, SW7 2BB. Tel: (020) 7594 8060. Fax: (020) 7594 8065.
E-mail: president@ic.ac.uk

GENERAL

Jam sandwiched between The Natural History Museum and The Royal Albert Hall in South Kensington, just 1½ miles from Trafalgar Square, is Imperial College. Imperial was formed when in 1907 The Royal School of Mines, City & Guilds College and The Royal College of Science merged, with the Medical School coming along in the late 80s. *The main building is what Prince Chas would call a 'carbuncle' - a towering, oversized portakabin of aluminium, smoked glass and concrete.* The two new buildings, The Alexander Fleming and the other one (not yet named), were designed by Foster and Partners. Inside it's well ordered - echoing walkways with glass displays and cabinets full of scientific paraphernalia *which all adds to the sense of awesome scientific knowledge.* Overshadowing all this is the Queen's Tower, which has now been locked off. *Allegedly, too many frustrated finalists were flinging themselves from the parapet, knowing at least enough physics to realise it was a sure fire way of getting out of exams.* Apart from the campus at South Kensington and the various hospital sites, Imperial has a mine at Truro in Cornwall and a 260-acre site at Silwood Park, near Ascot, mainly for scientific fieldwork. There's been a recent merger with Wye College which specialises in farming and environmental courses.

Sex ratio(M:F): 67%:33%	Founded: 1907
Full time u'grads: 6,747	Part time: 0
Postgrads: 2,694	Non-degree: 244
Ave course: 3/4 yrs	Ethnic: n/a
Private school: n/a	Flunk rate: 6.2%
Mature students: n/a	Overseas students: 34%
Disabled students: 4%	

ATMOSPHERE:
Just because Imperial's students are overwhelmingly male and all studying science, technology or medicine, doesn't mean they're all

geeks. There are a few nerds, spods, boffins and dweebs as well. No, that's not really fair, but they do work very hard, on a nine-to-five basis mostly, and academic standards are world-renowned. Outside college hours they know how to chug a pint and there's a substantial sporty set as well. Relations with the immediate locals (posh Kensingtonians) are next to non-existent. With the sex ratio at two to one, the main problem for Imperial's (straight) males, of course, is intense sexual frustration.

THE SITES:
Medical students spend their first 2 years at the main South Kensington site, after which they study at one of the other 4 sites in West London:

St Mary's: (190 students) 2 miles from Imperial, in Paddington, is the medical school *and if you thought the scientists worked hard, the doctors-to-be do even more*. Despite this, they have time to use the recreation centre on site, as well as the swimming pool and bar.

Royal Brompton: (140 students) What used to be known as the National Heart and Lung Institute is now the Royal Brompton site in Chelsea, a mile from the main site. *Apart from academic facilities, fun-time is restricted to a sarnie shop.*

Charing Cross: (225 students) Not, despite its name, anywhere near Charing Cross, this site is 3 miles from the main site, in Hammersmith. There's a bar and a café.

Hammersmith: (347 students) Formerly the Royal Postgraduate Medical School, this site is mostly for postgraduates. There are two new sites, both non-medical:

Wye: formerly Wye College, 1,129 students, 50 miles from the main campus in the quiet little village of Wye (*surprise, surprise*). Parts of Biology and the TH Huxley School are also based here.

Silwood Park: 81 postgrad students.

THE CITY: see University of London

SOUTH KENSINGTON:
The area immediately surrounding the College is a *prim quad* with privet hedges in the *relative peace* of South Kensington. Kensington itself is *a well-to-do area* with Harrods just round the corner in Knightsbridge (*although we don't recommend students use it for their weekly shop*). The area's full of expensive boutiques and delicatessens. *Even the kebab joints have French names round here.* It's also an *erudite* part of London, brimming with museums and libraries and educational institutions. It's *pricey* to live in South Kensington itself; *Shepherd's Bush or Earl's Court are a likelier bet.* However, it's well connected for the West End and ULU only takes 20 minutes by tube or slightly longer by bus.

TRAVEL: see University of London
Trains: The nearest mainline BR stations are Paddington and Victoria, each about 1½ miles away.
Buses: 9, 10, 14, 51, 74 and C1. Night buses: N14 and N97.
Car: Parking at the college is limited to those with disabilities.
Underground: Gloucester Road and South Kensington (both on the District, Circle and Piccadilly Lines).

CAREER PROSPECTS:
• Careers Service • No of staff: 3 full/2 part
• Unemployed after 6mths: 2.7%

Potential employers, particularly in scientific and technical areas, regard Imperial as a goldmine of bright bods.

SPECIAL FEATURES:
Imperial's mascot is a 185lb micrometer, *which avoids the trend among London colleges of stealing each other's mascots.*

FAMOUS ALUMNI:
Mary Archer (Lord Jeff's wife); Sir Roger Bannister (4-minute miler); Alexander Fleming (discovered penicillin); Rajiv Gandhi (former Indian Prime Minister); WG Grace (cricketer); David Irving (revisionist 'historian'); David Livingstone (explorer); Brian May (large-haired Queen guitar hero); Trevor Phillips (Deputy London Mayor); Joan Ruddock MP (Lab); Simon Singh (Author 'Fermat's Last Theorem'); HG Wells (writer); JPR Williams (rugby player); Francis Wilson (weatherman).

FURTHER INFO:
Prospectuses for undergrads and postgrads, website (www.ic.ac.uk) and an alternative prospectus from SU.

ACADEMIC

Academic standards are renowned worldwide and 20% of students get 1st class degrees. It's famous for its science and technology work, but does a few arts and language courses too. Imperial College, as a college of the University of London, is basically independent, but the degrees awarded are University of London degrees. The College can award diplomas. Some graduates can also end up with unusual letters after their names (such as ARCS, ARSM and ACGI) showing they're now associates to various professional bodies. 99% of the teaching staff have PhDs and through the Undergraduate Research Opportunities Programme (UROP) gives students the opportunity to take part in the research activities of College academic staff and postgraduates.

Participation is voluntary and enables you to do what research is all about and get practical experience of some of the College's research facilities. You can also follow up your own interests (*no bombs and stuff though*). In addition, you may be able to get your name on scientific publications before you even graduate (*impressive for sure*). There may also be possibilities for final year project work.

In addition to the opportunities available during term time, there is also a substantial amount of activity during vacations. In the summer vacation, you could be paid a bursary based on the level of those paid to postgraduates. UROP bursaries are tax-free and do not attract a national insurance charge. Summer vacation UROP work has proved to be particularly popular with overseas students who do not need work permits for UROP projects.

A directory describing the UROP scheme is available, free of charge, from the UROP Office, Level 3, in the Mechanical Engineering Building or see the website www.hu.ic.ac.uk/urop/

staff/student ratio: 1:10
Range of points required for entrance: 340-260
Percentage accepted through clearing: 4%
Number of terms/semesters: 3
Length of terms/semesters: 11wks
Research: 5.9

LIBRARIES:
- Books: 1,235,000 (including 4,000 electronic journals)
- Study places: 2,500

There are 20 libraries in all, including the Medical School and departmental libraries.

COMPUTERS:
- Computer workstations: 1,500

Unsurprisingly, computer provision is better than average but the facilities still can't keep up with the eager little mouse-wielders.

ENTERTAINMENT

IN LONDON: see University of London

SOUTH KENSINGTON:
South Kensington has a fair level of entertainments of its own, but it's mainly wine bars and posh clubs, although the Queen's Arms is popular. The West End is within a stroll's distance and many of the areas around Kensington offer some thrills and spills (Notting Hill, Earl's Court, Hammersmith, Chelsea, Fulham, Putney). Local pubs with a Pushplug include: The Queen's Arms, Rat & Parrot and Finnegan's Wake.

COLLEGE:
- Price of a pint of beer: £1.40 • Glass of wine: £1.50

Bars: There are 5 bars at the main site, including Da Vinci's *(still looks like a Butlin's leisure lounge despite having been done up)*, Southside *(pipe 'n' slippers pub)*, Union Bar *(also pubby, popular with rugby gorillas)*, and dBs *(venue bar, womb-like)*.

Theatres: Imperial has 2 halls, *which are both eminently suitable as theatres for the strangely strong dramatic contingent*, including medical opera and drama societies. Not only do they take shows to the Edinburgh Fringe, they rent a theatre and sub-let it to other groups.

Cinemas: Imperial has the largest student cinema screen in the country and shows 2 mainstream films a week.

Clubs/discos: Several clubs every week: the mainstream Pop Tarts; Common People (indie); Hedonizm (dub); Shaft (70s) and more.

Music venues: The Great Hall has a capacity of 600 and there's also the Concert Hall (450) and dBs (450). Names to appear recently include Branden Block, Noel Fielding and Chris Addison.

Cabaret: Once a fortnight, in the Union building, there's a comic on the bill, Phil Nichol being a recent example.

Food: Basics pizzeria at Southside is run-of-the-mill. Da Vinci's Café Bar offers a *wide-ranging edible spread*. QT in the Sherfield Building sells snacks in the daytime as well as the Main Dining Hall which serves slightly more substantial scoff. dBs does baguettes. There's also a café in the new Alexander Fleming building *(watch out for the penicillin experiments - it's a type of mould, don't you know?)*

Others: 2 big balls a year, occasionally in posh London hotels. Also Christmas and departmental *binges* and 3 carnivals a year.

The law department at Warwick University has admitted the former military director of Sierra Leone.

SOCIAL & POLITICAL

IMPERIAL COLLEGE STUDENTS' UNION:
• 6 sabbaticals • Turnout at last ballot: 13%
The Union is politically independent, even of the NUS. *It exists to provide services to its members, who lap them up when they can tear themselves away from work. Urging the students into any political activity is harder than learning Gujurati from a Martian.* Only 30 of them attended a recent fees rally. **Also ULU:** see University of London.

SU FACILITIES:
The Union has facilities at the main site, St Mary's and Charing Cross. At South Kensington, the Union building, called Beit Quad, is on the other side of the road. In all, the Union offers bars, a cafeteria, sandwich bar, travel agency, resources centre, 2 shops, minibus hire, photo booth, video and games machines, juke boxes, cinema and fax service. There's a new centre housing advice, welfare, chaplaincy services, a media centre, store and library.

CLUBS (NON SPORTING):
Amateur Radio; Arabic; Best; Book; Cypriot; Exploration; Finance; ICUWWW; Indian; Italian; Japanese; Junior Enterprise; Korean; Latin American; Lebanese; Newspaper; Persian Gulf; Quiz; Radio Modellers; St John Ambulance; Scandinavian; Sikh; Singapore; Spanish; Sri Lankan; Thai; Turkish; Wargames.

OTHER ORGANISATIONS:
'Felix' is the Union's weekly newspaper and there's also a radio station (Imperial College Radio) and a TV station (STOIC - Student Television of Imperial College). *Imperial College's Rag is very energetic, although as much energy goes into oh-so-wacky stunts as into actual fund-raising.* There's the annual tiddlywink race down Oxford Street and legends abound of the naked parachute leap which ended in nude students being bundled out of a van at Harrods. 'Felix' claims to have photos.

RELIGIOUS:
The West London Chaplaincy handles all Christians, whatever the denomination. Daily prayer meetings are held in the Islamic Society prayer room and Regent's Park Mosque (one of the country's largest) is nearby. **Religion in London:** see University of London.

PAID WORK:
Imperial students can appeal to the firms constantly vying for their talents for vacation work or there's Imperial's UROP scheme where they help lecturers with their research work and can expect to earn anything up to £120 a week *and many brownie points*.

SPORTS

• Recent successes: across the board
Bearing in mind that Imperial students are entitled to use ULU and the University's facilities as well as their own excellent amenities, they've got the world at their feet like a football. Imperial is top of the London colleges in the student sports league.

SPORTS FACILITIES:
Imperial has 60 acres of playing fields at Harlington (15 miles from Kensington) which are also used for practice by Chelsea Football Club, 50 acres at Cobham in Kent with 3 tennis courts, and 12.5

acres at Teddington with 4 tennis courts. The College lays on buses 2 days a week to get there so that students can use the pitches, including an all-weather pitch, and the pavilion. Meanwhile, over the road from the South Kensington ranch, Imperial has a sports centre which *is a fabulous feat of architecture. It is built underground to save space with only a transparent tardis visible on the surface. The cavern down below looks like something from The Man from U.N.C.L.E.* and includes a 25m pool, 4 squash courts, weights room and multigym, jacuzzi, projectile hall, health suite and studio. It's hired out to the public to subsidise student use. Back above ground, Imperial has 2 tennis courts, a shooting range, martial arts centre and a boat-house at Putney. What's more, the SU provides 3 training halls, 2 tennis courts and a free weights room. Charges for other facilities are minimal (40-50p). A new sports centre is opening soon.

SPORTING CLUBS:
Billiards; Jiu Jitsu; Rowing; Snooker.

ATTRACTIONS: see University of London

ACCOMMODATION

IN COLLEGE:
• Catered: 3% • Cost: £64-83 (34wks)
• Self-catering: 32% • Cost: £43-95 (34-51wks)

Availability: Imperial accommodates all of its 1st years either in their own halls or intercollegiate halls, but college housing is limited for other students. There are 11 halls in all and 5 so-called student houses, the largest of which, *Bernard Sunley House, we'd call large enough to be a hall*. Women have to apply to the University for intercollegiate rooms if they want all-female housing. *A whopping 32% of students in college accommodation have to share rooms, sometimes even in triple rooms, but they are charged less*. The halls are mostly around South Kensington, but also spread throughout West London. Some self-catered places are in flats in South Ealing. Swipe card entry and security guards in some halls.

Catering: The kitchens shared by 8 students on average *are usually pretty well equipped and cleaned every day*. Catered places offer a meal a day, ranging from bad to edible.

Parking: Only if you have a disability, *a considerable disposable income or a magic laser-rifle that dissolves traffic wardens and clamps.*

EXTERNALLY: see University of London
Hammersmith is the closest location *for those who haven't struck lucky on the scratch cards*. The Union has a Housing Advice scheme and the Student Accommodation Office provides housing lists.

```
UCL has removed the preserved head of
philosopher Jeremy Bentham from its display
case after a group of King's College students
'borrowed' it for a game of football.
```

WELFARE

SERVICES:
- Nursery • Nightline • Mature SA • Overseas SA
- Lesbian & Gay Society (aka Imperial Queers)
- Minibus • Women's Officer • Self-defence classes

The Health Centre is home to 6 doctors, 4 nurses, a dentist and 1 full-time and 2 part-time counsellors.

Women: *With less than one woman to every two men, the most severe problem is solitude, although the increasing number of medical students is levelling the figures out. The College is trying to encourage female applicants. Attack alarms are available and there's a minibus.*

Disabled: Actively refurbishing older buildings to supply disabled access and the new buildings have good facilities. There is specially designed accommodation for wheelchair users and hearing- and sight-impaired students. There is also a Disabled Students' Association which supports students with seen and unseen disabilities including dyslexia. The College employs a Disabilities Officer. There are hearing loops in some lecture theatres and lifts around the main building.

FINANCE:
- Access fund: £452,918 • Successful applications: 864

Many scholarships and sponsorships are available.

'I just didn't have anything in common with students. I thought that the people I knew in my home town were brighter.'
- Rob Newman.

Goddes kechyl, or a tryp of chese,
elles what yow list, we may nat
cheese

Goddes halpeny, or a mass peny,
yif us of youre brawn, if ye have en
dagon of youre blanket—leeve dame
re suster dere—lo, heere I write yo
name

con or beef, or swich thyng as ye fy
A sturdy harlot wente ay hem bihyn
at was hir hostes man, and bar a sa
d what men yaf hem, leyde it on hi
d whan that he was out of dore, an
planed away the names everichon
at he biforn hadde writen in his table
served hem with nyfles and with fa

"Nay, ther thou lixt, thou Somonou
the F

"Pees, quod oure hoost, "for Crist
good eere, tellyng of
told thy tale, and spare it nat at
"So thryve I, quod this Somonour,

So longe he wente, hous by hous, ti

KCL see King's College, London

Keele University

University of Kent at Canterbury

Kent Institute see Other Institutions

King Alfred's see Other Institutions

King's College, London

King's Hospital see King's College, London

Kingston University

KCL

see King's College, London

Keele University

Keele University, Keele, Staffordshire, ST5 5BG.
Tel: (01782) 584005. Fax: (01782) 632343.
E-mail: aaa20@admin.keele.ac.uk
Keele University Students' Union, Keele, Staffordshire, ST5 5BG.
Tel: (01782) 711411. Fax: (01782) 712671.
E-mail: sta15@kusu.keele.ac.uk

GENERAL

Keele University is situated near the city of Stoke-on-Trent and Newcastle-under-Lyme in the north midlands *but at the same time manages to feel like a million miles from anywhere. It's a set of geometric blocks in a square mile of parkland, mostly modern but including the beautiful Keele Hall, the oldest building (19th-century) on the estate.* It gained a reputation in the post-war expansion of higher education for its (at the time) unique flexibility of study, which many institutions have since copied, and its communal atmosphere. These are still true to an extent but the *isolation is also an important consideration either for or against.* Most students do joint honours degrees.

Sex ratio(M:F): 41%:59%	Founded: 1949
Full time u'grads: 4,600	Part time: 250
Postgrads: 747	Non-degree: 2,924
Ave course: 3/4yrs	Ethnic: 5%
Private school: n/a	Flunk rate: 9.8%
Mature students: 6%	Overseas students: 7%
Disabled students: 4%	

ATMOSPHERE:
Keele is a small, friendly and busy University, with 70% of students and many of the staff and their families living on campus. It's important that it should be friendly because escape to Newcastle-under-Lyme or even Stoke-on-Trent is hardly freedom. Social life is important and so often takes precedence over all else. The place can get to people and start to feel like a 600-acre ivory tower made by IKEA, from time to time most students just have to get away.

LOCAL AREA:
• London: 147miles • Manchester: 34miles • Birmingham: 43miles
Keele only just classes as a village. The area around Keele was built on the 19th-century pottery industry, hence the *cunning* name, The Potteries. Wedgewood, Spode and Royal Doulton pottery all came from round here *(Habitat and Tupperware didn't)*. Local facilities in the old market town of Newcastle are *a tad limited* but there is a development of new shops to try. *However, there's more than enough to get by* – all the major banks and *a fair few* shops (not after 10pm, though). For more of the trappings of commercialism, Hanley (one of the six towns that make up the city of Stoke-on-Trent) *is better equipped*. The Potteries Shopping Centre is full of all the national traders. Local attractions include all the various Pottery Museums, the once industrial, but now leisure canals, Festival Park (shops, cinema, dry ski slope), the Stoke City Museum & Art Gallery and Alton Towers, the theme park, half an hour down the road.

TRAVEL:
Trains: There's no station at Keele or at Newcastle (*that's the little one nearby*). Trains from Stoke-on-Trent go to London (£24.10), Manchester (£5.00), Newcastle (that's the big one up North – £31.30) and all over.
Coaches: National Express doesn't go to Keele either, the nearest service being Stoke, from where there are services to London (£12) and Manchester (£3.80).
Car: *The M6 is within smelling distance of the campus* – in fact it runs along the southern edge of the park. The A525 runs right past the campus and the A34, A50, A52, A53 and A531 are all nearby.
Hitching: Hitchers need to get to the M6 junctions (by bus), *which is quite hopeful.*
Local: Buses run between the campus and the surrounding towns every 10 minutes and as far afield as Chester and Sheffield. The SU runs a free bus service for off campus students.
Taxis: Plenty of taxis which charge up to £3 to Newcastle.
Bicycles: *Bikes are a useful way of getting around the campus although the landscaped hills are bumptious. Off-campus, there are hazardous roundabouts.*

CAREER PROSPECTS:
• Careers Service • No of staff: 3 full-time
• Unemployed after 6mths: 5.4%

SPECIAL FEATURES:
Unique course structure (see academic section below).

FAMOUS ALUMNI:
Don Foster MP (Lib Dem); Michael Mansfiel QC (Barrister); Lord Melchett (Greenpeace leader and nothing to do with Blackadder); Alun Michael MP (Secretary of State for Wales); Nick Partridge (AIDS campaigner); Jack Straw MP (Lab); Adelaide Tambo (ANC official).

FURTHER INFO:
Prospectuses for undergrads and postgrads, departmental leaflets and a video. 'The handbook' acts as an unofficial prospectus and guide and is available from the SU (£3). Check out the websites: www.keele.ac.uk (Uni) or www.kusu.net (SU).

ACADEMIC

Flexible study is generally the name of the game and most students do joint honours degrees. It is compulsory to take a cross faculty subsidiary course in the first year – for example, if you study an arts subject, you'll have to do a science subsidiary. *The result is that students get an insight into matters they might have otherwise completely ignored.*

staff/student ratio: n/a
Range of points required for entrance: 300-220
Percentage accepted through clearing: 5%
Number of terms/semesters: 2
Length of terms/semesters: 16wks
Research: 4.1

LIBRARIES:
• Books: 500,000 • Study places: 900

COMPUTERS:
• Computer workstations: 160
There is a general sense of angst around the shortage of computers, *but all students should leave knowing how to use some kind of keyboard*, since all final year coursework has to be typed *(and the University charges for printer paper – clever if a little harsh on the computer hopeless).*

ENTERTAINMENT

TOWN:
• Price of a pint of beer: £2.00 • Glass of wine: £1.50
Since students usually have to venture beyond Keele itself if they want off-campus adventure, some go the whole hog and stray as far as Birmingham and Manchester.
Pubs: *There are 2 pubs within stumbling distance of the campus:* the Golfer's Arms (owned by the SU) and the Sneyd Arms. *Other Pushplugs: O'Neill's; Scruffy Murphy's; Firkin.*
Cinemas: There's a *massive* new Warner Brothers multiplex in Newcastle and the Stoke Film Theatre shows left-field, art and international films. Stoke also has one further cinema.
Theatres: There are 5 theatres locally, in particular, the Theatre Royal in Hanley and the New Vic Rep in Newcastle offer a wide ranging selection.
Clubs/discos: There are numerous clubs around the towns. Monday tends to be student night. *Pushplugs: The Place (cheesy pop); Valentino's (Bonk, free bus from SU); Void (Hanley); Golden.*
Music venues: Stoke is the epicentre of live sounds, especially guitar-based – recently, Sleeper, Paul Weller, Radiohead. *Pushplugs: The Stage; Trentham Gardens.*
Eating out: *A better selection than might be expected. Pushplugs:*

Dylans (veggie) in Hanley; Hungry Horse and Golfer's Arms (pub grub); Shalimar's (Indian); Azzuri (Italian); Pablo Frankies (Spanish); Sukhota (Thai).

UNIVERSITY:
•Price of a pint of beer: £1.50   •Glass of wine: £1.30
Bars: (6) The main SU-run bars, all with late licences, are the Gallery, BJs (non-smoking) and Baldwin's (sporty and non-smoking in the evenings).
Theatres: The University gives financial support to the strong drama society which puts on about 5 major productions a year.
Cinema: 4 films a week, mainstream and world cinema.
Clubs/discos: 3 club nights a week in the Ballroom (capacity 1,100) and the Club (450), events with names like Luvshack (70s & 80s), Underground (indie), Cheeky Half (cheese) and Shag (80s retro, does exactly what it says on the tin). *Top DJs have been lured,* including LTJ Bukem and Judge Jules.
Music venues: The Ballroom plays host to various bands such as, recently, Lo-Fidelity, Allstars, Chicane, Ian Brown.
Cabaret: Fortnightly, top comedy turns in the Nightclub, courtesy of the Carlsberg Ice Comedy Network.
Food: Multiple munch outlets across campus, the Diner (meat & 2 veg) being run by the SU and others by the University. *All offer sound value for money. Harvey's is a continental-style veggie cafe, and Keele Hall restaurant does Binge till you Burst for a fiver.*
Others: Termly (at least) balls and various theme nights.

SOCIAL & POLITICAL

KEELE UNIVERSITY STUDENTS' UNION:
•4 sabbaticals   •Turnout at last ballot: 69%   •NUS member
Politically, the Union is full of wide-eyed interest, but very few party affiliations. The SU is a source of pride to students, who are unafraid to stand up to the University on welfare and other issues. Recently Keele held a national day of action by constructing a cardboard city and soup kitchen. *The SU places a lot of emphasis on its welfare role and is currently at odds with Hospitality who take care of the conferences and are felt to neglect student needs as soon as the academic term is over and those fat corporate money-bags move in.*

SU FACILITIES:
The Union Building in the middle of the campus has bars, a cafeteria and restaurant, travel agency, a bank and 2 cash machines (NatWest, Halifax), general shop, Endsleigh Insurance office, discos, print service and photocopying, 2 minibuses, arts studio, vending machines and video games, photo booth, pool tables, bookshop, video rental, Wednesday market, juke box and function rooms.

CLUBS (NON SPORTING):
Arcana; Chapel Choir; Clubbers; Concert Band; Duke of Edinburgh; Film; Folk; Hellenic; Klas (role-playing); Fantasy Football; Sword and Sorcery; Writers; Wargames.

OTHER ORGANISATIONS:
The student newspaper, 'Fuzzy Duck', comes out every month and the 'Grapevine' comes out weekly. The charity Rag raises pretty big bucks, considering the location. Keele's radio station KUBE broadcasts on two FM monthly licences a year. They are also trying to get a permanent AM licence.

RELIGIOUS:
- 3 chaplains (CofE, RC, Free Church).

The big inter-denominational Christian chapel is a bizarre grey brick structure, rectangular with 2 cylindrical turrets at one end. Muslim prayer room provided on campus. In Newcastle and Stoke, apart from various churches, there are places of worship for Muslims, Sikhs and Buddhists.

PAID WORK:
The Keele jobshop does its best despite the few opportunities in the local towns. The good news is that the Union employs 200-300 staff.

- Recent successes: skiing, cross country

A fairly good level of facilities and involvement. There is a small charge for some facilities if not organised through the sporting clubs.

SPORTS FACILITIES:
Close to the principal parts of the University (the halls of residence, the Union and the main teaching areas) are the sports facilities spread over 46 acres including playing fields, cricket squares, an all-weather floodlit pitch and netball and tennis courts. In the adjacent sports centre, there's an upgraded gym, sports hall, multigym, fitness centre, 7 squash courts and a climbing wall. Also, based in the sports centre, there's a sports shop and *strangely*, a pizza take-away and a hairdresser. The towns add extra choice including a golf course, ski slope, a swimming pool, lake and bowling green.

SPORTING CLUBS:
Aeroball; Caving; Frisbee; Kung Fu; Lacrosse; Rock Climbing; Ultimate Frisbee; Water-skiing.

ATTRACTIONS:
Locally, there's Stoke City and Port Vale Football Clubs, Uttoxeter Race Course, the Potteries marathon and, most years, the Lombard Rally. Keele is also host to the National Karate Championships.

IN COLLEGE:
- Self-catering: 77% • Cost: £39-64(33-51wks)

Availability: Living in is the norm. *It's one of the big things about Keele as far as Keele is concerned. 1st years actually have to apply to live out rather than to live in. As a consequence, they are almost all housed in the University's four halls on campus. Conditions vary depending on how much you pay, eg in the cheaper halls you might have to share a kitchen with 30 people.* They are all self-catering (some have pay-as-you-eat refectories and snack bars, though). They vary in size from 400 to 800 places and have a minimum of 2 single and mixed sex blocks each. 2 halls are blocks of flats for 4 students each, sharing a kitchen and bathroom, although these are mainly for 2nd and 3rd years and finalists, 95% of whom live in. 25% live out for their 2nd year. There are phone and computer links in most rooms. Some space is available on campus specially for mature students and a few single parents. Off campus, the University owns houses which can accommodate up to 99 students in groups of 4 to 6.

Car parking: At present there's limited permit parking (£10 per year) on campus although this could be raised to £50 to fund new car parks. Visitors (including mums and dads) have to pay and display.

EXTERNALLY:
- Ave rent: £35

Availability: The University is expanding and may have to reduce its proportion of students living in which may well create problems in the local housing market. *At the moment Newcastle or Silverdale are the preferred options, being on a handy bus-route, although Hanley and parts of Stoke are also options. Knutton and Cobridge are a bit rough and Parkside is getting worse. When living out a car wouldn't go unused, unless students are on the main bus routes.*
Housing help: The University's Accommodation Office has 3 full-time officers, a vacancies newsletter and a housing approval scheme.

WELFARE

SERVICES:
- Creche • Nightline • Lesbian & Gay Society • Mature SA
- Overseas SA • Minibus • Women's Officer • Self-defence classes

The Keele General Practice is based on campus and employs a male and a female doctor and two nurses. As well as normal health care, it offers a psychiatry clinic. The mental even keel of Keele is also maintained by the 2 full-time counsellors of the University's Counselling Service (the chaplains also help out). The Union runs an independent Advice Unit with 4 counsellors who can offer a free and confidential listening service, financial and legal advice, help for overseas students, drugs information, jobshop with local vacancies and support for lesbian and gay students.

Women: The health centre has a well woman clinic and the Union has a women's resources centre and a women's officer.

Disabled: *Facilities for hearing- and sight-impaired students and for those with dyslexia look good but there have been complaints that they're just left to get on with it themselves. Things are hard for wheelchair users*, but there is at least a Disability Services Co-ordinator.

FINANCE:
- Access fund: £370,765   • Successful applications: 578

Help is provided by the International Loan Fund, the Lindsay Loan Fund and the Emergency Hardship Fund. The SU and chaplains have similar arrangements.

University of Kent at Canterbury

The University of Kent at Canterbury, The Registry, Canterbury, Kent, CT2 7NZ. Tel: (01227) 764000. Fax: (01227) 452196. E-mail: admissions@ukc.ac.uk
Students' Union, University of Kent, Canterbury, Kent, CT2 7NW. Tel: (01227) 765224. Fax: (01227) 464625. E-mail: union@ukc.ac.uk

GENERAL

Kent is the so-called Garden of England, full of hop fields, oast-houses and ruminating cows. Well actually, Canterbury, an ancient city and the seat of the Church of England, *is more than a quaint slice of ye olde heritage industrie. It's still surrounded by rolling Kent countryside and little villages of pretty ivy-covered cottages, but nowadays trendy cafés* and an increasing number of big chain stores have joined the long stretches of 13th- and 14th-century city walls to the south and east of the city. The University is 1½ miles from the city, based on a very large campus (300 acres) with 4 University colleges. *For those who like ornate architecture the University doesn't offer much.* The buildings are a plain collection of redbrick with *more than enough concrete*, set amidst a green, landscaped campus *which has the bizarre effect of magnifying weather conditions: when the sun comes out it's baking and as soon as it goes away, it might as well be Siberia.*

Sex ratio(M:F): 45%:55%	**Founded: 1965**
Full time u'grads: 6,306	**Part time: 196**
Postgrads: 997	**Non-degree: 2,005**
Ave course: 3yrs	**Ethnic: 14%**
Private school: n/a	**Flunk rate: 14.5%**
Mature students: 19%	**Overseas students: 25%**
Disabled students: n/a	

ATMOSPHERE:
The collegiate system at Kent tends to encourage cliques and students remain faithful to their particular college throughout their University careers. However, the 4 colleges (each about 1,250 undergrads) aren't that different from one another and students don't normally express a preference in their application (nor is it a particularly good idea). Like most collegiate universities, the strength of the colleges and the Junior College Committees (JCCs – mini SUs) detracts from the University-wide Students' Union. Students seeking a full social life need to look for it. Since many of the students come from the Home Counties, a lot go home at the weekends. Those who stay behind have lots of fun behind the others' backs, particularly at the Venue which has improved the social life no end.

THE CITY:
- Population: 54,500 • London: 56miles
- Dover: 16miles • Maidstone: 26miles

Canterbury has all the local amenities of a city with *the advantage of still being a small place amidst beautiful surroundings*. Not least of these are the many historical buildings, the medieval city walls and the *overbearing, but impressive*, ancient Cathedral. There has been a cathedral here (not the same one) since the end of the 6th-century, staking an early claim to become the centre of the Anglican Church. Urban decay can be spotted on the way out of the city, although there's also a good deal of modern development and big chain stores based on the outskirts. Students (including those from various other nearby colleges) make up more than 25% of the local population.

TRAVEL:
Trains: Although Canterbury West is closer, Canterbury East is the station with the mainline connections to London (£14.15) and Dover and connections to Edinburgh, Birmingham and Bristol.
Coaches: National Express services all over the country.
Car: The A2 and, some way up the road, the M2 connect London with Canterbury while the A28 runs to the south coast.
Ferries: From Dover and Folkstone to France and Belgium.

Hitching: *The A2 and A28 should be good bets, but drivers are pretty possessive about their upholstery in Kent.*
Local: Buses from town to campus every 15 minutes and student bus cards are available.
Taxis: £2 for the mile from the campus to Canterbury.
Bicycles: Many bikes – despite the fact the campus is on a huge hill.

CAREER PROSPECTS:
- Careers Service • No of staff: 4 full
- Unemployed after 6mths: 2.7%

FAMOUS ALUMNI:
Paul Ackford (rugby player and journalist); Alan Davies (comedian); Gavin Esler (journalist); Anna Hill (broadcaster); Kazuo Ishiguro (writer); Wayne Otto (karate champ); Paul Ross (TV presenter); Ramon Tikaram (Ferdie in 'This Life'); David Walsh (historian); Charles Wigoder (mobile phone entrepreneur); Tom Wilkinson (actor).

FURTHER INFO:
Prospectuses for undergrads and postgrads. Website (www.ukc.ac.uk).

ACADEMIC

There are three faculties comprising 19 departments offering courses in humanities, science, technology and medical studies, social sciences and other bits 'n' bobs. There is also a Law clinic which handles real cases and enables law students to gain some practical experience of casework.

staff/student ratio: 1:10
Range of points required for entrance: 320-240
Percentage accepted through clearing: n/a
Number of terms/semesters: 3
Length of terms/semesters: 12wks
Research: 4.9

LIBRARIES:
- Books: 1,000,000 • Study places: 1,300

In addition to the Templeman Library, the colleges have their own small collections and the University looks after the running of the Cathedral Library, which isn't available for general academic purposes.

COMPUTERS:
- Computer workstations: 600

The campus computer network is available 24 hours a day, 7 days a week.

ENTERTAINMENT

THE CITY:
- Price of a pint of beer: £2.20 • Glass of wine: £1.60

Cinemas: (1) The Cannon has 2 screens, *but the flicks in Whitstable is less fleapitty.*
Theatres: (1) The Marlowe Theatre is the city's only permanent theatre although TS Eliot's verse play 'Murder in the Cathedral' was written for and first performed in Canterbury Cathedral.

Pubs: In some parts of Kent the air is thick with the *cornflakey* stench of hops and brewing. Not all this local brew gets transported out of the county and Canterbury is full of pubs that serve a *mean* brew or two. *Testing the local tastes is a major student pastime.* Pushplugs: Simple Simons (14th-century); Three Compasses (packed, wild and brash); Black Griffin; Falstaff & Tap; Franklin & Firkin.
Clubs/discos: (2) Canterbury is not club city but Churchill's and Alberry's are worth a try.
Music venues: Classical concerts are held in the Cathedral and the Marlowe Theatre, which also has folk music. Cuba specialises in jazz and Latin. For local bands and indie, there's the Penny Theatre and Cardinal's Cap. Otherwise, a trip to Metronome or Leas Cliff Hall in Folkestone (over 14 miles away) or Whitstable Labour Club (6 miles) is in order, but it's still mostly local bands.
Food: Local scoff shops are geared to the student and tourist trade and there are plentiful Indian, Italian, pizza, Chinese, French and vegetarian restaurants, as well as various fish'n'chip shops and other takeaways. Pushplugs: Pinnochio's (Italian); Café des Amis, which, is, of course, Mexican; Ask (gorgeous pizzas); Caesar's (big portions). Students who need to stuff something down their throats late at night can resort to curries and kebabs until about 1am.

UNIVERSITY:
- Price of a pint of beer: £1.60 • Glass of wine: £1.20

The ents side of things has improved with the opening of the long-awaited The Venue serving up a 1,200-capacity nightclub compete with bistro.
Bars: (8) The SU building has 3 bars, one of which is part of 'The Venue'. *The Theatre bar is trendy.* The colleges also run their own bars.
Theatres: The Gulbenkian Theatre on campus (cap 342) *is very well equipped, but there's a price to be paid for that* – it's not for the exclusive use of students. It plays host to many touring productions, the annual Canterbury Festival and concerts of all sorts. The University does, however, have the largest drama department in the country. Students put on productions in makeshift theatres in the colleges when the Gulbenkian's booked.
Cinemas: Cinema 3 shows commercial and occasional arty stuff, and the cinema club shows three films a week.
Clubs/discos/music venues: There's a different theme night every night in The Venue. Recent gigs include: Grooverider; DJ Luck & MC Neat; LTJ Bukem; DJ Judge Jules.
Food: Catering is based in individual colleges while the new bistro provides an all day *nosh-fest*.
Cabaret: 2 or 3 funsters per term including, recently, Adam Bloom.
Others: Apart from college and society dos, there's at least 1 major event a term, culminating in the Grand Summer Ball. An ents card (£25) gives discounts on all SU events.

UNIVERSITY OF KENT AT CANTERBURY STUDENTS' UNION:
- 6 sabbaticals • Turnout at last ballot: 12% • NUS member

The Union is based in the small Mandela Building and things tend to have a collegiate, rather than University, feel. The SU strikes a good relationship between the University and students. Recently, the rewriting of the constitution went down well, 'cause it made the Student Council more representative.

SU FACILITIES:
The new Virginia Woolf building contains the jobshop and the campus shop. The Nelson Mandela building contains: minibus; travel agency; printing; Endsleigh Insurance office; general shop; secondhand bookshop; pool table; juke box; vending machines; TV lounge; meeting room; launderette; stationery shop; photocopier; photobooth; van hire. Also banks with cashpoints on campus.

CLUBS (NON SPORTING):
Adventure Gaming; Amateur Radio; Anglican; Ballroom Dancing; Belly Dancing; Buddhist Meditation; Chess; Chinese; Comic; Creative Expression; Critical Lawyers; Film-Making; Scandinavian; Sci-Fi; Shiatsu; Singapore; Space; Spanish; Sri Lanka; Star Trek; Wine.

OTHER ORGANISATIONS:
'Kred' is the student newspaper, produced by the Union. 'Propaganda' is a handy ents listing sheet, out every fortnight. UKC Radio broadcasts across campus on FM. There is a charity Rag and the student community organisation works with local help projects.

RELIGIOUS:
• <u>7 chaplains (CofE, RC, Baptist, Methodist, Quaker, Buddhist, Orthodox, Jewish)</u>
The Eliot Chapel is the campus prayer place although there are various makeshift worship shops in the colleges as well as a Muslim prayer room. In town, there's the Cathedral, of course, *but Christians who fancy something a little less lofty don't have to worry about any kind of theological drought. Non-Christians may get a bit more spiritually thirsty.*

PAID WORK:
During the summer, the Garden of England offers a monumental set of gardening tasks such as hop and fruit picking. There's a new jobshop on campus, *but even so there isn't a lot going.* A foreign language is handy for touristy Canterbury and it's also possible to find jobs teaching English as a foreign language.

SPORTS

• <u>Recent successes: basketball, karate</u>
Intercollegiate rivalries come into the open when sportsmen and women get into gear but Kent's reputation in national competitions is on the up as well. The facilities are all on campus and shared between colleges. Sports bursaries worth £500 are available.

SPORTS FACILITIES:
Playing fields; sports centre including sports hall; archery range; cricket nets; gym; 2 multigyms; weights; boxing ring; sauna and solarium; 6 squash courts; athletics field; tennis courts; floodlit all-weather pitch; climbing wall; running track. The city adds a croquet lawn, swimming pool and golf course and the coast isn't too far away.

SPORTING CLUBS:
American Football; Boxing; Caving; Handball; Kendo; Lacrosse; Motorcycling; Mountaineering; Paintball; Street Hockey; Tennis; Ten Pin Bowling; Ultimate Frisbee.

ATTRACTIONS:
Dog racing track and windsurfing at Whitstable.

ACCOMMODATION

IN COLLEGE:
- Catered: 26% • Cost: £60-77 (30wks)
- Self-catering: 28% • Cost: £42-47 (37wks)

Availability: Whether or not students live in, they remain members of their colleges throughout their University careers. 1st years are guaranteed accommodation if they want it. 5% share. In general, the self-catering accommodation in University Houses and Park Wood Courts – a small village of terraced purpose-built student houses on campus – is used by students beyond their 1st year. Beckett Court is 5-star, spacious accommodation. *Eliot and Keynes are popular, but other housing is a bit run down.* Catered here means B+B. As a rule, demand for on-site accommodation outstrips supply.

Car parking: Free but limited, provided you live off-campus.

EXTERNALLY:
- Ave rent: £50-55

Availability: *Students have to keep their eyes, ears and cheque books open if they're going to find anywhere to live in Canterbury.* An increasing number are moving out to Herne Bay and Whitstable (5 to 7 miles north), where rents are cheaper, places are more plentiful and life more dull. For those who are bed-wettingly keen for something closer to the action, Wincheap, Downs Road and Sturry Road are the places to aim for.

Housing help: The University Accommodation Office employs 4 staff who try to place students, especially 1st years, but its main concern is allocating places on campus. *Big hint – get in early.*

WELFARE

SERVICES:
- Creche • Nightline • Lesbian & Gay Society • Mature SA
- Overseas SA • Postgrad SA • Minibus • Women's Officer
- Self-defence classes

There is a 24-hour counselling service based in Darwin which employs 4 part-time members of staff and a medical centre complete with residential sick-bay. There are campus escorts and new lamps are being installed all over. An Overseas Group and newsletter also operates.

Disabled: There's parking, lifts and ramps in most buildings and there's a new Disability Support Officer. *A committee also does a lot of talking.*

FINANCE:
- Access fund: £145,000 • Successful applications: 1,200

Sports and music bursaries are available.

Kent Institute

see Other Institutions

King Alfred's

see Other Institutions

King's College, London

- *The College is part of University of London and students are entitled to use its facilities.*

King's College London, University of London, The Strand, London, WC2R 2LS. Tel: (020) 7836 5454. Fax: (020) 7836 1799.
King's College London Students' Union, Macadam Building, Surrey Street, London, WC2R 2NS. Tel: (020) 7836 7132. Fax: (020) 7379 9833. E-mail: enquiries@kclsu.org

GENERAL

King's was founded by King George IV and the Duke of Wellington in 1829 and is one of the two oldest colleges of the University of London. At one end of The Strand is Trafalgar Square and at the other is King's College, among other things. Those other things include the Thames, the beginning of Fleet Street, Somerset House (which was home to the Inland Revenue *but they've since been kicked out to make way for more public space*, but does house the Courtauld Institute), Aldwych (a 5-lane crescent curving round Bush House, the HQ of the BBC World Service), the LSE and the *handsome* Wren church St Mary's-in-the-Strand. *The 70s front of the King's College main building is in stark contrast to the more traditional buildings that surround it. It's concrete, glass and grey and even has a giant internet screen in reception. Hidden away at the back of the building, overlooking the Thames, is much finer Georgian architecture, but once that far into the building it's hard to find your way out again.* In addition to the Strand site there are several further sites including the Waterloo, Guy's and St Thomas' Hospital sites just across the river, and King's College Hospital in Camberwell in South London. King's also has halls of residence all over central London (both north and south) *in some of the capital's most exciting, not to say valuable, locations.*

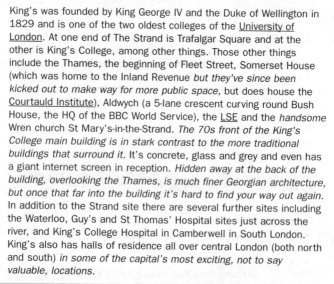

Sex ratio(M:F): 40%:60%	Founded: 1829
Full time u'grads: 12,228	Part time: 1,400
Postgrads: 2,599	Non-degree: 77
Ave course: 3yrs	Ethnic: 42%
Private school: n/a	Flunk rate: 9.7%
Mature students: 30%	Overseas students: 14%
Disabled students: 5%	

ATMOSPHERE:
It's a pulsating, multicultural social mix with, since a recent merger, a big focus being placed on the three main sites to create a tighter student body, community and atmosphere. Many students feel proud to be studying here, although this is usually expressed in rivalry with University College, London. The Strand site is ideally placed for enjoyment of all that London cares to offer (and attendant costs) but those based at some of the outlying sites tend to experience less of the action.

THE SITES:
The Strand: (humanities, law, physical sciences, engineering) This is the eastern end of the West End. *There's a million ways to spend money but not, however, any places to live, or many places to do the weekly shopping without your daily bread costing more than your dough.* The SU is based at this site and the nearest college halls are just a 10-minute walk away.
Waterloo: (4,507 students – management, education, nursing and midwifery, health and life studies) ½ mile from the Strand site on the other side of Waterloo Bridge on the Thames' South Bank. Café bar, common room, K4 Fitness centre.
Guy's: (3,000 students – biomedical sciences, medicine and dentistry) A *Georgian-style* collection of buildings close to London Bridge. From the top of the very tall Guy's Tower there is an *incredible view across the city*; it's 2 miles from the Strand site on the Thames' South Bank. There is also a fairly new complex at Guy's Hospital offering a teaching base and facilities, a new Student Union building and welfare centre.

Medical/Dental Schools: (2,700 students – dentistry and medicine) There are 3 hospitals at which teaching takes place:
St Thomas': (aka Tommy's) ¾ mile from Trafalgar Square, opposite the Houses of Parliament on the south side of the Thames is Tommy's modern 70s development with open plan, bright and clean inter-connected buildings.
Denmark Hill: King's College Hospital in Camberwell. *A different kettle of cod altogether,* Camberwell is in South London and, *almost necessarily, shabbier as a result. It's not London's safest area (or its worst – London gets much worse), but it's cheap, residential and good for shopping. It's also got streets and squares. Camberwell may not have a great deal by way of entertainment itself, but is very well connected for the West End. The hospital has its own social life, anyway.*

THE CITY: see University of London

TRAVEL: see University of London
Trains: Charing Cross is the nearest mainline station for the Strand site and Waterloo for the Waterloo site (funny that). Denmark Hill station is the best way of getting to King's Hospital, while Guy's is closest to London Bridge.
Buses: Denmark Hill: 12, 35, 40, 45, 68, 171, 176, 185; Night Buses N12, N62, N72, N176, N82 & N86. p11, 108, 501 and 133 go near Guy's and Waterloo and 77 and 507 go to Tommy's.
Underground: Temple (District & Circle Lines) or Holborn (Piccadilly and Central) for the Strand site. Northern and Bakerloo lines for Waterloo; London Bridge (Northern line) for Guy's; Lambeth North (Bakerloo line) for Tommy's. The Jubilee line serves students based at both Guy's and Waterloo.
Bicycles: *Quite a popular form of transport although pollution and fatal injury aren't big selling points.*

CAREER PROSPECTS:
- Careers Service •No of staff: 6 full/1 part
- Unemployed after 6mths: 4%

SPECIAL FEATURES:
A relic of the College's religious foundations, KCL runs an optional course for all students, covering ethics and philosophy as well as theology – successful completion gets you the AKC (Associate of King's College) certificate.

FAMOUS ALUMNI:
Rory Bremner (impressionist); Anita Brookner (novelist); George Carey (Archbishop of Canterbury); Arthur C Clarke (sci-fi writer); John Eliot Gardner (composer/conductor); Susan Hill (novelist); Hanif Kureishi (writer); Chapman Pincher (writer/journalist); Ian Shaw (jazz singer); Desmond Tutu, Njongonkulu Winston Ndungane (past and present Archbishops of Cape Town); Maurice Wilkins (Nobel Laureate DNA Scientist).

FURTHER INFO:
Prospectuses for undergrads and postgrads, and website (www.kcl.ac.uk).

ACADEMIC

staff/student ratio: 10%
Range of points required for entrance: 340-240
Percentage accepted through clearing: 13%
Number of terms/semesters: 2
Length of terms/semesters: 14wks
Research: 5.2

LIBRARIES:
• Books: 800,000   • Study places: 2,800
There are 3 main libraries and 2 smaller ones. The Strand libraries will be moved to a new site on Chancery Lane and will *hopefully* provide the *long awaited* extended opening hours.

COMPUTERS:
• Computer workstations: 1,200

ENTERTAINMENT

IN LONDON: see University of London

COLLEGE:
• Price of a pint of beer: £1.55   • Glass of wine: £1.10
Bars: The Strand site has 3 bars, the Waterfront (cap 350, *hip & happening*), Tutu's (620) which concentrates on events and the Reach Bar, at the top of Tutu's (view over the Thames). There's also the Penthouse at Denmark Hill and bars at Guy's and Thomas'.
Theatres: *There are very strong drama societies*, particularly The Kings Players, who put on shows in the theatre at the Strand site and go to the Edinburgh Fringe (3 shows taken last year).
Clubs/discos/music venues: There are regular club nights at the Strand. The Penthouse Bar at Denmark Hill expands into the next room (cap 300) and makes *a hot spot to trot*. Regular club nights in Guy's bar (cap 400). Tutu's is used for band nights. Recent names to perform include Greenday, Toploader and Beth Orton.
Food: The College-run *scoff stops* at the Strand are B1 (refectory) and the Terrazza complete with cappuccino bar and patisserie while King's Hospital at Denmark Hill *has a less than enthralling monicker for its eaterie – 'hospital canteen'. Still it's the food you eat, not the names*. The SU runs a deli at the Strand in the Waterfront Bar and Tutu's sells cheap pizzas, baked spuds, pasta, curry and breakfast.
Others: The SU keeps trotting out a host of hoots well-attended by

students on each site: weekly bar quizzes, karaoke. Each year there's a *thoroughly formal Summer Ball at a posh hotel.*

SOCIAL & POLITICAL

KING'S COLLEGE LONDON STUDENTS' UNION (KCLSU):
• 6 sabbaticals • Turnout at last ballot: 12% • NUS member
KCLSU has a tiny political core and does its little bit for student representation, but is essentially a slick organiser of student ents, bars and clubs. SU is beginning to become amalgamated over the different sites with two officers permanently based at Guy's.

SU FACILITIES:
Strand: The Macadam Building (named after NUS's first president) houses bars, cafés, nightclub, shop, travel agency, Waterstones, insurance agent, cashpoint and financial advice centre (Barclays).
Guy's Hospital: Bar, MacDonalds, ballroom, Blackwells, cashpoint. The new complex will have an SU building.
Denmark Hill: Meeting room, TV and games room, Union offices.

CLUBS (NON SPORTING):
Afro-Caribbean; Ballroom Dancing; Chinese; Debating; Film; Filmakers; Hellenic; Hindu; Japanese; Jazz; Juggling; Liberation; Malaysian & Singapore; Musical Theatre; Salsa; Sikh; Windband.

OTHER ORGANISATIONS:
There's 'Roar', a *fair to average SU mag which includes listings. King's charity Rag does all the normal stupid and occasionally illegal things that students get up to in the name of charity. Beer races with UCL go down well and London colleges have a penchant for pinching each other's mascots. King's mascot was Reggie, a ¼ -ton red copper lion, until he was stolen by City & Guilds who castrated him. A new mascot was then filled with concrete, making it such a challenge that it was quickly stolen with the aid of trucks and winches. Now they've got a copper lion again, which is just asking for it.*

RELIGIOUS:
• 4 chaplains (CofE, Orthodox, RC, Free Church)
Chapels at the Strand and Guy's, Muslim prayer rooms are located on various campuses.

PAID WORK: see University of London

SPORTS

• Recent successes: jiu jitsu, athletics
They're a sporty lot at King's, *surprisingly so considering the outdoor facilities are at Berrylands in Mitcham, about 9 miles south of the Strand. 40% of University of London team members are King's students.*

SPORTS FACILITIES:
Some indoor facilities are on site, including a shooting range at the Strand. The K4 fitness centre at the Waterloo site has qualified trainers. There is a 6-acre ground in Dulwich, 2 miles from the St Thomas' Hospital and a sports ground at New Malden. Guy's has a swimming pool.

SPORTING CLUBS:
Aerobics; Aerosports; Boat; Boxing; Bujinkan; Capoira; Lacrosse; Polo; Rifle & Pistol; Shaolin Kung Fu; Thai Boxing; Water Polo; Yoga.

ATTRACTIONS: SEE University of London

ACCOMMODATION

IN COLLEGE:
•Catered: 6% •Cost: £98-121(30wks)
•Self-catering: 25% •Cost: £62-£68(36-50wks)
Availability: King's has 8 halls of residences dotted around London, all within a 4-mile radius of the Strand, with halls attached to each of the other sites. *Some are very expensive, but are correspondingly lavish.* About 11% of students share. The provision is sufficient to offer places to most 1st years who request them but over 35% do live out, *albeit out of choice. The most spirited of King's residences is Hampstead Hall, King's College Hall is a little less desirable.*
Car parking: Almost impossible at almost all the halls.

EXTERNALLY: see University of London
Housing help: The College has its own Accommodation Office as well as the University's excellent service.

WELFARE

SERVICES:
•Nursery •Lesbian & Gay Society •Overseas SA
•Minibus •Self-defence classes
For most services, the University's provisions are more extensive than those available in the College. However, KCLSU offers a Welfare Department and the College runs a Counselling and Medical Centre, employing 10 full-time staff, including trained counsellors, 4 doctors, 3 nurses, 1 counsellor and a psychotherapist. *The personal tutor system also operates in a caring kind of way.*
Disabled: Hit and miss wheelchair access.

FINANCE:
•Access fund: £636,000 •Successful applications: 496
Overseas Students' Hardship Fund.

King's Hospital
see King's College, London

Kingston University

• *Formerly Kingston Polytechnic*
Kingston University, Student Enquiry and Applicant Services,
Cooper House, 40-46 Surbiton Road, Kingston Upon Thames, Surrey,
KT1 2HX. Tel: (020) 8547 2000. Fax: (020) 8547 7080.
E-mail: admissions-info@kingston.ac.uk
Kingston University Students Union, Penrhyn Road, Kingston upon Thames, Surrey, KT1 2EE. Tel: (020) 8547 8868.
Fax: (020) 8547 8862. E-mail: president@kingston.ac.uk

GENERAL

The address may say Surrey, but don't be fooled – London doesn't stop between the suburban streets of Kingston and Trafalgar Square, 10 miles to the north east. But Kingston is one of London's pleasantest parts with 2 large parks breaking up the alternating streets of homes and shops. Local highlights include the famous Hampton Court, one-time home of Henry VIII and its deer-infested park. But to get to such delights from Kingston University, a trip across Kingston's handsome bridge is required. The University is based on 4 main sites all within 4 miles of each other, two of which are in Kingston town centre. They are composed of a *mangled mix* of different buildings, from the new Roehampton Vale site to the white-washed charm of the Kingston Hill site (the slightly separate one) set in 50 acres of parkland. There are old and new. *There are ugly blocks and attractive towers.*

Sex ratio(M:F): 49:51%	Founded: 1971
Full time u'grads: 11,204	Part time: 1,142
Postgrads: 866	Non-degree: 603
Ave course: 3yrs	Ethnic: 40%
Private school: 10%	Flunk rate: 16.8%
Mature students: 33%	Overseas students: 11%
Disabled students: 3.9%	

ATMOSPHERE & SITES:
Each site has its own distinct characteristics (and different faculties are based at each one). Although there is a stronger identity than most split-site colleges, it's not easy to pin it down – 'well-to-do and largely from the South' would be a bit too harsh. Penrhyn Road, the largest site with 7,500 students, for example, is lively and noisy – lots of drinking and prankish japes, any excuse to dress up and get wasted. Knight's Park (2,000 students), though, is much more sober and sombre, full of trendy arty-types in the throes of creativity. Roehampton Vale (500 students) has the engineers who work hard and when they're not working hard, they're sitting around just chatting. Kingston Hill (6,000 students) is the only one with halls of residence on site and so has a much stronger community unity – Sloanier too.

THE CITY: see University of London

KINGSTON:
Kingston upon Thames is about as historic as places get in this country *(if it were any older, it'd have to be nearer Rome)*. Its *village-like character is alive and well* and living in the centre of the town where there's an old daily market. But *time has left its ticks and tocks on Kingston* and recently it has been swamped by new developments: a huge shopping centre; a great many car parks and even more cars. In retaliation, many of its streets have been pedestrianised and now it has a monster one-way system (one way in – no way out). Still, it does offer a trolleyful of shops (including a bookshop in Brook Street) and a wacky sculpture consisting of old red telephone boxes toppling each other like dominoes.

TRAVEL: see University of London

CAREER PROSPECTS:
- Careers Service • No of staff: 1 full/3 part
- Unemployed after 6mths: 3.6%

FAMOUS ALUMNI:
Glenda Bailey (editor, American 'Marie Claire'); Angie Bowie (Dave's 1st wife); Lawrence Dallaglio (rugby player); Trevor Eve (actor); Patrick Forge (DJ); Carolyn Franklin (TV presenter); Richard James (the Aphex Twin); Graeme Le Saux (footballer); Steve Mason (Gene guitarist); John Richmond, Helen Storey (fashion designers); Stella Tennant (posh model).

FURTHER INFO:
Free video or audio tape. Prospectus and website (www.kingston.ac.uk).

All undergraduate courses have a modular format and flexible learning patterns mean that you can study courses on either a full- or part-time basis. Most courses offer periods of study in industry or commerce. Courses tend to be mainly assessed by continual assessment and project-based work. Entry to courses is possible without formal qualifications – if you're 21 or over, alternative qualifications or appropriate experience will be considered.

staff/student ratio: 1:14
Range of points required for entrance: 360-80
Percentage accepted through clearing: n/a
Number of terms/semesters: 3
Length of terms/semesters: 13wks
Research: 2.6

LIBRARIES:
- Books: 558,930 • Study places: 1,262

There are 4 libraries, one on each site, devoted to the faculties based there. *The weekend opening hours have improved.*

COMPUTERS:
- Computer workstations: 1,400

TOWN:
- Price of a pint of beer: £2.10 • Glass of wine: £1.90

Cinemas: In Kingston, there's a multi-screen cinema and a 14-screen cinema and leisure complex is under development by Kingston Station.
Theatres: 1,100-seat theatre is currently being built by the market place.
Pubs: *Many of the local pubs, which have much more local charm than most in London, host live music.* Pushplugs: Porter Black's; Kingston Mill; Gazebo.
Clubs/discos: *The Works is the student-friendly club, along with Bacchus (indie/dance in a dingy cellar – better than it sounds) and McCluskey's (all sorts of music).*
Eating out: Pushplugs: Wagamama; Pizza piazza; Mantana (Thai).

Others: Kingston offers many *pastoral pastimes* such as boat trips on the Thames, which can be booked for evening parties.

UNIVERSITY:
- Price of a pint of beer: £1.60 • Glass of wine: £1.30

Bars: (4) *Penrhyn Road is the liveliest.*
Comedy: *Every other Tuesday, comics struggle to get a drunken audience's attention.*
Clubs/discos/music venues: *Abysmal* music scene sees some bands live in the bar at Penrhyn Rd (600); Gorillaz and Divine Comedy have played there recently. The Works (cap 2,000) in town hosts the weekly student stomp.
Food: All sites have canteens and sandwich bars.
Balls: Several balls every term run by clubs and the Guild.

SOCIAL & POLITICAL

KINGSTON UNIVERSITY STUDENTS' UNION:
- 4 sabbaticals • Turnout: 5% • NUS member

The union is a lot more active than it is radical, more into clubs than clubbing policemen, more into bars than barricades.

SU FACILITIES:
The *portacabinesque* Union Building is based at Penrhyn Road and offers bars with TVs, pool tables and games machines, a travel office, bookshop, photocopying and printing. Each Site has its own Union office and bar (except for Roehampton).

CLUBS (NON-SPORTING):
Architecture; Chinese & Far Eastern; Debating; DJ Mixing; Film & Cult TV; Hellenic; International; Kingston Kidney Choir; Malaysian; Music and Design; Salsa; Sikh.

OTHER ORGANISATIONS:
The weekly Union-run broadsheet 'Rhubarb' *(not bad at all)* is filled with student contributions. There's also the once a term mag, 'Tsar'. Students and staff do a fair deal of community work arranging, among other things, an Xmas dinner for OAPs and an appeal for Romanian Orphans. Rag raised £5,500 last year.

RELIGIOUS:
- 3 chaplains (ecumenical)

PAID WORK:
The many local fast food joints always need new blood (not literally) as does the union. There's a job centre desk in the Uni for part-time work and many students get work in a wide variety of all the regular *fun-filled* occupations.

One of the proposed name-changes for the old Polytechnic South West was the New University of Devon Institute of Science and Technology (NUDIST).

SPORTS

- <u>Recent successes: hockey, badminton, rowing</u>
The Uni runs a 'Talented Sportsperson Scheme' which helps to support students competing at a national and international level. Currently, there are 21 students on the scheme.

SPORTS FACILITIES:
The playing fields are a couple of miles away at Tolworth in Surbiton where there are also tennis courts. Other facilities are spread around the sites: a gym at Kingston Hill; and a fitness centre and aerobics studio at Penrhyn Road. There's also a local public leisure centre and swimming pool.

SPORTING CLUBS:
Caving; Gaelic Football; Jui Jitsu; Kung Fu; Motor Bike; Mountaineering; Parachute; Rowing; Surf; Ten Pin Bowling.

ATTRACTIONS:
Rugby at Twickenham is close and there's racing at Sandown Park. Wimbledon for the tennis after summer exams and, of course, all of London's sports ports.

ACCOMMODATION

IN COLLEGE:
- <u>Self-catering: 20%</u> • <u>Cost: £53-63(40wks)</u>

Availability: The University can house all 1st years who apply in time if they meet all the conditions set out in the Uni prospectus – *so beware (picky, picky)*. Mature students are offered 'quiet flats' *(it's no good pretending you're responsible, you just need to be over 25)*. There are 2,286 places in 5 purpose-built halls and 450 places run under a head tenancy scheme, all at pretty reasonable prices. Nobody needs to share.

Car parking: Free parking *but some students complain that there's not nearly enough*. The Uni offers a free bus service linking most halls and the main campus.

EXTERNALLY:
- <u>Ave rent: £68</u>

Availability: *It's quite difficult to find local accommodation at an affordable price. Surbiton and Berrylands are popular areas, but in Kingston, landlords are reluctant to rent to rowdy students.*

Housing help: The University and Students' Union offer a joint Accommodation Service with vacancy bulletins and info on the net.

```
The grounds of Heriot-Watt University
contain a disused ticket office, all that
remains of Edinburgh's proposed underground
train system.
```

WELFARE

SERVICES:
- Creche • Lesbian & Gay Society
- International Students' Society • Minibus

The Union runs an *impressive* welfare service and employs a full-time welfare caseworker. An advice and information 'one stop shop' has just opened for financial, career and housing matters while the University employs 6 full-time counsellors and has a medical centre at Penrhyn Rd with a visiting doctor and a nurse. There are lots of *rather nice* services including acupuncture, aromatherapy, relaxation sessions, sexual health clinic, reflexology, food and feeling group, stress clinic, hypnotherapy, sport therapy, osteopathy and chiropody clinics and free dental health checks.

Disabled: *Access and facilities are okay-ish. Students with dyslexia are particularly well served.*

FINANCE:
- Access fund: £570,969 • Successful applications : 627

Merton College, Oxford, has an annual 'Time Ceremony'. When the clocks are turned back at 2am, students walk backwards in academic dress around the Fellows' Quad.

La Sainte Union see University of Southampton

Lampeter, University of Wales

Lancashire see University of Central Lancashire

Lancaster University

University of Leeds

Leeds Metropolitan University

University of Leicester

Leicester Poly see De Montfort University

University of Lincolnshire and Humberside

University of Liverpool

Liverpool Hope University College see Other Institutions

Liverpool John Moores University

Liverpool Poly see Liverpool John Moores University

University of London

London College of Fashion see The London Institute

London College of Printing see The London Institute

London Guildhall University

The London Institute

London School of Economics see LSE

London School of Jewish Studies see SOAS

Loughborough University

LSE

University of Luton

La Sainte Union

see University of Southampton

> A group of 45 students at Leeds Metropolitan University claims to be the most unlucky Lottery syndicate ever after paying out £2,880 and winning nothing.

Lampeter, University of Wales

- *Formerly St David's College*
- *The College is part of <u>University of Wales</u>*

University of Wales, Lampeter, Ceredigion, SA48 7ED. Tel: (01570) 422351. Fax: (01570) 423423. E-mail: admissions@lampeter.ac.uk
Ty Ceredig, University of Wales Lampeter, Lampeter, Ceredigion, Wales, SA48 7ED. Tel: (01570) 422619. Fax: (01570) 422480. E-mail: union@vax.acs.lampeter.ac.uk Website: www.lamp.ac.uk

GENERAL

Deep in south-west Wales, where valleys meet, is a little market town called Lampeter, so remote it doesn't even have a train station and quite a way from Carmarthen, the nearest town with anything approaching excitement. In this virtual village just round the corner from nowhere, is the appropriately small college. Set in its own grounds, the elegant stone buildings of Wales's oldest university college almost engulf the town. Beyond the town's borders, *you're immediately plunged into the beautifully rugged hills* from which the stones of Stonehenge were cut and 13 miles away, the town of Aberaeron on Wales's west coast.

Sex ratio(M:F): 50%:50%	Founded: 1822
Full time u'grads: 1,000	Part time: 300
Postgrads: 80	Non-degree: 15
Ave course: 3yrs	Ethnic: 8.9%
Private school: n/a	Flunk rate: 17.8%
Mature students: 49%	Overseas students: 9.7%
Disabled students: 5%	

ATMOSPHERE:
Students (a strange mixture of sensible country folk and Lampeter zonked-out Swampy lookalikes) are happy enough to make their own entertainment. After all, since there's little alternative. Everyone knows each other and the local community came to terms with the College about a century ago. Students who find themselves here by accident, through UCAS clearing or whatever, can have a problem adjusting but most find this extended chill-out zone a great way to spend three years.

THE TOWN:
- <u>Population: 2,000</u> • London: 180 miles • <u>Aberystwyth: 30 miles</u>
- <u>Swansea: 45 miles</u>

It depends what you consider to be the local town. Lampeter has about 20 shops *and there the excitement ends* (outside the SU, of course), so most students look on Aberystwyth as the local big-time *even though that's pretty titchy as well* (see <u>Aberystwyth, University of Wales</u>). Carmarthen is 22 miles away and smaller (pop 8,500); it's a *good* shopping town serving quite a large catchment area where there are more sheep than people. The surrounding area is *rich* in tourist attractions: the Roman gold mine; castles; Talley Abbey; Pembrokeshire National Park; and the famous Devil's Bridge.

TRAVEL:
Trains: From Carmarthen you can get mainline trains to London (£27.70), Cardiff (£10.30) and Birmingham (£24.25). Aberystwyth station is better for northbound journeys.
Coaches: Lampeter is now on a National Express route to London via Cardiff (£30.60), Cardiff (£12.10) and Birmingham via Swansea (£26.15).
Car: *Now there's a good idea. If you can afford it, get a car, or, failing that, a turbo-powered lawn mower. In Lampeter, it makes a big difference to the quality of life. Day trips and shopping become feasible.* 18 miles (½ hr) off the A40.
Hitching: *Without any major roads, it ain't easy. Allow a day to get anywhere and take a sleeping bag just in case, because it's not worth thinking, 'I can always catch a bus' – you can't, there probably won't be one.*
Local: The buses stick to the timetables, one every hour till about 5.30pm. It's £3.50 return to Carmarthen with a similar service to Aberystwyth.
Taxis: *Sure, there are taxis, but frankly, students can't afford the cost anywhere – It's about £20 to Carmarthen. Maybe worth it to have a night out in town if four share the ride back.*
Bicycles: There are sheds, not too many hills and virtually no theft, *but without motorised legs, most places are out of cycle reach.*

CAREER PROSPECTS:
• Careers Service • No of staff: 2part-time
• Unemployed after 6mths: 9.6%
Although there aren't many big employers on the doorstep the careers service arranges trips to Cardiff for the milk round.

FAMOUS ALUMNI:
Jack Higgins (thriller writer); Anthony Hopkins (*colossally great* actor); TE Lawrence (of Arabia).

FURTHER INFO:
Prospectus for undergrads; alternative prospectus from SU. Also, a website (www.lamp.ac.uk) and a video loan service. An open day is usually held in March or April.

ACADEMIC

staff/student ratio: 1:20
Range of points required for entrance: 240-160
Percentage accepted through clearing: 7.2%
Number of terms/semesters: 3
Length of terms/semesters: 10 wks
Research: 3.7

LIBRARIES:
• Books: 230,000 • Study places: 200
There are two libraries: the Founder's Library (with 20,000 historical books, documents and manuscripts) and the Main Library. *Both adhere to slightly archaic opening hours*: 9am – 9.45pm weekdays; 9am – 3.45pm Saturdays; 2pm – 4.45pm Sundays.

COMPUTERS:
• Computer workstations: 84

ENTERTAINMENT

TOWN:
- Price of a pint of beer: £1.70 • Glass of wine: £1.35

Pubs/clubs/music/theatre: There are 14 pubs within a 1½ mile radius, Cumann Tavern is *popular with students for its live music.* Felinfach Theatre is about 15mins away by car and puts on mostly Welsh language productions. *Occasional music in the pubs but for anything else you need to get out of town.*
Food: *Not a great deal.* Pushplugs: Lloyds (fish & chips); Shapla (Indian).

UNIVERSITY:
- Price of a pint of beer: £1.50 • Glass of wine: £1.10

Bars: (2) Students and staff *mix socially and sociably* in the Main SU Bar (cap 365) and the Extension Bar (350).
Theatres: The Arts Hall (450) is used for events of all sorts, including student theatre productions.
Cinemas: The film club shows major films and cult pics every Wednesday.
Clubs/discos/music venues: Popular bops three nights a week in the Union Extension. Local bands play on Tuesdays. Saturday bands are free. NoWaySis and Dust Junkies have played here in the past, *but no one knows why.* There's also a comedy show every week (£2).
Food: The Refectory offers basic school dinnery stuff, but the portions are generous. Pooh's Corner and the Pizza Bar in the SU are more likely to tempt jaded palates.
Other: Three balls a year.

SOCIAL & POLITICAL

LAMPETER STUDENTS' UNION/TY CEREDIG:
- 2 sabbaticals • Turnout at last ballot: 40% • NUS member

Being such a small institution, it's not hard to maintain a high level of involvement in the SU and (almost) unanimous consent. This is because no one gets too party political at Lampeter. It's all pretty liberal and tolerant. Having said that, Lampeter students will stand up and be counted *as the recent anti-fees campaign showed over 60% of the student body turned out to protest.*

SU FACILITIES:
The SU building, Ty Ceredig, has a bar, cafeteria, restaurant, printing and photocopying, general shop, travel service, TV room, function room, pool table, juke box and vending machines and minibus hire. The Union Extension provides a dancefloor, bar, nightclub facilities and a conference suite.

CLUBS (NON SPORTING):
Battle Re-enactment; Cymdeithas Cymreig (Welsh); Dyslexia; Fluffy; Hellenic; Hunt Sabs; ICT; Inter-Faith Dialogue; Masquerade; Media; Meditation; Methodist; Music; Pagan; Rave; Swedish; TocH; Warpsoc.

OTHER ORGANISATIONS:
Three times a term the SU publishes 'Union News' (union stuff and politics). '1822' is the College's satirical magazine four times a term and there's a gay publication, 'Absolutely Campus'. There is no student community group – *good relations make it unnecessary* – but there are clubs that do voluntary work.

RELIGIOUS:
- Chaplains (Christian)

The College has a chapel and Muslim prayer room and there are local churches. *Other religions will find it a bit tougher.*

PAID WORK:
The SU employs some student staff and there's a local organic farm, *but we're not talking major opportunities here.*

- Recent successes: karate, squash

The Uni has the oldest rugby playing institution in Wales and *generally there's a high level of participation with the emphasis on fun, not competitiveness.*

SPORTS FACILITIES:
There is a *stark* modern sports hall, 5 acres of playing fields, squash and tennis courts, an all-weather pitch, swimming pool, multi-gym and croquet lawn. The river (Afon Teifi) is *useful for some sports but isn't large enough for any aquatic Olympics.* Around town, there's a golf course and pony trekking and the mountains *are excellent* for rambling and hill walking, climbing and mountaineering, hang-gliding and getting cold.

SPORTING CLUBS:
Boxing; Darts; Karate; Keep-Fit; Pool; Surf; Watersports; Womens Rugby.

IN COLLEGE:
- Catered: 9% • Cost: £66 (30wks) • Self-catering: 29%
- Cost: £38-44 (35-36wks)

Availability: All 1st years who want to live in can do, along with 45% of the finalists. There's a mix of catered and self-catering halls on campus and there's also a complex of ex-holiday bungalows *which works out cheaper but residents need a car to make it worthwhile.* A surplus of accommodation means that students can live in over vacation time – very popular with the finalists. *Note though, accommodation tends to vary in quality.* 24-hour porterage.

Car parking: Parking is free with a permit *and there's enough for the moment, although the situation will deteriorate as numbers expand.*

EXTERNALLY:
- Ave rent: £38

Availability: Lampeter offers a mix of shared rented houses, bedsits and digs (with a live-in landlord/lady), mostly okay. If you've got wheels, of course, out in the country there are dinky little cottages aplenty, although some hippies have been known to disappear completely.

Housing help: Help is at hand from the College's Accommodation Office which has two full-time staff offering standard contracts, advice and a vacancies board.

```
Saggy old cloth cat Bagpuss has an honorary
degree from the University of Kent.
```

WELFARE

SERVICES:
- Creche • Nightline • Lesbian & Gay Society • Mature SA
- Overseas SA • Postgrad SA • Women's Officer
- Self-defence classes

Most welfare provision is handled by the SU, with no professional support and limited resources. The University has three part-time counsellors. New additions include a student support officer and an after-school club. There's also a nursery with 30 places for kids between just born (ish) babies to four-year-olds.

Disabled: *There are a few special rooms for wheelchair users and there is wheelchair access to most buildings. Although there's a wheelchair lift in the library, the aisles between books are too narrow. Structural changes are taking place slowly. To be fair, facilities for hearing-impaired students are good.*

FINANCE:
- Access fund: £128,500 • Successful applications n/a

Lancashire

see University of Central Lancashire

Lancaster University

Lancaster University, University House, Lancaster, LA1 4YW.
Tel: (01524) 65201. Fax: (01524) 846243.
E-mail: ugadmissions@lancaster.ac.uk
Lancaster University Students' Union, Bailrigg, Lancaster, LA1 4YW.
Tel: (01524) 593765. Fax: (01524) 846732.

GENERAL

The historic county town of Lancaster is a few miles south of the *luscious* Lake District. It dates from Roman times and much remains of the *splendid honey-coloured* limestone Georgian architecture. Hemmed by countryside on most sides, it reaches out to Morecambe and Heysham on the north-west coast, 4 miles away as well as the *beautiful* Forest of Bowland (but don't be surprised if you don't see any trees. This is a forest under the original definition – crown property for hunting). The University is 2 miles from Lancaster and is situated on a *large greenfield* campus on a hill. *Many of the buildings were put up during the 60s and are now looking decidedly naff.* However, many buildings were put up in the 90s including the Rushkin Library which won the Best Educational Building Architectural Award in 1999. At the centre of the campus is Alexandra Square, a large paved area with a few trees and surrounded by light-coloured brick buildings. Spread around this square, there are 250 acres of *spacious* landscaped woods, parkland and fields as well as geometric buildings, including the University's nine colleges.

Sex ratio(M:F): 50%:50%
Full time u'grads: 6,999
Postgrads: 1,269
Ave course: 3yrs
Private school: 35%
Mature students: 12%
Disabled students: 4.9%

Founded: 1964
Part time: 140
Non-degree: 0
Ethnic: 18%
Flunk rate: 14.8%
Overseas students: 14%

ATMOSPHERE:
The most important factor is the small 'communities within a community' in which most students live: the colleges. The colleges don't conduct admissions (although students can voice a preference), which means that, in atmosphere, they don't differ enormously. The main difference between them is size, varying from 450 to 800 undergrads. The college system is not as strong as, say, Oxbridge. They're not that much more than glorified halls of residence, although most teaching is based in college and; they each do have a JCR and an SCR. The system, combined with the high proportion of privately educated students who come here to avoid inner city life, means that Lancaster sometimes feels like a boarding school as much as a university. The lack of an on-campus ents facility doesn't help, but most students think the hike into town is worth it. However, fun-seekers can look forward to Extravs (Extravaganza's) which occurs each summer – basically, a festival in each college for a night.

THE CITY:
- **Population:** 50,000 • **London:** 250 miles • **Manchester:** 48 miles
- **Blackpool:** 20 miles

Lancaster is a *quaint tourist centre dominated* by the Ashton Memorial on one hill and the castle and priory on another. At the moment, parts of the castle are used as a prison. Some parts of it are open to the public, including the dungeons, but not the prison cells, *naturally*. The rest of the city goes up and down all over the place and is battered by wind and rain, but is lovely when the sun dares to shine. It has the usual facilities like a public library, supermarkets, late night shops, bookshops and the Maritime Museum. Marketgate and the St Nicholas Arcade are the *favoured* shopping haunts.

TRAVEL:
Trains: Lancaster station, 3 miles from the campus, has direct connections to London (£36.35), Manchester (£8.50), Birmingham (£26.95) and further afield.
Coaches: National Express services from the campus all over the country including London (£23.50), Manchester (£7.50) and Birmingham (£16.00).
Car: The M6 bypasses Lancaster from north to south slicing past the edge of the campus. The A6 and A683 go right into the centre. *A car is useful around town, especially for students who live out.*
Ferries: Service from Heysham to Douglas on the Isle of Man.
Hitching: *Students have set up a great hitching system. There is a special shelter on the campus and an established point in town for pick ups for trips to and from the University.* For longer journeys the M6 is a good bet.
Local: There is a *reliable* double-decker bus service to campus every 10 minutes (£1.10 return) and a minibus from campus to the station. Bus passes covering the Lancaster area cost £120 for a year.
Taxis: There are ranks at the rail and bus stations, *but they work out expensive.*

Bicycles: *A bike is even better than a car (the fuel is free unless you count burgers and chips) although the squash factor from traffic is high. A cycle path runs from campus to town.*

CAREER PROSPECTS
- Careers Service • No of staff: 10 full/3 part
- Unemployed after 6mths: 6.3%

FAMOUS ALUMNI:
Richard Allinson (DJ); Anna Lawson (actor); Oly Marsden (skier); Kieron McCaffrey (fisherman); Gary Waller MP (Con); Alan Milburn MP (Lab); Peter Whalley and Marvin Close (Coronation Street writers); Jason Queally (cycling Olympic gold medallist); Simon Smith (rugby player).

FURTHER INFO:
Prospectuses for undergrads, postgrads and mature students (all also available on audio tape), as well as a video. Alternative Prospectus available from SU Welfare Department. Websites (www.lancs.ac.uk and www.lancs.ac.uk/lusu). Check out the open days in August – you need to pre-book.

ACADEMIC

The 1st year of study is very flexible; students study three subjects. By the 2nd year, many do a course other than the one for which they originally applied.

staff/student ratio: 1:10
Range of points required for entrance: 340-220
Percentage accepted through clearing: 10%
Number of terms/semesters: 3
Length of terms/semesters: 11 wks
Research: 4

LIBRARIES:
- Books: 1,000,000 plus • Study places: 900 plus

The Library has recently been extended.

COMPUTERS:
- Computer workstations: 1,500

Computer provision gets a thumbs-up.

ENTERTAINMENT

THE CITY:
- Price of a pint of beer: £1.70 • Glass of wine: £1.50

Lancaster has a high proportion of nearly-deads. The liveliest entertainment is student-centred.

Cinemas: There are two cinemas including arty movies at The Dukes Theatre Arts Centre. New 4-screen Apollo at Morecambe.

Theatres: (2) The Dukes Theatre also hosts touring companies. The Grand Theatre is mainly amateur and shows also go on at the Gregson Centre.

Pubs: *Plenty of real ale and friendly olde worlde pubs. Pushplugs: Water Witch (on the canal, best in summer); Merchants; Blob Shop; It's a Scream; Penny Bank; Gallon Drunk Club; Paddy Mulligan's. Avoid Lanky's where there's hostility to studility.*

Clubs/discos/music venues: The Sugarhouse (see below) is the main venue in town. Otherwise, there's Brookes and the Warehouse (mainstream), the Carleton (indie/dance), Springs, Elemental (trendy bar), the Alex (rock) and the club Liquid (mainstream).
Eating out: Not a vast selection, but all bar the pickiest palates will be satisfied. Pushplugs: Nawaab Tandoori (excellent value balti); Sultan's (Indian, in a converted church); Paulo Gianni's (Italian, student discounts); Whaletale Café (veggie); Marco's; Icky's; Bodrums.

UNIVERSITY:
- Price of a pint of beer: £1.30 • Glass of wine: £1.30

Bars: Each college has a bar, *popular* with its own students. Cross-fertilisation only usually happens when there's an event on somewhere or students do 'Bar Golf' (a pint in each college bar (9 in all), some only do the 9, but others do the 9 twice (18 holes)).
Theatre: The Nuffield Studio is a *flexible* theatre space for *strong* student productions and visiting companies.
Cinemas: Blockbusters and more are shown 4 times a week by one of the biggest and best equipped student film clubs in the country.
Clubs/disco: The centre of all action is the Sugarhouse (cap 1,000), owned and run by the Union but situated in town. Three nights a week the place quakes to some sound sounds, from the indie of Star to the hard house of Lust which has attracted *serious guest DJs* such as Carl Cox. Time Tunnel is a retro night every other Friday.
Music venues: Again, the Sugarhouse stands out against the *culturally bleak* landscape luring such names as Shed Seven, Mansun, the Shire Horses and Hot Chocolate.
Food: Students are spoiled for choice: there's the Wibbly Wobbly Burger Bar *(we kid you not)* open till midnight, plus Pizetta Republica, Moonlight's Kebabs, Diggles sandwiches, curries, chips and *even real food on the go all day.*
Others: Most weeks, there's something in at least one of the college bars (competitions, theme parties, comedy, etc). College balls at Christmas and a Graduation Ball in June. The last week of the summer term is 'Extrav Week' – major party time, culminating in a 'Summer Extrav' at each college (6pm to 6am, drink, bands, DJs, drink, karaoke, food and drink).

SOCIAL & POLITICAL

LANCASTER UNIVERSITY STUDENTS' UNION (LUSU):
- 6 sabbaticals • Turnout at last ballot: 25% • NUS member

LUSU has the ground floor of the *plush*, Slaidburn House to administer *its little empire*. Representation, ents and services are also provided on a college level through Junior Common Rooms (JCRs). *Students here are more politically aware than some we could mention and the SU rouses rabbles on their behalf.*

SU FACILITIES:
LUSU provides two general shops, a second-hand bookshop, drugstore and, of course, the Sugarhouse. Also around the campus there are banks, a post office, petrol station, bookshops (new and second-hand), hairdresser, chemist, newsagent, supermarket, bakery, travel agency and a few smaller shops. Each college also has a JCR.

CLUBS (NON SPORTING):
Buddhist; Chinese; Finnish; Jugglers; Motoring; Poetry.

OTHER ORGANISATIONS:
'SCAN' (Student Comment And News) is the Union-published student newspaper, with a sabbatical editor, and Bailrigg FM broadcasts around campus. There's also a full-time Rag co-ordinator – events include the *infamous* Lancaster-Paris hitch.

RELIGIOUS:
• 3 Chaplains (Anglican, Methodist, RC)
Two chapels (Anglican and Roman Catholic) as well as rooms for the Jewish community with a Kosher kitchen. There is a non-denominational Chaplaincy Centre on campus, which hosts visits from ministers of most religions, and a Muslim prayer room. There are various places of worship in town, including a number of different churches and a mosque.

PAID WORK:
Nothing unusual except some tourist jobs in summer. The SU job-shop has a minimum wage policy.

• Recent successes: fencing, hockey
One of the clearest expressions of college differences is through the intercollegiate sporting competitions for the Carter Shield. When they gang up and take on other universities the story is less impressive, but not disastrous. Every year the University fights for the Roses Cup with York University. Lancaster has the best record.

SPORTS FACILITIES:
18.2 acres of playing fields *(which allegedly provide a fine harvest of magic mushrooms in season)*; all-weather pitches; sports hall; 8 tennis and 8 squash courts; croquet lawn; bowling green; 25m swimming pool; climbing wall; gymnasium; multi-gym; sauna & solarium; gym; weights rooms (male and female); dance studio; athletics area; golf practice area; archery range; floodlit hard playing area; and the University's Lake Carter. Locally, a golf course and the River Lune (where the University has a boat house). The Sailing Club uses the Glasson Dock marina.

SPORTING CLUBS:
American Football; Caving; Freefall; Frisbee; Korfball; Lacrosse; Rowing; Water polo, Windsurfing.

IN COLLEGE:
• Self-catering: 52% • Cost: £40-61 (31-38wks)
Availability: All 1st years live in their colleges, although there are no guarantees for students coming through clearing. Nearly half of finalists also live in but 2nd years are almost entirely on their own. Corridors in the colleges are split into single sex areas. There are 176 rooms with en suite bathrooms at Cartmel College (costing £47 a week) – most are taken by overseas students. Alexandra Hall in town is used by postgrads. A head tenancy scheme provides 430 places too. There are plans to give all campus accommodation on-line access within the next year.
Car parking: *Limited* free parking 5 to 10 minutes from the colleges.

Even more limited permit parking nearer, but 1st years are not allowed to bring cars.

EXTERNALLY:
• Ave rent: £40
Availability: *The best places are Bowerham (convenient), Galgate (10 mins walk) and around Blade and Dale Streets (studentsville), but the Marsh Estate and Rylands should be avoided. Accommodation in Lancaster has become much easier to find.*
Housing help: The Accommodation Office is run jointly by the University and LUSU and provides a vacancy board, a list of recommended landlords, newsletter, approval scheme and standard contracts.

SERVICES:
• Creche • Nightline • Nursery • Mature SA • Overseas SA
• Minibus • Women's Officer

LUSU's Welfare Officer works in conjunction with University staff to provide help and advice with all manner of tear-jerkers. The University provides a counselling service with 7 part-time staff and a campus clinic with a medic. The Union has four counsellors. The nursery has 30 places for under 2's and 72 places for 2–5-year-olds.
Disabled: *The University has worked wonders in improving access on campus,* earning itself a Queen's Anniversary Award for special needs provisions. There are ramps all over the place, taped information available for sight-impaired students and a loop system in lecture halls for the hearing-impaired.

FINANCE:
• Access fund: £505,992 • Successful applications: 455
Each college administers its own hardship fund for loans and gifts. There's also a good selection of scholarships and bursaries for academic merit. There are also 4 debt counsellors to provide commiseration.

University of Leeds

The University of Leeds, Leeds, LS2 9JT. Tel: (0113) 243 1751. Fax: (0113) 233 3991. E-mail: prospectus@leeds.ac.uk
Leeds University Union, PO Box 157, Leeds, LS1 1UH. Tel: (0113) 231 4254. Fax: (0113) 244 8786. E-mail: comms@union.leeds.ac.uk

From the top of the *virginally* white Parkinson Building clock tower, which is the University's landmark, it's possible to see Leeds City Centre, the tidy terraces of the inner city, the *sprawling, crawling* suburbs and the *tangled spaghetti* of bypasses, ring roads and the M1. Casting eyes beyond the city boundaries, the southern edge of the Yorkshire moors *loom* to the north. To the south and west, there are few green spaces separating Leeds from Bradford, Wakefield and Sheffield. Although founded in the late 19th century, the University has undergone *spasmodic periods of growth, mainly in the 30s and 60s, creating a campus which is the architectural equivalent of Bombay Mix.* Together with Leeds Metropolitan University, the University forms a massive 'student-land' conurbation of homes, halls and other academic buildings.

Sex ratio(M:F): 47%:53%
Full time u'grads: 17,904
Postgrads: 5,563
Ave course: 3yrs
Private school: 23%
Mature students: 14%
Disabled students: 8.2%

Founded: 1887
Part time: 4,066
Non-degree: 2,500
Ethnic: 8.4%
Flunk rate: 8.7%
Overseas students: 16%

ATMOSPHERE:
With so many examples, it's difficult to draw a very exact picture of the Leeds University student. In such a vibrant, frantic city (Leeds' serious social scene battles with London for UK top spot), the prevailing relaxed attitude is odd. A scepticism, bordering on apathy, abounds in virtually epidemic proportions and an observer more cruel than Push might suggest that *few students consider anything deeper than the bottom of their glass.* But appearances can be deceptive and the large Union Building is always busy.

THE CITY:
• <u>Population: 674,400</u> • <u>Manchester: 40 miles</u> • <u>London: 189 miles</u>
Although the bombs of the second-world war missed the city, the 60s developers and town planners didn't and Leeds' one-way system provides *endless entertainment. On tour, the frustrated driver will trundle round in circles,* passing *glorious* Victorian civic buildings – the Town Hall, City Museum, Henry Moore Gallery and The Grand Theatre (home to Opera North). The driver, however, will miss the semi-pedestrianised, *bustling* main street, known as the Briggate – *the site of every local amenity a student could ever want and many they wouldn't.* Soft Southerners shouldn't write Leeds off as a home to coal-munching whippet breeders. It's a vibrant, youthful city, with some of the best clubs and venues in the country and even its own branch of Harvey Nick's. Fabulous, dahling.

TRAVEL:
Trains: Leeds station is the centre of the *very efficient* West Yorkshire metro train network which serves all the local Yorkshire towns (Bradford, Wakefield, Sheffield and York). Many direct services operate further afield to, for example, London (£38.30), Manchester (£9.10) and more.
Coaches: National Express to London (£16.75), Manchester (£7), Edinburgh (£22.50) and other destinations. Also served by Blueline.
Car: 10 mins off the M1 and on the M62 to Manchester. *A car is unnecessary for local travel, thanks to the good public transport.*
Air: Leeds/Bradford Airport for inland and European flights.
Hitching: *Excellent prospects for long distance on the M1 and M62, but as ever, there are safer ways of getting around.*
Local: *Very reliable, frequent* trains and buses (the maximum off-peak fare is 80p). A monthly student Metrocard (bus and train) is £39.50 while the Student First travel card (£34 per month) is valid on bus routes from the uni through to the city centre.

Taxis: *Quick and efficient but never cheap.*
Bicycles: There are cycle paths in many areas, *but the place is too hilly and fume-filled and has too many light-fingered locals.*

CAREER PROSPECTS:
• Careers Service • No of staff: 24 full
• Unemployed after 6mths: 3.5%
There's the *highly efficient* Careers Service.

FAMOUS ALUMNI:
Steve Bell (cartoonist); Barry Cryer (writer/comedian); Paul Dacre (former Daily Mail editor); Andrew Eldritch (Sisters of Mercy); Gavin Esler (BBC journalist); David Gedge (Wedding Present); Andy Kershaw (DJ); Mystic Meg (who only got a 2(ii), *so she obviously didn't foresee her exam questions*); Mark Knopfler (Gomez); Nick Owen (BBC presenter); Gerald Ratner (former 'crap' jeweller); Clare Short MP (Lab); Jack Straw MP (Lab, ex-SU president); Nicholas Witchell (BBC newscaster, once editor of 'Leeds Student').

FURTHER INFO:
Prospectuses (official and alternative) for undergrads and postgrads, a guide for mature students and an extensive website www.leeds.ac.uk. Open days in June and September.

ACADEMIC

staff/student ratio: 1:16
Range of points required for entrance: 360-180
Percentage accepted through clearing: 4%
Number of terms/semesters: 3
Length of terms/semesters: 10 wks
Research: 4.6

LIBRARIES:
• Books: 2,600,000 • Study places: 8,000
There are 2 main libraries and 7 departmental ones.

COMPUTERS:
• Computer workstations: 2,393
24-hour access to computers for postgrads only.

ENTERTAINMENT

CITY:
• Price of a pint of beer: £2.05
Check out the 'Leeds Student' free sheet for listings.
Cinemas: (5) 2 independent single-screen *flea pits*, 3 multiplex.
Theatres: (4) Everything from opera at the Grand to Alan Ayckbourn and amateur dramatics. The West Yorkshire Playhouse is an *excellent* modern repertory theatre complex.
Pubs: This is the home of Yorkshire bitter *and there are few local pubs that don't serve a decent pint. Serious imbibers should contemplate the Otley Run, a 14-pub crawl of mythical proportions, including The Eldon, The Skyrack, The Original Oak and The Dry Dock (on a boat). Or try the Royal Park, the Arc, and Headingley Taps.*

Clubs/discos: Leeds is an all-night city thanks to a tolerant council licensing policy. It's also home to some *great* clubs, if you can squeeze past the queues. *The Push posse is on the guest-list for: Funky Mule at the Warehouse; The Hi Fi Club; Majestyk.*

Music venues: Leeds is a compulsory stop shop for touring bands from big names to the biggest and there's a thriving live scene. Pushplugs: T&C; Duchess of York; Irish Centre (indie).

Eating out: Somewhere as large and cosmopolitan as Leeds is guaranteed to have grubstops to satisfy all palates and pockets. Pushplugs: Theo's (kebabs and the best lentil burgers in the world); Zacks (pizza/pasta buffet £4); Sala (good value Thai); Salvos (Italian), Baraka (Moroccan); Original Oak (pub lunches); Clock Café; Grove Café; Manuela's; Dino's; Fujihiro (cheap Japanese food).

UNIVERSITY:

- Glass of wine: 80p • Price of a pint of beer: £1

Bars: With five bars in the Union and at least one in most of the halls, students are in little danger of dying of sobriety. All are popular, especially the brand new Terrace Bar (cap 1,000). The Harvey Milk Bar doubles as the main club venue.

Cinemas: Two mainstream movies a week.

Theatres: (3) *Leeds holds its own among thespians with a workshop theatre and a selection of other potential venues. The Edinburgh Fringe is a regular summer jaunt for students' shows with 5 shows making the trek this year.*

Clubs/discos/music venues: The Harvey Milk Bar (cap 450, £3) hosts club nights three nights a week, from 70s to hiphop via goth, there are plans for a new 1,000 capacity venue hosting club nights. *The live band scene isn't quite as pumping as the one at their upstart neighbours (*Leeds Metropolitan University*), probably because they can't sell beer in the gig venue.* However, Toploader, James, Placebo and the Levellers have played in recent months in the cavernous Refectory.

Food: *The Refectory's the best bet for full and filling meals,* while the Mouat Jones coffee bar deals with all snack requirements. The bars also serve up a *good* range of eats.

Cabaret: Comedy often in Harvey's Milk Bar from the likes of Mark Lamarr, Rhona Cameron and Rolf 'can you tell what it is yet' Harris.

Others: Balls bounce all over the place, the biggest being the *one of the largest* graduation shindigs in the country (5,000 people) and the Freshers' do in October.

SOCIAL & POLITICAL

LEEDS UNIVERSITY UNION (LUU):

• 13 sabbaticals • Turnout at last ballot: 8% • NUS member

Many other students would be delighted to have an operation on the scale of LUU to represent them, but size brings its own problems, not least remoteness for the average non-hack. Still, as long as the beer's cheap and the ents are entertaining, most are happy with the set-up. Political activity is high on the agenda. Funnily enough, Jack Straw (former LUU President) was banned from the Union building.

SU FACILITIES:

Every facility but the kitchen sink – oh, no, there's one of those too: bars; a coffee bar; darkroom; opticians; minibus & car hire; ABTA travel agency; book/stationery shops; Lloyds Bank with cashpoint;

hair salon; photocopying; photo booth; games and video machines; TV lounges; cash-back facilities at shops; meeting rooms; launderette and dry-cleaning. A new extension to the Union building will add a 1,000 cap venue and, 2 more bars.

CLUBS (NON SPORTING):
Action for Animals; AIESEC; Arts; Backstage; Ballet; Ballroom Dancing; Bangin' and Mashed; Black Lodge; Breakdance; Boardgames and Wargames; Buddhist Meditation; Caballe and Meditation; Chamber Choir; Chao Thai; CHAOS (Physics & Astronomy); Chinese; Christian Focus; Creative Journal; Danceband; Debating; DJ; Finnish; Fire International; Egyptian; Film; Free Speech; Hellenic; Hiking; Hindu; Iranian; Juggling; Kabal; Role Playing; LSR (student radio); LUST (theological, funnily enough); Malaysian; Massoc; Model UN; Modern Dance; Motorcycle; Monkeyhouse; Music Theatre; Pakistani; Pelicans (creative writing); Real Ale; Revelation Rock Gospel; Scottish Dance; Scout & Guide; Singaporean; Soka Gokai Buddhist; Speleological; Spurs Supporters; Stage Musical; Tibet Support; Welsh.

OTHER ORGANISATIONS:
'Leeds Student' is the award-winning University and <u>Leeds Metropolitan University</u> joint weekly newspaper, with a sabbatical editor and 50,000 readers. The award-winning radio station (LSR FM) broadcasts several times a year. The charity Rag is also a co-production with Leeds Met. Leeds Student Community Action runs 60 effective local help projects.

RELIGIOUS:
There are *excellent facilities* for 99 different denominations and religions and the largest Jewish student community outside Manchester.

PAID WORK:
There's the usual bar work and stewarding at Union ents and a job-link scheme run by the SU, a noticeboard and an on-line joblink.

SPORTS

- Recent successes: karate, rifle, gymnastics

The facilities are there for sporting success and there are more than enough healthy hopefuls with lycra bottoms. Participation is fairly high.

SPORTS FACILITIES:
The Leeds Sports Centre provides facilities for everything from weight training to ballet and from table tennis to martial arts, all in a large sports centre. The Weetwood playing ground, 4 miles away, has 15 soccer, 5 hockey, 4 rugby, 1 American Football, 2 Lacrosse and 5 cricket pitches. There's also an astroturf football pitch, 6 tennis courts and the Lawnswood playing fields. The Sports Centre has a climbing wall, but the Yorkshire Dales offer the real thing. *The solarium, however, is the most reliable sunshine source round here.*

SPORTING CLUBS:
Aikido; American Football; Archery; Athletics; Badminton; Basketball; Boat; Boxing; Canoe; Cricket; Cross Country; Cycling; Darts; Fencing; Football; Golf; Gymnastics and Trampoline; Hang Gliding; Hockey; Horse Riding; Judo; Karate; Korfball; Lacrosse; Netball; Orienteering; Paragliding; Rifle; Rowing; Rugby League; Rugby Union; Sailing; Samurai Jiu Jitsu; Ski; Snooker; Sport Parachute; Squash; Swimming and Waterpolo; Table Tennis; Ten Pin Bowling; Triathlon; Ultimate Frisbee; Volleyball; Windsurfing.

ATTRACTIONS:
In the heartland of rugby league, with Leeds United at Elland Road, international cricket at Headingley and swimming facilities *only a paddle away,* Leeds is fully equipped with all the mod cons.

ACCOMMODATION

IN COLLEGE:
• Catered: 11% • Cost: £58-109 (33wks) • Self-catering: 28%
• Cost: £27-65 (40wks)
Availability: All 1st years who want to can live in a variety of *highly comfortsome* halls. The older halls, such as Bodington and Devonshire (both catered), require about 10% of their students to share (for whom rents are lower). The self-catering flats hold between 4 and 14 students. *Students do complain about odd restrictions (against posters, in some cases) and cleaners who arrive at inopportune moments.*
Car parking: *Expensive, unnecessary and in short supply.*

EXTERNALLY:
• Ave rent: £43
Most students stick to the large quantity of late 19th-century back-to-back terraced housing in variable condition. The Unipol code of practice has sorted out a few problems with unscrupulous landlords. *Favourite areas for Students are Headingley, Woodhouse and Hyde Park, not so for Chapeltown which can get a bit rough.*
Housing help: UniPol *(which should change its name to UniUni)* – the joint University and Leeds Metropolitan University SUs' housing service – provides lots of help and advice with a code of standards and an *excellent* Internet search service. It also keeps tabs on the worst landlords. With 10 full- and 4 part-time staff, *it's a dream scheme.*

WELFARE

SERVICES:
• Nursery • Lesbian & Gay Society • Women's Minibus
• Overseas SA • Women's Officers • Self-defence classes

The student health service is now ensconced in its very own mini hospital (10 doctors, 7-bed sick bay and even a minor operation suite). There are also 7 full-time and 9 part-time counsellors. There's also a nursery *for the people of baby variety,* 60 places for kids 6 months up to 5 years old. *This makes the University extremely well equipped, but somewhere this size needs to be.*

Disabled: The University and Union *are making efforts to improve access and have shown a willingness to make changes* like adapting rooms, providing equipment, introducing a buddying scheme and so on. The new Union building has been designed with disabled students in mind. *However, despite all these efforts, the campus does not lend itself to easy access, what with being on a hill with many steps and level changes.*

FINANCE:
• Access fund: £875,000 • Successful applications: 1,000

The Union offers emergency loans of up to £100, the usual bursaries and welfare funds and there's a range of budgeting advice, debt counselling and even help with bankruptcy.

'It looks like bleedin' Marbella' –unidentified visitor to an HE Fair, upon seeing an aerial photo of Swansea.

Leeds Metropolitan University

- **Formerly Leeds Polytechnic**

Leeds Metropolitan University, Calverley Street, Leeds, LS1 3HE.
Tel: (0113) 283 3113. Fax: (0113) 283 3114.
E-mail: course-enquiries@lmu.ac.uk
Leeds Metropolitan University Students' Union, Calverley Street, Leeds, LS1 3HE. Tel: (0113) 209 8413. Fax: (0113) 234 2973.

GENERAL

Right in the middle of Leeds there is a university. Right next-door is another one. Somewhere one ends and the next begins, but it's not easy to tell where. Like its more elderly neighbour, the Met's buildings are a jumble of old and new, but it centres on 7 ugly concrete tower blocks. The central building is a 60s block with a recently redesigned front entrance, much like the colour and character of Bridget Jones's big pants, with the fresh addition of a small stain. It's a crying shame that the site cannot be shifted en-masse to the Beckett Park Campus, 3 miles out in a *picturesque* wooded site arranged *tastefully* around a cricket square.

Sex ratio(M:F): 48%:52%	Founded: 1970
Full time u'grads: 10,812	Part time: 3,665
Postgrads: 796	Non-degree: 1,355
Ave course: 3yrs	Ethnic: 12%
Private school: 7%	Flunk rate: 20%
Mature students: 19%	Overseas students: 4%
Disabled students: 5%	

ATMOSPHERE:
Not a place to take itself too seriously, Leeds Met students know the meaning of fun (n. enjoyment, amusement, or light-hearted pleasure – Oxford Dictionary) and there's a hectic party atmosphere often lacking in institutions with such a high proportion of part-time students.

THE SITES:
City Centre: Brunswick and Calverley sites, 300 yards from the civic centre and 200 yards from the most *unattractive supermarket* outside Moscow.
Beckett Park Campus: 3 miles from the city campus, Beckett Park is in 100 acres of woodland and parkland, affording panoramic views across Leeds. The main building dates back to 1913. Beckett Park houses various departments (including business, education, IT, law, sports sciences and languages), and the University's main sports facilities. There's a bus service between here and the city campus every 6 to 10 minutes.

THE CITY: see University of Leeds

TRAVEL: see University of Leeds

CAREER PROSPECTS:
- Careers Service • No of staff: 2 full/4 part
- Unemployed after 6mths: 8%

The busy but welcoming Careers Service runs development workshops, offering help job applications and finding work experience.

FAMOUS ALUMNI:
Marc Almond (singer); Glen Baxter (cartoonist); Betty Boothroyd (former Speaker of the Commons); Peter Cattaneo (film director); Sir Henry Moore (sculptor); Ron Pickering (sports commentator); Eric Pickles MP (Con); Keith Waterhouse (writer).

FURTHER INFO:
Prospectus for undergraduates and postgrads. Website (www.lmu.ac.uk).

ACADEMIC

Vocational lead degree structure. The business school recently scored well on the quality of teaching and is strong in Hospitality, Leisure, Recreation, Sport and Tourism. 13-week autumn and spring terms allow students to get away with a 3rd term of just 8 weeks hard labour in the summer.

staff/student ratio: 1:10
Range of points required for entrance: 300-120
Percentage accepted through clearing: 22%
Number of terms/semesters: 3
Length of terms/semesters: 11wks
Research: 1.9

LIBRARIES:
- Books: 400,000 • Study places: 2,300

There are 3 main libraries. The Learning Centre at Beckett Park has a selection of sports and leisure volumes, as well as the more academic stuff.

COMPUTERS:
- Computer workstations: 1,578

Computer facilities are *good*.

ENTERTAINMENT

THE CITY: see University of Leeds

UNIVERSITY:
- Price of a pint of beer: £1.70 • Glass of wine: £1.25

Bars: (3) The Kirkstall Bar (capacity 1,000) spreads over 2 floors and there's also the Becketts (450, *popular for post-match celebrations/sorrow-drowning*), the City Bar (1,400) which has a late licence 3 nights a week.
Theatre: There's a University-run studio theatre.
Clubs/discos: The Star and The Bop.
Music venues: Recently in the Ents Hall: Coldplay, Badly Drawn Boy and Moby. *Leeds Met has a deserved reputation as a major indie tour date, overshadowing its more staid neighbour.* Local bands play free gigs at Beckett Park.
Cabaret: The SU occasionally attracts some *top-notch giggle jugglers*: Craig Charles and Rob Newman have packed out the Ents Hall. Mark & Lard and Howard Marks have also appeared.
Food: *The main refectory 'The Depot' offers good value for limited dosh and the SU coffee bar deals with the munchies.* The Grapevine

is a posher affair where the lecturers hang out. There's also a refectory at Beckett Park, also confusingly called 'The Depot'.

SOCIAL & POLITICAL

LEEDS METROPOLITAN UNIVERSITY STUDENTS' UNION:
• 6 sabbaticals • Turnout at last ballot: 10% • NUS member
Abject apathy rules supreme, although the University's decision to close the Health Faculty provoked a few concerned noises. Students really aren't that bothered who's running things, though. They're more concerned with who scored the winning try and whose round it is.

SU FACILITIES:
The main facilities are at the City campus where there are 2 bars, 5 coffee bars, 2 print rooms, Lloyds Bank and cash-point, games machines, health & fitness suite and 2 shops. At Beckett Park, there's not just another bar, but also a cafe, bank, photo booth, games and video machines, pool tables, TV lounge, disco and a juke-box. Look out for 3 new internet cafes across the city.

CLUBS (NON SPORTING):
International; Law; Malaysian; Motorclub; Music.

OTHER ORGANISATIONS:
The SU produces a fortnightly newsletter, 'Headliner'. The award-winning and widely read 'Leeds Student' newspaper, run jointly with University of Leeds Union along with the radio station, deserves both to win awards and to be widely read. The Rag is also a joint effort and the Action group, headed by a sabbatical officer, *does all manner of good stuff in the local community.*

RELIGIOUS:
There are two Muslim prayer rooms and Islamic and Jewish advisors while students can share 6 other chaplains with University of Leeds.

PAID WORK:
The *excellent* job shop has filled well over 2,000 vacancies.

SPORTS

• Recent successes: football, rugby league
This lot play to win. To use facilities there's a single charge of £25 per year.

SPORTS FACILITIES:
The *excellent* facilities (all at Beckett Park) include the new Centre of Excellence for Tennis, Carnegie Regional Gymnastics Centre, a swimming pool, squash courts, athletics and playing fields including 12 football pitches, 4 rugby, 1 lacrosse, 2 synthetic floodlit and 1 5-a-side pitch, a multi-gym, weights room, running track, tennis courts and regular aerobics classes. These facilities were acquired through lottery funding, which means that they are also open to the public. The city has its own leisure centre, pool, sauna, ski slope, a lake and river, a bowling green and golf course.

SPORTING CLUBS:
Boxing; Gymnastics; Kung Fu; Lacrosse, Mountaineering; Tai Chi; Waterskiing.

ATTRACTIONS: see University of Leeds

ACCOMMODATION

IN COLLEGE:
• Self-catering: 16% •Cost: £41-63 (41-43wks)
Availability: With the addition of the Kirkstall Brewery complex 60% of 1st years can be accommodated. The rest are handled by Unipol, not an international crime-fighting agency, but the Leeds universities' *first-rate* joint student property management scheme.
Car parking: Parking is very limited at Beckett Park, and non-existent at the city campus. Students are advised not to bring their cars to the city campus.

EXTERNALLY: see University of Leeds
Housing help: See University of Leeds for details of Unipol. Leeds Met also has its own Accommodation Office which has in the past *successfully* avoided any students-on-gym-floors scenarios.

WELFARE

SERVICES:
• Lesbian & Gay Society • Mature SA • Minibus
•Women's Officer • Self-defence classes

The University's student health centres at Beckett Park are staffed by nurses. There are also 5 full- and 2 part-time counsellors, with additional specialists for disability, finance and other issues. The university also provides fact sheets for every conceivable emergency. A nightline service is available.
Disabled: Despite a fine array of Equal Opportunity policies and a Disability Support service, some buildings cannot be adapted for wheelchair users. Unipol (see above) makes an extra effort to accommodate students with disabilities. There's a full-time dyslexia support officer and induction loops at Beckett Park.

FINANCE:
• Access fund: £990,000 • Successful applications: 800
Debt counselling is available from the Budget Advisor and 2 part-timers. Emergency fund for overseas students.

University of Leicester

University of Leicester, Admissions and Student Recruitment, University Road, Leicester, LE1 7RH. Tel: (0116) 252 5281.
Fax: (0116) 252 2200. E-mail: admissions@le.ac.uk
University of Leicester Students' Union, Percy Gee Building, University Road, Leicester, LE1 7RH. Tel: (0116) 223 1111.
Fax: (0116) 223 1123.

> Because of an architect's error, the Psychology building at Exeter University was built back-to-front.

GENERAL

Leicester (along with Nottingham to the north and Northampton to the south) is one of the principal cities of the East Midlands. *But it doesn't really feel all that big. It's something about the attitude of the people, which is generally full of small-town small-talk friendliness. The suburbs are attractive, but the centre, steeped in history, has a few dodgy areas.* Parts have been pedestrianised, mainly the shopping areas. A mile from the centre, opposite a large cemetery and the rather pretty Victoria Park, is the city's older University. It's a mixture of pleasant old architecture, such as the original Georgian building and *new-fangled* post-war bits. Three of these are particularly prominent on the skyline: the Attenborough Building, 18 storeys high, which won a design award (but then, France won the 1998 World Cup); the 10-storey Charles Wilson Building; and the Engineering block, *which looks like it's got a crane sticking out of the top* and is Grade II listed (having won an award in the 1960s for its use of aluminium).

Sex ratio(M:F): 49%:51%
Full time u'grads: 6,800
Postgrads: 1,479
Ave course: 3yrs
Private school: 13%
Mature students: 8%
Disabled students: 5.5%

Founded: 1921
Part time: 62
Non-degree: n/a
Ethnic: n/a
Flunk rate: 6%
Overseas students: 7%

ATMOSPHERE:
Students are into having a good time, whether on the playing fields or in the bars. The campus is surrounded by much greenery, heightening the impression that the University is slightly divorced from the rest of town, physically as well as socially.

THE CITY:
• Population: 300,000 • London: 98 miles • Birmingham: 33 miles
• Nottingham: 21 miles

Leicester is large enough to have all the local amenities *that a student grant can bear, yet small enough to have some kind of homeliness.* Apart from the 700-year old market place, local highlights include a bookshop on Market St, the largest open-air market in Europe (for clothes, fruit and veg, fish and so on), the second-hand clothes stalls in Silver Arcade, Malcolm Arcade and Silver St, and Gary Lineker's dad's fruit stall. A more touristy tour takes in the Newarke House Museum, the City Museum & Art Gallery, Snibston Discovery Park and Rutland Water *(very popular with students in summer)*. The National Space Centre is an encouragement to students to put a little aside for a trip to the moon. *There's a large Asian population,* adding further variety to the culinary and sartorial availables. Leicester may not be the hottest nightspot in the land, but Nottingham and even London are close enough for day trips.

TRAVEL:
Trains: Leicester Station operates many services direct all over the Midlands and the rest of the country, including London (£23.45), Sheffield (£19.80), Edinburgh (£53.60), Leeds and beyond.
Coaches: National Express and other services to London (£13.25), Sheffield (£8.50), Edinburgh (£32.75) and elsewhere.

Car: The M1 skirts the edge of Leicester and the M69 connects with the A5 from the city's outskirts. Also, the A6, A46, A47, A50 and A607.
Air: Flights from East Midlands Airport (16 miles away) inland and to Europe.
Hitching: *Excellent* for London or Birmingham. Catch a bus out to near the M1 or M69 motorway junctions.
Local: *Buses are reliable, cheap (60p from campus to town), well used and run until 11pm.*
Taxis: £3 for an average journey.
Bicycles: Leicester, 'Britain's First Environmental City', is steadily introducing cycle ways and there are racks on campus.

CAREER PROSPECTS:
- Careers Service • No of staff: 8 full/2 part-time
- Unemployed after 6mths: 6%

Jobshop, workshops and help from advisors.

FAMOUS ALUMNI:
Malcolm Bradbury (writer); Sue Cook (TV presenter); Heather Couper (TV astronomer); Carol Galley (city whizzkid); Michael Jack MP (Con); Bob Mortimer (comedian); Pete McCarthy (comedian, TV presenter); Michael Nicholson (ITN newscaster); Andrew Taylor (chief exec McDonalds); Tony Underwood (rugby player); Sir Alan Walters (economist).

FURTHER INFO:
Prospectuses for undergrads and postgrads. CD-Rom and website (www.le.ac.uk). There are open days in May and September.

ACADEMIC

Mostly traditional courses, taught well.

staff/student ratio: 1:14
Range of points required for entrance: 340-240
Percentage accepted through clearing: 10%
Number of terms/semesters: 2
Length of terms/semesters: 15 wks
Research: 4.4

LIBRARIES:
- Books: 1,100,000 • Study places: 1,500

The University has 3 main libraries: the Main Library, Clinical Science and School of Education.

COMPUTERS:
- Computer workstations: 965

Some computers are accessible 24-hours and all terminals have Windows 2000.

ENTERTAINMENT

TOWN:
- Price of a pint of beer: £2.00 • Glass of wine: £1.70

Cinemas: (12) *The 8-screen Odeon and the Cannon (for mainstream movies and the occasional Indian film), a Warner multiplex, the Phoenix Arts centre (for arthouse flicks) and Capital Cinema (for Asian epics).*

Theatres: (2) The Haymarket hosts populist productions and touring companies and, again, the Phoenix for fringe and cult productions.
Pubs: Pushplugs: Fullback & Firkin; O'Neill's; Bar Gaudi (cocktails); The Globe; Loaded Dog. Don't bother with the Braunstone (anti-student) or the Angel (unless you support Leicester City FC).
Clubs/discos: Leicester has enough clubs to suit all but the most ardent tail feather shaker although some aren't up to much. Pushplugs: Planet (trance/acid, big queues); le Palais de Danse (charty, hired by SU for Happy Mondaze and Mega on Fridays); Attik (ambient/drum n bass); The Fan Club and Alcatraz (indie); Streetlife (gay); Junction 21 (hip hop, dub); Mosquito Coast (NUS night indie/retro).
Comedy: *The comedy scene here is funtastic;* check out Club Jongleurs and the Leicester Comedy Festival which is the biggest in GB attracting over 40,000 giggle-meisters.
Music venues: De Montfort Hall, *an important indie venue,* shouldn't be confused with De Montfort University, which is also *a good sound spot.* The Charlotte, Half Time Orange and the Shed have smaller indie bands.
Eating out: Leicester's a vindaloo hot favourite for curry fiends. Among the dozens of cumin attractions Akash, Shireen and Manzel's stand out, but there are plenty more. Other Pushplugs: Que Pasa (Mexican); The Good Earth (veggie); Lynn's Café (greasy spoon); Café Brussels; Bread & Roses (veggie); Dino's (Italian); Fat Cat Café.
Other: Leicester's numerous ethnic communities add to the fun with annual Caribbean and Mela (Asian) carnivals and Diwali (Hindu) celebrations.

UNIVERSITY:
- Price of a pint of beer: £1 • Glass of wine: £1.50

Bars: There are 4 main bars: Redfearn Bar (cap 500, popular at lunchtimes); Element (cap 300); Mirage and the Oasis Bar in the Venue (total cap 2,000). Also 7 hall bars.
Theatres: *Student drama is strong,* with three productions a year and the outdoor Shakespeare festival in summer. A thespian marathon held by the students, for all things bard-produced, is being considerd for the world record.
Clubs/discos: The Venue (1,700) *is the jumpingest joint.* Rock and indie take it in turns each Saturday, and once a month it's house. Recent guest DJs have included Ronny Size.
Music venues: The Venue is the boogie box with regular nights including 80s on Wednesdays (£1.50 only, 80p drinks), 90s sounds at Blair's, 60s at Lollipop, 70s at Locomotion, gay nights and Cheesecake (funky). Entry is usually under £3. Bands to have played recently include Ash and Henry Rollins.
Food: The University offers a discount card for food bought on campus. Scoff stops include: Snappers Diner; Loafer's for fast food at lunchtimes; Piazza 2 go (pizza); the Venue Food Court *does cheap and cheerful fare* while the Café Piazza has *a pricey continental style.*
Others: The union boasts plenty events a week. Regular balls run through the year, culminating in the Graduation do (be-do).

Chuck Berry's 1972 hit 'My Ding-a-Ling' was recorded at Lanchester College, now part of Coventry University.

SOCIAL & POLITICAL

UNIVERSITY OF LEICESTER STUDENTS' UNION:
• 5 sabbaticals • Turnout at last ballot: 17% • NUS member

The SU enjoys a good relationship with the University administration and with the students. It concentrates on organising successful services. Issues revolve around awareness and information and, rarely gets over political.

SU FACILITIES:
The Percy Gee Building contains a general shop, two bars, travel agency, Queen's Hall (cap 800), second-hand bookshop, development area, TV rooms (including satellite), launderette, snooker room, two banks with cashpoints, print shop, Elements nightclub, gym, weekly market stalls, video machines, squash court, mature and overseas students' rooms.

CLUBS (NON SPORTING):
Afro-Caribbean; Anglican; Arab; Asian; Astronomy; Biological; Change; Choral; Geology; Gospel choir; Islamic; Jewish; Juggling; Orchestral; Modern Dance; Politics; Science-fiction and Fantasy; Sikh; Street Jazz; Theatre; Wind Band.

OTHER ORGANISATIONS:
Apart from 'Ripple', the independent student newspaper (fortnightly), there's also Leicester University Student Television or LUST for short and LUSH FM. The charity Rag has a full-time sabbatical organiser which explains the £55,000 raised recently. 'Contact' is the student community group, which runs about 10 local help projects with up to 400 student volunteers.

RELIGIOUS:
• 9 chaplains

The Gatehouse Chaplaincy Centre welcomes students of all denominations. One chaplian has specific responsibility for international students. A Muslim prayer room has opened. Locally, there are churches and places of worship for every brand of god-fearer including a Jain Centre, unique outside the Indian sub-continent. There are also 7 faith advisors.

PAID WORK:
The Union-run jobshop sorts out the students with casual work and, failing that, there's always the Walkers Crisps factory. There is also a Student Employment Centre and you can even look it up on the web: www.susec@le.ac.uk

SPORTS

• Recent successes: rowing, football, shooting, Jiu Jitsu

The sports facilities are worth checking out. To do so, students have got to get a Sports Card (£35). *The athletics union is one of the best funded around.* Loughborough University, 10 miles up the A6, *takes most of the honours round here, but this lot can pull the odd rabbit or two out of the hat when required. (Didn't realise that was a competitive sport but never mind.)*

SPORTS FACILITIES:
The main sports ground is at the Oadby halls of residence, where there is also a sports hall and a gym. In addition, there is a sports hall a fitness centre and a boat club on the main campus. Between them, they provide 25 acres of playing fields, athletics track, two sports halls, an all-weather pitch, gym complex, football pitches,

14 tennis courts and a health and fitness club. Leicester adds a croquet lawn/bowling green, 7 swimming pools, 4 squash courts, hockey pitch, sports injury clinic, snooker and pool facilities, roller-blading rink, health and fitness club, golf course, basketball centre, sauna and solarium, and the River Soar. A new sports pavilion should be finished soon.

SPORTING CLUBS:
American Football; Fell-walking; Jiu Jitsu; Lacrosse; Mountaineering; Netball; Rowing; Smallbore Rifle; Table Tennis; Ultimate Frisbee;

ATTRACTIONS:
Apart from Leicester City FC, there are the Tigers (rugby), the Riders (basketball), the Panthers (American Football), Leicestershire Cricket Club, Cannons sports complex *(very expensive though)*, a Cycling Stadium and racecourse (horses).

ACCOMMODATION

IN COLLEGE:
- Catered: 27% • Cost: £60-95 (30wks)
- Self-catering: 22% • Cost: £45-53 (39-52wks)

Availability: 1st years are guaranteed a place in University accommodation if they want it. About 25% stay in for their 2nd year and a few finalists. The choice is between the 5 catered halls at Oadby, 2½ miles from the campus (60s blocks and Edwardian houses *beautifully* set in the University's Botanical Gardens), the hall at Knighton (halfway to Oadby) or the self-catering student houses, mainly at Knighton, but some nearer the campus. The Gilbert Murrey Hall has recently been fully refurbished. 10% of students in halls have to share rooms and all halls are mixed, although sexes are split into corridors. The rooms themselves are a decent size – some are very new and have en-suite facilities and the halls are well equipped with bars and so on. About half of all halls have computer rooms. The houses have single rooms and each is single sex but groups of houses are mixed. Some halls have night porters, wardens or postgrads who live on site.

Car parking: Limited free parking at all halls.

EXTERNALLY:
- Ave rent: £38

Availability: *A decent standard at pretty reasonable prices, if you look around. The best places to look are the Tudor Road and Narborough Road areas Clarendon, Knighton and the cosmo-trendy Evington with its cultural mix. The City centre is also good. Highfields is the dodgy district, so only try it if you want the seedy ambience or like being stalked at night. Parking is about as difficult as getting a needle through the eye of a camel without the RSPCA complaining.*

Housing help: The University has the obligatory accommodation service while the Union-run Accommodation Office provides a vacancy board and help and advice in the great home hunt.

A former Vice-President of John Moores Students' Union was hypnotised on 'Richard & Judy' by a dog called Oscar.

WELFARE

SERVICES:
- Nightline • Gay and Bisexual Society • Mature SA
- International SA • Postgrad SA • Minibus
- Women's Officer • Self-defence classes

Both the Union and University provide welfare help and advice. The University employs 2 full and 2 part-time counsellors and the Union also has a Legal Advice Centre. The Student Health Centre has 7 doctors, 3 sisters and a nurse and, what's more, there's 24-hour care at the Hugh Binnie sick bay *(that name alone should make you feel better)*. There's no nursery but the Uni has arrangements with an affiliated nursery which offers reductions for students *(their kids only, the parents have to find other amusements)*.

Women: There's a Women's Committee with reps from the halls and the city and a safety minibus.

Disabled: There's the Richard Attenborough Centre for Disability and the Arts, a disability co-ordinator and an Accessibility Centre for students with specific difficulties. The University also publishes its prospectus in Braille.

FINANCE:
- Access fund: £532,472 • Successful applications: 1,500

Numerous hardship funds exist, some for specific groups (mature students, overseas students, etc), scholarships for physics, engineering and sports bursaries. The SU gives hardship loans up to £100 and special needs students are given priority.

Leicester Poly

see De Montfort University

University of Lincolnshire and Humberside

- *Formerly Humberside Polytechnic, University of Humberside*

(1) Humberside Campus, Cottingham Road, Kingston-upon-Hull, HU6 7RT. Tel: (01482) 440550. Fax: (01482) 463310.
E-mail: marketing@humber.ac.uk
University of Lincolnshire and Humberside Students' Union, Barmston House, Inglemere Lane, Hull, HU6 7LU Tel: (01482) 440550.
Fax: (01482) 463310. E-mail: union@humber.ac.uk
(2) Lincoln University, Marketing Department, Brayford Pool, Lincoln, LN6 7TS. Tel: (01522) 882000. Fax: (01522) 882088.
E-mail: marketing@lincoln.ac.uk
Students' Union, Lincoln Campus, PO Box 182, Lincoln LN2 4YF.
Tel: (01522) 882000. Fax: (01522) 886142.
E-mail: union@lincoln.ac.uk

The library at Queen Mary and Westfield is built on top of a cemetery.

GENERAL

Now concentrate, this could get confusing. In 1983, the higher education colleges in Hull and Grimsby combined to create Humberside Poly. Seven years later, it turned into the University of Humberside. Then Nottingham Trent University (which used to be Trent Poly - *still with us?*) dropped out of a deal to set up a new campus 44 miles from Hull in Lincoln (see De Montfort University – which used to be Leicester Poly – *do try to keep up*). So the University of Humberside stepped in and changed its name to the University of Lincolnshire and Humberside, now based in two towns, as the Grimsby site has now closed. There, simple, isn't it? Who threw that? The Hull site is by far the biggest *although Lincoln is flexing its muscles and trying to prove it can stand on its own two feet.* It has recently opened an impressive £5.4Mn science facility.

Sex ratio(M:F): 50%:50%	Founded: 1983
Full time u'grads: 6,386	Part time: 1,307
Postgrads: 148	Non-degree: 1,200
Ave course: 3yrs	Ethnic: 7%
Private school: n/a	Flunk rate: 19.8%
Mature students: 40%	Overseas students: 11%
Disabled students: 4%	

ATMOSPHERE:
The two separate sites without cast iron links and the proportion of mature students conspire to slow down any party potential. Some students (particularly those at the Cottingham site) pop round the corner to Hull University for a social life. Lincoln has lots of eager types, keen to better themselves in a development that looks more like a conference centre than an academic facility. *Oops, there goes a judgement.*

THE SITES:
Hull: Cottingham Road is the University's *largest and most elegant site*, next door to Hull University. It is constructed of brick with grass quads in front with a *few flash additions* like the modern Polygon building and the Language Centre. Many of the University's overseas students are based on this site. There's also Queen's Gardens, the city centre site, about 2 miles from Cottingham Road.
Lincoln: *This modern but not gruesome,* £32Mn development on the edge of an ancient harbour in the historic city of Lincoln is primed for continued expansion and the Learning Resource Centre has already opened for business.

LINCOLN:
• London: 132 miles • Hull: 44 miles • Population: 83,500
Lincoln's a *beautiful* cathedral city surrounded by *flat, peaceful, boring* countryside but despite the presence of two universities in its midst (see De Montfort University) local amenity providers are only just waking up to the (allegedly lucrative) student market.

HULL TRAVEL: see University of Hull

LINCOLN TRAVEL:
Trains: The station, a few minutes walk from the campus, has services to London (£27.70), Birmingham (£16.65), Edinburgh (£51.30) and more.
Car: The A1 runs nearby, intersecting with the A46 at Newark and the A57 near Retford. Lincolnshire has no motorways.
Bicycles: *Flat beyond your dreams. Get pedalling.*

CAREER PROSPECTS:
• Careers Service • No of staff: 4 full
• Unemployed after 6mths: 11.8%

SPECIAL FEATURES:
• It runs one of the largest and most successful international exchange schemes in the country with connections with 64 institutions.

FAMOUS ALUMNI:
Elliott Morley MP (Lab); Mary Parkinson (TV presenter); Dean Watling (Lincoln FC footballer).

FURTHER INFO:
Prospectuses for full- and part-time and overseas students, plus a separate publication for the Lincoln campus. Video and CD-Rom and websites (www.humber.ac.uk and www.lincoln.ac.uk) and plenty of open days.

ACADEMIC

The Cottingham Road campus offers courses in business, engineering, info and tech, social/professional studies. Queen's Gardens has art & design, architecture and social/professional studies. The Lincoln site has taken over the Grimsby courses and now offers courses at the new Learning Resource Centre as well as applied science, food & fisheries. Many courses include a sandwich year working in industry.

staff/student ratio: 1:24
Range of points required for entrance: 240-160
Percentage accepted through clearing: 25%
Number of terms/semesters: 2
Length of terms/semesters: 16 wks
Research: 2.7

LIBRARIES:
• Books: 231,000 • Study places: 1,541
The libraries in Hull are inadequate for the numbers of students, though provision has improved in Lincoln following its recent expansion. Problems are inevitable though, with the sites sharing books and not having had all that long to build up a collection.

COMPUTERS:
• Computer workstations: 1,510
Still no 24-hour access for computers but the Uni is pulling its pants up, just a bit.

ENTERTAINMENT

HULL: see University of Hull

LINCOLN:
• Price of a pint of beer: £1.80 • Glass of wine: £1.40
Lincoln is slowly getting used to these strange student creatures and new ways to spend your money are popping up all the time.
Cinemas: (2) Both mainstream. *There's a new multiplex cinema almost within popcorn throwing distance of the Lincolnshire campus.*

Pubs: *The Jolly Brewer is the only one that could reasonably be labelled a student haunt.* Other Pushplugs: Varsity; Green Dragon; Cheltenham Arms; Cornhill Vaults (alternative); Barge; Edward's; Yate's; Martha's; the Falcon.
Music venues: Grafton House and O'Rourke's host local indie wannabes and O'Rourke's also has jazz nights.
Clubs/discos: *Lincoln is hardly awash with club venues.* Pushplugs: Klubhopping at Ritzy (chart dance); Milligan's (house/techno); Baracudas; the Sugar Club.
Eating out: *A decent range of eateries, although not all of them are student oriented (or priced).* Pushplugs: Restaurant Italia; The Mint; Spinning Wheel, Wig & Mitre (for rich parents); Raj Duth (very good Indian, free if you can prove it's your birthday); Damon's Motel; the Barge does decent pub grub.

UNIVERSITY:
• Price of a pint of beer: £1.50 • Glass of wine: £1.40
Bars: (2) The Cottingham Road Flyer's Bar *is the most lively* and doubles as an ents venue (500). The new bar at Lincoln (cap 360) has DJ nights and live bands.
Cinema: The film society shows a film a week, sometimes mainstream, sometimes course-related, at Cottingham Road.
Clubs/discos/music venues: Cottingham Road bops to the sounds four nights a week, ranging from 70s retro to local name DJs. Live music (apart from local bands) *are more rare but not unknown*. Straw, Soul Time and Mutley played here recently. *Yet, stage-diving enthusiasts are more likely to find their human launch-pads at Hull University. It's said that the new sports hall at Lincoln will make a groovy venue for live bands – only time will tell, then Push will tell you.*
Food: The SU Café at Cottingham Road serves up *cheap 'n' cheerful* stuff and both campuses have won awards for healthy eating and non-smoking facilities *(but healthy salad n' stuff is not a bonus if you have a hangover, to be fair). The main Refectory is usually packed* but overall everyday nosh seems to be better at Lincoln.
Others: Occasional balls, often of a sporty nature. *The Hull Music and Drama soc do productions, to much acclaim.* Fancy a bit of Little Women? – well, these are your guys.

UNIVERSITY OF LINCOLNSHIRE AND HUMBERSIDE STUDENTS' UNION:
• 6 sabbaticals • Turnout at last ballot: 30% • NUS member
The SU has suffered over the years from a bad case of spreading themselves too thin over different sites. Four of the six sabbaticals are based at Hull; which has meant a struggle to unify the masses. Recent campaigns have included a anti-tuition fees demo which attracted 500 protesters.

SU FACILITIES:
The Union building at Hull, the Strand, *is something of a shell*. All the available funds have been sucked up by the building itself, leaving a skeleton staff and few facilities. There are offices, two bars (one at Cottingham Road) *and not much else. However, this is positively sumptuous when compared with Lincoln. Still, it's early days yet.*

CLUBS (NON SPORTING):
Belgian Beer; Clubbing; Hellenic; International Students; Law; Malaysian; Warsoc; Wine.

OTHER ORGANISATIONS:
There's a student magazine, 'The Bridge', and Siren FM which broadcasts for a month every year.

RELIGIOUS:
Two full-time ecumenical chaplains at each site.

PAID WORK: see University of Hull

SPORTS

- Recent successes: nothing special

The sports facilities are still too feeble to propel Humberside into the big time, or even among the alsorans, but they've improved in recent years. Where there are shortfalls, students make use of University of Hull.

SPORTS FACILITIES:
A new £5Mn sports centre was opened by Trevor Brooking last Winter. There's also a sports hall, gym, all-weather pitch, gravel hockey pitch, three football pitches, multi-gym, solarium and health & fitness club.

SPORTING CLUBS:
Gendo Kai Karate.

ATTRACTIONS: see University of Hull

ACCOMMODATION

IN COLLEGE:
- Catered: 2% • Cost: £60-65 (38wks) • Self-catering: 15%
- Cost: £53 (38wks)

Availability: 85% of first years are accommodated in halls. 13% who want to be, can't. The spaces in Hull are mostly based at Cottingham Road (including the all-female Johnson Hall) and the new Pacific Court development, near Queen's Gardens. Two new private halls have also opened. There are also 1,000 places in a direct lettings scheme, where accommodation is allocated by the accommodation service. Lincoln has 1,044 self-catering places, *adequate for the current number of undergrads but liable to be outstripped if things progress as quickly as they'd hope.*
Car parking: Free permit parking, *but insufficient.*

EXTERNALLY: see University of Hull

LINCOLN:
- Ave rent: £35

Because Lincoln isn't yet swamped with house-hungry students there's enough private accommodation going, especially the relatively cheap Victorian houses around Monks Road and West Parade. The areas near the football ground are somewhat grimmer.

> New entertainment facilities at the University of Paisley are being built in a disused bingo hall.

WELFARE

SERVICES:
• Nightline • Lesbian & Gay Society • Overseas SA
• Women's Officer • Self-defence classes
The University Advice Office, with 3 full-time counselling staff, deal with most problems that life can throw up. There are also new welfare drop-in sessions on both campuses but for severed limbs try the Student Health Service, staffed by 3 nurses.
Disabled: Poor wheelchair access, but some loops, braille printers, etc for hearing- and sight-impaired students. The Division of Assistive Resources and Technology supports students with special needs.
Women: A safe room is available. Women outnumber men 2:1 at Lincoln.

FINANCE:
• Access fund: £500,000 • Successful applications: 1,500
The University waives fees for part-time undergraduates on income support. The cost of living in Hull is low.

University of Liverpool

The University of Liverpool, Liverpool, L69 3GD. Tel: (0151) 794 2000. Fax: (0151) 794 5602. E-mail: ugrecruitment@liv.ac.uk
The Guild, The University of Liverpool, PO Box 187, 160 Mount Pleasant, Liverpool, L69 7BR. Tel: (0151) 794 6868. Fax: (0151) 794 4174.

GENERAL

If, when you think of Liverpool, you think of The Beatles, Bill Shankly and Brookside, you're not far wrong. Of course, the Beatles and Bill are no more and Brookie can get a bit ridiculous at times, but Liverpool lives on as one of Britain's youth culture capitals. It's always taken an independent stand politically and it is rich with culture and art, but it's more exciting just strolling the streets. The Mersey cuts through the city, dividing it from the Wirral and skirting the jumble of streets, full of art-deco and post-industrialist architecture. Liverpool is unique, the seaway for the North West. Considering how big it is, *it seems odd that it's so close to Manchester (28 miles) – but with two great cities for the price of one, who's complaining?* What's more, there is a massive programme of redevelopment in the city.
Liverpool's first university (joined in 1992 by Liverpool John Moores University) is the original 'redbrick' university. The word was coined to describe the University's Victoria Building on Brownlow Hill. Many of the other buildings are redbrick too but others are more modern (60s and 70s), based on a 100-acre site (big for an inner city campus) in the Mount Pleasant area of town, on top of a hill.

Liverpool

Sex ratio(M:F): 50%:50%	Founded: 1881
Full time u'grads: 10,946	Part time: 3,771
Postgrads: 1,952	Non-degree: 3,829
Ave course: 3yrs	Ethnic: 11%
Private school: 7%	Flunk rate: 10.2%
Mature students: 13%	Overseas students: 17%
Disabled students: 2%	

ATMOSPHERE:
Liverpool University is down-to-earth, unpretentious and the students enjoy good relations with the local community. Not bad for starters from a town few respect for anything but its music and football. Scousers and the University students defend their city to the hilt and it's hard not to have a good time in Liverpool so, in your best Harry Enfield voice, 'Caaalm down'.

THE CITY:
- Population: 448,300 • London: 189 miles
- Manchester: 28 miles • Glasgow: 213 miles

Liverpool was once a prosperous merchant town, doing deals on the docks, touting for trade inland. It still bears the legacy of former times with grand Victorian houses and old streets built for carriages, such as Princes Road lined with tall houses, but it's seen some rough times. *Some areas, such as Toxteth, had developed a reputation for being notoriously run-down and violent, but with a number of students making the area their home.* The Albert Dock development is just one part of a face-lift programme *that makes Michael Jackson's nasal amendment look subtle by comparison. The richness and contrast of architectural styles is being revitalised and is beginning to reflect the spirit of the people, a spirit that never dwindled.* There are nightclubs everywhere and *bohemian bustle is bubbling away*. Supermarkets, shops and markets abound and there's more for tourists to do than visit Penny Lane and Strawberry Fields. There's the Liverpool Museum, the Museum of Labour History, the Walker Art Gallery (the largest art collection in the UK outside London), the Tate Gallery in Albert Dock and Liverpool University's own art gallery on campus.

TRAVEL:
Trains: Mainline links with many destinations including London Euston (£31.80), Manchester (£6.10) and Birmingham (£15.85).
Coaches: National Express to most destinations including London (£17) and Manchester (£5).
Car: M53, M56, M57, M58 and M62 (good for North West and Wales).
Air: Flights inland and to Europe from Liverpool Airport, 7 miles from the city centre. *Easyjet can be very cheap*, Liverpool to London (Luton) from £7.50 single.
Ferries: This is the main port for Belfast and there are other regular ferries to Ireland. *And, of course, there's the ferry 'cross the Mersey.*
Hitching: *Good connections and many long-haul drivers who sympathise, especially round the M62.*
Local: *Efficient bus services. Student fares are 60p, but it works out cheaper to get a term bus pass.* A University bus service runs between halls all day (£1). Merseyrail runs for those who prefer trains.

Taxis: Many black cabs.
Bicycles: Cycles lanes are being developed, *but it's generally too smoggy and large and chances are the bike'll get nicked.* The city came last once in a 'New Cyclist' magazine survey.

CAREER PROSPECTS:
- Careers Service • No of staff: 4 full/2 part
- Unemployed after 6mths: 5%

FAMOUS ALUMNI:
Steve Coppell (footballer/manager); Hugh Jones (marathon runner); Chris Lowe (Pet Shop Boy); Phil Redmond (TV mogul, writer and inventor of 'Brookside', 'Grange Hill' and 'Hollyoaks'); Patricia Routledge (actress); Jon Snow (ITN reporter).

FURTHER INFO:
Prospectuses for undergrads and postgrads and an alternative prospectus available from the SU (£2). Website (www.liv.ac.uk).

ACADEMIC

The English Department runs a science fiction course.

staff/student ratio: 1:11
Range of points required for entrance: 360-60
Percentage accepted through clearing: n/a
Number of terms/semesters: 2
Length of terms/semesters: 15 wks
Research: 4.5

LIBRARIES:
• Books: 1,500,000 • Study places: 1,500
The Sydney Jones Library is the largest, but the Harold Cohen Library would be *big enough for most universities.* There are also 13 department libraries. *Facilities are excellent.*

COMPUTERS:
• Computer workstations: 1,600 • 24-hour access.

ENTERTAINMENT

CITY:
• Price of a pint of beer: £1.80 • Glass of wine: £1.40
Cinemas: (5) including 2 Odeons, UCL, Crosby Plaza and Showcase.
Theatres: (4) The Empire is a national touring venue for subsidised companies where you can see shows before they transfer to London's West End. Also, there are the *often controversial and innovative, but financially threatened* Everyman Theatre, the Neptune and the *small, but beautiful* Unity Theatre which hosts an *unconventional* array of drama, dance and comedy.
Pubs: Liverpool's pubs can vary from Berni Inn style drop-outs to shrines like Ye Cracke (Lennon and crew drank here). Smithdown Road is the prime student crawl route. Pushplugs: Magnet & Modo; Baa Bar (trendy); The Philharmonic (Grade II listed loos); The Rose; Eurobar (by Liverpool John Moores University).
Clubs/discos: Cream at The Nation attracts trendhoppers from across the UK and beyond. Other Pushplugs: Voodoo (techno);

Liquidation (indie); student nights at the Cavern (next door to where the original was); L2; No Fakin' at Zanzibar; indie at Krazy House and the Razz.
Music venues: The premiere venues are: the Empire (mainstream and classical); The Royal Court for top bands; the Zanzibar and L2 for bands; the Lomax (indie bliss). The Flying Picket next to John Moores has smaller local bands.
Eating out: The Baa Bar is terminally hip, but not overpriced. Other Pushplugs: El Macho (Mexican); The Egg; Everyman Bistro; Uncle Sam's; No 7 (fat portions without a fat bill); Caesar's Palace; Royal Tandoori. Chinatown keeps sizzling until 4am.
Other: If none of the above appeals and you've checked that you still have a pulse, why not try the bowling alley or live poetry at the Everyman or one of the many cabaret venues (especially the Neptune) where the legendary Scouse wit lives on.

UNIVERSITY:

- Price of a pint of beer: £1   • Glass of wine: £1.25

Bars: There are 8 bars around the Guild and the University. The most notable are the Liver Bar (pink and purpleness), the Ken Saro Wiwa (named after the Nigerian political prisoner) and the 3 lounge bars. All are open during clubs and events.

Theatres: There are 2 theatres in the University: the Stanley Theatre in the Guild and the University Theatre. Most years they manage to muster a production for the Edinburgh Fringe.
Cinemas: The Guild has a large screen in the Stanley Theatre and shows a film every week.
Clubs/discos: The Time Tunnel is the Saturday night retro fest now in its eight-year (*for students who think they're George Michael when they're pissed*) and Double Vision on Mondays. Guest DJs have included Paul Oakenfold and Ministry of Sound tour.
Music venues: Mountford Hall (1,530) is the main venue but the Courtyard and some of the bars are equipped for live gigs too. Recent appearances include Reef, David Grey, The Bluetones.
Cabaret: The Guild organises the fortnightly Uncle Piehead's Comedy Parlour, usually featuring top japesters such as Harry Hill, Martin BigPig and Craig Charles.
Food: The bars all serve food of some description. The Lounge Food Court in the Ken Saro Wiwa bar rustles up a *respectable range at a reasonable rate* and this is bolstered by various fast food outlets, the Courtyard Café and new addition Reilly's Cafe which serves up all day breakfasts and hot meals.
Others: All the major academic departments and halls arrange balls at least once a year (adm £8-£25).

SOCIAL & POLITICAL

THE UNIVERSITY OF LIVERPOOL GUILD OF STUDENTS:
• 4 sabbaticals   • Turnout at last ballot: 10%   • NUS member

The Guild is the second largest students' union building in Europe (the biggest is in Paris) and so it's not surprising that it offers some pretty good facilities, but also being so big, it's often difficult to fill it. Still, it's a bit rich to start complaining that the Guild's facilities are too big while too many students' unions have to go without. The Guild enjoys a love-in with the students and most think that the body does an excellent job. Recent action includes an 85% turn-out against tuition fees and a 1,000-signature petition for the student rights charter.

SU FACILITIES:
Bars: cafeterias; print shop; general shop; photographers; optician; 'Little Cohen' Library with study area; travel agency; prayer room; international lounge; launderette; hair-dresser; table tennis; snooker; Mountford Hall; Monday market (clothes, CDs, plants, etc); theatre; dark room; band practice room; function rooms; photo booth; games and vending machines; film-making facilities; photocopying.

CLUBS (NON SPORTING):
Amateur DJs; Astronomy; Band; Change Ringers; Hellenic; Hindu; Juggling; Life; Links; Liverpool University Show Troupe; Mountaineering; Music; Politics; Radio; Welsh; Wine.

OTHER ORGANISATIONS:
'Liverpool Student' city-wide publication, circ 50,000, in conjunction with <u>John Moores</u> and <u>Liverpool Hope Institution</u>. The Guild executive produces a newsletter ('Blurb') and plans are being made for a radio station. The Community Action group has a full-time paid worker who co-ordinates many local help projects including play schemes and soup runs.

RELIGIOUS:
• <u>2 chaplains (CofE, RC); 1 rabbi</u>
There's a Muslim prayer room in the Union and an Anglican chaplaincy on campus. There are 2 cathedrals in town, Catholic and Anglican, in *strongly contrasting* architectural styles, and both within praying distance of the Union. There are plenty of churches, more synagogues than in any other English town this size and a few mosques, as well as temples for Hindus, Buddhists and Hare Krishnas.

PAID WORK:
There is high unemployment in Liverpool, so there's lots of competition for the few places in bakeries, shops and bars. The Business Bridge scheme helps students find local placements.

• <u>Recent successes: rugby, ten pin bowling</u>
Membership of the Athletics Union costs £24, about 1 in 3 students cough up and there are minimal charges for facilities. *The facilities are excellent, including one of the best pools in any UK university – in fact, with an infrastructure like this, it's surprising sport isn't more important to the students.*

SPORTS FACILITIES:
There are 2 main sports centres on the campus, including one with a pool, sports hall, 4 squash courts, a climbing wall, dance studio, multi-gym and solarium. There are 3 more sports grounds near the halls, the main one with floodlit artificial pitches, tennis courts, lacrosse pitch and cricket squares and, naturally, a bar and café. The sports fields at Wyncote Allerton are 4 miles from the campus but not too far from the halls. Further away, there are more grounds at Maryton Grange and Widnes served by University minibuses. Added extras include the boat house at Knowsley Park and the outdoor activity centre in Snowdonia in North Wales. *The town and area make up for the few shortcomings in the University provisions.* Apart from

the Mersey for water sports, there are a number of sports and leisure centres, some of *which are excellent* (Toxteth, Everton, Kirkby, among others).

SPORTING CLUBS:
Ballroom; Boating; Dancing; Diving; Hang Gliding; Jiu Jitsu; Kung Fu; Lacrosse; Rifle; Surf; Table Tennis; Ten Pin Bowling; Water Polo; Windsurfing.

ATTRACTIONS:
Liverpool FC is still one of the legendary teams of world footie (honours include 18 league, 6 FA, 4 European and 3 UEFA - the most successful English club), but don't forget Everton (not as successful as Liverpool, but still the fourth most successful English club, *but you wouldn't think so from recent years*) or, indeed, the *feisty* Tranmere Rovers. There's Aintree Race Course and many other sporting gems.

ACCOMMODATION

IN COLLEGE:
- Catered: 20% • Cost: £78 (32wks)
- Self-catering: 9% • Cost: £48-54 (40-52wks)

Availability: Students who accept an offer by May and apply for accommodation before September are sorted for their 1st year – about 9% can't live in for one reason or another. The halls, *which are of a high standard with good amenities and truly edible food*, are on two *pleasant* green sites, both about 3 miles from campus. The larger, *with a strong community atmosphere*, is Carnatic, with 6 halls of about 250 spaces each. The other is Greenbank *with a social life all of its own* and 2 halls of about 500 each. Buses go to and from the halls in the mornings and evenings. one hall is all-female, but otherwise they're mixed.

Car parking: Limited permit parking on campus.

EXTERNALLY:
- Ave rent: £38

Availability: There's enough housing to make it possible to get something considerably cheaper than £38, if students are prepared to take what's going. The real competition is to find somewhere close to your place of study but nobody's left miles away. Some areas have developed as decidedly student, such as Wavertree (a veritable student ghetto), Sefton Park (more expensive, but arty, converted flats), Allerton, Mossley Hill, Aigburth, Old Swan and the famous Penny Lane. Some areas are less salubrious, such as Toxteth and Walton, but students do live there quite happily. Car parking depends very much on the area: further out of the city, it becomes easier, but public transport is fine.

Housing help: The Accommodation Office keeps a vacancy list and provides advice. The 2 universities are running a scheme called 'Liverpool Student Homes' helping students find housing and providing grants for modernisation and building.

WELFARE

SERVICES:
- Creche • Lesbian & Gay Society • Mature SA
- Overseas SA • Minibus • Women's Officer
- Self-defence classes • Nursery

The Guild operates a good Welfare Advice Centre where students can drop in and consult advisers, including 16 counsellors. The University provides a further 2 full- and 3 part-time advisers. For bruised knees and severed limbs, the doctors, sister and nurses at the Health Centre can help. The nursey has places for 68 little ones.

Women: There are women-only swimming lessons at the pool and they have priority on the minibus.

Drugs: *The trade in Liverpool isn't as nasty as it was but there are still lots of drugs about.*

Disabled: *Access isn't so good*, but there's been *serious* investment towards ramps and lifts in some campus buildings. There is a Disabled Students' Working Party as well as particular provisions for hearing-impaired and students with dyslexia.

FINANCE:
- Access fund: £690,000 • Successful applications: 938

Also Vice Chancellor's Hardship Fund (mainly for overseas students); Hillsborough Trust Memorial Bursaries (£500; must come from Merseyside); John Lennon Fund (£1,000, for environmental interests); Clare Hansen fund (vets).

Liverpool Hope University College
see Other Institutions

Liverpool John Moores University

- *Formerly Liverpool Polytechnic*

Liverpool John Moores University, Enquiry Management Team, Roscoe Court, 4 Rodney Street, Liverpool, L1 2TZ. Tel: (0151) 231 5090. Fax: (0151) 231 3194. E-mail: recruitment@livjm.ac.uk
Liverpool John Moores Students' Union, The Haigh Building, Maryland Street, Liverpool, L1 9DE. Tel: (0151) 794 1900. Fax: (0151) 708 5334. www.livjm.ac.uk

GENERAL

Liverpool John Moores University is built on 17 sites. Or four. Or maybe only three. Or possibly over 20. *In fact, it's so spread out that it's hard to say exactly how many sites there are and none of them can be said to be the main one.* The University definitely used to be four separate colleges *and you can still detect the cracks where the merger took place back* in the 60s. As a result, some of the University buildings are modern purpose-built constructions while others, such as the Fine Art Department, are *fine* examples of Georgian and Victorian architecture. The sites are clustered in the city centre, near Liverpool University, and further out in some of the *less kempt* areas of Liverpool's urban edges.

Sex ratio(M:F): 47%:53%
Full time u'grads: 13,188
Postgrads: 631
Ave course: 3/4yrs
Private school: n/a
Mature students: 29.25%
Disabled students: 4.8%

Founded: 1970
Part time: 4,294
Non-degree: 4,043
Ethnic: 6.5%
Flunk rate: 19.7%
Overseas students: 7.5%

ATMOSPHERE:
Students at Liverpool's newer university love their city, many being locals anyway. They're also proud of their university (if not its name) and despite the separate sites the students are united by their SU and its building, the Haigh, which is the hub of an electric social life.

THE SITES:
Although JMU can be divided into four main chunks, Mount Pleasant and Byrom Street each have numerous smaller annexes. There are also associated institutions throughout Merseyside and Cheshire.

Mount Pleasant: (4,000) The main building is old with lots of gargoyle type things, next door to the Haigh. There's a huge new Learning Resources Centre here.

Byrom Street: (8,000) A 60s *carbuncle* and the *more attractive* Georgian Mountford Building in the city's shopping district, 2 mins from the centre.

IM Marsh: (1,000) 3 miles from the city centre, on the *ruralish* outskirts of Aigburth. *Usually swarming with sporty types.*

THE CITY: see University of Liverpool

TRAVEL: see University of Liverpool

CAREER PROSPECTS:
- Careers Service • No of staff: 5 full-time
- Unemployed after 6mths: 6.1%

SPECIAL FEATURES:
- Phil Redmond – TV mogul and deviser of such series as 'Grange Hill', 'Brookside' and, um, 'Hollyoaks' – is an Honorary Professor of the University.
- In a ballot of students when it was still Liverpool Poly, 60% opposed 'Liverpool John Moores University' as the new name. Nevertheless, it was named after the bloke behind Littlewoods Pools.

FAMOUS ALUMNI:
Caroline Aherne (Mrs Merton, Royle family); Stephen Byers (MP and former SU president); Julian Cope (musician); Bill Drummond (KLF); Phil Gayle (Big Breakfast newsreader and former SU president); Debbie Greenwood (ex-Miss England & TV presenter); Jim King (Cream club runner); John Lennon, Stu Sutcliffe (dead Beatles); Martin 'Chariots' Offiah (Rugby League). Liverpool and Everton FCs have honorary degrees.

FURTHER INFO:
Prospectuses for undergrads, postgrads and overseas students. Also videos, a website (www.livjm.ac.uk) and open days in July and September – don't forget to pre-book. Call (0151) 231 5090 for details.

ACADEMIC

Across its different sites the Uni offers courses including: business, design, law, modern languages, social work, architecture, built environment, art, media, bioscience, computing, engineering, maths, pharmacy, health, social and human sciences, education, sports, dance. *The fashion courses have a good reputation* and former students are now selling to Donna Karan and Ralph Lauren.

staff/student ratio: 1:16
Range of points required for entrance: 240-160
Percentage accepted through clearing: 13%
Number of terms/semesters: 2
Length of terms/semesters: 15 wks
Research: 2.9

LIBRARIES:
- Books: 655,511 • Study places: 1,634

Students are *pretty satisfied* with the facilities at the three libraries, also known as Learning Resource Centres. (*Why not 'Information in Tiny Silicon Objects and Bound Papery Things General Containment Facilitation'? What was wrong with 'library'?*)

COMPUTERS:
- Computer workstations: 1,150

Jan 2001 saw the arrival of 24-hour access to computers, *so students can leave their assignments even later.*

ENTERTAINMENT

CITY: see University of Liverpool

UNIVERSITY:
- Price of a pint of beer: £1.45 • Glass of wine: £1.25

Bars: (4)There are two bars in the Haigh (the SU building), Scholars and The Cooler – *both very popular.* IM Marsh and Byrom Street each have a boozer.

Theatres: 2 theatre venues around the University, plus the facilities at the Liverpool Institute of Performing Arts (LIPA).

Cinemas: The SU shows weekly films for free, in the Moore Dome, in The Cooler (Sundays), mostly recent mainstream releases and *surefire student hits (ones where the director's first name begins with 'Q').*

Clubs/discos/music venues: The Cooler (300) is the prime dance site most nights of the week, Shine On (indie), Fever Pitch (dance), Time Out (party tunes), Breezeblock (hip hop/big beat) and the Loveshack (60s, 70s, 80s and er, 90s – well yeah, the lot), Disco Inferno, Popgun, Deliverance (house/dance). It's also the venue for mainly local bands and recent names to play include Steve Lamacq, Primal Scream and the Essential Selection Tour. All nights have free entry and beer promos.

Food: All the bars double as food stops. Scholars does pub lunches, *while the Cooler gets top marks for value.*

Others: Black tie events throughout the year.

SOCIAL & POLITICAL

LIVERPOOL STUDENTS' UNION:
• 6 sabbaticals • Turnout at last ballot: 20% • NUS member
The SU manages to pull off the tricky balancing act of getting on okay with the University authorities and maintaining a level of political radicalism, most of which passes the students by completely. The 'Aintree campaign' stirred up students in protest against the University's decision to hold exams at Aintree 7 miles away without providing free transport. Oh and membership fees for clubs and socs were abolished by LSU in 1999 *so you're free to join as many as you like without shelling out any beer money during Freshers Week but you still won't go to half of them.*

SU FACILITIES:

In The Haigh: The Cooler; Scholars Bar; travel agency; shop; solarium; print shop; minibus hire; meeting rooms; Barclays Bank cash dispenser; 'Unitemp' jobshop; JMV counselling service; games room and vending machines; juke box; photo booth; photocopying. There are bars and smaller shops (including an art shop) at the other sites.

CLUBS (NON SPORTING):
Chinese; Circus; Debating; DJ and Dance Music; Real Ale; Role Play; St Johns Ambulance; Welsh; Wine Tasting.

OTHER ORGANISATIONS:
JMU has joined forces with Liverpool University and Liverpool Hope to produce a fortnightly publication covering all three institutions. Shout FM Radio broadcasts intermittently. No Rag but there are one-off charity events like Children in Need.

SPORTS

• Recent successes: rugby league, Gaelic football
Lycra and studs tend to be donned more for pleasure than for glory, although the Uni won the rugby league European Student Championships last year. *Students at IM Marsh take it all more seriously than those at other sites.*

SPORTS FACILITIES:
At the IM Marsh site there are two gyms, two dance studios, a renovated sports hall, indoor swimming pool, five playing fields and an all-weather athletics track. Students at the other sites can choose to make the trek to IM Marsh or use The B2 at the St Nicholas Building near the City Centre, which has various fitness programmes and classes, a gym, dance studio, sports hall and massage facilities. Or they can try public facilities (for which they can get a £15 discount pass) or those at Liverpool University.

SPORTING CLUBS:
Gaelic Football; Hang Gliding; Kickboxing; Mountainbiking; Parachuting; Rowing; Waterpolo.

ATTRACTIONS: see University of Liverpool

The new offices of Nottingham Trent SU were opened in 1995 by Torvill and Dean but the plaque spelled their names wrong.

ACCOMMODATION

IN COLLEGE:
• Self-catering: 10%   • Cost: £44-59 (40wks)
Availability: Students only stand any chance of living in during their 1st year with only around 40% getting places. The choice is between Cathedral Campus, self-catering flats for three people, or houses for five at Parkside Hall in Aigburth. *The houses are pleasant and very well situated* in the centre near the Anglican Cathedral. The flats in Lime Street *are also good* and *swish* private residences have recently been completed. All accommodation has CCTV 24-hour security and entry-phones.
Car parking: *Easy enough at the houses, harder at the halls, very hard at the flats* and the Northwestern Hall has none at all.

EXTERNALLY: see University of Liverpool
Housing help: Liverpool Student Homes is run jointly by JMU and the University of Liverpool and offers legal help and advice, lists of recommended landlords and safety checks.

WELFARE

SERVICES:
• Nursery   • Nightline   • Lesbian & Gay Society   • Mature SA
• Overseas SA   • Minibus   • Women's Officer   • Self-defence classes
The University provides 3 medical centres and 3 counsellors. Each student has an academic tutor called a 'counsellor' and the SU Welfare Unit's 4 welfare advisers and 3 financail advisors are equipped to provide counselling, legal and financial advice.
Disabled: Some buildings have been adapted for improved access and, *while there are still some major problems, the University's record is better than most*. Some older parts such as Hamwemann Building have no access at all, whereas others (eg Josephine Butler House) are *excellent*. There is a loop system in some lecture halls. There is a disabled student charter, awareness training for staff and a full-time Disabilities Welfare Advisor.

FINANCE:
• Access fund: £847,622   • Successful applications: 2,272
Various bursaries, scholarships, a hardship fund and emergency loans. The SU Hillsborough Fund offers help to disadvantaged students.

Liverpool Poly

see Liverpool John Moores University

```
When mad Romantic poet Percy Shelly was at
University College, Oxford he wired up his
door-handle in an attempt to electrocute his
scout.
```

University of London

- *The information, which follows, refers to the University of London as an amorphous blob. The services described are those provided centrally by the University and by ULU, the Students' Union. The colleges and individual unions of the University provide services themselves, and Push covers these in individual entries. Similarly, the general comments about London apply on the whole to the central area, close to ULU itself, and these are of equal relevance to the many institutions which are in the city but not part of London University itself. For more specific discussion of the differences between Norf 'n' Sarf, Hackney 'n' Hampstead, look at the individual entries.*

The University of London, Senate House, Malet Street, London, WC1E 7HU. Tel: (020) 7862 8000. Fax: (020) 7862 8358.
University of London Union, ULU Building, Malet Street, London, WC1E 7HY. Tel: (020) 7664 2000. Fax: (020) 7436 4604.
E-mail: general@ulu.ucl.ac.uk

GENERAL

The capital is a big place. A very big place. Just under 10 million people live within the boundary of the M25 (150 miles of 8-lane car park). If you've got the idea that London is basically Big Ben, Buckingham Palace and a few big shops, go back to square one. It is mile after mile of urban flood *and there is so much diversity, it is pointless even to attempt to describe the place briefly. Push may provide good value for money, but there are limits.* Students who don't know London, but are serious about wanting to study there should get hold of one of the less touristy guides. Most years, 'Time Out' – the essential magazine to what's on in the capital (and they haven't paid us to say that) – produces a London Students' Guide (priced under £5).

Suffice it to say that since the days of the little Roman village of Londinium on the banks of the Thames, London has come a long way, becoming the country's centre of politics, finance, arts, heritage, tourism, media, pornography, crime, bagel production and so on... Appropriately, the University of London is also big. One in 10 of the country's entire higher education population is at one of London University's 39 colleges and associated institutions. *However, students rarely get a sense of the University as a whole especially since some of the larger constituent colleges, such as King's, Imperial and UCL, are big enough to be fairly sizeable universities on their own.*

The University's headquarters are in the *magnificent* art deco Senate House in Bloomsbury about a mile from Trafalgar Square. *Push* features entries for most of the undergraduate colleges, so read this and read the separate colleges' entries too *because they vary as much as if they were different universities.* We don't cover postgraduate-only institutions and a medical school or other institution which is part of an individual college (e.g. King's College Hospital) will be mentioned under the college heading. For the record, here are those London colleges in full:

FEATURED IN PUSH:

Birkbeck College
Goldsmiths College
Imperial College
LSE
Royal Academy of Music
Royal Veterinary College
SOAS (School of Oriental & African Studies)
Courtauld Institute of Art
Heythrop College
King's College London
Queen Mary
Royal Holloway
St George's Hospital Medical School
School of Pharmacy
University College London

Sex ratio(M:F): 50%:50%
Full time u'grads: 48,746
Postgrads: 19,082
Mature students: 20%
Founded: 1836
Part time: 16,176
Ave course: 3yrs
Overseas students: 19%

THE CITY:
- Population: 6,377,900
- Birmingham: 106miles
- Manchester: 172miles
- Edinburgh: 423miles

Samuel Johnson wrote 'When a man is tired of London, he is tired of life; for there is in London all that life can afford.' More recently it's been dubbed 'the coolest city on the planet' and the relaxation of licensing laws, the resurgence of the UK fashion and film industries and the dance phenomenon have combined to create a city that's buzzing like a wasp on spiked lager. It's easy to feel that you're not making the most of London if you're not spending every waking minute at the theatre, ballet, opera or cinema, in clubs or fashionable markets, in museums and galleries, sports grounds and parks. It's a bit like the salad counter in Pizza Hut – it's up to you to make a selection from the vast selection of goodies and pile them on your plate however you like, but you might end up face-down in a puddle of sweetcorn and thousand island dressing, while the waiters have a good laugh. Not everyone likes the pace or the impersonal atmosphere that many find in London. It's easy to be lonely, even when it's hard to be alone. London can be oppressive and if you're not streetwise, or at least street sensible, it can be a dangerous place. The traffic can be manic as well and it's sometimes hard to discern the capital's charms beneath the grime.

And it costs, if not the earth, then a sizeable pile of mud. There are a number of responses to the high cost of living in London: (1) burst into tears; (2) mug someone; (3) live on credit; (4) ask daddy for lashings of cash. Alternatively, if these don't appeal, you can always use the following methods: (1) Limit your spending by only going out when and where you can afford it (ULU fits the bill, offering cheap events for students). (2) Buy second-hand – for books, there's ULU, Charing Cross Road and Waterloo and, for clothes, try Camden Market, Greenwich, Brick Lane and Portobello Road. (3) Get a job – more London students have part-time jobs than anywhere else. If you find yourself in London in your teens or twenties, you'd be a fool not to take advantage of the situation – but don't use this as an excuse to go on a spree. You can live within a budget, but it's bloody tempting to forget this when the view from your college bar looks like the latest edition of 'The Face' and people from New York, Paris and Tokyo are telling you how lucky you are to be living at the centre of the universe.

TRAVEL:

Trains: London is the centre of the network: Birmingham (£12); Manchester (£16); Leeds (£34); Bristol (£21); Glasgow (£42.50) – anywhere you like, *provided the whole system hasn't completely disappeared up its own shunting yard by the time you read this.*

Coaches: London is also the centre of the National Express system and a whole variety of other national bus services (Green Line, Blue Line and so on) letting you ride to Birmingham (£13), Manchester (£21) and so on.

Local Trains: Local over-ground trains are a *speedy and sometimes pleasant way to travel and are moderately efficient. The main problems are ease of use (a fair level of understanding is necessary), the high fares (although Travelcards are valid) and the early closing (last trains between 11pm and 1am). Trains are often the best bet south of the river.*

Underground: The 'Tube' is the largest underground train system in the world and generally, *it's okay and takes you just about anywhere you want to go, although south-east London is a bit hard done by.* However, *it is often crowded, shuts down around midnight, it's often disrupted by strikes and breakdowns, though bomb scares are less common these days, and it's expensive (students in full-time education are entitled to a 30% discount, which makes it only somewhat expensive). Talking to other tube passengers is tantamount to threatening their mother – the only people who do it are tourists and people who want to talk to you about Jesus.* Also, the London Underground is in the midst of a massive rebuilding phase, which will put whole stretches of track into mothballs for months on end, not to mention a funding crisis *which seems to have gone on longer than the escalator at Tottenham Court Road.* Nearest tube to Senate House/ULU Building: Goodge St (Northern Line).

Local Buses: *In the Tube you can't see the real sights, so why not take the buses which are just as efficient, offer even more destinations and are slightly cheaper (70p minimum). But buses are slow and, until you know your way around, it's difficult to know which ones take you where.* After midnight, buses come into their own – Night Buses are London's only form of all-night public transport and *if you don't mind how long it takes,* you can go almost anywhere within 10 miles of the centre.

Travelcards: All London students now get 30% off all tube and bus fares. Travelcards, which can be used on all London buses, tubes and trains, are available at £4.30 for a daily pass for zones 1 to 4 of the network (most of inner London) or, much more cost-effective, £27.60 for a weekly and £108.20 for a monthly, although the 30% off takes the sting out of current prices and any future rises.

Taxis: There are 2 types: the classic black cabs, *which are well regulated and enormously expensive, and dodgy merchants in Ford Escorts, which are almost as expensive.* There are now also some run by and for women. *Basically though, forget all taxis, except late at night when all else fails and/or you're in a party of 4 or more.*

Car: Parking in Central London is impossible, and, although there is only one rush hour every day it lasts from 6 in the morning until midnight. Nutters only need apply (and do).

Air: Served by 4 airports – Gatwick, Standstead, Luton and Heathrow, the world's busiest. Regular flights to Paris (£72), Belfast (£79), Prague (£129), New York, Timbuktu, anywhere else you care to pluck out of your WH Smith School Atlas.

Hitching: *Not possible from Central London, but get out a little way on to the city's escape routes or beyond the M25 and a thumb's a first class ticket.*

Bicycles: *A popular form of student travel given the pros: it's cheap and you can get through traffic. But there are the cons: London is big, full of exhaust fumes, lacking in cycle lanes and a Houdini-proof lock is advisable. It's also an easy way to die.*

CAREER PROSPECTS:
• Careers Service • No of staff: 25 full
The University careers service is well used and even offers job lists, careers fairs etc to non-London students for a small fee.

FURTHER INFO:
The University produces the *glossy* 'Guide to the University of London' which covers all the colleges. There's also an accommodation pamphlet and a Student Guide from ULU. For further details, see the websites (www.lon.ac.uk and www.ulu.ucl.ac.uk).

LIBRARIES:
• Books: 2,000,000 • Study places: 650
There is a vast central library at Senate House but individual colleges also have their own facilities. Check out www.ull.ac.uk/ull for up-to-date details.

COMPUTERS:
• Computer workstations: 950
Most of the individual colleges provide their own computers for student use – *not always enough*.

IN LONDON:
• Price of a pint of beer: £2.20 • Glass of wine: £2.50
For a weekly guide to the Capital's entertainments, 'Time Out' magazine (£2.20) is a must, but if you're brassic you can get the free Hot Tickets guide in Thursdays Evening Standard, or The Guide in Saturday's Guardian.
Pubs: *Some London pubs water down their ridiculously expensive beer, but you can often find a decent pint of Young's or Fuller's, or a good selection of guest ales (the Weatherspoon chain is a reliable starting point). Beyond that, every variety of drinking den, from Irish to Jamaican, from sports bars to wine bars, from plush chrome extravaganzas serving Belgian banana beer with a free half-hour on the 'net to rough dives that serve phlegmy Carlsberg and a filthy look to any outsiders, you've got the lot. Pushplugs in Bloomsbury area: Jeremy Bentham; Marlborough Arms; University Tavern; Rising Sun.*
Cinemas: *Many repertory cinemas offer student discounts and The Prince Charles Cinema just off Leicester Square shows films from £1.99. Pushplugs; Ritzy (Brixton); Everyman (Hampstead); Riverside (Hammersmith); NFT (South Bank); the Gate (Notting Hill, the only one where you can still smoke); the Odeon in Leicester Square has student discounts for some screenings.*
Theatres: *Student standby tickets are sometimes available for West End shows, but they're still around £12. The National Theatre on the South Bank and the RSC at the Barbican are cheaper and feature some of the country's top talent. Also, don't forget the Fringe (the*

collective title for all the smaller theatres around town, ranging from back rooms at pubs to full-size auditoria) *where you can often see high quality at low cost.*
Clubs/discos: *Although London clubs are always at the very hub of any fashion scene, you pay for the privilege.* At top nightspots, admission starts at around £10 and drinks can be anything up to 5 times pub prices. There is, however, an ever-changing set of cheaper hang-outs where the latest sounds are available without the latest prices. *Pushplugs: Turnmills; 93Feet East, Bagleys Studios (vast warehouse); Club Aquarium (check out the pool); Heaven (gay); Fabric (very cool); 333; School Disco (does exactly what it says on the tin)* The Ministry of Sound, The Fridge. These are the venues – individual events move between clubs and disappear like clichés in the night, so we won't recommend any beyond saying there's anything from jungle to swingbeat, gabba to goth, to places where you can chill out and play Connect 4 while listening to Shirley Bassey, so if you can't find something to move to, you might ask yourself whether you've left your legs on the bus.
Music venues: Many of the country's biggest and most famous, including Wembley Arena, Labatt's Apollo, The Forum, The Astoria, Docklands Arena, Shepherds Bush Empire, Brixton Academy *(big Pushplug)*, 2 major opera houses and dozens of classical music venues. *As ever, though, it's the smaller, less publicised venues that provide for the real connoisseur,* whether it's the latest lofi sensation in the back room of the Camden Falcon or an uplifting cello recital in a church hall in Kensington. *If it makes a noise, you can go and hear it, sometimes even for free.*
Cabaret: *London is a hot-bed of alternative laugh-mongers. Pushplugs: There's the Comedy Store near Piccadilly Circus or, more cheaply, Jongleurs (Camden, Battersea, Shepherds Bush), Acton Banana, Hackney Empire and many, many more. Also, keep a look out for free tickets to TV and radio show recordings.*
Eating out: Nowhere in the country, possibly the world, has a broader choice of eateries. There is every kind of café, restaurant and fast food and then some. *Not everywhere is bank-busting either. Head for Soho and Chinatown for affordable food and late night nibbles. For budget fare in the West End, our Pushplugs: Pollo's (madhouse Italian); Stockpot (school dinners, but superb value); Gaby's (friendly deli); Poon's (Chinese); Wagamama (Japanese noodles); Pret á Manger (imaginative sarnie chain); Cranks and Food for Thought (veggie without stodge); Bar Italia (Frith St, open till 7am); etc, etc, etc.* These are ours, go find your own – and if you run out of places to eat, you probably need to go on a diet.

ULU:
• Price of a pint of beer: £1.50   • Glass of wine: £2.00
Bars: (3) Gallery Bar/Diner (*very popular all day*); Duck & Dive (*café bar*); Bar 101 (chrome design, for gigs, clubs etc); Palms (events only).
Clubs/discos: The chartier 'Beano' on Saturdays with other nights during the week.
Music venues: The refurbished Room 101 (cap 700) is probably the best college venue in London and attracts some pretty big names, mostly of an indie persuasion, recently, for example Coldplay, Asian Dub Foundation and JJ72.
Food: *The Gallery Diner provides all a hungry student could desire, from spuds to fry-ups to, well, spuds, really.* Macmillans at Senate

House offers *decent value* meat 'n' 2 veg in a gorgeous art deco setting. Sandwich shop 'Lunchbox' is very popular for quick bites and snacks.

Others: Quite apart from the individual colleges' events there are annual balls (the Purples Ball is the main event of the year), regular quiz nights, casinos and cultural and international social nights.

SOCIAL & POLITICAL

UNIVERSITY OF LONDON UNION (ULU):
- 5 sabbaticals

The individual colleges' SUs affiliate separately to NUS and are automatically part of ULU which offers *the most extraordinary level* of facilities at the building in Bloomsbury, open to 11pm or later when hosting an event. ULU (which is pronounced 'yooloo') is also the students' central representative body and has *effective* officers on most of the University's important committees. Almost all ULU staff are students and *it's not unusual to find security staff that speak 5 languages and study politics. It is a politically balanced union and isn't a NUS member, works with activists from most parties.* ULU now elects its officers through an on-line system giving all the students a chance to vote meaning the officers have the backing of quite a few students. They're *a very cosmopolitan crowd* with a large percentage of mature and part-time students. Recent campaigns have included the successful 30% discount on London transport, an anti-tuition fees demo (5,000 turn out) and action against facism. ULU itself isn't a member of NUS, but most individual college unions are.

SU FACILITIES:
The Union building (ULU Building) contains: 3 bars; cafeteria; general shop; sports shop; print shop and photocopying; travel agent; banks (Barclays and Halifax) with cashpoints; Endsleigh Insurance office; opticians; vending machines; games and gambling machines; fax service; creche; snack bar; sandwich shop; full-size swimming pool; fitness centre; gymnasium; squash and badminton courts; launderette; theatre hall; offices and meeting rooms; *and a partridge in a pear tree*. ULU also provides training for staff and student officers of all the member colleges' SUs and handbooks and publications about all aspects of London student life. The basement of the ULU building is being demolished to build a new sports centre. (Won't the rest fall down though?).

CLUBS (NON SPORTING):
AEGEE; Afro Caribbean; Arabic; Arts; Ballroom and Latin Dance; Bridge; Campaign for Free Education; Caving; Chamber Choir; Chinese; Chorus; Debating; French Jive; Games; Hindu; Indian Dance; Jidokwan Taekwondo; Krishna; Lifesaving; Marxist; Meditation; Methodist; Muslim Women; Opera; Refugee Support; Salsa; Scandinavian; Shaolin; Singapore; Slavonic; Starfleet; Tai Chi; Zhuan Shu Kuan. Colleges of the University also have their own clubs.

OTHER ORGANISATIONS:
The award-winning student newspaper, 'London Student', is published by ULU but is editorially independent. It has a sabbatical editor and is aimed at all London students both in and outside the University. *Editorially and stylistically it's more 'The Sun' than 'The Guardian' but does hit more targets than it misses.*

RELIGIOUS:
London has religious groups for every denomination from Muslims to Moonies, Jews to Jains. *If you can't find spiritual solace here, please direct your complaint upwards.*

PAID WORK:
Vacancy lists are posted up in the Union and ULU usually has vacancies. There are more opportunities in London for part-time work than anywhere else, but there are also more people trying to get those jobs. Students find work quite easy in all the usual places like bars and restaurants and also in theatres, offices and shops.

SPORTS

- Recent successes: karate, rowing, lacrosse, rifle

There being so many students in London, certain features are inevitable – there are some very high sporting standards and some peerless facilities. The high standard doesn't put off beginners though, and the facilities mean that sport is an important social focus for students of all abilities. There are certain areas where London has been particularly successful, notably rowing (they've beaten both Oxford and Cambridge repeatedly over the last 10 years). Many competitions are run between the University's colleges.

SPORTS FACILITIES:
At the ULU Building, there are all the amenities mentioned above (the swimming pool, gym, fitness centre, squash court and so on). 31 acres of playing fields, a floodlit artificial pitch, 6 grass tennis courts and a hard court can be found at Motspur Park sports ground in New Malden just outside London, which, despite having been sold off, can still be used by students. ULU has sailing facilities at the Welsh Harp reservoir in North London and a boathouse at Chiswick on the Thames.

SPORTING CLUBS:
Canoe; Gymnastics; Jitsu; Korfball; Kung Fu; Lacrosse; Polo; Rifle; Rowing; Ski and Snowboarding; Sub Aqua; Table Tennis; Tai Chi Chuan; Ten Pin Bowling; Water Polo; Windsurfing; Zhuan Shu Kuan.

ATTRACTIONS:
There is no end to London's sporting attractions: from tennis and strawberries at Wimbledon to football and fighting at Millwall; from cricket at Lords to croquet at Hurlingham; from athletics at Crystal Palace to rugby at Twickers; from... *well, as we said, there's no end.*

ACCOMMODATION

IN UNIVERSITY:
- Catered: 31%   • Cost: £77-102 (30wks)

Availability: The percentage of London students living in college accommodation varies enormously from college to college, but for those that the colleges don't accommodate, there's a limited number of catered places in the University's 8 intercollegiate halls and 500 places in self-catered flats and houses. The halls are mainly mixed but there are 2 (Canterbury and College) for women only, (Connaught) for men and International Hall mainly for overseas students.

Amenities: Conditions in each hall are different but, mostly, it's single rooms with shared bathrooms and minimal cooking facilities. There is also a selection of other amenities including bars, TV rooms, telephones in every room, function, meeting and study rooms, libraries, launderettes, payphones and so on. Depending on the hall, students may be able to enjoy the delights of a squash court, darkroom, music room, bike sheds, gardens, videos and in College Hall there is a hairdressing salon. In some halls, there is the chance

to share rooms, sometimes even for mixed couples.
Car parking: *Not recommended. Spaces are limited – get yourself a scooter (not one of those rubbish toy things, a proper cool mover with engine and seat).*

EXTERNALLY:
- Ave rent: £75

London Transport (buses, tube and trains) splits the city into several 'zones' which are concentric circles from the centre. Zone 1, for example, is the area within a radius of about 2 miles of Trafalgar Square. Zone 2 is the next 3 miles and so on. Obviously, rents get cheaper in the outer zones, but then travel costs to the centre go up accordingly.

Availability: *Contrary to popular belief, it's really not that difficult to find accommodation in London, just buy a copy of the Evening Standard or Loot and there are hundreds of places. It is, however, a challenge of epic proportions to find anywhere that is both affordable and inhabitable. There's very little housing in Zone 1 even for yuppies, and students come a lot lower in the pecking order. Zone 2 is a bit better, particularly for single rooms in shared flats or houses in places like Wandsworth, Putney and Fulham and wherever the tube system is lacking. Zone 3 is relatively promising, but the catch is that it can take an hour to get to the centre. Zone 4 and beyond are not popular for the same reason, but, as they say, homeless students can't be choosers. Although there are many thousands of people living in cardboard boxes on London's streets, they aren't students. In fact, many students manage to find very comfortable flats for almost reasonable rents. There is also a number living in squats. To be safe, students coming to London should work out where they're going to stay first. Hammersmith, Camberwell and Finsbury Park all have student ghettos but it obviously depends where in the city you need to get to every day.*

Housing help: The University Accommodation Office with 8 full-time staff is a *formidable* service with the *formidable task of handling the external housing requirements of the University's students*. It offers a bulletin board, vacancies list and accommodation counselling. Larger colleges also have their own services.

WELFARE

SERVICES:
- Creche • Lesbian & Gay Society • Women's Officer • Minibus
- Self-defence classes • International SA • Anti Racism SA

ULU runs the above services as well as playing host to an optician in the ULU Building and producing an *excellent* annual Welfare Handbook. Students usually go to the University's Central Health Centre in Gower Street (Bloomsbury again), where counselling and health and dental treatment are on offer. *Generally, London students tend to use their own colleges' provisions, the local public health services, the Citizens Advice Bureau or else they suffer in silence.*

Drugs: *Many Londoners live for years in the capital without ever encountering them. Others, however, walk around with their eyes open. Every drug you've heard of and a great many beside are readily available on the streets and in the pubs and clubs of London. Cannabis is perpetually prevalent and ecstasy currently has a high profile. Heroin is more common than in most English cities and the* abuse/use of crack is spreading, especially in the South. They're often more expensive than elsewhere, but that shouldn't be regarded as any guarantee of quality – dangerous mixtures are common and the risks are your own. There are a number of help centres (including Narcotics Anonymous 020 7351 6066) and the authorities usually take a progressive but firm attitude.

Women: Anyone who isn't familiar with London, but particularly women, should remember that the diversity of the capital has a nasty slant – it's easy to turn a corner from a delightful residential area and suddenly find yourself in considerably less attractive surroundings. ULU's self-defence classes are not laid on as anybody's idea of a good joke. Without being sensational, in London there are risks it's best to avoid. Free attack alarms are available from ULU.

Lesbian, gay & bisexual: Far more than most places, it's possible to be out in London without experiencing constant prejudice (although that still doesn't make coming out easy and there are plenty of sad bigots around as well). The gay community in London is sizeable and proud, and has marked out a large chunk of Soho as pretty much its own. As a result, there are plenty of entertainments which don't conform to heterosexist stereotypes and a few London boroughs make special housing provisions. Many of the best clubs have gay nights or even, for a change, straight nights. And don't forget the Pride March and Festival, every summer.

Disabled: College facilities vary. The ULU building has a front ramp and lifts to all floors. Getting around London can be hellish even for those who are fully mobile, but plenty have learned to cope.

FINANCE:

College arrangements vary but if all else fails, there's the Vice-Chancellor's Hardship Fund or the ULU fund, sponsored by Waterstone's bookshop.

London College of Fashion

see The London Institute

London College of Printing

see The London Institute

London Guildhall University

- **Formerly City of London Polytechnic**

London Guildhall University, 31 Jewry Street, London, EC3N 2EY. Tel: (020) 7320 1000. Fax: (020) 7320 1163. E-mail: enqs@lgu.ac.uk
London Guildhall University Students' Union, 2 Goulston Street, London, E1 7TP. Tel: (020) 7247 1441. Fax: (020) 7247 0618.

GENERAL

London Guildhall University is based at, well, 7 places, really. And

London Guildhall

they're all in the City – the financial and corporate centre of London and the UK (with the 'EC' postcodes). Except for the sites in the East End (with just 'E' postcodes). Anyway, they're all around there and they're all *fairly drab* concrete constructions. Err, except for some of them, like the building at Moorgate, which is built in *elegant* grey stone, or the Jewry Street building (which has remains of London Wall running through the basement), both Grade II listed. The City, the famous square mile from about ¾ to 2 miles east of Trafalgar Square, is not one of London's shopping areas, nor is it residential – we're talking big business and big buildings. *The East End is well-known enough because of a certain TV soap. Ironically for an institution so intimately situated in the heart of financial derring-do,* London Guildhall has suffered the odd financial, since then, they've been turning over a tidy profit, thank you very much.

Sex ratio(M:F): 49%:51%	**Founded: 1970**
Full time u'grads: 7,712	**Part time: 462**
Postgrads: 482	**Non-degree: 1,607**
Ave course: 3yrs	**Ethnic: 38%**
Private school: 5%	**Flunk rate: 33.2%**
Mature students: 59%	**Overseas students: 13%**
Disabled students: 5%	

ATMOSPHERE:
For such a dispersed college in the centre of London, the University has a surprisingly united identity as an open, unpretentious place, possibly because so many of the students are locals. They manage to achieve some semblance of solidarity by quite a hefty emphasis on ents, which, compared to London's bright lights, are *something of a sputtering candle.*

THE SITES:
Not all the sites, *but the most prominent* (some students are based at more than one site):
Central House: (1,513 students – art, design, jewellery) A grey 60s block *with a laid back atmosphere,* about 2 minutes walk from Calcutta House, *one of the University's most essential student ports of call.*
Moorgate: (2,744 – law, economics, accountancy, business studies, financial services) A 19th-century building, *looking vaguely important, but very easy going.* 15 minutes walk from Calcutta House.
Tower Hill: (921 – computing, civil aviation) Opposite the Tower of London, but being 60s concrete, *hardly a reflection of its glory. Quiet with a serious work ethic.* 3 minutes from Calcutta House.
Commercial Rd: (1,500 – design, furniture, manufacture, music, technology) Another 60s building, 8 minutes from Calcutta House.
Calcutta House: (2,174 – languages, politics, modern history and psychology) Once an old tea warehouse.

THE CITY: see University of London

THE CITY & EAST END:
T*he City of London is full of people busy making money in phallic towers and as a result lots and lots of expensive wine bars, theme pubs, shops and sandwich bars for them to spend money in during the week but it's as quiet as the proverbial grave at weekends, which can be rather nice.*
The East End is closer to reality. Traditionally, it is the home of London's dispossessed: first, Jews; nowadays, Asians and yuppies. It

has a lively community atmosphere, which is hard to find elsewhere in inner city London. The market in Petticoat Lane may be a bit more gimmicky than once upon a time, but Brick Lane is a massive overdose for the shopaholic, even late into the night. The University's protestations that they're not near the East End are belied by the jellied eel vendor making a killing outside the Union building.

TRAVEL: see University of London
Local Trains: Liverpool St and Fenchurch St mainline stations are both within 10 minutes walk of almost all the University's sites.
Buses: The City and East End are well served by an enormous number of buses and you must be kidding if you think we're going to list them all, but here are the ones to catch to the SU building: 8; 15; 15B; 25; 40; 67; and 253. Night buses: N6; N8; N16; N76; N95; N97; and N98.
Car: *Parking? Yeah, right, as if.*
Underground: Moorgate (Northern, Metropolitan, Circle and Hammersmith & City Lines), Aldgate (Metropolitan and Circle), Aldgate East (Hammersmith & City and District), Tower Hill (District and Circle) and Tower Gateway (on the Docklands Light Railway) are all local. No two sites are further than 1½ miles apart so any of these stations will do for most sites.

CAREER PROSPECTS:
- Careers Service • No of staff: 7 full/1 part
- Unemployed after 6mths: 9%

FAMOUS ALUMNI:
Sonya Aurora Madan (Echobelly); Joy Gardner (victim of extradition procedures); Kate Hoey MP (Lab, ex-Spurs physio); Jools Holland (the prince of piano); Michael Jackson (TV executive, rather than King of Pop); Nick Leeson (disgraced bank bloke); Terry Marsh (former boxing champ); Alison Moyet (chanteuse); Anna Nolan ('Big Brother' lesbian nun); Vic Reeves (comedian); Mark Thatcher (Maggie's pride and joy).

FURTHER INFO:
Prospectus and individual course leaflets, and a mature students' guide. Website (www.lgu.ac.uk).

ACADEMIC

Many of the courses have vocational links, some taking advantage of local money meddling, but there are also plenty with a more arts 'n' crafts leaning.

staff/student ratio: 1:24
Range of points required for entrance: 280-60
Percentage accepted through clearing: 28%
Number of terms/semesters: 3
Length of terms/semesters: 11 wks
Research: 2.4

LIBRARIES:
- Books: 291,640 • Study places: 500

In all there are 3 libraries, closed on Sundays. Same old grumbles: *not enough books.*

COMPUTERS:
- Computer workstations: 1,500

ENTERTAINMENT

IN LONDON: see University of London

UNIVERSITY:
• Price of a pint of beer: £1.50 • Glass of wine: £1.15
Students tend to stick with the SU for fun, if only because the immediate vicinity is so expensive (although Brick Lane is very close).
Bars: (3) The main supping spot is on the 1st floor of the SU building, *in relaxing shades of candy blue and banana*. There's also the *dingy* Sub Bar (cap 450), mainly used for ents (*dead when it's not*) and there's a *more relaxed* place at Commercial Road.
Music venues/clubs/discos: The Sub Bar hosts 3 club nights a week (R & B, retro, hiphop), open DJ spots and jam sessions and occasional bands, most recently *the old school* De La Soul.
Cabaret: *Occasional selection of comics,* recent acts include Junior Simpson, *but then, where hasn't he played?*
Food: The SU Diner doles out hot and cold food from 12 to 8, *leaving a much saner bill than you'd get at any nearby café*. The SU Bars do pizzas.
Others: At least 3 balls a year.

SOCIAL & POLITICAL

LONDON GUILDHALL UNIVERSITY STUDENTS' UNION:
• 4 sabbaticals • Turnout at last ballot: 10% • NUS member
The SU has facilities at 4 sites, but its main centre is the freshly renovated Joy Gardner House in Goulston Street. *Getting this lot interested in politics would be harder than a concrete ox. The SU offered free transport to an anti-fees demo and only two students turned up.*

SU FACILITIES:
In the SU Building there are 2 bars, a diner, print shop and satellite TV. Elsewhere the SU runs a bar at Calcutta House, a snack bar and 3 stationery shops.

CLUBS (NON SPORTING):
Bangladeshi; Hindu; Kurdish; Media; Musicians; Vegetarian.

OTHER ORGANISATIONS:
There's a mag, 'G:Echo', (*Gecko, get it? No, oh well.*) which comes out every 6 weeks. The Community Action Group is very active. No Rag but various charity events raise a few quid.

RELIGIOUS:
• 2 chaplains (RC, CofE)
There's an ecumenical chaplaincy and a multi-faith 'quiet area', mainly used by Islamic students as a prayer room. The East End is a multi-ethnic area with Judaism and most Asian religions well represented.

PAID WORK: see University of London

The Central computer system of the University of Wales crashed recently, when a student downloaded too much hardcore pornography.

SPORTS

- Recent successes: football

Split sites mean that it's hard to maintain an overall level of athletic bravado. There's a new fitness centre, but the outdoor facilities are quite a trek by train or tube. By the time students get there, they're often too knackered to play.

SPORTS FACILITIES:
The fitness centre has a gym and activities rooms for exercise classes such as yoga and funky step (*we didn't like to ask*). There's a gym on the top floor at Tower Hill. The University also has a sports ground at Beckenham (20 acres of playing fields and tennis courts), 7 miles away.

SPORTING CLUBS:
Abseiling; Pool; Tai Chi; Yoga.

ATTRACTIONS: see University of London

ACCOMMODATION

IN COLLEGE:
- Self-catering: 6% • Cost: £58-75 (38wks)

Availability: There are only 461 places in the University's accommodation, procured through an arrangement with an independent housing association, in Sir John Cass Hall, a purpose built self-catered building in Hackney (4 miles from the City), and in 2 blocks of self-catering flats. No one is guaranteed a place and about 50% of first years who want to can't get one. *The students who are lucky enough to get such accommodation,* get single rooms in mixed blocks or the single sex flats. Between 3 and 5 students share cooking and cleaning facilities. *Security is good* with pin number entry, wardens and ground floor barriers.

Car parking: Limited permit parking space at the flats, *but students can forget any thoughts of driving to the University.*

EXTERNALLY: see University of London
Housing help: Students appeal to the Accommodation Service and private letting firms for help in finding housing. *Leyton and Hackney are recommended areas for budget and proximity.*

WELFARE

SERVICES:
- 2 Creches • Lesbian & Gay Society • Mature SA
- Overseas SA • Equal Ops Officer

The Student Advice Centre has 3 full-time counsellors at Calcutta House where a nurse provides medical cover and a doctor drops in for 3 sessions a week. The University runs health-related workshops, including stress management and controlling eating disorders.

Women: The Fawcett Library (soon to move to a new building and be renamed The Women's Library includes banners and unique archive material). The University also has a number of links with other organisations promoting women's educational opportunities.

Disabled: The University encourages advance visits for applicants with disabilities and has its own Equal Opportunities Adviser. *Most buildings have reasonably good access and the University goes a fair distance to make its education open to all.* There are supplementary workshops and an Equal Opportunities Adviser based at Calcutta House. The University also runs a dyslexia support group.

FINANCE:
• Access fund: £900,000 • Successful applications: 1,080
The University targets the access fund at students with special needs (ie. self-funding students and those with children or disabilities). Other bursaries and scholarships are available.

The London Institute

(1) The London Institute, 65 Davies Street, London, W1Y 2DA.
Tel: (020) 7514 6127. Fax: (020) 7514 6131.
E-mail: marcom@linst.ac.uk
London Institute Students' Union, 2-6 Catton Street, Holborn, London, WC1R 4AA. Tel: (020) 7514 6270 Fax: (020) 7514 6284.
(2) Camberwell College of Arts, Peckham Road, London, SE5 8UF.
(3) Central Saint Martin's College of Art and Design, Southampton Row, London, WC1B 4AP.
(4) Chelsea College of Art and Design, Manresa Road, London, SW3 6LS.
(5) London College of Fashion, 20 John Princes Street, London, W1M 0BJ.
(6) London College of Printing & Distributive Trades, Elephant & Castle, London, SE1 6SB.

GENERAL

Despite its *somewhat clinical* name, the London Institute is the largest art school in Europe, comprising five separate institutions, all of which have excellent reputations in their own right and attract students the world over. Although the Institute awards the degrees, students apply to the individual colleges.

Sex ratio(M:F): 31:69%	Founded: 1989
Full time u'grads: 6,337	Part time: 491
Postgrads: 503	Non-degree: 1,360
Ave course: 3yrs	Ethnic: 37%
Private school: 1.5%	Flunk rate: 16.6%
Mature students: 65%	Overseas students: 35%
Disabled students: 6%	

ATMOSPHERE:
Not only is the Institute the sum of five separate colleges, but these are in turn fragmented into 24 different sites all over London, which means the chance of overall social cohesion is pretty much non-existent. The only generalisations possible are the students' tendency to trendiness and a strong level of commitment to their

courses. The days of self-conscious artists wallowing in an existential mire of absinthe and syphilis may have passed, but many want to keep the image going (if not the reality).

THE SITES:
Camberwell: A large mixed modern/Victorian building, next to the South London Art Gallery, with two annexes up to 15 minutes walk away. This part of South London is *shabby, but friendly enough and relatively cheap.*
Central Saint Martin's: (2,579 students) HQ in Holborn, near Bloomsbury; further sites at Clerkenwell (shared with LCP, see below) nearer the City, in Covent Garden and on the Charing Cross Road.
Chelsea: (880 students) 3 sites in and around *Sloane country*, with a fourth further west at Lime Grove.
London College of Fashion: (1,365 students) 3 sites around the western, *posher* stretch of Oxford Street. 2 more in the City, *among the financial whizzkids.*
London College of Printing: (3,405 students) LCP is based at the Elephant & Castle (see South Bank University) with other bits at Clerkenwell.

THE CITY: see University of London

TRAVEL: see University of London
All the sites have plenty of buses. Nearest Underground/rail links:
Camberwell: Peckham Rye and Denmark Hill over-ground stations.
C St Martin's: Holborn (Central and Piccadilly lines) for Southampton Row. Farringdon (Circle, Hammersmith & City) for Clerkenwell. Covent Garden (Piccadilly) for Long Acre. Tottenham Court Road (Central and Northern) for Charing Cross Rd.
Chelsea: Manresa Rd: South Kensington (Circle, District, Piccadilly Lines). Bagley's Lane and Hugon Rd: Putney Bridge (District). Lime Grove: Shepherd's Bush (Central).
LCF: Oxford Circus (Central, Bakerloo, Victoria and Northern) or Bond Street (Central and Jubilee) for Oxford Street sites. Barbican (Circle and Hammersmith & City) or Old Street (Northern) for City sites.
LCP: Elephant & Castle (Bakerloo and Northern, also over-ground and Thameslink). Clerkenwell: Farringdon (Circle, Hammersmith & City).

CAREER PROSPECTS:
• Careers Service • No of staff: 3 full/2 part
• Unemployed after 6mths: 12.5%
The Careers Service publishes a monthly job list. These arty subjects, though – they're not easy career courses. LCP is quite vocational though.

FAMOUS ALUMNI:
Lionel Bart (composer); Quentin Blake (illustrator); Dirk Bogarde (actor, writer); Neville Brody (graphic designer); Jarvis Cocker (Pulp); Terence Conran (entrepreneur); Nicole Farhi, John Galliano, Katherine Hamnett, Stella McCartney, Alexander McQueen, Bruce Oldfield, Rifat Ozbek, Zandra Rhodes (fashion designers); Mike Flowers (of Pops fame); Gilbert & George (artists); Mike Leigh (film director); Henry Moore (sculptor); Chris Ofili (painter and Turner Prize winner); Alexei Sayle (comedian); Vivian Stanshall (eccentric musician); Mark Wallenger (sculptor)..

FURTHER INFO:
Prospectuses, videos, leaflets from the central Communications and Marketing Office. Website (www.linst.ac.uk).
E-mail for prospectus: prospectus@linst.ac.uk

ACADEMIC

The various sites offer a range of arts courses including: graphics, the dramatic arts, fine art and graphic design, fashion, footwear and accessories, media, business, retail and printing. Each site specialises in just a few of these already specialist areas and *they all have pretty good reputations in what they do. CSM, for instance, is especially respected for fine art.*

staff/student ratio: 1:17
Range of points required for entrance: n/a
Percentage accepted through clearing: 5%
Number of terms/semesters: 3
Length of terms/semesters: 11 wks
Research: 2.8

LIBRARIES:
• Books: 310,000 • Study places: 900
There are 9 libraries in all, dotted between the various sites. *Library facilities get the thumbs up.*

COMPUTERS:
• Computer workstations: 1,000
Computers – thumbs down, not enough and not adequate.

ENTERTAINMENT

IN LONDON: see University of London
COLLEGES:
• Price of a pint of beer: £1.70 • Glass of wine: £1
The ents side of things suffers greatly from the lack of a main venue and any kind of collective thought from the Union as to what entertainments at a university should involve. They do however sometimes have a go and host Nights at Home nightclub, if you get their drift. They also have two black tie events per year at Xmas and graduation. *When students get a serious urge to party as a collective mass, they take over Heaven and the Ministry of Sound* (see University of London).
Bars: *There are 6 bars, the biggest and best of which is the Boiler Room at LCP where most events take place.* One is at the Clerkenwell site, another at the Furzedown halls of residence in Tooting and one at Chelsea.
Food: The LCP and Camberwell bars serve jacket potatoes and other such nosh. *Catering on all sites is handled by an outside contractor to less than universal approval.*

SOCIAL & POLITICAL

LONDON INSTITUTE STUDENTS' UNION (LISU):
• 4 sabbaticals • Turnout at last ballot: 12.2% • NUS member
Each college has its own SU, under the umbrella of LISU. *Because of the fragmented nature of the Institute (and even of some of the component bodies) and probably the lack of a SU venue, there is absolutely no cohesion and students often become aware of their Union only when something goes wrong. LISU has been described as one colossal, inadequate mess, or is that art?*

SU FACILITIES:
There are probably more facilities at the newsagents around the corner. At LISU; photocopier; payphones; weekly on-line job vacancy bulletin which covers temp and full-time stuff.

OTHER ORGANISATIONS:
The LISU newsletter, 'Blue', comes out monthly, *a wonderful example of the triumph of style over content. But then they're into style, aren't they? No Rag but there is a voluntary group called Fact and Focus but what it actually does, nobody knows.*

RELIGIOUS: see University of London

PAID WORK: see University of London

SPORTS

• Recent successes: not a lot
Those students and their creative urges tend to steer clear of competitive team stuff.

SPORTING CLUBS:
Men's Football; Women's Football.

ATTRACTIONS: see University of London

ACCOMMODATION

IN COLLEGE:
• Catered: 3% • Cost: £102-106 (39-52wks) • Self-catering: 10%
• Cost: £55-106 (39-52wks)
Five blocks of mostly 60s design, split between Battersea (200 catered places, *bearable*) or Tooting (380 self-catering) with preference given to 1st years from outside SE England. 16% of first years are unlucky and don't get the place they're after. There's no single-sex accommodation. Students can book accommodation over the summer if they need to look for rented places. *Criticism of the accommodation ranges from awful to expensive and very overpriced.* Security is *good* and there's 24-hour coverage. Car parking is available and there's also a bike store.

EXTERNALLY: see University of London
The College Accommodation Service offers housing lists and a Find-a-Flatmate service.

WELFARE

SERVICES:
• Nursery – 35 places (six months to five years)
One full- and one part-time counsellor are employed by Student Services. LISU has 9 full- and 4 part-time advisers.
Disabled: *Access is poor in some areas but facilities overall are pretty good. There is a lot of support for dyslexia as apparently a high proportion of artists are sufferers.* There's also a Deaf Students Soc.

FINANCE:
• Access fund: n/a • Successful applications n/a
Finalists at Camberwell, Central St. Martin's or Chelsea can apply to the Nancy Baker Fund.

London School of Economics
see LSE

London School of Jewish Studies
see SOAS

Loughborough University

Loughborough University, Loughborough, Leicestershire, LE11 3TU.
Tel: (01509) 263171. Fax: (01509) 223905.
E-mail: admissions@lboro.ac.uk
Loughborough Students' Union, Ashby Road, Loughborough,
Leicestershire, LE11 3TT. Tel: (01509) 217766. Fax: (01509)
235593. E-mail: lsu.kiosk@lboro.ac.uk

GENERAL

Loughborough, pronounced 'Lufbra' by the locals and 'Loogabarooga' by the crazy and/or drunk, is a small, industrial market town, set among wandering countryside and small suburban villages of the East Midlands. The University is set about a mile west of the town centre in *green and pleasant* parkland. It became a university in 1966. The campus buildings are mainly *inoffensive,* low-rise blocks on a landscaped, 223 acre site. It's *perfect* for the various playing fields and sporting facilities, *the University's chief extracurricular preoccupation.*

Sex ratio(M:F): 62%:38%	Founded: 1966
Full time u'grads: 8,778	Part time: 156
Postgrads: 1,090	Non-degree: 322
Ave course: 3/4yrs	Ethnic: 14%
Private school: 18%	Flunk rate: 6%
Mature students: 7%	Overseas students: 8%
Disabled students: 4%	

ATMOSPHERE:
Don't believe what they say about 'it's not the winning but the taking part'. At Loughborough University, it's the winning that matters, and the training beforehand and the celebration, analysis, recriminations and loud drinking games afterwards. If you're not particularly interested in sport one way or another, don't be dismayed – there's plenty else to do, plus the influx of new arty types in the wake of the merge with Loughbough College of Art and Design. However, for those who are allergic to track suits and become apoplexic at the hint of exertion, applying here could be construed as a little perverse.

THE TOWN:
• Population: 51,000 • London: 100miles
• Leicester: 13miles • Nottingham: 17miles

Loughborough is not big enough to fit in more than a few sites of historic interest, but it gives its money's worth, including a few old churches and museums (eg. the Bell Foundry Museum – which makes bells – the Military Museum and the Ancient Monuments Museum). Apart from all the usual shops and public amenities, there is a twice-weekly street market, some *good* independent record stores and some ethnic jewellery shops. The town is surrounded by the ancient Charnwood Forest – *so ancient that there's not much forest left* – and various waterways flow through the area. Of local note is the Great Central Railway, still steaming its way cross-country and there's the Quorn Hunt *who victimise foxes, look silly and fall off horses.*

TRAVEL:
Trains: Loughborough station, 2 miles from the campus on the mainline north from London St Pancras (£25.10) to Edinburgh (£58.30).
Coaches: Served by local coach company Paul Winson and National Express – London (£13.25), student special – Nottingham (£2).
Car: The A6 goes straight through Loughborough and the M1 is less than 2 miles west of the campus.
Air: East Midlands Airport (inland and European flights) is 5½ miles from the campus.
Hitching: *The M1 is good, but it's a bus ride to the junction.*
Local: Local buses run between campus and town. For 65p students can get across town to the station.
Taxis: £3 from the campus to the station (2 miles).
Bicycles: *Useful for getting into town (and the campus and its sports fields). The theft situation is improving, but don't bring an expensive mountain bike – you won't take it back.*

CAREER PROSPECTS:
- Careers Service
- No of staff: 8 full/4 part
- Unemployed after 6mths: 4%

FAMOUS ALUMNI:
Steve Backley (javelin chucker); Sebastian Coe (runner); Michael Fabricant MP (Con); Lorna Fitzsimons MP (Lab, former NUS president); Tanni Grey (Para Olympic athlete); Barry Hines (wrote Kes); Jason Lee (England hockey player); David Moorcroft (athlete); Carole Tongue MEP (Lab); Bob Wilson (commentator, ex-Arsenal goalie).

FURTHER INFO:
Prospectuses for undergrads, postgrads and individual departments. Website (www.lboro.ac.uk). There are open days in June and September.

ACADEMIC

The Uni has its origins as a technical college dating back to 1909. It continues to evolve and now offers humanities and arts courses due to the merger with Loughborough College of Art & Design in August 1998.

staff/student ratio: 1:14
Range of points required for entrance: 320-240
Percentage accepted through clearing: 5%
Number of terms/semesters: 2
Length of terms/semesters: 15 wks
Research: 4.6

LIBRARIES:
- Books: 600,000   • Study places: 500

The large white library is in the centre of the campus. *Good weekend opening hours.*

COMPUTERS:
- Computer workstations: 250

Some 24-hour access to computers.

ENTERTAINMENT

TOWN:
- Price of a pint of beer: £1.80   • Glass of wine: £1.60

Cinemas: (1) The six-screen Curzon.
Theatres: Amateur and touring shows in the Town Hall.
Pubs: *Local pubs are popular with students who live out or want to get off campus, but Loughborough generally suffers from an embarrassing lack of swinging student spots.* Pushplugs: The Griffin and The Paget (*as studenty as any round here*); The Swan (live bands and real ale); Barleymow; Phantom & Firkin; Tap & Spile; Blacksmith's Arms; The Warehouse; Matts Bar; Orange Tree.
Clubs/discos/music venues: *The town's mainstream clubs, Pulse and Club XS, which everyone still knows by their former names 'Crystals' and 'Echos' respectively, along with Discoteca all compete for student trade.* Pubs, The Swan, Bar 32 and the Town Hall have occasional bands but Leicester and Nottingham are better bets for any form of entertainment.
Eating out: *Again, it's necessary to go out of town for serious tastebud tingles but a few establishments are worth a look.* Pushplugs: Bar Europa (good, cheap pizza); Cactus Café (Mexican); Mr Chans (cheap chinese). There are numerous Indian, Chinese and takeaway places, some open till at least 2am.

UNIVERSITY:
- Price of a pint of beer: £1.50   • Glass of wine: £1.40

Bars: (12) There are nine bars around campus, three in residential halls, one on campus and eight in the Union Building, *which are always lively, especially on event nights and when there's something sporty to celebrate.*
Theatres: Regular presentations in the Arts Centre and a Union-funded troupe.
Cinemas: The film society shows pics and flicks twice a week and a film festival every year.
Clubs/discos: 2 club nights a week in Rattlers *but students tend to shake their butts on the fields more than on the dance floor.* For those who need some ents-style exercise, the Saturday Selection rotates 70s, 80s, charity and club nights.
Music venues: The Main Auditorium tempts up-and-coming acts. There's also a regular comedy night.
Cabaret: Weekly cabaret in the Union Building.
Food: In the Union and the Student Village students can find something edible *(and legal)* to put in their mouths from 10am to 3am. There's an *imaginative* selection, from the Purple Onion pizza/burger delivery service to Al's Diner breakfast outlet.
Other: Freshers' week is a blur of ents from surf simulators to bucking broncos and at the other end of a student's stint is the Graduation ball (this year, Atomic Kitten, Dum Dums, Black Ledgend,

Chicane and Right Said Fred, a casino and that bloody bronco again). Occasional bingo.

SOCIAL & POLITICAL

LOUGHBOROUGH STUDENTS' UNION (LSU):
• 8 sabbaticals • Turnout at last ballot: 25% • NUS member
Politics is a non-issue for most students – radical it ain't, but awareness campaigns go down well. LSU represents students from the University, Loughborough College and the RNIB Vocational College. Although the Union remains part of NUS, *it holds the national body at arm's length.*

SU FACILITIES:
A general shop (complete, of course, with sports gear section); 8 bars; 4 catering outlets; travel agency; printing facilities; bookshop (Blackwells); market stalls; 3 banks; 'Employment Exchange' jobshop; an insurance office; photocopier; photo booth; games and vending machines; pool tables; juke box; meeting rooms; auditorium; optician; dentist; hairdresser; accommodation letting agency, taxi hire; suit hire.

CLUBS (NON SPORTING):
Aerospace; CD Library; Chemical Engineering; Clubbing; Cocktail; Hellenic; Hiking and Hostelling; Indian; Malaysian; Mature; Music Club; Real Ale; Role Play; Stage; Wargames; Welsh.

OTHER ORGANISATIONS:
The remarkable Rag raised a stonking £235,000 last year and is about the only thing that distracts anyone from sporting pursuits. There's a new £1.4Mn Media Centre with professional quality recording studio, radio station and video editing suite. There's also a Student Community Action group. Student media includes the *pukka* 'The Label', a weekly newspaper financed by the Union, but run independently, and the radio station which is 25 years old this year.

RELIGIOUS:
There's an ecumenical Christian chaplaincy, a Muslim prayer room and an Islamic library.

PAID WORK:
There's a *very successful* employment agency with a job database for students.

SPORTS

• Recent successes: it'd be quicker to list the ones they didn't win
Did we mention that Loughborough University is big on sport? Applicants who think that running around a field in shorts, chasing/catching/kicking/throwing a ball is stupid should keep quite quiet about it if they go to Loughborough, unless they want to see grown men and women cry. The University enjoys a vast range of sporting facilities, virtually unmatched by any other, let alone by a university this size. Success in most sports has been phenomenal – they've won the British Universities Sports Association women's championship for the last 22 consecutive years and the men's version for the last 20. *(Perhaps they're all bionic or clones, has anybody actually checked?)*

SPORTS FACILITIES:
All sports clubs are fully insured against accidents, which makes them relatively pricey to join – even table tennis costs £8. But many would argue that the facilities are worth it. Four sports centres geared up for all manner of indoor exertion; 2 gymnasia; dance studio; two swimming pools; 7 squash courts; 2 floodlit all-weather areas; an all-weather athletics stadium (run jointly with the town); many acres of playing fields; the Dan Maskell tennis centre; and equipment for indoor sports of all sorts such as a multi-gym, martial arts dojo, badminton courts and so on and so on...

The town doesn't really need to add anything, but the surrounding area does make outdoor sports, such as fell walking and water-sports, possible. If you can believe this, there is soon to be a National Institute of Sport to be based here. Millions of quids are going to be spent on even more facilities. What can we say?

SPORTING CLUBS:
Aerobics; American Football; Gliding; Hot Air Balloon; Jiu Jitsu; Karting; Kickboxing; Kung Fu; Lacrosse; Paragliding; Rifle; Rowing; Speleological (caving); Sport Parachuting; Surf; Table Tennis; Ten Pin Bowling; Tetsudo; Thai Boxing; Triathlon; Ultimate Frisbee; Water Skiing; Windsurfing

ATTRACTIONS:
Formula 3 motor racing, motorcycle racing and the Grand Prix at Donington.

ACCOMMODATION

IN COLLEGE:
- <u>Catered: 37%</u> • Cost: £56-88 (31-38wks) • <u>Self-catering: 21%</u>
- <u>Cost: £39-54 (35-50wks)</u>

Availability: There are 10 catered and 6 self-catering halls, all of which are gradually being upgraded. They are all mixed (although some blocks or corridors are single sex) and accommodate between 150 and 650 students. This is enough to house all 1st years who request it and a good number of finalists. 11% of rooms are shared. They are all on or adjacent to campus except one en route to town ½ mile away. All halls are now networked at a charge of £3 per week for unlimited surfing (wahay). There are also self-catering flats arranged in courts or in the student village. Between 6 and 8 students share each kitchen.

Car parking: Limited permit parking for 2nd and 3rd years only.

EXTERNALLY:
- <u>Ave rent: £40</u>

Availability: It's a renter's market and you're unlikely to be left on the pavement. The best places, plucked by the early birds, are around Ashby Road and Storer Road, between the campus and Sainsbury's.

Housing help: The Union runs an advice service and the University's Student Accommodation Service holds an accommodation list and offers handy suggestions to new and bemused students. Also see the letting agency in the SU.

Bishop Grosseteste College is named after the 13th-century scientist and first ever Chancellor of Oxford University, Bishop Big Head.

WELFARE

SERVICES:
- Nursery • Lesbian & Gay Society • Mature SA • Overseas SA
- Postgrad SA • Nightbus • Women's Officer

The University Counselling Service has 2 full- and 2 part-time counsellors and there's a medical centre on campus, providing a sick bay, a doctor on call 24 hours a day and a physiotherapy clinic for sportspersons who exert themselves that bit too much. There's a harrassment council and the SU also runs a student advice centre with 5 advisers. The SU runs a nursery for kiddies aged 6 months to 5 years, they've got 100 places.

Disabled: *Access is reasonably good to most buildings*, even though the campus isn't entirely flat. Support is also available for students with sight and hearing difficulties and there's a tutor for students with special needs.

FINANCE:
- Access fund: £500,000 • Successful applications: 1,300

There is a hardship fund and over 200 scholarships and bursaries, 70 of which are sports-related.

LSE

- **The School is part of University of London and students are entitled to use its facilities.**

The London School of Economics & Political Science, Houghton Street, London, WC2A 2AE. Tel: (020) 7955 7124/5. Fax: (020) 7955 6001. E-mail: ug-admissions@lse.ac.uk

LSE Students' Union, East Building, LSE, Houghton Street, London, WC2A 2AE. Tel: (020) 7955 7158. Fax: (020) 7955 6789. E-mail: su-gen-sec@lse.ac.uk

GENERAL

Hot in the heartland of London's throbbing core, between the end of the Strand and the beginning of Fleet Street, is one of the *bull's eyes in the world's economic and political darts board*. LSE may have an international reputation for the E part of its name, but studies extend to social sciences of all sorts. *The buildings themselves don't live up to expectations, being a cross between the old and austere and your modern cake-tin type blocks.* The buildings are clustered – well, *squashed actually* – onto the pavement just opposite the BBC's Bush House, less than a mile down the road from Trafalgar Square, and just round the corner from King's College London and the Courtauld Institute. *The place is cramped and busy – not a good place to start swinging cats because you'll either (a) hit a wall, (b) hit a person, or (c) get caught by the RSPCA.*

LSE

Sex ratio(M:F): 54%:46%
Full time u'grads: 3,384
Postgrads: 3,100
Ave course: 3yrs
Private school: 37%
Mature students: 13%
Disabled students: n/a

Founded: 1895
Part time: 34
Non-degree: 0
Ethnic: n/a
Flunk rate: 4.3%
Overseas students: 54%

ATMOSPHERE:
It's a hectic hive of intellectual pressure, attracting the brightest social scientists from around the world. A combination of the high proportion of overseas and postgrad students and the fact that they can get very ambitious, career-minded and academically competitive tempers the potential for youthful exuberance but there are still enough traces of the radicalism for which the School was renowned in the 1960s to keep things electric. If you want to chill for 3 years, don't come to the LSE.

THE CITY: see University of London

ALDWYCH:
Spit east and it'll land in the eye of a businessman in the City. Spit west and you'll hit either a theatre, a restaurant, a café or a cinema in the West End. Spit north and you'll have dampened the cardboard home of one of the many homeless who live on the streets around Lincoln's Inn Fields (London's largest square). Spit south and it'll go deservedly straight back in your face because the Thames is about 100 yards in that direction and the wind will probably be blowing from there. For more details where to spit, look up either the Courtauld Institute, King's College London or University of London.

TRAVEL: see University of London

CAREER PROSPECTS:
• Careers Service • No of staff: 1 full/2 part
• Unemployed after 6mths: 7%
A high proportion of students go on to further training or higher degrees.

SPECIAL FEATURES:
• LSE has students from 136 countries. That's more than the World Bank and almost as many as the UN.

FAMOUS ALUMNI:
Sir David Attenborough (biologist and broadcaster); Cherie Booth QC (wife of you know who); Carlos the Jackal (terrorist); Ekow Eshun (editor, 'Arena' magazine); Clare Francis (yachtswoman, author); Loyd Grossman (foodie TV presenter); Mick Jagger (Stone); Judge Jules (DJ); John F Kennedy (dead US president); Robert Kilroy-Silk (smoothie chat-show host); Bernard Levin (journalist); Malcolm Maclaren (ex Sex Pistols manager); Mat Osman (Suede); Romano Prodi (President, European Commission); Maurice Saatchi (advertising guru); George Soros (financier).

FURTHER INFO:
Prospectuses for undergrads and postgrads, alternative prospectus from the SU, video (£6) plus a website (www.lse.ac.uk).

ACADEMIC

staff/student ratio: 1:9
Range of points required for entrance: 360-300
Percentage accepted through clearing: n/a
Number of terms/semesters: 3
Length of terms/semesters: 10 wks
Research: 5.9

LIBRARIES:
- Books: 4,000,000 • Study places: 1,600

LSE's huge main library goes under the *appropriately grand* title of the British Library of Political & Economic Science. There are also several small departmental libraries. *Fair to good facilities in all with unusually good opening hours.*

COMPUTERS:
- Computer workstations: 600

Some 24-hr access to computers.

ENTERTAINMENT

IN LONDON: see University of London

COLLEGE:
- Price of a pint of beer: £1.50 • Glass of wine: £1.25

Bars: (3) The Three Tuns Bar (cap 700) is *pretty popular*. The Underground (120) is primarily an events venue and the Beavers Retreat, *which looks as if it's been furnished courtesy of MFI, is expensive and only really popular with the academics.*
Cinemas: The film club shows the occasional flick or buses everyone off to a local cinema.
Theatres: *Brimming with luvvies, LSE may not be,* but it does have a theatre which hosts at least 3 productions a year.
Clubs/discos/music venues: The Underground goes overboard for its Friday night disco 'Crush' and the Quad is used for bands, most recently Bis and Cornershop.
Cabaret: Every Saturday the Chuckle Club chucks up comics, the *excellent* Stewart Lee being a recent example.
Food: The Union runs a café, *which is unusually good for vegetarian and vegan grub, with furniture from the next decade and trendy murals.* It also runs a pizzeria and restaurant.
Others: Student society events (eg tequila and dance nights) and multi-cultural goings-on. Annual Rag and Graduation Balls (last year's Grad Ball was at the Savoy).

SOCIAL & POLITICAL

LSE STUDENTS' UNION:
- 4 sabbaticals • Turnout at last ballot: n/a • NUS member

The SU still veers leftwards, but not at the break-neck angle it once did. It has weekly general meetings and occasionally threatens to disaffiliate from the NUS, but the fact that it attracts major political speakers from the UK and abroad is of more interest to the political junkies who infest the place. Recent campaigns for better library/computer facilities and against tuition fees.
Also ULU: see University of London

SU FACILITIES:
The SU has 3 floors and the basement in the *cramped and slightly claustrophobic* East Building where The Three Tuns bar is based as well as the café, travel agent, advice centre, general shop, printing and photocopying service. The School also has a bookshop on its grounds.

CLUBS (NON SPORTING):
Aid for Bosnia; Animal Aid; Arabic; Bridge; Catholic; Central/Eastern European; Chinese; Christian; Conservative; Cypriot; Dr Bike; Drama; European; Grimshaw Club; Hayek; Hellenic; Historical Materialism; Human Rights of Women; Indian; Italian; Jelly Baby; Mauritian; Mexican; Music; Modern Dance; Peace; Pakistan; Pyschology; Scandinavian; Schapiro Government Club; Stop the Fees; Student Industrial; Theatre Appreciation; Vedic.

OTHER ORGANISATIONS:
The weekly student newspaper 'The Beaver' is published by the SU. PuLSE FM (geddit) broadcasts on campus permanently and temporarily for a month in London.

RELIGIOUS:
- 4 chaplains (RC, CofE, Free Church, Jewish)
Also Buddhist and Muslim facilities.

PAID WORK: see University of London

- Recent successes: football

Most of LSE's greatest sporting moments are reserved for the Rugby Club Ball. The Aldwych is obviously not the place for vast playing fields but a hardy few make the 40-minute train journey to the School's 25 acres of playing fields at Berrylands near New Malden way out west. Students can, of course, use ULU's facilities.

SPORTS FACILITIES:
On site, LSE offers 3 squash courts, a badminton court, a fitness centre, multi-gym, snooker table and a circuit room. At Berrylands, 10 miles away, there are playing fields, tennis courts, a croquet lawn, pavilion, bar and restaurant.

SPORTING CLUBS:
Badminton; Basketball; Boxing; Cricket; Football; Hapkido; Hockey; Judo; Karate; Kung Fu; Muay Thai Boxing; Netball; Rock Climbing; Rowing; Rugby; Squash; Table Tennis; Tae Kwon Do.

ATTRACTIONS: see University of London

IN COLLEGE:
- Catered: 23% • Cost: £48-108 (31-52wks) • Self-catering: 11%
- Cost: £76-110 (40-52wks)

Availability: Students can use the University's intercollegiate housing (see University of London) so all 1st years from outside Greater London are guaranteed accommodation. Although students from inside Greater London cannot be guaranteed accommodation, they are still encouraged to apply. The accommodation itself is in 1 set of self-catering flats and 4 catered (pay-as-you-eat) halls spread out between 1 and 4 miles from the School, from Holborn to Docklands. 16% of places are shared, some even in triple rooms and some flats

are available for single parents or married couples. None of the School's own housing is single sex although the University offers some. In some rooms heating and/or lighting is not included. All rooms now have personal telephones. Security wise, CCTV is in all halls while 24-hour security guards and swipe cards are in use in the majority of halls.
Catering: As well as kitchens shared between 6 students, there are refectories operating a pay-as-you-eat scheme in some self-catering halls and, in catered housing, dining halls.
EXTERNALLY: see University of London
Housing help: The SU runs the student advice centre where they can help with housing problems.

WELFARE

SERVICES:
- Creche • Lesbian & Gay Society • Mature SA • Overseas SA
- Minibus • Women's Officer • Post Grad Officer
- Self-defence classes

The School has 4 full-time counsellors and the Union 3 part-time advisers, who provide assistance to students in need. The Health Service provides medical support. There is a student Parents' Society. Other services are available through the Union and London University.
Disabled: There are lifts aplenty, but often you have to climb stairs to get to them. There's also a Society for the Enlightenment of Able-Bodied Students, as well as a disabled support officer, Braille and recording facilities, induction loops on some telephones and plans for voice synthesisers on library PCs. A disabled students' fund is available.

FINANCE:
- Access fund: £157,500 • Successful applications: 167

Generous hardship funds and scholarships ease the way more than a little. Maybe *the economists help everyone to budget more successfully than at other colleges. Maybe not.*

University of Luton

- **Formerly Luton College of Higher Education**

University of Luton, Park Square, Luton, Bedfordshire, LU1 3JU.
Tel: (01582) 734111. Fax: (01582) 743400.
E-mail: admissions@luton.ac.uk
Luton University Students' Union, Europa House, Vicarage Street, Luton, Bedfordshire, LU1 3HZ. Tel: (01582) 489366. Fax: (01582) 457187. E-mail: info@ulsu.org.uk

GENERAL

For years, Luton has had a hard time living down the image of dropped aitches and having a local Vauxhall car factory as its most interesting feature. This perception is becoming increasingly outdated, however, and Luton is metamorphosing into a lively, growing place with 150 acres of pleasant greenery (winner of Britain in Bloom 97, *the highest accolade in the world, ever*), not far from the Chiltern hills and London (½ an hour by train). The University of Luton is now one of the *most exciting* features and sure is going some on the expansion front, having grown unrecognisably since 1976, when it became a college of higher education rather than a technical college. It became a university in 1993.

Sex ratio(M:F): 40%:60%
Full time u'grads: 6,386
Postgrads: 998
Ave course: 3yrs
Private school: 5%
Mature students: 45%
Disabled students: 1%

Founded: 1976
Part time: 1,478
Non-degree: 3,472
Ethnic: 30%
Flunk rate: 27.1%
Overseas students: 18%

ATMOSPHERE:
A high proportion of students are here simply because it's their local university and a good chunk had little choice in the matter, being sucked in through clearing. That said, once they find their feet, most seem quite happy with their lot, provided they see a degree course primarily as a means to a job. Everything else, especially politics, can disappear down the cracks in the concrete.

THE SITES:
Park Square: (main site) The harsh architecture of the Park Square site is rather appropriate to the utilitarian philosophy of the courses taught here, although it has been tempered somewhat by the very swish award-winning Learning Resources Centre.
Castle Street: (humanities) 5 minutes walk from the main site, this is another *not terribly attractive* example of 60s office block architecture, although it does house some *nifty* multimedia equipment.
Putteridge Bury: (management) 3 miles away, this is a *much more aesthetically pleasing site*, although much of it is devoted to conferences and research, so few undergraduates get to benefit (*typical*).

THE TOWN:
- Population: 167,300 • London: 28miles • Bedford: 25miles
- Birmingham: 80miles

Luton, which started as the centre of the hat and lace industry – *don't knock it* – is now a *busy* business town, not suffering the high unemployment that some are. It's the largest town in Bedfordshire, which doesn't say much since Bedford is just about the only competition. Nevertheless, it has *all the cosmopolitan paraphernalia* like shops, libraries, banks, markets and the rest in *plentiful* supply. *Worth a particular mention* are the *massive* modern Arndale Shopping Centre, right by the University and the Galaxy Centre, which offers music, TV and multimedia facilities, cinema, art gallery, restaurant and café.

TRAVEL:
Trains: Luton is the nearest station, 5 minutes walk from the University with trains to, among other places, London King's Cross

(£21.00), Bedford, Milton Keynes and east coast mainline services all the way to Edinburgh (£58.90).
Coaches: Green Line and National Express services (London £8, Birmingham £12).
Car: Luton is on the edge of the M1 at the junction where it splits with the A6 which goes straight through the town. The A1 is only 5 miles east and the end of the A5 is 2 miles south.
Air: Luton Airport is the home of budget airline Easyjet and offers inland and international services to Europe, Ireland and the USA.
Hitching: *Despite the good connections, it's easier to pick up the white lines on the road than pick up a lift in the Home Counties. It's none too safe either, but a few students try anyway.*
Local: Little 'hopper' buses scuttle round the town *reliably although not particularly cheaply* and not late. No local trains around the town, but an excellent link into London which students often use for a day trip. *However, the last train's all too early and easy to miss.*
Taxis: *Not cheap, but worth using at night because Luton's not too big or congested.*
Bicycles: *Although Luton is flat, not many students bike it. Maybe because about three heavy padlocks are needed to hang on to a bike for more than a week, but there's no denying it would be useful for the many students who don't live on site.*

CAREER PROSPECTS:
- Careers Service
- No of staff: 4 full/1 part
- Unemployed after 6mths: 1.6 %

FAMOUS ALUMNI:
Ian Dury, Sir David Plaston (industrialist), Paul Young (singer).

FURTHER INFO:
Prospectuses for undergrads, postgrads and part-time students, 'on course' newsletter, course leaflets, video and websites (Uni: www.luton.ac.uk and SU: www.ulsu.org.uk). Open days are held in February, April and July or in fact anytime if you make an appointment.

ACADEMIC

The last few years have seen a huge increase in degree students and expenditure of over £50Mn on buildings. The University is rated in the top 10 of the new universities for academic standards. There are various work-placement schemes (paid and un-paid) to help students offer practical skills to future employers as well as their studies.

staff/student ratio: 1:19
Range of points required for entrance: 240-180
Percentage accepted through clearing: 30%
Number of terms/semesters: 2
Length of terms/semesters: 15 wks
Research: 1.9

LIBRARIES:
- Books: 200,000
- Study places: 1,100

The main library is in the Learning Resources Centre at Park Square and *is listed by the Borough Council as a stop on the sightseeing tour of Luton.* There's also a smaller library at Putteridge Bury. *Major gripe, though, not enough books.*

COMPUTERS:
- Computer workstations: 800

The Learning Resource Centre houses many of the Uni's computers. Students lament the shortage of available computers.

ENTERTAINMENT

TOWN:
- Price of a pint of beer: £2 • Glass of wine: £1.60

Cinemas: The new Galaxy multiplex has 11 screens while the Cannon has 3.

Theatres: St George's Theatre (cap 256) plays host to local professional and amateur productions, occasional music and *even the RSC when on tour*. The Arts Centre has a small theatre studio, *a good events programme and a congenial atmosphere*.

Pubs: *Pubs have started waking up to the student trade.* Pushplugs: Yates; Dog & Donut; the Cock; Newt & Cucumber; Brewery Tap. Avoid Mr Bumbles.

Clubs/discos: *The Beach is popular, but can get rough at the weekend. The Zone is a better bet.*

Cabaret: Cabaret venue in Guildford Street.

Music venues: *The Arts Centre has a bit of everything,* especially jazz and minor league indie. The Beach has regular live bands, as do the Colliseum, Brannigans and Artezium. O'Shea's has live Irish bands free six nights a week.

Eating out: *The Arndale Centre has a wide variety of scoff stops and Leagrave Road has the best Indian restaurants in town. Arab and Caribbean cuisine are also popular.* pushplugs: Cork & Bull for good pub fayre; Brooks Café Bar.

Others: The new Galaxy complex has a cinema, bowling alley and food court. There's a Fair at Wardown Park, an annual Beer Festival in High Town (*a studenty area*).

UNIVERSITY:
- Price of a pint of beer: £1.50 • Glass of wine: £1.00

Bars: (3) *2 smallish, hot, loud and busy bars,* including the Subclub venue, and a quieter one. The main SU bar has just had a £100,000 refurb and the other two have had new sound-systems put in.

Cinema: Film society has weekly showings *veering between cult and mainstream.*

Clubs/discos/music venues: Swaying to sounds and moving to music 3 or 4 nights a week in the Subclub (cap 360): Fridays is Disco Inferno and Saturdays rotate between indie, dance and soul and swing. Recent live acts include: DJ Brandon Block, Atomic Kitten, EZ.

Food: The University has two refectories on Church St and Vicarage St and a restaurant. Mary's Coffee Bar *is popular for its value for money.* In the halls, for the few livers-in, there are canteens dishing up grub and the Union provides snack machines and titbits from behind the bar.

Others: The enormous May Ball claims to be the biggest in the country. Last year's effort lured 6,000 punters to the Luton Hoo stately home with acts such as Dodgy and Tim Westwood. Cabaret from the likes of Alan Parker once a month.

SOCIAL & POLITICAL

UNIVERSITY OF LUTON STUDENTS' UNION:
• 4 sabbaticals • Turnout at last ballot: 26% • NUS member
There are no political parties (by choice, not by policy), and specifically student issues such as Learning Resources Centre opening times take centre stage. The Union does an okay job with limited resources, especially on the ents front.

SU FACILITIES:
The Union has its own building, Europa House, right next to the Park Square building, containing bars, nightclub, photocopier, juke boxes, video games, pool tables, vending machines, function rooms, and minibus hire.

CLUBS (NON SPORTING):
Asian; Baha'i; Club Rev (dance); Hellenic; Hindu; Italian; Moving Image; Sikh; Student Action.

OTHER ORGANISATIONS:
Luton FM is the campus radio station while the SU magazine, 'L'Uni', comes out monthly. The Rag raised £2,000 recently – *not much, but every penny blah, blah.*

RELIGIOUS:
Ecumenical chaplaincy. Luton is abundantly furnished with places of worship including churches, a synagogue, 2 mosques, several Sikh and Buddhist temples.

PAID WORK:
The airport sometimes needs part-time staff. The Brook Street employment agency is on campus.

SPORTS

• Recent successes: football
The emphasis is on taking part and *pecs are flexed by a good few*. The University's own facilities are virtually negligible, but Vauxhall and Lucozade have recently laid on the use of recreational facilities for students and the public, *which has improved opportunity no end,* and Luton is now climbing the student sports league and were finalists last year. The students also have the use of the nearby Vauxhall training ground and sports facilities. Students could even bump into the odd Western Samoan team player they have been known to train here.

SPORTS FACILITIES:
At Park Square: fitness suite; gym; multi-gym; sauna and sun-bed. There are 4 sports centres in Luton, 6 swimming pools, a running track, 2 golf courses and a boating lake. At Luton Regional Sports Centre (a public leisure centre 15 minutes away by bus) the University has a club room and squash club and has arranged a scheme for using other facilities.

SPORTING CLUBS:
Aerobics; Boxing; Gaelic football; Kick Boxing; Terra Firma (Parachuting); Weight Training; Windsurfing.

ATTRACTIONS:
Luton's biggest sporting non-attraction are 'the Hatters' (Luton FC) who for years cheated with their plastic so-called 'pitch', until they were finally made to get rid of it and then started to slide down one division per season.

ACCOMMODATION

IN COLLEGE:
• Self-catering: 23% • Cost: £55-59 (40wks)
Availability: There are 20 halls in all, ranging from terraced houses to tower blocks. Most 1st years who want University accommodation can get it, provided they apply in time. The University also has a head tenancy scheme where it rents houses from landlords and lets them on to students, currently providing 391 places on better terms than the open market. Some single sex accommodation is also available. Security in halls has improved with CCTV and the launch of Campus Watch, a crime prevention and safety initiative.
Car parking: Limited parking, a permit is needed.

EXTERNALLY:
• Ave rent: £50
Availability: *For the moment, there's no shortage of appropriate housing around Luton, although the beginning of the year panic is becoming a regular 'mare. The best areas are High Town, Folly Hill, Park Town, New Town and the Town Centre, which are all within walking distance of the University. Bury Park (especially Crawley Rd) is not that safe.*
Housing help: The University Accommodation Office allocates the places in college and in the head tenancy scheme (see above) as well as providing vacancy lists and advice.

WELFARE

SERVICES:
• Lesbian & Gay Society • Mature SA • Overseas SA • Minibus
• Women's Officer
The University places considerable emphasis on its student support. Counselling and advice are available from the 12 full- and 2 part-time counsellors at the Student Advisory Service. The University has an on-site nurse from the NHS Health Centre 200 metres from Park Square. The Union also offers a *busy* advice service with 3 advisers. A minibus runs between all three campuses until 2.30am every night, 50p per journey.
Disabled: *The various new buildings take disabled students' needs into consideration, which is more than can be said for the older ones, although they are being adapted slowly.* A local sponsor with a huge heart has recently given the Uni several thousand smackers to improve facilities. A Disability Officer and Dyslexia Officer are available as are note-takers.

FINANCE:
• Access fund: £636,000 • Successful applications: 83%
There are several bursaries, scholarships and trust funds. Funds are also available for members of specific groups, eg. ethnic minorities, mature students, local students.

```
Huddersfield University is building a teaching
and accommodation block on the site of the
largest psychiatric hospital in Europe.
```

Photos

NATIONAL UNION OF STUDENTS

Students Union
Vauxhall College

AFFILIATED TO NUS 91/92

NAME DAVID EYRES
ADDRESS 149 GEORGE LANE
LONDON SE13 6HW
COURSE STUDIO SUB YEAR 1st
SIGNATURE
F

Magee see University of Ulster

University of Manchester

University of Manchester Institute of Science & Technology see UMIST

Manchester Metropolitan University

Metropolitan University see Leeds Metropolitan University

Metropolitan University see Manchester Metropolitan University

Middlesex University

Milton Keynes see De Monfort University

Moores University see Liverpool John Moores University

Moray House see University of Edinburgh

Magee

see University of Ulster

University of Manchester

University of Manchester, Oxford Road, Manchester, M13 9PL.
Tel: (0161) 275 2000.
Manchester University Students' Union, Oxford Road, Manchester, M13 9PR. Tel: (0161) 275 2930. Fax: (0161) 275 2936.
E-mail: info@umu.man.ac.uk

GENERAL

Welcome to the 25-hour party town, the battered but mad-for-it sprawl of Britain's second largest city and the capital of the North-West. It's a big place with a big student population. Including the surrounding towns of the hub, such as Salford, there are well over 50,000 higher education students living in Manchester and the University accounts for the lion's share. It's one of the biggest universities in the country with buildings spread around a campus about a mile from the city centre. The campus is surrounded by other colleges – UMIST, Manchester Metropolitan University, teaching hospitals and so on – which together form the largest educational complex in western Europe. The buildings themselves range from the grand Victorian main building to *drab* blocks from the 60s and 70s and then to the stark towers of *Thatcherite* architecture.

Sex ratio(M:F): 46%:54%	Founded: 1851
Full time u'grads: 16,836	Part time: 809
Postgrads: 3,762	Non-degree: 490
Ave course: 4yrs	Ethnic: 38%
Private school: 24%	Flunk rate: 8.5%
Mature students: 22%	Overseas students: 12%
Disabled students: 4%	

ATMOSPHERE:
The University is big enough and compact enough to give its students the best of both worlds: city life and a campus community. They're a vibrant and diverse bunch, who often seem to think of themselves as the archetypal student. Although facilities are top-rate, the sheer size and bustle of the place can put all but the most confident individuals into the shade. Relations with the locals are variable but there is safety in numbers if things get unpleasant.

BEING A STUDENT IN MANCHESTER:
Manchester's late 80s heyday as youth capital of the Universe is nowt but a dim, baggy-topped memory these days but the city is still buzzing like very few others and, it can still churn out music-makers and style-setters to trample over everyone else. A job's pretty handy (there are a few about but many hunters) because life ain't cheap here. Although not on a London scale of urban extortion, there are too many temptations to look after the pennies and the pounds end up playing follow the leader. However, Manchester has very little of the crowded loneliness of London or its impersonality. The people are friendly (Paul Calf isn't representative of all locals) and, among students, local pride is a virus. At the end of term, students from the south frequently return (to their mothers' horror) sporting 'Born in the North – Die in the North' T-shirts. While the city sprawls for about 10 miles in all directions, its centre is relatively small which makes getting out and about a cruise. With so much to do around town, there's no excuse for a Saturday night on the sofa. A bar or a club on the other side of town is only 20 minutes walk and, since the student residential areas tend to be inner-city districts, even a minicab home won't be bank-busting. At the very core, indeed, the hard core of the Manchester Scene is ecstasy. This and other, harder, drugs are readily available in the clubs, pubs and on the streets of Manchester. Manchester students' attitudes to drugs obviously vary enormously between individuals and although use of E, acid (LSD), cocaine and dope (cannabis) is perhaps more widespread than the norm, the pressure to partake is small and those old standbys of cigarettes and alcohol are still far more common.

THE CITY:
- Population: 2,454,800 • London: 167 miles
- Liverpool: 28 miles • Birmingham: 72 miles

Manchester, although it's been around since the days *when Caesar took his stroll in the forum*, was really built out of cotton during the Industrial Revolution. Out of the money from cotton, that is. *Industry flooded Manchester and the canals drained it*, making the city one of the all-time boom towns. But it didn't last and Manchester found depression pretty depressing, scarring the city with slums. Some of these, such as Moss Side and Burnage, remain pretty bleak, but many areas have been redeveloped and its chequered history has left Manchester rich in culture. Being a student here is to be rocking in the free world with every facility under the sun, from theatres to Afflecks, from museums to Old Trafford.

TRAVEL:
Trains: Not one but two mainline stations, Manchester Piccadilly for London and the South, and Manchester Victoria for just about everywhere else. Routes go all over, including London (£29.70), Birmingham (£14.90), Edinburgh (£36.65) and more.
Coaches: All sorts of coach services to, among most other places, London (£15.75), Birmingham (£8), Edinburgh (£15) and beyond.
Car: From the north, M6 (then M61 or M62), A6 or M66; from the east, M62, A58, A62; from the south, M6, A6, A523, A34; and from Wales, the M56. *Parking may well be a problem in central Manchester, but, for the lazy and environmentally carefree, a car doesn't go amiss.*
Air: Manchester Airport is one of the UK's big ones – flights all over the world as well as inland.
Hitching: *Not possible from central Manchester, but quite good on arterial routes out of the city.*
Local: Manchester has a major bus network, running all over town, especially up and down Oxford Road. Trains are a quicker alternative, especially for the outskirts. The Metrolink tram service trundles around helpfully.

Taxis: Manchester's centre, being relatively small, means taxi trips are a viable resort. The black cabs which screech to a halt as you hail them are a lot more expensive than the private traders who are only supposed to pick up phone callers and drop-ins.
Bicycles: *Manchester's quite bike-friendly (flat with a fair few bicycle lanes), but theft is rife. A mountain bike will identify you as a drug pusher, especially if you're about 12.*

CAREER PROSPECTS:
• Careers Service • No of staff: 10 full/7 part
• Unemployed after 6mths: 3%
The careers service operates jointly with UMIST and is open office hours all year round.

SPECIAL FEATURES:
• Being so close, Manchester University has strong ties, both official and unofficial, with other local institutions, particularly Manchester Metropolitan University and UMIST. Students join each others' clubs and societies, use each others' facilities and go to each others' ents, toilets, beds and therapy sessions.
• Manchester degrees are also awarded at the Institute of Advanced Nursing Education in London, Stockport College of Further & Higher Education and University College, Warrington.

FAMOUS ALUMNI:
Sir Rhodes Boyson (ex-Con MP); Nick Brown MP (Lab); Anthony Burgess (writer); Adrian Edmonson, Ben Elton, Rik Mayall (comedians); Anna Ford (broadcaster); Peter Maxwell Davies (composer); Austin Mitchell MP (Lab); Sir Maurice Oldfield (MI6); Christabel Pankhurst (suffragette); Justin Robertson (DJ); Louise Wener (Sleeper).

FURTHER INFO:
Prospectuses for undergrads and postgrads. Alternative prospectus from the SU (£3.20). Website: (www.man.ac.uk). SU website: www.umu.man.ac.uk

ACADEMIC

staff/student ratio: 1:14
Range of points required for entrance: 340-240
Percentage accepted through clearing: n/a
Number of terms/semesters: 2
Length of terms/semesters: 16wks
Research: 5.1

LIBRARIES:
- Books: 3,750,000 • Study places: 2,500

Despite the vast acreage of reading material, there's still a panic run on valuable books around exam time.

COMPUTERS:
- Computer workstations: 1,000

Computer provision is more than adequate.

ENTERTAINMENT

CITY:
- Price of a pint of beer: £1.50 • Glass of wine: £1.30

Manchester is a cultural jamboree, bringing together the brightest and the best in theatre, food, nightlife and, most *recently, music to this corner of the country. In fact, you could say the city's a bit of an Oasis.*

Cinemas: A multiplicity of multiplexes and sundry cinemas, everything from the 8-screen Salford Quays multiplex and the cool and trendy Cornerhouse (3 screens) which shows many an arty flick. With a gallery and café thrown in, *it's a poser's paradise.*

Theatres: The old Cotton Exchange is now the nationally renowned Royal Exchange Theatre - some of the country's best shows for under a fiver on student standbys. The Palace and Opera House do good pantos while the Green Room is more experimental.

Pubs: *Manchester has historic pubs in the truest tradition of the working men's dive but there's everything from real ales to obscure liqueurs to weak lemon drinks. If you must be a poseur, pose in Manto and Dry 201 but, for those living somewhere in reality, Pushplugs go to the central Rocket Bar, Jabes Clegg, the Queen Of Hearts (Fallowfield), Retro Bar and Joshua Brooks (both near <u>UMIST</u>).*

Clubs/discos: *A student night out is often a euphemism for dancing and a curry and the only problem is listing the best bop spots. The music is alive and the clubs come and go – The Hacienda, alas, continues only in spirit. Read 'City Life' for the latest. Pushplugs: Temptation at Home (Weds); the Rock 'n' Roll Bar (indie); Hallelujah at the Paradise Factory; and Thursday night is student night at the hysterically tacky Royale. Check for the cheaper NUS-only nights and watch also the flyers for the alighting points of fly-by-night clubs.*

Music venues: The Manchester Evening News Arena lures the hugest names, *if binocular-rock's your game.* The Apollo, by most towns' standards, would be a best bet, however, all over town there are live venues of every size. Among the many others: The Academy (run by Manchester University SU); Boardwalk (indie); Jilly's (rock); Band on the Wall (rootsy); Chorlton Irish Club (folk); P J Bells (jazz); The Bridgewater Hall and the Royal Northern College of Music (classical). Many of these clubs also stage live bands.

Cabaret: *Manchester is a breeding ground for stand-up talent. Live comedy lives and is usually high octane fun. Bernard Manning is a local boy. Well, the exception that proves the rule, eh?*
Eating out: *OK, there may not be many places in the running for the Michelin Guide but if you want it good, quick, tasty and cheap, you've come to the right place.* Chinatown (the oldest in Europe) is stacked with noodleries and Rusholme has half a mile of end-to-end Indian restaurants. There's the usual artery-full of kebab and burger dens but the *Pushplugs go to: Generation X; Amigo's (Oxford Road, Mexican); Barca (tapas); Sangam, Shezan (Indian); Green Room (hip veggie with slack service); Dalton Café (greasy spoon and then some).*
Others: *Millionaire students, or at least lucky or stupid ones, will, no doubt, not want to miss Manchester's many casinos.* The more cultured will find many a fond hour to spend in some of the city's splendid galleries (The City Gallery, The Cornerhouse and The Whitworth). The Lowry Centre has a theatre and gallery with some of LS Lowry's most famous paintings. As for shopping, head for the Trafford Centre (the mega-mall of the north-west).

UNIVERSITY:
• Price of a pint of beer: £1.35   • Glass of wine: £1.05
The Union itself is one of Manchester's main entertainment venues – no mean feat round here.
Bars: (3) The Hop & Grape pub (cap 300) at the top of the SU building is also a music venue. The Main Debating Hall (cap 400) and of course, the Academy (cap 2000) also have bars.
Theatres: (2) The University's Contact Theatre (revamped to the tune of £4.45m) has its own resident professional company, but also provides an *impressive and versatile venue* for regular student productions and recent productions at the Edinburgh Fringe *have been very successful.* The Drama Department has its own studio theatre (Stephen Joneo Studio) and there is a drama festival featuring student plays.
Cinemas: The University has its own excellent film club for blockbusters and cult/foreign faves, 2-3 times a week.
Clubs/discos: There are 2 or 3 nights a week, chart and nostalgia efforts such as Tuesdays' Club Trop (80s), with occasional guest nights (eg Megadog, Paul Oakenfold) for *more serious clubbers.*
Music venues: In addition to The Academy, *one of the top live venues in the north west*, live bands also feature at the Union's Hop & Grape pub (300), the Burlington Rooms (150) and the MDH (the Union's main hall, 450). Recent band appearances: Arabstrap, David Bowie, Mel C, Embrace, Faithless, Robbie Williams, Kula Shaker, Beck, Mansun, Reef, Jamiroquai, Kenickie, Divine Comedy, Pavement, Cardigans, the Shirehorses, slipknot, Space, Chemical Brothers, Bis, Lemonheads, The Orb, Placebo, Boo Radleys, CJ Bolland, Super Furry Animals, 3 Colours Red and that's just a small selection. Imagine, 100 gigs in the first semester alone.
Cabaret: Occasional stand-up.
Food: The University Food Court and the SU coffee bar provide an *unimaginative* selection of burgers, sandwiches and chips *but portions are substantial and nobody's complained about the value for money.* The Café Express in the Union does light lunches. The bars also do grub.
Others: *Among the other delights are* quizzes, multi-cultural events and all-night balls.

SOCIAL & POLITICAL

MANCHESTER UNIVERSITY STUDENTS' UNION:
• 6 sabbaticals • Turnout at last ballot: 12% • NUS member
The Union is well organised and has left-wing tendencies which are *probably stronger than the overall view of the student body. The punters, however, are happy enough with the Union as it is, so long as it keeps on offering the bevvy of brilliant facilities in the Steve Biko Building as the Union Building is officially called – well, it's more original than Nelson Mandela.*

SU FACILITIES:
In the *impressively big* art deco Union Building there are: a general shop; a bookshop (second-hand); an opticians; travel agency; hairdresser; customised night clubs and discos; photocopiers; coffee and snack bar; 2 burger bars; 2 bars and a pub (with satellite TV); Barclays and Halifax cashpoints; taxi freephone; video, vending and games machines; TV room; meeting and function rooms; societies resource centre; showers; sauna and solarium; photo booth.

CLUBS (NON SPORTING):
How long have you got? Students are also entitled to join UMIST clubs and societies and vice versa. Active performance; Anti-bloodsports; Bangladesh; Buddhist; Campaign for Free Education; Chamber Music; Chinese; Cocktail; Cuba; Debating; Expedition; Japanese; Meditation; Spanish. If your own particular passion isn't covered there's probably enough people around to find a few fellow fetishists to set something up.

OTHER ORGANISATIONS:
A new paper 'Student Direct' is up and running, and if that's not enough for the student journo, there are plenty of other opportunities including a city-wide radio station. The Manchester Universities Charities Association employs a full-time co-ordinator. Rag pulled in over £70,000 one year. A community action group does nice things for kids and OAPs.

RELIGIOUS:
• 3 chaplains (Anglican, RC, Jewish)
The University has both Anglican and Catholic chapels and a Muslim prayer room. *The huge Jewish Society is social as much as religious and is a strong political force.* The city caters for most creeds' needs: local cathedrals, churches, temples, mosques, synagogues and almost all the usual places of worship.

PAID WORK:
Because Manchester's such a big centre for entertainment there are lots of part-time jobs in bars, clubs and restaurants – but, of course, there are lots of people chasing them. Still, the situation's better than in some other parts of the North-West. The Careers Service advertises temporary vacancies.

SPORTS

• Recent successes: yachting, women's rugby
Quite apart from *excellent* facilities (not 1, but 2 sports centres), the University's size means more than a fair share of sporting stars. *But choice abounds giving even the hardiest couch potato the chance to uproot and branch out into a sprouting of sports.* There is a charge for the sports centres *but its mini (like pence).*

SPORTS FACILITIES:
On campus there's the McDougall Centre offering, a sports hall, a small gym, multigym, 4 squash courts, 2 fives courts, rifle range, climbing wall, sauna, solarium and outside basketball/netball court. A small admission fee is charged. There are also facilities at a variety of other centres. The Wythenshawe Ground is the largest: 60 acres of playing fields (10 acres more, shared with UMIST, are within 4 miles from the campus), 6 tennis courts and a pavilion. Firs Athletic Ground at Fallowfield in South Manchester has 31 acres of playing fields, 8 tennis courts, an all-weather pitch and a large pavilion, all near the main student halls of residence. Nearby, the Fallowfield Stadium has amenities for track and field events and a soccer pitch. The Armitage Centre provides a sports hall, a climbing room, sauna and solarium, 2 martial arts dojos, table tennis and a fitness room, all for a small charge. The new Commonwealth pool (the Manchester Aquatics Centre) has been built in the middle of Oxford Road (with fund from Manchesters 4 universities) and is home to the universities swimming teams. The University is also hosting judo, squash and wrestling events for the 2002 Commonwealth Games.

SPORTING CLUBS:
Aikido; Jiu Jitsu; Karting; Korfball; Nin Jitsu; Rifle; Speleology (caving); Table Tennis; Ten Pin Bowling; Water-Polo; Yachting.

ATTRACTIONS:
Can you identify 3 football teams with swear-words in their names? Answer: Arsenal, Scunthorpe and *F***in' Manchester United. Real Mancs (like Oasis) tend to support the less successful, but less-despised Man City.* For Test and County Cricket, there's Old Trafford and golf at the Golf Club. Basketball (The Giants) and ice hockey (The Storm) at the Manchester Evening News Arena, speedway at Broadhurst Park, rugby at Swinton, Salford and Trafford Borough, volleyball at Sale. Manchester is hosting the Commonwealth Games in 2002 and the resulting facilities, such as the new Olympic sized swimming pool, are pretty special. The Manchester Aquatics Centre offers lovely discounts for student water-babies.

ACCOMMODATION

IN COLLEGE:
- Catered: 17% • Cost: £60-105 (31-51wks)
- Self-catering: 23% • Cost: £46-69 (31-52wks)

Availability: The University and UMIST bundle all their accommodation in one hat and pull it out together. As a result, the options vary from small houses owned by the University and shared by as few as 8 students to massive complexes of flats and rooms, providing over 1,000 places in the case of Owens Park. All 1st years who want to can live in halls (with less than 1% sharing) and there's space for plenty of other years as well. *The demand exceeds the supply, but the opportunities are better than most places.* Out of 14 halls – all within 2½ miles of the campus – 1 is all male (156 places in Ashburne Hall), one is for women only (131 places in St. Anselm) and in all, only about 150 first years have to share a room. *Apart from this, just about everything depends on the individual hall and the variety is broad: fabulous facilities to bare necessities (usually good, though).* Some have car parking, though charges vary, but *most accommodation is very central and within easy walking distance of* the campus. CCTV and entry-phones make it hard to get in if you've lost your keys.

EXTERNALLY:
• Ave rent: £38
Availability: *It's not too difficult to find housing without resorting to damp-ridden dives and rents are rarely extortionate. Fallowfield, Victoria Park and Withington are the studey ghettos. Didsbury is a bit more suburban but quite accessible. Rusholme can be quite rough but is improving. Hulme and Moss Side should be treated with caution, although some hardy souls do settle there and rumour has it that things are getting better here too.*
Housing help: The University Accommodation Office offers vacancy lists, emergency housing and help with landlord problems. Manchester Student Homes, run in association with UMIST and Manchester Metropolitan University, can lend a hand.

WELFARE

SERVICES:
• Creche • Nightline • Mature SA • Overseas SA
• Lesbian Gay & Bisexual Society • Postgrad SA • Minibus
• Women's Officer • Self-defence classes

The Union's Advice Centre is *extremely effective* and is one of the students' main sources of welfare support. Its Welfare sabbatical, 2 professional advisers and weekly legal sessions will this year see over 10,000 students. The University also runs a counselling service employing trained counsellors and a health centre for students. *The Union has a particularly positive attitude to gays, lesbians and bisexuals, who are a powerfully vocal force amongst the students. (Manchester as a whole is a bit of a gay mecca).*

Women: The Union has a strong policy (often promoting positive discrimination) on women's issues and representation. Attack alarms are provided.

Disabled: Some ramps around campus and lifts in many buildings (including the Union), but, *generally, access really isn't up to scratch, especially considering how good other facilities are.* There is a study skills room with dyslexia software and tuition. Also some dyslexia software on the network.

FINANCE:
• Access fund: £902,642 • Successful applications: 1,498
In future the University will distribute the access fund by giving smaller amounts to a larger number of applicants. The Union lends up to £100 (interest-free) in emergency cases. They say that no one will be turned away. The Uni also gives short-term loans to students with cash-flow problems (*everybody then?*) repayable after six to eight weeks, with no interest.

University of Manchester Institute of Science & Technology

see UMIST

403 Manchester Metropolitan

Manchester Metropolitan University

- *Formerly Manchester Polytechnic*

Manchester Metropolitan University, All Saints, Oxford Road, Manchester, M15 6BH.
Tel: (0161) 247 2000. Fax: (0161) 247 6390.
E-mail: prospectus@mmu.ac.uk
MMU Students' Union, 99 Oxford Road, Manchester, M1 7EL.
Tel: (0161) 273 1162. Fax: (0161) 273 7237.
E-mail: mmsu@mmu.ac.uk

GENERAL

The main cluster of Manchester Metropolitan University at the All Saints sites is centred on the biggest educational complex in western Europe, which also includes the Manchester University and UMIST. There are, however, further sites along the A34, in the Didsbury area and, some distance out of the city, in Crewe. The University was originally Manchester Poly, which was in turn set up in 1970 from a number of smaller colleges.

Sex ratio(M:F): 41%:59%	Founded: 1970
Full time u'grads: 17,111	Part time: 2,268
Postgrads: 1,668	Non-degree: 5,268
Ave course: 3yrs	Ethnic: 19%
Private school: n/a	Flunk rate: 18.4%
Mature students: 18%	Overseas students: 6%
Disabled students: 3%	

ATMOSPHERE:
MMU is a pretty vibrant environment being part of a huge student village. Many students admit to picking the place for the city's party-till-you-puke atmosphere, but nearly half the students are returners to education and some feel that entertainments are aimed too specifically at the young, groovy and beautiful element.

THE SITES:
The Business School: ½ mile from All Saints and with 4,400 students, it's one of the largest business schools in the UK.
John Dalton: Based in Chester Street, 100 yards from the All Saints sites, 5,500 students in the science engineering and technology departments do cool stuff with petri dishes and capacitors and all that gubbins.
Geoffrey Manton: (3,500 students) ½ a mile from All Saints, various Humanities and Social Science departments are sited here.
Hollings: (1,700 students) The clothing, food and hospitality & tourism management courses are based here in Fallowfield, a 3-mile bus ride from All Saints. There's a training restaurant run by students.
Didsbury: Nearly 4,000 students in the community studies, law and education faculty are based here, about 5 miles from the city centre. *It's a leafy site with lively* restaurants and bars and *good* public transport to All Saints.

Elizabeth Gaskell: (3,500 students) About 1 mile from the main site, psychology, speech pathology and health care are taught here and more law and community studies. Walking distance to the main site is (10-15 minutes).

Crewe: (3,300 students) 28 miles south-west of Manchester, we find business studies and trainee teachers.

Alsager: This site is about 34 miles from Manchester, near Stoke-on-Trent (see Staffordshire University), with 1,592 students on a variety of arts, humanities and sports science courses. *Despite coach trips to Manchester, students at these last two sites don't really feel like part of the MMU experience and those applying to the University for the bright lights should check where they're going to be based; Crewe and Alsager are less than dazzling.*

THE CITY: see University of Manchester

TRAVEL: see University of Manchester

CAREER PROSPECTS:

- Careers Service • No of staff: 5 full/4 part
- Unemployed after 6mths: 5%

FAMOUS ALUMNI:
Terry Christian (ex-'Word' presenter and Oasis biographer); Bernhard Hill, David Threfall, Julie Walters (actors); Steve Coogan, John Thompson (comedians); Mick Hucknall (Simply Red soul dwarf); LS Lowry (painter); Min Patel (cricketer); Bryan Robson (footballer).

FURTHER INFO:
Prospectuses covering undergrad, postgrad, professional and 'post-experience' courses; also a website (www.mmu.ac.uk and www.mmsu.com).

ACADEMIC

staff/student ratio: 1:18
Range of points required for entrance: 280-60
Percentage accepted through clearing: n/a
Number of terms/semesters: 3
Length of terms/semesters: 12wks
Research: 2.8

LIBRARIES:
- Books: 1,000,000 • Study places: 3,420

There are 7 libraries in all, including those at Crewe and Alsager.

COMPUTERS:
- Computer workstations: 2,500

Computers tend to get clogged although things are improving and students make use of Manchester University's even more generous provision.

> Surrey Rag covered the University's geodesic dome in red sheets for Comic Relief, creating the world's largest red nose.

ENTERTAINMENT

CITY: see University of Manchester

UNIVERSITY:
• Price of a pint of beer: £1.00 • Glass of wine: £1.30
Bars: (4) The bars in the main All Saints building are *large, noisy, popular* and open from 11.30am until chucking-out/falling-over time. There's a smaller, quieter affair at Didsbury as well as facilities at Crewe and Alsager.
Theatre/cinema: The Horniman Theatre is based at Didsbury. Performance students at Crewe have their own studio. A mix of 3 films per week keep 'em cinematographically sussed.
Clubs/discos: 3 or 4 times a week, it's club night in the K-two bar (cap 900 and revamped to the tune of £92K; adm £2-£3, mainly indie, chart and retro) in the Union's main building. Revival offers cheese galore, Shebang has pop and the groovy Soul Vibe gives you alternative drum 'n' base. Gay-Two has the longest running gay night in the country – 21 years (not all in one go).
Music venues: K-two is also the site for gigs including Eagle Eye Cherrie, Trevor Nelson, Phats and Small, the Chemical Brothers, Dreem Team and Space. MMU students also slope off to Manchester University for their live kicks.
Food: The University Refectory is open 11am-3pm but the SU coffee bar *has a more interesting selection and more sensible opening hours.*
Other: Academic departments have their own balls and the annual Athletic Union bash is popular. Craig Charles *played here as well, so he could get a full house of every bloody university in the world in his own private bingo game.* Thursday night is comedy night in association with local comedy clubs.

SOCIAL & POLITICAL

MMU STUDENTS' UNION:
• 7 sabbaticals • Turnout at last ballot: 5½% • NUS member
The Union's main building on Oxford Road has variously been named after Nelson Mandela, Martin Luther King and Bruce Forsyth, *which gives some idea of the level of political commitment round these parts. Party political allegiances aren't that strong and the only thing that gets the students really worked up is money (or lack of it).*

SU FACILITIES:
The Union has facilities on three sites. In the main building there are two bars, two cafés, travel agency, shop, Barclays and Link cash machines, a bakery, vending and games machines, pool tables, photo booth, launderette, TV lounge, 2 minibuses, function rooms and recycling facilities.

CLUBS (NON SPORTING):
Arts & galleries; Capital; Dechen Buddhist; Muslim Heritage; Role-playing; Sikh.

OTHER ORGANISATIONS:
'Pulp' (no, not them) is the award-winning student mag (with a sabbatical editor) and the Athletics Union has its own weekly bulletin. 'Student Direct' is a new publication covering the whole of Manchester (not literally, of course).

RELIGIOUS:
The multi-faith chaplaincy for anyone seeking spiritual solace.

PAID WORK: see University of Manchester
The student jobshop 'Steam' has close links with local job networks.

SPORTS

- Recent successes: tennis, badminton

As with most things at MMU, keeping up with course work and having a quick half in the bar tends to take precedence over busting a gut on the track, court or pitch but there are a few brave souls prepared to strain the odd ligament in pursuit of laurels.

SPORTS FACILITIES:
There are sports halls and Sugden sports centre and at All Saints. Didsbury has a sports hall, squash and tennis courts and weight training and is a joint venture with UMIST. There is also a sports hall and astroturf at Alsager. The best outdoor facilities, however, are at the Crewe & Alsager sites, where there are 32 acres of playing fields and an outdoor swimming pool. You can even get to play on hallowed turf (for some) at Man City's Platt Lane Football Training Centre.

SPORTING CLUBS:
Aikido; Aerobics; Floorball; Hung Kuen; Jiu Jitsu; KSBO; Links; Mountaineering; Rowing; Rugby League; Ski & Snowboard; Surf; Ultimate Frisbee; Walking; Women's Football & Rugby.

ATTRACTIONS: see University of Manchester

ACCOMMODATION

IN COLLEGE:
- Catered: 4% • Cost: £70-73 (34wks)
- Self-catering: 10% • Cost: £45-60 (40-44wks)

Bearing in mind the proportion of locals, who are mostly set up elsewhere, things aren't as bad as the stats might appear, since many live in Manchester's other universities' halls. Generally students are impressed with the quality and value of halls. CCTV, some entry-phones and night porters watch their flocks.

EXTERNALLY: see University of Manchester
Housing help: The Accomodation & Welfare Office keeps vacancy lists, checks properties and contracts and attempts to resolve disputes. There is a housing service run by UMIST, Manchester Metropolitan and the University of Manchester.

WELFARE

SERVICES:
- Creche • Nightline • Lesbian & Gay Society • Mature SA
- Minibus • Women's Officer • Self-defence classes

In the case of medical emergencies or more moderate malaise, students can rush to the University's Health Centre at All Saints or the daily clinics at Broomhurst Hall, Didsbury and Loxford Hall. There are 3 full-time counsellors and 2 at Crewe and Alsager, which also have their own medical facilities. The University also employs a Learning Skills Co-ordinator and learning support for returners to education.

Women: The Women's Officer is a sabbatical post and there are *regular activity-packed* Women's Weeks.
Disabled: Not only are there ramps and lifts in most places and a Disability Adviser, but the disabled access policy has genuinely helped. *Didsbury and Elizabeth Gaskill can prove awkward for disabled access.* A guideline publication is produced specially for students and applicants with disabilities and the SU has a specialist officer. *Other universities take note.*

FINANCE:
- Access fund: £1,076,881 • Successful applications: 1,428

The SU can give loans of up to £75 (or higher in exceptional circumstances), but they want the money back by the end of the year, thank you.

Metropolitan University
see Leeds Metropolitan University

Metropolitan University
see Manchester Metropolitan University

Middlesex University

- **Formerly Middlesex Polytechnic**

Middlesex University, White Hart Lane, London, N17 8HR.
Tel: (020) 8411 5000. Fax: (020) 8411 5649.
E-mail: admissions@mdx.ac.uk
Middlesex University Students' Union, Trent Park, Bramley Road, London, N14 4YZ. Tel: (020) 8362 6450. Fax: (020) 8440 5944.

GENERAL

Middlesex used to be a county, now it only really exists as a postal district, a cricket team and an abstract band down the western side of London, which *roly-poly* TV starman Russell Grant is campaigning to return to county status. *The location of Middlesex University is equally non-specific.* It's based on 6 major and 3 minor teaching 'campuses', 4 Hospitals and several one-off buildings throughout London. There's also the Bedford campus which used to be misleadingly known as the London College of Dance. The London sites range from White Hart Lane campus – an urban, industrial area – to Trent Park – a series of blocks on a campus in country grounds around an old manor house, 15 miles from Central London. Maintaining the dance motif, one minor site is in an old house in Golders Green that belonged to Anna Pavlova, the famous ballerina and pudding.

```
Led Zeppelin played their first gig at
Surrey University.
```

Middlesex

Sex ratio(M:F): 40%:60%
Full time u'grads: 12,442
Postgrads: 1,028
Ave course: 4yrs
Private school: n/a
Mature students: 41%
Disabled students: 2.5%

Founded: 1973
Part time: 1,130
Non-degree: 4,545
Ethnic: 40%
Flunk rate: 22.2%
Overseas students: 20%

ATMOSPHERE:
Having lots of mature students puts a different emphasis on things and being so spread out leads to a lack of cohesion between sites. Students, especially from Bound's Green and Hendon, are loyal to their own campus rather than to the University as a whole. With facilities all over the place, it's hard to know what's available and, once discovered, it can be a hassle getting to it.

THE SITES:

Bounds Green: (2,034 – computing, environmental, business) *It feels like a degree factory in the ugliest building in the world.*
Cat Hill: (1,924 – textiles, product design, electronic arts) In Barnet, facilities include a bar and a multigym.
Enfield: (3,907 – social science, health studies) includes ents venue the Forum.
Health 'Campus': (2,097 full-time equivalent – nursing) Teaching facilities spread across 4 North London hospitals *(so it can hardly be called a campus).*
Hendon: (4,958 – business school) The largest site in terms of numbers, 13 miles from Tottenham.
Ivy House: (163 – Drama) Due to close by Autumn 2002.
Quicksilver Place: (277 – fine art).
Tottenham: (2,924 – humanities, business, law) The main admin site *(if there is such a thing).*
Trent Park: (2,924 – arts, education, humanities) *The main SU site and the only place the students seem really satisfied.*

THE CITY: see University of London

TRAVEL: see University of London
Car: *Parking is slightly easier than in other universities closer to the centre of London, but it's still not really necessary.*

CAREER PROSPECTS:
- Careers Service • No of staff: 4 full/3 part
- Unemployed after 6mths: 7%

Careers advisers travel between sites.

FAMOUS ALUMNI:
Adam Ant (singer); Ray Davies (Kinks mainman); Nick Harvey MP (LibDem); James Herbert (novelist); Alison Lloyd and Jomo Platt (Ally Capellino fashion house); Anish Kapoor (artist); Matthew Marsden (Corrie); Helen Mirren (actress); Omar (singer); Stephen Seargeant (sailor); Rianna Scipio (TV presenter); Vivienne Westwood (designer); Johnny Vegas (funny man); Arabella Weir ('does my bum look big in this?').

FURTHER INFO:
Prospectuses for undergrads and postgrads. Rough Cuts for Students. Video. There's also a website (www.mdx.ac.uk).

ACADEMIC

Middlesex was the first university to offer a degree course in herbal medicine.

staff/student ratio: 1:24
Range of points required for entrance: 240-160
Percentage accepted through clearing: n/a
Number of terms/semesters: 2
Length of terms/semesters: 15 wks
Research: 2.9

LIBRARIES:
- Books: 600,000 • Study places: 1,650

COMPUTERS:
- Computer workstations: 1,850

ENTERTAINMENT

IN LONDON: see University of London

UNIVERSITY:
- Price of a pint of beer: £1.70 • Glass of wine: £1.35

Bars: 4 are run by the SU on separate campuses, 3 others by the University. The Enfield set-up is the biggest, with a combined capacity of 800 across 2 bars. There are others at Trent Park, Tottenham and Bounds Green.

Theatres/cinema: The Simmonds Theatre (cap 400) is the larger of two. Middlesex has one of the largest drama departments in Europe, but it's currently suffering serious cutbacks. 1 mainstream film a week.

Clubs/discos/music venues: The 3 venues offer entertainments ranging from weekly discos and dance events to talent shows and comedy nights.

Food: Most catering outlets are now operated by Scholarest an external contractor. *The canteen at Tottenham leaves a lot to be desired.*

Others: *Middlesex is big on balls.* The Summer extravaganza usually lasts 36 hours and last year's Freshers' do took place in The Forum at Enfield with appearances by the likes of Dannii Minogue, Steps and Faithless. Lures to lubrication in the *often under-used* bars include Bar FTSE where the beer prices fluctuate with demand.

SOCIAL & POLITICAL

MIDDLESEX UNIVERSITY STUDENTS' UNION:
- 6 sabbaticals • Turnout at last ballot: 2% • NUS member

The SU is about services, representation and ents, rather than tearing down the barricades and guillotining the University administration. They've suffered for this though: the inter-site bus service was stopped last year and the students are a little annoyed about this, especially as the chance they had to prevent it through the Union was squandered through non-attendance.

SU FACILITIES:
The SU has facilities on all campuses. There are 5 bars, 3 snack bars, 6 shops, a printing service, games machines, photo booths,

function rooms, prayer room, art shop, DJ equipment, TV lounges and a minibus for hire. The Trent Park facilities have been recently refurbished. And a sculpture of Posh Spice, made of Dairylea triangles. Also all ents are SU run, *prolific and very good*. By the way, we lied about the sculpture.

CLUBS (NON SPORTING):
Life-drawing; Malaysian; Millennium; Poetry, Traditional Chinese Medicine.

OTHER ORGANISATIONS:
The SU magazine is called 'Mud' and is *better than the previous efforts*. A successful 4-week radio jaunt into FM means it might happen again one day. Soon. Ish.

RELIGIOUS:
There is an ecumenical chaplaincy based at the Tottenham campus. At Bound's Green and Hendon (large Jewish community), there is a Muslim prayer room in college, an Islamic society, a Jewish society.
Religion in London: see University of London.

PAID WORK:
Apart from bar and ents work, the SU has work for about 100 students, including decorating and so on during the holidays. The national headquarters of the Small Press Association are at the Tottenham campus. There are about 5,000 members and work placements often come up for students.
Paid Work in London: see University of London.

SPORTS

• Recent successes: table tennis, karate, volleyball.
The same old problems of divergent sites and students with other things on their minds means that Middlesex is never going to be kicking serious butt, although they're not sofa spuds either. Karate champions for the last 15 years, *apparently. No arguments*.

SPORTS FACILITIES:
The University has 5 sports halls and 3 playing fields. There are indoor and outdoor tennis courts, a sauna, 6 multigyms, swimming pools, a hockey and an all-weather pitch, real tennis courts at Hendon and climbing walls at Bounds Green. Recent expansion has been helped by Lottery funding.

SPORTING CLUBS:
Table tennis.

ATTRACTIONS:
Spurs at White Hart Lane and various sports, including ice skating at Alexandra Palace.

ACCOMMODATION

IN COLLEGE:
• Self-catering: 10% • Cost: £58-69 (40wks)
Availability: There's accommodation for 75% of 1st years. There are 7 halls on separate campuses not far from most of the teaching sites. Kitchens are shared between up to 14 students. *There have been cases where students have had to live at one site when their course is taught at another. Doh.* CCTV is watching over the entry-phones and night porters.

Car parking: Parking is free with a permit, *although there's not enough.*

EXTERNALLY: see University of London
• Ave rent: £60

Availability: *Most students must find their own housing and a lot live at home. It's not difficult to find somewhere decent since the sites are far enough from the city centre. Palmers Green is popular and convenient. Wood Green and Turnpike Lane are also handy.*

Housing help: The University runs an accommodation service which produces a vacancies sheet, housing database, lists of recommended landlords and they can give legal help and advice.

WELFARE

SERVICES:
• Creche • Lesbian & Gay Society • Overseas SA • Postgrad SA

Services include various counselling groups with 1 full- and 9 part-time counsellors. There is a parents' group, 3 health advisors. The creche, which caters for littl'uns 6 months to 5 year-olds may get privatised. *Poor provision for bewildered overseas students has left some feeling a bit lost.*

Disabled: *Major improvements in access over the last 4 years, mainly facilitated by the very impressive Able Centre. Induction loops installed, dyslexia support.*

FINANCE:
• Hardship fund: £1,113,787 • Successful applications: 1,114

Scholarships, loans and part-time fee remission.

Milton Keynes

see De Monfort University

Moores University

see Liverpool John Moores University

Moray House

see University of Edinburgh

'What's wrong with the University of Oxford? President Clinton went there and failed to inhale; Tony Blair didn't even put his fingers to the smouldering sin.' - Julian Barnes.

Napier University

Nene University College see University College Northampton

NESCOT see Other Institutions

University of Newcastle

Newcastle Poly see University of Northumbria at Newcastle

UWC Newport see Other Institutions

North East London Poly see University of East London

North East Wales Institute see Other Institutions

University of North London

North Wales see Bangor, University of Wales

University College Northampton

Northern College see Other Institutions

University of Northumbria at Newcastle

Norwich see University of East Anglia

University of Nottingham

Nottingham Trent University

Napier University

- *Formerly Napier Polytechnic*

Napier University, Craiglockhart Campus, 219 Colinton Road, Edinburgh, EH14 1DJ. Tel: 0500 353570. Fax: (0131) 455 6333. E-mail: info@napier.ac.uk
Napier Students' Association, 12 Merchiston Place, Edinburgh, EH10 4NR. Tel: (0131) 229 8791. Fax: (0131) 228 3462.

GENERAL

For general information about Edinburgh: see Edinburgh University.
Napier is one of the new universities and, like many others, it is growing at a rip-roaring pace and based on a number of sites. 5 major sites in fact, and with the exception of Sighthill Court, they're all spread around a *pleasant*, predominantly middle-class area a couple of miles to the west of Edinburgh city centre.

Napier

Sex ratio(M:F): 48%:52%
Full time u'grads: 7,725
Postgrads: 881
Ave course: 4yrs
Private school: n/a
Mature students: 33%
Disabled students: 7.5%

Founded: 1964
Part time: 1,957
Non-degree: 1,835
Ethnic: n/a
Flunk rate: 23.4%
Overseas students: 10%

ATMOSPHERE:
Most students come from the local area and pride themselves on not having the self-consciously 'studenty' attitudes that sometimes bedevil older institutions. However, the seriously over-stretched facilities mean there's not much scope for such behaviour anyway. It's a pretty functional place with a distinct lack of social glue and, as a former Student President has said, 'People tend to come to get a job, not to hobnob with Henriettas and other Hoorays.'

THE SITES:
The problem with overcrowding has been made worse by the fact that students have to be shunted from site to site for many classes and lectures, often not knowing where they're supposed to be. A new bus service that runs between the sites helps matters.

Merchiston: (3,700 students – science, engineering, arts, social sciences, Photography, film & TV) Although most of the main campus consists of a large modern block, a paved square and a converted house for NSA, the focus is the ancient Tower of Merchiston in the centre. This is where John Napier – the mathematician and inventor of logarithms, after whom the University is named – was born in 1550.

Craiglockhart: (1,300 – central services, electrical engineering, maths, computing) The buildings here include the 19th century administrative building, an accommodation block, swimming pool and a few other sports facilities set in *pleasant* terraced grounds 1½ miles from Merchiston. From here it's possible to see the Forth Bridge.

Sighthill: (2,000 – business) This is an *ugly great* 6-storey tower block with an even more modern extension, a sports dome and another NSA centre, all on the edge of the city near a *dodgy* housing estate, 3 miles east of Merchiston. *It's not so bad on the inside.*

Craighouse: (1,000 – music, hospitality and tourism, media) This is a new site, 2 miles from Merchiston. It's on a hill *with some of the best views in town*. It also used to be a lunatic asylum – *the locals still think it is.*

Canaan Lane: (nursing/midwifery) The former Lothian College of Health Studies, about 1½ miles from Merchiston.

THE CITY: see University of Edinburgh

TRAVEL: see University of Edinburgh
Local Trains: The closest stations are: Haymarket for Merchiston, Redwood House; Waverley for Marchmont; Slateford for Craiglockhart; Wester Hailes or South Gyle for Sighthill.
Buses: Public buses offer good services between the sites and into the city centre from 50p upwards. *The inter-site buses are too small, too infrequent and their drivers are best described as 'relaxed'.*
Bicycles: There's a big bike rack at Merchiston and at other sites.

CAREER PROSPECTS:
- Careers Service • No of staff: 7 full/2 part
- Unemployed after 6mths: 6%

FAMOUS ALUMNI:
Mark Goodier (Radio 1 DJ); Greg Kane (of has-beens Hue & Cry); Derrick Lee (Scottish rugby player); Kenny MacAlpine (Supernaturals); Alison Paton (Siren the Gladiator); Jane Franchi, Bill McFarlan, Malcolm Wilson, Cathy McDonald and Jim White (all Scottish TV presenters).

FURTHER INFO:
Prospectuses for undergrads, postgrads and part-timers and a website (www.napier.ac.uk and www.napierstudents.com).

ACADEMIC

Many courses are geared towards jobs and include lots of real-life projects and work placements.

staff/student ratio: 1:17
Range of points required for entrance: 240-140
Percentage accepted through clearing: n/a
Number of terms/semesters: 2
Length of terms/semesters: 15 wks
Research: 3.6

LIBRARIES:
• Books: 250,000 • Study places: 1,268
There are 8 libraries, the largest being at Merchiston, Sighthill and Craiglockhart.

COMPUTERS:
• Computer workstations: 1,400
New computer facility under construction at Merchiston Campus, *which is nice*.

ENTERTAINMENT

THE CITY: see University of Edinburgh

UNIVERSITY:
• Price of a pint of beer: £1.50 • Glass of wine: £1.60
Bars: (4). The most popular drinking den is at Merchiston (cap 200), known as 'Twelve'. There are also bars at Sighthill (500) and Craiglockhart (125). All the bars are closed at weekends, except at Craighouse.
Theatres: *3 active drama groups and trips to the Fringe.*
Clubs/discos/music venues: NSA's club/music has *a huge venue-shaped problem. Sighthill is big enough, but it's miles out of the way.* However, there is live music at 'Twelve' and regular DJ slots and there's also a monthly meander to a club in the city – *but that's about it.*
Food: The SA bars do fast food at all sites. New venue called Triangle opened at Merchiston. *The Asylum manages fresh rolls.*
Others: There are several balls a year *but they've suffered from a low turnout recently.*

Sussex University has the sunniest campus in Britain.

SOCIAL & POLITICAL

NAPIER STUDENTS' ASSOCIATION (NSA):
• 3 sabbaticals • Turnout at last ballot: 12% • NUS member

To encourage democratic participation, NSA (aka 'Byker Grove' for some reason) did resort to beer raffles to entice voters for a while, *but things are improving. Bribery aside, NSA concentrates on doing the best it can to provide services, given its limited facilities.*

SU FACILITIES:
Merchiston Avenue is NSA's converted house and corporate headquarters housing a bar/snack bar, common room, print shop, job shop, general shop, photocopier, DTP facilities, games rooms, pool table, juke box, games machines, vending machine, function room and car park. NSA has shops, pool tables and bars at Sighthill and Craiglockhart.

CLUBS (NON SPORTING):
Swedish.

OTHER ORGANISATIONS:
The mag, *pretentiously* called 'Veritas', *is floundering in an act of pretentious justice.*

RELIGIOUS:
• 10 chaplains (every hue of Christianity)

There is a large inter-denominational chapel and chaplaincy centre at Craiglockhart, which used to be a Catholic teaching college. Also chaplains representing the major Christian faiths.
Religion in Edinburgh: see Edinburgh University

PAID WORK:
The SA runs a job-shop, which has policies of minimum wages. There's also a net-based job-bank. See University of Edinburgh.

SPORTS

• Recent successes: snowboarding, kayaking

Sport facilities aren't up to much and there isn't the thigh-slapping, cold-showering enthusiasm for active activities that is often found elsewhere. However, balls are kicked and hamstrings are... whatever it is that happens to hamstrings.

SPORTING CLUBS:
Aikido; Canoe polo; Jiu Jitsu; Kayaking; Kuk sool win; Sailing; Snow Sports; Windsurfing; Women's football.

SPORTS FACILITIES:
The dome at Sighthill includes a sports hall, multi-gym, climbing wall and tennis courts. At Craiglockhart, there's the swimming pool (*which could better be descibed as a large bath*) and a putting green. Other facilities must be hired.

ATTRACTIONS: see University of Edinburgh

```
Central St martin's (London Institute) is
mentioned in Pulp's 'Common People'.
```

ACCOMMODATION

IN COLLEGE:
• Self-catering: 14% • Cost: £34-57 (33-39wks)
Availability: There are 714 places in a hall at Craiglockhart, West Bryson Road and Morrison Circus, enough for most non-local freshers to be housed if they want, but 10% who want to be, can't. If they do get a place, there's a 10% chance it'll be shared. Halls are split into single sex corridors with kitchens for every 5 or 6 students. Some CCTV and entry-phones.

EXTERNALLY: see University of Edinburgh
Housing help: NSA's Student Services employs a full-time accommodation officer who keeps a list of vacancies, who helps match students and landlords and who advises generally on housing and contracts. *Private agencies are also worth contacting.*

WELFARE

SERVICES:
• Lesbian & Gay Society • Mature SA
• Equal Opportunities Officer • Self-defence classes
The University employs 3 part-time counsellors to help students with problems more serious than an overdue essay. Each site has a welfare room. The Health Centre at Craiglockhart has a nurse and an occupational therapy service is available.
Women: The Women's Group deals with family planning, rape counselling and invites speakers. There's a Men's Group, but they discuss men's attitudes to feminism more than beer and football.
Disabled: *Acess is generally poor*, but improvements are underway.

FINANCE:
• Access fund: £500,000 • Successful applications: 1,200
NSA has a hardship fund of £3,000 (or 50p per undergrad), which it dishes out as £30 loans to the desperate. £15,000 nursery relief fund.

Nene University College

see University College Northampton

NESCOT

see Other Institutions

University of Newcastle

University of Newcastle, 6 Kensington Terrace, Newcastle upon Tyne, NE1 7RU. Tel: (0191) 222 6000. Fax: (0191) 222 6139.
E-mail: admissions-enquiries@ncl.ac.uk

Newcastle University Union Society, King's Walk, Newcastle upon Tyne, NE1 8QB. Tel: (0191) 232 3900. Fax: (0191) 222 1876. E-mail: union.society@ncl.ac.uk

GENERAL

Set in the *stunning* Northumbrian countryside, and at the heart of England's Geordie country, is Newcastle upon Tyne, *the unofficial capital of the North East and, as far as the Geordies are concerned, the world*. It is most of the way up the A1, the largest town north of Leeds and south of Edinburgh. As you might expect from a city that can boast the likes of the *splendid* Alan Shearer, as well as the *tiresome* Sting, Viz Comic and Ant & Dec, Newcastle has two sides: *on the one hand it is a buzzing cosmopolitan city, with more shops, pubs and clubs than you can shake a bus-load of Texans at*, and, *on the other, it is in parts riddled by crime and unemployment. It has been a victim of economic strife, but never lost its vitality, style, spirit or pride*. Its outer areas are arranged in eras – *some quite run down*, such as Byker (of 'Byker Grove' fame), *some still remaining quite posh*, such as Jesmond, known for its nightlife ('Jesmond Grove' just didn't cut it). The heart of the city is laced with gorgeous Georgian and Victorian architecture, alongside *uninspiring* 60s shopping centres. There are two universities in town: <u>Northumbria University</u> and Newcastle University, a classic redbrick campus on a 45-acre site in the city centre. The buildings are mostly 19th-century constructions formed into *attractive* blocks arranged around paved squares, but there are also some concrete additions *with little to offer the aesthete*.

Sex ratio(M:F): 51%:49%	Founded: 1834
Full time u'grads: 10,231	Part time: 134
Postgrads: 2,072	Non-degree: 0
Ave course: 3yrs	Ethnic: 8%
Private school: 29%	Flunk rate: 6%
Mature students: 11.7%	Overseas students: 14%
Disabled students: 3%	

ATMOSPHERE:
The atmosphere is buzzing and friendly but cliquey. Despite the city's rough diamond image, the student body is predominantly middle class. Nearby is Durham, with whose students there is an intense rivalry. The cost of living round here is quite low and so students can almost afford to enjoy Newcastle's bright lights. Haweey the ladz!

THE CITY:
• Population: 263,000 • London: 255miles
• Edinburgh: 94miles • Manchester: 112miles

There have been loads'a developments including at the Quayside with the new Millennium footbridge (wobble-free of course), the new Modern Art Gallery – the biggest outside London – and the Centre for Life. Oh yes, and there's a blue carpet square being laid outside the Laing Art Gallery (quality Axminster, we trust). The River Tyne runs through Newcastle towards the North Sea, just 8 miles away. The city itself is the *fun hub* of the Tyne & Wear area and its shopping centre too. Among the modern additions to the city centre are the Haymarket Metro Station and the Eldon Square Centre, a huge shopping mall. The *trendiest* areas for shops are High Bridge Street and

Old Eldon Square. There are *endless* banks, late-night shops and bookshops. Among the many museums and galleries, there's the Laing Art Gallery, where students can pick up arty posters a bit different from Jennifer Lopez or men cuddling babies. A little bit south is the town of Gateshead, where the vast Metro Centre is based. It's more of a shopping town than a centre (the largest in Europe) with expanses of shops, a ten-screen cinema, a bowling alley, funfair and ten *humongous* car parks.

TRAVEL:
Trains: The station's about 10 mins' walk from the city centre, or 2 mins by Metro. Direct lines to London (£37.60), Sheffield (£17.80), Edinburgh (£17.30) and all over the country.
Coaches: Several coach companies, including Clipper, Blue Line and National Express, offer services to many other destinations, for example London (£26), Sheffield (£17.75), Edinburgh (£15.25) and so on.
Car: The A1 proper hooks round the edge of the city. The A69, A692, A696, A189 and A19 *are all useful.*
Air: Newcastle Airport, 6 miles from the centre, has many inland and European flights.
Hitching: Good prospects from the routes out of the city, especially on the A1.
Local: Bus routes through the city are regular, *reliable and cheap.*
Underground: *The best underground system in the world is Tokyo's, but Newcastle's Metro comes a close second – clean, cheap, reliable and easy to use. It's noisy and not as extensive as it could be, but it serves all the essential areas for students.*
Taxis: *Cheaper than in most towns.*
Bicycles: *The city's hilly and full of traffic. There's nowhere to leave bikes off-campus and with the high theft rate, you need somewhere.*

CAREER PROSPECTS:
• Careers Service • No of staff: 31 full-time
• Unemployed after 6mths: 2.9%
Supposedly, international employers are looking to recruit from Newcastle as an alternative to Oxford and Cambridge. Yeah, right.

SPECIAL FEATURES:
• The University has appointed its first Writer in Residence (based in the medical school), Carol Clewlow, who wrote 'A Woman's Guide to Adultery'.

FAMOUS ALUMNI:
Kate Adie (BBC flak-jacketed überbabe); Rowan Atkinson (comedian, who reportedly spent three years in his room); Ed Coode (Olympic rower); Bryan Ferry (Roxy Music); Richard Hamilton (artist); Debbie Horsfield (TV writer); Miriam Stoppard (TV doctor); Paul Tucker (Lighthouse Family).

FURTHER INFO:
Extensive prospectuses for undergrads and postgrads and an alternative prospectus from the SU. Video available to schools and careers libraries. Websites (www.ncl.ac.uk and www.union.ncl.ac.uk).

```
Staffordshire University has pioneered the use
of sewage for making bricks and floor tiles.
```

ACADEMIC

The Uni was voted UK Centre of Excellence for the teaching of Medicine and was also The Sunday Times University of the Year 2000 *(based on all sorts of pointless and spurious criteria).*

staff/student ratio: 1:7
Range of points required for entrance: 320-220
Percentage accepted through clearing: 12%
Number of terms/semesters: 3
Length of terms/semesters: 12wks
Research: 4.3

LIBRARIES:
- Books: 1,000,000
- Study places: 2,000

The comfy, well-stocked Robinson Library has a Relative Humidity of 50%±10%, *just in case you were wondering.*

COMPUTERS:
- Computer workstations: 1,600

ENTERTAINMENT

TOWN:
- Price of a pint of beer: £1.95
- Glass of wine: £1.70

Newcastle is as happening a city as any, running a close race with the likes of Manchester, Leeds and London. The club and music scene is massive, both mainstream and underground. To keep a check on what's on, pick up a free copy of 'Crack' or 'Paint it Red'.

Cinemas: There's a ten-screen Warner cinema, a four-screen Odeon and the *excellent* Tyneside Arts Cinema (two screens), all within walking distance of the Uni. There's also a multiplex at the Metro Centre, *though this isn't used much by students since it's further out.*

Theatres: Among other theatres, there's the Theatre Royal (a regular venue for the Royal Shakespeare Company), the Tyne Theatre & Opera House, the Newcastle Playhouse and the Gulbenkian.

Pubs: Newcastle has many, many pubs, some rougher than students might like, but plenty serve a welcome brew, not least a pint of the ubiquitous 'dog' – Newcastle Brown. *The Bigg Market in the city centre is popular, but this is town territory at weekends and a bit more down-market than the Quayside, which has been redeveloped over the last few years and is now a vibrant place to hang out. Pushplugs: Offshore; Dobson's; Ramjam's; Chase Bar; Pitcher & Piano; Luckies; Bar Oz; New Pacific.*

Clubs/discos: Club life is part of the Geordie way of being. *Pushplugs (among others): Riverside (dance and indie); Ikon, Planet Earth and Legends for cheap cheese; Rockshots for clubheads; Tuxedo Royale (revolving dance floor on a boat, student night Mondays).*

Music venues: The Telewest Arena houses the biggest bands but there's also the Riverside (indie), City Hall (classical and pop), the Jazz Café near the station (music and cheap food) and Mayfair (mainstream/indie). Whitley Bay Ice Rink and Gateshead are easily reachable on the Metro.

Cabaret: Newcastle nurtures many a comic talent in pubs and clubs. Pushplug: Hyena Café.

Eating out: *Newcastle's got the lot, from posh restaurants to impress your lust objects, through to bacterium bhuna in a bun.* Somewhere between these extremes, Pushplugs: Marco Polo's & Don Vito's (Italian); Cradlewell (all-day breakfasts); Charlie's Chinese (£5 for as much as you can eat). The Playhouse and the Tyneside Coffee Rooms are the places to pose and Stowell Street is good for Chinese food.

UNIVERSITY:
- Price of a pint of beer: £1.50 • Glass of wine: £1.20

Bars: The vast Union building has seven *excellent and popular* bars. The Mens Bar is not for men only, but named after the Uni motto, 'Mens agitat molem' ('*subterranean rodent creating havoc in the gents*' or something). However, it does retain a pretty laddish, sporty atmosphere. The Cochrane Lounge is *comfy* and smoke-free, Twisters is the games bar; the Global has a continental café style and *the Irish Bar is singularly un-Irish.* The vast Bassment is mainly for gigs, but it's also open at lunchtime.

Theatres: NUTS (Newcastle University Theatre Society) does regular jaunts to the Edinburgh Fringe.

Clubs/discos: The Bassment Club in the Union Building (cap 1,850, adm £1) is the dance venue *to end them all.* Friday Night Positive and Saturday Night Fever and Eclectic *get hips hooplahing.* Recent guests have included Paul Oakenfold and Ian Brown.

Music venues: The Bassment (cap 1,200) is big enough to attract some *pretty impressive* names including recently: Goldie; Coldplay; Badly Drawn Boy; Embrace; Judge Jules. Global Café (cap 280) for dance events and bands.

Cabaret: Regular *giggles* at the comedy night with names such as Ed Byrne, Simon Day and Tony Burgess.

Food: *The Bassment eating area looks like a school dining hall but the food provokes no complaints.* The bars also come up with the goods, gulletwise.

Others: At least four balls a year plus a five-day freshers' binge.

SOCIAL & POLITICAL

NEWCASTLE UNIVERSITY UNION SOCIETY:
- 6 sabbaticals • Turnout at last ballot: 13% • NUS member

When it comes to services, the Union is not only as frantic as Coxy on ProPlus, but also owns its own building and so is free to do what it blimmin' well likes with it. Political activity extends to awareness campaigns, but not much further.

SU FACILITIES:
There's a whole floor of franchise outlets, currently hosting a travel shop and others. There's also the union shop (including a post office), advice centre, print shop, training room, education unit, second-hand bookshop, music rooms, bars, restaurant, hot food counter, salad bar, TV lounge, games, photo booth and function rooms.

CLUBS (NON SPORTING):
Duke of Edinburgh; Fellwalking; Gilbert & Sullivan; Jazz; Juggling; Link; Norwegian; NOMAD (Gap year travellers).

OTHER ORGANISATIONS:
The award-winning student newspaper 'Courier' is published by the Union and there's also an Ents guide. Newcastle Student Radio is aired jointly with Northumbria University. The charity Rag raises loads of cash. SCAN (Student Community Action Newcastle) has a very high profile and has 500 volunteers, helps with local projects, has a full-time staff member, its own fund-raising shop and minibuses.

RELIGIOUS:
- Four chaplains (CofE, RC, Baptist, United Reformed)

There is a mosque on campus. If not in Newcastle itself, most denominations are represented on the Tyne & Wear conurbation.

PAID WORK:
The Union runs a jobshop, upon registering students receive an induction on job-related issues, and it continually monitors conditions and pay. There are opportunities to augment coffers in bars, the theatres and tedious work at the Metro Centre.

SPORTS

- Recent successes: football, hockey, volleyball

There are reasonable sporting facilities both on and off campus and some impressive achievements. However, participation is not as broad as it could be (not for lack of opportunity).

SPORTS FACILITIES:
On campus, there are facilities in the Claremont Sports Hall (sports hall, squash courts) on the edge and in the Centre for PE & Sport at the newly-refurbished Kings Walk Sports Centre with two gyms, weights room and two squash courts. There are outdoor amenities on five sites: Heaton (medic's playing fields); Close House (10 miles out, 18-hole golf course, hockey pitches); Cochrane Park (playing fields); Longbenton (more playing fields); and Newburn Boat House on the Tyne for rowers. Just six acres of playing fields in all, though.

SPORTING CLUBS:
American Football; Clay Pigeon Shooting; Hang Gliding; Lacrosse; Parachute; Real Tennis; Rugby League; Surfing; Table Tennis; Ten-pin Bowling.

ATTRACTIONS:
You may have heard of Newcastle United FC and their not unenthusiastic fans, the Toon Army. If not, bone up before you get here. 'Alan who?' will not be tolerated. There's also the rugby union club, Gateshead International Stadium and racing at Gosforth. Whitley Bay Ice Rink is close as well.

ACCOMMODATION

IN COLLEGE:
- Catered: 15% • Cost: £62-84 (up to 52wks)
- Self-catering: 18% • Cost: £39-63 (up to 52wks)

Availability: All those who return accommodation forms in time will be housed and even students who get in at the last minute, via clearing, will usually do okay for their 1st year. There is also space for about 20% of other students. The three Castle Leazes halls *(60s Swedish prison design)*, Richardson Road (self-catered flats) and Windsor Terrace (converted Georgian) are five minutes' walk from the

campus, the others are 2 and 3 miles away. Castle Leazes and Henderson Hall are catered, offering two meals a day. There are self-catering flats in four main blocks in shared sets for up to six to a flat. Finally, there are 300 student houses at Leazes Terrace, converted Georgian houses, a ¼ mile from the campus. *Flats seem to be preferable to halls, mainly because the food in catered accommodation is pretty dire.* Only about 2% need to share. The University also operates a head tenancy scheme housing 292 students in local private accommodation. Night porters and some entryphones repel ruffians.
Car parking: Free.

EXTERNALLY:
- Ave rent: £45

Availability: *There's not much problem about finding housing in Newcastle and students can afford to be choosy. The best places to look are in Fenham (good for parties, bad for burglary), Jesmond (safe & leafy) and Heaton. Avoid Benwell and Scotswood (burnt out cars). The West End has a high crime rate and lots of drug taking – in fact, some students would be surprised if they didn't get offered something. However, with cheap accommodation elsewhere, students can afford not to bother with such areas.* Car parking is restricted around the city centre and it's not really worth having a car.
Housing help: The University Accommodation Service approves houses and flats on its lists, runs a landlord accreditation scheme and provides help, advice and standard contracts.

WELFARE

SERVICES:
- Nightline • Lesbian & Gay Society • Mature SA • Overseas SA
- Minibus • Women's Officer • Postgrad SA

Both the Union and University have welfare departments. There are two full- and three part-time counsellors.
Women: There's a clause in the Union's constitution to provide women-only space.
Disabled: *With many 19th-century buildings, access is bound to be limited, but the Union is a good example of an old building adapted to provide access to every level. The library's pretty good as well.* The Uni has a disability unit providing help, support and advice, there is also a wheelchair route around campus.

FINANCE:
- Access fund: £598,166 • Successful applications: 1,505

Debt is still a problem but the relatively low cost of living takes a few ounces of pressure off. Plus the usual dept bursaries and a part time fee waiver fund.

Newcastle Poly
see University of Northumbria at Newcastle

UWC Newport
see Other Institutions

North East London Poly
see University of East London

North East Wales Institute
see Other Institutions

University of North London

- *Formerly Polytechnic of North London*
University of North London, 166-220 Holloway Road, London, N7 8DB.
Tel: (020) 7753 3355. Fax: (020) 7753 3271.
E-mail: admissions@unl.ac.uk
University of North London Students' Association, 166-220 Holloway Road, London, N7 8DB. Tel: (020) 7753 3200.
Fax: (020) 7753 3201.

GENERAL

Most of the University of North London is concentrated on a cluster of buildings on the Holloway Road, dominated by the mirror-glass Learning Centre containing the main computing and library facilities. *The new building containing a language centre and computing facilities is described by the University as 'architect-designed', which Push finds most reassuring.* The University has a policy to double as a community resource as well as an educational institution. As a result, over 70% of students are real live Londoners, with a very high proportion of mature students, many on part-time courses.

Sex ratio(M:F): 45%:55%	Founded: 1896
Full time u'grads: 8,778	Part time: 2,743
Postgrads: 1,213	Non-degree: 2,717
Ave course: 3/4yrs	Ethnic: 53%
Private school: n/a	Flunk rate: 38.1%
Mature students: 52%	Overseas students: 25%
Disabled students: 4.5%	

ATMOSPHERE:
UNL has got over some of the inevitable problems of split-site universities with limited resources and has managed to develop an overall sense of unity. However, the high proportion of locals and mature students means that there are many people for whom 'student life' isn't the be-all and end-all and wacky student hijinks don't figure much.

THE CITY: see University of London

TRAVEL: see University of London
Trains: The nearest mainline station is King's Cross. Local stations near the sites include Highbury & Islington and Drayton Park.

Buses: Many bus routes to all sites and between them.
Car: *Cars are unparkable and really not necessary – clamps will work out just as expensive as London public transport.*
Underground: Nearest stations – Holloway Road and Caledonian Road (both on the Piccadilly Line) and Highbury & Islington (Victoria).

CAREER PROSPECTS:
• Careers Service • No of staff: 5 full-time
• Unemployed after 6mths: 12.1%

FAMOUS ALUMNI:
Miki Berenyi (Lush); Jake Chapman (artist); Garth Crooks (journalist, ex-Spurs star); David Kossof (actor); Martyn Lewis (newsreader); Stephen Platt (editor, New Statesman & Society); Sinead O'Connor (singer); Peter Tatchell (gay activist); Neil Tennant (Pet Shop Boy); Jamie Theakston (TV presenter).

FURTHER INFO:
Prospectuses for undergrads and postgrads, 'Informed Choice' booklet and a website (www.unl.ac.uk).

ACADEMIC

staff/student ratio: 1:25
Range of points required for entrance: 240-140
Percentage accepted through clearing: 36%
Number of terms/semesters: 3
Length of terms/semesters: 13wks
Research: 2.7

LIBRARIES:

• Books: 395,365 • Study places: 1,388
There are libraries on 2 sites.

COMPUTERS:
• Computer workstations: 1,650

ENTERTAINMENT

IN LONDON: see University of London

CAMDEN & ISLINGTON:
Pubs: Lots of Irish theme pubs, *which at least means three things: they know how to run a good pub, serve a good pint and play good music.* Pushplugs: The Tappit (close with good grub); Hobgoblin; Coronet; the George; Liar Maguire; Salmon & Compasses. Avoid the Highbury Barn near Ladbroke House.
Clubs/discos/music venues: Many bands in local pubs and on the streets. The Electric Ballroom, Megadog; HQ's, the Garage and the Forum are all nearby.
Eating out: *A wide range, particularly ethnic specialities.* Pushplugs: Delhi Diner; Steve's Nest (Greek).

The Queen's College, Oxford, is allowed to shut down the High street for archery parctice.

UNIVERSITY:
• Price of a pint of beer: £1.50   • Glass of wine: £1.10
Bars: 2 *dark and buzzy* boozers at the Student Centre.
Clubs/discos/music venues: There are events most evenings at the Rocket (capacity 1,000, *lime green with chairs and tables that look like giant smarties*) in the Student Centre (voted second best student venue by Live Awards), the main venue for visits from *noteworthy* DJs and recent acts like Bentley Rhythm Ace and Jazzy B. Heaven on Earth is a regular 10pm to 6am event. *Club culture overall is better represented than spotty rock-boys with guitars.*
Food: There are 6 refectories (new Rocket Coffee Shop) and 2 restaurants (1 training) *all at what would be sensible prices if the food were any good.*
Other: Regular May Ball. Wednesday night is Big Fish night where *strange foamy wrestling occurs.*

SOCIAL & POLITICAL

UNIVERSITY OF NORTH LONDON STUDENTS' ASSOCIATION:
• 3 sabbaticals   • Turnout at last ballot: 12%   • NUS member
SU elections for this year's sabbaticals were postponed and were unlikely to be decided before the start of next academic year. Possibly the weakest, least effective SU in the country.

SA FACILITIES:
Shop; 2 bars; Rocket venue; vending machines; pool tables; common rooms.

CLUBS (NON SPORTING):
Chinese; Scandinavian; Sikh.

OTHER ORGANISATIONS:
The new student magazine, 'Big Fish', is published monthly by the SA. It's also online – (for a taster try www.unl.ac.uk/su). Rag has finally gotten off the ground after a long absence.

RELIGIOUS:
• 1 full-time, 4 part-time chaplains
There are prayer rooms for student use for any religion.
Religion in London: see University of London.

PAID WORK: see University of London
An internet-based job-shop can e-mail student vacancies.

SPORTS

• Recent successes: boxing, footie, tennis
The sporting record and facilities can be described as adequate, though things should improve with the new Sports Council and the recent development of a gym and dance studio.

SPORTS FACILITIES:
New 22-acre sports ground with 3 football pitches; 1 rugby; astroturf; 2 gyms; fitness room; sports hall; dance studio; weights room.

SPORTING CLUBS:
Aerobics; Box-fit; Boxing; Circuit training; Jazz dance; Powercise; Power-lifting; Rowing; Table tennis; Women's football; Yoga.

ATTRACTIONS:
Arsenal & Tottenham are the local teams, *but it is considered bad manners to support them both.*

ACCOMMODATION

IN COLLEGE:
• Catered: 3% • Cost: £80 (39-50wks)
• Self-catering: 8% • Cost: £68 (39-50wks)
Availability: Most 1st years who want accommodation can be housed but most are already sorted. They live in the purpose-built blocks and Victorian houses around Tufnell Park, the Caledonian Road and Holloway Road. *High* levels of security including CCTV, video-phones, swipe cards and the like.
Car parking: None.

EXTERNALLY: see University of London
Availability: *Islington, Wood Green, Camden and Kentish Town especially are the best areas to look*, but the majority of students are locals anyway.
Housing help: The Uni provides newsletters, vacancy lists and landlord blacklists, emergency housing and general advice.

WELFARE

SERVICES:
• Nursery • Lesbian & Gay Society • Mature SA
• Overseas SA • Minibus • Women's Officer
The University runs a Counselling & Advisory Service employing 2 full- and 3 part-time counsellors, publishing an annual welfare help book. There are advisers to cover the whole spectrum of personal and academic problems.
Disabled: *Access is average, but improving.* Special arrangements include adjustable timetables, dyslexia support unit and a special needs co-ordinator.

FINANCE:
• Access fund: £872,810 • Successful applications: 1,600
The Student Hardship Fund provides small emergency loans. There are limited amounts for postgrads and mature students and a bursary fund is being set up.

North Wales

see Bangor, University of Wales

'The people who went into politics were those who couldn't get in the Footlights or were no good at journalism.' - Peter Cook on his Cambridge contemporaries. college of medicine

University College Northampton

- *Formerly Nene College*

(1) University College Northampton, Park Campus, Boughton Green Road, Northampton, NN2 7AL. Tel: (01604) 735500.
Fax: (01604) 722083. E-mail: admissions@northampton.ac.uk
University College Northampton Students' Union, Boughton Green Road, Northampton, NN2 7AL. Tel: (01604) 712071.
Fax: (01604) 719454.
(2) University College Northampton, Avenue Campus, St George's Avenue, Northampton, NN2 6JD. Tel: (01604) 735500.

GENERAL

Northampton's a *pleasant* market town, slap bang between Brum and London, *a bit too far east to be properly in the Midlands and too far north to be in the Home Counties*. Its nearest neighbour is the *deservedly maligned* Milton Keynes, but there's some *lovely* countryside nearby to get lost in. Historically, it's the centre of the British shoe industry (this is where your DMs came from) and, more recently, Carlsberg UK has set up shop here. *Northampton – probably the most Northampton-ish town in the world.* Now we've got the town placed, University College Northampton is about 2½ miles away on 2 landscaped campuses, with modern building developments, *tastefully arranged*. It's allowed to award its own degrees and in early 1999 was granted 'University College' status (*neither a university, nor a college, but something in between*).

Sex ratio(M:F): 40%:60%	Founded: 1975
Full time u'grads: 7,300	Part time: 1,530
Postgrads: 217	Non-degree: 1,295
Ave course: 3yrs	Ethnic: 12%
Private school: 2%	Flunk rate: 21.4%
Mature students: 20%	Overseas students: 3%
Disabled students: 4%	

ATMOSPHERE:
The Park Campus is a smattering of high-tech architecture and rolling greenery and the student body is similarly mixed-up, a broad blend of all accents and ages. They're a friendly lot too, although relations with the locals are as chummy as you could wish for from people who avoid each other religiously.

AVENUE CAMPUS:
Arts, technology and marketing departments co-exist, 2½ miles from the main campus. There's a sports hall and SU bar and this is the site of regular club nights and arts events.

NORTHAMPTON:
- Population: 200,000 • London: 63miles
- Birmingham: 52miles • Manchester: 137miles

Northampton has managed to maintain its ancient market square (the largest in Britain) in *something approaching good nick* and there are some *lovely* examples of Georgian and Victorian architecture around the city centre. *Some of the outer reaches are closer to prefab hell, however.* In amongst the urban planning exercise, you can find the usual array of banks, malls, supermarkets, book shops (new and second-hand), art galleries and museums, *although the Leather Museum isn't as much fun as it potentially could be.* Other attractions include regular hot-air balloon festivals (*why don't they get together with the museum people and make a leather balloon?*) and one of the *best-preserved* Norman round churches in the country.

TRAVEL:
Trains: Northampton station is about 4 miles from the Park Campus, offering mainline services to London (£23.15), Birmingham (£8.05), Manchester (£23.95) and beyond.
Coaches: Midland Fox and National Express services to, among others, London (£9) and Birmingham (£4).
Car: The M1 goes right past Northampton, although there's about 3 miles of wiggling before you get to the college. There's also the A45, A50, and A43.
Hitching: *Hitching is reasonably easy near the M1 junctions.*
Local: *Buses are reliable*, running every 15 mins between the Park campus and the town (90p one way). There's also a free (*but unreliable*) bus between the 2 UCN campuses.
Taxis: Westbridge and Favell companies offer student discounts.
Bicycles: There are some bike lanes, but not throughout town, and the roads are pretty busy. Park Campus has locked sheds (so how do you get your bike in? Ha-ha-ha).

CAREER PROSPECTS:
• Careers Service • No of staff: 5 full-time
• Unemployed after 6mths: 5%

SPECIAL FEATURES:
• There was a University in Northampton in 1261 but it only lasted 3 years.
• The School of Leather Technology has on display a fine specimen of a blue whale's foreskin.
• Park Campus was a mental institution in the 19th and 20th Century.

FAMOUS ALUMNI:
Daniel Ash, David J (Bauhaus/Love & Rockets); Lord Hesketh (Formula 1 team manager); Jonn (Ned's Atomic Dustbin); Des O'Connor (TV celeb); Derek Redmond (athlete); Jonathan Waller (artist).

FURTHER INFO:
Prospectuses for undergrads and part-timers and a video. More info on the website (www.northampton.ac.uk and www.ucnu.org.uk).

ACADEMIC

staff/student ratio: 1:17
Range of points required for entrance: 220-80
Percentage accepted through clearing: 20%
Number of terms/semesters: 3
Length of terms/semesters: 11 wks
Research: 2

Northampton

LIBRARIES:
- Books: 210,742 • Study places: 1,000

Libraries on each campus. *Weekend library access could be better.*

COMPUTERS:
- Computer workstations: 2,000

24-hour access to some computer facilities.

TOWN:
- Price of a pint of beer: £2.20 • Glass of wine: £2

Northampton has had a bit of a renaissance recently and there are actually things to do now.

Cinemas: There's a multi just outside town. The 10-screener at Milton Keynes is popular as well.

Theatres: (3) The Royal puts on traditional stuff, mainly rep. The Derngate is a flexible, multi-purpose venue and the Roadmender puts on experimental stuff.

Pubs: *A sudden surge of studenty swig-spots.* Pushplugs: Chicago Rock; Sunnyside; Moon & Square; Bar Soviet. Stay away from the Keep and the Prince of Wales.

Clubs/discos: *The revelry revival has yet to colonise the club scene.* Pushplugs: Visage (student night on Monday); the Lounge for a Saturday night bop.

Music venues: The Roadmender is a *fair-to-middling* indie stop-off and the Racehorse pub offers *lesser lights.*

Eating out: Northampton has the usual range of eateries, including burgers and pizzas till 4am; *Wellingborough Road is the best bet, for value and variety.* Pushplugs: Papa Luigi; Giggling Sausage; Rat & Parrot; Imran's Balti (3 courses for a fiver).

COLLEGE:
- Price of a pint of beer: £1.60 • Glass of wine: £1.00

Bars: (4) The Venue (cap 600) is open late on Thursdays and Saturdays. The Pavilion Bar is a non-smoking area. George's (300) is the Avenue Campus boozer. There's also a new café bar in the Park Campus Union.

Theatre/cinema: The Black Box theatre hosts shows by the luvvy contingent. 1 free film a week.

Clubs/discos: *There've been complaints that the ents aren't big or alternative enough.* That said, Cult Addiction (cult movie tunes) on Thursdays at the Venue is popular and DJs to stop off here have included Dave Pearce, Yomanda, Bongo Ted (?), Judge Jules and Boy George.

Music venues: The Venue and George's are used *for local bands.*

Food: *The bars are the main food stops and the value's okay.*

Others: 3 balls a year, plus the Pavilion 2-night festival.

UNIVERSITY COLLEGE NORTHAMPTON STUDENTS' UNION:
- 3 sabbaticals • Turnout at last ballot: 20% • NUS member

The SU actually managed to fill the sabbatical posts this year, which is something of a triumph. Still, there are grumble rumbles about ents but communication by the Union is improving.

SU FACILITIES:
Bars, cafeterias, minibus hire, payphones, photo machine, video machine, pool table, juke box and TV lounge.

CLUBS (NON SPORTING):
Chess; Games; Scout & Guide.

OTHER ORGANISATIONS:
The SU newspaper is 'Wave'. Rag rakes in some cash relief.

RELIGIOUS:
There's an interdenominational chaplaincy centre. Northampton is big enough to support all but the most esoteric spiritual requirements.

PAID WORK:
The SU and the University's Student Services unit between them run Jobs Junction which links up with local employers.

- Recent successes: rugby, footie, lacrosse, netball

Enthusiasm outstrips the facilities and trophy collection. Outside sponsorship has perked things up, though successes are mostly down to the women.

SPORTS FACILITIES:
The Park Campus has: sports hall; 25 acres of fields; pavilion. Nothing at Avenue. Access to the swimming pool in the school next door and to the River Nene.

SPORTING CLUBS:
Aerobics; Exiles; Kick-boxing; Lacrosse; Parachute; Rowing; Women's basketball & football.

ATTRACTIONS:
Northampton Rugby Club *are local heroes*. Northampton FC (*known, not entirely inaccurately, as 'The Cobblers'*). Nene Whitewater Centre.

IN COLLEGE:
- Self-catering: 23% • Cost: £30-57 (40wks)

There are around 1,600 places in purpose-built halls and blocks on campus. All 1st years can be accommodated. No other years live in. 6% overall share. It's mostly mixed-sex but there's one all-female hall with 90 spaces. Security guards wander round.

EXTERNALLY:
- Ave rent: £40

Student Services offer a placement service – it's intended that each 1st year should have an address at the beginning of the year. *The fact that they have to state that intention doesn't bode well. Local housing is pretty good and reasonable, although the hike between town and campus can get a little wearisome. Kingsthorpe and Abington are your best bet. Semilong is the red-light district but whether that's a bad thing is down to your personal predilections.*

> The original Alice in Wonderland was the daughter of the Dean of Christ Church, Oxford.

WELFARE

SERVICES:
• Creche • Lesbian & Gay Society • Mature SA • International SA
Student Services employs 2 full-time and 1 part-time counsellors and there are 2 nurses and a visiting GP in the health service.
Disabled: All SU buildings are wheelchair-accessible *and access as a whole is pretty good.*

FINANCE:
• Access fund: £486,555 • Successful applications: 660
Short-term loans of up to £100 are available from the Extreme Hardship Fund. Bursaries for student nurses and a childcare fund.

Northern College
see Other Institutions

University of Northumbria at Newcastle

• *Formerly Newcastle Polytechnic*
(1) University of Northumbria at Newcastle, Ellison Place, Newcastle upon Tyne, NE1 8ST. Tel: (0191) 232 6002. Fax: (0191) 227 4017.
University of Northumbria Students' Union, Sandyford Lane, Newcastle upon Tyne, NE1 8SB. Tel: (0191) 227 4757.
Fax: (0191) 227 3760. E-mail: studentsunion@unn.ac.uk
(2) University of Northumbria, Longhirst Campus, Longhirst Hall, Longhirst, Morpeth, Northumberland, NE61 3LL.
Tel: (01670) 795000. Fax: (01670) 795021.
(3) University of Northumbria, Carlisle Campus, 45 Paternoster Row, Carlisle, Cumbria, CA3 8TB. Tel: (0191) 227 4550.
Fax: (0191) 227 4820. E-mail: carlisle.admin@unn.ac.uk

GENERAL

The name of Newcastle's newer university draws attention to its intentions to expand beyond its birthplace. The main site and one other are in Newcastle (see University of Newcastle), but there are two other campuses, 15 and 57 miles away.

Sex ratio(M:F): 44%:56%	Founded: 1969
Full time u'grads: 11,556	Part time: 1,465
Postgrads: 3,249	Non-degree: 5,369
Ave course: 3yrs	Ethnic: 5%
Private school: n/a	Flunk rate: 16.9%
Mature students: 49.8%	Overseas students: 7.9%
Disabled students: 2%	

ATMOSPHERE:
The architecturally oppressive environment doesn't dampen the enthusiasm of the students, even though many are mature, often with outside commitments. Any shortcomings in the Uni are more than offset by Newcastle's ultrabright lights. Local relations are good, unsurprisingly as many students are local, although things can get a bit hairy on a Friday or Saturday night.

THE SITES:
City Campus: (13,118 students – most courses) The main site is a mixture of 1880s municipal buildings, such as the original redbrick Sutherland Building, and 60s concrete architecture. *Being just a continuation of buildings and no greenery, it's fairly difficult to tell exactly where the town stops and the campus starts.* In Ellison Place, the University has many *attractive* examples of early 19th-century buildings.

Coach Lane: (5,647 – education, health, behavioural studies) 3 miles from the main site in Benton (*quite a rough suburb*) is the Coach Lane site, a modern campus, *clean and green*.

Longhirst Hall: (606 – business) A stately home 15 miles north of Newcastle, in Morpeth, *which Newcastle students regard as a bit like being sent to the middle of nowhere (God knows what they'd make of Cornwall)*. Many postgrad courses.

Carlisle: (350 – business) Opened in October 1992, this is a set of converted buildings, many of which are listed, in the town centre (60 miles from the main site). For example, the library building used to be a tea warehouse. *Carlisle itself is an attractive city with a long heritage*, not far from the Lake District, Eden Valley, the west side of the North Pennines and the Solway Firth. The site is intended as a business school for local students, but anyone can apply.

THE CITY: see University of Newcastle

TRAVEL: see University of Newcastle
Carlisle: Served by National Express coach services and by many trains on the mainline from Glasgow to London Euston. The Uni runs buses between sites and a free late-night bus for clubbing nuts (not cashews, mind).

CAREER PROSPECTS:
- Careers Service • No of staff: 4 full
- Unemployed after 6mths: 5%

FAMOUS ALUMNI:
Emmanuel Bajyewv (Lighthouse Family); Jeff Banks (fashion designer/former Clothes Show presenter); Steve Bell (cartoonist); Sarah Blackwood (Dubstar); Steve Cram (athlete); Robson Green (of '& Jerome' fame); Vaughan Oliver (artist/designer); Sting (*pompous* pop star); Kevin Whateley (actor).

FURTHER INFO:
Prospectuses for undergrads, postgrads and part-timers, Guide for overseas students, CD-rom and a website: www.northumbria.ac.uk, there are also taster days in the summer.

Lincoln College, Oxford, suffered a 10-year ban from 'University Challenge' for stripping the set bare.

ACADEMIC

The Uni has been named 'best new university' for the last three years running by Sunday Times Education, which begs the question, 'Best for whom?'

staff/student ratio: 1:22
Range of points required for entrance: 300-60
Percentage accepted through clearing: 33%
Number of terms/semesters: 2
Length of terms/semesters: 17wks
Research: 2.5

LIBRARIES:
• Books: 500,000 • Study places: 1,200 at City Campus
The main library is a brick and concrete structure with small arrow-slit windows on the edge of a quadrangle in the City Campus. *As student numbers have rocketed over the last few years, book provision hasn't kept up.* There are four libraries in total.

COMPUTERS:
• Computer workstations: 5,500

ENTERTAINMENT

CITY: see University of Newcastle

UNIVERSITY:
• Price of a pint of beer: £1.35 • Glass of wine: £1.70
Bars: There are 3 bars at the main centre: Reds (cap 500) which has had a recent revamp; the Northumbria (150, *mainly mature students*); the Venue (1,200, events only). Carlisle has two new bars and Coach Lane has one drinking den.
Theatre: *Periodic* performances at the Stage 2 theatre in the Union.
Clubs/discos: Four dance nights a week at Reds, from the cheesy sounds of Wiggle Wiggle to Wednesdays' 80s Footloose.
Music venues: Bands to visit recently include: Supergrass, Stereophonics and Catatonia.
Food: The Union runs four eateries, offering a *wide range* from filled stotties (baps, ooh er) to full breakfasts. The University has a refectory *doling out the usual greasy spoon fare*. There is a food cart on each campus (*but no straw or fluffy farm animals*).
Others: An *impressive* art gallery in the library building and occasional balls. Comedy every fortnight.

SOCIAL & POLITICAL

UNIVERSITY OF NORTHUMBRIA STUDENTS' UNION:
• 5 sabbaticals • Turnout at last ballot: 10% • NUS member
The Union ran into big debt a few years ago, but things are looking better now. Their building, situated on the main campus's central quadrangle opposite the library, is very big *with decent facilities. The students aren't the most politically committed, to put it mildly.*

SU FACILITIES:
Ballroom; theatre; function rooms; bars; small stationery/general

shop; bookshop; travel agent; employment office; launderette; photocopying; cafeteria. A new SU building with two bars has opened at Carlisle.

CLUBS (NON SPORTING):
Kiss (international); Radio; Après Ski.

OTHER ORGANISATIONS:
The fortnightly 'Newcastle Student' (*how long did it take them to think that one up?*) is *dull* and supplemented by some unofficial publications at the satellite sites. Newcastle Student Radio is produced jointly with Newcastle University. *It's rumoured that Rag might get off the ground after five years' absence.*

PAID WORK: see University of Newcastle

RELIGIOUS:
- 5 chaplains (CofE, Methodist, United Reformed, 2RC)

- Recent successes: rugby
As a poly, it had better facilities than most, but as a university, it doesn't rank with the seriously big boys, just the slightly chunky ones. Membership of the Sports Centre costs £7.50 a month.

SPORTS FACILITIES:
At the City Campus, there's the Lipman Sports Centre, the Wynne Jones Hall and a sports centre with new facilities including the Paramount Fitness Suite and squash courts. There are further provisions at Coach Lane. The 42-acre Bullockstead sports ground complete with new fitness suite, artificial turf, martial arts and aerobics studio, 5 miles from the City Campus. Other facilities cater for most sports including squash and tennis courts, sports halls, climbing wall, weights room, gym, multigym and 47 acres of playing fields. Of course, for Carlisle students the lakes offer *real* watery pursuits and mountains. Longhirst Campus has cricket, hockey and rugby pitches and a golf course. Bursaries for the elite sportsters.

SPORTING CLUBS:
Ice Hockey.

ATTRACTIONS: see University of Newcastle

IN COLLEGE:
- Catered: 5% • Cost: £76-81 (33-35wks)
- Self-catering: 13% • Cost: £48-54 (43wks)

Availability: The University halls are based on the main campus, at Coach Lane, in Jesmond and in Gosforth (a few miles from the city centre). Of the 1st years who request accommodation, 10% are turned down. A few rooms (4%) are shared. The halls are 60s highrise blocks in an *unattractive blend of grey concrete and grey concrete. Students complain that they are poorly maintained and that showers never work.* The University also acts as a *benevolent* landlord, running a head tenancy scheme and allocating 450 places in houses and flats, none too far from the city centre. New for 2002 is a new building of en-suite rooms and some *swanky* studio-style appartments for three plus.

Car parking: Free permit parking.

EXTERNALLY: see University of Newcastle

Housing help: The University Accommodation Office has six staff who operate an extensive advertising service including newsletters and providing help, information and advice. An accreditation scheme is set up with Newcastle University to lend a hand.

WELFARE

SERVICES:
- Nursery • Nightline • Lesbian & Gay Society
- Mature SA • Overseas SA • Postgrad SA
- Minibus • Women's Officer • Self-defence classes

The Union has a welfare officer and the University employs six full-time counsellors. There are three nurses at the Health Centre, two at City and one at Coach Lane campuses. The Walksafe scheme provides escorts across campus at night.

Disabled: *Access is a mixed bag – some courses aren't suitable for wheelchair-users because the relevant buildings aren't. However, there are some halls specially designed for wheelchair access.* There are facilities for sight- and hearing-impaired students and a Dyslexia Support Group.

FINANCE:
- Access fund: £220,000 • Successful applications: 709

Assistance with part-time fees is available and there are also specialist bursaries.

Norwich

see University of East Anglia

University of Nottingham

(1) University of Nottingham, University Park, Nottingham, NG7 2RD.
Tel: (0115) 951 5151. Fax: (0115) 951 3666.
E-mail: undergraduate-enquiries@nottingham.ac.uk
University of Nottingham Union, Portland Building, University Park, Nottingham, NG7 2RD. Tel: (0115) 935 1100.
Fax: (0115) 935 1101.
(2) University of Nottingham, School of Biological Science, Sutton Bonington, Nr Loughborough, Leicestershire, LE12 5RD.
Tel: (0115) 951 5151.

GENERAL

'Robin Hood - Prince of Thieves' would have you believe that Nottingham is about ½ an hour by horse from Kent, but it is, actually, in the East Midlands. In fact, the East Midlands' largest city. As with most cities in the Midlands, it's come a long way since the days of the evil Sheriff (*and Michael Praed was better than Kev Costner any*

day). It grew rich during the Industrial Revolution then got poorer again when that finished. But Nottingham didn't let a slight change of fortune get it down, not in the same way that, for instance, Birmingham did. It remained and remains a *busy, cultural, beautiful city*, about ½ an hour by horse from the Peak District. About 3 miles from the city centre is the University Park Campus, 330 *hugely spacious* acres of *charming* views, parkland, lake and a mixture of *majestic* old buildings (such as the main administrative centre and the Union) and newer blocks (such as the white concrete *flying saucer* which disguises itself as the Hallward Library). 10 miles south, at Sutton Bonington near Loughborough (see Loughborough University for general details), the University has another self-contained campus, a *huger* 400 acres, devoted to the School of Biological Science.

Sex ratio(M:F): 45%:55%	Founded: 1881
Full time u'grads: 13,349	Part time: 4,780
Postgrads: 2,737	Non-degree: 6,367
Ave course: 4yrs	Ethnic: 5%
Private school: n/a	Flunk rate: 5.5%
Mature students: 21%	Overseas students: 7.7%
Disabled students: 6.5%	

ATMOSPHERE:
The buzz and hum on the campus is like a hive of bees on speed. The social life flows with honey and the clubs milk the efforts of almost all students. Yet, a staggering proportion of students still gets involved in the successful Rag and Community Action group. Undiluted essence of life is bottled and served in large quantities at centres around the campus and it would take considerable effort to be bored.

THE SITES:
Sutton Bonington: (600 students) This site has its own Student Guild (funded by the Union) which runs a shop and some social events. *The site is self-contained and has all the basic necessities for life*, but escape into Loughborough or Nottingham is easy if it all gets too claustrophobic.

New Campus: This as yet unnamed site is being developed 2 miles from the main campus on the western edge of the city. It will be the base for business, computing and education students and will have accommodation and other facilities including a library, 24 hour computer access and a canteen.

THE CITY:
- Population: 261,500 • London: 117miles
- Birmingham: 47miles • Loughborough: 13miles

Nottingham is big enough to have all the amenities a social animal could desire but small and cosy enough to avoid urban angst. It has its *dank and squalid corners*, but the main areas with shops galore and developments like the Victoria Centre are *clean, spacious and filled with beautiful* Victorian buildings. *The city centre has been rejuvenated with huge cosmopolitan bars*. Areas such as Hockley, among others, offer *trendy* little bars, *trendy* little designer shops and *trendy* big second-hand markets. Some of the *daintiest* features include the Goose Fair every October (the largest temporary fun fair in Europe), the famous old lace market (an old quarter of the city where lace is still sold wholesale), Nottingham Castle (more of a mansion really), Slab Square for sitting amidst pigeons, and 'Ye Olde

Trip to Jerusalem' and 'Salutation Inn', two of the country's oldest pubs. Students particularly enjoy 'The Tales of Robin Hood', a heritage centre aimed at kids of all ages.

TRAVEL:
Trains: Nottingham Station offers services all round the country (north and south are simpler than east and west), including London (£28.05), Birmingham (£9.85), Manchester (£18.15) and Edinburgh (£51.90).
Coaches: National Express services to, among other places, London (£15.75), Birmingham (£5.75) and Glasgow (£31.25).
Car: Nottingham is 5 minutes off the M1 and is also easily reached by the A6, A47, A52 and the A1 (20 miles away).
Air: East Midlands Airport, 12 miles outside town, has flights inland and to Europe.
Hitching: *The M1 is a goody for wild rovers.*
Local: Buses run every 15 minutes from the campus into the city centre until 9pm and cost around 75p.
Taxis: *Pretty reasonable rates in the city centre.*
Bicycles: *Flat with cycle lanes, but laxity with locks can leave legs with little to lever.*

CAREER PROSPECTS:
• Careers Service • No of staff: 6 full-time
• Unemployed after 6mths: 3.7%

SPECIAL FEATURES:
• The University makes a big deal out of the fact that DH Lawrence was a student here and is the foremost centre for research into his works, although Lawrence's attitude to the University was, to say the least, ambivalent.
• The University claims to have more applications per place than any other UK university (but others make the same claim).

FAMOUS ALUMNI:
Matthew Bannister (ex-controller, Radio 1); DH Lawrence (writer); Brian Moore (former England rugby player); Tim Robinson (cricketer); Sultan Raja Azlan Shah (King of Malaysia).

FURTHER INFO:
Prospectuses for undergrads and postgrads, video for schools loan and a website (www.nottingham.ac.uk).

ACADEMIC

staff/student ratio: 1:16
Range of points required for entrance: 360-200
Percentage accepted through clearing: 3%
Number of terms/semesters: 2
Length of terms/semesters: 15 wks
Research: 5.9

LIBRARIES:
• Books: 1,500,000 • Study places: 2,856
There are 7 libraries (two of which are specialist interest collections) including a library on the Sutton Bonington site.

COMPUTERS:
• Computer workstations: 1,000
The Cripps Computing Centre is the base of the University network.

ENTERTAINMENT

THE CITY:
- Price of a pint of beer: £2.20 • Glass of wine: £2

Cinemas: Nottingham has a 16-screen multiplex as well as 3 four-screen cinemas. The Nottingham Film Theatre shows arty pics and the Broadway offers student discounts. The Savoy is a rare instance of a cinema you can smoke in and also has seats for 2 and an ice cream lady.

Theatres: The Royal Theatre is Nottingham's largest theatre and shows mainstream stuff, as well as opera and ballet. The Playhouse offers *top* rep and the Lace Market and Co-op Theatres host amateur local dramatics and fringe shows.

Pubs: The local brew is Shipstones. *Pushplugs: Bag O' Nails; Old Peacock; Rubber Duck; Revolution; Via Fossa; the Waterfront; Ye Olde Trip to Jerusalem (the country's oldest pub). Some boozers in Beeston aren't that student friendly.*

Clubs/discos: *For the discerning clubber, Nottingham has many sweaty cattle markets where students can bop their socks off. Pushplugs: for the more discerning, student nights at the Isis; Lost Weekend and Options (house); Cookie Club and The Zone (jazz); Beatroot (speed garage, jazz & house); Palais (70s and fancy dress nights); Marcus Garvey for D'n'B and techno; the Lenton and the Bomb do student nights.*

Music venues: Rock City is Nottingham's main indie/rock venue. The Royal Concert Hall has classical concerts, and more mainstream ents and Sam Fay's stages reggae events. Robbie Williams and Massive Attack did Nottingham recently.

Cabaret: The Mad Dog Comedy Club at the Malt Cross Music Hall stars such wits as Dylan Moran, Jo Brand and Lee Hurst every Saturday.

Eating out: *Plenty to satisfy the most jaded palate, including the usual run of franchises and dodgy kebabberies. Pushplugs: Tequila, Muchacha's (Mexican); Severez, Sapnars (Indian); Mayflower (Chinese); San Rimo's, Antibo's (Italian); Fat Cats (gorgeous potato skins); Baltimore Exchange (for that parental visit); Wok-u-like (bad name, good food).*

UNIVERSITY:
- Price of a pint of beer: £1.35 • Glass of wine: £1

Bars: (17) There are well-patronised bars in the halls of residence and the sports centre but the focal points are the Buttery and DH Lawrence bars. Campus 14 is a tried and tested bar crawl around halls which still goes on *despite being outlawed by the sheriffs of Nottingham University.*

Theatres: The New Theatre is used for 7 productions each term, as are the Main Hall and Studio. 3 student shows made it to the Edinburgh Fringe last year.

Cinema: 1 or 2 films a week in a converted lecture theatre.

Clubs/discos/music venues: There are 2 club nights a week and the Buttery Bar has been adapted for live music. Lightning Seeds, De La Soul, Steps and Rialto were recent visitors.

Cabaret: Titterworthy turns every two weeks.

Food: The bars do *reasonable* sarnies to soak up the booze. The University-run Lakeside Diner and Food Court have a wider range *but they're a bit pricey*. The Ballroom is a *rather swanky Continental-style* café and the Portland Dining Room has a *good* veggie variety.

Others: Several balls a year including the Graduation extravaganza and the Snowflake Ball for Rag. The University has its own art galleries, art bookshop, museum and a cafeteria (Café Lautrec).

SOCIAL & POLITICAL

UNIVERSITY OF NOTTINGHAM STUDENTS' UNION:
• 6 sabbaticals • Turnout at last ballot: 25% • NUS member
It's a very moderate union, concentrating on slickly-run services rather than identifiable political commitment, though demos have been more successful here than elsewhere. Relations between the Union and the University authorities are very good.

SU FACILITIES:
1 bar; travel agent; 3 shops; advice centre; jobshop; theatre; rehearsal room; print shop and photocopying; record/CD/video library; car and minibus hire; NatWest and HSBC Banks (with cashpoints); games and vending machines; Endsleigh Insurance office; library; photo booth; pool table; juke box; TV lounge; 8 meeting rooms; and car parking.

CLUBS (NON SPORTING):
Action For Earth; AIESEC; American; Amnesty; Arab; Baha'i; Bands; Bassic; Bell Ringing; Blowsoc; Bouncy castle; BUNAC; Catholic; Chess & Backgammon; Chinese; Chocolate; Classic & Cult Film; Classical; Cocktail; Conservation; Cymsoc (Welsh); Cyprus; Dance; Debating; Duke of Edinburgh; Feast; Football Supporters; Funk; Gaba (Going Abroad, Being Abroad); Gilbert & Sullivan; Guinness; Hedonizm; Hellenic; High; Hispanic; Indian; Juggling; Kebab; Korean; Latin & Ballroom Dancing; Law; Malaysian & Singapore; Music; Mutant; New Lit; Pakistan; Photographic; Politics; Rock Music; Role play; Russian; Scout & Guide; Scribble; Seventies; Sikh; Slavonic; Soul; Star; Taiwan; Thai; Turkish; Wine.

OTHER ORGANISATIONS:
'Impact' and 'Grapevine' are the University's student magazines. University Radio Nottingham is constantly winning national prizes. Also Karnival, the charity Rag, is the country's biggest student-run (ie non-sabbatical) Rag, with a turnover of more than £230,000 last year. The University's *tremendously successful* Community Action group involves nearly 2,000 students in 75 projects *and can claim some responsibility for the excellent student/community relations.*

RELIGIOUS:
• 8 chaplains (CofE, RC, Methodist, Baptist, Jewish, Muslim)
There's a chapel and Muslim prayer room in the Portland Building. Locally, the city offers churches for most Christian denominations and worship shops for Muslims, Jews, Sikhs, Hindus and Buddhists.

PAID WORK:
The Union runs a job agency, 'Nucleus'. Apart from the usual money scrambles, students have been known to sell themselves as guinea pigs at the medical school (£120 for 3 days).

SPORTS

• Recent successes: football
The SU has arranged blanket sponsorship for all sporting activities. Facilities are outstanding and involvement and standards are high despite bad organisation.

SPORTS FACILITIES:
Most outdoor facilities are at Grove Farm, 1 mile from the campus, but some are also on campus. In all, there are 220 acres of playing

fields, including a floodlit artificial hockey pitch and a croquet lawn/bowling green. There's also the University lake, a 2,000m rowing course near the campus and the University boathouse on the Trent. The sports centre on campus has the biggest and *most efficient* sports hall in the country, a 25m pool, 2 tennis courts, indoor sports courts, a smaller hall, 7 squash courts, a climbing wall, fitness room, table tennis, snooker room, bar and coffee shop. The membership fee is £20 a year and there are bursaries for the best.

SPORTING CLUBS:
Aikido; American Football; Archery; Bat Polo; Boat; Boxing; Caving; Exploring; Gliding; Hand Ball; Hang Gliding; Jiu Jitsu; Korfball; Kung Fu; Lacrosse; Lifesaving; Mountaineering; Motorsport; Munro; Nin Jutsu; Parachuting; Paragliding; Polo; Rambling; Rifle & Pistol; Rugby League; Snowsports; Surfing; Tai Chi; Ten Pin Bowling; Triathlon; Water Polo; Water Skiing; Weight Training; Windsurfing; Yawara Ryu.

ATTRACTIONS:
In addition to Nottingham Forest and Notts County FCs, the Rugby Club and the County Cricket, there are geegees and woof-woofs racing at Colwick, the ice rink (where Torvill and Dean learned their craft) and the National Watersports Centre.

ACCOMMODATION

IN COLLEGE:
- Catered: 22% • Cost: £80-93 (31wks)
- Self-catering: 5% • Cost: £40-93 (44wks)

Availability: Every 1st year is offered the opportunity to live in college accommodation in one of the catered halls or self-catering flats (there are 300 places at the Sutton Bonington site). 80% of 1st years take up the opportunity, leaving space for about 20% of other students. 2% have to share. *The community atmosphere in halls is very strong and there is always a friendly rivalry with inter-hall competitions and so on.* 4 halls are single sex only (2 men's, 2 women's). In self-catering flats, each kitchen is shared by 5 students. Use of network points in all rooms costs £20/term. A campaign is afoot to add CCTV to the current measures of key-pads and 24-hour security guards after recent thefts.

Car parking: At Sutton Bonington there is some parking, but elsewhere a permit is needed and this is never allocated to 1st years.

EXTERNALLY:
- Ave rent: £42

Availability: *The bad news is that finding suitable housing in Nottingham is not easy. The good news is it is possible.* Lenton and Dunkirk (not that Dunkirk) are good places to look, lying as they do between the campus and the city. Beeston is also a student spot, but slightly further out. Stapleford and Ilkeston are a bit far and Radford is none too safe.

WELFARE

SERVICES:
- Nursery • Nightline • Lesbian & Gay Society • Mature SA
- International SA • Postgrad SA • Minibus • Women's Officer
- Self-defence classes

The Students' Union Student Advice Centre and its 2 counsellors are its pride and joy, co-ordinating all its welfare work from advice and

help for students to the International Students Bureau. It also offers the Union solicitors for consultation (free for the first session). The University employs 4 full- and 5 part-time counsellors in the Student Counselling Service. Cripps Health Centre has 4 doctors, an occupational health specialist and nurses and offers extra care for a £12 annual subscription. Physiotherapists are based in the Sports Centre. Free attack alarms are available to first years, £1 to others.
Disabled: There is a special mobility van and facilities for both hearing- and sight-impaired students, *but despite good intentions, access is a mixed bag. There is good learning support for students with dyslexia.*

FINANCE:
• Access fund: £278,234   • Successful applications: 807
The Registrar's Necessitous Student Fund can offer limited assistance to anyone who can say 'necessitous' and the University gives £50 loans when needed.

Nottingham Trent University

• *Formerly Nottingham Polytechnic, Trent Polytechnic*
The Nottingham Trent University, Burton Street, Nottingham, NG1 4BU. Tel: (0115) 941 8418. Fax: (0115) 848 6503.
E-mail: marketing@ntu.ac.uk
The Nottingham Trent University Union of Students, Byron House, Shakespeare Street, Nottingham, NG1 4GH. Tel: (0115) 848 6200. Fax: (0115) 848 6201.

GENERAL

Once upon a time there was Trent Poly, then it became Nottingham Poly, and now it's in its third incarnation as a university. There are three campuses: the City site in the city centre, the largest site and, *if the truth be known*, the main one; the more modern Clifton site, 4 miles from the centre, and next to Clifton Hall, a *stunning* large Georgian manor which houses the new education block; and a third site at Brackenhurst 14 miles from the city centre.

Sex ratio(M:F): 50%:50%	Founded: 1970
Full time u'grads: 14,045	Part time: 3,810
Postgrads: 1,917	Non-degree: 3,302
Ave course: 3/4yrs	Ethnic: 11.5%
Private school: n/a	Flunk rate: 16.4%
Mature students: 21%	Overseas students: 6.4%
Disabled students: 3.6%	

ATMOSPHERE:
It's a right old mix of ages and backgrounds. Students are scattered geographically, because most live out and because they're spread across both sites. But students from the three sites mingle, despite the fact that both can look after themselves very well, thank you.

THE SITES:
City Site: (art and design, business, environment, law, economics, social sciences, computing and engineering) Just on the edge of the city centre, the University's main campus is a jumble of *lovely* converted three- and four-storey terraces, slabs of *clean* concrete and tower blocks (such as the main Newton Building) with *sparse* green areas between. The Union's main centre is in a block designed as a swimming pool complex. *It's an ugly building, but the lively atmosphere endears it to the regulars.* The Waverly Building, housing the School of Art and Design, has just had a £2.2Mn renovation.
Clifton Campus: (4,916 students – humanities, education, mathematics and science) 4 miles away on a hill overlooking the River Trent and its valley, near where D H Lawrence set 'Sons & Lovers', Clifton is a *small, friendly, modern site with so much to offer that students can get isolated from city life.*
Brackenhurst Campus: (100 students – Land-based studies) 14 miles away from the main site, *eager* students live at this site with some catering facilities, library, sports facilities, SU and bar, all set in *tranquil (aka dull)* farmland and woods.

THE CITY: see University of Nottingham

TRAVEL: see University of Nottingham
Nottingham Station is 1 mile from the City site. Buses cost between 50p and 80p (£1 return) from the City site to Clifton, with several companies running regular services. There's also a new inter-campus bus service which also covers late-night *cavorting*.

CAREER PROSPECTS:
- Careers Service • No of staff: 6 full/11 part
- Unemployed after 6mths: 2.2%

FAMOUS ALUMNI:
Jonathan Glazner (Sexy Beast and Guinness Surfer Ad director); Simon Hodgkinson (rugby player); Paul Kaye (aka Donnie Pennis); Dame Laura Knight (artist); Paul Ratcliffe (Olympic silver medallist canoeing); Alan Simpson MP (Lab, former Union President); Steve Trapmore (Olympic gold medallist rower).

FURTHER INFO:
Prospectuses for undergrads and postgrads, CD-rom, video and a website (www.ntu.ac.uk). More info on (0115) 848 6410. The dept of land, art and design and the main Uni all have different open days for which you gotta book.

Newcastle SU produced a caricature of Liz Hurley saying 'Please Don't Suck My Grant' for their anti-poverty campaign. The actress asked for it to be withdrawn but she was so nice about it that the Union is pushing for her to have an honorary degree.

ACADEMIC

staff/student ratio: 1:18
Range of points required for entrance: 300-120
Percentage accepted through clearing: 16.9%
Number of terms/semesters: 3
Length of terms/semesters: 10wks
Research: 3.1

LIBRARIES:
• Books: 443,000   • Study places: 2,800
There are three libraries at the City and Brackenhurst. The third library, at Clifton, has been renovated and extended, *but it's still short on books.*

COMPUTERS:
• Computer workstations: 1,500
There are Computer Centres at each site, some are available 24-hours.

ENTERTAINMENT

THE CITY: see University of Nottingham

UNIVERSITY:
• Price of a pint of beer: £1.50   • Glass of wine: £1.45
Bars: (4) At the City site, the Glo Bar is *fairly popular* during the day but Le Metro downstairs *seems to close unexpectedly from time to time.* Clifton's bar, 'The Point', 'has recently been refurbished.
Theatre: One customised theatre and two lecture rooms with stages. Shows at both sites from the *uninspiring* drama society.
Clubs/discos/music venues: Once a week at Clifton and twice at the City site, Shipwrecked washes the faithful safely to shore with its blend of charty, dancey, techno stuff. Clifton bar also has a comedy night once a month, while Trolleyed gets them trolleyed. Tease in the Sub Bar. The Acoustic Café in Le Metro *sounds good. Things may be on the up on the band front as Judge Jules, Atomic Kitten and, er, Dane Bowers are on the bill for this year (we said 'may be').* Most nights, entry will set you back £3 to 4 *big ones*, however, at Pounded at Clifton, entry is £1 and drinks are £1 (*double Ribenas, all round, then*).
Food: The Sports Diner, Sandwich City and Chaucer Late deal with all fast food requirements – *the school dinner efforts at the Uni's Legoland-like Refectory pale by comparison.*
Others: Balls are mostly organised by societies but the SU does the big summer affair.

In 1953, just before the Coronation, students from Glasgow University pinched the Stone of Scone from Westminster Abbey, and took it back to Scotland. Sure beats traffic cones.

SOCIAL & POLITICAL

NOTTINGHAM TRENT UNIVERSITY UNION OF STUDENTS (NTUUS):
• 6 sabbaticals • Turnout at last ballot: 28% • NUS member
NTUUS shuns politics, preferring to stress its position as a commercial organisation. Seen as friendly and helpful but politically emasculated. A jolly eunuch, then.

SU FACILITIES:
NTUUS has facilities on both sites: in Byron House on the City site and in the Benenson Building at Clifton. Byron provides two bars, café, two minibuses, one car, travel agent, photocopying, a shop, games and vending machines, pool tables, juke box, bank, recycling facilities, meeting and conference rooms, HSBC bank, Endsleigh Insurance and STA Travel. Clifton offers a bar, coffee bar, shop, bookshop, printing service, pool tables, recycling facilities and games machines. Employment store and ticket agency at both sites.

CLUBS (NON SPORTING):
Chinese Christian; Cocktail; Cult fiction; Bad Poets; Film foundation; Ghanian; Hindu; Human rights; Pirates; Sikh; Soul and dance; Wargames and role-play; Wine-tasting.

OTHER ORGANISATIONS:
'Platform', the weekly NTUUS student newspaper, is distributed free in conjunction with the local 'Evening Post'. Fly FM transmits for 1 month twice a year. The Student Festival Week raises cheques for charity, while the SCAG does noble things in the wider world.

RELIGIOUS:
• 6 chaplains (CofE, RC, Free Church)
The Christian Union is extremely forthright and influential. Muslim prayer 'space'. Societies include: Islamic, Students, Jewish, Sikh, CU, Catholic.
Religion in Nottingham: see University of Nottingham.

PAID WORK: see University of Nottingham
The Employment Store can help to find work with a registration scheme which matches skills to jobs.

SPORTS

• Recent successes: cricket, rugby, hockey, swimming
The primary responsibility for the co-ordination of athletic endeavour is in the hands of NTUUS and goes under the title of 'recreation' rather than sports, *placing the emphasis on fun and fitness rather than trophy-winning.* There is a fee of £5 per year to use facilities, but thereafter charges are nominal. A new annual Varsity cricket match with University of Nottingham starts this year.

> 'Always plan for practice fire alarms at 3 in the morning: extra bodies in a hall of residence are difficult to explain.'
> – Michael Fish, weatherman.

SPORTS FACILITIES:
There are facilities on both sites.
City: A large sports hall; indoor cricket nets; climbing wall; badminton & volleyball courts; fitness suites; 2 squash courts; gym. Enthusiasm is sapped as access to pitches is a bit of a pain.
Clifton: Sports hall; 2 gyms; multigym; 2 squash courts; playing fields; all-weather sports pitch and another new one; athletics track; cricket pitch.

SPORTING CLUBS:
American football; Duke of Edinburgh; Gliding; Hiking; Jiu Jitsu; KSBO; Motorcycle; Mountaineering; Paintball; Rowing; Rugby league; Sky-diving; Snowboarding; Surf; Table tennis; Ultimate frisbee; Water-ski; Women's football; Yawara Ryu.

ATTRACTIONS: see University of Nottingham

ACCOMMODATION

IN COLLEGE:
• Self-catering: 15% • Cost: £50-57 (39wks)
Availability: Only 75% of 1st years live in. Most halls are near the City site (or on the main road that leads to it), with one at Clifton. Very few have to share. *Students who hope to get a place in college would be wise to apply early. Peverill is the most popular digs choice on campus as it's got en-suite facilities.* Brackenhurst site offers places for 100 at £45 per week and limited catering facilities. There's also a University-run head tenancy scheme for 600 students.
Car parking: Parking permits for the limited spaces for a few really deserving cases.

EXTERNALLY: see University of Nottingham
Housing help: The University Accommodation Service has an office on each site and employs five full- and two part-time staff keeping a register of houses, helping with contracts and running a landlord accreditation scheme. NTUUS runs an introduction course to house-hunting for 1st years.

WELFARE

SERVICES:
• Nursery • Nightline • Lesbian, Gay and Transgender Society
• Overseas SA • Minibus • Self-defence classes

The University offers a full counselling service. The medical centres (on both sites) have four doctors and nurses. There are day nurseries on both sites with 87 places (1-5 years) and a holiday play scheme

---

Great exam excuses of our time - students at Anglia Poly University had their exams postponed because the hall didn't have enough desks to go round.

for 5-14 year olds.
Disabled: There is a Disabled Students Society and the self-catering hall in Peel Street has suitable accommodation for students with wheelchairs, students are advised to contact the universities Disability Support Service to ensure barrier free learning. *However, with notable exceptions, access to most buildings is poor.*
Women: Free alarms available to all women.

FINANCE:
• Access fund: £1,013,556 • Successful applications: 992
There's an Emergency Hardship Fund to which students can appeal and the Hillsborough Memorial Bursary is for part-time students.

The Kipper Memorial Prize For Contribution To College Atmosphere at Clare, Cambridge has been set up to commemorate late lamented college cat.

Open University

Oriental Studies see SOAS

University of Oxford
Balliol College, Oxford
Brasenose College, Oxford
Christ Church, Oxford
Corpus Christi College, Oxford
Exeter College, Oxford
Greyfriars Hall, Oxford
Harris Manchester College, Oxford
Hertford College, Oxford
Jesus College, Oxford
Keble College, Oxford
Lady Margaret Hall, Oxford
Lincoln College, Oxford
Magdalen College, Oxford
Mansfield College, Oxford
Merton College, Oxford
New College, Oxford
Oriel College, Oxford
Pembroke College, Oxford
The Queen's College, Oxford
Regent's Park College, Oxford
St Anne's College, Oxford
St Catherine's College, Oxford
St Edmund Hall, Oxford
St Hilda's College, Oxford
St Hugh's College, Oxford
St John's College, Oxford
St Peter's College, Oxford
Somerville College, Oxford
Trinity College, Oxford
University College, Oxford
Wadham College, Oxford
Worcester College, Oxford

Oxford Brookes University

Oxford Poly see Oxford Brookes University

Open University

The Open University, Walton Hall, Milton Keynes, MK7 6AA.
Tel: (01908) 653231. Fax: (01908) 654806.
E-mail: ces-gen@open.ac.uk
Open University Students' Association (OUSA), PO Box 397,
Walton Hall, Milton Keynes, MK7 6BE. Tel: (01908) 652045.
Fax: (01908) 654326. E-mail: ousa@open.ac.uk

Open University

GENERAL

The Open University or 'the OU' to those in the know was set up to provide the opportunity for anyone, regardless of other qualifications, to take a degree through 'distance learning'. *This doesn't mean holding books at arm's length*, nor is it just a correspondence course. Distance learning, as the OU runs it, is a range of teaching media such as TV and radio programmes, computer software, the internet, books and tapes – all providing students with the chance to study for a degree in their own time and in their own homes. There's no campus as such, although there are tutorial rooms and very limited facilities in 350 study centres around the UK and overseas where students and tutors meet. Most students are in their 20s, 30s or 40s and, although they only study part time, OU degrees are as valuable as any others. *They must be doing something right* – plenty of other institutions have started providing distance learning facilities, *but the OU is the original and probably the best at this kind of education*.

Sex ratio(M:F): 46%:54%
Full time u'grads: 0
Postgrads: 29,007
Ave course: 4/6yrs
Private school: n/a
Mature students: 99%
Disabled students: 5%

Founded: 1969
Part time: 129,707
Non-degree: 2,634
Ethnic: 4.5%
Flunk rate: n/a
Overseas students: 5%

ATMOSPHERE:
The old image of middle-aged housewives watching strange men with greasy trousers and flared corduroy hair demonstrating thermodynamics at 3 in the morning is well out of date. The lecturers have cut their hair and the TV programmes are dead trendy. Still, the OU is not, and doesn't attempt to be, like conventional colleges. Most students are studying while they continue to work or raise a family or serve jail sentences or whatever it is they normally do. *OU students are usually very committed to their studies and talk about the increased confidence and opportunities afforded them. Everything is very flexible* and even doing a whole degree is optional. Shorter courses are available as refreshers (for teachers, doctors, business people and so on), for professional qualifications or just for fun. *All this, inevitably, is at the expense of a more conventional student life*. The contact between students is confined to seminars at the study centres and week-long summer schools (not confined to summer), while personal contact and support comes through locally based tutors. *Those who become active in the Students' Association (the exception rather than the rule) see each other a bit, but basically, as the car stickers say, OU students do it on their own.* The OU's unique approach lends itself especially to students that bit older than your standard spotty teenager. Maybe they've got other commitments, like jobs or children, or just don't fancy spending 3 years in an institution. Many OU students left school at 16 and have very few qualifications, so wouldn't be able to study elsewhere even if they wanted to. The OU has nibbled a special niche for itself among students with disabilities, who may have access difficulties elsewhere.

TRAVEL:
Working at home is a distinct advantage when it comes to travel, but the cost of travel to the local study centre for seminars and often long distances to 'summer schools' comes out of the student's pocket. National Express decided that OU students are real students and so deserve discounts. ISIC and rail operators haven't been so generous.

CAREER PROSPECTS:
The OU solves the problem of how to take a degree and pursue a career at the same time. Over 80% of students are in full-time employment and *their employers are often extremely encouraging, particularly for students in the OU's Business School.*

FAMOUS ALUMNI:
Connie Booth (actress/writer, Polly in 'Fawlty Towers'); Julie Christie (actress); Micky Dolenz (ex-Monkee); Lord Gardiner (former Lord Chancellor); Sheila Hancock (actress); Matthew Kelly (stars in his eyes); Dave Sexton (football manager); Susan Tully (ex-'EastEnders' actress). The Chancellor is Betty Boothroyd, former *excellent* Speaker of the House of Commons.

FURTHER INFO:
Various free course guides, brochures and website (www.open.ac.uk).

ACADEMIC

In March 2000 the OU held the world's first Virtual Degree Ceremony, 24 students in 8 different countires received their MAs on-line, all their work and study was also done on-line.

staff/student ratio: 1:18
Range of points required for entrance: n/a
Percentage accepted through clearing: n/a
Number of terms/semesters: n/a
Length of terms/semesters: n/a
Research: 4.3

LIBRARIES AND COMPUTERS:
OU students may find this a particular problem, because, without a campus, the OU is without a library except for a 400,000 volume collection at the OU headquarters in Milton Keynes *which is great for those who can get to it (incidentally, Milton Keynes is strictly for those who think that life as a Fisher Price toy would be paradise).* But there are also 350 study centres around the UK and 4 overseas and OUSA has agreements with students' unions at other colleges so that OU students can use their libraries and other services. *Good* electronic learning facilities including a new on-line library service providing access to 4,000+ journals and core reference books (www.oulib1.open.ac.uk/lib) and a *fantastic* electronic conferencing system which allows students in over 150 courses to join in discussion forums. Many students make their own arrangements with local colleges (for which they often have to pay) or rely on public libraries and *excellent* course aids. The number of courses requiring computer access is increasing and students usually have to find their own – 100,000 students are currently studying on-line with OU.

Social & Political

OPEN UNIVERSITY STUDENTS' ASSOCIATION:
• Turnout at OUSA National Conference: 400-500 delegates
OUSA is not really a political union and most of its campaigns relate directly to academic and welfare issues as they affect OU students (OUSA's pushing for creche facilities at regional centres, for example). The NUS won't accept OU students as members. Of more than 80,000 students, about 12,000 apply for their SA membership cards, but few are genuinely active. OUSA is run by student volunteers and 17 full-time staff.

SA FACILITIES:
OUSA's main role is a campaigning and representative one and there is no union building, although they do sell stationery and other products by mail and organise a few handy services such as societies, back exam papers and ents at the Summer Schools.

CLUBS (NON SPORTING):
Change Ringers; London; London Arts; Music; OU Graduates; Poetry; Postal Chess; Remote Students; Shakespeare.

OTHER ORGANISATIONS:
OUSA staff publish 'OU Student' and the University publishes 'Sesame', which both feature students' contributions. 'Open Graduate' has been relaunched as 'Open Eye'. Students raise OUSET funds and this takes the place of any Rag organisation.

Welfare

SERVICES:
• Lesbian & Gay Society • Postgrad SA
OUSA offers some advisers and there are full-time senior counsellors at the 13 regional centres and at the Summer Schools.

FINANCE:
• Access fund: £804,720 • Successful applications: 4,435
Students wanting to take OU degrees often have to fork out about £500 a year in fees themselves. Many turn to their employers who often look on it as an investment, some take out loans (government student loans aren't available). Last year the University paid out £6,496,545 in bursaries to 12,619 students. Students on certain benefits can have their fees waived.

Oriental Studies

see SOAS

> A petition against a proposed hall of residence at Royal Holloway claimed that local businesses would decline as students do not require anything except cheap food.

University of Oxford

University of Oxford, University Offices, Wellington Square,
Oxford, OX1 2JD. Tel: (01865) 270207. Fax: (01865) 270208.
E-mail: undergraduate.admissions@admin.ox.ac.uk
Oxford University Student Union (OUSU), New Barnett House,
28 Little Clarendon Street, Oxford, OX1 2HU.
Tel: (01865) 270777. Fax: (01865) 270778.
E-mail: president@ousu.ox.ac.uk

GENERAL

The oldest university in Britain and, along with Cambridge, probably the most famous in the world. It is split into 39 colleges and 6 private halls, which all have their own unique features – hence, Oxford's catch-phrase: '...except for some of the colleges'. Each college is self-managing, though applications are co-ordinated centrally and the University also provides many central facilities. In addition to the colleges described here (those who admit undergraduates) there are 6 private halls and 7 graduate colleges – for further info about these, contact the University at the above address.

The citizens of Oxford manage to avoid virtually all contact with students despite their influence. It's a bit like one of those Escher drawings where faceless wraiths walk up and down the same set of stairs, but are completely ignorant of each other's existence. It is, however, impossible to ignore the stunning elegance of Oxford, the city of the 'dreaming spires' of the colleges' chapels. Around every unassuming corner is a scene from everyone's stereotypical image of Oxford with the River Cherwell or the Thames (or Isis, as it's called around here) completing the picture. The buildings in the city centre date from every century since the years reached 4 figures. They are all connected with the University, but these are interspersed with shops, supermarkets, houses and all things civic. Just 10 miles out of the city are the villages and hills of the Cotswolds.

Sex ratio(M:F): 57%:43%	**Founded: c1150**
Full time u'grads: 10,993	**Part time: 0**
Postgrads: 4,901	**Non-degree: 492**
Ave course: 3yrs	**Ethnic: 16%**
Private school: 50%	**Flunk rate: 1.4%**
Mature students: 6%	**Overseas students: 32%**
Disabled students: 4%	

BEING A STUDENT IN OXFORD:
If someone says s/he's a student at Oxford, people will immediately think of intellectual superiority, gowns, punts, teddy-bears, jugs of Pimm's and re-runs of 'Inspector Morse'. The stereotypes are – as are most stereotypes – true in part.
Oxford is indeed a hive of tradition – it is the elephant's tusk from which the original ivory tower of academia was carved. It is full of pomposity and circumstance and some of the students are as intelligent, and some are as arrogant, as the myths tell. On the other hand, some are not so special nor so intimidating and nobody should

assume that everyone will be brainier or posher or more deserving than them. The legends of excellence mainly spring from an utter intensity of activity. At Oxford, it is just not 'the done thing' to concentrate on your degree to the exclusion of all else. No one should underestimate the work involved but Oxford students are also constantly active in other ways too: in politics, debating, sports, drama, the media or worm-breeding. They almost all find some untrivial pursuit.

Life for many is centred around their colleges. Unless students live out, they eat, sleep, play and work in their college. In theory, it would actually be possible to avoid ever leaving and rumour has it that this is what some dons – as tutors are called (but not by students) – have been doing for centuries. Students, however, usually find the colleges, which range in size from 15 (Campion Hall) to over 615 (Keble), are altogether too claustrophobic for 24 hours a day. The atmosphere varies enormously from college to college, from the supposedly stuffy Magdalen to the tentatively trendy Wadham. It would be almost as big a mistake to apply to any old college (or new college, for that matter), as it would be to apply to just any university without discretion and preparation. Features worth watching for are whether the college does the course you want to do, how big it is, the sex ratio, the accommodation, where it is and how it's designed (St Catherine's buildings are uncommonly modern for Oxford, and New College is, ironically, very old).

THE CITY:
- Population: 146,100
- London: 55miles
- Bristol: 55miles
- Birmingham: 55miles

If tourists want to 'do' England properly, they must 'do' Oxford. They *must* tour the colleges, go for a punt on the river and possibly drop in to one of the city's many museums, especially the famous Ashmolean and Pitt Rivers Museums. However, it's not all atmospheric shots from 'Morse'. Real people do also live in Oxford and for them there are plenty of shops (including 2 shopping malls), banks, a market, public libraries and enough new and second-hand bookshops *to fill a village on their own*. On the seedier side, there are also 2 brothels in Jericho, North Oxford – *it being one of the more gentrified and richer parts of the city. Also, amongst Oxford's more dubious honours*, the city has one of the worst homelessness problems outside London.

TRAVEL:
Trains: Trains draw up at Oxford Station, close to the steps of the city's most central colleges. Mainline services to London (£11.20), Bristol (£17.80), etc.
Coaches: As well as National Express serving London (£7), Bristol (£12) and all points beyond, there are other coach companies (Oxford Express) serving London only, with City Link also going to and from Heathrow and Gatwick. For London, the bus is much cheaper than the train *and not much slower*.
Car: 10 mins off the M40. Also on the A40, A34, A423, A43 and A420. However, there is very *restricted access* to the city centre and parking is either limited or expensive. Car theft is also a problem – remember the University is only a few miles from the infamous joyriders of Blackbird Leys.
Hitching: *Pretty good on the M40 or the larger local A roads, but get out of the city by bus.*
Local: Several local bus companies with *frequent and cheap* services

(40p to get as far as digs in Jericho), *but they're not really worth it for shorter trips.*
Taxis: *Enough of them, but they cost a lot.*
Bicycles: *Ah yes. Paradise on pedals.* Oxford is flat, some roads are closed to cars and most colleges have sheds. *Two words of warning: (i) a good lock and a cheap bike is the safest defence against theft and (ii) pedestrians, beware of pedal-powered hell's angels. That's 21 words.*

CAREER PROSPECTS:
- Careers Service • No of staff: 11 full-time
- Unemployed after 6mths: 3%

There is a theory that certain fields of employment won't take anyone unless they've been to Oxford (or maybe Cambridge). The professions particularly pinpointed include politics, the civil service, journalism (the BBC especially), law and high finance. *Some say this is just paranoia, but that doesn't mean they're not out to get the non-Oxbridge types.* Whatever the truth, the Careers Service is *big* and offers a variety of services including vacancy lists, careers library, talks, counselling and so on.

SPECIAL FEATURES:
- *Oxford is full of ritual*, especially when it comes to exams where students have to dress in subfusc and *look like batman on the way to the Oscars*. It is a well-known myth that once a student turned up for his finals exams and demanded a glass of sherry in accordance with an ancient rite. After the exam, he was fined a shilling by his college authorities for not wearing his sword during his exam – another forgotten statute. *Rites like these seem positively sane when compared with some of the continuing traditions.*

FURTHER INFO:
Prospectuses for undergrads and postgrads. Also available are the Alternative Prospectus (£4.65 inc p&p) and the Oxford Handbook (£6.85) from OUSU – *both excellent*. Most colleges produce their own prospectuses and some JCRs also cobble together their own alternative guides. University and SU websites (www.ox.ac.uk and www.ousu.ox.ac.uk) and most colleges and departments also have their own.

ACADEMIC

Oxford has terms of just 8 weeks, *though it would be a tragic error to think that means long lazy days of vacant vacation.* Exams such as 'mods' *(nothing to do with parka-wearing bike-riding Paul Weller fans)*, 'collections' *(nothing to do with church plates and small change)* and 'prelims' await students' return. The new Begbroke Business & Science Park has integrated science research with business start-ups. There's also the new Said Business School.

staff/student ratio: 1:3
Range of points required for entrance: 360-340
Percentage accepted through clearing: 0%
Number of terms/semesters: 3
Length of terms/semesters: 8wks
Research: 6.3

LIBRARIES:
- Books: 6,000,000 • Study places: 2,507+

Contrary to popular belief, Oxford students tend to spend more time in libraries than pubs. This isn't just because the opening hours are longer, but also because the choice of libraries is virtually unparalleled. The famous Bodleian Library is the collective title given to the University's main research libraries (including the Radcliffe Science Library, Bodleian Law Library and Indian Institute Library, mainly housed in the Old and the New Library Buildings, and all the *marvellous* others). It is one of the country's 5 copyright libraries which means that it can demand a copy of any book published in this country and, as a consequence, it has over 6 million books, including The Push Guides. 948,000 of these – yup, a mere 948,000 – are on open shelves and most of them can't be borrowed, *though students can view them if they ask nicely.* In fact, Oxford students don't have the right to use the Bodleian until they've undergone one of the University's many *bizarre* initiation rituals. Like so many others, this one involves wearing a gown and swearing oddly practical oaths such as agreeing not to set fire to the buildings. *Nude dancing and sacrificing virgin goats is not usually an essential part of this ceremony.* Each college and University department also has its own library, most of which lend books.

COMPUTERS:
- Computer workstations: 2,405

The story for computer facilities is less impressive although most colleges have woken up to the idea of an IT revolution and upgraded from their clapped-out Amstrads. There is also the Computer Teaching Centre with 100 networked terminals and the Computer Service which provides support for students' research where their departments fall short. 24-hour access during term-time and many college rooms have free access to the University network and internet.

ENTERTAINMENT

IN TOWN:
- Price of a pint of beer: £2.50 • Glass of wine: £2.10

Cinemas: For standard blockbusters there are 2 ABC Cinemas (3 screens and 1 screen) *and for the slightly higher brow,* The Phoenix (2) in Jericho and The Ultimate Picture Palace in Cowley.

Theatres: The Apollo has standard family entertainment with pantos at Xmas and summer specials after the end of term. Occasionally it also hosts concerts. The Oxford Playhouse hosts more thespian offerings, including a few student productions. The Pegasus Theatre is on the fringe in every sense with experimental productions and a bit of a trek to get there. It also shows student productions. The Old Fire Station also hosts theatrical endeavours.

Pubs: *Although expensive, Oxford's pubs have ubiquitous old world charm and the advantage of not being monopolised by students. It would be unfair not to mention a few of Oxford's most studenty haunts, although it's also unfair to mention only these:* The King's Arms ('The KA' as it's affectionately known); The Turf; The Bullingdon Arms; The Lamb & Flag (now owned by St John's); The Horse and Jockey; The Eagle and Child (CS Lewis and Tolkien used to quaff there). The Jolly Farmers is the main gay haunt.

Clubs/discos: *Most clubs go for the lowest common denominator and then work downwards.* Pushplugs: Club Zoo; Safari at Club Latino (indie); The Studio and The Coven II are also popular.

Music venues: *The music scene is booming, with dozens of hopefuls taking a lead from local boys made good Radiohead and Supergrass.* Oxford also has Oxygen FM, the first UK student radio station to get a permanent FM licence (on 107.9FM). Check out the free mag 'Nightshift' for details of gigs etc. Pushplugs: The Apollo (big, mainstream); The Pub Oxford; The Zodiac (indie).

Eating out: There are various kebab vans *open till they run out of domestic animals or 3am whichever is sooner.* Cowley Road in general is good for cheap eats. Pushplugs: Brown's (perfect parent parlour); Jamal's (Indian); Queen's Lane Coffee House; George and Davis (ice cream); Radcliffe Arms (pub grub); La Cappanina (Italian, *Supergrass ate here*).

UNIVERSITY:
• Price of a pint of beer: £1.20 • Glass of wine: £1.20

Bars: Each college has its own bar (see college entries following), some of which serve only their own students – officially, that is. *It is in these bars that students find their college identity. Some also find themselves talking to God and seeing indigo meerkats, but that's what comes of cheap alcohol.* 'The Union' (see later) has a bar – again, officially only for members, but Push managed to get served.

Balls: No, not an unsubtle insult – each college (except for some – spot the Oxford catch-phrase) has an annual ball, which is a big dinner with everyone in posh frocks and penguin suits with loads of live bands, discos, cabarets, casinos, hypnotists, karaoke, in fact anything that becomes a lot more fun when completely pissed. *Sounds great? Well, for some, it's the lark of a lifetime. For others, balls are a sickening Sloane-swamped waste of about £80 in one night.* Either way, balls are an Oxbridge institution. Some colleges have a cheaper alternative called an 'event', which usually doesn't involve the get-up or the grub and costs nearer £20.

Theatres: If a room is large enough to fit in more audience than cast members, then the likelihood is that it has been, is being, or will be used as a theatre for student productions. In particular, there's the customised Burton-Taylor Theatre (above The Playhouse) and the larger Newman Rooms. In summer, there are also outdoor productions in many College gardens.

Clubs/discos: Frequent bops pop in almost every college.

Cabaret: Every week The Oxford Revue (student comedy group *which for several years now has out-jested Cambridge Footlights*) performs stand-up and impro at the Comedy Cellar at 'the Union' (see later) and does other special shows.

Music venues: The twice weekly Purple Turtle at 'the Union' has live jazz, but a capacity of only 80. Student bands play in any room large enough – bars usually – and the Sheldonian Theatre and Holywell Music rooms host classical concerts. However, because the University has no single big venue, it doesn't often attract big names, except at college balls *when old has-beens crawl out of their coffins, for example Desmond Dekker, Shawaddywaddy and so on. Crumblies they may be, but most of them have still got what it takes.*

Food: Oxford tends to go for formal meals in a *big way*, although the frequency, quality and number of *ludicrous* rituals differs from college to college. There are cafeterias, often known (*in true boarding school fashion*) as 'butteries'. Apart from these, there are few University facilities – no central refectory, although some faculties have caffs.

SOCIAL & POLITICAL

OXFORD UNIVERSITY STUDENT UNION (OUSU):
• 6 sabbaticals • Turnout at last ballot: 33%

The big thing about OUSU is that it doesn't have a union building. Well, they feel really insecure about it anyway. Being a strongly collegiate University, the colleges provide most of the services that Students' Unions offer elsewhere. The purpose of OUSU is largely to step in at a University-wide level on representation and campaigning. It also provides a soap box for students who find their college's Junior Common Room ('JCRs' are mini Students' Unions) too parochial. The JCRs affiliate to OUSU and give it much of its funding. OUSU isn't a member of NUS, but some JCRs are. Confused? Well, don't worry, it's not important. The important thing to know is that every student is a member of OUSU, but, like anywhere else, it is run by a collection of hack activists. It is also worth noting the phenomenal number of clubs OUSU co-ordinates and their excellent publications such as the Oxford Handbook, the Alternative Prospectus (see above), Freshers' Guide, a variety of handbooks and so on. Politically, OUSU is a bit to the left of many Oxford students.

CLUBS (NON SPORTING):
Acoustic Music; Air Squadron; Alice (Lewis Carroll Appreciation); Alternative Classical; Apathy; Arcadian Singers (unaccompanied singing); Archaeological; Architectural; Art; Arthurian; Artificial Intelligence; Arts; Astronomical; Australia; Bach Choir; Ba'hai; Ballroom Dancing; Bell Ringing; Black Caucus; Bonn (Oxford's German twin town); Book-Lovers; Bow Group (Conservative ideology); Brazilian; Buddhist; Caledonian (Scottish dancing); Friends of Cambodia; Campaign for an Independent Europe (anti- EU); Canadian; Central America Support; Ceroc (French-style jive dancing); Chamber Choir; Champagne Socialists; Choice (teacher & pupil support); Christian Aid; Student Christian Movement; Christian Science; Classical; Classical Drama; Colombian; Comedy Cellar; Comic Books; Community Church; Computing; Contemporary Music; Cranmer (Anglican Christian); Creative Writing; Cribbage; CS Lewis Appreciation; Cypriot; Dangerous Sports; Diplomatic (tactical board games); Dr Who; Douglas Adams ('Hitch Hikers' Guide to the Galaxy'); Early Music; East Asian Research; Educational Exchange (studying abroad); English-Speaking Union; Enterprise; Esperanto; European Community; Exploration; Film Foundation; Alternative Film; Food & Wine; Freedom (dance music); French; Gamelan (Javanese percussion); German; Gilbert & Sullivan; Go (oriental game); Greek; Guitar; History; History Alive!; Homeless Action; Hong Kong; Humanist; Hunt Sabs; Indie Music; Inner Temple (Law); International Political Economy; Investment; Israel; Italian; Japanese; Juggling; Kites; Laissez-Faire Dining (individual freedoms and food); Latin American; Law; L'Chaim (Jewish cultural); Legal Aid; Light Entertainment; Links (St John Ambulance); Literary Society; Living Marxism; La Maison Française (French cultural); Malaysia-Singapore; Malaysian; Middle-East; Middle Temple (Law); Monty Python Appreciation; Motor Drivers; Natural History; Natural Philosophy; New Testament; Numismatic (Coins); Ockham (philosophical); Opera; Ornithology; Pacific Rim; Past & Present Historical; Pastorate (Christian); Peripheral Vision (film/Third World issues); Club de Pétanque (French game); Philharmonia; Plough (bio-environmental); Poetry; Polish & Central European; Politics; Pooh Sticks (A A Milne appreciation); Practical Arts; Psychology; Railway; Reformed Church; Role-Playing Games; Russian; Save the Children; Schola Cantoram (Chamber Choir); Scientific; Scottish Dance; Scout & Guide; Sherlock Holmes; Sinfonietta (chamber orchestra); Soul Appreciation; Soviet Jewry Campaign; Space Exploration; Spanish; Star Trek; Strategic Studies; Tawney (discussion); Theatre-Going; Tolkein; Tory Reform; Turf (horse-racing & gambling); UNICEF; Upfront (soul/hip-hop/house disco); Vedic (Indian); Vegetarian; Visual Productions (film/video); Wagner (appreciation); Wargaming; Welsh; John Wesley (Christian); Wheatsheaf (pub philosophy); Wind Orchestra; Wine; WWF; Wychwood Warriors (dark ages); Yank (Americans).

OTHER ORGANISATIONS:
Students who spend their days at Oxford doing nothing but their degrees are made to feel like David Beckham at a Mensa meeting. There are plenty of fields of endeavour to choose from including various sports, OUSU and college JCRs as well as the following:
The Oxford Union Society: Not to be confused with OUSU (the Students' Union), 'The Union' is Oxford's world famous debating

society. Ted Heath, Edwina Currie and Benazir Bhutto are among the many, many famous ex-presidents. Its high profile has attracted some of the world's most famous speakers to take part in debates and discussions, from Yasser Arafat to Vinny Jones, JFK to Kermit the Frog. 'The Union' is also their HQ building which offers a social scene, a bar, restaurant, the Comedy Cellar, a library and all the paraphernalia of traditional gentlemen's clubs, but women can join too. *That's the good news. The bad news is that it costs £100 and The Union is a nest for some of the University's most arrogant and obnoxious knob-ends.*

Oxford University Dramatic Society (OUDS): Almost every day of every term, the population of Oxford is faced with a choice of several student theatrical performances. Thesps visit each other's productions and thus the shows go on. *The standard often reaches a thoroughly professional level, but sometimes, well, it doesn't, and the selection is as diverse as any legal experience in a theatre can get.* Whether the star of Spielberg's last pic or the third sheep in the primary school nativity effort, new talent is welcomed to auditions with open arms, kisses on both cheeks and the words 'lovely, daaarling'. The post-audition reception is more discriminating and bitter cries of 'clique!' have echoes of truth, although drama at Oxford is so widespread that even the most wooden pretenders get a chance to try their board-treading technique. Meanwhile, there are just as many opportunities to play the non-singing part of unsung hero backstage. OUDS is the organisational body which co-ordinates and supports this plague of plays and runs the Cuppers drama competition.

The Media: Magazines come and go as fast as the tourists in Oxford but there are several long-standing publications *with excellent reputations*. Primarily, there's 'Cherwell', Oxford's award-winning weekly student newspaper. Last of the newspapers and least, is OUSU's 'Oxford Student'. For magazines, there's 'Isis', the students' answer to 'Vogue' and verbosity, and various others such as 'International Review', 'Amazon' (women's), 'Phoenix' (termly magazine of student writing, both poetry and prose) and a recycling binfull of college gossip/scandal rags and societies' newsletters.

Music: *It would be unfair not to mention Oxford's many student bands and classical music groups, so now, we've mentioned them.*

Rag: With its own sabbatical co-ordinator, Rag raises over £50,000 a year with all the standard pranks, stunts and events.

Student Volunteer Action: *The relationship between the students and the locals can't be described as nasty – they just tend to misunderstand or ignore each other.* Volunteer Action links students up with nearly 40 help groups both in the University and the local community, *going some way to improve matters in the process.* All sorts of other activities incude KEEN which works with kids and young adults with special needs.

RELIGIOUS:

Put any group of self-consciously intellectual people together – such as Oxford students – and within minutes they'll have established as many different religious groups as they can invent and then some. The fervour for activity amongst Oxford students extends to religion as much as anything else. Many of the colleges owe their existence to funding from Christian sinners in fear of hell and the religious rock rolls on.

Christianity: Students at Christ Church who say they're popping down to the college chapel are talking about Oxford's Anglican cathedral.

The other colleges have less 'high church' chapels and most have at least one chaplain. Other Christian denominations are also catered for around town: Catholics, Baptists, Evangelicals, Methodists, URC, Seventh-Day Adventists, Christian Scientists, Pentecostals, Unitarians, Quakers, Orthodox, Cliff Richard Fan Club and so on. The Inter-Collegiate Christian Union (OICCU) brings these Christian groups together *(Ireland could do with them)*.
Islam: Mosque and prayer room at the Islamic Studies centre.
Jews: Local synagogue and large Jewish student population.

PAID WORK:
With nearly 25,000 students (including <u>Oxford Brookes University</u>) competition could be an issue, but with the hectic pace of academic and social life at Oxford, many find it hard to find the time anyhow, although some students earn a bob in shops and college bars. *If you really need the cash, rob a bank.*

SPORTS

- <u>Recent successes: boat race, rugby, cross channel swim</u>

One of the highest accolades in university sport (apart from being able to drink a pint of beer in under 3 seconds) is an Oxbridge 'blue'. To earn one of these, you've got to be selected for one of the University's major sports teams. These teams often compete on a first class level, which doesn't necessarily mean that they're better than all the other university teams, just they're highly respected and they expect highly. There are those of a cruel and malicious disposition who claim that the University admissions procedure becomes a whole lot more flexible if you have an international sporting reputation. Push would (for legal reasons) like to distance itself from any suggestion of the sort. Suffice it to say that the University places emphasis and funding on its impressive record in sports both minor and major. Sport at a college level is more geared to fun and fitness and is very welcoming, even to students who aren't quite Olympians.

SPORTS FACILITIES:
All colleges have their own facilities to varying degrees and the University has an *excellent* range of central amenities: floodlit all-weather hockey pitch; playing fields; sports halls; squash courts; athletics field; bowls and croquet in the quads; tennis courts; gym (with multi-gym); and, of course, the rivers Isis and Cherwell. The town also has a golf course, ice rink and 2 swimming pools.

SPORTING CLUBS:
Aerobics; Aikido; American Football; Board Sailing; Boxing; Bridge; Croquet; Gliding; Gymnastics; Hang Gliding; Ice Hockey; Kayak; Korfball; Lacrosse; Mountain Bike; Pentathlon; Pistol; Polo; Rambling & Hill-walking; Real Tennis; Rifle; Rowing; Rugby League; Shoringo Kempo; Squash; Sul Ki Do; Table Football; Tiddlywinks; Triathlon; Water Polo; Yachting.

ATTRACTIONS:
The Combined Oxford Universities Cricket team is a joint effort with <u>Oxford Brookes</u>. Oxford United Football Club are the local round-ballers and the city also has its own ice hockey team.

```
Get Your money's worth... read 'Pushover: how
to use Push' at the front of the book.
```

ACCOMMODATION

IN COLLEGE:
• Catered: 87%
Availability: One of the best features of the Oxford colleges is that accommodation is guaranteed in college rooms *(often of an excellent standard)* for all 1st years. Most colleges also provide for finalists and so, if they want, students can usually stay in college for all but one of their years – though some can even stay in for their whole university career. What's more, rooms are cleaned, beds are made and *sleeping partners are frowned upon* by 'bedders' or 'scouts' in most colleges. Each college has its own quirks and quiddities, for example, St Hilda's is all-female and in some colleges most 1st years have to share, but all this stuff varies from college to college and details can be found in the entries following. Centrally, the University has no accommodation other than a few flats – about 390 places – for families, couples and single graduates, *but you can offer to snog the Chancellor to get them and it still won't help*.

EXTERNALLY:
• Ave rent: £55
Availability: *Most housing is organised by letting agencies which have a nasty policy of panicking students into snapping up property months before they need to move in – the agencies then suck up the interest from their hefty deposits. The flipside is that quality's pretty good – at their prices, it should be.* Cowley Road and Jericho are the preferred locations but everywhere's expensive – nearly as much as London.
Housing help: *The best way of finding a house is to get friendly with someone who's got one the year before you need it.* You can also turn to agencies who'll charge a supplement, or to ads on notice-boards around the colleges. The University-run Accommodation Office with 4 full-time staff, a vacancies list and bulletin board usually points students in the right direction. The local Housing Rights Centre is much frequented by students, but, like OUSU, they can only offer free advice and don't have any vacancies to dish out.

WELFARE

SERVICES:
• 2 Nurseries • Lesbian & Gay Society • Minibus
• Women's Officer • Self-defence classes
The academic and social pressures of Oxford can seem overwhelming but the University is onto the problem. The University operates a central counselling service with 3 full- and 7 part-time staff and some individual colleges have their own arrangements. The OUSU Welfare Officer can advise and refer students with most problems. Law students give free advice at OUSU 2 days a week. 2 nurseries for 94 of those loud little 4 months–5 year-olds, plans for a third.
Women: St Hilda's is the last all-female college. *Life in the male-dominated colleges can often be just that.* The University has a harassment code, to deal with the worst macho excesses. A nightwalk service accompanies women walking alone at night and there's a women-only bus.

Disabled: Over the past 8 centuries, access for people with disabilities has not been given a high priority by architects and Oxford suffers as a result. Things are improving and efforts include OUSU's disabled access guide, a disability co-ordinator and Taylor House, an accommodation block with special facilities. Some colleges have Braille machines, etc.

FINANCE:
- Access fund: £625,931
- Successful applications: 78% of applicants are successful

The University operates the central Access Fund, while other hardship funds are run by the College. *Some of them are very well off and can provide support in the form of loans, grants, bursaries or prizes to a pocket-popping extent.*

Balliol College, Oxford

- *The College is part of <u>University of Oxford</u> and students are entitled to use its facilities.*

Balliol College, Broad Street, Oxford, OX1 3BJ. Tel: (01865) 277748.
Fax: (01865) 277730. E-mail: admissions@balliol.ox.ac.uk
Junior Common Room, Balliol College, Oxford, OX1 3BJ.
Tel: (01865) 277744. Fax: (01865) 240152.
E-mail: jcr.admissions@balliol.ox.ac.uk
Website: www.balliol.ox.ac.uk

Balliol is one of the oldest, largest, *famous-est and central-est* colleges, just 350 metres from the Carfax chippy. *Academic standards are high, yet the atmosphere remains relatively relaxed, with a cosmopolitan flavour lent by the proportion of international students. Descriptions of the buildings range from 'idiosyncratically Gothic' through 'silly Disney' to 'unpleasant and stripey'.*

Sex ratio(M:F): 60%:40%	Founded: 1263
Full time u'grads: 406	Postgrads: 140
Private school: 35%	Mature students: 1%
Overseas students: 25%	Disabled students: 0

2 bars; 2 or 3 *sweaty* bops per term in JCR Norway Rm (cap 250); May Event (<u>not</u> Ball) has a big-name band, but no penguin suits. Recitals in dining hall (cap 450) and free student bands in bar; cabaret and karaoke. 'John de Balliol' weekly news sheet in loos. Anglican chapel. Library (110,000 books); 30 computers, 24hr access. *Good* sports facilities and *does okay in a variety of sports;* sports fields 5 mins away. College tortoise – Rosa. All students live in except 75% of 2nd years; pay-as-you-eat self-service; *legendary* JCR pantry. Hardship funds, living-out grants; doctor, nurse. Taxi fund, rape alarms and free tampons.

FAMOUS ALUMNI:
Rabbi Lionel Blue (writer, broadcaster); Richard Dawkins (scientist); Graham Greene (writer); Sir Edward Heath (former Con PM); Gerard Manley Hopkins (poet); Aldous Huxley (writer); Lord Jenkins (Oxford University Chancellor); Howard Marks (dope evangelist); Adam Smith (economist); Algernon Swinburne ('perverse' poet); Stephen Twigg MP (Lab, Portillo-slayer); Hugo Young ('The Guardian').

Brasenose College, Oxford

- **The College is part of <u>University of Oxford</u> and students are entitled to use its facilities.**
Brasenose College, Radcliffe Square, Oxford, OX1 4AJ. Tel: (01865) 277510. Fax: (01865) 277520. E-mail: brasinfo@brasenose.ox.ac.uk
Junior Common Room, Brasenose College, Oxford, OX1 4AJ.
Tel: (01865) 277510. Fax: (01865) 277520.
Website: www.bnc.ox.ac.uk

Brasenose College is named after its brass door knocker (made in 1279 and now hanging over the high table) which is shaped like an animal's face with a pronounced snout (ie. brazen nose). *The College is ideally situated at the heart of the University in Radcliffe Square and 300 metres from Carfax. The College is very sporty, with a bit of a rugby-lad feel to the place, but they're tolerant with it and an arty side is emerging strongly Law, PPE, History and English along with an increasing number of scientists.* The students also provide the University with a steady stream of journalists for 'Cherwell' and so on.

Sex ratio(M:F): 60%:40%	Founded: 1509
Full time u'grads: 355	Postgrads: 120
Private school: 55%	Mature students: 1%
Overseas students: 14%	Disabled students: 1%

Excellent bar (cap 120). Student bands in the dining hall (200), JCR (100) and a basement room (100); bops 3 times per term, quizzes and karaoke; annual drama and arts mini-festival; biennial ball. New publication 'Sanesober'. Anglican chapel. 2 libraries (60,000 books); 20 computers, 24hrs. Oldest rowing club, strong in rugby, hockey; sports fields 5 mins bike ride away. All 1st and 3rd years live in; some cooking facilities for finalists. CCTV, entry-phones; doctor, nurse; attack alarms issued.

FAMOUS ALUMNI:
Lord Jeffrey Archer (briefly); Colin Cowdrey (cricketer); Stephen Dorrell MP (Con); William Golding (writer); Field Marshall Earl Haig (WW1); Michael Palin ('Monty Python', etc); Lord Runcle (former Archbishop of Canterbury); Lord Saville (Law Lord); Andrew Lindsay (Olympic Gold Medallist).

Christ Church, Oxford

- **The College is part of <u>University of Oxford</u> and students are entitled to use its facilities.**
Christ Church, St Aldate's, Oxford, OX1 1DP.
Tel: (01865) 276181. Fax: (01865) 286583.
E-mail: tutor.admissions@christ-church.ox.ac.uk
Junior Common Room, Christ Church, Oxford, OX1 1DP.
Tel: (01865) 276166. Fax: (01865) 286335.
Website: www.chch.ox.ac.uk

Christ Church ('The House'), just 200 metres from Carfax, is the home of Oxford's Anglican cathedral. *When people dream about the dreaming spires of Oxford, the spires of Christ Church are the ones they remember when they wake up. There are 5 fine quads and a meadow stretching down to the river. The architecture and tradition*

can be quite daunting to outsiders, but the natives are friendly, often arty or thespian with a high involvement in Oxygen FM.

Sex ratio(M:F): 57%:43%	Founded: 1525
Full time u'grads: 426	Postgrads: 154
Private school: 52%	Mature students: 2%
Overseas students: 5%	Disabled students: 7%

Bar; occasional theme discos in the 'Undercroft' (cap 120) or JCR with occasional student bands; annual Ball; own picture gallery with works by Michelangelo and Raphael. *JCR steers clear of political debate.* 'Chit Chat' bogsheet. 2 libraries (160,000 books and other treasures); 12 computers, 24hrs. *Quality* sports fields 5 mins away, swimming success. Everyone lives in; *spacious* rooms; vacation accommodation feasible; evening meal either formal *(gown and tie with Latin and bigwigs sitting at high table),* or *the standard scoff scuffle;* veggie option. CCTV. *Generous* hardship fund; nurse, doctor and counsellor. *Limited* access for disabled students, *but they try.*

FAMOUS ALUMNI:
WH Auden (poet); Lewis Carroll (writer); Alan Clark (late Con MP, diarist); David Dimbleby (broadcaster); Einstein (briefly); 13 Prime Ministers including William Gladstone; Lord Hailsham (ex-Lord Chancellor); Lord Nigel Lawson (slimming guru and ex-Chancellor); Anna Pasternak (Di 'n' Hewitt hack); Sir Robert Peel (founder of the police); Auberon Waugh (controversialist).

Corpus Christi College, Oxford

- **The College is part of University of Oxford and students are entitled to use its facilities.**

Corpus Christi College, Merton Street, Oxford, OX1 4JF. Tel: (01865) 276737. Fax: (01865) 276767. E-mail: college.office@ccc.ox.ac.uk
Junior Common Room, Corpus Christi College, Merton Street, Oxford, OX1 4JF. Tel: (01865) 276693. Fax: (01865) 793121.
Website: www.ccc.ox.ac.uk

500 metres from Carfax is one of Oxford's smallest colleges – *classic dreaming spire-type* buildings from the 16th, 18th, 19th and 20th centuries, around *standard pretty paved* quads backing onto Christ Church meadow. At the front of the College is a famous Pelican sundial and the main quad is bordered by an *elegant* Tudor building. *Corpus has a strong academic reputation but by no means is it stuffy or dull.*

Sex ratio(M:F): 63%:37%	Founded: 1517
Full time u'grads: 220	Postgrads: 106
Private school: 51%	Mature students: 1%
Overseas students: 11%	Disabled students: 1%

The Beer Cellar Bar (cap 150, closed Saturday nights); 'sweaty bops' every fortnight; theme nights and gigs in the bar, concerts in new music room; annual 'Mayhem' event; Burns night with haggis and pipes. 16th century library (60,000 books); reading rooms; 16 computers, 24hrs. 'Smallprint' magazine and weekly newsletter; music and drama increasingly popular; annual tortoise race with Balliol for charity. Playing fields (5 acres) 15mins walk; shares a boathouse; *emphasis on participation and fun rather than sporting* honours but football's strong. Everyone can live in college in *pretty good* rooms on site and shares the *plush* Liddell housing complex in Iffley Rd with Christ Church; phone/internet points in all rooms; *excellent* food, veggie option. Doctors and nurse; dentist; *excellent* welfare.

FAMOUS ALUMNI:
Dr Arnold (of Rugby fame); Sir Isaiah Berlin (writer); Robert Bridges (Poet Laureate); Brough Scott (racing commentator); Vikram Seth (novelist); William Waldegrave MP (Con).

Exeter College, Oxford

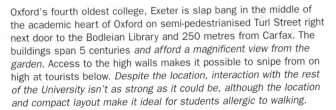

- **The College is part of <u>University of Oxford</u> and students are entitled to use its facilities.**
Exeter College, Turl Street, Oxford, OX1 3DP. Tel: (01865) 279660. Fax: (01865) 279630. E-mail: admissions@exeter.ox.ac.uk
The Stapledon Society, Exeter College, Turl Street, Oxford, OX1 3DP. Tel: (01865) 279600. Fax: (01865) 279645.
Website: www.exeter.ox.ac.uk

Oxford's fourth oldest college, Exeter is slap bang in the middle of the academic heart of Oxford on semi-pedestrianised Turl Street right next door to the Bodleian Library and 250 metres from Carfax. The buildings span 5 centuries *and afford a magnificent view from the garden. Access to the high walls makes it possible to snipe from on high at tourists below. Despite the location, interaction with the rest of the University isn't as strong as it could be, although the location* and compact layout make it ideal for students allergic to walking.

Sex ratio(M:F): 60%:40%	Founded: 1314
Full time u'grads: 333	Postgrads: 136
Private school: 50%	Mature students: 1%
Overseas students: 10%	Disabled students: <1%

Subterranean, medieval bar; bops 3 times a term – mostly free, mostly house/cheese (cap 200); *thriving* music soc; *popular* christmas review (sketches); student bands occasionally; annual black-tie ball. Library (70,000 books); 15 computers, 24hrs. Anglican chapel. Sports fields and boathouse 1½ miles; lots of successes. All 1st years live in; most others are placed in college-owned accommodation; veggie option, self-catering *(if you don't mind sharing a single stove with 333 bean-eaters)*. Doctor, nurse; hardship fund, travel grants.

FAMOUS ALUMNI:
Tariq Ali (journalist, activist); Martin Amis, Alan Bennett, Will Self, JRR Tolkein (writers); Roger Bannister (4 minute miler); Richard Burton (actor); William Morris (designer & socialist pioneer); Russell Harty, Robert Robinson, Ned Sherrin (broadcasters); Imogen Stubbs (actress).

> In 1969 the SOAS Union disaffiliated itself from NUS (because it was too reactionary and allied itself to the Black Panthers).

Greyfriars Hall, Oxford

- **The College is part of University of Oxford and students are entitled to use its facilities.**
Greyfriars Hall, Iffley Road, Oxford, OX4 1SB. Tel: (01865) 250667. Fax: (01865) 727027.
Junior Common Room, Greyfriars Hall, Iffley Road, Oxford, OX4 1SB. Tel: (01865) 246665.
Website: www.greyfriars.ox.ac.uk

Greyfriars, surrounded by *gorgeous* Oxfordshire countryside, offers a number of places for academically successful lay candidates, but apart from them the students are Franciscans, members of other orders and priests. *There is a strong family atmosphere, and the body of students is so small that they can all go for a sedate drink in the pub together.* Most keen athletes attach themselves to Balliol or Keble for lively pursuits, although they do have a rugby team. They accepted women for the first time in 1992.

Sex ratio(M:F): 58%:42%	Founded: 1953
Full time u'grads: 31	Postgrads: 5
Private school: 50%	Mature students: 0
Overseas students: 1%	Disabled students: 0

No bar just 1 *poorly* stocked shelf of drinks and free Pimms at the summer party; 1 bop/year, but regular 'parties' in the basement. Pool table, Sky TV, weights room. Catholic church. *Well-equipped* specialist library (10,000 volumes); 3 computers. Smart formal dinner every evening. Women's officer.

Harris Manchester College, Oxford

- **The College is part of University of Oxford and students are entitled to use its facilities.**
Harris Manchester College, Mansfield Road, Oxford, OX1 3TD. Tel: (01865) 271006. Fax: (01865) 271012.
E-mail: college.office@hmc.ox.ac.uk
Junior Common Room, Harris Manchester College, Mansfield Road, Oxford, OX1 3TD. Tel: (01865) 271006.
Website: www.hmc.ox.ac.uk

Harris Manchester is an 18thC institution but only came to Oxford in 1889. The buildings are mainly late Victorian Gothic and there's some *lovely* pre-Raphaelite stained glass in the chapel. *Its atmosphere is distinct from other Oxford colleges,* originally because of its Nonconformist Christian roots and more recently because it only accepts mature students. The students are *friendly* and have varied backgrounds *and there's still a liberal, worldly ethos.* The college was named not after His Rolfness, *sadly,* but after Lord Harris of Peckham, *who's doubtless an excellent bloke but probably can't play the wobble-board.*

Sex ratio(M:F): 57%:43%	Founded: 1786
Full time u'grads: 89	Postgrads: 16
Private school: n/a	Mature students: 100%
Overseas students: 20%	Disabled students: 3%

Small bar; film club; ball every 3 years; 3 libraries (40,000 books); 6 computers, 24hrs; *cordial staff/student relations;* 'Village Voice' college newspaper. Unitarian chaplain. Recent emergence in University football and cricket. All who wish to can live in, *excellent food,* veggie option, 2 formals a week. Poor wheelchair access; CCTV; doctor; hardship fund; Women's and LGB officers, chaplain.

Hertford College, Oxford

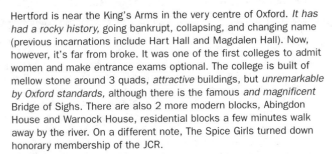

- **The College is part of <u>University of Oxford</u> and students are entitled to use its facilities.**

Hertford College, Catte Street, Oxford, OX1 3BW. Tel: (01865) 279404. Fax: (01865) 279466.
E-mail: admissions@hertford.ox.ac.uk
Junior Common Room, Hertford College, Catte Street, Oxford, OX1 3BU. Tel: (01865) 279400.
Website: www.hertford.ox.ac.uk

Hertford is near the King's Arms in the very centre of Oxford. *It has had a rocky history,* going bankrupt, collapsing, and changing name (previous incarnations include Hart Hall and Magdalen Hall). Now, however, it's far from broke. It was one of the first colleges to admit women and make entrance exams optional. The college is built of mellow stone around 3 quads, *attractive* buildings, but *unremarkable by Oxford standards,* although there is the famous *and magnificent* Bridge of Sighs. There are also 2 more modern blocks, Abingdon House and Warnock House, residential blocks a few minutes walk away by the river. On a different note, The Spice Girls turned down honorary membership of the JCR.

Sex ratio(M:F): 48%:52%	Founded: 1282
Full time u'grads: 370	Postgrads: 160
Private school: 31%	Mature students: <1%
Overseas students: <1%	Disabled students: 0

Bar; *strong* drama and music; Baring Room (cap 250) *is one of the best venues in any Oxford college*; bop cellar Saturday nights; floating black-tie party on Thames. College magazine 'Simpkins' (after the college cat); JCR considering affiliation to NUS. Anglican chapel. Library (47,000 books); 16 computers, 24hrs. *Sporty,* excelling in football; multi-gym, squash courts, boathouse 10 mins by bike. All accommodated; all rooms have network points; self-catering available; cafeteria, new coffee bar. CCTV; doctor & nurse; Women's, LGB and 2 Welfare officers; *good security.*

FAMOUS ALUMNI:
John Donne (poet); David Elleray (football referee); Charles James Fox (18th century politician); Thomas Hobbes (philosopher); Jonathan Swift (writer); William Tyndale (translator of international best-seller 'The Bible'); Evelyn Waugh (writer).

Chris Tarrant is rumoured to have been kicked out of Birmingham's hall of residence for cruelty to geese.

Jesus College, Oxford

- **The College is part of <u>University of Oxford</u> and students are entitled to use its facilities.**
Jesus College, Turl Street, Oxford, OX1 3DW. Tel: (01865) 279720.
Fax: (01865) 279769. E-mail: admissions.tutor@jesus.ox.ac.uk

Junior Common Room, Jesus College, Turl Street, Oxford, OX1 3DW.
Tel: (01865) 279270. Fax: (01865) 279687.
Website: www.jesus.ox.ac.uk

Jesus is just 250 metres from both Carfax and the Bodleian. It was founded by Queen Elizabeth (the first one) and traditionally it was rumoured to be full of Welsh students *(still a little true)* and Old Etonians *(less true)*. Nowadays, students from *all social backgrounds and levels of fondness for daffodils* sunbathe and revise (allegedly) in the small second quad.

Sex ratio(M:F): 56%:44%	Founded: 1571
Full time u'grads: 344	Postgrads: 120
Private school: 41%	Mature students: n/a
Overseas students: 4%	Disabled students: <1%

Bar (cap 150), *usually packed;* happy hours and quizzes; hosts bops every Friday, usually themed, and occasional local bands; new ents pavilion underway; Friday night socials; annual event; lots of one-off events and trips; Thames boat cruise. Drinking and dining clubs; 'Sheepshagger' for gossip; *fortnightly JCR meetings popular, possibly due to the free booze.* 'Lizzie's' banned drinking soc which carries on in secret *regardless.* Interdenominational chapel. Library (36,000 volumes); 45 computers, 24hrs. *Excellent* sports facilities 1½ miles from college, pavilion with multigym, conference rooms and bar; *good reputation in rugby, hockey, rowing and football.* All can live in, 10% share; daily formals; food on a credit system and self-catering is available as are flats for couples. CCTV; doctor, nurse and LGB officer; hardship grants, scholarships.

FAMOUS ALUMNI:
Paul Jones (singer); TE Lawrence (of Arabia); Sian Lloyd (weatherperson); Magnus Magnusson ('Mastermind' inquisitor); Lord Wilson (former PM).

Keble College, Oxford

- **The College is part of <u>University of Oxford</u> and students are entitled to use its facilities.**
Keble College, Parks Road, Oxford, OX1 3PG. Tel: (01865) 272727.
Fax: (01865) 272705. E-mail: admissions@keb.ox.ac.uk

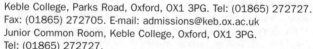

Junior Common Room, Keble College, Oxford, OX1 3PG.
Tel: (01865) 272727.
Website: www.keble.ox.ac.uk

Keble is just under ½ mile north of Carfax, right next to the University Science Area. It's very convenient for students in that faculty and also well placed for OUSU, 'The Lamb & Flag' and the *excellent* Maison Blanc patisserie. It's a big and relatively modern college – a mere 129 years old. The main buildings are Victorian redbrick, *some of them resembling vast Battenburg cakes.* These buildings contrast *almost violently* with the spaceship which landed one night in the rear quad and claimed it was the bar and Middle Common Room. *Students get out and about and are often involved in high profile University activities, especially sports, despite being fairly laid-back.*

Sex ratio(M:F): 60%:40%
Full time u'grads: 438
Private school: 40%
Overseas students: 10%
Founded: 1870
Postgrads: 190
Mature students: 2
Disabled students: 0

Large *popular* purpose-built bar; bop room under JCR, 2 or 3 themed a term, Loveboat *popular*; big ball every other year; weekly ents eg. karaoke, paintball. *Active* Rag and *strong* drama. Library (40,000 books); 25 computers, 24hrs. Anglican chapel. 'The Brick' weekly for college news. *Very sporty* (loads of 'Blues') and *excellent* sports facilities, but most over 1 mile away. *Especially strong at rugby and hockey.* Keble can house most of its many undergrads due to new *conference-type* rooms; catered pay-as-you-eat credit system (you have to buy 30 meals in advance) and limited self-catering; 6 formals a week (no alternative), network points in all rooms. Nurse, doctor, LGB, Women's and welfare officers; scholarships, bursaries, hardship fund.

FAMOUS ALUMNI:
Michael Croft (founder, National Youth Theatre); Imran Khan (cricketer); Rev Chad Varah (founder of the Samaritans); Andreas Whittam Smith (founder of 'The Independent') – *yes, Keble's your college if you're planning to found something.*

Lady Margaret Hall, Oxford

• **The College is part of <u>University of Oxford</u> and students are entitled to use its facilities.**
Lady Margaret Hall, Norham Gardens, Oxford, OX2 6QA.
Tel: (01865) 274300. Fax: (01865) 274257.
Junior Common Room, Lady Margaret Hall, Oxford, OX2 6QA.
Tel: (01865) 274277.
Website: www.lmh.ox.ac.uk

Lady Margaret Hall is a 19thC redbrick 'River' College set in extensive gardens. Two purpose-built 5-floor residential blocks *slightly damage the idyllic setting and the handsome architecture, but they're really popular with them inside.* Being ¾ mile from Oxford's centre doesn't put a dampener on University-level involvement. They are pretty informal and down to earth as Oxford goes.

Sex ratio(M:F): 50%:50%
Full time u'grads: 415
Private school: 53%
Overseas students: 4%
Founded: 1878
Postgrads: 140
Mature students: 3%
Disabled students: 0

Bar (cap 200); Talbot Hall (120) and Toynbee (100) for student bands/discos; 3 bops a term; quizzes; rowing cocktail party. 2 libraries (1 for law only, 60,000 books total); 25 computers, 24hrs. Anglican chapel. Strong drama. Sports facilities 1 mile away, (multigym, squash and tennis on-site); *strong on netball, hockey and rowing.* 1st years and finalists live in and most 2nd years; pay-as-you-eat dining hall and weekly formal hall dinner; *food excellent.* Doctor/nurse; First Year, Welfare and Women's Officers.

FAMOUS ALUMNI:
Benazir Bhutto (ex-President, Pakistan); Caryl Churchill (writer); Lady Antonia Fraser (historian); Eglantyne Jebb (founder, Save the Children); Barbara Mills (Director of Public Prosecutions); Diana Quick (actress); Matthew Taylor MP (Lib Dem); Lady Warnock (educationalist); Anne Widdecombe MP (Con, still a virgin).

Lincoln College, Oxford

• **The College is part of <u>University of Oxford</u> and students are entitled to use its facilities.**
Lincoln College, Turl Street, Oxford, OX1 3DR. Tel: (01865) 279800. Fax: (01865) 279802. E-mail: admissions@lincoln.ox.ac.uk.
Junior Common Room, Lincoln College, Oxford, OX1 3DR.
Tel: (01865) 724122. Fax: (01865) 240094.
Website: www.lincoln.ox.ac.uk

200 metres from Carfax is Lincoln, *a miniature version of a picture-book Oxford college, though they consider themselves to be 'forward-looking'. Its small, old stone quads are just dreamy.* Students tend to stick to college affairs and this helps to maintain the impressive academic standard.

Sex ratio(M:F): 60%:40%	Founded: 1427
Full time u'grads: 275	Postgrads: 180
Private school: 45%	Mature students: 2%
Overseas students: 1%	Disabled students: <1%

Annual pantomime; discos in Deep Hall Bar (cap 200) 4 times a term; biennial ball. 'Imperative' newsletter. Library (30,000); 22 computers, 24hrs. Anglican chapel. *Rowing and croquet are popular;* sports fields 10 mins bike ride away. Everyone lives in and eats the formal and/or informal dinners; *best food in Oxford; self-catering is limited.* Trained undergraduate peer supporters Nurse; Women's Tutor; harassment support; *generous* financial support; book grant.

FAMOUS ALUMNI:
John le Carré (writer); Bill Cash MP (Con, Europhobe); Manfred von Richtofen (the Red Baron); Dr Seuss (writer); Edward Thomas (poet); John Wesley (founder of Methodism).

Magdalen College, Oxford

• **The College is part of <u>University of Oxford</u> and students are entitled to use its facilities.**
Magdalen College, High St, Oxford, OX1 4AU. Tel: (01865) 276063. Fax: (01865) 276094. E-mail: admissions@magd.ox.ac.uk
Junior Common Room, Magdalen College, Oxford, OX1 4AU.
Website: www.magd.ox.ac.uk

Magdalen (pronounced 'Maudlin') is one of Oxford's biggest, richest colleges. Its *superb* buildings, ½ mile from Carfax, are set in 100 acres of grounds, which include over a mile of riverside walks, as well as a deer park. The surroundings attract a plague of tourists and plenty of film crews. The *old-fashioned* bar (crossed oars, etc) overlooks the river. The Magdalen May Morning celebration *is especially enchanting,* coming to a climax when the choir welcomes summer from the top of Magdalen Tower. *The students are a tolerant and friendly bunch, hard-working but not overly so.*

Sex ratio(M:F): 58%:42%
Full time u'grads: 402
Private school: 50%
Overseas students: 7%
Founded: 1458
Postgrads: 182
Mature students: <1%
Disabled students: 1.5%

Bar (cap 200, *has a debit scheme – max OD:* £10) and JCR (150) used for student bands; classical concerts in the chapel (200); fortnightly bops and cocktail parties; Commemoration Ball every 3 years, *one of the biggies;* new auditorium. 5 libraries (100,000 books); 20 computers, 24hrs. *Drama strong.* Anglo-Catholic chapel *(isn't that heresy?).* Weekly bogsheet, 'The Stag'. Great sports fields 10mins walk; 4 squash courts in College; excellent gym; *women's squash strong, as are hockey, tennis, football and rowing.* Almost everyone lives in; most rooms have network points; 27 kitchens for undergrads, *food not great – better in the bar but bring your garibaldi biscuits, anyway.* Doctor and nurse, free condoms; LGB officer and Equal Opportunities Committee. College is *responsive to students' problems.* Free attack alarms provided. Hardship funds, scholarships, book and travel grants.

FAMOUS ALUMNI:
John Betjeman (poet, sent down); Edward Gibbon (historian, described his time here as 'idle and unprofitable'); Darius Guppy *(fraudster)*; William Hague MP (Con Leader), John Redwood MP (Con); Ian Hislop (editor, 'Private Eye'); CS Lewis (writer); Dudley Moore (comedian/actor/pianist); Desmond Morris (socioanthropologist); David Rendel MP (LibDem); AJP Taylor (historian); Oscar Wilde (*great writer, great wit*); Cardinal Wolsey.

Mansfield College, Oxford

• **The College is part of <u>University of Oxford</u> and students are entitled to use its facilities.**
Mansfield College, Mansfield Road, Oxford, OX1 3TF.
Tel: (01865) 270999. Fax: (01865) 282910.
Junior Common Room, Mansfield College, Oxford, OX1 3TF.
Tel: (01865) 270889.
Website: www.mansfield.ox.ac.uk

The main Victorian buildings are set around the huge circular lawn. Outside it *looks inspiring and spacious. Rowing is popular* and the College has its own boathouse, indeed Mansfield was the home of *True Blue and meaty rower* Donald McDonald; most sports amenities are run jointly with <u>Merton College</u>. Mansfield was once a Free Church centre *and prides itself on its liberal tradition and on being the source of many a minister. The atmosphere is friendly and down-to-earth and there's a strong tradition of supplying hacks to the SU and journos to Cherwell.*

Sex ratio(M:F): 53%:47%
Full time u'grads: 192
Private school: 30%
Overseas students: 10%
Founded: 1886
Postgrads: 58
Mature students: 1%
Disabled students: 2%

'Black Bottle' Bar, packed at the weekend; 2-3 bops termly and bands in the JCR (cap 225); cabaret; Sky TV; jazz & cocktail parties. Weekly bogsheet. 3 libraries (28,000 volumes); 15 computers, 24hrs. URC chapel. Sport: rugby, hockey, football and basketball. *Varied* accommodation for all 1st and 3rd years/finalists; students eat in college dining halls; 3 kitchens. CCTV; 1 room for a wheelchair user; doctor and nurse; counselling team; Women's and LGB officers.

FAMOUS ALUMNI:
CH Dodd and Albert Schweitzer (theologians); Donald McDonald (mutinous rower); Von Trott (who tried to kill Hitler).

Merton College, Oxford

• *The College is part of <u>University of Oxford</u> and students are entitled to use its facilities.*
Merton College, Merton St, Oxford, OX1 4JD. Tel: (01865) 276329. Fax: (01865) 286500.

E-mail: undergraduate-admissions@merton.ox.ac.uk
Junior Common Room, Merton College, Oxford, OX1 4JD. Tel: (01865) 276300. Fax: (01865) 286495. E-mail: president@merton.ox.ac.uk
Website: www.merton.ox.ac.uk

Merton is *one of Oxford's prettier colleges,* 600 metres from Carfax, with *magical* gardens (where Tolkien wrote 'Lord of the Rings'), a *beautiful* chapel and bizarre *gargoyles*. The Mob Quad is the oldest quad in Oxford and home of the library (the oldest in England), which is supposedly haunted and contains Chaucer's Astrolabe. *The atmosphere is laid-back but standards are high and students have made their mark in University journalism, drama and music.* Odd traditions include walking backwards around the quad drinking port for an hour when the clocks go back.

Sex ratio(M:F): 62%:38%	Founded: 1264
Full time u'grads: 293	Postgrads: 139
Private school: 44%	Mature students: 1%
Overseas students: 12%	Disabled students: 1%

Friendly bar; student bands and fortnightly bops in JCR (cap 200); Xmas Ball; *strong* Choral Society; 'Merton News' weekly paper and *charmingly named* termly mag 'The Phelcher'. 3 libraries (80,000 volumes); 20 computers, 24hrs. Interdenominational chapel. Sports facilities (10 mins walk) shared with <u>Mansfield College</u>; *korfball is strong; emphasis on sports participation rather than achievement.* JCR no longer has a Squirrel Rep who worked tirelessly to protect trees in the Merton garden *(bring him/her/it back)*. Almost everyone lives in; many *elegant* rooms; daily formals, *excellent* food. Entry-phones; shared doctor and nurse, 2 LGB officers; hardship fund.

FAMOUS ALUMNI:
Frank Bough (broadcaster); Howard Davies (deputy Governor, Bank of England); TS Eliot (poet); Kris Kristofferson (singer); Robert Morley (actor); Crown Prince Naruhito (Japanese heir apparent); John Wycliffe (theologian).

> 'Blur are Chas and Dave for students' - Owen Morris, Oasis Producer.

New College, Oxford

- **The College is part of <u>University of Oxford</u> and students are entitled to use its facilities.**
New College, Oxford, OX1 3BN. Tel: (01865) 279555.
Fax: (01865) 279590.
E-mail: admissions@new.ox.ac.uk
Junior Common Room, New College, Oxford, OX1 3BN.
Tel: (01865) 279577.
Website: www.new.ox.ac.uk

New College, *ironically* one of the oldest colleges, is *so prettily Gothic that it wouldn't look out of place in Disneyland*, with the city wall running through its *pleasant* grounds. The College is 600 metres from Carfax, but it's hidden to a certain extent from the swarms of tourists. The social scene rotates around the Beer Cellar, a refurbished medieval cave attracting students from all over Oxford.

Sex ratio(M:F): 50%:50%	Founded: 1379
Full time u'grads: 430	Postgrads: 170
Private school: 52%	Mature students: 1%
Overseas students: 10%	Disabled students: 0.5%

Bar (cap 200); classical music in Anglican chapel; bops, jazz and student bands in the Long Room (200); student DJ nights *popular*, open to non-college members; *big ball*, 'social event of the year' according to 'The Times'. *Strong music and theatre; famous choir.* Fortnightly bogsheet. Rugby champions 99/00. Library (70,000 books & 30,000 antiquarian items); 45 computers, 24hrs. 8 acres of playing fields on site. Everyone can be housed in college. All students eat in hall; daily formal dinner; self-catering in new buildings. Doctor, nurse; LGB, Women's and Harassment Officers – *good welfare*.

FAMOUS ALUMNI:
Tony Benn (former Lab MP); Angus Deayton (*before he was famously annoying*); John Fowles, John Galsworthy (writers); Hugh Grant (er, er, um, er, actor); Bryan Johnston (former *effusive* cricket commentator, after whom the pavilion is named); Naomi Woolf (feminist writer).

Oriel College, Oxford

- **The College is part of <u>University of Oxford</u> and students are entitled to use its facilities.**
Oriel College, Oriel Square, Oxford, OX1 4EW. Tel: (01865) 276555.
Fax: (01865) 286548. E-mail: admissions@oriel.ox.ac.uk
Junior Common Room, Oriel College, Oxford, OX1 4EW.
Tel: (01865) 276555.
Website: www.oriel.ox.ac.uk

One of the oldest and smallest Colleges, Oriel is 300 metres from Carfax *and despite the popular stereotype, it's no more of a public school stronghold than the rest of Oxford. Its quiet and closed quads and tight, friendly communal spirit can be a bit suffocating.* It's had a reputation for sporting obsessions, but this is waning. The bar, however, is great to hang out in if you're into pool, darts or table football. There is an *excellent* choir *and a famed* drama society.

Sex ratio(M:F): 65%:35%	Founded: 1326
Full time u'grads: 271	Postgrads: 128
Private school: 50%	Mature students: <1%
Overseas students: 5%	Disabled students: 0

Student bands and bops in the bar (cap 160); regular cabaret, cocktail and jazz night; ball every 3 years. Various news sheets and college mags. Library (100,000 books); 12 computers. Anglican chapel. 6½ acres of playing fields 1 mile off site; ideally positioned for the river, rowing very strong, plus cricket, rugby and hockey. All students live in; students eat in the dining hall; *moderate* food, but eat-as-much-as-you-like breakfasts. Doctor, nurse; separate male and female welfare officers; LGB. Scholarships, book and travel grants and *lots of* prizes.

FAMOUS ALUMNI:
Beau Brummel (dandy); Cardinal Newman; Sir Walter Raleigh (Armada basher and bowls enthusiast); Cecil Rhodes (dodgy imperialist); AJP Taylor (historian).

Pembroke College, Oxford

• *The College is part of <u>University of Oxford</u> and students are entitled to use its facilities.*
Pembroke College, Pembroke Square, Oxford, OX1 1DW.
Tel: (01865) 276412. Fax: (01865) 276418.
Junior Common Room, Pembroke College, Oxford, OX1 1DW.
Tel: (01865) 276427.
Website: www.pembroke.ox.ac.uk

Pembroke's quads, 300 metres from Carfax, range from *medieval marvels to modern misdemeanours*, but even Alan Titchmarsh could get some tips from their gardens. They're also known for sporting prowess and political hackery but academic achievement hovers around the 'adequate' mark (in Oxford terms). Still, as long as there's beer flowing, they're a happy bunch.

Sex ratio(M:F): 58%:42%	Founded: 1624
Full time u'grads: 459	Postgrads: 106
Private school: 50%	Mature students: 2%
Overseas students: 20%	Disabled students: <1%

Bar (cap 120) and *refurbished* JCR (150) used for student bands; ball every 2 years (cap 1,000); regular bops (180) and karaoke. 2 newpapers: 'Broadsheet' *(run by wimmin)* and 'Endeavour' *(raucous)*; yearbook. Library (40,000 books); 10 computers, 24hrs. Anglican chapel; music room. *Thriving* sports; high proportion of University sports players, *excellent rowing*. 1st and 3rd years guaranteed accommodation; no sharing; some single sex staircases; creeping 'conference effect' means rooms are gradually being tarted up; formal dinner in dining hall, *pretty much compulsory for 1st years*; food *pretty good*. Good disabled access in Geoffrey Arthur Building, where all finalists are guaranteed rooms. Doctor, nurse; hardship fund; Rowland bursaries; *enormous* art fund.

FAMOUS ALUMNI:
Denzil Davies MP (Lab); Michael Heseltine (former Con MP, arboriculturist); Samuel Johnson (writer, lexicographer); James Smithson (founded Smithsonian Institute).

The Queen's College, Oxford

- **The College is part of <u>University of Oxford</u> and students are entitled to use its facilities.**
The Queen's College, High Street, Oxford, OX1 4AW. Tel: (01865) 279167. Fax: (01865) 790819. E-mail: admissions@queens.ox.ac.uk
Junior Common Room, The Queen's College, Oxford, OX1 4AW.
Website: www.queens.ox.ac.uk

Queen's is steeped in history and tradition. For example, under ancient lore, students have the right to send servants to the cellar to fetch them beer. Its *superb* buildings *dominate* the High Street, 600 metres from Carfax. The cupola and quad designed by Hawksmoor are *impressive*. Queen's isn't typical of Oxford colleges. There is a larger northern contingent among the students than at most colleges and the atmosphere is refreshingly unpretentious. They don't often go beyond their own doorstep for entertainment.

Sex ratio(M:F): 55%:45%	Founded: 1341
Full time u'grads: 300	Postgrads: 100
Private school: 46%	Mature students: n/a
Overseas students: 12%	Disabled students: 1.5%

Bar – The Beer Cellar (150) – with 'the friendliest bar manager in the world'. Queen's was the last college to brew its own beer; Queen's Hall (cap 350) and JCR (75) used for ents as above and bands, cabaret and fortnightly groove in The Beer Cellar; also slap-up dinners preceeded by trumpet fanfare, afternoon tea. Library (170,000 books); 12 computers, 24hrs. Anglican chapel. *Participation in sport stressed rather than success, but they're dead good at darts;* 6½ acres of playing fields, ¾ mile from College. Everyone lives in and eats either in the dining hall (*food edible*) or in new self-catering facilities. Doctor, nurse; bursaries and hardship fund.

FAMOUS ALUMNI:
Rowan Atkinson (comedian, 'Blackadder'); Jeremy Bentham (philosopher); Tim Burners-Lee (invented the www); Edmund Halley (as in comet); Henry V (king); Gerald Kaufman MP (Lab); Oliver Sacks (writer, psychiatrist); Brian Walden (journalist).

Regent's Park College, Oxford

- **The College is part of <u>University of Oxford</u> and students are entitled to use its facilities.**
Regent's Park College, Pusey Street, Oxford, OX1 2LB.
Tel: (01865) 288120. Fax: (01865) 228121.
Junior Common Room, Regent's Park College, Pusey Street, Oxford, OX1 2LB. Tel: (01865) 288120.
Website: www.rpc.ox.ac.uk

Regent's Park is a very small college in the heart of town and its *unassuming* entrance, a door off the street, is typical of the whole College. It was originally established in London to train Baptist ministers and missionaries, *but it's not solely for the spiritual - it has its fair share of typical Oxford rowers and hacks* and attracts many visiting students from the USA and elsewhere. The College has a *homely atmosphere* and welcomes those with families. *Techie boffins*, however, need not apply, as you can only read arts subjects at Regent's Park. Lots of bursaries for the *theologically inclined*.

Sex ratio(M:F): 50%:50%
Full time u'grads: 80
Private school: 45%
Overseas students: 2%
Founded: 1810
Postgrads: 40
Mature students: 12%
Disabled students: 0

Bar (*tiny*); 30s Helwys Hall (cap 300) and JCR (60) for bands, cabaret termly and discos 2 times a term; lots of ad hoc ents, quiz nights, picnics, punting parties; mini ball. *The JCR is very active and votes about everything. Good relations with staff; drama and charitable urges strong.* 2 libraries (25,000 books) – *good for theology, poor for anything else;* 5 computers, 24hrs. Baptist chapel. Snooker table, but no sports fields. Everyone lives in. *Food is cheap* and *chompable*. Swipe cards; poor disabled access; nurse.

FAMOUS ALUMNI:
The bloke who directed 'Spiceworld'.

St Anne's College, Oxford

• **The College is part of <u>University of Oxford</u> and students are entitled to use its facilities.**
St Anne's College, Woodstock Road, Oxford, OX2 6HS.
Tel: (01865) 274825. Fax: (01865) 274899.
E-mail: enquiries@st-annes.ox.ac.uk
Junior Common Room, St Anne's College, Oxford, OX2 6HS.
Tel: (01865) 274870
Website: www.stannes.ox.ac.uk

St Anne's is 10mins walk from the town centre. The main building is made of *warm* Cotswold stone with a battlement top and was built in the 30s. Most of the others were constructed *with a little less care for beauty* in the 50s and 60s as well as a new building finished in 1992. *The students are a no-nonsense bunch - not much petty student politicking. They prefer to put their energies into charity Rag events or the wealth of drama societies.* St Anne's claims to be particularly open to applications from minorities and its students are reputed to be 'normal'. Well, that's comforting.

Sex ratio(M:F): 55%:45%
Full time u'grads: 455
Private school: 50%
Overseas students: 4%
Founded: 1878
Postgrads: 168
Mature students: 0
Disabled students: 0

Bar; big lecture theatre with screen and collapsible stage (cap 150); bops, bands in JCR (150); *fab* discos in dining hall (300); cabarets 1-3 times a term. 'Double Standards' and 'Agent Orange' mags; 'Bogsheet' for news/gossip; TV room; library (110,000 books); 30 computers, 24hrs. *Successful* sport this year; sports fields shared with St John's ½ mile away. Everyone lives in; meal card system, veggie option; *good* self-catering. Doctor, nurse; student counsellor. *Good* disabled access.

FAMOUS ALUMNI:
Maria Aitken (actress); Sister Wendy Beckett (art nun); Edwina Currie (ex-Mp and romance writer); Penelope Lively, Iris Murdoch (writers); Libby Purves (broadcaster); Simon Rattle (conductor); Victor Ubogu (former rugby player).

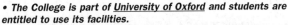

St Catherine's College, Oxford

- **The College is part of University of Oxford and students are entitled to use its facilities.**
St Catherine's College, Manor Road, Oxford, OX1 3UJ. Tel: (01865) 271703. Fax: (01865) 271768. E-mail: admissions@stcatz.ox.ac.uk
Junior Common Room, St Catherine's College, Oxford, OX1 3UJ.
Website: www.stcatz.ox.ac.uk

Catz, as St Catherine's is known, is a modernist brick, glass and concrete environment 1 mile from Carfax. *The relatively progressive architecture doesn't look like an Oxbridge college, and the same is true of the forward-looking, unstuffy atmosphere inside.* There are lots of ents and bops which pull in the crowds. It's very big and has all the mod cons: warm rooms, showers, kitchens, purpose-built bar, even a grassy amphitheatre and water gardens. *For students who want to go to Oxford for the academic kudos, but want to steer clear of the Ivory Tower mentality, Catz is a good bet. It still has that one big happy family feel, though, mainly because of its comparatively detached setting.*

Sex ratio(M:F): 73%:27%	Founded: 1962
Full time u'grads: 427	Postgrads: 140
Private school: 48%	Mature students: 1%
Overseas students: 5%	Disabled students: n/a

Lively bar; 2 theatres; JCR (cap 400), Bernard Sunley theatre (250) and the Music House (30) used for bands; May ball; *very popular* air-conditioned weekly bops in JCR and MCR (250). Library (56,500 books); 40 computers, 24hrs. Some on-site sports facilities (gym, squash courts), the rest 15 mins walk away. Most 1st years and finalists, plus 20% of 2nd years, can live in; formal dining hall in the evenings; cafeteria; buttery. Doctor and nurse; hardship fund. *Good* disabled access.

FAMOUS ALUMNI:
John Birt (former DG, BBC); Phil De Glanville (former England rugby captain); Joseph Heller ('Catch 22' author); Richard Herring (of Lee & Herring fame); Peter Mandelson MP (Lab); AA Milne ('Winnie-the-Pooh' author) Matthew Pinsent (three-time Olympic gold – rowing); Jeanette Winterson (writer).

St Edmund Hall, Oxford

- **The College is part of University of Oxford and students are entitled to use its facilities.**
St Edmund Hall, Queen's Lane, Oxford, OX1 4AR.
Tel: (01865) 279005.
Junior Common Room, St Edmund Hall, Oxford, OX1 4AR.
Tel (01865) 279000.
Website: www.seh.ox.ac.uk

Small, cute and cuddly, Teddy Hall, officially St Edmund Hall, is a blend of old and new buildings, 650 metres from Carfax. The buildings include a Norman church (now the library) and its attached graveyard. *The students radiate freedom of spirit and intimacy and definitely know how to paaarty.* They're strong in journalism, drama and, especially, sport, but always with an emphasis on 'team spirit'.

For anyone particularly concerned about the punyness of their pounds, college charges are *uniquely* linked to the retail price index. *Isn't that interesting?*

Sex ratio(M:F): 55%:45%	Founded: 1263
Full time u'grads: 420	Postgrads: 120
Private school: 30%	Mature students: 10%
Overseas students: 5%	Disabled students: 0

Excellent tiny bar; bands and bops in Wolfson Hall, old dining hall (150) and the 2 JCR party rooms (100); 2 black tie dinners a term; theatre trips; annual summer Event. College mag 'Closet Chronicles' and *informative* 'Hall Happenings' newsletter. Library (50,000 books); 20 computers, 24hrs. Anglican chapel. Sports facilities 5 mins from site, rugby and fencing strong. All 1st and 3rd years live in; students eat in dining hall, *pricey* food; optional Sunday formal meal; *good* self-catering (microwaves). 'Unique' JCR butler who serves 'Chaps Tea' of toasted tea-cakes and other 'goodies' every weekday in the coffee bar: *smokin'*. CCTV; doctor, nurse; hardship fund; 1 room equipped for wheelchair user.

FAMOUS ALUMNI:
Sir Robin Day (broadcaster); Nicholas Evans ('Horse Whisperer' author); Terry Jones ('Monty Python' – his room is now a toilet); Graham Kentfield (former Chief Cashier, Bank of England).

St Hilda's College, Oxford

- **The College is part of University of Oxford and students are entitled to use its facilities.**
St Hilda's College, Oxford, OX4 1DY. Tel: (01865) 276884.
Fax: (01865) 276816. E-mail: college.office@sthildas.ox.ac.uk
Junior Common Room, St Hilda's College, Oxford, OX4 1DY.
Tel: (01865) 276846.
Website: www.sthildas.ox.ac.uk

St Hilda's College, almost a mile from Carfax, is the last all-female college in Oxford. The *mish-mash* of detached buildings is not arranged around quads or linear corridors, but dotted about beside the river. *This is no nunnery; most students have come to an environment where macho attitudes don't impinge on academic life, but they don't object to associating with blokes after hours – after all, the only ones around have been hand picked.* The high proportion of foreign students adds to the fun mix. There's a 'sister' programme, whereby each fresher 'Hildabeast' is assigned to a student on the same course in the year above.

Sex ratio(M:F): 0%:100%	Founded: 1893
Full time u'grads: 412	Postgrads: 72
Private school: 36%	Mature students: 4%
Overseas students: 28%	Disabled students: 0

Bar; dining room (cap 200) and JCR (100) for student bands and jazz nights, theme bops; cheapest annual ball; annual arts festival week; new music building. Termly mag 'Hilda Guardian' and weekly 'Loo News'; *keen* recycling policies. 2 libraries (65,000 books); 16 computers, 24hrs. Non-denominational chapel. Near Iffley Road Sports Centre; a few sports facilities on site, including punts, new boathouse; *strong on rowing, netball, rugby.* A new accommodation block is under construction; all 1st and 3rd years/finalists live in; students eat in buttery and dining room; *damn fine food;* optional weekly formal meal; self-catering kitchens on most floors. CCTV; 2 doctors; nurse; hardship fund, travel grants.

FAMOUS ALUMNI:
Zeinab Badawi (newscaster); Helen Jackson MP (Lab); Susan Kramer (London mayorial candidate, Lib); Rosalind Miles (writer); Kate Millett (writer, victim of live TV snog from Ollie Reed); Barbara Pym (writer); Gillian Shephard MP (Con). Jacqueline du Pré (cellist) was an Honorary Fellow and the music building is named after her.

St Hugh's College, Oxford

- *The College is part of <u>University of Oxford</u> and students are entitled to use its facilities.*

St Hugh's College, St Margaret's Road, Oxford, OX2 6LE.
Tel: (01865) 274910. Fax: (01865) 274912.
E-mail: admissions@st-hughs.ox.ac.uk
Junior Common Room, St Hugh's College, Oxford, OX2 6LE.
Tel: (01865) 274425.
Website: www.st-hughs.ox.ac.uk

St Hugh's red brick buildings are a mile from Carfax. The College was founded *almost by accident* by Elizabeth Wordsworth. It's known for its garden parties, firework party and ball, its big booze ups at the start of each term *and its general penchant for revelry, larks and laughs.* Having survived for a century without them, St Hugh's admitted men in 1987. This apparently resulted in an increase of rugby songs and associated lewdness in the bar – though the women's football team give as good as they get – and the college is welcoming with a community atmosphere. Hugh's students plague almost every activity at a University level.

Sex ratio(M:F): 60%:40%	Founded: 1886
Full time u'grads: 421	Postgrads: 160
Private school: 45%	Mature students: 10%
Overseas students: 15%	Disabled students: 2%

Bar; Wordsworth Room (cap 50), functions at Lee House (50) and Mordan Hall theatre (300); frequent, *popular* ents events in JCR (250). 2 libraries (88,503 books); 36 computers, 24hrs. *Strong squash, rugby and basketball;* some sports facilities on site; joint college sports fields with <u>Wadham</u> ½ mile off site. All can live in; buttery for *good* food; hall food; formal meal in dining hall weekly. CCTV; visiting doctor, nurse and counsellor; interdenominational chapel.

FAMOUS ALUMNI:
Baroness Barbara Castle (former Labour MP); Emily Davidson (suffragette martyr); Ruth Lawrence (mathematical prodigy); Mary Renault (historical novelist); Aung San Suu Kyi (Burmese human rights activist); Joanna Trollope (Aga saga writer).

Mick Jagger, who dropped out of LSE, is now honorary President of the SU.

St John's College, Oxford

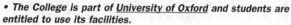

- **The College is part of <u>University of Oxford</u> and students are entitled to use its facilities.**

St John's College, St Giles', Oxford, OX1 3JP. Tel: (01865) 277317. Fax: (01865) 277640. E-mail: admissions@sjc.ox.zc.uk

Junior Common Room, St John's College, Oxford, OX1 3JP. Website: www.sjc.ox.ac.uk

St John's, one of the oldest and richest colleges in Oxford, is half a mile from Carfax. Its 15th-, 17th- and 18th-century buildings are arranged around 6 quads, for the public gaze, *and the largest garden in Oxford*. Meanwhile, like poor relations, the modern additions are kept wisely out of sight. The only sounds during the day are the busy jottings, the page-flicking or the pencil-chewing of diligent students. At night, though, students remove their thinking caps, let their hair down and get down to the bar, already full of the women rowers (alias 'The Sirens'). Its reputation as an academically snooty workhouse isn't entirely justified.

Sex ratio(M:F): 56%:44%	Founded: 1555
Full time u'grads: 392	Postgrads: 174
Private school: 37%	Mature students: 1%
Overseas students: 6%	Disabled students: 1%

Auditorium for St John's Mummers; student bands in *post-modern* Basement (cap 80), Prestwich Room (40) and Larkin Room (40); 4 bops a term; balls every 3 years. Library (75,000 books); 40 computers, 24hrs. Anglican chapel. Squash courts; 10 acres of sports fields 1 mile. Everyone lives in (*high standard*); most eat in hall once a day; formal hall daily; *reasonable* self-catering. Doctor, nurse, counsellor. Money available for those who need/deserve it.

FAMOUS ALUMNI:
Sir Kingsley Amis, Robert Graves, Philip Larkin, John Wain (all writers and/or poets); Tony Blair (PM).

St Peter's College, Oxford

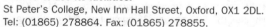

- **The College is part of <u>University of Oxford</u> and students are entitled to use its facilities.**

St Peter's College, New Inn Hall Street, Oxford, OX1 2DL.
Tel: (01865) 278864. Fax: (01865) 278855.
E-mail: admissions@spc.ox.ac.uk

Junior Common Room, St Peter's College, Oxford, OX1 2DL.
Tel: (01865) 278876.
Website: www.spc.ox.ac.uk

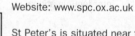

St Peter's is situated near to Carfax and Oxford's main High Street. It's small and cosy, with buildings from a variety of *modern* architectural styles arranged around 4 grass quads. The large JCR, *ideal for entertainments,* is on the ground floor of a 70s building, where some of the 1st years live, and next to the modern bar and deli, which spills over onto a terrace, overlooking Oxford. *St Peter's is a friendly and relaxed college.*

Sex ratio(M:F): 60%:40%	Founded: 1929
Full time u'grads: 347	Postgrads: 92
Private school: 50%	Mature students: 1%
Overseas students: 10%	Disabled students: 0

Bar; student bands and 3 bops per term in the JCR (cap 200); concerts in chapel (250); JCR sometimes hires local clubs in Oxford; black-tie dinners each term and ball every other year. 'The Peterphile' college *rag*. 2 libraries (40,000 books) open 24hrs; 15 computers, 24hrs. Anglican chapel. *Sporty*; college shares a sports ground with Exeter and Hertford colleges; *women's sport strong*. 1st years and 90% of 3rd years live in; 3 female-only corridors in 1st yr block; no self-catering; everyone eats in dining hall; optional formal dinners. CCTV; nurse, doctor; LGB, Women's officers; *disabled access okay except in the library*.

FAMOUS ALUMNI:
Rev W Awdry (writer of 'Thomas the Tank Engine'); Simon Beaufoy (wrote 'The Full Monty'); Lord Condon (former Met Police commissioner) Ken Loach (film director); Peter Wright (author, 'Spycatcher') .

Somerville College, Oxford

- **The College is part of University of Oxford and students are entitled to use its facilities.**
Somerville College, Woodstock Road, Oxford, OX2 6HD.
Tel: (01865) 270600. Fax: (01865) 270620.
Junior Common Room, Somerville College, Oxford, OX2 6HD.
Tel: (01865) 270593.
Website: www.som.ox.ac.uk

Somerville is ½ a mile from the town centre. The architecture is mixed *and the gardens are very peaceful*. The small bar, *with its merry happy hours, bonds the bits other bars cannot reach*. Men are a recent addition *but the atmosphere hasn't become as blokey as some hoped/feared*. Informality and tolerance is the rule and Somervillians spout out of some of Oxford's dafter traditions, although they are ubiquitous in positions of authority across the University. *Clearly the college to choose if your ambition is to be a Baroness when you grow up*.

Sex ratio(M:F): 50%:50%	Founded: 1879
Full time u'grads: 360	Postgrads: 80
Private school: 50%	Mature students: 1%
Overseas students: 15%	Disabled students: 0

Bar; Wolfson Hall (cap 200) for bands; summer event; ball every 3 years. Weekly bogsheet. Library (100,000 books); 20 computers, 24hrs. Shares sports facilities with Wadham College; netball *strong*. All 1st yrs and finalists live in; *varied, but generally spacious rooms; lack of college houses a bone of contention;* 20% of rooms have network access; students eat in the cafeteria with formal dinners weekly in dining hall. Multi-denominational chapel. CCTV; doctor, nurse; hardship fund.

FAMOUS ALUMNI:
Sunethra Bandaranaike (Sri Lanka's former PM); Indira Ghandi (India's former PM); Dorothy Hodgkin (Nobel Prize winner); Iris

Murdoch (writer); Baroness Park (spymaster); Esther Rantzen (TeethV celeb); Dorothy L Sayers (writer); Baroness Maggie Thatcher (former PM); Baroness Shirley Williams.

Trinity College, Oxford

- **The College is part of <u>University of Oxford</u> and students are entitled to use its facilities.**
Trinity College, Broad Street, Oxford, OX1 3BH. Tel: (01865) 279910. Fax: (01865) 279911.
Junior Common Room, Trinity College, Oxford, OX1 3BH.
E-mail: jcr@tri.ox.ac.uk
Website: www.trinity.ox.ac.uk

Trinity College sits *very prettily* in extensive gardens, 400 metres from Carfax and within easy walking distance of the University's main facilities, libraries, other colleges and shops. *The college is a generally moderate one (size, sporting and political activity, cost), though it has a keenly academic tilt.* Trinity has its fair share of *journos, politicos and thespos on the University scene too.*

Sex ratio(M:F): 55%:45%	Founded: 1555
Full time u'grads: 288	Postgrads: 120
Private school: 50%	Mature students: 0
Overseas students: 8%	Disabled students: 1%

Bar; student bands and 3 bops a term in Beer Cellar (cap 150); small weekly ents events; ball every 3 years; drinking and dining socs. 1 library (52,000 books); 15 computers, 24hrs; internet access in all rooms. 5 acres of shared sports fields 1½ miles away, *which puts students off sport a bit – though resurgent boat club, strong in football and athletics.* All students live in college or college-owned housing and eat in the dining hall or in the Beer Cellar; *good veggie options* ; *one kitchen for self-catering.* CCTV; doctor, nurse; Anglican chapel.

FAMOUS ALUMNI:
Richard Burton (explorer, not the actor); Sir Kenneth Clark (art historian); Ross & Norris McWhirter (right-wing twins of 'Record Breakers' fame); Cardinal Newman (theologian); William Pitt and Lord North (ex-PMs); Terence Rattigan (playwright).

University College, Oxford

- **The College is part of <u>University of Oxford</u> and students are entitled to use its facilities.**
University College, High Street, Oxford, OX1 4BH. Tel: (01865) 276602. Fax: (01865) 276790. E-mail: college.office@univ.ox.ac.uk
Junior Common Room, University College, Oxford, OX1 4BH.
Tel: (01865) 276606. E-mail: jcr.president@univ.ox.ac.uk
Website: www.univ.ox.ac.uk

University College, the oldest Oxford College, claims to have been founded by King Alfred the Bad Cook in the 9th century. It presents an *imposing* facade to the High Street, but is *pleasantly habitable inside* with the massive marble Shelley memorial lurking down one of its quieter corridors. *The friendly environment tempts students not to stray too far from their college, which has tended towards insularity in*

the past. A tolerable level of things sporty and dramatic complement the strong academic record and JCR meetings are well attended.

Sex ratio(M:F): 63%:37%	Founded: 1249
Full time u'grads: 430	Postgrads: 112
Private school: 53%	Mature students: <1%
Overseas students: 11%	Disabled students: 5%

Bar (cap 150); 3 sweaty bops per term; jazz evenings; *strong* drama soc puts on panto and annual revue; music soc performs regularly. JCR newsletter and 'News & Screws'. 2 libraries (Main, Law: 50,000 books); 35 computers, 24hrs. Inter-denominational chapel. *Strong in sports, women's teams especially;* 7 acres of sports fields and boat-house 1½ miles away; gym, squash court. 1st and 2nd yrs live in, 70% of 3rds, finalists *in a distant annexe; generally comfortable rooms; limited self-catering.* Nurse; *reasonable disabled access.*

FAMOUS ALUMNI:
Clement Attlee, Harold Wilson (former Labour PMs); Bill Clinton (US President); Bob Hawke (former Australian PM); Stephen Hawking (physicist/cosmologist); Armando Ianucci (comedian, writer); Richard Ingrams (founder 'Private Eye', editor 'The Oldie'); VS Naipaul (writer); PB Shelley (poet); Peter Snow (BBC 'swingometer' guru); Prince Youssoupov (Rasputin's murderer).

Wadham College, Oxford

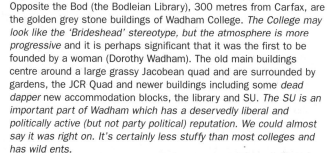

• **The College is part of <u>University of Oxford</u> and students are entitled to use its facilities.**
Wadham College, Parks Road, Oxford, OX1 3PN.
Tel: (01865) 277900. E-mail: admissions@wadham.ox.ac.uk
Wadham College Student Union, Parks Road, Oxford, OX1 3PN.
Tel: (01865) 277969.
Website: www.wadham.ox.ac.uk

Opposite the Bod (the Bodleian Library), 300 metres from Carfax, are the golden grey stone buildings of Wadham College. *The College may look like the 'Brideshead' stereotype, but the atmosphere is more progressive* and it is perhaps significant that it was the first to be founded by a woman (Dorothy Wadham). The old main buildings centre around a large grassy Jacobean quad and are surrounded by gardens, the JCR Quad and newer buildings including some *dead dapper* new accommodation blocks, the library and SU. *The SU is an important part of Wadham which has a deservedly liberal and politically active (but not party political) reputation. We could almost say it was right on. It's certainly less stuffy than most colleges and has wild ents.*

Sex ratio(M:F): 48%:52%	Founded: 1610
Full time u'grads: 454	Postgrads: 151
Private school: 35%	Mature students: 1%
Overseas students: 11%	Disabled students: 1%

Bar; theatre; King's Arms pub almost in grounds; classical concerts in Holywell Music Room (cap 150); fortnightly top bops, cabaret, bands and other regular events in the JCR (200); 'Wadstock' festival every summer. 'Wadham Sound' news sheet; 'Wadwords' termly slag mag. Library (40,000 books); 30 computers, 24hrs. Chapel. 6 acres of playing fields 1½ miles away; some sports facilities on site; *strong* badminton and women's tennis. All 1st years and finalists live in, and 20% of 2nd years; *good* self-catering amenities; livers in eat in cafeteria; informal meals in dining hall. CCTV; college counsellors; nurse; minorities group; free safety alarms; tampon coop; women's room.

FAMOUS ALUMNI:
Melvyn Bragg (writer, bore-caster); Alan Coren (columnist); Cecil Day Lewis (poet, Daniel's grandad); Michael Foot (former Labour leader); Earl of Rochester (libertine, poet); Christopher Wren (architect).

Worcester College, Oxford

• The College is part of <u>University of Oxford</u> and students are entitled to use its facilities.
Worcester College, Worcester Street, Oxford, OX1 2HB.
Tel: (01865) 278391. Fax: (01865) 278303.
E-mail: admissions@worcester.ox.ac.uk
Junior Common Room, Worcester College, Oxford, OX1 2HB.
Tel: (01865) 278300.
Website: www.worcester.ox.ac.uk

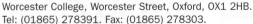

Worcester is a *beautiful* college, half a mile from Carfax, with both medieval and modern buildings, some of which are *splendid and spacious,* all surrounded by *stunning* gardens, complete with a lake and ducks. *They're sporty and serious about music but still concentrate on having a good time. The JCR reflects this attitude by not mentioning the P-word (politics)* and offering weekly bops and regular bands instead.

Sex ratio(M:F): 54%:46%	Founded: 1714
Full time u'grads: 419	Postgrads: 147
Private school: 61%	Mature students: 1.5%
Overseas students: 6%	Disabled students: 1%

Cellar bar (cap 100); For bops: the Hall (150), JCR (100), Morley Fletcher Room (100); soundproof room; ball every 3 years; termly boat club cocktail party. Worcester Buskins drama soc. Newsletter 'The Worcester Source' fortnightly. 2 libraries (100,000 books); 22 computers, 24hrs. Anglican chapel. 12 acres of sports fields on site; boathouse; *strong* women's football, cricket, athletics and rugby. 1st and 2nd years live in, 20% of final years; *varied* rooms – en suite showers in new block; Ethernet and phone in all rooms, most eat in Hall; *limited* self-catering; buttery sells snacks. CCTV; doctor, nurse; *limited* wheelchair access.

FAMOUS ALUMNI:
Richard Adams (bunny writer); Sir Alistair Burnett (newscaster); Rupert Murdoch (media mogul); John Sainsbury (of supermarket fame).

> The original site of Reading University was the back yard of the Huntley and Palmer biscuit factory.

Oxford Brookes University

- **Formerly Oxford Polytechnic**

Oxford Brookes University, Gipsy Lane, Headington, Oxford, OX3 0BP.
Tel: (01865) 484848. Fax: (01865) 483616.
E-mail: query@brookes.ac.uk
Oxford Brookes University Students' Union, Helena Kennedy
Student Centre, Headington Hill Campus, Oxford, OX3 0BP.
Tel: (01865) 484750. Fax: (01865) 484799.
E-mail: obsu@brookes.ac.uk

GENERAL

Oxford Brookes is unlike its famous neighbour in many ways. Despite being in the same city of ivory towers and dreaming spires, Oxford Brookes dodges any of the dusty stuffiness of Oxford University. The students, however, are just as partial to punting, falling in the river and strolling through Christchurch meadows. It has 4 campuses as well as a site based at the John Radcliffe Hospital. The main site at Gipsy Lane is a mile outside Oxford's centre in the suburbs, away from that hazy churn of academic ritual. It is compressed into a cramped 11 acres of 60s blocks of glass and concrete *(but is not as bad as it sounds)*; the media centre is based here. A recent site is Headington Hill, a 15-acre estate which used to belong to the dodgy Robert Maxwell, just across the road from Gipsy Lane. The Wheatley site houses the education and business courses on its 65 acres, 5 miles further out into the countryside. There's also a newly acquired campus called Harcourt Hill which offers a home to the Westminster Institute of Education.

Sex ratio(M:F): 43%:57%	Founded: 1865
Full time u'grads: 8,000	Part time: 2,160
Postgrads: 3,200	Non-degree: n/a
Ave course: 3yrs	Ethnic: 13%
Private school: 20%	Flunk rate: 15.6%
Mature students: 45.2%	Overseas students: 20.4%
Disabled students: 8%	

ATMOSPHERE:
Unlike many 'new' universities, there's a high proportion of phone-wielding, privately-educated, GTi-driving students from the Home Counties, possibly drawn by the 'Oxford' name-tag (without such rigorous entry requirements). That said, there are plenty of mature students and others who don't necessarily fit the mould, and everyone is included in the sporty, boozy party that is social life at Brookes.

THE CITY: see University of Oxford

TRAVEL: see University of Oxford
The University provides free buses between the Gipsy Lane, Harcourt and Wheatley sites, and the Cowley Centre and the John Radcliffe Hospital, every ½ hour, both of which take about 15–25 minutes. The modular course structure means that some students have academic commitments on more than one site.

CAREER PROSPECTS:
- Careers Service • No of staff: 3 full/5 part
- Unemployed after 6mths: 2.3%

Those students who know the careers service exists are quite happy with it and employment rates are excellent.

SPECIAL FEATURES:
- There's a no-smoking rule in all areas of the University, except the SU Bars.
- The University's Chancellor is Jon Snow (Channel 4 News Presenter).

FAMOUS ALUMNI:
Andrew Logan (creator of Alternative Miss World); John Pilkington (BBC); Tim Rodber (rugby player).

FURTHER INFO:
Prospectuses for undergrads and postgrads. There's also a web site (www.brookes.ac.uk).

ACADEMIC

staff/student ratio: 1:12
Range of points required for entrance: 320-80
Percentage accepted through clearing: 12.5%
Number of terms/semesters: 3
Length of terms/semesters: 10 wks
Research: 2.9

LIBRARIES:
- Books: 350,000 • Study places: 1,100

Library provision is one of the many areas where Brookes is in the shadow of its famous neighbour.

COMPUTERS:
- Computer workstations: 850

24-hour computer provision, but it's still not good enough.

ENTERTAINMENT

IN TOWN: see University of Oxford

UNIVERSITY:
- Price of a pint of beer: £1.40 • Glass of wine: £1.20

Bars: (5) Morals Café bar at Morrell Hall is the largest bar (cap 550) and it doubles as a club venue. Hart's Lounge Bar (350) – so-called because it was opened by Tony Hart – and the Mezzanine Bar at Headington Hill are also popular.

> University of Kent Radio began as a pirate station in 1967, broadcasting through the radiators in Rutherford College.

Theatres: The 2 drama societies are pretty popular, with at least one show usually going to the Edinburgh Fringe Festival each year.
Cinema: Mainstream and cult movies every week on a big digital screen.
Clubs/discos: The week is dominated by Crunchy (the biggest club night in Oxford) on Fridays at Headington Hill (1,200). *The charty/dance mix may not win any plaudits for originality or cool, but it's the biggest club night in Oxford.* However the summer will see it undergoing a refurbishment including a change in style. There are two discos a week at Morals. Newly updated lighting and sound systems have done groovy things and DJs such as Pete Tong have also spun their stuff at the Uni recently.
Music venues: Headington Hill can also attract some *decent* live acts such as, recently, Judge Jules, Tall Paul, Coldplay, David Gray, Toploader, Bluetones and Mansun. On Thursdays there's a new bands' night.
Food: The University's refectory, contracted out to an external caterer, refects at lunchtime and early evenings. *Most students' thoughts about the food are unprintable, but suffice to say it's overpriced and revolting, though the portions are mercifully tiny.*
Others: Three balls a year.

SOCIAL & POLITICAL

OXFORD BROOKES UNIVERSITY STUDENTS' UNION:
• 7 sabbaticals • Turnout at last ballot: 12% • NUS member

The Students' Union based in the Helena Kennedy Students' Centre is surprisingly politically active for such a middle-class set. Recently they've been locked in arguments with the University authorities who they feel are encouraging only rich kids to apply and in the restructuring of the academic year. There are also 2 full and 2 part time advice staff, to, well, advise you really.

SU FACILITIES:
Ents venue; shops; bars; vending and games machines; pool tables; photocopying; minibus; TV room; insurance; travel agents; monthly jobsheet.

CLUBS (NON SPORTING):
Anime Unlimited; Arabic; BND; CHAOS (Choral and Orchestral); Chinese; Club Caribbean; Corkscrew; Dregs (alternative rock); Dyxies; Fortune Players; Hellenic; Immoral; Italian; Latino; Japanese; Jazz; Juggling; Malaysian; MOLES (environmental); ORBS (radio station); Pakistan; Poetry; Pooh; Rag; Residential Assistants; Scandinavian; Sprogs; Taiwanese; Turkish; Underground Dance; WARP (war games).

OTHER ORGANISATIONS:
The SU publishes 'O.B.SCENE' every three weeks.

Past competitors on 'University Challenge' include Stephen Fry, David Mellor, Clive James, John Simpson and Malcolm Rifkind.

RELIGIOUS:
- 9 chaplains (CofE, RC, Methodist, Baptist, Russian Orthodox)

Prayer provisions in the University for Christians and Muslims.

PAID WORK:
The SU runs a jobshop with specialist staff filling over 1,500 vacancies a year.

- Recent successes: rowing

Sport is one of the few things that can drag students out of the bar. Standards are pretty good and facilities are superb, especially by comparison with other former polys.

SPORTS FACILITIES:
There's a *superbly equipped* sports centre at Headington, including an astroturf pitch, gym, sports hall, climbing room and *plush* bar and social areas. Outdoor sports facilities including a golf course are based at the Wheatley site. The Uni is building a new weights room, rebuilding the Boathouse and adding a swimming pool and another golf course.

SPORTING CLUBS:
Aerobics; Go-karting; Jiu Jitsu; Soma.

ATTRACTIONS: see University of Oxford

IN COLLEGE:
- Catered: 11% • Cost: £85 (42wks)
- Self-catering: 19% • Cost: £36-66 (42wks)

Availability: The University can house 70% of 1st years but no other students. *Although a tad pricey, almost all the accommodation is of a high standard and* includes 12 meals in the price (in the catered halls obviously), *conveniently in or near the Headington campus with good amenities.* Very few have to share rooms *and it's only ever for the start of term when everyone turns up and for some reason the University hasn't managed to allocate rooms properly.* There are plans to build accommodation for couples and there's already some single sex accommodation for female overseas students. Entry-phones and keypads attempt to keep out the ghouls in some halls, although some students complain about the standard of security as well as the delays if you need repairs doing.

```
According to York University regulations
students can be chucked out if they eat the
ducks that live on the campus lake.
```

Car parking: Permit parking at three halls only.
EXTERNALLY: see University of Oxford
Housing help: Places in the University are allocated by pot luck, but those 1st years and other students who need to go it alone can get help from the University Accommodation Office which has a number of full-time staff providing bulletin boards and an approval scheme to check for roaches.

WELFARE

SERVICES:
• Lesbian & Gay Society • Mature SA • Overseas SA
• Minibus • Women's Officer • Self-defence classes
The Health Centre on the Headington campus has 4 doctors and nurses and there are 8 part- and 6 full-time counsellors. There is a policy to help disadvantaged minorities and so there are support groups for dyslexia and students with eating disorders, local helplines and specialist advisers for mature, disabled and overseas students.
Women: Safety bus and Officer, and rape alarms given out free by SU. One or two *dingy lanes* near some of the halls of residence.
Disabled: There is a rolling programme of improvements to access including lifts and ramps and *all new developments are excellent*.

FINANCE:
• Access fund: £255,000 • Successful applications: 445
A small hardship fund is set aside, used mainly for those disadvantaged minorities (in particular, part-time and overseas students). There's also a debt counsellor and child care grants.

Oxford Poly
see Oxford Brookes University

One of the entrances to Loughborough University is nicknamed 'The Bastard Gates' because they were presented by sir William Bastard, a former chairman of the University governors.

University of Paisley

PCL see University of Westminster

Pharmacy School see School of Pharmacy, London

University of Plymouth

PNL see University of North London

University of Portsmouth

Preston Polytechnic see University of Central Lancashire

Printing see The London Institute

University Paisley

- *Formerly Paisley College*

(1) University of Paisley, Paisley, PA1 2BE. Tel: 0800 027 1000. Fax: (0141) 848 3000. E-mail: uni-direct@paisley.ac.uk
University of Paisley Students' Association, 17 Hunter Street, Paisley, PA1 1DN. Tel: (0141) 889 9940.
(2) University of Paisley, Ayr Campus, Beech Grove, Ayr, KA8 0SR. Tel: (01292) 260321. Fax: (01292) 611705.

GENERAL

Paisley, 5 miles to the west of central Glasgow, is a town *in manufacturing decline, but business growth* – long gone are those 18th- and 19th-century days when it had a great weaving industry. The town used to produce so many shawls, that it even invented its own pattern – the familiar 'paisley', venerated by millions of suburban golfers. (*Here they're more likely to be playing 'urban golf', an altogether different and deleterious game where one doesn't need be a member, wear paisley or play on greens or fairways.*) Spread around the centre of town is the University campus, mostly concrete blocks, joined by walkways, *scoring zero on the eyeability scale*, but also including lecture halls in converted churches. The second campus is in Ayr, a coastal town about 30 miles away to the south-west.

Sex ratio(M:F): 45%:55%	Founded: 1897
Full time u'grads: 5,728	Part time: 2,764
Postgrads: 705	Non-degree: 904
Ave course: 4yrs	Ethnic: 4%
Private school: n/a	Flunk rate: 25%
Mature students: 26%	Overseas students: 4.5%
Disabled students: 5.5%	

ATMOSPHERE:
Most students are drawn from Paisley and the surrounding area which creates a tight-knit community, a level-headed bunch, concentrating on their vocationally oriented degrees and not leaving much time for hedonism. They occasionally suffer from a slight but unwarranted inferiority complex due to the 3 big brother unis in Glasgow, 7 miles away. In the past, the party people had to head out to Glasgow to get their kicks, but these days the Glaswegians are popping over to Paisley.

AYR CAMPUS:
1,300 full-time students are at the Ayr Campus, 30 miles away and the home of Robbie Burns. Education, business, media and nursing courses are taught here. A Management Centre has been set up and a new union building is being built.

PAISLEY:
- Population: 100,000
- London: 371 miles
- Glasgow: 7 miles
- Edinburgh: 51 miles

You can't spend centuries making fine swirling shapes without a fair amount of artiness rubbing off on you. And indeed, despite everything else, Paisley remains a thriving arts centre. Right opposite the University are the town's museum and art gallery. Along with shops and the like, there are Paisley Abbey (parts of which date back to the 12th century), the Coats Observatory and the Weaver's Cottage, *but Paisley isn't one of Scotland's tourist draws. It's a noted drugs blackspot and the Students Union is in one of the more notorious areas.*

THE CITY: see University of Glasgow

TRAVEL:
Trains: The nearest mainline station is 5 minutes' walk from Gilmour St. Regular direct services to Glasgow (£1.65 return) with the last train at night at 11.46pm. London (£50.80).
Coaches: Served nationally by Scottish Citylink, via Glasgow. London (£27); Glasgow (£1.70).
Car: The M8 is 1 mile from the town, also the A737 and A726.
Taxis: Relatively cheap. There's a huge rank by the station.
Hitching: *Generally not recommended.*
Local: Buses allow easy short hops: at 85p, a single fare to Glasgow is cheaper than the train and is available till 3am.
Bicycles: *Quite hilly* and nowhere to store bikes on campus, but quite a few students give it a go.

CAREER PROSPECTS:
- Careers Service
- No of staff: 5 full/1 part
- Unemployed after 6mths: 12%

FAMOUS ALUMNI:
Gavin Hastings (rugby/American football legend); Graeme Obree (cyclist).

FURTHER INFO:
Undergrad & postgrad prospectuses available free on 0800 027 1000. Course leaflets. Website (www.paisley.ac.uk).

Researchers at De Montfort University have perfected a technique for turning pig manure into energy.

493 Paisley

ACADEMIC

The main reason students are here is to improve their career chances. As a result, the courses reflect the jobsy slant.

staff/student ratio: 1:20
Range of points required for entrance: 240-100
Percentage accepted through clearing: 21%
Number of terms/semesters: 2
Length of terms/semesters: 15wks
Research: 2.1

LIBRARIES:
- Books: 262,000   • Study places: 1,120

The Robertson Trust Library and Learning Resource Centre have improved the *previously inadequate internet facilities*.

COMPUTERS:
- Computer workstations: 2,000

ENTERTAINMENT

THE CITY: see University of Glasgow

PAISLEY:
- Price of a pint of beer: £1.80   • Glass of wine: £1.50

Cinemas: The CAC has 2 screens (adm £3.50) and the Arts Centre has regular screenings (£2).
Theatres: Paisley Arts Centre hosts popular touring companies.
Pubs: *Pushplugs: Café Borgia; Cellar Bar (very close to University); Fiddlers Green, O'Neill's and Paddy Malarkey's (Irish); Vodka Wodka (Scotland's first vodka bar).*
Clubs/discos: *Shag at Furry Murry's, Toledo (student nights are popular) and Utopia are the real booty-shakers.*
Music venues: *The Arts Centre is the only real hot-spot.*
Eating out: *Pub lunches are a reliable source of sustenance. Other Pushplugs: Café Borgia in the Arts Centre (again); A Taste of Europe (bargain lunches); Kaldi's Coffee House; Vodka Wodka (excellent value at £2 for 2 colossal courses).*

UNIVERSITY:
- Price of a pint of beer: £1.60   • Glass of wine: £1.70

Bars: (3) The Buroo is the most popular quaff-stop and there's also the Subway and the Association.
Films: 1 film a week along arthouse and world cinema lines.
Clubs/discos/music venues: Friday night is charty dance night at the Union, Saturdays is live music night, although for anything beyond local and tribute bands Paisleyites have to go to Glasgow.
Food: The refectory fare hardly deserves the name 'food' but nosh from the SU and The Buroo is cheap and cheerful.
Others: 1 formal ball a year and a big bash at a nightclub in Glasgow once a term. Major sports events every week in the Union. Comedy nights are quite popular.

```
Cranfield is the first University to hire out
its own security guards.
```

SOCIAL & POLITICAL

UNIVERSITY OF PAISLEY STUDENTS' ASSOCIATION:
• 3 sabbaticals • Turnout at last ballot: 12% • NUS member

The SA, based in a run-down building, is solidly left-wing, with strong nationalist tendencies, although this isn't reflected so strongly in the student body. The most motivating campaign so far this year concerned the price of Guinness...

SU FACILITIES:
2 bars; café; a shop; Bank of Scotland cashpoint; pool tables; photocopiers; games and video machines; juke box; vending machines; TV lounge; a meeting room; advice centre; stationery shop; customised night club; launderette.

CLUBS (NON SPORTING):
Hellenic; Landing Party; SNP; Star Trek.

OTHER ORGANISATIONS:
The SA has revamped 'The Associate', called it 'AM' and given it a glossy *cover to make it seem less like one of those earnest left-wing rags that intense people sell in shopping-centres.* The student TV club uses the Educational Development Unit's Studio to produce programmes by and for students. For Rag, *lunatics jump out of aeroplanes with nothing but a large carefully arranged piece of silk. Stranger still, people give them money to do it.*

RELIGIOUS:
• 9 chaplains (6 at Paisley, 3 at Ayr)

The multi-faith chaplaincy at the Thomas Coats Memorial Church has CofE, RC, Baptist, Methodist, Muslim prayer room, Episcopalian and lay preachers plus links with the local rabbi and Muslim leaders. The town provides various Christian worship shops.

PAID WORK:
The Student Advisory Service lists vacation vacancies and term-time tasks, *but the openings aren't out of the ordinary.*

SPORTS

• Recent successes: nothing special

Sport isn't a major obsession, but the Robertson Trust Sports Centre gets a few people dragging their Green Flash out of the closet, if only to lose that beer-belly.

SPORTS FACILITIES:
The Sports Centre, 2 miles from campus, includes rugby and football pitches, a sports hall and a fitness room. *Extensive* local facilities and reciprocal agreements with other educational establishments nearby, mean students also have access to a lake, swimming pool, golf course, squash and tennis courts, croquet lawn, sauna/solarium and ice rink.

SPORTING CLUBS:
Aikido; Gaelic Football.

ATTRACTIONS:
The local football heroes are St Mirren.

ACCOMMODATION

IN COLLEGE:
- Self-catering: 15% • Cost: £32-40 (31wks)

Availability: The University has 940 places accommodating 70% of 1st years, although 10% of new students who want to live in, can't. Most places are within 10 minutes of the campus, such as Underwood Residence, which has 171 places (165 single rooms). *Thornly Park is sociable and desirable.* Security guards over the weekends, and security systems on doors.

EXTERNALLY:
- Ave rent: £35

Availability: *It is reasonably easy to find accommodation in Paisley and the standard is usually okay.* West End Park should be avoided on safety grounds and Ladylane and Storie Street are best left alone too, not because they're rough, but because the houses have mould growing in them.

Housing help: The Residential Accommodation Unit employs 3 full-time staff, offering residential places when available, a register of local private accommodation and gas safety checks.

WELFARE

SERVICES:
- Nursery • Lesbian & Gay Society
- Overseas SA • Women's Officer

Various help organisations: the Student Advisory Service employs 4 counsellors; Student Welfare Association; the Student Health Service with nurse; another counsellor and a full-time welfare adviser in the SA. The nursery costs £3.50/session to students.

Drugs: Paisley is one of the hard drug blackspots of the UK *but problems haven't really filtered into the University.*

Disabled: *Standard of access and special facilities are pretty average, but with the appointment of a Special Needs Adviser things are improving. Facilities for the visually and hearing impaired are very good* and there's a dyslexia support group.

FINANCE:
- Access fund: £123,000 • Successful applications: 1,468

Bursary system and hardship fund (£10,000) from Student Welfare for those who wouldn't get other help. Loans (but not grants) from the access fund available in as little as 48 hours.

PCL

see University of Westminster

Pharmacy School

see School of Pharmacy, London

```
Hitler planned to make Oxford the capital of
the UK, with Christ Church as his palace.
```

University of Plymouth

- *Formerly Polytechnic South West*

(1) University of Plymouth, Drake Circus, Plymouth, PL4 8AA.
Tel: (01752) 232232. Fax: (01752) 232141.
E-mail: admissions@plymouth.ac.uk
University of Plymouth Students' Union, Drake Circus, Plymouth,
PL4 8AA Tel: (01752) 663337. Fax: (01752) 251669.
E-mail: union@upsports.plym.ac.uk
(2) Faculty of Arts & Education, University of Plymouth, Earl Richards
Road North, Exeter, EX2 6AS. Tel: (01392) 475022. Fax: (01392)
475012. E-mail: fae-admissions@plym.ac.uk
(3) Faculty of Arts & Education, University of Plymouth, Douglas
Avenue, Exmouth, EX8 2AT. Tel: (01395) 255309. Fax: (01395)
255303.
(4) Seale-Hayne Faculty of Agriculture, Food & Land Use, University of
Plymouth, Newton Abbot, Devon, TQ12 6NQ. Tel: (01626) 325606/7.
Fax: (01626) 325605.

GENERAL

If Plymouth were any further south-west, it would be Cornwall. If it were any further south it'd be in the English Channel. As it is, it's a port around the Plymouth Sound (the bay) on the south coast of Devon near *wild and windy* Dartmoor. It was from here that Sir Francis Drake sailed to whip the Spanish Armada's butt – according to the myth, Frankie psyched himself up by playing bowls on the Hoe, a patch of greenery by the sea. The Hoe's still there near the city centre and not far from the main site of the University. The University's old name, Polytechnic South West, was more accurate geographically, because, in fact, it has six sites spread around south: Plymouth, Exeter, Exmouth, Seale-Hayne, Taunton and Poole. *To be fair, Plymouth does provide the focal point for the University.* However, all the sites have some of their own facilities.

Sex ratio(M:F): 46%:54%
Full time u'grads: 15,520
Postgrads: 612
Ave course: 3yrs
Private school: n/a
Mature students: 42.7%
Disabled students: 5%

Founded: 1970
Part time: 3,463
Non-degree: 3,723
Ethnic: 2.4%
Flunk rate: 15.3%
Overseas students: 8.6%

ATMOSPHERE:
The South-West as a whole is a pretty mellow place but Plymouth students are capable of perking up when it comes to work (there's lots of careerist zeal) and drinking unfeasible quantities of beer. The smaller sites have their own quirks.

THE SITES:
Plymouth: This is the main site housing 5 out of the University's 7 faculties and nearly 7,500 of the students. It's a city centre campus and *concrete is much in evidence.*

Exeter: The campus is redbrick, 2 miles from the city centre, next to the hilly countryside that surrounds Exeter. It was purpose-built as Exeter Art College. For a more detailed low-down on the ups and downs of Exeter, see University of Exeter, which, *for students who are willing to mix with the Sloanes, is a social life-saver.* There are 732 students based here.

Exmouth: The town of Exmouth is, unsurprisingly, at the mouth of the river Exe on the east bank of the wide estuary. *This is a small town, a bit of a baby brother to Exeter, 8 miles upstream. Exeter is very important for students who want more from life than pretty sea views.* There are 2,814 students at Exmouth.

Seale-Hayne: 3 miles outside the tiny town of Newton Abbot, 30 miles from Plymouth, 16 from Exeter, and just round the corner from the middle of nowhere, Seale-Hayne houses around 1,000 students in *beautiful stately* buildings in *magnificent* countryside. *But the site is self-contained and, since travelling around is a major hassle, it's very close-knit. Some students find it a bit suffocating, others love the close and closeted lifestyle.*

PLYMOUTH:
- Population: 238,800 • London: 200 miles
- Exeter: 37 miles • Bristol: 106 miles

Apart from a few buildings which date from the days of Drake, most of Plymouth has been rebuilt since the last World War, when it was trashed by bombing raids. *As a result, it has a great deal less rural charm than most West Country towns* and consequently fewer tourists. Instead, it's a functional city with amenities serving a large catchment area. The Hoe and Quay are *pleasant enough* and students wanting a little aesthetic distraction might stroll across the road to the City Art Gallery and Museum, or even go to the National Aquarium with its shark theatre and deep reef tank *to ooh and ah at.*

EXETER: see University of Exeter

TRAVEL:
Trains: Plymouth is the nearest station to the main site which is only about 5 minutes away or, if crawling, a tad longer. Services to London (£29.70), Bristol (£21.10) etc. Most stop at Newton Abbot and Exeter (on the same line).
Coaches: National Express and Western National services from Plymouth to London (£26.75) and beyond.
Car: The A38 links Plymouth with Newton Abbot and Exeter.
Air: Flights inland and to Ireland from Plymouth airport.
Ferries: Services from Plymouth to France and Spain.
Hitching: *Okay along the A38 for he (and she) that wait, as long as you're not up the Cornwall end.*
Local: Devon buses aren't as cheap as they used to be.
Taxis: *Plenty and they're comprehensive, but pricey.*
Bicycles: *Plymouth is a bit hilly. At Seale-Hayne, a bike is handy for getting into Newton Abbot.*

CAREER PROSPECTS:
- Careers Service • No of staff: 4 full/2 part
- Unemployed after 6mths: 6.3%

FAMOUS ALUMNI:
David Braine (BBC weatherman); Jules Leaver (Founder of the Face clothing company); Didi Osman (Sleeper bassist); Pam St Clement (Pat in 'EastEnders'); Peter Winterbottom (rugby player).

FURTHER INFO:
Prospectuses for undergrads and postgrads, guides for overseas and mature students and a CD-Rom. Website (www.plymouth.ac.uk).

ACADEMIC

The Uni offers some very unusual courses including the only perfumery course in Europe and even Surf Studies, dude. Other *potentially less fascinating* courses include Business, Human Sciences, Science, Technology, Art and Design, Health Studies, Arts & Education, Agriculture and Food & Land Use. There's also a planetarium for all aspiring or indeed current space-cadets and the Uni also has a Diving and Sailing Centre of which it's very proud the only uni in the UK to have its very own.

staff/student ratio: 1:18
Range of points required for entrance: 280-140
Percentage accepted through clearing: 18.3%
Number of terms/semesters: 2
Length of terms/semesters: 15 wks
Research: 2.6

LIBRARIES:
• Books: 480,335 • Study places: 1,096
There are libraries at each site. *Many students still find book facilities limited – except when it comes to marine biology for which they have one of the best libraries in the country.*

COMPUTERS:
• Computer workstations: 500
Major investment has improved computer provision.

ENTERTAINMENT

PLYMOUTH:
• Price of a pint of beer: £2.10 • Glass of wine: £1.45
Cinemas: The Warner Village has 15 screens, the ABC has 4, The Drake Odeon (*independent flea-pit*) has 5 and there are arty pics at Plymouth Arts Centre.
Theatres: (4) There's the Theatre Royal, which had the RSC in residence last year, and experimental productions at the Arts Centre, the Drum and Barbican Theatre.
Pubs: *Pubs range from the friendly and welcoming (some even sponsor sports teams) to those in Devonport where identifiably studenty behaviour isn't recommended. Pushplugs: Caffeine Club (pretentious); Bar Italia; Goodbodies (60s rather than necessarily good bodies); Hogshead.*
Clubs/discos: *Plymouth has more clubs than, by all rights, a city of its size should and, with admission costing around £2, most are worth checking out. Apart from the Quay Club (Jelly Jazz), the clubs are all down Union Street. Thursday is student night. Pushplugs: Millennium (cap 1,500, very popular, a beach bar with real sand, often live music, adm £1-2, what more could you ask for?); The Dance Academy; Zeroes.*

Music venues: Classical at the Theatre Royal and Guildhall, pop at the Plymouth Pavilions. Recently: James, the Corrs. Try the Cooperage for local bands. *On second thoughts...*

Eating out: Apart from the usual chains *Pushplugs: Cafés Cuba and Rouge; Bomb Shelter Café; Cap'n Jasper's; Caffeine Club (chilled filling post). Exmouth's speciality is seafood.*

UNIVERSITY:
- Price of a pint of beer: £1.45 • Glass of wine: £1.15

Most of the University entertainments are at Plymouth.

Bars: The Main Bar at Plymouth is open until 2am at the weekend but fills up shortly after 10. *Four Union bars are nameless, which makes arranging to meet there a little hard.* There are smaller bars at the outlying sites.

Clubs/discos: The SU (cap 1,400) pounds to house and indie sounds twice a week (£1.50); Sub Sub Club Fridays & Saturdays at the Union, plus occasional funk. Clubs in town are often booked as well.

Music venues: The Pavilions in the town centre is the site for sore ears, names to have played recently include the Artful Dodger and Freestylers.

Theatre/cinema: Free film night every Sunday. Musical Theatre Group put on Grease last year, despite the lack of either a theatre or *John Travolta's cheddar grin.*

Eating out: There's a total of eight University-run refectories around the sites. A new sandwich bar, Loafers2, was voted best for food.

Others: Balls galore, especially the Babs Valentine Ball.

SOCIAL & POLITICAL

UNIVERSITY OF PLYMOUTH STUDENTS' UNION:
- 10 sabbaticals • Turnout at last ballot: 25% • NUS member

The Union has facilities on all sites, usually in a building shared with the University. The notable exception is Plymouth where the Union building is a largely subterranean, modern maze. Apathy reigns like a rainy Sunday (sorry), except when it comes to fees.

SU FACILITIES:
Four bars; advice centre at four main sites; games & vending machines; Union shop; sandwich bar; launderette; showers; pool tables; PO; print, fax and photocopying; meeting room; juke box; reprographics unit; photobooth; ticket agency; welfare office.

CLUBS (NON SPORTING):
DJ; Juggling; Little Goblins; Motorcycle; Terminal.

OTHER ORGANISATIONS:
'Fly', the fortnightly student newspaper, is produced by the SU. Charity Rag and student Community Action Group with over 300 volunteers and links with other organisations, eg The Big Issue.

RELIGIOUS:
- 10 chaplains (1 full ecumenical, 9 part-time)

A range of churches in Plymouth and a synagogue.

PAID WORK:
Apart from the usual bar work and all that, there are a few tourist and maritime based jobs in Plymouth. *The SU's employment register can be fruitful, as can hopping over the Tamar to Cornwall in the summer.*

SPORTS

- Recent successes: sailing, surfing

The sports situation is going from good to gripeworthy despite students' efforts. Housing shortages mean halls are planned on the site of Exmouth's facilities and a campaign to stop Wednesday afternoon lectures was rejected by the University. *The sporting spirit is considerably dampened. For shame.*

SPORTS FACILITIES:
Plymouth: Fitness room; squash courts; sports hall; playing fields; 7-hole golf-course; watersports centre. The city provides facilities for watersports, a bowling green, swimming pools and ski slope and ice skating.
Exmouth: 13 acres of fields; netball/tennis courts; multigym.
Seale-Hayne: Playing fields; sports hall; squash/tennis courts.
Exeter: Facilities are mainly hired.

SPORTING CLUBS:
Aikido; Boxercise; Caving; Chinese Kung-Fu; Flying; Jiu Jitsu; Kick-boxing; Life-saving; Mountain bike; Mountaineering; Octopush; Paintball; Shooting; Sky Diving; Snowriders; Surf; Ultimate Frisbee; Water-polo; Water-Skiing; Windsurfing.

ATTRACTIONS
Plymouth Argyle for footie, gee-gees at Newton Abbot, regattas at Plymouth. Plymouth is one of the UK's big surf spots.

ACCOMMODATION

IN COLLEGE:
- Self-catering: 14%   • Cost: £40-92 (39wks)

Availability: Across all sites, 50% of 1st years have a place in college accommodation, but 10% can't live in. 400 new en suite rooms are being built to redress this. Less than 1% have to share. At Plymouth the halls are all within 3 miles of the campus – *Gilwell and Radnor are popular, but the latter expensive.* There are further places at Seale-Hayne and 145 places in head tenancy schemes in Exeter. The university plans to build more halls at Exmouth.
Car parking: Very, very, very limited but free with permit.

EXTERNALLY:
- Ave rent: £40

Availability in Plymouth: *There's just about enough for those who are quick off the mark, but students who bend down to tie their laces or check the mirror for zits may look round to find, to mix a metaphor or two, they've missed the boat.* Recommended areas include Mutley, Greenbank, Stoke, Peverell and St Judes.
Housing help: The University runs an efficient accommodation office on each site with 16 staff, offering computerised vacancy lists and an approval scheme.

In 1881, the entire student body of University College, Oxford, was sent down, after the Dean's Room was screwed shut (with the Dean inside).

WELFARE

SERVICES:
- Nursery • Lesbian & Gay Society • Mature SA • Overseas SA
- Minibus • Women's Officer • Self-defence classes

There are two full- and one part-time counsellors overall, as well as a GP and nurse on each site. SU welfare office and a family planning unit, which gives out free condoms and pregnancy tests. Late minibuses run you home.

Disabled: *Access could be better around the Plymouth campus, including the Union.* There are induction loops.

FINANCE:
- Access fund: £845,387 • Successful applications: 730

Small loans and vacation funds are available.

PNL

see University of North London

University of Portsmouth

- *Formerly Portsmouth Polytechnic*

University of Portsmouth, Winston Churchill Avenue, Portsmouth, PO1 2UP. Tel: (023) 9284 8484. Fax: (023) 9284 2733.
E-mail: info.centre@port.ac.uk
University of Portsmouth Students' Union, Alexandra House, Museum Road, Southsea, Hants, PO1 2QH. Tel: (023) 9284 3640. Fax: (023) 9284 3675.

GENERAL

Portsmouth sits by the Solent just a shortish row off the Isle of Wight. Built on Portsea Island, it is one of Europe's most densely populated cities and, for 400 years, one of Britain's foremost naval ports. *The maritime influence is unavoidable. However where the Navy once ruled students have made the city their own.* The other main campus, at Milton, is 2½ miles from the Guildhall site.

Sex ratio(M:F): 56%:44%	Founded: 1969
Full time u'grads: 11,238	Part time: 2,062
Postgrads: 879	Non-degree: 3,450
Ave course: 3yrs	Ethnic: 8%
Private school: n/a	Flunk rate: 18.2%
Mature students: 25%	Overseas students: 6%
Disabled students: 6%	

ATMOSPHERE:
The transition from polydom has been less stressful than with many of the other new universities. Student life still revolves around the

battle of beer and brains with occasional sporting interludes. Horizons are firmly fixed on getting a good job.

THE SITES:
The Guildhall campus is definitely the dominant site and students at Milton, which merged with the then Poly in 1976, can feel like lesser cousins (business studies and information science are based there).

TOWN:
- Population: 174,700 • London: 70 miles
- Southampton: 21 miles

Portsmouth is compact, if not bijou. Small enough to walk around town, down to the beach or to pay a visit to all sorts of maritime sights: HMS Victory; The Mary Rose; The Warrior; The Royal Marines Museum and so on. *More useful but much more ugly*, there's the Cascades shopping centre. You can find most major branch stores here and in the other shopping streets and centres. Gunwharf Quays has over 70 factory outlets from Levis to Ralph Lauren. There's also a daily fruit and veg market, plenty of supermarkets and late-night corner shops. Millennium projects in the town include £112Mn redevelopment of the harbour including shops, bars, restaurants and houses and, *Term,* a tower. *Town/gown relations are a bit scary, especially when it comes to parking.*

TRAVEL:
Trains: Mainline connections to, among other places, London Waterloo (£13.35), So'ton (£4.30) and Liverpool (£42.75).
Coaches: National Express services to many destinations including London (£13), So'ton (£3.50) and Liverpool (£33).
Car: The A27, which runs along the south coast, becomes the M27 between Portsmouth and Southampton. The A3 connects the town with London.
Air: Southampton Airport is 22 miles away.
Ferries: Regular ferries to the Isle of Wight, Spain and France (St Malo, Cherbourg, Caen, Le Havre), and the Isle of Wight hovercraft.
Hitching: *Good opportunities from lorry drivers coming off the ferries on to the A3.*
Local: *Buses are decent, but most distances are walkable.*
Taxis: *An unnecessarily extravagant way of getting around, but it doesn't work out too expensive since the town's so small.*
Bicycles: *A bike loan scheme and Lottery-funded cycle lanes make for two wheels pretty good.*

CAREER PROSPECTS:
- Careers Service • No of staff: 4 full/6 part
- Unemployed after 6mths: 4%

Efficient, effective but underused service at Guildford Walk on the Guildhall campus and an information room in Milton.

FAMOUS ALUMNI:
David Chidgey MP (Lib Dem); Shirley Conran (writer); Ron Davies MP (Lab); Ben Fogle (Castaway chap); Nicky Wire (Manic Street Preachers) dropped out because he was 'having a thoroughly miserable time'.

FURTHER INFO:
Prospectus, departmental brochures, mature students' guide, video, information leaflets (tel: (023) 9284 2705) and a website (www.port.ac.uk).

ACADEMIC

staff/student ratio: 1:18
Range of points required for entrance: 300-140
Percentage accepted through clearing: 8%
Number of terms/semesters: 2
Length of terms/semesters: 15 wks
Research: 3.5

LIBRARIES:
• Books: 600,000 • Study places: 800
The Frewen Library is on the main site; smaller Goldsmith Library at Milton; three other subject-based libraries.

COMPUTERS:
• Computer workstations: 710

ENTERTAINMENT

THE CITY:
• Price of a pint of beer: £1.80 • Glass of wine: £1.50
Cinemas: (3) UCI 6-screener and 14 screen Warner for blockbusters, one for arty films and one for student discounts. There are historic cinemas at Southsea and in the Theatre Royal.
Theatres: The King's Theatre and the Theatre Royal are *decent mainstream thespitoria*. There's also the Southsea Arts Centre.
Pubs: *More than enough to turn a pub crawl into a night in the gutter and all friendly, especially in Old Portsmouth and along Albert Road (Southsea). Gales HSB, a local brew, is worth a tongue trial, if you're not doing anything the next day.* Pushplugs: Wetherspoon's (near the Guildhall); Fuzz & Firkin; The Hogshead; Havana Café; Wine Vaults; Owtback bar (Australian theme); Great Goose (student); Green Goose. *Any pub packed with jolly jack tars is best avoided.*
Clubs/discos: Plenty of clubs, particularly around the South Parade Pier. *Pushplugs: Scandals (indie/house); Maggie Thatcher Experience (80s) at Time; EQ (funk/acid jazz); Route 66.*
Music venues: Portsmouth's premiere venue is the Guildhall *which hosts big old names and currently groovy popsters*. The Wedgewood Rooms is a *solid* indie haunt, which also hosts comedy, and the Pyramids adds further to the aural palette.

When 'Mastermind' was filmed at Ulster University, students kidnapped the Black Chair. When the BBC refused to pay a ransom, the chair was pushed into the River Bann.

Eating out: There's more than enough in the way of fish'n'chip shops and burger joints, as well as curry houses (including balti) by the furnace-full. *Pushplugs: Bombay Express; The Vaults (pub grub); Café Citrus; Fistful of Tacos (Mexican); Rickshaws (Mongolian); Big Kev's (post-club munchies).*

Other: Portsmouth is by the sea! So it has piers and fairs, etc.

UNIVERSITY:
• Price of a pint of beer: £1.60 • Glass of wine: £1.10

Bars: (4) The Lighthouse (cap 1,100) at Alexandra House is the main dive throughout the day. The Ranch House (300) *is quieter and more pubby* while the Garage (600) is used for ents. There are also Bar Zest and The Foster at the Milton site and a bar at the halls in Langstone.

Music venues: The Garage has recently coped with Judge Jules, Billie (Mrs Evans herself) and the Artful Dodger.

Clubs/discos: Five club nights a week from the Amnesia (disco) in the Lighthouse to Contrast (dance), Shaft (70s) and the Latin American Carnival.

Cabaret: Recent comedy has seen Lee Mack, Dave Gorman, Phil Nicholl and Ian Cognito at the Garage.

Food: The SU runs the Globe Bistro and the Pitstop at the main site. Alternatively Al's snack bar and the Milton Café Olé do snackular stuff.

Other: Several balls, including the Freshers', Alternative Xmas, Valentine and Graduation which can pull in 3,000 plus punters and punteresses.

SOCIAL & POLITICAL

UNIVERSITY OF PORTSMOUTH STUDENTS' UNION:
• 6 sabbaticals • Turnout at last ballot: 10% • NUS member

The SU's main strength is social – political posturing rarely comes into the frame. Relations between the SU and the University administration are practically at the snogging stage, a closeness which some students find peculiar. Recent successes on that front include a direct debit scheme for fee-payers and Wednesday afternoons being freed up for sport. There are SU facilities on each site.

'Go to St Andrew's for the golf if nothing else. It is one of the town's best, and, of course, most famous attractions. Perhaps, however, I spent a little too much time playing golf, especially late at night.'
– Alex Salmond MP, former leader SNP.

SU FACILITIES:
Alexandra House contains bars, café, canteen, cash machines, Endsleigh Insurance office, employment bureau, travel agency, shop, ents halls, print shop, lift-sharing scheme, photo booth and fax.

CLUBS (NON SPORTING):
American Beats; Big Band; Hellenic; Malaysian; Rhymes and Basslines.

OTHER ORGANISATIONS:
'Pugwash' is the SU's magazine, *and it means something rude in Australia, apparently*. Pure FM is the radio station currently without a licence and 'Purple Wednesdays' is the weekly clubs & societies newsletter. Rag raises readies and the SCAG gets involved in aid convoys to Croatia.

RELIGIOUS:
• 3 chaplains (CofE, RC, Free)
Most religions represented in town (mosques and synagogues) where there are also Anglican and Catholic cathedrals.

PAID WORK:
What with the ferries, the bars, Southsea being a holiday resort and all, there's a better than average chance of finding something to line students' pockets during vacations. A jobshop at Alex House puts students in touch with temp employers.

SPORTS

• Recent successes: swimming, volleyball
University sports are pretty well organised by the SU and jockish attitudes are quite prevalent. Bursaries are available for rugby, hockey and sailing.

SPORTS FACILITIES:
On the main site, there's the Nuffield Sports Centre with cricket bays, a gym, two weights rooms with multigym, netball, squash and tennis courts and a climbing wall. Near the halls, there are 4 acres of sports fields by Langstone Harbour. The University also has a host of facilities to be used on the Solent, *a flood of fun for those whose appetite is whetted by water sports*. Locally there are sports centres, tennis courts, golf courses, a swimming complex and sailing and windsurfing in the Solent.

Students at Wye College are convinced that the H & G blocks in the College's accommodation are haunted, due to the odd tapping sound which rattle through the pipes. Allegations that these sounds are created by drunken jokers in the druids club are fiercely denied.

SPORTING CLUBS:
Aerobics; Boxing; Canoe; Jiu Jitsu; Gymnastics; Lacrosse; Motorcycle; Paintball; Rowing; Self-protection; Sky-diving; Snow-boarding; Surf; Tai Chi; Ten Pin Bowling; Triathlon; Ultimate Frisbee.

ATTRACTIONS:
Portsmouth FC *(Pompey) is the biz, alroight?* Also in town there's Hampshire Cricket Club's second ground and a dog track.

ACCOMMODATION

IN COLLEGE:
- Catered: 6% • Cost: £64-78 (38-52wks)
- Self-catering: 12% • Cost: £38-44 (38wks)

Availability: ¾ of the 1,778 places in 10 halls are reserved for 1st years, but that only houses half of them. Seven of the halls are self-catering with some limited provisions for students with children. A head tenancy scheme also provides 700 places.

Car parking: Only feasible at QEQM and then a permit is needed. Bateson has an NCP car park opposite, but that costs. *Otherwise, it's virtually impossible throughout Portsmouth.*

EXTERNALLY:
- Ave rent: £42

Availability: *All students will find something given time, but some graduate first.* The most appropriate places are in the large Victorian houses which have been split into tenement flats and bedsits, usually shared by two to four people. *Many aren't worth the cost, but what can you do, eh?* The best places are Southsea, Fratton and North End. Eastney, Somerstown and Paulsgrove are too rough to be worth it.

Housing help: The Accommodation Office publishes a daily bulletin, as well as assisting individual students. The University and SU run a 'Secure a Home' Day before the first year.

'He'd got into Aberdeen University, and found the course easy, but was forced to leave mid-way through the first year after blowing his grant money an drugs and prostitutes.'

- Irvine Welsh, Trainspotting.

WELFARE

SERVICES:
• Creche • Lesbian & Gay Society • Postgrad SA
• Ethnic Minorities SA • Mature SA • Overseas SA • Minibus
University sick bay and two local NHS practices. *Very good* University Welfare Service has a team of counsellors and a weekly solicitor's visits and there's the SU Rights & Advice Centre. There is a late-night minibus for the traditional queasy ride home.
Disabled: *Wheelchair access is good in the newer, purpose-built areas, less so in the older parts.* The library has a braille computer and there's some accommodation for students with special needs, as well as a new Disability Co-ordinator.

FINANCE:
• Access fund: £907,968 • Successful applications: 1300
Short-term loans (£1K max) are available and financial workshops and debt counselling are organised.

Preston Polytechnic

see University of Central Lancashire

Printing

see The London Institute

'When I started at Cambridge, I was anxious to be Prime Minister but uncertain through which political party this might best be arranged. I therefore joined the Liberals, the Labour Party and the Conservative Party as it seemed wise not to put all my eggs in one basket.'
- Matthew Parris, journalist and ex-MP.

Queen Margaret College, Edinburgh

Queen Mary & Westfield College, London

Queen's College, Glasgow see Glasgow Caledonian University

The Queen's University of Belfast

Queen Margaret University College, Edinburgh

(1) Queen Margaret University College, Corstorphine Campus, Edinburgh, EH12 8TS. Tel: (0131) 317 3000. Fax: (0131) 317 3248. E–mail: admissions@mail.qmuc.ac.uk
Queen Margaret Students' Association, Clerwood Terrace, Edinburgh, EH12 8TS. Tel: (0131) 317 3401. Fax: (0131) 317 3402. E–mail: union@qmuc.ac.uk
(2) Queen Margaret University College, Leith Campus, Duke Street, Leith, Edinburgh, EH6 8HF.
(3) Queen Margaret University College, Gateway Theatre, Leith Walk, Edinburgh.

GENERAL

QMC is based on 3 campuses, one in the Corstorphine area of Edinburgh, located at a 24-acre greenfield site with mature gardens, 4 miles from the city centre and the other in Leith, a mile from the East End, and one on Leith Walk. The college specialises in business, theatre and healthcare subjects. The drama department is based at the new *state-of-the-art* drama centre, which includes The Gateway Theatre, only 5 minutes walk from the city centre.

Sex ratio(M:F): 20%:80%	Founded: 1875
Full time u'grads: 4,000	Part time: 733
Postgrads: 42	Non-degree: 0
Ave course: 4yrs	Ethnic: 4.5%
Private school: n/a	Flunk rate: 15.8%
Mature students: 49%	Overseas students: 8%
Disabled students: 5.4%	

ATMOSPHERE:
It's a friendly, quite intimate place and the fact that some of the buildings conjure up the worst excesses of 60s comprehensive school architecture doesn't dampen the students' enthusiasm. Men are severely outnumbered, which can be an advantage or extra pressure for them (depending what mood they're in and whether they're an arse or breast man).

LEITH CAMPUS:
The Leith site, which houses 600 students on physiotherapy, occupational therapy, radiography and podiatry courses, is 7 miles from Corstorphine. *Apart from a café, facilities are limited, but the ethos here is work–oriented anyway.*

LEITH CAMPUS:
The Gateway Theatre is home to 200 students and is a brand new learning facility with a working theatre combined with modern classrooms.

THE CITY: see University of Edinburgh

TRAVEL: see University of Edinburgh

CAREER PROSPECTS:
- Careers Service • No of staff: 1 full
- Unemployed after 6mths: 5.9%

This must be the only institution where the Careers Adviser is described (by students) as 'lovely', 'brilliant' and 'everyone's mum'.

FAMOUS ALUMNI:
David Crystal (linguistics guru); Kevin McKidd (Tommy in Trainspotting); Lloyd Quinan (Scottish weatherman); Andy Gray (actor).

FURTHER INFO:
Undergrad and postgrad prospectuses, student association handbook, video, websites (www.qmuc.ac.uk and www.qmuc.ac.uk/union).

ACADEMIC

staff/student ratio: 1:15
Range of points required for entrance: 320-120
Percentage accepted through clearing: 16%
Number of terms/semesters: 2
Length of terms/semesters: 15 wks
Research: 2.9

LIBRARIES:
• Books: 100,000 • Study places: 400

COMPUTERS:
• Computer workstations: 250
Not enough to go round.

ENTERTAINMENT

THE CITY: see University of Edinburgh

COLLEGE:
• Price of a pint of beer: £1.50 • Glass of wine: £1.30
Bar/music venue/club: The Union Bar (cap 350) is open from 9am till late, Mon–Sat. It's the only place in college where smoking is allowed. The bar doubles (triples?) as a disco and gig venue (local and student bands only).
Cinema: The SA shows arthouse to mainsteam flicks and the occasional theme night like horror or halloween.
Theatre: It's one big theatre love in. Lots of Queen Margaret

students study drama while The Absolute Drama Collective puts on productions at the College theatre. QMC doubles as a Fringe venue during the festival in the summer. All students are encouraged to participate in theatre.

Food: The College provides 2 dining halls and a fast food bar *but it's mostly of a stodgy nature*. The Union bar serves up baguettes, danishes, cappuccinos and espressos from 9 till 9.

Others: Karaoke, comedy and quiz nights, graduation ball in June, Christmas ball at er, well, you know when, as well as various departmental beanos.

SOCIAL & POLITICAL

QUEEN MARGARET'S STUDENTS' ASSOCIATION:
• 2 sabbaticals • Turnout at last ballot: 25% • NUS member

Political activity has increased, unsurprisingly since a) it was dead before and b) the introduction of tuition fees stirred things up. Recent campaigns have enjoyed good support including a demo against student hardship and a staged walkout of lectures. Internally, the SA enjoys good relationships with the college and students.

SU FACILITIES:
Bar; general shop; Royal Bank of Scotland; photocopier; payphone; pool table; jukebox; TV lounge; meeting rooms.

OTHER ORGANISATIONS:
'EH12' is the SA-organised newsletter coming out fortnightly, also FSM the student newspaper. The SA employs a charity convenor and community relations are discussed with local reps twice a year.

RELIGIOUS:
A new room has recently been provided for meetings of any persuasion.

PAID WORK: see University of Edinburgh. Also a job-shop.

SPORTS

• Recent successes: rugby, football

Sport comes a poor second to drama. Sports provisions are limited at the moment, especially at Leith. They're better at Carstorphine.

SPORTS FACILITIES:
Sports hall; pool; multigym; squash courts; all-weather playing field.

SPORTING CLUBS:
Tai Chai.

ACCOMMODATION

IN COLLEGE:
• Catered: 6% • Cost: £67 (31wks)
• Self-catering: 14% • Cost: £42–51 (38wks)

Rather chaotic and disorganised with double bookings known in the past. About half of the 1st years can live in, but very few others. The Guthrie-Wright Halls are all-female, have single study bedrooms and offer 10 meals a week. *The fact that all catered accommodation is reserved for women is either a very right-on statement about domestic sex roles, a wry piece of irony or a cock-up. Although by the end of the year most are sick of what's on offer.* The self-catering halls and flats have kitchens shared between 3 and 13. Grainger Stewart hall is particularly popular, *although that's probably due to its recent refurbishment.* There's also a head tenancy scheme, for those who want private housing without the hassle of finding it.

EXTERNALLY: see University of Edinburgh
The Accommodation Office is very helpful. Dalry, Corstorphine and Haymarket are the most popular areas for students to rest their heads. Flats are cheaper and more plentiful in Leith.

SERVICES:
• Lesbian & Gay Society • Overseas SA • Women's officer
• Equal Opportunities Officer

The new welfare centre comes with a full-time counsellor and nurse plus 20 voluntary advisers who have their own room.
Disabled: *Access is slowly improving:* the main building has installed a stairlift, but there are still *narrow, sloping* paths and *too many* stairs. Lecture theatres have induction loops.
Women: There's an *increasingly active women's* group campaigning for improved provision.

FINANCE:
• Access fund: £150,000 • Successful applications: 300
Some bursaries and emergency loans from the Union.

Queen Mary, University of London

• *Used to be known as Queen Mary & Westfield College, London.*
• *The College is part of University of London and students are entitled to use its facilities.*

(1) Queen Mary, University of London, Mile End Road, London, E1 4NS. Tel: (020) 7882 5555. Fax: (020) 7975 5500.
Queen Mary Students' Union, Mile End Site, 432 Bancroft Road, London, E1 4DH. Tel: (020) 7882 5390. Fax: (020) 8981 0802.
E-mail: su-genoff@qmw.ac.uk
(2) Barts and the London Queen Mary University, University of London, Biomedical sciences, Mile End Road, London, E1 4NS. Tel: (020) 7882 5555. Fax: (020) 7882 5500

Set in the multi-cultural melee of the East End, QM is surrounded by the *bursting and buoyant* areas of Bethnal Green and Whitechapel, very close to Brick Lane Market and loads of East End pubs. QM is the only campus college in London University – *a sprawling mass* of buildings from many different periods – from the fine old Queens' Building (complete with clock tower) to some 50s art deco and 60s *eyesores*, and strangely, a Jewish cemetery (which still has room for more residents). With 19th-century origins, Queen Mary College was set up as a philanthropic institution for the education of East Enders, while Westfield (now dropped from the name) was a pioneering college for women. It's a 15 minute tube journey from the College to the city centre.

Sex ratio(M:F): 50%:50%
Full time u'grads: 7,219
Postgrads: 1,120
Ave course: 3yrs
Private school: 18%
Mature students: 25%
Disabled students: 2%
Founded: 1915
Part time: 100
Non-degree: 611
Ethnic: 52%
Flunk rate: 12.7%
Overseas students: 20%

ATMOSPHERE:
The multi-racial, multi-national mix alone can be a learning experience and its situation, in the bizarre bazaar that is the East End, is worth something in itself. This rubs off on the students who mix with each other (and with the locals) whiskey in an Irish Coffee.

THE MEDICAL SCHOOL:
The medical schools of Barts and the London Hospital now form one school within QM, but with two sites.

Whitechapel: (170 students) *Friendly and approachable (at least by comparison with some other med schools),* London Hospital is right opposite Whitechapel Tube in an *impressive* brick edifice, ½ mile from the main QM site.

West Smithfield: (730) Bart's Hospital is housed in a *lovely* Georgian-fronted building near Smithfield meat market *(don't bother, they've heard all the jokes about where the corpses end up).* It's got something of a reputation as a public school bastion, *but the merger with QM has toned this down a bit.* It's a mile from QM's main campus. Students at both med school sites are entitled to use the facilities at the main Mile End campus if they've got the time.

THE CITY: see University of London

TRAVEL: see University of London
Trains: Liverpool Street and Limehouse Stations are very close.
Buses: Numbers 339, 25, 106 and Night buses N25, N8 and N15.
Underground: Nearest tubes are Mile End (Central, District, Jubilee, Hammersmith & City Lines) and Stepney Green (District, Hammersmith & City peak times only). Whitechapel (District, East London Line, Hammersmith and City) for the London Hospital, St Paul's and Barbican for Bart's.

CAREER PROSPECTS:
• Careers Service • No of staff: 3 full/3 part
• Unemployed after 6mths: 4%
There is now a careers reference library, *which is handy in a careers office.*

FAMOUS ALUMNI:
Dr Barnardo (of nice-to-kids fame); Bernard Butler (indie guitar deity); Graham Chapman (Monty Python); Bruce Dickinson (ex–Iron Maiden); Malcolm Bradbury, Eva Figes, Ruth Prawer Jhabvala, Andrea Newman (writers); Peter Hain MP (Lab); Sir Roy Strong (former Director, V&A Museum); David Sullivan (football/porn baron); Frederick Treves (treated the Elephant Man).

Queen Mary 514

FURTHER INFO:
Prospectuses for undergrads and postgrads and a website (www.qmw.ac.uk).

ACADEMIC

Law, medical, medical and more medical courses. All students can study a language with their degree and all should become computer literate.

staff/student ratio: 1:8
Range of points required for entrance: 340-200
Percentage accepted through clearing: n/a
Number of terms/semesters: 2
Length of terms/semesters: 12wks
Research: 4.8

LIBRARIES:
- Books: 570,000 • Study places: 1,444

The Law and Medical libraries are pretty impressive, the general one is not bad either, considering it's won awards and stuff, but has poor opening hours.

COMPUTERS:
- Computer workstations: 700

Computer availability is good although the opening hours are again poor.

ENTERTAINMENT

IN LONDON: see University of London
Local: *Pub prices in the East End are less ludicrous than in the centre of town but it still ain't cheap. A new cinema is open on the Mile End Road and Lee Hurst's Backyard comedy club is there to make you giggle. Bow Wharf – a resto and bar complex is also definitely worth a look.*

COLLEGE:
- Price of a pint of beer: £1.60 • Glass of wine: 90p

Bars: The SU runs four bars. *The e1 Venue Bar, unsurprisingly, comes into its own when there are ents on. The main focus for elbow-lifting is the Drapers Arms* (capacity 350). There's also the Association Bar (Whitechapel), Barts Bar (Smithfield), Club 0181 (South Woodford).
Cinema: (1) Mainstream films shown every fortnight.
Theatres: The *strong* drama department, the QM Players from history and the medic drama society make good use of the Harold Pinter Drama Studio. Shows regularly make it to the Edinburgh Fringe by the students at the main campus.
Clubs/discos/music venues: The e1 nightclub *serves a slamming selection of prime cuts* (Time Tunnel – 60s/70s/80s) and is also the base for guest DJs such as Jeremy Healey and Moorcheeba. The Drapers Bar hosts *lower-key gigs.*
Cabaret: Top acts twice a term courtesy of QM's new pals at Jongleurs, the famous comedy club (10 minutes walk away).
Food: *The college refectory spreads over three floors, quality and value*

are good. The SU has a noodle bar in e1. The Griddle in the Draper's Arms does all-day breakfasts, curries and baked potatoes. Balcony Bar does baguettes and soup, as does the Octagon and Bar Med.
Others: *The annual Valentine's Ball is very successful.* There is a gallery in the College which exhibits local artists' work.

SOCIAL & POLITICAL

QUEEN MARY UNIVERSITY OF LONDON STUDENTS' UNION:
• 5 sabbaticals • Turnout at last ballot: 12% • NUS member
The SU is hard-working and popular with the students, but hardly radical. A recent health awareness campaign went down far better than the anti-tuition fees campaign. The SU building has recently undergone a much needed £2Mn facelift.

SU FACILITIES:
The recently improved SU building has a main shop; societies resource centre; gym; games room; coffee bar; advice centre; bars; photocopying; video games; cashpoint.

CLUBS (NON SPORTING):
Astrological; English; Hellenic; Hispanic; Law; Malaysian; Thinking.

OTHER ORGANISATIONS:
'CUB' is the monthly student newspaper, shortlisted recently for the 'Guardian' student newspaper of the year. The Community Action group is the biggest in London and there's Rag, which is huge at Barts.

RELIGIOUS:
One full- and two part-time chaplains. Muslim prayer room.

PAID WORK: see University of London

SPORTS

• Recent successes: fencing, football
Sport is one of the few activities that binds the student body together and, for an inner-city college, QM's record is pretty sound.

SPORTS FACILITIES:
In the SU Building there's a gym, weights room, squash courts, snooker room, sauna and multigym. The Union has facilities Chistlehurst and there are watersports at Docklands. There are, as always, University of London's facilities.

SPORTING CLUBS:
Aikido; Boating; Polo; Wu Shu Kwan.

ATTRACTIONS:
West Ham is the local footie team. There's Leyton Orient as well, *but Andrew Lloyd Webber supports them, so there's always a catch.* There's also a dog track, indoor climbing wall and ice rink.

ACCOMMODATION

IN COLLEGE:
• Catered: 15% • Cost: £80-95 (31wks) • Self-catering: 18%
• Cost: £69-83 (38wks)

Availability: The College's own accommodation includes 855 catered and about 900 self–catered places. Another 142 find a roof in the University's inter–collegiate halls. All 1st years who apply in time can live in (5% have to share) and over 22% of finalists. The accommodation at Mile End is newish and *good looking* with a view of the Regent's Canal *but some of the other sites are depressing and too far away. It's expensive, even for London, and the food in catered halls is dreadful.*
Car parking: Parking only available South Woodford.

EXTERNALLY: see University of London
Housing help: The College Accommodation Office offers full-time staff and a bulletin board. *The East End is fun but quality can be variable and not all parts are safe.*

SERVICES:
- Creche • Lesbian & Gay Society • Postgrad SA • Mature SA
- Overseas SA

The College provides 5 full-time and 2 part-time counsellors and the SU has 2 welfare officers. There's a Health Centre with 2 doctors, a senior nurse and a visiting psychiatrist. The Union have a new Student Support Centre with a welfare suite
Disabled: *Access in University accommodation is okay, but it's variable in some of the other buildings.* There's a part-time dyslexia support worker and induction loops in all lecture halls.

FINANCE:
- Access fund: £260,000 • Successful applications: 641

There are undergraduate bursaries of £1,500 pa for the lucky few.

Queen's College, Glasgow

see Glasgow Caledonian University

The Queen's University of Belfast

(1) The Queen's University of Belfast, University Road, Belfast, BT7 1PE. Tel: (028) 9024 5133. Fax: (028) 9024 7895.
Queen's University of Belfast Students' Union, University Road, Belfast, BT7 1PE. Tel: (028) 9023 6900. Fax: (028) 90322 4803.
E-mail: s.union@qub.ac.uk
(2) The Queen's University at Armagh, 39 Abbey Street, Armagh, BT61 7EB. Tel: (028) 3750678. Fax: (028) 3751 0679.

On the River Lagan, where Belfast Lough opens out into the Irish Sea, lies Belfast, the largest city in Northern Ireland. The queen of Queen's University was the *unamused* Queen Vic and the *tasteful*

University buildings date from her time to ours. The University has taken over much of the surrounding prosperous Belfast suburb, so that the houses of the nearby Victorian terraces are more likely to contain one of the University's faculties (or Schools) than any Victorians. Given the surrounding greenery – many parks and the nearby Botanical Gardens – it can be hard to believe that Belfast city centre is only ½ mile away, with the Shankill and Falls Roads ½ mile beyond that.

Sex ratio(M:F): 40%:60%	Founded: 1845
Full time u'grads: 9,862	Part time: 1,402
Postgrads: 1,952	Non-degree: 6,162
Ave course: 3yrs	Ethnic: 1%
Private school: n/a	Flunk rate: 9.6%
Mature students: 9%	Overseas students: 8%
Disabled students: 3.6%	

ATMOSPHERE:
It's beyond the scope of Push to comment in depth on the Northern Ireland situation. At the time of going to press the peace process was still struggling on, but the days when we'll see a big street party with all the factions dancing a conga still seem a little way off. But whatever the state of play, it's fair to say that the worst of 'The Troubles' has bypassed students at Queen's, especially since it's in a prosperous suburb of South Belfast, away from the profoundly sectarian parts. 87% of Queen's students are locals and 7% are from the Republic of Ireland with a healthy mix of Catholic and Protestant students. Most of the tension on campus is reserved for essays and exams rather than sectarianism. The rest is reserved for being rude about <u>Ulster University</u> and hardcore drinking.

OUTREACH SITES:
Queen's also has two subsidiary sites, one in Armagh, about 40 miles south-west of Belfast and one in Portaferry, also 40 miles from Belfast. Further Outreach sites are planned and will concentrate on serving the local population, especially returners to education.

THE CITY:
- Population: 300,000

The first impression of Belfast city centre is of a collection of *earthy* Victorian civic buildings, with a *monstrously* modern shopping centre at its heart. Belfast lies in an *attractive* bay ringed by mountains and when the rain clears *(twice a year if you're lucky)*, it's quite possible to enjoy the city's gifts: shopping malls; supermarkets; new and second-hand bookshops; the Ulster Museum on campus and the banks (mainly Irish). *The debris of the Troubles (murals, protection rackets) lingers on but the locals are a really friendly bunch almost as if they're making up for politics and there are fun and games to be had, with clubs and pubs doing a roaring trade. Ironically perhaps,* the overall crime rate is among the lowest in the UK.

TRAVEL:
Trains: All of Ireland's main cities and towns, north and south, are just a Northern Ireland Railways' journey away, including (London)Derry (£7.20) and Coleraine. A fast train, the Enterprise, goes to Dublin (£21).

Coaches: Translink serve most destinations in Northern Ireland and the Republic, but it's somewhat difficult to catch a bus direct from Britain what with the Irish Sea and all. National Express runs a service to London (£60).

Car: *The centre of Belfast is a pain for driving in, although parking's easy enough.*
Air: *Regular flights from all over Britain and Europe to Belfast City and Aldergrove Airports, including London (£69). The Airbus service runs from Belfast to the airport (£7.50).*
Ferries: *Services to Stranraer, Holyhead and Liverpool in Britain and a fast, new Sea Cat. Unfortunately you can't go out on deck, which is all part of the necessary fun – perhaps they think you would be blown off, which to be fair would only be fun for on-lookers.*
Hitching: *Better than most places in the UK, particularly heading south or west, but not to the ports or airport. The worst bit is heading for a crossing from the mainland and invariably being asked about The Troubles.*
Local: *Frequent local buses provide a 10-minute journey into the city centre for 50p.*
Taxis: *Plenty of taxis and black cabs, minimum fare of £2.50.*
Bicycles: *Theft's not a problem, but the weather is dreadful.*

CAREER PROSPECTS:
- Careers Service • No of staff: 12 full
- Unemployed after 6mths: 3.5%

FAMOUS ALUMNI:
Dr John Alderdice (leader, Alliance Party); Simon Callow, James Ellis, Liam Neeson, Stephen Rea (actors); Seamus Heaney (Nobel-winning poet); Patrick Kielty (comedian); Mary McAleese (President of Ireland); Bernadette McAliskey (née Devlin, former MP); Dr Brian Mawhinney MP (Con); Ian Paisley Jr (chip off the old mouth); Dawson Stelfox (mountaineer), David Trimble MP (1st Minister).

FURTHER INFO:
Prospectuses for undergrads and postgrads, newsletter for schools, CD-Rom. The SU is starting up an alternative prospectus. Website (www.qub.ac.uk).

ACADEMIC

staff/student ratio: 1:16
Range of points required for entrance: 360-200
Percentage accepted through clearing: 3%
Number of terms/semesters: 2
Length of terms/semesters: 15wks
Research: 4.1

LIBRARIES:
- Books: 1,100,000 • Study places: 2,530

Students are more than a little grumpy about limited book availability despite the five libraries and a quantity of books most unis would kill for.

COMPUTERS:
- Computer workstations: 2,000

There are usually sufficient computers to go round but they're not necessarily the most powerful or up-to-date models.

```
Members of Newcastle University rugby club
appeared naked in Margi Clarkes's Good Sex Guide.
```

ENTERTAINMENT

CITY:
- Price of a pint of beer: £1.80 • Glass of wine: £1.80

Most Belfast nightlife takes place in the Golden Mile that stretches from Queen's to the city centre. For up-to-the-minute details, catch the bi-monthly 'Buzz' magazine, or 'That's Entertainment'.

Cinemas: (3) Two multiplexes and the arty Queen's Film Theatre.

Theatres: (7) Plenty of choice including the *legendary* Belfast Grand Opera House and regular major touring productions including the Royal Shakespeare Company and An Culturlann, an *innovative* Irish language theatre company.

Pubs: *What better reason for coming to Ireland than for a pint of stout strong enough to stand a pencil in?* Guinness from any of the local hostelries will have a head you can draw a broad smile in or, as they do, a shamrock. Pushplugs: Botanic (aka The Bot); Lavery's Gin Palace (v. friendly and alternative); The Fly. The Parliament Bar and the Crow's Nest are the main gay venues.

Clubs/discos: *Belfast is developing quite a reputation as a clubbers' paradise.* Pushplugs: Limelight (indie, retro and jazz nights); The Brunswick (soul and hardcore, four separate floors); Network Club (dance/hip-hop); M Club (student nights); Thompson's Garage (house); the new Storm in Lisburn is the largest club in NI, 5 miles from Belfast.

Music venues: Ulster Hall for big names, Empire Music Hall for medium-sized and comedy nights, the newish Waterfront Hall (anything from Robbie Williams to The Sofia Philarmonic) and innumerable smaller-scale gigs in pubs and clubs.

Eating out: *Plenty of eating experiences good and cheap enough to make Gary Rhodes' hair lie flat.* Locals spend more on eating out than in any other UK city. Lisburn Road, close to the campus, has lots of *decent* cafés, patisseries, Chinese and Indian takeaways. Pushplugs: Bishops (chippie); Speranza's (pizzas, a student institution); The Other Place (bring your own booze); Oasis (cheap); the Mad Hatter; Which Sandwich (guess). Many of the pubs are good for a bite, too.

UNIVERSITY:
- Price of a pint of beer: £1.60 • Glass of wine: £2

Bars: The Union's two main bars, the Bunatee Bar (cap 300) and the Speakeasy (550, recently refurbished), are packed by 7pm.

Cinema: The QFT (Queen's Film Theatre) offers an *excellent* mix of arty, culty and left-field celluloid.

Clubs/discos: The Mandela Hall *(with the best sound system in Ireland)* quivers to a variety of sounds, *the most impressive being the Saturday 'Shine' house/hip-hop event which attracts big-name guest DJs (and punters from across the water).*

Music venues: The Speakeasy has recently hosted Roni Size.

Cabaret: Every fortnight the Speakeasy is taken over by *some nutter or other* as part of the National Comedy Network.

Food: *The Speakeasy undercuts the opposition when it comes to price but the range leaves a bit to be desired.* The University also has several fuelling stations.

Other: Up to 7 balls a year, including Freshers', Rag and St Paddy's bashes. Most faculties also have some kind of formal. The annual Queen's International Arts Festival is now second only to Edinburgh, with a bit of everything – ballet, theatre, alternative comedy and the alternative to alternative comedy.

SOCIAL & POLITICAL

QUEEN'S UNIVERSITY OF BELFAST STUDENTS' UNION/ AONTAS NA MAC LÉINN OLLSCOIL NA BANRIONA:
• 5 sabbaticals • Turnout at last ballot: 10% • NUS/USI member
Most strands of political thought, NI-based or not, are represented, which tends to balance things out, though nationalists are in the majority. Recent introduction of bilingual signs had a mixed response. The incestuous nature of the SU's internal politics have alienated some students but the majority, of course, just regard the SU as a source of cheap booze. An Ents Officer has finally been appointed to ensure stability and progress (presumably just in the area of entertainments).

SU FACILITIES:
Bars; refectories; advice centre; Bank of Ireland (with cashpoint); launderette; showers; supermarket; writing room; second-hand bookshops; sports shop; Endsleigh Insurance office; travel centre; computer shop; hairdresser; snooker room; games room; vending/games machines; photocopier; function rooms.

CLUBS (NON SPORTING):
Accounting; African; Amnesty; Ballroom Dancing; Biological; Bridge; Celtic Supporters; Chess; Chinese; Christian Union; Conservation; Conservative; CS Lewis; Dragon Slayers; Economics; English; European; Finance; French; Green; Hare Krishna; Hispanic; Historical; Internet; Irish Studies; Islamic; Juggling; Labour; Law; Malaysian; Music; Photographic; Republican; Rock; SDLP; Skipping; Sociology; Ulster; Wine; Yoga.

OTHER ORGANISATIONS:
Queen's students run two newspapers: 'Gown' and 'Banter'. The charity Rag clocks along actively, raising £36,000 last year. *The Community Workshop does its bit for town/gown relations.*

RELIGIOUS:
There are 16 chaplaincies at Queen's, from Catholic and Church of Ireland to facilities for 5 flavours of Presbyterians, Muslims and Jews and even a Church for the Deaf. Belfast fills in any gaps there might be, including Mormons, Seventh Day Adventists and Hare Krishnas.

PAID WORK:
The new jobshop helps to place over 200 registered students in on/off-campus work.

SPORTS

• Recent successes: gaelic football, judo, hockey
Sport is very popular at Queens. The University's PE Centre has all the mod cons to get students shaking their tail feathers. Blues are awarded, on the Oxbridge model, for sportsters who represent the University.

SPORTS FACILITIES:
Apart from the many indoor facilities of the PE centre on campus, Queen's is proud of the Mary Peters Track (named after the Olympic athlete), *but it's 400m long and goes round in circles like everyone else's.* The track and 16 playing fields (four all-weather) are a 2-mile bus ride away. The town offers a further sprinkling of leisure centres and golf courses. *Worthy of special mention* is the Dundonald Ice Bowl. The Malone Sports Facility (known as 'The Dub') *is good for outdoor stuff.*

SPORTING CLUBS:
Caving; Gaelic Football; Handball; Hurling; Jiu–Jitsu; Motor–Cycle; Parachute; Racquet Ball; Road Bowls; Snooker; Sub–Aqua; Surf; Table–Tennis; Waterpolo; Waterski; Wing Chun Kung Fu.

ACCOMMODATION

IN COLLEGE:
- Catered: 7% • Cost: £54-62 (32wks)
- Self–catering: 13% • Cost: £39–50 (38–50wks)

Availability: 48% of 1st years live in, with half of them sharing, mainly in 10-storey blocks ½ mile from campus in *attractive surrounds*. All 1st years who wish to, can live in. *Queen's* Elms has a *groovy* 1,100 rooms, with catered and self-catering accomodation, and Riddell is all-female. There are also a few places in associated halls (two with religious links) and flats for married couples.

Car parking: *Plentiful and permitless, if you really need wheels.*

EXTERNALLY:
- Ave rent: £40

Availability: *Many students are locals. For home-hunters who look early in summer, there is little difficulty in finding accommodation, although by September the task is harder. Most student areas offer good quality terraced housing with high class amenities, particularly Stranmillis, Malone Rd, Holylands and Lisburn Rd. Queen's is popular but expensive. Some areas are obviously best avoided, but previously untouchable parts, such as the Ormeau Road, are becoming increasingly popular, mainly because they're so cheap.*

Housing help: The Union Welfare Office and the University Accommodation Office are the roofing specialists, that is to say, they help make sure students have one over their heads, and keep tabs on vacant rooms and houses. There are also a number of Housing Associations who accept students.

WELFARE

SERVICES:
- Nursery • Nightline • Lesbian, Gay & Bi Society • Mature SA
- Overseas SA • Minibus • Women's Officer • Outreach officer
- Self–defence classes • Post Grad SA

The Union's small counselling service meets most immediate needs for troubled souls, while troubled bodies are mended by the Student Health Centre. The legally troubled can ask the advice of the solicitor who visits 4 afternoons a week. There are also officers with responsibility for mature and overseas students. A new Sports Injury Clinic has started up.

Women: There are *excellent* services for women including the support magazine 'Shrewd' and a women's night–time minibus.

Disabled: *Ramps are all over the place, lifts less so. Serious efforts are being made to tackle some of the older buildings.* The hearing-impaired are particularly well catered for with the JUDE Centre (Joint Universities Deaf Education) which employs 3 people.

Drugs: *Apart from the usual dangers, the drug trade has paramilitary connections, so watch it.*

FINANCE:
- Access fund: £762,250 • Successful applications: 901

There are several scholarships, including 15 Guinness sports bursaries.

University of Reading

RMCS see Cranfield University

Robert Gordon University

Roehampton Institute see Other Institutions

Rose Bruford see Other Institutions

Royal Academy of Music

Royal Agricultural College see Other Institutions

Royal College of Music

Royal Holloway, London

Royal Military College of Science see Cranfield University

Royal Veterinary College, London

> Space at Luton University is so tight that some exams have taken place in a disused lorry factory in Dunstable.

University of Reading

University of Reading, Whiteknights, PO Box 217, Reading, Berks RG6 6AH. Tel: (0118) 931 6586. Fax: (0118) 931 8924.
E-mail: Schools.liason@reading.ac.uk
University of Reading Students' Union, Whiteknights, Reading, Berks RG6 6AZ. Tel: (0118) 986 0222. Fax: (0118) 975 5283.
E-mail: rusu-exec@rdg.ac.uk

GENERAL

Reading is unfortunately pronounced 'redding' which scuppers the jokes from friends of students' parents such as, 'So, what are you reading at Reading?'. *Apart from the potential for jokes about the name, there is little remotely remarkable about the town. It's a nondescript place* close enough to London to be popular with commuters. *The surrounding area is more attractive, lots of pleasant Thames-side villages and small towns,* such as Henley, Hurley and Goring. The University is based on the large Whiteknights campus, just under 2 miles from the town centre, set in 300 acres of parkland, lake and wood. The buildings are a varied mixture, ranging from 19th-century houses to the new microbiology building. There is a small second campus about 1½ miles away at Bulmershe, housing about 2,000 students in the departments of Education and Film & Drama. *It has a closer-knit community atmosphere, but fewer facilities.*

53% ♀	Sex ratio(M:F): 47%:53%	Founded: 1892
♀ ♀ ♀ ♀ ♂ ♂ ♂ ♂ ♂ 47%	Full time u'grads: 7,615	Part time: 3,475
	Postgrads: 5,222	Non-degree: 0
	Ave course: 3yrs	Ethnic: 3%
	Private school: n/a	Flunk rate: 10.8%
	Mature students: n/a	Overseas students: 18.4%
	Disabled students: n/a	

ATMOSPHERE:
The University is cosy, sporty and self-contained with a large proportion of students living on the green and quiet campus, or close to it. The students tend to be middle-class and from south-east England, but there are plenty who buck the trend. The campus empties at the weekend.

THE TOWN:
- Population: 122,600 • London: 40 miles
- Oxford: 25 miles • Bristol: 74 miles

The University often seems more fun than it really is, because the town's pretty bland and is dead on week nights. It is a large country town *with little more to recommend it than good shopping and opportunities for business.* There's a vast range of supermarkets, bookshops (including a very big Blackwells) and plenty of shops open into the night. Reading does have tourist attractions – *well, there has to be something to do on rainy bank holidays* – 3 museums (English Rural Life *(a pre-eminent museum of hand-ploughs and things)*, Reading Museum and Blakes Lock Museum) and the River Thames, the Kennet and Avon Canal and Reading Abbey ruins.

TRAVEL:
Trains: Reading station, about 1½ miles from campus, offers direct services to London Paddington and Waterloo (£6.40) and most points west.
Coaches: National Express services all over the country. There are also the Reading-London Link (Reading Transport, £7) and Bee-Line Coaches.
Car: The M4 and A4 run west out of London. The M25 and M40 lead onto the M1.
Air: 45-minute coach trip every half hour to Heathrow International Airport, the busiest airport in the world.
Hitching: *The SU doesn't recommend it after attacks in the past.*
Local: Buses between the University and town are reasonable (£1 rtn).
Taxis: Many taxi companies, *but beware of those offering so-called 'student fares' – they can be even more expensive.*
Bicycles: *The campus is bikeably flat. Bikes are especially useful for early morning lectures or for getting to Bulmershe.*

CAREER PROSPECTS:
- Careers Service • No of staff: 9 full/10 part
- Unemployed after 6mths: 11%

The Univeristy runs a jobshop supported by the Union.

FAMOUS ALUMNI:
Suzanne Charlton (BBC weatherperson, daughter of Sir Bobby); Nigel de Gruchy (general secretary, NASUWT); Glynn Ford MEP (Lab); Andy McKay (Roxy Music saxophonist). Gustav Holst, the composer of 'The Planets Suite', lectured here.

FURTHER INFO:
Prospectuses for undergrads, postgrads, part-timers and mature students, a handbook for students with special needs and a website (www.rdg.ac.uk).

ACADEMIC

A flexible 1st year course structure is operated, giving students in some faculties a chance to experience other subjects and even change. *1st years get very wound up about their FUEs (First University Exams) and, unlike most universities, the 1st year is as academically demanding as any other.* However, many students don't see another exam paper till their finals.

staff/student ratio: 1:15
Range of points required for entrance: 320-200
Percentage accepted through clearing: 15%
Number of terms/semesters: 2
Length of terms/semesters: 10 wks
Research: 4.6

LIBRARIES:
• Books: 1,000,000 • Study places: 400
Apart from the main University Library at Whiteknights there's another at Bulmershe and various departmental libraries (eg Music, Education and Agriculture). Students are pretty happy with their facilities.

COMPUTERS:
• Computer workstations: 500

ENTERTAINMENT

THE TOWN:
• Price of a pint of beer: £2.30 • Glass of wine: £2
Cinemas: (5) Including two multiplexes, the 12-screen Show Case, the new Oracle and the *excellent and varied* Reading Film Theatre.
Theatres: The Hexagon stages everything from snooker to ballet, panto to opera as does the Millstream, on a smaller scale. For alternative drama, try the Progress Theatre.
Pubs: *Apart from the ridiculous prices, several pubs are a tad unwelcoming to students.* Pushplugs: Monk's Retreat; Rising Sun; Pavlov's Dog; Newt and Cucumber; College Arms; Queen's Head.
Clubs/discos: *Reading doesn't have the hottest club scene in the world, in fact it's tepid.* Purple Turtle and RGI do the straightforward chart/dance business and Level 1 does regular student nights.
Music venues: Alleycat Live is a *good* indie venue and the Rivermead Centre has regular bands. It's also been the site of the WOMAD Festival in recent years.
Eating out: All the usual chains and franchises you'd expect are present and politically incorrect *but Reading isn't exactly a gustatorial centre of excellence.* Pushplugs: JD Wetherspoons; Monk's Tree (cheap and cheerful); Muswell's (American-style diner); College Arms (good pub food); TGI Friday's (good for parties, but the joke wears thin eventually).

Other: The new Oracle shopping centre housing a multiplex cinema, shops, pubs and a bowling alley. The Reading Festival, *the No 2 hang-out (after Glastonbury) for all blitzed party people*, is held on the flood bank of the Thames over the August bank holiday weekend.

UNIVERSITY:
- Price of a pint of beer: £1.50 • Glass of wine: £1.30

Bars: The main Mojo's (cap 450) doubles as a small band venue and has a late licence till 2am for most of the week. The alternative, Nelson's (180) *is a bit dingy*. There are others in each hall and at Bulmershe there's Legends Bar, which is the main social meeting place. Also Café Mondial and the Pavillion, busy on Wednesdays.

Clubs/discos: There are 3 club nights a week in the Main Hall (cap 770). Extra-Time (Wed's £2) including Candy Club (Sat £2, disco and cheese) and Café Mondial gives up the coffee stuff for cocktails when it becomes a club at night, plus occasional specialist nights and guest DJs such as LTJ Bukem.

Cinema: The Fim theatre shows 3-4 flicks a week.

Theatre: The drama society put on major productions, most recently 'Fiddler on the Roof' *(which incidentally is not the true life story of Nick Leeson contemplating suicide on his prison roof)*.

Music venues: The Main Hall (cap 1,400) is also the scene of live action from, recently, Shed Seven, Utah Saints, LTJ Bukem, Terrorvision.

Food: *There is an okay choice of chomping on campus* including Fresh Start (sandwiches, snacks, drinks), The Buttery or, *slightly better*, the pre-packed platters in the Blue and Orange Rooms. Most faculties have their own refectories, open all day. The SU provides the Servery and Mojo's does *cheap* hot food at lunchtime.

Other: Several balls, Karaoke on Thurs.

SOCIAL & POLITICAL

READING UNIVERSITY STUDENTS' UNION (RUSU):
- 6 sabbaticals • Turnout at last ballot: 18% • NUS member

RUSU has facilities at both the Bulmershe and Whiteknights sites, where it has its own big building with damn fine amenities. Students seem quite happy with things but they're probably more concerned with sport than anything else. More people turned out for a university football match than a protest against tuition fees, held on the same day.

SU FACILITIES:
Travel shop; welfare office; 3 bars; stationery shop; bookshop; general/wholefood shop; Endsleigh Insurance office and other services such as photocopying and vending machines; launderette. SU has £1.2 million to re-develop its main venue *(should be good)*.

OTHER ORGANISATIONS:
There is an independent weekly colour newspaper, 'Spark' (also online at spark@rdg.ac.uk). Junction 11 (j11@hotmail.com) is the very popular radio station. There's the charity Rag and the student Community Action group runs projects for children and people with disabilities.

PAID WORK:
The jobshop is run by the union and sponsored by Barclays Bank *(that's one way of making sure they get overdrafts paid back)*. All jobs have to offer the minimum wage to be included.

RELIGIOUS:
There is a Chaplaincy centre on campus serving Christians and a Muslim centre. In town, there are prayer places for Muslims, Hindus, Sikhs, Jews and most Christians.

- Recent successes: hockey, rowing

The University has *good* facilities, mostly on campus attached to the Wolfendon Sports Centre although the Thames is *handy for watersports*. After an initial payment of £4.50 each year, there is only a nominal fee for some facilities. *Standards are especially high in women's sports.*

SPORTS FACILITIES:
On campus the Wolfendon Sports Centre provides facilities for badminton, archery, basketball, cricket, fencing, five-a-side football, hockey, martial arts, netball, table tennis, trampolining and tennis, gym and a brand new astroturf pitch. There's also a squash centre, gym and weights room at Bulmershe. Outdoor facilities include an athletics pavilion, playing fields for cricket, football and rugby, an all-weather surface and running track. In town, there are numerous swimming pools and rowing and sailing on the river.

SPORTING CLUBS:
Jiu Jitsu; Mountaineering; Polo; Rifle & Pistol; Surf; Weights.

ATTRACTIONS:
Henley Regatta; Ascot; Windsor Races; Newbury Races; Reading Football Club.

IN COLLEGE:
- Catered: 30% • Cost: £74-93 (30wks)
- Self-catering: 16% • Cost: £41-60 (30wks)

Availability: All 1st years that apply in time are accommodated (by June, ie that excludes students arriving through clearing). Only 1% have to share. 45 flats are available for married couples with or without children. There is a £60 reduction for prompt payment of hall fees. With the exception of Sibly (self-catering) and Mansfield (owned by a Japanese college, but not housing exclusively Japanese students), all halls are within a mile of the Whiteknights site. They range from self-catering blocks to the redbrick Oxbridge-style Wantage Hall and Grade II-listed St Andrew's Hall. Many of the newest ones offer en suite facilities. There is accommodation for 465 students at Bulmershe.

Car parking: A permit is needed for limited parking on campus and 1st years are dissuaded from bringing cars.

EXTERNALLY:
- Ave rent: £55

Availability: *With the help of the accommodation office, it is quite easy to find accommodation, although the quality varies from lucky luxury to dingy dives. There's a fair amount of housing available within a mile of campus – Donnington Gardens, Addington Road and Wokingham Road having the best selection. The rough stuff between London Road and the Railway and around Oxford Road is worth giving a miss.*

Housing help: The University Accommodation Office is willing to do a cockroach check on accommodation within a mile of campus. The Welfare Office will also give contracts the once over. *The best places though, are usually passed down through generations of students via RUSU's notice board.*

WELFARE

SERVICES:
• Nursery • Mature SA • Overseas SA • Minibus
• Women's Officer • Self-defence classes

Advice and help can be obtained from tutors or the Welfare Office. The Health Centre has 5 doctors, 2 dentists, a physiotherapist, various nurses and 6 full- and 5 part-time counselling staff, but it charges annually for registering (although this entitles students to reduced rates for vaccinations and medical examinations). Nursery for 40 (3mths-5yrs). The union runs a 24-hour nightline.

Women: Priority on the late night minibus.

Disabled: The thought's there – there are 2 Special Needs Co-ordinators, a handbook, hearing and induction loops and some accommodation is specifically adapted for wheelchair users. *However, there are still gaps.*

FINANCE:
• Access fund: £350,188 • Successful applications: 571

Emergency loans fund, scholarships and various departmental prizes.

RMCS
see Cranfield University

The Robert Gordon University

• *Formerly Robert Gordon Institute of Technology*
The Robert Gordon University, Schoolhill, Aberdeen, AB10 1FR.
Tel: (01224) 262180. Fax: (01224) 262185.
E-mail: i.centre@rgu.ac.uk
Robert Gordon University Students' Association, 60 Schoolhill, Aberdeen, AB10 1JQ. Tel: (01224) 262262. Fax: (01224) 262268.
E-mail: rgusa@compuserve.com

GENERAL

The old Robert Gordon Institute *(but you can call it Bob's or Flash)* became a university in 1992. The student population of the city is large and *RGU's students mix affably with all the others. Perhaps this is helped by where they're situated*, because RGU is spread across 5 sites around the city. Apart from the main site on Schoolhill in the city centre, the sites are on the outskirts, but all are within 3½ miles of the centre and set in small parks or gardens.

Sex ratio(M:F): 50%:50%	Founded: 1881
Full time u'grads: 5,451	Part time: 771
Postgrads: 734	Non-degree: 1,715
Ave course: 4yrs	Ethnic: 7%
Private school: 8.3%	Flunk rate: 19.7%
Mature students: 32%	Overseas students: 11%
Disabled students: 5%	

ATMOSPHERE:
This is no ivory tower, more of a modest formica bungalow – a damn sight more realistic but it can be a bit soul-destroying. The Union is the focus for social and political activity and is the bonding agent between slightly disparate sites. Students make the most of the limited facilities, but when they don't meet their needs, they're quick to take advantage of Aberdeen University's attractions and those of the wider city. The emphasis on hard work (mostly vocational courses), however, is never dropped completely. Students are referred to as 'customers' but they shouldn't have undue expectations about the level of services this entails.

THE SITES:
Schoolhill/St Andrew Street: (2,500 students – applied sciences, engineering, electronics, computing, maths, pharmacy). The largest site and home of the Union.
Garthdee: (3,500 students – art, architecture, design, surveying, management, business & librarianship). The furthest site from Schoolhill, 3 miles to the south west, *but possibly the most attractive* – a large mansion overlooking the River Dee and encompassed by rolling parkland. A new building has opened containing a library and IT and video conferencing facilities. *The site is less convenient, but peaceful and conducive to contemplative study.*
Kepplestone: (800 students – applied social studies, food & consumer studies, hotel, tourism and retail management, nutrition & dietetics). A set of modern blocks surrounded by playing fields and landscaped grounds, 1¾ miles west of Schoolhill. *Largely residential with an amiable ambience.*
Hilton: (1,500 students – school of nursing). ½ mile from Schoolhill.
Woolmanhill: (400 – occupational therapy, radiography, physiotherapy). In the centre of town.

THE CITY: see University of Aberdeen

TRAVEL: see University of Aberdeen
Aberdeen Station is a mile south of Schoolhill. Buses run every 20 minutes to most sites, *but feet are the most effective way of getting around.*

CAREER PROSPECTS:
• Careers Service • No of staff: 2 full/1 part
• Unemployed after 6mths: 2%
Vocational degrees make for excellent job prospects, as do industrial placements and careers advice within courses.

FAMOUS ALUMNI:
Ena Baxter (maker of wholesome and nutritious soups); Donnie Munro (Runrig singer).

FURTHER INFO:
Prospectuses for undergrads and postgrads, school brochures, CD-Rom, website (www.rgu.ac.uk).

ACADEMIC

The emphasis is firmly on vocational courses and transferable job skills.

staff/student ratio: 1:16
Range of points required for entrance: 320-100
Percentage accepted through clearing: 15%
Number of terms/semesters: 2
Length of terms/semesters: 15 wks
Research: 2.6

LIBRARIES:
• Books: 217,568 • Study places: 1,021
There are 5 libraries around the sites including a new library at Garthdee.

COMPUTERS:
• Computer workstations: 300
Computer facilities have improved considerably since the opening of the Garthdee site.

ENTERTAINMENT

THE CITY: see University of Aberdeen

UNIVERSITY:
• Price of a pint of beer: £1.35 • Glass of wine: 85p
Bars/music venues/clubs/discos: There are two *small but friendly* SA-run bars, but there's no club or music venue.
Theatre: The main theatre group Rogues put on the odd production.
Food: Café bar *offers variants on fast food and meat 'n' 2 veg (ie chips).*
Others: TV room for sport, general television and even Playstation competitions. *But students are tending to drift away from the Union, preferring the increasingly groovy entertainments in town or maybe sneaking in to see what* Aberdeen University *has to offer. Creative types have the additional option to stay put and live awhile in their heads.*

SOCIAL & POLITICAL

ROBERT GORDON UNIVERSITY STUDENTS' ASSOCIATION:
• 3 sabbaticals • Turnout at last ballot: 5% • NUS member
The Student Association is the representative body and the co-ordinating group for student activities and the Union is the building where the Association and its facilities are based. *The SA is suffering from a severe lack of funds which does not make it popular. When students do take an interest in SA affairs they complain about the lack of entertainment faciliities. They did manage to rake enough money together to provide free sandwiches at the Garthdee site following complaints that the site caterers were overcharging.*

SU FACILITIES:
Bar; cafeteria; general shop; photocopying; vending and games machines; pool table; launderette; showers; TV room with cable TV; cashpoint (Clydesdale bank); 2 meeting rooms.

CLUBS (NON SPORTING):
Duke of Edinburgh; Norwegian; Nursing; Scottish Explorers; Self Defence.

OTHER ORGANISATIONS:
There's a monthly paper, 'Cogno'.

RELIGIOUS:
Multi-denominational chaplaincy.

PAID WORK: see University of Aberdeen

- Recent successes: athletics

Finally, something that gets students interested. Well, some of them. Sometimes. A bit.

SPORTS FACILITIES:
Sports facilities vary from site to site. Students have access to 4 acres of playing fields, 2 sports halls and tennis courts. Some use of the Council facilities.

SPORTING CLUBS:
Curling; Rowing; Surfing; Underwater Hockey; Zhoan Su Huan.

ATTRACTIONS: see University of Aberdeen

IN COLLEGE:
- Self-catering: 15% • Cost: £49-63 (36wks)

Availability: About 70% of all 1st years and 30% of others live in. Blocks of self-catering flats make more space at the Woolmanhill and Kepplestone sites and at the Mearns all-male block near the harbour, ½ mile from Schoolhill. There is a head tenancy scheme. Parking is available but costs £6 per week.

EXTERNALLY: see University of Aberdeen
Housing help: The University Accommodation Office has 6 staff who help by offering a bulletin board and advice on contracts.

SERVICES:
- Nursery • Lesbian & Gay Society • Overseas SA
- Minibus • Self-defence classes

The Student Counselling Service (SCS), which employs 1 full-time and 2 part-time counsellors *(and is especially helpful for students from minorities and special needs groups)*, is the main source of comfort for students with problems of all sorts. *The SA's welfare department is willing to listen* and *will do what little it can*. The Medical Advisory Service has nurses and administrative staff and links with local GPs.

Women: Subsidised attack alarms. The Women's Officer is now the Equal Opportunities Officer, *which means the men complained, presumably.*

Disabled: *Changes have been taking place and most buildings are more-or-less accessible to wheelchair-users. Some flats have been adapted and one flat has been set up for the hearing-impaired.*

FINANCE:
- Access fund: £175,000 • Successful applications: 336

The hardship fund offers small short-term loans and there are a few scholarships and trust funds.

Roehampton Institute
see Other Institutions

Rose Bruford
see Other Institutions

Royal Academy of Music

- **The Academy is part of University of London and students are entitled to use its facilities.**

Royal Academy of Music, Marylebone Road, London, NW1 5HT.
Tel: (020) 7873 7373. Fax: (020) 7873 7374.
E-mail: registry@ram.ac.uk
Royal Academy of Music Students' Union, Marylebone Road, London, NW1 5HT. Tel: (020) 7837 7337. Fax: (020) 7873 7334

Just south of Regent's Park, along Marylebone Road from Madame Tussaud's, stands the *striking Edwardian edifice* that houses the Royal Academy of Music (RAM to its many friends). *It's one of the pre-eminent music schools in the country, probably in the world, with the notes of current budding geniuses harmonising with the echoes of greats from the past.* The place is steeped in history and musical tradition, *with big names from the musical world liable to pop in at any minute.* Current professors include early music specialist Christopher Hogwood and conductor Sir Colin Davis and the *excellent* instrument collection includes Wagner's old piano. *The RAM is proudly elitist, in the best possible sense, but the students are as financially down-trodden as any in London. The college is small, so everybody knows everyone else. It's friendly and frenetic but with a sense of purpose. This is vocational training for the cut-throat classical music biz, not art for art's sake.* The Academy is near Baker Street tube, with easy access to Paddington, Euston and King's Cross mainline stations.

Sex ratio(M:F): 45%:55%	Founded: 1822
Full time u'grads: 334	Part time: 0
Postgrads: 262	Non-degree: 0
Ave course: 4yrs	Ethnic: 20%
Private school: 25%	Flunk rate: 10.5%
Mature students: 5%	Overseas students: 43%
Disabled students: 6.7%	Staff/student ratio: n/a
Clearing: 0%	

Library (125,000 volumes, 29 study places, 10 computers) *which students consider pretty good* and modem link to the more substantial facilities of King's College, London; Development Office runs 'Music Box' for career-related help and advice – employment figures are hard to ascertain as most graduates go freelance immediately. *Small, cosy and comfy*, RAM bar (beer £1.60, wine £1.40, cap 100) open until 11pm every night except weekends; *much entertainment centres around 'proper' music* and there are countless recital and concert rooms geared up for this; RAMSU also lays on discos, termly balls, international nights, regular jazz nights and everything from karaoke to didgeridoo workshops and even belly dancing; College-run cafeteria (8am-6pm) *serves up a high standard of grub which compares favourably for value with the local cafés and sarnie bars*. SU (one sabb) apolitical – *most students wave batons, not banners*; pool table, microwave oven and *rather comfy* TV lounge (with Sky TV); twice termly 'SU News'; Rag week enjoys a good turn-out. Students can steward at concerts or get box office work with the big London concert halls and opera houses and there's also help in obtaining paid performance and freelance tuition work. No sports facilities or accommodation of its own – *the lack of halls is a bone of contention among many students who feel that first years miss out on getting to know each other*; access to the Accommodation Offices at King's College, London and the University of London and the Academy advertises in London papers for landlords who are sympathetic to students – *presumably the ones with thick walls and double-glazing. As the local Kensington area is so mega expensive most students head for the west and south-west areas of London.* Counsellor shared with King's College; RAMSU can provide another and course tutors are also available; links to medical specialists dealing with problems related to musical performance *(such as supporting Aston Villa and saying 'monstah' when you really come from the Home Counties)*; poor disabled access (the main building is listed) although there's a lift to all floors and good support for dyslexia; access fund £47,000 (56 successful applications); average debt per year £600.

CLUBS (NON SPORTING):
Tai Chi.

FAMOUS ALUMNI:
Sir John Barbirolli (conductor); Johnny Dankworth (jazz musician); Lesley Garrett (opera singer); Evelyn Glennie (percussionist); Dame Myra Hess (pianist); Sir Elton John *(wig-wearer extraordinaire)*; Graham Johnson (pianist); Aled Jones (former chorister, *grans loved him*); Annie Lennox (ex-Eurythmic); Joanna McGregor (pianist); Simon Rattle (conductor); Sir Arthur Sullivan (Gilbert and...); Mark Wigglesworth (conductor).

FURTHER INFO:
Prospectus. Website (www.ram.ac.uk).

Royal Agricultural College
see Other Institutions

> 20% of the medals won by Britain in the 1996 Olympics went to Loughborough University graduates.

Royal College of Music

Royal College of Music, Prince Consort Road, London, SW7 2BS.
Tel: (020) 7589 3643. Fax: (020) 7589 7740.
E-mail: admissions@rcm.ac.uk
Students' Association, Royal College of Music, Prince Consort Road, London, SW7 2BS. Tel: (020) 7584 8195.

Right next to the Albert Hall, over the road from Kensington Gardens (where Peter Pan lives, honest) is the *imposing* Victorian edifice of the Royal College of Music. It was founded by the Prince of Wales who went on to become the chubby, popular Timothy West lookalike Edward VII. He also had it off with numerous actresses, *but we're drifting from the point.* We're talking music, not drama here. The RCM has a worldwide reputation, especially for chamber music. The college also runs a unique joint honours Physics and Music degree in conjunction with Imperial College and exchange schemes are in place with the Universities of California and Western Ontario and numerous European conservatoires. *Things are quite laid-back (although the workload isn't) and the whole college shuts down at weekends. Students are unified by a love of music, but little else.* The nearest tubes are South Kensington, Gloucester Road and Knightsbridge and the nearest rail station is Paddington.

Sex ratio(M:F): 57%:43%	Founded: 1882
Full time u'grads: 380	Part time: 0
Postgrads: 172	Non-degree: 11
Ave course: 4yrs	Ethnic: 10%
Private school: 35%	Flunk rate: 2.3%
Mature students: 37%	Overseas students: 33%
Disabled students: 2.5%	Staff/student ratio: 1:3
Clearing: 0%	

Library (300,000 volumes, 82 study places, 13 computers). Careers Service with 2 full-time staff and new vocation advice unit 'Woodhouse Centre' offering advice and info on the music business. *Small, shabby but lively* bar (beer £1.60, wine £1.40); *students can also use the facilities at* Imperial College *next door*; 3 halls for concerts and recitals; *great* opera theatre; jazz evenings; *students have been known to indulge in spontaneous bursts of musical virtuosity just like the Kids from Fame*; theme nights; summer ball; the college refectory. Students' Association (1 sabb, 32% turnout), *party politics is, if not a dirty word, a bit grubby round the edges*; photocopier; games machines; pool table; TV lounge; the College publishes 'The Note', a termly newsletter, and Rag week. Sports facilities and clubs are shared with Imperial College, London. All 1st years who want to can be housed in College Hall (a converted bank) and about 20% of other students (47% total, self-catering, £48-79, 43wks); single-sex accommodation for girls at Queen Alexandra House, next door to the Royal Albert Hall; car parking – *expensive and hard to find;* soundproofed practice suite, *to allow for the sort of spontaneous, nocturnal virtuosity that doesn't go down too well in a rented flat (some students complain that it's a bit crap and noisy.*

College welfare officer holds details of appropriate accommodation (such as landlords who don't mind musical instruments) and maintains a notice board. Chaplain; counsellor; 3 Alexander Technique therapists; student health centre at Imperial College with 4 doctors; *disabled access is mixed* with lifts and ramps in the theatre and concert halls, but no ramp at the main entrance; access fund £46,979 (86 successful applications); ave debt per year £1,500; scholarships, study support grants and other financial resources, including an instrument loan fund.

FAMOUS ALUMNI:
Janet Baker, Peter Pears, Joan Sutherland (singers); Julian Bream (guitarist); Benjamin Britten, Gustav Holst, Michael Tippet, Mark Anthony Turnage, Ralph Vaughan Williams (composers); Colin Davis, Neville Marriner (conductors); Barry Douglas (pianist); James Galway (flautist); Vanessa-Mae (*nymphet* violinist); Rick Wakeman (*weirdy beardy* keyboard bloke); Lord Lloyd Webber (*provide your own description*).

FURTHER INFO:
Prospectuses and video (£4) from the Registry, plus a website (www.rcm.ac.uk).

Royal Holloway, London

- **The College is part of University of London and students are entitled to use its facilities.**
Royal Holloway, Egham, Surrey, TW20 0EX. Tel: (01784) 434455.
Fax: (01784) 471381. E-mail: liaison-office@rhul.ac.uk
Royal Holloway Student Union, Egham, Surrey, TW20 0EX.
Tel: (01784) 477003. Fax: (01784) 486312.

GENERAL

Royal Holloway is part of London University, despite being 20 miles away from the capital, a mile from Egham in Surrey, near Thorpe Park and Windsor. It is sometimes called London's country campus – *it's certainly as green as the University gets, even if it is all manicured and tamed splendour.* The *extensive* park grounds on a *steep* hill on the fringe of Windsor Park set off the College's *astoundingly beautiful* Founder's Building, an ornate red brick and stone structure, based on the Château Chambord in the Loire Valley in France, arranged as a square around grass courtyards with turrets, domes and ornamental carvings all over.

Sex ratio(M:F):60%:40%	Founded: 1886
Full time u'grads: 5,700	Part time: 51
Postgrads: 1,300	Non-degree: 250
Ave course: 3yrs	Ethnic: n/a
Private school: n/a	Flunk rate: 9.1%
Mature students: 10%	Overseas students: 20%
Disabled students: 5%	Staff/student ratio: 1:15
Clearing: 14%	

ATMOSPHERE:
Royal Holloway is starting to shrug off its right-wing past and become much more open and multi-cultural, though still somewhat middle-class. It's just the right size and location (small but not claustrophobic, close to London but still green) for fun and friendship and most of the students seem glad to be here.

THE CITY: see University of London

EGHAM:
The closest town to the campus is Egham, about a mile away. *It's a typically small, suburban, commutery-type place and it cannot truthfully be described as either groovy or student-oriented. Staines is nearby too, which is where Ali G's posse hangs.*

TRAVEL: see University of London

TRAVEL: EGHAM:
Trains: Trains to Waterloo from Egham every ¼ hour (£3.65).
Buses: *They are infrequent and dear* – 90p single for a 5min journey to the station – but there's a College service every 15 minutes or so (35p for the same trip) and the SU bus is 50p to livers-out after 10pm.
Coaches: Egham's just a hop from Heathrow *(useful if you want to catch a plane anywhere, oddly enough)*. Coaches cost £2.50 to the airport and from there they go anywhere in the UK.
Car: Egham is just outside the M25 London ring road, north of where the M3 crosses it on the way south west. The A30 goes right through the town. *A car is obviously handier than at other London sites but there are clampers on campus.*
Bicycles: *If cycling up the slight hill doesn't put students off, bikes are useful.*

CAREER PROSPECTS:
• Careers Service • No of staff: 3 full-time
• Unemployed after 6mths: 5%

SPECIAL FEATURES:
• Royal Holloway owns some of Britain's most valuable works of art. In 1993, amidst much controversy, it flogged a Turner painting to the Getty Museum in the USA for £11million. This money has been put in a trust and the interest will be used to pay towards the up-keep of the *beautiful* Founder's Building. They've sold other works too because they're just expensive to look after and, besides, they needed the dough. However the selling spree's over for now.
• The Drama Department has the only stage for Japanese Noh theatre in the UK.

FAMOUS ALUMNI:
David Bellamy (naturalist); Richmal Crompton (writer, 'Just William'); Emma Freud (broadcaster and Mrs Richard Curtis); Felicity Lott, Susan Bullock (opera singers); Francis Wheen (journalist).

FURTHER INFO:
Prospectuses for undergrads and postgrads, departmental brochures, SU handbook, video loan, guide for mature students, guide for international students, website (www.rhul.ac.uk). Open days in March, June and October.

```
The Vice-Chancellor of Staffordshire University
is a leading authority on Elvis Presley.
```

Royal Holloway

ACADEMIC

staff/student ratio: 1:15
Range of points required for entrance: 340-240
Percentage accepted through clearing: 14%
Number of terms/semesters: 3
Length of terms/semesters: 12 wks
Research: 4.9

LIBRARIES:
- Books: 548,815 • Study places: 634

There are three libraries, Bedford, Founders and Music. *Facilities are pretty good but students feel an itsy bit like there's still room for improvement.*

COMPUTERS:
- Computer workstations: 580

24-hour computer access is available with a swipe card.

ENTERTAINMENT

EGHAM:
- Price of a pint of beer: £2.20 • Glass of wine: £1.50

Egham is about as lively as a flattened hedgehog, although the Happy Man pub is aptly named, and run by ex-students. *The new Monkey's Forehead, opposite the college is worth a go,* it also employs loads of students. *The Tap & Spile and Bar 163 are also worth a gargle.* There's an okay selection of eateries here and in Englefield Green. Pushplugs: Beehive; Holly Tree; Armstrong Gun; Don Beni (Italian); Rengal Brasserie (Indian). There's a cinema in Staines and theatres in Windsor but students looking for the high life go into London instead.

CITY: see University of London

COLLEGE:
- Price of a pint of beer: £1.70 • Glass of wine: £1.20

Bars: There are six bars in all *(it's rumoured that the Queen Mum once had a sneaky pint in one of them).* The busiest drink-spot being the recently refurbished Tommy's *(perhaps because it's on the ground floor of the SU and not such an effort to reach),* the Stumble Inn and the Union Bar. Holloway's is popular with the sporty set.
Theatres: Not one, but two theatres, including a Japanese one. The drama soc puts on regular plays and productions in London. The Musical Theatre Soc goes to Edinburgh.
Cinemas: The SU puts on a film a week, *usually mainstream.*
Clubs/discos/music venues: 4 or 5 nights a week there are all flavours of clubbing in the SU (cap 1,250), attracting big name DJs like Judge Jules and Boy George. Occasional bands play here, recent examples being Billie Piper, Brandon Block and Jamiroquoi.
Cabaret: About twice a term chuckle monsters like Ali G and Shaun Lock *cause ribs to pop out at Holloways or the Union.*
Food: The SU-run TWZO's offers *the best range (including a decent vegetarian selection) but some find it a bit pricey.* Students who live on campus tend to prefer the University dining halls. Café Jules provides chic and sophisticated dishes.

Others: *Since there's little else to do around this part of the world*, the SU runs ents on virtually every night of the week. Clubs and societies hold functions and there are film nights and everything comes to a star-speckled, champagne-filled head at the Summer Ball (2,000 people, tickets £60 a throw).

SOCIAL & POLITICAL

ROYAL HOLLOWAY STUDENTS' UNION:
• 4 sabbaticals • Turnout at last ballot: 18% • NUS member

The SU has good reason to smile. It's finally lost the right wing tag that dogged it for so many years and is now considered a very fair and democratic union by many. It has a warm relationship with the university with whom it regularly co-operates and collaborates on many issues and it even enjoys massive student support, something that most SU's would trade their grannies for.

SU FACILITIES:
Second-hand book stall; bars; coffee bar; satellite TV; photobooth; function halls; three minibuses and vans; games machines; bus service; NatWest bank on campus; uni-run shop.

CLUBS (NON SPORTING):
Acid Jazz; Battle Re-enactment; Chinese; Chocoholics; James Bond; Touring Theatre; Wines & Spirits

OTHER ORGANISATIONS:
The *spankingly good* 'The Orbital', nominated for the Guardian student mag of the year, is published by the students. The student radio station 'Insanity' *has been well received, to put it mildly* and has been granted a five-year AM licence, which isn't surprising as the station has been nominated for four BBC Radio One awards. There is a Community Action Group and the Rag usually does alright. (It raised over £15,000 recently.)

RELIGIOUS:
• 3 chaplains (CofE, RC, Free Church)

Within college there are a non-denominational chapel and a Muslim prayer room, as well as facilities for Jewish and other persuasions.

PAID WORK:
The SU has vacancies for 350 students and provides a job training scheme with vocational certificates. The University administration employs casual envelope stuffers and the careers office helps temp job-seekers.

SPORTS

• Recent successes: too many to mention

Enthusiasm and results are excellent. It also helps that there's a new sports centre with a fully equipped gym, offering classes day and night *for all energy addicts. The Royal Holloway has been declared London's best sporting college by the* University of London Union (ULU).

SPORTS FACILITIES:
There are playing fields on the campus, tennis and netball courts, rugby and cricket fields, fitness room and a small gym and a sports hall and at Kingswood Halls of Residence there are squash courts. The nearby Thames and Datchet Reservoirs provide sailing and

watersport opportunities. Students can purchase a cheap sports card for local leisure centres and are, of course, entitled to use ULU facilities although they're a bit far. There are sporting bursaries for the especially talented.

SPORTING CLUBS:
Many including: Caving; Lacrosse; Mountaineering; Ninjutsu; Rowing; Sky-Diving; Thai Boxing.

ATTRACTIONS:
Horsey types can visit Ascot or watch polo in Windsor Great Park. Wentworth and Sunningdale are easy travelling distance too.

ACCOMMODATION

IN COLLEGE:
- Catered: 40% • Cost: £45-80 (30-38wks)
- Self-catering: 4% • Cost: £65-70 (38-50wks)

Availability: All 1st years and about half the finalists can live in, but very few 2nd years. There are big and modern halls or, for *spacious rooms and kudos*, there are rooms in the Founder's Building. 6% have to share (only in Founder's and Kingswood). In Reid Hall, solely for finalists, rooms have en suite showers and loos. Self-catering (for 3rd years and postgrads only) in the recently extended Runnymede Hall and Penrose Court. Students must vacate most rooms during the holidays so the College can host the lucrative conference trade. Parking is by permit only and clampers are used. *Students are on the whole happy with the accommodation although they do feel it's too pricey.*

EXTERNALLY:
- Ave rent: £55-70

Availability: *Students must expect to look early to find anywhere decent, but, for a price, there is just about enough. Englefield Green is the most convenient area but many go as far as Staines (4 to 5 miles) for the better social life it offers – better than Egham, that is.*

Housing help: The College Accommodation Service provides vacancy sheets and standard contracts.

WELFARE

SERVICES:
- Nightline • Lesbian & Gay Society • Mature SA
- Overseas SA • Self-defence classes

There are four counsellors employed by the College and the SU has a Welfare Officer. There is a nursery for 2-8 year-olds, but there is a waiting list for places. Other services include a legal aid solicitor, drug counselling, minibus and attack alarms.

Disabled: *Access is pretty bad in some parts of the campus – the older parts mainly. The receipt of a major grant has improved things with for example, more ramps are being installed, but potential applicants are encouraged to contact the registrar before submitting an application, they have also employed an Educational Support Officer. There is accommodation for disabled students and facilities for the hearing-impaired.*

FINANCE:
- Access fund: £190,813 • Successful applications: 215

Loans from the Principal's Hardship Fund have to be repaid before students are allowed to graduate. Also scholarships and bursaries for travel, instrumental students and sports.

Royal Military College of Science
see Cranfield University

Royal Veterinary College, London

- **The College is part of University of London and students are entitled to use its facilities.**

The Royal Veterinary College, Royal College Street, London, NW1 OTU. Tel: (020) 7468 5000. Fax: (020) 7388 2342.
Royal Veterinary College Union Society, Hawkshead Campus, Hawkshead Lane, North Mimms, Hatfield, Herts, AL9 7TA. Tel: (01707) 666310. Fax: (01707) 652090.

GENERAL

You won't be surprised to learn that RVC (as its chums call it) only teaches students how to be vets. It's all to do with training people to make the sort of decisions that have Rolf Harris in floods of tears, *so if you can't hack 5 years of that, stop reading now*. The College's main site is 1¼ miles from Trafalgar Square in Camden, *one of the trendiest, buzziest areas of London*. The redbrick College buildings here are home to the pre-clinical teaching and administration. The College's Hawkshead campus, a couple of miles from Hatfield, is set in the *relaxed, commuter belt* countryside (see University of Hertfordshire). It is a large self-contained green site with low buildings accommodating clinical students. In other words, students spend 2 years at Camden, *enjoying city life*, and then move out to almost tediously tranquil Hawkshead, *which is beautiful even if much of it smells of animal poo. The atmosphere is quite intense and geared to studying, although there is also a lot of sport going on.*

Sex ratio(M:F): 70%:30%	Founded: 1791
Full time u'grads: 674	Part time: 0
Postgrads: 106	Non-degree: 0
Ave course: 5yrs	Ethnic: n/a
Private school: n/a	Flunk rate: 1.4%
Mature students: 14%	Overseas students: 17%
Disabled students: 2%	

THE CITY: see University of London

TRAVEL: see University of London
Trains: Nearest stations are King's Cross, St Pancras, Euston and Camden Road for the Camden site. Two trains every hour between King's Cross and Potter's Bar (£4) for Hawkshead. Taxis from the station to Hawkshead cost £3.50, *otherwise it's a long hike*.

541 Royal Veterinary

Buses: Numbers 46 and 214 pass close to the Camden site.
Car: A lot of students have cars at Hawkshead.
Underground: Camden Town or Mornington Crescent (Northern Line).
Bicycles: Racks are provided on both sites.
Hawkshead: See University of Hertfordshire.

CAREER PROSPECTS:
Students can use the careers facilities of University of London.

FURTHER INFO:
Undergrad/postgrad prospectus, website (www.rvc.ac.uk).

ACADEMIC

During vacations in the 1st and 2nd years, students have to work on farms. The college has just been AVMA approved which means that any graduate wanting to work in America does not now have to spend 2-3 years having to train in the States.

staff/student ratio: 1:6
Range of points required for entrance: 360
Percentage accepted through clearing: 0
Number of terms/semesters: n/a
Length of terms/semesters: n/a
Research: 6

LIBRARIES:
• Books: 16,000 • Study places: 30
Library facilities are no more than *adequate*, open till 8pm on Sundays for serious swotting.

COMPUTERS:
• Computer workstations: 50
Recently been updated, *better than adequate - agreeable even*.

ENTERTAINMENT

IN LONDON: see

University of London

CAMDEN & HAWKSHEAD:
Obviously there is a lot more going on near Camden than Hawkshead, but prices are higher. The famous weekend market is still pretty cool, especially for young, slightly alternative Japanese tourists. If you're not one, it can get a bit samey. Pushplugged pubs at Hawkshead: The Bridge; The Maypole; avoid Williots. In Camden: Prince Alfred; Lord John Russell.

```
A candidate for the Presidency of Cardiff
Student's Union was forced to withdraw when it
was revealed that his campaign t-shirts were
sponsored by the 'Sunday Sport'.
```

COLLEGE:
- Price of a pint of beer: £1.30 • No wine, stick to beer

2 bars, one at each site. 1 ball a year at each site. A boogie bus runs from the Hawkshead site stopping at several pubs and a club in Enfield or Hatfield. Serious clubbers at the Camden site head into town or the West End. ULU facilities are open to RVC students. Hawkshead has a small theatre production company which puts on an annual production. Both Hawkshead and Camden have refectories open from 10.30am to 2.30pm – *quality and choice is good but expensive.*

SOCIAL & POLITICAL

ROYAL VETERINARY COLLEGE UNION SOCIETY:
- Turnout at last ballot: 90%

The Union is *rather good considering* it's not affiliated to the NUS, but membership is due soon. The Union has been putting a recent emphasis on welfare and stress management following a rising number of drop-outs in the 3rd year. They have also been plugging away for a new sports/examinations/social hall *which the college is steadfastly refusing on financial grounds*. It provides welfare services, a shop, a pool table and a minibus but there are very few non-sporting societies. There is, however, a Rag week, a jobs notice board and a online newspaper called the 'Weekly Dose'. *For religious advice one reverend is willing to help worshippers of any persuasion with matters ecumenical or snooker-related (apparently he's quite good).*

CLUBS (NON SPORTING):
Clinical Science Club; Zoological Soc.

SPORTS

- Recent successes: women's rugby, netball

This is a very sporty place. Being a vet keeps you fit and a liking for the great outdoors is second nature. It's a shame that nobody's discovered a way to make sticking your fist up a cow's bum a competitive sport. Sports provision is good. Camden has a gym but Hawkshead is the winner with tennis and squash courts, a football pitch, rugger pitch, netball court and a heated pool.

SPORTING CLUBS:
Polo; Water Polo; Rowing.

```
'Spice' the Cardiff SU Dance night, was
closed down when all the sweaty bodies set
off the fire alarms  and nobody paid any
attention because they thought it was a
techno record.
```

ACCOMMODATION

IN COLLEGE:
- Catered: 11% • Cost: £73 (45wks)
- Self-catering: 6% • Cost: £53 (32-45wks)

Availability: In Camden students stay in London University accommodation for 2 years *so the real scenario is a little better than the figures above might suggest.* In all, 85% of 1st years are housed and 10% of finalists can also live in. The catered accommodation at Hawkshead has pool and snooker tables and computers on site. All accommodation is in single rooms. New houses have been built 2 minutes from college.

Car parking: *Parking is a real problem in Camden,* but in Hawkshead it's free *and there is plenty of it.*

EXTERNALLY: see University of London
Camden: *Most Camden students live in Kentish Town which is a bit cheaper than Camden.* The College and SU keep details of housing and run lectures on the pitfalls of letting.
Hawkshead: *Potter's Bar is the best place to look for a place,* but students have to compete with students from University of Hertfordshire.

WELFARE

SERVICES:
The SU and the College go halves on a bought-in counselling service. Free rape alarms are available from the SU. ULU runs a nightline service and there's the extremely popular snooker playing chaplain to talk to.

FINANCE:
- Access fund: £24,000 • Successful applications: 20

The Chancellor of the University of East London is Lord (Brian) Rix, famous for a) his charity work on behalf of people with learning disabilities and b) innumerable appearances on stage and screen without his trousers.

University of St Andrews

St David's University College see Lampeter, University of Wales

St George's Hospital Medical School, London

St Mark & St John see Other Institutions

St Martin's College see Other Institutions

St Martin's College of Art see The London Institute

St Mary's College see Other Institutions

St Mary's Hospital see Imperial College, London

St Thomas's Hospital see King's College, London

University of Salford

Scarborough University College see Other Institutions

School of Economics see LSE

School of Oriental & African Studies see SOAS

School of Pharmacy, London

School of Slavonic & East European Studies see UCL

Scottish College of Textiles see Heriot-Watt University

University of Sheffield

Sheffield City Poly see Sheffield Hallam University

Sheffield Hallam University

Shrivenham see Cranfield University

Silsoe see Cranfield University

Slavonic & East European Studies see UCL

SOAS

University of Southampton

Southampton Institute of Higher Education

South Bank University

South West Poly see University of Plymouth

Staffordshire University

University of Stirling

Stockton see University of Durham

continued next page

University of Strathclyde

University of Sunderland

University of Surrey

Surrey Institute of Art & Design

University of Sussex

Swansea Institute see other Institutions

Swansea, University of Wales

> The Sutra rave at BUWE is so popular that one punter, denied entry, tried to ram-raid the venue – in his own car.

University of St Andrews

University of St Andrews, Admissions Office, 79 North Street,
St Andrews, Fife, KY16 9AJ. Tel: (01334) 462150.
Fax: (01334) 463388. E-mail: admissions@st-andrews.ac.uk
University of St Andrews Students' Association, St Mary's Place,
St Andrews, Fife, KY16 9JZ. Tel: (01334) 462700.
Fax: (01334) 462740. E-mail: union@st-andrews.ac.uk

GENERAL

The city of St Andrews is situated on the east coast of Scotland. St Andrews, the University, is the oldest in Scotland, the third oldest in the UK (after Oxford and Cambridge) and, *quite naturally,* tradition plays a large part in the lives of the students. The University buildings reflect the heritage, dating from the 15th century until the modern day, with many *tasteful* examples from the 16th and 17th centuries. *Neither the city nor the University are very big – in fact, more than a ¼ of the local population are students. Apart from making this a university city (as opposed to a city with a university),* it means that, although the University buildings are scattered all over the place, they are all still within walking distance of each other.

Sex ratio(M:F): 48%:52%	Founded: 1410
Full time u'grads: 4,965	Part time: 54
Postgrads: 104	Non-degree: 262
Ave course: 4yrs	Ethnic: 6%
Private school: n/a	Flunk rate: 9.5%
Mature students: 11%	Overseas students: 19%
Disabled students: 6%	

ATMOSPHERE:
Everywhere there are rituals, ceremonies, customs and students wearing groovy red gowns. Relations between students and the local population are generally good, partly because the University is the major local employer. Among students themselves, there's a happy atmosphere – even the state school/private school and English/Scottish divides are expressed more as healthy rivalry than as bitter antagonism. To top it all, Prince William is now a student.

THE CITY:
- Population: 16,000 • London: 371miles • Edinburgh: 45miles
- Dundee: 13miles

Never mind Florida, this is the world's golfing capital. There's not only the Royal & Ancient Golf Club, the oldest in the world, but five other courses, attracting thousands of people *in peach and purple plaid pants.* It's not just golfers who come here, though; it's a natural tourist town, like a theme park, with museums, *enchanting* architecture *and scenery to die for.* The cathedral and castle are the most famous of St Andrews' many historic buildings. For the tourist trade, there are many *quaint shops and cafés, but nothing of particular note aimed at students.* The city consists of three main streets with interlocking alleys and side streets. *It's all fairly isolated, enclosed by a rock coast to the north, sandy beaches to the east and countryside the rest of the way round.*

TRAVEL:
The University Travel Service provides info and sells tickets.
Trains: Leuchars station is 5 miles from the main group of the University buildings with direct lines to London (£53.45), Dundee and Edinburgh. For other services, passengers *(sorry, customers)* must change at Edinburgh or Dundee.
Coaches: National Express coaches run from Dundee, 13 miles away, to London (£32), Glasgow (£11) and beyond.
Car: A915 south, A91 west to M90 (to Edinburgh).
Hitching: *Difficult to get from St Andrews to anywhere. Better from Edinburgh (A1) or Dundee if thumbsters can get there.*
Local: Buses every ½ hour but rarer at night, *although they're quite cheap (£1.40). In general, St Andrews is small enough to walk around.*
Taxis: *A taxi ride into Leuchars is very expensive at £8, although some firms offer student discounts.*
Bicycles: *The best way to get around short of a chauffeur-driven limo. St Andrews is small and quite flat with limited traffic.*

CAREER PROSPECTS:
- Careers Service • No of staff: 3 full/1 part
- Unemployed after 6mths: 3.4%

SPECIAL FEATURES:
- Students get free admission to the castle while wearing their gowns.

FAMOUS ALUMNI:
Sir James Black (Nobel Prize scientist); Crispin Bonham-Carter (actor); Hazel Irvine (sports presenter); Edward Jenner (discovered vaccination for smallpox); John McAllion (MP for Dundee); Madsen Pirie (Adam Smith Institute); Siobhan Redmond (actress); Alex Salmond MP (SNP); Fay Weldon (writer). Former Rectors (elected by students) include Rudyard Kipling and John Cleese, who advised students not to let their degrees get in the way of their education.

FURTHER INFO:
Prospectuses for undergrads and postgrads, video loans. CD-Rom and website (www.st-andrews.ac.uk).

ACADEMIC

staff/student ratio: 1:11
Range of points required for entrance: 340-240
Percentage accepted through clearing: n/a
Number of terms/semesters: 2
Length of terms/semesters: 15 wks
Research: 5

LIBRARIES:
• Books: 950,000 • Study places: 1,150
University Library is the main library with well over 750,000 books – a lot *for a university this size*. There are also several other libraries spread across the university.

COMPUTERS:
• Computer workstations: 620
24-hour computer facilities are available.

ENTERTAINMENT

TOWN:
• Price of a pint of beer: £1.90 • Glass of wine: £1.60
Cinemas: One single-screen cinema, The Picture House.
Theatres: Two *small* theatres, The Crawford Art Centre and The Byre Theatre. The Castle sometimes doubles up.
Pubs: *Pubs tend to be geared towards the summer tourist trade more than students. Some (such as Ma Bell's) are monopolised by the privately educated yahs.* Pushplugs: The Cellar Bar; Lizard Lounge; Whey Pat Tavern; Bert's Bar; Ogston's; The Central.
Music venues: Jazz swings its stuff at Younger Hall and the Vic Café, which also hosts blues and folk music. Ogston's has live bands every Thursday.
Eating out: *Considering the city's size, the range and quality is impressive – again, this has much to do with the tourist trade. Pubs are often a good bet.* Pushplugs: Babur (Indian); Vine Leaf (*for romantic liaisons à deux*); Ziggys (*decent burgers and pizza*); North Point (*tea shop*); Coffee House (*15 blends and hotly tipped bacon sarnies*); The Doll's House (vfm).

UNIVERSITY:
• Price of a pint of beer: £1.50 • Glass of wine: £1.35
Bars: (3) The Union's *groovily* decorated Main Bar *provides the cheapest eating and drinking in town.* The Beer Bar is used as a venue. The Fraser Suite is *quieter and more intimate*.
Cinema: *Three film clubs show a range of flicks from arty to mainstream and Manga.*
Theatres: *There's an immense selection of thespian goings on going on (mostly in the Union Theatre, cap 500) and every student is automatically a member of the Mermaids University Dramatic Society which usually performs at the Edinburgh Fringe, the National Student Drama Festival and the Scottish Drama Festival.*

Clubs/discos: The city doesn't have any real nightclubs *and so the Union's two weekly club nights do wonders for local relations. Friday night is the very popular cheesy pop Bop and Saturdays rotate between dance and Drum 'n' Bass.*
Music venues: When the Union Theatre isn't being used for discos, plays or *whatever*, it's often used for live music – recently: Toploader, Steps tribute band (live-ish music). Visiting DJs have included Ministry of Sound and Miss Moneypennys.
Cabaret: *A major stopover for touring talent,* such as Craig Charles and Rob Newman.
Food: The Main Bar includes a restaurant which *doles out everything from snacks to full feasts which can only be described as canteen style.* The Old Union coffee bar also deals in nibbles.
Others: *These posh student types love their balls – the black tie variety – and so they have over a dozen a term, some of them full Scottish kilt-and-sporran jobs.*

SOCIAL & POLITICAL

UNIVERSITY OF ST ANDREWS STUDENTS' ASSOCIATION:
• 4 sabbaticals • Turnout at last ballot: 24%
The Students' Association is made up of two parts, the Student Representative Council (SRC), which does all the shouting, and the Students' Union, which dishes out services. The SRC opted out of NUS in 1979. *Political stances tend to be supine, although a proposed switch to a semesterised calender was successfully fought off recently.*

SU FACILITIES:
The Union has facilities at St Mary's Place: three bars; cafeteria; travel agency; general shop; Clydesdale cashpoint; TV lounge; launderette; photocopying; photo booth; fax service; two minibuses for hire; sexual health clinic; games and vending machines; pool table; juke box; five meeting rooms; two conference halls; parking.

CLUBS (NON SPORTING):
Amnesty; Archaeological; Astronomy; Ballroom Dancing; Boys Dentistry; Catholic; Chinese; Cocktail; Comedy; Christian Music and Drama; Conservative Unionist; Dead Parrots; Drinking; French; Girls Drinking; Hindu; Islamic; Italian; Internet; James Bond; Labour; Left Wing; Live Music; Marxist Alliance; Medical; Model United Nations; One World; Pooh Bear; Real Ale; Rocksoc; Scottish Hellenic; Tree and Frog; War-games; Wired; Women in Art; Wine.

OTHER ORGANISATIONS:
'The Saint' is the *readily readable read*. A radio station is planned. The *very active* Student Voluntary Service (SVS) has won an award for being the best in Scotland. The Rag, Scotland's *most successful*, raises at least £35,000 every year, there's also the Kate Kennedy Club (named after the niece of the University's founder), an all-male charitable club which raised an additional £3,000 last year. There's also the Union Debating Society, a *(pompous) talk shop*.

RELIGIOUS:
• 1 chaplain
The University chaplaincy, city churches and cathedral cater for most versions of Christianity. A rabbi is also available occasionally as he's based in Glasgow. There's also a Muslim prayer room.

PAID WORK:
A University-organised jobs databank is available and the Student Support Service has a job club. Most vacancies are in the local

tourist and golfing trade – hotels, golf bars and so on. *Caddying isn't as easy as you'd think, though.*

SPORTS

- Recent successes: golf, lacrosse, rugby, squash

Excellent facilities (especially for golf) considering that, as far as universities go, this ain't one of the big boys. Participation and enthusiasm remain high despite the introduction of nominal fees for the facilities.

SPORTS FACILITIES:
Sports halls; 45 acres of playing fields; squash courts; croquet lawn; floodlit astroturf, track and all-weather tennis courts; multigym; gym; cricket nets; boat house (sailing and rowing facilities); sauna; and, *of course*, a reduced fee for the golf course. Locally, there's also the sea, hills for hilly-type sports, ski slopes and five golf courses.

SPORTING CLUBS:
Aikido; Canoe; Cricket; Clay Pigeon; Fencing; Football; Gaelic; Karate; Korfball; Mountaineering; Orienteering; Parachute; Riding; Rifle; Shinty; Soaring; Trampolining; Ultimate Frisbee; Volleyball; Waterpolo; Windsurfing.

ATTRACTIONS:
There's golf, watersports, golf, walking, golf, climbing, golf. Oh, and golf, for which students pay only the same as local residents (less than £100 a year). Other amenities include nearby riding schools and skiing.

ACCOMMODATION

IN COLLEGE:
- Catered: 38% • Cost: £67-89 (31-50wks)
- Self-catering: 17% • Cost: £32-55 (36-50wks)

Availability: All 1st years who want to live in can do so and there's room for nearly half of other years. 23% of students have to share rooms. A head tenancy scheme is available with 121 places. *There's a large mixture of old and new buildings,* including the self-catered flats in Fife Park and Albany Park (on the beach). New Hall is very popular as every room has a double bed, en suite bathroom and Sky TV.

EXTERNALLY:
- Ave rent: £55

Availability: *There are no specific student areas because it's so small. The available places are generally good, a reflection of local prosperity.* Student houses tend to be rented out over the summer so *conditions are pretty good* and you only have to pay rent for 9/10 months of the year. *It's slightly easier to sell condoms in a convent than to park in St Andrews – even in the residential areas it is fairly bad. Bikes are recommended.* A few students resort to local villages.

Housing help: Help is available from the Head of University Accommodation which employs four staff to help with house hunting *and the problems that inevitably will occur, even to the most optimistic. After all, the difference between an optimist and a pessimist is that an optimist isn't in possession of all the facts.*

10% of London's young homeless are graduates.

WELFARE

SERVICES:
- Creche • Playgroup • Nursery • Lesbian & Gay Society
- Mature SA • Overseas SA • Equal Opportunities Officer
- Disability adviser • Self-defence classes

The SA Welfare Adviser helps with legal, financial and academic problems. As does the University's three part-time student counsellors and the Director of Student Support Services (welfare/discipline officer). The local health centre has a dedicated student practice. There's a befriending scheme for overseas students.

Disabled: *Access is good in the more modern buildings but pretty hopeless in the listed ones. Residences are better.* Dyslexia sufferers get extra exam time, one-to-one proof reading and special computers. There is a Special Needs Co-ordinator and disability co-ordinators in each academic school.

Women: *Although female students are now in the majority, many feel that this is still a male-dominated enclave and that specific welfare provision is limited.* Subsidised alarms are available.

FINANCE:
- Access fund: £280,694 • Successful applications: 658

In addition to the access fund, bursaries and scholarships, the University can provide interest-free loans in extreme cases through the Director of Student Support Services.

St David's University College

see Lampeter, University of Wales

St George's Hospital Medical School, London

- **The Medical School is part of University of London and students are entitled to use its facilities.**

St George's Hospital Medical School, Cranmer Terrace, Tooting, London, SW17 0RE. Tel: (020) 8672 9944. Fax: (020) 8725 5919.
E-mail: adm-med@sgnms.ac.uk
St George's School Club, Cranmer Terrace, Tooting, London, SW17 0RE. Tel: (020) 8725 5201. Fax: (020) 8767 0841.
E-mail: sgms203@sghms.ac.uk

6 miles from Trafalgar Square is St George's Hospital, situated in the Tooting district of South London, *famed for 'Citizen Smith' and, well, not a lot else.* The Medical School is in a 1970s redbrick building, adjoined by other older buildings. *George's has a much more relaxed feel and informal atmosphere than the other London medical schools and the students miss it when they're sent off on assignments in other hospitals.* Because of the teaching structure, there is also

much better mixing between years. Undergraduates are less alienated from the rest of the hospital than those in other medical schools, but are distanced from the rest of the University of London. The Theatre is the local night spot with a student night, *but little else going for it*, while JJ Moon's, part of the Wetherspoon operation, is a *good* local boozer; *prices are cheaper than elsewhere in town but for any variety of thrills, students head to Clapham, Brixton or, better still, the city centre.* Lots of students have bikes *and theft is rare – racks are available at the hospital and sheds at the halls of residence.* For longer journeys and non-peddle pushers, the nearest stations are Tooting and Earlsfield, Tooting Broadway (Northern Line) for the underground, or bus numbers 44, 57, 77, 131, 133, 155, 270, 264, 280, 355, N77 and N44.

Sex ratio(M:F): 48%:52%	**Founded:** 1751
Full time u'grads: 1,275	**Part time:** 0
Postgrads: 50	**Non-degree:** 0
Ave course: 3/6yrs	**Ethnic:** 45%
Private school: 40%	**Flunk rate:** n/a
Mature students: 10%	**Overseas students:** 12%
Disabled students: <1%	

Library (40,000 volumes, 400 study places); 150 computers with 24-hour access. 2 full-time careers advisers. Bar (beer £1.25, wine 70p, cap 650) stages live music, regular discos, student DJ nights and lunchtime food, with regular cut-price promotions; 400-seat theatre for the thesps – musicals are popular; 1 cult film or recent release every week in a lecture theatre; 7 black tie extravaganzas a year; *the hospital canteen is ok but not great and the Queen Vic over the road usually soaks up the resulting hungry custom.* School Club (2 sabbs, 38% turnout, NUS member) *is apolitical, maybe even conservative (but with a small 'c') with emphasis more on student services than campaigning and politicising;* Rag always raises huge amounts (£102,000 last year); fortnightly newsletter *revelling compellingly in its lack of political correctness;* slightly more reverent 'Gazette'.

Sport tends to be a social thing and isn't an all-consuming passion, though there have been several minor successes recently (cricket, badminton); 35 acres of playing fields; sports hall, climbing wall, 6 squash courts and multigym on site; free entry to Tooting Leisure Centre swimming pool. 90% of 1st years and a few of the others live in college accommodation (25% total, self-catering, £60/wk, 30-50wks); *rooms are clean and modern and set in large grounds;* no female students are housed on the ground floor; *loads of free parking, but only because no one uses it; overall the accommodation is popular, partly due to the intimacy of some of the buildings and partly due to the cost, which is very reasonable for London;* local accommodation *slightly cheaper and easier to find than in Central London, but some of it's a bit grotty.* 3 full-time counsellors for students' non-physical ailments; free, women-only taxi service for big events; self-defence classes; access fund £46,880 (51 successful applications); bursaries, grants and prizes all over the place.

CLUBS (SPORTING & NON SPORTING):
Curry Club; Gaelic Football; Hurling; Medicaid; Paintball; Real Ale.

FAMOUS ALUMNI:
Henry Gray (author, Gray's Anatomy); Harry Hill (neckless comic); Edward Jenner (invented smallpox vaccination); Edward Wilson (accompanied Scott to the Antarctic); Mike Stroud (Antarctic explorer).

FURTHER INFO:
Prospectuses for undergrads and postgrads and an alternative prospectus (all available from the Registry). Website (www.sghms.ac.uk).

St Mark & St John
see Other Institutions

St Martin's College
see Other Institutions

St Martin's College of Art
see The London Institute

St Mary's College
see Other Institutions

St Mary's Hospital
see Imperial College, London

St Thomas's Hospital
see King's College, London

University of Salford

University of Salford, Salford, M5 4WT. Tel: (0161) 295 5000.
Fax: (0161) 295 5999. E-mail: ug.prospectus@salford.ac.uk
University of Salford Students' Union, University House,
The Crescent, Salford, M5 4WT. Tel: (0161) 736 7811.
Fax: (0161) 737 1633.

GENERAL

At the western end of Manchester is the city of Salford, *but screw up your eyes and you can't see the join. Salford isn't magically different, nor is it sufficiently far to make it properly distinct and so everything we said about Manchester* (see University of Manchester) *applies equally to Salford.* After all, it's only 2 miles to the centre of Manchester. *It's certainly not the posh end of Manchester,* but the 34-acre site of the University is quite green *and less ugly than many modern campuses.* With a few redbrick exceptions, the buildings have all been built in the last 20 years.

Salford

Sex ratio(M:F): 52%:48%
Full time u'grads: 11,527
Postgrads: 2,371
Ave course: 3-4yrs
Private school: n/a
Mature students: 33%
Disabled students: n/a

Founded: 1967
Part time: 3,257
Non-degree: 6,222
Ethnic: 17%
Flunk rate: 19.4%
Overseas students: 8.5%

ATMOSPHERE:
The University's strong local links provide a real community identity for students. Students get the best of both worlds: a campus university in a small neighbourhood town at the same time as the metropolitan high life of Manchester, although the latter tends to overshadow any specifically Salfordian local colour. There's a good mix of ages and backgrounds.

THE SITES:
Peel Park, Frederick Road and Adelphi: (2,000 students) The majority of students are based at these three campuses, all within 10 minutes walk of each other. There's also Irwell Valley, a further 10 minutes from Frederick Road, near the Castle Irwell Student Village.
Eccles and Bury: Nursing and midwifery are taught at Eccles, 3 miles from the main site, and Bury, 8 miles away.

THE CITY: see University of Manchester

SALFORD:

- Population: 217,900

Salford has its own small and friendly community. Occasionally, it looks somewhat like a Lowry painting, full of matchstick men and matchstick cats and dogs, factory gates and the rest of it. Not surprising, really, since this is Lowry's home town. There's a spectacular gallery to show off his work. *Occasionally, Salford also looks like a scene from 'Coronation Street'.* Again, no surprise, chuck, as this is where it is set. But far more often, it is the rebuilt Salford that shows its face, the docklands have been developed and right in the heart of the North are all sorts of new constructions: high rise blocks; shopping malls and supermarkets; libraries; book shops; banks; and everything else a town needs, including three museums, an 'urban heritage park' and its own nightlife.

TRAVEL: see University of Manchester
Local: Salford is covered by Manchester's bus and train networks which are *reliable, comprehensive and generally cheap*. Salford Crescent station is actually on the campus, although for national services it may be necessary to change at one of Manchester's stations (trains every 15 mins). Buses go to Manchester city centre every 3 minutes.

CAREER PROSPECTS:
- Careers Service • No of staff: 5 full-time
- Unemployed after 6mths: 9%

FAMOUS ALUMNI:
Bill Beaumont (ex-England rugby captain); John Cooper Clarke (poet); Christopher Ecclestone (actor); Ieuan Evans (rugby player); Peter Kay (loud-mouthed northern comedian); LS Lowry (artist); Jonathon Morris (actor); Norman Whiteside (ex-Man Utd footballer); Murray Lachlan Young (poet).

FURTHER INFO:
Prospectuses for undergrads and postgrads, video, part-time course brochures and a website (www.salford.ac.uk).

ACADEMIC

The University has strong links with industry, particularly local firms, *which can be kind of handy for arranging decent work-placements and the like.*

staff/student ratio: 1:22
Range of points required for entrance: 320-120
Percentage accepted through clearing: 10%
Number of terms/semesters: 2
Length of terms/semesters: 15 wks
Research: 4.4

LIBRARIES:
• Books: 474,102   • Study places: 1,380
There are 7 libraries in all, the weekend opening hours are pretty weak though (3 hours on Saturday, 6 on Sunday).

COMPUTERS:
• Computer workstations: 820

ENTERTAINMENT

CITY: see University of Manchester
SALFORD:
• Price of a pint of beer: £1.70   • Glass of wine: £1.50
Cinemas: Even Mancunians leave their more local cinemas to come to the eight-screen multiplex at Salford Quays.
Pubs: The real Coronation St has been demolished long since, *but the spirit of 'The Rover's Return' continues in many a local, although many are quite rough and you don't get Detty's hotpots or Natllle Barnes' warm welcome.* Pushplugs: The Old Pint Pot; The Crescent; The Black Horse; Wallness Tavern.
Food: Pushplugs: *Hanrahan's and Frankie & Benny's at Salford Quays; Punter's Bistro.*

UNIVERSITY:
• Price of a pint of beer: £1.55   • Glass of wine: £1.20
Bars: The Pavilion ('Pav', cap 900) and the Wallness Tavern ('Walley') are the main all-day drinking dens. The Lowry is pretty packed at lunchtimes. There's also the Sub Club Bar, mainly used for ents.
Cinemas: The 'Culture Club' shows the latest mainstream DVDs three times a week. Free entry for members, 50p everyone else.
Clubs/discos/music venues: The Pav is the Union's customised club venue with regular club nights: Tuesday – Flair, Thursday – Destiny and Friday – Top Banana. Live music tends to be local and/or cover bands but Atomic Kitten and er, Chesney Hawks have played here recently.
Food: There's a restaurant, 6 cafeterias and 2 sandwich bars and the bars also do snacky type things. Other grub spots include: the Wallness Tavern and the Pavilion, both offering *cheap and cheerful munchies. While it's not going to earn a Michelin star, the customers seem quite happy with the quality and cost.*

Others: Regular quiz nights, talent spots, live football in the Pav. Also there's a gallery, sometimes exhibiting student work and a campus pottery. Five balls a year.

SOCIAL & POLITICAL

SALFORD STUDENTS' UNION:
• 4 sabbaticals • Turnout at last ballot: 15% • NUS member
The Union's main thrust is its professionally handled services and entertainments. It even has its own company, SUPER Services, which runs the student pub among other things. The SU have been pushing for better sporting facilities while other campaigns have included a health drive against smoking, drinking and lack of exercise. *Yea, right, that's sure to go down well with students.* They also support charities including Children in Need and Breast Cancer Awareness.

SU FACILITIES:
The Union has *felicitous* facilities on three sites and a main Union building, University House. The total gamut of provisions includes: 4 bars and a pub; travel agency; print shop; 3 shops (stationery, groceries and second-hand books); hairdressers; computer shop; opticians; mortgage advisory service *(that's a unique one);* Interflora service; Endsleigh Insurance; disco; cafeterias and snack bars; 2 minibuses (for hire); vending, video and games machines; photo booth; juke box; launderette; TV and function rooms. There's also a HSBC Bank on campus.

CLUBS (NON SPORTING):
Chinese & Hong Kong; Christian; Cyprus; Hellenic; Malaysian; Rag; Singapore; Theatre; Turkish.

OTHER ORGANISATIONS:
The Union publishes the *better than average* weekly newspaper, 'Student Direct'. MSTV is the campus television station. The charity Rag is part of MUSA (the umbrella spongers for all Manchester's universities). The Community Services Group involves a *healthy* 200 or so students in a range of local help projects and has a permanent member of staff.

RELIGIOUS:
• 4 chaplains (CofE, RC, Methodist, URC)
There is a chaplaincy in the main lecture hall building, a Muslim prayer room on campus and Manchester's two rabbis act as chaplains to Jewish students in the area.

PAID WORK: see University of Manchester
The jobshop has part-time and casual vacancies within the University as well as Salford and Manchester.

SPORTS

• Recent successes: hockey, squash
While Salford may not be nationally famous for its sporting record, enthusiasm and facilities are above average. A campaign by the students successfully won them floodlights for their playing fields while an on-going SU-led campaign is plugging away for even more sports stuff.

SPORTS FACILITIES:
There's a leisure centre right next to the Union building including a

gym, sports hall, multi-gym, four squash courts and a snooker room. Oh, and the *best* student climbing wall in the country. On the campus, there are floodlit playing fields and all-weather pitches including astroturf; new swimming pool with sauna, jacuzzi and sunbeds. The Union employs an Outdoor Pursuits Officer who takes responsibility for encouraging involvement in the kinds of sports which make thermal pants popular, like canoeing, mountaineering and so on.

SPORTING CLUBS:
Caving; Climbing; Fencing; Kung Fu; Motor; Paintball; Parachuting; Scuba; Shooting; Tai Chi; Water Polo; Wing Chun.

ATTRACTIONS: see University of Manchester

ACCOMMODATION

IN COLLEGE:
• Catered: 2% • Cost: £71-81 (33wks)
• Self-catering: 22% • Cost: £39-51 (39-50wks)

Availability: None of the accommodation blocks is too far from the campus. All 1st years who apply in time are guaranteed accommodation and, if self-catering, there's a choice of blocks of rooms, blocks of flats, courts of blocks of flats or rooms and the large Student Village (1,612 places in terraced single sex houses on the old race course at Castle Irwell). Catered accommodation is available at Peel Park. Nobody has to share. *Security is very tight* with security guards, barriers and regular patrols conspicuous on campus.

Car parking: Although a permit is needed, *there's generally adequate free parking around the student accommodation.*

EXTERNALLY: see University of Manchester
Students who can't find anything closer than Eccles are not looking hard enough. The Union-run Accommodation Office can help students find housing with a vacancies board and newsletter. *Avoid Ordsall and Higher Broughton.*

WELFARE

SERVICES:
• Nightline • Lesbian & Gay Society • Mature SA • Overseas SA
• Minibus • Equal Opportunities Officer • Self-defence classes

The Union runs its own advice centre with a visiting solicitor every Thursday. The University Health Centre has male and female doctors, 3 nurses as well as 3 full-time counsellors. Overseas students can turn to the Overseas Student Secretary or the University's Overseas Students Counsellor for problems which relate particularly to them.

Disabled: All new buildings have ramps and *facilities are improving gradually.* There's a Learning Support Co-ordinator who helps with special needs.

FINANCE:
• Hardship fund: £873,468 • Successful applications: 577

Scarborough University College
see Other Institutions

School of Economics
see LSE

School of Oriental & African Studies
see SOAS

School of Pharmacy, London

- **The College is part of University of London and students are entitled to use its facilities.**
The School of Pharmacy, 29 Brunswick Square, London, WC1N 1AX.
Tel: (020) 7753 5831. Fax: (020) 7753 5827.
E-mail: registry@ulsop.ac.uk
School of Pharmacy Student Union, 29 Brunswick Square, London, WC1N 1AX. Tel: (020) 7753 5809.

Close to Russell Square, ¾ mile from Trafalgar Square, is the School of Pharmacy, an *attractive* brown brick building with *huge imposing windows and an art deco interior in the main entrance. The atmosphere is as much like a school as a university college. There is a strong work ethic and the really wild social animals have to look to ULU or UCL for a crazyfest. There's an unusually high proportion of women for a science-based college and there are also lots of students of Asian origin.* The nearest tube station is Russell Square (Piccadilly line) and Euston, King's Cross & St Pancras stations are all pretty close. Bus nos 17, 45, 46, 68 and 168 pass near by. Bike stands are provided *but the traffic is mad and the NCP car parking that is available is very expensive and the Uni offers nada.*

Sex ratio(M:F): 40%:60%	Founded: 1842
Full time u'grads: 550	Part time: 0
Postgrads: 85	Non-degree: 0
Ave course: 4yrs	Ethnic: 85%
Private school: 30%	Flunk rate: 4.9%
Mature students: 23%	Overseas students: 20%
Disabled students: 1%	Staff/student ratio: 1:13
Clearing: 1%	

The library is *book-worm friendly* (65,000 volumes, 75 study places, 50 computers) but only open weekdays and *computer provision could be better,* though students can use UCL's facilities and the Royal Society in Lambeth. There's no formal careers services although the Registry helps out and London University's facilities are available and there's little unemployment in this sector (1% grads unemployed after 6mths). *Smoky* JCR bar – *you'd think this lot would be anti-nicotine zealots* – open till midnight on Fridays for discos (beer £1.50, wine £2); occasional comedy and jazz but ULU is pretty close; annual formal ball in a posh hotel; boat parties twice a year; popular cafeteria (8.30am-4pm, no food 2-3pm) *serves cheap, institutional food* and is the hang-out for students during the day while the bar's closed. SU (no sabbs, 30% turnout). Games room and limited ents; *completely apolitical stance; surprisingly productive* Rag raises loads of cash for good causes. Playing fields in Enfield (rugby, hockey, football, tennis, netball) shared with the Royal Free Hospital. No accommodation of its own but, with the University's intercollegiate housing, most 1st years from outside London can be housed, along with a *good number of* finalists. Pastoral care scheme run by the Registrar who doubles as Welfare Officer; personal tutors available to give help; other welfare services provided by ULU and the University Health Service; *limited wheelchair access* due to old building *but there are lifts and ramps in places;* Hardship fund £29,500 (78 successful applications); some postgraduate scholarships available.

CLUBS (SPORTING & NON SPORTING):
British Pharmaceutical Student Association (BPSA); Entertainment; Football; Kabbadi.

FURTHER INFO:
Prospectuses covers undergrads and postgrads. Website (www.ulsop.ac.uk).

School of Slavonic & East European Studies
see UCL

Scottish College of Textiles
see Heriot-Watt University

University of Sheffield

The University of Sheffield, 14 Favell Road, Sheffield, S3 7QX.
Tel: (0114) 222 2000. Fax: (0114) 222 8032.
E-mail: ug.admissions@sheffield.ac.uk
University of Sheffield Union of Students, Western Bank, Sheffield, S10 2TG. Tel: (0114) 222 8500. Fax: (0114) 275 2506.
E-mail: union@sheffield.ac.uk

GENERAL

Sheffield, England's fourth largest city, is the closest city to the north-east corner of the Derbyshire Peak District and one of the furthest places from the coast in the whole of Britain. *Most people immediately connect it with the steel industry – knives, forks and razor blades. Fair enough, that's what made the place famous* and, to the east, there's still a *stark* reminder of industrial demise. Now the city is a *busy and bustling but friendly place* with a modern centre and compact Victorian suburbs. The University is 15 minutes walk (1 mile) due west from the city centre on a campus extending over about a mile of buildings massaged into the surrounding urban setting. Almost all the buildings are less than a century old and *have been constructed with some thought and care.* Mostly they're *attractive* redbrick buildings, although there are a few more modern structures – the arts tower and library, which are Grade II listed, are *quite appealing* glass high rises.

Sex ratio(M:F): 50%:50%	Founded: 1905
Full time u'grads: 13,242	Part time: 2,703
Postgrads: 2,513	Non–degree: 0
Ave course: 3/4yrs	Ethnic: n/a
Private school: n/a	Flunk rate: 5%
Mature students: 20%	Overseas students: 16%
Disabled students: 4.45%	Staff/student ratio: 1:13
Clearing: n/a	

ATMOSPHERE:
Nearly quarter of students stay in Sheffield after graduation which can't be bad. That's probably because, unlike some cities, being a student in Sheffield is to 'live' here for three years rather than just 'stay' here. The University accommodation has its limitations in that only a small number live in after the first year so students go out into the community which welcomes them. It also means students form family groups for the purpose of sharing a house, so they form strong friendships. Student life is hectic and full of opportunities – the SU is wide awake – throbbing with a heady mix of town and gown activities. Sheffield has a good cultural and racial mix which is reflected among the students, who willingly jump head-first on to any bandwagon in the belief that their actions might actually make a difference (good for them).

THE CITY:
- Population: 499,700 • London: 147 miles
- Manchester: 35 miles • Birmingham: 67 miles

'WELCOME TO SHEFFIELD, THE HOME OF BRITISH CUTLERY' reads a sign on the outskirts of the city but, *honestly, it's got a hell of a lot more than that, being the cultural core of a wide catchment, offering all sorts of ents and diversions.* Cars are diverted from pedestrian parts of the modern city centre. *It's a hilly, clean, litterless city*, threaded by three rivers. The old industrial area has been redeveloped and Sheffield is *so well set for leisure and sports facilities* that it's now known as the city of sport. The suburbs in the south-west, where the University accommodation is based, were described by John Betjeman as one of 'England's prettiest suburbs'. *As far as amenities are concerned, Sheffield has it all, or almost: local luxuries* like late-night shops, 52 parks, street markets, museums and galleries (the City Museum, the Mappin Art Gallery and so on). Four big bookshops plus many second-hand. *Special mention must go to the vast Meadowhall Shopping Centre, one of Europe's largest. It's known as Meadow-hell to some, but its sheer range and size is astonishing.*

TRAVEL:
Trains: Sheffield Station offers services to London (£27.70), Birmingham (£15.65), Edinburgh (£43.55) and more.
Coaches: Sheffield is served by South Yorkshire Transport as well as National Express, whose services go to London (£14.50), Birmingham (£11.50) and other destinations.
Car: 10 mins off the M1, Sheffield is also visited by the A57, A61, A616 and A631. 20 mins off the end of the M18.
Air: Sheffield's own brand new airport is now open.
Hitching: *For getting out to the M1 a bus is needed, but then*

students can cruise by the rule of thumb.
Local: Local buses run all day and all night and are *frequent, reliable and quite cheap. The local minibuses are even better because they go everywhere. The Supertram is best of all, though, 'cos it's fun and cheap* (£1.90 all-day pass, Megarider seven-day pass £6.30) and the University is on the tram route.
Taxis: *Worthy wheels for after 11pm.* Private companies are cheaper than the black cabs. Either way it's over £1 per mile.
Bicycles: Some *but Sheffield is quite hilly and pedal pinchers prowl.*

CAREER PROSPECTS:
- Careers Service • No of staff: 19 full/8 part
- Unemployed after 6mths: 5.1%

FAMOUS ALUMNI:
Carol Barnes (newsreader); David Blunkett MP (Lab); Stephen Grabiner (Managing Director, Daily Telegraph group); Eddie Izzard (comedian); Amy Johnson (aviator); Harry Kroto (Nobel prize winning scientist); Sir Peter Middleton (Chairman Barclays Bank); Jack Rosenthal (writer); Richard Roberts (another Nobel prize-winning scientist); Helen Sharman (Britain's first astronaut); Ann Taylor MP (Lab); Dave Weatherall (footballer).

FURTHER INFO:
Prospectuses for undergrads and postgrads. Departmental booklets. Further info on the websites (www.shef.ac.uk and www.shef.ac.uk/~union).

ACADEMIC

staff/student ratio: 1:14
Range of points required for entrance: 340-240
Percentage accepted through clearing: n/a
Number of terms/semesters: 2
Length of terms/semesters: 15 wks
Research: 4.9

LIBRARIES:
- Books: 1,300,000 • Study places: 2,230

There are three main libraries and 10 of the 73 departments also have their own mini collections.

COMPUTERS:
- Computer workstations: 1,000+

The computer hardware includes 100 Apple Macs.

ENTERTAINMENT

THE CITY:
- Price of a pint of beer: £1.75 • Glass of wine: £1.85

Cinemas: Four mainstream (The Virgin is one of the largest in the country) and *two less so* (the Showroom and the Union).
Theatres: The Crucible may be famous for the World Snooker Championship, but also features top shows in its main theatre (cap 1,000) and more alternative productions in its studio. The Lyceum also hosts many plays and concerts. Both offer student discounts. There are some smaller community theatres and several arts centres and galleries.

Pubs: With over 500 pubs, café bars and wine bars there's no excuse to go thirsty. The SU runs a couple of pubs itself, but Push would also like to shove in some quick plugs: the Frog & Parrot ('strongest beer in the world'), the Cavendish; Bar Coast, the Forum and the Halcyon (cool-as-fridge pre-club hangouts), and Scruffy Murphy's. Overall, 'Irish' pubs such as O'Neill's are in the ascendant and Devenshire Street and West Street are the areas of biggest concentration.

Clubs/discos: The grooves are cut deep in the streets of Sheffield although the usual mob of lager-swilling bullet-heads might want to get in your way (see 'Mis-Shapes' by local wordsmith J Cocker Esq for full sociological analysis). Pushplugs: Club Wow (free buses courtesy of SU); Step On (indie) at the Leadmill; My Sushi at the Unit; Delirious (happy house) at Niche; Double Decade (retro) at Millionaires; Disco 2000 and Gatecrasher at Republic; and many more...

Music venues: The Arena and Don Valley Stadium deal with the sort of acts *punters are happy to watch through binoculars.* City Hall copes with the mainstream. The Leadmill, the Roundhouse and Hallamshire Hotel are the major indie venues. The Speakeasy and the Legion have local bands while Ecclesall Non-Pots is the local jazz club – *nice.*

Eating out: As might be expected in a place this size, there's the usual range of fast grease franchises and BSE vans until the small hours but Pushplugs for the more discerning budget gourmet go to: Balti King and Butlers Balti Bar; Blue Moon (veggie); Fat Jack's (burgers). The Italian restaurants down West Street are also very popular.

UNIVERSITY:
- Price of a pint of beer: £1.40 • Glass of wine: £1.75

Bars: Bar One is one of the largest student bars in the country. *It's packed out most of the time especially in summer due to its monster beer garden.* The Interval bar is *slightly more laid back* and is marketed as 'an eating and drinking experience'. The SU also runs the Fox & Duck in Broomhill and there are five other bars for gigs and other events.

Theatres: The *busy* University Theatre Company puts on 50 concerts and 15 plays a year in the University Drama Studio (cap 200).

Film: Four films a week in the new 400-seat auditorium – *a good mix of mainstream, old faves and alternative movies.*

Music venues: Concerts are held in the *fantastic* Octagon Centre (cap 1,500) – not only an eight-sided building, *but also an arts venue to run with the best.* Recent names include: Placebo, David Gray, Badly Drawn Boy, Robbie Williams.

Clubs/discos: Five club events a week including the *brazenly naff, astonishingly popular* Pop Tarts retro night, the Massive Loveshack Party Night (chart), Bleach and Fuzzclub (indie). *For those keen to hang onto their cred,* visiting clubs and DJs have included Grooverider, Alex P and LTJ Bukem.

Cabaret: The SU hosts cabaret nights three or four times a term in the Auditorium.

Food: The University-run Food Court supplies *satisfying* school dinners and Bar One has burgers, chips and pizza *while the Interval does posh pasta and salady type stuff.* Loxely's does a *fab* English breakfast for £1.55. These, and the numerous other eateries around the place, offer excellent value.

Other: Balls and annual beer festival.

SOCIAL & POLITICAL

UNIVERSITY OF SHEFFIELD UNION OF STUDENTS:
• 8 sabbaticals • Turnout at last ballot: 12% • NUS member
The SU's facilities are enough to have other unions drooling at the sweetshop window but they don't lounge on their laurels. The exec is efficient and proactive and commited to ethical issues and 'grants not fees'.

SU FACILITIES:
5 bars; 2 pubs; 2 snack bars; pizza kiosk; travel agent; general shop; advice centre; NatWest Bank; Co-op Bank; 5 cash machines; quiet room; study space; Endsleigh Insurance; cinema; sandwich kiosk; café bar; ticket agency; prayer rooms; nursery; studio shop; TV lounge; pool and snooker tables; daily stalls and Thursday market; formal wear hire shop; print shop; computer suite; photocopiers; video games; juke boxes; vending machines; launderette and conference facilities.

CLUBS (NON SPORTING):
Anime Anonymous; Assassins Guild; Ballroom and Latin American; Bond; Catholic Chaplaincy; Chess; Comedy; Debating; Everton Supporters; Hindu; Iranian; Italian; Korean; Malaysian; Mileage Marathon; Medieval; Music; North American; Pagan; Portuguese Speaking; Radio; Real Ale; Sound; Sri Lankan; Star Trek; Student Christian; Turkish; Wargames.

OTHER ORGANISATIONS:
'Steel Press' is the free, fortnightly newspaper published by, but independent of, the SU which also produces the weekly 'What's On'. 'Sure' is the Campus radio station. SHEP (Sheffield Electronic Press) was the UK's first online student newspaper. The Students' Charity Fund has a full-time member of staff and raise whopping amounts of cash. The Student Community Action group is *big*, involving nearly 800 students in all sorts of community work (teaching English, helping the elderly, etc).

RELIGIOUS:
• 8 chaplains
There are centres for both Jews and Muslims in the SU. In town, there is no shortage of places to pray including two cathedrals (Anglican & Catholic).

PAID WORK:
Sheffield may offer a lot of things to students, but employment is often hard to come by. The university jobshop does its best finding vacancies in bars, shops and restaurants.

SPORTS

• Recent successes: too numerous to list
The amenities are possibly the best in the country but the prevailing attitude is that beginners and casual participants should be encouraged as well as thronging supermen and wonder-women. Sheffield is nationally renowned for rock climbing with 4 climbing walls and some of the best crags in England nearby.

SPORTS FACILITIES:
There are 3 world class sports centres in Sheffield: Ponds Forge, offering an Olympic pool, the indoor Sheffield Arena and the Don Valley Stadium. The University's facilities include 2 astroturf pitches,

indoor swimming pool, large sports hall and 40 acres of sports fields. The River Don provides for most water sports with Ogston reservoir (20 miles away) making up the weight. The Peak District covers rambling, mountaineering, caving and all that stuff. *The biggest challenge facing Sheffield students is finding a sport which isn't catered for.*

SPORTING CLUBS:
Athletics; Badminton; Basketball; Diving; Fencing; Golf; Gymnastics; Hang Gliding; High Peaks; Hockey; Jiu-Jitsu; Korfball; Ladies Cricket; Mountaineering; Orienteering; Rowing; Scuba-diving; Skydiving; Ten pin bowling; Walking; Windsurfing.

ATTRACTIONS:
The local football clubs are well known: Sheffield Wednesday and United. Sheffield Eagles (rugby), Steelers (ice hockey), Sharks (basketball), speedway at Owlerton Stadium. Also locally: Europe's biggest dry ski slope, the Peak District for hang gliding, ballooning and rock climbing.

ACCOMMODATION

IN COLLEGE:
• Catered: 21% • Cost: £74-95 (31wks)
• Self-catering: 14% • Cost: £45-58 (38wks)
Availability: Nearly all 1st years live in *but the rapid expansion in recent years has put pressure on this provision.* 17% of the rest of students get places in college, *but they realise the score early on and can start looking at their options.* The halls of residence are collections of large brick buildings each housing between 380 and 670 students in the *leafy* south-west of the city and 20 minutes walk from the University. 4% have to share. There are 183 family flats available and there are also 39 units leased from the city council. The halls at Endcliffe Vale have won awards *but this is scant compensation for the price of a room.* Security is tight on campus with porters, swipe cards and alarm systems at every hall.
Car parking: *Barely adequate (permits for the most needy).*

EXTERNALLY:
• Ave rent: £40
Availability: *There is little difficulty in finding accommodation,* usually in shared terraced houses for four or more, *especially in Crookes, Hunter's Bar, Broomhill, Crookesmoor and Ecclesall Road. Car parking isn't a problem except in the city centre, partly because there's little need for a car to get around.*
Housing help: The University accommodation office does its best to check out houses and match them up with students. The advice centre provides a recommended contract for tenants. Most students use word of mouth, notice boards in the Union and ads in shops.

WELFARE

SERVICES:
• Nursery • Lesbian & Gay Society • Mature SA • International SA • Postgrad SA • Minibus • Women's Officer • Self-defence classes
The SU has 5 full-time advisers while the University employs 3 counsellors. The Health Service employs 4 doctors, 2 nurses and a dentist and has 16 beds and in-patient facilities. There is a student

advice centre and an information and listening service which runs throughout the night.
Women: There's a women-only room, sabbatical officer, subsidised alarms and a women's safety bus.
Disabled: The policy is, of course, to encourage applications from disabled students, *but access is poor and in some cases restricted to certain departments and services.* Sheffield's hills can give wheelchair users the hump, but the Supertram is well equipped for them. The Union is 100% wheelchair accessible though, and the library is well equipped for students with hearing – and sight – impairment. There's a range of services for those with dyslexia.

FINANCE:
- Access fund: £644,000 • Successful applications: 263

Short term loan scheme and trust funds. Hardship funds are available *without too much difficulty* and instalment payment schemes can be arranged for hall fees.

Sheffield City Poly

see Sheffield Hallam University

Sheffield Hallam University

- *Formerly Sheffield City Polytechnic*

Sheffield Hallam University, City Campus, Howard Street, Sheffield, S1 1WB. Tel: (0114) 225 5555. Fax: (0114) 225 2159.
Sheffield Hallam University Union of Students, Nelson Mandela Building, City Campus, Pond Street, Sheffield, S1 2BW.
Tel: (0114) 255 4111. Fax: (0114) 255 4140.
E-mail: hallam-union@shu.ac.uk

GENERAL

Sheffield Hallam's main site is built around a glass atrium on the City Campus with 2 other campuses in town. Different departments are based at *each site and each is pretty much self-sufficient.* Students don't need to hop constantly between sites *but it's not that difficult to do.* Applicants should check on which site their course would be based.

Sex ratio(M:F): 55%:45%	Founded: 1969
Full time u'grads: 15,510	Part time: 2,849
Postgrads: 4,693	Non-degree: n/a
Ave course: 4yrs	Ethnic: 13.5%
Private school: n/a	Flunk rate: 15.2%
Mature students: 60%	Overseas students: 7.9%
Disabled students: 2%	

ATMOSPHERE:
The proportion of mature and local students gives a special flavour to

the student body: Sheffield's their home patch – they don't need to prove anything to anybody and they enjoy themselves how they blimmin' well want. Meanwhile, many courses involve placements, which make a change from academia and keep students' livelier interests alive.

THE SITES:
City Campus: (most subjects and SU) Main city centre site, at Pond Street.
Collegiate Crescent: (health, education) The second largest site with 3,500 students, green space and a mix of buildings. The Union runs a shop in the Pearson Building. Also sports facilities, 3 halls (housing 520 students) and 65 houses.
Psalter Lane: (cultural studies, art, design, film) This is a little community of over 2,000 students, *generally artists and weirdos (the two are far from exclusive)*, 3 miles from City Campus. It has a Union Bar and a few facilities, including a library and a hall (cap 300) for discos.

TOWN: see University of Sheffield

TRAVEL: see University of Sheffield
Campuses are close enough to walk between but there is also well served public transport between most of them.

CAREER PROSPECTS:
- Careers Service • No of staff: 5 full/7 part
- Unemployed after 6mths: 7%

FAMOUS ALUMNI:
David Kohler (footballer); Bruce Oldfield (fashion designer); Nick Park (animator, 'Wallace & Gromit', *big cheese*); Howard Wilkinson (FA bigwig and ex-England coach for a week).

FURTHER INFO:
Prospectuses for undergrads, postgrads, part-time and mature students from the Customer Services Office; free CD-Rom, website (www.shu.ac.uk).

ACADEMIC

Many courses include a year's placement for work experience and the University offers more sandwich courses than any other.

staff/student ratio: 1:16
Range of points required for entrance: 280-140
Percentage accepted through clearing: 25%
Number of terms/semesters: 2
Length of terms/semesters: 16 wks
Research: 3.3

LIBRARIES:
- Books: 549,000 • Study places: 1,950

Very good library and computer facilities. There's a library on each site with a 'Learning Centre' (the Adsetts Centre) at City Campus including TV recording studios, photography units and lecture theatres. The Collegiate Crescent Campus Learning Centre has recently been expanded and modernised.

COMPUTERS:
- Computer workstations: 800

ENTERTAINMENT

TOWN: see University of Sheffield

UNIVERSITY:
- Price of a pint of beer: £1.20 • No wine, stick to beer

Bars: (3) The main union bar is The Hub. The Cooler Bar in the union is mainly a snack bar during the day and is non-smoking during this time. The Furnace is used for comedy nights and other small events. The Works (cap 1,000) opens for bigtime ents.

Clubs/discos: The Works hosts club nights across the board, Stardust (60s, 70s etc), Rollercoaster (mainstream), Lyrics 2000 (international), Dissolution (goth), Ballistic (alternative rock and big beat).

Music venues: The Works has recently hosted Trevor Nelson, True Steppers and the Dream Team

Food: The Union's main food stop is Hub Grub and there's The Full Works *where the chip butties come particularly recommended*. The Uni runs three cafés: The Cutting Edge (continental), The Heartspace Bar (healthy) Tappers Snack Bar (salads).

Others: Annual Graduation, School and Sports Balls.

SOCIAL & POLITICAL

SHEFFIELD HALLAM UNIVERSITY UNION OF STUDENTS:
- 6 sabbaticals • Turnout at last ballot: 12% • NUS member

Student interest in SU affairs is on the rise, no doubt helped by recent high profile incidents like the 'can't pay, won't pay' campaign for free education. The Union are also campaigning against what they call NUS bureaucracy.

SU FACILITIES:
4 bars; 1 cafeteria; 3 snack bars; photo booth; shop; Endsleigh Insurance office; travel agency; disco; gay room; ticket office; video games; minibus hire; vending machines; photocopier; function rooms.

CLUBS (NON SPORTING):
African Caribbean; Alchemists; Chinese; Computer and Internet; Debating; Drama; Degree Show Catalogue; Environmental; Ekistics (art); Entropists (physics); Halo Art; Hellenic; Hindu; Islamic; International; Jewish; Law; Malaysian; Overseas Chinese; Role-Play; SHUXI (catholic); Student Industrial; SWSS.

OTHER ORGANISATIONS:
'S-Press' is the SU run magazine. More than 500 students get involved in direct community help through the Community Action group. *The group is nationally renowned* and even employs a professional support worker.

RELIGIOUS:
- 2 chaplains

A network of associate chaplains and religious advisers are available from Sheffield's religious communities.

PAID WORK: see University of Sheffield
There is a Network-Student Employment Service at the City Campus

SPORTS

- Recent successes: rugby, volleyball

Participation, facilities and the silverware collection are more than adequate, if slightly overshadowed by the other University in town.

SPORTS FACILITIES:
The University relies on the hire of local amenities (see Sheffield University), *but it also has a fair few facilities of its own for a range of indoor and outdoor sports, 3 fitness suites, 2 fitness studios, squash courts, tennis, astro-turf pitch, 23 acres of playing fields and 3 sports halls. For £40 a year students have access to all the University's facilities.*

SPORTING CLUBS:
Aikido; American Football; Board Sailing; Circuit Training; Fitness Assessments; Lacrosse; Rowing; Self Defence; Table Tennis; Water Skiing; Weight Training; Yoga.

ATTRACTIONS: see University of Sheffield

ACCOMMODATION

IN COLLEGE:
- Catered: 7% • Cost: £60-77 (33wks)
- Self-catering: 13% • Cost: £60-77 (39wks)

Availability: At the moment 80% of 1st years can be housed. 20% of 1st years who want to, can't. The halls are outside the city centre and some have been purpose-built (modern brick – *boring but comfy enough*). Most rooms are single and the halls are mixed. Most of the self-catering accommodation is in converted houses or recently converted or constructed complexes in and around the city centre. Some spaces are reserved for single-sex groups. One conversion, Truro Works, boasts its own pub and car hire centre. Good security with night porters, CCTV, security patrols and 24-hour telephone helpline. A new 800 space hall is planned.
Car parking: *Permits required for limited parking.*

EXTERNALLY: see University of Sheffield
Housing help: The University runs the Accommodation Office and advice service with 7 full-time staff. Packed notice boards and contract negotiation.

WELFARE

SERVICES:
- Creche • Lesbian & Gay Society • Mature SA • Overseas SA
- Postgrad SA • Minibus • Women's Officer • Self-defence classes
- Nursery

The Union Advice Centre and Financial Support Office offer free help to students. The University employs 6 counsellors and the Union 3 advisers. At the City Campus there is a student health centre with 3 doctors and a number of nurses. There are also daily surgeries at 2 sites.
Women: There's a sabbatical officer, a group, a room and a priority minibus. Women-only fitness sessions twice a week.
Disabled: *Most of the more modern buildings (including the Union) have excellent access and there is some assistance available. The*

welfare unit gives out financial advice, the specialist disability team, advice and support. The University sets out to recruit a minimum number of disabled students per year. Special facilities for hearing-impaired students.

FINANCE:
• Access fund: n/a   • Successful applications: 1,691
Hillsborough Trust memorial bursaries, international prize, scholarships and hardship funds. Also a loan of £50 cash or food vouchers is available in extreme emergencies to be repaid as soon as possible.

Shrivenham
see Cranfield University

Silsoe
see Cranfield University

Slavonic & East European Studies
see UCL

• **The College is part of University of London and students are entitled to use its facilities.**
School of Oriental & African Studies, Thornhaugh Street, Russell Square, London, WC1H 0XG. Tel: (020) 7637 2388.
Fax: (020) 7436 3844. E-mail: registrar@soas.ac.uk
SOAS Students' Union, Thornhaugh Street, Russell Square, London, WC1H 0XG. Tel: (020) 7580 0916. Fax: (020) 7636 8376.
E-mail: sunion@tropicalstorm.com

SOAS is part of the central complex of London University in Bloomsbury, *which makes it convenient for students wanting to wallow in the luxury of the* University of London Union's (ULU's) *services*. Directly over the road is the University's Senate House and Birkbeck College is just round the corner. The whole caboodle is on the roads parallel to Tottenham Court Rd, bang in the middle of London. SOAS itself is a 30s brick building, *hyper-depressingly uniform* and overshadowed by the vast Brunei Gallery opposite, a gift from the *well-loaded* Sultan of Brunei. It's not called the School of Oriental & African Studies for nothing and courses all concentrate on subjects that fit the description. It was originally a training ground for those about to go off to look after the British Empire, *but the general tone now is definitely post-Imperial and right-on, although not as much as some students would wish.*

SOAS 570

Sex ratio(M:F): 50%:50%	Founded: 1916
Full time u'grads: 1,460	Part time: 0
Postgrads: 1,500	Non-degree: n/a
Ave course: 3yrs	Ethnic: 60%
Private school: n/a	Flunk rate: 29.3%
Mature students: 45%	Overseas students: 40%
Disabled students: n/a	

ATMOSPHERE:
SOAS is small enough for everyone to know everyone else, by sight at least. There's a wide mix of religious and ethnic backgrounds, a fascinating example of multi-culturalism. ULU offers an escape from the potential pressure cooker, as well as being the main facilitator of extra-curricular activity.

THE CITY: see University of London

TRAVEL: see University of London

CAREER PROSPECTS:
• Careers Service • No of staff: 3 full • Unemployed after 6mths: 7%

FAMOUS ALUMNI:
Zeinab Badawi (newsreader); Jomo Kenyatta (ex-President of Kenya); Enoch Powell (former MP); Paul Robeson (singer); Princess Sirindhorn of Thailand.

FURTHER INFO:
Undergrad and postgrad prospectuses, video, website (www.soas.ac.uk), also (Union website www.soasunion.org.uk).

ACADEMIC

staff/student ratio: 1:12
Range of points required for entrance: 340-220
Percentage accepted through clearing: 0
Number of terms/semesters: 3
Length of terms/semesters: 10 wks
Research: 6

LIBRARIES:
• Books: 900,000 • Study places: 600
The main library is *impressive* (housing a *well-stocked* section on Oriental and African music), *though provision for undergrads is a source of much complaint, as is the overall organisation of the library.* Many departments have their own smaller libraries.

COMPUTERS:
• Computer workstations: 150

ENTERTAINMENT

IN LONDON: see University of London

COLLEGE:
• Price of a pint of beer: £1.70
Bars: (1) *During the day, the bar is relaxed and informal and provides a good melting pot for all the varying cultures at the university. Evenings are a dead loss as it shuts up shop at 8.30pm but what the*

hell, the whole of London's out there.
Clubs/discos/music venues: The bar (100), the Assembly Hall (500) and the SU building (250) host the occasional bands.
Food: *The JCR Snack Bar is the best value* but there's also a Refectory, another snack bar and a posh café in the Brunei Gallery.
Others: Many of the international student clubs provide ents which attract many people from outside college. There have been Indonesian Gamelan recitals, Laotian dancing, an African drum and dance group, Capoeria shows, Ghanian drumming, food and music evenings and so on, plus 2 or 3 balls a year.

SOCIAL & POLITICAL

SOAS STUDENTS' UNION:
• 2 sabbaticals • Turnout at last ballot: 40% • NUS member
The SU has endured rather poor relations with the college authorities after being rapped on the knuckles and losing its bar. Nor is it on best buddies terms with its own students, who view the SU with distrust. Recent campaigns have included the anti-UCL merger (or collaboration) campaign, the Stephen Lawrence report demo and a free education campaign *but even these have failed to whip up any semblance of wide support.* However, election turnouts show that at least the students feel something – even if it's only disgruntlement.
Also ULU: see University of London.

SU FACILITIES:
A shop; snack bar; newspaper outlet; creche; jukebox; pool tables; games machines.

CLUBS (NON SPORTING):
Arab; Black and Proud; Chinese; Indian; Indonesian; Pakistan; Palestinian; Thai; Korean; South African; Burma, Vietnamese, Buddhist meditation, Pakistan, Model United Nations.

OTHER ORGANISATIONS:
'The New Spirit' is published independently, a website and radio station are at the planning stage.

RELIGIOUS:
• 2 chaplains (CofE, RC)
Muslim prayer room.

PAID WORK: see University of London

SPORTS

• Recent successes: nothing special
Budget and facilities are scarce – there are squash courts and a gym, but most make use of ULU. *The emphasis is on sport for enjoyment but most students find that anyway in their fags and beer.*

ACCOMMODATION

IN COLLEGE:
• Self-catering: 23% • Cost: £85 (30wks)
Availability: SOAS has an allocation of University of London places, which means that 50% of 1st years and 20% of other students can be housed. *Accommodation can seem prison-like, with the addition that it's expensive,* much like a prison, except unlike a real prison it's

expensive to its inhabitants, not the tax payer.
EXTERNALLY: see University of London
Housing help: The Student Accommodation Adviser helps those with roof-over-head related traumas and there's always ULU.

WELFARE

SERVICES:
• Lesbian & Gay Society • Mature SA • Overseas SA • Minibus
• Women's Officer • Self-defence classes

The college offers 2 part-time counsellors, the Union one full-time.
Disabled: New Disabilities Officer has *improved things. Physical access is okay, but there are a lot of annoying little oversights. For instance, library shelves are too high for students in wheelchairs and you need to get a key from the porter to use the modified toilets.*
Drugs: CCTV and undercover police have been introduced to help in toning down SOAS's reputation as a soft drugs den.

University of Southampton

University of Southampton, Southampton, SO17 1BJ.
Tel: (023) 8059 5000. Fax: (023) 8059 3037.
E-mail: prospenq@soton.ac.uk
Southampton University Students' Union, Highfield, Southampton, SO17 1BJ. Tel: (023) 8059 5200. Fax: (023) 8059 5252.
E-mail: pres@soton.ac.uk

GENERAL

The chunk of the southern coast that fell off and became the Isle of Wight left a hole which was filled by a channel of water called The Solent. In the niche on the mainland to the north of the Solent is Southampton. During the 2nd World War the Luftwaffe decided to pay a visit and drop a few hundred tonnes of explosives all over the place. Despite destroying just about everything else, the bombs somehow managed to miss most of the 12th-century city wall and various other historic relics. The University – *typical of the rest of the city* – has redbrick buildings that survived the war, along with post-war geometric blocks that won awards in the 60s and *look pretty cruddy now,* mostly on a landscaped campus, 2 miles from the city centre. The main site is dotted with *bizarre Henry Moore-style* sculptures. (Some actually are by Henry Moore.)

Sex ratio(M:F): 48%:52%	Founded: 1952
Full time u'grads: 12,803	Part time: 869
Postgrads: 2,290	Non-degree: 0
Ave course: 3/4yrs	Ethnic: 2.5%
Private school: n/a	Flunk rate: 9.7%
Mature students: 21%	Overseas students: 8%
Disabled students: n/a	

ATMOSPHERE:
It's probably fair to say that white, English, middle-class students aren't exactly thin on the ground. This doesn't, of course, mean that people who don't fall into these groups will come to any grief – indeed on arrival at Southampton students tend to turn into unpretentious, vaguely scruffy types no matter what their background.

THE SITES:
Boldrewood: (1,000 students – medicine) Less than a mile from the main campus is this large, *squat Lego-box* building. *Even though it's within easy walking distance this is a separate community where the student medics make their own entertainment.*
Southampton Oceanography Centre: (600 – School of Ocean and Earth Science) A purpose-built site taking advantage of Southampton's natural environment. It's 3 miles from the main campus but there's a regular shuttle bus service.
Avenue Campus: (3,000 – Faculty of Arts) New development, a short walk from the main campus, served by the uni-link bus service, housing most arts students, except musicians and...
Winchester School of Art: (1,000 art students) This member of the Southampton family merged with the University in August 96. It's in the historic city of Winchester (12 miles from Southampton) and maintains its own separate identity, but is well served by the uni-link bus creative and predominantly female.

THE CITY:
• Population: 194,400 • London: 74 miles • Portsmouth: 16 miles
Southampton used to revolve around its port, *but since its pretty functional reconstruction after the war it's become a city that's there simply because a lot of people were all in the same place at the same time. The centre is thoroughly modern and great for loan-losing sprees. But Southampton has more to recommend it than the opportunity to buy anything from a continental quilt to those things you put eggs in to boil them in a microwave.* There is a *small bohemian* quarter with *good* pubs and shops, and the outlying districts are *quaint and worth exploring* for cream teas and antiques. The town boasts a *very good* music and book library, various supermarkets and a few late night shops around the student areas. The docks are being developed and are *worth a look.* The city contains many parks, archaeological digs and 5 museums of varying size and obscurity of content. *Rumours that this is a cultural desert are probably put around by jealous people from Bognor or snooty Londoners. They're not to be believed.*

TRAVEL:
Trains: Southampton Central offers services to London (£15.45), Bristol (£19.80), Manchester (£38.60) and others.
Buses: National Express services all over the country, including London (£9.50), Manchester (£26.50) and all points beyond.
Car: The A27 splits for a brief spell into the M27 and the continuing A27 around Southampton. There's also the A31, A33, A36 and A336 and the M3.
Air: Flights inland, to Europe, Ireland and the Channel Islands from Southampton Airport.
Ferries: To France, the Isle of Wight and the Channel Islands.
Hitching: *Good prospects to London, Oxford, the Midlands and Wales from the petrol station at the end of the A33. The Union also offers a lifts board for cadging off other students.*

Local: *Buses are cheap and reliable, but infrequent.* Local trains are *regular* with connections all over Hampshire and there are 7 stations around the city, *but it's not the cheapest or most practical way of getting around.* The University has its own bus service, 'uni-link', linking the city and the campuses.
Bicycles: *Good cycling, despite a couple of big hills.*

CAREER PROSPECTS:
- Careers Service • No of staff: 5 full/3 part
- Unemployed after 6mths: 7.6%

FAMOUS ALUMNI:
Roger Black (athlete turned BBC athletics commentator); John Denham MP (Lab, ex-SU President); Jeremy Hardy (comic); John Inverdale (BBC TV/radio sports presenter, the new Des Lynham); Jenni Murray (Radio 4, Woman's Hour); Chris Packman ('Really Wild Show'); John Sopel (BBC correspondent); Kathy Tayler (ex-athlete, TV non-personality); Lord Tonypandy (former speaker of House of Commons).

FURTHER INFO:
Prospectuses for undergrads, postgrads and part-timers and a website (www.soton.ac.uk).

ACADEMIC

staff/student ratio: 1:14
Range of points required for entrance: 340-240
Percentage accepted through clearing: 5%
Number of terms/semesters: 2
Length of terms/semesters: 15 wks
Research: 4.8

LIBRARIES:
- Books: 1,000,000+ • Study places: 1,921

7 libraries – the main one is the Hartley Library in the centre of the campus. *Facilities are considered fair to good, with very good opening hours.*

COMPUTERS:
- Computer workstations: 900+

ENTERTAINMENT

CITY:
- Price of a pint of beer: £1.80 • Glass of wine: £1.30

Nightlife is dominated by the vast Ocean Village complex but there's plenty of other fun for the more discerning student. Latest addition to Southampton's scene is Leisure World incorporating a cinema, clubs and a bowling alley – beware of teenagers, well, those wearing white trainers and trackie bottoms.
Cinemas: (3) A 7-screen multiplex at Ocean Village. New 14-screen multiplex at Leisure World.
Theatres: (3) The Nuffield specialises in modern drama, the Mayflower in the touring blockbusters and the Gantry in arty and experimental theatre.

Pubs: *A wide selection,* many with extended opening. *Pushplugs: Hobbit; Gordon Arms; Talking Heads; The Hogshead and Hedgehog; Greenhouse; O'Malley's; The Mitre. The Stoneham Arms is best avoided.*

Clubs/discos: Southampton is trying to shake off its reputation as 'the arse end of our dance nation' ('Sky' magazine) and has a fair few nights to satisfy even the more trend-conscious booty-shaker. Ocean Village is a mainstay of mainstream glitz and Leisure World has added two new clubs. *Pushplugs: Academy, Ikon, Magnum, Kaos (pop/chart); Rhinos, University of Sound, Menage-a-Trois at the Chantry (house/garage/techno).*

Music venues: The Joiners for middling indie, The Gantry for jazz and folk and The Mayflower and the Guildhall for bigger names.

Eating out: *Apart from several excellent pub-lunchy type places, Pushplugs: Boozy Rouge, Bon Gusto (French/Italian); New Orleans (cajun); Rose of India; Mustang Sally's; Fatty Arbuckles.* There are also some *bearable* restaurants in the Ocean Village development. The kebab shops in Bedford Place keep on turning till 4am.

Others: The 'Bitterne Bowl' has hi-tech ten pin bowling and you can zap your pals at the Quasar Studio at Ocean Village.

UNIVERSITY:
- Price of a pint of beer: £1.32 • Glass of wine: 70p

Bars: (6) The main Union Bar (cap 400) is *fairly pubby*. There's also a sports bar with board games and *Twister for those who need to flex their competitive instincts.* The bar at the School of Art at Winchester has just been refurbished with rubbish skips and there are 3 additional University-run bars.

Theatres: (3) Two of the theatres are temporary spaces used for between 1 and 3 weeks a term. The third is The Nuffield, a professional theatre used once a year by students. There are regular trips to Edinburgh.

Cinemas: 6 movies a week are shown by the award-winning Union Films Society with *extremely cheap* admission, only £10 for the whole year. It's a *very active* club with regular cult movie nights and there are film-making opportunities as well.

Clubs/discos/music venues: The University's largest venue is the West Refectory (800) but the Bar and the Ballroom (400 each) can cope with smaller events. 1 or 2 club nights a week, cover the spectrum from indie to jungle. Recent live appearances include Terrorvision, Space, N-Trance, Alison Limerick, Embrace and Catatonia.

Cabaret: Most Sundays, there's a comedy gig on the go.

Food: The Union runs the coffee bars and Gordon's, *offering excellent quality and VFM (value for money).* The University's refectories are good on the quality and selection front (Chinese, Indian, Vegetarian) but portions are small, prices high. The Piazza does *good value* food, mostly pizza, jacket potatoes, burgers and chicken.

Other: At least 7 annual balls.

SOCIAL & POLITICAL

SOUTHAMPTON UNIVERSITY STUDENTS' UNION:
- 5 sabbaticals • Turnout at last ballot: 15% • NUS member

The Tories are the largest society and although the majority of students prefer their conservatism with a small 'c', Southampton *isn't the ideal place to foment a proletarian uprising. The Union is trying valiantly to shake out the apathy but it's like trying to jumpstart a tub of butter.*

SU FACILITIES:
Dry cleaners; hairdressers; guarded cloakroom; lockers; photo booth; pottery studio; minibus; 2 bars; café; cheap driving school; showers and baths; launderette; market stalls each Monday; sports equipment and hire service; Lloyds Bank with cashpoint; TV rooms; Interflora; darkroom; meeting rooms; customised disco; ballroom; retail centre with a shop; travel agency; and sports shop.

CLUBS (NON SPORTING):
Well over 100 including: AIESEC; Archaeology; Afro Caribean; Art; Asian; Astronomical; Buddhist; Concert Band; Hellenic; Hindu; Juggling; Lodge; Malaysian; Massage; Radio; Singapore; Students Against NUS; Students For NUS; Wessex Films; Wine; Women's Safety.

OTHER ORGANISATIONS:
The SU produces the 'Wessex Scene' newspaper. New College publishes 'Disclosure'. Other campus media includes the Glen Eyre Hall radio station and 'Wessex Films' which makes films and documentaries. Rag raised £15,000 last year. The Community Interaction group runs 12 local projects from helping disabled kids to soup kitchens.

RELIGIOUS:
- <u>3 chaplains (CofE, RC, Free)</u>

There's a chapel for regular worship or private hire. Muslim prayer room in the Union. Just about every religion is catered for in Southampton.

PAID WORK:
The University-run job shop 'Openings' places students with part-time and temporary work. The boat show in summer offers some opportunities not available elsewhere.

SPORTS

- <u>Recent successes: hockey, sailing, polo</u>

The SU President says 'sport for all', unfortunately some students say 'elitist and cliquey'. Having said that, the University enjoys sports successes on a regular basis. There are good facilities for most activities on or near the campus.

SPORTS FACILITIES:
On campus there's a large sports hall, multigym, 6 squash courts, climbing wall (outdoors), judo room, table tennis, aerobics room, tennis courts, snooker room and after all that, an injuries clinic. Off campus there are 90 acres of playing fields, a rifle range and a boatyard. The city adds a golf course, dry ski slope, bowling green and a cycle track.

SPORTING CLUBS:
Aikido; American Football; Baseball; Boat; Boxing; Caving; Equestrian; Frisbee; Gliding; Gymnastics; Hang Gliding; Hung Leng Kuen Kung Fu; Jiu Jitsu; Kick Boxing; Lacrosse; Life Saving; Mantis; Motor; Mountain Bike; Mountaineering; Ninjutsu; Orienteering; Parachute; Polo; Pushing Hands; Rambling; Rifle; Rollerblading; Shorinji Kempo; Shotokai Karate; Shotokan Karate; Snooker; Surf; Table Tennis; Ten Pin Bowling; Triathlon; Volleyball; Water Polo; Waterskiing; Weightlifting; Windsurf.

ATTRACTIONS:
Southampton FC, *Saints to their friends, Scummers to others,* will never again be relegated from the Dell, coz they've moved to a

spanking new stadium, *who's name has far too many syllables.* There's also Hampshire County Cricket ground. Cowes Week, when lots of people go messing about in boats on the Solent, is one of the major events of the sailing calendar, *but, sadly, few cows attend – can they swim?*

ACCOMMODATION

IN COLLEGE:
- Catered: 9% • Cost: £74-93 (39-50wks)
- Self-catering: 31% • Cost: £39-61 (30-50wks)

Availability: Almost all 1st years live in, but very few others can. 7 of the 17 halls are catered (13 meals a week), just under a mile from the campus. The kitchens in the self-catering halls are shared by between 6 and 20 students. All halls are mixed, but sexes are split into floors or corridors according to each hall's layout. 6 halls are en suite. 69 flats are available for families or couples. *All the rooms are broadly similar with basic furnishings and fittings.* Security is tight with CCTV, keypad entry systems, night patrols, mobile security and wardens. *Students who think the grass is significantly greener on the other side of the hall fence can switch without hassle.*

Car parking: Permit needed, 1st years not allowed cars.

EXTERNALLY:
- Ave rent: £40

Availability: *It's very easy to find accommodation – two days search max to find somewhere (if it takes longer, don't come crying to us). Good standard housing can be found, particularly around Portswood, Highfield and Inner Avenue, within staggering distance of the best student pubs. Avoid Bassett Green and Bitterne which are less welcoming than the Strangeways reception committee. Students should also avoid letting anyone convince them to sort it out too long in advance. Landlords shove up prices and charge for renting over the summer. It takes guts, but this is the time to wait and hold on till the landlords are a little more anxious to fill their places – don't worry, there are enough.*

Housing help: The University Accommodation Office in Winchester is developing a full private rented sector property service. In Southampton all landlords are asked to produce safety certificates before they can have their property advertised. The Union has a vacancies board.

WELFARE

SERVICES:
- Creche • Nightline • Lesbian & Gay Society • Mature SA
- Overseas SA • Postgrad SA • Minibus • Women's Officer
- Outreach SA • Self-defence classes

For all manner of problems, SUSU has a Student Advice & Information Centre and the University runs a counselling service with 1 full- and 5 part-time counsellors who not only arrange help on a individual basis, but also run group sessions on study skills, relaxation and so on. There are 2 University health centres with psychotherapists and 5 doctors running various clinics for family planning and sports injuries. Nursery has places for 68 little ones, students need not apply. There is an eating disorders support group and SUSU gives

attack alarms to students, as well as running a Night Bus.
Disabled: *Access is improving all the time.* Most buildings have lifts and there's a residential hall for students who need care assistance. There are a number of specialist computer workstations with equipment for students with a variety of disabilities. The Learning Differences Clinic provides support for students with dyslexia.

FINANCE:
- Access fund: £672,000 • Successful applications: 1,458

In addition to the access fund, the University runs a hardship fund for people whose circumstances change mid-course. SUSU also gives short-term emergency loans.

Southampton Institute of Higher Education

Southampton Institute, East Park Terrace, Southampton, SO14 0YN.
Tel: (023) 80 319000. Fax: (023) 80 222259.
E-mail: er@solent.ac.uk
Southampton Institute Students' Union, East Park Terrace, Southampton, SO14 0YN. Tel: (023) 80 232154.
Fax: (023) 80 235248.

GENERAL

Southampton is one of the largest and most important cities on the south coast with a history firmly rooted in maritime trade. Although it was bombed heavily by *Fritz* in 1940 there remains much of the medieval town including most of the 12th-century city wall and medieval timber-framed buildings. There is much to explore in the surrounding area – the Isle of Wight is only a short ferry hop across The Solent, to the south; to the west lies the *ancient* New Forest which covers an area of 145 sq miles; beyond the forest is the city of Bournemouth, which includes an *excellent* sandy beach; to the north lies the ancinet cathedral towns of Salisbury and Winchester; and to the east lies Portsmouth and the South Downs. The Institute is located at a modern campus in the heart of Southampton. The campus is expanding fast and is now the largest HE institution that still isn't a university (or part of one). The second site is 9 miles up the coast at Warsash.

Sex ratio(M:F): 58%:42%	Founded: 1984
Full time u'grads: 7,930	Part time: 420
Postgrads: 288	Non-degree: 3,542
Ave course: 3yrs	Ethnic: 8%
Private school: 7%	Flunk rate: n/a
Mature students: 46%	Overseas students: 9%
Disabled students: 7%	

ATMOSPHERE:
The Institute is busy and friendly and a bit less cramped than it was. The students are a good friendly mix, from crazed skateboarders to

mature returners to education, all united in a vocational dream. Despite the size of the place, everyone seems to know everyone else.

WARSASH SITE:
This site is a 20-acre campus with about 800 undergraduates and its own pier. An old naval college was based here, overlooking the River Hamble in a *beautiful* landscaped setting, *quietly tucked out of town.* Departments of maritime study and engineering are based at this site, *which is essentially self-contained and maintains a completely separate existence from the main site.* Entertainment is lacking and regular trips into town are needed to stave off boredom, unless you enjoy talking to old people about their time in the navy.

THE CITY: see University of Southampton

TRAVEL: see University of Southampton

CAREER PROSPECTS:
• Careers Service • No of staff: 3 full/1 part
• Unemployed after 6mths: 5%

FURTHER INFO:
General and part time prospectuses, free video, website (www.solent.ac.uk).

ACADEMIC

Southampton Institute feels that it really should become a university. So much so that *it received a rap across the knuckles for describing itself as such in an advert a couple of years ago.*

staff/student ratio: 1:21
Range of points required for entrance: 260-140
Percentage accepted through clearing: 18%
Number of terms/semesters: 3
Length of terms/semesters: 11 wks
Research: 2.2

LIBRARIES:
• Books: 175,000 • Study places: 1,113
The Mountbatten Library and Design Library are on the city campus. Warsash houses the *best* nautical/maritime library in the country.

COMPUTERS:
• Computer workstations: 600
The Mountbatten Library has a new IT suite.

ENTERTAINMENT

TOWN: see University of Southampton

INSTITUTE:
• Price of a pint of beer: £1.50 • Glass of wine: £1.50
Bars: There are three bars, one on top of the other, each with a capacity of 750. Biffa's and Bilbo's have DJs. The Brass Tap is a sports bar *and the beer's better.*
Clubs/discos/music venues: Two free club nights a week, open DJ spots and karaoke. *Quite a few decent acts* such as Terrorvision, Louise, Artful Dodger and The James Taylor Quartet have stopped off here recently.

Food: Bilbo's dishes out breakfast, lunch and tea at *rock-bottom prices*. The Institute refrectory serves up the usual refectory nosh.
Others: The SU organises five balls a year.

SOCIAL & POLITICAL

SOUTHAMPTON INSTITUTE STUDENTS' UNION (SISU):
• 5 sabbaticals • Turnout at last ballot: 10% • NUS member
SISU has facilities in the Student Union building on the main site and in another small building at Warsash. *Student officers are basically apolitical and the students themselves are apathy personified. Not even the merest sniff of a recent campaign.*

SU FACILITIES:
City: 3 bars; 4 minibuses for hire; advice centre; 2 shops (books, stationery, sweets); cash machines (Barclays, NatWest); photo booth; games and vending machines; pool tables; juke boxes; 2 meeting rooms; satellite TV. **Warsash:** Shop; bar; refectory.

CLUBS (NON SPORTING):
2d Painting; Hindu; Karting; Postgrad; Record; Roleplay; Sculpture.

OTHER ORGANISATIONS:
'Havit' is a three-weekly mag. 'Sin Radio' broadcasts one month of the year. There's a student community organisation (arranging youth clubs, decorating flats and helping at local special needs schools).

RELIGIOUS:
• 1 chaplain (Anglican)
A prayer room is available for all denominations.

PAID WORK:
There's the usual jobs offered by the SU such as bar work and stewarding, plus a jobshop on campus. Also see University of Southampton.

SPORTS

• Recent successes: windsurfing, sailing
Overall participation is greater than the somewhat thin facilities might suggest.

SPORTS FACILITIES:
Main site: Sports hall; a health suite; sailing facilities; fitness centre; multigym; circuit training; 12 acres of playing fields 3 miles away; use of squash and tennis courts. **Warsash:** Small sports hall; multigym; sailing/water sports on the Hamble and Itchen.

SPORTING CLUBS:
Lacrosse; Snowboarding; Surfing; Windsurfing.

ATTRACTIONS: see University of Southampton

ACCOMMODATION

IN COLLEGE:
• Self-catering: 29% • Cost: £40-77 (39-48wks)
Availability: 60% of 1st years are accommodated *but the large proportion of local and mature students means that this is pretty*

much everyone who wants it. Tight security with wardens, CCTV's and code entry systems. *The newer halls appear to be pretty good although they're very expensive. It can actually be cheaper to live out.*
Car parking: With a permit (£215/year).

EXTERNALLY: see University of Southampton
Students tend to gravitate to the Polygon/Bedford Place area of the city to live. It's safe and lively and contains clubs, bars and restaurants. It's also only 10 minutes from the Institute.
Housing help: The Institute has a huge Accommodation Office with 14 full-time staff, providing a vacancies notice board, safety checks, emergency housing and listings.

WELFARE

SERVICES:
• Lesbian & Gay Society • Mature SA • Overseas SA • Minibus
• Women's Officer • Self-defence classes

The Institute has four full-time counsellors. There is an NHS medical practice near the city campus and a visiting nurse. Warsash has its own nurse and visiting doctor. Each site has a 'student assistance base' to provide help with revision, time management and other study problems.
Women: Free attack alarms and self-defence classes.
Disabled: 75% of the Institute is wheelchair accessible. There are specialist IT equipment, induction loops and a Disabilities Co-ordinator. A dyslexia tutor is also available.

FINANCE:
• Access fund: £852,000 • Successful applications: 1,000
The SU provides hardship loans up to £30 and the Principal's Discretionary Fund (£10,000) lends £150 to students waiting for their loans to arrive.

South Bank University

• *Formerly South Bank Polytechnic*
South Bank University, 103 Borough Road, Elephant & Castle, London, SE1 0AA. Tel: (020) 7815 8158. Fax: (020) 7815 8273.
E-mail: registry@sbu.ac.uk
South Bank Students' Union, Keyworth Street, Elephant & Castle, London, SE1 0AA. Tel: (020) 7815 6060. Fax: (020) 7815 6061.

GENERAL

Southwark, in south London, is not London's most beautiful borough. And the Elephant & Castle, 2½ miles from Trafalgar Square, is not Southwark's most beautiful part. It is grey and drab until the garish red shopping centre assaults your gaze. Apart from the precinct, the Elephant consists of 2 large roundabouts, surrounded by an indoor leisure pool, the enormous Metropolitan Tabernacle Church and various offices, shops and a halfway house for released criminals.

But it's not all urban psychosis – the South Bank complex, a honeytrap for culture cravers, is within walking distance and some of the local residential areas are very upwardly mobile. The main site of South Bank University is just north of the Elephant, there's another site on the Wandsworth Road, just under 3 miles away. It houses the faculty of the Built Environment, *but doesn't set a very good example, looking rather like a big breeze-block.*

Sex ratio(M:F): 49%:51%	Founded: 1970
Full time u'grads: 8,600	Part time: 1,200
Postgrads: 1,000	Non-degree: 3,500
Ave course: 3yrs	Ethnic: 50%
Private school: n/a	Flunk rate: 29.8%
Mature students: 38%	Overseas students: 20%
Disabled students: 3%	

ATMOSPHERE:
Once you've shown your pass to get inside, South Bank is smart, upbeat and busy. Students, many of whom are returning to education, are down to earth and realistic – this is gritty south London stuff and they're proud of it. The University has a strong cosmopolitan flavour with a broad ethnic and social mix so, in theory at least, nobody should feel out of place. It has been expanding, so resources are starting to feel the pinch.

THE CITY: see <u>University of London</u>

ELEPHANT & CASTLE:
The Old Kent Road costs just £60 on a Monopoly Board and is the cheapest property available. It starts at the Elephant & Castle. *This tells you something about the area.* The roundabouts are among the *busiest* London has to offer. Within a stone's throw there are shops and more shops, a council estate and some *quite nice* Georgian terraced streets. *Local communications are good, for those who can find them.* The BR train connection involves a walk via the upstairs of the red shopping centre and the tube is hidden in a *cave-like* entrance. The whole area's scheduled for *fairly awesome* redevelopment and by 2015 *it might be quite nice.*

TRAVEL: see <u>University of London</u>
Local Trains: Elephant & Castle (ThamesLink) or for a mainline station, Waterloo.
Buses: Numbers 3, 44, 12, 45, 59 and 68 pass nearby the main site. College minibus runs every ½ hour between sites.
Underground: Elephant & Castle (Bakerloo, Northern Lines).

CAREER PROSPECTS:
- <u>Careers Service</u> • <u>No of staff: 7 full/3 part</u>
- <u>Unemployed after 6mths: 15%</u>

FAMOUS ALUMNI:
Ben Arogundade (editor, 'Extract'); Jimeoin (comedian); Norma Major (former PM's wife); Umer Rashid (cricketer); Greg Searle (Olympic oarsman).

FURTHER INFO:
Undergraduate and postgrad/post-experience prospectuses.
Free video. Website (www.sbu.ac.uk).

ACADEMIC

Most courses have a vocational element and there are close links with business and industry.

staff/student ratio: 1:17
Range of points required for entrance: 240-140
Percentage accepted through clearing: 30%
Number of terms/semesters: 2
Length of terms/semesters: 15wks
Research: 2.9

LIBRARIES:
- Books: 300,000 • Study places: 1,500
4 libraries in all.

COMPUTERS:
- Computer workstations: 950

The Learning Resource Centre on Borough Road runs IT courses available to all students. *Computer facilities are a bone of contention, not nearly enough terminals and even those available are always breaking down.*

ENTERTAINMENT

IN LONDON: see University of London

ELEPHANT & CASTLE:
Avoid the Elephant & Castle. The Goose & Firkin, J D Wetherspoons and Ruby Tuesdays are safer options. There's the IMAX cinema, the NFT and all the other attractions of the South Bank arts complex, including The National Theatre and Royal Festival Hall. For music lovers, the Brixton Academy, the Fridge and the Vox are just a couple of miles down the road and Ministry of Sound is around the corner. *There are many good, cheap cafés around this part of London and some of the ones around the South Bank arts complex are excellent.*

UNIVERSITY:
- Price of a pint of beer: £1.50 • Glass of wine: £1

Bars: (6) The most popular bars are in the SU at Keyworth Street. Upstairs is the Tavern which is *pubby, smoky and backgammony,* while downstairs is the Isobar *in resplendent* chrome. Union bar on Wandsworth Rd near main Southwark Campus. The Arc has a late licence twice a week.

Clubs/discos/music venues: The Isobar is the SU venue, while the Arc is run by the University. There are 2 club nights a week (Wednesdays disco, Fridays karoke and student DJs), and monthly specials (like Raise the Roof – garage or Blackpepper – rap). Recent visiting DJs have included Renagade, Drez and Lisa Pinup and there's the occasional unknown band (recently Brit Connection, Rollercoaster).

Food: There are canteens and snack bars all over. The Tavern is *tops* for snacks, the Isobar for fast food and there's the European Coffee Lounge in Borough Road. *But the best bet for actual sustenance is the refectory.*

Others: 2 balls a year and at least 2 mirth-makers a term.

SOCIAL & POLITICAL

SOUTH BANK UNIVERSITY STUDENTS' UNION (SBUSU):
• 5 sabbaticals • Turnout at last ballot: 20% • NUS member
SBUSU has had a hard few years, what with political in-fighting, limited resources and even limited interest from the student body who feel they should do more on the ents side. The SU has attempted to woo students back with recent campaigns, the student charter and the Wednesday timetable campaign.

SU FACILITIES:
6 bars; cafés; 3 shops; HSBC Bank; Endsleigh Insurance; Campus Travel; recreation and common rooms.

CLUBS (NON SPORTING):
Chinese; Friends of the Earth; Gaelic; Industrial; Law; Music; Secret Jazz.

OTHER ORGANISATIONS:
The SU magazine, 'Scratch' comes out monthly. The Rag is under serious review and nothing is planned for this year.

RELIGIOUS:
• 2 chaplains (CofE, RC)
Catholic masses held on site. Muslim prayer room. Religion in London: see University of London

PAID WORK: see University of London

SPORTS

• Recent successes: hockey, football
Interest in all things sporting have increased with the establishment of an AU.

SPORTS FACILITIES:
The 21-acre fields in Dulwich offer: 4 football; 2 rugby and 3 cricket pitches; a bar; pavilion; changing facilities and new scrummage machines. At the other 2 sites there is a sports hall, gymnasium and weights. A swimming pool is planned.

SPORTING CLUBS:
Aikido; Chinese Boxing; Dominos & Games; Jiu Jitsu; Paintballing; Hang-gliding; Mountain Biking; Self Defence; Surfing.

ATTRACTIONS:
The Elephant & Castle pool is too small for any serious swimming (unless treading water becomes an Olympic event) but is excellent fun with slides and a wave machine. The huge plastic elephant in the middle of the pool, unsurprisingly, causes problems. The Oval Cricket Ground is within a bowling distance of the Elephant.
Sports in London: see University of London.

ACCOMMODATION

IN COLLEGE:
• Self-catering: 16% • Cost: £64-78 (42wks)
Availability: *Housing is not a serious problem,* since the majority of students are already sorted, though 5% of those who want to live in can't. Places are distributed according to who lives furthest away.

New accommodation opening soon (late 2001). The prices are high (you can get a better deal locally) *and there's been a fuss over room priority for foreign students.* There are security gates, 24 hour wardens and site managers at all halls.
Car parking: Limited, *to say the least.*

EXTERNALLY: see University of London
Availability: *It's easier to find accommodation in South London than north of the river (The Thames) and it's cheaper. Camberwell, Kennington and Peckham are popular although some streets and estates are a little dodgy.*
Housing help: The *excellent* service offers 3 housing advice workers to help with house hunting. There are daily accommodation vacancy lists, often as long as 70 pages.

SERVICES:
• Creche • Lesbian & Gay Society • Overseas SA • Postgrad SA • Women's Officer

The University employs 2 full- and 2 part-time counsellors and an adviser and the Union has an Advice Bureau with 3 full-time advisers. All students have personal tutors assigned to them. 2 full-time nurses work on site in term-time.
Disabled: *Access is not very good* and only the Union building has ramps to the entrance and lifts. A booklet is available, 'Enabling You'. There are induction loops plus a Dyslexia Support Group.
Women: There's always a female member of the welfare team available.

FINANCE:
• Access fund: £750,000 • Successful applications: 1,500
The University distributes a charitable fund of £12,000, mainly to those who wouldn't otherwise get financial assistance, such as part-time and overseas students, *but that kind of amount doesn't go very far.* The Access fund offers £100 awards. Student Services also provides a Money Management Guide and gives out £50,000 in Fee Remissions so that those who pay their own tuition costs can finish their courses.

South West Poly
see University of Plymouth

    Students at Lancaster claim that Alex Square
    on campus is named after Alex 'Hurricane'
    Higgins the bad boy of snooker. Sadly, it's
    really named after Princess Alexandria, the
    University Chancellor.

Staffordshire University

* *Formerly Staffordshire Polytechnic*

(1) Staffordshire University, College Road, Stoke-on-Trent, ST4 2DE.
Tel: (01782) 294000. Fax: (01782) 745422.
E-mail: admissions@staffs.ac.uk
Staffordshire University Union of Students, College Road,
Stoke-on-Trent, ST4 2DE. Tel: (01782) 294629.
Fax: (01782) 295736. E-mail: theunion@staffs.ac.uk
(2) Staffordshire University, Beaconside Campus, Stafford,
ST18 0AD. Tel: (01782) 294000. Fax: (01782) 745422.

GENERAL

Staffordshire University is named after the county not the town of Stafford – students might find themselves in either of two towns depending on where their course is based. Stafford is one of them and Stoke the other and *never the twain shall meet. They may as well be separate institutions, having their own identities and loyalties. Both look down on the other,* but what they have in common is that they are towns in the north-west Midlands, 17 miles apart. The Stafford campus is on a greenfield site in the outskirts of the small and *pretty* county town. It is a former technical college made of 1960s concrete. *It's a bit bleak in winter, but great for lazy days in summer marred only by the looming doom of exams.* The Stoke part of the University is on two sites at College Road and Leek Road in the town centre of Stoke-on-Trent. *Leek Road has more of the feeling of a self-contained campus with playing fields and accommodation on site.*

Sex ratio(M:F): 53%:47%	Founded: 1970
Full time u'grads: 9,787	Part time: 5,192
Postgrads: 1,784	Non-degree: 4,255
Ave course: 3yrs	Ethnic: 11%
Private school: n/a	Flunk rate: 15.4%
Mature students: 29%	Overseas students: 2.6%
Disabled students: 0.8%	

ATMOSPHERE:
Many students are on part-time or professional courses and the University as a whole is developing very rapidly. *Stoke and Stafford have totally different atmospheres despite plucky attempts by the University to unite them: Stoke is proactive and radical, while Stafford is dominated by male engineers with more interest in study and beer than anything more creative or political.*

THE SITES:
Stoke: (11,345 students – social sciences, business, art & design, sciences, law) 2 sites of tightly packed post-war buildings. *They have less of the closeness of a community than Stafford although the snack bars are busy and bustling.*
Stafford: (5,066 students – engineering, computing, business, health) *The site is small and students mix between subject groups and across other boundaries often imposed elsewhere. It can get claustrophobic since there's nowhere much to escape to.*

Staffordshire

STOKE-ON-TRENT:
- Population: 244,800 • London: 165miles
- Birmingham: 44miles • Manchester: 38miles

Stoke has suffered for the last couple of decades from urban decline and the closure of many local industries, *but never mind, it's also the hometown of Anthea Turner and Robbie Williams.* In Hanley, there is a fair-sized shopping centre and Festival Park, once the site of the National Garden Festival, an *excellent* swimming pool and various other attractions. *Most Stoke students love it, but they didn't apply for the scenery – whoever painted this place forgot to wash his brush out between colours.* See also Keele University.

STAFFORD:
- Population: 117,000 • London: 131miles • Birmingham: 32miles

Stafford is a market town. The livestock has all gone though and been replaced by an indoor market instead. There are *a couple of pleasant streets, but much of the town has been ruined by a blight of town planning.* A new complex of shops near the church has brought in *more attractions for trendy young things.*

TRAVEL:
Trains: Stafford and Stoke are on the Merseyside and Manchester services to London (£19.45). The main Stoke site is right next to the station.
Coaches: National Express services from both towns include London (£12) and more.
Car: The M6 and A34 connect the 2 towns. Stafford is also served by the A518 and A513. The A50 provides handy links to Derby and Nottingham.
Hitching: *In Stoke a hike may be hitched from the nearby ringroad and the M6 provides a launch pad for both towns.* The University and SU discourage this, though, for safety reasons.
Local: The University runs a free minibus between sites 6 times a day but priority goes to staff and it's impossible to get to a 9am lecture. *The 20-minute train journey might offer better odds.* Local buses run by the bizarrely named PMT are also handy and cheap.
Taxis: *With many firms working in both towns, prices are competitive. Some offer student discounts which is worth remembering for late nights.*
Bicycles: *For those with thighs like tree trunks, or consciences like Greenpeace activists, bikes are useful.*

CAREER PROSPECTS:
- Careers Service • No of staff: 4 full/10 part-time
- Unemployed after 6mths: 7.2%

SPECIAL FEATURES:
- Any student under 21 who is resident in Staffordshire, Shropshire or Cheshire is guaranteed an offer, provided they meet the normal entry requirements.
- Staffordshire recently became the first University in the UK to open an Art Gallery in New York, which the kids in Stoke and Stafford will doubtless appreciate enormously.

FAMOUS ALUMNUS:
Jim Davies (auxiliary Chemical Brother).

FURTHER INFO:
Prospectuses for undergrads, postgrads and part-timers. Also a video guide and website (www.staffs.ac.uk/welcome.html).

ACADEMIC

staff/student ratio: 1:21
Range of points required for entrance: 280-160
Percentage accepted through clearing: 5.7%
Number of terms/semesters: 3
Length of terms/semesters: 12wks
Research: 2.2

LIBRARIES:
- Books: 314,811 • Study places: 1,331

3 libraries: Leek Rd, College Rd and Beaconside (Stafford). *There's a severe lack of books and limited opening times at the weekends means there's a Friday stampede.*

COMPUTERS:
- Computer workstations: 2,420

Computing facilities at Stafford are excellent.

ENTERTAINMENT

TOWNS:
- Price of a pint of beer: £1.80 • Glass of wine: £1.40

Pubs: Stafford has a slight edge on Stoke as far as variety goes. Most pubs are student-friendly but the general rule is, the closer to the University, the safer. Pushplugs: Stoke: The Terrace; Fawn & Firkin; Corner Cupboard; the Roebuck. Stafford: Bird in Hand; Hogs Head; Telegraph; Wagon & Horses; Potterhouse.

Cinemas: Two in Stoke (9 screen Odeon and 3 screen Cannon), one in Stafford.

Theatres: The Royal in Hanley, the Stoke Repertory Theatre, the New Vic in Newcastle-under-Lyme near Stoke and the Gatehouse in Stafford *are the prime spots for luvvie-viewing.*

Clubs/discos: *The University is probably the best place for serious clubbing but Pushplugs go to the Sugarmill on Fridays and Swoon (hardcore rave) at the Void (Stafford).*

Music venues: The Sugarmill, the Royal and the Victoria Hall (Hanley) all have *decent* touring indie bands stopping off. *Nothing to speak of in Stafford but the Talbot pub in Stoke has regular local or up and coming bands.*

Eating out: *Not a bad selection, especially for curry-nuts.* Pushplugs: Al Sheikh's (balti); Shaka's (Indian); Dylan's (veggie).

UNIVERSITY:
- Price of a pint of beer: £1.20 • Glass of wine: £1.10

Bars: 4 SU-run bars. The Leek Road Venue doubles as the prime ents venue; the green-and-blue Odyssey (cap 500) at College Road is an alternative. Stafford has Sleepers (350), the day-to-day boozer, and Legends (550), a nightclub bar.

Cinemas: The Stoke regional film theatre on the College Road site puts on 3 films a week of a art/culty nature. The Stafford campus has a Cult TV society that 'unofficially' shows films.

Theatre: The *small but moderately active* drama society puts on 2 productions a semester and a panto a year, helped, no doubt, by the drama and theatre arts course.

Clubs/discos: *Club highlights include Scandal Wax (jungle/funk) at*

the Odyssey, Shag on Fridays at Leek Road and the monthly Clock (breakbeat/funk) at Legends. Guest DJ's like Danny Rampling have appeared at Leek Road.
Music venues: All the bars double as venues of some description but Leek Road is the obvious choice for major acts. Recent bands: Shed Seven, Lightning Seeds and Space.
Cabaret: Every Thursday Odyssey is turned over to the funnyfolk.
Food: The SU and University compete for the tastebuds of students across the sites. There are *traditional* refectories as well as the Universe-City fast food operation (Leek Road) and the *smart* Terrace Café and American Graffiti for fast food (Stafford). The bars can also fill an 'ole.
Others: Jazz nights and quiz nights have been introduced at the Odyssey and apart from club and society dos there are 3 major events crammed together at the end of the year – the May, Summer and AU balls.

SOCIAL & POLITICAL

STAFFORDSHIRE UNIVERSITY UNION OF STUDENTS:
• 7 sabbaticals • Turnout at last ballot: 11% • NUS member
University, Union and student body appear to operate on a level of mutual respect; the University consults the SU on all main developments while the SU focuses most of its attention on providing for its students. It's just one big love-in.

CLUBS (NON SPORTING):
Art About; BABS; Computer; Classic Cars; Cult TV; Environmental Protection; Ernest Borgnine Film Society; HIV/Aids Awareness; Hard Rock Beer Drinking; Kebab; Krishna; Malaysian; Melvyn Bragg; Multicultural; Northern Bastards; Pagan; Performing Musicians; Role-Playing; Star Trek; Swinging Sculptors; Vampire; Vinyl Only; Wargames; Welsh.

OTHER ORGANISATIONS:
The 'Get Knotted' newspaper has twice been shortlisted for a 'Guardian' award. The radio station Zone has been granted a licence to broadcast 28 days a year.

RELIGIOUS:
The University has a Christian Chaplaincy and both towns have churches for all the main denominations. A Muslim prayer room is available at Stafford and there are places of worship in Stoke for Jews, Muslims, Hindus and Sikhs.

PAID WORK:
Locally there's the usual kind of shop work and the University hires students for work such as mailing and decorating. Union Ents employs 100 students.

SPORTS

• Recent successes: rowing, cross country
Sport is a major preoccupation for some. A Sport & Recreation degree is offered at Stoke and consequently, the facilities are much better than at Stafford. There are small charges for some of the newest facilities (eg 50p).

SPORTS FACILITIES:
Stoke: 40 acres of fields; 5 floodlit synthetic pitches; sports hall; squash courts; activities studio; fitness suite.

Stafford: 30 acres of fields; 2 synthetic pitches; sports hall; squash court; fitness suite.

SPORTING CLUBS:
American Football; Boxing; Equestrian; Lacrosse; Parachute; Power Lifting; Rollerskate; Rowing; Table Tennis.

ATTRACTIONS:
Stoke City FC (*City were good for about 5 mins in the 1970s*); Port Vale FC; Crewe Alexandra FC; Uttoxeter Race Course; Northwood Stadium for international athletics.

ACCOMMODATION

IN COLLEGE:
• Self-catering: 15%   • Cost: £27-56 (40wks)
Availability: Half of the 1st years can be housed, but still very few from other years. 10% of new undergrads don't get a place, but many of the local, mature and part-time students aren't interested anyway. At least 5% have to share a room. The University runs a head tenancy scheme offering 30 places. Even though the accommodation is self-catering, for an extra £20 a week all meals can be provided. *Security is good* with 24-hours security patrols and wardens. All residences are floodlit.
Car parking: There are limited spaces, but at least it's free. Permits are needed in Stoke.

EXTERNALLY:
• Ave rent: £36
Availability: Hanley and Shelton are popular areas for Stoke students and Highfields is convenient for the Stafford site. Stafford is marginally more expensive than Stoke but still very affordable.
Housing help: Each site has an Accommodation Office which keeps registers of landlords.

WELFARE

SERVICES:
• Nurseries • Nightline • Lesbian & Gay Society • Mature SA
• Overseas SA • Women's Officer • Disability Officer
• Self-defence classes

There is a University-run counselling service with 2 full- and 3 part-time helpful counsellors and a student advice centre run by the Union which gives advice on almost anything. There's also an on-site GP, a harassment network and legal advice.
Women: There's a Women's Group and free attack alarms.
Disabled: *Access is excellent in Stoke and in Stafford it's vastly improved* (new lifts, etc). 19 rooms are adapted for mobility-impaired students, 12 rooms have trembler alarms for hearing-impaired students and every reception area has minicom phones. Main lecture theatres have induction loops with portable loops in smaller rooms. A support team is available on 24-hour call and a support worker scheme provides non-medical care for students with disabilities.

FINANCE:
• Access fund: £524,248   • Successful applications: 267

University of Stirling

University of Stirling, Stirling, FK9 4LA. Tel: (01786) 467046.
Fax: (01786) 446800. E-mail: s-c-liason@stir.ac.uk
Stirling University Students' Association, SUSA office, The Robbins Centre, University of Stirling, Stirling, FK9 4LA. Tel: (01786) 467166.
Fax: (01786) 467190. E-mail: susa-president@stir.ac.uk

GENERAL

Stirling is nestled in the centre of Scotland, surrounded by the Highlands and Trossachs. The castle, on a cliff face, dominates the landscape and was the royal home in Scotland until 1600. Much of the historic architecture survives in the Old Town. The University is 2 miles out of town and, like Stirling itself, is small. The students, who account for 1 in 8 of the local population, have a campus reputed to be the second most beautiful in Europe. *Which begs two questions: which is the most beautiful? and how do you measure?* It's set in 350 acres of landscaped grounds, complete with Airthrey Castle (another castle - *the place is plagued with them*), a golf course and a loch with a bridge, separating the residences from the academic buildings and providing a home for wild fowl *and a fun feature for wild students. The University buildings are less impressive than the setting, apart from the castle* which is used by University departments and offices. Most of the buildings are grey or white flat-topped oblongs, usually 3 or 4 floors high, but shaded with trees, *they blend in somehow.* Meanwhile, the towering Wallace Monument (dedicated to William 'Braveheart' Wallace) presides over the goings on. (*Note to high-jinx students/Mel Gibson fans: the monument could do with a bit of blue face paint.*)

Sex ratio(M:F): 42%:58%	Founded: 1967
Full time u'grads: 5,538	Part time: 849
Postgrads: 723	Non-degree: 1,300
Ave course: 4yrs	Ethnic: n/a
Private school: n/a	Flunk rate: 14.9%
Mature students: 13%	Overseas students: 3%
Disabled students: 4%	

ATMOSPHERE:
There's a busy, bustling feel to the place, as if everyone knows exactly where they're going, although they're always prepared to take a detour for a coffee (read beer) and a slice of gossip (read preferred sex). The campus is self-sufficient and the relatively small student body is cosy and welcoming. As a result many students rarely feel the need to leave.

THE SITES:
There are two other sites which are both part of the Department of Nursing and Midwifery.
Highland Campus: (370 students) On the outskirts of Inverness in the grounds of Raigmore Hospital is the medical school. There is a regular bus service into Inverness.

Western Isles Campus: (60 students) *Somewhat isolated* (you can only reach it by boat), this site is a part of Lewis Hospital in Stornoway on the island of Lewis. Its purpose is to serve the Western Highlands and almost all students are locals.

THE TOWN:
- Population: 35,000 • London: 378 miles • Glasgow: 27 miles
- Edinburgh: 33 miles

The University is placed between a very small town, Bridge of Allan, and Stirling itself. Lots of 17th- and 18th-century architecture, craft and antique shops *give Stirling that historical feel.* There's also an indoor shopping centre and all the essential shops. *It has a small town atmosphere (maybe because it is).*

TRAVEL:
Trains: Stirling Station, 2 miles from the campus, has direct services to London (£47.25) and Edinburgh (£3.15) which is a good place to change for most Scottish destinations.
Coaches: National Express services to London (£16), Edinburgh (£5), Newcastle (£12.50) and all points beyond.
Car: Just off the A9 and M9.
Hitching: *Fairly easy to Edinburgh, if you start from the outskirts of town.*
Local: *A cheap bus service runs till midnight between the campus and the town centre, but the timetables appear to have been created by someone with a somewhat tenuous grasp on reality.*
Taxis: Stirling is a *taxi-infested* town, but they're no cheaper than most places (£2.50ish city–campus).
Bicycles: *Except for the strong wind and rain there are no good reasons why students shouldn't cycle. Then again, there's no good reason why they should (except – cheap, green transport, fun, keep fit – enough).*

CAREER PROSPECTS:
- Careers Service • No of staff: 4full/3part
- Unemployed after 6mths: 5.3%

FAMOUS ALUMNI:
Iain Banks (writer); Michael Connarty MP, John Reid MP (Lab); Stuart Hepburn, Shelley Jofre, Andrew Miller (TV personalities); Shirley Standstead Tarquin-Scrot (fisherman); Tommy Sheridan (poll tax campaigner); Gordon Sherry (golfer). The current rector is ex-Avenger Diana Rigg aka Emma Peel.

FURTHER INFO:
Prospectuses for undergrads and postgrads, course leaflets, website (www.stir.ac.uk).

ACADEMIC

Stirling was the first UK university to operate a semester system where there are 2 terms (semesters) of 15 weeks each year. There's also a continuous assessment policy. Both these ideas have been taken up by many other universities since.

> Liverpool University awarded Arthur C Clarke an honorary degree by satellite link to Sri Lanka.

staff/student ratio: 1:10
Range of points required for entrance: 300-220
Percentage accepted through clearing: 10%
Number of terms/semesters: 2
Length of terms/semesters: 15 wks
Research: 4.3

LIBRARIES:
• Books: 500,000 • Study places: 1,000
Main library and Pathfoot education library (5,000 books). Facilities are *good if a little congested.*

COMPUTERS:
• Computer workstations: 950
24 hour access, *handy for doing an essay the night before.*

TOWN:
• Price of a pint of beer: £1.70 • Glass of wine: £1.75
Before you judge harshly, remember Edinburgh and Glasgow are only an hour away.
Cinemas: 1, Alm Park with 2 screens, *but it's not up to much.*
Theatres: 2 theatres providing anything from panto to opera.
Pubs: Quite a few are tolerant of, even friendly to students, but some, such as the Rob Roy and the Caperceidlh, *deserve a wide berth.* Pushplugs: The Meadow Park; Hog's Head; O'Neill's; Courtyard.
Clubs/discos: A couple of *tacky* clubs in town. *The FU Bar and Rocks have student nights on Thursdays.*
Music venues: Stirling Council have finally realised that castles can be fun. Stirling Castle now hosts open air concerts, recently Ocean Colour Scene, with more planned. Several pubs have folk nights and the Albert Bar hosts jazz.
Eating out: The best food in town is probably to be found in the pubs but there's the standard range of Indian, Italian and fast food feeders as well. Pushplugs: Pacos; Smilin' Jack's (both Mexican); Littlejohns (American); Riverhouse (*classy joint owned by Carol Smiley's husband*); The Bistro.

UNIVERSITY:
• Price of a pint of beer: £1.50 • Glass of wine: £1.10
Artistic yearnings tend to be focused on the MacRobert Arts Centre, *a cultural nexus for aesthetes from all over central Scotland, when it's not showing blockbusters, that is.*
Bars: (6) In the Robbins Student Centre there's a choice of floors upon which to fall face down (remember the recovery position – *nothing to do with sex*): the Alehouse (*rustic/pubby,* no music); Shankies (disco bar, events-driven); Long Bar (newly refurbished); Maisies (*good food*); the refurbished *but still sweaty* Gannochy (sports bar) and the new Cocktail Lounge.
Cinemas: The MacRobert Arts Centre on campus shows 2-4 films a week, *from Jackie Brown to Chitty Chitty Bang Bang.*
Theatres: The drama society put on productions in Stirling's Tollbooth Theatre. The MacRobert has a *very well-equipped* 450-seat theatre and smaller studio (140), both open to the people of Stirling as well as students. It has performances from touring companies rather than student productions.

Clubs/discos: New *'state of the art'* club Glow, also Shankies which plays party host 3 times a week: Weds Stomp (Drum and Bass); Fri (60s/70s/80s music) and Indie or dance on alternating Saturdays.
Music venues: Robbins, the small bar (cap 200) and the Union bar throb with the vibes of mostly cover bands, but also original bands including Freestylers, Dan Bailey and Idle Wild. The MacRobert hosts classical and jazz nights.
Food: McBob, the university canteen, serves *unexciting but cheap* grub. The Alehouse does pies, Oscars does snacks, Julienne's Vegetarian Café at the Gannocky Sports Centre does – you guessed it – veggie food.
Others: The Freshers Week Four Pack allows students to choose 4 events on the MacRobert programme for only £10. There are also 3 balls a year and the *anarchic* 'Final Fling'.

SOCIAL & POLITICAL

STIRLING UNIVERSITY STUDENTS' ASSOCIATION:
• 4 sabbaticals • Turnout at last ballot: 15% • NUS member
After a spell of frost, relations between the SA and the University administration are quite positive again. Political interest is on the up – Labour is the dominant political group with a substantial SNP presence. Recent campaigns have included a free education demo and a referendum on NUS membership – 74% voted in favour.

SU FACILITIES:
6 bars, 3 serving food; a disco; general shop; academic support centre; photocopying; photo booth; 2 meeting rooms.

CLUBS (NON SPORTING):
Birding; Chinese; Film Circle; Hellenic; Japanese; Laughing Fiddler; Maisie's Fold Music; Malaysian; SNP; Strategy Games; Tap and Dance; Wildwatchers.

OTHER ORGANISATIONS:
There's a monthly student paper, 'Brig', that is independent but works with the Union. SUSA runs Airthrey 963 which is Scotland's only campus radio station. It broadcasts daily from 11am to 11pm. The resurrected Rag holds events like a raft race across Loch Ness, a bean-eating contest using tooth picks and a slave auction conducted by rector, Diana Rigg.

RELIGIOUS:
• 6 chaplains (Baptist, Methodist, Anglican, RC, Congregationalist, C of S)
There's a Christian chaplaincy on campus and a Muslim prayer room. In town there are 9 holy watering holes for those thirsty for Christianity. There's a Jewish chaplain in Glasgow.

PAID WORK:
Usual stuff in Stirling, but limited. During vacations, try Glasgow or Edinburgh, a daily train journey away. Within SUSA, there's bar work and the University sometimes needs gaps filled in the library.

SPORTS

• Recent successes: Women's hockey, basketball
Stirling offers a successful sports bursary scheme, which has brought many honours to the University, although the campus isn't infected by the insanely competitive zeal that occurs in some other

successful universities. Nevertheless sport is part of everyday life on campus. One of SUSA's 4 sabbaticals runs the Sports Union which offers *excellent* sports facilities, including the loch, *which, although it's mainly there to look pretty, does very well for canoeists, sailors, anglers and skinny dippers (actually it's a bit too chilly for that).* The Scottish National Tennis Centre is also on campus. At the last Commonwealth Games, the University had 8 students in competition for medals.

SPORTS FACILITIES:
23 acres of playing fields; sports hall; squash courts; athletics field; loch; croquet lawn/bowling green; swimming pool (new Olympic pool under construction); tennis courts; all-weather pitch; multigym; running track; 9-hole golf course; sauna & solarium. Jogging routes are situated around the campus. The town adds a curling and skating rink, ten pin bowling and the River Forth. Skiing facilities are close by.

SPORTING CLUBS:
Aikido; American Football; Croquet; Gaelic Football; Lacrosse; Mountaineering; Rowing; Ten Pin Bowling.

ATTRACTIONS:
The local teams are, for rugby, Stirling County, and for football, Stirling Albion. There's also local greyhound racing.

ACCOMMODATION

IN COLLEGE:
• Self-catering: 70% • Cost: £46-62 (30-37wks)
Availability: The refurbished campus accommodation consists of 4 halls: 3 mixed sex and one divided into single sex sections. *They are all blessed with unimaginative* breeze blocks, which quickly get smothered in posters. This is enough to house all the 1st years who want to live in. Over 50% of 3rd years, finalists and postgrads can be housed as well, but 2nd years are more likely to fend for themselves. Overseas students can live in for the whole of their course if they want. Only 2% have to share and there are facilities for married couples, mainly in the 130 off-campus flats maintained by the University. There's also a flat for women only. Rent increases are expected once the refurbishments are completed. There is 24 hour campus security from what are known as the 'Green Meanies'. After 11pm on campus, students must show their student ID.
Car parking: Free and *sufficient*.

EXTERNALLY:
• Ave rent: £45
Availability: *Stirling is a small place and it ain't easy to find housing locally. Bridge of Allan is the best nest. Raploch, Caperceilidh and Cornton can be scary. A car can be parked, but students won't need one unless they fancy regular jaunts to the Highlands.*
Housing help: Help is at hand from 7 full- and 3 part-time staff. They provide a vacancies newsletter advertising lodging listings and bulletin boards and they vet all recommended gaffs.

> Every year, a tortoise race takes place between Corpus Christi and Balliol Colleges, Oxford.

WELFARE

SERVICES:
- Equal Ops SA • Nightline • Lesbian & Gay Society • Overseas SA
- Minibus • Women's Officer • Self-defence classes

The University employs 2 counsellors. There's a Student & Staff Health Centre, which employs a sister and consulting doctor, and a medical practice on campus. The University will pay half the fees towards the town's Beehive nursery. Late-night shuttle bus, free attack alarms, free condoms. The women's group meets every week.
Disabled: The campus is one of the few designed with disabled access in mind. Rooms and facilities have been adapted, new lifts have been installed and doorways have been widened. There are induction loops in lecture theatres and help is available for students with dyslexia. S*tudents with severe disabilities may still face problems but the Disabilities Officer irons out many creases.*

FINANCE:
- Access fund: £139,900 • Successful applications: 365

Twenty £1,000 bursaries are available for local and UK/EU students. Ten £2,000 academic bursaries for overseas students used against fees. Thirty sports scholarships.

Stockton

see University of Durham

University of Strathclyde

University of Strathclyde, McCance Building, 16 Richmond Street, Glasgow, G1 1XQ. Tel: (0141) 548 2426. Fax: (0141) 552 5860. Strathclyde University Students' Association, 90 John Street, Glasgow, G1 1JH. Tel: (0141) 567 5000. Fax: (0141) 567 5050.

GENERAL

Strathclyde University is situated on a number of hills in the middle of Glasgow, right in the city's central business district. The campus is modern *and fairly ugly, but blends inconspicuously with the rest of this part of the city.* The original University building, an o*ut of place redbrick affair, is rather lost* among the more modern structures built since the 1960s. The *compact* campus consists of *large* department buildings and tower blocks and is being developed quickly. *But when it comes to greenery, you wouldn't find much less in an underground car park* (however, the University gardens did win an award in 1994 from the Incorporation of Gardeners of Glasgow). The 'merger' with Jordanhill College created a second site housing the Faculty of Education.

597 Strathclyde

Sex ratio(M:F): 48%:52%
Full time u'grads: 10,900
Postgrads: 2,400
Ave course: 4yrs
Private school: 10%
Mature students: 16%
Disabled students: 5%
Founded: 1796
Part time: 250
Non-degree: 0
Ethnic: 10%
Flunk rate: 14.5%
Overseas students: 6%

ATMOSPHERE:
Strathclyde was originally a non-residential University and the students all lived locally. There's still a high proportion of Glaswegians who regard the University as an extension of school and don't hang around more than is necessary. Despite this and the uninspiring architecture, there's a lot of fun to be had, a large proportion of it generated by the SA.

JORDANHILL:
The Faculty of Education at Jordanhill has 2,000 students. *In cheesey-chalk contrast with the main campus 5 miles away, it's a pleasant leafy site, lovely in summer.* It has good sports facilities and accommodation for 180 students. *Students don't really need to travel between sites*, but it's possible anyway by free University bus.

THE CITY: see University of Glasgow

TRAVEL: see University of Glasgow
Strathclyde University is 5 minutes walk from Queen Street Station and 10 minutes from Central Station.

CAREER PROSPECTS:
• Careers Service • No of staff: 4 full/3 part
• Unemployed after 6mths: 3%

FAMOUS ALUMNI:
Malcom Bruce MP (Lib Dem); Michael Connarty, Ian Davidson, Maria Fyfe, John McFall, Jim Murphy (Labour MPs); Dougie Donnelly (sports commentator); James Kelman (Booker-winning author); Helena Kennedy QC; Lord Reith (founder of the BBC); Elaine Smith (actress); Teenage Fanclub (band).

FURTHER INFO:
Undergrad prospectuses and departmental leaflets. CD-Rom and websites (www.strath.ac.uk and www.strath.ac.uk/ussa).

ACADEMIC

Strathclyde has a longer academic year than most – 33 weeks.

staff/student ratio: 1:17
Range of points required for entrance: 360-120
Percentage accepted through clearing: 10%
Number of terms/semesters: 2
Length of terms/semesters: 17 wks
Research: 4.3

LIBRARIES:
• Books: 900,000 • Study places: 2,100
There all 5 libraries in all, the Andersonian being the main one.

COMPUTERS:
- Computer workstations: 950

Computing standards are good but there aren't enough to go round.

ENTERTAINMENT

THE CITY: see University of Glasgow

UNIVERSITY:
- Price of a pint of beer: £1.65 • Glass of wine: £1.95

Bars: There are 5 bars in the *vast* Union Building. The *pubby* Barony Bar *is the most popular*. The others include the Cavern (baguettes by day, bops by night) and the Dark Room.

Theatres: The Eclipse drama group presents 3 or 4 productions a year in the Drama Centre and performs at the Edinburgh Fringe.

Clubs/discos: The Dark Room is the main venue, with 3 club nights a week. There are also regular visits from *big name* DJs such as Paul Oakenfold, Leftfield and the Propellerheads.

Music venues: The Union has a *good reputatio*n, especially for giving a kick-start to local bands and it's also hosted the likes of Toploader and Brandon Block. Every bar in the Union building is equipped for big sounds.

Food: The Food Court in the Dark Room offers traditional stodge and curries, while Delice de France does *healthy* baguettes. *The best bet* is the Cavern which does baked spuds and the like *at great value for money.*

SOCIAL & POLITICAL

STRATHCLYDE UNIVERSITY STUDENTS' ASSOCIATION:
- 6 sabbaticals • Turnout at last ballot: 25% • NUS member

The Union is very well organised and provides a phenomenal number of commercial services. Political activists might feel a little aghast but then you can't have everything.

SU FACILITIES:
5 bars; 5 cafeterias; travel agency; printing shop; 3 general shops; bank and cash machines; Endsleigh Insurance office; TV lounge; photocopier; free playgroup (for offspring of students, *sadly*, not the students themselves); games and vending machines; snooker and pool tables; juke box; nightclub; launderette; 8 meeting and function rooms including LGB room; 2 conference rooms.

CLUBS (NON SPORTING):
AIESEC; Andersonian Chemistry; ANSA Glasgow; Architecture; Building/Environmental; Christian; Debating; EEE; EME; Graduates; Hellenic; Highland; Hong Kong; Indonesian; Invention; Kilt; Korean; Lifesaving; Malaysian; Mountaineering; Orienteering; Spanish; Thai; Third World; Turkish; Websoc; Winnie-the-Pooh.

OTHER ORGANISATIONS:
'Telegraph' is the student newspaper published by, but editorially independent of, the Union. There are also a University radio station, and a charity Rag called 'Outrageous' which recently raised £55,063.

RELIGIOUS:
There is a team of chaplains who cater to most shades of biblical taste, as well as Jewish and Muslim persuasions.
Religion in Glasgow: see University of Glasgow

PAID WORK: see University of Glasgow

SPORTS

- Recent successes: badminton, basketball, yachting

The University has provided much for the energetic type – sport has become quite a social as well as a physical activity – many of those who can't bring themselves to compete are quite prepared to yell from the sidelines. Nature has also been quite generous, throwing in the River Clyde for watersports. There are 5 golf scholarships, each worth £1,250 a year.

SPORTS FACILITIES:
45 acres of playing fields; sports centre; 2 small gyms; 2 swimming pools; all-weather pitch; squash courts; climbing wall; weight-training room and multigym.

SPORTING CLUBS:
Archery; Canoe; Chinese Boxing; Hockey; Paragliding; Rowing; Sub-Aqua; Windsurfing.

ATTRACTIONS: see University of Glasgow

ACCOMMODATION

IN COLLEGE:
- Catered: 5% • Cost: £63 (35wks)
- Self-catering: 18% • Cost: £43-67 (37-50wks)

Availability: 46% of 1st years can live in and then 17% of 2nd years. 11% of 1st years in halls have to share. Baird Hall, 20 minutes from the campus, is the only catered hall and houses mainly 1st years. The University provides housing for some married couples, but it's 15 miles away. Self-catered flats make up the student village next to the campus. *There have been complaints about the size of rooms and the fact that it's impossible to control the heating.* The most expensive self-catered places are in new blocks where rooms have en suite facilities and TVs. The other self-catered flats, not far from the student village, *can suffer from a lack of social mingling because they are separated into flats – they are a bit stuffy and lacking in character, even the Waterfront ones, in Yuppieville.*

EXTERNALLY: see University of Glasgow
Housing help: The Accommodation Office has 7 full- and 1 part-time staff who keep lists of vacancies and recommended and blacklisted landlords. Help also from the SA.

WELFARE

SERVICES:
- Nursery • Lesbian & Gay Society • Nightline • Mature SA
- Overseas SA • Postgrad SA • Minibus • Finance SA
- Women's Officer • Self-defence classes

The University Student Advisory & Counselling Service provides 1 full- and 5 part-time counsellors. The Student Health Service runs a daily clinic on campus with a consultant psychiatrist. There are student advisers and the Welfare Officer at the SA Welfare Office. There's also a Centre for Academic Practice for academic advice and an International Office for overseas students. All these bodies work closely together.

Women: Attack alarms and CCTV on campus help on the security front.

Disabled: *The hilly campus is a problem for access.* Individual arrangements can be made with the part-time adviser. The Union Building has disabled access to 6 of its 10 levels and there's a Co-ordinator for Special Needs. For sight-impaired students, there's a support group ('Outreach') and a Braille translator/transcriber.

FINANCE:
- Access fund: £800,000 • Successful applications: 1,000

University of Sunderland

- *Formerly Sunderland Polytechnic*

University of Sunderland, Student Recruitment, Edinburgh Building, Chester Road, Sunderland, SR1 2SD. Tel: (0191) 515 3000. Fax: (0191) 515 3805. E-mail: student-helpline@sunderland.ac.uk
University of Sunderland Students' Union, Wearbank House, Charles Street, St Peter's Campus, Sunderland, SR6 0DD.
Tel: (0191) 515 3584. Fax: (0191) 514 2499.
E-mail: su.president@sunderland.ac.uk

GENERAL

Sunderland is a port forming part of the Tyne & Wear conurbation. The city centre is changing fast: the Stadium of Light, the National Glass Centre, Sunderland Marina, Riverside Regeneration, Winter Gardens, the Metro, Crowtree Leisure Centre *phew*. The other buildings almost all date from the 60s and onwards and the buildings in the centre are *only just old enough to have started to look shabby.* Although it is industrial, the Northumbrian coast and moors and the rural city of Durham to the south-west are all close, as are two of Europe's largest shopping complexes – the Metro Centre in Gateshead and Eldon Square in Newcastle (see Newcastle University). The University has 3 areas that you might call campuses, but, in fact, has splinters all over the city – more than 40 buildings in all. The Chester Road campus in the city centre is composed of early 60s tower blocks *which match most of the city's architecture in style and complete lack of aesthetic appeal.* The St Peter's campus, by the river, is more attractive.

Sex ratio(M:F): 49%:51%	Founded: 1860
Full time u'grads: 8,141	Part time: 1,624
Postgrads: 866	Non-degree: 599
Ave course: 3yrs	Ethnic: 9%
Private school: 3%	Flunk rate: 26%
Mature students: 33%	Overseas students: 11%
Disabled students: 4%	

ATMOSPHERE:
The University makes a specific point of attracting local students and for many in this once deprived corner of the country, it can be a life-changing experience. Neither the city nor the Uni will win any beauty

contests (they've won architecture awards, but that's something different altogether) but they make up for it in friendliness and enthusiasm.

ST PETER'S CAMPUS:
4,000 students in the Business and IT departments are based here, a mile from the main site. *It's a far more attractive setting for study, being a coherent mix of wood and concrete.* The University hope to base 60% of students here.

THE CITY:
- <u>Population: 286,800</u> • <u>London: 257miles</u> • <u>Newcastle: 10miles</u>
- <u>Durham: 13miles</u>

No-one would claim this is an architecturally appealing city – unless they were architects. It doesn't have a wide range of shops – although the Bridges shopping centre has recently doubled in size – just repetitive branch stores, Newcastle and the Metro Centre are also a *godsend for shoppers*. There are two museums, some *interesting* bridges and, a little way inland, the Penshaw Monument, *a massive thingy that looks like a Greek temple* and can be seen for miles around. An ongoing £200m development programme is beginning to make a difference.

TRAVEL:
Trains: Sunderland station is 10 minutes walk from the Chester Road campus. There are direct trains to Newcastle, Middlesbrough (£3.95) and London (£47.50) and connections to the rest of the country. There's also the Metro Link in Newcastle.
Coaches: Blueline and National Express services to many destinations including London (£25.50) and Manchester (£17.50).
Car: 8 miles off the A1(M) on the A123, A19 and A690.
Air: Newcastle International and Teesside Airports are both under an hour's drive away.
Ferries: The nearest ferries are from Newcastle and Hull, serving Europe and Scandinavia.
Hitching: *Good prospects once out of Sunderland, particularly on the A1 heading north or south.*
Local: The buses are cheap (fares from 20p) *and quite reliable.* A free campus bus service runs between all key University buildings and halls of residence. Development of an underground system is imminent. There's also a *shiny* new bus/Metro station.
Taxis: *Sunderland is small, so taxi fares are pretty cheap. The Union has struck a deal with Station Taxis where if you hand over your Union card to the driver, the Union is billed the next day. Pay back your fare and get your Union card back.*
Bicycles: There are bike lanes between Consett and the coast and between Sunderland and Whitehaven in Cumbria. *Problems with theft are decreasing, but there aren't many secure places to leave bikes in town.*

CAREER PROSPECTS:
- <u>Careers Service</u> • <u>No of staff: 3 full-time</u>
- <u>Unemployed after 6mths: 5%</u>

FAMOUS ALUMNI:
Steve Cram (ex runner); Ortis Deley (CBBC presenter); Ian Wilson (swimmer). Sunderland FC has a collective honorary degree.

FURTHER INFO:
Prospectus, course literature, leaflets, web site (www.sunderland.ac.uk), open days.

ACADEMIC

One of Sunderland's founder colleges was the first in England to introduce the sandwich course (the fillings and wrapping courses came much later).

staff/student ratio: 1:18
Range of points required for entrance: 300-140
Percentage accepted through clearing: 18%
Number of terms/semesters: 3
Length of terms/semesters: 12 wks
Research: 2.9

LIBRARIES:
- Books: 500,000 • Study places: 1,900

The main libraries are on the Chester Road and St Peter's Campus and there are further departmental libraries.

COMPUTERS:
- Computer workstations: 2,500

24-hour access to computer facilities.

ENTERTAINMENT

THE CITY:
- Price of a pint of beer: £1.85 • Glass of wine: £1.50

Newcastle is more of a wonderland than Sunderland (see Newcastle University) but the place does have its fans.

Cinemas: A 3-screen mainstream house and a new 12-screen Virgin cinema 10 miles out of town.

Theatres: (2) The Empire shows mainstream plays, pantos and concerts. The Royalty is for local offerings. The Seaburn Centre hosts visits from the RSC.

Pubs: *Cheap, cheerful and mostly friendly. Pushplugs: Fitzgeralds; Stone Bridge; Baroque, a huge gothic style pub; Royalty Museum Vaults; Ivy House (very student friendly); The Windsor Castle is a cool gay hang-out.*

Clubs/discos/music venues: Not too many clubs, but the *Pushplugs* go to *The Palace (charty, free bus transport included), KU Club (Indie), Annabels (dance/retro) and Pzazz (Britpop). There are live jazz jives at the Ground Floor Café.*

Eating out: *Fancy food isn't a Sunderland speciality but, apart from a large selection of burger bars and kebab joints, Pushplugs go to: Marcello's, Capanella (Italian; NUS discount); Ming Dynasty II (cheap Chinese); Johnny Ringo's.*

UNIVERSITY:
- Price of a pint of beer: £1.35 • Glass of wine: £1.05

Bars: (4) The Manor Quay Bar is the main ents venue. The new Bonded Warehouse at Panns Bank has two floors and gets packed on a Saturday night. The Roker Bar at St Peter's and the Wearmouth Bar at Chester Road are the daytime haunts.

Cinema: The University has an 'occasional cinema', presumably showing occasional films, in the 400-seater Sir Tom Cowie lecture theatre.

Theatre: *Strong* performing arts courses and access to the Sunderland Empire.

Clubs/discos: Manor Quay (cap 1,200) gets somewhat funky three nights a week (Weds chart/dance, Fri 70s/80s, Sat Indie) and it can lure the likes of Judge Jules and Boy George as guests. There's a termly LGB night too.

Music venues: Manor Quay is a *good* source of live sounds, recently: Shed 7 and Asia Dub Foundation.

Food: The University provides foodstops at all sites, the Bonded Warehouse does *good* hot food (Sunday lunches are *excellent and cheap* – £2.95) and the Roker and Wearmouth bars provide sustenance as well. A new addition is the Cybernet Connection on the Chester Road campus with fast food next to online access.

Others: The Bonded Warehouse has got TVs linked to playstations and videos to watch, borrowed from behind the bar. The clubs and societies dinner dance is held at Sunderland FC (not on the pitch though) and there's a regatta every May. The Summer Ball is popular *but they don't tend to go for the old dinner-jacket-and-strawberries-with-champagne-darling thing round these parts.*

SOCIAL & POLITICAL

UNIVERSITY OF SUNDERLAND STUDENTS' UNION (USSU):
• 6 sabbaticals • Turnout at last ballot: 10% • NUS member

The Union arranges enough to keep a large number of the students busy and motivated, but it's ents and events, not politics. Recent campaigns that have hit the wall of apathy include the NUS students rights charter and breast cancer awareness.

SU FACILITIES:
Bars; pool tables; games machines; vending machine; quiet room; shops; travel agency; jobshop; advice centre; minibus service; photocopier; print shop. There's also a shop in the Bonded Warehouse.

CLUBS (NON SPORTING):
Duke of Edinburgh; First Aid; Games; Hellenic; National Hat Society; Real Ale.

OTHER ORGANISATIONS:
'Degrees North' is the monthly student newspaper, with a sabbatical editor. There's also a charity Rag and a student Community Action group.

RELIGIOUS:
• 1 chaplain (CofE)

The Islamic Society has its own mosque. Most brands of Christianity, as well as Judaism, have outlets in town.

PAID WORK:
Unemployment in the area has dropped substantially since the days of grim recession. There is now a USSU-run jobshop and the Union has about 150 casual posts to offer.

SPORTS

• Recent successes: basketball, squash

Not a particularly sporty place but there are plenty of sports-related clubs for those who want it. The University has an okay range of sporting clubs and the council facilities compensate for any gaps. £5 membership fee to use all facilities.

SPORTS FACILITIES:
The sports centre on Chester Road has a 25m pool, sports hall and 2 gyms. St George's House has a dance studio and training room. There are 10 acres of playing fields at Seaburn and Hendon. The town adds squash, badminton and basketball courts, a dry ski-slope, football, rugby and cricket pitches. The local Crowtree Centre also has a pool, ice skating and hockey and boxing facilities. Silksworth outdoor complex has a tennis centre, dry ski-slope, running track, lake and orienteering courses. Sunderland Marina for water sports.

SPORTING CLUBS:
American Football; Caving; Gaelic Football; Ice Hockey; Surfing.

ATTRACTIONS:
Support for Sunderland FC (*and loathing for their Newcastle neighbours*) is endemic. There are also ice hockey and basketball teams.

ACCOMMODATION

IN COLLEGE:
- Catered: 3% • Cost: £49-58 (40wks)
- Self-catering: 25% • Cost: £36-53 (40-52wks)

Availability: All 1st years who want University accommodation can have it (1 in 4 say no, ta) and about 20% of other undergraduates *should be in luck*. No one has to share. The facilities range from purpose-built halls to tower blocks to *swish* self-catering flats with en suite facilities. There are also 800 places under the head tenancy scheme. Security is *good* with 24-hour watch on all sites, CCTV, swipe card entry systems and mobile and foot patrols.
Car parking: Permit parking, £30 a year (free to the disabled).

EXTERNALLY:
- Ave rent: £35

Availability: *As the University grows quickly, it's becoming harder to find decent affordable housing. Unfortunately, as with most things in life you get what you pay for. Recommended areas include Millfield, Ashbrooke, Chester Road and Hylton Road. Avoid Hendon, Pennywell and Ford.*
Housing help: The University's accommodation service provides a list of private landlords.

WELFARE

SERVICES:
- Creche • Nightline • Lesbian Gay & Bisexual Society • Mature SA
- Overseas SA • Late-night minibus • Women's Officer
- Holiday Playscheme • Self-defence classes

Help is at hand from Student Services and the welfare department, which has two counsellors (one full-time and one part-time), two health advisers, a nurse and a legal service provided by a local solicitor. Two bobbies from Northumbria Police are permanently attached to the campus *but not by electrodes to the genitals or Copydex glue or anything*. The Union adds five full-time welfare and academic advisers. A free four-week English language summer school is available for overseas students.
Women: There is a lot of concentration on careers for women and there's also a female-only minibus.

Disabled: Wearmouth Hall has been made wheelchair accessible. *The older buildings are not wheelchair-friendly* but efforts are being made to adapt them. There's a three-person disability support team and special course modules for students with dyslexia.

FINANCE:
• Access fund: £756,029 • Successful applications: 1,400
Student Services has debt counsellors and financial help-books. Some bursaries are available, hardship fund and loans.

University of Surrey

University of Surrey, Guildford, Surrey, GU2 5XH.
Tel: (01483) 300800. Fax: (01483) 300803.
E-mail: information@surrey.ac.uk
University of Surrey Students' Union, Union House, University of Surrey, Guildford, Surrey, GU2 7XH. Tel: (01483) 879223. Fax: (01483) 534749. E-mail: su-comms@surrey.ac.uk

GENERAL

On the edge of the North Downs, in the heart of London's commuter country is the town of Guildford. Around the outskirts, *it's a post-war invasion* of modern architecture (not least the cathedral, where Gregory Peck met a sticky end in 'The Omen') and shopping malls, but the city centre is a *quaint* old place with its cobbled main street and *rural feel*. The University campus is on Stag Hill, 10 minutes walk away. It was built in the late 60s, before which the University had been Battersea Poly. *The campus is a bit cramped and confusing and looks a bit like a sandy grey Lego set.* However, new buildings *have sprouted which improve things loads,* built by the architects who did the Eurostar station at Waterloo International. From certain viewpoints over the man-made lakes and landscape gardening, it's just about possible to hide the concrete with greenery and occasional migrant wildlife (rabbits, ducks and the like).

Sex ratio(M:F): 43%:57%	Founded: 1966
Full time u'grads: 5,285	Part time: 62
Postgrads: 1,575	Non-degree: 743
Ave course: 4yrs	Ethnic: 23%
Private school: n/a	Flunk rate: 15.6%
Mature students: 22%	Overseas students: 21%
Disabled students: 5%	

ATMOSPHERE:
Being campus-based and with such a large proportion of students living in, the University of Surrey is a close-knit community, which from the outside seems insular, but is friendly enough from within. There are some seriously career-minded individuals around and a fairly business-like attitude to study. They do, however, loosen up a bit when night falls.

THE TOWN:
- <u>Population: 122,500</u> • <u>London: 30 miles</u>
- <u>Southampton: 45 miles</u> • <u>Birmingham: 106 miles</u>

One of the best things about Guildford is that it is close to London but the town itself does offer pretty decent shopping options. It's also good for your other daily needs, as Guildford is well equipped with supermarkets (a Tesco's within walking distance of the campus), banks with cashpoints, bookshops (including second-hand), public libraries and a street market. The Spectrum Leisure Centre has an ice rink, bowling alley, pool and gym. Guildford also offers the River Wey, two museums and the castle keep.

TRAVEL:
Trains: From Guildford Station (½ mile from campus) mainline connections to London Waterloo (£7 – including travelcard for Underground and buses). Trains every hour.
Coaches: National Express from Guildford to London (£7.50) and elsewhere.
Car: 5 minutes from A3 (look for the mortar board sign posts), A25 and Junction 10 of the M25 also near.
Air: ½ an hour by car to both Heathrow & Gatwick.
Hitching: *Okay for the A3 for London or to the M25 if you can find somewhere to stand.*
Local: *Good* bus service around town, including a minibus every 12 mins from campus to the centre (70p return). The Uni has recently joined up with a local bus company to offer a decent service throughout the area and a *super lovely* season ticket offer (£100).
Bicycles: *Not too hilly*, there's a cycle path and shower facilities *so you've no excuse to be stinky.*

CAREER PROSPECTS:
- <u>Careers Service</u> • <u>No of staff: 4 full/3 part</u>
- <u>Unemployed after 6mths: 1.1%</u>

Excellent drop-in centre and *there's never a problem getting an appointment to see a careers adviser*. The University boasts the lowest graduate unemployment rate in the country.

FAMOUS ALUMNI:
Ian Eldridge (CEO of Pizza Express); Alec Issigonis (designed the Mini); Nabil Shaban (actor, founder Greae Theatre).

FURTHER INFO:
Prospectuses for undergrads and postgrads, alternative prospectus from the SU, course guides and brochures, a video, CD-Rom and a website (www.surrey.ac.uk).

ACADEMIC

Surrey originally specialised in science and engineering but recently performing arts, social studies and nursing and midwifery have expanded greatly, *taming a previously bloke-heavy atmosphere* that now 58% of students are women. Most courses are four years with most of one year (usually 3rd) or two half-years spent on professional placements. Although optional, it's generally seen as an advantage. Students (regardless of their own course) are encouraged to learn a language for which extra classes are laid on.

staff/student ratio: 1:13
Range of points required for entrance: 320-240
Percentage accepted through clearing: 12.5%
Number of terms/semesters: 2
Length of terms/semesters: 15wks
Research: 4.6

LIBRARIES:
- Books: 400,000 • Study places: 900

COMPUTERS:
- Computer workstations: 626

The new IT labs provide 24-hour access to all computer facilities.

TOWN:
- Price of a pint of beer: £2.20 • Glass of wine: £2

Pubs: In the city, the pubs represent a fairly broad and uninspired mix, although around the local countryside, pubs are a sight more real – real ale, real log fires, real pub grub. Pushplugs: The Hogshead; Bar Med; Scruffy Murphy's; The Forger & Firkin; Star Inn; George Abbott. Avoid the less than student-friendly Robin Hood.

Cinemas: (2) Odeon with 10 screens (has student rates) and an arthouse.

Theatres: (2) The Yvonne Arnaud Theatre is sometimes a springboard for West End shows and the Electric Theatre stages am dram.

Clubs/discos: (3) Bojanglez, Cinderellas, The Drink and Bar Mambo are the main outlets for dance insanity *but none of them can be described as cutting-edge.*

Music venues: The Civic Hall hosts everything from Harry Hill to Mansun.

Eating out: There's an *okay* range of cosmopolitan eateries, as well as the usual greasebuckets. Pushplugs: Bombay Spice (Indian); Bamboo Garden (Chinese); Mississippi Exchange (diner); TGI Friday's; King's Head; Cafés Uno; Rouge; Cambio (Italian) and Tote.

UNIVERSITY:
- Price of a pint of beer: £1.39 • Glass of wine: £2.50

Bars: (5) The vast Union Bar is open lunchtimes and evenings *and is the main drinking den.* The refurbished Chancellors *is plusher* and the Helyn Rose Bar is mainly used for functions. The Varsity Centre Bar is popular with the sporty crowd, *probably due to the widescreen TV.*

Theatres: (1) The well-equipped Performing Arts Technology studios play host to productions such as the annual international week which includes dance and theatre from around the world.

Cinemas: The film club shows mainstream cinema at least once a week.

Clubs/discos: The huge Union bar is the biggest club venue in the area. Three discos every week: Confusion (Trance, D&B), Outrage (Cheese) and the Friday Night Out (Dance).

Music venues: The Union has recently hosted the likes of Space, Hepburn, Lightining Seeds, Daphne and Celeste and Louise as well as top DJ's Paul Oakenfold, Dave Pearce, Judge Jules, and Alex Patterson.

Cabaret: The Helyn Rose bar has recently hosted acts from The Comedy Network, later broadcast on Channel 4.

Food: The University refectory is the main face-filler but there's more besides. The Helyn Rose Bar does pasta, chilli, curry, burgers, salads, lasagne. A Pizza Plus takeaway is at the Union and the Seasons Complex, Chancellors and the Lakeside and restaurants are run by Hotel and Catering Management undergraduates.

Balls: Apart from the annual Graduation Ball, the Colours Ball celebrates sports awards and the Charter Ball celebrates the granting of the University's charter and is used to announce the results of Union elections.

SOCIAL & POLITICAL

UNIVERSITY OF SURREY STUDENTS' UNION:
• 6 sabbaticals • Turnout at last ballot: 15% • NUS member

Students have a good level of say within the University through USSU which has representatives on most major committees, partly because the University can rest assured the students aren't likely to get militant. There are no political societies and everyone stands for election on an independent slate. Recent campaigns have been against tuition fees and to keep Wednesday afternoons free for sport.

SU FACILITIES:
5 bars; 2 cafeterias; 7 minibuses (for hire); travel agency; photocopying; market stalls; pizza takeaway; photo booth; pool and snooker tables; juke box; vending machines. NatWest bank with cash machine on campus.

CLUBS (NON SPORTING):

Afro Caribbean; Asian; Astronomy; Amateur Radio; Arabic; Amnesty; Ballroom; Biker; Bio; Catholic; Christian Union; Chemical Engineering; Chemistry; Chess; Chinese; Civil Engineering; Computer Games; Conker; Conservative; Cyprus; Ears; Economics; Electrical Engineering; Friends of Asia; Game; German; Green; Hellenic; Hong Kong; Iranian; Islamic; Japanese; Jewish; Korean; Labour; Law; LGB; Liberty; Malaysian; Maths and Computing; Mechanical Engineering; Nordick; Norwegian; Origins of Sound; Robot; Russian; Singapore; Sri Lankan; SOMSS; Taiwanese; Turkish; UOS; Wind Band; Yoga and Meditation.

OTHER ORGANISATIONS:
The student newspaper 'Bare Facts', magazine 'Phased' and GU2 is the award-winning student radio station based on campus. There's a Rag committee organising charity events throughout the year.

RELIGIOUS:
There is a meditation centre on site and a prayer room for the Islamic faith. Right next to the campus is the famous modern cathedral. Hindus and Sikhs are also catered for locally.

PAID WORK:
The careers service helps out with work in the local area – mostly bar, shop and restaurant work.

SPORTS

• Recent successes: women's football

The University tasted success not so long ago in the 1998 Commonwealth Games winning two gold and a bronze medal in fencing and gymnastics. The top class sports facilities are used by athletes Roger Black, Paul Johnson and the England Rugby Union squad. Students can buy a sports and classes card for £30 a year which gives them annual use of the extensive facilities. It's also £30 annually for the Quantum Fitness Club or £40 for both services.

Surrey

SPORTS FACILITIES:
Sports hall; 60 acres of playing fields; sports injury clinic; squash courts; astroturf; croquet lawn; tennis courts; climbing wall; gymnasium; multigym; sunbeds and the River Wey (suitable for a variety of water sports). The city also has a swimming pool, the Spectrum Leisure Centre (offers student deals) and athletics field.

SPORTING CLUBS:
American Football; Archery; Athletics; Backgammon; Badminton; Basketball; Boxing; Boat; Chess; Cricket; Cross Country; Fencing; Football; Freestyle Karate; Golf; Hiking; Hockey; Jiu Jitsu; Judo; Karate; Kung Fu; Lacrosse; Mountain Biking; Netball; Parachute; Riding; Rifle; Running; Sailing; Scout and Guide; Ski; Squash; Swimming; Table Tennis; Taijitsu; Trampolining; Volleyball; Water Polo; Windsurfing.

ATTRACTIONS:
Sandown Park Race Course is near enough for a day's outing, as are Ascot and Twickenham.

ACCOMMODATION

IN COLLEGE:
• Self-catering: 60% • Cost: £35-67 (30/38wks)
Availability: All 1st years and most (70%) of finalists have the chance to live in. 3rd years, who for the most part are on placements, don't really need to. *That only leaves the 2nd years to fend for themselves.* On campus there are seven 'courts' which are accommodation blocks of a *generally good* standard. Between them they house 2,608 students in single rooms with shared kitchens, sometimes even an en suite bathroom (*very popular*). A further 208 places are available about 2½ miles away at Hazel Farm which are, in effect, terraced houses for six to seven students let by the University. Students share 'KUBs' (Kitchen/Utility/Breakfast rooms with fridge/freezers and cookers) with about a dozen others, *great for coffee* and gossip.
6% of 1st years have to share split level rooms. Some floors and houses are single sex, but it's mostly mixed. There are a few flats for married students. A shuttle bus runs to and from Hazel Farm when the Union shuts at night. The University have been installing phone and e-mail connections in all rooms.
Car-parking: Parking is only available to students living off-site and then at a cost of £68 a year.

EXTERNALLY:
• Ave rent: £62
Availability: *There is accommodation to be found out there but it's expensive. Favourite areas include Bellfields, Stoughton and Park Barn and which are reasonably close but pricey. Guildford is commuter land and this is reflected in the price.*
Housing help: To the rescue comes the University-run Accommodation Office to guide students through the vacancy bulletin board and standard renting contracts.

> The first person to be caught for speeding in a Sinclair C5 was a student at the University of Kent.

WELFARE

SERVICES:
- Lesbian & Gay Society • Mature SA • Overseas SA • Postgrad SA
- Minibus • Women's Officer • Self-defence classes

USSU's Student Advice and Information Service employs 5 staff including a welfare advice officer. The University health centre has doctors, nurses and 2 full- and 5 part-time counsellors, as well as a 24-hour sick bay.

Disabled: *Wheelchair access isn't much cop* – the campus is on a hill and covered in steps. Some provision can be made with prior notice. USSU employ a disability officer, there is also a special needs clinic, learning support tutors, an assistive technology centre and special hearing equipment.

FINANCE:
- Access fund: £233,850 • Successful applications: 715

The access fund is largely used to help with accommodation problems. Up to £1,000 is available for undergrads and mature students in need. Sports bursaries and various scholarships are available.

Surrey Institute of Art & Design

- *Formerly West Surrey College of Art and Design*

(1) Surrey Institute of Art and Design, Falkner Road, Farnham, Surrey, GU9 7DS. Tel: (01252) 722441. Fax: (01252) 892616.
E-mail: registry@surrart.ac.uk
Students' Union, Surrey Institute of Art and Design, Falkner Road, Farnham, Surrey, GU9 7DS. Tel: (01252) 710263.
Fax: (01252) 713591. E-mail: su@surrart.ac.uk
(2) Surrey Institute of Art and Design, Epsom Campus, Ashley Road, Epsom, Surrey, KT18 5BE. Tel: (01372) 728811.
Fax: (01372) 726233.

GENERAL

Farnham, on the home counties trail from London to Southampton, is an old rural market town, *full of quaint shops and beige jackets*. Not all, but many of those who live here commute to the big city and *give the town a suburban (rather than a village) feel*. Epsom is 32 miles away, *but a Martian would be hard-pressed to spot the difference*. The main Farnham site is on a small redbrick, prefabricated, *well-equipped*, campus with a village on one side and gently rolling fields on the other. (There's also an further education site on the main campus.) The Epsom building, designed by the same bloke, holds 451 undergrads and 301 other students in the Faculty of Fashion and Communication.

```
Keele is Old English for 'Cow Hill'.
```

Surrey Institute

- Sex ratio(M:F): 40%:60%
- Full time u'grads: 2,375
- Postgrads: 16
- Ave course: 3yrs
- Private school: n/a
- Mature students: 27%
- Disabled students: 9%
- Founded: 1969
- Part time: 95
- Non-degree: 527
- Ethnic: 16%
- Flunk rate: 19.5%
- Overseas students: 14%

ATMOSPHERE:
Like all art colleges, the students are utter trend monsters. To dress unobtrusively is a fashion faux pas. Nerds are few and far between and everybody is friendly. Local reactions are a bit mixed. This is green welly/commuter country and the concept of purple-haired, multiply-pierced arty farties doesn't really appeal to some. Farnham is quite buzzy socially, but at Epsom work seems to come first.

FARNHAM:
- London: 42 miles • Reading: 19 miles • Southampton: 31 miles

Farnham has a weekly street market and a large arts centre (the Maltings). It also provides the regular panoply of suburban amenities (public library, supermarket, bookshops, major banks, cashpoints, a shopping mall, etc).

EPSOM:
Epsom is close enough to London to feel a bit like a suburb of the Big Smoke. The area's nothing to get excited over but with the city so accessible, who needs local excitement?

TRAVEL:
Trains: Farnham station is ¾ of a mile from the College, on the line to London (£7.15) and Guildford. Epsom station is 5 minutes walk from the Institute site – a return trip to London costs a *miserly* £3.05.
Coaches: Services to London (£7.50), Birmingham (£20.75), Manchester (£27.50), among others.
Car: *Both towns are bedevilled by one-way systems.* Farnham is best approached from the A325, Epsom from the A24.
Air: Heathrow and Gatwick both less than 30 miles.
Hitching: *Don't bother, no one's going anywhere useful even if they would give you a lift.*
Local: Local buses in Farnham are fairly regular, Epsom, being closer to London, has more co-ordinated services.
Bicycles: No hills, lots of places to leave bikes *and only small amounts of theft.*
Others: Just west of Farnham is Alton, where the Watercress Line steam trains run in the summer. *Very pretty, but useless if you actually want to go anywhere.*

CAREER PROSPECTS:
- Careers Service • No of staff: 4 part
- Unemployed after 6mths: 18%

FAMOUS ALUMNI:
Daniel Greaves (animator); Alex Keshishian (director who got 'In Bed with Madonna'); Sadie Lee (artist); Nick Park (Oscar-laden animator).

FURTHER INFO:
Prospectuses for undergrads and postgrads, alternative prospectus 'The Gospel' from the Union and a website (www.surrart.ac.uk).

ACADEMIC

The Institute provides the only Animation degree course in Europe.

staff/student ratio: 1:27
Range of points required for entrance: 220-180
Percentage accepted through clearing: 5%
Number of terms/semesters: 2
Length of terms/semesters: 15wks
Research: n/a

LIBRARIES:
- Books: 77,000 • Study places: 314

There's a library at Epsom and at Farnham. *Library facilities are fair to middling although a Sunday opening would go down well.*

COMPUTERS:
- Computer workstations: 245

ENTERTAINMENT

TOWN:
- Price of a pint of beer: £2.10 • Glass of wine: £1.80

There isn't really much happening in Farnham, nor really in Aldershot (4 miles up the road). Guildford (11 miles) has 3 nightclubs, a smattering of pubs, a cinema and a leisure centre (see University of Surrey). London's not too far, especially for Epsom students.

Pubs: Many local boozers are bunged up by old buffers in Barbours but some are equally stuffed with students. Pushplugs: The Plough, Ye Ol Flyer, The Hogshead (Farnham); Rising Sun (Epsom).

Cinemas: Multiplex in Guildford, none in Farnham or Epsom.

Theatres: No theatre in Farnham. The Playhouse in Epsom hosts comedy, films and concerts as well as some *low-brow* theatre.

Clubs/discos/music venues: The Maltings and The Chicago Rock Café in Epsom field local tunesters. *For serious clubbing (or any clubbing, really) Guildford's the nearest option*, as clubs in Farnham are rarer than hen's teeth. *In Epsom, Greens provides mild doses of almost-hedonism (disco/house/garage).*

Food: There are cheap Italian pizza and pasta stops in Farnham. Epsom has a Pierre Victoire and the Rising Sun for pub grub, *but that's about it.*

COLLEGE:
- Price of a pint of beer: £1.45 • Glass of wine: £1.20

Bars/venues: (2) *The Glasshouse (cap 750) is the centre of social life.* Big faves include Vodka promotions, 50p a shot. Epsom's bar is called The Retreat.

Theatre: There is a fledgling drama society.

Cinemas: 3 film societies in College – 'Image Appreciation Society', 'CU Next Thursday' and 'Epsom Film Society' – *all three tending to culty/mainstream showings.*

Music venues/clubs/discos: 3 dance nights a week in the bar, ranging from house to 90s sounds. Drum'n'bass nights once a month. This is also the site for live noise of a *congenial calibre* (e.g. Sash, St Etienne).

Cabaret: 3 or 4 doses of chuckle a term in the Grapes.

Food: *Not much choice, there's the Farnham canteen but that's only open from 10am-4.30pm.*
Other: *3 balls a year, plus a Leavers' Event.*

SOCIAL & POLITICAL

SURREY INSTITUTE OF ART AND DESIGN STUDENTS' UNION:
• 3 sabbaticals • Turnout at last ballot: 47% • NUS member
The SU stays out of the bigger political picture preferring instead to concentrate on student services. When it does campaign, though, students are enthusiastic and get involved. Recently the SU campaigned to keep Wednesday afternoons free and it has been lobbying the University to increase the number of disabled and overseas students.

SU FACILITIES:
In a shared building the SU runs the bar, fax service, cafeteria, games, video and vending machines.

CLUBS (NON SPORTING):
International Students; Life Drawing; Role Playing; Women's Society.

OTHER ORGANISATIONS:
'Velvet' magazine comes out monthly and is produced by the SU. The Rag raised just £3,000 last year.

RELIGIOUS:
There are 2 chaplains who cover all denominations. Also local CofE and Baptist churches.

PAID WORK:
The jobs notice board is updated regularly. The College employs students as cleaners and security staff and the SU takes them on in the bar.

SPORTS

• Recent successes: football, rugby
Students are quite sporty considering that this is an arts college and that the only facility is an indoor games hall, which, it has to be said, is free to use. *Local facilities are better:* a sports centre (where Jet from 'Gladiators' is an instructor) and playing fields, a swimming pool, golf course, squash and tennis courts, a sauna and solarium.

SPORTING CLUBS:
Aerobics; Kick Boxing; Skateboarding; Surfing; Tayitsu.

ATTRACTIONS:
Local rugby team. Epsom has, as you may have heard, a race course. Local schoolkids often get a half-day holiday for the Derby.

ACCOMMODATION

IN COLLEGE:
• Self-catering: 16% • Cost: £32-58 (38wks)
Availability: 94% of 1st years can be accommodated, spread between 2 halls and the popular award-winning student village. Bridge House is not so sought after as it's a bit run down. 1% have to share

and 5% of 1st years who want to live in can't. There's no Institute-owned housing at Epsom.
Car parking: For disabled students only.

EXTERNALLY:
• Ave rent: £50
Availability: *Suitable, cheap accommodation can be hard to find. Wrecclesham, Upper Hale and Tilford Road are all convenient. Even though walking to College may be a schlep, a car really is an unnecessary luxury. Some even move out to Aldershot where accommodation is in more abundant supply and cheaper – be warned, though, it has a dodgy reputation.*
Housing help: The Accommodation Office has offices at Epsom and Farnham.

WELFARE

SERVICES:
• Lesbian & Gay Society • Minibus • Mature SA • International SA
• Women's Officer
There are 3 full-time and 2 part-time counsellors, provided by the University.
Disabled: *Access is fair in some parts, pretty poor in others.* There's a Disabled Students' Officer, who provides lots of literature. BSL interpreters are also available. Dyslexia sufferers are given study support.

FINANCE:
• Access fund: £98,000 • Successful applications: 299
£14,500 hardship fund for first years and a small (*and we mean small*) SU welfare fund.

University of Sussex

University of Sussex, Falmer, Brighton, BN1 9RH.
Tel: (01273) 606755. Fax: (01273) 678545.
E-mail: ug.admissions@sussex.ac.uk
University of Sussex Students' Union, Falmer House, Falmer, Brighton, BN1 9QF. Tel: (01273) 678555 Fax: (01273) 678875.
E-mail: ussu@sussex.ac.uk

GENERAL

3½ miles inland from Brighton town centre, before the land rises on to the Downs, is the *thoroughly modern*, 200-acre campus of Sussex University, set in rolling green land near the village of Falmer. The Basil Spence design of courtyards, arches, concrete pillars and redbrick buildings *could so easily have been yuck, but, in context, it works – it really does –* and it has awards to prove it. Certain buildings were even designed to look specifically like certain objects from the air, Falmer House is a camera, the arts building a bug. *(Cool, huuh? – if you're a seagull.)* The campus *is isolated, but virtually self-sufficient* with a chemist, greengrocer, health centre and so on, all on site.

Sussex

Sex ratio(M:F): 44%:56%
Full time u'grads: 6,759
Postgrads: 1,561
Ave course: 3yrs
Private school: 17.5%
Mature students: 24%
Disabled students: 7%

Founded: 1961
Part time: 122
Non-degree: 1,701
Ethnic: 12%
Flunk rate: 18.1%
Overseas students: 24%

ATMOSPHERE:
It's a laid-back campus and people tend to allow a good time to happen to them – the SU obliges and then some. For further fun, Brighton's nearby-ish, although a few find the 7-mile round trip too much of an effort.

TOWN: see University of Brighton

TRAVEL: see University of Brighton
Falmer is the closest station with frequent trains into Brighton and providing a *comprehensive* local service (£8.25 to London). *Local buses are reliable both when it comes to turning up and when it comes to taking the longest route into town and charging a quid for the privilege.* There are late night buses until 2am.

CAREER PROSPECTS:
• Career Development Unit   • No of staff: 5 full/8 part-time
• Unemployed after 6mths: 3.4%

FAMOUS ALUMNI:
Rob Bonnet (BBC news reporter); Simon Fanshawe (comedian); Brendan Foster (athletic commentator); Peter Hain MP (Lab); Hattie Hayridge (female Holly off Red Dwarf); Billy Idol *(bleached rock prat)*; Ian McEwan (writer); Simon Jenkins (journalist); Bob Mortimer *(the sexier one)*; Andrew Morton (writer); Dermot Murnaghan (ITN reporter); Nigel Planer (Neil from 'The Young Ones'); Julia Somerville (newsreader); Virginia Wade (the last female Briton to win a Wimbledon singles title).

FURTHER INFO:
Prospectuses for undergrads and postgrads, alternative prospectus from the SU, a video and a website (www.sussex.ac.uk).

ACADEMIC

staff/student ratio: 1:14
Range of points required for entrance: 320-120
Percentage accepted through clearing: 11%
Number of terms/semesters: 3
Length of terms/semesters: 10 wks
Research: 4.9

LIBRARIES:
• Books: 750,000   • Study places: 1,000
The library has recently been extended.

COMPUTERS:
• Computer workstations: 1,000
There's 24-hour computer access.

ENTERTAINMENT

TOWN: see University of Brighton
UNIVERSITY:
• Price of a pint of beer: £1.50 • Glass of wine: £1
Bars: (6) The East Slope (cap 280) *is the most popular*. Park Village Bar (100) is usually packed as well; The Falmer Pub *is more relaxed*; *the Grapevine Bar is open 365 days of the year*.
Theatres: The Gardner Arts Centre hosts student productions and touring shows. It also displays art exhibitions.
Cinema: There's a *thriving* Film Society and the Gardner Arts Centre also shows *non-mainstream* flicks.
Clubs/discos: The Hothouse (250 cap) keeps the tunes churning.
Music venues: The Mandela Hall, the largest music venue, recently hosted Ash and Red Snapper among others. The East Slope has local and student bands and jazz nights while Park Village does open mic and jam sessions for budding musos.
Food: The refectory food outlet, Pitstop, does burgers, chips and bagettes. The Downs and Laines restaurants put on standard fare and curry nights once a week and each school of study has a snack bar. There's also Falmer Bar (pasta).
Others: There are two balls a year Freshers and Summer.

SOCIAL & POLITICAL

UNIVERSITY OF SUSSEX STUDENTS' UNION:
• 6 sabbaticals • Turnout at last ballot: 25% • NUS member
Relations with the University are gradually improving after past animosity, although the SU still complain that they do not get enough money and claim that they are one of the worst funded unions in the country. There's a frosty atmosphere with students who are dissatisfied with the organisation and promotion of events, clubs and societies. The SU has its own trading company which runs the commercial services.

SU FACILITIES:
In USSU's Falmer House, there's a bar; a print shop and photocopying; welfare service; employment office; general shop; second-hand bookshop; photo booth; kids' club; volunteer bureau and games room. There's another bar in Mandela Hall.

CLUBS (NON SPORTING):
Arts; Blue Trees (Circus); Creative Writing; Cuba Solidarity; Film Making; Literature & Philosophy; SMUTS (Sussex Musical Theatre); SUDS (Sussex University Drama Society); SUFS (Sussex University Film Society).

OTHER ORGANISATIONS:
'Badger' is the weekly newspaper, produced by the SU and the Guardian award winning 'Pulse' magazine comes out every term. URF (University Radio Falmer) is also an award winner, picking up a gong from Radio 1.

RELIGIOUS:
• Four chaplains (CofE, RC, Free Church, Jewish)
Interdenominational Meeting House chapel and an Islamic prayer room.
Religion in Brighton: see University of Brighton.

PAID WORK:
The University has a Student Employment Office, providing part-time and vacation work for students locally.

- Recent successes: Hockey, Rowing

The facilities are good and conveniently placed on campus but there are *small* charges for using them (eg 60p for the badminton court). *Sport isn't an all-enveloping obsession.*

SPORTS FACILITIES:
The Falmer Sports Complex contains: 2 floor gym; cardiovascular and resistance equipment; dance studio; 2 sports halls; fitness room with multigym; 4 squash courts; sauna & solarium; café bar; sports shop; injury clinic with physiotherapists. Outdoor facilities include 14 acres of playing fields, a floodlit training area, a floodlit all-weather pitch, 6 tennis courts and 5 more squash courts.

SPORTING CLUBS:
Aikido; Canoe; Fencing; Golf; Judo; Karate; Kickboxing; Kung-Fu; Mountaineering; Ski & Snowboard; Sub-Aqua; Squash; Surf; Ultimate Frisbee; Windsurfing.

ATTRACTIONS: see University of Brighton

IN COLLEGE:
- Self-catering: 41% • Cost: £48-63 (30/38wks)

Availability: The University is able to accommodate all 1st years who request a place and about 30% of the others. The campus accommodation is in halls, houses and flats in groups of between 5 and 12 rooms. 105 flats cater for families. 10% of rooms are shared and there are some segregated areas for female Muslims. *Very good* security: night porters, entry-phones, CCTV, door chains/keyholes, phones in every room and two security offices.

Car parking: Parking is free for students, however even the lecturers have trouble finding a space

EXTERNALLY: see University of Brighton

Housing help: The University allocates students into the places they manage but also helps in the general home hunt, *which is increasingly fraught.* Lewes Road and London Road (near the train station) *are favoured haunts. Several local agencies also make a quick buck getting in on the act.*

SERVICES:
- Creche • Nightline • Mature SA • Overseas SA • Postgrad SA
- Late-Night Minibus • Women's Officer • Self-defence classes

USSU runs a Welfare Advice Unit with two welfare advisers complementing the University-run counselling service which employs 7 counsellors and 2 advisers. The NHS runs the University health service on campus with doctors, nurses, maternity care and family planning and a dentist.

Disabled: *Wheelchair access is fairly good and arrangements are made for the special needs of students with most forms of disability. Falmer House is being refitted so should be disability-friendly when it's finished. Kulukundis House is specially adapted accommodation for disabled students.*

FINANCE:
- Access fund: £557,078 • Successful applications: 1,125

There's the hardship fund and students can also apply for a Vice-Chancellor's Loan of £100 if their grants are late.

Swansea Institute
see Other Institutions

Swansea, University of Wales

- **The College is part of University of Wales and students are entitled to use its facilities.**

University of Wales Swansea, Singleton Park, Swansea, SA2 8PP.
Tel: (01792) 205678. Fax: (01792) 295897.
E-mail: admissions@swan.ac.uk
Swansea Students' Union, Singleton Park, Swansea, SA2 8PP.
Tel: (01792) 295466. Fax: (01792) 206029.
E-mail: sugenoff@swan.ac.uk

GENERAL

Swansea, Wales's second largest city, site of the invention of instant custard and home of the world's only commercial leech farm, squats on the south coast on the Gower peninsula – the country's first designated Area of Outstanding Natural Beauty and a *cool place to have beach parties*. The city centre's not bad – a modern and *not unpleasant* selection of slate and stone houses and brick and concrete shopping malls. Out west is *better still*, for there, about 2½ miles out of town, among the rolling parkland overlooking the bay *(which looks good from a distance)* is the University of Wales, Swansea. Its buildings are a mix of red brick and concrete blocks with concrete paths interspersed with yet more concrete. But the surrounding park is *very pleasant* and about 350 yards on the other side of the coast road (which runs through the park) is the sandy beach with dunes stretching into the distance (as far as the sea, anyway). *Meanwhile, the climate's mild but wet.*

Sex ratio(M:F): 42%:58%	Founded: 1920
Full time u'grads: 6,200	Part time: 375
Postgrads: 1,190	Non-degree: 590
Ave course: 3yrs	Ethnic: 4%
Private school: n/a	Flunk rate: 11.1%
Mature students: 11%	Overseas students: 8%
Disabled students: 5%	

ATMOSPHERE:
The seafront campus affords incredible sunrises across the beach and Bristol Channel, but they're missed by everyone most of the time, except those still out from the night before and gull's. There's a laid-back atmosphere that can feel like a holiday camp at half-term – when the weather is nice. Relations with the locals are perfectly cordial and most thrill-seeking goes on in town.

THE CITY:
- Population: 182,100 • London: 160miles • Cardiff: 40miles
- Bristol: 60miles

Dylan Thomas described Swansea as the 'graveyard of ambition' because people just never bring themselves to leave and pursue their wilder dreams – *they love it here too much. Although Swansea itself may not be a tourist attraction, the surrounding countryside is beautiful and brings in the holiday trade.* They have to be fed and housed and so Swansea does the business. *The locals are very friendly and will talk you into the next world if you let them. There's a good level of tourist facilities* as well as all the amenities for the local residents: shops (some open till midnight); new and second hand bookshops; supermarkets; 3 large shopping malls; banks; a market and a street market once a week; libraries and museums (notably the Swansea Museum). In the summertime, tourists and students descend to bask on the beaches near The Mumbles, the *oddly named but pretty* village on the Gower peninsula 1½ miles west of the campus. *But beware – you may never leave.*

TRAVEL:
Trains: Direct trains from Swansea station, 3 miles from the campus, to Cardiff (£9.05), London (£23.70), Shrewsbury and beyond.
Coaches: Services to London (£22.75), Cardiff (£6.50), Manchester (£27.50).
Car: A465, A48 and 5 miles off the M4.
Hitching: *Catch a bus to the M4 and then lifts are pretty easy.*
Local: Regular buses between the student village and the town centre (£1.55) and from the town to the railway station (55p).
Taxis: Free phone at the campus for students with flammable cash – *not as expensive as in many towns.*
Bicycles: *The hills inland from the coast have some crazy contours (beware of double arrows), but for the journey between campus and the city centre, a bike's an asset.*

CAREER PROSPECTS:
- Careers Service • No of staff: 6 full-time/2 part-time
- Unemployed after 6mths: 3%

The careers service is *very well-organised,* friendly and pretty efficient. They arrange job-link and work shadowing schemes.

SPECIAL FEATURES:
- The campus includes the 'Egypt Centre', containing a considerable collection of Egyptian artefacts.

FAMOUS ALUMNI:
Donald Anderson MP (Lab); Ian Bone (founder of Class War); Richey Edwards, Nicky Wire (Manics); Nigel Evans MP, Rod Richards MP (Con); Robert Howley, Paul Thorburn (Welsh rugby players); Mavis Nicholson (TV interviewer).

FURTHER INFO:
Prospectuses for undergrads and postgrads, video, websites (www.swan.ac.uk and www.swansea-union.co.uk) and an annual 6th form newsletter called 'Baywatch'.

ACADEMIC

Over half of those *putting pen to exam paper*, get a 2:1 or better. What's more, any student can submit his or her exam scripts in Welsh.

staff/student ratio: 1:15
Range of points required for entrance: 320-160
Percentage accepted through clearing: 15%
Number of terms/semesters: 3
Length of terms/semesters: 10 wks
Research: 4.1

LIBRARIES:
• Books: 750,000 • Study places: 1,000
4 libraries, *which students say are overcrowded, although book provision is good.*

COMPUTERS:
• Computer workstations: 950
Generally satisfactory (see old school reports for meaning of 'satisfactory').

ENTERTAINMENT

TOWN:
• Price of a pint of beer: £1.50 • Glass of wine: £1.20
Cinemas: Apart from the 10-screen multiplex, the Taliesin (on campus) and Ty Llen arts centres provide less mainstream celluloid.
Theatres: The Grand Theatre *is very popular and successful, if not exactly radical.*
Pubs: Pubs along the 'Mumbles Mile' and Wind Street are very popular with students *and there are very few hostile ones in town.* Pushplugs: Smokin' Dog (indie hang-out); Indigo; Hogshead; Ice Bar; Fineleg & Firkin; Rhydding's; Rasputin.
Clubs/discos: *Swansea is something of a clubber-magnet in an area ill-served for dance fans. Serious party punters come from all over South Wales.* Pushplugs: Escape (Top DJs and Indie hangoat at weekends); Time; Jumpin Jacks; Uropa (drum 'n' bass); Quids (cheese).
Music venues: Apart from the campus refectory, Swansea doesn't have a major venue but dozens of pubs and clubs put on smaller-scale gigs, so there's always something on. *Pushplugs: Coach House (local rockers); Ellington's (jazz and blues); Singleton, Mumbles Fishing Club and Celtic Pride (indie); Duke of York (jazz and blues).*
Eating out: *Come the evening, all your wildest greeds are catered for. The Indian restaurants, in particular on St Helens Rd, are worth a mention. The range, quality and price are second only to Bradford, Rusholme and Delhi. Night-time nibbles are available till at least 2am and deliveries till midnight, but only 10pm in The Mumbles.* Pushplugs: Café Mambo (Mexican); Baguette du Jour (sandwich bar); Mozart's (Austrian); Viceroy (Indian); Slow Boat (Chinese); Angellettos (Italian).

UNIVERSITY:
• Price of a pint of beer: £1.40 • Glass of wine: £1.20
The Taliesin Arts Centre is the *crown of the campus* with a whole

host of entertainment facilities (from exhibitions to film and music). *It makes up in part for the city's musical and arty cultural limitations.* Most of the events aren't exclusively by or for students even though the College owns the place. In October it's the focus of the Swansea Fringe Festival – the second biggest in Britain after Edinburgh. *However, unlike Edinburgh it has the advantage of being during term-time.* There are plans to build a 2,000 cap nightclub and music venue on campus.

Bars: (2) The main SU bar is Diva's (capacity 400) and Idols (cap 400). There is also a bar in the Taliesin Arts Centre.

Theatres: The theatre in the Taliesin has a capacity of 350 where student productions get a look-in between the touring pros. *The Drama Society is a hotbed of actors acting actively,* with a major production every term and an annual panto.

Cinemas: Each week the Taliesin shows 2 or 3 films mostly foreign/minority and the odd mainstream flick. There's also a gay film season.

Clubs/discos: Most of the fun revolves around Diva's but there is action is in town where the SU hires out Time and Escape.

Music venues: The Refectory is the largest venue (800) playing host, recently, to Jools Holland and the Honeyz. Brangwyn Hall is also used for gigs.

Food: Angles Food Hall offers *good value and a wide selection,* including an *extensive* veggie range. *Diva's looks like a glamourous fish and chip shop and is less easy on the pocket.* Salad Bowl does salads, soups and baked potatoes and there's also an internet café called Impressions, but it only has 6 workstations.

Others: Several major balls, culminating in the midsummer bash at, of all places, Swansea Airport. Five marquees are set up on one of the runways.

SOCIAL & POLITICAL

SWANSEA STUDENTS' UNION/ UNDEB Y MYFYRWYR:
• <u>5 sabbaticals</u> • <u>Turnout at last ballot: 22%</u> • <u>NUS member</u>
The SU wags the ear of the college administration and manages to keep the punters fairly happy at the same time – no mean achievement. Fun and facilities abound as if their genes were fused with rabbits.

SU FACILITIES:
There are 3 bars; travel agency, café; media centre; TV lounge; general shop (including second-hand books); print shop, nursery; Endsleigh Insurance; launderette; 4 pool tables; photo booth; video and vending machines; NatWest cashpoint; Lloyds cashpoint and bank and pay phones. It also has the Student Amenities Centre at Hendrefoilan Student Village which has a general shop, a bar, licensed diner, vending machines, a launderette and pay phones.

CLUBS (NON SPORTING):
Arsenal Supporters; Ballroom Dancing; Choral; Cult TV; Journalists; Juggling; Kite Flyers; Musicians; Plaid Cymru; Role Playing; Travel and Expedition; UN Society; Welsh language.

OTHER ORGANISATIONS:
The *rather good* 'Waterfront' is the student newspaper; Xtreme 963 radio can be heard across Swansea (not because it's played loudly, but just coz it can – if you have a radio receiver). SSCA (Swansea Students Community Action) has over 500 people involved and a

full-time co-ordinator organising 24 projects run every week with the young, the old, the disabled and the deprived.

RELIGIOUS:
• 6 chaplains (CofE, RC, URC, Methodist, Baptist and Orthodox)
On campus there's an inter-denominational chapel, mosque and, in town, churches of most orientations and places of worship for Jews and Jehovah's Witnesses.

PAID WORK:
The careers centre runs a job surgery called 'Worklink'. Students looking for work often end up in bars, *but only sometimes working there*. Engineers and select scientists may find a little vocational vacation work in the local oil industry, but otherwise it's tourism that brings in the loot.

SPORTS

• Recent successes: rugby, surfing
The College has attractive facilities and has achieved a considerable level of success on a national level *as well as creating an enjoyable diversion from studies for those with less Olympian – Olympic, even – talents*. Sports scholarships of £700 per year are available for applicants with an extraordinary prowess or potential in a particular sport. There is a £3 annual fee to join the Athletics Union which organises student sports and has well over 3,000 members. Thereafter, there are minimal charges (eg 50p for the sports centre) to use facilities.

SPORTS FACILITIES:
On and around the campus: 20 acres of playing fields; astroturf pitch; fitness suite; weightlifting equipment; athletics track and field; sports hall; swimming pool; 5 squash; 6 tennis and 2 netball courts; gymnasium and multigym; climbing wall; rifle range and a lake. Off campus the College offers another 70 acres. The city supplements all this with several repetitions and a bowling green, an excellent dry ski slope, golf course, leisure centre and sauna and solarium. There's sailing at the Mumbles and surfing on the Gower peninsula.

SPORTING CLUBS:
Aquidic; Chinese Kickboxing; Lacrosse; Lifesaving; Jiu Jitsu; Rowing; Water Polo; Windsurfing.

ATTRACTIONS:
Within just 2 miles of the campus, students can watch rugby at St Helens and can see Swansea City FC at Vetch Field.

ACCOMMODATION

IN COLLEGE:
• Catered: 15% • Cost: £58-72 (31wks)
• Self-catering: 26% • Cost: £40-62 (40-51wks)
Availability: 90% of freshers are accommodated and some other students with 12% sharing. The 2 Clyne Halls are very popular and provide nearly 350 catered places a mile further west out of town. One *prize* feature is the student village at Hendrefoilan which accommodates 989 students in *attractive* purpose-built houses, often split into flats. All these places are self-catering with between 4 and 11 people sharing a kitchen and bathroom in *noisy harmony*.

The Clyne Halls and Hendrefoilan are very much self-contained communities with some of their own amenities and organisations.
Car parking: No student parking on campus, the nearest is 5 minutes away at St Helens Rugby ground. *At the other halls and at Hendrefoilan, though, it's not a problem.*

EXTERNALLY:
- Ave rent: £40

Availability: *Most students who end up looking for their own accommodation find it without too much difficulty,* usually sharing in the Victorian terraced houses and flats on the west side of town or in The Mumbles if you're willing to travel that little bit further. *Other good areas include Brynmill, Uplands and Sketty although the east side of town is a bit too distant.*

Housing help: The 11 full-time staff of the Accommodation Office offer lists of recommended vacancies, a bulletin board, contract negotiation and an approval scheme. The SU produces its own accommodation handbook to help avoid *unscrupulous* landlords.

WELFARE

SERVICES:
- Creche • Nursery • Nightline • Lesbian & Gay Society
- Mature SA • Overseas SA • Postgrad SA • Minibus
- Women's Officer • Self-defence classes

The University-run Health Centre and Counselling Service employs a medical officer, a sister, receptionist and 2 full-time and 2 part-time counsellors providing help with all sorts of personal and health problems.

Women: *Active* women's group, offering free alarms, women-only room, etc, although they've had to battle to keep the SU Women's Officer. *Avoid Singleton Park at night unless you want to get flashed at.*

Disabled: There are some specific modifications which help things along, such as a recording centre for visually-impaired students (opened by David Blunkett MP). Most buildings have wheelchair access. There are induction loops, guaranteed places in halls and helpers for hearing- and sight-impaired students. Also weekly classes and support for dyslexia sufferers.

FINANCE:
- Access fund: £201,339 • Successful applications: 882

£700 per annum sports and cultural scholarships.

'I met a girl who was going to Oxford. I said to her, "Why can't you read bloody Pride and Prejudice in the f***ing kitchen? Why do you have to go to Oxford?" No Answer.'

- Jeffrey Bernard, writer and bon viveur.

625 Teesside

University of Teesside

Textiles see Heriot-Watt University

Thames Poly see University of Greenwich

Thames Valley University

Trent University see Nottingham Trent University

Trinity & All Saints see Other Institutions

Trinity College, Carmarthen see Other Institutions

Trinity College of Music see Other Institutions

University of Teesside

- *Formerly Teesside Polytechnic*

University of Teesside, Middlesbrough, TS1 3BA.
Tel: (01642) 218121. Fax: (01642) 342067.
E-mail: h.cummins@tees.ac.uk
University of Teesside Students' Union, Borough Road,
Middlesbrough, TS1 3BW. Tel: (01642) 342234.
Fax: (01642) 342241. E-mail: s.judd@utu.org.uk

GENERAL

On the edge of the *glorious* Yorkshire moors, on the north-east coast of England and not far from the ancient city of Durham, lies Cleveland, which was only created as a county in 1974 and was abolished again in the early 90s. It's a large industrial conurbation encompassing the towns of Middlesbrough, Stockton, Redcar and Hartlepool, squeezing in over a million people. *One of Middlesbrough's newer attributes is the University,* with the 'Campus 2000' expansion project which includes a new School of Health building and the Centre for Enterprise.

Sex ratio(M:F): 46%:54%	Founded: 1930
Full time u'grads: 7,663	Part time: 7,753
Postgrads: 1,594	Non-degree: 6,578
Ave course: 3/4yrs	Ethnic: 9%
Private school: 3%	Flunk rate: 20.2%
Mature students: 34.5%	Overseas students: 6%
Disabled students: 7%	

ATMOSPHERE:
It's very much a local university – the campus has a village-like air, and the locality is generally friendly and cheap.

MIDDLESBROUGH:
- Population: 143,600 • London: 256 miles • York: 49 miles
- Newcastle: 39 miles

Middlesbrough's a true northern town: mile upon mile of back-to-back Victorian terraces; massive (now largely silent) industrial plants; *strangely,* still active docks; and an *inconsistent* football team. Furthermore, the town's large enough to provide more shopping opportunities than any student can reasonably afford, including a sprinkling of bookshops and 3 shopping malls. *Potential students will be uninterested to note that the town's most attractive building is the 19th-century Central Library, and probably they couldn't care less that Teesside was the birthplace of the railway* (Stockton-Darlington, 1825). *Unless they like trains.*

TRAVEL:
Trains: Middlesbrough station offers direct links to Newcastle (£5.15), Manchester (£18.15) and other major interchanges. For London (£42.25) change at Darlington.
Coaches: Coach services courtesy of Blue Line, City Link, Swiftline and National Express to London (£21), Manchester (£11.75) and all over.
Car: The A19 south to York and north to Newcastle runs straight through Middlesbrough. Also, there's the A66, cross country to the lakes and the A1 runs through Darlington, 15 miles to the west.
Air: Teesside airport, 12 miles away – domestic flights and to Europe and Scandinavia.
Local: *Buses are cheap* (50p max) *and fairly regular* but stop running after 11pm. Trains run *regularly* all over the Teesside conurbation.
Taxis: *Reasonably priced* (£2 across town) *and readily available.*
Bicycles: *The town is flat, but small enough to render pedalling purely recreational.*

CAREER PROSPECTS:
- Careers Service • No of staff: 3 full-time
- Unemployed after 6mths: 7.7%

FAMOUS ALUMNI:
David Bowe and Steve Hughes (MEPs); Paul Marsden (MP); Skin (singer, Skunk Anansie).

FURTHER INFO:
Prospectuses for undergrads, part timers and postgrads, newsletters, parent guide and booklets, video, websites (www.tees.ac.uk and www.utu.org.uk).

ACADEMIC:

The emphasis on business, health and vocational courses has attracted career-oriented students who appreciate the opportunities to study part-time or on sandwich courses and don't mind the *unattractive surroundings.*

staff/student ratio: 1:12
Range of points required for entrance: 260-140
Percentage accepted through clearing: 15%
Number of terms/semesters: 2
Length of terms/semesters: 15wks
Research: 1.6

LIBRARIES:
- Books: 300,000 • Study places: 1,300

The new Learning Resource Centre is *visually and qualitatively impressive, but students complain that there just aren't enough books in the place.*

COMPUTERS:
- Computer workstations: 1,500

THE CITY:
- Price of a pint of beer: £2.00 • Glass of wine: £2.00

Cinemas: In addition to the 4-screen Odeon in Middlesbrough and the arts cinema in Stockton, there's the Teesside Park development which includes a 14-screen multiplex and a new multiplex close to campus.

Theatres: *The Little Theatre is mostly mainstream but Dovecot Arts Centre offers a wider range.* The Arc arts complex in nearby Stockton contains 3 theatres, a cinema, dance and recording studios, bars and a health club.

Pubs: *Pushplugs: Dickens Inn; Cornerhouse; The Crown; Scruffy Murphy's; Star & Garter. The Zetland is definitely to be avoided.*

Clubs/discos: *It would be unfair to say that all of Middlesbrough's large selection of clubs are tacky, but as generalisations go, it's fair enough.* Grudging Pushplugs are awarded to: Liquid (mainstream); Empire.

Music venues: The Town Hall stages everything from popular to classical, country to more country. It's had the sublime (Kula Shaker) to the ridiculous (Steps). Sessions Jazz Bar does exactly what it says on the tin.

Eating out: *The choice is surprisingly good,* including several value veggie joints and any number of curry houses. *Above all, Roy's Café is a student institution – Roy is an honorary life member of the SU.* Further Pushplugs: Jo Rigatonoies (Italian); Royal Palace and Khan's (Indian).

UNIVERSITY:
- Price of a pint of beer: £1.55 • Glass of wine: £1.45

Bars: (3) Union Central (capacity 600) has a pub-like atmosphere with Sky TV and pool hall.

Cinema: University Cinema (that's its name) shows a blockbuster a week on a big screen.

Clubs/discos: Club One (1,000) is also the venue for shaking your body down and swinging it all around. Friday is party night with Saturday offering nights of 60s, 70s and 80s, Britpop and Dance. The SU promotes the Monday night bash at the Cornerhouse and Wednesdays at Liquid in town.

Music venues: Club One hosts occasional bands and DJs, such as Fragma, The Freestylers and Seb Fontaine. Other nights have seen such *musical giants* as Chesney Hawkes.

Food: The Central Café, the Coffee Stop and the Gallery Restaurant all provide *decent if unexciting food at sensible prices.*

Others: *The Graduation and May Balls are the biggest event in the social calendar, attracting up to 1,500 people each, but there are several other dos that require more sartorial effort than putting on a clean T-shirt.*

SOCIAL & POLITICAL

UNIVERSITY OF TEESSIDE STUDENTS' UNION:
• 4 sabbaticals • Turnout at last ballot: 8% • NUS member
Once a militant left organisation, the SU now sees itself as apolitical and concentrates instead on providing good services for its students. The SU building is very big and well-equipped, virtually a cube and looks from the outside as if it's made of plastic. The students are largely unaware of the SU as anything other than this pseudo-box-cum-beer-dispenser. Recent campaigns have included safety awareness, safer sex and the obligatory anti-tuition fees campaign.

SU FACILITIES:
There are 3 bars, 1 cafeteria, general shop, cash machine (HSBC), Endsleigh Insurance, advice centre, new activities and skills centre, pool tables, vending machines, market stalls and other general services such as phones, photocopiers and photo booths.

CLUBS (NON SPORTING):
Cultural; First Aid; Hellenic; Irish; Photography; Rock; Wine.

OTHER ORGANISATIONS:
The SU produces the monthly 'U2U' magazine and the weekly 'Teesguide' newsletter. The Rag raised the grand total of £11,000 last year, which is not bad for starters.

RELIGIOUS:
In Middlesbrough there's the cathedral and Christians, Muslims and Jews are well served locally.

PAID WORK:
The Union-run Job-shop Unitec has found 2,200 jobs for students in the last year ranging from security to advertising.

SPORTS

• Recent successes: rugby, football, American football
Teesside was a major player among the polytechnics and its standing has improved within BUSA competitions. With a sports card (£25), almost all facilities are free. The University offers an honours degree in Sports and Exercise and Leisure Management.

SPORTS FACILITIES:
The University's on-site sports facilities include a sports hall, tennis courts, an all-weather pitch, a climbing wall and gym. There are 65 acres of playing fields but these are off site, although a free bus will take you there. Overall, $1/3$ of the block grant goes on sport.

SPORTING CLUBS:
American Football; Cheerleading; Gaelic Football; Horse Riding; Netball; Outdoor Pursuits; Rowing; Rugby; Parachuting; Roller Hockey; Sailing; Swimming.

ATTRACTIONS:
Middlesbrough FC *(a team of human yo-yos get another go at the top)*; West Hartlepool Rugby Union; horse-racing at Redcar; speedway at Stockton. Tees Barrage is an 11-mile stretch of *worldclass* white-water for rafting and canoeing.

Vimto was invented at UMIST.

ACCOMMODATION

IN COLLEGE:
• Self-catering: 11% • Cost: £30-52 (37wks)
Availability: All accommodation is reserved for 1st years and 20% of the rooms are shared. *The University accommodation, if not plentiful or pretty, is cheap and weatherproof,* and there are also 546 places on a head tenancy scheme. Improved security on campus *means students might even find their room in one piece when they go back to it.*
Car parking: Free (well for a £20 deposit) within the accommodation blocks, although a £40 permit is required for university parking.

EXTERNALLY:
• Ave rent: £35
Availability: The large mature and local student population tends to live at home and *the private sector is far from saturated. It's pretty easy to find a place and some nice houses are available. Anywhere within the town centre is liable to be suitable. The area near the station probably isn't.*
Housing Help: The Accommodation Office has 6 staff who negotiate rent levels, inspect accommodation, produce lists of vacancies.

WELFARE

SERVICES:
• Nursery • Lesbian & Gay Society • Mature SA • Overseas SA
• Minibus • Women's Officer • Equal Ops Committee
• Self-defence classes

The University employs 3 full-time and 1 part-time counsellors and 10 advisers, but most students with problems call first at the Union's *very good* Advice Centre. The campus has CCTV and a late-night minibus.
Disabled: Most new buildings have decent access and lifts. There is also specially adapted accommodation, computing rooms and a dedicated Disability Adviser. Induction loops are being installed.

FINANCE:
• Hardship fund: n/a • Successful applications: 815
There are short-term emergency loans.

Textiles

see Heriot-Watt University

Thames Poly

see University of Greenwich

```
The Sex Pistols played their first proper
gig at St Martin's College (Now part of
London Institute).
```

Thames Valley University

- **Formerly Polytechnic of West London, Ealing College.**
(1) Thames Valley University, St Mary's Road, Ealing, London, W5 5RF. Tel: (020) 8579 5000. Fax: (020) 8566 1353.
E-mail: learning.advice@tvu.ac.uk
Thames Valley University Students' Union, St Mary's Road, Ealing, London, W5 5RF. Tel: (020) 8231 2276. Fax: (020) 8231 2589.
E-mail: students.union@tvu.ac.uk
(2) Thames Valley University, Wellington Street, Slough, Berkshire, SL1 1YG. Tel: (01753) 534585.

GENERAL

In 1991, Ealing College, Thames Valley College Slough, London College of Music and Queen Charlotte's College of Healthcare Study amalgamated to form the Polytechnic of West London, which consequently had 4 sites. A year later it changed again and became Thames Valley University. There was a bit of fuss about this – a considerable faction preferred the name 'University of West London' *(Push preferred 'Kylie', but no-one asked us)*. The University has a strong commitment to the local area and to encouraging entry through non-traditional routes. Most students are in Ealing, 10 miles from Trafalgar Square, with Slough (pronounced to rhyme with 'cow'), currently housing 40% of courses.

Sex ratio(M:F): 36%:64%
Full time u'grads: 3,859
Postgrads: 415
Ave course: 3yrs
Private school: n/a
Mature students: 81%
Disabled students: 2.5%

Founded: 1992
Part time: 1,755
Non-degree: 4,660
Ethnic: 53%
Flunk rate: 32.7%
Overseas students: 8%

ATMOSPHERE:
TVU's a real melting pot, taking in a high proportion of mature students and reflecting the local ethnically diverse community. There's also a large number of students on part-time, day-release and evening courses and plenty who rolled in off the roulette wheel of clearing, so it's quite far removed from many people's perception of a 'normal' university. Students always seem to be going somewhere, as if standing still makes them a target for paintball snipers.

> The Cannabis Awareness Society at UEA arranges fact-finding tours to Amsterdam, and has appeared on Radio 4 to promote the alleged benefits of the weed.

THE SITES:
Ealing: The airport *lounge-style reception area is just a front for interiors that resemble the High School in 'Grease'*.
Slough: (hotel & catering, science, computing, accounting, business & finance) The Slough site, 17 miles away, has the new Paul Hamlyn Learning Resource Centre. There is much more available space and fewer students on this site than Ealing, though Slough itself, a commuter satellite town, *is probably best described by John Betjeman: 'Come friendly bombs and fall on Slough. It's not fit for humans now'*.

THE CITY: see University of London

EALING:
Ealing is a usefully accessible part of West London. It is mostly affluent with designer dress shops and patisseries alongside the more sensible, basic shops. This part of town is renowned as a haunt for would-be celebs – the National Film & Television School is just opposite the University. South Ealing, however, is much less well-to-do. The main campus is between these two parts, *a busy private estate, which has led to a bit of local friction.* Matters have improved following a threatened ents and bar ban by the University authorities.

TRAVEL: see University of London
Local travel: The nearest tube stations are Ealing Broadway (District and Central Lines) and South Ealing (Piccadilly Line).

CAREER PROSPECTS:
• Careers Service • No of staff: 8 full/2 part-time
• Unemployed after 6mths: 10%
Careers centres at both sites and careers tutors in each School.

FAMOUS ALUMNI:
Emma Anderson (Lush guitarist); John Bird (Big Issue bloke); Holly Hotlips (Chris Evans' posse pal, *one of those who clap and applaud imperishably, try Coxy 97-99 fm)*; Jay Kay from Jamiroquai (the cat in the hat); James Larlett (previous British hockey captain); Alan Lee (illustrator); Freddie Mercury (of Queen, *again try 97-99 fm, but if you like try the Holly Hotlips show thingy)*; Robert Rankin (writer); Pete Townshend (of The Who); Alan Warner (writer); Ron Wood (of The Rolling Stones). Honorary Professorships have been awarded to figures as diverse as David Frost, Neil Kinnock and Alexei Sayle; but not Billie Piper yet.

FURTHER INFO:
Undergrad and postgrad prospectuses, fact sheets for all courses, website (www.tvu.ac.uk).

The Sloane Ranger Handbook list of approved UK universities is: Oxford, Cambridge, Bristol, Exeter, Durham, the Courtauld, UCL, Reading, St Andrews, UEA and Edinburgh.

ACADEMIC:

An 'electronic campus' has been created, with its central hub at the new Paul Hamlyn LRC in Slough, designed to facilitate distance learning. *Many students were afraid this might mean they were to be taught by robots, until Tony Blair's appearance at the opening when he blustered forth inane platitudes about it being something 'new', which of course meant that it would be the same as what they'd had for 18 years before but with a different name.*

staff/student ratio: n/a
Range of points required for entrance: 180-140
Percentage accepted through clearing: 19%
Number of terms/semesters: 2
Length of terms/semesters: 15wks
Research: 2.5

LIBRARIES:
• <u>Books: 221,000</u> • <u>Study places: 767</u>
There are 5 libraries in all. The two main libraries are the *all-singing-all-dancing* Paul Hamlyn Learning Resource Centre at Slough *(which looks like a railway station, but obviously a lot more quiet)* and the Ealing Learning Resource Centre.

COMPUTERS:
• <u>Computer workstations: 550</u>

ENTERTAINMENT

IN LONDON: see <u>University of London</u>

EALING:
• <u>Price of a pint of beer: £2.20</u> • <u>Glass of wine: £2</u>

Students tend not to bother with central London that often (it's more expensive and hassle to get back from late). Ealing itself offers quite enough by way of entertainments, pricey though they can be.
Cinemas: 3 local mainstream cinemas (Virgin, 3 screens, and Warner, 8) and the Bellevue Asian cinema is nearby.
Theatres: Questors is the nearest (about 5 minutes) hosting quality rep. Also the *unpretentious, but arty* Waterman's Centre (Brentford).
Pubs: *Pushplugs:* The Better Half; Yates; The Townhouse; Old Orleans; Crispian's; Old Goa.
Clubs/discos/music venues: The Broadway Boulevard is Ealing's *classiest* venue, with a student night on Tuesdays. Live music is mainly pub-based but the Labbats Apollo (Hammersmith) and the Shepherds Bush Empire are within easy reach.

The architect who designed the Rutherford accommodation building at the University of Kent was also responsible for the H-block prisons in Northern Ireland.

Food: *Ealing has a good multi-cultural mix of food foundries.* Pushplugs: Nando's (Mexican); Pizza on the Green (Italian); La Cucina (sandwiches); Tandoori Villa; Minsky's (American diner).

UNIVERSITY:
• Price of a pint of beer: £1.50 • Glass of wine: £1

Bars: The Studio and Artwoods Hall, the dance venue. 2 bars in Slough.

Clubs/discos/music venues: Artwoods Hall (cap 800) hosts grooving and gigs *(mostly tribute bands)*.

Balls: Each site holds an annual ball.

Food: *The Dinermite canteen scores highly for value nosh but rather blows it on the sensible name front.* There are also 3 training restaurants at Slough and another at Ealing, *for above average scoff at below average prices.*

Other: Cultural societies stage events at the SU throughout the year. Annual May Ball is a 10-hour *extravaganzathon*.

SOCIAL & POLITICAL

THAMES VALLEY UNIVERSITY STUDENTS' UNION:
• 4 sabbaticals • NUS member

Slough and Ealing have separate facilities and sabbaticals, *but seem united in not taking politics too seriously.* The University is good at listening though and holds open meetings with the departmental student reps and the Student Council.

SU FACILITIES:
The main SU building is a converted Victorian grammar school. A bar; 2 minibuses; photocopying; printing facilities; catering facilities; vending and games machines.

CLUBS (NON SPORTING):
Law; Music Industry; Sikh; Video Production.

OTHER ORGANISATIONS:
The bi-monthly student magazine, 'Undergrad', was shortlisted for a 'Guardian' award after only 3 issues. TUBE radio station has a temporary licence. 'Tomfoolery' published twice a year for Rag.

RELIGIOUS:
• 3 chaplains (CofE, RC, Jewish)

The chaplains are based at the chaplaincy part-time. *So if you're a part-time believer...*

PAID WORK:
TVU Temps offers part-time and temp vacancies to students including word-processing BBC scripts.

```
The University of East London forced the BBC
to announce that the university in
'Eastenders' is entirely fictional, and that
no member of staff at UEL has ever slept a
fictional character.
```

SPORTS

- Recent successes: Rugby, rowing, football

A growing interest in sporting pursuits is hampered by the lack of facilities.

SPORTS FACILITIES:
Apart from one football field, squash courts and a gym at Slough, the University has to hire facilities. The gym, *however, is amazing*: piped music videos all day, fitness and toning and heavy duty rooms, trained staff, indoor jogging track, exercise bikes, rowing machines, saunas, sunbeds, a masseur and osteopath. Locally, there is an all-weather pitch, golf course, squash, tennis and swimming baths.

SPORTING CLUBS:
Ladies' and Mixed Basketball; Ladies' Football; Ladies' and Mixed Hockey; Ladies' Rugby; Rowing; Skiing; Snowboarding; Softball; Tennis.

ATTRACTIONS:
Locally: Brentford FC; QPR FC; Wasps Rugby Union.

ACCOMMODATION

IN COLLEGE:
TVU has no accommodation although limited reserved places are available at Ealing YMCA. *This isn't quite as disastrous as it may seem, when you consider the number of local students.*

EXTERNALLY: see University of London
- Ave rent: £70

Ealing: *South Ealing, Hanwell and Acton are popular and cheapish.*
Slough: *There are worse places to live than Slough – such as Mars. Windsor is close by but very expensive.*
Housing help: The Administration Department runs an *excellent* accommodation service with 4 full-time officers. They have contacts with over 600 local landlords and last year housed about 1,500 students within 4 miles.

WELFARE

SERVICES:
- Lesbian & Gay Society • Minibus • Women's Officer
- Self-defence classes

There are nurses at both sites and a visiting doctor and the University employs 2 part-time counsellors, *a reduction in service which has left it inadequate.* A minibus runs between each campus.

Anthrozoologists at Southampton University have discovered that one of the most immature and antisocial dog breed is the cocker spaniel.

Women: The women's group is called the Betty Boothroyd Appreciation Society.
Disabled: *Wheelchair access is excellent.* There are induction loops in all lecture and seminar rooms, dyslexia support and a special needs suite in the Paul Hamlyn LRC. A guide to disabled facilities is produced each year.

FINANCE:
• Access fund: £240,000 • Successful applications: 411
There are bursaries of up to £500 and some funding for overseas students.

Trent University
see Nottingham Trent University

Trinity & All Saints
see Other Institutions

Trinity College, Carmarthen
see Other Institutions

Trinity College of Music
see Other Institutions

> The JCR of Balliol College, Oxford once sent Prince Charles a letter applauding him over his environmental but then sent him another one taking it all back because they'd forgotten their standing policy against the monarchy.

UCE see University of Central England

UCL see University College, London

University of East Anglia

UEL see University of East London

University of Ulster

UMDS see King's College, London

UMIST

United Medical & Dental Schools see King's College, London

University College, London

University College, Stockton see University of Durham

UNL see University of North London

Uxbridge see Brunel University

UCE

see University of Central England

UCL

see University College, London

University of East Anglia, Norwich, NR4 7TJ. Tel: (01603) 593 967.
Fax: (01603) 458 596. E-mail: admissions@uea.ac.uk
Union of UEA Students, Union House, University of East Anglia,
Norwich, NR4 7TJ. Tel: (01603) 503711. Fax: (01603) 250144.
E-mail: comms@su.uea.sk

GENERAL

East Anglia is mostly flat as a pancake (but not as flat as neighbouring Lincolnshire). Norfolk, the northern half, also has the Broads: canals and rivers running all over the county *like golden syrup.* The county's largest city is Norwich, which a couple of hundred years ago was also the second biggest in England and, by East Anglian standards is really quite hilly. *It was somewhat left behind by the Industrial Revolution and, while other cities cottoned on to cotton or coined it in with coal,* Norwich developed a mustard industry, still thriving today. Now Norwich is a tourist attraction, market town and administrative centre for Norfolk. The University's 270–acre campus, known as University Plain, is 2½ miles from the city centre between a 1940s council estate and the Yare Valley conservation area. Most of the buildings are concrete, *but it's not a jungle.* In fact, the campus is very green, and even has its very own Norfolk Broad (or lake).

Sex ratio(M:F): 45%:55%	Founded: 1963
Full time u'grads: 8,635	Part time: 4,097
Postgrads: 2,184	Non–degree: 197
Ave course: 3yrs	Ethnic: 14%
Private school: 21%	Flunk rate: 8.7%
Mature students: 31%	Overseas students: 9%
Disabled students: 4%	

ATMOSPHERE:
There's an easy-going, informal atmosphere, but cliques still exist in this largely white, middle-class environment. Those who can overcome this, the lousy weather and the morgue-like atmosphere that descends at weekends, will find it a great place to work and play. If it does get a bit claustrophobic, however, the town's only a short bus or cycle ride. This is a greenfield campus in the truest sense. *Don't come looking for cutting edge street style. Quite clever people having fun in a pleasant environment is closer to the mark.*

TOWN:
- Population: 120,700 • London: 103 miles
- Birmingham: 139 miles • Cambridge: 62 miles

Local people insist that Norwich is a city not a town. It does, after all, have two cathedrals and contains all the usual amenities such as a whole range of supermarkets, late-night shops, bookshops, banks and well-located cashpoints. As well as the Cathedral, tourist attractions include a Norman Castle, which has been converted into a museum and art gallery, and a small agricultural museum. *For UEA students, Norwich is like a warm duvet, nice and cosy, without masses else to offer. The town's also far from an ethnic melting pot.*

TRAVEL:
Trains: Nearest BR station is Norwich, 3 miles from the University campus. Direct services to London (2hrs, £19.95) and change there for most other destinations.
Coaches: Services to, among other places, London (£15.25) and Glasgow (£42.50).
Car: The A11, A47, A140 and A146 go via Norwich.
Air: Flights inland and also to Amsterdam from Norwich Airport.
Local: *Buses are reliable and wide ranging.* Campus to town centre £1.70 return.
Taxis: *Many students have problems with taxis not arriving, but use them quite a lot anyway (relatively speaking).*
Bicycles: Some provision of cycle lanes near UEA, *but it's advisable to wear a gas mask on the ring road.* Otherwise, it's good territory for two–wheelers, since Norfolk is, as Noël Coward remarked, flat.

CAREER PROSPECTS:
- Careers Service • No of staff: 5 full/1 part
- Unemployed after 6mths : 5%

FAMOUS ALUMNI:
Jenny Abramsky (Radio 5 Live controller); Trezzo Azopardi, Martyn Bedford, Kazuo Ishiguro, Toby Litt, Ian McEwan, Clive Sinclair, Rose Tremain (writers); Jack Davenport (actor); Charlie Higson, Arthur Smith (comedians); Selina Scott (TV celebrity).

FURTHER INFO:
Official prospectuses from Admissions Office, alternative prospectus from the SU. There's also a web site (www.uea.ac.uk/welcome.html) and a CD-ROM.

ACADEMIC

UEA is particulary renowned in two areas. The first is English and American studies including the world famous MA in writing (see alumni above). The other is in environmental studies, which although it includes meteorology and the like, isn't quite as green as it sounds. Lots of genetic modification goes on at the John Innes centre.

staff/student ratio: 1:20
Range of points required for entrance: 360-200
Percentage accepted through clearing: 14%
Number of terms/semesters: 3
Length of terms/semesters: 9wks
Research: 4.5

LIBRARIES
• Books: 800,000 • Study places: 250
The library has 'Silence Is Golden' plastered all over the walls. Which is nice.

COMPUTERS:
• Computer workstations: 2,000
Students are content with computer facilities, although a free palm-top for all would obviously be preferable.

ENTERTAINMENT

TOWN:
• Price of a pint of beer: £2.10 • Glass of wine: £1.85
Cinemas: (4) A multiplex, a Cannon, an Odeon and the *more cool and interesting* Cinema City.
Theatres: The Theatre Royal is the largest with a capacity of 2,000, *providing mainstream fare, opera and Shakespeare. The Norwich Playhouse is a bit more radical and Norwich Arts Centre is yet more diverse.*
Pubs: *Norwich has a massive choice of pubs; over 300 in all. The best concentration is in the Golden Triangle, the main student area.* Pushplugs: Garden House; Unthank Arms; Belle Vue; Café Da (vodka bar); Mad Moose (rugger buggers). *Best to avoid hostelries on some of the less friendly estates (eg West Earlham and the Larkman).*
Clubs/discos: A varied selection, *which is nurturing Norwich's hitherto lame nightlife.* Pushplugs: Liquid (Tues is student night with free entry); Zoom (indie/garage); Marvel (hip-hop/acid jazz) and Gas Station (soul/funk) at The Loft; Ikon (student nights); Mojo's Club

(trip-hop/drum'n'bass); Time.
Music venues: The Arts Centre (cap 350) offers an eclectic selection and indeed comedy, *but the University is probably the best venue in East Anglia.*
Eating out: Again, *nothing too extraordinary, but who cares when you're out to celebrate, pull, or just soak up the beer?* Pushplugs: Tree House (wholefood); Café Rouge; Anchor Quay; Pedro's (Mexican); Earlham Café and Unthank Kitchen (greasy spoons).

UNIVERSITY:
• <u>Price of a pint of beer: £1.60</u> • <u>Glass of wine: £1.40</u>
Bars: (4) The Hive is open all day, although The Pub is the main watering hole. Others are the Back Bar and the LCR but that only opens when there's an event on.
Theatres: The UEA Studio (cap 200) is the site of *some damn fine work* by the drama and non-drama students and small touring productions.
Cabaret: Live in the Hive buzzes (sorry) with regular comedy and the occasional hypnotist.
Cinemas: Three mainstream and art films each week are shown in a lecture theatre. The Film Soc manages to get movies very soon after release.
Music venues: The LCR is a major tour date for some of the top name bands, such as, in the past year, Paul Wellar, Mel C, David Gray, Toploader. Local and *obscure* indie bands play the SU-run Waterfront in the city. Uni (cap 1,440); Studio (cap 700). For more classical and *conventional* tastes, the site for sound is the small concert hall (cap 150) in the University Music Centre.
Clubs/discos: LCR every Thursday night is the big club event, held, funnily enough, in the LCR. The Su also runs the Waterfront, *a major cred* nightspot in town.
Food: On campus there are eight main food stops, ranging from the *cheap and cheerful* fast food in The Diner to the *right-on (but still reasonable)* SASSAF sandwich bar, from which all profits go to charity. All outlets are run by the University except for one *wee* pizza bar. The best cappuccinos are in the Sainsbury Centre café.
Other: The *incredible* Sainsbury Centre for Visual Arts on campus has a *very impressive* array of tribal modern and other art, built in 1978 by the guy who owns the supermarkets. *Fortunately,* it's got a different colour scheme. There are also Latin parties and two balls a year.

SOCIAL & POLITICAL

THE UNION OF UEA STUDENTS:
• <u>4 sabbaticals</u> • <u>Turnout at last ballot: 14%</u> • <u>NUS member</u>
UEA has lost its past reputation as a left-wing hotbed. *The apathy ague* (mistaking indifference for impartiality) has spread. Relations with the uni administration are as icy as a freezer which has never been defrosted, and frankly never will be.

SU FACILITIES:
In Union House and elsewhere on campus: 5 bars; the campus convenience store; newsagent; a post office; travel shop; second-hand bookshop; Waterstone; games room; common rooms; print room; darkroom; photocopying; advice centre; women's room; snack-bar; vending machines; minibus hire; snooker tables; launderette; ticket agency; banks with cashpoints (Barclays, Lloyds).

CLUBS (NON SPORTING):
AIESEC; Alternative Music; Art; Bell–ringing; Bird Club; Brew; Bridge; Buddhist; Chess; Chinese; Cult Film; Football Supporters; French; Games; German; Greek; Hellenic; History/Archeology; Italian; Jazz & Blues; Juggling; Kite; Klustaflux (comedy); Latin; Law; Malaysian; Motorcycle; Music; Oxfam; Peace; Photo; Politics; Skan Clan (Scandinavian); Spanish; Travel & Exploration; Turkish; Wine; Young European.

OTHER ORGANISATIONS:
'Concrete', the fortnightly newspaper, is a regular award-winner and there's also the termly mags 'Retarded Scholaire' and 'Bucket of Tongues'. Livewire Radio has also picked up gongs *but Nexus TV is hampered by the fact it can only be seen in The Hive bar.* There's the Student Community Action group and SASSAF (South African Student Support and Aid Fund).

RELIGIOUS:
There is a non-denominational chaplaincy on campus and a worship room for Muslims. In the city, there is a splendid Anglican Cathedral and another for Catholics, as well as prayer areas for Jews, Muslims and Buddhists.

PAID WORK:
The jobshop is jointly run by the SU and the University. There's less unemployment in East Anglia than in most of the country and apart from the usual bar work, students can get better paid jobs in local government and other areas.

SPORTS

- Recent successes: rowing, volleyball

The campus is big enough to support sports facilities to stretch eyes as well as limbs and athletic activity is a mass participation thing. The SU has a 'sports for all' policy but some are put off by the cliqueyness of the sports clubs.

SPORTS FACILITIES:
Most facilities are on campus, including a *fantastic* new sports hall, gym, badminton courts, multigym, weight-training and indoor football facilities, swimming pool, baseball diamond, six squash courts (for which there's a small charge), 12 tennis courts, cricket nets, artificial pitch, the county athletics track and two newish hockey pitches. On the edge of University Plain are 30 acres of playing fields. Locally, there are the Norfolk Broads for water sports and the city provides a pool and golf course.

SPORTING CLUBS:
American Football; Athletics; Badminton; Basketball; Billiards & Snooker; Boat; Cricket; Cycling; Fell and Cave; Fencing; Football; Golf; Hockey; Kayak; Korfball; Lacrosse; Mountaineering; Netball; Parachute; Riding; Rock Climbing; Rowing; Rugby; Sailing; Shi Kon Karate; Skate; Ski; Squash; Sub Aqua; Surf; Swimming; Table Tennis; Tae Kwon Do; Trampoline; Volleyball; Windsurfing.

ATTRACTIONS:
A few miles from the University is the massive Norwich Sports Village – a multi-million quid sports centre. There's a dry ski slope at Trowse (4 miles away) and an indoor kart club, snooker hall, ten pin bowling and Quasar laser skirmish in the city. Norwich City FC (with Delia Smith and hubby on the board).

```
Imperial College, London, has its own nuclear reactor.
```

ACCOMMODATION

IN COLLEGE:
• Self-catering: 35% • Cost: £40–58 (34-39wks)
Availability: All 1st years (so long as they normally live further than 12 miles away) can live in and about a quarter of other years have a chance. Overseas and disabled students have priority for all three years. Most rooms are on campus in mixed halls (ground floors rooms are all male) and no-one has to share. *Don't bring a cat, there isn't room to swing one in most rooms (and it's cruel, anyway)*, but Norfolk and Suffolk Terraces (*which won awards from architects who don't actually have to live there*) have *great* views of the University Broad (the lake, not the *local floozy*). Waverley Terrace is older and a less good deal. 24-hour security, CCTV and emergency phones are in use on campus.
Car parking: A hi-tech card (for which there is a £10 refundable deposit) and barrier system operates but (and there's always a but) it's only available for 1st years living at home who have to travel and for the disabled.

EXTERNALLY:
• Ave rent: £40
Availability: *Students can usually find accommodation in Norwich.* An area known as the Golden Triangle is marked out by Unthank Road, Earlham Road and Dereham Road. *It's a bit of a yuppie ghetto but that's where the good pubs and the 24-hour shops are, so, funnily enough, that's where the students go. Avoid the estates at Larkham and West Earlham.*
Housing help: The Housing Bureau operated by the SU keeps details of vacancies, a property index and offers advice on contracts.

WELFARE

SERVICES:
• Nursery • Nightline • Lesbian & Gay Society • Mature SA
• Overseas SA • Minibus • Women's Officer
The University provides 3 full-time counsellors and one part-time. There's a 24-hour Health Centre on campus, including GPs, a dentist and a psychiatrist. Race Awareness Society.
Women: Subsidised personal alarms, women's group and delayed fare system for those without the taxi fare home.
Disabled: *Wheelchair access is pretty good, mainly because the campus is quite flat, but there are also plenty of lifts and ramps and all that good stuff, as well as a Special Needs Awareness society.* There's a dyslexia support service and HEFCE funding (£203,000) for the 'Support for Learning' project for students with dyslexia and hearing problems.

FINANCE:
• Access fund: £306,755 • Successful applications : 405
There are five hardship funds, the VC's fund, a Nursery Fund and tuition fees scholarships for undergrad and overseas students.

The Athletics Union at York is sponsored by Vaseline.

UEL

see University of East London

University of Ulster

(1) The University of Ulster (Coleraine), Cromore Road, Coleraine, BT52 1SA. Tel: (028) 7034 4141. Fax: (028) 7034 0947.
Students' Union, South Buildings, The University of Ulster at Coleraine, Cromore Road, Coleraine, BT52 ISA.
Tel: (028) 7035 6321. Fax: (028) 7033 24915.
(2) The University of Ulster (Jordanstown), Shore Road, Newtownabbey, Co Antrim, BT37 0QB. Tel: (028) 9036 5131.
Students' Union, The University of Ulster (Jordanstown), Co Antrim, BT37 0QB. Tel: (028) 9036 5121. Fax: (028) 9036 2817.
(3) The University of Ulster (Belfast), York Street, Belfast, BT15 1ED. Tel: (028) 9032 8515.
(4) The University of Ulster (Magee College), Northland Road, Londonderry, BT48 7JL. Tel: (028) 7137 1371.
Fax: (028) 7137 5410.

GENERAL

Once upon a time, there was a University and a Polytechnic in Northern Ireland. Then, in 1984, they merged and became one large University with four distinctly different sites, thinly spread across three of the six counties. The largest is Jordanstown – the former poly site on the hills above Belfast overlooking the Lough (bay) – and the smallest (housing art & design) is in the city centre. The University *HQ* is on the outskirts of Coleraine, nearly 60 miles north of Belfast (as the crow with a compass flies) on the *beautiful* Antrim coast. 30 miles to the west of that, is the 4th site, Magee College in (London)Derry. Each site is distinct and retains its own atmosphere and administration. *Indeed, all that Jordanstown and Coleraine seem to have in common are a beautiful isolated setting and monstrously ugly modern concrete buildings.*

Sex ratio(M:F): 41%:59%	Founded: 1968
Full time u'grads: 10,668	Part time: 3,307
Postgrads: 1,394	Non–degree: 1,216
Ave course: 3yrs	Ethnic: 1%
Private school: n/a	Flunk rate: 12.5%
Mature students: 75%	Overseas students: n/a
Disabled students: 7%	

ATMOSPHERE & SITES:
We're dealing with four different sites here, which despite the University's best efforts towards integration are still stubbornly up to 80 miles apart. Failing divine intervention, they will remain geographically distinct so that's the way to treat them.

Jordanstown: (11,900 students) The largest site is attended by over half the University's students and is still expanding fast. Belfast, 7 miles away, is the nearest town of any size, and *students can be known to complain of isolation, but the campus is well-connected and the attractive grounds, buildings and views over the Lough provide some compensation.* Anyway, 80% of the students go home each weekend, so there's no room for claustrophobia. *Relaxed and vacant just about sums up Jordanstown.*

Coleraine: (5,400 students) The original site of the University and its HQ. The campus is on the edge of the *small, bland and quiet (as a bored mouse)* market town of Coleraine and less than 5 miles from the coastal resorts *(in the loosest sense)* of Portrush and Portstewart, where most students live. The campus is surrounded by green countryside and nearby the Giant's Causeway reaches out across the Irish Sea towards Scotland. *It is a peaceful place if a bit dull.* It would be unfair to describe the students as apathetic (well, not that unfair) but every night at 6pm the campus dies completely – and we mean dies. This is true for weekends too (so if you're after a blinding Saturday night better be inventive). *The students can, however, be moved to groove in the nightclubs of the nearby seaside resorts of Portrush and Portstewart.*

Magee: (3,000 students) An *attractive* campus on the River Foyle, just north of the old walled city of (London)Derry.

Belfast: (970) Art and Design students are housed on York Street just a mile away from <u>Queen's University</u>, *whose facilities they share and which is the focus of their social life.*

CITY: see <u>Queen's University Belfast</u>

TOWNS:
Coleraine/Portrush/Portstewart: The three towns form a triangle with the two ports to the north providing accommodation, jobs and *random* nightlife, and Coleraine at the southern tip providing what class as amenities. A town of 20,721 give or take a few, Coleraine has a *fair sprinkling of cheapy* supermarkets, Irish and UK banks and bookshops. *It's an isolated, parochial, coastal (touristy) outpost.*

(London)Derry: It's an ancient and *scenic city* and Northern Ireland's second largest. The city walls show a *different concern for security from those that trouble the city today,* but as you might expect, people's lives are ruled not by terrorism, but the more mundane concerns of life. They are immensely friendly. (NB. Use of the prefix 'London' labels a person as pro-Unionist to the largely Catholic locals. Calling the city simply 'Derry' ruffles feathers the other way. *Either way, students are stuffed. No wonder* most of the students are from Northern Ireland – *at least they understand the questions, even if they don't know the answers.*)

TRAVEL: see <u>Queen's University Belfast</u>
Trains: Direct lines from Coleraine to Belfast and (London)Derry only on Northern Ireland Railways, frequent and *frequently dirty* trains. Trains from (London)Derry to Belfast and most other local destinations, and to Dublin from Belfast.
Coaches: Goldline Express and Ulsterbus link Belfast, Coleraine and (London)Derry regularly.
Air: Flights to the UK mainland and the rest of Europe from Belfast International. Prices do vary from £69 from Luton up to £300 return from Cardiff but there are many prices in between. Also other flights to the UK mainland from Belfast City Airport and Derry airport in the north-west. Check out Buzz, Go and Ryannair to see whose doing the latest budget offers.

Hitching: *Okay between Coleraine and the ports, otherwise only with the greatest care. A bad idea to the airport or ferries.*
Local: *Comprehensive, but expensive* local buses, but half-price fares for students around Coleraine. Ulsterbus offer an all-day £5 rambler ticket.
Taxis: *Readily available and very cheap if shared.*
Bicycles: *With hills and inclement weather, cycling's only for the most hardy although theft is not a problem.*

CAREER PROSPECTS:
• Careers Services • No of staff: 15 full/2 part
• Unemployed after 6mths: 9%
The Jordanstown, Coleraine and Magee sites all have their own careers advisory services.

SPECIAL FEATURES:
• *Travel between sites is rarely needed,* but for those occasions when the gap has to be bridged, a video-conferencing facility is available currently linking three campuses with further extension planned to the Belfast site.
• Almost everyone goes home at the weekends – *beware.*

FAMOUS ALUMNI:
Gerry Anderson (radio presenter); Brian Friel (playwright); Kate Hoey MP (Lab); Brian Keenan (ex-hostage); Brian Robinson (Irish rugby player).

FURTHER INFO:
Prospectuses for undergrads, part-timers, and postgrads and a video. Also website (www.ulst.ac.uk).

ACADEMIC

staff/student ratio: 1:18
Range of points required for entrance: 340-180
Percentage accepted through clearing: 14%
Number of terms/semesters: 3
Length of terms/semesters: 10wks
Research: 3.9

LIBRARIES:
• Books: 646,808 • Study places: 1,914
There are libraries on all campuses and loans can be made between sites from the Arts collection at Belfast (35,000 books) or the Irish collection at Magee (70,000 books).

COMPUTERS:
• Computer workstations: 1,476
Each faculty has its own computing facilities and there are up to four computer centres on each campus. 24-hour access to computers except at Belfast.

ENTERTAINMENT

CITY: see Queen's University Belfast
(LONDON)DERRY:
Cinemas: Two, including a multiplex.

Pubs: (London)Derry has three parallel streets running from Magee to the town centre and they're all lined with pubs. *Pushplugs: The Gweedore/Peadar O'Donnell's (two pubs in one, very studenty, traditional music every week); The Strand (very close to the Uni); The Anchor (more locals).*

Clubs/discos/music venues: The Rialto and the Guildhall sometimes host big name bands. The only purpose-built club is Squires but many of the pubs have upstairs rooms *for a bit more than an Irish jig.*

Eating out: *Pushplugs: Paolo's Pizza; Leprechaun (coffee shop); Mandarin Palace.*

COLERAINE:
- <u>Price of a pint of beer:</u> £1.80   • <u>Glass of wine:</u> £2.30

Coleraine itself is far from the beating heart of the fun rhythm and what there is, is jealously guarded by the locals (not the most student-friendly bunch). Any so-called nightlife is in Portrush and Portstewart where the majority of students live.

Cinemas: Four screens at the *dead* Jet Centre in Coleraine and The Playhouse in Portrush.

Pubs: *Burberry's is the only pub of note in Coleraine itself but The Derry and the Harbour Inn in Portrush and The Anchor and O'Hara's in Portstewart are pretty student-friendly.* The Bushmills distillery is nearby and does guided tours *(whoopee).*

Clubs/discos: *Pushplugs: in Portrush, Trax (Student meat-market on Mondays).*

Music venues: Many of the bars and clubs host bands, *some are less promising than others such as those who play Snappers in Portstewart. Pushplugs: O'Hara's in Portstewart (traditional music).*

Eating out: *Portrush and Portstewart have all the chips and candyfloss you'd associate with seaside resorts but only really during the summer season. Pushplugs: Morelli's in Portstewart (for ice cream).*

UNIVERSITY:
- <u>Price of a pint of beer:</u> £1.55   • <u>Glass of wine:</u> £1.23

Bars: Jordanstown has three bars, including the newly renovated Arthur's; Club Bar at Coleraine; Bunker Bar at Magee; Conor Hall at Belfast.

Theatres: The School of Performing Arts is due to re-locate to the Magee campus. *There's also a lovely theatre (only architecturally speaking) – the Riverside – which has had a lot of problems recently. It's so bad that even bored students don't go there.* There are trips to the Belfast International Festival and a small drama society at Jordanstown.

Music venues: *Jordanstown comes out best with its Assembly Hall but Coleraine's Biko Hall ain't bad either. Recent rockers include The Saw Doctors and Mansun.*

Clubs/discos: The Saturday night raves at Conor Hall (Belfast) *are very popular, despite the lack of air-conditioning,* and are open to non-students. *Big-time* DJs such as DJ Griff are regular attractions. Club Bar hosts 'Chaos' every fortnight and club nights every Tues and Thurs. There's usually something, *however low-key,* going on at all campuses every week night.

Food: All sites except Belfast have *cheap but basic* (burger & chips variants) canteens run by the SU. Belfast has no catering outlets, *much to the consternation of skint and starving students.* Banside canteen at Coleraine serves *revolting tuck.*

SOCIAL & POLITICAL

UNIVERSITY OF ULSTER STUDENTS' UNION:
• 9 sabbaticals • NUS/USI member
Politics isn't really an issue with the apathetic student body. The SU co-ordinates ents and facilities across all the sites, but can seem distant and unapproachable to the point that many students think the SU is just a bar and stuff. There are three global sabbaticals and each site has one or two of its own as well.

SU FACILITIES:
All sites have bars and snack bar or caféteria facilities as well as music venues, clubs and societies. Also in the South Building at Coleraine: a general shop; cashpoint; travel agent; hairdresser; launderette and printing facilities. At Jordanstown: a shop; travel agency; cashpoint; insurance office; second-hand bookshop; car and van hire; photobooth and photocopying. At Belfast: an art shop; games room and free shuttle after SU ents. There's a general shop, photocopier and photobooth in the new SU building at Magee.

CLUBS (NON SPORTING):
There are different clubs on each campus but many duplicate and all are open to all Ulster students, whatever site. Accounting; An Cumann Gaelach; Bio-chemical; Chemistry; Chinese; Christian; Craft & Art; Cross-Cultural; Dalriada; Divine Harmony; Environment; Euro; Film; International; Literary; Mature; Musicians; Nursing; Nutrition; Parents; Peace People; Pro Choice; Pro Life; Role-Playing; Silversmiths; Spanish; Stimulus; Stork; Transport; Vedic.

OTHER ORGANISATIONS:
Each campus has its own magazine and there's an all-site publication called – *wait for it* – 'Foursite', as well as the Coleraine-based publication 'Ufouria'. The combined charity Rag raises vast sums each year with wacky stunts and students do many good works in the local communities surrounding each of the sites.

RELIGIOUS:
• Chaplains (Christian)
Non-Christians must go into town for a wider choice of gods and creeds. Non-denominational prayer rooms are available.

PAID WORK:
The usual bar jobs and so on in Coleraine and the tourist trade brings summer opportunities with the National Trust among others. The Union employs 70 to 80 students on a casual basis.

SPORTS

• Recent successes: pool, gaelic football, canoeing
Sport is an enthusiasm on a campus basis, rather than University-wide. The best facilities are inevitably centred on Jordanstown and Coleraine. Ten £500 bursaries are available for sports players.

SPORTS FACILITIES:
Coleraine and Jordanstown offer 40 acres of playing fields (collectively), sports centres, athletic tracks, steam rooms and squash and tennis courts. In addition, at Coleraine there are floodlit hockey and soccer pitches, a new fitness suite and the Antrim coast offers plenty of opportunities for scenery-destroying golf courses, sinking and swimming, bobbing and boating. At Jordanstown, there's an *excellent* swimming and diving pool.

SPORTING CLUBS:
Bahai; Camogie; Gaelic; Gymnastics; Hurling; Jiu Jitsu; Kung Fu; Martial Arts; Mountaineering; Parachuting; Rock Climbing; Rowing; Snooker; Surf; Table Tennis; Tae Kwondo.

ACCOMMODATION

IN COLLEGE:
• Self-catering: 12% • Cost: £33-36(32-37wks)
Availability: *The figures look a bit limited but remember that a high proportion of students are locals.* All 1st years who require accommodation will be housed. Jordanstown has 6-bedroom houses and flats. Meanwhile Coleraine offers 4 halls; and Magee has 3 blocks and a student village. Belfast art students have to find their own *bohemian garrets*. There's a head tenancy scheme with 649 places.

EXTERNALLY:
• Ave rent: £29
Availability: Most students at Coleraine actually live in Portrush or Portstewart *where housing is exceptionally cheap,* although more affluent students can choose to spend up to £50 per week on a single flat. *Most are more than happy with a comfortable room in a shared house.* The University's renting scheme SHAC (Student Housing Association) provides 37-week leases (66 places at Coleraine, 4 at Magee) with Portrush and Portstewart houses being surrendered to tourists over the summer. *Cars make life a little simpler at Coleraine and parking presents few problems.*
Belfast: see Queen's University Belfast
Housing help: Both the SU and Accommodation Office are ready with advice. The accommodation list can be helpful to those housed in cardboard, *but SHAC is the real life-saver.*

WELFARE

SERVICES:
• Creche • Nightline • Lesbian & Gay Society • Mature SA
• Overseas SA • Minibus • Women's Officer • Self–defence classes
There's a Parent Support group and the University is *justifiably* proud of its child-care provision with *well-run* creches at all sites. It also employs 7 counsellors and the SU adds 2 welfare officers. The SU solicitor is on hand once a week with free legal advice. The chaplains run a non-alcoholic bar at Jordanstown.
Disabled: Two new bodies have been set up. CODAR (Coalition for Disability Awareness) dealing with access and facilities, and JUDE (Joint Universities Deaf Education). *There is a concerted effort to improve facilities and they're getting there, but things still aren't that great.*

FINANCE:
• Access fund: £227,000 • Successful applications : 1,709
Financial help is also available from the Hardship Fund, Endowment Awards, Disabled Student Allowance and the Hardship Loan Fund.

UMDS

see King's College, London

UMIST

University of Manchester Institute of Science & Technology, PO Box 88, Manchester, M60 1QD. Tel: (0161) 236 3311. Fax: (0161) 228 7040. E-mail: ug.admissions@umist.ac.uk
UMIST Students' Association, UMIST, PO Box 88, Sackville Street, Manchester, M60 1QD. Tel: (0161) 200 3270. Fax: (0161) 200 3268. E-mail: president@umist.ac.uk

GENERAL

UMIST, the University of Manchester Institute of Science & Technology, occupies a 16-hectare site in Western Europe's largest education precinct. UMIST and its students have informal links with the University of Manchester, although recently, the two institutions have formally separated (*but they're still good friends and Neil Morrisey is not Involved*). UMIST's Main Building, which was built in 1902 just before it was first allowed to award degrees, is an art nouveau redbrick block. But most of the architecture is 60s and 70s concrete blocks, white fronts, straight lines and glass. *Useful rather than beautiful.* Once upon a time, it was only possible to study sciences and engineering, but these days, social sciences and even arts are available, but still it's test tubes and all that stuff which dominate.

Sex ratio(M:F): 69%:31%	Founded: 1824
Full time u'grads: 5,093	Part time: 0
Postgrads: 1,679	Non–degree: 0
Ave course: 3/4yrs	Ethnic: n/a
Private school: n/a	Flunk rate: 19.0%
Mature students: 19%	Overseas students: 21%
Disabled students: 3%	

ATMOSPHERE:
UMIST students are a hard-working crowd, with their noses in books or their faces reflected in computer screens as often as not. Non-science courses have been introduced alongside the techie stuff for which UMIST is famous, but it's probably fair to say that those blessed by trendiness or creative style don't tend to make this their first choice. It's overwhelmingly male and, dare we say it, a bit nerdy. Still, they're a nice bunch and everyone seems to appreciate a pint or seven.

THE CITY: see University of Manchester
TRAVEL: see University of Manchester

CAREER PROSPECTS:
• Careers Service   • No of staff: 10 full/7 part
• Unemployed after 6mths: 3%
The careers service is one of the biggest in the country probably because it's shared with Manchester University. *A phenomenal proportion of UMIST students are sponsored by companies to study there.*

FAMOUS ALUMNI:
Margaret Beckett MP, David Clark MP (Lab cabinet ministers); Sir John Cockcroft (scientist); John Dalton (chemist – not the type that stocks condoms); Keith Edelman (Chief Executive, Storehouse); Ian Gibson (Chief Executive, Nissan); Sophie Grigson (TV cook); Terry

Leahy (Chief Executive, Tesco); Geoff Mulcahy (Chief Executive, Kingfisher Group); Keith Oates (Chief Executive, M&S); Sir Arthur Whitten-Brown (trans–Atlantic pilot).

FURTHER INFO:
Prospectuses for undergrads and postgrads, departmental, accommodation and course information and website (www.umist.ac.uk).

ACADEMIC

staff/student ratio: 1:13
Range of points required for entrance: 320-240
Percentage accepted through clearing: 5%
Number of terms/semesters: 2
Length of terms/semesters: 16wks
Research: 5.2

LIBRARIES:
• Books: 311,000 • Study places: 839

COMPUTERS:
• Computer workstations: 1,000
There are enough computers to go round but sometimes they're just not powerful enough for the academic hoops the students make them jump through.

ENTERTAINMENT

TOWN: see University of Manchester

UNIVERSITY:
• Price of a pint of beer: £1.50 • Glass of wine: £1.50
The two local universities (Manchester and Manchester Metropolitan) host some pretty swinging times and UMIST students often take their funky stuff strutting off to them. In return, other students often strut down to UMIST ents.
Bars: (2) Harry's Bar and new Paddy's Lounge.
Theatre: The Renold Theatre hosts productions.
Clubs/discos/music venues: Club Underground (cap 600) hosts various nights from Rock to Cheese to Sub-Tub Manchester's biggest hip-hop and drum and bass night.
Food: The Refectory offers a *wide* choice at lunchtimes (including halal food). Cyber café '@campus' lets you munch and surf. Renold Tavern is open from 11am–4pm and the Café does snacks and butties until 9pm.
Other: Freshers' Ball.

SOCIAL & POLITICAL

UMIST ASSOCIATION:
• 3 sabbaticals • Turnout at last ballot: 5%
UMIST Union's main impact on the student in the 'hood is through the clubs and services it runs rather than its representative role. Politics just doesn't intrude – even to the extent that in 1999 UMIST

disaffiliated itself from the NUS because it felt that the NUS was, and still is, too politically motivated and irrelevant to students at the university.

ASSOCIATION FACILITIES:
In the Barnes Wallis Building (named after the Michael Redgrave look-alike who invented the bouncing bomb and was immortalised in 'The Dambusters'), UMIST Association offers: 2 bars; a general shop; print shop; travel centre; darkroom; Barclay's cashpoint; T-shirt printing service; lounge; and pool tables.

CLUBS (NON SPORTING):
Students are also entitled to join University of Manchester clubs and societies and vice versa.
African-Caribbean; Asian; Chinese; Choir; Cyprus; Dance; First; Gilbert & Sullivan; Hellenic; Indonesian; Industrial; Korean; Malaysian; Management; Mandarin; Mexican; New Music; Norwegian; Pakistan; Palestinian; Party Physics; Rally Club; Role Playing; Singapore; Storm; Student Chemistry; Textiles; Thai; Turkish.

OTHER ORGANISATIONS:
The professional looking 'GRIP' magazine comes out monthly and can also be found online. The Rag (raised £35,000 last year) organises the annual Bogle Stroll, a 55-mile sponsored walk. The Community Action group employs permanent staff as well as enlisting student volunteers.

RELIGIOUS:
3 chaplains are available (Catholic, Methodist, Orthodox) plus 2 rabbis. UMIST shares religious facilities with Manchester University, but does also have a Muslim prayer room of its own, as well as a quiet room.
PAID WORK: see University of Manchester

- Recent successes: rowing
Students are entitled to use Manchester University's facilities, *so they have some mean amenities at their disposal. On their own, UMIST competitions and involvement aren't quite so pulse-straining.* Students can play for Manchester University's teams in sports where UMIST hasn't got a team of its own.

SPORTS FACILITIES:
Most facilities are shared with Manchester University and Manchester Metropolitan. At Fallowfield, 2½ miles from the campus, UMIST has a 10-acre sports ground called MUTECH, *which sounds frighteningly like something you might find on a used hanky* and where students can use the various playing fields, the tennis courts, the pavilion and its bar. Rowing facilities are being developed. On the campus, on the top floor of the Main Building, there are facilities for 5-a-side football, badminton and basketball. At the Sugden Sports Centre just a short sprint from the campus, there's more sporty gear, including a multigym, squash and tennis courts and more 5-a-side football. A *frighteningly* flash pool (£1.50 entry) has been opened for the Commonwealth Games in 2002 and is *on campus as luck would have it.*

SPORTING CLUBS:
Athletics; Basketball; Fencing; Gliding; Hiking and Mountaineering; Motor; Rowing; Ski and Snowboarding; Water Polo; Windsurfing.

ATTRACTIONS: see University of Manchester

ACCOMMODATION

IN COLLEGE:
• Catered: 12% • Cost: £60-105 (31-51wks) • Self-catering: 38%
• Cost: £46-49 (31-52wks)
Availability: All 1st years are guaranteed housing in halls and a few finalists come back as well. An *unlucky* few have to share rooms. UMIST pools its accommodation resources with Manchester Uni – for more on the score, see University of Manchester.
EXTERNALLY: see University of Manchester

WELFARE

SERVICES:
• Creche • Lesbian & Gay Society • Mature SA
• Overseas SA • Minibus • Equal Opportunities Officer
Apart from the joint University counselling service, help is available from the SA advice centre.
Disabled: UMIST has a Special Needs tutor and *the general provision for students with all kinds of disabilities is positive* – ramps, hearing induction loops in some rooms, adapted rooms and computer suites for sight-impaired students.

FINANCE:
• Access fund: £250,000 • Successful applications : 500
The Association-employed adviser points students in the right direction with financial, housing and welfare problems. Bursaries, scholarships and a hardship fund.

United Medical & Dental Schools

see King's College, London

University College, London

• *The College is part of The University of London and students are entitled to use its facilities.*
University College London, Gower Street, London, WC1E 6BT.
Tel: (020) 7679 3000. Fax: (020) 7679 3001.
E-mail: degree-info@ucl.ac.uk
University College London Union, 25 Gordon Street, London, WC1H 0AH. Tel: (020) 7679 3611. Fax: (020) 7383 3937.

GENERAL

University College London, or 'UCL', is the largest college in the University of London (*big enough to be a whopper university on its own*). Faculties and accommodation are concentrated in Bloomsbury, *so this is the nearest thing the University of London has to a campus*

in the city. It was founded by a group of worthies influenced by the ideas of Jeremy Bentham, the famous Utilitarian philosopher (*but, of course, you knew that already*), to promote equality and the crossing of class barriers. It had no religious leanings – which was unique in those days – and was also the first university college to admit women. The main building is *very beautiful* with steps leading to an *impressive* portico at the main entrance. The library dome can be seen behind it. Three stone cloisters edge a big grass lawn. It's all a bit like an inner city stately home. *Unfortunately, the other buildings, humdrum brick, aren't all that.*

Sex ratio(M:F): 49%:51%	
Full time u'grads: 10,694	Part time: 203
Postgrads: 4,060	Non-degree: 581
Ave course: 3yrs	Ethnic: 30%
Private school: 30%	Flunk rate: 7.7%
Mature students: 13%	Overseas students: 21%
Disabled students: 3%	
Founded: 1826	

ATMOSPHERE:
There's a hectic atmosphere consisting mainly of drinking beer, contemplating navels and putting off that library stint for another hour. The size of the college and its proximity to all the temptations of the West End combine to dilute any specific 'college spirit', but it's not an unfriendly place. A recent survey of international students carried out by the Uni, asked them to sum up UCL in three words. They came up with 'friendly, international, great, vibrant, funky, quality and prestigious' (*they can't count though*).

THE SITES:
Royal Free and University College Medical School: the Royal Free Hospital site (582 undergrads, about 4 miles away in Hampstead), and the Whittington Hospital site (at Archway). The Royal Free Hospital, an early 70s concrete building, is based in the *very upmarket and trendily wealthy* London district of Hampstead. It's a relaxed environment and students demonstrate a team spirit which is usually put into practice on the sports field. The School of Slavonic and East European Studies (SSEES) has c. 400 undergrads and merged with UCL in 1999 – it is based in Bloomsbury. Space science and astronomy students have access to sites in Mill Hill (London) and Dorking (Surrey) with specialist Observatories and equipment.

THE CITY: see University of London
TRAVEL: see University of London

CAREER PROSPECTS:
• Careers Service • No of staff: 7 full • Unemployed after 6mths: 3%
UCL's careers service is separate from the University's, but students can use either.

SPECIAL FEATURES:
• UCL includes the Slade School of Fine Art – *dead prestigious and nothing to do with a cuppa-soup-loving yob-rock quartet from Wolverhampton.*

FAMOUS ALUMNI:
Brett Anderson (Suede); Rabbi Lionel Blue (writer/ broadcaster); Raymond Briggs (writer/illustrator); AS Byatt (novelist); Tom Courtney (actor); Jonathan Dimbleby (broadcaster); Ken Follet (writer); Sir Norman Foster (architect); Justine Frischmann (Elastica);

Hugh Gaitskell (dead former Labour leader); Mahatma Gandhi; David Gower (cricketer); Margaret Hodge MP (Lab); Derek Jarman (film director); Dr Hilary Jones (TV doctor); Jonathan Miller (writer and director); Sir Eduardo Paolozzi (artist/sculptor); Dr Mark Porter (yet another TV doctor); Stanley Spencer (artist); Marie Stopes (birth control pioneer); all of Coldplay (John Buckland, Guy Berryman, Will Champion and Chris Martin).

FURTHER INFO:
Prospectuses for undergrads and postgrads from Admissions Enquiries. Websites (www.ucl.ac.uk and www.uclu.org).

ACADEMIC

Students at UCL's Barlett School (which runs courses in architecture, planning and built environment) won the top undergrad and postgrad awards from Royal Institute of British Architects for 1999. Across the whole of UCL, research income is one of the largest of any Uni in the UK (*not that undergrads see much of it*).

staff/student ratio: 1:3
Range of points required for entrance: 360-240
Percentage accepted through clearing: 9%
Number of terms/semesters: 3
Length of terms/semesters: 10wks
Research: 5.8

LIBRARIES:
• Books: 1,500,000 • Study places: 1,514
Apart from the Main and Science libraries there are 12 specialist book barns and another at the Royal Free.

COMPUTERS:
• Computer workstations: 900
Advance booking for computers and some 24-hour access.

ENTERTAINMENT

IN LONDON: see University of London

COLLEGE:
• Price of a pint of beer: £1.70 • Glass of wine: £1.85
Bars: There are 8 bars around the campus and in its halls of residence, the central one being the *pub-like* Phineas. Others include the *sporty* 2nd floor Bar, the vast Windeyer and Gordon's Café Bar. Another three bars are at the Royal Free site – the Doctors', Students' and Hospital Bars.

> The Greenwich University Rag was banned when students blocked the Dartford Tunnel with the cannon from Woolwich barracks.

Cinema: Two films a week, *a good mix* of art films, golden oldies and blockbusters only recently in the West End.
Theatre: The Bloomsbury Theatre (cap 550) hosts UCL productions for 10 weeks a year and the Drama Society makes regular trips to the Edinburgh Fringe. *Opera and musical theatre are also strong.*
Clubs/discos: There's something of the dance variety every night, major events being the Thursday Cocktails night and the Windeyer Bar, with guest DJs, such as recently, DJ Swing and Brian Norman. The SU at the Royal Free throws a *cheesy* party every two-three weeks (but no crackers).
Music venues: There are occasional theme nights (eg salsa) with live bands. Recent names to play include Atomic Kitten, Grooverider and Tim of the Westwood Variety. The Royal Free has the New JCR (cap 200) for live bands and the Peter Samuel Hall for classical music.
Cabaret: Shows at the Bloomsbury Theatre have recently featured Richard Whiteley and Stewart Lee.
Food: There are three University refectories *but students tend to prefer the SU facilities,* which include snack and sandwich bars and food served in 6 of the bars as well as cafés in some departments. There's also the hospital canteen, bars and a servery at the Royal Free.
Others: At least 3 balls a year, drinks promotions, quizzes.

Social & Political

UCL UNION (UCLU):
• 6 sabbaticals • Turnout at last ballot: 9% • NUS member
UCLU is not renowned for its political activity but it is very close to ULU, so those desperate for a soap box or frantic for fantastic facilities don't have far to go. The Union was involved in the successful campaign for cheaper travel in London which put a smile on most people's faces – except the University registry who complained about the extra work involved. The Union at the Royal Free site has merged with UCL.

SU FACILITIES:
In UCLU's main building: 4 bars; fast food and sandwich bars; 2 shops including a 'Bear Necessities' (general shop); a print shop; travel agency; advice centre; HSBC cashpoint; hairdresser; games machines and pool tables. There's a shop; various games; pool table; Lloyds cashpoint and satellite TV at the Royal Free site.

CLUBS (NON SPORTING):
Afro-Caribbean; Arabic; Bangla; Bloomsbury TV; Chess; Chinese; Debating; Hindu; Human Powered Flight; Japan; Jazz; Music; Pakistani; Photographic; Stage Crew; Singapore Students; Spectrum (helping special-needs children); Taiwanese.

> The official name of Jesus College, Cambridge, is the college of the Blessed Virgin Mary, Saint John the Evangelist and the Glorious Virgin Saint Radegund.

OTHER ORGANISATIONS:
'PI' is the official mag. The award-winning Bloomsbury TV is broadcast by the Union at least once a week and Rare FM broadcasts throughout the year on www.rarefm.co.uk. 'Union Volunteers' organise voluntary placements in the local community. At the Royal Free there's 'Spectrum' community action group and a Rag week.

RELIGIOUS:
Despite UCL's godless foundations, the Christian Union is one of London's largest. In the Union there is a multi-purpose meditation room and the University's church (the Church of Christ the King) is in Byng Place.

SPORTS

• Recent successes: hockey, fencing, tennis

All faculties keep Wednesday afternoons free for sports, although facilities are not so free – there's an annual charge for the Bloomsbury Fitness Centre. *Royal Free has a strong sporting reputation among the London medical schools.*

SPORTS FACILITIES:
In the Bloomsbury Fitness Centre, which is also open to the public, there are squash courts, aerobics, fencing and dance halls and weights gym. The sports centre at Somers Town is 10 minutes' walk from campus. The UCLU sports grounds at Shenley in Hertfordshire provide good facilities and costs only £3 for the coach there and back and is home to Watford FC's training ground.

SPORTING CLUBS:
Cricket; Football; Kung Fu; Netball; Rowing; Skate Boarding; Wing Chun.
ATTRACTIONS: see University of London

ACCOMMODATION

IN COLLEGE:
• Catered: 12%   • Cost: £70-94(30wks)   • Self-catering: 20%
• Cost: £47-115(37wks)

Availability: All 1st years who apply in time get college accommodation, 15% of them sharing. 2nd years are almost certainly on their own, but a few finalists come back. Those who do get housed will be in one of UCL's halls of residence or in the University's inter-collegiate accommodation. There's also accommodation at the Royal Free. Catered halls provide breakfast and evening meals every day, except Ifor Evans which doesn't at weekends and has cooking facilities instead. *The food has a poor reputation though.* Self-catering halls have *good big* kitchens with a couple of cookers and fridges between 10 people. Parking is only available at Max Rayne, Ifor Evans and Langton Close.

```
Rabbits outnumber students on the University
of Essex campus.
```

EXTERNALLY: see University of London
Availability: Many UCL students live in Stoke Newington (the number 73 bus runs to UCL) and the Finsbury Park/Manor House ghetto or Camden *if they're feeling flush. The areas around the Royal Free are more expensive.*
Housing help: UCL keeps information on private and College accommodation and they publish a regular bulletin. The 30% discount from London Transport takes the sting out of commuting.

WELFARE

SERVICES:
- Lesbian & Gay Society • Mature Students' Officer
- Overseas Officer • Minibus • Women's Officer
- Post Grad Officer • Part-time Students' Officer • Disability Officer
- Self-defence classes

UCLU has a rights and advice centre with three advisers, offering advice on issues ranging from drugs to finance and legal matters. On campus is a health centre with three trained counsellors (and part-time psychiatrists). The Dean of Students is responsible for student welfare.

Women: Two advisers to women students can be consulted by any female students. A women's awareness week is held every year.
Disabled: *Provision varies greatly depending on departments* and some changes can be made if required on an individual basis. The Disability Co-ordinator and IT Trainer for disabled students provide support before application and after enrolment.

FINANCE:
- Access fund: £660,411 • Successful applications: 917: 844

The SU has a hardship fund of £30,000. Further bursaries are available through the college

University College, Stockton

see University of Durham

UNL

see University of North London

Uxbridge

see Brunel University

'When I was a student I couldn't wait to be a proper grown-up. A few years after graduating, I couldn't wait to be a student again.'
— Zeinab Badawi, newsreader.

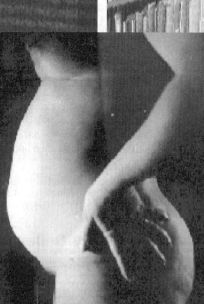

University of Wales

University of Wales College of Medicine

Wales Poly see University of Glamorgan

University College Warrington see Other Institutions

University of Warwick

West London Poly see Thames Valley University

University of the West of England see Bristol, University of the West of England

West Surrey College of Art & Design see Surrey Institute of Art & Design

Westfield see Queen Mary & Westfield College, London

Westhill College of HE see Other Institutions

University of Westminster

Westminster College, Oxford see Other Institutions

Wimbledon School of Art see Other Institutions

Winchester College of Art see University of Southampton

University of Wolverhampton

University College, Worcester see Other Institutions

Writtle College see Other Institutions

Wye College see Imperial College, London

'I bleed for these students' unions that have been hijacked by a bunch of lefties. We're sick of them wasting our money on their pathetic marches, demos and women's things. We should tell students to go stuff themselves.' - Brian Hitchens, former editor of the 'Daily Express' and profound educational philosopher.

University of Wales

University of Wales, University Registry, Cathays Park, Cardiff,
CF1 3NS. Tel: (01222) 382656.

GENERAL

The University of Wales is the 3rd largest in the country after Open University and University of London, and like these, it's rather unusual. It's a federal university, a collection of 6 colleges which operate almost entirely independent of each other. *Many students in Wales don't even realise that their colleges aren't, technically, fully fledged universities.* Interested students shouldn't start writing off to the University of Wales for its prospectus or wondering why they can't find the campus on the map. They should instead investigate the main constituent colleges, which are, of course, included elsewhere in *Push*, as follows:

Aberystwyth, University of Wales
Bangor, University of Wales
Cardiff, University of Wales
Lampeter, University of Wales
Swansea, University of Wales
University of Wales College of Medicine

Some of the colleges in the 'Other Institutions' chapter also award University of Wales degrees. UCAS applications are made to the individual colleges.

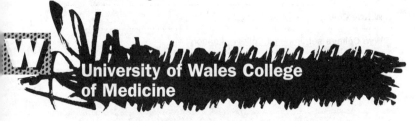

University of Wales College of Medicine

• *The Medical College is part of University of Wales and students are entitled to use its facilities.*
University of Wales College of Medicine, Heath Park, Cardiff,
CF14 4XN. Tel: (029) 2074 2027. Fax: (029) 2074 2914.
UWCM Students' Club, Neuadd Meirionnydd, Heath Park, Cardiff,
CF14 4YS. Tel: (029) 2074 2125. Fax: (029) 2074 4170.

GENERAL

UWCM is on the outskirts of Cardiff with the countryside in sight but still no more than 3 miles from the city centre. Being a medical school, the College is attached to a hospital next door and only offers courses in healthcare subjects. *The College is made up of low-rise 70s blocks and is small with few student facilities of its own.* If students want more, they get down to the larger and completely separate Cardiff, University of Wales, whose facilities they're allowed to use.

Wales College of Medicine

Sex ratio(M:F): 30%:70%	Founded: 1931
Full time u'grads: 1,394	Part time: 177
Postgrads: 177	Non-degree: 896
Ave course: 5yrs	Ethnic: n/a
Private school: n/a	Flunk rate: n/a
Mature students: 16%	Overseas students: 10%
Disabled students: 4%	

ATMOSPHERE:
Medical types take a professional, serious-minded and quiet attitude to study, working closely together and with hospital staff. The SU says that as 20% of students are Muslim, there's less drinking by the student population as a whole. The College trots along on a friendly plane, but it's small (notwithstanding being the third largest hospital college in the UK) and a tad cliquey. Escape into town is possible and students can take a less quiet attitude to fun there. Locals like to stay on the right side of those who may be stitching them up or fiddling with their most valued body parts in the future.

THE CITY: see Cardiff, University of Wales
TRAVEL: see Cardiff, University of Wales
Heath High Level and Heath Low Level stations are $^3/_4$ mile away. Reliable local buses (Nos 8 & 9) run from the city centre through the campus every 20 mins till around midnight. Taxis to or from the city centre cost about £4.

CAREER PROSPECTS:
Unemployment is always rare for graduates from any medical school, but there is a careers service, operated by staff from the postgraduate departments. Nurses should bear in mind the fact that cash will be ludicrously tight.

SPECIAL FEATURES:
All 4th-year medical, dental and Bachelor of Nursing students do an 'elective' – an opportunity to spend time on a research project for 6 to 8 weeks, often abroad.

FAMOUS ALUMNI:
Prof Bernard Knight (Home Office pathologist, crime writer); Dr Thomas Stamps (Health Minister, Zimbabwe).

FURTHER INFO:
Prospectuses for undergrads and postgrads and loan of a video. Website for the Uni (www.uwcm.ac.uk) and SU (www.uwcmsu.org).

ACADEMIC

As the only medical school in Wales the College is attached to a hospital next door and only offers courses in healthcare subjects. Academic courses include medicine, nursing, dentistry, physiotherapy, radiography, and occupational therapy.

staff/student ratio: 1:3
Range of points required for entrance: 340-220
Percentage accepted through clearing: n/a
Number of terms/semesters: 2
Length of terms/semesters: 18 wks
Research: 4

LIBRARIES:
- Books: 150,000 • Study places: 582

7 libraries. 24-hour reading room.

COMPUTERS:
- Computer workstations: 110

24-hour access to computers

ENTERTAINMENT

THE CITY: see Cardiff, University of Wales

COLLEGE:
- Price of a pint of beer: £1.30 • Glass of wine: £1.50

Bars: (2) The students-only Med Club Bar (cap 500) *is the hub of all social activity, especially on Friday nights.* The Sports & Social Club on the hospital site, is used by hospital staff as well as students, although it charges a £15 annual membership fee.

Clubs/discos/venues: Discos every Thursday and Friday in the Med Club and occasional tribute bands and DJs.

Cabaret: Occasional hypnotists and contortionists.

Food: The food in the refectories *is pretty dull but cheap.* The hospital canteen is open all day *and the food is always hospital food.*

Others: At least 5 balls a year, beer fests, toga parties and other spiritually and intellectually uplifting pastimes.

SOCIAL & POLITICAL

UNIVERSITY OF WALES COLLEGE OF MEDICINE STUDENTS' CLUB:
- 1 sabbatical • Turnout at last ballot: 30% • NUS member

Med Club is the home of (among other things) the Students' Club, which is apolitical and then some. Apart from its representative role, it's mainly ents-based.

SU FACILITIES:
In the Med Club, which has been recently refurbished: Bars (with TV); pool table; big screen TV; extended games room; disco area with equipment; games and video machines. The Students' Club also has 3 minibuses for student clubs to hire and a snooker room. The hospital has several shops and a NatWest Bank.

CLUBS (NON SPORTING):
St John's Ambulance.

OTHER ORGANISATIONS:
The independent student paper is called 'Leech', or 'Y Gelen' to its Welsh fans. It can also be found online (www.uwcm.ac.uk/uwcmsc/leech). Charity Groups Revue organises marathons, charity balls, theatre productions and bed pushes.

RELIGIOUS:
- 6 chaplains (CofW, RC, Free Church)

The hospital chapel caters for all denominations.

Bradford University offers the country's only degree course in Yorkshire Studies.

SPORTS

- Recent successes: Rugby, men's and women's
Med Club runs about 20 clubs and despite its size, the College has its own facilities (which students can use by joining The Sports & Social Club at £15 a year) and sports teams *who enjoy reasonable success*. The men's rugby won the National Medical School Championship and the girlies won the universities' women's rugby quarter finals.

SPORTS FACILITIES:
A sports hall; squash courts; swimming pool; 2 gyms; badminton court; weights room. Students can also use the facilities of Cardiff, University of Wales.

ACCOMMODATION

IN COLLEGE:
- Self-catering: 11% • Cost: £38-43 (to 46wks)

Availability: All 1st years are housed, many of them in Cardiff, University of Wales's accommodation – single study bedrooms in *modern* purpose built halls with 8 people to a kitchen and single sex corridors. After the 1st year, about 20% of students get places, often in College-owned flats and houses. The Medical School accommodation, Neuadd Meirionnydd, is *a pretty basic 70s tower block, overlooking the Med Club bar*. 24-hour porters operate security.
Car parking: *Inadequate* permit parking space.
EXTERNALLY: see Cardiff, University of Wales
Housing help: The Accommodation Office provides lists of landlords and houses.

WELFARE

SERVICES:
- Creche • Nightline • Overseas SA • Postgrad SA

There are 2 independent counsellors and an occupational health service on site. A sexual health awareness group is being set up too (called SHAG – *how appropriate*).
Disabled: *While access is good – patients need to get in as well as students – medicine is not a profession in which there are many opportunities for students with disabilities.*

FINANCE:
- Access fund: £150,00 • Successful applications: 170

There's an emergency loan fund of £8,000. Selective scholarships.

Wales Poly

see University of Glamorgan

University College Warrington

see Other Institutions

University of Warwick

University of Warwick, Coventry, CV4 7AL. Tel: (02476) 523709.
Fax: (0870) 1269902. E-mail: ugadmissions@admin.warwick.ac.uk
University of Warwick Students' Union, Coventry, CV4 7AL
Tel: (02476) 572777. Fax: (02476) 572759.
E-mail: enquiries@sunion.warwick.ac.uk

GENERAL

Warwick University isn't actually in Warwick. In fact, Warwick, just over 9 miles south, isn't even the nearest town. Royal Leamington Spa is bigger than Warwick and only 7 miles away. Coventry, bigger still, is just 3 miles north, or there's Kenilworth about 1½ miles west. *But the University of Somewhere-In-The-South-East-Midlands was a bit of a mouthful and, under the title that was chosen, it's earned a very good name for itself.* It's on a 500-acre site *hiding from Leamington Spa and Coventry amidst rolling hills and it is deceptively remote*, although Birmingham is within 25 miles. *The campus looks extraordinary: wildly modern with lots of sculptures and 3 man-made lakes, all surrounded by nature. The buildings are white or as brightly coloured as children's play-blocks and just as weirdly shaped. It's not unpleasant, so long as you don't mind living in an episode of 'The Jetsons'.* The smaller Westwood campus is about 10 minutes walk away and houses the Institute of Education and some halls.

Sex ratio(M:F): 52%:48%	Founded: 1965
Full time u'grads: 8,555	Part time: 305
Postgrads: 5,100	Non-degree: 1,460
Ave course: 3/4yrs	Ethnic: 15%
Private school: n/a	Flunk rate: 5.7%
Mature students: 10%	Overseas students: 20%
Disabled students: 2.6%	

ATMOSPHERE:
Although it's a favourite with middle-class southern students, in no way is Warwick a cliquey den of snobbery. In fact, it's a buzzing, friendly campus with students who can balance high academic standards with having a good time, whether on the gym floor, the dance-floor or the pub floor. In the summer the whole site turns into one big sun lounge.

LEAMINGTON SPA:
Many Warwick students live in Leamington Spa – more than in Coventry, although this trend is changing as Coventry gets cheaper. *Leamington Spa is an attractive little town, belonging more to the Cotswolds to the south than to the Midlands, which might be a more accurate geographic description.* It has enough by way of shops for daily fodder, but foraging for clothes or major purchases, Coventry or even Birmingham would be a better bet. It's not too hot on local entertainments either.

COVENTRY: see Coventry University

TRAVEL:
Trains: The nearest main station is 2½ miles away in Coventry, but there is a line that runs south through to Leamington Spa and Warwick.
Cars: *Cars are not the answer to Warwick's isolation (the suburbs of Coventry are pretty isolated). As the University is quick to point out, they're less environmentally friendly than public transport. This is a genuine concern, but it also happens to coincide conveniently with a need to reduce pressure on the campus' limited parking.* Only 70 residents are allowed permits for overnight parking, but during term, up to 1,000 cars can park on campus during the day and permits for off-campus students cost £80.
Local: From the bus stops on campus, the numbers 12, 12A, 12B, 12C and 112 run into Coventry centre via the train station every 15 mins until 11pm (50-72p) and other services go to other parts of town. There are similar services to Leamington (£1.60) and Kenilworth (70p). Late night services during term time.
Taxis: *At some point as a student living out at Warwick University, most students are likely to get caught on campus after the last bus and without a lift. Then it's time to dig deep in the pocket for £6 to Coventry or £10-£12 to Leamington.*
Bicycles: *Quite handy for getting around the campus, especially for students who live in, but think of that ride twice a day for the students living in Leamington. A big lock's a good idea, as are big legs.*

TRAVEL: see Coventry University

CAREER PROSPECTS:
- Careers Service • No of staff: 10 full/5 part
- Unemployed after 6mths: 3%

SPECIAL FEATURES:
- The University does a roaring trade in conferences, which means there are some *excellent* facilities and accommodation manages to be better at a cheaper rate. *It also means students can feel like they're an inconvenience stuck between the real business of travelling salesmen's piss-ups and dandruffy, navel-gazing academics reading logarithms at each other.*
- Warwick has over 14,000 students doing Open Studies Certificates and post-experience training, but no HND courses.

FAMOUS ALUMNI:
Jenny Bond (BBC correspondent); David Davis MP; Timmy Mallett (hammer-wielding TV prat); Simon Mayo (DJ); Sheila McKechnie (campaigner); Dave Nellist (Militant ex-MP); Stephen Pile (writer); Jeff Rooker MP (Lab); Frank Skinner (comedian); Gary Sinyor & Vadim Jean (filmmakers); Sting (for a term); Tony Wheeler (author, 'Lonely Planet' guides).

FURTHER INFO:
Prospectuses for undergrads, postgrads and part-timers, video and website (www.warwick.ac.uk). Alternative prospectus (£1) from SU.

> 'Get off your backsides and do something!' - Eco-activist Swampy, when asked if he had a message to students.

ACADEMIC

Quite a few really strong departments and courses for both teaching and research.

staff/student ratio: 1:16
Range of points required for entrance: 360-280
Percentage accepted through clearing: 24%
Number of terms/semesters: 3
Length of terms/semesters: 10 wks
Research: 5.2

LIBRARIES:
• Books: 900,000 • Study places: 1,890
Library facilities have come in for some student criticism over space, book availability and the cost of photocopying.

COMPUTERS:
• Computer workstations: 1000
24-hour access to computers.

ENTERTAINMENT

COVENTRY: see Coventry University

LEAMINGTON:
• Price of a pint of beer: £1.70 • Glass of wine: £1.40
The excellent facilities on campus compensate for Leamington's deficiencies.
Pubs: Pushplugs: Benjamin Satchwell's, Jug & Jester, Robin's Well and Scholars (made for students). Don't win on the bandit in The Guardsman – it upsets the locals.
Cinemas: 2, with 7 screens between them. *The Rubin Cinema is a bit artier than the Apollo.*
Theatre: The Royal Spa is a *standard* regional rep house but Leamington is on a direct rail route to Stratford-upon-Avon.
Clubs/discos/music venues: Sugar is the new club on the scene; Mirage has a Thursday student night; Brown's Cow attracts bands and DJs from out of town.
Eating out: *Again, not a huge deal, although, this being the Midlands, there's a number of excellent value balti houses.* Pushplugs: Mongolian Wok Bar in Coventry (£7.50 buffet lunch); Ali Baba (balti). Spun End Balti does deliveries to campus.

UNIVERSITY:
• Price of a pint of beer: £1.60 • Glass of wine: £1.50
Bars: (8) The principal bars are Cholo's (cap 750) and the Cooler (850) which doubles as a club. Others include Lynam's Lounge (300, no smoking), Grumpy John's (270, pub-like), Zippy's (270, mainly used by societies), South Central (bottle bar) and two relatively new places: Xanana, a café bar, and the Airport Lounge *(as dull as it sounds)*. There are also supping stops at the Arts Centre, in the Sports Pavilion and some University bars, *which tend to be frequented more by staff.*
Arts Centre: *The Arts Centre on campus is fantastic in every respect – it looks as though it's sprung from some futuristic fantasy and has facilities to dream about:* 2 theatres; conference hall; film theatre; art gallery; sculpture court; concert hall; music centre and bookshop.

Bars: (8) The principal bars are Cholo's (cap 750) and the Cooler (850) which doubles as a club. Others include Lynam's Lounge (300, no smoking), Grumpy John's (270, pub-like), Zippy's (270, mainly used by societies), South Central (bottle bar) and two relatively new places: Xanana, a café bar, and the Airport Lounge *(as dull as it sounds)*. There are also supping stops at the Arts Centre, in the Sports Pavilion and some University bars, *which tend to be frequented more by staff.*
Arts Centre: *The Arts Centre on campus is fantastic in every respect – it looks as though it's sprung from some futuristic fantasy and has facilities to dream about:* 2 theatres; conference hall; film theatre; art gallery; sculpture court; concert hall; music centre and bookshop.

Theatres: (3) In the Arts Centre, the main theatre (cap 570) attracts touring companies (drama, dance, opera, etc), as well as big student shows. The studio theatre (200) lends itself to smaller scale productions. *Students enter into the dramatic fray with thespian gusto,* including some productions that have gone to Edinburgh Fringe and won prizes. Last year 9 shows were taken to Edinburgh and the comedy sketch show 'Ubersausage' received five star reviews.
Cinemas: The Cinema Society shows classics and blockbusters, *while the Arts Centre provides a less commercial counterbalance.*
Clubs/discos: *The Cooler is developing quite a name for clubular antics.* There are 6 events a week, from the acid jazz of Mojo, via Decadance's 80s throwback, to Saturday night's Culture, Quench which takes over the Market Place as well with its blend of tance and dance sounds. Guest DJs have included Carl Cox, Paul Oakenfold, Fabio and Danny Rampling.
Music venues: The Union's Market Place is the vastest venue, featuring names such as, recently, the Bluetones, Space, Lo-fidelity and Allstars. Butterworth Hall (1,500) in the Arts Centre features a variety of music, mostly classical, attracting top international performers. The University Chorus and orchestra, among other University and student music groups, perform here *in between world tours.*
Food: *Grub served at Xanana's (baguettes and meals), Kaleidoscope, Viva (Pret-a-Manger-like), Eat Eat Eat (expensive), Rootes, Air Fair (junk) and the Cooler – if you can't find what you want in there you never will.* If all else fails there's always the Costcutter supermarket.
Cabaret: Comedy every other Sunday in Zippy's, *recent funsters include Stewart Lee, Ross Noble and Mighty Boosh.*
Others: At least 7 balls a year, February Real Ale Festival, One World Week Festival (*with carnivals, drinking and dancing from around the world*) and plenty more debauchery.

SOCIAL & POLITICAL

UNIVERSITY OF WARWICK STUDENTS' UNION:
• 7 sabbaticals • Turnout at last ballot: 23% • NUS member
Hacks are swinging towards green here, with the SU having successfully campaigned against the threat of compulsary laptops for students . In this post-80s culture, commercialism is the principle prong – sabaticals are board members with the 19 exec members being trustees in the company which is their Union, but they are also social satellites to its solar services which stay open late. As for clubs and societies, there are just so many.

SU FACILITIES:
In the new Union Building and elsewhere: bars; cafeteria; 2 coffee bars; restaurants; shopping parade; welfare centre; resource centre; 3 minibuses and a car for hire; travel agency; print shop; DTP suite; darkroom; bookshop; Costcutter supermarket; computer and typewriters for sale; all 4 major banks with cash machines; Endsleigh Insurance office; photocopying; fax; photo booth; games and vending machines; pool tables; juke boxes; 5 TVs; 5 meeting rooms; conference hall; customised nightclub; launderette; opticians; hairdresser; post office; snooker tables.

CLUBS (NON SPORTING):

Absynth; Ach Deutschland; African and Caribbean; Almost Teachers; Anime and Manga; Amnesty; Amateur Radio; Art; Asian; Bahai; Bandsoc; Bellringing; Band; Blues & Roots; Boar; Brass Soc; Break dancing; Bridge; Cannabis Decriminalisation; Change Ringing; Cheemu; Chess; Cheerleaders; Chill Out; Chinese; Clubland; Codpiece (theatrical); Comedy; Community Action; Computing; Contemporary Dance; Christian Action; CU; Cypriot; Da Muthafunkas; Debating Forum; Deck Masters; Dirty Fat Beatz Crew; Disability Rights; Earth First!; E-commerce; Euro-talk; Fat Wreck Chords; Fine Tea; Film-making; Fresh Blood Theatre; G-Force; GLOW; Guild of Assassins; Greek Cypriot; Hellenic; Hindu; Jubilee; Juggling; La Petite Grenouille; Landrover; Laissez faire; LARPS (live action replay); Life Group; Malaysian; Millionaires; Monty Python; Motobike; Nightline; Offbeat; Oikos; Pagan; Phat Stylz Crew; Poetry; Portuguese-speaking; Pottery; RAW (radio); Radio drama; Real Ale; Revelation; Saville Row; Scandinavian; Shaft; Stockbrokers; Strictly Business; Shopaholics; Sikh; Singapore; Sri Lankan; Stockbroker; Role-play; Strictly Breaks; Synergy; Taiwan; Tapdancing; Tech crew; Theatre4All; Tibet Support; Tribe of the Trout; UoW Chorus; United Nations; Warwick pride; Welsh; Wine.

OTHER ORGANISATIONS:

There's the *award-hogging* 'Warwick Boar' student newspaper, a magazine called 'The Word' and the radio station, RAW, broadcasting 18hrs a day. The Warwick Boar is online (www.warwickboar.co.uk). The charity Rag *raises plenty of cash.* The Community Volunteers Group gets students involved in local help projects and owns Dippy, an inflatable dragon *(it has more uses than you might think).*

RELIGIOUS:
- 6 chaplains (CofE, RC, Free Church, Jewish)

Multi-faith chaplaincy on campus and Muslim prayer room.

PAID WORK:

At such a major conference venue there's plenty of vacation work. The Union runs a service publishing an opportunities list and linking students with jobs and vice versa both on and off campus. The Union itself employs over 300 students on a casual basis and the University runs a Temp Agency.

SPORTS

- Recent successes: badminton, rugby, netball

Plenty of clubs and goings on. *Almost all sport is based on campus, split into 2 areas. 40% take part in regular activity.*

SPORTS FACILITIES:

There are 2 sports centres with 7 squash courts, a new pavilion, 2 swimming pools, 2 sports halls, fitness room, weights, dance studios, 2 gyms/activities rooms, climbing wall and a sauna. The playing fields include: 2 all weather pitches, 7 football, 1 ladies' football, 4 netball, 1 American football and 4 rugby pitches, 3 cricket squares, 9 tennis courts, 1 lacrosse pitch and an athletics track. There's also a climbing centre which recently hosted the British Climbing Championships.

SPORTING CLUBS:

Aerobics; Aikido; American Football; Autosport; Ballroom & Latin Dance; Baseball; Canoe Polo; Christians in Sport; Eskrima; Five-a-Side Football; Hang-gliding; Inline Skating; Lacrosse; Life Saving; Kempo Jiu Jitsu; Ken Yu Kiai Karate; Knockdown Sport Budo; Life-saving; Mountain Bike; Mountaineering; Parachute; Paragliding; Pool; Rifle; Rowing; Rugby League; Samurai Jiu Jitsu; Shotokan Karate; Snooker; Snowboarding; Street Hockey; Surf; Table tennis; Tai Chi; Taiji Quan; Ten Pin Bowling; Thai Boxing; Triathlon; Ultimate Frisbee; Waterpolo; Windsurfing; Wing Chun Athletic; Women's football and rugby; Yoga; Zhuan Shu Khan.

ATTRACTIONS: see Coventry University

ACCOMMODATION

IN COLLEGE:
- Catered: 4% • Cost: £68 (30wks)
- Self-catering: 36% • Cost: £43-56 (30-39wks)

Availability: Almost everyone lives in during their 1st year, usually in the 10 halls (4% in shared rooms) although the few students who enter through clearing aren't guaranteed a place. About 50% of finalists are also allowed back in. *Some of the accommodation is very nice: luxury rooms with en suite bathrooms, not built for the better comfort of students but to attract conference guests – still, students can't complain, except that rents for the better rooms are higher.* There may be problems, however, if they want to stay over the vacation. There are also 1,642 – places off campus, organised by the University under head tenancy arrangements. The Uni has three purpose-built postgraduate residences (Claycroft, Lakeside and Tocil) all located on the central campus and which provide accommodation for new postgraduates. All new single overseas postgraduates who apply for accommodation before the start of the academic year have a guarantee of a room on campus. Security arrangements include CCTV, entry-phones and 24-hour porters.

EXTERNALLY: see Coventry University
Central Leamington is the preferred roost for the majority but South Coventry and Earlsdon are cheap and near enough to be worthy of consideration.

Housing help: The Accommodation Office has 14 staff who approve vacancies on their list and help negotiate contracts. The SU can also assist.

WELFARE

SERVICES:
- Creche • Nightline • Lesbian & Gay Society • Mature SA
- Overseas SA • Minibus • Women's Officer • Anti-racism SA
- Ethnic Minorities SA • Self-defence classes

The Union runs an effective Advice and Welfare Centre with 4 staff and a student sabbatical Welfare and Equal Opportunities Officer. The University has 4 part-time counselling staff of its own and further help with personal problems can be found through Nightline's phone and drop-in service. Each hall has a resident tutor, *who often isn't a tutor at all, so you don't need to worry about doing your homework before looking for some sympathy.*

Women: Personal alarms are available and there's a minibus to get around campus at night.

Drugs: *There has been fairly strong dope (cannabis) culture at Warwick. The University is very tough on users if they're discovered.*

Disabled: Wheelchair access is among the best in the country including lifts in the Union. There are induction loops and accommodation for carers if necessary. The SU and the newer academic buildings also have Braille signs.

FINANCE:
- Access fund: £400,000 • Successful applications: 300

There's also a hardship fund, as well as postgrad bursaries and music scholarships.

West London Poly
see Thames Valley University

University of the West of England
see Bristol, University of the West of England

West Surrey College of Art & Design
see Surrey Institute of Art & Design

Westfield
see Queen Mary & Westfield College, London

Westhill College of HE
see Other Institutions

University of Westminster

- *Formerly Polytechnic of Central London*

University of Westminster, 309 Regent Street, London, W1B 2UW.
Tel: (020) 7911 5000. Fax: (020) 7911 5192.
E-mail: Admissions@wmin.ac.uk
University of Westminster Students' Union, 32-38 Wells Street,
London, W1P 4DJ. Tel: (020) 7636 6271. Fax: (020) 7911 5192.
E-mail: supresi@wmin.ac.uk

General

The University was founded as the Royal Polytechnic Institute to give lectures on science and engineering to the general public. It's changed a bit since then – there are four main sites plus numerous additional buildings, built in a real mixture of old and new architectural styles. They are mostly in the 2 miles north of Trafalgar Square *so all that London's West End has to offer is within easy reach*. The exception is the site at Harrow, which used to be the separate Harrow College of HE, 9 miles away or ½ hour by tube.

Sex ratio(M:F): 46%:54%	Founded: 1838
Full time u'grads: 8,990	Part time: 2,502
Postgrads: 1,565	Non-degree: 4,085
Ave course: 3yrs	Ethnic: 53%
Private school: n/a	Flunk rate: 20.4%
Mature students: 40%	Overseas students: 16%
Disabled students: 3%	

ATMOSPHERE:
The students are a mixed crowd with a great ethnic diversity and a high proportion of mature students. Although the campuses are relatively close together, students tend to stick to their own site's bars and facilities and there's little sense of one big cohesive family. Still, with all the fun of the West End on their doorsteps, nobody's got any excuse to be bored. Jimmy Hendrix played here and Cherie Blair taught at the law school (so there). The ethnic diversity is seen as one of the strengths of the Uni.

HARROW SITE:
Over 5,000 full-time and part-time students are based here, studying Communications, Design & Media, Management and Computer Science. Major investment has been ploughed into the site: recent additions have included two TV/film studios, a new computer centre, four radio production suites, accommodation for 400 students - oh, and a bar.

THE CITY: see University of London

TRAVEL: see University of London

Trains: Euston station is closest.
Buses: If you think we're going to list all the buses that go to all the sites, you've got another bus coming.
Underground: Baker Street (Bakerloo, Circle, Jubilee, Metropolitan and Hammersmith & City Lines), Oxford Circus (Bakerloo, Victoria and Central Lines) and so on... For Harrow, Northwick Park (Metropolitan) and Kenton (Bakerloo).

CAREER PROSPECTS:
• Careers Service • No of staff: 5 full/2 part
• Unemployed after 6mths: 8%
The careers service is very efficient.

FAMOUS ALUMNI:
Baroness Chalker (Tory peer); the Emmanuels (designers who rustled up Princess Di's wedding frock); Lisa I'Anson (TV presenter, DJ); Michael Jackson (Channel 4 controller, not Wacko); Julian Metcalfe (sandwich entrepreneur); some of Pink Floyd; Lord Puttnam (film director); Timothy West (actor); Vivienne Westwood (fashion designer).

FURTHER INFO:
Prospectuses for undergrads and postgrads, website (www.wmin.ac.uk) and SU website (www.uwsu.com).

ACADEMIC

The Uni offers mostly job-related courses ranging from International Relations to Biosciences and Urban Design. More than three-quarters of undergraduates do 'enterprise' activities as an assessed part of their courses. *Sadly, this does not involve learning Klingon, how to set your phasers on 'stun' or making corsets for William Shatner.* More generally, despite its ex-poly reputation, the University has done relatively well in recent quality assessments. Psychology was singled out as excellent.

```
Wallace and Gromit are honorary members of the
University of Lancaster SU.
```

staff/student ratio: 1:14
Range of points required for entrance: 340-40
Percentage accepted through clearing: 30%
Number of terms/semesters: 2
Length of terms/semesters: 17wks
Research: 3.3

LIBRARIES:
- Books: 400,000 • Study places: 1,900

There are four libraries distributed around the campuses, plus an Information Resource Centre (*which is the same thing really*) at Harrow.

COMPUTERS:
- Computer workstations: 1,700

IN LONDON: see University of London

UNIVERSITY:
- Price of a pint of beer: £1.20 • Glass of wine: £1.10

Bars: Around the University sites, there are 7 bars of which 3 are run by students and the rest are run by outside caterers, *making them more expensive*. The Studio Bar and Area 51 have opened at Harrow, while the Dragon Bar on Wells St has a new look, *hoping to attract a new funky crowd*.

Cinemas: There's a big screen at Harrow. Student-made films are often shown *and Manga flicks are pretty popular*.

Clubs/discos/music venues: There are two dance nights a week, one at each bar, for most cheese/house/garage/D'n'B tastes. Recent gigs: Spiller, Dream Team and Atomic Kitten.

Food: The University offers contract catering at each site. *Students complain about the cost but it tastes okay.*

Others: The Union runs three big events a year, including a Freshers' extravaganza at the Ministry of Sound nightclub and irregular comedy *(that's not often, not a new type of comedy)*. There are two club nights: Fire it up hits the Dragon Bar with R&B, hip hop and garage; and Toast, at Area 51, offers lovely, tasty cheese.

UNIVERSITY OF WESTMINSTER STUDENTS' UNION:
- 5 sabbaticals • Turnout at last ballot: 12% • NUS member

The exec tends to be hardworking and prepared to stand up to the administration but the students don't seem to know or care what's going on. The SU is trying to address this by revamping its style, but the students still find them slightly distant. The sabbatical officer for ents has been dropped for a professional, although functions still seem to be few and far between nonetheless.

SU FACILITIES:
The Union building is part of the main student and staff centre in Wells St near Regent's Park. It provides a bar, common rooms and vending and games machines. Harrow has a bar, shop and common room. There are Union offices on all sites.

CLUBS (NON SPORTING):
Chinese; Future Medic; Hellenic; Hempology (study of cannabis – *as if they'd ever write up their research*); Internet Radio; Real Ale; Reggae.

OTHER ORGANISATIONS:
The fortnightly 'Smoke' student mag is *pretty damn good*, plus there's the Metropolis radio station which broadcasts intermittently. A new Rag is also being set up.

RELIGIOUS:
• 1 chaplain (CofE)

PAID WORK: see University of London
A jobshop is run by the Union. Part-time jobs are regularly posted on the internet.

• Recent successes: cross country

Bearing in mind the urban location of the University and the lack of cohesion between sites, sporting success is nowhere near as lame as you might have expected.

SPORTS FACILITIES:
The Regent Street site has badminton, snooker, a gym, a sauna, solarium and multigym. At Harrow there's a fitness centre and a sports hall. There's a sports ground at Chiswick, complete with running track, boathouse, bar and 55 acres of pitches. There's also a gym and all-weather pitches.

SPORTING CLUBS:
Rowing; Kick-Boxing; Parachuting; Roller-blading; Rowing; Skate Boarding; Water Polo.

ATTRACTIONS: see University of London

IN COLLEGE:
• Self-catering: 12% • Cost: £63-75 (38-60wks)
Availability: *Accommodation on site is fairly limited and it is not possible to offer digs to all 28% of first years who want it. However, the high proportion of local students should put this into perspective.* There are 8 halls, with kitchens shared by 6 to 12 students and single sex flats are available. Entry-phones and night security keep out the prowlers.

EXTERNALLY: see University of London
Housing help: The University advisery scheme at the Marylebone Road and Harrow sites provides a notice board, newsletter, an approval scheme and advice on various housing matters. Temporary accommodation is available in September while students house hunt.

SERVICES:
• Creche • Nightline • Lesbian & Gay Society • Mature SA
• Overseas SA • Women's Officer
The Student Services Department provides 4 part-time and 3 full-time counsellors and the SU also offers advisers and help. A nurse and

doctor are assigned to the Bolsover Street site and to Harrow. An International Student Officer helps overseas students. There's also an Exam Anxiety Group - *other universities, take note*.
Disabled: Toilets, ramps and lifts are provided, *although the lifts often don't work. Access is pretty poor, although Harrow's okay*. Dyslexia advice is available.

FINANCE:
- Access fund: £500,000 • Successful applications: 807

A booklet called 'Housing & Money Matters' is distributed free to students. There are also short-term loans available.

Westminster College, Oxford
see Other Institutions

Wimbledon School of Art
see Other Institutions

Winchester College of Art
see University of Southampton

University of Wolverhampton

- *Formerly Wolverhampton Polytechnic*

(1) University of Wolverhampton, Wulfruna Street, Wolverhampton, WV1 1SB. Tel: (01902) 322222. Fax: (01902) 322680.
E-mail: enquiries@wlv.ac.uk
University of Wolverhampton Students' Union, Wulfruna Street, Wolverhampton, WV1 1LY. Tel: (01902) 322021.
Fax: (01902) 322020. E-mail: uwsu@wlv.ac.uk
(2) University of Wolverhampton, Telford Campus, Shifnal Road, Priorslee, Telford, Shropshire, TF2 9NT. Tel: (01902) 323900.

GENERAL

It will probably offend every one of Wolverhampton's 269,000 inhabitants to say that it's a sprawling mass sprouting out of the north west of Birmingham. From the centre of Wolves (as it's called) to the centre of Brum (as it's called) is 13 miles, with Walsall, Dudley and West Bromwich in between and no break in the urban crush and crawl. *For pretty bits, head towards Telford and Shropshire. Each of these towns in The Birmingham Conurbation is distinctly different: for example, Wolves is more residential and has a slower pace than Brum itself.* As for the University, Wolves is simply one of its bases. Humanities, Languages & Social Sciences are based on a campus in Dudley, and Education is on the Walsall Campus. And even further flung, is the University's Business School half in Telford, a town of 28,000 souls, 16 miles away and the other half in Compton.

Wolverhampton

Sex ratio(M:F): 43%:57%
Full time u'grads: 12,981
Postgrads: 788
Ave course: 3yrs
Private school: 1%
Mature students: 77.8%
Disabled students: 3.1%

Founded: 1983
Part time: 6,589
Non-degree: 6,334
Ethnic: 26.5%
Flunk rate: 24.9%
Overseas students: 14.8%

ATMOSPHERE:
There's a high proportion of mature, local and non-degree students, many with their own lives and responsibilities beyond the University. *One survey identified this part of the Midlands as the least popular UK region for prospective applicants, but the locals are still flocking in and they don't need anybody else, ta very much.* So many students from the local area means town/gown relations are unusually mellow.

THE SITES:
Wolverhampton City Campus: This is the main campus, consisting of a number of modern buildings. It may not be too ugly, but the main building is seriously big and does look distinctly institutional, as if it used to be a hospital. Inside, *the floors are so clean there's not a skirt or trouser leg you can't look up. The reception looks like the entrance to a law court or something similarly official and smart.* Being in the centre of Wolves, it is useful for the shopping centre and other civic amenities.

Compton Park Campus: (Business Studies) *Business Schools always get the best-looking site and this is not an exception. This is the smart, leafy part of Wolves,* 1½ miles from the main site, but connected by public transport and free university shuttle buses.

Dudley Campus: (Humanities, Social Sciences, Continuing Education) 7 miles from the main site, this campus is just under a mile from Dudley town centre in a *pleasantly green suburb. The best things about this campus are the facilities and the real ale in the local pubs,* but it is not so good for shops or transport connections. Dudley itself is a small market town dominated by a castle.

Walsall Campus: (Education, Health, Sport, Performing Arts, Leisure) 9 miles from the main site, this campus is about ¾ of a mile from Walsall town centre – *more of a suburb of Brum than a town in itself* – but is okay for shops and stuff like that. The campus, a set of geometric modern purpose-built blocks, also has a few facilities of its own for sports and fun.

Telford: (Business, Engineering, Social Work) Out on a limb, 16 miles from Wolverhampton, this site was set up for students who wanted to live and study locally. It's the smallest and newest site. It's based around a stately home, *but is lacking a lot by way of atmosphere or facilities.*

WOLVERHAMPTON:
For so long in the shadow of the Brum Beast, it's now possible to buy decent clothes and records, get your hair cut, have a pint or two somewhere without sawdust on the floor and then go to a nightclub and tongue-wrestle with someone half-decent looking all within the (ill-defined) town limits. Recent renovations mean that Wolverhampton has new bars and clubs popping up, while it retains its laid-back air. Of course, if you want to do something really spectacular, Birmingham's just down the road.

THE CITY: see University of Birmingham

TRAVEL:
Trains: Wolverhampton Station is 5 minutes' walk from the main site and operates services all over the country and into Brum (£3.80). Other destinations include London (£18.50), Manchester (£12.85) and Edinburgh (£30.70). There are also British Rail stations at Walsall and Telford.
Coaches: National Express services to London (£13.50), Manchester (£8.50), Edinburgh (£27.75) and beyond.
Car: Wolverhampton, Walsall and Dudley can be reached on the M5, M54, M6. The A41 and M54 also connect with Telford.
Local: *The many cheap buses are the best way of getting anywhere and connect with Brum too, although there are the unreliable trains too.* The *supertram* service is called The Metro and links Wolverhampton with Birmingham (£2.60 return). The University also provides a free, *popular, but less than dependable*, inter-site shuttle bus for staff and students, between all the sites.
Bicycles: Secure bike sheds on the main campus. *Unless you're in training for the Tour de France, cycling between the sites is not on.*

THE CITY: see University of Birmingham

CAREER PROSPECTS:
- Careers Service • No of staff: 6 full
- Unemployed after 6mths: 5.3%

FAMOUS ALUMNI:
Trevor Beattie (advertising guru, so they say); Sir Terence Beckett (deputy chairman, CEGB); Jenny Jones; Michael Foster (MPs); Vernie (Eternal).

FURTHER INFO:
Full-time, part-time and postgrad prospectuses, video, alternative prospectus, Uni website (www.wlv.ac.uk) and SU website (www.wlv.ac.uk/su).

ACADEMIC

Apart from a typical range of degrees and diplomas, the Uni has some bizarre professional courses, such as Complementary Therapies, Virtual Reality, Automotive Design and Multimedia, Virtual Reality Design, Digital Product Modelling, E-Commerce and even an online degree in Business Administration. Courses are mostly vocational and the University also arranges work placements, which may soon be accredited on courses. Courses can be full- or part-time as anything from a short taster to a postgrad degree.

staff/student ratio: 1:18
Range of points required for entrance: 300-120
Percentage accepted through clearing: 4%
Number of terms/semesters: 2
Length of terms/semesters: 17wks
Research: 2.5

LIBRARIES:
- Books: 514,943 • Study places: 2,280

There's a library on each site – including the main Wolverhampton Learning Centre (a recent multi-million pound development *which has improved working conditions no end, but failed to address limited book availability*).

COMPUTERS:
- Computer workstations: 650

Wolverhampton Learning Centre also houses most of the computer service.

TOWN:
- Price of a pint of beer: £1.80 • Glass of wine: £1.59

Cinemas & theatres: There's a number of theatres and cinemas in Wolves, most notably the Grand Theatre, *the fringe-ish* Arena Theatre on campus, 10-screen multiplexes at Dudley's Merry Hill Centre (*great for shopping too*) and at Walsall and Telford, and *the arty* Lighthouse Arts & Media Centre.

Pubs: *Cheap and cheery, putting the real back into real ale. Pushplugs: Varsity; Posada. The students' own bars are more popular, given that the Uni is hard by the Wanderer's Molyneux Park soccer ground.*

Clubs/discos: There's a choice of student clubs. *Pushplugs: student night at the Canal Club (dance and alternative); the Beach and Atlantis do student nights; Blast Off at the Civic Hall (indie).*

Music venues: T*he Varsity is getting onto the map as a damn fine indie hangout, pulling in the kids from Brum.* The Civic/Wulfrun Hall (2 venues under one roof) *has sounds to stomp to, as does JBs in Dudley.*

Eating out: *The multi-ethnic mix of the whole West Midlands effects Wolves restaurants as much as anywhere else, but, as with most things, for serious choice of eats it's best to go closer to the centre of Brum. Pushplugs: Dilshad Tandoori; Gondola (Italian); Moon Under Water; John's Balti; J's Café.*

Others: The West Midlands Safari & Leisure Park *is a relief to those who like seeing animals so long as they're not behind bars, unlike the zoo in Dudley. Boating on the canal is good cleanish fun for all.*

CITY: see University of Birmingham

UNIVERSITY:
- Price of a pint of beer: £1.40 • Glass of wine: £1.40

Bars: 4 bars around the SU's sites, *the most important being Fat Mick's at the main site.*

Clubs/discos: *Some sort of dance thang somewhere every night;* regulars include Delicious (free) and the Saturday alternative night.

Music venues: Fat Mick's and Dudley host live gigs, recent examples being Chaz n Dave, Emma B.

Theatre & cinema: Screwed Up & Clueless Theatre Group is run by drama students and is making a splash. *Free video showings once a week.*

Cabaret: There's occasional cabaret at Fat Mick's.

Food: *The University Refectory offers a good range but at a price.* The SU café does snacks.

Others: Rag and SU Balls at each site. The University has been granted lottery money to build a new arena/theatre thing in the Union.

UNIVERSITY OF WOLVERHAMPTON STUDENTS' UNION:
- 7 sabbaticals • Turnout at last ballot: 5% • NUS member

The SU does its best on the welfare and ents fronts, within the constraints of pretty limited resources. Politics is usually either strongly left-wing or non-existent, with non-existent well on top, despite the efforts of the SU exec to rouse the masses.

SU FACILITIES:
Most facilities are in the SU Building on the main campus and at the Dudley campus, but the SU also has centres at Walsall, Compton and Telford. In all, the SU offers 5 bars, 5 minibuses, a travel agency, printing & photocopying services, 4 shops, library, games, vending & video machines, photo developing, pool tables, juke box, TV lounge, nightclub, function rooms (cap 600) and conference facilities.

CLUBS (NON SPORTING):
Asian; Bhangra; Biko Trust; Brunei; Chaplaincy; Creative Aid; Cult TV; Dance; Eastern; Great Escape; Hunt Sabs; Jazz; Juggling; Malaysian; Pagan; Punjabi; Real Ale; Role Playing; Sikh; Singapore; Signing; Vegan and Vegetarian; War Games.

OTHER ORGANISATIONS:
'Cry Wolf' is the monthly SU mag. A Student Community Action group is emerging as if by magic, while Rag hosts circus acts, theme nights and beach parties – *though where they find the beaches, Push doesn't know.* The SU has started up a Skills Training Scheme which covers useful potential CV fillers.

RELIGIOUS:
• 4 chaplains (CofE, RC Free Church)

SPORTS

• Recent successes: basketball

Most sites have their own facilities, which add up to an okay level of service, but since they're spread out, there's very little focus for sporting activity. Recent additions to the trophy cabinet may galvanise things a bit, though. A Sports Card costs £12 per year and with one of these you get access, coaching and insurance.

SPORTS FACILITIES:
Main campus: sports hall; multigym; squash courts. **Compton Park:** local public sports centre, tennis courts. **Dudley:** playing field; sports hall; tennis courts. **Walsall:** swimming pool; playing fields; gym; floodlit tennis courts; running track; dance studio. **Telford:** football; basketball; netball; tennis facilities.

SPORTING CLUBS:
Aikido; Extreme Sports; Kung Fu; Wrestling.

ATTRACTIONS:
Apart from the famous Wolverhampton Wanderers FC, 100 yards from the SU building, and the nearby West Bromwich Albion (the Baggies) at Walsall, there's a race course, a dog track and a local athletics club.

ACCOMMODATION

IN COLLEGE:
• <u>Self-catering: 18%</u> • Cost: £40-43 (38wks)
Some students have felt let down by allegedly misleading college brochures.
Availability: *All sites have some form of accommodation.* What there is gets snapped up mostly by 1st years, accommodating about 13% of them *(usually most of those who want it).* However, 90% of undergrads do not live in college accommodation. The prompt

payment discount *is worth pursuing*. CCTV and 24-hour porters keep watch. **Main campus:** 1,075 single self-catering rooms. **Compton Park:** 130 single self-catering rooms. **Dudley:** 360 rooms with some meals catered, mostly single, but some shared. **Walsall:** 380 single rooms with evening meals only during the week. **Telford:** 300 new single rooms with en suite facilities (£38/wk). All halls have shared kitchens and bathrooms and single sex corridors.
Car parking: Free, *but inadequate.*

EXTERNALLY:
- Ave rent: £36-45

Availability: *No problem about finding a place in Wolves and the prices aren't extortionate. Walsall and Dudley are less easy and more expensive, but still well under £40. Whitmore Reans is the studenty ghetto. The University has about 100 places in 40 houses and flats, which it also rents to students on a private basis, but on more sympathetic terms than the open market.*

Housing help: The University Residential Services at the main campus run by the University, help find and arrange student housing for almost all students who don't get hall places as well as providing lists of recommended landlords.

WELFARE

SERVICES:
- Nursery • Lesbian & Gay Sector • Mature SA • Overseas SA
- Minibus • Women's Officer • Self-defence classes

The University has 6 counsellors and the chaplains are also to hand. Medical problems are dealt with by the health centres near each of the main 4 sites. At the main Wolves site, the health centre is within the campus bounds. The nurseries are based at the main campus and Dudley. The University provides free rape/attack alarms for all students. *The subway between the North and South sides of Wolves campus is rather dingy and dangerous but new lighting should improve things.*

Disabled: There is a Disabilities Officer based at Dudley and a Disabled Students' Council providing advice and representation. For more practical help, there are lifts, ramps and *generally okay access to most places, although accommodation is a little lacking.* Good facilities for students with hearing impairment.

FINANCE:
- Access fund: £330,500 • Successful applications: 1,529

Hardship Funds are appallingly advertised and therefore undersubscribed. Go get that cash! Also bursaries and a fund for black South African students.

University College, Worcester

see Other Institutions

Writtle College

see Other Institutions

Wye College

see Imperial College, London

University of York

York St John see Other Istitutes

University of York

University of York, Heslington, York, YO1 5DD. Tel: (01904) 433533.
Fax: (01904) 433538. E-mail: admissions@york.ac.uk
York University Students' Union, The Daw Suu Centre, Goodricke
College, Heslington, York, YO1 5DD. Tel: (01904) 433724
Fax: (01904) 433724. E-mail: su-web@york.ac.uk

GENERAL

The Romans came to York. So did the Vikings and Dick Turpin. The builders of *magnificent* Minsters also came and the cathedral they left dominates the city *both culturally and physically.* However, all this historical importance has more to do with the fact that York, coursed by the *beautiful* River Ouse, is midway between London and Edinburgh, 35 miles from the coast, than with the University, because that didn't pop up until 1963. It is 2 miles south-east of the city centre at the village of Heslington. It is a largely concrete campus around a man-made lake, complete with ducks, a stately manor and some *pleasant* landscaping, *albeit with a giant replica UFO in the middle of it all.* It was designed as a 'concept' campus – the concept in question being 'discovery around every corner', *which explains why everywhere looks the same and it's easy to get lost.*

Sex ratio(M:F): 49%:51%	Founded: 1963
Full time u'grads: 5,702	Part time: 1,021
Postgrads: 1,392	Non-degree: 571
Ave course: 3yrs	Ethnic: 5%
Private school: 16%	Flunk rate: 5.5%
Mature students: 14%	Overseas students: 10%
Disabled students: 4%	

ATMOSPHERE:
York is a collegiate University – cynics claim this is an unsuccessful attempt to copy Oxbridge. There are 8 colleges, each with 900–1,000 members, which don't vary enormously. Students don't get to choose their own college, but it's not difficult to switch if they feel the need. The collegiate system isn't all that strong (especially compared to Oxbridge) – college spirit can mostly be found when served with ice in college bars. The University may not be enormously happening (and positively moribund at weekends), but it's cosy and friendly (some find it almost suffocating) and many find it hard to leave. Anybody who's seen 60s cult TV show 'The Prisoner' will have an idea. The town swarms with graduates, which must mean something positive.

THE CITY:
- Population: 175,000 • London: 205miles • Edinburgh: 205miles
- Leeds: 23miles

Apart from London, York is Britain's top tourist city and offers a host of traps and treats, including museums such as the Jorvik Viking Centre (free admission with a Blue Peter badge). *It is quaint in the extreme* with city walls, tea shops, a castle and what claims to be the oldest street in Britain, The Shambles. The shortest street in the city also has the longest name: Whip–ma–Whop–ma Gate. In York, as locals love to explain to American visitors, streets are called 'gates', city gates are called 'bars' and bars are called 'pubs', of which there are a *huge* number. Got that? There is also a daily market, supermarkets and numerous bookshops (new and second-hand), but there's not much for the late night shopper.

TRAVEL:
Trains: Mainline connections from York Station (2 miles from the campus) to many destinations including London King's X (£29.70), Glasgow (£27.05) and Birmingham (£16.85).
Coaches: National Express to most destinations, including London (£19), Newcastle and beyond.
Car: A64; 10 miles from the A1, M1 and 20 from the M62.
Air: Nearest airport of any size is Leeds/Bradford (40 minutes by car) and there is a direct train link to and from Manchester Airport.
Hitching: *Good north/south, once hitchers reach M1 or A1.*
Local: York is too small and compact for local trains except regionally to Leeds, Hull and Bradford. Frequent bus services run everywhere (90p from campus to city centre) but they don't run late at night.
Taxis: *Unreliable and expensive despite some companies offering student discounts, although students still use them for late night journeys.*
Bicycles: *Pretty good, flat with plenty of cycle lanes, but also a few light–fingered would–be bike owners.*

CAREER PROSPECTS:

- Careers Service • No of staff: 3 full/1 half
- Unemployed after 6mths: 6%

FAMOUS ALUMNI:
Tony Banks MP, Harriet Harman MP, Oona King MP (all Lab); Greg Dyke *(the man who gave us Roland Rat. Thanks. Now Director General of BBC);* Harry Enfield (comedian); Jung Chang (writer); Christine Hamilton (loyal Tory spouse); Mark Laity (BBC reporter); Denise O Donohue (MD of Hat Trick TV); Victor Lewis–Smith (comedian/journalist); Genista McIntosh (theatre director); Dominic Muldowney (composer); John Witherow (editor, Sunday Times).

FURTHER INFO:
Prospectuses for undergrads and postgrads, alternative prospectus 50p from SU and website (www.york.ac.uk).

```
Wye college is home to the Druids, a secretive
drinking society of practical jokers who leave
sheep in odd places.
```

ACADEMIC

staff/student ratio: 1:17
Range of points required for entrance: 360-240
Percentage accepted through clearing: 4.8%
Number of terms/semesters: 3
Length of terms/semesters: 10wks
Research: 2.9

LIBRARIES:
- Books: 800,000 • Study places: 1,000

Main JB Morrell Library – smaller specialist outposts and individual college libraries are being closed and centralised. Students are mostly satisfied with library facilities.

COMPUTERS:
- Computer workstations: 510

Computer provisions are slow, crash too often and do not provide enough net and e-mail access.

ENTERTAINMENT

THE CITY:
- Price of a pint of beer: £1.80 • Glass of wine: £2

Cinemas: A choice of 4, ranging from a 12–screen multiplex to the *arty* City Screen.
Theatres: (4) *Mostly quite straight but the Arts Centre makes up for it with weirder stuff.*
Pubs: Supposedly, there's a pub *(mostly student–friendly)* for every day of the year, playing hosts to such Yorkshire favourites as the 3 Smiths – Samuel, John and Tom – as well as Theakston's, Tetley and Timothy Taylor. *Enough to make any southern blouse renounce his/her lager shandy past. Pushplugs: The Charles; Rose & Crown; The Firkin; The Lowther; The Deramore Arms.*
Clubs/discos: There's a number of popular nights *with mainstream student leanings:* Mondays at The Gallery (70s/80s); Tuesdays at Toffs (indie); weekends at the Arts Centre *(bohemian posing and dancing).* Also new clubs Icon and Divas. *There's an underground rave scene in York and nearby Selby but students don't tend to get involved. For serious clubbers though the nearest prime site is Leeds.*
Music venues: *Not a great deal.* Fibbers is a fair–to–middling indie hang-out. The De Gray Rooms are popular.
Eating out: *A good range of cheap eats, including some excellent Indians, if nothing to get you really drooling puddles. Other Pushplugs:* Oscar's wine bar; Caesar's (Italian); Rubicon (pricey veggie); Fellini's (Italian); The Cello (café); The Willow (Chinese restaurant becomes cheesy disco at midnight).

UNIVERSITY:
- Price of a pint of beer: £1.40 • Glass of wine: £1.50

Bars: 8 bars in all, 6 in colleges, one in the central hall (only open when events are on) and one in the sports centre. *Vanbrugh and Goodricke college bars get quite groovy.*
Theatres: (2) The Drama Barn hosts regular productions.
Cinema: York Student Cinema show mainstream films 2–3 times a week.

Clubs/discos/music venues: *The SU has had trouble enticing big name acts, but things have improved.* Lightening Seeds, Terrorvision, Artful Dodger and Utah Saints are recent players.
Cabaret: Fortnightly comic capers, Dave Gorman, Mark Lamarr and Bill Bailey.
Food: Each college has a snack bar and most have a dining hall, *a fair bet for daytime nosh and natter.* Vanburgh does expensive sandwiches, Langwith has a veggie snack bar and Alcuin is noted for its hot chocolate – *is that food or drink? Answers on a Cadbury's Options sachet, please.*
Others: Annual balls in colleges.

SOCIAL & POLITICAL

YORK UNIVERSITY STUDENTS' UNION:
• 6 sabbaticals • Turnout at last ballot: 20% • NUS member

YUSU survived for many years without its own building and it still lacks a central SU bar or music venue. Because of the collegiate system, many students operate day-to-day without much awareness of the SU, but it's there when they want it. YUSU is not as radical as it used to be, although it still makes the effort for the big campaigns (anti-tuition fees for instance) and those closer to home (like the campaigns for improved portering, against rent increases and for health awareness).

SU FACILITIES:
A shop; second-hand bookshop; cashpoint (Link); essay bank; vending machines; minibus hire; printing and typing services.

CLUBS (NON SPORTING):
Astronomy; Ballroom and Latin American Dancing; Bloke Soc; Campus Bands; Cassoc Christis; Concert; Conservation; Conservative/Unionist; Debating; Duke of Edinburgh; Gilbert & Sullivan; Juggling; Labour; Liberal Democrats; Lunatic Fringe; Links; Methodist–Anglican; Multimedia; Natural History; Outdoor; Physics; Radio; Rock; Scout and Guides; Socialist Worker; Spooky; Television; Theatre; Wine.

OTHER ORGANISATIONS:
Two independent student newspapers, 'Nouse' (inevitably nicknamed 'no use') and 'Vision', which compete for the top student journo hacks. There are also 4 mags (feminist, arts, Christian and environmental). The University radio station (URY) was one of the first *and is among the most respected.* YSTV – the award-winning television station – broadcasts to snack bars and JCRs across campus and its SU election night specials are *enough to get Peter Snow fidgeting with his swingometer.* The York Rag raised over £56,000 last year, the Rag week has stunts such as soaking – students pay to have their friends, or strangers even, squirted with water. *This goes on for a very long week.* The Community Action Project (known as 'CAP'), organised by a dedicated sabbatical officer, runs over 30 community projects, especially holidays for disadvantaged kids.

> One of Bristol University's accommodation blocks used to be a Berni Inn.

RELIGIOUS:
- 7 chaplains

For Anglicans, the Minster, home to one of England's two Archbishops, *has an inspiring influence, which has rubbed off on other Christian denominations.* Following an incident involving a Jewish massacre nearly 1,000 years ago, there is no synagogue in York, but there is a Jewish Centre on campus for meetings and prayers which also provides accommodation for 4 people.

PAID WORK:
Plenty of pubs and a few restaurants during term-time and the conference trade brings opportunities during vacations. 'Unijobs' is a university run one-stop job shop for students seeking work in the local area. The SU has a vacancy board.

- Recent successes: women's rowing, basketball

It's not up with the really big boys and girls but plenty muck in and keep trim. The 'roses' events between York and Lancaster can bring out the killer competitive instinct though. The Athletics Union – which, including membership of the sports centre, costs £10 to join – has its own sabbatical officer.

SPORTS FACILITIES:
57.5 acres of playing fields; new sports pavilion and new Astroturf pitch; sailing boats; trampolines; climbing wall; gym; multigym; sports hall; sauna; 6 tennis courts; athletics track. The city also has 3 public swimming pools and the River Ouse.

SPORTING CLUBS:
Aikido; Archery; Athletics; Badminton; Basketball; Ben Lairig; Boating; Bridge; Canoe; Canoe Polo; Caving & Potholing; Cricket; Cycling; Fencing; Football; Gliding; Golf; Hang Gliding; Hockey; Jiu-Jitsu; Judo; Karate; Lacrosse; Mountaineering; Netball; Octopush; Orienteering; Parachuting; Riding; Rifle and Pistol; Rugby; Sailing; Ski; Squash; Sub Aqua; Swimming; Tae Kwon Do; Table Tennis; Trampoline; Volleyball; Windsurfing.

ATTRACTIONS:
York Race Course, Rugby League or York FC *(if you can call them an attraction).*

IN COLLEGE:
- Self-catering: 59% • Cost: £47-52 (30-38wks)

Availability: All 1st years can be accommodated, in the *Stalinist* grey blocks by the lake, as can 30% of all finalists. *The major problem with living on campus is having to ensure you don't fall in the lake*

> The Fine Art Building at Staffordshire University was painted bright pink and covered with song lyrics as a final year project.

when drunk, the duck droppings in it reach toxic levels. About 1% of residents have to share rooms. Security on campus is *very good* with night porters, keypad access and security chains/peepholes on all apartment doors.

Car parking: No students can have cars on campus, unless medically necessary. Firing weapons in halls is also prohibited, apparently.

EXTERNALLY:
- Ave rent: £45

Availability: *Finding accommodation is easy enough, especially in Fulford and Heslington, but some council estates are best avoided. Cars are difficult to park around town and unnecessary for getting around.*

Housing help: The University Accommodation Office runs a Property Rental Scheme, where inspected houses are tied to a recommended rent. There are housing lists and tenancy advice on offer from the welfare office while the SU keeps informal reports on accommodation.

WELFARE

SERVICES:
- Access Officer • Creche • Nightline • Racial Equality Officer
- Lesbian, Gay & Bisexual Society • Minibus • Women's Officer
- Nursery • Self-defence classes

There is a health centre and students can always register with local NHS practices. The University employs a Welfare Information Officer and 5 part-time counsellors. The SU can arrange a free consultation with a solicitor. Special provisions for those with dyslexia.

Women: The SU maintains a right to choose fund, free attack alarms and the night bus gives priority to women. *Some dark/poorly lit areas on the fringes of campus should be avoided at night.*

Disabled: James College was built with disabled access in mind *and generally the campus is pretty good with almost every building having a lift.* There is a new Disability Officer and some hearing loops have been installed.

FINANCE:
- Access fund: £480,000 • Successful applications: 381

Overseas student scholarships, mature students bursaries, sponsorship and YUSU hardship loans.

York St John

see Other Institutes

> 'Have you seen how many people have gone back to school now? It just keeps the unemployment figures down and produces millions of half educated old coots.' - Mark E Smith (The Fall) holds forth on mature students.

Other Institutions

OR EVEN MORE PLACES TO CONFUSE YOU...
In addition to the main institutions in *Push*, there are a number of other colleges, usually those that don't award their own degrees but confer them on behalf of a larger university. *It shouldn't be presumed that these colleges are in any way inferior to the other institutions but they do tend to have certain things in common. They're usually smaller, which can create a sense of community and/or claustrophobia according to the mood you're in.* Several have links to particular Christian denominations, although they all accept applications from people of any religious background or none. Many have a high proportion of students training to be teachers – this tends to affect the gender balance and in many of these colleges men are heavily outnumbered.

DEPTH WARNING
A word of warning – unlike the colleges and universities in the main chapters, these institutions have not been visited by our gallant band of push researchers and most of the data comes direct from the colleges themselves. It's as accurate as we can make it but the entries are, by definition, not as in-depth as those in other chapters.

Bishop Grosseteste College

Canterbury Chirst Church University College

University of Wales Institute, Cardiff

Chester College

University College Chichester

Dartington College of Arts

Edge Hill College of Higher Education

Falmouth College of Arts

Farnborough College of Technology

Harper Adams University College

Kent Institute of Art & Design

King Alfred's, Winchester

Liverpool Hope University College

NESCOT

University of Wales College, Newport

North East Wales Institute of HE

Northern College

Rose Bruford College

Royal Agricultural College

University College of St Mark & St John

St Martin's College

St Mary's College

Swansea Institute of HE

Trinity & All Saints

Trinity College, Carmarthen

Trinity College of Music

University College, Warrington

Wimbledon School of Art

University College Worcester

Writtle College

York St John

> When Philip Larkin was librarian at Hull University, he used to lock himself in his office to listen to his jazz records, and abuse anybody who tried to disturb him.

Bishop Grosseteste College

Bishop Grosseteste College, Newport, Lincoln, LN1 3DY.
Tel: (01522) 527347. Fax: (01522) 530243.
E-mail: registry@bgc.ac.uk Website: www.bgc.ac.uk

Formerly Lincoln Training College, until it changed its name in 1962, Bishop Grosseteste College is set on a single site in the centre of Lincoln. The College specialises in initial teacher training but also offers courses in drama in the Community, Heritage Studies and English Literature. Teaching has a firmly practical bent and the college has strong links with local primary schools. For information about being a student in Lincoln, see the University of Lincolnshire & Humberside.

Sex ratio(M:F): 13%:87%	Founded: 1862
Full time u'grads: 853	Part time: 0
Postgrads: 59	Non-degree: 0
Ave course: 3/4 yrs	Ethnic: 0.6%
Private school: n/a	Flunk rate: 10.1%
Mature students: 78%	Overseas students: 1%
Disabled students: 18%	Staff/student ratio: 1:22
Clearing: 14%	

Library (140,000 volumes, 150 study places, open 7 days); 56 PCs; (17% grads unemployed after 6 months). Refurbished SU Bar (12noon-11pm and 7pm-11pm); college dining hall (7.45am-6.45pm); theatre/cinema (cap 230); TV lounge; SU ents (discos, bands) most nights. SU (1 sabb, NUS member); facilities include bookshop, function, laundry and TV rooms; Rag. Refurbished gym; tennis courts; football pitches; local Sports & Leisure Centre 5 minutes' walk away. All 1st years accommodated (200 catered places, 60, 34wks, 3 meals a day, 5 days a week); local rents £35/wk. Accommodation officer; counsellor; disability co ordinator; CofE chaplain; nurse; LGB group; access fund £54,511 (88 successful applications); cathedral scholarships. Undergrad and postgrad prospectuses, course leaflets, 2 student and 2 family open days a year.

Canterbury Christ Church University College

Canterbury Christ Church University College, Canterbury, Kent, CT1 1QU. Tel: (01227) 767700. Fax: (01227) 470442. E-mail: admissions@cant.ac.uk Website: www.cant.ac.uk

CCCUC is in the centre of Canterbury, near the cathedral. There are 3 other local sites, none more than 20 minutes' walk from the main one, and also a site at Broadstairs, 15 miles from Canterbury. As with many colleges, it was originally a teacher training college and a quarter of 1st degree students are still on education courses but its main academic selling point is its combined honours system – TV and tourism, anyone? 40% of students are locals. For local info see University of Kent.

Sex ratio(M:F): 35%:65%	Founded: 1962
Full time u'grads: 3,800	Part time: n/a
Postgrads: 700	Non-degree: 34
Ave course: 3yrs	Ethnic: 5%
Private school: n/a	Flunk rate: n/a
Mature students: 35%	Overseas students: 3%
Disabled students: 5%	Staff/student ratio: n/a
Clearing: 8%	

Library (231,000 volumes, 374 study places, open 7 days) and access to University of Kent facilities; 440 computers. 2 bars; price of a pint of beer £1.40, glass of wine £1.80; good ents; SU bar doubles as music/club venue (cap 400) hosting 3 club nights a week (dance, retro, party), live bands (Bluetones and Robbie W played recently) and comedians. SU (3 sabbs, turnout at last ballot: 5%,

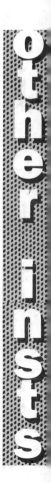

NUS member); student paper, 'Eye Eye', radio and TV stations; Rag. *Strong* sport (football, rugby, cricket, hockey); 12 acres playing fields; all-weather pitch; multigym; tennis courts; fitness centre. 38% of 1st years in hall (£50-80), boosted by a number of head-leases. Chapel; 2 counsellors; medical centre; Overseas SA; Postgrad SA; Welfare Officer; access fund £77,059 (340 successful applications). Undergrad and postgrad prospectuses.

University of Wales Institute, Cardiff

University of Wales Institute Cardiff, Western Avenue,
PO Box 377, Llandaff, Cardiff, CF5 2SG. Tel: (029) 2050 6070.
Fax: (029) 2050 6928.
E-mail: uwicinfo@uwic.ac.uk Website: www.uwic.ac.uk

On six sites, all within a four-mile radius of the centre of Cardiff, *we find* UWIC – offering a mixed palette of courses, all with a vocational edge. The sites are all linked by the college bus service – Business, Leisure and Food courses are based at the Colchester Avenue campus; Education and Sport at the Cyncoed Campus; Community Health Sciences at the Llandaff Campus; and Art, Design & Engineering at Llandaff and Howard Gardens campuses. There are 2 other sites which house halls of residence – Plas Gwyn is home to approximately 400 students, all accommodated in self-catered, en suite single rooms, and Fairwater is used for student accommodation (catered) and conferences. The SU has recently bought a local nightclub (Reds) and bar (Bar Ice) in the city. For more details on the local area, see Cardiff, University of Wales.

Sex ratio(M:F): 55%:45%	Founded: 1976
Full time u'grads: 4,755	Part time: 193
Postgrads: 644	Non-degree: 893
Ave course: 3yrs	Ethnic: n/a
Private school: n/a	Flunk rate: n/a
Mature students: 28%	Overseas students: n/a
Disabled students: 5%	Staff/student ratio: 1:15
Clearing: 11%	

4 libraries (244,010 volumes, 712 study places); 300 computers; both 6 days. 2 full-time, 1 part-time careers advisers (11% grads unemployed after 6 months). 3 bars – Taffy's *is the main bar*, Tommys (cap 300) *is more alternative*; Dum Dums and Keith Harris and Orville have played recently ('I wish I could fly'). SU (3 sabbs, NUS member, 8% turnout); new SU block with bar, café and gym; shop and café at each campus; monthly magazine, 'Retro'. *Excellent* sports facilities: astro-turf pitch; tennis centre; 2 rugby and 2 football pitches; swimming pool; squash courts; new indoor athletics centre. 90% of 1st years accommodated (£48-67, 39wks catering and self-catering, some en suite), no one shares a room; CCTV; accommodation office. Chaplain, chapel and mosque; jobshop during term-time; 3 counsellors; nursery (40 places, 0-5 yrs); welfare officer; health clinic; access fund £115,362, sports scholarships.
Prospectus, course leaflets, CD-Rom, video.

Chester College

Chester: A College of the University of Liverpool, Parkgate Road, Chester, CH1 4BJ. Tel: (01244) 375444. Fax: (01244) 392821. E-mail: enquiries@chester.ac.uk Website: www.chester.ac.uk

Chester, home of Hollyoaks and Mansun, is 25 miles from Liverpool, near the Welsh border. *Apart from smug bad actors and second rate indie bands* there's the College, a compact 30-acre campus containing a mix of Victorian and modern buildings, about 10 minutes' walk from the city centre. A number of undergraduates are trainee teachers, with the rest on various science and humanities courses, often with a vocational emphasis, and 20% are locals. Liverpool and Manchester *aren't too far for those after brighter lights than Chester can muster*, as are the *stunning* Welsh hills *if even Chester's subdued attractions get too much*.

Sex ratio(M:F): 32%:68%	Founded: 1839
Full time u'grads: 2,912	Part time: 135
Postgrads: 1247	Non-degree: 157
Ave course: 3yrs	Ethnic: 2.7%
Private school: n/a	Flunk rate: 10.4%
Mature students: 17.9%	Overseas students: 0.3%
Disabled students: 6.4%	Staff/student ratio: n/a
Clearing: 7%	

Library (196,557 volumes, 484 study places, open seven days) and access to University of Liverpool facilities (25 miles away); 500 computers; 2 full-time careers advisers (8% grads unemployed after six months). The recently revamped 'Max 250' bar with big screen TV and pool tables; promo nights, DJs, special events, local bands, film nights; new SU building with 1,000 cap venue planned; Molloy Hall is the college-run venue for higher-brow stuff and the drama society puts on regular productions; *plenty of eateries* including two college dining halls, SU Bistro and several coffee bars. SU (two sabbs, 12% turnout); SU-run monthly paper 'The Collegian' and 'The Sun' weekly newsletter; Action into the Community group; Rag raised £40,000 recently. *Good reputation in sport* helped by *strong* PE Department; sports hall; pool; multigym; squash and tennis courts; athletics field; all-weather pitch; climbing wall; the local area adds an ice rink, dry-ski slope; bowling alley and the Welsh mountains. Accommodation for most 1st years who want it; bar a few who get in via Clearing; also a few students from other years can live in college housing; 360 catered, £70-80, 40wks, in all 350 self-catered, £34-45, 40wks, 3 or 4 to a kitchen; 10% share; CCTV; also head tenancy scheme run by *good* accommodation office; local rents £40-65/wk. Jobshop; 2 chaplains, chapel, muslim prayer room; 2 counsellors; nursery (0-5yrs); Medical Centre; late-night minibus through local Women's Safe Transport Scheme; good disabled facilities; overseas, postgrad and LGB groups. Access fund. Undergraduate and postgraduate prospectuses, including the alternative variety from the SU.

University College Chichester

(1) University College Chichester, Bishop Otter Campus,
College Lane, Chichester, West Sussex, PO19 4PE.
(2) University College Chichester, Bognor Regis Campus,
Upper Bognor Road, Bognor Regis, West Sussex, PO21 1HR.
Tel: (01243) 816000. Fax: (01243) 816080.
E-mail: admissions@chihe.ac.uk Website: www.chihe.ac.uk

Despite the name, only one of this college's 2 sites is in Chichester itself. The Bishop Otter Campus, named after the 19th-century religious leader and aquatic mammal, is a 38-acre site just outside the centre of this *pretty* cathedral city, 20 miles from Portsmouth, founded in 1839 as Bishop Otter College. The other campus dates from 1947 and is centred on a Georgian mansion terrace in the seaside resort of Bognor Regis, 6 miles away. They merged in 1977 and both sites have several modern additions. Nearly half the students are on teaching-related courses and Sports Studies and arts are also popular options. The College now validates its own degrees.

Sex ratio(M:F): 30%:70%	Founded: 1977
Full time u'grads: 2,900	Part time: 300
Postgrads: 200	Non-degree: 0
Ave course: 3/4 yrs	Ethnic: 10%
Private school: 5%	Flunk rate: n/a
Mature students: 40%	Overseas students: 10%
Disabled students: 10%	Staff/student ratio: 1:30
Clearing: 20%	

Library at Bognor; Learning Resources Centre at Bishop Otter (200,000 volumes in all, open 7 days); 100 computers; full-time careers officer. Free shuttle bus between sites. 2 bars, weekly discos, quizzes, bands (recently Dum Dums) and comedians (recently Craig Charles); drama and music socs; film club with regular mainstream/arty showings; College refectory at each campus, burger/pizza bar. SU (2 sabbs; NUS member; 25% turnout), *emphasis on social/ents rather than politics but good support for recent anti-tuition fees campaigns*; 'A259' magazine and the alternative 'Cartlaridge'; community action group; Rag week, which includes a beer race around Bognor. *Strong on sport and arts, boosted by relevant courses and attendant facilities.* 35% of 1st years accommodated (330 catered, £61-83, 36wks, 12 meals/wk) but no others; more rooms being added at Bognor; local rents £50/wk. Accommodation office; Jobshop; 4 counsellors; chaplain, chapel (Bishop Otter) and prayer room (Bognor); nurse on each site; dyslexia support officer; women's mature/postgrad, overseas and LGB groups; nursery at Bognor; access fund £75,000 (350 successful applicants), various loans and a rugby scholarship.

Dartington College of Arts

Dartington College of Arts, Totnes, Devon, TQ9 6EJ.
Tel: (01803) 862224. Fax: (01803) 863569.
E-mail: registry@dartington.ac.uk Website: www.dartington.ac.uk

The *dinky* (pop 7,020) townlet of Totnes is on the South Devon coast and 2 miles away, by the River Dart, is the *beautiful* Dartington Hall estate, the site of this unique college. Dartington concentrates on contemporary visual & performance arts and arts management and has a high academic reputation in these areas, with its teaching described with *uncharacteristic enthusiasm* by inspectors as "inspirational" and "charismatic". All students study the same core programme, including arts management for artists, and there are 4 specialist subject areas available (music, performance writing, visual performance and theatre). *The location is relatively isolated and Totnes doesn't have that much to offer crazy funseekers, though it has the usual market town accoutrements* of supermarkets, leisure centre, pubs and restaurants. However, Dartington Arts, a year-round programme of concerts, exhibitions, film and more, together with its famous International Summer School of Music, is on the same estate, and *Dartington's creative students are more than capable of making their own entertainment. For those after more conventional student kicks* the cities and universities of Exeter and Plymouth are less than 30 miles away in each direction.

Sex ratio(M:F): 45%:55%	Founded: 1961
Full time u'grads: 371	Part time: 0
Postgrads: 10	Non-degree: 0
Ave course: 3yrs	Ethnic: 7%
Private school: n/a	Flunk rate: n/a
Mature students: 55%	Overseas students: 3%
Disabled students: 13%	Staff/student ratio: 1:12
Clearing: 20%	

Library (46,000 volumes, 50 study places, open 7 days); 36 computers. SU's Higher Close Club Bar serves snacks; BFI supported cinema on campus; the Barn Theatre and Great Hall for live performances of all varieties plus *more workshops, studios and practice rooms than you can poke a stick at* including digital audio and video suites. Famous alumni: Josie Lawrence (actress); Yolande Snaith (Dancer). *The SU provides social rather than political focus. As un-sporty as you'd expect* but there's a squash court and open air swimming pool (summer term only, *surprise, surprise*).
No accommodation of its own, but the Dartington Hall Trust offers 70 self-catered places on campus; local rents £40/wk. Welfare issues tackled on an individual basis; counsellor; a disability officer, welfare & accommodation officer; health centre (nurse; doctors twice weekly); academic counselling; women's officer; access fund £38,550 (119 successful applicants) plus a few bursaries to help with instrumental tuition. Undergraduate prospectus, course leaflets.

Edge Hill College of Higher Education

Edge Hill College of Higher Education, St Helen's Road, Ormskirk, Lancashire, L39 4QP. Tel: (01695) 575171. Fax: (01695) 579997. E-mail: enquiries@edgehill.ac.uk Website: www.edgehill.ac.uk

About 17 miles from Liverpool is the market town of Ormskirk and on the edge of that is the 45-acre site of Edge Hill. The buildings are mainly brick, with a few concrete blocks and some *interesting* wrought iron sculptures. A third of undergraduates are trainee

teachers and the rest are on nursing courses or modular degrees. Professional courses are based in Chorley, 17 miles away, and the health studies and nursing programmes take place in Aintree, near Liverpool. Both <u>Manchester</u> and <u>Liverpool</u> *are just about close enough to provide excitement.*

Sex ratio(M:F): 31%:69%	Founded: 1885
Full time u'grads: 4,391	Part time: 2,140
Postgrads: 515	Non-degree: 845
Ave course: 3yrs	Ethnic: 3%
Private school: 3%	Flunk rate: 15.9%
Mature students: 36%	Overseas students: 0.2%
Disabled students: 3.9%	Staff/student ratio: 1:19.3
Clearing: 20%	

One library (225,000 volumes, open 7 days); 600 computers. 5% of graduates unemployed after six months. SU bar; discos drop-off bus service when the bar closes etc with food in SU bar (burgers and pizzas), Terrace Café and Sages Restaurant. SU (no sabbs, NUS member); Community Action group and RAG. Recent £4Mn sports development 'Sporting Edge' *(boom! boom!)* adding playing fields, running track, weights room, squash, five-a-side (won the cup last year) and badminton courts; pool on campus. All 1st years who want to can live in (around 80%) but only a handful of others (302 catered, £66, 38wks, two meals/day; 351 self-catered, £36-52, 38wks); 2 all-female halls; 24-hour security; local rents £40/wk. 3 part-time counsellors; multi-faith prayer room; creche (2-5yrs, 20 places); 2 Financial/Welfare Rights Officers; ethnic minorities and LGB groups; *okay* wheelchair access; access fund £336,041 (431 successful applications). Undergraduate and postgraduate prospectuses, video loan.

Falmouth College of Arts

Falmouth College of Arts, Woodlane, Falmouth, Cornwall, TR11 4RA. Tel: (01326) 211077. Fax: (01326) 211205.

In the *remote, close-knit* town of Falmouth, almost at the *pointiest* bit of Cornwall, sits this large college, now affiliated to <u>Plymouth University</u>. Originally founded as an Art School, Falmouth now covers various aspects of media and journalism as well as painting and stuff. There's an annexe at Redruth, about 9 miles away. *Falmouth can be a bit of a tourist trap in summer, but this does help swell the facilities.* There's a *decent* live music venue, the Pirate (recent melody makers include Ash, Reef, Dodgy and the Supernaturals), and the Paradox nighclub provides the sounds every night (dance, indie, retro, party) including a *popular* student-night on Wednesdays. The nearest cinema is the Old Regal in Redruth, *but we're not talking 12-screen multiplex here.*

> Cilla Black declined an honorary fellowship of Liverpool John Moores University, after students objected.

Sex ratio(M:F): 40%:60%	Founded: 1938
Full time u'grads: 453	Part time: 0
Postgrads: 58	Non-degree: 864
Ave course: 3yrs	Ethnic: 1.5%
Private school: 4%	Flunk rate: n/a
Mature students: 10%	Overseas students: 1%
Disabled students: 1%	Staff/student ratio: 1:22
Clearing: 5%	

Library (20,000 volumes); 140 computers; neither accessible on Sundays. Refectory/bar (food 10am-7pm Mon-Thurs, 10am-5pm Fri; booze 12.30-1.30pm and 6-11pm; beer £1, glass of wine £1.35) doubles as *decent* club/music venue (cap 240); comedians termly; 1 or 2 films a week, either in a lecture theatre (cap 120) or in the refectory/bar/venue. SU (1 sabb, NUS member) *active for its size*; SU-run paper, 'Mouth'; Flavour Radio broadcasts at lunchtimes to the refectory (*slightly bizarrely* through TV sets). No sports facilities of its own, though students can use local facilities which, what with *Falmouth being on the coast, are especially good for watersports*; women's football won all matches last year. No accommodation of its own either, *and local rents aren't the cheapest (£45/wk), but it's usually possible to get something within walking distance of campus*. Accommodation, welfare and counselling are handled by Student Services; 1 full-time and 2 part-time counsellors; nurse; creche; *limited* wheelchair access; *good* dyslexia support; access fund £37,000. Prospectus.

Farnborough College of Technology

Farnborough College of Technology, Boundary Road, Farnborough, Hants, GU14 6SB, Tel: (01252) 405555. Fax: (01252) 407041. E-mail: info@farn-ct.ac.uk Website: www.farn-ct.ac.uk, www.fcotsu.co.uk

35 miles from London is the commuter town of Farnborough. The College of Technology is mainly inhabited by non-degree students (A-levels, HND etc) but it offers degree courses in various vocational areas, including business, computing, engineering and media technology, all on a concrete-and-glass site about 500 metres from the town centre. *Its claim to fame is that* it boasts a couple of Gladiators among its famous offspring (Jet and Trojan *if you really must know*). Farnborough offers enough for a *basic* night-out (pubs, restaurants) with a cinema, bowling alley and dry-ski slope 4 miles away and the teeming metropolis *just a short but usually packed* train-ride up the mainline to Waterloo.

Sex ratio(M:F): 47%:53%	Founded: 1957
Full time u'grads: 520	Part time: 115
Postgrads: 39	Non-degree: 5,810
Ave course: 3yrs	Ethnic: 9%
Private school: n/a	Flunk rate: n/a
Mature students: 40%	Overseas students: 3.1%
Disabled students: 3%	Staff/student ratio: 1:15
Clearing: n/a	

Two libraries (45,000 volumes, 400 study places, open six days); 300 computers; recent Teaching and Learning Technologies Resources Centre. SU building with *top quality* club/music venue (cap 300) with recent visits from DJ Punk Roc, Lisa Pinup and Euphoria. Oh, and a Playstation. Student-run newspaper, 24-hour radio station one month a year and Genesis TV; film club. Life Fitness is the completely refitted and doubled-in-size gym; *pretty hot* at soccer. Accommodation for 30% of 1st years, 25% of 2nd years and a few finalists (200 catered, £55-80, 33wks, half-board), with a few students sharing rooms and *mumblings about quality; commuter-belt rents* (£50/wk). 2 counsellors; chaplains; occupational health nurse; nursery (40 places, 6mths-5yrs); Disabilities Co-ordinator; access fund £33,500, Sky TV sponsorships, bursaries for locals. Prospectuses, accommodation pack, video.

Harper Adams University College

Harper Adams University College, Newport, Shropshire, TF10 8NB.
Tel: (01952) 815000. Fax: (01952) 814783.
E-mail: admissions@harper-adams.ac.uk
Website: www.harper-adams.ac.uk

Harper Adams, in the heart of rural Shropshire, offers courses related to land-based industries. 37% of undergrads are studying agriculture including topics such as animal science, business and marketing, countryside and land management, engineering and food studies. The college also offers such *oddities* as an HND in golf course management and courses in environmental protection as well as the *more standard stuff*. It's a huge 500-acre site, with its own 236-hectare working farm, 2 miles outside Newport and 36 from Birmingham. 95% of students are on sandwich courses and 10% come from Northern Ireland or the Irish Republic. It's a bit isolated and the nearest train station is 10 miles away in Telford, *so a car comes in handy*.

Sex ratio(M:F): 58%:42%	Founded: 1901
Full time u'grads: 1,545	Part time: 51
Postgrads: 55	Non-degree: 563
Ave course: 4yrs	Ethnic: 0.2%
Private school: 35%	Flunk rate: 11.3%
Mature students: 15.5%	Overseas students: 8%
Disabled students: 0.1%	Staff/student ratio: 1:15
Clearing: 5%	

Library (41,000 volumes, 40 study places, open seven days); 117 computers. Two bars; Harper Adams Café open all day, including weekends; regular club nights and *grand* end of session ball. SU; student paper, 'Cat-a-Mountain'; Rag; pheasant-shooting society. *Strong* sporting reputation, regularly taking on *sporting giants like Loughborough and Durham*, especially at rugby; 40 acres playing fields; sports hall; pool; multigym; squash and tennis courts; athletics field; climbing wall; croquet pitch *for the more sedate*; the local area adds plenty for climbers, hikers, canoeists, horse-riders and other outward-bound folk. All 1st years and most finalists accommodated (500 catered, £66-90, all meals Mon-Fri, 180 en-suite; 20 places self-catering £40); security guards and CCTV. Jobshop; Student Services provides accommodation and welfare advice; a counsellor; doctor's surgery; access fund £27,000 (22 successful applications). Undergraduate and postgraduate prospectuses, video; national sixth form conference (£15) and open days.

Kent Institute of Art & Design

Kent Institute of Art & Design, Oakwood Park, Maidstone, Kent, ME16 8AG. Tel: (01622) 757286. Fax: (01622) 621100. E-mail: kiadmarketing@kiad.ac.uk Website: www.kiad.ac.uk

KIAD was formed from the merger of 3 art colleges and different courses are based at each one: Canterbury (65 miles from London) for Fine Art and Architecture; Rochester (40 miles) for 3D Design, Jewellery, Fashion and Photography; Maidstone (45 miles) for Graphic Design, Illustration and Visual Communication. All sites are concrete constructions amidst *pleasant greenery* on the outskirts of town. Canterbury has a built-in student population from the University of Kent which validates all degrees; *the other areas are quieter*.

Sex ratio(M:F): 44%:56%	Founded: 1987
Full time u'grads: 1,580	Part time: 148
Postgrads: 70	Non-degree: 675
Ave course: 3yrs	Ethnic: 5%
Private school: n/a	Flunk rate: n/a
Mature students: 14%	Overseas students: 13%
Disabled students: 12%	Staff/student ratio: 1:21
Clearing: 2%	

Library at each site (70,000 volumes, 150 study places between them, closed weekends); 35 PCs in library. SU bar/canteen facilities at each site. SA organises events and sport; student paper 'Impress/Express'. No sports facilities but access to local facilities with student discounts. 52% of 1st years housed in college-owned or managed housing plus a fair few from other years (438 self-catered, £57, 43wks, 5-7 share *good* kitchens; 130 head tenancy); local rents above average (£45/wk) but *not bad for commuter-country* and there's enough of it. Careers adviser; 3 part-time counsellors; Welfare Officers; wheelchair access *improving*; access fund £64,836 (192 successful applications), small number of bursaries. Undergrad and postgrad prospectus, course leaflets, video.

King Alfred's, Winchester

King Alfred's College Winchester, Sparkford Road, Winchester, Hants, SO22 4NR. Tel: (01962) 841515. Fax: (01962) 842280. E-mail: a.childs@wkac.ac.uk Website: www.wkac.ac.uk

King Alfred (who burned the cakes) not only had his HQ in Winchester, 10 miles from Southampton, he also lent his name to the College, about ½ mile from the town centre. King Alf's was originally set up as a teacher training college and there's still a sizeable chunk of BEd students, although a wide range of arts, humanities, media and business subjects are on offer too. Health and Community Studies have a base in the North Hampshire Hospital, 20 miles up the M3 in Basingstoke.

Sex ratio(M:F): 28%:72%
Full time u'grads: 3,252
Postgrads: 140
Ave course: 3yrs
Private school: n/a
Mature students: 34%
Disabled students: 4%
Clearing: 10%

Founded: 1840
Part time: 1,321
Non-degree: 1,164
Ethnic: 8%
Flunk rate: n/a
Overseas students: 3%
Staff/student ratio: 1:33

New award-winning library (200,000 volumes, 450 study places, open 7 days); 400 computers; a careers adviser (3.2% graduates unemployed after 6 months). 3 bars (open all day); John Stripe theatre for luvvies (both student and pro), also new Drama/Cultural Studies building. SU (3 sabbs); student paper, 'Harder Times'; radio station; Rag; SU-run Job Shop. *Limited* sports facilities including sports hall, squash courts, athletics field, gym and dance studio; 4 balls a year. 78% of 1st years accommodated but few others (234 catered, £82, 30wks, £30 worth of meals a week; 793 self-catered, £61-68, 40wks); a devilish 666 places in the student village with 24-hr security (*armed with holy-water?*); local rents £60pw; accommodation officer. Famous alumni: John McIntyre (reporter); Lenny Beige (comedian). Anglican chaplain, chapel and Muslim facilities; nurse; a counsellor; 3 full-time welfare advisers; nursery (20 places, 3 months-4 years); late-night minibus; Disability Adviser and dyslexia tutors; access fund £200,000 (140 successful applications), some bursaries. Undergrad, postgrad and part-time prospectuses, video, course leaflets and accommodation brochure.

Liverpool Hope University College

Liverpool Hope University College, Hope Park, Liverpool, L16 9JD.
Tel: (0151) 291 3295. Fax: (0151) 291 3048.
Website: www.livhope.ac.uk

4 miles (*or a cheap bus ride*) from the centre of Liverpool is the city's third higher education institution, formerly Liverpool Institute and *(by the sound of the new name) rather 'Hope'-ful to gain University status soonish.* In the meantime its degrees are validated by Liverpool University. Appropriately in this *strongly ecumenical* city, it was formed from the federation of 3 colleges, 1 Anglican and 2 Catholic, with roots in the 19th-century, and theology is still a *strong* subject area, as is teacher training (25% of students). In all, 16 degree courses are on offer. The Anglican Bishop and the Catholic Archbishop of Liverpool alternate as chairs of the Governing Council. Architecturally, it's a mix of 30s and 60s styles with several modern additions, *kind of George Formby does Britpop.*

Sex ratio(M:F): 28%:72%
Full time u'grads: 3,497
Postgrads: 737
Ave course: 3yrs
Private school: n/a
Mature students: 33%
Disabled students: 8%
Clearing: 18.5%

Founded: 1980
Part time: 379
Non-degree: 250
Ethnic: 4%
Flunk rate: 19.7%
Overseas students: 1.7%
Staff/student ratio: 1:20

New learning resources centre (225,000 volumes, 500 study places, open 7 days); 65 computers. 2 bars; refectory (9am-5pm), snack bar (10am-3pm, 8-11pm, Mon-Thurs) and pizza kitchen (8-11pm); the massed entertainments of Liverpool *are practically on your doorstep.* SU (2 sabbs, NUS member, 30% turnout); student paper; community action group. *Good at sport* (especially rugby and football); new sports complex; health and fitness centre; flood-lit astro-turf; squash courts; 2 football pitches; sports injury clinic and 2 scientific sports laboratories; outdoor pursuits centre in N Wales. Accommodation for nearly 40% of 1st years, with priority to non-Liverpudlians who make Hope their first choice (822 catered, £59, 31wks, 12 meals/wk; 12 self-catered, £45, 31wks); 188 en suite self-catering rooms planned for new Everton campus. 2 counsellors; nurse; twice weekly GP surgery; 2 chaplains (1 RC, 1 Anglican); multi-faith prayer room; *good wheelchair access,* disability officer; welfare advice from SU; access fund £70,000 (239 successful applications), Hillsborough Bursary for local students, subject specific prizes and bursaries, hardship fund and loans. Undergrad and postgrad prospectuses, programme and subject leaflets, quarterly mag 'Hope Direct'.

NESCOT

NESCOT, Reigate Road, Ewell, Epsom, Surrey, KT17 3DS.
Tel: (020) 8394 1731. Fax: (020) 8394 3030.
E-mail: info@nescot.ac.uk. Website: www.nescot.ac.uk

Based near Epsom, about 15 miles from Central London, is the former North East Surrey College Of Technology, now called NESCOT *(which sounds like a whisky-flavour milkshake, but don't worry). It's a classic example of the way the Higher Ed market has exploded in the last few years*: it offers everything from GCSEs to postgrad qualifications and the vast majority of the degree-level students are local returners to education. It's *strongly* vocational in emphasis with courses in technology, business, design and performing arts. *Epsom* (also home to part of Surrey Institute of Art & Design) *cannot truthfully be called the entertainment capital of the UK, but it's close enough to London to keep serious withdrawal symptoms at bay.*

Sex ratio(M:F): 51%:49%	Founded: 1953
Full time u'grads: 488	Part time: 723
Postgrads: 3	Non-degree: 4,264
Ave course: 3yrs	Ethnic: 24%
Private school: n/a	Flunk rate: n/a
Mature students: 66%	Overseas students: 8.6%
Disabled students: 1%	Staff/student ratio: 1:20
Clearing: n/a	

Library (45,000 volumes, 200 study places, closed at weekends); 60 PCs (24 hours); one career adviser. Bar doubles as club/music venue (cap 400); refectory (10am-8.30pm); Adrian Mann theatre; visual and performing arts centre. SU (no sabbs, NUS member, 25% turnout) provides snack bar, shop, pool table, photocopier, jobs board and video games. Sports hall; fitness suite; outdoor pitches; multigym; tennis courts; athletics field and running track; Epsom Races in summer. Hardly any accommodation of its own and *extortionate* local rents (up to £100/wk); accommodation office *does its best.* Jobs

noticeboard; 2 part-time counsellors; CofE chaplain; nurse; visiting doctor; Welfare & Student Services for welfare, legal and other advice; wheelchair access to most areas and tuition for dyslexia sufferers; access fund £85,000 (100 successful applications), college trust fund, hardship fund. Open days, prospectus and course sheets available.

University of Wales College, Newport

University of Wales College, Newport, Campus, PO Box 101, Newport, NP18 3YH. Tel: (01633) 432432. Fax: (01633) 432850
E-mail: uic@newport.ac.uk Website: www.newport.ac.uk

UWCN is on two main sites, 5 miles apart, in the town of Newport, SE Wales. It is affiliated to the University of Wales. Caerleon, the larger campus, is a village on the outskirts of the town *which was a pretty happening place in Roman times.* It houses the administration and accommodation buildings and much of the teaching premises, except for 3 departments (Business & Management, Health & Social Care and Engineering) which are in Allt-yr-yn in the town centre. *Newport itself is looking pretty happening these days, with local boyz 60ft Dolls, Catatonia, Manics and Super Furry Animals generating a load of hype.* Overall, art, design and media students provide the single biggest chunk of the full-time undergraduates with another 19% on teacher training courses, but if you include part-timers, business and management comes top.

Sex ratio(M:F): 48%:52%
Full time u'grads: 2,858
Postgrads: 121
Ave course: 3yrs
Private school: n/a
Mature students: 41%
Disabled students: 11%
Clearing: 30%

Founded: 1975
Part time: 5,114
Non-degree: 460
Ethnic: 8%
Flunk rate: n/a
Overseas students: 1%
Staff/student ratio: n/a

Libraries at each site (150,000 volumes, 130 study places in all, open 7 days); 100 computers. TV studio; SU bar, cyber café at Caerleon. College is home to the new International Film School, Wales. Famous alumni: Justin Kerrigan (director, 'Human Traffic'). Recent sporting success in men's rugby and women's cross country; sports centre at Caerleon site. 39% of 1st years accommodated (643 self-catered, £43-52, 37wks, up to 16 share a kitchen, 447 en suite) but around 50% of undergrads live at home; free car parking. Unemployed after 6 months: 3%, 2 careers advisers. 3 part-time counsellors; medical service (doctor, 2 nurses); Student Support Services; creche available at half-term only, disability co-ordinator. Access fund £319,508 (480 successful applications). Prospectus.

North East Wales Institute of HE

North East Wales Institute of Higher Education, Plas Coch Mold Road, Wrexham, LL11 2AW. Tel: (01978) 290666. Fax: (01978) 290008.
E-mail: admission@newi.ac.uk
Websites: www.newi.ac.uk and www.newi.ac.uk/sunion

NEWI is in the centre of Wrexham, a town of 123,000 people near the English/Welsh border, 30 miles from Liverpool. Most departments are based at Mold Road with the School of Art & Design (350 students) just 500 yards away. There's a bilingual policy in the Institute and the SU, although the vast majority of students have English as a first or only language. 21% of students are trainee teachers.

Sex ratio(M:F): 49%:51%
Full time u'grads: 2,011
Postgrads: 337
Ave course: 3yrs
Private school: 1%
Mature students: 40%
Disabled students: 3%
Clearing: 10%

Founded: 1975
Part time: 437
Non-degree: 1,058
Ethnic: 3%
Flunk rate: n/a
Overseas students: 5%
Staff/student ratio: 1:11

Library (102,000 volumes, 230 study places, open 6 days); 400 computers; 4 careers advisers (5% grads unemployed after 6 months). Bar; SU (2 sabbs, NUS member); student paper; Rag. 40% of 1st years and a few finalists accommodated in self-catering hostels (450 places, £41-53, 37wks), 40% en suite, 15% shared; local rents £38/wk. New sports centre including astroturf. Welfare and accommodation services provided by Information & Student Support; 2 counsellors; nurse; GP surgery 1 day/wk; disability co-ordinator; nursery (24 places); SU also offers welfare advice; access fund £45,000 (170 successful applications). Undergrad and postgrad prospectuses.

Northern College

Northern College of Education, Aberdeen Campus, Hilton Place, Aberdeen, AB24 4FA. Tel: (01224) 283500. Fax: (01224) 283900. Website: www.norcol.ac.uk
Dundee Campus, Gardyne Road, Dundee, DD5 1NY. Tel: (01382) 464000. Fax: (01382) 464900.

Northern College was formed by the merger of the teacher training colleges in Aberdeen and Dundee. The resulting two-site college still specialises in initial teacher training and also offers courses in community education and social work. Many of its courses are validated by the Open University and there is a strong programme of off-campus, distance learning and professional development studies. Most courses, however, are based at one of the two campuses with the exception of community education, which is based at Dundee, and the BEd in Music, which is based at Aberdeen. For information about the towns, see Aberdeen University and Dundee University.

Sex ratio(M:F): 20%:80%
Full time u'grads: 960
Postgrads: 200
Ave course: 4yrs
Private school: n/a
Mature students: 20%
Disabled students: 1%
Clearing: 30%

Founded: 1987
Part time: 0
Non-degree: 0
Ethnic: 2%
Flunk rate: n/a
Overseas students: 2%
Staff/student ratio: 1:22

Library on each site (160,000 volumes, 230 study places, open 6 days); 350 computers; careers adviser (5% grads unemployed after 6 months). Bar on each site (pint of beer £1.50, ½ bottle wine £2.50); canteen, refectory, vending machines. SU (2 sabbs, 30% voted in last ballot, NUS member). Pool, football pitch and sports hall on each site, gymnasium and squash courts at Dundee. About 45% of 1st years live in plus 10-25% from other years (135 catered, £63, 33wks; 145 self-catered, £47-69, 33wks); night porter, swipe cards. 2 chaplains; chapel (Dundee); counsellor; nursery (Dundee, 24 places, 0-5 years); medical officer; range of disabled facilities; access fund £86,509 (260 successful applicants). Undergrad prospectus, course brochures.

Rose Bruford College

Rose Bruford College, Burnt Oak Lane, Sidcup, Kent, DA15 9DF.
Tel: (020) 8300 3024. Fax: (020) 8308 0542.
E-mail: admiss@bruford.ac.uk

In a green commuter-belt setting, 25 minutes by train from central London, stands the main site of Rose Bruford College, which is entirely concerned with offering degrees (validated by University of Manchester) related to all aspects of the theatre, including the only opera studies degree course in Europe. Ex-Doctor Who Tom Baker, Gary Oldman (*Hollywood bad-guy extraordinaire* and *top* Brit director) and Pam St. Clements (Pat in Eastenders) are among its former students. There's another site in Deptford, 8 miles away, based in a former secondary school (see Goldsmiths and Greenwich for details of the local area).

Sex ratio(M:F): 43%:57%	Founded: 1950
Full time u'grads: 589	Part time: 274
Postgrads: 10	Non-degree: 12
Ave course: 3yrs	Ethnic: 25%
Private school: n/a	Flunk rate: n/a
Mature students: 40%	Overseas students: 16%
Disabled students: 15%	Staff/student ratio: 1:17
Clearing: 2%	

Libraries on each site (38,000 volumes in all, 73 study places), 16 computers, neither accessible at weekends. 15% unemployment after 6 months. *Limited* SU facilities (no bar). 26% of 1st years housed in University of Greenwich accommodation. Counsellor and welfare officer; access fund £37,970 (132 successful applicants). Prospectus.

Royal Agricultural College

The Royal Agricultural College, Stroud Road, Cirencester, Gloucestershire, GL7 6JS. Tel: (01285) 652531. Fax: (01285) 650219.
E-mail: admissions@royagcol.ac.uk Website: www.royagcol.ac.uk

About a mile from the county town of Cirencester is the (other) RAC, the world's oldest agricultural college and, since 1995, the first to award its own degrees. It's a private institution, so full fees are payable (£3,282 to £6,291 for undergrads). The College farms 1,800 acres nearby, to which students have access. College alumni between them are said to own, manage or administer over 80% of the UK. *Conspiracy-theorist heaven or what?*

Sex ratio(M:F): 66%:34%
Full time u'grads: 464
Postgrads: 59
Ave course: 3yrs
Private school: 75%
Mature students: 18%
Disabled students: 0
Clearing: 1%

Founded: 1845
Part time: 40
Non-degree: 67
Ethnic: 2%
Flunk rate: n/a
Overseas students: 11%
Staff/student ratio: 1:13

Library (31,000 volumes, 160 study places, open 6 days); 56 PCs; careers adviser (8% grads unemployed after 6 months). SU common room and bar (open 12.30-2pm, 7-11pm); 5 balls a year; disco till 2am on Fridays; canteen (8.30am-4pm, 7.30-10pm). *Strong* sports ethos (particularly rugby, polo and other equestrian sports); 20 acres of playing fields; all-weather pitch; tennis and squash courts; multigym; clay-pigeon shooting range. 98% of 1st years in catered halls (245 places, £70-120, 52wks, 3 meals/day, cleaning, some en suite). Counsellor; nightline; GP surgery (4 days); access fund £90,000 (40 successful applications); hardship fund (£40,000 available), scholarships. Undergrad and postgrad prospectuses, video, 'The Cirencester Experience' brochure.

University College of St Mark & St John

University College of St Mark and St John, Derriford Road, Plymouth, PL6 8BH. Tel: (01752) 636827. Fax: (01752) 636849.

Quick quiz: Marjon is (1) A Chinese version of dominoes, (2) how some people like their toast, or (3) the popular name for an Anglican college 5 miles from the centre of Plymouth, pretty close to the airport and the *gorgeous wilderness* of Dartmoor. Although the constituent colleges were founded in London over 150 years ago, and merged in 1923, Marjon has only been in Plymouth since 1973. It's still primarily a teacher training college, with 44% on related courses – the others are studying for modular BA degrees. For information on the local area, see University of Plymouth.

Sex ratio(M:F): 33%:67%
Full time u'grads: 2,200
Postgrads: 274
Ave course: 3yrs
Private school: n/a
Mature students: 30%
Disabled students: 8%
Clearing: 79%

Founded: 1840
Part time: 31
Non-degree: 1,300
Ethnic: 5%
Flunk rate: n/a
Overseas students: 13%
Staff/student ratio: 1:20

Learning Resources Centre (131,412+ volumes, 250 study places); 225 computers, 25 available 24 hours. 3 bars and own pub; disco every Thursday, live music every Friday (recently Abba Gold), canteen, snack bar. SU (no sabbs, NUS member), café, shop; 'Subscribe' magazine run by SU; radio station; Rag. *Good sports facilities and results.* 85% of 1st years accommodated and 5% of finalists (£48-58/wk). 3 counsellors; chapel; access fund £90,000. Union guide, prospectus and video.

St Martin's College

St Martin's College, Bowerham Road, Lancaster, LA1 3JD.
Tel: (01524) 384444. Fax: (01524) 384567.
E-mail: admissions@ucsm.ac.uk Website: www.ucsm.ac.uk

A mile from the centre of Lancaster is this 'college for the caring professions', specialising in teacher-training and health-based courses. Degrees are validated by Lancaster University, but apart from the odd student relationship that's the only connection between them. There's also a site in Ambleside, 35 miles away in the *beautiful* Lake District, and the college has training venues in towns all around the region, mainly for nursing students. Claims to fame include having its own maze *modelled* on *Chartres Cathedral* (which you can still explore), and former student, Postman Pat – creator, John Cunliffe. For town details, see Lancaster University.

Sex ratio(M:F): 25%:75%	**Founded: 1963**
Full time u'grads: 4,500	**Part time: 5,000**
Postgrads: 1,000	**Non-degree: 1,226**
Ave course: 3/4yrs	**Ethnic: 5%**
Private school: n/a	**Flunk rate: n/a**
Mature students: 20%	**Overseas students: 1%**
Disabled students: 1.1%	**Staff/student ratio: 1:21**
Clearing: 20%	

7 libraries (237,427 volumes, 475 study places, open 6 days) and access to Lancaster Universitys' library; 160 computers (24hrs); 3 careers advisers (10% grads unemployed after 6 months). 2 bars (open 6-11pm); 2 dining rooms; 2 snack bars; various ents every week night at Lancaster plus 4 major events a year; *good* student drama. SU (NUS member, 20% turnout at last ballot); fortnightly paper, 'The Saint', with its own sabb editor; charity group; SU-run jobshop. *Strong* sports; sports hall; multigym; squash and tennis courts; all-weather pitch; gym; new £1.4Mn sports complex under development. 95% of 1st years accommodated plus a few finalists (640 catered, £63-74, 34wks, all meals; 89 self-catered, £40-43, 42wks; 86 head tenancies); 25% have to share; 24-hour security. 3 counsellors; accommodation office; SU welfare officer; late-night minibus; creche (44 places, 2-4yrs); access fund £67,956 (148 successful applications); bursaries and scholarships. Undergrad prospectus, department and course leaflets.

St Mary's College

St Mary's College, Waldegrave Road, Strawberry Hill, Twickenham, TW1 4SX. Tel: (020) 8240 4000. Fax: (020) 8240 4255.

Apart from being the HQ of English rugby union, Twickenham, in the *attractive and wealthy* London borough of Richmond, is the site of St

Mary's, a Catholic college of the University of Surrey, based in a Grade I listed Gothic mansion originally built by the 18th-century writer, Horace Walpole. Trainee teachers make up 33% of the student body with the remainder on modular courses in various arts and science subjects. The college counts *the damn fine* Pete Postlethwaite among its alumni.

Sex ratio(M:F): 32%:68%
Full time u'grads: 2,470
Postgrads: 18
Ave course: 3yrs
Private school: n/a
Mature students: 14%
Disabled students: n/a
Clearing: 15%
Founded: 1850
Part time: 184
Non-degree: 0
Ethnic: n/a
Flunk rate: n/a
Overseas students: 11%
Staff/student ratio: 1:21

1 library (146,000 volumes, 274 study places, open 7 days), 380 computers (24 hours); 2 careers advisers (4.1% grads unemployed after 6 months). Most 1st years accommodated (11% have to share), but under 10% of other years (£63-85/wk). Access fund £70,000; 2 counsellors; chapel, 2 RC chaplains. Prospectus.

Swansea Institute of HE

Swansea Institute of Higher Education, Registry, Mount Pleasant, Swansea, SA1 6ED. Tel: (01792) 481000. Fax: (01792) 481085. E-mail: enquiry@sihe.ac.uk Website: www.sihe.ac.uk

Athrofa Addysg Uwch Abertawe, as it's known by some, is based on two main sites on the west side of Wales's second largest city (see Swansea, University of Wales for more details) and is an associate college of the University of Wales. The Townhill site houses the artists and trainee teachers while Mount Pleasant is for computer boffins, lawyers, engineers and the rest. It was the first college in Europe to offer a motorsport design and engineering degree.

Sex ratio(M:F): 55%:45%
Full time u'grads: 2,198
Postgrads: 76
Ave course: 3yrs
Private school: n/a
Mature students: 55%
Disabled students: 4.6%
Clearing: n/a
Founded: 1976
Part time: 458
Non-degree: 3,262
Ethnic: 59%
Flunk rate: n/a
Overseas students: 5.3%
Staff/student ratio: 1:18

3 libraries (130,000 volumes between them, open 6 days); 450 computers; careers adviser, 7% of students unemployed 6 months after graduating. Small bar (open 12-2pm, 7-11pm); 3 college refectories (8.30am-6pm); 2 SU coffee bars (9am-4pm); main hall (cap 350) for live bands; no club nights; student drama coming on, with one show heading Fringe-wards last year. SU (3 sabbs, NUS member, 20% turnout); input into Swansea University paper. Surfing team regularly reach universities' finals; multigym and fitness suite. 25% of 1st years live in self-catering halls (350 places, £41-49, 33wks, some en-suite; 1 all-female hall; one hall was Dylan Thomas' grammar school). 2 counsellors; chapel; prayer rooms 'by

arrangement'; nurse; SU welfare service; accommodation office; access fund £258,969, 147 successful applicants; emergency fund. Prospectus.

Trinity & All Saints

Trinity & All Saints College, Brownberrie Lane, Horsforth, Leeds, LS18 5HD. Tel: (0113) 283 7123. Fax: (0113) 283 7321.
E-mail: s.sellars@tasc.ac.uk Website: www.tasc.ac.uk

6 miles from the centre of Leeds is the northern suburb of Horsforth and on a rural 43-acre campus is Trinity & All Saints, a Catholic foundation and a college of the University of Leeds. The college concentrates on combining academic and vocational subjects; 44% of undergraduates are on media-related courses, 24% are studying towards teaching qualifications while 32% are studying management.

Sex ratio(M:F): 35%:65%	Founded: 1966
Full time u'grads: 2,073	Part time: 7
Postgrads: 263	Non-degree: 0
Ave course: 3/4yrs	Ethnic: 10%
Private school: n/a	Flunk rate: 15.4%
Mature students: 8%	Overseas students: 2%
Disabled students: 3.4%	Staff/student ratio: 1:21
Clearing: 15%	

Library (129,000 volumes, 200 study places, open 7 days) plus access to University of Leeds facilities; 250 computers; 2 careers advisers (2% grads unemployed after 6 months). College bar (10am-2pm, 5.30-11.00pm) serves food; SU discos and live bands (cap 300). SU (2 sabbs, NUS member, 25% turnout); SU-run paper, 'Saint & Sinner'; Rag. Gym; football, rugby and all-weather pitches; squash and tennis courts; athletics field; multigym. 70% of 1st years live in (520 catered, £62, 34wks, all meals, some en suite); accommodation officer helps the rest; CCTV, entry codes, porters. 2 p-t counsellors; RC chaplain; nursery (20 places, 2-5yrs); surgery; some wheelchair access and adapted rooms, induction loops, support for dyslexia; access fund £95,000 (300 successful applicants); a range of bursaries, scholarships and hardship fund. Prospectus.

Trinity College, Carmarthen

Trinity College, Carmarthen, Carmarthenshire, SA31 3EP.
Tel: (01267) 676791. Fax: (01267) 676766.
E-mail: registry@trinity-cm.ac.uk

Carmarthen's a market town in West Wales, about 25 miles from Swansea, with a population of 18,000 and good access to the *splendid* countryside of the Gower Peninsula, Pembrokeshire and the *surf-friendly* Carmarthen Bay. There's also, a mile outside town, Trinity College, mainly a teacher-training college (60% of undergraduates) with a special emphasis on Welsh language education. The main building dates from the College's Victorian foundation, while various modern additions are dotted around the green campus.

Sex ratio(M:F): 40%:60%	Founded: 1848
Full time u'grads: 1,200	Part time: 900
Postgrads: 159	Non-degree: 0
Ave course: 3yrs	Ethnic: 2.5%
Private school: n/a	Flunk rate: n/a
Mature students: 35%	Overseas students: 3%
Disabled students: 1%	Staff/student ratio: 1:16
Clearing: 30%	

2 libraries (110,000 volumes, 132 study places, open 7 days); 81 computers; careers adviser (8% grads unemployed after 6 months). 2 bars, *big* dance floor (cap 500), regular bands (biggies have included Republica, but also Tony Blackburn and Graham Green?) and balls; Halliwell Theatre. *Strong* sports, especially 5-a-side football and rugby. 95% of 1st years live in, plus some 2nd years and 75% of finalists (266 catered, £68.50, 34 wks, 2 meals/day Mon-Fri; 288 self-catered, £54-68, 34 wks); local rents £40/wk; accommodation officer. Anglican chapel; chaplains; part-time counsellor, *good* wheelchair access, nursery for 9 of the little smelly ones. IT facilities for dyslexia sufferers; access fund £92,950, bursaries. Prospectus, dept leaflets.

Trinity College of Music

Trinity College of Music, 11 Mandeville Place, London, W1M 6AQ. Tel: (020) 7935 5773. Fax: (020) 7224 6278. E-mail: info@tcm.ac.uk Website: www.tcm.ac.uk

Currently in the heart of London's West End, close to Oxford Street (there are plans to move to Greenwich very soon), Trinity is the oldest music college in the UK, offering four-year degree courses in all areas of classical music. There are practice rooms in Blandford Street and the library and academic studies centre are in Bulstrode Place, each a few minutes' walk away. As with all music colleges, students get one-to-one tuition on their chosen instrument.

Sex ratio(M:F): 42%:58%	Founded: 1872
Full time u'grads: 373	Part time: 0
Postgrads: 114	Non-degree: 47
Ave course: 4yrs	Ethnic: 18%
Private school: n/a	Flunk rate: 6.6%
Mature students: 18%	Overseas students: 26%
Disabled students: 5%	Staff/student ratio: 1:3
Clearing: n/a	

The planned move to Greenwich *should bring big changes* including full wheelchair access, a canteen in the SU, accommodation, better library facilities and 78 practice rooms. Library (115,000 volumes, 64 study places, open 5 days); 12 PCs (5 days). SU common room, the odd do or party is thrown, often jointly with other music colleges; no food outlets. SU (one sabb, NUS member, 10% turnout); Rag week. *Virtually no sport.* No college accommodation but advice

available from College and SU. Methodist chaplain and chapel; 1 counsellor; women's officer; doctor; some wheelchair access, IT facilities for the visually impaired and dyslexia; osteopathy and physiotherapy sessions; scheme for employing students within the college; SU provides hardship and instrument loans; access fund £31,600 (56 successful applications); limited bursaries and scholarships. Prospectus.

University College, Warrington

University College Warrington, Higher Education Registry, Padgate Campus, Crab Lane, Warrington, WA2 0DB.
Tel: (01925) 494494. Fax: (01925) 494289.
E-mail: registry.he@warr.ac.uk Website: www.ucw.warr.ac.uk

Equidistant (20 miles) from Manchester and Liverpool is the town of Warrington and 3 miles from the city centre, on the site of a WW2 air force base, is The College Formerly Known As Warrington Collegiate Institute and, before that, North Cheshire College. Its main academic concentration is in joint degrees, all with a business and management component to which students can add media, leisure, performing arts or sports studies. Padgate Campus is supposedly haunted with spooky goings on. The college has *strong* links with employers (media courses are run in assocation with Granada TV) and work placements are done by all in their second year.

Sex ratio(M:F): 50%:50%	Founded: 1946
Full time u'grads: 814	Part time: 117
Postgrads: 8	Non-degree: 383
Ave course: 3yrs	Ethnic: 5.4%
Private school: n/a	Flunk rate: n/a
Mature students: 21%	Overseas students: 1.5%
Disabled students: 2.4%	Staff/student ratio: 1:18
Clearing: 17%	

2 libraries (100,000 volumes, 200 study places, open 6 days); 134 computers; careers adviser (3.7% grads unemployed after 6 months). 2 bars (open lunchtimes and evenings); *lots of* eateries for a range of tastes and pockets; 1 video a week on a big screen; NOMADS drama and ents group; theatre. SU (3 sabbs, NUS member, 15% turnout); SU-paper, 'Shrapnel'; online paper, 'Xpansion'; student radio; Rag. *Good* reputation in rugby, hockey and football; *national-standard* facilities including sports hall, fitness centre, football, rugby and hockey pitches and sports laboratories. Self-catered accommodation for 24% of 1st years and finalists (480 places, £28-38, 34wks, 16 share a kitchen); 24-hour security and CCTV; local rents £56/wk. Student services for welfare advice, accommodation and job-hunting; 4 counsellors; 3 chaplains (CofE, RC, Methodist); 2 nurseries (34 places, 0-5yrs); wheelchair access to 95% of buildings; access fund £70,000; bursaries from Granada TV for media courses; emergency fund. Undergrad and postgrad prospectuses, SU alternative prospectus, course leaflets.

Wimbledon School of Art

Wimbledon School of Art, Merton Hall Road, London, SW19 3QA.
Tel: (020) 8408 5000. Fax: (020) 8408 5050.
E-mail: registry@wimbledon.ac.uk Website: www.wimbledon.ac.uk

Situated in suburbia, but a half-hour train or tube ride to central London, Wimbledon includes the country's largest centre for Theatre Design degree courses as well as Fine Art courses. A mile from the main site is the Terry Bruen Building where foundation courses are based. Degrees are awarded by Surrey University. For more information about being a student in London, see University of London.

Sex ratio(M:F): 30%:70%
Full time u'grads: 429
Postgrads: 138
Ave course: 3yrs
Private school: n/a
Mature students: 36%
Disabled students: 10%
Clearing: 1%
Founded: 1890
Part time: 92
Non-degree: 235
Ethnic: 5.1%
Flunk rate: n/a
Overseas students: 15%
Staff/student ratio: 1:9

Library (29,000 volumes, 40 study places, open 5 days); 40 computers (9am-5pm). Careers advice. *State-of-the-art* theatre/workshop and studio; new SU building, no bar; college canteen. No college accommodation. Welfare office; counsellor; wheelchair access; dyslexia unit; hardship fund £42,000. Prospectus, course information sheets.

> UMIST's collection of modern art includes a sculpture of Pacioli, the hugely interesting creator of double-entry book-keeping.

University College Worcester

University College Worcester, Henwick Grove, Worcester, WR2 6AJ.
Tel: (01905) 855111. Fax: (01905) 855132.
Website: www.worc.ac.uk

Worcester College is on a single site in a rural setting, 2 miles from the city centre. Worcester has a number of *student-friendly* pubs, a 7-screen Odeon and Thursday night is the night to try out the 2 local clubs. *It's within easy reach of glorious countryside but any gaps in entertainment have to be met by Birmingham, 30 miles away.*

Worchester

Sex ratio(M:F): 31%:69%
Full time u'grads: 2,320
Postgrads: 249
Ave course: 3yrs
Private school: n/a
Mature students: 38%
Disabled students: 5%
Clearing: n/a

Founded: 1946
Part time: 1,435
Non-degree: 989
Ethnic: 1.8%
Flunk rate: 14.6%
Overseas students: 2.5%
Staff/student ratio: 1:23

Library (200,000 volumes, 630 study places, open 6 days); 160 computers (6 days); careers adviser (5.6% of grads unemployed after 6 months). 2 SU bars, Hanger bar (12noon-11pm) doubles as club/music venue (cap 634); smaller Sports bar opens some nights; Henwicks college canteen (8.30am-7.30pm) and SU-run Snack Attack (11am-3pm, 9pm-11.30pm) for *cheap eats*; drama studio; 2 films a week in SU bar; sports awards ball. SU (3 sabbs, NUS member, 30% turnout), *active but apolitical*; Student Community Action; Rag raised £25,000 last year. *Good showing in rowing, football, women's hockey, table tennis*; tennis courts; gym; all-weather pitch. 50% of 1st years and 25% of finalists live in self-catered accommodation (582 places, £35-49, 35-38wks), cheaper rooms have no cooking facilities, otherwise 5/6 to a kitchen; some sharing at the start of the year; 24-hour security, some entry phones; local rents £50/wk. Counselling service; prayer room; 5 chaplains; accommodation office; nursery (36 places, 3mths-5yrs); SU welfare advice and help; equal opportunities co-ordinator; wheelchair access to most of campus; minicoms and induction loops; *good support* for dyslexia; access fund £173,478 (299 successful applicants); bursaries and sports scholarships. Prospectus, course leaflets, video.

> 'It was a time when the number of times one could get laid was exceeded only by the number of job opportunities – a state of affairs which applies only in the House of Commons. And to think we did it on local authority grants'
> – Tony Banks MP on his student days.

other insts

Writtle College

Writtle College, Chelmsford, Essex, CM1 3RR.
Tel: (01245) 424200. Fax: (01245) 420456.
E-mail: postmaster@writtle.ac.uk Website: www.writtle.ac.uk

2 miles west of Chelmsford lies the historic village of Writtle, where, if you take a right at the village green, you will also find the 220-hectare estate of Writtle College which specialises in vocational courses for the land, countryside, amenity and related industries. Its degrees are validated by the University of Essex, with which the College has strong links. For information on the attractions of Chelmsford see Anglia Polytechnic University.

Sex ratio(M:F): 44%:56%	Founded: 1893
Full time u'grads: 1,012	Part time: 80
Postgrads: 90	Non-degree: 332
Ave course: 3yrs	Ethnic: n/a
Private school: n/a	Flunk rate: n/a
Mature students: n/a	Overseas students: 5%
Disabled students: 7%	Staff/student ratio: 1:12
Clearing: n/a	

Library (50,000 volumes, open 6 days), 180 computers (7 days). Career Adviser (8% students unemployed after 6 months). Recreation Centre with refurbished bar, new sound system, jukebox, snooker and pool tables, TV lounge and big screen; some live bands plus promo nights and balls; the *wittily named* Writz, Writtle Chef and Cow Watering Café for food. SU (no sabbs, NUS member, 28% voted in last ballot); Rag committee. Large indoor hall for sport; 2 squash courts; fitness room and multigym; playing fields; pitches for rugby, football, hockey and cricket; several tennis courts. Around 75% of 1st years and 20% from other years can live-in (410 catered, £71-86, 37wks, 10 meals a week in term-time); half the rooms en suite; basic cooking facilities. Student Support Unit; accommodation office; 3 chaplains (Anglican, RC, free church); chapel; counsellor; nursery (100 places, 3mths-4yrs); wheelchair access to most buildings; access fund £92,300 (320 successful applications); hardship fund, special support fund for part-time and overseas students. Undergrad and postgrad prospectuses, video.

'If you go straight (to College) from school, unfortunately you turn into a student, and you go on pyjama jumps and talk in that student voice.'
- Jarvis Cocker.

York St John

* *Formerly the College of Ripon and York St John*
York St John, Lord Mayor's Walk, York, YO31 7EX.
Tel: (01904) 716850. Fax: (01904) 616921.
E-mail: i.waghorn@ucrysj.ac.uk Website: www.ucrysj.ac.uk

York St John is in the centre of historic York right by its *impressive* medieval walls (see University of York for local info) and has had to change its name since the closure of the Ripon campus, it awards degrees from the University of Leeds. The College was historically a centre for teacher training and education courses still make up 25% of the student body, although the College has expanded its brief to cover creative and performing arts, health & life sciences and humanities courses as well.

Sex ratio(M:F): 35%:65%	Founded: 1841
Full time u'grads: 2,919	Part time: 10
Postgrads: 141	Non-degree: 0
Ave course: 3yrs	Ethnic: 0.1%
Private school: 4%	Flunk rate: 10.3%
Mature students: 22%	Overseas students: 1%
Disabled students: 1%	Staff/student ratio: 1:21
Clearing: 20%	

Library (200,000 volumes, 300 study places in all, open 6 days); 200 computers. 2 careers advisers (7.6% grads unemployed after 6 mths). SU bars at both sites, club/music venue (cap 200), live bands and 2 club nights a week; 2 snack bars (9am-4pm); health food shop drama (fringe regulars) and musical production (non-luvvies) socs; theatre; 1 film a week. SU (3 sabbs, NUS member, 26% turnout); SU-run paper, 'Scoop'; Rag on each site. *Good* sports record; sports hall; pool; playing fields; multigym; tennis courts; athletics field and running track; climbing wall; gym; access to University of York facilities. Most 1st years can live in plus around 15% from other years (371 catered, £65, 31wks, 21 meals/wk; 497 self-catered, £43, 48wks). CCTV, 24-hr porters; accommodation office. Jobshop; 3 full-time and 7 part-time counsellors; Health Centre; chapel and chaplain at each site; new buildings have wheelchair access; access fund £54,000 (296 successful applications). Leeds Uni prospectus, course leaflets.

> In the mid-70s smarty pants at University College, Oxford who won too many times were banned from competing in University Challenge.

PUSH, of course

How to use *'Push,* of course':

CHOOSING A COURSE
For every different student, there's probably a different way to choose a course. Many take one look at the list of courses available and run screaming into the night. Others stick to their 'best' subject at A level, without giving a thought to the fact that maths at A level and maths as a degree can be about as similar as watching a Formula 1 car race and standing in front of one.

Others pick a degree based on the career they want to follow. This is usually sound but don't forget that you can get a career in the media without a Media Studies degree and not all accountants studied Accountancy at university.

The safest bet is always to pick a course you'll enjoy. If you enjoy it, it'll be worthwhile and you'll do better.

Check out a uni you like the sound of, visit or phone the relevant departments of the subjects you're considering then talk to the students who're studying it and the tutors who teach it to find out what it's all about.

Choose carefully – you can sometimes change your course once you've started it but at some universities it's about as difficult, exhausting and painful as listening to Britney Spears and trying to have a good time.

JOINT HONOURS COURSES
Forget any notion of lazy, hazy sunday afternoons – these are degrees where you study 2 subjects instead of just the one, usually in two seperate departments of the University.

Most universities offer combinations of courses. Obvious ones are language courses (eg French and German), but more adventurous bods may want to tackle something less likely – physics and music, anyone?

Don't presume, however, that just because two separate subjects are available at one institution that you can do both. Check with the prospectus and/or in the UCAS listings.

How the courses are combined also varies. Some are 'interdisciplinary' (meaning you do a course which combines stuff from both subjects) and some are independent of each other – in effect you're doing two separate half-courses.

Just to confuse you even more, some mix 50% of each course and others offer the option of picking one subject as a 'major' (though you usually don't have to decide which until after your first year).

Some students find the workload on joint courses is heavier than on single honours equivalents and that communication levels between departments seem to pre-date the telephone. As a result, their organisational skills need to be as watertight as dinghy in shark-infested seas. But at the end of it all you should have a wider range of skills, be less likely to be fed up with your subjects and have had the chance to make loads more friends.

For those who really like to live on the edge (or who can't make up their minds and pick just one course), there are combined honours courses where you study not two, but three subjects.

MODULAR COURSES

Most universities now offer modular courses. This means you can pick and choose a range of options across the academic spectrum. You go through university life successfully completing (hopefully) individual 'modules' in different subject areas and collecting credits. When you've got enough credits, you can trade them in for a degree. This system is particularly good for students with outside commitments, since you can often accumulate credits, go back to full-time work for a year and then pick up again where you left off. It's also great for people who don't know at the time of application what sort of subjects will interest them.

LENGTH OF COURSE

Most full-time degrees are three years in length while some – eg. Engineering, most languages – tend to take a wee while longer being four years. That's not to say that 'all' Engineering and language courses are four years in duration nor that all other courses are only three. Push probes where others fear to smell, but we all have limits, so contact the college or university in question to find out the exact length of the course you're interested in.

The difference often depends on the letters at the beginning of the course name – BA/BSc will usually be three years of hard and fruitful graft and make you a 'bachelor' of your subject. Meanwhile MA/MSc/MEng/etc will be a four-year course (if not five) and mean you are a 'master' ('...but only a master of evil, Darth').

Most English undergraduate courses are bachelor courses, but in Scotland, they usually head to masters degrees and so tak an extra year.

For added relish, 'sandwich' courses are four years in length, but get you a bachelor degree. A sandwich course contains some time (usually a year, but often in more than one bit) doing a work placement (and getting paid for it) or studying abroad, usually betwen your second and final year, in a country, industry or bed related to your degree.

Medicine, Dentistry and Veterinary Science are just far too long for all but the mad, dedicated, perverted or rich, being a whacking five or six years of studenthood.

Accountancy/Accounting and Finance

Aberdeen, Abertay, Aberystwyth, Anglia, Aston, Bangor, Birmingham, Bolton, Bournemouth, Brighton, BUWE Cardiff, C England, C Lancs, De Montfort, Durham, E London, Essex, Exeter, Glamorgan, Glasgow, Glasgow Cal, Guildhall, Huddersfield, Kingston, Leeds, Leeds Met, Liverpool, Liverpool JM, Luton, Manchester, Man Met, Middlesex,

Napier, Newcastle, Newport, Northampton, Northumbria, N London, Nott Trent, Oxford Brookes, Paisley, Plymouth, Portsmouth, Queen's Belfast, Robert Gordon, Sheffield, Sheffield Hallam, Southampton Inst, Staffs, Stirling, Strathclyde, Sunderland, Swansea Inst, Teesside, Thames Valley, Ulster, Wolves
see also Business Studies; Economics; Europe – European Financial Management

Agriculture

Aberdeen, Aberystwyth, Bangor, C Lancs, Edinburgh, Harper Adams, Newcastle, Imperial, Nottingham, Plymouth, Queen's Belfast, Reading, Royal Agric, Writtle
see also Environmental Science; Natural Resources

American Studies

Aberystwyth, Birmingham, Brunel, C Lancs, Derby, Dundee, UEA, Essex, Hull, Kent, King Alfred's, Lampeter, Lancaster, Leicester, Liv Hope, Man Met, Middlesex, Northampton, Nottingham, Queen's Belfast, Reading, Sheffield, Staffs, Swansea, Warwick, Wolves
see also Humanities; Literature

Ancient History

Birmingham, Bristol, Cardiff, Durham, Edinburgh, Exeter, Lampeter, Newcastle, Nottingham, Oxford, Queen's Belfast, Reading, Royal Holloway, St Andrews, Swansea, UCL
see also Archaeology; Classics; History

Anthropology

Aberdeen, Durham, E London, Edinburgh, Goldsmiths, Hull, Kent, Lampeter, LSE, Manchester, Queen's Belfast, Roehampton, SOAS, St Andrews, Swansea, UCL
Cultural Social Anthropology Kent, Leeds Met, Liv Hope, Man Met, Staffs
see also Geography - Social; Social Science; Third World Studies

Archaeology

Birmingham, Bradford, Bristol, Edinburgh, Exeter, Glasgow, King Alfred's, Lampeter, Leicester, Liverpool, Manchester, Newcastle, Nottingham, Queen's Belfast, Reading, Southampton, Trinity Carmarthen, York
see also Ancient History; Classics; History

Architecture

Bath, Brighton, Cambridge, Cardiff, C England, De Montfort, Derby, Dundee, E London, Edinburgh, Glasgow, Greenwich, Heriot-Watt, Huddersfield, KIAD, Kingston, Leeds Met, Lincs & Humbs, Liverpool, Liverpool JM, Luton, Manchester, Man Met, Newcastle, NEWI, N London, Nottingham, Nott Trent, Oxford Brookes, Plymouth, Portsmouth, Queen's Belfast, Robert Gordon, Sheffield, South Bank,

Strathclyde, UCL, Westminster
Building Anglia, Bolton, Brighton, BUWE, C Lancs, Coventry, Glamorgan, Glasgow Cal, Heriot-Watt, Liverpool, Nott Trent, Oxford Brookes, Paisley, Portsmouth, Salford, Southampton Inst, Staffs, Wolves

ARTS

Ceramics and Glass Canterbury Christ Church, De Montfort, Leeds, NEWI
Creative/Performing Dartington, De Montfort, Derby, Glasgow, Herts, King Alfred's, Liv Hope, Luton, Man Met, Middlesex, N London, Northampton, Northumbria, Nott Trent, Roehampton, Salford, Staffs
Dance Birmingham, Bretton Hall, Chester, Coventry, De Montfort, Herts, Liverpool JM, Middlesex, Northumbria, Roehampton, Scarborough, Surrey
Design Studies Anglia, Bath Spa, Bolton, Bucks Chilterns, Derby, Goldsmiths, Greenwich, KIAD, Liv Hope, Guildhall, London Inst, Luton, Man Met, Napier, Nott Trent, Plymouth, Salford, Southampton, Staffs, Westminster, Wolves
Fashion De Montfort, London Inst, Man Met, Heriot-Watt
Fine Art Bath Spa, Brighton, Bucks Chilterns, Canterbury Christ Church, Cardiff Inst, C England, C Lancs, Chester, Chichester, Coventry, De Montfort, Derby, Falmouth, Goldsmiths, Herts, KIAD, Kingston, Lancaster, Leeds Met, Lincs & Humbs, Guildhall, London Inst, Man Met, N London, Northampton, Northumbria, Oxford, Plymouth, Salford, Scarborough, St Martin's, Southampton Inst, Staffs, Sunderland, Surrey Inst, Swansea Inst, Wolves
History of Art Aberdeen, Anglia, Brighton, Bristol, Cambridge, Cardiff Inst, C Lancs, Courtauld, De Montfort, Derby, E London, Edinburgh, Glasgow, Goldsmiths, Kent, Leeds, Leicester, Manchester, Middlesex, Nottingham, Oxford Brookes, SOAS, Sheffield Hallam, Southampton, St Andrews, UCL, Warwick, York
Industrial Design Bournemouth, Brighton, Cardiff Inst, C England, C Lancs, Coventry, De Montfort, Falmouth, Huddersfield, KIAD, Leeds Met, Loughborough, Luton, Man Met, Middlesex, NEWI, Plymouth, Robert Gordon, Salford, Sheffield Hallam, Staffs, Surrey Inst, Swansea Inst, Teesside, Wolves
Textiles Bolton, E London, Man Met, Napier, Heriot-Watt
see also Drama; Humanities; Media Studies; Music

Astronomy

C Lancs, Herts, QMW, Sussex, UCL
Astrophysics Cardiff, C Lancs, Edinburgh, Herts, Keele, Liverpool, Liverpool JM, Newcastle, QMW, Royal Holloway, St Andrews, UCL
see also Physics

Biology

Aberdeen, Aberystwyth, Anglia, Bangor, Bath, Birmingham, Bolton, Bristol, Cardiff, Chester, Derby, Dundee, Durham, UEA, Edinburgh, Essex, Exeter, Glamorgan, Hull, Imperial, Keele, Kent, Lancaster, Leeds, Leicester, Liverpool, Luton, Manchester, Man Met, Newcastle, NEWI, N London, Northumbria, Nottingham, Oxford, Oxford Brookes, Paisley, Plymouth, Portsmouth, QMW, Queen's Belfast, Reading, Royal Holloway, Salford, Southampton, St Andrews, Stirling, Sussex,

Swansea, Ulster, UCL, Warwick, York
Applied Biology Aston, Bath, BUWE, Brunel, Cardiff, C Lancs, Chester, Coventry, De Montfort, E London, Glasgow, Greenwich, Herts, Imperial, Kingston, Leeds, Liverpool, Liverpool JM, Newcastle, Nescot, Nott Trent, South Bank, Staffs, Sunderland, Westminster
Anatomy/Physiology Bristol, Cardiff, Dundee, E London, Edinburgh, Glasgow, Greenwich, Herts, King's Coll, Leeds, Liverpool, Manchester, Newcastle, Oxford, Queen's Belfast, Sheffield, Southampton, St Andrews, UCL, Westminster
Biotechnology Aberdeen, Birmingham, Cardiff, De Montfort, E London, Glamorgan, Greenwich, Herts, Imperial, King's Coll, Leeds, Nescot, Oxford Brookes, Paisley, Portsmouth, Reading, South Bank, Teesside, UCL, Westminster, Wolves, Writtle
Botany Aberdeen, Aberystwyth, Bangor, Bristol, Dundee, Durham, Edinburgh, Glasgow, Imperial, Leicester, Liverpool, Manchester, Plymouth, Reading, Royal Holloway, Sheffield, Southampton
Ecology Bradford, Brighton, Coventry, Durham, Edinburgh, Herts, Liverpool JM, QMW, Sheffield, Staffs, Strathclyde, UCL, Westminster, Wolves, York
Genetics Aberdeen, Aberystwyth, Birmingham, Cardiff, Edinburgh, Glasgow, King's Coll, Leeds, Leicester, Liverpool, Manchester, Newcastle, Nottingham, QMW, Queen's Belfast, Sheffield, Swansea, UCL, York
Immunology E London, Edinburgh, Glasgow, King's Coll, UCL
Marine Biology Aberystwyth, Bangor, Essex, Glasgow, Heriot-Watt, Hull, Liverpool, Newcastle, Plymouth, Portsmouth, QMW, Queen's Belfast, St Andrews, Stirling, Swansea
Microbiology Aberdeen, Aberystwyth, Anglia, Birmingham, Bradford, Bristol, Cardiff, C Lancs, Dundee, UEA, E London, Edinburgh, Glamorgan, Glasgow, Heriot-Watt, Herts, Huddersfield, Imperial, Kent, King's Coll, Leeds, Leicester, Liverpool, Manchester, Newcastle, Nescot, N London, Nottingham, Queen's Belfast, Reading, Sheffield, South Bank, Surrey, Teesside, UCL, Wolves
Physiology Aberdeen, Bristol, Cardiff, Dundee, E London, Edinburgh, Glasgow, Greenwich, Herts, King's Coll, Leeds, Liverpool, Manchester, Newcastle, Oxford, Queen's Belfast, Sheffield, Southampton, St Andrews, UCL, Westminster
see also Environmental Science; Medicine; Natural Resources; Nutrition; Psychology - as a Biological Science; Veterinary Science; Zoology

Business Studies

Aberdeen, Abertay, Aberystwyth, Anglia, Aston, Bath, Bath Spa, Bolton, Bournemouth, Bradford, Brighton, BUWE, Buckingham, Bucks Chilterns, Cardiff, Cardiff Inst, C England, C Lancs, Chelt & Gloucs, Chester, City, Coventry, De Montfort, Derby, E London, Farnborough, Glamorgan, Glasgow Cal, Greenwich, Harper Adams, Heriot-Watt, Herts, Huddersfield, Hull, Imperial, Kent, Kingston, Lancaster, Leeds Met, Lincs & Humbs, Liverpool JM, Guildhall, Luton, Manchester, UMIST, Man Met, Middlesex, Napier, Newport, Nescot, N London, Northampton, Northumbria, Nott Trent, Oxford Brookes, Plymouth, Portsmouth, Reading, Robert Gordon, Roehampton, Heriot-Watt, Salford, Scarborough, Sheffield, Sheffield Hallam, St Martin's, Southampton Inst, South Bank, Staffs, Stirling, Sunderland, Swansea, Swansea Inst, Teesside, Thames Valley, Ulster, Westminster, Wolves
Business and Management Aberdeen, Abertay, Anglia, Aston,

Birmingham, Bolton, BUWE, Brunel, Bucks Chilterns, C England,
Lancs, Chelt & Gloucs, Chester, City, De Montfort, Derby, UEA, Essex,
Exeter, Glamorgan, Glasgow, Glasgow Cal, Herts, Huddersfield, Hull,
Kent, King's Coll, Lampeter, Lancaster, Leeds, Lincs & Humbs,
Liverpool JM, LSE, Loughborough, UMIST, Man Met, Middlesex,
Napier, Newcastle, NEWI, Nottingham, Nott Trent, Paisley, Plymouth,
Queen's Belfast, Robert Gordon, Royal Agric, Royal Holloway,
Sheffield Hallam, St Martin's, Southampton, Southampton Inst, St
Andrews, Stirling, Sunderland, Swansea, Teesside, Warwick,
Westminster, Worcester, Writtle
Human Resource Management Anglia, Bolton, Bucks Chilterns,
C England, C Lancs, Chelt & Gloucs, Coventry, De Montfort, Derby,
Edge Hill, Lancaster, Luton, UMIST, Middlesex, Northumbria,
Southampton Inst, South Bank, Staffs, Stirling, Sunderland, Teesside,
Wolves
Industrial Organisation Aberdeen, Abertay, Aberystwyth, Anglia,
Aston, Bath, Bath Spa, Bolton, Bournemouth, Bradford, Brighton,
BUWE, Buckingham, Bucks Chilterns, Cardiff, Cardiff Inst, C England,
C Lancs, Chelt & Gloucs, Chester, City, Coventry, De Montfort, Derby,
E London, Edge Hill, Farnborough, Glamorgan, Glasgow Cal,
Greenwich, Harper Adams, Heriot-Watt, Herts, Huddersfield, Hull,
Imperial, Kent, Kingston, Lancaster, Leeds Met, Lincs & Humbs,
Liverpool JM, Guildhall, Luton, Manchester, UMIST, Man Met,
Middlesex, Napier, Newport, Nescot, N London, Northampton,
Northumbria, Nott Trent, Oxford Brookes, Plymouth, Portsmouth,
Reading, Robert Gordon, Roehampton, Heriot-Watt, Salford,
Scarborough, Sheffield, Sheffield Hallam, St Martin's, Southampton
Inst, South Bank, Staffs, Stirling, Sunderland, Swansea, Swansea
Inst, Teesside, Thames Valley, Ulster, Westminster, Wolves
Recreation Management Bucks Chilterns, C Lancs, De Montfort,
Luton, Surrey, Warrington
Tourism Abertay, Anglia, Bath Spa, Bolton, Bournemouth, Brighton,
Bucks Chilterns, Cardiff Inst, C Lancs, Coventry, Derby, Glasgow Cal,
Herts, Leeds Met, Lincs & Humbs, Luton, Napier, Northumbria,
Paisley, Plymouth, Queen Margaret, Salford, South Bank, Sunderland,
Swansea Inst, Thames Valley, Wolves
see also Computer Science - Business Computing; Europe – European
Business Management; Law – Business Law; Media Studies –
Marketing/Market Research; Media Studies – Public Relations

Chemistry

Aberdeen, Anglia, Aston, Bangor, Bath, Birmingham, Bradford, Bristol,
Cardiff, Dundee, Durham, UEA, Edinburgh, Exeter, Glamorgan,
Glasgow, Greenwich, Heriot-Watt, Herts, Huddersfield, Hull, Imperial,
Keele, Kent, King's Coll, Kingston, Lancaster, Leeds, Leicester,
Liverpool, Liverpool JM, Loughborough, Manchester, UMIST, Man Met,
Newcastle, N London, Northumbria, Nottingham, Nott Trent,
OxfordPaisley, QMW, Queen's Belfast, Reading, Salford, Sheffield,
Sheffield Hallam, Southampton, St Andrews, Stirling, Strathclyde,
Surrey, Sussex, Swansea, Teesside, UCL, Warwick, York
Chemical Engineering Aston, Bath, Birmingham, Bradford, Edinburgh,
Heriot-Watt, Imperial, Leeds, Loughborough, UMIST, Newcastle,
Nottingham, Oxford, Paisley, Queen's Belfast, Sheffield, South Bank,
Strathclyde, Surrey, Swansea, Teesside, UCL
see also Pharmacy; Science (Combined or General)

Classics

Birmingham, Bristol, Cambridge, Durham, Edinburgh, Exeter, King's Coll, Lampeter, Leeds, Liverpool, Manchester, Newcastle, Nottingham, Oxford, Queen's Belfast, Reading, Royal Holloway, Swansea, UCL
Classical Greek Edinburgh, Glasgow, Leeds, Manchester, Royal Holloway, St Andrews
Latin Birmingham, Durham, Edinburgh, Exeter, Glasgow, Lampeter, Leeds, Manchester, Nottingham, Reading, Royal Holloway, St Andrews, Swansea
see also Ancient History; Languages

Computer Science

Aberdeen, Abertay, Aberystwyth, Anglia, Aston, Bangor, Bath, Bolton, Bradford, Brighton, Bristol, BUWE, Brunel, Buckingham, Bucks Chilterns, Cambridge, Canterbury Christ Church, Cardiff, C England, C Lancs, Chelt & Gloucs, Chester, City, Coventry, De Montfort, Derby, Durham, UEA, E London, Edinburgh, Essex, Exeter, Farnborough, Glamorgan, Glasgow, Glasgow Cal, Greenwich, Heriot-Watt, Herts, Huddersfield, Hull, Imperial, Keele, Kent, King's Coll, Kingston, Lancaster, Leeds, Leeds Met, Leicester, Lincs & Humbs, Liverpool, Liverpool JM, Loughborough, Luton, Manchester, UMIST, Man Met, Middlesex, Napier, Newcastle, Newport, Nescot, NEWI, N London, Northampton, Northumbria, Nottingham, Nott Trent, Oxford, Oxford Brookes, Paisley, Plymouth, Portsmouth, QMW, Queen's Belfast, Reading, Robert Gordon, Royal Holloway, Salford, Sheffield, Southampton, Southampton Inst, South Bank, St Andrews, Staffs, Stirling, Strathclyde, Sunderland, Sussex, Swansea, Teesside, Ulster, UCL, Warwick, Westminster, Wolves, York
Artificial Intelligence Derby, Durham, Essex, Herts, Imperial, Luton, Manchester, UMIST, Oxford Brookes, Staffs, Sussex, Westminster
Business Computing Bolton, Bournemouth, Bradford, BUWE, City, Herts, Leeds Met, Northumbria, Roehampton, Staffs, Stirling, Swansea Inst, Teesside, Westminster
Computer Systems Engineering Bolton, C England, City, UEA, Hull, Liverpool JM, Luton, Manchester, Napier, Newcastle, Nottingham, Nott Trent, Oxford Brookes, Paisley, Plymouth, Portsmouth, Sheffield, Sheffield Hallam, Southampton Inst, Staffs, Swansea Inst, Westminster
Digital Systems Engineering Anglia, Bangor, Birmingham, Bournemouth, BUWE, Brunel, C Lancs, Coventry, Durham, Edinburgh, Essex, Herts, Hull, Kent, Liverpool, Loughborough, Luton, Manchester, UMIST, N London, Northumbria, Nottingham, Nott Trent, Oxford Brookes, QMW, Salford, Sheffield, Sheffield Hallam, Southampton, Sunderland, Sussex, Ulster
see also Engineering – Electronic Engineering; Microelectronics

Criminology

Aberdeen, Anglia, Bangor, BUWE, Bucks Chilterns, C Lancs, Coventry, UEA, E London, Essex, Glamorgan, Herts, Keele, Kent, Lancaster, Lincs & Humbs, Luton, Portsmouth, Sheffield, Southampton Inst, Strathclyde, Sussex, Wolves
see also Law

Drama

Aberystwyth, Bishop Grosseteste, Bristol, Brunel, Chester, Chichester, UEA, E London, Edge Hill, Exeter, Glamorgan, Hull, King Alfred's, Liverpool JM, Loughborough, Manchester, Middlesex, Northumbria, Queen Margaret, Queen's Belfast, Salford, St Mary's, Wolves
Theatre Studies Birmingham, Bretton Hall, Coventry, Dartington, Goldsmiths, Huddersfield, Kent, Lancaster, Reading, Roehampton, Rose Bruford, Royal Holloway, Scarborough, Trinity Carmarthen, Ulster, Warwick
Acting Bretton Hall, C Lancs, Herts, Man Met, Middlesex, Queen Margaret, Rose Bruford
see also Arts – Creative/Performing

Economics

Aberdeen, Abertay, Aberystwyth, Anglia, Bangor, Bath, Birmingham, Bradford, Bristol, BUWE, Brunel, Buckingham, Cambridge, Cardiff, C England, City, Coventry, De Montfort, Dundee, Durham, UEA, E London, Edinburgh, Essex, Exeter, Heriot-Watt, Herts, Huddersfield, Hull, Kent, Kingston, Lancaster, Leeds, Leeds Met, Leicester, Lincs & Humbs, Liverpool, Guildhall, LSE, Loughborough, Manchester, Man Met, Middlesex, Newcastle, Northumbria, Nottingham, Nott Trent, Plymouth, Portsmouth, QMW, Queen's Belfast, Reading, Royal Holloway, Salford, SOAS, Sheffield, Southampton, St Andrews, Staffs, Stirling, Sunderland, Surrey, Swansea, Teesside, Ulster, UCL, Warwick, York
Finance Abertay, Anglia, Birmingham, Bournemouth, BUWE, Buckingham, Cardiff, C England, C Lancs, Chelt & Gloucs, City, Dundee, E London, Glasgow Cal, Lancaster, Guildhall, Loughborough, Manchester, Man Met, Middlesex, Northumbria, Nott Trent, Oxford Brookes, Paisley, Portsmouth, Queen's Belfast, Reading, Sheffield Hallam, Southampton Inst, Stirling, Ulster
see also Accountancy/Accounting and Finance; Business Studies; Europe - European Financial Management; Politics, Philosophy & Economics

Education

Cardiff, Herts, King Alfred's, Lancaster, Liverpool JM, Luton, Northumbria, Plymouth, Sheffield Hallam, St Martin's, York
Physical Education Canterbury Christ Church
see also Sports Science

Engineering

Aberdeen, Abertay, Aston, Birmingham, Bolton, Brighton, BUWE, Brunel, Cambridge, C Lancs, Coventry, De Montfort, Durham, E London, Edinburgh, Exeter, Huddersfield, Hull, Lancaster, Leeds, Leeds Met, Leicester, Lincs & Humbs, Liverpool, Liverpool JM, Loughborough, Man Met, Northampton, Oxford, Oxford Brookes, Plymouth, Portsmouth, QMW, Reading, Salford, Sheffield Hallam, Southampton, Staffs, Surrey, Swansea, Swansea Inst, Teesside, Warwick, Wolves
Aeronautical Engineering BUWE, City, Coventry, Farnborough,

Glasgow, Herts, Imperial, Kingston, Lincs & Humbs, Loughborough, Manchester, UMIST, Queen's Belfast, Salford, Southampton
Aerospace Engineering Bath, BUWE, City, Cranfield, Kingston, Liverpool, QMW, Salford, Sheffield, Southampton
Automated Engineering Design Bangor, Bolton, Brunel, Bucks Chilterns, C England, C Lancs, E London, Glasgow Cal, Herts, Huddersfield, Hull, Liverpool JM, Luton, Middlesex, Northumbria, Oxford Brookes, Paisley, Sheffield Hallam, South Bank, Staffs, Wolves
Civil Engineering Aberdeen, Abertay, Aston, Bath, Birmingham, Bolton, Bradford, Brighton, Bristol, Cardiff, City, Coventry, Cranfield, Dundee, Durham, E London, Edinburgh, Exeter, Glamorgan, Glasgow, Glasgow Cal, Greenwich, Heriot-Watt, Herts, Imperial, Kingston, Leeds, Leeds Met, Liverpool, Liverpool JM, Loughborough, Manchester, UMIST, Napier, Newcastle, Nottingham, Nott Trent, Oxford, Oxford Brookes, Paisley, Plymouth, Portsmouth, Queen's Belfast, Salford, Sheffield, Sheffield Hallam, Southampton, South Bank, Strathclyde, Surrey, Swansea, Ulster, UCL, Warwick, Westminster, Wolves
Electrical Engineering Aberdeen, Bangor, Cranfield, De Montfort, Durham, Edinburgh, Greenwich, Herts, Imperial, Liverpool, Nottingham, Oxford, Sheffield, Southampton, Staffs, Teesside, Warwick
Electronic Engineering Aberdeen, Abertay, Anglia, Bangor, Birmingham, Bolton, Bournemouth, Bradford, Brighton, Bristol, BUWE, Cardiff, Cardiff Inst, C England, C Lancs, Cranfield, De Montfort, Durham, UEA, E London, Edinburgh, Essex, Exeter, Glamorgan, Glasgow Cal, Greenwich, Herts, Huddersfield, Hull, Kent, King's Coll, Lancaster, Leeds, Liverpool, Manchester, UMIST, Man Met, Middlesex, Newcastle, N London, Northumbria, Nottingham, Nott Trent, Oxford Brookes, Plymouth, Portsmouth, QMW, Reading, Salford, Sheffield, Sheffield Hallam, Southampton, Southampton Inst, Staffs, Sussex, Swansea Inst, Teesside, Warwick, Westminster, York
Mechanical Engineering Aberdeen, Abertay, Aston, Bath, Birmingham, Bolton, Bradford, Brighton, Bristol, BUWE, Brunel, Cardiff, C England, C Lancs, City, Coventry, Cranfield, De Montfort, Dundee, Durham, Edinburgh, Exeter, Glamorgan, Glasgow, Greenwich, Heriot-Watt, Herts, Huddersfield, Hull, Imperial, Kingston, Lancaster, Leeds, Leicester, Lincs & Humbs, Liverpool, Liverpool JM, Loughborough, Manchester, UMIST, Man Met, Middlesex, Napier, Newcastle, Northumbria, Nottingham, Nott Trent, Oxford, Oxford Brookes, Paisley, Plymouth, Portsmouth, QMW, Queen's Belfast, Reading, Robert Gordon, Salford, Sheffield, Sheffield Hallam, Southampton, South Bank, Staffs, Strathclyde, Sunderland, Surrey, Sussex, Swansea, Teesside, Ulster, UCL, Warwick, Westminster
Production/Manufacturing Engineering Birmingham, Bradford, Brunel, Cardiff, Coventry, De Montfort, Durham, E London, Exeter, Glamorgan, Herts, Hull, Leeds Met, Middlesex, Newport, Nott Trent, Portsmouth, Salford, Sunderland, Wolves
see also Chemistry - Chemical Engineering; Computer Science - Computer Systems Engineering; Computer Science - Digital Systems Engineering; Environmental Science - Environmental Technologies; Maritime Technology

English

Aberdeen, Aberystwyth, Anglia, Bangor, Bath Spa, Birmingham, Bishop Grosseteste, Bolton, Bretton Hall, Bristol, BUWE, Brunel, Buckingham, Cambridge, Cardiff, C England, C Lancs, Chester, Chichester, De Montfort, Dundee, Durham, UEA, Edge Hill, Edinburgh, Essex, Exeter, Glamorgan, Glasgow, Goldsmiths, Greenwich, Herts, Huddersfield, Hull, Kent, King Alfred's, King's Coll, Kingston, Lampeter, Lancaster, Leeds, Leicester, Lincs & Humbs, Liverpool, Guildhall, Loughborough, Luton, Manchester, Man Met, Middlesex, Newcastle, NEWI, N London, Northumbria, Nottingham, Nott Trent, Oxford, Oxford Brookes, QMW, Queen's Belfast, Reading, Roehampton, Royal Holloway, Salford, Scarborough, Sheffield, Sheffield Hallam, St Martin's, Southampton, South Bank, St Andrews, St Mary's, Staffs, Stirling, Sunderland, Swansea, Teesside, Trinity Carmarthen, Ulster, UCL, Warwick, Westminster, Wolves, Worcester, York
see also Humanities; Linguistics; Literature; Media Studies – Journalism

Environmental Science

Aberdeen, Abertay, Aberystwyth, Anglia, Bangor, Bath Spa, Birmingham, Bolton, Bournemouth, Bradford, Brighton, BUWE, Brunel, Canterbury Christ Church, C Lancs, Chester, Colchester Institute, Coventry, De Montfort, Derby, Dundee, Durham, UEA, E London, Edge Hill, Exeter, Glamorgan, Glasgow, Herts, Huddersfield, Hull, Imperial, Kingston, Lancaster, Leeds, Lincs & Humbs, Liverpool, Liverpool JM, Luton, Manchester, Man Met, Middlesex, Napier, Newport, N London, Northumbria, Nottingham, Nott Trent, Paisley, Plymouth, Portsmouth, QMW, Reading, Robert Gordon, Roehampton, Royal Holloway, Salford, Scarborough, Sheffield, Sheffield Hallam, Southampton, Southampton Inst, South Bank, Staffs, Stirling, Sunderland, Sussex, Swansea Inst, Ulster, Wolves, Worcester, Writtle
Conservation Aberystwyth, Bangor, UEA, E London, Greenwich, Harper Adams, Imperial, Lincs & Humbs, Roehampton, Sheffield Hallam, South Bank, Sunderland, Writtle
Environmental Technologies Bolton, C England, C Lancs, Chelt & Gloucs, Dundee, Greenwich, Heriot-Watt, Kingston, Leeds Met, Man Met, Staffs, Writtle
see also Agriculture; Biology – Botany; Biology – Ecology; Biology – Marine Biology; Geography; Natural Resources

EUROPE

European Business Management Abertay, Brighton, BUWE, Canterbury Christ Church, Cardiff Inst, Chelt & Gloucs, Coventry, De Montfort, Derby, E London, Edinburgh, European Business School London, Glamorgan, Glasgow, Glasgow Cal, Greenwich, Heriot-Watt, Herts, Hull, Imperial, Kent, Lancaster, Lincs & Humbs, Loughborough, UMIST, Man Met, Middlesex, Newcastle, N London, Northumbria, Oxford Brookes, Plymouth, Portsmouth, Royal Agric, Salford, Southampton Inst, Staffs, Sunderland, Swansea, Teesside, Ulster, Warwick, Westminster, Wolves
European Community Studies Birmingham, Brighton, Brunel, C England, C Lancs, De Montfort, Essex, Glamorgan, Hull, Kent, Leeds,

Lincs & Humbs, Guildhall, LSE, Luton, Manchester, Man Met, Newcastle, Northumbria, Nottingham, Paisley, Robert Gordon, Sheffield Hallam, St Martin's, Teesside
European Financial Management Brighton, City, Glamorgan, Greenwich, Portsmouth
East European Studies Glasgow, SSEES
see also History – European History; Law – European Law; Languages

French

Aberdeen, Aberystwyth, Aston, Bangor, Bath, Birmingham, Bradford, Bristol, Cardiff, UEA, E London, Edinburgh, Exeter, Glasgow, Goldsmiths, Hull, Kent, King's Coll, Kingston, Lancaster, Leeds, Leicester, Liverpool, Guildhall, Luton, Newcastle, N London, Northumbria, Nottingham, QMW, Queen's Belfast, Reading, Royal Holloway, Sheffield, Southampton, St Andrews, Stirling, Swansea, UCL, Warwick, Wolves
see also Europe; Languages; Linguistics

Geography

Physical Aberdeen, Brunel, Cranfield, Edge Hill, Hull, Keele, Lancaster, Liverpool JM, QMW, Reading, Wolves
Social Aberdeen, Aberystwyth, Anglia, Birmingham, Bristol, BUWE, Brunel, Cambridge, Canterbury Christ Church, Chichester, Dundee, Durham, Edge Hill, Edinburgh, Exeter, Glasgow, Greenwich, Huddersfield, Hull, King's Coll, Kingston, Lampeter, Leeds, Leicester, Liverpool, Liverpool JM, LSE, Manchester, Man Met, Middlesex, Newcastle, Newport, Northumbria, Nottingham, Oxford, Plymouth, Portsmouth, QMW, Queen's Belfast, Roehampton, Royal Holloway, Salford, Sheffield, St Martin's, Southampton, St Andrews, Sunderland, Swansea, UCL, Westminster, Wolves, Worcester
Geology Aberdeen, Birmingham, Bristol, Cardiff, Derby, Durham, Edinburgh, Exeter, Glasgow, Greenwich, Herts, Imperial, Keele, Kingston, Leeds, Leicester, Liverpool, Luton, Manchester, Oxford Brookes, Plymouth, Portsmouth, Royal Holloway, Southampton, Staffs, UCL
Urban Studies BUWE, Edge Hill, Glamorgan, Liverpool JM, Northumbria, Nott Trent, Sheffield Hallam, Westminster, Wolves
see also Environmental Science; Natural Resources; Social Science; Third World Studies

German

Aberdeen, Aston, Bath, Birmingham, Bradford, Bristol, Cardiff, UEA, E London, Edinburgh, Exeter, Glasgow, Goldsmiths, Hull, Kent, King's Coll, Lancaster, Leeds, Liverpool, Guildhall, Luton, Middlesex, Newcastle, Nottingham, QMW, Queen's Belfast, Reading, Royal Holloway, Sheffield, Southampton, St Andrews, Stirling, Sussex, Swansea, UCL, Warwick
see also Europe; Languages; Linguistics

History

Aberdeen, Aberystwyth, Bangor, Bath Spa, Birmingham, Bishop Grosseteste, Bolton, Bristol, BUWE, Brunel, Cambridge, Canterbury Christ Church, Cardiff, C Lancs, Chester, Chichester, De Montfort, Derby, Durham, UEA, E London, Edge Hill, Edinburgh, Essex, Exeter, Glamorgan, Glasgow, Goldsmiths, Greenwich, Herts, Huddersfield, Keele, Kent, King Alfred's, King's Coll, Kingston, Lampeter, Lancaster, Leeds, Trinity & All St, Leicester, Lincs & Humbs, Liverpool, LSE, Luton, Manchester, Man Met, Middlesex, Newcastle, NEWI, N London, Northampton, Northumbria, Nottingham, Nott Trent, Portsmouth, QMW, Reading, Roehampton, Royal Holloway, SOAS, Sheffield, Sheffield Hallam, St Martin's, Southampton, St Andrews, St Mary's, Staffs, Stirling, Sunderland, Swansea, Teesside, Trinity Carmarthen, UEA, UCL, Warwick, Westminster, Wolves, Worcester, York
European History Aberdeen, Aberystwyth, Bangor, Birmingham, Cardiff, UEA, Edinburgh, Essex, Glasgow, LSE, St Andrews, Stirling, Trinity Carmarthen, Ulster, UCL
Economic and Social History Aberystwyth, Birmingham, Bristol, Edinburgh, Glasgow, LSE, Portsmouth, Sussex
Irish History Ulster
Jewish History SOAS
Scottish History Aberdeen, Edinburgh, Glasgow, St Andrews, Stirling
Welsh History Aberystwyth, Bangor, Cardiff, Trinity Carmarthen,
see also Ancient History; Archaeology; Arts - History of Art; Classical Studies

Humanities

Aberdeen, Essex, Leeds Met, Southampton
see also American Studies; English; History; Languages; Literature

Information Science

Abertay, Aberystwyth, Leeds Met, Loughborough, Northumbria, Queen Margaret, Queen's Belfast, Sheffield

Italian

Birmingham, Bristol, Cardiff, Edinburgh, Exeter, Glasgow, Hull, Leeds, Luton, Reading, Royal Holloway, Sussex, Swansea, UCL
see also Europe; Languages; Linguistics

Languages

African Birmingham, SOAS
Arabic Exeter, Leeds, Oxford, Salford, SOAS, St Andrews
Asian C Lancs, Hull, SOAS, Sheffield
Celtic Aberdeen, Aberystwyth, Edinburgh, Glasgow, Queen's Belfast
Czech Glasgow
Chinese Durham, Edinburgh, Leeds, Oxford, SOAS
Dutch Hull, UCL
European Languages Aberdeen, Aberystwyth, Anglia, Aston, Bangor, Bradford, Cardiff, Coventry, Derby, Dundee, Durham, UEA, E London, Edge Hill, Goldsmiths, Herts, Huddersfield, Hull, Kent, Kingston,

Lancaster, Leeds, Liv Hope, Liverpool JM, Loughborough, Luton, N London, Northumbria, Nottingham, Portsmouth, Queen's Belfast, Reading, R&Y St John, Royal Holloway, Salford, Southampton, South Bank, SSEES, Stirling, Sunderland, Thames Valley, UCL
Japanese Edinburgh, Oxford, SOAS, Sheffield, Stirling
Latin American Aberdeen, Essex, Liverpool, Middlesex, Newcastle, Portsmouth, Wolves
Scandinavian UEA, Edinburgh, Hull, UCL
Modern Middle-Eastern Languages Durham, Lampeter, Manchester
Modern (other) Aston, Cambridge, C Lancs, Derby, Durham, UEA, Edinburgh, Essex, Exeter, Hull, Kent, Leeds Met, Leicester, Liverpool, Nottingham, Oxford, Sheffield, SOAS, SSEES, St Andrews, Surrey, Ulster
Russian Birmingham, Bradford, Bristol, Durham, Glasgow, Leeds, QMW, Sheffield, SSEES, St Andrews, Sussex
see also Europe; French; German; Italian; Linguistics; Spanish; Classical Studies

Law

Aberystwyth, Anglia, Birmingham, Bristol, BUWE, Brunel, Buckingham, Cambridge, Cardiff, C England, C Lancs, City, Coventry, De Montfort, Derby, Durham, UEA, E London, Essex, Exeter, Glamorgan, Greenwich, Herts, Huddersfield, Hull, Kent, Kingston, Lancaster, Leeds, Leeds Met, Leicester, Lincs & Humbs, Liverpool, Liverpool JM, Guildhall, LSE, Luton, Manchester, Man Met, Middlesex, Newcastle, N London, Northampton, Northumbria, Nottingham, Nott Trent, Oxford, Oxford Brookes, Plymouth, QMW, Queen's Belfast, Reading, SOAS, Sheffield, Sheffield Hallam, Southampton, Southampton Inst, South Bank, Staffs, Sussex, Swansea, Swansea Inst, Teesside, Thames Valley, UCL, Warwick, Westminster, Wolves
Business Anglia, Aston, Bournemouth, Brunel, City, Guildhall, NEWI, Stirling
French Aberdeen, UEA, Essex, Glasgow, Kent, King's Coll, Kingston, Lancaster, LSE, Manchester, Northumbria, Oxford, Reading, UCL, Warwick, Westminster
German Aberdeen, UEA, Glasgow, Kent, King's Coll, Kingston, Liverpool, UCL
Scots Aberdeen, Edinburgh, Glasgow, Napier, Strathclyde
European Aberdeen, Anglia, Bangor, BUWE, Bucks Chilterns, C Lancs, Coventry, UEA, E London, Essex, Glamorgan, Herts, Keele, Kent, Lancaster, Lincs & Humbs, Luton, Portsmouth, Sheffield, Southampton Inst, Strathclyde, Sussex, Wolves
Welsh Aberystwyth, Bangor, Cardiff, Lampeter, Swansea, Trinity Carmarthen
see also Criminology

Linguistics

Bangor, BUWE, UEA, Edinburgh, Essex, Herts, Lancaster, Leeds, Luton, Manchester, Newcastle, Reading, Thames Valley, Ulster, UCL, York
see also Languages

Literature

Bolton, Bradford, Derby, UEA, E London, Glasgow, Kent, Leeds Met, Luton, Northampton
see also American Studies; English; Humanities

Maritime Technology

Liverpool JM, Plymouth, Southampton Inst, Strathclyde
see also Engineering – Aeronautical Engineering

Mathematics

Aberdeen, Aberystwyth, Bangor, Bath, Birmingham, Bolton, Brighton, Bristol, Brunel, Cambridge, Cardiff, C Lancs, City, Coventry, De Montfort, Dundee, Durham, UEA, Edinburgh, Essex, Exeter, Glamorgan, Glasgow, Goldsmiths, Heriot-Watt, Herts, Hull, Imperial, Keele, Kent, King's Coll, Kingston, Lancaster, Leeds, Leicester, Liverpool, Loughborough, Manchester, UMIST, Man Met, Middlesex, Newcastle, N London, Northumbria, Nottingham, Nott Trent, Oxford, Plymouth, Portsmouth, QMW, Queen's Belfast, Reading, Royal Holloway, Salford, Sheffield, Sheffield Hallam, Southampton, St Andrews, Stirling, Strathclyde, Surrey, Sussex, Swansea, Teesside, UCL, Warwick, Westminster, York
Applied Mathematics Cardiff, Derby, Dundee, Glasgow, Man Met, Newcastle, QMW, Reading, Southampton, St Andrews, Stirling, Swansea
Other Mathematical and Informatics Sciences BUWE, Chester, Coventry, Derby, Greenwich, Portsmouth, QMW
Statistics Aberdeen, Bath, BUWE, C Lancs, Glasgow, Glasgow Cal, Heriot-Watt, Lancaster, Liverpool, Newcastle, Nott Trent, Portsmouth, QMW, Reading, St Andrews, Strathclyde, Sussex, Swansea, UCL

Media Studies

Birmingham, Chelt & Gloucs, Coventry, De Montfort, UEA, E London, Glamorgan, Huddersfield, Lincs & Humbs, Liverpool JM, London Inst, Luton, Paisley, Sheffield Hallam, Southampton Inst, Staffs, Stirling, Sunderland, Thames Valley, Ulster, Warrington, Worcester
Communications Anglia, Bangor, Bournemouth, Cardiff, C England, Coventry, E London, Glamorgan, Leeds, Leicester, Lincs & Humbs, Middlesex, Napier, Nott Trent, Queen Margaret, Robert Gordon, Sheffield Hallam, Southampton Inst, Sunderland, Ulster, Wolves
Graphic Communication Anglia, Brighton, Bucks Chilterns, Cardiff Inst, C England, Chelt & Gloucs, Coventry, De Montfort, Derby, Falmouth, Glamorgan, Herts, Huddersfield, KIAD, Leeds Met, Lincs & Humbs, London Inst, Loughborough, Luton, Man Met, Napier, Newport, NEWI, Northampton, Plymouth, Reading, Salford, Sheffield Hallam, Southampton Inst, Staffs, Sunderland, Surrey Inst, Swansea Inst, Teesside, Westminster, Wolves
Journalism Bournemouth, C Lancs, Falmouth, Lincs & Humbs, Liverpool JM, London Inst, Napier, Nott Trent, Sheffield, Southampton Inst, Staffs, Surrey Inst
Marketing/Market Research Abertay, Anglia, Aston, Bolton, Bournemouth, BUWE, Bucks Chilterns, Cardiff Inst, C England,

C Lancs, Chester, Coventry, De Montfort, Derby, Farnborough, Glamorgan, Greenwich, Herts, Huddersfield, Lancaster, Lincs & Humbs, Luton, Man Met, Middlesex, NEWI, N London, Northampton, Oxford Brookes, Paisley, Plymouth, Southampton Inst, South Bank, Staffs, Stirling, Swansea Inst, Teesside, Wolves, Writtle
Media Production Bucks Chilterns, C England, Herts, Luton
Public Relations Chelt & Gloucs, Luton, Southampton Inst, Ulster
Publishing Napier, Oxford Brookes, Robert Gordon
see also Arts – Design Studies; Arts – Fashion

Medicine

Aberdeen, Birmingham, Bristol, Cambridge, Dundee, Edinburgh, Glasgow, Imperial, King's Coll, Leeds, Leicester, Liverpool, Manchester, Newcastle, Nottingham, Oxford, QMW, Queen's Belfast, Sheffield, Southampton, St Andrews, St George's, UCL, Wales Coll Med
Dentistry Birmingham, Bristol, Dundee, Glasgow, King's Coll, Leeds, Liverpool, Manchester, Newcastle, QMW, Queen's Belfast, Sheffield, Wales Coll Med
Health Studies Brunel, C Lancs, Chichester, De Montfort, Leeds Met, Lincs & Humbs, Luton, Man Met, Middlesex, Napier, Newport, St Martin's, Staffs, Thames Valley, Worcester
Other subjects related to medicine Birmingham, Bournemouth, BUWE, Canterbury Christ Church, Cardiff Inst, Greenwich, King's Coll, Leeds Met, Man Met, Middlesex, N London, Nott Trent, Roehampton, St Martin's, South Bank, Teesside, Trinity Carmarthen, Ulster, Wolves
see also Biology; Nutrition; Nursing; Pharmacy; Psychology; Veterinary Science

Microelectronics

Anglia, Bangor, Birmingham, Bournemouth, BUWE, Brunel, C Lancs, Coventry, Durham, Edinburgh, Essex, Herts, Hull, Kent, Liverpool, Loughborough, Luton, Manchester, UMIST, N London, Northumbria, Nottingham, Nott Trent, Oxford Brookes, QMW, Salford, Sheffield, Sheffield Hallam, Southampton, Sunderland, Sussex, Ulster
see also Computer Science – Computer Systems Engineering; Computer Science – Digital Systems Engineering; Engineering – Electronic Engineering

Music

Anglia, Bangor, Bath Spa, Birmingham, Bretton Hall, Bristol, Brunel, Cambridge, Canterbury Christ Church, Cardiff, Chichester, City, Coventry, Dartington, Durham, UEA, Edinburgh, Exeter, Glasgow, Goldsmiths, Huddersfield, Hull, King's Coll, Kingston, Lancaster, Leeds, Liverpool, Manchester, Middlesex, Napier, Newcastle, Northampton, Nottingham, Oxford, Oxford Brookes, Queen's Belfast, Reading, Roehampton, RAM, RCM, Royal Holloway, Salford, SOAS, Sheffield, Southampton, Strathclyde, Surrey, Thames Valley, Trinity Coll Music, Ulster, Westminster, Wolves, York
Technology Bath Spa, Brighton, Bucks Chilterns, Edinburgh, Glasgow Cal, Herts, Leeds Met, Rose Bruford, Salford, Scarborough, Staffs, Surrey
see also Arts – Creative/Performing

Natural Resources

Aberystwyth, Bangor, UEA, E London, Greenwich, Harper Adams, Imperial, Lincs & Humbs, Roehampton, Sheffield Hallam, South Bank, Sunderland, Writtle
see also Agriculture; Biology; Environmental Science; Geography

Nursing

Abertay, Anglia, Bangor, Birmingham, Bournemouth, Brighton, BUWE, Brunel, Bucks Chilterns, Canterbury Christ Church, C England, City, De Montfort, UEA, Edinburgh, Glamorgan, Glasgow, Glasgow Cal, Herts, Hull, King's Coll, Leeds Met, Liverpool, Liverpool JM, Luton, Manchester, Middlesex, NEWI, N London, Northampton, Northumbria, Nottingham, Oxford Brookes, Plymouth, Reading, Robert Gordon, Salford, Sheffield Hallam, St Martin's, South Bank, Sunderland, Swansea, Thames Valley, Ulster, Wales Coll Med
see also Medicine

Nutrition

Cardiff Inst, Coventry, Glasgow Cal, Greenwich, King's Coll, Kingston, Leeds Met, Liverpool JM, Luton, N London, Nottingham, Oxford Brookes, Queen Margaret, Robert Gordon, Roehampton, Southampton, South Bank, Surrey, Ulster, Westminster
Food Science Anglia, Bournemouth, Cardiff Inst, Dundee, Leeds, Lincs & Humbs, Nottingham, Plymouth, Queen's Belfast, Reading, South Bank
see also Biology; Medicine

Pharmacy

Aston, Bath, Bradford, Brighton, Cardiff, Coventry, De montfort, Greenwich, Hertfordshire, Huddersfield, King's, Liverpool JM, Manchester, Nottingham, Portsmouth, Queen's Belfast, Robert Gordon, School of Pharmacy, Strathclyde, Sunderland
Pharmocology Aberdeen, Bath, Bradford, Bristol, Cardiff, Dundee, E London, Edinburgh, Glasgow, Herts, King's Coll, Leeds, Liverpool, Luton, Manchester, Newcastle, Nescot, Portsmouth, Sheffield, Southampton, Sunderland, UCL
Pharmaceutical Chemistry Abertay, Anglia, Aston, Coventry, De Montfort, Dundee, UEA, Glamorgan, Greenwich, Heriot-Watt, Herts, Huddersfield, Imperial, Kent, Kingston, Leeds, Liverpool JM, Loughborough, UMIST, Newcastle, N London, Nott Trent, Paisley, QMW, Salford, Sheffield Hallam, Southampton, Sussex, Teesside, UCL, Warwick, York
see also Chemistry; Medicine

Philosophy

Aberdeen, Anglia, Birmingham, Bolton, Bradford, Bristol, Cambridge, Cardiff, Dundee, Durham, UEA, Edinburgh, Essex, Glasgow, Greenwich, Herts, Heythrop, Hull, Kent, King's Coll, Lampeter, Lancaster, Leeds, Liverpool, LSE, Manchester, Man Met, Middlesex, N London, Nottingham, Queen's Belfast, Reading, Sheffield,

Southampton, St Andrews, Staffs, Stirling, Swansea, Ulster, UCL, Warwick, Wolves, York
see also Politics, Philosophy & Economics; Religious Studies/Theology

Physics

Aberdeen, Aberystwyth, Bath, Birmingham, Bristol, Cardiff, C Lancs, Dundee, Durham, Edinburgh, Exeter, Glasgow, Heriot-Watt, Herts, Hull, Imperial, Keele, Kent, King's Coll, Lancaster, Leeds, Leicester, Liverpool, Loughborough, Manchester, UMIST, Newcastle, Nottingham, Nott Trent, Oxford, Paisley, Portsmouth, QMW, Queen's Belfast, Reading, Royal Holloway, Salford, Sheffield, Sheffield Hallam, Southampton, St Andrews, Staffs, Strathclyde, Surrey, Sussex, Swansea, UCL, Warwick, York
Applied Physics Bath, C Lancs, Dundee, Durham, Heriot-Watt, Herts, Hull, Northumbria, Nottingham, Nott Trent, Portsmouth, Robert Gordon, Royal Holloway, Salford, Strathclyde, Sussex, UCL
see also Astronomy - Astrophysics; Engineering; Science (Combined or General)

Politics

Aberdeen, Aberystwyth, Birmingham, Bradford, Bristol, BUWE, Cardiff, De Montfort, Dundee, Durham, UEA, E London, Edinburgh, Essex, Exeter, Glasgow, Greenwich, Herts, Huddersfield, Hull, Kingston, Lancaster, Leeds, Leeds Met, Leicester, Lincs & Humbs, Liverpool, Luton, Manchester, Man Met, Newcastle, N London, Northumbria, Nottingham, Nott Trent, Plymouth, Portsmouth, QMW, Queen's Belfast, Royal Holloway, SOAS, Sheffield, Southampton, Southampton Inst, South Bank, Staffs, Stirling, Sunderland, Swansea, Teesside, Warwick, Westminster, Wolves, York
International Politics Aberystwyth, Birmingham, Bradford, C Lancs, Essex, Glamorgan, Hull, Keele, Kent, Lancaster, Leeds, Lincs & Humbs, Guildhall, LSE, Luton, Middlesex, Nott Trent, Plymouth, Portsmouth, Reading, St Andrews, Staffs, Swansea, Ulster
see also Politics, Philosophy & Economics

Politics, Philosophy & Economics

Brunel, Buckingham, UEA, Essex, Hull, Keele, Lancaster, Guildhall, Oxford, Salford, Stirling, Teesside, York
see also Politics; Philosophy; Economics

Psychology

as a Biological Science Aberdeen, Abertay, Anglia, Bangor, Birmingham, Bolton, Bristol, BUWE, Brunel, Cardiff, C Lancs, City, Coventry, Dundee, Durham, E London, Edge Hill, Edinburgh, Essex, Exeter, Glasgow, Goldsmiths, Greenwich, Herts, Hull, Kent, Lancaster, Leeds, Leicester, Lincs & Humbs, Liverpool, Loughborough, Manchester, Middlesex, Newcastle, NEWI, Northampton, Northumbria, Nottingham, Nott Trent, Plymouth, Portsmouth, Queen's Belfast, Reading, Royal Holloway, Sheffield, Southampton, Southampton Inst, South Bank, St Andrews, Staffs, Stirling, Surrey, Sussex, Swansea, Thames Valley, UCL, Warwick, Westminster,

Wolves, York
as a Social Science Aston, Bradford, Bristol, Bucks Chilterns, Cardiff Inst, Chester, De Montfort, Dundee, Edinburgh, Exeter, Glamorgan, Glasgow Cal, Huddersfield, Leeds Met, Luton, Man Met, R&Y St John, Roehampton, Sheffield Hallam, St Martin's, Sunderland, Swansea, Teesside, Worcester
Occupational/Clinical Psychology Derby, Hull, Kent
see also Medicine; Social Science

Religious Studies/Theology

Aberdeen, Bangor, Bath Spa, Birmingham, BUWE, Cambridge, Canterbury Christ Church, Cardiff, Chelt & Gloucs, Chester, Chichester, Durham, Exeter, Glasgow, Heythrop, Hull, King Alfred's, King's Coll, Lampeter, Trinity & All St, Manchester, Middlesex, Nottingham, Oxford, Queen's Belfast, R&Y St John, Roehampton, St Martin's, St Andrews, St Mary's, Sunderland, Westhill, Wolves
see also Philosophy

Science (Combined or General)

Aberdeen, Anglia, Bath, Bolton, Brunel, Canterbury Christ Church, Cardiff, C Lancs, De Montfort, Derby, Dundee, Durham, E London, Glasgow, Glasgow Cal, Greenwich, Heriot-Watt, Herts, Huddersfield, Leeds, Trinity & All St, Leicester, Liverpool, Luton, Man Met, Napier, Newcastle, Newport, N London, Nott Trent, Oxford Brookes, Paisley, Plymouth, Royal Holloway, Heriot-Watt, Salford, Sheffield, Sheffield Hallam, St Martin's, St Andrews, Strathclyde, Teesside, UCL, Wolves
see also Astronomy; Biology; Chemistry; Engineering; Medicine; Nutrition; Physics; Veterinary Science; Zoology

Social Policy

Anglia, Bath, Birmingham, Bradford, Brighton, Bristol, Cardiff, C Lancs, E London, Goldsmiths, Herts, Hull, Leeds Met, Lincs & Humbs, LSE, Loughborough, Luton, Manchester, Middlesex, Newcastle, N London, Nottingham, Plymouth, Portsmouth, Roehampton, Salford, Sheffield Hallam, Southampton, South Bank, Stirling, Swansea, Teesside, Ulster, Wolves
Social Policy and Administration Anglia, Bath, Birmingham, Bradford, Brighton, Bristol, Cardiff, C Lancs, E London, Goldsmiths, Herts, Hull, Leeds Met, Lincs & Humbs, LSE, Loughborough, Luton, Manchester, Middlesex, Newcastle, N London, Nottingham, Plymouth, Portsmouth, Roehampton, Salford, Sheffield Hallam, Southampton, South Bank, Stirling, Swansea, Teesside, Ulster, Wolves
see also Geography - Social; Social Science; Social Work; Third World Studies

Social Science – Combined or General

Edinburgh, Essex, Glasgow, Leeds Met, Liverpool, Liverpool JM, Manchester, Newport, Northumbria, Nott Trent, Roehampton, Salford, Staffs, Sussex, Ulster, Westminster
see also Anthropology; Geography - Social; Psycology - as a Social

Science; Social Policy; Social Work; Sociology; Third World Studies

Social Work

Anglia, Bath, Bournemouth, Bradford, Brunel, Bucks Chilterns, Cardiff Inst, C England, Chelt & Gloucs, Coventry, De Montfort, Dundee, E London, Edge Hill, Edinburgh, Glasgow Cal, Greenwich, Herts, Huddersfield, Kingston, Lancaster, Lincs & Humbs, Man Met, Middlesex, NEWI, N London, Northampton, Northern Coll, Northumbria, Nott Trent, Oxford Brookes, Salford, Sheffield Hallam, St Martin's, Southampton Inst, Stirling, Strathclyde, Teesside, Ulster, Westhill, Worcester
see also Social Policy; Social Science

Sociology

Aberdeen, Abertay, Anglia, Bangor, Bath, Bath Spa, Birmingham, Bradford, Bristol, BUWE, Brunel, Bucks Chilterns, Cardiff, C England, C Lancs, City, Coventry, De Montfort, Derby, Durham, UEA, E London, Edge Hill, Edinburgh, Essex, Exeter, Glamorgan, Glasgow, Goldsmiths, Greenwich, Herts, Huddersfield, Hull, Kent, Kingston, Lancaster, Leeds, Leeds Met, Leicester, Liverpool, Liv Hope, Guildhall, LSE, Loughborough, Luton, Manchester, Man Met, Middlesex, NEWI, Northampton, Northumbria, Nottingham, Plymouth, Portsmouth, Queen's Belfast, Reading, Roehampton, Salford, Sheffield, Sheffield Hallam, Southampton, South Bank, St Mary's, Staffs, Stirling, Sunderland, Surrey, Swansea, Teesside, Thames Valley, Ulster, Warwick, Westminster, Wolves, Worcester, York
Applied Sociology Brunel, Canterbury Christ Church, Edge Hill, King Alfred's, Leeds Met, Luton, N London, Northumbria, Oxford Brookes, Paisley, Plymouth, Sheffield Hallam, St Martin's, Southampton, Sunderland
see also Geography – Social; Social Science

Spanish

Aberdeen, Aberystwyth, Birmingham, Bradford, Bristol, Cardiff, E London, Edinburgh, Exeter, Hull, King's Coll, Leeds, Luton, Middlesex, Newcastle, Nottingham, Queen's Belfast, Sheffield, Southampton, St Andrews, Stirling, Swansea, UCL, Wolves
see also Languages

Sports Science

Aberdeen, Anglia, Bangor, Birmingham, Bolton, Brighton, BUWE, Brunel, Bucks Chilterns, Canterbury Christ Church, Cardiff Inst, C Lancs, Chelt & Gloucs, Chester, Chichester, Coventry, Durham, Edge Hill, Essex, Exeter, Glamorgan, Glasgow, Greenwich, Herts, Hull, King Alfred's, Kingston, Leeds, Leeds Met, Liverpool JM, Man Met, NEWI, N London, Plymouth, Portsmouth, R&Y St John, Sheffield Hallam, St Martin's, South Bank, St Mary's, Staffs, Stirling, Strathclyde, Sunderland, Swansea, Teesside, Trinity Carmarthen, Westminster
see also Education - Physical Education

Third World Studies

Bradford, C Lancs, UEA, E London, Greenwich, Leeds, Middlesex, St Andrews, Swansea
see also Anthropology; Geography

Veterinary Science

Bristol, Cambridge, Edinburgh, Glasgow, Liverpool, Royal Vet
see also Biology; Medicine; Zoology

Zoology

Aberdeen, Aberystwyth, Bangor, Birmingham, Bristol, Cardiff, Dundee, Durham, E London, Edinburgh, Glasgow, Imperial, Leeds, Leicester, Liverpool, Manchester, Newcastle, Nottingham, QMW, Queen's Belfast, Reading, Roehampton, Royal Holloway, Sheffield, Southampton, Swansea, UCL
see also Biology; Veterinary Science

Push in: Entrance Requirements

However much you might like to choose from every university in this book, not every one will have you. The best way of knowing in advance which ones would welcome you with open arms and which would give you the finger is to check out the entrance requirements.

Who they'll accept is usually based largely on points that students collect by passing exams and qualifications. A levels, obviously, but also Highers, AS levels, NVQs and any one of the new bits of paper that pass for proof of intelligence.

Each grade in each qualification is worth a different number of points and, in theory, once you've got enough points for a particular course, you should stand a good chance of being accepted. The whole 'UCAS point tariff' looks like this

A Levels		Highers		Advanced Highers		Vocational A Levels		AS Levels		Key Skills	
Grade	Pts	Grade	Pts	Grade	Pts	Grade	Pts	Grade	Pts	Level	Pts
A	120	A	72	A	120	AA	240	A	60	4	30
B	100	B	60	B	100	BB	200	B	50	3	20
C	80	C	48	C	80	CC	160	C	40	2	10
D	80					DD	120	D	30		
E	40					EE	80	E	20		

However, it's not that simple. (Is it ever?) All points are supposed to be equal, but some are a lot more equal than others.

First off, it matters what qualification you've got. Whatever the points score says, universities don't take AS levels or vocational A levels quite as seriously as an equal number of points at A level.

Then there's the subject you've studied. In practice, points gained in a relevant subject count for more than points in something completely unrelated. For example, if you want to do a science degree, but all you've got is arts A levels, only universities desperate for students aren't going to look at your application and snigger.

The whole system of points is more than a bit dubious at the edges, not least because many mature students will be accepted without traditional qualifications and the set-up of modular courses throws a spanner in the works. Besides, come Clearing, universities with vacancies to fill will throw their list of requirements out the window and take what they can get.

Heed that huge health warning and the additional advice that it's best to check with the actual department you're applying to what grades they'd be likely to want from you given the subjects and qualifications you're taking.

Having said that, here's Push's exclusive guide to grades.

The attached is a Gant Diagram, but you already knew that if you're studying statistics, right? It's a quick reference diagram to help you narrow down where to study, depending entirely on what points you already have or expect to get.

The diagram is a good tool for seeing the range of points required to get into where you want, but you'll need to contact the college to get a better idea what grades they want for your chosen course.

Some univerisities offer a narrow range of points. For example, Cambridge and Oxford expect you to have a minimum of 340 points (AAB) for most courses. With anything from 240 to 340 (CCC to AAB), Manchester's courses span a wider range of abilities and at Kingston, the spread is even wider – from just 60 up to 300 (from a D up to BBB).

Of course, remember that these are the minimum requirements for their various courses. If you've got four As and if it were down to grades alone, you'd be able to get in pretty much anywhere.

Points table 736

Institution	Points range
University of Aberdeen	320–below 240
University of Abertay Dundee	280–below 240
Aberystwyth	300–below 240
Anglia Polytechnic University	320–below 240
Aston University	340–280
Bangor	300–below 240
University of Bath	340–below 240
Bath Spa	
University of Birmingham	340–260
Bolton Institute	
Bournemouth University	300–below 240
University of Bradford	320–below 240
University of Brighton	320–below 240
University of Bristol	360–340
Bristol, W of E	320–below 240
Brunel University	320–below 240
University of Buckingham	260–below 240
Buckinghamshire	
University of Cambridge	360–340
Cardiff	340–260
University of Central England	260–below 240
University of Central Lancashire	below 240
Cheltenham & Gloucester CHE	260–below 240
City University	340–below 240
Coventry University	320–below 240
Cranfield	280–below 240
De Montfort University	320–below 240
University of Derby	260–below 240
University of Dundee	320–below 240
University of Durham	340–260
University of East London	300–below 240
University of Edinburgh	340–below 240
University of Essex	320–below 240
University of Exeter	320–below 240
University of Glamorgan	320–below 240
Glasgow University	340–below 240
Glasgow Caledonian University	320–below 240
Goldsmiths College	300–below 240
University of Greenwich	260–below 240
Heriot-Watt University	280–below 240
University of Hertfordshire	320–below 240
Heythrop College, London	280–260
University of Huddersfield	300–below 240
University of Hull	320–below 240
Imperial College, London	340–280

737 Points table

Points table

Institution	Points range
Keele University	300–230
University of Kent & Canterbury	330–260
King's College London	350–260
Kingston University	360–230
Lampeter, University of Wales	250–230
Lancaster University	340–230
University of Leeds	360–230
Leeds Metropolitan University	300–240
Leicester University	350–230
University of Lincs & Humbs	250–230
University of Liverpool	360–230
Liverpool John Moores University	360–230
London Guildhall University	290–250
Loughborough University	320–260
LSE	360–330
Luton University	—
University of Manchester	340–260
Manchester Metropolitan University	290–230
Middlesex University	250–230
Napier University	250–230
University of Newcastle	360–230
University of North London	250–230
University College, Northampton	—
University of Northumbria	300–230
University of Nottingham	360–230
Nottingham Trent University	300–230
University of Oxford	360–350
Oxford Brookes University	330–230
University of Paisley	—
University of Plymouth	290–230
University of Portsmouth	310–230
Queen Margaret College	330–230
Queen Mary & Westfield College	360–230
Queen's University Belfast	360–230
University of Reading	330–230
Robert Gordon University	330–230
Royal Hollaway, London	330–260
Royal Vetinary College, London	360
University of St Andrews	340–260
University of Salford	330–230
University of Sheffield	350–260
Sheffield Hallum	290–230
SOAS	350–230
University of Southampton	330–260
Southampton Institute	260–230

739 Points table

Points table 740

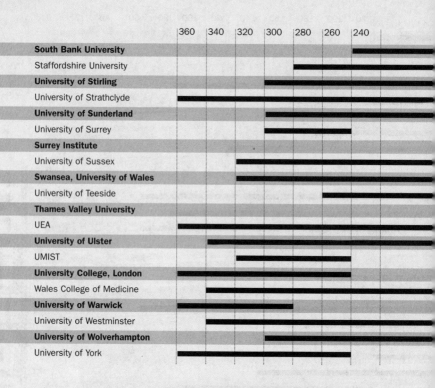

741 Points table

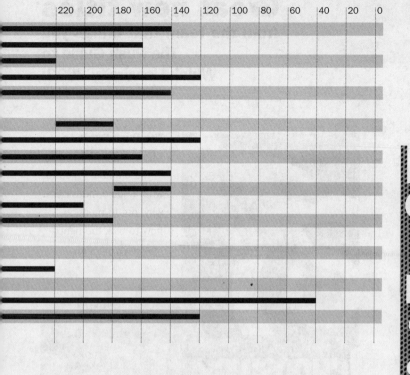

Great new titles
from the team that brings you The Push Guide to Which University 2002:

The Push Guide to Choosing a University is the ultimate guide to what should matter and why, not to mention how to pick the right university for you.

The Push Guide to Money 2002 is the in-depth student survival guide, detailing what you'll have to spend, what you'll have to spend it on and how it differs at every UK university.

Push tables

Where would education be without tables? There is a great tradition from the the Periodic Table, times tables, time-tables, log tables, until most recently, the government's own league tables. And, of course, school desks, which are tables. Sort of.

Never one to buck a trend, push introduces the tables to end all tables - the crucial guides to clubs and sports and the controversial reality of hard facts.

CLUBS
Some clubs and societies are available at most colleges. So, rather than bore you rigid listing them in every college profile, *Push* has detailed them in the following pages (756 to 761), so you can see if there's rock at Reading or karate at Keele.

VITAL STATISTICS
What you want to do is get those colleges up against the wall and see how they look side by side. So on pages 762 to 767 *Push* has distilled its finest facts and charted them: the sex ratio; the founding year; the student numbers; the level of care; the numbers who enter through clearing; the numbers who flunk; the cost and availability of housing; the cost of booze (average cost of a pint of beer/glass of wine); the employment prospects; and the bill of debt at the end of the day (including student loans).

NB Some smaller colleges have been left out of the clubs tables because they've hardly got any anyway. For a fuller explanation of the statistical data see 'How to use Push' (page 8).

TOP 10S
Top 10s are top eye-candy – found everywhere from Top of the Pops to Viz, recording everything from the biggest-selling records to the world's fastest slugs. They're also an easy way to decode information without having to do much at all apart from raise the occasional eyebrow.
Push's Top 10s shouldn't be taken too seriously. Anyone choosing a university solely on the basis that it tops the charts for cheap beer has maybe not made a full and rounded decision. But all else being equal, it's as good a clincher as any.
Furthermore, taken together our Top 10s tell you quite a bit. Every university has it's good and bad points and we help you pinpoint the strongest strengths and the weakest weaknesses. (It also provides a quick guide to cheap rent, top totty and bargain beer.)

Clubs

	UNI OF ABERDEEN	UNI OF ABERTAY DUNDEE	ABERYSTWYTH UNI OF WALES	ANGLIA POLYTECHNIC UNI	ASTON UNI	BANGOR UNI OF WALES	BATH SPA UNI COLLEGE	UNI OF BATH	BIRKBECK COLLEGE, LONDON	UNI OF BIRMINGHAM	BOLTON INSTITUTE	UNI OF BOURNEMOUTH	UNI OF BRADFORD	UNI OF BRIGHTON	BRISTOL, UNI OF W OF ENGLAND	UNI OF BRISTOL	BRUNEL UNI	UNI OF BUCKINGHAM	BUCKINGHAMSHIRE UNI COLLEGE	UNI OF CAMBRIDGE	CARDIFF UNI OF WALES
NON-SPORTING																					
African-Caribbean	●	●	●	●	●	●		●		●		●	●	●	●	●	●		●	●	●
Amnesty		●			●			●		●			●		●		●			●	●
Animal Rights	●			●						●					●					●	●
Anti-racist/Anti-nazi										●					●						
Asian		●	●	●				●		●		●		●		●	●		●		●
BUNAC								●		●			●		●						
Catholic	●		●					●		●			●		●		●			●	●
Christian Union		●			●			●		●		●	●	●	●	●	●		●	●	●
Conservation								●		●			●		●					●	●
Conservative	●							●		●					●		●			●	●
Dance	●	●		●				●		●		●		●	●	●				●	●
Debating		●	●					●							●		●			●	●
Drama		●			●	●	●	●		●		●	●	●	●	●	●		●	●	●
Film making		●					●	●		●					●		●		●	●	●
Green/Environment	●		●	●				●	●	●		●	●	●	●	●	●		●	●	●
Industrial Society					●			●					●							●	●
Irish Society	●		●	●				●		●			●		●				●	●	●
Islamic	●		●	●	●	●		●		●			●		●	●	●		●	●	●
Jewish			●		●	●		●		●			●		●		●			●	●
Labour	●	●	●			●		●		●			●		●		●			●	●
Lesbian/Gay/Bisexual	●	●	●	●	●		●	●	●	●		●	●	●	●	●	●		●	●	●
Lib Dem		●						●							●		●			●	●
Orchestra(s)				●	●			●							●		●		●	●	●
Photography	●			●	●			●							●		●		●	●	●
Rock/Indie Music		●			●		●			●		●			●					●	●
SF & Fantasy	●	●								●					●		●				●
Socialist Worker (SWSS)										●					●					●	●
Third World First		●			●			●		●					●		●			●	●
SPORTING																					
Archery	●			●	●			●		●			●			●			●		
Athletics	●				●	●		●		●			●		●	●				●	
Badminton	●		●	●	●	●		●		●		●	●	●	●	●	●		●	●	●
Basketball	●	●	●	●	●	●		●		●	●	●	●	●	●	●	●		●	●	●
Canoeing	●		●	●	●			●		●		●		●	●	●	●			●	●
Chess		●						●		●			●		●		●			●	●
Climbing		●						●		●			●		●	●	●		●		
Cricket	●		●	●	●			●		●		●	●	●	●	●	●				
Cross country		●						●		●				●		●					●
Cycling	●			●	●	●		●		●			●		●	●	●			●	●
Fencing	●	●	●		●			●		●			●		●	●	●			●	●
Football	●	●	●	●	●	●	●	●	●	●		●	●	●	●	●	●	●	●	●	●
Golf	●		●	●		●		●		●			●		●		●			●	●
Hill-walking		●						●		●					●						●
Hockey	●		●	●	●	●		●		●		●	●	●	●	●	●		●	●	●
Horse-riding		●	●	●		●		●		●			●		●	●	●		●	●	●
Judo	●		●	●	●	●		●		●					●		●			●	●
Karate		●	●					●		●					●		●		●	●	●
Netball	●		●	●	●	●		●		●		●	●	●	●	●	●			●	●
Orienteering				●				●					●			●			●		
Rugby	●		●	●	●	●	●	●		●		●	●	●	●	●	●		●	●	●
Sailing	●		●	●	●			●		●		●	●	●	●	●	●		●	●	●
Skiing	●		●	●	●			●		●		●	●	●	●	●	●		●	●	●
Squash			●	●		●		●		●		●	●	●	●	●	●			●	●
Sub-aqua	●		●		●	●		●		●			●		●	●	●			●	●
Swimming			●	●		●		●		●					●	●	●			●	●
Tennis		●	●	●	●			●		●			●		●	●	●			●	●
Tae Kwan Do										●				●		●	●		●		
Trampolining	●		●					●		●					●	●	●		●	●	●
Volleyball	●		●	●	●			●		●		●	●	●	●	●	●		●	●	●

Clubs

	UNI OF CENTRAL ENGLAND	UNIV OF CENTRAL LANCASHIRE	CHELTENHAM & GLOUCESTER	CITY UNI	COURTAULD INSTITUTE, LONDON	COVENTRY UNI	CRANFIELD UNI	DE MONTFORT UNI	UNI OF DERBY	UNI OF DUNDEE	UNI OF DURHAM	UNI OF EAST LONDON	UNI OF EDINBURGH	UNI OF ESSEX	UNI OF EXETER	UNI OF GLAMORGAN	UNI OF GLASGOW	GLASGOW CALEDONIAN UNI	GOLDSMITH'S COLLEGE, LONDON	UNI OF GREENWICH	HERIOT-WATT UNI
NON-SPORTING																					
African-Caribbean				•		•		•	•	•	•	•	•	•				•	•	•	
Amnesty				•				•	•	•			•		•			•	•		•
Animal Rights												•	•		•				•	•	
Anti-racist/Anti-nazi										•										•	
Asian	•	•				•		•		•		•	•	•	•			•	•	•	•
BUNAC				•				•	•		•		•		•	•					•
Catholic			•					•		•	•		•		•						•
Christian Union	•	•	•			•		•	•	•	•	•	•	•	•			•		•	•
Conservation															•						•
Conservative								•		•	•		•		•						•
Dance																					•
Debating		•	•			•			•	•	•	•	•	•	•		•			•	•
Drama	•	•				•		•		•	•	•	•	•	•		•			•	•
Film making	•	•				•				•			•		•				•	•	•
Green/Environment						•		•		•			•		•				•	•	•
Industrial Society	•	•	•							•											
Irish Society										•			•		•						•
Islamic	•	•	•	•		•		•	•	•	•	•	•	•	•					•	•
Jewish	•			•							•		•		•			•			•
Labour		•											•								•
Lesbian/Gay/Bisexual	•	•		•		•		•	•	•	•	•	•	•	•		•			•	•
Lib Dem												•	•	•							
Orchestra(s)					•	•					•		•		•						•
Photography		•									•		•		•						•
Rock/Indie Music	•	•				•		•	•			•					•		•		•
SF & Fantasy		•								•			•	•							•
Socialist Worker (SWSS)	•	•	•			•				•								•			•
Third World First	•				•								•		•					•	
SPORTING																					
Archery			•					•		•			•		•			•		•	•
Athletics	•	•		•		•		•	•	•	•		•		•			•		•	•
Badminton	•	•	•			•	•	•	•	•	•	•	•	•	•		•	•		•	•
Basketball	•	•	•	•		•		•	•	•	•	•	•	•	•			•	•	•	•
Canoeing	•	•	•			•	•	•	•	•	•		•	•	•			•	•	•	•
Chess										•			•		•						•
Climbing	•			•		•	•	•		•	•		•	•	•			•	•		•
Cricket	•	•						•		•	•	•	•	•	•					•	•
Cross country							•												•		•
Cycling	•	•	•			•		•		•		•		•	•			•			•
Fencing																					•
Football	•	•	•			•	•	•	•	•	•	•	•	•	•		•	•	•	•	•
Golf					•																•
Hill-walking	•	•	•	•				•		•			•		•		•	•		•	•
Hockey		•	•				•	•	•	•	•	•	•	•	•		•				•
Horse-riding		•				•	•	•		•			•		•						•
Judo	•					•		•		•			•	•	•					•	
Karate	•	•											•							•	•
Netball		•	•			•			•			•		•			•				
Orienteering	•	•	•			•		•	•	•	•		•	•	•		•			•	•
Rugby		•	•					•	•	•	•	•	•	•	•						•
Sailing		•		•		•		•		•	•		•		•					•	•
Skiing		•	•	•				•		•			•		•			•		•	•
Squash							•										•			•	•
Sub-aqua										•		•			•						•
Swimming	•	•	•			•		•		•	•		•	•	•			•		•	•
Tennis	•	•	•							•	•		•		•			•		•	•
Tae Kwan Do		•				•			•				•							•	•
Trampolining		•				•							•		•						•
Volleyball		•	•			•	•	•		•		•	•	•	•			•		•	•

clubs

	Hertfordshire	Heythrop	Huddersfield	Imperial	Kent	Keele	King's	Kingston	Lampeter	Lancaster	Leeds Met	Leeds	Leicester	Lincs & Humbs	Liverpool JM	Liverpool	London Guildhall	London Inst	Loughborough
NON-SPORTING																			
African-Caribbean	•			•	•	•	•	•			•	•		•		•		•	•
Amnesty	•			•		•				•	•	•	•	•	•				•
Animal Rights			•		•							•						•	
Anti-racist/Anti-nazi			•									•							
Asian	•			•	•	•	•				•	•		•		•	•		•
BUNAC				•	•	•					•	•							
Catholic	•		•	•		•						•							
Christian Union	•	•		•	•	•	•	•	•	•		•	•	•		•		• •	•
Conservation			•			•		•				•							
Conservative			•	•	•	•					•	•		•		•			•
Dance			•		•	•	•				•	•		•		•			•
Debating				•			•					•	•	•		•			
Drama	•		•	•			•	•			•	•	•	•	•	•			•
Film making						•	•			•		•		•					
Green/Environment	•		•	•							•	•		•		•			
Industrial Society	•			•		•	•					•							
Irish Society				•					•	•						•			
Islamic	•	•	•	•	•		•	•			•	•	•	•	•	•	•		
Jewish	•			•			•					•				•			•
Labour				•		•	•			•		•		•		•	•		•
Lesbian/Gay/Bisexual	•	•	•	•	•	•	•	•		•	•	•	•	•		•	•	• •	•
Lib Dem				•		•						•				•			
Orchestra(s)			•	•	•	•	•				•			•		•		• •	•
Photography	•		•	•	•						•			•		•			
Rock/Indie Music	•			•														•	•
SF & Fantasy	•		•	•							•			•		•			•
Socialist Worker (SWSS)				•		•						•	•	•		•			
Third World First				•							•	•	•			•			
SPORTING																			
Archery	•				•			•				•		•		•		•	•
Athletics	•		•	•	•	•	•	•		•	•	•	•	•		•		•	•
Badminton	•		•	•	•	•	•	•	•	•	•	•	•	•	•	•	•	•	•
Basketball	•		•	•	•		•	•		•	•	•	•	•	•	•	•		•
Canoeing	•		•	•	•	•	•	•		•	•	•	•	•		•	•		•
Chess	•					•				•		•	•						
Climbing	•		•	•		•					•	•		•		•	•	• •	•
Cricket	•		•	•	•	•	•	•	•		•	•	•			•			•
Cross country	•		•	•		•					•	•	•	•		•			•
Cycling	•		•	•		•					•	•	•			•		•	•
Fencing	•			•	•	•	•	•		•	•	•	•	•		•	•		•
Football	•	•	•	•	•	•	•	•	•	•	•	•	•	•	•	•	•	• •	•
Golf	•			•	•	•					•	•	•	•		•		•	•
Hill-walking	•		•							•		•							
Hockey	•		•	•	•	•	•	•		•	•	•	•	•		•	•		•
Horse-riding	•		•							•		•	•	•	•	•			•
Judo	•		•	•		•		•			•	•	•	•	•	•			•
Karate	•		•	•	•	•					•	•	•	•	•	•			•
Netball				•		•	•				•		•			•			
Orienteering	•				•		•					•	•						
Rugby	•			•		•				•		•	•	•		•	•		•
Sailing	•		•		•	•	•	•			•	•	•	•		•	•	•	•
Skiing	•		•	•	•	•	•	•		•	•	•	•	•	•	•	•		•
Squash	•		•	•	•	•		•			•	•	•	•		•	•		•
Sub-aqua	•		•	•	•	•	•	•			•	•	•		•	•		•	•
Swimming	•			•	•	•	•	•		•	•	•	•	•		•	•	•	•
Tennis	•		•		•	•	•	•			•	•	•	•		•	•		•
Tae Kwan Do	•		•													•	•		•
Trampolining			•	•							•	•		•		•			
Volleyball			•	•	•	•	•	•	•	•	•	•	•		•	•	•	•	•

747

Clubs

	LSE	LUTON UNIVERSITY	UNIVERSITY OF MANCHESTER	MANCHESTER METROPOLITAN UNI	MIDDLESEX UNIVERSITY	NAPIER UNIVERSITY	NENE UNIVERSITY COLLEGE	UNIVERSITY OF NEWCASTLE	UNIVERSITY OF NORTH LONDON	UNIVERSITY OF NORTHUMBRIA	UNIVERSITY OF NOTTINGHAM	NOTTINGHAM TRENT UNIVERSITY	UNIVERSITY OF OXFORD	OXFORD BROOKES UNIVERSITY	UNIVERSITY OF PAISLEY	UNIVERSITY OF PLYMOUTH	UNIVERSITY OF PORTSMOUTH	QUEEN MARGARET COLLEGE	Q MARY & WESTFIELD COLLEGE	QUEEN'S UNIVERSITY BELFAST	UNIVERSITY OF READING	
																						NON-SPORTING
African-Caribbean	•	•	•	•				•	•			•					•		•		•	
Amnesty	•		•					•		•			•				•	•		•	•	
Animal Rights	•		•	•	•																•	
Anti-racist/Anti-nazi													•								•	
Asian	•		•	•	•				•		•		•		•		•		•	•	•	
BUNAC				•	•				•			•					•					
Catholic	•									•			•				•				•	
Christian Union	•	•	•	•				•		•			•		•		•		•	•	•	
Conservation	•		•					•					•						•		•	
Conservative	•		•	•	•			•					•	•							•	
Dance	•		•	•					•								•	•			•	
Debating	•								•												•	
Drama	•	•	•	•					•			•					•			•	•	
Film making		•	•	•					•	•							•			•	•	
Green/Environment	•			•	•		•						•						•		•	
Industrial Society	•			•	•																	
Irish Society	•			•	•	•													•			
Islamic	•	•	•	•	•	•		•		•	•	•	•	•					•	•	•	
Jewish		•	•										•							•	•	
Labour	•		•	•					•	•			•			•	•			•	•	
Lesbian/Gay/Bisexual	•		•	•				•	•				•				•		•	•	•	
Lib Dem									•				•								•	
Orchestra(s)	•		•									•	•								•	
Photography	•		•	•													•			•	•	
Rock/Indie Music			•																		•	
SF & Fantasy								•	•			•	•		•						•	
Socialist Worker (SWSS)	•	•	•					•				•			•						•	
Third World First	•		•		•			•													•	
																						SPORTING
Archery					•							•									•	
Athletics		•	•	•		•	•	•			•	•			•	•		•	•	•	•	
Badminton	•	•	•	•					•			•			•		•				•	
Basketball	•		•	•					•			•			•		•		•	•	•	
Canoeing			•	•					•			•			•		•				•	
Chess					•	•						•									•	
Climbing	•		•	•	•				•						•		•			•	•	
Cricket	•	•	•	•	•				•			•			•		•		•	•	•	
Cross country	•		•	•								•			•		•			•	•	
Cycling			•						•						•		•			•	•	
Fencing	•		•	•	•				•			•			•		•		•	•	•	
Football	•	•	•	•	•	•	•		•			•			•		•		•	•	•	
Golf			•	•					•			•			•			•			•	
Hill-walking				•	•													•				
Hockey	•		•	•	•				•			•			•		•			•	•	
Horse-riding			•									•			•						•	
Judo	•	•	•	•	•							•					•		•		•	
Karate	•	•	•	•	•	•	•		•			•			•		•		•	•	•	
Netball			•		•				•			•					•			•	•	
Orienteering												•									•	
Rugby	•		•	•	•				•			•			•		•		•	•	•	
Sailing		•	•		•				•			•			•		•				•	
Skiing		•	•	•		•			•			•			•		•				•	
Squash	•		•	•	•				•			•			•		•			•	•	
Sub-aqua		•	•	•	•	•						•			•		•		•		•	
Swimming		•	•	•	•		•	•	•		•	•			•		•			•	•	
Tennis	•		•						•			•			•		•			•	•	
Tae Kwan Do	•			•								•					•			•	•	
Trampolining					•			•							•						•	
Volleyball	•	•	•	•	•	•	•	•	•	•		•			•		•		•	•	•	

Clubs

Universities (columns, left to right): Robert Gordon University · Royal Academy of Music · Royal College of Music · Royal Free Hospital · Royal Holloway, London · Royal Veterinary College · University of St Andrews · St George's Hospital · School of Pharmacy, London · University of Salford · Sheffield Hallam University · University of Sheffield · University of Southampton · SOAS · Southampton Institute · South Bank University · Staffordshire University · SSEES · University of Stirling · University of Strathclyde · University of Sunderland

NON-SPORTING

Club	RGU	RAM	RCM	RFH	RH	RVC	StA	StG	SoP	Sal	SHU	Shef	Sou	SOAS	SI	SBU	Staf	SSEES	Stir	Strath	Sund
African-Caribbean					●					●		●	●	●		●					●
Amnesty					●		●			●	●	●	●	●		●	●			●	
Animal Rights					●							●		●	●				●		
Anti-racist/Anti-nazi													●	●						●	●
Asian					●					●	●	●	●			●				●	●
BUNAC	●						●					●						●		●	
Catholic					●							●	●		●	●	●	●		●	
Christian Union	●	●		●	●	●	●		●			●	●			●	●		●	●	●
Conservation						●															
Conservative							●						●								
Dance					●		●	●	●			●				●			●	●	
Debating					●		●	●					●	●		●		●		●	
Drama	●				●		●		●				●	●		●			●	●	●
Film making					●							●	●		●		●	●			
Green/Environment					●							●			●						
Industrial Society												●	●								
Irish Society					●								●			●			●	●	
Islamic	●			●	●		●		●	●	●	●	●	●		●	●			●	●
Jewish		●	●	●	●		●	●				●	●	●		●	●				
Labour					●								●			●				●	
Lesbian/Gay/Bisexual	●				●	●	●					●	●			●			●	●	
Lib Dem					●							●	●								
Orchestra(s)		●	●				●					●	●			●					
Photography					●								●						●	●	●
Rock/Indie Music	●						●					●							●	●	●
SF & Fantasy	●				●							●							●	●	
Socialist Worker (SWSS)					●								●	●	●					●	●
Third World First							●						●			●					

SPORTING

Club	RGU	RAM	RCM	RFH	RH	RVC	StA	StG	SoP	Sal	SHU	Shef	Sou	SOAS	SI	SBU	Staf	SSEES	Stir	Strath	Sund
Archery	●				●							●	●			●			●	●	●
Athletics	●			●			●			●		●	●			●			●	●	●
Badminton	●		●	●	●	●	●	●	●	●	●	●	●		●	●	●		●	●	●
Basketball	●	●	●							●	●	●	●		●	●	●		●	●	●
Canoeing	●								●			●	●			●	●		●	●	●
Chess	●				●		●		●			●	●			●	●				
Climbing	●			●	●	●	●					●	●			●			●		●
Cricket	●			●	●	●	●		●	●	●	●	●	●	●	●	●		●	●	●
Cross country						●		●				●	●			●			●	●	●
Cycling	●											●	●			●			●	●	●
Fencing				●	●		●					●	●			●	●			●	●
Football	●	●	●	●	●	●	●	●	●	●	●	●	●	●	●	●	●	●	●	●	●
Golf				●	●		●	●	●	●	●	●	●		●	●	●		●	●	●
Hill-walking	●				●		●					●	●			●	●		●	●	●
Hockey				●	●	●	●	●	●	●	●	●	●		●	●	●		●	●	●
Horse-riding	●				●	●	●									●	●		●		
Judo												●	●			●	●		●	●	●
Karate							●	●	●		●	●	●			●	●		●	●	●
Netball	●	●		●	●	●	●	●	●	●	●	●	●		●	●	●		●	●	●
Orienteering	●												●			●				●	
Rugby	●			●	●	●	●	●	●	●	●	●	●		●	●	●		●	●	●
Sailing							●			●		●	●		●	●	●		●	●	●
Skiing	●			●	●	●	●		●	●	●	●	●		●	●	●		●	●	●
Squash				●	●		●	●	●	●	●	●	●		●	●	●		●	●	●
Sub-aqua					●					●		●	●			●			●	●	●
Swimming	●				●		●	●	●	●	●	●	●			●	●		●	●	●
Tennis				●	●		●	●	●	●	●	●	●		●	●	●		●	●	●
Tae Kwan Do					●								●			●	●			●	
Trampolining											●	●			●	●	●			●	●
Volleyball				●	●	●						●	●		●	●	●		●	●	●

Clubs

Surrey	Surrey Inst	Sussex	Swansea	Teesside	Thames Valley	UEA	UMIST	Ulster	UCL	Wales Coll Medicine	Warwick	Westminster	Wolverhampton	Wye	York	**NON-SPORTING**
		•		•		•		•			•		•		•	African-Caribbean
•		•		•		•	•		•		•			•	•	Amnesty
		•		•			•		•		•				•	Animal Rights
		•			•		•		•	•					•	Anti-racist/Anti-nazi
		•					•		•		•				•	Asian
									•		•				•	BUNAC
•					•	•	•									Catholic
•	•	•		•	•	•	•	•	•	•	•	•		•	•	Christian Union
		•				•			•		•				•	Conservation
•		•		•		•			•		•				•	Conservative
		•				•			•		•				•	Dance
		•				•			•		•				•	Debating
	•	•		•		•		•	•	•	•				•	Drama
		•				•			•		•				•	Film making
•		•		•		•			•		•			•	•	Green/Environment
		•							•							Industrial Society
		•		•	•	•	•		•							Irish Society
•						•			•		•		•		•	Islamic
		•				•			•		•		•		•	Jewish
•		•		•		•			•						•	Labour
		•	•	•		•	•		•		•	•	•		•	Lesbian/Gay/Bisexual
		•				•			•		•				•	Lib Dem
		•				•	•		•		•				•	Orchestra(s)
		•		•		•			•		•				•	Photography
	•					•			•		•		•			Rock/Indie Music
		•		•		•			•		•				•	SF & Fantasy
		•		•		•					•				•	Socialist Worker (SWSS)
		•		•					•		•				•	Third World First
																SPORTING
•		•		•		•			•		•				•	Archery
•		•	•	•		•	•	•	•	•	•				•	Athletics
		•		•		•			•		•				•	Badminton
•		•	•	•		•	•	•	•		•		•		•	Basketball
•		•	•	•		•	•	•	•	•	•		•		•	Canoeing
•		•	•	•		•	•		•	•	•				•	Chess
		•	•	•		•	•		•		•				•	Climbing
•		•	•				•		•	•	•			•	•	Cricket
•			•				•		•		•					Cross country
		•	•	•		•	•	•	•	•	•				•	Cycling
•		•	•	•		•	•		•		•				•	Fencing
•	•	•	•	•		•	•	•	•	•	•	•	•	•	•	Football
•		•	•	•		•	•		•		•				•	Golf
•		•	•	•		•			•		•				•	Hill-walking
•		•	•	•		•	•	•	•	•	•		•		•	Hockey
	•	•	•			•			•		•				•	Horse-riding
•		•	•	•		•	•		•	•	•				•	Judo
•				•		•	•		•		•				•	Karate
•	•	•	•	•		•	•	•	•	•	•		•		•	Netball
								•	•		•				•	Orienteering
•		•	•	•		•	•	•	•	•	•		•		•	Rugby
•		•	•	•		•	•		•	•	•				•	Sailing
•		•	•	•		•	•	•	•	•	•		•		•	Skiing
•		•	•	•		•	•	•	•	•	•		•		•	Squash
		•	•	•		•	•		•		•				•	Sub-aqua
•		•	•	•		•	•	•	•	•	•				•	Swimming
•		•													•	Tennis
		•	•	•			•		•		•				•	Tae Kwan Do
		•	•			•	•		•		•				•	Trampolining
•		•	•	•	•	•	•		•	•	•		•		•	Volleyball

Vital statistics 750

	SEX RATIO	YEAR FOUNDED	NUMBER OF UNDERGRADS	NUMBER OF PART TIME STUDENTS	NUMBER OF POSTGRADS
University of Aberdeen	**48:52**	**1495**	**7,866**	**568**	**1,163**
University of Abertay Dundee	49:51	1994	3,448	374	386
Aberystwyth	**50:50**	**1872**	**5,500**	**400**	**780**
Anglia Polytechnic University	39:61	1989	7,563	2,077	532
Aston University	**51:49**	**1966**	**4,751**	**0**	**589**
Bangor	46:54	1884	5,408	156	902
University of Bath	**59:41**	**1966**	**8,482**	**0**	**1,179**
Bath Spa	30:70	1983	2,552	48	519
University of Birmingham	**49:510**	**1900**	**13,254**	**208**	**3,500**
Bolton Institute	52:48	1982	3,033	1,406	417
Bournemouth University	**43:57**	**1976**	**6,471**	**480**	**632**
University of Bradford	47:53	1966	6,161	1,708	705
University of Brighton	**38:62**	**1976**	**8,791**	**935**	**752**
University of Bristol	50:50	1876	9,989	32	2,179
Bristol, W of E	**44:56**	**1969**	**13,390**	**1,583**	**1,155**
Brunel University	53:47	1966	8,534	1,142	1,306
University of Buckingham	**45:55**	**1974**	**458**	**60**	**140**
Buckinghamshire	43:57	1893	5,990	2,282	187
University of Cambridge	**54:47**	**1284**	**11,495**	**0**	**4,819**
Cardiff	46:54	1883	12,014	0	3,329
Central England	**44:56**	**1971**	**8,236**	**2,419**	**1071**
University of Central Lancashire	43:57	1828	10,722	2,081	450
Cheltenham & Gloucester CHE	**43:57**	**1990**	**5,362**	**1,119**	**389**
City University	47:53	1894	4,741	515	1,785
Courtauld Institute of Art	**25:75**	**1932**	**116**	**0**	**174**
Coventry University	55:45	1970	11,096	3,218	627
Cranfield	**70:30**	**1948**	**744**	**0**	**595**
De Montfort University	47:53	1909	13,715	1,750	1,325
University of Derby	**47:53**	**1851**	**8,567**	**2,369**	**223**
University of Dundee	41:59	1967	7,452	1,018	669
University of Durham	**50:50**	**1832**	**8,822**	**66**	**1,403**
University of East London	50:50	1970	8,000	1,700	2,800
University of Edinburgh	**46:54**	**1583**	**15,604**	**599**	**2,375**
University of Essex	52:48	1964	4,600	0	1,395
University of Exeter	**52:48**	**1964**	**4,600**	**0**	**1,395**
University of Glamorgan	50:50	1913	19,915	5,501	632
Glasgow University	**44:56**	**1451**	**14,820**	**3,023**	**1,813**
Glasgow Caledonian University	60:40	1971	14,836	2,883	849
Goldsmiths College	**34:66**	**1891**	**4,074**	**1,021**	**1,095**
University of Greenwich	49:51	1890	7,999	1,727	1,160

751 Vital statistics

% IN VIA CLEARING	% OF MATURE STUDENTS	% OF OVERSEAS STUDENTS	AVERAGE COST OF ACCOMMODATION PER WEEK	% IN COLLEGE ACCOMMODATION	BOOZE INDEX	% OF GRADS UNEMPLOYED AFTER 6 MONTHS
10	19	14	£47.15	35	£1.75	4
5	35	10	£43.27	21	£1.80	2.3
19	12	8	£43.35	56	£1.45	5.8
24	40	16	£54.20	30	£1.68	5.4
9	8	5	£45.60	45	£1.67	3
13	16	7	£40.66	44	£1.85	5.6
2	10	13	£47.11	42	£1.82	3.2
n/a	43	5	£50.21	22	£1.78	10
1	11	10	£45.48	37	£1.62	3.6
10	72	15	£39.84	23	£1.63	36
15	22	7	£55.70	14	£1.67	18
20	20	17	£35.85	30	£1.55	6
5	27	18	£49.19	17	£1.63	6
1	10	15	£49.38	25	£1.75	3
12	15	7	£49.85	15	£1.90	5.5
24	23	7	£56.28	31	£1.97	4
n/a	33	74	£66.08	87	£1.19	17
19	48	10	£57.40	20	£1.86	8
n/a	6	11	£45.50	95	£1.34	4
2	12	17	£44.43	35	£1.62	5
10	30	12	£45.64	26	£1.61	6
20	45	7	£38.45	14	£1.52	5
13	40	31	£44.70	14	£1.90	6
18	43	26	£75.53	21	£2.23	3.9
4.5	14	9.5	£75.00	0	£2.35	n/a
n/a	37	17	£40.06	16	£1.77	16.0
1.5	23	10	£59.98	57	£1.64	0.0
27	25	7	£46.60	80	£1.49	4.0
20	40	5	£42.35	29	£1.60	10.0
10	32	8	£45.00	21	£1.80	2.0
10	11.5	10	£49.16	58	£1.47	6.0
n/a	80	19.5	£50.13	17.9	£1.96	11.0
5	13	10	£56.29	43	£1.92	4.2
15	20	32	£47.15	65	£1.33	3.0
15	20	32	£40.65	65	£1.49	3.0
13	37	10	£36.10	10	£1.66	7.2
2	11	8	£53.81	17	£1.70	5.0
n/a	38	n/a	£50.96	6.4	£1.72	10.5
13	55	15.9	£61.90	24	£1.65	5.0
38	40	16	£58.85	23	£2.13	14.0

stats

Vital statistics   752

	SEX RATIO	YEAR FOUNDED	NUMBER OF UNDERGRADS	NUMBER OF PART TIME STUDENTS	NUMBER OF POSTGRADS
Heriot-Watt University	**60:40**	**1966**	**4,494**	**133**	**843**
University of Hertfordshire	50:50	1952	13,000	3,000	2,900
Heythrop College	**60:40**	**1614**	**150**	**1**	**224**
University of Huddersfield	44:56	1841	7,764	4,140	936
University of Hull	**41:59**	**1927**	**6,695**	**513**	**1447**
Imperial College	67:33	1907	6,747	0	2,694
Keele University	**41:59**	**1949**	**4,600**	**250**	**747**
King's College, London	45:55	1965	6,306	196	997
King's College, London	**40:60**	**1829**	**10,846**	**1,400**	**2153**
Kingston University	49:51	1971	11,204	1,142	866
Lampeter	**50:50**	**1822**	**1000**	**300**	**80**
Lancaster University	50:50	1940	6,999	140	1,262
University of Leeds	**47:53**	**1887**	**15,666**	**683**	**3,185**
Leeds Metropolitan University	48:52	1970	10,812	3,665	796
University of Leicester	**52:48**	**1921**	**7051**	**62**	**1,389**
University of Lincs & Humbs	50:50	1983	6,386	1,307	148
University of Liverpool	**50:50**	**1881**	**10,946**	**3,771**	**1,952**
Liverpool John Moores	47:53	1970	13,188	4,294	631
London Guildhall University	**49:51**	**1970**	**7,712**	**462**	**482**
London Institute	31:69	1989	6337	491	503
Loughborough University	**62:38**	**1966**	**8,778**	**156**	**1,090**
LSE	54:46	1895	3,384	34	3,100
University of Luton	**40:60**	**1976**	**6,386**	**1,478**	**998**
University of Manchester	46:54	1851	16,836	809	3,762
Manchester Metropolitan	**41:59**	**1970**	**17111**	**2,268**	**1,168**
Middlesex University	40:60	1973	12,442	1,130	1028
Napier University	**48:52**	**1964**	**7,725**	**1,957**	**881**
University of Newcastle	51:49	1834	10,231	134	2,072
University of North London	**46:54**	**1896**	**8,778**	**2,743**	**1,213**
Northampton	40:60	1975	7,300	1,530	217
University of Northumbria	**41:59**	**1969**	**14,000**	**7,000**	**2,900**
University of Nottingham	45:55	1881	13,349	4,780	2,737
Nottingham Trent University	**51:49**	**1970**	**15,184**	**3,666**	**1,735**
University of Oxford	57:43	1,150	10,993	0	4,901
Oxford Brookes University	**43:57**	**1865**	**8000**	**2,160**	**3,200**
University of Paisley	45:55	1897	5,728	2,764	705
University of Plymouth	**46:54**	**1970**	**15,520**	**3,463**	**612**
University of Portmouth	56:44	1969	11,238	2,062	879
Queen Margaret College	**20:80**	**1875**	**2,588**	**733**	**42**
Queen Mary & Westfield College	50:50	1915	6,630	0	1045

753 Vital statistics

% IN VIA CLEARING	% OF MATURE STUDENTS	% OF OVERSEAS STUDENTS	AVERAGE COST OF ACCOMMODATION PER WEEK	% IN COLLEGE ACCOMMODATION	BOOZE INDEX	% OF GRADS UNEMPLOYED AFTER 6 MONTHS
7.7	15	17	£48.39	46	£1.75	5.6
15	55	10	£58.46	22	£1.93	5.2
15	20	6	£75.00	0	£2.35	n/a
16	30	5	£40.33	25	£1.65	4.9
13	25	8.3	£36.55	41	£1.52	3
4	n/a	34	£80.50	35	£2.04	2.7
10	6	7	£41.24	77	£1.48	5.4
n/a	19	25	£50.14	54	£1.63	2.7
13	30	14	£69.87	31	£2.03	4
n/a	33	11	£86.97	20	£1.89	3.6
7.2	49	9.7	£37.89	38	£1.44	9.6
10	12	14	£14.82	52	£1.50	6.3
4	n/a	7.2	£39.66	39	£0.98	4.5
22	7	4	£45.60	22	£1.12	8.2
9	9	9	£37.50	49	£1.56	6
25	40	11	£42.21	17	£1.57	11.8
5	13	17	£39.92	29	£1.50	5
13	29.25	7.5	£35.95	10	£1.58	6.1
28	59	13	£69.79	6	£1.74	9
5	65	35	£73.92	13	£2.22	12.5
5	7	9	£41.03	58	£1.56	4
n/a	13	54	£77.65	34	£2.01	7
30	45	18	£51.61	23	£1.67	1.6
n/a	22	12	£42.80	40	£1.32	3
n/a	18	6	£43.40	14	£1.37	5
n/a	441	20	£59.97	7	£1.77	19.4
n/a	33	10	£54.02	14	£2.11	6
12	11.7	14	£43.02	33	£1.67	2.9
36	53	25	£69.78	11	£2.23	12.1
20	20	3	£41.24	23	£1.92	5
33	53	14	£55.90	18	£1.77	4
3	21	7.7	£41.70	27	£1.85	3.7
14	22	6.4	£42.12	15	£2.01	1.3
n/a	6	32	£58.26	87	£1.34	3
12.5	45.2	20.4	£57.60	30	£2.03	2.3
21	26	4.5	£39.20	15	£1.65	12
18.3	42.7	8.6	£48.15	14	£1.71	6.3
8	25	6	£43.62	18	£1.60	7
16	49	8	£53.00	20	£2.04	5.9
n/a	18	20	£77.01	33	£1.99	4

Vital statistics 754

	SEX RATIO	YEAR FOUNDED	NUMBER OF UNDERGRADS	NUMBER OF PART TIME STUDENTS	NUMBER OF POSTGRADS
Queen's University, Belfast	45:55	1845	9,862	1,402	1,952
University of Reading	47:53	1892	7,615	3,475	5,222
Robert Gordon University	50:50	1881	5,451	771	734
Royal Academy of Music	45:55	1822	334	0	262
Royal College of Music	44:56	1882	380	0	172
Royal Holloway	50:50	1886	4,297	51	1,046
Royal Veterinary College	70:30	1791	674	0	106
University of Salford	49:51	1967	11,384	3,257	967
School of Pharmacy	40:60	1842	550	0	85
University of Sheffield	50:50	1905	13,242	2,703	2,513
Sheffield Hallam	55:45	1969	15,510	2,849	4,693
SOAS	50:50	1916	1,460	0	1,500
South Bank University	49:51	1970	8,600	1,200	1,000
University of Southampton	50:50	1952	12,803	869	2,290
Southampton Institute	58:42	1984	7,930	420	288
University of St Andrews	48:52	1,410	4,965	54	104
St George's Hospital	48:52	1,751	1,275	0	50
Staffordshire University	52:48	1970	9,787	5,192	1,784
University of Stirling	42:58	1967	5,538	849	723
University of Strathclyde	48:52	1796	10,9000	250	2,400
University of Sunderland	49:51	1860	8,141	1,624	866
University of Surrey	34:66	1966	5,324	62	0
Surrey Institute	40:60	1969	2,375	95	16
University of Sussex	44:56	1961	6,796	125	1,380
Swansea	42:58	1920	6,200	375	1,190
University of Teesside	42:58	1930	6,689	922	363
Thames Valley University	65:35	1992	3,859	1,755	415
UEA	45:55	1963	8,635	4,097	2,181
University of Ulster	41:59	1968	10,668	3,307	1,394
UMIST	69:31	1824	5,093	0	1,679
University College, London	48:52	1826	10,694	203	4,060
Wales College of Medicine	30:70	1931	1,394	177	177
University of Warwick	52:48	1965	8,555	305	5,100
University of Westminster	46:54	1838	8,990	2,502	1,565
University of Wolverhampton	44:56	1983	14,211	8,789	819
University of York	49:51	1963	5,702	1,021	1,392
UK Averages	47:53	n/a	7890	1362	1,353

755 Vital statistics

% IN VIA CLEARING	% OF MATURE STUDENTS	% OF OVERSEAS STUDENTS	AVERAGE COST OF ACCOMMODATION PER WEEK	% IN COLLEGE ACCOMMODATION	BOOZE INDEX	% OF GRADS UNEMPLOYED AFTER 6 MONTHS
3	9	8	£42.00	20	£1.80	3.5
15	n/a	18.4	£50.80	42	£1.84	11
15	32	11	£59.40	15	£1.74	1.5
0	5	43	£65.00	0	£2.35	n/a
0	37	33	£85.00	0	£1.95	n/a
14	10	28	£74.12	44	£1.67	54.9
0	14	17	£60.00	17	£2.06	n/a
10	27	10	£38.00	24	£1.55	5
1	23	20	£90.00	0	£2.35	n/a
n/a	20	16	£43.85	35	£1.72	6.4
25	60	7.9	£43.14	20	£1.56	7
0	45	40	£57.75	23	£2.01	7
30	38	20	£71.80	16	£2.17	15
5	21	8	£51.72§	14	£1.49	7.6
18	46	9	£64.20	29	£1.54	5
20	11	19	£43.42	55	£1.57	3.4
20	10	12	£57.00	25	£2.01	n/a
5.7	29	2.6	£36.83	15	£1.53	7.2
10	13	3	£51.30	70	£1.43	5.3
10	10	6	£49.66	23	£1.76	3
18	33	11	£39.38	28	£1.54	5
12.5	17	17	£56.60	60	£2.01	1.4
5	27	14	£54.20	16	£1.85	18
9	26	21.8	£53.26	41	£1.52	3.4
19	11	8	£48.14	44	£1.33	2.7
18	32	6	£35.44	11	£1.95	7.7
19	81	8	£70.00	0	£2.35	10
14	31	9	£40.00	35	£1.81	5
14	75	N/A	£29.72	12	£1.97	9
5	19	21	£44.00	50	£1.45	3
5	13	21	£75.00	32	£2.17	3
n/a	16	10	£42.90	11	£1.62	n/a
2.1	10	20	£40.58	40	£1.55	3
30	40	16	£74.34	12	£2.22	8
4	60	15	£36.80	18	£1.64	5.3
5	14	10	£46.43	59	£1.63	6
12.7	28.3	14.7	£51.51	29.7	£1.74	6.9

stats

Top ten

Cheapest Campus Pint
Bristol
Leeds
Leicester
Manchester Metropolitan University
St Hilda's College, Oxford
Central Lancashire
Emmanuel College, Cambridge
Queen's College, Oxford
Bolton Institute of Higher Education
Buckingham

Cheapest college accommodation
St Andrews
Paisley
Ulster
Abertay Dundee
Lampeter
Salford
University of Wales College of Medicine
Hull
Newcastle
Teeside

Lowest external rent
Ulster
Keele University
Bradford
Glamorgan
Hull
Leicester
Liverpool John Moores University
Teeside
Wolverhampton
Central Lancashire

Highest male sex ratio
Cranfield
Royal Veternary
UMIST
Imperial
Thames Valley
Loughborough
Glasgow Caledonian
Heythrop
Heriot-Watt
Southampton Institute

Highest female sex ratio
Queen Margaret
Courtauld
Bath Spa
University of Wales College of Medicine
London Institute
Goldsmiths
Surrey
Brighton
Northampton
Surrey Institute

757 Top ten

TOP 10 — Lowest unemployment after 6 months
- Nottingham Trent
- Surrey
- Robert Gordon
- Luton Dundee
- Oxford Brookes
- Abertay Dundee
- Imperial
- Swansea
- Bristol

TOP 10 — Highest proportion living in
- Cambridge
- Oxford
- Buckingham
- De Montfort
- Keele
- Stirling
- Exeter
- Essex
- Surrey
- Loughborough

TOP 10 — Best at student sport
- Loughborough
- Bath
- University of Wales Institute
- Exeter
- Birmingham
- Bristol
- Northumbria
- Durham
- Brunel
- Oxford

TOP 10 — Highest proportion living out
- Guildhall
- Glasgow Caledonian
- Middlesex
- Liverpool John Moores
- Glamorgan
- Teesside
- North London
- University of Wales College of Medicine
- Westminster
- Ulster

TOP 10 — Most politically active
- Keele
- SOAS
- Lampeter
- Oxford
- Cambridge
- Lincolnshire & Humberside
- Bath
- Nottingham Trent
- Glasgow
- Nottingham

TOP 10 — Highest % of female students
- Queen Margaret
- Wales college of medicine
- UEA
- Northampton
- Northumbria
- Ulster
- North London
- Nottingham
- Queen's
- Paisley

Glossary

In the world of higher education, there's a whole language of weird words and interminable terminology. Ever true to our no nonsense, cut-the-brown-smelly-stuff approach, The push Guide takes you on a ramble through the jargon jungle, explaining all the terms to help anyone pass themselves off as a student. We've even highlighted some of the more confusing course terms that don't tend to crop up in pre-university education – they're the ones in italics.

A Levels: Duh. A Levels are the exams most students take at the end of school or college (further education) in England and Wales. Usually students heading for university take three or four A levels and, unless there are other circumstances, finding a place will be tough with fewer than that. Those other circumstances might well include having other qualifications such as Highers in Scotland, others such as International Baccalaureate in other countries or some of the new qualifications such as vocational A levels and AS levels.

Accountancy/Accounting: Not a professional qualification, just a background course giving prospective accountants the necessary insight into finance, investment, tax, management and business. These courses do not, however, give you a life.

Admissions: The admissions office of any university or college handles the applications and enrolments, the 'admissions' if you will. That's the department to ask for when you phone up to talk about getting in.

Alumni: 'Old boys' and 'old girls', but they're not called that in case they don't give the university any money after they've left. Singular: alumnus. Feminine singular: alumna. Feminine plural: alumnae. Neuter ablative plural: go ask a Latin student.

American Studies: Often dismissed as a doss subject (eg 'you just watch films and listen to old jazz records') this is a multi-disciplinary subject, covering the culture (?), history and current affairs of the US. Usually includes a period spent in the States – a big draw for people who like Oreo cookies, country music and drive-by shootings.

Archaeology: You might think 3 years risking the wrath of disturbed Egyptian mummies is a cool way to spend a degree course, but archaeology courses are more 'Time Team' than 'Indiana Jones', using a combination of history, science, languages and other disciplines, as well as practical fieldwork.

Architecture: Architecture requires a combination of technical knowledge of forms and structures (sciencey) with creative and aesthetic talents (arty), as well as history, economics, environmental studies and upsetting Prince Charles.

Art(s): Arts subjects include pretty much anything creative. You know, painting, drama, music and all that. It often overlaps with humanities.

Athletics Union/Sports Union: The student organisation that runs student sports clubs and sometimes sports facilities. They're usually hot-beds of sexism, alcohol abuse and hairy chests... and that's just the women.

Awards: Most students get awards, but unfortunately there's no big Oscars-style ceremony because these awards are basically the new version of what used to be called grants. Students get awards from their local education authority or equivalent to pay towards their university tuition costs.

Bachelor: of... Arts, Science, Education, Engineering, etc. At English and Welsh universities, this is the degree most undergraduate students are heading for. When you get it, you can put BA, BSc, BEd, BEng or whatever else is appropriate at the end of your name, but if you feel you have to boast about it like that, most people will think you're a nob.

Balls: Big black-tie and posh frock parties. Why? What did you think I'd say? Many student balls include not only a slap-up dinner and much drinking, but also bands (often including quite big has-been names), discos, casinos, fun fairs, cabaret acts, fortune-tellers, snogging and vomiting. Hardy ball-goers often party all night and occasionally the event is rounded off with a champagne breakfast and 'survivors' photo' (not a pretty site).

Bops: A dance night more in the school disco style than a hardcore club night.

Botany: The plant bit of Biology.

Business Studies: The study of business, obviously (doh!), but it also includes maths and economics and, less predictably, bits of psychology and sociology. And what with Europe and all that stuff, languages are becoming increasingly unavoidable.

Campaign for Free Education: Unlike the NUS, whose policy commits them to trying to get rid of tuition fees (but in practice, they've accepted it now), these guys still campaign to get grants restored.

Campus: The area of land on which a collection of college buildings are built. So, a campus university is one built entirely or mainly on a single campus. A civic campus is a campus in a town. And a greenfield campus is not. Just to confuse things, some universities use 'campus' as a synonym for 'site' and vice versa, so it could mean anything from a single building to an almost entirely separate college.

Court: The Cambridge term for a quad.

Chaplain: Chaplains hang around universities offering religious guidance and support to those who want it. They usually come in a variety of religious flavours.

Clearing: Each year after the A levels are published, many students find they haven't got the place they wanted and many universities find they haven't filled their courses. Having participated in a sophisticated applications and admissions process up to then, the unis and students throw caution to the wind and try to shove square pegs into round holes. Clearing tends not to result in the best possible matches.

College: A vague word that could mean (a) a sixth form college where students do A levels, (b) a semi-self-contained unit in a collegiate university, (c) an institution of higher education that isn't allowed to call itself a university or (d) any university, college of higher education, its buildings and/or its administrative authorites.

Combined honours: An undergraduate degree course that involves several subject areas – usually three – in approximately equal parts (to start with at any rate).

Degree: A higher education qualification of a certain level. They split into undergraduate degrees or first degrees which are usually Bachelorships and various postgraduate degrees (masters, doctorates, PGCEs and so on). A university isn't a university if it doesn't teach degrees although some do other higher education qualifications too like Higher National Diplomas (HNDs).

Department: Most universities break down different subject areas into departments and students 'belong' to whatever department teaches their course. It gets more complicated if they study more than one subject, because they may end up in several departments. Some universities don't have departments, they have schools or faculties instead (or even as well), but they're basically the same thing.

Dons: Dons are Mafia bosses, but in the context of universities, particularly Oxbridge, they're more likely to be lecturers, tutors or other academics who do teaching.

Economics: Economists will tell you that their subject is 'the study of the allocation of scarce resources'. In fact, they mean it's about the way money changes hands, affecting society (and managing never to reach you and me).

Education: A Bachelor of Education degree trains teachers to teach, within a specialised field at any rate (usually determined by age group, academic subject, or both). Some take a 'normal' first degree (BA, BSc, etc) instead and study for a further year to get a Postgraduate Certificate of Education (PGCE). Either way, after four years of being a student, they know how to work for low pay and look moth-eaten.

Engineering: Engineering is the study of how to create things that make people's lives easier/healthier/safer/better. There are sub-divisions such as: Chemical Engineering (studying how materials change); Civil Engineering (transport, sewage, public buildings, etc); Electrical Engineering and so on. Engineers usually work phenomenally hard, play 'Quake' for hours, and tell you that their subject is 'really interesting, actually'.

Ents: Short for entertainments, which are usually run by the students' union and include such larks as gigs, hypnotists and, if you're unlucky, karaoke.

Environmental Studies: A relatively new discipline that takes bits of biology, chemistry, geology and social sciences and investigates how environmental problems occur, how to prevent them and how to chain yourself to a bulldozer.

European Studies: French, Spanish and Italian aren't just languages, nowadays there are courses which combine learning how to talk with learning something to talk about. A French course might include bits about French culture, business, law, history and David Ginola's diving techniques.

Faculty: Old lectures never die, they just lose their faculties. Universities are usually divided into departments (se above). Just in case these <u>departments</u> feel lonely, they're allowed to club together into faculties. So, the physicists join their chemistry and biology chums in a Science Faculty and the musicians get together with the drama luvvies in an Arts Faculty and everybody's happy. Except the lawyers, who usually have a Faculty on their own. Maybe they smell.

Finals/Finalists: Finals are the exams in the final year of study that decide whether or not the last 3 or 4 years have been worth living in abject poverty for. Hence, finalists are students in their final year with their heads on the exam block.

Flunking: To flunk is to drop out of university or fail. Hence the proportion of students who do it is the flunk rate.

Formals: Posh universities and colleges sometimes have formal dinners where students are supposed to dress up sometimes in black tie, sometimes in suits or sometimes in gowns over their combats and T-shirts. Such formals may be compulsory or voluntary or they may be so popular that students have to sign up to attend (especially if the formals followed by <u>ents</u> of some sort). Some places have formals every night, some have them only once a term.

Freshers: Freshers are first year students in their first few weeks – when the pace is faster than curry through a dog with diarrhoea and the main topics of conversation are home towns, <u>A level</u> grades and <u>UCAS</u> codes. During students' time as freshers, they are likely to spend 99% of their student loan, join student clubs whose events they never attend and get stupidly drunk most nights. After 3 weeks of this, they are hungover, broke and wiser – ie. fully-fledged students.

Freshers' Week: Also known as Week One, Orientation Week, <u>Intro Week</u> and 'Cyril' for all I know, this is the first week of the first term of the first year of a student's university career. It's packed with events and ents designed to help students settle in, make friends and to tell them everything they need to know about how the university and students' union work. In the process, they tend to both drink and spend too much, but have a damn good time. See also <u>Freshers</u> above.

Further education (FE): Further education is what comes after primary and secondary education. In other words it's usually what 16 to 18 year-olds do. In yet other words, it's <u>A levels</u>, <u>Highers</u> and the like. And in other, other, other words, it's what you have to do to be qualified to go on to higher education (universities and the like).

Gap year: Many students decide to take a year off – or a gap year – after school or college and before going to university. This is best not spent in front of the TV, but getting work experience, earning money, travelling or doing something exciting or mind-expanding. Or a mixture of all of the above.

Geology: Geologists study the structure of the earth and the rocks, fossils, minerals and all the general gunk that's in it.

Graduand: A student in the few months between finishing their course and being awarded their degree. It's from the Latin – the gerundive case or something.

Graduate: Someone who's successfully completed a degree. A graduate student is a glutton for punishment who's embarking on another degree, usually a postgraduate degree.

Grants: Once upon a time, students used to get grants which paid for their tuition and grants which paid towards their living costs. They still exist in Scotland for Scottish students only, but otherwise they are the stuff of myth and legend. Now students get far less generous 'awards'.

Guild of Students/Students' Guild: Another name for a students' union.

Hack: Not the sound of a bad cough or a lozenge to cure it, but a person who is utterly committed to their extra-curricular activities. Usually refers to those involved in SUs or student journalism. You can tell a hack because they are the ones claiming everyone else is apathetic.

Halls: At most colleges, when students talk about halls, they mean 'halls of residence', the accommodation blocks, which traditionally provide catered meals (but increasingly are becoming self-catered), cleaners, heat, light and electricity and a variety of amenities such as launderettes, common rooms and TV lounges. Oxbridge, of course, has to be different. At Oxford or Cambridge, halls are the formal dining rooms.

Head tenancy scheme: Rather than handing out cardboard boxes or have students cluttering up the gym floor, some colleges have started to do the house-hunting themselves. They get a group of landlords together, rent all their brick boxes that pretend to be homes and then sublet them to students, often at cheaper rates or on better terms.

Higher education (HE): After primary school, there's secondary school, then further education and, finally, higher education which takes place at universities, colleges of higher education and so on. HE includes undergraduate and postgraduate degrees, higher national diplomas (HNDs) and a few other things like certain vocational qualifications (such as LLBs for lawyers, for instance).

Highers: In Scotland, instead of A levels, students take Highers.

Honours degree: When people boast about having an *honours* degree, don't be too impressed. Most degrees are honours degrees. If a student does badly, but not quite badly enough to fail, that's when they might not get an honours degree, but an ordinary degree instead.

Humanities: The study of human creative endeavour, whether it's literature, art, music or whatever. It's arguable whether Richard & Judy counts, though. Humanities aren't quite the same as actually doing the creative bit, ie The Arts (which includes almost anything likely to get Lottery funding).

Intro Week: Another name for Freshers' Week.

Jobshop: A student employment agency usually run the students' union. Apart from advertising vacancies, jobshops are sometime more proactive and actually look for appropriate paid work for students. They also sometimes check that the employer's not a crooked slave-driver and impose minimum pay and conditions. Unlike most job agencies, they usually don't take a cut and often students get work in the jobshop or students' union itself.

Joint Honours: Not an honours degree in cooking big roasts or rolling spliffs, but, like a combined honours degree a course involving more then one subject. In this case, two subjects.

Junior Common Room (JCR): Another name for a students' union, but usually quite a modest affair such as in a Oxbridge college of a hall of residence. It's also usually a real common room too for undergrad students.

Law: An LLB course will not qualify a student to don a silly wig and act like Kavanagh QC. In theory, it teaches the workings of the legal system (usually the English one) and how laws are applied. It also includes the skills and methods that the legal profession requires (eg cross-examination). To actually become a barrister or solicitor requires further study at Bar or Law School.

Learning Resources Centre (LRC): In the old days (when there were Tories in Scotland) universities used to have libraries (which had books in them) and computer rooms (which had computers). Now they're just as likely to have LRCs which are vast buildings with books and computers.

Lecture: Someone once defined a lecture as the process of transferring words from the notes of the lecturer to the student without passing through the brain of either. Lectures are one of the main teaching mechanisms of universities. They tend to be larger than a regular school class and less interactive. (Seminars are closer to school classes.) Usually attendance is not compulsory, but missing them isn't likely to help your studies.

Lecturer: Apart from the obvious – ie. someone who gives a lecture – lecturers are academics at a certain level in the hierarchy well above postgraduates but below professors and deans.

Mature students: It is not necessarily true that mature students behave any more maturely than conventional ones. Nor are they necessarily old fogeys - some are as young as 21 - but, generally, they are older than most other students and are probably returning to education rather than being fresh out of school. (Having a year out counts as being fresh, having 10 years out living in a brothel doesn't.)

Means-testing: Local Education Authorities assess how much money students have at their disposal before handing out any money for their tuition fees. Similarly student loans are based on a means test. However it may seem, they're not called that because they're trying to see how mean they can be.

Media Studies: A heavily over-subscribed course, often by students who think (i) it'll get them straight into the BBC or Hollywood or (ii) it's a doss course. Both are wrong. Media courses usually cover practical and theoretical training in all areas of mass communication and while the experience and contacts might give students an edge in pursuit of a glittering career full of men with pony-tails, unfortunately, life-membership of the Groucho Club is not automatic and there are many other routes to media infamy.

Middle Common Room (MCR): Like a Junior Common Room, but for postgrads only.

Modular courses: A sort of pick'n'mix course comprising a number of components (modules), either within just one department or across a range of subjects.

Nightline: All students have times when the skin on the cup of cocoa of life is just a bit too thick and Nightline services, available in most colleges worth their salt, are there for those times. They are telephone counselling services, a bit like the Samaritans, run (usually) by students for students.

Non-completion/non-progression rate: A politer term for what we at *Push* call the flunk rate.

NUS: The National Union of Students, run by students who never grew up, provides research, welfare information and services to SUs which are affiliated. NUS is also the national body which represents and campaigns on behalf of students.

Open days: An opportunity for prospective students to be shown around the university. Beware only being shown the good parts and take the opportunity to talk to the inmates, er, students.

Ordinary degree: An 'ordinary degree' is somewhat less than ordinary, because most students get an honours degree. You only get an ordinary degree if either you decide to aim lower for some reasons or you fail an honours degree, but don't fail so badly you get nothing.

Oxbridge: The collective name for the two oldest universities in the country, Oxford and Cambridge, both collegiate, both traditional, both highly respected (not least by themselves). It's strange that Camford never caught on.

Personal Tutors/Moral Tutors: At many, if not most, universities, students are assigned to a personal tutor who is charged with responsibilities beyond the purely academic. The extent of their remit and of their usefulness varies enormously. Some have regular meetings to discuss everything from exams to sex, others introduce themselves to their tutees at the beginning of their college career with some Le Piat D'Or and limp cheese and don't see them again till graduation day. Sometimes they're called moral tutors, but expecting academics to give moral guidance is like asking a fish to run a marathon.

Philosophy: 'What is philosophy?' is a philosophical question, but, ever ready to ponder the even the deepest mysteries, Push's definition is that it's about asking the complex questions behind other subjects. Without necessarily expecting an answer. So, when philosophers ask 'Does God exist?', they're more interested in the ideas and argument involved, than His fax number (for that you want theology).

PGCE: A Postgraduate Certificate in Education is a one-year postgraduate course that graduates can take and which qualifies them to become teachers. At the moment, most students get six grand just for doing the course and might get their student loan paid off too if they go on to become a teacher in a subject where there's a shortage. A PGCE's not the only way to become a teacher – you can also do a four-year Bachelor of Education undergrad degree.

Politics: Of course, nobody with the intelligence and decency to read The Push Guide would want to become anything as vile as a politician, but you might wish to study how these creatures operate. Politics (aka Political Studies, Government, etc) uses elements of history, economics, statistics and more to investigate how people govern themselves and each other and whether Gordon Brown will ever smile.

Polytechnic: Once upon a time there was something called 'the binary divide' which distinguished between universities and polytechnics. It never meant much anyway and now it means nothing at all. Polytechnics tended to have a slant towards vocational courses and an often unfair reputation for lower academic standards than universities. Now they've all become universities themselves, but the old poly prejudices seem to linger about like last week's dirty socks, again somewhat unfairly.

Postgraduate/postgrad: A student doing a postgraduate degree, ie. they've already got one degree and now they're doing another higher one such as a masters degree, a doctorate (PhD) or a postgraduate certificate in education (PGCE).

Practical: A form of teaching, or probably more accurately, of learning, usually used in sciencey type subjects. It involves doing experiments and the like.

Professor: A big cheese in an academic department – often the head – but, at any rate, someone who has climbed the brain hierarchy.

Psychology: If, at university, you ever get pestered by students wielding clipboards and asking intimate questions about sexuality and your favourite colour, chances are they're either chatting you up or they're psychologists (or both). Psychology is the study of the way people think and behave, using elements of biology, sociology, maths and other disciplines. And sometimes they experiment on rats.

Quad: A square surrounded by buildings, usually covered in grass and commonly found in Oxbridge colleges. Only at Cambridge they call them courts, just to be difficult.

Rag: Rag is an excuse to dress up in stupid clothing and get up to wacky, irresponsible and often illegal antics – and all in the name of charity. Collectively, student charity Rags raise millions of pounds with stunts like parachute jumps, sponsored hitch-hikes and so-called Rag raids where students (usually dressed as rabbits, Spice Girls, characters from Rocky Horror, etc) accost strangers in the street and try to sell them 'Rag magazines'. Rag mags are tackily printed joke books, which usually fulfil one of two conditions: either, they are not very funny, or they're in appalling bad taste, or both.

Redbrick: A redbrick building or campus does not necessarily have to have a single red brick. Instead, it refers to a style of building, or a period from around the turn of the century through to the Second World War. What redbrick means is not very precise, but what it doesn't mean is easier to explain. A campus is described as redbrick if it isn't an Oxbridge rip-off or a modern concrete monstrosity.

Sabbatical: Every year at most colleges, a few students either take a year off their studies or hang around after them because they've got nothing better to do. In the meantime they are employed (sub-peanut wages) by various student bodies, such as SUs, Rags, newspapers, athletics unions and so on. Not just anyone can do this though – they almost always have to be elected by the other students, who then spend the rest of the sabbatical's year of office wondering why they ever voted for them. Just like real politics.

Sandwich course: Not a catering course (although, come to think of it, you could do a sandwich course in catering), but a course that involves vocational experience. So, the bread in a sandwich course is academic study and the filling is a work placement usually in business or industry. Usually it takes a year to fill a sandwich (as a result, most last 4 years), but there are thin and thick versions that involve different amounts of filling dispersed between different thicknesses of bread. Push eagerly awaits the introduction of toasted and club sandwich courses.

Semester: A semester is the American word for a term and is used in this country to describe American-style college terms that are longer (usually about 15 weeks) than British ones (between 8 and 11 weeks). Generally speaking, universities have either 2 semesters or 3 terms.

Seminar: A teaching class, overseen by a lecturer, in which anything from half a dozen to about 35 student discuss and maybe even do exercises. Sound familiar?

Senior Common Room (SCR): Like a Junior or Middle Common Room, but this is for the fully qualified academics and the emphasis is exclusively on the room itself and a few clubby activities rather than any kind of students' union or representative role.

Single honours: An undergraduate degree involving one main subject.

Social science: A social science is any subject which uses scientific methods to study human society, rather than the natural world. Originally regarded as a soft option, some social scientists can now earn big wads by going on the telly and talking lots.

Sociology: The study of how people operate within social groups (eg families, schools, football crowds). Sociologists have to use a variety of skills, such as dealing with data and statistics. Sociology still has an undeserved reputation as a dumping ground for left-wing under-achievers, but it's as intellectually rigorous (and attractive to employers) as any other social science subject.

Socs: Short for 'societies', these are the student clubs which range from serious political battlegrounds to sporting teams, from cultural groups to seriously silly socs, such as the Rolf Harris Appreciation Club and Up Shit Creek Without A Paddle Soc - both genuine.

Students' Association (SA): Just another name for a students' union really. Common in Scotland.

Students' Union (SU): Almost all colleges have a students' union and students are usually automatically members, though they can opt out if they wish. As a rule, an SU is usually a services and representative organisation run by students for students or the building in which such services are housed.
Students' Representative Council/Committee (SRC): Yet another name for a students' union or part of one, especially the part that focuses on representation.

SU: A students' union.

Subsidiary course: A course that acts as a side dish to the main course usually in a single honours course.

Tariff: The list of points you score for each of your further education qualifications. Collect enough points and you might have enough to get into a particular degree at a particular university. As it happens, the tariff is almost complete fiction because most universities only really take traditional A levels and Highers seriously.

Theology: The study of God, gods and religion. Often largely Christian-based, theology tends to attract Bible-bashers, ardent atheists and little in between.

Thesp: An arty-farty acting type.

Town/Gown: An expression which describes the juxtaposition of the local populace with the student and academic staff community. This is why people say 'town/gown', even though students these days are more at home in a Manics T-shirt and a pair of scuffed Vans than a gown and mortar board. Come Graduation Day, though, students are geared up in 'subfusc', as the outfit is called, and photos are taken of them. Embarrassment guaranteed.

Tutee: A student whose work (and/or well-being) is overseen by a particular tutor. It's pronounced more like 'chew tea' than like 'tutty'.

Tutor: An academic who oversees or supervises the work of individual students (tutees).

Tutorial: A small group of students – definitely no more then five otherwise it's a seminar whatever they claim – who meet up with a tutor and discuss their studies. If they're lucky, students get one-to-one tutorials which are a great opportunity to discuss individual ideas, thoughts and problems with work.

UCAS: The Universities & Colleges Admissions Service is the organisation that handles most university applications. Prospective students fill out a UCAS Form, send it to UCAS who send it to the universities the student wants to apply to. Various complications ensue, but eventually the student either gets accepted or not and UCAS oversees the process to check no one finds themselves with more than one place and to try to match students with vacancies as efficiently as possible.

Undergraduate: A student doing their first degree.

Union: Usually this is just another name for a students' union or the building in which the students' union and/or it's facilities and services are based. As such, it's often the students' main hang-out on campus. However, at Oxbridge (and various other universities that just have to be awkward), the Union might also be the Union Society, a bunch of mass debaters, er, I mean a debating club with some highly exclusive (even elitist) facilities attached.

University: Not nearly as easy to define as you might have thought, although officially a UK university has to be founded by Parliamentary Statute. There are plenty of places like certain university colleges and places like King's College London (and other colleges of London University) that deserve the name as much as many of the places that have it. The long and the short of it is that a university is a place to get a higher education.

University College: Officially, a college that has the power to award its own degrees, but isn't a fully-fledged university, or a college run by a fully-fledged university. HE Colleges which are independent, but whose degrees are rubber-stamped by a University, aren't allowed to use the 'University' bit, but to the student on the ground they're pretty much the same thing.

Vice-Chancellor: Aka principals, wardens, masters etc. These are the big cheeses - the Stilton amongst the Dairyleas of academia. Students rarely get to meet them, but basically they run the place. Where there are vice-chancellors, there are also chancellors, who are the token heads of the institutions but usually don't do much more than shake students' hands at the graduation ceremony. The allegations that vice-chancellors have anything to do with vice are entirely unfounded.

Vocational course: Any course that is intended at least to train students for a particular profession, career or job. They often involve practical experience in a work environment, such as placements, or doing projects similar to what goes on in real world jobs.

Women's Studies (aka Gender Studies): A multi-disciplinary subject that studies how women (and men) are treated in fields as diverse as law, history and health and the reasons for gender differences in behaviour, communication, pay and more. Oh, and men are allowed to apply.

Zoology: The animal bit of biology.

Abbreviations

The abbreviations used in *Push*:

AU:	Athletics Union
BUNAC:	British Universities North America Club
BUSA:	British Universities Sports Association
cap:	capacity
CDL:	Career Development Loan
CofE:	Church of England
CofS:	Church of Scotland
CVCP:	The Committee of Vice-Chancellors & Principals
DfEE:	Department for Education and Employment
ents:	entertainments
HND:	Higher National Diploma
HE:	higher education (ie degree/HND-level or above)
HESA:	Higher Education Statistics Agency
JCR:	Junior Common/Combination Room (usually Oxbridge)
LEA:	Local Education Authority
LGB:	Lesbian, Gay, Bisexual
LRC:	Learning Resources Centre
NHS:	National Health Service
NUS:	The National Union of Students
Poly:	Polytechnic
Postgrads:	postgraduates
RC:	Roman Catholic
SA:	Students' Association (usually Scottish)
sabb:	sabbatical officer
SCR:	Senior Common Room
SNP:	Scottish Nationalist Party
soc:	society or club
SRC:	Student Representative Council
SU:	Students' Union
SWSS:	Socialist Workers' Student Society
u'grads:	undergraduates
UCAS:	The Universities and Colleges Admissions Service
URC:	United Reform Church
USI:	Union of Students in Ireland

Pushing on

Where to go from here. A guide to useful publications, websites and other resources.

GENERAL
Push Online (www.push.co.uk) has loads of information for anyone thinking about going to university, links to university and college websites (plus a fair few student unions and student papers) and is just generally fab (though we probably would say that).
The Push Guide to Choosing a University,
  TSO, £7.99, ISBN 0117028347.
Everything you Need to Know About Going to University,
  Sally Longson, Kogan Page, £8.99.
Student Life: A Survival Guide,
  Natasha Roe, Student Helpbook Series, £8.99
The Complete Parent's Guide to Higher Education,
  Trotman/UCAS, £8.99. A condensed version is available free from UCAS.
The Sixthformer's Guide to Visiting Universities and Colleges,
  ISCO Publications, £5.95.
"The Times" Good University Guide 2002,
  John O'Leary, £9.99.
NatWest Student Book 2002.
www.nusonline.co.uk – the site of the National Union of Students'.
www.studentmagazine.com – a good lifestyle magazine site with articles including relationships, sex, drugs, housing and money.
www.studentuk.com – another useful lifestyle site.

TAKING A YEAR OFF/TRAVELLING
Taking a Year Off, Val Butcher, Trotman, £9.99.
The Gap Year Guide Book, Peridot Press, £9.95.
Taking a Gap Year, Susan Griffith, £11.95.
Planning your Gap Year, Mark Hempshall, How To Books, £9.99.
The Gap-Year Guidebook, www.gap-year.com, £9.95.
Work your Way around the World, Susan Griffith, £12.95.
Working Holidays Abroad, Mark Hempshall, Trotman, £9.99.
The Virgin Student Travellers' Handbook, Tom Griffiths, Virgin, £12.99.
Let's Go Guides.
Lonely Planet Guides. Website: www.lonelyplanet.com
Rough Guides. Many of their guide books are reproduced on their website (www.roughguides.co.uk).
www.gap-year.com
Opportunities in the Gap Year (ISCO).
A year off... a year on? Doe, T.Evans, H. £8.50 ISBN: 1902876016. Ideas on what to do, where to go and how to use your time constructively.
Working Holidays (Central Bureau of Educational Visits and Exchanges); if you can't find a copy in your local library contact the Bureau on 020 7389 4004.
UCAS can provide a free booklet called **'A Year Out'**.
The Year in Industry scheme – Contact: National Director, University of Manchester, Simon Building, Oxford Road, Manchester M13 9PL. Tel: 0161 275 4396. Email: enquiries@yini.org.uk, or visit their website for an online application form: www.yini.org.uk
Visit www.yearoutgroup.org/organisations.htm for a full list, including:
Academic Year in the USA and Europe: cultural exchange and study

abroad in USA, France, Germany, Spain and Italy for 3, 4, 5 or 9 months. Apply early. Tel: 020 8786 7711. Website www.aaiuk.org

Africa and Asia Venture: 4 and 5 month schemes offering great scope for cultural and interpersonal development in Kenya, Tanzania, Uganda, Malawi, Zimbabwe, India and Nepal. Mainly unpaid teaching work, with extensive travel and safari opportunities. Tel: 01380 729009. Website: www.aventure.co.uk

BUNAC (British Universities North America Club) offers an extensive range of work/travel programmes worldwide, varying from a few months to a whole year, depending on destination and programme. Tel: 020 7251 3472. Website: www.bunac.org

Community Service Volunteers (CSV) – full-time voluntary placements throughout the UK for people between 16 and 35. Allowance, accommodation and food provided. Freephone 0800 374 991. Website www.csv.org.uk

Gap Activity Projects (GAP) Ltd: an independent educational charity founded in 1972, which organises voluntary work overseas in 30 different countries. Tel: 0118 959 4914. Website: www.gap.org.uk

Gap Challenge/World Challenge Expeditions: Varied schemes for students 18-25, from voluntary conservation projects to paid hotel work in many different countries. Tel: 020 8537 7930. Website www.world-challenge.co.uk

Health Projects Abroad: various schemes in rural Africa. Tel: 01629 640051. E-mail: info@hpauk.org. Website: www.hpauk.org

Raleigh International: a charity-run scheme giving young people the opportunity to go on 3-month expeditions all over the world for varied project work. Over 20,000 young people (including Prince William) have taken part in a total of 168 expeditions in 35 countries since 1984. Tel: 020 7371 8585. Website www.raleigh.org.uk

If you fancy working on a kibbutz, contact: Kibbutz Representatives, 1a Accommodation Road, London NW11 8ED. Tel: 020 8458 9235. Also try Project 67, also based in London, on 020 7831 7626, email: project67@aol.com

Students Partnership Worldwide: Challenging and rewarding 4-9 month projects in developing countries. Tel: 020 7222 0138. Website: www.spw.org

Teaching & Projects Abroad: Foreign travel and experience in teaching English, conservation work, medicine and journalism among others. Countries include China, Ghana, India, Thailand, Mexico and South Africa. Tel: 01903 859911. Website: www.teaching-abroad.co.uk

UKSA – 'The Perfect Marriage of gap year, radical watersports and awesome experience.' Windsurfing, kayaking, sailing, professional crew and skipper training. Tel: 01983 203013. Website: www.uk-sail.org.uk/gapyear.html

For teaching opportunities (no formal training needed to take up a temporary position), contact Gabbitas Educational Consultants, Carrington House, 126-130 Regent Street, London W1R 6EE Tel: 020 7734 0161.

The Voluntary Service Organisation (VSO) runs special overseas youth programmes for under 25's. Contact VSO Enquiries: 020 8780 7500, or e-mail enquiry@vso.org.uk – You can apply online at www.vso.org.uk

ACADEMIC GUIDES & APPLICATIONS PROCEDURE

Individual colleges publish prospectuses for admissions and many students' unions produce alternative prospectuses. To get hold of a copy, use the contact details in the push entries or see your careers adviser/library.

The Big Guide (University & College Entrance: The Official Guide), UCAS, £22.95 (includes the StudyLink CD-ROM).

The COSHEP/UCAS Entrance Guide to Higher Education in Scotland, UCAS, £8.95.

How to Complete Your UCAS Form, Tony Higgins, Trotman, £9.99.

Choosing Your Degree Course & University, Brian Heap, Trotman, £16.99.

Degree Course Offers, Brian Heap, Trotman, £21.99.

The Best in University & College Courses, Brian Hep, Trotman, £12.99.

You want to study what?, Dianah Ellis, Trotman, £9.99.

The UCAS/Trotman Complete Guides Series, individual guides for various subject areas from engineering to performing arts, each is priced individually from £12.99 to £16.99.

The Laser Compendium of Higher Education, Laser, £25.99.

Clearing the Way, a guide to the Clearing system, Trotman, £8.99.

UK Course Discover, ECCTIS+, subscription CD and website (www.ecctis.co.uk), covering over 100,000 courses at universities and colleges in the UK. Available at schools, colleges, careers offices and training access points (TAP).

The UCAS website (www.ucas.com) has details of the application procedure, an order forms for books, forms and resources and a course search facility for finding which universities do the course you're after.

UCAS Directory 2002 Entry £6. ISBN: 0948241969.

UCAS/ Universities Scotland - Entrance Guide to Higher Education in Scotland 2002 Entry: £8.95. ISBN: 0948241942. Focuses solely on full-time degrees and diplomas at Scottish institutions.

For Scottish students: **'Scottish Higher Education for the 21st Century',** available from the Scottish Office on 0131 244 8075 or at www.scotland.gov.uk – For specific advice, call 0131 244 5823.

Student Awards Agency for Scotland (SAAS): www.student-support-saas.gov.uk Their address: SAAS, Gyleview House, 3 Redheughs Rigg, Edinburgh EH12 9HH.

For students from Northern Ireland: The Department of Higher and Further Education, Training and Employment (DHFETE) publishes its own version of 'Financial Support for Students in Higher Education 2001/2'. Call 02890 257 777 or visit www.dhfeteni.gov.uk Their address: Adelaide House, 39-49 Adelaide Street, Belfast BT2 8SD.

For Welsh-speaking students: contact National Assembly for Wales on 02920 825 111. Their address: FHEI Division, 4th Floor, Cathays Park, Cardiff CF10 3NQ. Or visit www.wfc.ac.uk/hefcw

Different arrangements for **hardship funds and bursaries** exist in Wales. Contact the Further and Higher Education Division of the National Assembly for Wales on 029 2082 6318.

The Best in University and College Courses, Brian Heap, £12.99.

British University and College Courses, The British Council, £10.95.

UCAS: Fulton House, Jessop Avenue, Cheltenham, Gloucs, GL50 3SH; Tel (voice) 01242 227788; Tel (minicom) 01242 544942; Fax 01242 544961; E-mail enq@ucas.ac.uk; www.ucas.com

Writing an Effective UCAS Personal Statement – Michael Senior, Paul Mannix: £25.00.

www.student.co.uk - good site for information on completing a UCAS form.

FINANCE, GRANTS AND SPONSORSHIP

The Push Guide to Money 2002: Student Survival, Johnny Rich and Mikki Goffin, TSO, £7.99, ISBN 0117028339.

Student Loans, Department for Education and Employment, Publications Centre, PO Box 2193, London, E15 ZEU. Tel: (020) 8 533 2000. The DfEE's riveting missives on student funding are also available on their website (www.dfee.gov.uk).
Sponsorships for Students, Hobsons, £8.99.
University Scholarships and Awards 2001, Brian Heap, £11.99.
The Sponsorship & Funding Directory 2002, £8.99.
The Educational Grants Directory by Sarah Harland (Directory of Social Change). Lists all sources of non-statutory help for students in financial need. As it states: "The £50 million available from sources in this guide is becoming increasingly important to higher education students who may find themselves getting deeper into debt as state support for them drops still further." Updated annually.
Students' Money Matters, Gwenda Thomas, Trotman, £10.99. This is an excellent reference book with details on just about everything concerning student finance, plus student case studies and 'thrift tips' throughout.
Balancing your Books, ECCTIS/CRAC, £5.99.
Form AB11 from the Department of Social Security has information about student entitlement to help with prescriptions, dental and eye care charges. Claims can be made on form AG1.
Scholarship Search UK (SSUK) at www.scholarship-search.org.uk was launched in April 2000 and is a free search facility for all undergraduate students. Constantly updated. You can search by subject, awarding body or region. Postal address: SSUK, The Old House, Church Lane, Claxton, Norwich, Norfolk NR14 7HY. Tel: 01508 480 327.
Also try www.freefund.com for info on all types of educational assistance. Check your own eligibility with the search facility. The Windsor Fellowship runs undergraduate personal and professional development programmes (such as sponsorships, community work and summer placements) – this is primarily for gifted black and Asian students. Their address: 47 Hackney Road, London E2 7NX. Tel: 020 7613 0373. Email info@windsor-fellow.demon.co.uk.
Education Grants Advisory Service (EGAS): 501-505 Kingsland Road, Dalston, London E8 4AU. (Enclose a stamped addressed envelope with you enquiry letter). Tel: 020 7249 6636.
A Guide to Scholarships and Awards, Brian Heap, Trotman. All the info you'll need, plus information for overseas students and a list of charitable and other awards. Each university is broken down with a list of awards they offer.
The Sponsorship and Funding Directory 2001, Hobsons. Available in most schools, colleges and public libraries. As above, also lists charities that offer educational sponsorships.
Engineering Opportunities for Students and Graduate (Institution of Mechanical Engineers). If you are studying any kind of engineering course, this book lists several sponsors and universities with sponsored courses. Call 020 7222 3337 or email education@imeche.org.uk
Student Life – A Survival Guide (Lifetime Careers 2001) £8.99.
Making the most of being a student by Judy Bastyra and Charles Bradley (Kogan Page, in association with Student Pages).
Know Your Rights: Students by Shirley Meredeen (How to Books).
The Independent Complete Parents' Guide to Higher Education (published by Trotman).
The Liberal Democrats petition regarding fees:
www.scraptuitionfees.com
www.studentuk.com - a general student guide including a good

money section.

www.times-money.co.uk/student

www.studentmoneynet.co.uk - this website offers a very good budget planner (Excel spreadsheet) as well as some sound advice and general financing info.

If you're looking for a job, check out www.studentjobs.org.uk

Also: www.ncwe.com or the student section of www.loot.com, both of which offer excellent info and details of companies who offer student placements. There is also a site called www.hotrecruit.co.uk and this has student-specific jobs nationwide.

www.jobpilot.co.uk/content/channel/student is another one to try and don't forget that The Guardian newspaper has student and graduate opportunities advertised regularly (especially in Saturday editions), or try www.guardian.co.uk/jobs

www.dti.gov.uk/er/pay.htm tells you about the national minimum wage and hours of employment and also has a 'young worker' section.

www.cujo.co.uk - launched in February 2000. Provides an online 'student supastore', help and advice for students; from special offers, classifieds, house shares including extensive student property search engine.

www.hotbeast.com – has been going since September 2000, designed to help students and graduates build networks.

www.student123.com – to help with all areas of student life.

www.studentsgetoff.com – providing discounts on books, booze, clubs, haircuts, mobiles, movies, travel...all a student could need. Except no winning lottery numbers unfortunately

www.studentswapshop.co.uk - speaks for itself!

www.books4beer.com - as above: cash in your old textbooks for a weekend of ethanolic fun.

www.uniservity.net - academic, social and financial web resources.

www.uniserveuk.com - offering lots of sound advice to students, with a great money section.

Other useful student websites: www.yoonee.co.uk and www.uni4me.com

OVERSEAS STUDENTS

Study UK Handbook, CRAC/Hobsons, £24.99.

British University & College Courses, UCAS/Trotman, £10.95.

The British Council website (www.britcoun.org.uk) has information on coming to university in Britain and a good 'virtual campus' to introduce you to life at UK universities.

EU students (non-UK) should contact: The European Team at the Department for Education and Employment (Department for Education and Employment, Mowden Hall, Staindrop Road, Darlington, Co. Durham DL3 9BG). Call 01325 391199 during office hours or visit www.dfee.gov.uk/eustudents

MATURE STUDENTS

The Mature Students' Guide, Getting Into Higher Education, Trotman, £7.95. A condensed version is available free from UCAS.

Studying for a Degree: How to Succeed as a Mature Student, Stephen Wade (How to Books).

POSTGRADUATE STUDY

How to Get a PhD, Open University Press, £14.99.

Directory of Postgraduate Studies, Hobsons, £109.99 (at that price, don't buy it, try the library).

Hobsons Postgraduate Student's Guides, 3 volumes by subject area

(Business Economics & Law; Engineering & Sciences; Arts, Humanities & Social Sciences), Hobsons, £6.50 each or £17.99 for all three.

Sources of Funding: The UK Research Councils – Biotechnology and Biological Sciences Research Council (BBSRC), Polaris House, North Star Avenue, Swindon SN2 1UH. Tel: 01793 413200. Website: www.bbsrc.ac.uk

Economic and Social Research Council (ESRC), Address as above, (Postcode SN2 1UJ). Tel: 01793 413000. Website: www.esrc.ac.uk

Engineering and Physical Sciences Research (EPSRC), Address as above (Postcode SN2 1ET) Tel: 01793 444000. Website: www.epsrc.ac.uk

Natural Environment Research Council (NERC), Address as above (Postcode SN2 1EU). Tel: 01793 411500. Website: www.nerc.ac.uk

Particle Physics and Astronomy Research (PPARC), Address as above (Postcode SN2 1SZ). Tel: 01793 442000, Website: www.pparc.ac.uk

Medical Research Council (MRC), 20 Park Crescent, London W1B 1AL. Tel: 020 7636 5422. Website: www.mrc.ac.uk

The Arts and Humanities Research Board (AHRB), 10 Carlton House Terrace, London SW1Y 5AH. Tel: 020 7969 5205 (Postgraduate Awards Division).

Council for the Central Laboratory of the Research Councils (CCLRC), Rutherford Appleton Laboratory, Chilton, Didcot, Oxfordshire OX11 0QX. Tel: 01235 821900. Website: www.cclrc.ac.uk

Further Postgraduate Sources: The Association of Graduate Careers Advisory Service (AGCAS), Armstrong House, Oxford Road, Manchester M1 7ED. Tel: 0161 277 5200. They publish a booklet called Postgraduate Management Education, this is free from your careers service.

Royal Society Research Fellowships, Research Appointments Department, 6 Carlton House Terrace, London SW1Y 5AG. Tel: 020 7451 2547. Website: www.royalsoc.ac.uk

STUDENTS WITH DISABILITIES

Higher Education & Disability, Skill, £1.50 to students.

Financial Assistance for Students with Disabilities in Higher Education, Skill, free. (This booklet contains information about social security entitlements).

Both available from: Skill, 336 Brixton Road, London, SW9 7AA. Tel: (020) 7 274 0565. Their website (www.skill.org.uk) offers information for students and carers and details of how to get hold of Skill publications.

The Disabled Students' Guide to University, Trotman, £14.99.

Action for Blind People, Grants Officer, 14-16 Verney Road, London SE16 3DZ. Tel: 020 7635 4821.

Association for Spina Bifida and Hydrocephalus, ASBAH House, 42 Park Road, Peterborough, PE1 2UQ. Maximum award £2,000.

The Dyslexia Institute Bursary Fund, 133 Gresham Road, Staines, Middlesex. TW18 2AJ. Tel: 01784 463851.

Snowdon Award Scheme, 22 City Business Centre, 6 Brighton Road, Horsham, West Sussex RH13 5BB. Helps disabled students aged 17-25 in further, higher or adult education.

For disabled students looking for work: Workable has loads of jobs across all sectors, and your university careers service or students' union will have their details. Alternatively, contact them direct: 67-71 Goswell Road, London EC1V 7EP. Tel: 020 7608 3161. Email: workableuk@aol.com

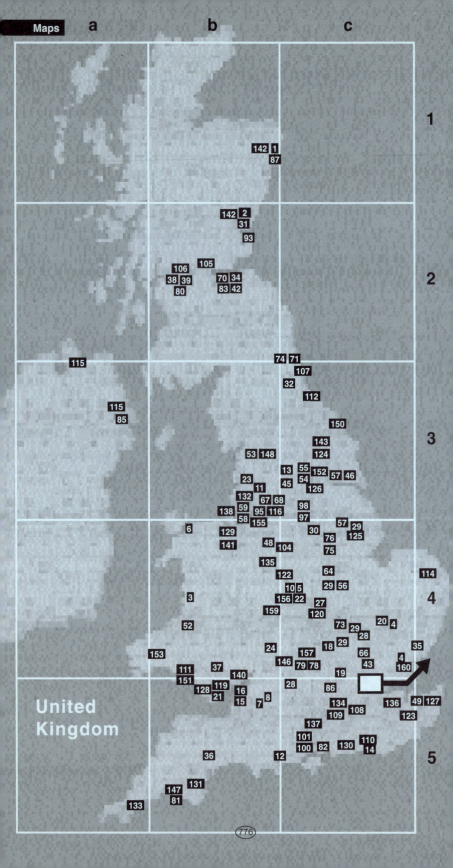

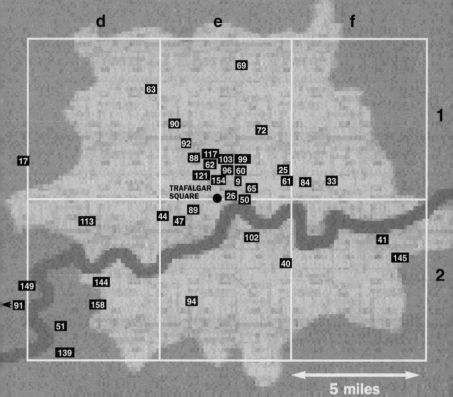

Greater London

#	Name	#	Name
1	University of Aberdeen b1	29	De Montfort University c4
2	University of Abertay Dundee b2	30	University of Derby c4
3	Aberystwyth, University of Wales b4	31	University of Dundee b2
4	Anglia Polytechnic University c4	32	University of Durham c3
5	Aston University c4	33	University of East London f1
6	Bangor, University of Wales b4	34	University of Edinburgh b2
7	University of Bath b5	35	University of Essex c4
8	Bath Spa University College b5	36	University of Exeter b5
9	Birkbeck College, London e1	37	University of Glamorgan b4
10	University of Birmingham c4	38	University of Glasgow b2
11	Bolton Institute b3	39	Glasgow Caledonian University b2
12	Bournemouth University b5	40	Goldsmiths College, London e2
13	University of Bradford b3	41	University of Greenwich f2
14	University of Brighton c5	42	Heriot-Watt University b2
15	University of Bristol b5	43	University of Hertfordshire c4
16	Bristol, Univ of the West of England b5	44	Heythrop College, London e2
17	Brunel University d1	45	University of Huddersfield c3
18	University of Buckingham c4	46	University of Hull c3
19	Buckinghamshire Chilterns UC c4	47	Imperial College, London e2
20	University of Cambridge c4	48	Keele University b4
21	Cardiff, University of Wales b5	49	University of Kent at Canterbury c5
22	University of Central England c4	50	King's College London e1
23	University of Central Lancashire b3	51	Kingston University d2
24	Cheltenham & Gloucester College b4	52	Lampeter, University of Wales b4
25	City University e1	53	Lancaster University b3
26	Courtauld Institute, London e1	54	University of Leeds c3
27	Coventry University c4		
28	Cranfield University c4, c5		

Continued on next page

Maps

Continued from last page

- **55** Leeds Metropolitan University *c3*
- **56** Leicester University *c4*
- **57** Univ of Lincolnshire & Humberside *c3, c4*
- **58** University of Liverpool *b3*
- **59** Liverpool John Moores University *b3*
- **60** University of London *e1*
- **61** London Guildhall University *e1*
- **62** The London Institute *e1*
- **63** The London School of Jewish Studies *d1*
- **64** Loughborough University *c4*
- **65** LSE *e1*
- **66** Luton University *c4*
- **67** University of Manchester *b3*
- **68** Manchester Metropolitan University *b3*
- **69** Middlesex University *e1*
- **70** Napier University *b2*
- **71** University of Newcastle Upon Tyne *b2*
- **72** University of North London *e1*
- **73** University College, Northampton *c4*
- **74** University of Northumbria at Newcastle *b2*
- **75** University of Nottingham *c4*
- **76** Nottingham Trent University *c4*
- **77** Open University *not marked on map*
- **78** University of Oxford *c4*
- **79** Oxford Brookes University *c4*
- **80** University of Paisley *b2*
- **81** University of Plymouth *b5*
- **82** University of Portsmouth *c5*
- **83** Queen Margaret College *b2*
- **84** Queen Mary & Westfield College *f1*
- **85** Queen's University Belfast *a3*
- **86** University of Reading *c5*
- **87** Robert Gordon University *b1*
- **88** Royal Academy of Music *e1*
- **89** Royal College of Music *e2*
- **90** Royal Free Hospital, London *e1*
- **91** Royal Holloway, London *d2*
- **92** Royal Veterinary College, London *e1*
- **93** University of St Andrews *b2*
- **94** St George's Hospital, London *e2*
- **95** University of Salford *b3*
- **96** School of Pharmacy, London *e1*
- **97** University of Sheffield *c3*
- **98** Sheffield Hallam University *c3*
- **99** SOAS *e1*
- **100** University of Southampton *c5*
- **101** Southampton Institute *c5*
- **102** South Bank University *e2*
- **103** SSEES *e1*
- **104** Staffordshire University *c4*
- **105** University of Stirling *b2*
- **106** University of Strathclyde *b2*
- **107** University of Sunderland *c3*
- **108** University of Surrey *c5*
- **109** Surrey Institute of Art & Design *c5*
- **110** University of Sussex *c5*
- **111** Swansea, University of Wales *b4*
- **112** University of Teesside *c3*
- **113** Thames Valley University *d2*
- **114** UEA *c4*
- **115** University of Ulster *a3*
- **116** UMIST *b3*
- **117** University College London *e1*
- **118** University of Wales *not marked on map*
- **119** University of Wales College of Medicine *b5*
- **120** University of Warwick *c4*
- **121** University of Westminster *e1*
- **122** University of Wolverhampton *b4*
- **123** Wye College, London *c5*
- **124** University of York *c3*
- **125** Bishop Grosseteste College *c4*
- **126** University College, Bretton Hall *c3*
- **127** Canterbury Christ Church UC *c5*
- **128** Cardiff UWI *b5*
- **129** Chester College *b4*
- **130** University College Chichester *c5*
- **131** Dartington College of Arts *b5*
- **132** Edge Hill University College *b3*
- **133** Falmouth College of Arts *a5*
- **134** Farnborough College of Technology *c5*
- **135** Harper Adams University College *b4*
- **136** Kent Institute of Art & Design *c5*
- **137** King Alfred's, Winchester *c5*
- **138** Liverpool Hope University College *b3*
- **139** NESCOT *d2*
- **140** Univ of Wales College, Newport *b4*
- **141** North East Wales Institute of HE *b4*
- **142** Northern College *b1, b2*
- **143** College of Ripon & York St John *c3*
- **144** Roehampton Institute, London *d2*
- **145** Rose Bruford College *f2*
- **146** Royal Agricultural College *c4*
- **147** University College of St Mark & St John *b5*
- **148** St Martin's College *b3*
- **149** St Mary's College, Twickenham *d2*
- **150** University College, Scarborough *c3*
- **151** Swansea Institute of HE *b4*
- **152** Trinity & All Saints *c3*
- **153** Trinity College, Carmarthen *b4*
- **154** Trinity College of Music *e1*
- **155** University College Warrington *b3*
- **156** Westhill College *c4*
- **157** Westminster College, Oxford *c4*
- **158** Wimbledon School of Art *d2*
- **159** University College, Worcester *b4*
- **160** Writtle College *c4*

Index

a
Aberdeen 35, 528, 701
Aberdeen, University of 35
Abertay Dundee, University of 41
Aberystwyth, University of Wales 44
abbreviations 769
African Studies 569
Anglia 49, 637
Anglia Polytechnic University 49
APU 49
Aston University 54

b
Balliol College, Oxford 462
Bangor, University of Wales 60
Bart's Hospital 512
Bath 65, 69
Bath, University of 65
Bath Spa UC 69
Bedford 191
Belfast 516, 643
Belfast, Queen's University 516
Birkbeck College, London 73
Birmingham 54, 74, 674
Birmingham Poly 161
Birmingham, University of 74, 161
Bishop Grosseteste UC 688
Bognor Regis 692
Bolton Institute 81
book list 770
Bournemouth University 85
Bradford, University of 90
Brasenose College, Oxford 463
Brighton 95, 614
Brighton, University of 95
Bristol 100, 106
Bristol, University of 100
Bristol, University of the West of England 106
Bristol Poly 106
Brookes University 485
Brunel University 110
Buckingham, University of 115
Buckinghamshire Chilterns UC 120

##
Caius College, Cambridge 143
Caledonian University, Glasgow 253
Camborne 128
Cambridge 49, 128
Cambridge, University of 128
Canterbury 304, 689
Canterbury Christ Church College 689
Cardiff 156, 660, 690

Cardiff Institute 690
Cardiff University 156
Carlisle 432
Carmarthen 706
Caythorpe 191
Central England, University of 161
Central Lancashire, University of 165
Central London Poly 670
Central St Martin's 375
Chalfont St Giles 120
Charing Cross 292
Chelmsford 49, 711
Chelsea College 375
Cheltenham & Gloucester College of HE 170
Chester College 691
Chichester, UC 692
Chilterns UC 120
Christ Church, Oxford 463
Christ's College, Cambridge 138
Churchill College, Cambridge 138
Cirencester 702
City of London Poly 370
City University 175
Clare College, Cambridge 139
clubs 744
Colchester 228
Coleraine 643
Corpus Christi College, Cambridge 140
Corpus Christi College, Oxford 464
courses 714
Courtauld Institute 179
Coventry 180, 664
Coventry University 180
Cranfield University 185

d
Dartington College 692
De Montfort University 191
Derby, University of 196
Derry 643
Downing College, Cambridge 140
Dudley 675
Dundee 41, 201, 701
Dundee Institute of Technology 41
Dundee, University of 201
Durham, University of 206

e
East Anglia 637
Eastbourne 95
East London, University of 215
Economics, London School of 384

Index

Edge Hill 693
Edinburgh 221, 267, 413, 509
Edinburgh, University of 221
Emmanuel College, Cambridge 141
Entrance requirements 734
Epsom 610, 699
Essex, University of 228
Exeter 234, 496
Exeter College, Oxford 465
Exeter, University of 234
Exmouth 496

Falmouth College 694
Farnborough College 695
Farnham 610
finance 18
Fitzwilliam College, Cambridge 142

Girton College, Cambridge 142
Glamorgan, University of 241
Glasgow 246, 253, 491
Glasgow, University of 246
Glasgow Caledonian University 253
glossary 758
Gloucester 170
Goldsmiths College, London 256
Gonville & Caius College, Cambridge 143
Gordon University, Robert 528
Greenwich, University of 261
Greyfriars Hall, Oxford 466
Grimsby 347
Guildhall University, London 370
Guildford 605
Guy's Hospital 310

Hallam University, Sheffield 565
Harper Adams 696
Harris Manchester College, Oxford 466
Hatfield 271
Heriot-Watt University 267
Hertford College, Oxford 467
Hertfordshire, University of 271
Heythrop College 278
High Wycombe 120
Holloway College 535
Homerton College, Cambridge 144
Huddersfield, University of 280
Hull 284, 346
Hull, University of 284
Humberside, University of Lincolnshire and 346

Imperial College, London 291

Jesus College, Cambridge 144
Jesus College, Oxford 468
John Moores University, Liverpool 357
Jordanstown 643

KCL 310
Keble College, Oxford 468
Keele University 299
Kent Institute 697
Kent, University of 304
King Alfred's, Winchester 697
King's College, Cambridge 145
King's College London 310
King's Hospital 310
Kingston University 314

Lady Margaret Hall, Oxford 469
Lampeter, University of Wales 322
Lancashire, University of Central 165
Lancaster 326, 704
Lancaster University 326
Leeds 331, 337, 706
Leeds, University of 331
Leeds Metropolitan University 337
Leicester 191, 340
Leicester, University of 340
Lincoln 191, 346, 688
Lincoln College, Oxford 470
Lincolnshire and Humberside, University of 346
Liverpool 351, 357, 691, 698
Liverpool, University of 351
Liverpool Hope UC 698
Liverpool John Moores University 357
London 73, 110, 175, 179, 215, 256, 261, 278, 291, 310, 362, 370, 375, 384, 407, 424, 512, 532, 534, 535, 540, 558, 569, 581, 551, 652, 670, 702, 707, 709
London, University of 362
London College of Fashion 375
London College of Printing 375
London Guildhall University 370
London Hospital 512
London Institute 375
London School of Economics 384
Londonderry 643
Loughborough University 379
LSE 384
Lucy Cavendish, Cambridge 146
Luton University 388

Magdalen College, Oxford *470*
Magdalene College, Cambridge *146*
Magee *643*
Maidstone *697*
Manchester *395, 403, 553, 649*
Manchester College, Oxford *466*
Manchester, University of *395*
Manchester Institute of Science & Technology, University of *649*
Manchester Metropolitan University *403*
Mansfield College, Oxford *471*
maps *776*
Marjon *726*
Merton College, Oxford *472*
Metropolitan University, Leeds *337*
Metropolitan University, Manchester *403*
Middlesbrough *625*
Middlesex University *407*
Milton Keynes *191, 449*
Moores University, Liverpool John *357*
Moray House *223*
Morpeth *432*

Napier University *413*
Nene College *428*
NESCOT *699*
New Hall, Cambridge *147*
New College, Oxford *473*
Newcastle upon Tyne *417, 432*
Newcastle upon Tyne, University of *417*
Newnham College, Cambridge *148*
Newport (Shropshire) *696*
Newport UWC *700*
Newton Abbot *496*
North East Wales Institute (NEWI) *700*
North London, University of *424*
Northampton, UC *428*
Northern College (of Education) *701*
Northern Ireland *516*
Northumbria, University of *432*
Norwich *637*
Nottingham *436, 442*
Nottingham, University of *436*
Nottingham Trent University *442*

Open University *449*
Oriel College, Oxford *473*
Oriental & African Studies *569*
Oxford *453, 485*
Oxford, University of *453*
Oxford Brookes University *485*

Paisley University *491*
PCL *670*
Pembroke College, Cambridge *149*
Pembroke College, Oxford *474*
Peterhouse, Cambridge *149*
Pharmacy, School of *558*
Plymouth *496, 726*
Plymouth University *496*
Pontypridd *241*
Poole *85*
Portsmouth, University of *501*
Preston *167*
Push *4, 6*

Queen Margaret College *509*
Queen Mary *512*
Queen's University, Belfast *516*
Queens' College, Cambridge *150*
Queen's College, Oxford *475*

RMCS *185*
Reading, University of *523*
Regent's Park College, Oxford *475*
Robert Gordon University *528*
Robinson College, Cambridge *151*
Rose Bruford College *702*
Royal Academy of Music *532*
Royal Agricultural College *702*
Royal College of Music *534*
Royal Free Hospital *653*
Royal Holloway *535*
Royal Military College of Science *185*
Royal Veterinary College *540*
Runnymede *110*

St Andrews, University of *546*
St Anne's College, Oxford *476*
St Bartholomew's Hospital *512*
St Catharine's College, Cambridge *151*
St Catherine's College, Oxford *477*
St David's College, Lampeter *322*
St George's Hospital *551*
St Edmund Hall, Oxford *477*
St Hilda's College, Oxford *478*
St Hugh's College, Oxford *479*
St John's College, Cambridge *152*
St John's College, Oxford *480*
St Mark & St John UC *703*
St Martin's College *704*
St Mary's College *704*
St Mary's Hospital *291*
St Peter's College, Oxford *480*
St Thomas's Hospital *310*
Salford, University of *553*

Index

School of Pharmacy 558
Scottish College of Textiles 268
Scotland 35, 41, 201, 221, 246, 253, 268, 413, 491, 509, 528, 546, 591, 596
Seale Hayne 496
Selwyn College, Cambridge 153
Sheffield 559, 565
Sheffield, University of 559
Sheffield Hallam University 565
Shrivenham 185
Sidcup 702
Sidney Sussex College, Cambridge 153
Silsoe 185
SOAS 569
societies 744
Somerville College, Oxford 481
South Bank University 581
South West Poly 496
Southampton 572, 578
Southampton, University of 572
Southampton Institute of HE 578
Stafford 586
Staffordshire University 586
statistics 750
Stirling, University of 591
Stockton, University College 206
Stoke-on-Trent 586
Strathclyde, University of 596
Sunderland, University of 600
Surrey, University of 605
Surrey Institute 610
Sussex University 610
Swansea 618, 705
Swansea Institute 705
Swansea, University of Wales 618

Teesside, University of 625
Telford 675
Thames Poly 261
Thames Valley University 630
Totnes 692
Top Ten 756
Treforest 241
Trent University, Nottingham 442
Trinity & All Saints 706
Trinity College, Cambridge 154
Trinity College, Carmarthen 706
Trinity College, Oxford 482
Trinity College of Music 707
Trinity Hall, Cambridge 155
Twickenham 110, 704

UCE 161
UCL 652
UEA 637
UEL 215
UKC 304
Ulster University 643
UMIST 649
United Medical & Dental Schools 311
University College London 652
University College, Oxford 482
University College Stockton 206
UWCM 660
UWE 106
UWIC 690
Uxbridge 111

Wadham College, Oxford 483
Wales 44, 60, 156, 241, 322, 618, 690, 700, 705, 707
Wales, University of 660
Wales College of Medicine 660
Wales Poly 241
Warrington, UC 708
Warwick, University of 664
West of England, University of the 106
West London Poly 630
Westminster, University of 670
Wimbledon School of Art 709
Winchester 573, 698
Wolverhampton, University of 674
Worcester, UC 709
Worcester College, Oxford 484
Wrexham 700
Writtle College 711

York 681, 712
York, University of 681
York St John 712

781 Index